# BOSCH

**Automotive
Handbook
6th Edition**

# BOSCH

# Automotive Handbook

## Imprint

**Published by**
© Robert Bosch GmbH, 2004
Postfach 1129,
D-73201 Plochingen.
Automotive Equipment Business Sector,
Department Product Marketing
Diagnostics & Test Equipment
(AA/PDT5).

6th edition
Completely revised and extended
October 2004

**Translation**
STAR Deutschland GmbH
Member of STAR Group

**Technical graphics**
Bauer & Partner,
Gesellschaft für technische Grafik mbH,
Leinfelden-Echterdingen.
Schwarz Technische Grafik, Leonberg.

All rights reserved.

Printed in Germany.
Imprimé en Allemagne.

**Distribution**
SAE Society of Automotive Engineers
400 Commonwealth Drive
Warrendale, PA 15096-0001
USA
CostumerService@sae.org

ISBN 0-7680-1513-8

The following companies kindly placed picture matter, diagrams, and other informative material at our disposal:

AUDI AG, Neckarsulm; Automotive Lighting Reutlingen GmbH; BASF Coatings AG, Münster; Behr GmbH & Co. KG, Stuttgart; BorgWarner Turbo Systems, Kirchheimbolanden; Brose Fahrzeugteile GmbH & Co. KG, Coburg; Continental AG, Hannover; DaimlerChrysler AG, Stuttgart; DaimlerChrysler AG, Sindelfingen; Dräxlmaier Systemtechnik GmbH, Vilsbiburg; J. Eberspächer GmbH & Co. KG, Esslingen; ETAS GmbH, Stuttgart; Filterwerk Mann + Hummel, Ludwigsburg; FHT Esslingen; Freudenberg Vliesstoffe KG, Weinheim; Institut für Betriebstechnik und Bauforschung der FAL, Braunschweig; Knorr-Bremse SfN GmbH, Schwieberdingen; MAN Nutzfahrzeuge AG, München; Mannesmann Kienzle GmbH, Villingen-Schwenningen; NBT GmbH, Hannover; Pierburg GmbH, Neuss; Dr. Ing. h.c. F. Porsche AG, Weissach; RWTH Aachen; SAINT-GOBAIN SEKURIT, Aachen; Siemens VDO Automotive AG, Villingen-Schwenningen; TNO Road-Vehicles Research Institute, Delft, Netherlands; VB Autobatterie GmbH, Hannover; Volkswagen AG, Wolfsburg; Zahnradfabrik Friedrichshafen AG, Friedrichshafen.

## Foreword to the 6th Edition

The history of the automobile's development is also an impressive documentation of technical innovations. New systems and detail enhancements make driving even safer and more comfortable, and continue to reduce the environmental impact by engine emissions and manufacturing processes. The 6th Edition of the "Automotive Handbook" reflects this development by including a number of new subjects and complete revisions of existing sections. Compared with the previous edition, the handbook has grown by about 270 pages.

The "Automotive Handbook" is an important reference work with worldwide distribution due to its up-to-date sections that are worded concisely. It is intended to provide an insight into the modern state of automotive technology for engineers and technicians, as well as those who are interested in technical matters.

The authors in the 6th Edition are experts from the Bosch corporation, universities, and the automotive industry. They have completely revised the contents of this handbook, brought it up-to-date, and expanded it with new subjects. We would like to take this opportunity of thanking all those involved for their cooperation.

In more than seven years the Automotive Handbook has grown from a calendar insert of 96 pages to an extensive work now with over 1,200 pages. In the meantime its circulation in several languages total more than a million copies.

The new edition has a revised page layout to provide better navigation for the reader. The left page title indicates the generic subject, while the right page title is the chapter heading. The redesigned and extended table of contents now contains all chapters and sections. This will help the reader to search for subjects more easily.

The Editors

## For your information

**The following subjects have been added since the 6th Edition:**
Hydrostatics ● Fluid mechanics ● Mechatronics ● Coating systems ● Frictional joints ● Positive or form-closed joints ● Engine lubrication ● Emission reduction systems ● Diagnosis ● Truck brake management as a platform for truck driver assistance systems ● Analog and digital signal transmission ● Mobile information services ● Fleet management ● Multimedia systems ● Developments methods and application tools for electronic systems ● Sound design ● Vehicle wind tunnels ● Environmental management ● Workshop technology.

**The following subjects have been totally revised and restructured:**
Basic equations used in mechanics ● Threaded fasteners ● Springs ● Air filtration ● Exhaust-gas measuring techniques ● Engine management for spark-ignition (SI) engines (including Motronic engine management) ● Diesel-engine management ● Car radio with auxiliary equipment ● Vehicle antennas ● Mobile and data radio ● Passenger-car driver-assistance systems.

**The following subjects have been updated, expanded and restructured:**
Acoustics ● Heat ● Electronics ● Substances ● Materials ● Corrosion ● Tribology ● Lubricants ● Fuels ● Antifreeze and brake fluid ● Chemicals ● Heat treatment ● Motor-vehicle dynamics ● Motor-vehicle requirements ● Internal-combustion engines ● Engine cooling ● Battery chargers ● Exhaust-gas system ● Alternative spark-ignition engine drive systems ● Hybrid drives ● Drivetrain ● Suspension ● Wheels ● Tires ● Braking systems ● Braking systems for passenger cars and commercial vehicles ● Vehicle stabilization systems for passenger cars and commercial vehicles ● Vehicle bodies for passenger cars and commercial vehicles ● Lighting technology (with cornering headlamps) ● Instrumentation ● Driver-information system ● Trip recorders ● Parking systems ● Navigation systems ● Traffic-control engineering ● Electromagnetic compatibility ● Occupant safety systems ● Comfort and convenience systems ● Starter batteries ● Alternators ● Starting systems.

# 6 Table of contents

## Contents

# 8 Table of contents

# 10 Table of contents

## Author in the 6th Edition

Unless otherwise stated,
the authors are employees
of Robert Bosch GmbH

**Basic Principles of Physics**
*Symbols, Units*
Dipl.-Ing. G. Brüggen

*Basic Equations Used in Mechanics*
Prof. Dr.-Ing. H. Haberhauer,
FHT Esslingen

*Vibrations and Oscillations*
Dipl.-Ing. J. Bohrer

*Optical Technology*
Dr.-Ing. F. Prinzhausen;
Dr. rer. nat. H. Sautter

*Acoustics*
Dipl.-Ing. H.-M. Gerhard,
Dr. Ing. h.c. F. Porsche AG, Weissach

*Hydrostatics, Fluid Mechanics*
Prof. Dr.-Ing. H. Haberhauer,
FHT Esslingen

*Heat*
Dr.-Ing. W. Volz

*Electrical Engineering*
Dr. rer. nat. W. Draxler;
Dipl.-Ing. B. Wörner

*Electronics*
Dr. rer. nat. U. Schaefer;
Dr. rer. nat. P. Egelhaaf;
Dr. rer. nat. U. Goebel;
Dr. rer. nat. M. Illing;
Dr. rer. nat. A. Zeppenfeld;
Dipl.-Ing. F. Raichle

*Mechatronics*
Dr.-Ing. K.-G. Bürger

*Sensors*
Dr.-Ing. E. Zabler

*Actuators*
Dr.-Ing. R. Heinz

*Electrical Machines*
Dr.-Ing. R. Schenk

**Mathematics and Methods**
*Mathematics*
Dipl.-Ing. G. Brüggen

*Strength of Materials*
Prof. Dr.-Ing. L. Issler, FHT Esslingen

*Finite-Element Method (FEM)*
Prof. Dipl.-Ing. P. Groth, FHT Esslingen

*Quality*
Dipl.-Ing. M. Graf;
Dr. rer. nat. H. Kuhn

*Reliability*
Dr. rer. nat. E. Dilger;
Dr. rer. nat. H. Weiler

*Technical Statistics,
Measuring Techniques*
Dipl.-Math. H.-P. Bartenschlager

*Control Engineering*
Dr. techn. R. Karrelmeyer

**Materials Science**
*Chemical Elements, Substances,
Materials*
Dr. rer. nat. J. Ullmann;
Dr. rer. nat. W. Draxler;
Director of Studies, K.-M. Erhardt,
Robert-Bosch-Schule, Stuttgart;
Dr.-Ing. D. Wicke;
Dipl.-Ing. F. Mühleder;
Dipl.-Ing. D. Scheunert,
DaimlerChrysler AG, Sindelfingen;
Dr. rer. nat. I. Brauer; F. Wetzl;
Dr. rer. nat. H.-J. Spranger;
Dr. rer. nat. H. P. Koch;
Dipl.-Ing. R. Mayer;
Dipl.-Ing. G. Lindemann;
Dipl.-Ing. (FH) W. Hasert; R.
Schäftlmeier; Dipl.-Ing. H. Schneider;
Dr. rer. pol. T. Lueb,
BASF Coatings AG, Münster

*Corrosion and Corrosion Protection*
Dipl.-Chem. B. Moro

*Coatings Systems*
Dr. rer. nat. U. Kraatz;
Dr. rer. nat. M. Rössler;
Dr. rer. nat. C. Treutler

*Tribology, Wear*
Dipl.-Ing. H. Schorr

*Lubricants*
Dr. rer. nat. G. Dornhöfer

*Fuels*
Dr. rer. nat. J. Ullmann

*Consumables,*
*Nomenclature of Chemicals*
Dr. rer. nat. D. Welting

**Machine Parts**
*Frictional, Positive, and Threaded-*
*Fastener Connections, Threads*
Prof. Dr.-Ing. H. Haberhauer,
FHT Esslingen; Dipl.-Ing. M. Nöcker

*Spring Calculations*
Prof. Dr.-Ing. H. Haberhauer,
FHT Esslingen

*Sliding Bearings and Rolling Bearings*
Dr.-Ing. R. Heinz

*Gears and Tooth Systems*
Dipl.-Ing. U. v. Ehrenwall

*Belt Drives*
C. Hansen

**Manufacturing Methods**
*Heat Treatment, Hardness*
Dr.-Ing. N. Lippmann

*Tolerances*
Ing. (grad.) J. Pfänder

*Sheet-Metal Processing*
U. Schröder, Volkswagen AG, Wolfsburg;
Dr.-Ing. M. Witt, Volkswagen AG,
Wolfsburg

*Joining and Bonding Techniques*
Dr.-Ing. M. Witt, Volkswagen AG,
Wolfsburg; Dipl.-Ing. R. Bald

**Influences in Motor Vehicles**
*Road-Going Vehicle Requirements*
Prof. Dr.-Ing. K. Binder,
DaimlerChrysler AG, Stuttgart

*Motor-Vehicle Dynamics*
Dipl.-Ing. G. Moresche,
DaimlerChrysler AG, Stuttgart;
Dr. rer. nat. L. Dragon,
DaimlerChrysler AG, Stuttgart;
Prof. Dr.-Ing. habil. E.-C. v. Glasner,
DaimlerChrysler AG, Stuttgart;
Dipl.-Math. J. Pressel,
DaimlerChrysler AG, Stuttgart;
Dr.-Ing. J. Brunotte, Institut für Betriebs-
technik und Bauforschung der FAL,
Braunschweig

*Environmental Stresses*
Dipl.-Ing. W. Golderer

**Internal-Combustion Engines**
Prof. Dr.-Ing. K. Binder,
DaimlerChrysler AG, Stuttgart;
Prof. Dr.-Ing. H. Hiereth,
DaimlerChrysler AG, Stuttgart

**Engine Peripherals**
*Engine Cooling*
Dipl.-Ing. S. Rogg,
Behr GmbH & Co. KG, Stuttgart

*Engine Lubrication, Oil Filtration*
Dipl.-Ing. M. Kolczyk, Filterwerk
Mann + Hummel, Ludwigsburg

*Air Filtration*
Dr.-Ing. M. Durst, Filterwerk
Mann + Hummel, Ludwigsburg

*Chargers*
Dipl.-Ing. A. Förster, BorgWarner
Turbo Systems, Kirchheimbolanden

*Emission Reduction Systems*
Dipl.-Ing. C. Köhler; Dr. rer. nat. M. Streib

*Crankcase Ventilation*
Dr.-Ing. P. Trautmann,
Filterwerk Mann + Hummel, Ludwigsburg

*Exhaust-Gas Systems*
Dr. rer. nat. R. Jebasinski,
J. Eberspächer GmbH & Co. KG,
Esslingen

**Emission-Control and Diagnosis Legislation**
*Exhaust Emissions*
Dr.-Ing. W. Polach

*Emission-Control Legislation and Measuring Techniques*
Dr.-Ing. M. Eggers; Dr.-Ing. S. Becher;
Dr.-Ing. T. Eggert;
Dipl.-Phys. M.-A. Drühe;
Dipl.-Ing. A. Kreh;
Dipl.-Ing. (FH) H.-G. Weißhaar

*Fault Diagnosis*
Dr.-Ing. M. Knirsch; Dr.-Ing. G. Driedger;
Dipl.-Ing. W. Schauer

**Engine Management for Gasoline Engines**
*Description of Engine Management System, Cylinder Charge, Mixture Formation, Carburetor, Intake-Manifold Injection, Gasoline Direct Injection*
Dipl.-Ing. A. Binder;
Dr.-Ing. T. Landenfeld;
Dr. rer. nat. A. Schenck zu Schweinsberg;
Dr.-Ing. J. Thurso;
Dipl.-Ing. (FH) T. Allgeier;
Dr.-Ing. D. Großmann, Neuss

*Fuel Supply, Fuel Filters*
Dr.-Ing. T. Frenz;
Dipl.-Ing. S. Fischbach;
Dipl.-Ing. H. Rembold;
Dr.-Ing. G.-M. Klein, Filterwerk
Mann + Hummel, Ludwigsburg

*Ignition*
Dipl.-Ing. W. Gollin;
Dipl.-Ing. W. Häming;
Dipl.-Ing. (FH) U. Bentel;
Dipl.-Ing. (FH) M. Weimert;
Dipl.-Ing. E. Breuser

*Motronic Engine Management*
Dipl.-Ing. B. Mencher

*Development of Fuel-Injection Systems*
Dipl.-Ing. G. Felger; Dipl.-Ing. M. Lembke;
Ing. (grad.) L. Seebald

*History of Coil-Ignition Systems*
Dipl.-Ing. W. Gollin

*Minimizing Pollutants in SI Engines*
Dr. rer. nat. M. Streib;
Dipl.-Ing. E. Schnaibel

**Alternative Spark-Ignition Engine Operation**
*Engines Fueled by LPG*
J. A. N. van Ling,
TNO Road-Vehicles Research Institute,
Delft, Niederlande

*Natural Gas, Alcohol, and Hydrogen Drives*
Dipl.-Ing. (FH) T. Allgeier;
Dr.-Ing. T. Landenfeld

**Diesel-Engine Management**
*Fuel Supply, Diesel Fuel-Injection Systems, Fuel Filters*
Dipl.-Ing. K. Krieger;
Dr.-Ing. W. Polach;
Dr.-Ing. G.-M. Klein, Filterwerk
Mann + Hummel, Ludwigsburg;
Dr. rer. nat. W. Dreßler

*Minimizing Pollutants in Diesel Engines*
Priv.-Doz. Dr.-Ing. J. K. Schaller

**Alternative Drives**
*Electric Drives, Traction Batteries*
Dr.-Ing. R. Schenk;
Dipl.-Ing. D. Übermeier, VB Autobatterie
GmbH, Hannover; Dr. rer. nat. U. Köhler,
NBT GmbH, Hannover

*Hybrid Drives*
Prof. Dr.-Ing. C. Bader,
DaimlerChrysler AG, Stuttgart

*Fuel Cells*
Dr. rer. nat. U. Alkemade;
Dr. rer. nat. A. Häbich

**Drivetrain**
Dipl.-Ing. P. Köpf,
Zahnradfabrik Friedrichshafen AG;
Dr. rer. nat. M. Schwab,
Zahnradfabrik Friedrichshafen AG

**Chassis Systems**
*Suspension, Suspension Linkage*
Prof. Dr.-Ing. H. Wallentowitz,
RWTH Aachen,
Institut für Kraftfahrzeugwesen

*Wheels*
Ing. (grad.) D. Renz,
DaimlerChrysler AG, Sindelfingen;
Prof. Dr.-Ing. habil. E.-C. v. Glasner,
DaimlerChrysler AG, Stuttgart

*Tires*
Dipl.-Ing. B. Meiß,
Continental AG, Hannover;
Prof. Dr.-Ing. habil. E.-C. v. Glasner,
DaimlerChrysler AG, Stuttgart

*Steering*
Ing. (grad.) D. Elser, Zahnradfabrik
Friedrichshafen AG, Schwäbisch Gmünd

**Vehicle Safety Systems**
*Braking Systems*
Dr. rer. nat. J. Bräuninger;
Prof. Dr.-Ing. habil. E.-C. v. Glasner,
DaimlerChrysler AG, Stuttgart

*Braking Systems for Passenger Cars
and Commercial Vehicles
SBC, ELB*
Dipl.-Ing. (FH) K.-H. Röß,
DaimlerChrysler AG, Stuttgart;
Prof. Dr.-Ing. habil. E.-C. v. Glasner,
DaimlerChrysler AG, Stuttgart;
Dipl.-Ing. B. Kant;
Dipl.-Ing. G. Klein, Knorr-Bremse SfN,
Schwieberdingen;
Dipl.-Ing. (FH) R. Klement, Knorr-
Bremse SfN, Schwieberdingen

*Vehicle Stabilization Systems*
Dipl.-Ing. (FH) H.-P. Stumpp;
Dr.-Ing. A. van Zanten; Dipl.-Ing. G. Pfaff;
Dr.-Ing. R. Erhardt;
Dipl.-Ing. F. Schwab, Knorr-Bremse SfN,
Schwieberdingen;
Dr.-Ing. F. Hecker, Knorr-Bremse SfN,
Schwieberdingen

*Electronic Commercial-Vehicle Brake
Management as the Platform for
Driver-Assistance Systems*
Prof. Dr.-Ing. habil. E.-C. v. Glasner,
DaimlerChrysler AG, Stuttgart

**Vehicle Bodies**
*Road-Vehicle Systematics*
Dipl.-Ing. D. Scheunert,
DaimlerChrysler AG, Sindelfingen

*Vehicle Bodies, Passenger Cars and
Light Commercial Vehicles*
Dipl.-Ing. D. Scheunert,
DaimlerChrysler AG, Sindelfingen;
Dipl.-Ing. H. Winter,
DaimlerChrysler AG, Stuttgart

*Lighting*
Dr.-Ing. M. Hamm, Automotive Lighting
Reutlingen GmbH; Dipl.-Ing. D. Boebel,
Automotive Lighting Reutlingen GmbH;
Dipl.-Ing. T. Spingler, Automotive Light-
ing Reutlingen GmbH

*Automotive Windshield and
Window Glass*
Dr. rer. nat. D. Linnhöfer,
SAINT-GOBAIN SEKURIT, Aachen

*Windshield Washer Systems*
Dipl.-Ing. (FH) A. Geis

*Heating, Ventilation and Air Conditioning*
Dipl.-Ing. G. Schweizer,
Behr GmbH & Co, Stuttgart;
J. Fath, Freudenberg Vliesstoffe KG,
Weinheim;
Dipl.-Ing. P. Reiser, J. Eberspächer
GmbH & Co. KG, Esslingen

**Automotive Electrical Systems**
*Vehicle Electrical Systems,
Starter Batteries, Alternators*
Ing. (grad.) R. Leunig;
Dr.-Ing. G. Richter, VB Autobatterie
GmbH, Hannover; Dipl.-Ing. R. Meyer

*Starting Systems*
Dipl.-Ing. C. Krondorfer; Dr.-Ing. I.
Richter

*Symbols and Circuit Diagrams*
Editorial Staff

*Conductor Dimensions*
Dipl.-Ing. A. Kerber, DST Dräxlmaier
Systemtechnik GmbH, Vilsbiburg;
Dipl.-Ing. M. Gentzsch, DST Dräxlmaier
Systemtechnik GmbH, Vilsbiburg

*Connectors*
Dipl.-Ing. W. Gansert

*Electromagnetic Compatibility (EMC)*
Dr.-Ing. W. Pfaff

**Vehicle Locking Systems**
*Acoustic Signaling Devices*
Dipl.-Ing. (FH) MBA J. Bowe

*Central Locking System*
A. Walther

*Locking systems*
Dr.-Ing. B. Kordowski

**Safety and Convenience**
*Occupant Safety Systems*
Dipl.-Ing. B. Mattes

*Power Windows, Power Sunroofs*
Dipl.-Ing. R. Kurzmann

*Seat and Steering-Column Adjustment*
Dr.-Ing. G. Hartz

*Biometric Systems*
Dr.-Ing. J. Lichtermann

*Driver-Assistance Systems*
Prof. Dr.-Ing. P. Knoll

*Adaptive Cruise Control (ACC)*
Dr. rer. nat. H. Winner;
Dr. rer. nat. H. Olbrich;
Dr.-Ing. H. Schramm, Knorr-Bremse SfN,
Schwieberdingen

**Information and Communication**
*Data Processing and Communication
Networks in Motor Vehicles*
Dr. rer. nat. V. Denner;
Dr. rer. nat. J. Maier;
Dr. phil. nat. D. Kraft;
Dipl.-Ing. G. Spreitz

*Instrumentation*
Prof. Dr.-Ing. P. Knoll;
Dr.-Ing. B. Herzog

*Vehicle Information Systems*
Dipl.-Ing. H. Kauff

*Trip Recorders*
Dipl.-Wirtschaftsingenieur T. Förster,
Siemens VDO Automotive AG,
Villingen-Schwenningen

*Parking systems*
Prof. Dr.-Ing. P. Knoll

*Analog Signal Transmission*
Dr.-Ing. J. Passoke

*Digital Signal Transmission*
Dipl.-Ing. G. Spreitz

*Car Radios with Auxiliary Equipment,
Vehicle Antennas*
Dr.-Ing. J. Passoke; B. Knerr;
E. Neumann

*Mobile and Data Radio*
Dr.-Ing. J. Wazeck

*Mobile Information Services*
Dipl.-Ing. (FH) M. Heßling

*Navigation Systems,
Traffic Telematics*
Dipl.-Ing. E. P. Neukirchner

*Fleet Management*
R. Hoechter

*Multimedia Systems*
Dipl.-Ing. G. Spreitz

**Development Methods and Processes**
*Development Methods and Application Tools for Electronic Systems*
Dipl.-Ing. J. Schäuffele, ETAS

*Sound Design*
Dipl.-Ing. R. von Sivers,
Dr. Ing. h.c. F. Porsche AG, Weissach

*Vehicle Wind Tunnels*
Dipl.-Ing. M. Preiß,
Dr. Ing. h.c. F. Porsche AG, Weissach

*Environmental Management*
Dipl.-Ing. B. Martin, AUDI AG,
Neckarsulm

**Workshop Technology**
R. Heinzmann;
Dipl.-Ing. (FH) F. Zauner;
Dipl.-Wirtsch.-Ing. S. Sohnle;
Dipl.-Ing., MBE, R. Nossek;
H. Weinmann;
Dipl.-Ing. T. Spingler,
Automotive Lighting Reutlingen GmbH;
Dipl.-Betriebsw. (BA) U. Peckolt, Automotive Testing Technologies GmbH, Kehl;
G. Mauderer;
G. Lemke;
Dipl.-Ing. C. Probst;
Dipl.-Ing. (FH) H.-G. Weißhaar

**Motorsports**
Dipl.-Red. U. Michelt;
Dipl.-Ing. T. Nickels,
MAN Nutzfahrzeuge AG, München

**Automotive Hydraulics and Pneumatics**
*Automotive Hydraulics*
Dipl.-Ing. H. Lödige; Dipl.-Ing. K. Griese;
Ing. (grad.) D. Bertsch; Dipl.-Ing. W. Kötter;
Dipl.-Ing. M. Bing;
Dipl.-Ing. (FH) W. Steudel;
Dipl.-Ing. G. Bredenfeld

*Automotive Pneumatics*
Ing. (grad.) P. Berg, Knorr-Bremse SfN,
Schwieberdingen

**Appendices**
*International Registration Plates*
Editorial Staff

*Alphabets and Numbers*
Editorial Staff

# Quantities and units

## SI units

SI means "Système International d'Unités" (International System of Units). The system is laid down in ISO 31 and ISO 1000 (ISO: International Organization for Standardization) and for Germany in DIN 1301 (DIN: Deutsches Institut für Normung – German Institute for Standardization).

SI units comprise the seven base SI units and coherent units derived from these base SI units using a numerical factor of 1.

### Base SI units

| Base quantity and symbols | | Base SI unit Name | Symbol |
|---|---|---|---|
| Length | $l$ | meter | m |
| Mass | $m$ | kilogram | kg |
| Time | $t$ | second | s |
| Electric current | $I$ | ampere | A |
| Thermodynamic temperature | $T$ | kelvin | K |
| Amount of substance | $n$ | mole | mol |
| Luminous intensity | $I$ | candela | cd |

All other quantities and units are derived from the base quantities and base units. The international unit of force is thus obtained by applying Newton's Law:

force = mass $\times$ acceleration
$F = m \cdot a$

where $m$ = 1 kg and $a$ = 1 m/s², thus
$F$ = 1 kg · 1 m/s² = 1 kg · m/s² = 1 N (newton).

### Definitions of the base SI units

1 meter is defined as the distance which light travels in a vacuum in 1/299,792,458 seconds (17th CGPM, 1983)[1]. The meter is therefore defined using the speed of light in a vacuum, $c$ = 299,792,458 m/s, and no longer by the wavelength of the radiation emitted by the krypton nuclide $^{86}$Kr. The meter was originally defined as the forty-millionth part of a terrestrial meridian (standard meter, Paris, 1875).

1 kilogram is the mass of the international prototype kilogram (1st CGPM, 1889 and 3rd CGPM, 1901)[1].

1 second is defined as the duration of 9,192,631,770 periods of the radiation corresponding to the transition between the two hyperfine levels of the ground state of atoms of the $^{133}$Cs nuclide (13th CGPM, 1967)[1].

1 ampere is defined as that constant electric current which, if maintained in two straight parallel conductors of infinite length, of negligible circular cross-sections, and placed 1 meter apart in a vacuum, will produce between these conductors a force equal to 2 x 10$^{-7}$ N per meter of length (9th CGPM, 1948)[1].

1 kelvin is defined as the fraction 1/273.16 of the thermodynamic temperature of the triple point[2] of water (13th CGPM, 1967)[1].

1 mole is defined as the amount of substance of a system which contains as many elementary entities as there are atoms in 0.012 kilogram of the carbon nuclide $^{12}$C. When the mole is used, the elementary entities must be specified and may be atoms, molecules, ions, electrons, other particles, or specified groups of such particles (14th CGPM, 1971)[1].

1 candela is the luminous intensity in a given direction of a source which emits monochromatic radiation of frequency 540 x 1,012 hertz and of which the radiant intensity in that direction is 1/683 watt per steradian (16th CGPM, 1979)[1].

---

[1] CGPM: Conférence Générale des Poids et Mesures (General Conference on Weights and Measures).

[2] Fixed point on the international temperature scale. The triple point is the only point at which all three phases of water (solid, liquid and gaseous) are in equilibrium (at a pressure of 1,013.25 hPa). This temperature of 273.16 K is 0.01 K above the freezing point of water (273.15 K).

### Decimal multiples and fractions of SI units

Decimal multiples and fractions of SI units are denoted by prefixes before the name of the unit or by prefix symbols before the unit symbol. The prefix symbol is placed immediately in front of the unit symbol to form a coherent unit, such as the milligram (mg). Multiple prefixes, such as microkilogram ($\mu$kg), may <u>not</u> be used. Prefixes are not to be used before the units of angular degree, minute and second, the units of time, minute, hour, day, and year, and the unit of temperature, degree Celsius.

| Prefix symbol | Prefix of ten | Power | Name |
|---|---|---|---|
| atto | a | $10^{-18}$ | trillionth |
| femto | f | $10^{-15}$ | thousand billionth |
| pico | p | $10^{-12}$ | billionth |
| nano | n | $10^{-9}$ | thousand millionth |
| micro | $\mu$ | $10^{-6}$ | millionth |
| milli | m | $10^{-3}$ | thousandth |
| centi | c | $10^{-2}$ | hundredth |
| deci | d | $10^{-1}$ | tenth |
| deca | da | $10^{1}$ | ten |
| hecto | h | $10^{2}$ | hundred |
| kilo | k | $10^{3}$ | thousand |
| mega | M | $10^{6}$ | million |
| giga | G | $10^{9}$ | milliard[1] |
| tera | T | $10^{12}$ | billion[1] |
| peta | P | $10^{15}$ | thousand billion |
| exa | E | $10^{18}$ | trillion |

## Legal units

The Law on Units in Metrology of 2 July 1969 and the related implementing order of 26 June 1970 specify the use of "Legal units" in business and official transactions in Germany[2]. Legal units are:
– the SI units
– decimal multiples and submultiples of the SI units
– other permitted units; see the tables on the following pages

Legal units are used in the Bosch Automotive Handbook. In many sections, values are also given in units of the technical system of units (e.g. in parentheses) to the extent considered necessary.

## Systems of units not to be used

### The physical system of units

Like the SI system of units, the physical system of units used the base quantities length, mass and time. However, the base units used for these quantities were the centimeter (cm), gram (g), and second (s) (CGS System).

### The technical system of units

The technical system of units used the following base quantities and base units:

| Base quantity | Base unit Name | Symbol |
|---|---|---|
| Length | meter | m |
| Force | kilopond | kp |
| Time | second | s |

Newton's Law,
$$F = m \cdot a,$$
provides the link between the international system of units and the technical system of units, where force due to weight $G$ is substituted for $F$, and acceleration of free fall $g$ is substituted for $a$.

In contrast to mass, acceleration of free fall, and therefore force due to weight, depend on location. The standard value of acceleration of free fall is defined as $g_n = 9.80665 \, \text{m/s}^2$ (DIN 1305). The approximate value is generally acceptable in technical calculations:
$$g = 9.81 \, \text{m/s}^2$$

1 kp is the force with which a mass of 1 kg exerts pressure on the surface beneath it at a place on the earth: where
$$G = m \cdot g$$
thus
$$1 \, \text{kp} = 1 \, \text{kg} \cdot 9.81 \, \text{m/s}^2 = 9.81 \, \text{N}$$

---

[1] In the U.S.A.: $10^9$ = 1 billion, $10^{12}$ = 1 trillion.

[2] Also valid: "Gesetz zur Änderung des Gesetzes über Einheiten im Meßwesen" dated 6 July 1973; "Verordnung zur Änderung der Ausführungsverordnung" dated 27 November 1973; "Zweite Verordnung zur Änderung der Ausführungsverordnung .." dated 12 December 1977.

## Quantities and units

Overview (from DIN 1301)

The following table gives a survey of the most important physical quantities and their standardized symbols, and includes a selection of the legal units specified for these quantities. Additional legal units can be formed by adding prefixes (P. 23). For this reason, the column "Others" only gives the decimal multiples and submultiples of the SI units which have their own names. Units which are not to be used are given in the last column together with their conversion formulas. Page numbers refer to conversion tables.

| Quantity and symbol | Legal units | | | Relationship | Remarks and units not to be used, incl. their conversion |
|---|---|---|---|---|---|
| | SI | Others | Name | | |
| **1. Length, area, volume** (P. 29 to 31) | | | | | |
| Length $l$ | m | | meter | | $1\,\mu$ (micron) $= 1\,\mu m$ |
| | | nm | international nautical mile | 1 nm = 1,852 m | $1\,\text{Å}$ (Ångström) $= 10^{-10}$ m $1$ X.U. (X-unit) $\approx 10^{-13}$ m $1$ p (typographical point) $= 0.376$ mm |
| Area $A$ | m² | | square meter | | |
| | | a | Ar | 1 a = 100 m² | |
| | | ha | hectare | 1 ha = 100 a = $10^4$ m² | |
| Volume $V$ | m³ | | cubic meter | | |
| | | l, L | liter | 1 l = 1 L = 1 dm³ | |
| **2. Angle** (P. 31) | | | | | |
| (Plane) angle $\alpha, \beta$ etc. | rad [1] | | radian | $1\text{ rad} = \dfrac{1\text{ m arc}}{1\text{ m radius}}$ | |
| | | ° | degree | 1 rad = 180°/π $= 57.296° \approx 57.3°$ $1° = 0.017453$ rad | $1\,L$ (right angle) $= 90°$ $= (\pi/2)$ rad $= 100$ gon $1g$ (centesimal degree) $= 1$ gon |
| | | ′ | minute | $1° = 60′ = 3,600″$ | $1c$ (centesimal minute) $= 1$ cgon |
| | | ″ | second | 1 gon = (π/200) rad | $1cc$ (centesimal second) $= 0.1$ mgon |
| | | gon | gon | | |
| Solid angle $\Omega$ | sr | | steradian | $1\text{ sr} = \dfrac{1\text{ m}^2 \text{ spherical surface}}{1\text{ m}^2 \text{ sphere radius}^2}$ | |
| **3. Mass** (P. 32 to 33) | | | | | |
| Mass (weight) [2] $m$ | kg | | kilogram | | $1\,\gamma$ (gamma) $= 1\mu g$ |
| | | g | gram | | 1 quintal $= 100$ kg |
| | | t | ton | 1 t = 1 Mg = $10^3$ kg | 1 Kt (karat) $= 0.2$ g |

---

[1] The unit rad (P. 31) can be replaced by the numeral 1 in calculations.
[2] The term "weight" is ambiguous in everyday usage; it is used to denote mass as well as weight (DIN 1305).

| Quantity and symbol | Legal units | | | Relationship | Remarks and units not to be used, incl. their conversion |
|---|---|---|---|---|---|
| | SI | Others | Name | | |
| Density $\varrho$ | kg/m³ | | | $1 \text{ kg/dm}^3 = 1 \text{ kg/}l$ $= 1 \text{ g/cm}^3$ $= 1,000 \text{ kg/m}^3$ | Weight per unit volume $\gamma$ (kp/dm³ or p/cm³). Conversion: The numerical value of the weight per unit volume in kp/dm³ is roughly equal to the numerical value of the density in kg/dm³ |
| | | $\dfrac{\text{kg}}{\text{dm}^3}$ | | | |
| | | kg/$l$ | | | |
| | | g/cm³ | | | |
| Moment of inertia (mass moment, 2nd order) $J$ | kg·m² | | | $J = m \cdot i^2$ $i$ = radius of gyration | Flywheel effect $G \cdot D^2$. Conversion: numerical value of $G \cdot D^2$ in kp · m² = 4 x numerical value of $J$ in kg · m² |

## 4. Time quantities (P. 38)

| Time, duration, interval $t$ | s | | second[1] | | In the energy industry, one year is calculated at 8,760 hours |
|---|---|---|---|---|---|
| | | min | minute[1] | 1 min = 60 s | |
| | | h | hour[1] | 1 h = 60 min | |
| | | d | day | 1 d = 24 h | |
| | | a | year | | |
| Frequency $f$ | Hz | | hertz | 1 Hz = 1/s | |
| Rotational speed (frequency of rotation) $n$ | s⁻¹ | | | 1 s⁻¹ = 1/s | r/min (revolutions per minute) is still permissible for expressing rotational speed, but is better replaced by rpm (1 r/min = 1 rpm) |
| | | rpm 1/min | | 1 rpm = 1/min = (1/60)s⁻¹ | |
| Angular frequency $\omega = 2\pi f$ | s⁻¹ | | | | |
| Velocity $v$ | m/s | km/h | | 1 km/h = (1/3.6) m/s | |
| | | kn | knot | 1 kn = 1 sm/h = 1.852 km/h | |
| Acceleration $a$ | m/s² | | | acceleration of free fall $g$ P.13 | |
| Angular velocity $\omega$ | rad/s [2] | | | | |
| Angular acceleration $\alpha$ | rad/s² [2] | | | | |

## 5. Force, energy, power (PP. 34 to 35)

| Force $F$ Force due to weight $G$ | N N | | newton | 1 N = 1 kg · m/s² | 1 p (pond) = 9.80665 mN 1 kp (kilopond) = 9.80665 N ≈ 10 N 1 dyn (dyne) = 10⁻⁵ N |
|---|---|---|---|---|---|

[1] Clock time: h, min, s written as superscripts, example: 3ʰ 25ᵐ 6ˢ
[2] The unit rad can be replaced by the numeral 1 in calculations.

| Quantity and symbol | Legal units | | | Relationship | Remarks and units not to be used, incl. their conversion |
|---|---|---|---|---|---|
| | SI | Others | Name | | |
| Pressure, gen. $p$ | Pa | | pascal | $1\ Pa = 1\ N/m^2$ | 1 at (technical atmosphere) = 1 kp/cm² |
| Absolute pressure $p_{abs}$ | | bar | bar | $1\ bar = 10^5\ Pa$ $= 10\ N/cm^2$ $1\ \mu bar = 0.1\ Pa$ $1\ mbar = 1\ hPa$ | = 0.980665 bar ≈ 1 bar 1 atm (physical atmosphere) = 1.01325 bar[1]) 1 mm W.C. (water column) |
| Atmospheric pressure $p_{amb}$ Gage pressure $p_e$ $p_e = p_{abs} - p_{amb}$ | Gage pressure, etc. is no longer denoted by a unit symbol, but rather by a formula symbol. Vacuum is given as negative gage pressure. Examples: previously now 3 atg $p_e$ = 2.94 bar ≈ 3 bar 10 ata $p_{abs}$ = 9.81 bar ≈ 10 bar 0.4 atu $p_e$ = −0.39 bar ≈ −0.4 bar | | | | = 1 kp/m² = 0.0980665 hPa ≈ 0.1 hPa 1 torr = 1 mm Hg (mercury column) = 1.33322 hPa dyn/cm² = 1 μbar |
| Mechanical stress $\sigma, \tau$ | N/m² | | | $1\ N/m^2 = 1\ Pa$ | 1 kp/mm² = 9.81 N/mm² ≈ 10 N/mm² 1 kp/cm² ≈ 0.1 N/mm² |
| | | N/mm² | | $1\ N/mm^2 = 1\ MPa$ | |
| Hardness (P. 310) | Brinell and Vickers hardness are no longer given in kp/mm². Instead, an abbreviation of the relevant hardness scale is written as the unit after the numerical value used previously (including an indication of the test force, etc., where applicable). | | | | Examples: previously now HB = 350 kp/mm² 350 HB |
| | | | | | HV30 = 720 kp/mm² 720 HV30 |
| | | | | | HRC = 60 60 HRC |
| Energy, work $E, W$ | J | | joule [dschul] | $1\ J = 1\ N \cdot m = 1\ W \cdot s$ $= 1\ kg\ m^2/s^2$ | 1 kp · m (kilopondmeter) = 9.81 J ≈ 10 J |
| Heat, quantity of heat $Q$ (P. 27) | | W · s | watt-second | | 1 HP · h (HP hour) = 0.7355 kW · h ≈ 0.74 kW · h 1 erg (erg) = 10⁻⁷ J |
| | | kW · h | kilowatt-hour | $1\ kW \cdot h = 3.6\ MJ$ | 1 kcal (kilocalorie) = 4.1868 kJ ≈ 4.2 kJ |
| | | eV | electron-volt | $1\ eV = 1.60219 \cdot 10^{-19} J$ | 1 cal (calorie) = 4.1868 J ≈ 4.2 J |
| Torque $M$ | N · m | | newton-meter | | 1 kp · m (kilopondmeter) = 9.81 N · m ≈ 10 N · m |
| Power $P$ Heat flow $\dot{Q}, \Phi$ (P. 27) | W | | watt | $1\ W = 1\ J/s = 1\ N \cdot m/s$ | 1 kp · m/s = 9.81 W ≈ 10 W 1 HP (horsepower) = 0.7355 kW ≈ 0.74 kW 1 kcal/s = 4.1868 kW ≈ 4.2 kW 1 kcal/h = 1.163 W |

## 6. Viscosimetric quantities (P. 37)

| Dynamic viscosity $\eta$ | Pa · s | | pascal-second | $1\ Pa \cdot s = 1\ N\ s/m^2$ $= 1\ kg/(s \cdot m)$ | 1 P (poise) = 0.1 Pa · s 1 cP (centipoise) = 1 mPa · s |
|---|---|---|---|---|---|
| Kinematic viscosity $\nu$ | m²/s | | | $1\ m^2/s$ $= 1\ Pa \cdot s/(kg/m^3)$ | 1 St (stokes) = 10⁻⁴ m²/s = 1 cm²/s 1 cSt (centistokes) = 1 mm²/s |

---

[1]) 1.01325 bar = 1013.25 hPa = 760 mm mercury column is the standard value for atmospheric pressure.

| Quantity and symbol | | Legal units | | | Relationship | Remarks and units not to be used, incl. their conversion |
|---|---|---|---|---|---|---|
| | | SI | Others | Name | | |

## 7. Temperature and heat (S. 36)

| Quantity and symbol | | SI | Others | Name | Relationship | Remarks |
|---|---|---|---|---|---|---|
| Temperature | $T$ $t$ | K | | kelvin | $t = (T - 273.15\ \text{K})\,\dfrac{°C}{K}$ | |
| | | | °C | degree Celsius | | |
| Temperature difference | $\Delta T$ $\Delta t$ | K | | kelvin | $1\ \text{K} = 1\,°C$ | |
| | | | °C | degree Celsius | | |
| | | In the case of composite units, express temperature differences in K, e.g. kJ/(m · h · K); tolerances for temperatures in degrees, for example, have the following notation: $t = (40 \pm 2)\,°C$ or $t = 40\,°C \pm 2\,°C$ or $t = 40\,°C \pm 2\,K$. | | | | |

Refer to 5. for quantity of heat and heat flow.

| Quantity | | SI | | | | Remarks |
|---|---|---|---|---|---|---|
| Specific heat capacity (spec. heat) | $c$ | $\dfrac{J}{kg \cdot K}$ | | | | 1 kcal/(kg · grd) = 4.187 kJ/(kg · K) ≈ 4.2 kJ/(kg · K) |
| Thermal conductivity | $\lambda$ | $\dfrac{W}{m \cdot K}$ | | | | 1 kcal/(m · h · grd) = 1.163 W/(m · K) ≈ 1.2 W/(m · K) 1 cal/(cm · s · grd) = 4.187 W/(cm · K) 1 W/(m · K) = 3.6 kJ/(m · h · K) |

## 8. Electrical quantities (P. 70)

| Quantity | | SI | Others | Name | Relationship | Remarks |
|---|---|---|---|---|---|---|
| Electric current | $I$ | A | | ampere | | |
| Electric potential | $U$ | V | | volt | $1\ \text{V} = 1\ \text{W/A}$ | |
| Electric conductance | $G$ | S | | siemens | $1\ \text{S} = 1\ \text{A/V} = 1/\Omega$ | |
| Electric resistance | $R$ | $\Omega$ | | ohm | $1\ \Omega = 1/\text{S} = 1\ \text{V/A}$ | |
| Quantity of electricity, electric charge | $Q$ | C | | coulomb | $1\ \text{C} = 1\ \text{A} \cdot \text{s}$ | |
| | | | A · h | ampere-hour | $1\ \text{A} \cdot \text{h} = 3{,}600\ \text{C}$ | |
| Electric capacitance | $C$ | F | | farad | $1\ \text{F} = 1\ \text{C/V}$ | |
| Electric flux density, electric displacement | $D$ | C/m² | | | | |
| Electric field strength | $E$ | V/m | | | | |

| Quantity and symbol | | Legal units | | Name | Relationship | Remarks and units not to be used, incl. their conversion |
|---|---|---|---|---|---|---|
| | | SI | Others | | | |

## 9. Magnetic quantities (P. 70)

| Quantity and symbol | | SI | Others | Name | Relationship | Remarks and units not to be used, incl. their conversion |
|---|---|---|---|---|---|---|
| Magnetic flux | $\Phi$ | Wb | | weber | $1\ Wb = 1\ V \cdot s$ | 1 M (maxwell) = $10^{-8}$ Wb |
| Magnetic flux density, induction | $B$ | T | | tesla | $1\ T = 1\ Wb/m^2$ | 1 G (gauss) = $10^{-4}$ T |
| Inductance | $L$ | H | | henry | $1\ H = 1\ Wb/A$ | |
| Magnetic field strength | $H$ | A/m | | | $1\ A/m = 1\ N/Wb$ | 1 Oe (oersted) $= 10^3/(4\,\pi)$ A/m $= 79.58$ A/m |

## 10. Photometric quantities and units (P. 49)

| Quantity and symbol | | SI | Others | Name | Relationship | Remarks and units not to be used, incl. their conversion |
|---|---|---|---|---|---|---|
| Luminous intensity | $I$ | cd | | candela [1]) | | |
| Luminance | $L$ | cd/m² | | | | 1 sb (stilb) = $10^4$ cd/m² <br> 1 asb (apostilb) = $1/\pi$ cd/m² |
| Luminous flux | $\Phi$ | lm | | lumen | $1\ lm = 1\ cd \cdot sr$ (sr = steradian) | |
| Illuminance | $E$ | lx | | lux | $1\ lx = 1\ lm/m^2$ | |

## 11. Quantities used in atom physics and other fields

| Quantity and symbol | | SI | Others | Name | Relationship | Remarks and units not to be used, incl. their conversion |
|---|---|---|---|---|---|---|
| Energy | $W$ | | eV | electron-volt | $1\ eV = 1.60219 \cdot 10^{-19}$J <br> $1\ MeV = 10^6$ eV | |
| Activity of a radioactive substance | $A$ | Bq | | becquerel | $1\ Bq = 1\ s^{-1}$ | 1 Ci (curie) = $3.7 \cdot 10^{10}$ Bq |
| Absorbed dose | $D$ | Gy | | gray | $1\ Gy = 1\ J/kg$ | 1 rd (rad) = $10^{-2}$ Gy |
| Dose equivalent | $Dq$ | Sv | | sievert | $1\ Sv = 1\ J/kg$ | 1 rem (rem) = $10^{-2}$ Sv |
| Absorbed dose rate | $\dot{D}$ | | | | $1\ Gy/s = 1\ W/kg$ | |
| Ion dose | $J$ | C/kg | | | | 1 R (röntgen) $= 258 \cdot 10^{-6}$C/kg |
| Ion dose rate | $\dot{J}$ | A/kg | | | | |
| Amount of substance | $n$ | mol | | mol | | |

---

[1]) The tonic stress is on the second syllable: can<u>de</u>la.

## Conversion of units

### Units of length

| Unit | | X.U. | pm | Å | nm | μm | mm | cm | dm | m | km |
|---|---|---|---|---|---|---|---|---|---|---|---|
| 1 X.U. | ≈ | 1 | $10^{-1}$ | $10^{-3}$ | $10^{-4}$ | $10^{-7}$ | $10^{-10}$ | $10^{-11}$ | $10^{-12}$ | $10^{-13}$ | — |
| 1 pm | = | 10 | 1 | $10^{-2}$ | $10^{-3}$ | $10^{-6}$ | $10^{-9}$ | $10^{-10}$ | $10^{-11}$ | $10^{-12}$ | — |
| 1 Å | = | $10^{3}$ | $10^{2}$ | 1 | $10^{-1}$ | $10^{-4}$ | $10^{-7}$ | $10^{-8}$ | $10^{-9}$ | $10^{-10}$ | — |
| 1 nm | = | $10^{4}$ | $10^{3}$ | 10 | 1 | $10^{-3}$ | $10^{-6}$ | $10^{-7}$ | $10^{-8}$ | $10^{-9}$ | $10^{-12}$ |
| 1 μm | = | $10^{7}$ | $10^{6}$ | $10^{4}$ | $10^{3}$ | 1 | $10^{-3}$ | $10^{-4}$ | $10^{-5}$ | $10^{-6}$ | $10^{-9}$ |
| 1 mm | = | $10^{10}$ | $10^{9}$ | $10^{7}$ | $10^{6}$ | $10^{3}$ | 1 | $10^{-1}$ | $10^{-2}$ | $10^{-3}$ | $10^{-6}$ |
| 1 cm | = | $10^{11}$ | $10^{10}$ | $10^{8}$ | $10^{7}$ | $10^{4}$ | 10 | 1 | $10^{-1}$ | $10^{-2}$ | $10^{-5}$ |
| 1 dm | = | $10^{12}$ | $10^{11}$ | $10^{9}$ | $10^{8}$ | $10^{5}$ | $10^{2}$ | 10 | 1 | $10^{-1}$ | $10^{-4}$ |
| 1 m | = | — | — | $10^{12}$ | $10^{10}$ | $10^{9}$ | $10^{6}$ | $10^{3}$ | $10^{2}$ | 10 | 1 | $10^{-3}$ |
| 1 km | = | — | — | — | $10^{12}$ | $10^{9}$ | $10^{6}$ | $10^{5}$ | $10^{4}$ | $10^{3}$ | 1 |

Do not use X.U. (X-unit) and Å (ångström)

| Unit | | in | ft | yd | mile | n mile | mm | m | km |
|---|---|---|---|---|---|---|---|---|---|
| 1 in | = | 1 | 0.08333 | 0.02778 | — | — | 25.4 | 0.0254 | — |
| 1 ft | = | 12 | 1 | 0.33333 | — | — | 304.8 | 0.3048 | — |
| 1 yd | = | 36 | 3 | 1 | — | — | 914.4 | 0.9144 | — |
| 1 mile | = | 63,360 | 5,280 | 1,760 | 1 | 0.86898 | — | 1,609.34 | 1.609 |
| 1 n mile [1]) | = | 72,913 | 6,076.1 | 2,025.4 | 1.1508 | 1 | — | 1,852 | 1.852 |
| 1 mm | = | 0.03937 | $3.281 \cdot 10^{-3}$ | $1.094 \cdot 10^{-3}$ | — | — | 1 | 0.001 | $10^{-6}$ |
| 1 m | = | 39.3701 | 3.2808 | 1.0936 | — | — | 1,000 | 1 | 0.001 |
| 1 km | = | 39,370 | 3,280.8 | 1,093.6 | 0.62137 | 0.53996 | $10^{6}$ | 1,000 | 1 |

in = inch, ft = foot, y = yard, mile = statute mile, n mile = nautical mile

#### Other British and U.S. units of length
1 μin (microinch) = 0.0254 μm
1 mil (milliinch) = 0.0254 mm
1 link = 201.17 mm
1 rod = 1 pole = 1 perch = 5.5 yd
  = 5.0292 m
1 chain = 22 yd = 20.1168 m
1 furlong = 220 yd = 201.168 m
1 fathom = 2 yd = 1.8288 m

#### Astronomical units
1 l.y. (light year)
  = $9.46053 \cdot 10^{15}$ m (distance traveled by
  electromagnetic waves in 1 year)
1 AU (astronomical unit)
  = $1.496 \cdot 10^{11}$ m (mean distance from
  earth to sun)

1 pc (parsec, parallax second)
  = 206,265 AU = $3.0857 \cdot 10^{16}$ m
  (distance at which the AU subtends
  an angle of one second of arc)

#### Do not use
1 line (watch & clock making) = 2.256 mm
1 p (typographical point)
  = 0.376 mm
1 German mile = 7,500 m
1 geographical mile = 7,420.4 m
  (≈ 4 arc minutes of equator)

---

[1]) 1 n mile = 1 nm = 1 international nautical mile
≈ 1 arc minute of the degree of longitude 1 knot
= 1 n mile/h = 1.852 km/h

### Units of area

| Unit | | in² | ft² | yd² | acre | mile² | cm² | m² | a | ha | km² |
|---|---|---|---|---|---|---|---|---|---|---|---|
| 1 in² | = | 1 | | – | – | – | 6.4516 | – | – | – | – |
| 1 ft² | = | 144 | 1 | 0.1111 | – | – | 929 | 0.0929 | – | – | – |
| 1 yd² | = | 1,296 | 9 | 1 | – | – | 8,361 | 0.8361 | – | – | – |
| 1 acre | = | – | – | 4,840 | 1 | 0.16 | – | 4,047 | 40.47 | 0.40 | – |
| 1 mile² | = | – | – | – | 6.40 | 1 | – | – | 259 | 2.59 | |
| 1 cm² | = | 0.155 | – | – | – | – | 1 | 0.01 | – | – | – |
| 1 m² | = | 1,550 | 10.76 | 1.196 | – | – | 10,000 | 1 | 0.01 | – | – |
| 1 a | = | | 1,076 | 119.6 | – | – | – | 100 | 1 | 0.01 | – |
| 1 ha | = | – | – | – | 2.47 | – | – | 10,000 | 100 | 1 | 0.01 |
| 1 km² | = | – | – | – | 247 | 0.3861 | – | – | 10,000 | 100 | 1 |

in² = square inch (sq in)
ft² = square foot (sq ft)
yd² = square yard (sq yd)
mile² = square mile (sq mile)

### Paper sizes
(DIN 476)

Dimensions in mm

| | | | | |
|---|---|---|---|---|
| A 0 | 841 x 1189 | | A 6 | 105 x 148 |
| A 1 | 594 x 841 | | A 7 | 74 x 105 |
| A 2 | 420 x 594 | | A 8 | 52 x 74 |
| A 3 | 297 x 420 | | A 9 | 37 x 52 |
| A 4 | 210 x 297[1] | | A 10 | 26 x 37 |
| A 5 | 148 x 210 | | | |

### Units of volume

| Unit | | in³ | ft³ | yd³ | gal (U.K.) | gal (U.S.) | cm³ | dm³(l) | m³ |
|---|---|---|---|---|---|---|---|---|---|
| 1 in³ | = | 1 | – | – | – | – | 16.3871 | 0.01639 | – |
| 1 ft³ | = | 1,728 | 1 | 0.03704 | 6.229 | 7.481 | – | 28.3168 | 0.01639 |
| 1 yd³ | = | 46,656 | 27 | 1 | 168.18 | 201.97 | – | 764.555 | 0.02832 |
| 1 gal (U.K.) | = | 277.42 | 0.16054 | – | 1 | 1.20095 | 4,546.09 | 4.54609 | 0.76456 |
| 1 gal (U.S.) | = | 231 | 0.13368 | – | 0.83267 | 1 | 3,785.41 | 3.78541 | – |
| 1 cm³ | = | 0.06102 | – | – | – | – | 1 | 0.001 | – |
| 1 dm³ (l) | = | 61.0236 | 0.03531 | 0.00131 | 0.21997 | 0.26417 | 1,000 | 1 | 0.001 |
| 1 m³ | = | 61,023.6 | 35.315 | 1.30795 | 219.969 | 264.172 | 10⁶ | 1,000 | 1 |

in³ = cubic inch (cu in)
ft³ = cubic foot (cu ft)
yd³ = cubic yard (cu yd)
gal = gallon

### Other units of volume

*United Kingdom (U.K.)*
1 fl oz (fluid ounce) = 0.028413 *l*
1 pt (pint) = 0.56826 *l*
1 qt (quart) = 2 pt = 1.13652 *l*
1 gal (gallon) = 4 qt = 4.5461 *l*
1 bbl (barrel) = 36 gal = 163.6 *l*

Units of dry measure:
1 bu (bushel) = 8 gal = 36.369 *l*

---

[1] Customary format in the U.S.A.: 216 mm x 279 mm

*United States (U.S.)*
1 fl oz (fluid ounce) = 0.029574 $l$
1 liq pt (liquid pint) = 0.47318 $l$
1 liq quart = 2 liq pt = 0.94635 $l$
1 gal (gallon) = 231 in³ = 4 liq quarts
= 3.7854 $l$
1 liq bbl (liquid barrel) = 119.24 $l$
1 barrel petroleum[1]) = 42 gal = 158.99 $l$

Units of dry measure:
1 bushel = 35.239 dm³

*Volume of ships*
1 RT (register ton) = 100 ft³
= 2.832 m³; GRT (gross RT) = total
shipping space, net register ton =
cargo space of a ship
GTI (gross tonnage index) = total volume
of ship (shell) in m³
1 ocean ton = 40 ft³ = 1.1327 m³

## Units of angle

| Unit[2]) | ° | ′ | ″ | rad | gon | cgon | mgon |
|---|---|---|---|---|---|---|---|
| 1° = | 1 | 60 | 3,600 | 0.017453 | 1.1111 | 111.11 | 1111.11 |
| 1′ = | 0.016667 | 1 | 60 | – | 0.018518 | 1.85185 | 18.5185 |
| 1″ = | 0.0002778 | 0.016667 | 1 | – | 0.0003086 | 0.030864 | 0.30864 |
| 1 rad = | 57.2958 | 3,437.75 | 206,265 | 1 | 63.662 | 6,366.2 | 63,662 |
| 1 gon = | 0.9 | 54 | 3,240 | 0.015708 | 1 | 100 | 1,000 |
| 1 cgon = | 0.009 | 0.54 | 32.4 | – | 0.01 | 1 | 10 |
| 1 mgon = | 0.0009 | 0.054 | 3.24 | – | 0.001 | 0.1 | 1 |

## Velocities

| | | | | |
|---|---|---|---|---|
| 1 km/h | = 0.27778 m/s, | | 1 m/s | = 3.6 km/h |
| 1 mile/h | = 1.60934 km/h, | | 1 km/h | = 0.62137 mile/h |
| 1 kn (knot) | = 1.852 km/h, | | 1 km/h | = 0.53996 kn |
| 1 ft/min | = 0.3048 m/min, | | 1 m/min | = 3.28084 ft/min |

$x$ km/h $\triangleq \dfrac{60}{x}$ min/km $\triangleq \dfrac{3{,}600}{x}$ s/km, $\qquad x$ mile/h $\triangleq \dfrac{37.2824}{x}$ min/km $\triangleq \dfrac{2{,}236.9}{x}$ s/km,

$x$ s/km $\triangleq \dfrac{3{,}600}{x}$ km/h

The <u>Mach number</u> $Ma$ specifies how much faster a body travels than sound (approx. 333 m/s in air). $Ma = 1.3$ therefore denotes 1.3 times the speed of sound.

## Fuel consumption

1 g/PS · h = 1.3596 g/kW · h,
1 lb/hp · h = 608.277 g/kW · h,
1 liq pt/hp · h = 634.545 cm³/kW · h,
1 pt (UK)/hp · h = 762.049 cm³/kW · h,

1 g/kW · h = 0.7355 g/PS · h
1 g/kW · h = 0.001644 lb/hp · h
1 cm³/kW · h = 0.001576 liq pt/hp · h
1 cm³/kW · h = 0.001312 pt (U.K.)/hp · h

$x$ mile/gal (U.S.) $\triangleq \dfrac{235.21}{x}$ $l$/100 km, $\qquad x$ $l$/100 km $\triangleq \dfrac{235.21}{x}$ mile/gal (U.S.)

$x$ mile/gal (U.K.) $\triangleq \dfrac{282.48}{x}$ $l$/100 km. $\qquad x$ $l$/100 km $\triangleq \dfrac{282.48}{x}$ mile/gal (U.K.)

---

[1]) For crude oil.
[2]) It is better to indicate angles by using only one of the units given above, i.e. not $\alpha = 33° 17′ 27.6″$ but rather $\alpha = 33.291°$ or $\alpha = 1{,}997.46′$ or $\alpha = 119{,}847.6″$.

## Units of mass

(colloquially also called "units of weight")

### Avoirdupois system (commercial weights in general use in the U.K. and the U.S.)

| Unit | gr | dram | oz | lb | cwt (U.K.) | cwt (U.S.) | ton (U.K.) | ton (U.S.) | g | kg | t |
|---|---|---|---|---|---|---|---|---|---|---|---|
| 1 gr = | 1 | 0.03657 | 0.00229 | 1/7000 | – | – | – | – | 0.064799 | – | – |
| 1 dram = | 27.344 | 1 | 0.0625 | 0.00391 | – | – | – | – | 1.77184 | – | – |
| 1 oz = | 437.5 | 16 | 1 | 0.0625 | – | – | – | – | 28.3495 | – | – |
| 1 lb = | 7,000 | 256 | 16 | 1 | 0.00893 | 0.01 | – | 0.0005 | 453.592 | 0.45359 | – |
| 1 cwt (U.K.)[1] = | – | – | – | 112 | 1 | 1.12 | 0.05 | 0.05 | – | 50.8023 | – |
| 1 cwt (U.S.)[2] = | – | – | – | 100 | 0.8929 | 1 | 0.04464 | 0.05 | – | 45.3592 | – |
| 1 ton (U.K.)[3] = | – | – | – | 2,240 | 20 | 22.4 | 1 | 1.12 | – | 1016.05 | 1.01605 |
| 1 ton (U.S.)[4] = | – | – | – | 2,000 | 17.857 | 20 | 0.8929 | 1 | – | 907.185 | 0.90718 |
| 1 g = | 15.432 | – | 0.03527 | – | – | – | – | – | 1 | 0.001 | – |
| 1 kg = | – | – | 35.274 | 2.2046 | 0.01968 | 0.02205 | – | – | 1,000 | 1 | 0.001 |
| 1 t = | – | – | – | 2204.6 | 19.684 | 22.046 | 0.9842 | 1.1023 | $10^6$ | 1,000 | 1 |

### Troy system (used in the U.K. and the U.S. for precious stones and noble metals), and Apothecaries' system (used in the U.K. and the U.S. for drugs)

| Unit | gr | s ap | dwt | dr ap | oz t = oz ap | lb t = lb ap | Kt | g |
|---|---|---|---|---|---|---|---|---|
| 1 gr = | 1 | 0.05 | 0.04167 | 0.01667 | – | – | 0.324 | 0.064799 |
| 1 s ap = | 20 | 1 | 0.8333 | 0.3333 | – | – | – | 1.296 |
| 1 dwt = | 24 | 1.2 | 1 | 0.4 | 0.05 | – | – | 1.5552 |
| 1 dr ap = | 60 | 3 | 2.5 | 1 | 0.125 | – | – | 3.8879 |
| 1 oz t = 1 oz ap = | 480 | 24 | 20 | 8 | 1 | 0.08333 | – | 31.1035 |
| 1 lb t = 1 lb ap = | 5,760 | 288 | 240 | 96 | 12 | 1 | – | 373.24 |
| 1 Kt = | 3.086 | – | – | – | – | – | 1 | 0.2000 |
| 1 g = | 15.432 | 0.7716 | 0.643 | 0.2572 | 0.03215 | 0.002679 | 5 | 1 |

## Mass per unit length

SI unit kg/m

1 lb/ft = 1.48816 kg/m, 1 lb/yd = 0.49605 kg/m

Units in textile industry (DIN 60905 and 60910):

1 tex = 1 g/km, 1 mtex = 1 mg/km

1 dtex = 1 dg/km, 1 ktex = 1 kg/km

Former unit (do not use):

1 den (denier) = 1 g/9 km = 0.1111 tex, 1 tex = 9 den

## Density

SI unit kg/m³

1 kg/dm³ = 1 kg/$l$ = 1 g/cm³ = 1,000 kg/m³

1 lb/ft³ = 16.018 kg/m³ = 0.016018 kg/$l$

1 lb/gal (U.K.) = 0.099776 kg/$l$, 1 lb/gal (U.S.) = 0.11983 kg/$l$

°Bé (degrees Baumé) is a measure of the density of liquids which are heavier (+°Bé) or lighter (−°Bé) than water (at 15 °C). Do not use the unit °Bé.

$\varrho = 144.3/(144.3 \mp n)$

$\varrho$ Density in kg/$l$, $n$ hydrometer degrees in °Bé.

°API (American Petroleum Institute) is used in the U.S.A. to indicate the density of fuels and oils.

$\varrho = 141.5/(131.5 + n)$

$\varrho$ Density in kg/$l$, $n$ hydrometer degrees in °API

Examples:

−12 °Bé = 144.3/(144.3 + 12) kg/$l$ = 0.923 kg/$l$

+34 °Bé = 144.3/(144.3 − 34) kg/$l$ = 1.308 kg/$l$

28° API = 141.5/(131.5 + 28) kg/$l$ = 0.887 kg/$l$

---

U.K. = United Kingdom, U.S. = U.S.A.

gr = grain, oz = ounce, lb = pound, cwt = hundredweight

1 slug = 14.5939 kg = mass, accelerated at 1 ft/s² by a force of 1 lbf

1 st (stone) = 14 lb = 6.35 kg (U.K. only)

1 qr (quarter) = 28 lb = 12.7006 kg (U.K. only, seldom used)

1 quintal = 100 lb = 1 cwt (U.S.) = 45.3592 kg

1 tdw (ton dead weight) = 1 ton (U.K.) = 1.016 t

The tonnage of cargo ships (cargo + ballast + fuel + supplies) is given in tdw.

s ap = apothecaries' scruple,

dwt = pennyweight,

dr ap = apothecaries' drachm (U.S.: apothecaries' dram)

oz t (U.K.: oz tr) = troy ounce

oz ap (U.K.: oz apoth) = apothecaries' ounce

lb t = troy pound

lb ap = apothecaries' pound

Kt = metric karat, used only for precious stones [5]

[1] Also "long cwt (cwt $l$)".

[2] Also "short cwt (cwt sh)".

[3] Also "long ton (tn $l$)".

[4] Also "short ton (tn sh)".

[5] The term "karat" was formerly used with a different meaning in connection with gold alloys to denote the gold content: pure gold (fine gold) = 24 karat; 14-karat gold has 14/24 = 585/1,000 parts by weight of fine gold.

## Units of force

| Unit | N | kp | lbf |
|---|---|---|---|
| 1 N (newton) = | 1 | 0.101972 | 0.224809 |
| Do not use | | | |
| 1 kp (kilopond) = | 9.80665 | 1 | 2.204615 |
| 1 lbf (pound-force) = | 4.44822 | 0.453594 | 1 |

1 pdl (poundal) = 0.138255 N = force which accelerates a mass of 1 lb by 1 ft/s².
1 sn (sthène)* = $10^{3}$ N

## Units of pressure and stress

| Unit¹) | Pa | µbar | hPa | bar | N/mm² | kp/mm² | at | kp/m² | torr | atm | lbf/in² | lbf/ft² | tonf/in² |
|---|---|---|---|---|---|---|---|---|---|---|---|---|---|
| 1 Pa = 1 N/m² = | 1 | 10 | 0.01 | $10^{-5}$ | $10^{-6}$ | – | – | 0.10197 | 0.0075 | – | – | – | – |
| 1 µbar = | 0.1 | 1 | 0.001 | $10^{-6}$ | $10^{-7}$ | – | – | 0.0102 | – | – | – | – | – |
| 1 hPa = 1 mbar = | 100 | 1,000 | 1 | 0.001 | 0.0001 | – | – | 10.197 | 0.7501 | – | 0.0145 | 2.0886 | – |
| 1 bar = | $10^{5}$ | $10^{6}$ | 1,000 | 1 | 0.1 | 0.0102 | 1.0197 | 10,197 | 750.06 | 0.9869 | 14.5037 | 2,088.6 | – |
| 1 N/mm² = | $10^{6}$ | $10^{7}$ | 10,000 | 10 | 1 | 0.10197 | 10.197 | 101,972 | 7,501 | 9.8692 | 145.037 | 20,886 | 0.06475 |
| Do not use | | | | | | | | | | | | | |
| 1 kp/mm² = | – | – | 98,066.5 | 98.0665 | 9.80665 | 1 | 100 | $10^{6}$ | 73,556 | 96.784 | 1,422.33 | – | 0.63497 |
| 1 at = 1 kp/cm² = | 98,066.5 | 980,665 | 980.665 | 0.98066 | 0.0981 | 0.01 | 1 | 10,000 | 735.56 | 0.96784 | 14.2233 | 2,048.16 | – |
| 1 kp/m²= 1 mmw.g. = | 9.80665 | 98.0665 | 0.0981 | – | – | $10^{-6}$ | $10^{-4}$ | 1 | 13.5951 | 0.00132 | 0.01934 | 0.2048 | – |
| 1 torr = 1 mmHg = | 133.322 | 1,333.22 | 1.33322 | – | – | – | 0.00136 | 13.5951 | 1 | 0.00132 | 0.01934 | 2.7845 | – |
| 1 atm = | 101,325 | – | 1,013.25 | 1.01325 | – | – | 1.03323 | 10,332.3 | 760 | 1 | 14.695 | 2,116.1 | – |
| British and U.S. units | | | | | | | | | | | | | |
| 1 lbf/in² = | 6,894.76 | 68,948 | 68.948 | 0.0689 | 0.00689 | – | 0.070031 | 703.07 | 51.715 | 0.06805 | 1 | 144 | – |
| 1 lbf/ft² = | 47.8803 | 478.8 | 0.4788 | – | – | – | – | 4.8824 | 0.35913 | – | 1 | 1 | – |
| 1 tonf/in² = | – | – | – | 154.443 | 15.4443 | 1.57488 | 157.488 | – | – | 152.42 | 2,240 | – | 1 |

lbf/in² = pound-force per square inch (psi), lbf/ft² = pound-force per square foot (psf), tonf/in² = ton-force (U.K.) per square inch
1 pdl/ft² (poundal per square foot) = 1.48816 Pa
1 barye* = 1µbar; 1 pz (pièce)* = 1 sn/m² (sthène/m²)* = $10^{3}$ Pa
Standards: DIN 66 034 Conversion tables, kilopond – newton, newton – kilopond, DIN 66 037 Conversion tables, kilopond/cm² – bar,
bar – kilopond/cm², DIN 66 038 Conversion tables, torr – millibar, millibar – torr

\* French units.

¹) See PP. 25 and 26 for names of units.

## Units of energy
(units of work)

| Unit[1] | J | kW · h | kp · m | PS · h | kcal | ft · lbf | Btu |
|---|---|---|---|---|---|---|---|
| 1 J = | 1 | $277.8 \cdot 10^{-9}$ | 0.10197 | $377.67 \cdot 10^{-9}$ | $238.85 \cdot 10^{-6}$ | 0.73756 | $947.8 \cdot 10^{-6}$ |
| 1 kW · h = | $3.6 \cdot 10^{6}$ | 1 | 367,098 | 1.35962 | 859.85 | $2.6552 \cdot 10^{6}$ | 3,412.13 |
| **Do not use** | | | | | | | |
| 1 kp · m = | 9.80665 | $2.7243 \cdot 10^{-6}$ | 1 | $3.704 \cdot 10^{-6}$ | $2.342 \cdot 10^{-3}$ | 7.2330 | $9.295 \cdot 10^{-3}$ |
| 1 PS · h = | $2.6478 \cdot 10^{6}$ | 0.735499 | 270,000 | 1 | 632.369 | $1.9529 \cdot 10^{6}$ | 2,509.6 |
| 1 kcal[2] = | 4,186.8 | $1.163 \cdot 10^{-3}$ | 426.935 | $1.581 \cdot 10^{-3}$ | 1 | 3,088 | 3.9683 |
| **British and U.S. units** | | | | | | | |
| 1 ft · lbf = | 1.35582 | $376.6 \cdot 10^{-9}$ | 0.13826 | $512.1 \cdot 10^{-9}$ | $323.8 \cdot 10^{-6}$ | 1 | $1.285 \cdot 10^{-3}$ |
| 1 Btu[3] = | 1,055.06 | $293.1 \cdot 10^{-6}$ | 107.59 | $398.5 \cdot 10^{-6}$ | 0.2520 | 778.17 | 1 |

ft lbf = foot pound-force, Btu = British thermal unit
1 in ozf (inch ounce-force) = 0.007062 J, 1 in lbf (inch pound-force) = 0.112985 J
1 ft pdl (foot poundal) = 0.04214 J
1 hph (horsepower-hour) = $2.685 \cdot 10^{6}$ J = 0.7457 kW · h
1 thermie (France) = 1,000 frigories (France) = 1,000 kcal = 4.1868 MJ
1 kg C.E. (coal equivalent kilogram)[4] = 29.3076 MJ = 8.141 kWh
1 t C.E. (coal equivalent ton)[4] = 1,000 kg C.E. = 29.3076 GJ = 8.141 MWh

## Units of power

| Unit[1] | W | kW | kp m/s | PS* | kcal/s | hp | Btu/s |
|---|---|---|---|---|---|---|---|
| 1 W = | 1 | 0.001 | 0.10197 | $1.3596 \cdot 10^{-3}$ | $238.8 \cdot 10^{-6}$ | $1.341 \cdot 10^{-3}$ | $947.8 \cdot 10^{-6}$ |
| 1 kW = | 1,000 | 1 | 101.97 | 1.35962 | $238.8 \cdot 10^{-3}$ | 1.34102 | $947.8 \cdot 10^{-6}$ |
| **Do not use** | | | | | | | |
| 1 kp · m/s = | 9.80665 | $9.807 \cdot 10^{-3}$ | 1 | $13.33 \cdot 10^{-3}$ | $2.342 \cdot 10^{-3}$ | $13.15 \cdot 10^{-3}$ | $9.295 \cdot 10^{-3}$ |
| 1 PS = | 735.499 | 0.735499 | 75 | 1 | 0.17567 | 0.98632 | 0.69712 |
| 1 kcal/s = | 4,186.8 | 4.1868 | 426.935 | 5.6925 | 1 | 5.6146 | 3.9683 |
| **British and U.S. units** | | | | | | | |
| 1 hp = | 745.70 | 0.74570 | 76.0402 | 1.0139 | 0.17811 | 1 | 0.70678 |
| 1 Btu/s = | 1,055.06 | 1.05506 | 107.586 | 1.4345 | 0.2520 | 1.4149 | 1 |

hp = horsepower
1 ft · lbf/s = 1.35582 W
1 ch (cheval vapeur) (France) = 1 PS = 0.7355 kW
1 poncelet (France) = 100 kp · m/s = 0.981 kW
Continuous human power generation ≈ 0.1 kW

Standards: DIN 66035 Conversion tables, calorie – joule, joule – calorie
DIN 66036 Conversion tables, metric horsepower – kilowatt,
kilowatt – metric horsepower
DIN 66039 Conversion tables, kilocalorie – watt-hour,
watt-hour – kilocalorie

---

[1] Names of units, see P. 26.
[2] 1 kcal ≈ quantity of heat required to increase temperature of 1 kg water at 15 °C by 1 °C.
[3] 1 Btu ≈ quantity of heat required to raise temperature of 1 lb water by 1 °F. 1 therm = $10^{5}$ Btu.
[4] The units of energy kg C.E. and t C.E. were based on a specific calorific value $H_u$ of 7,000 kcal/kg of coal.

## Units of temperature

°C = degree Celsius, K = Kelvin,
°F = degree Fahrenheit,
°R = degree Rankine.

### Temperature points

$$T_K = (273.15\,°C + t_C)\,\frac{K}{°C} = \frac{5}{9}\,T_R$$

$$T_R = (459.67\,°F + t_F)\,\frac{°R}{°F} = 1.8\,T_K$$

$$t_C = \frac{5}{9}\,(t_F - 32\,°F)\,\frac{°C}{°F} = (T_K - 273.15\,K)\,\frac{°C}{K}$$

$$t_F = (1.8\,t_C + 32\,°C)\,\frac{°F}{°C} = (T_R - 459.67\,°R)\,\frac{°F}{°R}$$

$t_C$, $t_F$, $T_K$ and $T_R$ denote the temperature points in °C, °F, K, and °R.

### Temperature difference
1 K = 1 °C = 1.8 °F = 1.8 °R

Zero points: 0 °C ≙ 32 °F, 0 °F ≙ − 17.78 °C
Absolute zero:
0 K ≙ − 273.15 °C ≙ 0 °R ≙ − 459.67 °F.

International practical temperature scale:
Boiling point of oxygen −182.97 °C, triple point of water 0.01 °C[1]), boiling point of water 100 °C, boiling point of sulfur (sulfur point) 444.6 °C, setting point of silver (silver point) 960.8 °C, setting point of gold 1,063 °C

---

[1]) That temperature of pure water at which ice, water, and water vapor occur together in equilibrium (at 1,013.25 hPa). See also footnote[2]) on P. 22.

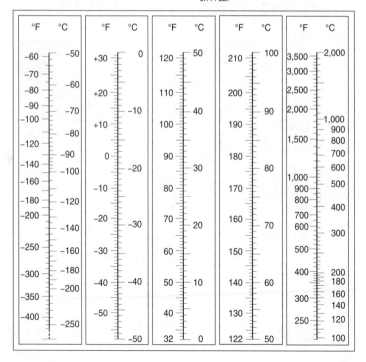

### Units of viscosity

<u>Legal units</u> of kinematic viscosity $v$
$1\ \text{m}^2/\text{s} = 1\ \text{Pa} \cdot \text{s}/(\text{kg/m}^3) = 10^4\ \text{cm}^2/\text{s}$
$= 10^6\ \text{mm}^2/\text{s}$

<u>British and U.S. units</u>
$1\ \text{ft}^2/\text{s} = 0.092903\ \text{m}^2/\text{s}$
RI seconds = efflux time from Redwood-I viscometer (U.K.)
SU seconds = efflux time from Saybolt-Universal viscometer (U.S.)

<u>Do not use:</u>
St (stokes) = $\text{cm}^2/\text{s}$, cSt = $\text{mm}^2/\text{s}$

<u>Conventional units</u>
E (Engler degree) = relative efflux time from Engler apparatus DIN 51560
For $v > 60\ \text{mm}^2/\text{s}$, $1\ \text{mm}^2/\text{s} = 0.132\ \text{E}$

At values below 3 E, Engler degrees do not give a true indication of the variation of viscosity; for example, a fluid with 2 E does not have twice the kinematic viscosity of a fluid with 1 E, but rather 12 times that value.

A seconds = efflux time from flow cup DIN 53211

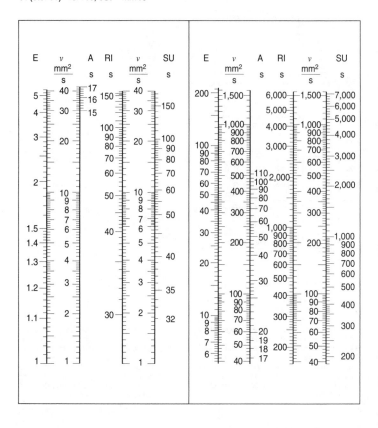

## Units of time

| Unit[1]) | | s | min | h | d |
|---|---|---|---|---|---|
| 1 s[2]) (second) | = | 1 | 0.01667 | $0.2778 \cdot 10^{-3}$ | $11.574 \cdot 10^{-6}$ |
| 1 min (minute) | = | 60 | 1 | 0.01667 | $0.6944 \times 10^{-3}$ |
| 1 h (hour) | = | 3,600 | 60 | 1 | 0.041667 |
| 1 d (day) | = | 86,400 | 1,440 | 24 | 1 |

1 civil year = 365 (or 366) days = 8,760 (8,784) hours (for calculation of interest in banking, 1 year = 360 days)
1 solar year[3]) = 365.2422 mean solar days = 365 d 5 h 48 min 46 s
1 sidereal year[4]) = 365.2564 mean solar days

## Clock times

The clock times listed for the following time zones are based on 12.00 CET (Central European Time)[5]):

| Clock time | Time-zone meridian | Countries (examples) | Clock time | Time-zone meridian | Countries (examples) |
|---|---|---|---|---|---|
| | West longitude | | | East longitude | |
| 1.00 | 150° | Alaska. | 12.00 | 15° | Central European Time (CET): Austria, Belgium, Denmark, France, Germany, Hungary, Italy, Luxembourg, Netherlands, Norway, Poland, Sweden, Switzerland, Spain; Algeria, Israel, Libya, Nigeria, Tunisia, Zaire. |
| 3.00 | 120° | West coast of Canada and the U.S.A. | | | |
| 4.00 | 105° | Western central zone of Canada and the U.S.A. | | | |
| 5.00 | 90° | Central zone of Canada and the U.S.A., Mexico, Central America. | | | |
| 6.00 | 75° | Canada between 68° and 90°, Eastern U.S.A., Ecuador, Colombia, Panama, Peru. | 13.00 | 30° | Eastern European Time (EET): Bulgaria, Finland, Greece, Romania; Egypt, Lebanon, Jordan, South Africa, Sudan, Syria. |
| 7.00 | 60° | Canada east of 68°, Bolivia, Chile, Venezuela. | 14.00 | 45° | East Africa, Iraq, Saudi Arabia, Turkey, Western Russia. |
| 8.00 | 45° | Argentina, Brazil, Greenland, Paraguay, Uruguay. | | | |
| | | | 14.30 | 52.5° | Iran. |
| 11.00 | 0° | Greenwich Mean Time (GMT)[6]): Canary Islands, United Kingdom, Ireland, Portugal, West Africa. | 16.30 | 82.5° | India, Sri Lanka. |
| | | | 18.00 | 105° | Cambodia, Indonesia, Laos, Thailand, Vietnam. |
| | | | 19.00 | 120° | Chinese coast, Philippines, Western Australia. |
| | | | 20.00 | 135° | Japan, Korea. |
| | | | 20.30 | 142.5° | Northern and Southern Australia. |
| | | | 21.00 | 150° | Eastern Australia. |

---

[1]) See also P. 25.
[2]) Base SI unit, see P. 22 for definition.
[3]) Time between two successive passages of the earth through the vernal equinox.
[4]) True time of revolution of the earth about the sun.
[5]) During the summer months, in countries in which daylight saving time is observed, clocks are set ahead by 1 hour (from approximately April to October north of the equator and October to March south of the equator).

[6]) = UT (Universal Time), mean solar time at the 0° meridian of Greenwich, or UTC (Coordinated Universal Time), defined by the invariable second of the International System of Units (P. 22). As the period of rotation of the earth about the sun is gradually becoming longer, UTC is adjusted to UT from time to time by the addition of a leap second.

# Basic equations used in mechanics

## Symbols and units

| Quantity | | Unit |
|---|---|---|
| $A$ | Area | m² |
| $E_k$ | Kinetic energy | $J = N \cdot m$ |
| $E_p$ | Potential energy | $J = N \cdot m$ |
| $E_{rot}$ | Rotational energy | $J = N \cdot m$ |
| $F$ | Force | N |
| $F_G$ | Weight | N |
| $F_m$ | Mean force during impulse period | N |
| $F_z$ | Centrifugal force | N |
| $H$ | Rotational impulse | $N \cdot m \cdot s = kg \cdot m^2/s$ |
| $I$ | Force impulse | $N \cdot s = kg \cdot m/s$ |
| $J$ | Moment of inertia | $kg \cdot m^2$ |
| $L$ | Angular momentum | $N \cdot m \cdot s$ |
| $M_t$ | Torque | $N \cdot m$ |
| $M_{t,m}$ | Mean torque during impulse period | $N \cdot m$ |
| $P$ | Power | $W = N \cdot m/s$ |
| $V$ | Volume | m³ |
| $W$ | Work, energy | $J = N \cdot m$ |
| $a$ | Acceleration | m/s² |
| $a_z$ | Centrifugal acceleration | m/s² |

| Quantity | | Unit |
|---|---|---|
| $d$ | Diameter | m |
| $e$ | Base of natural logarithms ($e = 2.781$) | – |
| $g$ | Acceleration of free fall ($g = 9.81$) | m/s² |
| $h$ | Height | m |
| $i$ | Radius of gyration | m |
| $l$ | Length | m |
| $m$ | Mass | kg |
| $n$ | Rotational frequency | 1/s |
| $p$ | Linear momentum | $N \cdot s$ |
| $r$ | Radius | m |
| $s$ | Length of path | m |
| $t$ | Time | s |
| $v$ | Velocity | m/s |
| $\alpha$ | Angular acceleration | rad/s² |
| $\beta$ | Wrap angle | rad |
| $\mu$ | Coefficient of friction | – |
| $\varrho$ | Density | kg/m³ |
| $\varphi$ | Angle of rotation | rad |
| $\omega$ | Angular velocity | 1/s |

## Rectilinear and rotary motion

A uniform motion exists when velocity $v$ or rotational frequency $n$ is constant. In this case, acceleration ($a$ or $\alpha$) equals zero. A motion is uniformly accelerated if acceleration is constant. In the case of negative acceleration, the motion is decelerated or braked.

| **Rectilinear motion** (translation) | | **Rotary motion** (rotation) | |
|---|---|---|---|
| **Mass** | | **Moment of inertia** (P. 41) | |
| $m = V \cdot \varrho$ | | $J = m \cdot i^2$ | |
| **Path** | | **Angle** | |
| $s = \int v(t) \cdot dt$ | | $\varphi = \int \omega(t) \cdot dt$ | |
| $s = v \cdot t$ | $[v = \text{const.}]$ | $\varphi = \omega \cdot t = 2\pi \cdot n$ | $[n = \text{const.}]$ |
| $s = \frac{1}{2} \cdot a \cdot t^2$ | $[a = \text{const.}]$ | $\varphi = \frac{1}{2} \cdot \alpha \cdot t^2$ | $[\alpha = \text{const.}]$ |
| **Velocity** | | **Angular velocity** | |
| $v = ds(t)/dt$ | | $\omega = d\varphi(t)/dt$ | |
| $v = s/t$ | $[v = \text{const.}]$ | $\omega = \varphi/t = 2\pi \cdot n$ | $[n = \text{const.}]$ |
| $v = a \cdot t = \sqrt{2 \cdot a \cdot s}$ | $[a = \text{const.}]$ | $\omega = \alpha \cdot t = \sqrt{2 \cdot \alpha \cdot \varphi}$ | $[\alpha = \text{const.}]$ |
| | | **Peripheral velocity** | |
| | | $v = r \cdot \omega$ | |
| **Acceleration** | | **Angular acceleration** | |
| $a = dv(t)/dt$ | | $\alpha = d\omega(t)/dt$ | |
| $a = (v_2 - v_1)/t$ | $[a = \text{const.}]$ | $\alpha = (\omega_2 - \omega_1)/t$ | $[\alpha = \text{const.}]$ |
| | | **Centrifugal acceleration** | |
| | | $a_z = r \cdot \omega^2$ | |

| Rectilinear motion (translation) | Rotary motion (rotation) |
|---|---|
| **Force** $F = m \cdot a$ | **Torque** $M_t = F \cdot r = J \cdot \alpha$ |
| | **Centrifugal force** $F_z = m \cdot r \cdot \omega^2$ |
| **Work** $W = F \cdot s$ | **Rotational work** $W = M_t \cdot \varphi$ |
| **Translation energy** $E_k = {}^1\!/_2 \cdot m \cdot v^2$ | **Rotational energy** $E_{rot} = {}^1\!/_2 \cdot J \cdot \omega^2$ |
| **Potential energy** $E_p = F_G \cdot h$ | |
| **Power** $P = F \cdot v$ | **Power** $P = M_t \cdot \omega = M_t \cdot 2\pi \cdot n$ |
| **Force impulse** $I = F_m \cdot (t_2 - t_1)$ | **Rotational impulse** $H = M_{t,\,m} \cdot (t_2 - t_1)$ |
| **Linear momentum** $p = m \cdot v$ | **Angular momentum** $L = J \cdot \omega = J \cdot 2\pi \cdot n$ |

## Laws of projectile motion

Ignoring aerodynamic drag, a body projected vertically upward at a positive projection velocity $v_0$ will result in a uniform decelerated motion. At the reversal point, the velocity $v = 0$.

When a body is projected obliquely upwards at the angle of throw $\alpha$ and at a positive initial velocity $v_0$, a uniform rectilinear motion with free fall is superimposed.

| | Body thrown vertically upward | Oblique throw |
|---|---|---|
| **Upward velocity** | $v = v_0 - g \cdot t = v_0 - \sqrt{2 \cdot g \cdot h}$ | $v = \sqrt{(v_0 \cdot \cos\alpha)^2 + (v_0 \cdot \sin\alpha - g \cdot t)^2}$ |
| **Height of throw** | $h = v_0 \cdot t - \dfrac{1}{2} \cdot g \cdot t^2 = \dfrac{v_0^2}{2 \cdot g}$ | $h = \dfrac{v_0^2 \cdot \sin^2\alpha}{2 \cdot g}$ |
| **Range of throw** | $s = 0$ | $s = \dfrac{v_0^2 \cdot \sin 2\alpha}{g}$ |
| **Duration of throw** | $t = \sqrt{\dfrac{8 \cdot h}{g}} = \dfrac{2 \cdot v_0}{g}$ | $t = \dfrac{s}{v_0 \cdot \cos\alpha} = \dfrac{2 \cdot v_0 \cdot \sin\alpha}{g}$ |

## Free fall

Free fall ignoring aerodynamic drag is a uniform accelerated motion.

If an allowance is made for aerodynamic drag, the result will be a nonuniform accelerated motion. The velocity of fall approaches a limit velocity $v_g$ at which the aerodynamic drag $F_L = {}^1\!/_2 \cdot \varrho \cdot c_d \cdot A \cdot v_g^2$ is as great as the weight $F_G = m \cdot g$ of the falling body. At air density $\varrho$ and drag coefficient $c_d$, the limit speed

$$v_g = \sqrt{\frac{2 \cdot m \cdot g}{\varrho \cdot c_d \cdot A}}$$

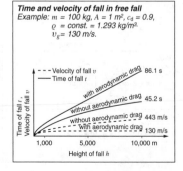

***Time and velocity of fall in free fall***
*Example: $m = 100\ kg$, $A = 1\ m^2$, $c_d = 0.9$,*
$\varrho = const. = 1.293\ kg/m^3$.
$v_g = 130\ m/s$.

- - - Velocity of fall $v$
— Time of fall $t$

with aerodynamic drag    86.1 s
without aerodynamic drag   45.2 s
without aerodynamic drag   443 m/s
with aerodynamic drag    130 m/s

Time of fall $t$, Velocity of fall $v$

1,000     5,000     10,000 m
Height of fall $h$

|  | **Free fall without air resistance** | **Free fall with aerodynamic drag** |
|---|---|---|
| **Velocity of fall** | $v = g \cdot t = \sqrt{2 \cdot g \cdot h}$ | $v = v_g \sqrt{1 - 1/\varkappa^2}$ where $\varkappa = e^{g \cdot h/v_g^2}$ |
| **Height of fall** | $h = \frac{1}{2} \cdot g \cdot t^2 = \frac{1}{2} \cdot v \cdot t = \frac{1}{2} \cdot \frac{v^2}{g}$ | $h = \frac{v_g^2}{2 \cdot g} \cdot \ln \frac{v_g^2}{v_g^2 - v^2}$ |
| **Time of fall** | $t = \frac{2 \cdot h}{v} = \frac{v}{g} = \sqrt{\frac{2 \cdot h}{g}}$ | $t = \frac{v_g}{g} \cdot \ln \left( \varkappa + \sqrt{\varkappa^2 - 1} \right)$ |

## Moments of inertia

| **Type of body** | **Moments of inertia** <br> $J_x$ about the $x$-axis [1], $J_y$ about the $y$-axis [1] |
|---|---|
| Rectangular parallelepiped, cuboid | $J_x = m \dfrac{b^2 + c^2}{12}$ <br><br> $J_y = m \dfrac{a^2 + c^2}{12}$     Cube with side length $a$: <br><br> $J_x = J_y = m \dfrac{a^2}{6}$ |
| Circular cylinder | $J_x = m \dfrac{r^2}{2}$ <br><br> $J_y = m \dfrac{3\,r^2 + l^2}{12}$ |
| Hollow regular cylinder | $J_x = m \dfrac{r_a^2 + r_i^2}{2}$ <br><br> $J_y = m \dfrac{r_a^2 + r_i^2 + l^2/3}{4}$ |
| Circular cone | $J_x = m \dfrac{3\,r^2}{10}$ <br><br> Envelope of cone (excluding end base) $J_x = m \dfrac{r^2}{2}$ |
| Circular circular cone | $J_x = m \dfrac{3\,(R^5 - r^5)}{10\,(R^3 - r^3)}$ <br><br> Envelope of cone (excluding end faces) $J_x = m \dfrac{R^2 + r^2}{2}$ |
| Pyramid | $J_x = m \dfrac{a^2 + b^2}{20}$ |
| Sphere and hemisphere | $J_x = m \dfrac{2\,r^2}{5}$ <br><br> Surface area of sphere $J_x = m \dfrac{2\,r^2}{3}$ |
| Hollow sphere   $r_a$ Outer sphere radius <br> $r_i$ Inner sphere radius | $J_x = m \dfrac{2\,(r_a^5 - r_i^5)}{5\,(r_a^3 - r_i^3)}$ |
| Torus | $J_x = m \left( R^2 + \dfrac{3}{4} r^2 \right)$ |

---

[1] The moment of inertia for an axis parallel to the $x$-axis or $y$-axis at a distance $a$ is $J_A = J_x + m \cdot a^2$ or $J_A = J_y + m \cdot a^2$.

## Transmission of force

Mechanical machines for the transmission of force can be reduced to the "lever" and "wedge" principles.

### Lever laws

A system is in equilibrium when the sum of the moments is equal to zero. Ignoring friction, the following applies:

$$M_{f1} = M_{f2} \qquad F_1 \cdot r_1 = F_2 \cdot r_2$$

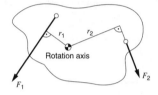

### Forces on the wedge

Depending on the wedge angle $\alpha$, small forces (insertion forces $F$) can be translated into large normal forces $F_N$. Without allowing for friction, the following applies:

$$F_N = \frac{F}{2 \cdot \sin \frac{\alpha}{2}}$$

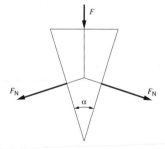

## Friction

When touching bodies move relative to each other, friction acts as mechanical resistance acting in the opposite direction to the motion. The force of resistance, known as frictional force $F_R$, is proportional to the normal force $F_N$. Static friction exists as long as the external force is less than the frictional force and the body remains at rest. When static friction is overcome, and the body is set in motion, frictional force is governed by Coulomb's law of sliding friction:

$$F_R = \mu \cdot F_N$$

### Friction on the wedge

Allowing for friction, the forces on the wedge are governed by:

$$F_N = \frac{F}{2 \cdot \sin \frac{\alpha}{2} + \mu \cdot \cos \frac{\alpha}{2}}$$

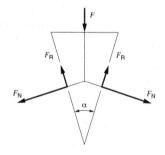

### Rope friction

Sliding friction occurs in the event of relative motion between rope and pulley (belt brake, bollard with running rope). Static friction exists when rope and pulley are at rest relative to each other (belt drive, belt brake as holding brake, bollard with rope at rest). The coefficient of sliding friction $\mu$ or static friction $\mu_H$ must be applied accordingly.

According to Euler's rope-friction formula

$$F_2 = F_1 \cdot e^{\mu \cdot \beta}$$

Frictional force is calculated as

$$F_R = F_2 - F_1$$

and the transmittable friction torque as

$$M_R = F_R \cdot r$$

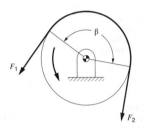

**Coefficient of friction**
The coefficient of friction always denotes a system property and not a material property. Coefficients of friction are, among other things, dependent on material pairing, temperature, surface condition, sliding velocity, the surrounding medium (e.g. water or $CO_2$, which can be adsorbed by the surface), and on the intermediate material (e.g. lubricant). For this reason, coefficients of friction always fluctuate between limit values and may have to be calculated experimentally. Static friction is generally greater than sliding friction. In special cases, the friction coefficient can exceed 1 (e.g. with very smooth surfaces where cohesion forces are predominant or with racing tires featuring an adhesion or suction effect).

**Reference values for coefficients of static and sliding friction**

| Material pair | Coefficient of static friction $\mu_H$ | | Coefficient of sliding friction $\mu$ | |
|---|---|---|---|---|
| | Dry | Lubricated | Dry | Lubricated |
| Iron – iron | | | 1.0 | |
| Copper – copper | | | 0.60...1.0 | |
| Steel – steel | 0.45...0.80 | 0.10 | 0.40...0.70 | 0.10 |
| Chrome – chrome | | | 0.41 | |
| Nickel – nickel | | | 0.39...0.70 | |
| Al alloy – Al alloy | | | 0.15...0.60 | |
| Steel – copper | | | 0.23...0.29 | |
| Steel – babbitt metal | | | 0.21 | |
| Steel – gray cast iron | 0.18...0.24 | 0.10 | 0.17...0.24 | 0.02...0.21 |
| Brake lining – steel | | | 0.50...0.60 | 0.20...0.50 |
| Leather – metal | 0.60 | 0.20 | 0.20...0.25 | 0.12 |
| Polyamide – steel | | | 0.32...0.45 | 0.10 |
| PTFE – steel | | | 0.04...0.22 | |
| Ice – steel | 0.027 | | 0.014 | |

# Vibrations and oscillations

## Symbols and units

| Quantity | | Unit |
|---|---|---|
| $a$ | Storage coefficient | |
| $b$ | Damping coefficient | |
| $c$ | Storage coefficient | |
| $c$ | Spring constant | N/m |
| $c_\alpha$ | Torsional rigidity | N · m/rad |
| $C$ | Capacity | F |
| $f$ | Frequency | Hz |
| $f_g$ | Resonant frequency | Hz |
| $\Delta f$ | Half-value width | Hz |
| $F$ | Force | N |
| $F_Q$ | Excitation function | |
| $I$ | Current | A |
| $J$ | Moment of inertia | kg · m² |
| $L$ | Self-inductance | H |
| $m$ | Mass | kg |
| $M$ | Torque | N · m |
| $n$ | Rotational speed | 1/min |
| $Q$ | Charge | C |
| $Q$ | Resonance sharpness | |
| $r$ | Damping factor | N · s/m |
| $r_\alpha$ | Rotational damping coefficient | N · s · m |
| $R$ | Ohmic resistance | Ω |
| $t$ | Time | s |
| $T$ | Period | s |
| $U$ | Voltage | V |
| $v$ | Particle velocity | m/s |
| $x$ | Travel/displacement | |
| $y$ | Instantaneous value | |
| $\hat{y}$ | Amplitude | |
| $\dot{y}$ ($\ddot{y}$) | Single (double) derivative with respect to time | |
| $y_{rec}$ | Rectified value | |
| $y_{eff}$ | Effective value | |
| $\alpha$ | Angle | rad |
| $\delta$ | Decay coefficient | 1/s |
| $\Lambda$ | Logarithmic decrement | |
| $\omega$ | Angular velocity | rad/s |
| $\omega$ | Angular frequency | 1/s |
| $\Omega$ | Exciter-circuit frequency | 1/s |
| $\vartheta$ | Damping ratio | |
| $\vartheta_{opt}$ | Optimum damping ratio | |

Subscripts:

| 0 | Undamped |
|---|---|
| d | Damped |
| T | Absorber |
| U | Base support |
| G | Machine |

## Terms
(see also DIN 1311)

### Vibrations and oscillations
Vibrations and oscillations are the terms used to denote changes in a physical quantity which repeat at more or less regular time intervals and whose direction changes with similar regularity.

### Period
The period is the time taken for one complete cycle of a single oscillation (period).

### Amplitude
Amplitude is the maximum instantaneous value (peak value) of a sinusoidally oscillating physical quantity.

### Frequency
Frequency is the number of oscillations in one second, the reciprocal value of the period of oscillation $T$.

### Angular frequency
Angular frequency is $2\pi$-times the frequency.

### Particle velocity
Particle velocity is the instantaneous value of the alternating velocity of a vibrating particle in its direction of vibration. It must not be confused with the velocity of propagation of a traveling wave (e.g. the velocity of sound).

### Fourier series
Every periodic function, which is piecewise monotonic and smooth, can be expressed as the sum of sinusoidal harmonic components.

### Beats
Beats occur when two sinusoidal oscillations, whose frequencies do not differ greatly, are superposed. They are periodic. Their basic frequency is the difference between the frequencies of the superposed sinusoidal oscillations.

### Natural oscillations
The frequency of natural oscillations (natural frequency) is dependent only on the properties of the oscillating system.

### Damping
Damping is a measure of the energy losses in an oscillatory system when one form of energy is converted into another.

## Logarithmic decrement
Natural logarithm of the relationship between two extreme values of a natural oscillation which are separated by one period.

## Damping ratio
Measure for the degree of damping.

## Forced oscillations
Forced oscillations arise under the influence of an external physical force (excitation), which does not change the properties of the oscillator. The frequency of forced oscillations is determined by the frequency of the excitation.

## Transfer function
The transfer function is the quotient of amplitude of the observed variable divided by the amplitude of excitation, plotted against the excitation frequency.

## Resonance
Resonance occurs when the transfer function produces very large values as the excitation frequency approaches the natural frequency.

## Resonant frequency
Resonant frequency is the excitation frequency at which the oscillator variable attains its maximum value.

## Half-value width
The half-value width is the difference between the frequencies at which the level of the variable has dropped to $1/\sqrt{2} \approx 0.707$ of the maximum value.

## Resonance sharpness
Resonance sharpness, or the quality factor (Q-factor), is the maximum value of the transfer function.

## Coupling
If two oscillatory systems are coupled together – mechanically by mass or elasticity, electrically by inductance or capacitance – a periodic exchange of energy takes place between the systems.

## Wave
Spatial and temporal change of state of a continuum, which can be expressed as a unidirectional transfer of location of a certain state over a period of time. There are transversal waves (e.g. waves in rope and water) and longitudinal waves (e.g. sound waves in air).

## Interference
The principle of undisturbed superposition of waves. At every point in space, the instantaneous value of the resulting wave is equal to the sum of the instantaneous values of the individual waves.

## Standing waves
Standing waves occur as a result of interference between two waves of equal frequency, wavelength, and amplitude traveling in opposite directions. In contrast to a propagating wave, the amplitude of the standing wave is constant at every point; nodes (zero amplitude) and antinodes (maximum amplitude) occur. Standing waves occur by reflection of a wave back on itself if the characteristic impedance of the medium differs greatly from the impedance of the reflector.

## Rectification value
Arithmetic mean value, linear in time, of the values of a periodic signal.

$$y_{\text{rec}} = (1/T) \int_0^T \mid y \mid \, \mathrm{d}t$$

For a sine curve:
$$y_{\text{rec}} = 2\hat{y}/\pi \approx 0.637 \, \hat{y}.$$

## Effective value
Also known as the root-mean-square value. The square root of the time average of the square of a periodic signal.

$$y_{\text{eff}} = \sqrt{(1/T)\int_0^T y^2 \, \mathrm{d}t}$$

For a sine curve:
$$y_{\text{eff}} = \hat{y}/\sqrt{2} \approx 0.707 \, \hat{y}.$$

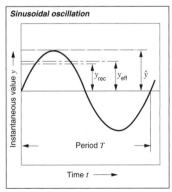

*Sinusoidal oscillation*

Instantaneous value $y$ — $y_{\text{rec}}$ — $y_{\text{eff}}$ — $\hat{y}$

Period $T$

Time $t$ ⟶

**Form factor** $= y_{eff}/y_{rec}$
For a sine curve:
$y_{eff}/y_{rec} \approx 1.111$.

**Peak factor** $= \hat{y}/y_{eff}$
For a sine curve:
$\hat{y}/y_{eff} = \sqrt{2} \approx 1.414$.

### Equations
The equations apply to the following simple oscillators if the general quantity designations in the formulas are replaced by the relevant physical quantities.

Simple oscillatory systems

| | Mechanical | | Electrical |
|---|---|---|---|
| | Transla-tional | Rotational | |
| | 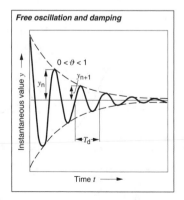 | | |
| Gen. desig-nation | Physical quantity | | |
| $y$ | $x$ | $\alpha$ | $Q$ |
| $\dot{y}$ | $\dot{x} = v$ | $\dot{\alpha} = \omega$ | $\dot{Q} = I$ |
| $\ddot{y}$ | $\ddot{x} = \dot{v}$ | $\ddot{\alpha} = \dot{\omega}$ | $\ddot{Q} = \dot{I}$ |
| $F_Q$ | $F$ | $M$ | $U$ |
| $a$ | $m$ | $J$ | $L$ |
| $b$ | $r$ | $r_\alpha$ | $R$ |
| $c$ | $c$ | $c_\alpha$ | $1/C$ |

*Free oscillation and damping*

### Differential equations
$a\ddot{y} + b\dot{y} + cy = F_Q(t) = \hat{F}_Q \sin \Omega t$
Period $T = 1/f$

Angular frequency $\omega = 2\pi f$

Sinusoidal oscillation (e.g. vibration displacement) $y = \hat{y} \sin \omega t$

### Free oscillations ($F_Q = 0$)
Logarithmic decrement
$\Lambda = \ln(y_n/y_{n+1}) = \pi b/\sqrt{ca - b^2/4}$

Decay coefficient $\delta = b/(2a)$

Damping ratio $\vartheta = \delta/\omega_0 = b/(2\sqrt{ca})$

$\vartheta = \Lambda/\sqrt{\Lambda^2 + 4\pi^2} \approx \Lambda/(2\pi)$
(low level of damping)

Angular frequency of undamped oscillation ($\vartheta = 0$) $\omega_0 = \sqrt{c/a}$

Angular frequency of damped oscillation ($0 < \vartheta < 1$) $\omega_d = \omega_0\sqrt{1 - \vartheta^2}$
For $\vartheta \geq 1$ no oscillations but creepage

### Forced oscillations
Quantity of transfer function

$\hat{y}/\hat{F}_Q = 1/\sqrt{(c - a\Omega^2)^2 + (b\Omega)^2}$
$= (1/c)/\sqrt{(1 - (\Omega/\omega_0)^2)^2 + (2\vartheta\Omega/\omega_0)^2}$
Resonant frequency $f_g = f_0\sqrt{1 - 2\vartheta^2} < f_0$
Resonance sharpness $Q = 1/(2\vartheta\sqrt{1 - \vartheta^2})$
Oscillator with low level of damping ($\vartheta \leq 0.1$):

Resonant frequency $f_g \approx f_0$

Resonance sharpness $Q \approx 1/(2\vartheta)$

Half-value width $\Delta f = 2\vartheta f_0 = f_0/Q$

## Vibration reduction

### Vibration damping
If damping can only be carried out between the machine and a quiescent point, damping must be at a high level (cf. "Standardized transmission function" figure).

### Vibration isolation

#### Active vibration isolation
Machines are to be mounted so that the forces transmitted to the base support are

**Standardized transmission function**

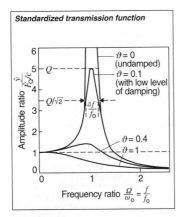

Amplitude ratio $\frac{\hat{v}}{\hat{F}_0/c}$

$\vartheta = 0$ (undamped)
$\vartheta = 0.1$ (with low level of damping)
$\vartheta = 0.4$
$\vartheta = 1$

$Q$
$Q/\sqrt{2}$
$\left| \frac{\Delta f}{f_0} \right|$

Frequency ratio $\frac{\Omega}{\omega_0} = \frac{f}{f_0}$

**Vibration isolation**
a Transmission function of machine,
b Structure of principle.

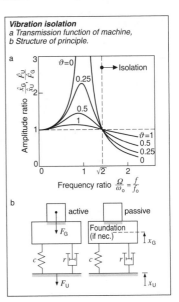

a

Amplitude ratio $\frac{\hat{x}_G}{\hat{x}_U}, \frac{\hat{F}_U}{\hat{F}_G}$

$\vartheta = 0$
0.25
0.5
1
Isolation
$\vartheta = 1$
0.5
0.25
0

Frequency ratio $\frac{\Omega}{\omega_0} = \frac{f}{f_0}$

b

active          passive
$F_G$
Foundation (if nec.)    $x_G$
$c$   $r$       $c$   $r$
$F_U$              $x_U$

small. One measure to be taken: The bearing point should be set below resonance so that the natural frequency lies below the lowest excitation frequency. Damping impedes isolation. Low values can result in excessively high vibrations during run-up when the resonant range is passed through.

Passive vibration isolation
Machines are to be mounted so that vibrations and shocks reaching the base support are only transmitted to the machines to a minor extent. Measures to be taken: same as for active isolation.

In many cases, flexible suspension or extreme damping is not practicable. To prevent the occurrence of resonance, the machine attachment should be so rigid that the natural frequency is far enough in excess of the highest excitation frequency which can occur.

**Vibration absorption**

Vibration absorber with fixed natural frequency
By tuning the natural frequency $\omega_T$ of an absorption mass with a flexible, loss-free coupling to the excitation frequency, vibrations acting on the machine are completely absorbed. Only the absorption mass still vibrates. The effectiveness of

the absorption decreases as the excitation frequency changes. Damping prevents complete absorption. However, appropriate tuning of the absorber frequency and an optimum damping ratio produce broadband vibration reduction, which remains effective when the excitation frequency changes.

Vibration absorber with varying natural frequency
Rotational oscillations with excitation frequencies proportional to the rotational speed (e.g. orders of balancing in IC engines, P. 455 onwards) can be absorbed by absorbers with natural frequencies proportional to the rotational speed (pendulum in the centrifugal-force field). The vibration absorption is effective at all rotational speeds.

Vibration absorption is also possible for oscillators with several degrees of freedom and interrelationships, as well as by the use of several absorption masses.

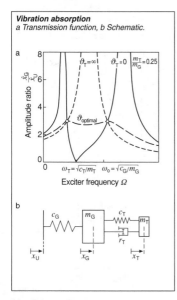

**Vibration absorption**
a Transmission function, b Schematic.

a

Amplitude ratio $\frac{\hat{x}_G}{\hat{x}_U}$

$\vartheta_T = \infty$   $\vartheta_T = 0$   $\frac{m_T}{m_G} = 0.25$

$\vartheta_{optimal}$

$\omega_T = \sqrt{c_T/m_T}$   $\omega_0 = \sqrt{c_G/m_G}$

Exciter frequency $\Omega$

b

$c_G$   $m_G$   $c_T$   $m_T$   $r_T$

$x_U$   $x_G$   $x_T$

## Modal analysis

The dynamic behavior (oscillatory characteristics) of a mechanical structure can be predicted with the aid of a mathematical model. The model parameters of the modal model are determined by means of modal analysis. A time-invariant and linear-elastic structure is an essential precondition. Oscillations are only observed at a limited number of points in the possible oscillation directions (degrees of freedom) and at defined frequency intervals. The continuous structure is then replaced in a clearly defined manner by a finite number of single-mass oscillators. Each single-mass oscillator is comprehensively and clearly defined by a characteristic vector and a characteristic value. The characteristic vector (mode form, natural oscillation form) describes the relative amplitudes and phases of all degrees of freedom; the characteristic value describes behavior in terms of time (damped harmonic oscillation). Every oscillation of the structure can be artificially recreated from the characteristic vectors and values.

The modal model not only describes the actual state, but also forms the basis for simulation calculations: In response calculation, the response of the structure to a defined excitation, corresponding, for instance, to test laboratory conditions, is calculated. By means of structure modifications (changes in mass, damping or stiffness), the vibrational behavior can be optimized to the level required by operating conditions. The substructure coupling process collates modal models of various structures, for example, into an overall model. The modal model can be constructed analytically. When the modal models produced by both processes are compared with each other, the modal model resulting from an analytical modal analysis is more accurate than that from an experimental modal analysis, due to the greater number of degrees of freedom in the analytical process. This applies in particular to simulation calculations based on the model.

### Analytical modal analysis
The geometry, material data, and marginal conditions must be known. Multibody-system or finite-element models provide characteristic values and vectors. Analytical modal analysis requires no specimen sample, and can therefore be used at an early stage of development. However, it is often the case that precise knowledge concerning the structure's fundamental properties (damping, marginal conditions) are lacking, which means that the modal model can be very inaccurate. As well as this, the error is unidentified. A remedy can be to adjust the model to the results of an experimental modal analysis.

### Experimental modal analysis
Knowledge of the structure is not necessary, but a specimen is required. Analysis is based on measurements of the transmission functions in the frequency band in question from one excitation point to a number of response points, and vice versa. The modal model is derived from the matrix of the transmission functions (which defines the response model).

# Optical technology

## Photometric quantities and units

(See P. 28 for names of units)

| Quantity | | Unit |
|---|---|---|
| $A$ | Area | m² |
| | $A_1$ Radiating area (surface) | |
| | $A_2$ Irradiated area (surface) | |
| $E$ | Illuminance | lx = lm/m² |
| $I$ | Luminous intensity | cd |
| $L$ | Luminance | cd/m² |
| $M$ | Luminous emittance | lm/m² |
| $P$ | Power | W |
| $Q$ | Luminous energy | lm · s |

| Quantity | | Unit |
|---|---|---|
| $r$ | Distance | m |
| $t$ | Time | s |
| $\varepsilon_1$ | Incident angle of radiation (with respect to surface normal) | ° |
| $\varepsilon_2$ | Angle of refraction | ° |
| $\varepsilon_3$ | Angle of reflection | ° |
| $\eta$ | Luminous efficiency | lm/W |
| $\Phi$ | Luminous flux | lm |
| $\Omega$ | Solid angle | sr |
| $\lambda$ | Wavelength | nm |

## Electromagnetic radiation

Propagated at the speed of light. Wave nature. Not deflected by electric or magnetic fields. Wavelength $\lambda = c/f$, $c$ = speed of light $\approx 3 \cdot 10^8$ m/s = 300,000 km/s, $f$ = frequency in Hz.

| Designation | Wavelength range | Origin and/or creation | Examples of application |
|---|---|---|---|
| Cosmic radiation | < 0.1 pm | Bombardment of Earth's atmosphere by cosmic elementary particles. | Nuclear-physics tests. |
| Gamma radiation | 0.1...10 pm | Radioactive decay. | Nuclear physics, isotope technology. |
| X-radiation | 10 pm...10 nm | X-ray tubes (bombardment of anticathode by high-energy electrons). | Materials testing, medical diagnosis. |
| Ultraviolet radiation | 10...380 nm | Gaseous-discharge lamps, lasers. | Skin therapy, photolithography in IC production. |
| Visible radiation | 380...780 nm | Gaseous-discharge lamps, incandescent lamps, lasers. | Optical technology, photography, automotive lighting. |
| Infrared radiation | 780 nm...1 mm | Thermal radiators, infrared diodes, lasers. | Therapy, motor-vehicle distance measurement. |
| EHF waves | 1...10 mm | | |
| SHF waves | 10...100 mm | | Satellite communications, microwave heating, traffic radar, television and radio broadcasting, radio services. |
| UHF waves | 100 mm...1 m | | |
| VHF waves | 1...10 m | Traveling-wave tubes, resonant circuits, quartz oscillators. | |
| HF waves | 10...100 m | | |
| MF waves | 100 m...1 km | | |
| LF waves | 1...10 km | | |
| VLF waves | 10...100 km | | |

## Geometrical optics

In many cases, the geometrical dimensions of the media, in which optical radiation propagates, are large in comparison to the wavelength of the radiation. In such cases, the propagation of radiation can be explained in terms of "light rays", and can be described by simple laws of geometry.

An incident ray of light is split into a refracted ray and a reflected ray at the boundary between two media.

The law of refraction applies to the refracted ray:

$$n_1 \cdot \sin \varepsilon_1 = n_2 \cdot \sin \varepsilon_2$$

The indices of refraction $n_1$ and $n_2$ of a vacuum and the so-called dielectric media (e.g. air, glass, and plastics) are real numbers; for other media, they are complex numbers. The indices of refraction of media are a function of the wavelength (dispersion). In most cases, they decrease as the wavelength increases.

The reflected ray behaves according to the following equation:

$$\varepsilon_3 = \varepsilon_1$$

The ratio of the intensity of the reflected ray to the intensity of the incident ray (reflectance) depends on the incident angle and the indices of refraction of the adjacent media. In the case of a ray of light passing through air ($n_1 = 1.00$) into glass ($n_2 = 1.52$) at an angle of 90° ($\varepsilon_1 = 0$), 4.3% of the energy of the ray is reflected.

If the ray emanates from the optically denser medium ($n_1 > n_2$), total reflection can occur if the angle of incidence $\varepsilon_1$ is equal to or exceeds the acceptance angle of total reflection $\varepsilon_{1max}$. According to the law of refraction:

$$\sin \varepsilon_{1max} = n_2/n_1$$

---

**Refraction and reflection**
a *Medium 1, refractive index $n_1$*, b *Medium 2, refractive index $n_2$*. 1 *Incident beam*, 2 *Refracted beam*, 3 *Reflected beam*.

---

**Indices of refraction $n_D$** (for yellow sodium light, wavelength $\lambda = 589.3$ nm).

| Medium | $n_D$ |
|---|---|
| Vacuum, air | 1.00 |
| Ice (0 °C) | 1.31 |
| Water (+20 °C) | 1.33 |
| Silica glass | 1.46 |
| Standard glass for optics (BK 7) | 1.51673 |
| Window glass, glass used for headlamp lenses | 1.52 |
| Polymethyl methacrylate | 1.49 |
| Polyvinyl chloride | 1.54 |
| Polycarbonate | 1.58 |
| Polystyrene | 1.59 |
| Epoxy resin | 1.60 |
| Gallium arsenide (dependent on doping level) | approx. 3.5 |

## Components

### Cylindrical lenses

Parallel rays are made to converge in a focal line by a cylindrical lens.

### Prisms

Prismatic elements are used for the purpose of deflecting a ray of light by a desired angle. Parallel rays remain parallel after deflection by a prism.

In a motor-vehicle headlamp, cylindrical lenses and prismatic elements are used in order to direct the light emanating from the reflector more favorably.

### Reflectors

The function of motor-vehicle lamp reflectors is to reflect as much light as possible from the headlamp bulb, to achieve as great a range as possible, and to influence the distribution of light on the road in such a way that legislative requirements are met. Additional demands are placed on the headlamps as a result of the design (for instance, when fitted in a fender).

Whereas paraboloids were used almost exclusively as reflectors, the above-mentioned requirements, which are, in some cases, mutually contradictory, can only be met today by the use of stepped reflectors, free-form surfaces, or new headlamp designs (PES = polyellipsoid system, see P. 705).

In general, the larger the lens aperture area, the greater the headlamp range. On the other hand, the greater the solid angle achieved by the reflector, the greater the luminous efficiency.

## Color filters

Motor-vehicle lamps must meet precise specifications with regard to chromaticity coordinates depending on their intended functions (turn-signal lamps, stop lamps). These specifications can be met through the use of color filters which weaken the light emitted in certain parts of the visible spectrum.

# Light sources

The outer electron shells of atoms of certain materials can absorb varying levels of energy by excitation (energy input). The transition from higher to lower levels may lead to the emission of electromagnetic radiation.

The various types of light source can be fundamentally distinguished by the nature of electron excitation (energy input).

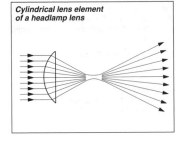

*Cylindrical lens element of a headlamp lens*

## Thermal radiators

In the case of this type of light source, the energy level is increased by adding heat energy. Emission is continuous across a broad wavelength range. The total radiated power is proportional to the power of 4 of the absolute temperature (Stephan Boltzmann's Law), and the distribution curve maximum is displaced to shorter wavelengths as temperature increases (Wien's Displacement Law).

### Incandescent lamps

Incandescent lamps, with tungsten glow filament (fusion temperature 3,660 K), are also thermal radiators. The evaporation of the tungsten and the resulting blackening of the bulb restrict the service life of this type of lamp.

### Halogen lamps

The halogen lamp allows the filament temperature to rise to close to the melting point of the tungsten. It is filled with a halogen gas (iodine or bromine). Close to the hot bulb wall, the evaporated tungsten combines with the filler gas to form tungsten halide. This is gaseous, light-transmitting and stable within a temperature range of 500 K to 1,700 K. It reaches the filament by means of convection, decomposes as a result of the high filament temperature, and forms an even tungsten deposit on the filament. In order to maintain this cycle, an external bulb temperature of approx. 300 °C is necessary. To achieve this, the bulb, made of fused silica (quartz), must surround the filament closely. A further advantage of this measure is that a higher filling pressure can be used, thereby providing additional resistance to tungsten evaporation. A disadvantage of these lamps is among others their low luminous efficiency.

## Gaseous-discharge lamps

Gaseous-discharge lamps are distinguished by their higher luminous efficiency. A gas discharge is maintained in an enclosed, gas-filled bulb by applying a voltage between two electrodes. The atoms of the emitted gas is excited by collisions between electrons and gas atoms. The atoms excited in the process give off their energy in the form of luminous radiation.

Examples of gaseous-discharge lamps are sodium-vapor lamps (street lighting), fluorescent lamps (interior illumination), and motor-vehicle headlamps ("Litronic", P. 917 onwards).

# Light and the physiology of vision

As the range of sensitivity to visible radiation varies from person to person, a general spectral-response function of the eye has been defined for photometric calculations and measurements and is contained, in table form for example, in DIN 5031, Part 3. This function $V(\lambda)$ was determined with test persons under daylight conditions ("light-adapted eye"), and can be used to calculate unambiguously the photometric values from objective physical values (see figure).

Definition of photometric quantities and units:

## Luminous flux $\Phi$
The radiant power emitted by a light source assessed on the basis of the spectral-response function of the human eye.

$$\Phi = K_m \cdot \int P_\lambda \cdot V(\lambda) d\lambda$$

$K_m$ Maximum value of luminosity factor of radiation for photopic vision $K_m = 683$ lm/W. $V(\lambda)$ Spectral-response function of the eye for a 2° visual field according to DIN 5031, Part 3. $P_\lambda$ Spectral radiant power.

## Luminous energy $Q$
The spectral radiant energy assessed on the basis of $V(\lambda)$. The following equation applies for temporally constant luminous flux:

$$Q = \Phi \cdot t$$

## Luminous intensity $I$
The ratio of luminous flux to a transilluminated solid angle.

$$I = \Phi/\Omega$$

## Illuminance $E$
The ratio of the incident luminous flux to the area of the illuminated surface.

$$E = \Phi/A_2$$

## Luminance $L$
The ratio of luminous intensity to the apparent (projected) area of the surface from which it is emitted.

$$L = I/(A_1 \cdot \cos \alpha)$$

where $\alpha$ is the angle between the ray direction and the surface normal.

## Luminous emittance $M$
The ratio of the luminous flux emitted by a luminous surface to the area of that surface.

$$M = \Phi/A_1$$

## Luminous efficiency $\eta$
The ratio of the emitted luminous flux to the power absorbed.

$$\eta = \Phi/P$$

Luminous efficiency can never exceed the maximum value for "luminosity factor of radiation" $K_m = 683$ lm/W at a wavelength of $\lambda = 555$ nm.

## Solid angle $\Omega$
The ratio of the transilluminated portion of the surface of a sphere concentric with the source of radiation to the square of the radius of the sphere. The total solid angle is:

$$\Omega = 4\pi \cdot sr \approx 12.56 \cdot sr$$

sr steradian

## Contrast
The ratio of the luminance values of two adjacent surfaces.

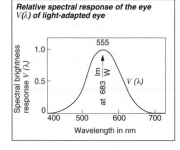

*Relative spectral response of the eye $V(\lambda)$ of light-adapted eye*

Spectral brightness response $V(\lambda)$

555

$\frac{lm}{W}$ at 683

$V(\lambda)$

Wavelength in nm

# Laser technology

Compared to other light sources, the laser has the following characteristic properties:
– High luminance, concentration of radiation on a diameter of a few light wavelengths
– Low beam expansion
– Monochromatic radiation
– Can be used for coherent measuring technology (high radiation coherence length)
– High power(in laser tools)

Light is generated in the laser is by induced emission in a specific laser material, which is brought to a state of excitation by the addition of energy (usually light). A resonator influences the beam geometry as required. Laser radiation emerges at the end of the resonator via a partly transparent mirror.

Examples of lasers in common use are:

| Laser type | Wavelength | Examples of application |
|---|---|---|
| Helium-neon-laser | 633 nm | Measuring technology |
| $CO_2$ laser | 10.6 μm | Material processing |
| YAG laser | 1,064 nm | Material processing |
| Semiconductor laser | e.g. 670 nm | Measuring technology |
| | e.g. 1,300 nm | Telecommunications |

---

**Laser principle**
*1 Pumping light source, 2 Resonator mirror, 3 Active laser material, 4 Partly transparent mirror, 5 Laser beam.*

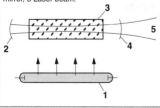

---

Laser measuring technology permits the noncontact, non-interacting testing of production tolerances of superfinished surfaces (e.g. fuel injectors). Resolutions in the nm range are achieved using interferometric methods. Further laser applications in technology are holography (spatial image information), automatic character recognition (bar-code scanners), information recording (CD scanning), material processing/machining, microsurgery, and transmitters for data transmission in optical waveguides.

Specific regulations are to be observed when handling laser products. Laser products are classified according to potential hazards. For details, see DIN 0837, "Radiation Safety of Laser Products".

# Optical fibers/waveguides

### Design

Optical fibers transmit electromagnetic waves in the ultraviolet (UV), visible, and infrared (IR) ranges of the spectrum. They are made of quartz, glass, or polymers, usually in the form of fibers or in channels created in transparent materials with a core whose refraction index is higher than that of the cladding. Thus, light launched into the core is retained in that area by means of refraction or total reflection. Depending on the refractive index profile, a distinction is made between three types of fiber (see figure):
– The step-index optical fiber, with a sharply-defined boundary between the core and the cladding
– The graded-index optical fiber, with parabolic refractive index profile in the core
– The monomode fiber with a very small core diameter

Step-index and graded-index fibers are multimode fibers, that is, light waves can be propagated along them at varying trajectories, generally at an oblique angle to the fiber axis. In the monomode fiber, propagation is only possible in the principal mode. Polymer fibers are always step-index fibers.

---

*Light propagation in optical fibers*
a *Fiber schematic*, b *Refractive index profile*.
*1 Step-index fiber, 2 Graded-index fiber,
3 Monomode fiber.*

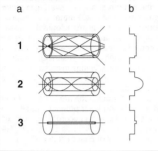

## Properties

Glass optical fibers have a high degree of transparency in the range from UV to IR. Attenuation is particularly low at wavelengths of 850 nm, 1,300 nm and 1,550 nm. Synthetic fibers absorb above 850 nm and below 450 nm.

They can only absorb light from a restricted angular range $\Theta$. The numerical aperture NA = SIN $(\Theta/2)$ serves as a basis for calculating this range (see table).

The differences in dispersion and propagation time of the various modes cause an increasing broadening of the light pulses as the length of the fiber increases, and thus restrict the bandwidth.

Optical fibers can be used within the temperature range of $-40\,°C$ to $135\,°C$; special versions can be used up to $800\,°C$.

## Areas of application

The main area of application is in data transmission. Synthetic fibers are preferred for use in the LAN (Local Area Network) field. Graded-index fibers are the most suitable for medium ranges. Only monomode fibers are used for long-distance data transmission. In fiber-optic networks, erbium-doped fibers serve as optical amplifiers. Optical fibers are being increasingly used in motor-vehicle lamps (P. 933) and sensors. Fiber-optic sensors generate neither stray fields nor sparks, and are themselves insensitive to that kind of disturbance. They are currently employed in potentially explosive environments, in medicine, and in high-speed trains (ICE).

Energy transport is at the forefront in the area of material processing with laser beams, in microsurgery, and in lighting engineering.

# Holography

In conventional image recording (photography, video cameras), a three-dimensional image is reduced to a two-dimensional representation. The spatial information contained in the image is lost when the image is stored. Spatial impressions gained when looking at the picture are based on sensory illusions.

With holography, three-dimensional information can be stored and also reproduced. For recording, coherent lightwave trains are necessary. In hologram imaging, a beam splitter divides the laser beam into an object beam and a reference beam. The resulting object and reference waves form an interference pattern on the recording medium (hologram plate), where the latter is stored as a diffraction grating.

## Characteristics of optical fibers (optical waveguides)

| Fiber type | Diameter Core μm | Diameter Cladding μm | Wavelength nm | Numerical aperture NA | Attenuation dB/km | Bandwidth MHz · km |
|---|---|---|---|---|---|---|
| Step-index fiber | | | | | | |
| Quartz/glass | 50...1,000 | 70...1,000 | 250...1,550 | 0.2...0.87 | 5...10 | 10 |
| Polymer | 200...>1,000 | 250...2,000 | 450...850 | 0.2...0.6 | 100...500 | <10 |
| Graded-index fiber | 50...150 | 100...500 | 450...1,550 | 0.2...0.3 | 3...5 | 200...1,000 |
| Monomode fiber | 3...10 | 100...500 | 850...1,550 | 0.12...0.21 | 0.3...1 | 2,500...15,000 |

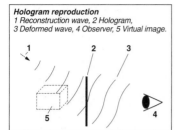

**Hologram reproduction**
1 Reconstruction wave, 2 Hologram,
3 Deformed wave, 4 Observer, 5 Virtual image.

The expanded beam of a laser illuminates the hologram plate and reconstructs the hologram. The diffraction grating on the hologram deforms the laser wave to such an extent that the observer has the impression that the holographically captured object is present behind the hologram plate.

Typical applications:
– Registration of minute path deviations
– Measurement of deformations and vibration amplitudes far below the wavelength of light by means of holographic interferometry
– Holographic measuring and testing methods in precision manufacturing (e.g. fuel-injection components)
– Production of forgery-proof documents
– Use of holographic elements for illustration purposes

# Display elements

The most important optical information displays are liquid crystal and light-emitting diode displays.

## Liquid crystal display

The liquid crystal display, or LCD (Liquid Crystal Display), is a passive display element. The contrast differences created are made visible by additional illumination. The most widely used type of LCD is the twisted nematic cell, or TN cell.

The liquid crystal substance is held between two glass plates. In the area of display segments, these glass plates are covered with a transparent conducting layer to which a voltage can be applied: An electric field is created between the layers. An additional orientation layer causes the plane of polarization of light passing through the cell to rotate. When polarizers acting at right angles to one another are added to both outside surfaces, the cell is initially transparent. In the area of the two opposed electrodes, the liquid crystal molecules are aligned in the direction of the electric field by applying voltage. Rotation of the plane of polarization is now suppressed and the display area becomes opaque.

Numbers, letters, and symbols are indicated in separately activated segment areas. LCD picture elements arranged in matrix form and individually activated by thin-film transistors (TFT) form the basis of TFT flatscreen displays.

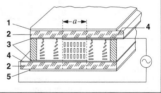

**Principle of operation of a liquid crystal display (nematic cell)**
1 Polarizer, 2 Glass, 3 Orientation and insulation layers, 4 Electrode, 5 Polarizer (and reflector). a Segment area.

## Light-emitting diodes (LEDs)

The Light-Emitting Diode, or LED, display is an active (self-luminous) display. It consists of a semiconductor element with PN junction. The charge carriers (free electrons and holes) recombine during operation in forward direction. With certain semiconductor materials, the energy which is released as a result is converted into electromagnetic radiation energy.

Frequently used semiconductor materials are: gallium arsenide (infrared), gallium arsenide phosphide (red to yellow), and gallium phosphide (green).

# Acoustics

## Quantities and units
(see also DIN 1332)

| Quantity | | SI unit |
|---|---|---|
| $c$ | Velocity of sound | m/s |
| $f$ | Frequency | Hz |
| $I$ | Sound intensity | W/m² |
| $L_I$ | Sound intensity level | dB |
| $L_{Aeq}$ | Equivalent continuous sound level, A-weighted | dB (A) |
| $L_{pA}$ | Sound pressure level, A-weighted | dB (A) |
| $L_r$ | Rating sound level | dB (A) |
| $L_{WA}$ | Sound power level, A-weighted | dB (A) |
| $P$ | Sound power | W |
| $p$ | Sound pressure | Pa |
| $S$ | Surface area | m² |
| $T$ | Reverberation time | s |
| $v$ | Particle velocity | m/s |
| $Z$ | Specific acoustic impedance | Pa · s/m |
| $\alpha$ | Sound absorption coefficient | 1 |
| $\lambda$ | Wavelength | m |
| $\varrho$ | Density | kg/m³ |
| $\omega$ | Angular frequency (= $2\,\pi f$) | 1/s |

## General terminology
(see also DIN 1320)

**Sound**
Mechanical vibrations and waves in an elastic medium, particularly in the audible frequency band (16 to 20,000 Hz).

**Ultrasound**
Mechanical vibrations above the frequency range of human hearing.

**Propagation of sound**
In general, sound propagates spherically from its source. In a free sound field, sound pressure decreases by 6 dB each time the distance from the sound source is doubled. Reflecting objects influence the sound field, and the rate at which the sound level is reduced as a function of the distance from the sound source is lower.

**Velocity of sound** $c$
The velocity of sound is the velocity of propagation of a sound wave.

## Sound velocities and wavelengths in different materials

| Material/medium | Sound speed $c$ m/s | Wave-length $\lambda$ m at 1,000 Hz |
|---|---|---|
| Air, 20 °C, 1,014 hPa | 343 | 0.343 |
| Water, 10 °C | 1,440 | 1.44 |
| Rubber (according to hardness) | 60...1,500 | 0.06...1.5 |
| Aluminum (rod) | 5,100 | 5.1 |
| Steel (rod) | 5,000 | 5.0 |

**Wavelength** $\lambda = c/f = 2\,\pi\,c/\omega$

**Particle velocity** $v$
Particle velocity $v$ is the alternating velocity of a vibrating particle. In a free sound field: $v = p/Z$. At low frequencies, perceived vibration is approximately proportional to the acoustic velocity.

**Sound pressure** $p$
Sound pressure is the alternating pressure generated in a medium by the vibration of sound. In a free sound field: $p = v \cdot Z$. It is usually measured as the effective value.

**Specific acoustic impedance** $Z$
Specific acoustic impedance is a measure of the ability of a medium to transmit sound waves. $Z = p/v = \varrho \cdot c$. For air at 20 °C and 1,013 hPa (760 torr) $Z$ = 415 Ns/m³, for water at 10 °C $Z$ = 1.44 · 10⁶ Ns/m³ = 1.44 · 10⁶ Pa · s/m.

**Sound power** $P$
Sound power is the power emitted by a sound source. Sound power of some sound sources:

| | |
|---|---|
| Normal conversation, average | $7 \cdot 10^{-6}$ W |
| Violin, fortissimo | $1 \cdot 10^{-3}$ W |
| Peak power of the human voice | $2 \cdot 10^{-3}$ W |
| Piano, trumpet | 0.2...0.3 W |
| Organ | 1...10 W |
| Kettle drum | 10 W |
| Orchestra (75 musicians) | up to 65 W |

**Sound intensity** $I$
(Sound intensity) $I = P/S$, i.e. sound power through a plane vertical to the direction of propagation. In a sound field:
$I = p^2/\varrho \cdot c = v^2 \cdot \varrho \cdot c$.

### Doppler effect
For moving sound sources: If the distance between the sound source and the observer decreases, the perceived pitch ($f'$) is higher than the actual pitch ($f$); as distance increases, the perceived pitch falls. The following relationship holds true if the observer and the sound source are moving along the same line: $f'/f = (c - u')/(c - u)$.
$c$ velocity of sound, $u'$ velocity of observer, $u$ velocity of sound source.

### Interval
The interval is the ratio of the frequencies of two tones. In the "equal-tempered scale" of our musical instruments (introduced by J. S. Bach), the octave (interval 2:1) is divided into 12 equal semitones with a ratio of $\sqrt[12]{2} = 1.0595$, i.e. a series of any number of tempered intervals always leads back to a tempered interval. In the case of "pure pitch", on the other hand, a sequence of pure intervals usually does not lead to a pure interval. (Pure pitch has the intervals 1, 16/15, 9/8, 6/5, 5/4, 4/3, 7/5, 3/2, 8/5, 5/3, 9/5, 15/8, 2.)

### Sound spectrum
The sound spectrum, generated by means of frequency analysis, is used to show the relationship between the sound pressure level (airborne or structure-borne noise) and frequency.

### Octave band spectrum
The sound levels are determined and represented in terms of octave bandwidth. Octave: frequency ranges with fundamental frequencies in a ratio of 1:2. Mean frequency of octave $f_m = \sqrt{f_1 \cdot f_2}$.
Recommended center frequencies: 31.5; 63; 125; 250; 500; 1,000; 2,000; 4,000; 8,000 Hz.

### Third-octave band spectrum
Sound levels are determined and represented in terms of third-octave bandwidth. The bandwidth referred to the center frequency is relatively constant, as in the case of the octave band spectrum.

### Sound insulation
Sound insulation is the reduction of the effect of a sound source by interposing a reflecting (insulating) wall between the source and the impact location.

### Sound absorption
Loss of sound energy when reflected on peripheries, but also for the propagation in a medium.

### Sound absorption coefficient $\alpha$
The sound absorption coefficient is the ratio of the non-reflected sound energy to the incident sound energy. With total reflection, $\alpha = 0$; with total absorption, $\alpha = 1$.

### Noise reduction
Attenuation of acoustic emissions: Reduction in the primary mechanical or electrodynamic generation of structure-borne noise and flow noises; damping and modification of sympathetic vibrations; reduction of the effective radiation surfaces; encapsulation.

### Low-noise design
Application of simulation techniques (modal analysis, modal variation, finite-element analysis, analysis of coupling effects of airborne noise) for advance calculation and optimization of the acoustic properties of new designs.

## Quantities for noise emission measurement

Sound field quantities are normally measured as RMS values, and are expressed in terms of frequency-dependent weighting (A-weighting). This is indicated by the subscript A next to the corresponding symbol.

### Sound power level $L_w$
The sound power of a sound source is described by the sound power level $L_w$. The sound power level is equal to ten times the logarithm to the base 10 of the ratio of the calculated sound power to the reference sound power $P_0 = 10^{-12}$ W. Sound power cannot be measured directly. It is calculated based on quantities of the sound field which surrounds the source. Measure-

ments are usually also made of the sound pressure level $L_p$ at specific points around the source (see DIN 45 635). $L_w$ can also be calculated based on sound intensity levels $L_I$ measured at various points on the surface of an imaginary envelope surrounding the sound source. If noise is emitted uniformly through a surface of $S_0 = 1$ m², the sound pressure level $L_p$ and the sound intensity level $L_I$ at this surface have the same value as the sound power level $L_w$.

**Sound pressure level $L_p$**
The sound pressure level is ten times the logarithm to the base 10 of the ratio of the square of the RMS sound pressure to the square of the reference sound pressure:
$p_0 = 20$ µPa. $L_p = 10 \log p^2/p_0^2$
or
$L_p = 20 \log p/p_0$.
The sound pressure level is given in decibels (dB).

The frequency-dependent, A-weighted sound pressure level $L_{pA}$ as measured at a distance of $d = 1$ m is frequently used to characterize sound sources.

**Sound intensity level $L_I$**
The sound intensity level is equal to ten times the logarithm to the base 10 of the ratio of sound intensity to reference sound intensity:
$I_0 = 10^{-12}$ W/m². $L_I = 10 \log I/I_0$.

**Interaction of two or more sound sources**
If two independent sound fields are superimposed, their sound intensities or the squares of their sound pressures must be added. The overall sound level is then determined from the individual sound levels as follows:

| Difference between 2 individual sound levels | Overall sound level = higher individual sound level + allowance of: |
|---|---|
| 0 dB | 3 dB |
| 1 dB | 2.5 dB |
| 2 dB | 2.1 dB |
| 3 dB | 1.8 dB |
| 4 dB | 1.5 dB |
| 6 dB | 1 dB |
| 8 dB | 0.6 dB |
| 10 dB | 0.4 dB |

## Motor-vehicle noise measurements and limits

The noise measurements employed to monitor compliance with legal requirements are concerned exclusively with external noise levels. The EC Directive 70/157/EEC enacted in 1970, together with its last revision 99/101/EEC in 1999, defines measurement procedures and limit values for noise emissions from stationary and moving vehicles. Due to the inadequate effectiveness of the statutory provisions in real traffic situations, EU legislators are currently working on revising the measurement procedure with the aim of better reproducing urban traffic situations in the test procedure. The Directive 01/43/EEC introduced in 2001 in addition to the type approval of vehicles limits the noise emissions by tires under constant-driving conditions in the 80 km/h speed range.

**Measuring noise emissions from moving passenger cars and trucks up to a permissible total weight of 3.5 t**
The vehicle approaches line AA, which is located up to 10 m from the microphone plane, at a constant velocity of 50 km/h. After the vehicle reaches line AA, it continues under full acceleration as far as line BB (placed 10 m behind the microphone plane), which serves as the end of the test section. Passenger cars with manual transmissions and a maximum of 4 forward gears are tested in 2nd gear. Consecutive readings in 2nd and 3rd gears are employed for vehicles with more than 4 forward gears, while sports cars are tested in 3rd gear in accordance with the definition in the Directive. Vehicles with automatic transmissions are tested in the D position. The noise-emissions level is defined as the maximum occurring sound level which is measured on the left and right sides of the vehicle at a distance of 7.5 m from the center of the lane. In a test in two gears, the noise-emissions level is the arithmetic mean from the measurement of both gears.

**Measuring noise emissions from moving trucks from a permissible total weight of 3.5 t**
The vehicle approaches line AA, which is located up to 10 m from the microphone plane,

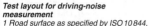

***Test layout for driving-noise measurement***
1 Road surface as specified by ISO 10 844,
2 Left microphone, 3 Right microphone.

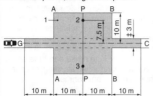

at a constant velocity. After the truck reaches line AA, it continues at full acceleration as far as line BB (also placed 10 m from the microphone plane), which serves as the end of the test section. The driving speed adopted is dependent on the gear tested and the rated engine speed. The choice of gears selected is based on the fact that at least the rated speed must be reached within the test section, however, the vehicle must pass through the test section without reaching the engine-speed limitation. The noise-emissions level is defined as the maximum occurring sound level from all the measurements.

### Noise emissions from stationary vehicles

Measurements are taken in the vicinity of the exhaust muffler in order to facilitate subsequent testing of motor-vehicle noise levels. Measurements are carried out with the engine running at $3/4$ the speed at which it develops its rated power output. Once the engine speed levels off, the throttle valve is quickly returned to its idle position. During this procedure, the maximum A-weighted sound-pressure level is monitored at a distance of 50 cm from the outlet at a horizontal angle of $(45 \pm 10)°$ to the direction of exhaust flow. The recorded level is entered in the vehicle documentation in dB(A) with the suffix "P" (making it possible to distinguish between this figure and levels derived using earlier test procedures). No limit values are specified in the type approval for measuring noise emissions from stationary levels.

### Interior noise level

There are no legal requirements pertaining to interior noise levels. The interior noise

### Limits and tolerances in dB (A) for noise emission from motor vehicles

| Vehicle category 92/97/EEC since Oct. 1995 | dB (A) |
|---|---|
| **Passenger cars** | |
| With spark-ignition or diesel engine | 74 + 1 |
| – with direct-injection diesel engine | 75 + 1 |
| **Trucks and buses** | |
| Permissible total weight below 2 t | 76 + 1 |
| – with direct-injection diesel engine | 77 + 1 |
| **Buses** | |
| Permissible total weight 2 t...3.5 t | 76 + 1 |
| – with direct-injection diesel engine | 77 + 1 |
| Permissible total weight above 3.5 t | |
| – engine power output up to 150 kW | 78 + 1 |
| – engine power output above 150 kW | 80 + 1 |
| **Trucks** | |
| Permissible total weight 2 t...3.5 t | 76 + 1 |
| – with direct-injection diesel engine | 77 + 1 |
| Permissible total weight above 3.5 t (German Road Traffic Licensing Regulations/CUR: above 2.8 t) | |
| – engine power output up to 75 kW | 77 + 1 |
| – engine power output up to 150 kW | 78 + 1 |
| – engine power output above 150 kW | 80 + 1 |

Off-road and AWD vehicles are subject to additional higher noise limits for engine brakes and pneumatic equipment.

level is measured, e.g. at constant speed or when gradually accelerating in the range from 60 km/h or 40% of the maximum driving speed, as the A-weighted sound-pressure level and then plotted as a function of the driving speed. One series of measurements is always to be made at the driver's seat; other measurement locations are selected in accordance with the passenger seating arrangement inside the vehicle. There are no plans to introduce a single value for indicating interior noise levels.

## Quantities for noise immission measurement

### Rating sound level $L_r$

The effect of noise on the human being is evaluated using the rating sound level $L_r$ (see also DIN 45645). This is a measure of the mean noise immission over a period of time (e.g. 8 working hours), and with fluctuating noises is either measured directly with integrated measuring instruments or calculated from individual sound-pressure-level measurements and the associated periods of time of the individual sound effects (see also DIN 45641). Noise immission parameters such as pulsation and tonal quality can be taken into account through level allowances (see table below for reference values).

The following standard values for the rating sound level (Germany; Technical Instructions on Noise Abatement, 16 July 1968) are measured outside the nearest residential building (0.5 m in front of an open window):

|  | Day | Night |
|---|---|---|
| Purely industrial areas | 70 dB (A) | 70 dB (A) |
| Areas with predominantly industrial areas | 65 dB (A) | 50 dB (A) |
| Mixed areas | 60 dB (A) | 45 dB (A) |
| Areas with predominantly residential premises | 55 dB (A) | 40 dB (A) |
| Purely residential areas | 50 dB (A) | 35 dB (A) |
| Health resorts, hospitals etc. | 45 dB (A) | 35 dB (A) |

**Equivalent continuous sound level $L_{Aeq}$**
In the case of noises which fluctuate in time, the mean A-weighted sound pressure level resulting from the individual sound pressure levels and the individual exposure times, equals the equivalent continuous sound level if it describes the mean sound energy over the entire assessment time period (see DIN 45641). The equivalent continuous sound level in accordance with the German "Aircraft Noise Abatement Law" is arrived at in a different manner (see DIN 45643).

# Perceived sound levels

The human ear can distinguish approximately 300 levels of acoustic intensity and 3,000...4,000 different frequencies (pitch levels) in rapid temporal succession and evaluate them according to complex patterns. Thus there is not necessarily any direct correspondence between perceived noise levels and (energy-oriented) technically defined sound levels. A rough approximation of subjective sound-level perception is provided by A-weighted sound levels, which take into account variations in the human ear's sensitivity as a function of frequency, the phon unit and the definition of loudness in sone. Sound-level measurements alone do not suffice to define the nuisance and disturbance potential of noise emanating from machinery and equipment. A hardly-perceptible ticking noise can thus be perceived as extremely disturbing, even in an otherwise loud environment.

**Loudness level $L_s$**
The loudness level is a comparative measure of the intensity of sound perception measured in phon. The loudness level of a sound (pure tone or noise) is the sound pressure level of a standard pure tone which, under standard listening conditions, is judged by a normal observer to be equally loud. The standard noise level is a plane sound wave at a frequency of 1,000 Hz impinging on the observer's head from the front. This is known internationally as the loudness level. A difference of 8 to 10 phon is perceived as twice or half as loud.

**Phon**
The standard pure tone judged as being equally loud has a specific sound pressure level in dB. This value is given as the loudness level of the tested sound, and has the designation "phon". As human perception of sound is frequency-dependent, the dB values of the tested sound for notes, for example, do not agree with the dB values of the standard pure tone (exception: reference frequency 1,000 Hz), however the phon figures do agree. See the graph below for curves of equal loudness level according to Fletcher-Munson.

**Loudness $S$ in sone**
The sone is the unit employed to define subjective noise levels. The starting point for defining the sone is: How much higher or lower is the perceived level of a particular sound relative to a specific standard.
Definition: sound level $L_s$ = 40 phon corresponds to a loudness level of $S$ = 1 sone. Doubling or halving the loudness is equivalent to a variation in the loudness level of approx. 10 phon.

There is an ISO loudness standard for calculating stationary sound using tertiary levels (Zwicker method). This procedure takes into account both frequency weighting and the screening effects of hearing.

### Pitch, sharpness

The spectrum of perceptible sound can be divided into 24 hearing-oriented frequency groups (bark). The groups define perceived pitch levels. The loudness/pitch distribution (analogous to the tertiary spectrum) can be used to quantify other subjective aural impressions, such as the sharpness of a noise.

## Engineering acoustics

### Measuring equipment for acoustics
- Sound-pressure recording with capacitor microphones, e.g. using sound-level meters in dB(A).
- Artificial-head recordings with ear microphones for faithful sound reproduction (with headphones).
- Measuring rooms for standard sound measurements are generally equipped with highly sound-absorbent walls.
- Vibrations, structure-borne noise: acceleration sensor (mass partly under 1 g), e.g. according to piezoelectric principle; laser vibrometer for rapid non-contacting measurement according to Doppler principle.

### Calculating methods in acoustics

Vibration/oscillation: FE modeling and natural-vibration calculation, adjustment with experimental modal analysis. Modeling of forces acting during operation enables calculation of operational vibration shapes. Thus optimization of design with regard to vibrational behavior.

Airborne noise, fluid-borne noise: Sound-field calculation e.g. of cabinet radiation or in cavities using FEM (finite-element method) or BEM (boundary-element method).

### Acoustic quality control

This is the evaluation, predominantly by human testers, of noise and interference levels and the classification of operating defects based on audible sound or structure-borne noise as part of the production process, e.g. in the runup of electric motors. Automated testers are used for specialized applications, but they are at present still unable to achieve human levels of flexibility, selectivity and learning ability. Advances have been made through the use of neural networks and combined evaluation of sound properties.

**Sound design** (see P. 1130 onwards).

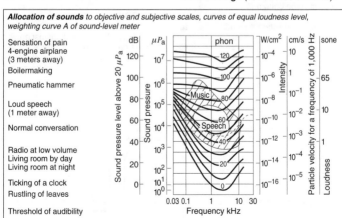

*Allocation of sounds to objective and subjective scales, curves of equal loudness level, weighting curve A of sound-level meter*

Sensation of pain
4-engine airplane (3 meters away)
Boilermaking
Pneumatic hammer
Loud speech (1 meter away)
Normal conversation
Radio at low volume
Living room by day
Living room at night
Ticking of a clock
Rustling of leaves
Threshold of audibility

# Hydrostatics

## Symbols and units

| Quantity | | Unit |
|---|---|---|
| $A$ | Cross-sectional area | m² |
| $A_B$ | Area of base | m² |
| $A_S$ | Area of side | m² |
| $F$ | Force | N |
| $F_A$ | Buoyancy force | N |
| $F_B$ | Force acting on bottom | N |
| $F_G$ | Weight | N |
| $F_S$ | Force acting on sides | N |

| Quantity | | Unit |
|---|---|---|
| $V_F$ | Volume of displaced fluid | m³ |
| $g$ | Acceleration of free fall | m/s² |
| | $(g = 9.81)$ | |
| $h$ | Depth of fluid | m |
| $m_F$ | Mass of displaced fluid | kg |
| $p$ | Pressure | Pa = N/m² |
| $\varrho$ | Density | kg/m³ |

## Density and pressure

Although fluids are compressible to a lesser extent, they can be viewed as being incompressible for most problems. In addition, since density is only slightly dependent on temperature, it can be taken as constant for many applications.

Pressure $p = \mathrm{d}F/\mathrm{d}A$ is non-directional in fluids which are at rest. If the pressure component produced by the difference in height (geodetic pressure) is negligible, the hydrostatic pressure is uniformly high everywhere (e.g. in a hydrostatic press).

### Static fluid in an open vessel

Pressure $\qquad p_{(h)} = \varrho \cdot g \cdot h$

Force acting on bottom $F_B = A_B \cdot \varrho \cdot g \cdot h$

Force acting on sides $F_S = 0.5 \cdot A_S \cdot \varrho \cdot g \cdot h$

## Hydrostatic press

Pressure $\qquad p = \dfrac{F_1}{A_1} = \dfrac{F_2}{A_2}$

Piston forces $F_1 = p \cdot A_1 = F_2 \cdot \dfrac{A_1}{A_2}$

$$F_2 = p \cdot A_2 = F_1 \cdot \frac{A_2}{A_1}$$

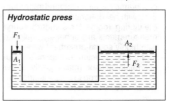

*Hydrostatic press*

## Buoyancy

Buoyancy is a force acting against gravity and acts on the center of gravity of the volume of the displaced fluid. It corresponds to the weight of the fluid displaced by the submerged body:

$$F_A = m_F \cdot g = V_F \cdot \varrho \cdot g$$

A body will float if $F_A = F_G$.

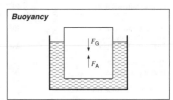

*Buoyancy*

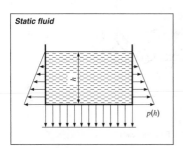

*Static fluid*

# Fluid mechanics

## Symbols and units

| Quantity | | Unit |
|---|---|---|
| $A$ | Cross-sectional area | m² |
| $F$ | Force | N |
| $F_A$ | Buoyancy force | N |
| $F_W$ | Resistance force | N |
| $L$ | Length in flow direction | m |
| $Q$ | Volumetric flow | m³/s |
| $Re$ | Reynolds number | – |
| $c_d$ | Aerodynamic drag | – |
| $d$ | Diameter | m |
| $g$ | Acceleration of free fall ($g = 9.81$) | m/s² |

| Quantity | | Unit |
|---|---|---|
| $h$ | Height | m |
| $m$ | Mass | kg |
| $\dot{m}$ | Mass flow | kg/s |
| $p$ | Pressure | Pa = N/m² |
| $t$ | Thickness | m |
| $?$ | Flow velocity | m/s |
| $\alpha$ | Contraction coefficient | – |
| $\eta$ | Dynamic viscosity | Pa·s = N·s/m² |
| $\mu$ | Discharge coefficient | – |
| $\nu$ | Kinematic viscosity | m/s² |
| $\varrho$ | Density | kg/m³ |
| $\varphi$ | Velocity coefficient | – |

## Basic principles

Since, in the case of gases with low flow velocities (up to 0.5 times the velocity of sound), compression is negligible in many flow processes, they are also governed by the laws of incompressible fluids.

An ideal fluid is incompressible and frictionless. This mean that no shear stresses occur in the fluid, and the pressure on a fluid element is uniform in all directions. In actual fact, however, a resistance must be overcome in fluids if deformations occur that are caused by displacement of fluid elements. The resulting shear stress complies with Newton:

$$\tau = \frac{F}{A} = \eta \cdot \frac{v}{h}$$

The proportionality factor $\eta$ is called the <u>dynamic viscosity</u> and is greatly dependent on temperature. A derived variable is the <u>kinematic viscosity</u>:

$$\nu = \frac{\eta}{\varrho}$$

Flows without turbulence, in which the individual fluid layers move separately in parallel and which are predominantly determined by viscosity, are known as <u>laminar flows</u>. If the flow velocity exceeds a limit value, adjacent layers start to swirl, resulting in a <u>turbulent flow</u>. In addition to the flow velocity, the transition point between laminar and turbulent flow is also dependent on the Reynolds number

$$Re = \frac{\varrho \cdot L \cdot v}{\eta} = \frac{L \cdot v}{\nu}$$

In the case of a flow within a pipe, the pipe diameter is used for $L$. Flow in a pipe becomes unstable or turbulent at $Re > 2,300$.

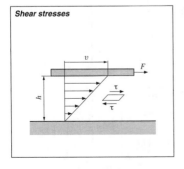

**Shear stresses**

## Continuity equation

In a steady state, mass conservation requires that the mass flow rate be of equal magnitude in each cross-section:

$$\dot{m} = \varrho \cdot A_1 \cdot v_1 = \varrho \cdot A_2 \cdot v_2 = \text{const.}$$

In the case of incompressible fluids ($\varrho$ = const.), the volumetric flow must also be constant:

$$Q = A_1 \cdot v_1 = A_2 \cdot v_2 = \text{const.}$$

## Bernoulli equation

From the continuity equation, it follows that an acceleration takes place between $A_1$ and $A_2$. This results in an increase in kinetic energy, which must be effected by a pressure drop, where $p_1 > p_2$. According to the law of conservation of energy, the sum of the static pressure $p$, kinetic pressure, and geodetic pressure is constant in a flowing fluid. Ignoring friction losses, the following applies accordingly to the flowing fluid in a non-horizontal pipe:

$$p_1 + \frac{1}{2} \cdot \varrho \cdot v_1^2 + \varrho \cdot g \cdot h_1 = p_2 + \frac{1}{2} \cdot \varrho \cdot v_2^2 + \varrho \cdot g \cdot h_2$$

## Discharge from a pressure vessel

Under the precondition that the cross-sectional area of the discharge end is very much smaller that that of the vessel (see diagram at the bottom of the facing page), the velocity $v_1$ is negligible according to the continuity equation. As derived from Bernoulli equation, the discharge velocity is governed by the following:

$$v_2 = \varphi \cdot \sqrt{\frac{2}{\varrho}\,(p_1 - p_2) + 2 \cdot g \cdot h}$$

The velocity coefficient $\varphi$ takes into account the losses that occur. The jet constriction must also be taken into account for the volumetric flow or the discharge volume. With the contraction coefficient $\alpha$, the following applies:

$$Q = \alpha \cdot \varphi \cdot A_2 \cdot \sqrt{\frac{2}{\varrho}\,(p_1 - p_2) + 2 \cdot g \cdot h}$$

Velocity coefficient and contraction coefficient are often expressed together as the discharge coefficient $\mu = \alpha \cdot \varphi$.

**Bernoulli equation**

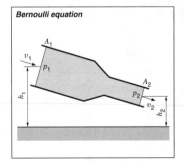

| Table 1 | | | |
|---|---|---|---|
| Orifice shape | Velocity coefficient $\varphi$ | Contraction coefficient $\alpha$ | Discharge coefficient $\mu$ |
| | 0.97 | 0.61...0.64 | 0.59...0.62 |
| | 0.97...0.99 | 1.0 | 0.97...0.99 |
| | 0.95...0.97 | $(d_2/d_1)^2$<br>0.4   0.6   0.8   1.0<br>0.87   0.90   0.94   1.0 | 0.82...0.97 |

## Resistance of bodies submerged in a fluid flow

A pressure differential occurs across a body submerged in a fluid flow, resulting in a resistance force

$$F_w = \frac{1}{2} \cdot c_d \cdot A \cdot \varrho \cdot v^2$$

Here, $A$ is the cross-sectional area of the body on which the fluid flow is acting and $c_d$ an undefined coefficient of resistance, which is dependent on the shape of the body submerged in the fluid flow.

As it is extremely complex to calculate exactly the resistance to flow even for simple bodies, resistance to flow is usually determined experimentally. If the dimensions are large, the measurements are taken on downscaled models. As well as geometrical similarity, the forms of energy that occur (kinetic energy, frictional work) in the original fluid flow and in the model flow must be proportional. This proportion is denoted by the Reynolds number.

Basically: Two flows are similar in fluid-dynamic terms if their Reynolds numbers are identical.

---

### Discharge from a pressure vessel

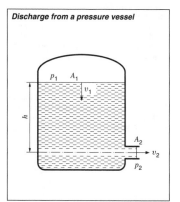

---

**Drag coefficients $c_d$**

| Body shape | | $c_d$ |
|---|---|---|
| Circular plate | | 1.11 |
| Open dish | | 1.33 |
| Sphere | $Re < 200,000$ | 0.47 |
| | $Re > 250,000$ | 0.20 |
| Narrow rotational body $L/t = 6$ | | 0.05 |
| Long cylinder | $Re < 200,000$ | 1.0 |
| | $Re > 450,000$ | 0.35 |
| Long plate $L/t = 30$ | $Re \approx 500,000$ | 0.78 |
| | $Re \approx 200,000$ | 0.66 |
| Long wing $L/t = 18$ | | 0.2 |
| $L/t = 8$ | $Re \approx 10^6$ | 0.1 |
| $L/t = 5$ | | 0.08 |
| $L/t = 2$ | $Re \approx 2 \cdot 10^5$ | 0.2 |

# Heat

## Symbols and units

See PP. 22 to 28 for names of units, P. 36 for conversion of heat units, and P. 232 onwards for thermal expansion, heat of fusion, and heat of evaporation.

| Quantity | | SI unit |
|---|---|---|
| $A$ | Cross-sectional area | $m^2$ |
| $c$ | Specific heat capacity | $J/(kg \cdot K)$ |
| | $c_p$ Isobaric (constant pressure) | |
| | $c_v$ Isochoric (constant volume) | |
| $k$ | Heat-transmission coefficient | $W/(m^2 \cdot K)$ |
| $m$ | Mass | kg |
| $p$ | Pressure | $Pa = N/m^2$ |
| $Q$ | Heat | J |
| $Q_i$ | Enthalpy (heat content) | J |
| $\dot{Q}$ | Heat flow $= Q/z$ | W |
| $R_m$ | Molar gas constant | $J/(mol \cdot K)$ |
| | $= 8.3145\ J/(mol \cdot K)$ | |
| | (same for all gases) | |
| $R_i$ | Special gas constant | $J/(kg \cdot K)$ |
| | $R_i = R_m/M$ ($M$ = molecular weight) | |
| $S$ | Entropy | $J/K$ |
| $s$ | Distance | m |
| $T$ | Thermodynamic temperature | K |
| | $T = t + 273.15$ | |
| $\Delta T$ | Temperature difference | K |
| | $= T_1 - T_2 = t_1 - t_2$ | |
| | $T_1, t_1$ higher temperature | |
| | $T_2, t_2$ lower temperature | |
| $t$ | Celsius temperature | °C |
| $V$ | Volume | $m^3$ |
| $v$ | Specific volume | $m^3/kg$ |
| $W$ | Work | J |
| $z$ | Time | s |
| $\alpha$ | Heat-transfer coefficient | $W/(m^2 \cdot K)$ |
| | $\alpha_a$ external, $\alpha_i$ internal | |
| $\varepsilon$ | Emissivity | – |
| $\lambda$ | Thermal conductivity | $W/(m \cdot K)$ |
| | (see P. 19 for values) | |
| $\varrho$ | Density | $kg/m^3$ |

**Conversion from outdated units**
(see also PP. 18 and 19)
1 kcal (kilocalorie) $= 4,186.8$ J
$\approx 4,200$ J $\approx 4.2$ kJ
1 kcal/(m $\cdot$ h $\cdot$ grd) $= 1.163$ W/(m $\cdot$ K)

## Enthalpy (heat content)

Enthalpy (heat content) $Q_i$ is the quantity of heat which a solid, liquid, or gaseous body of mass $m$ and specific heat capacity $c_p$ has at temperature $t$:

$$Q_i = c_p \cdot m \cdot t = c_p \cdot V \cdot \varrho \cdot t$$

## Heat transfer

Heat is transferred in three different ways:
<u>Thermal conduction</u>: Heat is conveyed inside a solid, liquid, or gaseous body by contact between the particles.
<u>Convection</u>: Heat is conveyed by the particles of a moving liquid or gaseous body. In natural or free convection, the state of motion is brought about by the effect of buoyancy; in forced convection, however, the motion is maintained artificially.
<u>Radiation</u>: Heat is transferred from one body to another by electromagnetic waves.

**Thermal conduction**
The heat flow in a body of constant cross-section $A$ between two parallel cross-sectional planes separated by a distance $s$ at a temperature difference $T = T_1 - T_2$ is

$$\dot{Q} = \frac{\lambda}{s} \cdot A \cdot \Delta T$$

**Thermal radiation**
Empty space and air are pervious to thermal radiation. Solid bodies and most liquids are impervious to thermal radiation, as are various gases at certain wavelengths.

The thermal radiation emitted by the area $A$ at temperature $T$ is:

$$\dot{Q} = \varepsilon \cdot \sigma \cdot A \cdot T^4$$

where $\sigma = 5.67 \cdot 10^{-8}$ W/(m² · K⁴) is the radiation constant of the black-body radiator[1]) and $\varepsilon$ is the emissivity of the surface area (see table on opposite page).

## Emissivity $\varepsilon$
up to a temperature of 300 °C (573 K)

| | |
|---|---|
| Black-body radiator[1] | 1.00 |
| Aluminum, unmachined | 0.07 |
| Aluminum, polished | 0.04 |
| Ice | 0.90 |
| Enamel paint, white | 0.91 |
| Glass | 0.93 |
| Cast iron, rough, oxidized | 0.94 |
| Cast iron, turned | 0.44 |
| Wood, smooth | 0.90 |
| Lime mortar, rough, white | 0.93 |
| Copper, oxidized | 0.64 |
| Copper, polished | 0.05 |
| Brass, matt | 0.22 |
| Brass, polished | 0.05 |
| Nickel, polished | 0.07 |
| Oil | 0.82 |
| Paper | 0.80 |
| Porcelain, glazed | 0.92 |
| Soot | 0.93 |
| Silver, polished | 0.02 |
| Steel, matt, oxidized | 0.96 |
| Steel, polished, oil-free | 0.06 |
| Steel, polished, oiled | 0.40 |
| Water | 0.92 |
| Bricks | 0.93 |
| Zinc, matt | 0.23 |
| Zinc, polished | 0.05 |
| Tin, polished | 0.06 |

### Transmission of heat through a wall
The heat flow through a wall of area $A$ and thickness $s$ at a temperature difference $\Delta T$ is:

$$\dot{Q} = k \cdot A \cdot \Delta T$$

The heat-transmission coefficient $k$ is calculated as follows:

$$1/k = 1/\alpha_i + s/\lambda + 1/\alpha_a$$

### Thermal resistance
Thermal resistance is composed of the thermal resistance of the individual layers of the wall:

$$s/\lambda = s_1/\lambda_1 + s_2/\lambda_2 + \ldots$$

See P. 234 for the thermal conductivity $\lambda$ of various materials.

## Heat-transfer coefficient $\alpha$
(convection + radiation)

| Type of material, wall surface, etc. | $\alpha_i$ or $\alpha_a$ W/(m² · K) |
|---|---|
| **Natural air movement in a closed room:** | |
| Wall surfaces, interior windows | 8 |
| Exterior windows | 11 |
| **Floors, ceilings:** | |
| from bottom upwards | 8 |
| from top downwards | 6 |
| **Forced air movement on a flat wall** | |
| Mean wind velocity $w = 2$ m/s | 15 |
| Mean wind velocity $w > 5$ m/s | $6.4 \cdot w^{0.75}$ |
| **Water on a flat wall** | |
| Still | 500...2,000 |
| Moving | 2,000...4,000 |
| Boiling | 2,000...6,000 |

## Thermal resistance of air layers $s/\lambda$
(conduction + convection + radiation)

| Position of air layer | Thickness of air layer mm | Thermal resistance $s/\lambda$ m²·K/W |
|---|---|---|
| **Vertical air layer** | 10 | 0.14 |
| | 20 | 0.16 |
| | 50 | 0.18 |
| | 100 | 0.17 |
| | 150 | 0.16 |
| **Horizontal air layer** Heat flow from bottom upwards | 10 | 0.14 |
| | 20 | 0.15 |
| | 50 | 0.16 |
| **Horizontal air layer** Heat flow from top downwards | 10 | 0.15 |
| | 20 | 0.18 |
| | 50 | 0.21 |

[1] A "black-body radiator" completely absorbs all radiation directed against it; therefore, when the black body is heated, it radiates the maximum amount of light which can be emitted by a body. An example of a black-body radiator is the opening in a carbon tube.

## Technical temperature measurement

(VDE/VDI Guideline 3511)

| Measurement system | Measurement range | Method of operation | Examples of application |
|---|---|---|---|
| **Liquid-in-glass thermometers** | –200... 1,000 °C | Thermal expansion of the liquid is visible in a narrow glass tube. Liquid: Pentane (–200...30 °C). Alcohol (–100...210 °C), Toluene (–90...100 °C). Mercury (–38...600 °C), Gallium (...1,000 °C). | For liquids and gases, for monitoring steam, heating and drying systems; refrigeration equipment; media flowing through pipes. |
| **Pressure-spring thermometers** | –50... 500 °C | Due to its expansion pressure (mercury, toluene) or vapor pressure (ether, hexane, toluene, xylene), a liquid in an immersion vessel actuates a pointer or a recording instrument via a Bourdon tube. | For monitoring and recording temperatures (including remote applications up to 35 m) in power plants, factories, heater systems, cold rooms. |
| **Solid expansion thermometers** | 0... 1,000 °C | Different thermal expansion of two metals (rod in tube). | Temperature regulators. |
| **Bimetallic thermometers** | –50... 400 °C | Curvature of a strip consisting of two different metals. | Temperature regulators. |
| **Resistance thermometers** | –220... 850 °C | Change in resistance caused by change in temperature Platinum wires –220...850 °C, Nickel wires –60...250 °C, Copper wires –50...150 °C, Semiconductors –40...180 °C. | Temperature measurements on machines, windings, refrigeration equipment. Remote transmission possible. |
| **Thermistors** | 0...500 °C (2,200 °C) | Sharp drop in electrical resistance as the temperature increases. | Measurement of minor temperature differences due to high sensitivity. |
| **Thermocouples** | –200... 1,800 °C | Thermoelectromotive force of two metals whose junctions are at different temperatures. | Temperature measurements on and in machines, engines, etc. Remote transmission possible. |
| **Radiation thermometers** (pyrometers, infrared cameras, high-speed pyrometers) | –100... 3,500 °C | The radiation emitted by a body is an indicator of its temperature. It is sensed by using either thermocouples or photocells, or by comparing luminance values. Emissivity must be observed. | Melting and annealing furnaces. Surface temperatures. Moving objects, thermogravimetry, extremely rapid response time. |
| **Temperature-sensitive paints, temperature-indicating crayons** | 40... 1,350 °C | Color changes when specific temperatures are exceeded. Paints and crayons are available with one or more color changes (up to 4). The new color remains after cooling. | Temperature measurements on rotating parts, in inaccessible places, in machining processes; warning of excessive temperature; material testing (cracks). |
| **Suction thermometers, pyrometers** | 1,800... 2,800 °C | Gas is extracted from the flame. | Measurement of flame temperature (delayed display). |

Other temperature-measurement methods: spectroscopy, interferometry, quartz thermometry, noise thermometry, liquid crystals, acoustic and magnetic thermometers.

# Thermodynamics

## First law of thermodynamics:
Energy can be neither created nor destroyed. Only the form in which energy exists can be changed, e.g. heat can be transformed into mechanical energy.

## Second law of thermodynamics:
Heat cannot be completely converted to another form of energy, e.g. mechanical work. All natural and synthetic energy transformation processes are irreversible and occur in a preferred direction (according to the probable state). On its own, heat passes only from warmer to colder bodies, the reverse is possible only if energy is supplied.

Entropy $S$ is a measure of the thermal energy in a system which is no longer capable of performing work. That proportion of energy available for work is referred to as exergy

For reversible processes, the sum of the entropy changes is equal to zero.

The greatest efficiency in the conversion of heat to mechanical work is achieved in a reversible process. The following then applies for thermal efficiency:
$$\eta_{th} = (Q_1 - Q_2)/Q_1 = (T_1 - T_2)/T_1$$
(Carnot cycle)

The maximum work to be gained here is:
$$W = Q_1 (T_1 - T_2)/T_1$$

# Changes of state for gases
(general equation of state: $p \cdot v = R_i \cdot T$)

| Change of state | Characteristics | Specific heat capacity [1] | Equations ($k$, $K$ are constants) [1] | Examples |
|---|---|---|---|---|
| **Isobaric** | Constant pressure | $c_p$ | $p = k$ <br> $v = K \cdot T$ | "Constant pressure" combustion in diesel engines; heating or cooling in once-through boilers. |
| **Isochoric** | Constant volume | $c_v$ | $v = k$ <br> $p = K \cdot T$ | "Constant volume" combustion in spark-ignition engines; heating or cooling in closed boilers. |
| **Isothermal** | Constant temperature | – | $T = k$ <br> $p \cdot v = K$ | Slow change of state (heat flows through partitions). |
| **Adiabatic** | Heat neither supplied nor dissipated | – | $P \cdot v^{\varkappa} = k$ <br><br> $T \cdot v^{\varkappa-1} = k$ | Compression or expansion stroke without cooling losses (the ideal condition which is virtually achieved in high-speed machines). |
| **Isentropic** | Adiabatic and frictionless (reversible) | – | | Theoretically optimum attainable comparison processes. |
| **Polytropic** | General change of state | $c = \dfrac{c_v (n - \varkappa)}{n - 1}$ | $P \cdot v^n = K$ <br> $T \cdot v^{n-1} = K$ <br> $T^n \cdot p^{1-n} = K$ | Compression and working strokes in internal-combustion engines, steam engines ($n = 1.2...1.4$). |

---

[1] $c_p$, $c_v$ and $\varkappa = c_p/c_v$ see P. 240, $n = \dfrac{\lg p_2 - \lg p_1}{\lg v_1 - \lg v_2}$

# Electrical engineering

## Quantities and units

| Quantity | SI unit |
|---|---|
| $A$ Area | m² |
| $a$ Distance | m |
| $B$ Magnetic flux density, induction | T = Wb/m² = V · s/m² |
| $C$ Capacitance | F = C/V |
| $D$ Electrical flux density, electric displacement | C/m² |
| $E$ Electric field strength | V/m |
| $F$ Force | N |
| $f$ Frequency | Hz |
| $G$ Conductance | S = 1/Ω |
| $H$ Magnetic field strength | A/m |
| $I$ Current intensity | A |
| $J$ Magnetic polarization | T |
| $k$ Electrochemical equivalent[1] | kg/C |
| $L$ Inductance | H = Wb/A = V · s/A |
| $l$ Length | m |
| $M$ Electric polarization | C/m² |
| $P$ Power | W = V · A |
| $P_s$ Apparent power[2] | V · A |
| $P_q$ Reactive power[3] | var |
| $Q$ Quantity of electricity, electric charge | C = A · s |
| $q$ Cross-sectional area | m² |
| $R$ Electrical resistance | Ω = V/A |
| $t$ Time | s |
| $r$ Radius | m |
| $U$ Electrical voltage | V |
| $V$ Magnetomotive force | A |
| $W$ Work, energy | J = W · s |
| $w$ Number of turns in winding | – |
| $X$ Reactance | Ω |
| $Z$ Impedance | Ω |
| $\varepsilon$ Dielectric constant | F/m = C/(V · m) |
| $\varepsilon_0$ Electric field constant $= 8.854 \cdot 10^{-12}$ F/m | |
| $\varepsilon_r$ Relative permittivity | – |
| $\Theta$ Current linkage | A |
| $\mu$ Permeability | H/m = V · s/(A · m) |
| $\mu_0$ Magnetic field constant $= 1.257 \cdot 10^{-6}$ H/m | |
| $\mu_r$ Relative permeability | – |
| $\varrho$ Resistivity[4] | Ω · m |
| $\sigma$ Electric conductivity $(= 1/\varrho)$ | 1/(Ω · m) |
| $\Phi$ Magnetic flux | Wb = V · s |
| $\varphi$ Phase displacement angle | ° (degrees) |
| $\varphi$ (P) Potential at point P | V |
| $\omega$ Angular frequency $(= 2 \cdot \pi \cdot f)$ | Hz |

Additional symbols and units are given in the text.

Conversion of obsolete units (see P. 19):
- Magnetic field strength $H$:
    1 Oe (oersted) = 79.577 A/m
- Magnetic flux density $B$:
    1 G (gauss) = $10^{-4}$ T
- Magnetic flux $\Phi$:
    1 M (maxwell) = $10^{-8}$ Wb

## Electromagnetic fields

Electrical engineering deals with electromagnetic fields and their effects. These fields are produced by electric charges which are integral multiples of the elementary charge. Static charges produce an electric field, whereas moving charges give rise to a magnetic field as well. The relationship between these two fields is described by Maxwell's equations. The presence of these fields is evidenced by the effects of their forces on other electric charges. The force between two point charges $Q_1$ and $Q_2$ is defined by <u>Coulomb's Law</u>:

$$F = Q_1 \cdot Q_2/(4\pi \cdot \varepsilon_0 \cdot a^2)$$

The force acting on a moving charge in a magnetic field is expressed by the <u>Lorentz force</u>:

$$F = Q \cdot v \cdot B \cdot \sin\alpha$$

$\varepsilon_0$ = electric field constant, $Q_1$ and $Q_2$ = charges, $a$ = distance between $Q_1$ and $Q_2$, $v$ = velocity of charge $Q$, $B$ = magnetic induction, and $\alpha$ = angle between direction of motion and magnetic field.

---

[1] The unit in common use is g/C.
[2] Apparent power is usually given in V · A rather than in W.
[3] Reactive power is usually given in var (volt-ampere reactive) rather than in W.
[4] The unit in common use is Ωmm²/m, where the wire cross-section is in mm² and wire length in m; conversion: 1 Ωmm²/m = $10^{-6}$ Ωm = 1 μΩm.

# Electric field

An electric field can be defined by the following quantities:

### Electric potential $\varphi$ (P) and voltage $U$

The electric potential $\varphi$ (P) at point P is a measure of the work required per charge to move the charge $Q$ from a reference point to point P:

$$\varphi (P) = W (P)/Q$$

The voltage $U$ is the potential difference (using the same reference point) between two points $P_1$ and $P_2$:

$$U = \varphi (P_2) - \varphi (P_1)$$

### Electric field strength $E$

The electric field strength at point P depends on the location P and its surrounding charges. It defines the maximum slope of the potential gradient at point P. The following equation applies to the field strength at a distance $a$ from a point charge $Q$:

$$E = Q/(4\pi \cdot \varepsilon_0 \cdot a^2)$$

The following force acts on a charge $Q$ at point P:

$$F = Q \cdot E$$

### Electric field and matter

Electric polarization $M$ and dielectric displacement density $D$

In a material which can be polarized (dielectric), an electric field generates electric dipoles (positive and negative charges at a distance $a$; $Q \cdot a$ is called the dipole moment). The dipole moment per unit volume is called the polarization $M$.

The dielectric displacement density $D$ indicates the density of the electric displacement flux, and is defined as follows:

$$D = \varepsilon \cdot E = \varepsilon_r \cdot \varepsilon_0 \cdot E = \varepsilon_0 \cdot E + M$$

where
$\varepsilon$: Dielectric constant of the material,
$$\varepsilon = \varepsilon_r \cdot \varepsilon_0$$
$\varepsilon_0$: Electric field constant (dielectric constant of vacuum)
$\varepsilon_r$: Relative permittivity (relative dielectric constant) $\varepsilon_r = 1$ for air, see PP. 273 to 275 for other materials

### Capacitor

Two electrodes separated by a dielectric form a capacitor. When a voltage is applied to the capacitor, the two electrodes receive equal but opposite charges. The following equation holds for the received charge $Q$:

$$Q = C \cdot U$$

$C$ is the capacitance of the capacitor. It is dependent on the geometric shape of the electrodes, the distance by which they are separated, and the dielectric constant of the dielectric.

Energy content of charged capacitor:

$$W = Q \cdot U/2 = Q^2/(2\ C) = C \cdot U^2/2$$

The force of attraction between two parallel plates (surface area $A$) at a distance $a$ is:

$$F = E \cdot D \cdot A/2 = \varepsilon_r \cdot \varepsilon_0 \cdot U^2 \cdot A/(2\ a^2)$$

## Capacitance $C$ of some conductor arrangements in F

| | | | |
|---|---|---|---|
| Plate capacitor with $n$ parallel plates | $C = (n - 1)\dfrac{\varepsilon_r \cdot \varepsilon_0 \cdot A}{a}$ | $\varepsilon_r, \varepsilon_0$<br>$n$<br>$A$<br>$a$ | See above<br>Number of plates<br>Surface area of one plate in m²<br>Distance between plates in m |
| Parallel conductors (twin conductors) | $C = \dfrac{\pi \cdot \varepsilon_r \cdot \varepsilon_0 \cdot l}{\ln\left(\dfrac{a-r}{r}\right)}$ | $l$<br>$a$<br>$r$ | Length of twin conductors in m<br>Distance between conductors in m<br>Conductor radius in m |
| Concentric conductor (cylindrical capacitor) | $C = \dfrac{2\pi \cdot \varepsilon_r \cdot \varepsilon_0 \cdot l}{\ln (r_2/r_1)}$ | $l$<br>$r_2, r_1$ | Length of conductor in m<br>Conductor radius in m, where $r_2 > r_1$ |
| Conductor to ground | $C = \dfrac{2\pi \cdot \varepsilon_r \cdot \varepsilon_0 \cdot l}{\ln (2\ a/r)}$ | $l$<br>$a$<br>$r$ | Length of conductor in m<br>Distance from conductor to ground in m<br>Conductor radius in m |
| Sphere with respect to distant surface | $C = 4\pi \cdot \varepsilon_r \cdot \varepsilon_0 \cdot r$ | $r$ | Sphere radius in m |

## Direct current (DC)

Moving charges give rise to a current $I$, which is characterized by its intensity and measured in amperes. The direction of flow and magnitude of direct current are independent of time.

### Direction of current flow and measurement

Current flowing from positive pole to negative pole outside of the current source is designated as positive (in reality, the electrons travel from the negative to the positive pole).

An ammeter (A) in the current path measures current flow; voltage is measured by a voltmeter (V) connected in shunt.

### Ohm's Law

Ohm's law defines the relationship between voltage and current in solid and liquid conductors.

$$U = R \cdot I$$

The proportionality constant $R$ is called ohmic resistance and is measured in ohms ($\Omega$). The reciprocal of resistance is called conductance $G$

$$G = 1/R$$

### Ohmic resistance[1])
Ohmic resistance depends on the material and its dimensions.
Round wire $R = \varrho \cdot l/q = l/(q \cdot \sigma)$
Hollow conductor $R = \ln (r_2/r_1)/(2\pi \cdot l \cdot \sigma)$
$\varrho$ Resistivity in $\Omega mm^2/m$
$\sigma = 1/\varrho$ electric conductivity
$l$ wire length in m
$q$ wire cross-section in $mm^2$
$r_2$ and $r_1$ wire radii, where $r_2 > r_1$
In the case of metals, resistance increases with temperature:

$$R_\vartheta = R_{20} [1 + \alpha (\vartheta - 20\,°C)]$$

$R_\vartheta$ resistance at $\vartheta°C$
$R_{20}$ resistance at 20 °C
$\alpha$ temperature coefficient[2]) in 1/K (= 1/°C)
$\vartheta$ temperature in °C
Near absolute zero (–273 °C), the resistance of many metals approaches zero (superconductivity).

### Work and power

In a resistor through which current passes, the following holds for the work produced or for the quantity of heat developed:

$$W = U \cdot I \cdot t = R \cdot I^2 \cdot t$$

and thus for power:

$$P = U \cdot I = R \cdot I^2$$

### Kirchhoff's Laws
First Law
The current flowing to each junction (node) in a circuit is equal to the current flowing away from that point.

Second Law
The algebraic sum of the voltage drops in any closed path in a circuit is equal to the algebraic sum of the electromotive forces in that path.

---

*Current and voltage measurement*
*R Load, A Ammeter in current path,*
*V Shunt-connected voltmeter.*

---

[1]) See P. 272 for table of $\varrho$ values.
[2]) See P. 272 for table of $\alpha$ values.

# Direct-current circuits

## Circuit with load
$U = (R_a + R_l) \cdot I$
$R_a$ = load
$R_l$ = line resistance

## Battery-charging circuit
$U - U_0 = (R_v + R_i) \cdot I$

$U$ line voltage, $U_0$ open-circuit voltage [1]) of battery, $R_v$ series resistance, $R_i$ internal resistance of battery.
Condition for charging: charging voltage > battery open-circuit voltage.

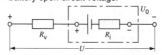

## Charging and discharging a capacitor
The time constant $\tau = R \cdot C$ is the decisive factor in the charging and discharging of a capacitor.

Charging
$I = U/R \cdot \exp(-t/\tau)$
$U_C = U[1 - \exp(-t/\tau)]$

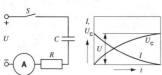

Circuit diagram, voltage and current curves

Discharging
$I = I_0 \cdot \exp(-t/\tau)$
$U_C = U_0 \cdot \exp(-t/\tau)$
$U$ charging voltage, $I$ charging current, $U_C$ capacitor voltage, $I_0$ initial current, $U_0$ voltage at start of discharge.

---

[1]) Formerly called electromotive force (emf).

## Series connection of resistors
$R_{total} = R_1 + R_2 + \ldots$
$U = U_1 + U_2 + \ldots$
The current is the same in all resistors.

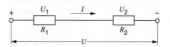

## Parallel connection of resistors
$1/R_{total} = 1/R_1 + 1/R_2$ or
$G = G_1 + G_2$
$I = I_1 + I_2; \; I_1/I_2 = R_2/R_1$
The voltage is the same across all resistors (Kirchhoff's second law).

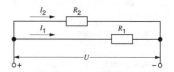

## Measurement of a resistance
A resistance can be measured by measuring current and voltage, by using a direct-reading ohmmeter or a bridge circuit, e.g. Wheatstone bridge. If sliding contact D is set so that Wheatstone bridge galvanometer A reads zero, the following equations apply:
$I_1 \cdot R_x = I_2 \cdot \varrho \cdot a/q$
$I_1 \cdot R = I_2 \cdot \varrho \cdot b/q$
thus: $R_x = R \cdot a/b$

*Wheatstone bridge circuit*
*$R_x$ Unknown resistance, R Known resistance, AB Homogeneous measuring wire (resistivity $\varrho$) with same cross-section $q$ at every point, A Galvanometer, D Sliding contact.*

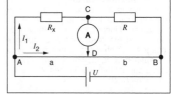

## Electrolytic conduction

Substances whose solutions or melts (salts, acids, bases) conduct current are called <u>electrolytes</u>. In contrast to conduction in metals, electrolytic conduction involves chemical decomposition at the electrodes. This decomposition is called <u>electrolysis</u> and the electrodes are termed anode (positive pole) and cathode (negative pole).

When dissolved, the electrolyte dissociates into various ions which move freely. When voltage is applied, the positive ions (cations) migrate toward the cathode and the negative ions (anions) migrate toward the anode. Cations include all metal ions, but also include ammonia ions ($NH_4^+$) and hydrogen ions ($H^+$). Anions comprise the ions of the nonmetals, oxygen, halogens, acid radical ions, and OH ions (see P. 968 onwards for use in batteries).

The ions are neutralized at the electrodes and precipitate out of solution. Faraday's laws describe the relationship between the amount of precipitated material and the transported charge:

1. The amount of precipitate is proportional to the current and time

$$m = k \cdot I \cdot t$$

$m$ mass in g, $I$ current in A, $t$ time in s, $k$ electrochemical equivalent in g/C. The electrochemical equivalent $k$ indicates how many g of ions are precipitated by 1 coulomb:

$$k = A/(F \cdot w) = 1.036 \cdot 10^{-5} A/w$$

$A$ atomic weight, see P. 212, $w$ valence (see table), $F$ Faraday constant with the value $F = 96{,}485$ C/g equivalent. The g equivalent is the mass in g which corresponds to the equivalent weight $A/w$.

2. When the same quantity of electricity is passed through different electrolytes, the masses of the precipitates are proportional to their equivalent weights.

## Electrolytic polarization

Ohm's law is also essentially applicable with electrolysis. In electrolysis, however, the so-called inconstant elements precipitate out at the electrodes and create a voltage $U_z$ which is opposite in polarity to the applied voltage. The following holds for the current in the cell of resistance $R$:

$$I = (U - U_z)/R$$

## Electrochemical equivalent $k$

| Substance | Valence $w$ | Electrochemical equivalent $k$ $10^{-3}$ g/C |
|---|---|---|
| **Cations** | | |
| Aluminum Al | 3 | 0.0932 |
| Lead Pb | 2 | 1.0735 |
| Chromium Cr | 3 | 0.1796 |
| Cadmium Cd | 2 | 0.5824 |
| Copper Cu | 1 | 0.6588 |
| | 2 | 0.3294 |
| Sodium Na | 1 | 0.2384 |
| Nickel Ni | 2 | 0.3041 |
| | 3 | 0.2027 |
| Silver Ag | 1 | 1.1180 |
| Hydrogen H | 1 | 0.01044 |
| Zinc Zn | 2 | 0.3387 |
| **Anions** | | |
| Chlorine Cl | 1 | 0.3675 |
| Oxygen O | 2 | 0.0829 |
| Hydroxyl OH | 1 | 0.1763 |
| Chlorate $ClO_3$ | 1 | 0.8649 |
| Chromate $CrO_4$ | 2 | 0.6011 |
| Carbonate $CO_3$ | 2 | 0.3109 |
| Manganate $MnO_4$ | 2 | 0.6163 |
| Permanganate $MnO_4$ | 1 | 1.2325 |
| Nitrate $NO_3$ | 1 | 0.6426 |
| Phosphate $PO_4$ | 3 | 0.3280 |
| Sulfate $SO_4$ | 2 | 0.4978 |

The change in the electrodes is called galvanic or electrolytic polarization. It can be largely avoided through the use of oxidizing chemicals (called depolarizers), e.g. manganese dioxide to prevent the formation of $H_2$.

## Galvanic cells

Galvanic cells convert chemical energy into electrical energy. They consist of two different metals in one or two electrolytic solutions. The open-circuit voltage of the cell depends on the electrode materials and the substance used as the electrolyte. Examples:

<u>Weston normal cell</u>
Electrodes: Cd + Hg( – ) and $Hg_2SO_4$ + Hg( + )
Electrolyte: $CdSO_4$
Voltage: 1.0187 V at 20 °C
<u>Leclanché cell</u> (dry cells)
Electrodes: Zn( – ) and C( + )
Depolarizer: $MnO_2$
Electrolyte: $NH_4Cl$
Voltage: 1.5 V

<u>Storage battery or battery</u> (see P. 971).

# Alternating current (AC)

Alternating current is a current whose magnitude and direction vary periodically (often sinusoidally). Its value lies in the fact that it is well suited to remote energy transmission because it can be stepped up to high voltages by means of transformers.

Standard frequencies for alternating-current power lines:
Africa: 50 Hz; most of Asia: 50 Hz; Australia: 50 Hz; Europe: 50 Hz; North America: 60 Hz; South America: 50/60 Hz.
Railroad power lines: Austria, Germany, Norway, Sweden, Switzerland: $16\,2/3$ Hz; U.S.A.: 20 Hz.

Electrolytic (galvanic) mean of sinusoidal alternating current.
This value is the arithmetic mean, i.e.

$$I_{galv} = 2\,\hat{\imath}/\pi = 0.64\,\hat{\imath}$$
$$U_{galv} = 2\,\hat{u}/\pi = 0.64\,\hat{u}$$

and has the same electrolytic effect as a direct current of this magnitude.

Root-mean-square values of sinusoidal alternating current:
$$I\,(= I_{rms}) = \hat{\imath}/\sqrt{2} = 0.71\,\hat{\imath}$$
$$U\,(= U_{rms}) = \hat{u}/\sqrt{2} = 0.71\,\hat{u}$$

---

*Alternating-current diagram*
*T Duration of one complete oscillation (period) in s, f Frequency in Hz (f = 1/T), $\hat{\imath}$ Peak value (amplitude) of current, $\hat{u}$ Peak value (amplitude) of voltage, $\omega$ Angular frequency in 1/s ($\omega = 2\pi \cdot f$), $\varphi$ Phase displacement angle between current and voltage (phase-displaced means: current and voltage reach their peak values or cross the zero axis at different times).*

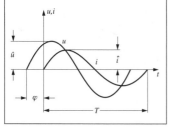

---

These equations indicate the magnitude of direct current which will generate the same amount of heat.

There are three kinds of power specified in an alternating-current circuit:

Active power   $P = U \cdot I \cdot \cos\varphi$
Reactive power $P_q = U \cdot I \cdot \sin\varphi$
Apparent power $P_s = U \cdot I$

The power factor $\cos\varphi$ indicates what percentage of the apparent power is useful as actual power. The remainder, called reactive power, is useless, and oscillates between the source and the load, but loads the lines.

In order to reduce the necessary size of the lines, the phase displacement angle $\varphi$ is kept as small as possible, usually by using phase shifters (e.g. capacitors).

# Alternating-current circuits

### Alternating-current circuit with coils

A coil of inductance $L$ (see P. 83) acts as a resistance of magnitude $R_L = \omega \cdot L$ (inductive resistance). As it consumes no energy, it is also called reactance. The induced countervoltage $U_L$ (see P. 82 for law of induction) lags the current by 90°, which in turn lags the applied voltage by 90°.

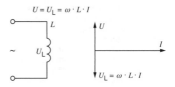

$$U = U_L = \omega \cdot L \cdot I$$

Inductance of coils connected in series and parallel:

| Coils connected in series | Coils connected in parallel |
|---|---|
| $L_{total} = L_1 + L_2$ | $\dfrac{1}{L_{total}} = \dfrac{1}{L_1} + \dfrac{1}{L_2} + \ldots$ |

### Alternating-current circuit with capacitor

A capacitor of capacitance $C$ acts as a resistance of magnitude $R_C = 1/(\omega \cdot C)$ (capacitive reactance); it also consumes no power (reactance). The countervoltage $U_C$ across the capacitor leads the current by 90°, which in turn leads the applied voltage $U$ by 90°.

$$U = U_C = I/(\omega \cdot C)$$

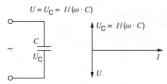

Capacitance of capacitors connected in series and parallel:

| Capacitor connected in series | Capacitor connected in parallel |
|---|---|
| $1/C_{total} = 1/C_1 + 1/C_2$ | $C_{total} = C_1 + C_2 + ...$ |

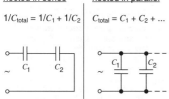

### Ohm's Law for alternating current

In an alternating-current circuit of ohmic resistance ($R$), coil (inductance $L$) and capacitor (capacitance $C$), the same laws apply to the electrical parameters of resistance, voltage and current as in a direct-current circuit.

In calculating the total resistance, the voltage, and the current in the circuit, however, the phase angle must also be considered, i.e. the vectors of the values must be added together. Vector diagrams are often used for this purpose.

Series connection

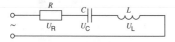

*Vector diagrams for determining U, Z and $\varphi$*

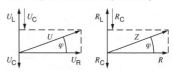

Ohm's law states that $U = Z \cdot I$

$Z$ is termed impedance and is the vector sum of the individual resistances.

$$Z = \sqrt{R^2 + X^2}$$

$R$ ohmic resistance, $X$ reactance.
$$X = \omega \cdot L - 1/(\omega \cdot C)$$
$\omega \cdot L$ is the inductive and $1/(\omega \cdot C)$ the capacitive component of reactance.

The following equation defines the phase displacement $\varphi$ between current and voltage:
$$\tan\varphi = [\omega \cdot L - 1/(\omega \cdot C)]/R$$

The maximum possible current ($I = U/R$) flows when the circuit resonates; the circuit will resonate if:
$$\omega^2 \cdot L \cdot C = 1 \text{ (i.e., X = 0)}$$

Parallel connection

*Vector diagrams for determining I, Y and $\varphi$*

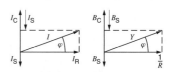

Current is determined by the following equation (Ohm's Law):
$$I = U \cdot Y$$
$Y$ is the complex admittance:
$$Y = \sqrt{G^2 + B^2}$$

$G$ (= $1/R$) is the conductance
$B$ [$= \omega \cdot C - 1/(\omega \cdot L)$] is the susceptance

The following equation describes the phase displacement between current and voltage:
$$\tan\varphi = R \cdot [\omega \cdot C - 1/(\omega \cdot L)]$$

As in the case of series connection, the circuit will resonate (minimum current flows in the main winding) if:
$$\omega^2 \cdot L \cdot C = 1 \text{ (i.e. } B = 0)$$

# Three-phase current

Three-phase alternating current in which the phases differ by 120° is called three-phase current. Three-phase current is generated by three-phase alternators which have three mutually independent windings which are displaced relative to one another by two-thirds of a pole pitch (120°).

The number of conductors carrying voltage is reduced from six to either three or four by linking the component voltages; customary conductor configurations are the star (Y) and delta connections.

Star (Y) connection
$$I = I_p$$
$$U = \sqrt{3} \cdot U_p$$

Delta connection
$$I = \sqrt{3} \cdot I_p$$
$$U = U_p$$

$I$ line current, $I_p$ phase current, $U$ line voltage, $U_p$ phase voltage.

The transmitted power is independent of the type of connection, and is determined by the following equations:

Apparent power:
$$P_s = \sqrt{3} \cdot U \cdot I = 3U_p \cdot I_p$$

Active power:
$$P = P_s \cdot \cos\varphi = \sqrt{3} \cdot U \cdot I \cdot \cos\varphi$$

Star (Y) connection

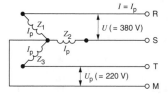

Delta connection

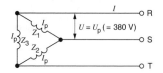

# Magnetic field

Magnetic fields are produced by moving electric charges, current-carrying conductors, magnetized bodies, or by an alternating electric field.

They can be detected by their effect on moving electric charges (Lorentz force) or magnetic dipoles (like poles repel, and unlike poles attract).

Magnetic fields are characterized by the vector of the magnetic flux density $B$ (induction). This vector can be determined by measuring either force or voltage, because a voltage is induced in a loop of wire by a changing magnetic field (see P. 82 for law of induction):
$$U = \Delta (B \cdot q)/t$$

$\Delta (B \cdot q)$ change in the product of magnetic induction (in T) and area of the conductor loop (in m²), $t$ time (in s). The following equations show the relationships between induction $B$ and the other field parameters:

Magnetic flux $\Phi$
$$\Phi = B \cdot q$$
$q$ = cross-sectional area in m²

Magnetic field strength $H$
In a vacuum:
$$B = \mu_0 \cdot H$$
$\mu_0 = 1.257 \cdot 10^{-6}$ H/m, magnetic field constant

**Magnetic field and matter**
In matter, induction $B$ theoretically consists of two components. One component comes from the applied field ($\mu_0 \cdot H$), and the other from the matter ($J$) (see also the relationship between electric displacement density and electric field strength).
$$B = \mu_0 \cdot H + J$$
$J$ is the magnetic polarization and describes that component of flux density contributed by the matter. In physical terms, $J$ is the magnetic dipole moment per unit volume, and is generally a function of field strength $H$. $J \ll \mu_0 \cdot H$ for many materials, and is proportional to $H$, so that:
$$B = \mu_r \cdot \mu_0 \cdot H$$
$\mu_r$ relative permeability. In a vacuum, $\mu_r = 1$.

Materials are divided into 3 groups according to their relative permeability values:

Diamagnetic materials ($\mu_r < 1$)
(e.g. Ag, Au, Cd, Cu, Hg, Pb, Zn, water, organic materials, gases)
$\mu_r$ is independent of magnetic field strength and smaller than 1; the values are within the range:
$$(1 - 10^{-11}) > \mu_r > (1 - 10^{-5})$$

Paramagnetic materials ($\mu_r > 1$)
(e.g. $O_2$, Al, Pt, Ti)
$\mu_r$ is independent of magnetic field strength and greater than 1; the values are within the range:
$$(1 + 4 \cdot 10^{-4}) > \mu_r > (1 + 10^{-8})$$

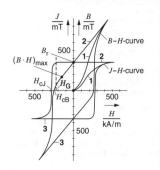

*Hysteresis loop (e.g. hard ferrite)*

The most important parameters of the hysteresis loop are:
– Saturation polarization $J_s$
– Remanence $B_r$ (residual induction for $H = 0$)
– Coercive field strength $H_{cB}$ (demagnetizing field strength where $B$ becomes equal to 0), or
– Coercive field strength $H_{cJ}$ (demagnetizing field strength where $J$ becomes equal to 0; of significance only for permanent magnets)
– Limiting field strength $H_G$ (a permanent magnet remains stable up to this field strength)
– $\mu_{max}$ (maximum slope of the rise path; significant only for soft magnetic materials)
– Hysteresis loss (energy loss in the material during one remagnetizing cycle, corresponds to the area of the $B-H$ hysteresis loop; significant only for soft magnetic materials)

Ferromagnetic materials ($\mu_r \gg 1$)
(e.g. Fe, Co, Ni, ferrites)
The magnetic polarization in these materials is very high, and its change as a function of the field strength $H$ is nonlinear; it is also dependent on hysteresis. Nevertheless, if, as is usual in electrical engineering, the relationship $B = \mu_r \cdot \mu_0 \cdot H$ is chosen, then $\mu_r$ is a function of $H$ and exhibits hysteresis; the values for $\mu_r$ are within the range $5 \cdot 10^5 > \mu_r > 10^2$.

The <u>hysteresis loop</u>, which illustrates the relationship between $B$ and $H$ as well as $J$ and $H$, is explained as follows:

If the material is in the unmagnetized state ($B = J = H = 0$) when a magnetic field $H$ is applied, the magnetization of the material follows the rise path (1). From a specific, material-dependent field strength, all magnetic dipoles are aligned and $J$ reaches the value of <u>saturation polarization</u> (material-dependent) which can no longer be increased. If $H$ is now reduced, $J$ decreases along section (2) of the curve and at $H = 0$ intersects the $B$ or $J$ axis at the remanence point $B_r$ or $J_r$ (in which case $B_r = J_r$). The flux density and polarization drop to zero only on application of an opposing field whose field strength is $H_{cB}$ or $H_{cJ}$; this field strength is called the coercive field strength. As the field strength is further increased, saturation polarization is reached in the opposite direction. If the field strength is again reduced and the field reversed, curve (3), which is symmetrical to curve section 2, is traversed.

# Ferromagnetic materials

Ferromagnetic materials are divided into soft and permanent magnetic materials. The chart on P. 268 shows a comparison of the range of magnetic characteristic values covered by the technically conventional, crystalline materials and the direction in which the materials are developed. What must be emphasized is the immense range of 8 powers of ten covered by the coercive field strength.

### Permanent-magnet materials
Permanent-magnet materials have high coercive field strengths; the values lie within the range:

$$H_{cJ} > 1 \ \frac{kA}{m}$$

Thus high demagnetizing fields $H$ can occur without the material losing its magnetic polarization. The magnetic state and operating range of a permanent magnet lie within the 2nd quadrant of the hysteresis loop, on the so-called demagnetiza-

tion curve. In practice, the <u>operating point</u> of a permanent magnet never coincides with the remanence point because a demagnetizing field is always present due to the intrinsic self-demagnetization of the magnet which shifts the operating point to the left.

The point on the demagnetization curve at which the product $B \cdot H$ reaches its maximum value, $(B \cdot H)_{max}$, is a measure of the maximum attainable air-gap energy. In addition to remanence and coercive field strength, this value is important for characterizing permanent magnets.

AlNiCo, ferrite, FeNdB (REFe), and SeCo magnets are currently the most important types of permanent magnets in terms of industrial applications; their demagnetization curves exhibit characteristics typical of the individual magnet types (see P. 266 for characteristics of permanent-magnet materials).

### Soft magnetic materials
Soft magnetic materials have a low coercive field strength ($H_C < 1,000$ A/m), i.e. a narrow hysteresis loop. The flux density assumes high values (large $\mu_r$ values) already for low field strengths so that, in customary applications $J \gg \mu_0 \cdot H$, i.e. in practice, no distinction need be made between $B(H)$ and $J(H)$ curves (see P. 260 for characteristics).

Due to their high induction at low field strengths, soft magnetic materials are used as conductors of magnetic flux. As they exhibit low remagnetization losses (hysteresis loss), materials with low coercive field strengths are particularly well-suited for applications in alternating magnetic fields.

The characteristics of soft magnetic materials depend essentially on their pretreatment. Machining increases the coercive field strength, i.e. the hysteresis loop becomes broader. The coercive field strength can be subsequently reduced to its initial value through material-specific annealing at high temperatures (magnetic final annealing). The magnetization curves, i.e. the $B–H$ relationships, are set out below for several important soft magnetic materials.

## Remagnetization losses

In the table below, P1 and P1.5 represent the remagnetization loss for inductions of 1 and 1.5 tesla respectively, in a 50 Hz field at 20 °C. These losses are composed of hysteresis losses and eddy-current losses. The eddy-current losses are caused by voltages which are induced (law of induction) in the magnetically soft circuit components as a result of changes in flux during alternating-field magnetization. Eddy-current losses can be kept low by applying the following measures to reduce electric conductivity:

– lamination of the core
– use of alloyed materials (e.g. silicon iron)
– use of insulated powder particles (powdered cores) in the higher frequency range
– use of ceramic materials (ferrites)

## The magnetic circuit

In addition to material equations, the following equations also determine the design of magnetic circuits:
1. Ampère's law (equation of magnetic voltage)
The following equation holds true for a closed magnetic circuit:

$$\sum_i H_i \cdot l_i = V_1 + V_2 + \ldots + V_i = I \cdot w \text{ or } 0,$$

depending on whether or not the circuit includes a current source.

$I \cdot w = \Theta$ ampere-turns
$H_i \cdot l_i = V_i$ magnetic potential difference ($H_i \cdot l_i$ is to be calculated for circuit components in which $H_i$ is constant).

| Type of sheet steel | Nominal thickness mm | Specific total loss W/kg P1 | P1.5 | $B$ (for $H$ = 10 kA/m) T |
|---|---|---|---|---|
| M 270 – 35 A | 0.35 | 1.1 | 2.7 | 1.70 |
| M 330 – 35 A | 0.35 | 1.3 | 3.3 | 1.70 |
| M 400 – 50 A | 0.5 | 1.7 | 4.0 | 1.71 |
| M 530 – 50 A | 0.5 | 2.3 | 5.3 | 1.74 |
| M 800 – 50 A | 0.5 | 3.6 | 8.1 | 1.77 |

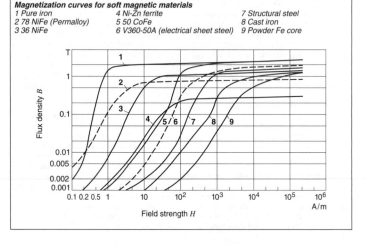

*Magnetization curves for soft magnetic materials*
1 Pure iron
2 78 NiFe (Permalloy)
3 36 NiFe
4 Ni-Zn ferrite
5 50 CoFe
6 V360-50A (electrical sheet steel)
7 Structural steel
8 Cast iron
9 Powder Fe core

Flux density $B$

Field strength $H$

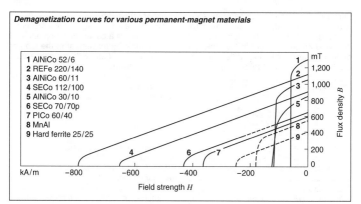

**Demagnetization curves for various permanent-magnet materials**

1 AlNiCo 52/6
2 REFe 220/140
3 AlNiCo 60/11
4 SECo 112/100
5 AlNiCo 30/10
6 SECo 70/70p
7 PlCo 60/40
8 MnAl
9 Hard ferrite 25/25

Flux density $B$ (mT): 1,200; 1,000; 800; 600; 400; 200; 0

Field strength $H$ (kA/m): −800; −600; −400; −200; 0

2. <u>Law of continuity</u> (equation of magnetic flux)

The same magnetic flux flows in the individual components of the circuit:

$\Phi (= B \cdot A)$:

$\Phi = $ const. or $\Phi_1 = \Phi_2 = ... = \Phi$

The quality of a circuit is determined by the amount of flux available in the working air gap. This flux is called *useful flux*; the ratio of useful flux to total flux (flux of the permanent magnet or electromagnet) is called the <u>leakage coefficient</u> $\sigma$ (practical values for $\sigma$ are between 0.2 and 0.9). The leakage flux – the difference between the total flux and the useful flux – does not pass through the working air gap and does not add to the power of the magnetic circuit.

## Magnetic field and electric current

Moving charges generate a magnetic field, i.e. conductors through which current flows are surrounded by a magnetic field. The direction in which the current flows ($\otimes$ current flow into the page, $\odot$ current flow out of the page) and the direction of the magnetic field strength form a right-handed screw. See the table on Page 82 for the magnetic field $H$ of various conductor configurations.

Two parallel conductors through which current flows in the same direction attract each other; if the current flows in opposite directions, they repel each other. The force acting between two conductors of length $l$ separated by distance $a$ and carrying currents $I_1$ and $I_2$ is governed by the equation:

$$F = \frac{\mu_0 \cdot \mu_r \cdot I_1 \cdot I_2 \cdot l}{2\pi \cdot a}[1]$$

In air, the approximate force is given by the equation:

$$F \approx 0.2 \cdot 10^{-6} \cdot I_1 \cdot I_2 \cdot l/a [1]$$

In a magnetic field $B$, a force is exerted on a current-carrying conductor (current $I$) of length $l$; if the conductor and the magnetic field form an angle of $\alpha$, the following applies:

$$F = B \cdot I \cdot l \cdot \sin\alpha [1]$$

---

[1] $F$ force in N, $I_1$, $I_2$ and $I$ current in A, $l$ and $a$ length in m; $B$ induction in T.

The direction of this force can be determined using the right-hand rule (when the thumb is pointed in the direction of current flow, and the index finger in the direction of the magnetic field, the middle finger indicates the direction of force).

---

*Three-finger rule*

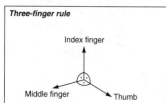

Index finger

Middle finger      Thumb

---

*Current-carrying conductors and associated lines of force* (H).
*a) A single current-carrying conductor with magnetic field. b) Parallel conductors attract each other if current flows in the same direction. c) Parallel conductors repel each other if current flows in opposite directions.*
*d) A magnetic field (B) exerts a force on a current-carrying conductor. The direction in which force is exerted is determined using the three-finger rule.*

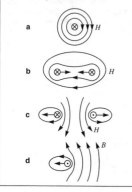

a

b

c

d

---

*Induction: B Magnetic field, C Direction of moving conductor, $U_i$ Induced voltage.*

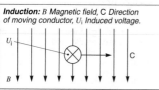

$U_i$

C

B

---

## Law of induction

Any change in the magnetic flux $\Phi$ around which there is a conducting loop, caused for example by movement of the loop or changes in field strength, induces a voltage $U_i$ in the loop.

A voltage $U_i$ going into the page is induced in a conductor moving in direction C through a magnetic field:

$$U_i = B \cdot l \cdot v$$

$U_i$ in V, $B$ in T, $l$ conductor length in m, $v$ velocity in m/s.

In a <u>direct-current machine</u>:
$$U_i = p \cdot n \cdot z \cdot \Phi/(60a)$$
$U_i$ in V, $\Phi$ magnetic flux generated by the excitation (field) winding in Wb, $p$ number of pole pairs, $n$ rotational speed in rpm, $z$ number of wires on armature surface, $a$ half the number of parallel armature-winding paths.

In an <u>alternating-current machine</u>:
$$U_i = 2.22 f \cdot z \cdot \Phi$$
$U_i$ in V, $\Phi$ magnetic flux generated by the excitation winding in Wb, $f$ frequency of alternating current in Hz = $p \cdot n/60$, $p$ number of pole pairs, $n$ rotational speed in rpm, $z$ number of wires on armature surface.

In a <u>transformer</u>:
$$U_1 = 4.44 f \cdot w \cdot \Phi$$
$U_1$ in V, $\Phi$ magnetic flux in Wb, $f$ frequency in Hz, $w$ number of turns on the coil which surround the flux $\Phi$.

The terminal voltage $U$ is smaller (alternator) or larger (motor) than $U_i$ by the ohmic drop in the winding (about 5%). In the case of alternating voltage, $U_i$ is the effective (rms) value.

## Self-induction

The magnetic field of a current-carrying conductor or a coil changes with the conductor current. A voltage proportional to the change in current is induced in the conductor itself and counteracts the current change producing it:

$$U_s = -L \frac{dI}{dt}$$

### Field strength $H$ of several conductor configurations

| | | | |
|---|---|---|---|
| Circular conductor | $H = I/(2a)$ at center of circle | $H$<br>$I$<br>$a$ | Field strength in A/m<br>Current in A<br>Radius of circular conductor in m |
| Long, straight conductor | $H = I/(2\pi \cdot a)$ outside of conductor<br>$H = I \cdot a/(2\pi \cdot r^2)$ inside of conductor | $a$<br>$r$ | Distance from conductor axis in m<br>Conductor radius in m |
| Cylindrical coil (solenoid) | $H = I \cdot w/l$ | $w$<br>$l$ | Number of turns on coil<br>Length of coil in m |

### Inductance $L$ of several conductor configurations

| | | | |
|---|---|---|---|
| Cylindrical coil | $L = \dfrac{1.257\,\mu_r}{10^6} \cdot \dfrac{w^2 \cdot q}{l}$ | $L$<br>$\mu_r$<br>$w$<br>$q$<br>$l$ | Inductance in H<br>Relative permeability<br>Number of turns<br>Coil cross-section in m²<br>Coil length in m |
| Twin conductor (in air, $\mu_r = 1$) | $L = \dfrac{4\,l}{10^7} \cdot \ln(a/r)$ | $l$<br>$a$<br>$r$ | Length of conductor in m<br>Distance between conductors in m<br>Conductor radius in m |
| Conductor to ground (in air, $\mu_r = 1$) | $L = \dfrac{2\,l}{10^7} \cdot \ln(2a/r)$ | $l$<br>$a$<br>$r$ | Length of conductor in m<br>Distance from conductor to ground in m<br>Conductor radius in m |

The inductance $L$ depends on the relative permeability $\mu_r$ which is constant and practically equal to 1 for most materials with the exception of ferromagnetic materials (see P. 79). In the case of iron-core coils, therefore, $L$ is highly dependent on the operating conditions.

### Energy of the magnetic field

$$W = L \cdot I^2/2$$

# Electric effects in metallic conductors

### Contact potential between conductors

Contact potential occurs in conductors, and is analogous to the triboelectricity or voltaic emf in insulators (e.g. glass, hard rubber). If two dissimilar metals (at the same temperature) are joined to make metal-to-metal contact with one another and are then separated, a contact potential is present between them. This is caused by: the different work functions of

### Contact potential values

| Material pair | Contact potential |
|---|---|
| Zn/Pb | 0.39 V |
| Pb/Sn | 0.06 V |
| Sn/Fe | 0.30 V |
| Fe/Cu | 0.14 V |
| Cu/Ag | 0.08 V |
| Ag/Pt | 0.12 V |
| Pt/C | 0.13 V |
| Zn/Pb/Sn/Fe | 0.75 V |
| Zn/Fe | 0.75 V |
| Zn/Pb/Sn/Fe/Cu/Ag | 0.97 V |
| Zn/Ag | 0.97 V |
| Sn/Cu | 0.44 V |
| Fe/Ag | 0.30 V |
| Ag/Au | – 0.07 V |
| Au/Cu | – 0.09 V |

the electrons. The magnitude of contact potential depends on the element positions in the electrode-potential series. If more than two conductors are so joined, the resulting contact potential is the sum of the individual contact potential values.

## Thermoelectricity

A potential difference, the <u>galvanic voltage</u>, forms at the junction of two conductors due to their dissimilar work functions. The sum of all galvanic voltages is zero in a closed conductor loop (in which the temperature is the same at all points). Measurement of these potentials is only possible by indirect means as a function of temperature (thermoelectric effect, Seebeck effect). The thermoelectric potential values are highly dependent on impurities and material pretreatment. The following equation gives an approximate value for thermoelectric potential in the case of small temperature differences:

$$U_{th} = \Delta T \cdot a + \Delta T^2 \cdot b/2 + \Delta T^3 \cdot c/3$$

where $U_{th}$ thermoelectric voltage

$\Delta T = T_1 - T_2$ temperature difference
$a, b, c$ material constants

The <u>thermoelectric series</u> specifies the differential thermoelectromotive forces referred to a reference metal (usually platinum, copper, or lead). At the hot junction, current flows from the conductor with the lower differential thermoelectromotive force to that with the higher force. The thermoelectromotive force $\eta$ of any pair (thermocouple) equals the difference of the differential thermoelectromotive forces.

The reciprocal of the Seebeck effect is the <u>Peltier effect</u>, in which a temperature difference is created by electrical energy (heat pump).

### Thermoelectric series
(referred to <u>platinum</u>)

| Material | Thermoelectric voltage $10^{-6}$ V/°C |
|---|---|
| Selenium | 1,003 |
| Tellurium | 500 |
| Silicon | 448 |
| Germanium | 303 |
| Antimony | 47...48.6 |
| Nickel chromium | 22 |
| Iron | 18.7...18.9 |
| Molybdenum | 11.6...13.1 |
| Cerium | 10.3 |
| Cadmium | 8.5...9.2 |
| Steel (V2A) | 7.7 |
| Copper | 7.2...7.7 |
| Silver | 6.7...7.9 |
| Tungsten | 6.5...9.0 |
| Iridium | 6.5...6.8 |
| Rhodium | 6.5 |
| Zinc | 6.0...7.9 |
| Manganin | 5.7...8.2 |
| Gold | 5.6...8.0 |
| Tin | 4.1...4.6 |
| Lead | 4.0...4.4 |
| Magnesium | 4.0...4.3 |
| Aluminum | 3.7...4.1 |
| Platinum | ±0 |
| Mercury | −0.1 |
| Sodium | −2.1 |
| Potassium | −9.4 |
| Nickel | −19.4...−12.0 |
| Cobalt | −19.9...−15.2 |
| Constantan | −34.7...−30.4 |
| Bismuth ⊥ axis | −52 |
| Bismuth ∥ axis | −77 |

### Thermocouples in common use[1]

| Material pair | Temperature |
|---|---|
| Copper/constantan | up to 600 °C |
| Iron/constantan | up to 900 °C |
| Nickel-chromium/constantan | up to 900 °C |
| Nickel-chromium/nickel | up to 1,200 °C |
| Platinum-rhodium/platinum | up to 1,600 °C |
| Platinum-rhodium/ platinum-rhodium | up to 1,800 °C |
| Iridium/iridium-rhodium | up to 2,300 °C |
| Tungsten/tungsten-molybdenum[2] | up to 2,600 °C |
| Tungsten/tantalum[2] | up to 3,000 °C |

---

[1] In addition to their use for measuring temperature, thermocouples are used as thermal generators. Efficiencies hitherto achieved: approx. 10% (application in satellites).

[2] In reducing atmosphere.

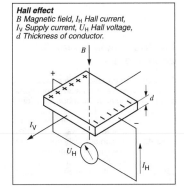

**Hall effect**
$B$ Magnetic field, $I_H$ Hall current,
$I_V$ Supply current, $U_H$ Hall voltage,
$d$ Thickness of conductor.

If current flows through an A-B-A series of conductors, one thermojunction absorbs heat while the other produces more heat than can be accounted for by the Joule effect. The amount of heat produced is governed by the equation:

$$\Delta Q = \pi \cdot I \cdot \Delta t$$

$\pi$ Peltier coefficient
$I$ current, $\Delta t$ time interval

The relationship between the Peltier coefficient and thermoelectromotive force $\eta$ is as follows:

$$\pi = \eta \cdot T$$

where $T$ is temperature.

Current flowing through a homogeneous conductor will also generate heat if a temperature gradient $\Delta T/l$ is maintained in the conductor (<u>Thomson effect</u>). Whereas the power developed by the Joule effect is proportional to $I^2$, the power developed by the Thomson effect is as follows:

$$P = -\sigma \cdot I \cdot \Delta T$$

$\sigma$ Thomson coefficient, $I$ current, $\Delta T$ temperature difference

The reciprocal of the Thomson effect is the <u>Benedicks effect</u>, in which an electric potential is produced as a result of asymmetrical temperature distribution (particularly at points where there is a significant change in cross-sectional area).

### Galvanomagnetic and thermomagnetic effects

Such effects are understood to be changes caused by a magnetic field in the flow of electricity or heat within a conductor. There are 12 different recognized effects which fall into this category, the most well-known of which are the Hall, Ettingshausen, Righi-Leduc and Nernst effects.

The <u>Hall effect</u> is of particular significance in industrial applications (see P. 114 for a discussion of the Hall-effect sensor). If a voltage is applied to a conductor located in a magnetic field perpendicular to the direction of applied voltage, a voltage is produced which is perpendicular to both the flow of current and the magnetic field. This voltage is called the Hall voltage $U_H$:

$$U_H = R \cdot I_V \cdot B/d$$

$R$ Hall constant, $I_V$ supply current, $B$ magnetic field, $d$ thickness of conductor

The Hall constant can be used to determine particle density and movement of electrons and holes. In ferromagnetic materials, the Hall voltage is a function of magnetization (hysteresis).

## Gas and plasma discharge

Gas discharge describes the process that occurs when electric current travels through a space containing a gas or vapor atmosphere.

The free charge carriers present in the gas accelerate within the field between the two charged electrodes, producing charge-carrier cascades and arcing due to impact ionization. This, in turn, results in the actual current discharge, which ignites with voltages of up to 100 million volts (atmospheric lightning), depending on the type of gas, the pressure, and the gap between electrodes. Self-discharge occurs when the excitation energy from the discharge frees electrons at the cathodes; the current flow is then maintained at sharply reduced spark voltages. Glow discharge generally takes place at low gas pressures.

The characteristic radiation of light is determined by the transport and reaction zones produced by field forces and ionic diffusion at low current densities. At higher currents, thermal ionization in the plasma concentrates the current flow, i.e. the discharge contracts.

Thermal electron emission from the cathode results in the transition to arc discharge. The current increases (limited by the external circuit). At temperatures of up to $10^4$ K, intense light is then emitted around the electrodes and from the bow-shaped (due to convection) plasma column located between them. The arc voltage drops to just a few volts. The discharge is terminated when voltage drops below the characteristic extinction potential for the specific momentary condition.

Industrial applications: spark-discharge gap as switching element, arc welding, spark ignition for the combustion of gases, discharge lamps, high-pressure arc lamps.

# Electronics

## Basic principles of semiconductor technology

### Electric conductivity in solid bodies

An individual material's capacity for conducting electricity is determined by the number and mobility of the free charge carriers which it contains. The disparities in the electric conductivities displayed by various solid bodies at room temperature extend through a range defined by 10 to the 24th power. Accordingly, materials are divided into three electrical groups (examples):

| Conductors, metals | Semi-conductors | Non-conductors, insulators |
|---|---|---|
| Silver Copper Aluminum | Germanium Silicon Gallium-arsenide | Teflon Quartz glass Aluminum-oxide |

### Metals, insulators, and semiconductors

All solid bodies contain approximately $10^{22}$ atoms per $cm^3$; they are held together by electrical forces.

In <u>metals</u>, the number of free charge carriers is extremely high (one to two free electrons per atom). The free carriers are characterized by moderate mobility and high conductivity. Conductivity of good conductors: $10^6$ siemens/cm

In <u>insulators</u>, the number of free charge carriers is practically nil, resulting in negligible electric conductivity. Conductivity of good insulators: $10^{-18}$ siemens/cm

The electric conductivity of <u>semiconductors</u> lies between that of metals and insulators. The conductivity of semiconductors varies from that of metals and insulators in that they are extremely sensitive to factors such as variations in pressure (affects the mobility of the charge carriers), temperature fluctuations (number and mobility of the charge carriers), variations in illumination intensity (number of charge carriers), and the presence of additives (number and type of charge carriers).

As they respond to changes in pressure, temperature and light intensity, semiconductors are suitable for application in sensors.

Doping (controlled addition of electrically active foreign substances to the base material) makes it possible to define and localize the semiconductor's electrical conductivity. This procedure forms the basis of present-day semiconductor components. Doping can be used for technically assured production of silicon-based semiconductors with conducting capacities ranging from $10^4$ to $10^{-2}$ siemens/cm.

### Electric conductivity of semiconductors

The following discussion focuses on the silicon-based semiconductor. In its solid state, silicon assumes the form of a crystal lattice with four equidistant contiguous atoms. Each silicon atom has 4 outer electrons, with two shared electrons forming the bond with the contiguous atoms. In this ideal state, silicon has no free charge carriers; thus it is not conductive. The situation changes dramatically with the addition of appropriate additives and the application of energy.

N-doping:

As only 4 electrons are required for bonding in a silicon lattice, the introduction of foreign atoms with 5 outer electrons (e.g. phosphorus) results in the presence of free electrons. Thus, each additional phosphorus atom will provide a free, negatively charged electron. The silicon is transformed into an N conductor: N-type silicon.

P-doping:

The introduction of foreign atoms with 3 outer electrons (e.g. boron) produces electron holes which result from the fact that the boron atom has one electron less for complete bonding in the silicon lattice. This gap in the bonding pattern is also called a hole.

As the latter designation indicates, these holes remain in motion within the silicon; in an electric field, they migrate in a direction opposite to that of the electrons. The holes exhibit the properties of a free positive charge carrier. Thus, every additional boron atom provides a free, positively charged electron hole (positive hole). The silicon is transformed into a P conductor: P-type silicon.

## Intrinsic conduction
Heat and light also generate free mobile charge carriers in undoped silicon; the resulting electron-hole pairs produce intrinsic conductivity in the semiconductor material. This conductivity is generally modest in comparison with that achieved by doping. Increases in temperature induce an exponential rise in the number of electron-hole pairs, ultimately obviating the electrical differences between the p and n regions produced by doping. This phenomenon defines the maximum operating temperatures to which semiconductor components may be subjected:

| | |
|---|---|
| Germanium | 90...100 °C |
| Silicon | 150...200 °C |
| Gallium arsenide | 300...350 °C |

A small number of opposite-polarity charge carriers is always present in both n-type and p-type semiconductors. These minority charges exert a considerable influence on the operating characteristics of virtually all semiconductor devices.

## The PN junction in the semiconductor
The area of transition between a p-type and an n-type zone within the <u>same</u> semiconductor crystal is referred to as the PN junction. The properties of this area exercise a major influence on the operating properties of most semiconductor components.

### PN junction without external voltage
The p-type zone has numerous holes (○), and the n-type zone has only very few. On the other hand, there are only an extremely limited number of electrons in the p-type zone, while in the n-type zone there are a very large number (●). Each type of mobile charge carrier tends to move across the concentration gradient, diffusing into the other zone (diffusion currents).

The loss of holes in the p-type zone results in a negative charge in this area, while electron depletion in the n-type zone produces a positive charge in this region. The result is an electrical potential (diffusion potential) between the p and n-type zones. This potential opposes the respective migration tendencies of the charge carriers, ultimately bringing the exchange of holes and electrons to a halt.

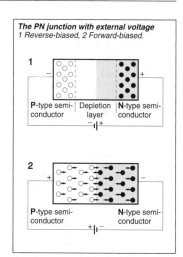

*The PN junction with external voltage*
*1 Reverse-biased, 2 Forward-biased.*

Result: A area deficient in mobile charge carriers is produced at the PN junction. This area, called the space-charge region or depletion layer, is characterized by both severely attenuated electrical conductivity and the presence of a strong electric field.

### PN junction with external voltage
Reverse state: The negative pole at the p-type zone and the positive pole at the n-type zone extends the space-charge region. Consequently, the flow of current is blocked except for a minimal residual current (reverse current) which stems from the minority charge carriers.

Forward state:
With the positive pole at the p-type zone and the negative pole at the n-type zone, the depletion layer is reduced and charge carriers permeate the PN junction, resulting in a large current flow in the forward direction.

Breakdown voltage:
This is the level of reverse-direction voltage beyond which a minimal increase in voltage will suffice to produce a sharp rise in reverse current.

Cause: Separation of bonded electrons from the crystal lattice in the space-charge region, either by high field strength (Zener breakdown), or due to accelerated electrons colliding with the bonded electrons and separating them from their valence bonds due to impact. This ultimately produces a dramatic rise in the number of charge carriers (avalanche breakdown).

# Discrete semiconductor devices

The properties of the PN junction and the combination of several PN junctions in a single semiconductor-crystal chip provide the basis for a steadily increasing array of inexpensive, reliable, rugged, compact semiconductor devices.

A single PN junction forms a diode, two PN junctions are used for transistors, and three or more PN junctions make up a thyristor. The planar technique makes it possible to combine numerous operating elements on a single chip to form the extremely important component group known as integrated semiconductor circuits. These combine the device and the circuitry in a single unit.

Semiconductor chips measure no more than several square millimeters and are usually installed in standardized housings (metal, ceramic, plastic).

## Diodes
A diode is a semiconductor device incorporating a single PN junction. Its specific properties are determined by the distribution pattern of the dopant in the crystal. Diodes which conduct currents in excess of 1 A in the forward direction are referred to as power diodes.

### Rectifier diode
The rectifier diode acts as a form of current valve; it is, therefore, ideally suited for rectifying alternating current. The current in the reverse direction (reverse current) can be approximately $10^7$ times lower than the forward current. It rises rapidly in response to increases in temperature.

### Rectifiers for high reverse voltages
At least one zone with low conductivity is required for high reverse voltages (high resistance in forward direction results in

generation of excessive heat). The insertion of a weakly doped zone (I) between the highly doped p- and n-type zones produces a PIN rectifier. This type of device is characterized by a combination of high reverse voltage and low forward-flow resistance (conductivity modulation).

### Switching diode
These devices are generally employed for rapid switching between high and low impedances. More rapid switching response can be achieved by diffusing gold into the material (promotes the recombination of electrons and holes).

### Zener diode
This is a semiconductor diode which, once a specific initial level of reverse voltage is reached, responds to further increases of reverse voltage with a sharp rise in current flow. This phenomenon is a result of a Zener and/or avalanche breakdown. Zener diodes are designed for continuous operation in this breakdown range.

### Variable-capacitance diode (varactor)
The space-charge region at the PN junction functions as a capacitor; the dielectric element is represented by the semiconductor material in which no charge carriers are present. Increasing the applied voltage extends the depletion layer and reduces the capacitance, while reducing the voltage increases the capacitance.

### Schottky barrier diode (Schottky diode)
A semiconductor diode featuring a metal-to-semiconductor junction. As the electrons move more freely from the n-type silicon into the metal layer than in the opposite direction, an electron-depleted layer is created in the semiconductor material; this is the Schottky barrier layer. Charges are carried exclusively by the electrons, a factor which results in extremely rapid switching, as the minority carriers do not perform any charge storage function.

### Photodiode
This is a semiconductor diode designed to exploit the photovoltaic effect. Reverse voltage is present at the PN junction. Incident light releases electrons from their lattice bonds to produce additional free

electrons and holes. These increase the reverse current (photovoltaic current) in direct proportion to the intensity of the light.

<u>Photovoltaic cell</u>
(see Solar cell, P. 91).

<u>LED (light-emitting diode)</u>
See "Optical technology", P. 49.

**Transistors**
Two contiguous PN junctions produce the transistor effect, a feature employed in the design of components used to amplify electrical signals and to assume switching duties.

<u>Bipolar transistors</u>
Bipolar transistors consist of three zones of varying conductivity, the configuration being either pnp or npn. The zones (and their terminals) are called: emitter E, base B, and collector C.

There are different transistor classifications, depending on the fields of application: small-signal transistors (power dissipation up to 1 watt), power transistors, switching transistors, audio-frequency transistors, high-frequency transistors, microwave transistors, phototransistors, etc. They are termed bipolar because charge carriers of both polarities (holes <u>and</u> electrons) are active. In the npn transistor, the base current's <u>positive</u> charge carriers (holes) control the flow of 100 times their number in <u>negative</u> charge carriers (electrons) from the emitter to the collector.

<u>Operation of a bipolar transistor</u>
(explanation based on the npn transistor)
The emitter-base junction (EB) is forward-biased. This causes electrons to be injected into the base region.

The base-collector junction (BC) is reverse biased. This induces the formation of a space-charge region with a strong electric field. Significant coupling (transistor effect) occurs if the two PN junctions lie in close proximity to each other (in silicon ≈ 10 μm). The electrons injected at the EB then diffuse through the base to the collector. On entering the BC's electric field, they are accelerated into the collector region, where they con-

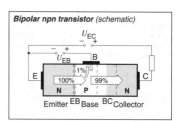

*Bipolar npn transistor* (schematic)

$U_{EC}$

$U_{EB}$  B

E                                              C

100%   1%   99%

N       P       N

Emitter EB Base BC Collector

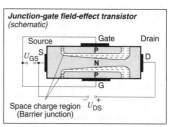

*Junction-gate field-effect transistor* (schematic)

Source                Gate            Drain

$U_{GS}$  S                                D

P

N

P

G

Space charge region   $U_{DS}$
(Barrier junction)

tinue to flow in the form of collector current. Thus, the concentration gradient in the base is retained, and additional electrons continue to migrate from the emitter to the collector. In standard transistors, 99% or more of all the electrons emanating from the emitter reach the space-charge region and become collector current. The few missing electrons are caught in the electron holes while traversing the p-doped base. Left to their own devices, these electrons would produce a negative charge in the base; almost immediately (50 ns), repulsive forces would bring the flow of additional electrons to a halt. A small base current comprised of positive charge carriers (holes) provides partial or complete compensation for this negative charge in the transistor. Small variations in the base current produce substantial changes in the emitter-collector current. The npn transistor is a bipolar, current-controlled semiconductor amplifier.

<u>Field-effect transistors (FET)</u>
In these devices, control of the current flow in a conductive path is exercised essentially by an electric field. The field, in turn, is generated with voltage applied at the control electrode, or gate. Field-effect transistors differ from their bipolar coun-

terparts in utilizing only a single type of charge carrier (electrons <u>or</u> holes), giving rise to the alternate designation "unipolar transistor". They are subdivided into the following classifications:
– <u>Junction-gate field-effect transistors</u> (junction FET, JFET).
– <u>Insulated-gate field-effect transistors, particularly MOS field-effect transistors (MOSFET)</u>, in short: MOS transistors.

MOS transistors are well suited for application in high-integration circuits. Power FETs represent a genuine alternative to bipolar power transistors in many applications. Terminals:
gate (G), source (S), drain (D).

## Operation of a junction FET
(applies to the n-channel FET)
DC voltage is present at the ends of an n-type crystal. Electrons flow from the source to the drain. The width of the channel is defined by two laterally diffused p-type zones and by the negative voltage present within them. Raising the negative gate voltage causes the space-charge regions to extend further into the channel, thereby constricting the current path. Thus, the current between source S and drain D is governed by the voltage at the control electrode G. Only charge carriers of one polarity are required for FET operation. The power necessary for controlling the current is virtually nil. Thus, the junction FET is a unipolar, voltage-controlled component.

## Operation of an MOS transistor
(applies to the p-channel enhancement device)
MOS represents the standard layer configuration: <u>M</u>etal <u>O</u>xide <u>S</u>emiconductor. If no voltage is applied to the gate electrode, then no current will flow between the source and the drain: the PN junctions remain in blocking mode. The application of negative voltage to the gate causes the electrons in the adjacent n-type region to be displaced toward the interior of the crystal, while holes – which are always present in n-type silicon in the form of minority charge carriers – are pulled to the surface. A narrow p-type layer forms beneath the surface: This is called the

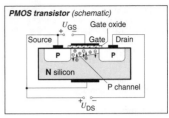

**PMOS transistor** *(schematic)*

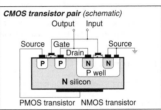

**CMOS transistor pair** *(schematic)*

PMOS transistor    NMOS transistor

P channel. Current can now flow between the two p-type regions (source and drain). This current consists exclusively of holes. As the gate voltage acts through an insulating oxide layer, no current flows in the control circuit: No power is required for the control function. In summary, the MOS transistor is a unipolar, voltage-controlled component.

## PMOS, NMOS, CMOS transistors
If a p-channel MOS transistor (PMOS transistor) is doped with a donor impurity rather than an acceptor impurity, it becomes an NMOS transistor. As the electrons in the NMOS transistor are more mobile, it operates more rapidly than the PMOS device, although the latter was the first to become available due to the fact that it is physically easier to manufacture.

It is also possible to employ complementary MOS technology to pair PMOS and NMOS transistors in a single silicon chip; the resulting devices are called <u>C</u>omplementary <u>MOS</u>, or CMOS transistors. The specific advantages of the CMOS transistor: extremely low power dissipation, a high degree of immunity to interference, relative insensitivity to varying supply voltages, suitability for analog signal processing, and high-integration applications.

### BCD hybrid technology

Integrated power structures are becoming increasingly important. Such structures are realized by combining bipolar and MOS components on a single silicon chip, thereby utilizing the advantages of both technologies. The BCD hybrid technology (Bipolar/CMOS/DMOS) is a significant manufacturing process in automotive electronics and also facilitates the manufacture of MOS power components (DMOS).

## Thyristors

Three consecutive PN junctions provide the thyristor effect, which is applied for components which act as multivibrators when triggered by an electrical signal. "Thyristor" is the generic term for all devices which can be switched from the forward (conducting) state to the reverse (blocking) state (or vice versa). Applications in power electronics: Control of frequency and rotational speed; rectification and frequency conversion; switching. In specialized usage, "thyristor" is understood to mean a reverse-blocking triode thyristor.

### Four-layer diode

DIN definition: A reverse-blocking diode thyristor. A semiconductor device with two terminals (anode A, cathode K), and switch characteristics. It has four layers of alternating doping. This device's electrical response is best understood by visualizing the four-layer structure as representing two transistor paths $T_1$ and $T_2$. Increasing the voltage between A and K induces a rise in the reverse currents of both transistors. At a specific voltage value of $U_{AK}$ (switched voltage), the reverse current of the one transistor increases to such a degree that it begins to exert a slight bias effect on the other transistor, resulting in conduction. Meanwhile, the second transistor operates in the same fashion. The mutual bias effect exerted by the two transistor units reaches such an intensity that the four-layer diode begins to act as a conductor: This is the thyristor effect.

### Thyristor with control terminal

DIN definition: triode thyristor (also SCR, silicon-controlled rectifier), a controllable device with switching characteristics. It consists of four zones of alternating conductivity type. Like the four-layer diode, it has two stable states (high resistance and low resistance). The switching operations between the respective states are governed via the control terminal (gate) G.

### GTO thyristor

DIN definition: gate turn-off (acronym: GTO) switch activated by positive trigger pulse, with deactivation via a negative trigger pulse at the same gate.

### Triac

DIN definition: bidirectional triode thyristor (triac = triode alternating current switch), a controllable thyristor with three terminals. It maintains essentially identical control properties in both of its two switching directions.

## Photovoltaic solar cells

The photovoltaic effect is applied to convert light energy directly into electrical energy.

---

**Four-layer diode and thyristor effect**
1 Four-layer structure, 2 Separated into two transistor paths.

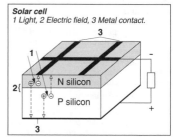

**Solar cell**
1 Light, 2 Electric field, 3 Metal contact.

Solar cells, consisting largely of semiconductor materials, are the basic elements of photovoltaic technology. Exposure to light results in the creation of free charge carriers (electron-hole pairs) in the semiconductor material due to the "internal photo-electric effect". If the semiconductor incorporates a PN junction, then the charge carriers separate in its electric field before proceeding to the metal contacts on the semiconductor's surface. Depending on the semiconductor material used, a DC voltage (photovoltage) ranging from 0.5 to 1.2 V is generated between the contacts. When a load resistor is connected, current starts to flow (photovoltaic current), e.g. 2.8 A at 0.58 V for an Si solar cell with a surface area of 100 cm$^2$.

The efficiency level with which radiated light energy is converted into electrical energy (indicated in percent) depends both on how well the semiconductor material is suited to the light's spectral distribution, and the efficiency with which the generated free charge carriers can be isolated and conducted to the appropriate surface contacts.

The paths within the semiconductor should be short (thin layers from several μm to 300 μm) to prevent the free charge carriers from recombining. The structure of the crystal lattices in the material must be as perfect as possible, while the material itself must be free of impurities. The manufacturing processes include procedures of the type employed for microelectronics components. Silicon is the most commonly used material for solar cells. It is used in single-crystal, polycrystalline, and amorphous modification. Typical efficiency levels achieved under laboratory conditions include:

| Silicon | – single crystal | 24.7% |
|---|---|---|
| | – polycrystalline | 19.8% |
| | – amorphous | 14.6% |
| CdTe | | 16.5% |
| CuInGaSe$_2$ | | 18.4% |
| GaAs [1] | | 27.6.% |
| GaInP/GaAs/Ge-Tandem [1] | | 34.0%. |

[1] Concentrated sunlight.

Average efficiency levels obtained from mass-produced solar cells are approximately one third lower. The "tandem cells" achieve their high efficiency by incorporating two solar cells – made of different materials – in consecutive layers; the unit is thus capable of converting light from various spectral ranges into charge carriers.

The individual solar cells are interconnected within a circuit to form solar modules. The output is always a DC voltage; an inverter can be used for conversion to AC (e.g. for discharge into the power supply network. The characteristic data of a module are its output voltage and power output in W$_P$ referred to full solar exposure ($\approx$ 1,000 W/m$^2$).

The ultimate objective is to develop inexpensive processes allowing the manufacture of large-area solar cells. Proven procedures include extracting crystals from molten mass, or cutting cast crystals into individual wafers and blocks. Research is now extending into new areas such as strip pulling, foil casting, and depositing of thin semiconductor layers. Although the energy generated by photovoltaic processes is still more expensive than that provided by conventional power stations, improvements in cell manufacturing techniques, increases in efficiency, and large-scale production will combine to allow further reductions in cost. For applications involving isolated systems (consumers without external power connections) and minimum power requirements (watches, pocket calculators), photovoltaics already represents the best solution. With a worldwide installed power output of 1,400 MW$_P$ in 2002, about 60% are connected to the power supply network. The photovoltaic market is growing at an annual rate of 300 to 400 MW$_P$ of new installed power.

## Monolithic integrated circuits

### Monolithic integration

Planar technology is based on the oxidation of silicon wafers, which is a relatively simple process, and the speed at which the dopants penetrate into silicon, which is exponentially greater than the speed at which they enter the oxide. Doping only occurs at locations where openings are present in the oxide layer. The specific design requirements of an individual integrated circuit determine the precise geometric configuration, which is applied to the wafer in a photolithographic process. All processing procedures (oxidizing, etching, doping, and depositing) progress consecutively from the surface plane (planar).

Planar technology makes it possible to manufacture all circuit components (resistors, capacitors, diodes, transistors, thyristors) and the associated conductor strips on a single silicon chip in a unified manufacturing process. The semiconductor devices are combined to produce monolithic integrated circuits IC: <u>I</u>ntegrated <u>C</u>ircuit.

This integration generally comprises a subsystem within the electronic circuit and increasingly comprises the entire system: <u>system-on-a-chip</u>.

Integration level
Either the number of individual functional elements, the number of transistors, or the number of gates on a single chip. The following classifications relate to the level of integration (and chip surface):
- <u>SSI</u> (<u>S</u>mall <u>S</u>cale <u>I</u>ntegration)
  Up to roughly 100 function elements per chip, mean chip surface area 3 mm², but can also be very much larger in circuits with high power outputs (e.g. smart power transistors).
- <u>MSI</u> (<u>M</u>edium <u>S</u>cale <u>I</u>ntegration)
  Roughly 100 to 1,000 function elements per chip, mean chip surface area 8 mm².

- <u>LSI</u> (<u>L</u>arge <u>S</u>cale <u>I</u>ntegration)
  Up to 100,000 function elements per chip, mean chip surface area 20 mm².
- <u>VLSI</u> (<u>V</u>ery <u>L</u>arge <u>S</u>cale <u>I</u>ntegration)
  Up to 1 million function elements per chip, mean chip surface area 30 mm².
- <u>ULSI</u> (<u>U</u>ltra <u>L</u>arge <u>S</u>cale <u>I</u>ntegration)
  Over 1 million function elements per chip (DRAM: more than 600 million transistors per chip), surface area up to 300 mm², very small structure size 80 nm.

Computer-aided simulation and design methods (CAE/CAD) are essential elements in the manufacture of integrated circuits. Entire function modules are used in VLSI and ULSI, otherwise the time expenditure and failure risk would make development impossible. In addition, simulation programs are used to detect any defects made.

**Classifications for integrated circuitry**
- According to transistor engineering:
  bipolar, MOS, mixed (bipolar/MOS, BiCMOS, BCD).
- According to circuit engineering:
  analog, digital, mixed (mixed signal)
- According to component families:
  analog, microcomponents (IC with microcomputer), memories, logic circuits
- According to application:
  standard IC, application-specific IC (ASIC, ASSP).

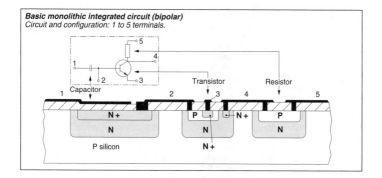

*Basic monolithic integrated circuit (bipolar)*
*Circuit and configuration: 1 to 5 terminals.*

**Integrated analog circuits**
- Basic structures:
  Stabilized-voltage supply, stabilized-current supply, differential amplifier components, switching elements, potential shift, output stages.
- Application-oriented classes:
  Operational amplifiers (OP), voltage regulators, comparators, timers, converters, interface circuits.
- Special analog ICs:
  Voltage references, wideband amplifiers, analog multipliers, function generators, phase-lock circuits, analog filters, analog switches.

**Integrated digital circuits**
The spectrum ranges from LSI (simple logic chips) through to ULSI (memories, microcomponents).

Several conditions must be met before logic chips can be combined within a single system: The power supply, logic level, the circuit speed, and the signal transit time must all be identical. This requirement is met within the respective circuit families. The most important are:
- Various bipolar types (e.g. TTL: Transistor-Transistor-Logic)
- MOS logic, in particular CMOS logic

MOS and CMOS chips make up more than 99% of the production of integrated digital circuits. Bipolar logic circuits are only used in exceptional cases. Here, too, CMOS devices are taking their place more and more.

**Semiconductor memories**
Data storage includes the following operations: recording (writing, entering), storage (data storage in the narrow sense), retrieval, and readout. The memory operates by exploiting physical properties that facilitate unambiguous production and recognition of two opposed states (binary information). In semiconductor memories, the states produced are "conductive/nonconductive" or "charged/discharged"; the latter state relies on special properties in the silicon/silicon oxide or silicon nitride/metal junction. In future magnetic memory chips (FDRAM) will also be used. They have small ferromagnetic areas integrated on the chip. The direction of the magnetic field is used to store information.

Semiconductor memories are divided into the two main categories of "volatile" and "non-volatile". Virtually all of them are manufactured according to CMOS technology.
- Volatile memories (short-term memories) can be read and over written any number of times, and are therefore referred to as RAMs (Random Access Memories); the information content is lost when the power supply is switched off.
- Non-volatile memory chips (long-term memories) retain their data even when the power supply is switched off; they are also referred to as ROMs (Read-Only Memory).

The chart on the facing page shows the relationships and classification of the most common types of memory chip.

**Microprocessors and microcomputers**
The microprocessor represents the integration of a computer's central processing unit on a single chip. Microprocessor design seeks to avoid individualization in the face of large-scale integration, and the units can be programmed to meet the varied requirements associated with specific operating conditions. There are two different main groups of processor. A PC (Personal Computer) uses CISC processors (CISC: Complete Instruction Set Computing). These processors are very versatile and user-programmable. A WS (work station) normally uses RISC processors (RISC: Re-duced Instruction Set Computing). These processors are very much faster for the specific tasks frequently associated with WS use, but are significantly slower for all other tasks. A microprocessor cannot operate by itself: it always acts as part of a microcomputer.

A microcomputer consists of:
- Microprocessor serving as CPU (central processing unit). The microprocessor contains the controller and the arithmetic-logic unit. The arithmetic and logic unit performs the operations indicated by its name, while the controller ensures implementation of the commands stored in the program memory.
- Input and output units (I/O), which control data communication with the peripherals.

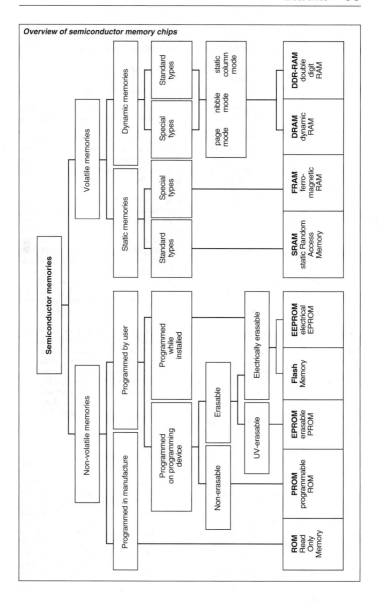

*Overview of semiconductor memory chips*

- Program memory which provides permanent storage for the operating program (user program), thus ROM, PROM, or EPROM.
- Data memory for the data being run at any given time. This data changes continuously; thus, the storage medium for this application is the RAM. Part of the RAM (cache) is integrated on the microcomputer since CPU speed would otherwise be drastically reduced due to the high data rates, and there would be no use in deploying a high-speed processor if the required data were always sent over external buses. SRAMs are always used in these cases owing to the low access times required.
- Clock generator and power-supply system.
- The bus system links the individual elements in a microcomputer.
- A clock generator makes sure that all the operations in the microcomputer take place within a specified timeframe.
- Logic circuits are chips that carry out special tasks, such as program interrupts, inserting intermediate programs, etc.
- The periphery includes input/output devices and external memories, e.g. the main memory (DRAM) or the hard disk.

The main components of a microcomputer are normally combined as separate components on printed-circuit boards. "Single-chip" computers are becoming used more and more for simpler tasks, e.g. internet access in wireless communications, which is a growing trend, or functions integrated on a single silicon chip (SoC: System on a Chip). The performance of these high-integration systems is limited by the relatively small amount of RAM which can be accommodated at reasonable expense on the chip.

A microcontroller includes at least the CPU function, read-only memory (ROM, EPROM, or EEPROM), input/output capability (I/O), and random-access memory (RAM) on a single chip. In some cases, analog functions are only integrated on the chip. In contrast to a microcomputer, the controller reacts with a specified program that provides particular output values depending on the input information. It is used to control self-governing systems, e.g. engine management.

The transputer is a special type of microprocessor which is especially useful for building parallel computer networks. In addition to the standard microprocessor components, the chip is also equipped with communications and processing hardware.

It has at least four serial bidirectional transmission channels (links), allowing extremely high-speed (> 1 Gbit/s per link) communications with many other transputers. As communications are completely asynchronous, distributed networks do not require a common clock circuit. Each link has its own DMA controller; once initialized by the CPU, it can carry out data transmission on its own. Thus, processing and communication are essentially parallel operations. Of particular significance are the extremely short process switchover and interrupt-response times of $\ll 1\ \mu s$. The transputer does not need a real-time operating system for this; instead, it has the necessary processing commands directly in its command set.

The transputer operates as a communication node within the parallel network, meaning that it serves as both computer and communications interface. The transputer can therefore be employed to avoid one of the gravest liabilities of many parallel systems, which is the inherent need to share a common bus. Maximum-performance computers are therefore built using transputers.

**Application-specific ICs**

Application-specific IC (ASIC: Application Specific Integrated Circuits or also ASSP: Application Specific Standard Product) are only designed for a single application, as opposed to standard ICs. ASICs are produced for, and sold only to, one customer. ASSPs are application-specific ICs which are sold to several customers for the same application. Both are the result of a successful cooperation between users who share special system experience, and producers who possess suitable technologies. The essential advantages of ASICs: fewer components, lower system costs, increased reliability, more difficult to copy.

The ASIC family is generally classified according to the development method which has been selected: chip-mounted circuitry, constructed from individual function elements (full-custom IC), provides the best results with regard to operation and packaging density. It is, however, only suited for large-volume applications (time and expense).

Standardized basic circuit functions (developed and tested in advance) represent one step towards rationalizing the development process. The circuits are incorporated in cells of varying sizes (ROM, RAM, computer core, or individualized, application-specific circuit groups). Depending on the number of available application-specific cells, this method can be employed to reduce development times without sacrificing efficient exploitation of the chip surface.

The next stage is the use of standardized, relatively complex basic functions which are developed in advance in standard cells of the same height and variable width. They are available in the form of cell libraries. These standard cells are automatically placed in series and then automatically connected with polysilicon and aluminum conductors. A dual or triple-layer metallic coating can be applied to achieve even better utilization of the surface area.

Gate arrays are predeveloped as far as the transistor/gate connection, and are manufactured in advance, leaving only the final masking operations for later completion. The connection with the application-specific circuit is then automatic. Rationalization is achieved by providing standard circuits for frequent basic computer functions (similar to a cell library). Special gate arrays designed for specific applications have particular advantages (e.g. pure computer-oriented digital circuits under the general conditions usual for computers).

Programmable logic devices (PLD) – completely preassembled transistor arrays – are programmed by the user in the same way as a special-application PROM. PLDs thus provide system developers with the option of producing silicon breadboard circuits within a short period of time. The production of complex systems in silicon is becoming increasingly important, as it allows the production of practical working models in the development phase.

### Smart-power ICs

Automotive and industrial systems rely upon electronics to govern numerous final-control elements and other loads. Circuit-breakers must be capable of assuming auxiliary functions extending beyond the control of circuit power: driver circuits for activating switching transistors, protective circuits for excess current, overvoltage, overtemperature, and fault acknowledgments in case of incorrect operation. Such bipolar or MOS-technology power ICs are generically termed smart-power ICs.

# Film and hybrid circuits, MCM

### Film circuits

The integrated film circuit features passive circuit elements – these include capacitors and inductors, as well as conductor tracks, insulators, and resistors. An integrated film circuit is produced by applying the layers which contain these elements to a substrate carrier. The terms "thin-film" and "thick-film" circuit derive from the fact that the film thickness was originally the determining factor for tailoring to specific performance characteristics; present technology employs a variety of manufacturing techniques to achieve the same end.

### Thin-film circuits

Integrated film circuits on which the individual layers are applied to glass or ceramic substrates, usually in a vacuum coating process. Advantages: fine structures (to approx. 10 µm) provide high circuit-element density, extremely good HF characteristics, and low-noise resistor elements. On the minus side are the relatively high manufacturing costs.

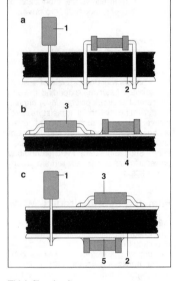

*Circuit-board technology, design options*
a) Insertion mounting (conventional),
b) SMD mounting on ceramic substrate
(hybrid technology), c) Mixed mounting.
1 Wired components, 2 Printed-circuit board,
3 Chips, 4 Ceramic substrate,
5 Bonding material.

## Thick-film circuits

Integrated film circuits in which the layers are usually applied to ceramic carriers in a screen-printing process before being fused on. Advantages: Multilayer construction provides high circuit-element density and good HF characteristics. A high degree of manufacturing automation is possible for large-scale production.

## Multilayer ceramic substrates

The base material for the multilayer ceramic substrate is the unfired ceramic foil to which conductor tracks are applied in a silk-screening process. In the next step, a number of these foils are laminated together to form a multilayer substrate. This device is then sintered at high temperature (850...1,600 °C) to form a hard ceramic device featuring integrated conductive paths. A metal paste is applied to the holes between the individual foils to form the interlayer electrical connections. Special materials are employed to integrate resistors and capacitors in the device. This process provides for substantially higher levels of circuit density than thick-film devices.

## Hybrid circuits

Integrated film circuits with additional discrete components, such as capacitors and integrated semiconductor circuits (ICs), which are applied by soldering or adhesive bonding. A high component density is achieved by using unpacked semiconductor chips which are contacted by means of "bonding", or SMD components (SMD: Surface Mounted Device). A multilayer ceramic substrate can be used to achieve extremely small hybrid control devices (microhybrids). Advantages: Good thermal dissipation allows high installation temperatures, while compact construction provides good vibration strength and HF response characteristics. Hybrid circuits are especially well-suited for automotive applications and for telecommunications.

## MCM

MCM (Multi-Chip Module) is used to identify an electronic component consisting of numerous "unpacked" integrated semiconductors (ICs). The basic element is the carrier substrate with its internal circuits. The ICs are unpacked and contacted by means of bonding, TAB, or flip-chip soldering. An MCM can also contain resistors and capacitors as required.

Classification is according to the selected substrate material:
– MCM-C multilayer ceramic substrate
– MCM-D thin-film design, generally on silicon
– MCM-L organic multilayer laminate

The MCM is generally selected to achieve compliance with specific operating requirements. It combines rapid switching response in processor cores with favorable EMC characteristics and extremely compact packages. The MCM is frequently employed to obtain electrical performance characteristics that would be either prohibitively expensive or totally impossible to obtain from current IC technology.

# Circuit-board technology, SMT

Basically, the circuits in an electronic system can be implemented in accordance with semiconductor, hybrid, and circuit-board technologies. Selection depends on such factors as economy (cost, production volumes), time (development time, service life), and ambient conditions (electrical, thermal, physical).

Circuit-board technology represents the classical process for producing an electrical circuit. On the most basic type of circuit board, the electronic components are mounted on a fiberboard or fiberglass-reinforced synthetic-resin carrier. A printing process is employed to apply the conductor tracks (copper foil) to the board (therefore the term "printed circuit"). An alternative is to etch the circuit from a copper-plated board. The component's contact pins are inserted through holes in the board and soldered in position on the conductor tracks. Meanwhile, surface mounting has become the standard process in modern volume production.

The rapid increase in the number of terminals (pins) was triggered by an increasing level of IC integration. This initiated the transition away from the conventional technology of insertion mounting and toward surface-mounting technology (SMT: Surface Mount Technology). In the meantime there is a very wide range of surface-mounted devices (SMD: Surface Mounted Devices) which are soldered flat on the printed-circuit board. These SMDs and their case forms (SOT, PQFP, PLCC, Flat Pack, CSP, etc.) are highly suitable for processing in automatic insertion machines. Many devices can only be subjected to an automatic process. Pin geometry has become so minute that manual assembly is practically impossible.

Inserting unpacked semiconductor components has now become the norm in surface-mounting technology. Here, there are two options, i.e. COB (Chip On Board) or Flip Chip. In COB assembly, the IC is placed with its processed side facing up on the substrate and it is connected to it by thin wires of gold or aluminum (wire bonding). In Flip Chip assembly, small quantities of solder are applied to the contact surfaces on the IC. The IC is then placed with its processed side facing down on a solder grid and soldered. The advantage of this assembly method is to minimize space requirements for the IC and it requires no packaging.

The most important application advantages provided by surface-mounting technology (SMT) include:
- Rationalized assembly production (high mounting speed and reliability).
- Low space requirements with identical function content, also achieved by mounting on both sides.
- Use of standard printed-circuit boards (e.g. epoxy fiberglass mat, FR4).
- No or fewer holes in each circuit board.
- Combinable with wired components.
- Increased reliability due to reduction of connection points.
- Improved circuit design, coupling and reproducibility.
- Better HF characteristics.

Surface-mounting technology is much more sensitive to the combination of processing techniques than is conventional insertion mounting. The advantages of SMT are directly proportional to the care with which components, circuit-board layout, automatic mounting, joining techniques, testing, repair, etc., are mutually adapted for optimal performance.

## Micromechanics

The term "micromechanics" is employed to denote the production of mechanical components using semiconductors (generally silicon) and semiconductor technology. This type of application exploits both the semiconducting and mechanical properties of silicon. The first micromechanical silicon pressure sensors were installed in motor vehicles at the beginning of the 1980s. Typical mechanical dimensions can extend into the micrometer range.

The mechanical characteristics of silicon (e.g. strength, hardness, and the modulus of elasticity, see Table) can be compared to those of steel. However, silicon is lighter and has greater thermal conductivity. Single-crystal Si wafers are used with almost perfect physical response characteristics. Hysteresis and creepage are negligible. Due to the brittleness of the single-crystal material, the stress-strain curve has no plastic range; the material ruptures when the elastic range is exceeded.

Two methods of manufacturing micromechanical structures in silicon have established themselves: bulk micromechanics and surface micromechanics.

Both methods use the standard procedures of microelectronics (e.g. epitaxial growth, oxidation, diffusion, and photolithography) together with some additional special procedures. To remove material, bulk micromechanics requires anisotropic etching with or without electrochemical etch stop, while surface micromechanics requires vapor-phase etching and deep trenching. Anodic bonding and seal-glass bonding are used to hermetically join two wafers (capping, inclusion of reference vacuum).

### Bulk micromechanics (BMM)

This method involves etching the entire wafer from the reverse side in order to produce the desired structure. The etching process takes place in alkaline media (caustic potash solution), in which the etching behavior of silicon demonstrates pronounced anisotropy, i.e. the etching rate is greatly dependent on the crystal direction. It is thus possible to represent the structure very accurately in terms of

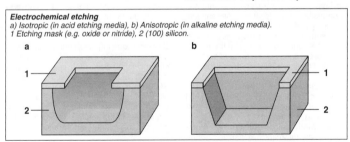

*Electrochemical etching*
*a) Isotropic (in acid etching media), b) Anisotropic (in alkaline etching media).*
*1 Etching mask (e.g. oxide or nitride), 2 (100) silicon.*

| Parameter | Unit | Silicon | Steel (max.) | Stainless steel |
|---|---|---|---|---|
| Tensile load | $10^5$ N/cm$^2$ | 7.0 | 4.2 | 2.1 |
| Knoop hardness | kg/mm$^2$ | 850 | 1,500 | 660 |
| Modulus of elasticity | $10^7$ N/cm$^2$ | 1.9 | 2.1 | 2.0 |
| Density | g/cm$^3$ | 2.3 | 7.9 | 7.9 |
| Thermal conductivity | W/cm · K | 1.57 | 0.97 | 0.33 |
| Thermal expansion | $10^{-6}$/K | 2.3 | 12.0 | 17.3 |

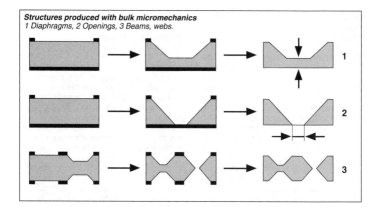

**Structures produced with bulk micromechanics**
1 Diaphragms, 2 Openings, 3 Beams, webs.

depth. When silicon wafers with (100) orientation are used, the (111) surfaces, for example, remain virtually unaffected. In the case of anisotropic etching, (111) surfaces develop and form a characteristic angle of 54.74° with the (100) surface.

In the simplest case, the etching process is stopped after a certain period of time while wafer thickness and etching rate are taken into consideration (time etching). However, for the most part, an electrochemical etch stop is used in which etching comes to a halt at the boundary of a PN junction. BMM can be used to produce diaphragms with typical thicknesses of between 5 and 50 µm for applications such as pressure sensors and air-mass meters.

#### Surface micromechanics (SMM)
In contrast to bulk micromechanics, SMM merely uses the silicon wafer as the substrate. Moving structures are formed from polycrystalline silicon layers which, similar to a manufacturing process for integrated circuits, are deposited on the surface of the silicon by epitaxial growth.

When an SMM component is made, a "sacrificial layer" of silicon oxide is first applied and structured with standard semiconductor processes. An approx. 10 µm thick polysilicon layer (epipoly layer) is then applied at high temperatures in an epitaxial reactor. The epipoly obtains the desired structure with the aid of a lacquer

mask and anisotropic, i.e. vertical etching (deep trenching). The vertical side walls are obtained by an alternation of etching and passivation cycles. After an etching cycle, the etched sidewall section is provided with a polymer during passivation as protection so that it is not attacked during the subsequent etching. Vertical side walls with a high representation accuracy are created in this way. In the last process stage, the sacrificial oxide layer beneath the

**Process stages in surface micromechanics**
1 Depositing and structuring the sacrificial layer, 2 Depositing polysilicon, 3 Structuring the polysilicon, 4 Removing the sacrificial layer and so producing freely moving structures on the surface.

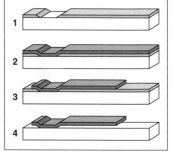

polysilicon layer is removed with gaseous hydrogen fluoride in order to expose the structures.

Among other things, SMM is used in the manufacture of capacitive acceleration sensors with movable and fixed electrodes for capacitive evaluation, and yaw-rate sensors with quasirotary oscillators.

### Wafer bonding

In addition to structuring the silicon, joining two wafers represents another essential task for micromechanical production engineering. Joining technology is required in order to hermetically seal cavities (e.g. inclusion of reference vacuum in pressure sensors), to protect sensitive structures by applying caps (e.g. for acceleration and yaw-rate sensors), or to join the silicon wafer with intermediate layers which minimize the thermal and mechanical stresses (e.g. glass base on pressure sensors).

With anodic bonding, a Pyrex-glass wafer is joined to a silicon wafer at a voltage of some 100 V and a temperature of approx. 400°C. At these temperatures, the alkaline ions in the Pyrex glass move. This creates a depletion layer at the boundary to the silicon, through which the applied voltage drops. A strong electrostatic attraction and an electrochemical reaction (anodic oxidation) result in a permanent hermetic bond between the glass and the silicon.

With seal-glass bonding, two silicon wafers are contacted by way of a glass-solder layer applied in the screen-printing process at approx. 400°C and under the exertion of pressure. The glass solder melts at this temperature and produces a hermetically sealed bond with the silicon.

## Analog/digital conversion

### Analog technology

Analog signals are electrical quantities whose amplitude, frequency, and phase convey information on physical variables or technical processes. This information can assume any intermediate value (value-continuous) within specific limits at any time (time-continuous). Analog technology provides means for processing these signals. Initial processing, consisting of filtering and amplification, can be supplemented by mathematical operations, such as addition, multiplication, and integration over time, etc. The operational amplifier (OP) is an integrated circuit of extreme importance in analog technology. Under ideal conditions, a relatively simple external circuit is sufficient for determining its operating characteristics (infinite amplification, no input current).

Analog units also have several disadvantages: the characteristic response curves of the various components alter with age, temperature fluctuations influence precision, and the manufacturing process must generally be supplemented by subsequent calibration.

### Digital technology

Analog-to-digital conversion entails a transition to discrete monitoring of both time and intensity, i.e. the analog signal is sampled with specific periodicity (sampling instants). The sampled values are assigned a numerical value in which the number of possible values, and thus the resolution, are limited (quantization).

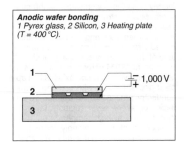

*Anodic wafer bonding*
*1 Pyrex glass, 2 Silicon, 3 Heating plate*
*(T = 400 °C).*

1 ⎓ 1,000 V

**Operational amplifier (OP)**
a) Inversion amplifier,
b) Differential amplifier.

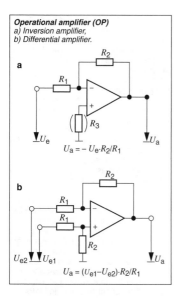

$$U_a = -U_e \cdot R_2/R_1$$

$$U_a = (U_{e1} - U_{e2}) \cdot R_2/R_1$$

**Digital conversion of an analog signal**
F Filter, S/H Sample-and-hold circuit,
A/D Analog/digital converter.

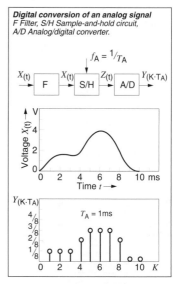

Instead of using the decimal system, digital technology uses the binary system which is easier for the computer to handle.
Example:
101 (binary) =
$1 \cdot 2^2 + 0 \cdot 2^1 + 1 \cdot 2^0 = 5$ (decimal).
The bit (position) with the greatest value is termed the MSB (Most Significant Bit), the lowest the LSB (Least Significant Bit). When represented as a two's complement, the MSB provides the prefix for the decimal number (1 ≙ negative, 0 ≙ positive). Values ranging from – 4 to + 3 can be represented with a 3-bit word.
Example: 101 =
$-1 \cdot 2^2 + 0 \cdot 2^1 + 1 \cdot 2^0 = -3$.

A word of n bits in length is able to represent $2^n$ different values. This becomes 256 values for 8 bits, and 65,536 values for 16 bits. An analog input voltage of ±5 V (FSR Full Scale Range) then has a resolution (LSB value) of 39 mV at 8 bits and 0.15 mV at 16 bits.
The bandwidth of the sampled time signal must be limited (anti-aliasing filter).

The highest signal frequency $f_g$ must be less than half the scanning frequency $f_A$ ($f_A > 2 \cdot f_g$). If a sample-and-hold circuit is not employed, the maximum allowable variation in input voltage during the A/D converter's conversion time (aperture time) is one LSB.
The transfer function illustrates how a single digital value is assigned to various input voltages. The maximum amplitude of the quantization error is $Q/2$ (rounding-off error) at $Q = FSR/(2^n) ≙ LSB$.
Quantization results in an overlay of quantization noise which contaminates the actual wanted signal. If a sine-wave signal is employed for full modulation in the A/D converter, the result is a signal-to-noise ratio which increases by about 6 dB for each additional bit of resolution. Real A/D converters display deviations from the ideal transfer characteristic. These are caused by offset, amplification, and linearity errors (static errors), as well as aperture inconsistency, and finite settling times (dynamic errors).

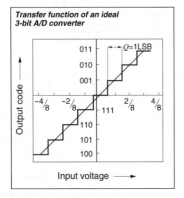

*Transfer function of an ideal 3-bit A/D converter*

**Basic principles of converters**
Converter architecture is basically determined by available performance features, such as "resolution", "maximum sampling rate" and "multiplexing capabiltiy".

A <u>flash converter</u> routes the analog input signal to a chain of comparators and compares it with all reference voltages within one cycle. A 10-bit converter requires 1,023 comparators with an identical number of concatenated reference voltages (voltage dividers).

Several flash converters (m bits), each supplemented by a sample-and-hold circuit and switched in series with an m-bit digital/analog converter, are referred to as <u>pipelined flash converters</u>. This architecture achieves higher resolutions with a low number of comparators. Parallel processing in single stages does not cause any losses in data throughput, but it does require a constant period length. As a result, it is only suitable for a variable sampling rate to a lesser extent (synchronous sampling of the crank angle).

Converters based on the <u>principle of successive approximation</u> have only one comparator and require 10 cycles for a word length of 10 bits until the event is defined. An analog signal is compared with the binary weights $1/2$ FSR through $(1/2)^n$ FSR in a similar way to the process of a beam balance.

The basic structure of a <u>sigma-delta comparator</u> consists of an integrator, a comparator, and a 1-bit digital/analog converter. It supplies a very high sampling rate with a 1-bit data stream (oversampling). Quantization noise is shifted in frequency bands outside of the wanted band owing to the feedback structure of the converter (noise shaping). A digital signal with a large word length is then obtainable after final digital filtering and a reduction in the sampling rate. A sigma-delta converter requires no additional analog anti-aliasing filter because of strong oversampling. There are disadvantages in the long propagation time of the filter and the restricted multiplexing capabilities.

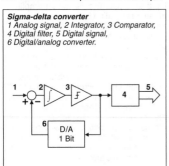

*Sigma-delta converter*
*1 Analog signal, 2 Integrator, 3 Comparator, 4 Digital filter, 5 Digital signal, 6 Digital/analog converter.*

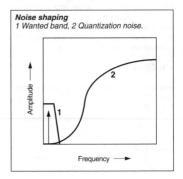

*Noise shaping*
*1 Wanted band, 2 Quantization noise.*

# Mechatronics

## Mechatronic systems and components

### Definition

The term "mechatronics" is a compound derived from the words me<u>cha</u>nisms and elec<u>tronics</u>, where electronics means "hardware" and "software", and mechanisms is the generic term for the disciplines of "mechanical engineering" and "hydraulics". It is not a question of replacing mechanical engineering by "electronification", but of developing a synergistic approach and design methodology. The aim is to achieve a synergistic optimization of mechanical engineering, electronic hardware and software in order to project more functions at low cost, less weight and installation space, and better quality.

A crucial factor governing the success of a mechatronic approach to solving problems is to regard the two previously separate disciplines as a single entity.

### Applications

Mechatronic systems and components are now used in practically all aspects of the automobile today, starting with engine management and fuel injection for gasoline and diesel engines, transmission-shift control, and electrical and thermal energy management, through to a wide variety of braking and vehicle-dynamic systems. It even includes communication and information systems, with many different requirements when it comes to operability. Besides systems and components, mechatronics are also playing an increasingly vital role in the field of micromechanics.

### Examples at system level

A general trend is emerging in the advanced development of systems for fully automated vehicle handling and guidance: In future, mechanical systems will be replaced to an increasing extent by "x-by-wire" systems.

One system that has been in existence for quite some time is "drive-by-wire", i.e. electronic throttle control.

"Brake-by-wire" is replacing the mechanical and hydraulic link between the brake pedal and the wheel brake. Sensors detect the driver's brake command and transmit this information to an electronic control unit. The unit then generates the required braking effect at the wheels by means of actuators.

A possible option for implementing "brake-by-wire" is the <u>electrohydraulic braking system</u>, SBC (<u>S</u>ensotronic <u>B</u>rake <u>C</u>ontrol). When the brake pedal is depressed, or when the <u>E</u>lectronic <u>St</u>ability <u>P</u>rogram (ESP) intervenes in the brake system to stabilize the vehicle, the SBC control unit calculates the required braking pressures for each of the wheels. Since the unit calculates the required braking pressures separately for each wheel and detects the actual values separately, it can also regulate the braking pressure to each wheel via the wheel-pressure modulators. The four pressure modulators each consist of an inlet and an outlet valve controlled by electronic output stages which together produce a finely metered pressure regulation.

In the <u>common-rail system</u>, pressure generation and fuel injection are separated from each other. A high-pressure accumulator, i.e. the common rail, stores constantly the fuel pressure required for each of the engine's operating states. A solenoid-valve-controlled injector with integrated nozzle assumes the function of injecting the fuel directly in the combustion chamber of each cylinder. The engine electronics constantly request data on accelerator-pedal position, rotational speed, operating temperature, fresh-air intake flow, and rail pressure in order to optimize the control of fuel metering as a function of the operating conditions.

### Examples at component level

Fuel injectors are crucial components in determining the future potential of Diesel-engine technology. <u>Common-rail injectors</u> are an excellent example of the fact that an extremely high degree of functionality and, ultimately, customer utility can only be achieved by controlling all the physical domains (electrodynamics, mechanical engineering, fluid dynamics) to which these components are subjected.

In-vehicle <u>CD drives</u> are exposed to particularly tough conditions. Besides wide temperature ranges, they must withstand extreme vibrations that have a critical impact on such precision-engineered systems.

The drives are usually equipped with a spring-damper system to isolate the playback unit from vibrations that occur when the vehicle is moving. Any considerations to reduce the weight and installation space of CD drives immediately raise questions concerning these spring-damper systems. If the damper system is eliminated from a CD drive, the main focus is on designing a mechanical system with zero clearances and producing additional reinforcement for the focus and tracking controllers at high frequencies.

Only by considering both measures from a mechatronic viewpoint is it possible to achieve an optimized vibration-proof solution for an automotive environment. Besides weight savings of about 15%, the installation height has also been reduced by about 20%.

The new mechatronic approach for <u>electrically driven coolant motors</u> is based on brushless, electronically commutated DC motors (BLDC). Initially, they are more expensive (motor with electronics) than previous DC motors equipped with brushes. However, the overall optimization approach has a positive tradeoff: BLDC motors can be used as "wet rotors" with a much simpler design. This reduces the number of single parts by roughly 60%. Taking the aggregate view, the sturdier design has double the service life, almost half the weight, about 40% less the overall length, while maintaining costs at a comparable level.

### Examples in the field of micromechanics

Another area of applications for mechatronics is the field of micromechanical sensors, with noteworthy examples such as hot-film air-mass meters and yaw-rate sensors.

The design of microsystems also requires an interdisciplinary approach owing to the close interaction between the subsystems involving individual disciplines such as mechanical engineering, electrostatics, fluid dynamics (where necessary), and electronics.

## Development methodology

### Simulation

The special challenges that designers face when developing mechatronic systems are the ever shorter development times and the increasing complexity of the systems. At the same time it is vital to ensure that the developments will result in useful products.

Complex mechatronic systems consist of a large number of components from a wide range of physical domains: hydraulics, mechanical engineering, and electronics. The interaction between these domains is a decisive factor governing the function and performance of the overall system. Simulation models are required to review key design decisions, especially in the early development stages when there is no prototype available.

Basic issues can often be clarified by producing relatively simple models of the components. If more detail is required, more refined component models are needed. The detailed models focus mainly on a specific physical domain:

- As a result, there are detailed hydraulic models of common-rail injectors. They are simulated using special programs whose algorithms are matched precisely to the hydraulic systems. For example, the requirements here would be to take cavitation phenomena into consideration.
- Detailed models are also needed to design the power electronics for activating the injectors. Again, this involves the use of simulation tools which must be developed specifically to design electronic circuits.

– Tools that are specially designed for this specific part of the overall system are also required to develop and simulate the control-unit software which controls the high-pressure pump and power electronics using signals from the sensors.

As the components in the overall system interact with each other, it is not sufficient to consider specific detailed models of the components in isolation. The optimum solution is also to take into account the models of other system components. In most cases, these components can be portrayed by much simpler models. For example, a system simulation focused on hydraulics only requires a simple model of the power electronics.

The application of various domain-specific simulation tools during the design of mechatronic systems is only efficient if there is some sort of support for exchanging models and parameters between the simulation tools. The direct exchange of models is highly problematic due to the specific languages used for describing the models of each of the tools.

However, an analysis of the typical components in mechatronic systems shows that they can be composed of a few simple elements specific to the domains.

These standard elements include, for example:
– in hydraulics: restrictor, valve, or pipe;
– in electronics: resistor, capacitor, or transistor;
– in mechanical engineering: mass with friction, transmission, or clutch (accordingly for micromechanics).

The preferable solution is that these elements should be stored in a central standard model library that is also decentrally accessible to product development. The kernel of the standard model library is a documentation of all the standard elements. For each element, this comprises:
– A textual description of the physical behavior.
– The physical equations, parameters (e.g. conductivity or permeability), and state variables (e.g. current, voltage, magnetic flux, pressure).
– A description of the associated interfaces.

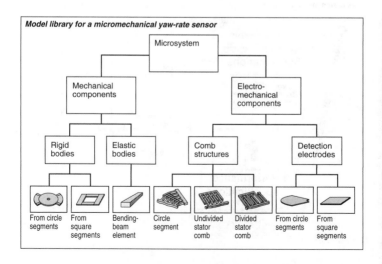

*Model library for a micromechanical yaw-rate sensor*

Microsystem

Mechanical components — Electro-mechanical components

Rigid bodies — Elastic bodies — Comb structures — Detection electrodes

From circle segments — From square segments — Bending-beam element — Circle segment — Undivided stator comb — Divided stator comb — From circle segments — From square segments

In addition, a major part of the environment is a reference model written in a modeling language that is independent of the tool. Ultimately, the library contains reference models from the domains of mechanical engineering, hydraulics, electronics, electrodynamics, and software.

## V model

The "V model" contains relationships between the various stages of product development, from the requirements definition and development, implementation, and test, through to system deployment. A project passes through three "top-down" levels during the development stage:
– customer-specific functions
– system
– components

A requirements specification (<u>what</u>) must first be produced at each level in the form of specifications. This is then used to produce the design specifications based on design decisions (the actual creative engineering output). The performance specifications describe <u>how</u> a requirement can be met. The performance specs form the

basis for a model description which allows a review (i.e. validation) of the correctness of each design stage together with previously defined test cases. This procedure passes through each of three stages, and, depending on the technologies applied, for each of the associated domains (mechanical engineering, hydraulics, fluid dynamics, electrics, electronics, and software).

Recursions at each of the design levels shorten the development stages significantly. Simulations, rapid prototyping, and simultaneous engineering are tools that allow rapid verification, and they create the conditions for shortening product cycles.

## Outlook

The driving force behind mechatronics is the continuous progress in microelectronics. Mechatronics benefits from computer technology in the form of ever more powerful integrated computers in standard applications. Accordingly, there is a huge potential for further increases in safety

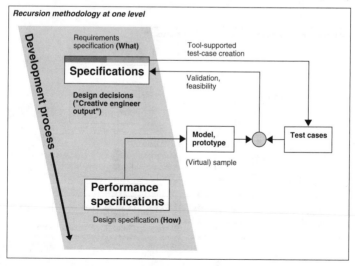

*Recursion methodology at one level*

Development process

Requirements specification **(What)**

**Specifications**

Design decisions ("Creative engineer output")

**Performance specifications**

Design specification **(How)**

Tool-supported test-case creation

Validation, feasibility

Model, prototype

(Virtual) sample

Test cases

and comfort in motor vehicles, accompanied by further reductions in pollutant emissions and fuel consumption. On the other hand, engineers face new challenges in mastering the new technologies for these systems.

Even in the event of a fault, future "x-by-wire" systems must continue to be capable of fulfilling a prescribed functionality without reverting to a mechanical or hydraulic fallback level. The condition for their implementation is a high-reliability and high-availability mechatronic architecture which requires a "simple" proof of safety. This affects both single components as well as energy and signal transmissions.

Besides "x-by-wire" systems, driver-assistance systems and their related man-machine interfaces are another field in which significant progress can be achieved for users and automotive manufacturers by the systematic implementation of mechatronic systems.

The design approaches of mechatronic systems should strive toward continuity in several aspects:

- Vertical:
  "Top-down" from system simulation, with the objective of overall optimization, through to finite-element simulation to achieve a detailed understanding, and "bottom-up" design engineering from component testing through to system testing.

- Horizontal:
  "Simultaneous engineering" across several disciplines in order to deal with all product-related aspects at the same time.

- Across corporate boundaries:
  The concept of a "virtual sample" is approaching gradually step by step.

Another challenge is training in order to further an interdisciplinary mindset and develop suitable DE processes and forms of organization and communication.

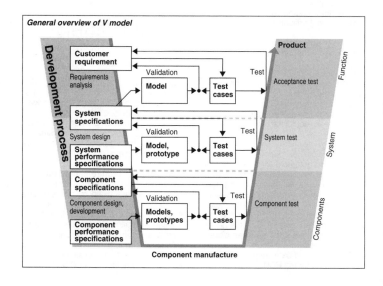

General overview of V model

# Sensors

## Basic principles

### Function
Sensors convert a physical or chemical (usually non-electrical) quantity into an electrical quantity (non-electrical intermediate stages may be employed).

### Classifications
1. Function and applications
- Operation (open-loop and closed-loop control circuits).
- Safety and backup.
- Monitoring and information.

2. Types of characteristic curve
- Continuous linear: control applications across a broad measurement range.
- Continuous nonlinear: closed-loop control of a measured variable within a narrow measurement range.
- Discontinuous multistage: Monitoring in applications where a signal is required urgently when a limit value is reached.
- Discontinuous dual-stage (with hysteresis in some cases): monitoring of correction thresholds for immediate or subsequent adjustments.

3. Type of output signal
Output signal proportional to:
- current/voltage, amplitude
- frequency/period
- pulse duration/pulse duty factor
Discrete output signal:
- dual stage (binary)
- multistage (irregular graduation)
- multistage (equidistant) or digital

### Automotive applications
In their function as peripheral elements, sensors and actuators form the interface between the vehicle with its complex drive, braking, chassis, suspension, and body functions (including guidance and navigation functions), and the usually digital-electronic control unit (ECU) as the processing unit. An adapter circuit is generally used to convert the sensor's signals into the standardized form (measuring chain, measured-data registration system) required by the ECU.

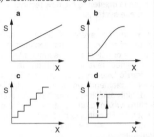

**Types of characteristic curve**
*S Output signal, X Measured variable.*
*a) Continuous linear, b) Continuous nonlinear, c) Discontinuous multistage, d) Discontinuous dual-stage.*

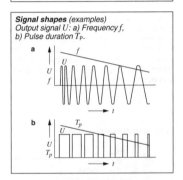

**Signal shapes** *(examples)*
*Output signal U: a) Frequency f, b) Pulse duration $T_P$.*

In addition, system operation can be influenced by sensor information from other processing elements and/or by driver-operated switches.

Display elements provide the driver with information on the static and dynamic status of vehicle operation as a single synergistic process.

### Main technical requirements, trends
The degree of stress to which the sensor is subjected is determined by the operating conditions (mechanical, climatic, chemical, electromagnetic influences) present at the installation location (for standard degrees of protection, see DIN 40050, Sheet 9).

According to application and technical requirements, automotive sensors are assigned to one of three reliability classes:

Class 1: Steering, brakes, passenger protection

Class 2: Engine, drivetrain, suspension, tires

Class 3: Comfort and convenience, information/diagnosis, theft deterrence

Miniaturization concepts are employed to achieve compact unit dimensions:
- Substrate and hybrid technology (pressure and temperature sensors)
- Semiconductor technology (monitoring rotational speed, e.g. with Hall-effect sensors)
- Micromechanics (pressure and acceleration sensors)
- Microsystem technology (combination of micromechanics, microelectronics, and possibly microoptics)

Integrated "intelligent" sensors

Systems range from hybrid and monolithic integrated sensors and electronic signal-processing circuits at the measuring point, through to complex digital circuits, such as A/D converters and microcomputers (mechatronics), for complete utilization of the sensor's inherent precision. These systems offer the following benefits and options:
- Reduction of load on the ECU
- Uniform, flexible, bus-compatible interface
- Multiple application of sensors
- Multisensor designs

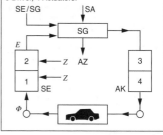

*Automotive sensors*
$\Phi$ Physical quantity, $E$ Electrical quantity, $Z$ Influencing quantities, AK Actuator, AZ Display, SA Switch, SE Sensor(s), SG Control unit (ECU).
1 Measuring sensor, 2 Adapter circuit, 3 Driver, 4 Actuators.

- By means of local amplification and de-modulation, very small quantities and HF signals can be processed.
- Correction of sensor deviations at the measuring point, and common calibration and compensation of sensor and circuit, are simplified and improved by storage of the individual correction information in PROM.

Fiber-optic sensors

Various physical factors can be employed to modify the intensity, phase (coherent laser light), and polarization of the light conducted in the optical fibers. Fiber-optic sensors are immune to electromagnetic

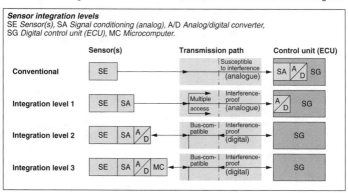

*Sensor integration levels*
SE Sensor(s), SA Signal conditioning (analog), A/D Analog/digital converter, SG Digital control unit (ECU), MC Microcomputer.

| | Sensor(s) | Transmission path | Control unit (ECU) |
|---|---|---|---|
| **Conventional** | SE | Susceptible to interference (analogue) | SA A/D SG |
| **Integration level 1** | SE SA | Multiple access \| Interference-proof (analogue) | A/D SG |
| **Integration level 2** | SE SA A/D | Bus-compatible \| Interference-proof (digital) | SG |
| **Integration level 3** | SE SA A/D MC | Bus-compatible \| Interference-proof (digital) | SG |

interference; they are, however, sensitive to physical pressure (intensity-modulation sensors), and, to some degree, to contamination and aging. Inexpensive plastic fibers are now available for application within some of the temperature ranges associated with automotive applications. These sensors require special couplers and plug connections.

<u>Extrinsic sensors</u>: The optical waveguide generally conducts light to an end point; it must emerge from the conductor to exert an effect.
<u>Intrinsic sensors</u>: The measurement effect occurs internally within the fibers.

## Sensor types

**Position sensors (displacement/angle)**
Position sensors employ both contact wipers and non-contacting (proximity) designs to detect displacement and angle.

Directly monitored variable quantities:
– Throttle-valve position
– Accelerator-pedal position
– Seat and mirror position
– Control-rack travel and position
– Fuel level
– Travel of clutch servo unit
– Distance: vehicle – vehicle or vehicle – obstacle
– Steering (wheel) angle

– Tilt angle
– Vehicle-course angle
– Brake-pedal position

Indirectly monitored variable quantities:
– Sensor-plate deflection angle (flow rate/FLR),
– Deflection of a spring-mass system (acceleration)
– Diaphragm deflection angle (pressure)
– Suspension compression travel (headlamp range adjustment)
– Torsion angle (torque)

<u>Wiper or film potentiometers</u>
The wiper potentiometer measures travel by exploiting the proportional relationship between the length of a wire or film resistor (conductor track) and its electrical resistance. This design currently provides the most economical displacement/angular-position sensors.

The voltage on the measurement track is usually routed through smaller series resistors $R_V$ for overload protection as well as for zero and progression-rate adjustments. The shape of the contour across the width of the measurement track (including that of individual sections) influences the shape of the characteristic curve.

The standard wiper connection is furnished by a second contact track consisting of the same material mounted on a low-resistance substrate. Wear and measure-

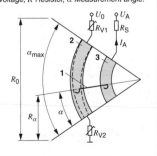

*Wiper potentiometer*
1 Wiper, 2 Potentiometer track, 3 Contact track. $U_0$ Supply voltage, $U_A$ Measurement voltage, R Resistor, $\alpha$ Measurement angle.

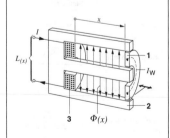

*Short-circuiting ring sensor*
1 Short-circuiting ring (movable),
2 Softmagnetic core, 3 Coil.
I Current, $I_W$ Eddy current, $L(x)$ Inductance and $\Phi(x)$ magnetic flux at travel x.

ment distortions can be avoided by minimizing the current at the tap ($I_A < 1\,\text{mA}$) and sealing the unit against dust.

## Short-circuiting ring sensors

Short-circuiting ring sensors consist of a laminated soft-magnetic core (straight/curved U- or E-shape), a coil, and a moving, highly-conductive short-circuiting ring made of copper or aluminum.

When an AC voltage is applied to the coil, a current $I$ is generated which is dependent on the inductance of the coil. The eddy currents produced in the short-circuiting ring limit expansion of the magnetic flux to the area between the coil and the ring itself. The position of the short-circuiting ring influences the inductance and thus the coil current. The current $I$ is therefore a measure of the position of the short-circuiting ring. Virtually the entire length of the sensor can be utilized for measurement purposes. The mass to be moved is very low. Contouring the distance between the sides influences the shape of the characteristic curve. Reducing the distance between the sides toward the end of the measuring range further enhances the good natural linearity. Operation is generally in the 5 ... 50 kHz range, depending on material and shape.

Half-differential sensors employ a moving measuring ring and a stationary reference short-circuiting ring to meet exacting demands for precision (on diesel distributor-type fuel-injection pumps, the rack-travel sensor for in-line units, and angular-position sensors in the injected-fuel-quantity actuator of distributor-type injection pumps); they measure by acting as:
- inductive voltage dividers (evaluation $L_1/L_2$ or $(L_1-L_2)/(L_1+L_2)$), or as
- frequency-definition elements in an oscillating circuit, producing a signal proportional to frequency (highly interference-proof, easy to digitize)

The measuring effect is fairly substantial, typically $L_{max}/L_{min} = 4$.

## Other sensor types

Solenoid plunger, differential-throttle and differential-transformer sensors operate based on the variation in the inductance of an individual coil and the proportional relationship of voltage dividers (supplied either directly or via inductive coupling) with moving cores. The overall length is often considerably greater than the measurement travel. This disadvantage is avoided by using a multistage winding in chambers of different dimensions. With this sensor, for angular measurement, the angle of rotation must be mechanically converted to a linear movement.

HF eddy-current sensors (electronics at the measuring point) are suitable, e.g. for non-contacting measurement of the throttle-valve angle and the accelerator-pedal

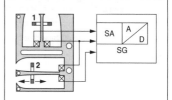

**Half-differential sensor**
1 Reference (fixed), 2 Short-circuiting ring (movable). A/D Analog/digital converter, SA Signal conditioning, SG Control unit (ECU).

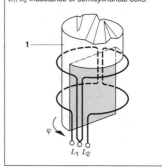

**Eddy-current pedal-travel sensor**
1 Spoiler. $\varphi$ Angle of rotation. $L_1$, $L_2$ Inductance of semicylindrical coils.

position. Here, the inductance of mostly nonferrous coils is modified by the approach of conductive formed parts (spoilers) or by variable overlapping with them. Due to the frequently high operating frequency (MHz range), the signal-processing circuits are mostly accommodated directly on the sensor. This is the case, for example, when two coils are wound onto a common cylinder (differential sensor) for measuring the throttle-valve angle. The same principle is used on sensors incorporating single lateral coils to measure clutch positions (70 mm measurement range) at substantially lower frequencies (approx. 7.5 kHz). The first of the above sensor types features a cylindrical aluminum spoiler with special recesses and is designed to pivot over the coil winding. The second concept monitors the penetration depth of an aluminum short-circuit tube within the sensor coil.

### Integrated Hall ICs

The Hall effect is a galvanomagnetic effect and is evaluated mainly by means of

thin semiconductor chips. When such a current-carrying chip is permeated vertically by a magnetic induction $B$, a voltage $U_H$ proportional to the field can be tapped transversely to the current direction (Hall effect), while the chip resistance simultaneously increases in accordance with a roughly parabolic characteristic (Gaussian effect, magnetoresistor). When silicon is used as the base material, a signal-conditioning circuit can be integrated on the chip at the same time. This makes such sensors very economical.

A disadvantage in the past proved to be their sensitivity to mechanical stress, which was inevitable due to packaging, and resulted in an unfavorable offset temperature coefficient. This disadvantage has been overcome by the application of the "spinning-current" principle. This made Hall ICs well suited for analog sensor applications. Mechanical interference (piezoresistive effects) is suppressed by rapid, electronically controlled rotation of the electrodes, or cyclical switching of the electrodes, and averaging of the output signal.

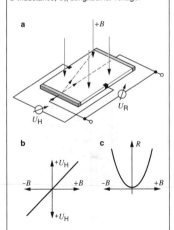

*Galvanomagnetic effects*
a) Circuit, b) Characteristic of Hall voltage $U_H$,
c) Increase in chip resistance $R$ (Gaussian effect).
$B$ Inductance, $U_R$ Longitudinal voltage.

*Hall sensor according to spinning-current principle*
a) Rotation phase $\varphi_1$,
b) Rotation phase $\varphi_2 = \varphi_1 + 45°$.
1 Semiconductor chip, 2 Active electrode,
3 Passive electrode.
$I$ Supply current, $U_H$ Hall voltage.

Such integrated Hall ICs are mainly suitable for measuring limited travel ranges in that they detect the fluctuating field strengths of a permanent magnet as a function of the IC. Larger angles up to 360° (e.g. for detecting the camshaft position) can be measured, e.g. with the configuration shown in the figure. The two Hall-effect sensors arranged at right angles supply sinusoidal/cosinusoidal signals which can be converted by means of the arctan function into the angle of rotation $\varphi$. In principle, the configuration can also be integrated in planar form with VHDs (<u>V</u>ertical <u>H</u>all <u>D</u>evices).

It is also possible with a rotating magnet ring and some fixed soft-magnetic conductors to obtain a linear output signal directly for larger angle ranges without conversion. In this case, the bipolar field of the magnet ring is passed through a Hall-effect sensor arranged between semicircular flux concentrating pieces. The effective magnetic flux through the Hall-effect sensor is dependent on the angle of rotation $\varphi$.

The disadvantage here is the persisting dependency on geometrical tolerances of the magnetic circuit and intensity fluctuations of the permanent magnet.

*Analog Hall sensor for 360°*
*a) Built from discrete Hall ICs,*
*b) Built from planar-integrated Hall ICs.*
*1 Signal-processing circuits, 2 Camshaft,*
*3 Control magnet.*
*B Inductance, I Current, U Voltage,*
*$U_A$ Measurement voltage.*

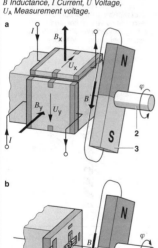

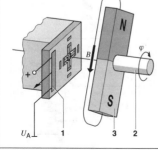

*Analog Hall angular-position sensor*
*with linear characteristic for angles up*
*to approx. 180°*
*a) Position a, b) Position b, c) Output signal.*
*1 Magnetic yoke, 2 Stator (1, 2 Soft iron),*
*3 Rotor (permanent magnet), 4 Air gap,*
*5 Hall-effect sensor. $\varphi$ Angle of rotation.*

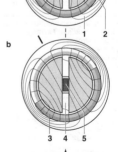

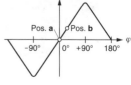

The simplest Hall ICs ("Hall-effect switches") also permit – in conjunction with a small working-point magnet – the construction of digital angular-position sensors up to 360°. For this purpose, for an $n$-bit resolution, $n$ Hall-effect switches are arranged equidistantly in a circle. A soft-magnetic code disk inhibits the field of the individual overlying permanent magnets, or enables it, so that, when the disk is rotated further, the Hall-effect switches in succession generate $n$ different code words. The Gray code is used to avoid large indication errors in intermediate states. To implement a steering-wheel angle sensor, for example, the code disk is connected to the steering spindle while the rest of the sensor is connected to the chassis. Multiple rotations can be recorded with an additional, simple 3-bit configuration whose code disk is moved by means of a reduction gear. The resolution of such configurations is mostly no better than 2.5°.

## Sensors of the future

Magnetoresistive NiFe thin-film sensors (AMR – anisotropic magnetoresistive thin-film NiFe, permalloy) provide extremely compact designs for non-contacting, proximity-based angular-position sensors.

The substrate consists of oxidized silicon wafers in which electronic signal-processing circuits can be incorporated as desired. The magnetic control field $B$ is usually generated by a pivoting magnet located above the sensor.

Magnetoresistive angular-position sensors in "barber's pole" configuration display serious limitations in both precision and measurement ranges (max. ±15°). Operation is based on the detuning of a magnetoresistant voltage divider consisting of longitudinal permalloy resistors with high-conductance lateral strips in gold.

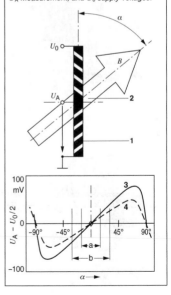

*Magnetoresistive angular-position sensor (barber's pole configuration)*
1 AMR, anisotropic magnetoresistive element (barber's pole), 2 Rotating permanent magnet with control inductance $B$, 3 Response curves for low, and 4 for high operating temperature. a Linear, b Effective measurement range. $\alpha$ Measurement angle, $U_A$ Measurement, and $U_0$ supply voltages.

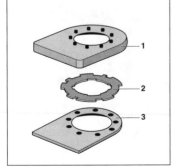

*Digital 360° Hall angular-position sensor with a circular, equidistant arrangement of simple Hall switches.*
1 Housing cover with permanent magnets, 2 Code disk (soft-magnetic material), 3 PCB with Hall switches.

Magnetoresistive angular-position sensors in "pseudo-Hall" configuration utilize the inherent precision in the sinusoidal pattern of signals monitored at the output terminals of a quadripolar planar sensor structure. A second element installed at 45° generates a supplementary cosinusoidal signal. From the mutual relationship of the two signal voltages, it is possible (e.g. using the arctan function) to determine the angle $\alpha$ (e.g. with a microcontroller or ASIC) with great accuracy over a range of 180°, largely irrespective of fluctuations in temperature and magnetic-field intensity (distance, aging).

The task of measuring various rotations of a rotating part (e.g. steering spindle) is solved with a dual configuration of

"pseudo-Hall angle-of-rotation sensors". Here the two associated permanent magnets are moved by the rotating part via a step-up gear train. However, as the two smaller driving gears differ to the tune of one tooth, their mutual phase angle is a clear measure of the absolute angular position. Each individual sensor also offers an indeterminate fine resolution of the angle of rotation. This configuration provides a resolution more precise than 1° for e.g. the entire steering-angle range of four full rotations.

Systems for monitoring vehicle-to-vehicle distance can use <u>ultrasonic transit-time processes</u> (close-range, 0.5...5 m), as well as processes based on transit-time and triangulation principles using short-range infrared <u>light</u> (lidar: mid-range measurements extending up to 50 m). Another option is electromagnetic <u>radar</u> (long-range operation, up to 150 m).

ACC systems (<u>A</u>daptive <u>C</u>ruise <u>C</u>ontrol) with just such a long-range radar sensor are vehicle-speed controllers with automatic detection of vehicles which are driving in front in a lane and where braking may be required. A working frequency of 76...77 GHz (wavelength approx. 3.8 mm) permits the compact design required for automotive applications. A Gunn oscillator (Gunn diode in the cavity resonator) feeds in parallel three

---

***Magnetoresistive angular-position sensor (pseudo-Hall version)***
*a) Measurement concept, b) Sensor structure.*
*1 Thin NiFe layer (AMR sensor), 2 Pivoting permanent magnet with inductive control $B$, 3 Hybrid, 4 ASIC, 5 Electrical connection.*
*$I_V$ Supply current, $U_{H1}$; $U_{H2}$ Measurement voltages, $\alpha$ Measurement angle.*

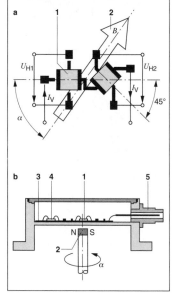

---

***AMR steering-angle sensor***
*1 Steering spindle, 2 Gear with $n > m$ teeth, 3 Gear with $m$ teeth, 4 Gear with $m+1$ teeth, 5 Magnets.*
*$\varphi$, $\psi$, $\theta$ Angles of rotation.*

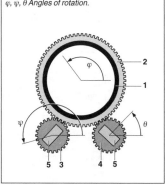

adjacently arranged patch antennas which also serve to receive the reflected signals. A plastic lens (Fresnel) set in front focuses the transmitted beam, referred to the vehicle axle, horizontally at an angle of ± 5° and vertically at an angle of ± 1.5°. Due to the lateral offset of the antennas, their reception characteristic (6 dB width 4°) points in different directions. As well as the distance of vehicles driving in front and their relative speed, it is also possible to determine the direction under which they are detected. Directional couplers separate transmitted and received reflection signals. Three downstream mixers transpose the received frequency down to virtually zero by admixing the transmit frequency (0...300 kHz). The low-frequency signals are digitized for further evaluation and subjected to a high-speed Fourier analysis to determine the frequency.

The frequency of the Gunn oscillator is compared continually with that of a stable reference oscillator DRO (Dielectric Resonance Oscillator) and regulated to a prespecified setpoint value. Here the supply voltage to the Gunn diode is modulated until it corresponds again to the setpoint value. This control loop is used for measurement purposes to increase and reduce the Gunn-oscillator frequency every 100 ms briefly in a saw-tooth wave shape by 300 MHz (FMCW Frequency Modulated Continuous Wave). The signal reflected from the vehicle driving in front is delayed according to the propagation time (i.e. in a rising ramp by a lower frequency and in a falling ramp by a frequency higher by the same amount). The frequency difference $\Delta f$ is a direct measure of the distance (e.g. 2 kHz/m). If, however, there is additionally a specific relative speed between the two vehicles, the received frequency $f_e$ is increased on account of the Doppler effect in both the rising and falling ramps by a specific, proportional amount $\Delta f_d$ (e.g. 512 Hz per m/s), i.e. there are two different difference frequencies $\Delta f_1$ and $\Delta f_2$. Their addition produces the distance between the vehicles, and their difference the relative speed of the vehicles. This

*Distance and velocity measurement with FMCW radar*
$f_s$ Transmit frequency, $f_e/f_e'$ Receive frequency without/with relative velocity, $\Delta f_d$ Frequency increase due to Doppler effect (relative velocity), $\Delta f_s /\Delta f_{1.2}$ Differential frequency without/with relative velocity.

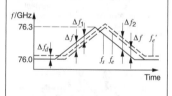

*ACC-sensor control unit (block diagram)*

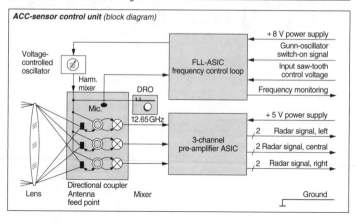

method can be used to detect and track up to 32 vehicles.

Magnetic-field sensors (saturation-core probes) can monitor the vehicle's direction of travel for general orientation and application in navigation systems.

**RPM/and velocity sensors**

A distinction is made between absolute rotating velocity in space and relative rotating velocity between two parts.

An example of absolute rotating velocity is the vehicle's yaw rate about its vertical axis ("yaw velocity"); this is required for the electronic stability program. Examples of relative rotating velocity are the crankshaft and camshaft speeds, the wheel speeds (for ABS/TCS) and the speed of the diesel fuel-injection pump. Measurements are mainly taken with the aid of an incremental sensor system comprising a gear and a rotational-speed sensor.

Recent applications:
- Bearing-integrated wheel-speed sensors (wheel bearings, Simmer shaft-seal module on the crankshaft)
- Linear velocity
- Vehicle yaw rate about the longitudinal axis ("roll velocity" for rollover protection)

Inductive sensors

The inductive sensor consists of a bar magnet with a soft-magnetic pole pin supporting an induction coil with two terminals. When a ferromagnetic ring gear (or a rotor of similar design) turns past this sensor, it generates a voltage in the coil which is directly proportional to the periodic variation in the magnetic flux. A uniform tooth pattern generates a near-sinusoidal voltage curve. The rotational speed is reflected in the periodic interval between the voltage's zero transition points, while the amplitude is also proportional to the rotating speed.

The air gap and the tooth dimensions are vital factors in defining the (exponential) signal amplitude. Teeth can still be detected without difficulty up to air-gap widths of one half or one third of a tooth interval. Standard gears for crankshaft and ABS wheel-speed sensors cover air gaps ranging from 0.8 to 1.5 mm. The reference point for the ignition timing is obtained ei-

ther by omitting a tooth or by closing a gap between teeth. The resulting increase in distance between zero transition points is identified as the reference point and is accompanied by a substantial increase in signal voltage (the system detects as apparently larger tooth).

Hall-effect sensors/vane switches

Semiconductor sensors utilize the Hall effect (P. 85) in the form of Hall vane switches, e.g. as ignition triggering sensors in ignition distributors (P. 654). The sensor and the electronic circuits for supply and signal evaluation are integrated on the sensor chip.

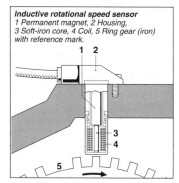

**Inductive rotational speed sensor**
1 Permanent magnet, 2 Housing,
3 Soft-iron core, 4 Coil, 5 Ring gear (iron) with reference mark.

**Hall vane switch (ignition distributor)**
1 Vane with width $b$, 2 Soft-magnetic conductors, 3 Hall IC, 4 Air gap.
$U_0$ Supply voltage, $U_S$ Sensor voltage.

This "Hall IC" (with bipolar technology for sustained temperatures of up to 150 °C and direct connection to the vehicle electrical system) is located within an almost completely insulated magnetic circuit consisting of permanent magnet and pole elements. A soft-magnetic trigger wheel (e.g. camshaft-driven) travels through the air gap. The trigger-wheel vane interrupts the magnetic flux (that is, it moves it past the sensor), while the gap in the trigger wheel allows it to travel through the sensor unimpeded.

The differential Hall-effect sensor of a system with electronic ignition distribution taps the camshaft position at a special, soft-magnetic segment disk.

### Recent sensors
Sensors of the future should satisfy the following criteria:
- static monitoring (e.g. zero rotational speed)
- larger air gaps
- independence from air-gap fluctuations (temperature-resistant 200 °C)

---

**Differential magnetoresistive sensor (radial)**
1 Magnetoresistor $R_1$, $R_2$, 2 Soft-magnetic substrate, 3 Permanent magnet, 4 Gear. $U_0$ Supply voltage, $U_A (\varphi)$ Measurement voltage at rotation angle $\varphi$.

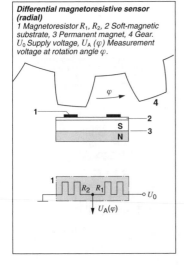

---

### Gradient sensors
Gradient sensors (e.g., based on Hall, differential, or differential magnetoresistive sensors) incorporate a permanent magnet on which the pole surface facing the gear is homogenized with a thin ferromagnetic wafer. Two galvanomagnetic elements (generic term for Hall-effect sensors and magnetoresistors) are located on each element's sensor tip, at a distance of roughly one half a tooth interval. Thus, one of the elements is always opposite a gap between teeth when the other is opposite to a tooth. The sensor measures the difference in field intensity at two adjacent locations on the circumference. The output signal is roughly proportional to the diversion of field strength as a function of the angle at the circumference; polarity is therefore independent of the air gap.

Gauss-effect <u>magnetoresistors</u> are magnetically controlled, bipolar semiconductor resistors (indium antimonide) with a design similar to that of the Hall-effect sensor. In the standard application range, their resistance is approximately proportional to the square of the field strength. The two resistors of a differential sensor assume the function of voltage dividers in the electric circuit; for the most part, they also compensate for temperature sensitivity. The substantial measurement effect makes it possible to dispense with local electronic amplifiers (output signal 0.1...1 V). Magnetoresistors for automotive applications withstand temperatures 170 °C (brief peaks 200 °C).

### Tangential sensors
Tangential sensors differ from gradient sensors by their reaction to variations in polarity and intensity in the components of a magnetic field located tangentially to the periphery of the rotor. Design options include AMR thin-film technology (barber's pole) or single permalloy resistors featuring full- or half-bridge circuits. Unlike the gradient sensor, the tangential unit does not need to be adapted for variations in tooth distribution patterns, and thus permits semi-punctiform configuration. Although the intrinsic measurement effect exceeds that of the silicon-based

Hall-effect sensor by a factor of approx. 1...2, local amplification is still required.

In the case of a bearing-integrated crankshaft speed sensor (Simmer shaft-seal module), the AMR thin-film sensor is mounted together with an evaluation IC on a common lead frame. For the purposes of space saving and temperature protection, the evaluation IC is bent at an angle of 90° and also located further away from the sensor tip.

<u>Oscillation gyrometers</u>
Oscillation gyrometers measure the absolute yaw rate $\Omega$ about the vehicle vertical axis (yaw axis), e.g. in systems for controlling a vehicle's dynamic stability (ESP, Electronic Stability Program) and for navigation. They are similar in principle to mechanical gyroscopes and for measurement purposes utilize the Coriolis acceleration that occurs during rotary motion in conjunction with an oscillating motion.

*Piezoelectric yaw-rate sensor*
Operating concept.
1 to 4 Piezoelectric elements, 8 Control circuit (fixed phase), 9 Bandpass filter, 10 Phase reference, 11 Rectifier (selective-phase).
$U_A$ Measurement voltage, $\Omega$ Yaw rate,
$U_{ref} = 0$ (normal operation),
$U_{ref} \cdot$ ("built-in" test).

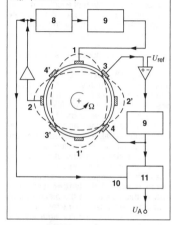

*AMR sensor (tangential)*
1 Gear (Fe), 2 Permanent magnet, 3 Sensor.
B Control field strength with tangential component $B_t$ and radial component $B_r$
(B' Initial position, $B_t = 0$), $R_1$, $R_2$ Permalloy thin-film resistors (AMR), $\varphi$ Rotation angle,
$U_0$ Supply voltage, $U_A$ Measurement voltage.

*Piezoelectric yaw-rate sensor*
Structure.
1 to 4 Piezoelectric element pairs,
5 Oscillating cylinder, 6 Base plate,
7 Connection pins. $\Omega$ Yaw rate.

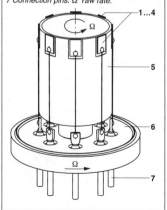

## Piezoelectric yaw-rate sensors

Two diametrically opposed piezoceramic elements (1-1') induce radial resonant oscillation in an oscillatory metallic hollow cylinder. A second piezoelectric pair (2-2') governs the cylinder to a constant oscillation amplitude with four axial nodes (45° offset to direction of excitation).

The nodes respond to rotation at a rate $\Omega$ about the cylinder axis with a slight peripheral displacement, inducing forces proportional to rotational speed in the otherwise force-free nodes. This state is detected by a third pair of piezoelectric elements 3-3'. The forces are then controlled down to a reference value $U_{ref} = 0$ by a fourth exciting pair (4-4') in a closed-loop operation. After careful filtering using phase-locked rectification, the required control value provides an extremely precise output signal. A controlled temporary change of the setpoint value to $U_{ref} \neq 0$ provides a simple means of testing the entire sensor system ("built-in" test).

A complex compensation circuit is required to deal with the temperature sensitivity of this sensor. As the piezoceramic elements' response characteristics also change with age, careful pretreatment (artificial aging) is also required.

## Micromechanical silicon yaw-rate sensors

provide an inexpensive and compact alternative to today's precision-engineered sensors. A combined technology is used to achieve the high precision needed in vehicle-dynamics systems: two thick paste plates worked from the wafer by means of bulk micromechanics (P. 100) oscillate in push-pull mode at their resonant frequency, which is determined by their mass and their coupling-spring stiffness (>2 kHz). Each of them is provided with an extremely small surface-micromechanical, capacitive acceleration sensor which measures Coriolis acceleration in the wafer plane perpendicular to the oscillation direction when the sensor chip rotates about its vertical axis at the yaw rate $\Omega$. They are proportional to the product of the yaw rate and the oscillation velocity, which is electronically regulated to a constant value. For drive purposes, there is a simple printed conductor on the relevant oscillation board which is subjected to a Lorentz force in a permanent-magnetic field perpendicular to the chip surface. A similarly simple, chip-surface-saving conductor is used to measure the oscillation velocity directly and inductively with the same magnetic field. The different physi-

*Micromechanical yaw-rate sensor with electrodynamic drive in combined technology form*
*(bulk and SMM micromechanics)*
*1 Oscillation direction, 2 Oscillating body, 3 Coriolis acceleration sensor, 4 Retaining/guide spring, 5 Direction of Coriolis acceleration. $\Omega$ Yaw rate, $\upsilon$ Oscillation velocity.*

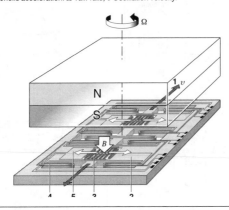

cal natures of the drive and sensor systems prevent unwanted crosstalk between the two parts. In order to suppress external acceleration (common-mode signal), the two opposing sensor signals are subtracted from each other (summation, however, can also be used to measure the external acceleration). The precise micromechanical structure helps to suppress the influence of high oscillation acceleration with regard to the Coriolis acceleration that is lower by several powers of ten (cross sensitivity well below 40 dB). The drive and measuring systems are mechanically and electrically isolated in rigorous terms here.

If the silicon yaw-rate sensor is manufactured completely in accordance with surface micromechanics (SMM) (P. 101), and the magnetic drive and control system is replaced at the same time by an electrostatic system, this isolation can be realized less consistently: Using "comb" structures, a centrally mounted rotary oscillator is electrostatically driven to oscillate at an amplitude which is constantly regulated by means of a similar capacitive tap. Coriolis forces force a simultaneous "out-of-plane" tilting motion whose amplitude is proportional to the yaw rate $\Omega$ and which is detected capacitively by electrodes located under the oscillator. To prevent this motion from being excessively damped, it is essential to operate the sensor in a vacuum. The smaller chip size and the simpler manufacturing process do indeed reduce the cost of such a sensor, but the reduction in size also diminishes the already slight measuring effect and thus the attainable accuracy. It places higher demands on the electronics. The influence of external accelerations is already mechanically suppressed here.

Radar sensors
Research focuses on simple (low-cost) Doppler radar systems for measuring the vehicle's linear velocity.

**Acceleration and vibration sensors**
These sensors are suitable for triggering passenger-protection systems (airbags, seat-belt tighteners, rollover bars), for knock control in internal-combustion engines, and for detecting lateral acceleration rates and velocity changes in four-wheel-drive vehicles fitted with ABS.

Hall acceleration sensor
In ABS-equipped vehicles with four-wheel drive and modern cars with electronic stability program, the wheel-speed sensors are supplemented by a Hall acceleration

Typical acceleration rates in automotive applications:

| Application | Range |
|---|---|
| Knock control | $1...10\,g$ |
| Passenger protection | |
| Airbag, seat-belt tightener | $50\,g$ |
| Rollover bar | $4\,g$ |
| Seat-belt inertia reel | $0.4\,g$ |
| ABS, ESP | $0.8...1.2\,g$ |
| Chassis and suspension control | |
| Design | $1\,g$ |
| Axle | $10\,g$ |

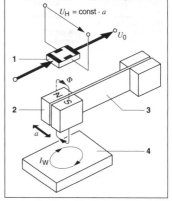

*Hall acceleration sensor*
*1 Hall-effect sensor, 2 Permanent magnet (seismic mass), 3 Spring, 4 Damping plate (Cu).*
*a Acceleration, $I_W$ Eddy currents, $U_H$ Hall voltage, $U_0$ Supply voltage, $\Phi$ Magnetic flux.*

sensor to monitor lateral and longitudinal acceleration rates. Deflection levels in the spring/mass system used in this application are recorded using a magnet and a Hall-effect sensor (measuring range: 1 $g$). The sensor is designed for narrowband operation (several Hz) and features electrodynamic damping.

## Piezoelectric sensors

### Piezoelectric bimorphous spring elements/ two-layer piezoceramics, are used for restraint-system sensors for triggering seatbelt tighteners, airbags, and rollover bars. Their intrinsic mass causes them to deflect under acceleration to provide a dynamic (not DC response pattern) signal with excellent processing characteristics (typical cutoff frequency: 10 Hz).

The sensor element is located in a sealed housing shared with the initial signal-amplification stage. It is sometimes encased in gel for physical protection.

The sensor's actuating principle can also be inverted. An additional actuator electrode makes it easy to check the sensor (on-board diagnosis).

### Longitudinal elements (knock sensors)

Longitudinal elements are employed as knock sensors (acceleration sensors) for ignition systems that feature knock control (P. 621 onwards). They measure (with low directional selectivity) the structure-borne noise at the engine block (measur-

ing range approx. 10 $g$ at a typical vibration frequency of 5...20 kHz). An unencapsulated, annular piezoceramic ring element measures the inertial forces exerted on a seismic mass of the same shape.

## Recent sensor concepts

### Capacitive silicon acceleration sensors

The first generation of micromechanical sensors relied on anisotropic and selective etching techniques to fabricate the required spring/mass system from the full wafer (bulk silicon micromechanics) and produce the spring profile.

Capacitive taps have proven especially effective for the high-precision measurement of this seismic-mass deflection. This design entails the use of supplementary silicon or glass wafers with counter-electrodes above and below the spring-held seismic mass. This leads to a 3-layer structure, whereby the wafers and their counter-electrodes also provide overload protection.

A precisely metered air cushion in the hermetically sealed oscillating system provides an extremely compact, yet efficient and inexpensive damping unit with good temperature response characteristics. Current designs almost always employ a fusion bonding process to join the three silicon wafers directly.

Due to variations in the thermal expansion rates of the different components, it is necessary to mount them on the casing base plate. This has a decisive effect on the desired measuring accuracy. Virtually straight-line mounting is used, with free support in the sensitive range.

This type of sensor is usually employed for low-level accelerations ($\leq 2\,g$) and relies upon a three-chip concept: (sensor chip + CMOS processing chip + bipolar protection IC). Conversion for extended signal evaluation triggers an <u>automatic reset</u>, returning the seismic mass to its base position and supplying the positioning signal as initial value.

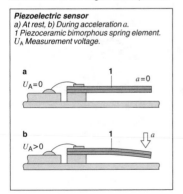

**Piezoelectric sensor**
a) At rest, b) During acceleration a.
1 Piezoceramic bimorphous spring element.
$U_A$ Measurement voltage.

**a**     1     $a=0$
$U_A=0$

**b**
$U_A>0$    1    $a$

For higher acceleration rates (passenger-protection systems), <u>surface-micromechanical sensors</u> with substantially more compact dimensions (typical edge lengths approx. 100 µm) are already in use. An additive process is employed to construct the spring/mass system on the surface of the silicon wafer.

In contrast to the bulk silicon sensors with capacitance levels of 10...20 pF, these sensors only have a typical capacitance of 1 pF. The evaluation electronics are therefore installed on a single chip along with the sensor (usually position-controlled systems).

### Pressure sensors

Pressure measurement is direct by means of diaphragm deflection or a force sensor. Typical applications:
– intake-manifold pressure (1...5 bar)
– braking pressure (10 bar), electropneumatic brakes
– air-spring pressure (16 bar), for vehicles with air suspension
– tire pressure (5 bar absolute), for monitoring and/or adjusting tire pressure
– hydraulic reservoir pressure (approx. 200 bar), ABS, power steering
– shock-absorber pressure (+200 bar), chassis and suspension-control systems
– refrigerant pressure (35 bar), air-conditioning systems
– modulation pressure (35 bar), automatic transmissions
– braking pressure in master- and wheel-brake cylinders (200 bar), automatic yaw-moment compensation, electronically controlled brake
– positive/vacuum pressure in fuel tank (0.5 bar) for on-board diagnostics (OBD)
– combustion-chamber pressure (100 bar, dynamic) for misfiring and knock detection

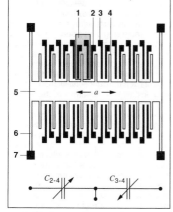

***Surface-micromechanical acceleration sensor***
*1 Elementary cell, 2, 3 Fixed wafers, 4 Movable wafers, 5 Seismic mass, 6 Spring shoulder, 7 Anchor.*
*a Acceleration, C Measurement capacitors.*

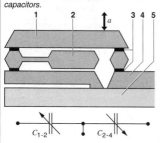

***Bulk silicon acceleration sensor***
*1 Si upper wafer, 2 Si center wafer (seismic mass), 3 Si oxide, 4 Si lower wafer, 5 Glass substrate. a Acceleration, C Measurement capacitors.*

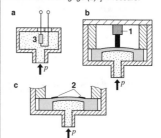

***Pressure measurement***
*a) Direct, pressure-sensitive resistor (3), b) with force sensor (1), c) via diaphragm deformation/strain gage (2). p Pressure.*

- diesel fuel-injection pump-side pressure (1,000 bar, dynamic), electronic diesel fuel injection
- common-rail pressure (1,500 to 1,800 bar), diesel engines
- common-rail pressure (100 bar) for spark-ignition (gasoline) engines

### Thick-film pressure sensors

The measurement diaphragm and its strain-gage resistors both use thick-film technology to measure absolute pressures of up to approx. 20 bar with a K factor (relative variation in resistance/expansion) of K = 12...15.

When the respective coefficients of expansion for the ceramic substrate and the ceramic cover film are correct, the diaphragm will form a dome-shaped bubble on cooling after bonding during manufacture. The result is a hollow chamber ("bubble") approx. 100 μm in height, with a diameter of 3...5 mm. After the application of additional thick-film strain-gage resistors, the unit is hermetically sealed with another ceramic glass coating. The residual gas remaining in the "bubble" provides partial compensation for temperature changes in the sensor.

The signal-amplification and correction components are separate from the measurement medium, but are located directly adjacent to the sensor on the same substrate.

The "bubble sensor" principle is not suitable for extremely high or low pressures; versions for these applications generally incorporate flat ceramic diaphragms.

### Semiconductor pressure sensors

The pressure is exerted against a silicon diaphragm incorporating pressure-sensitive resistors, manufactured using micromechanics technology. The K factor of the resistors diffused into the monocrystalline silicon is especially high, typically K = 100. So far the sensor and the hybrid circuitry for signal conditioning have been located together in a single housing. Sensor calibration and compensation can be continuous or in stages, and are performed either on an ancillary hybrid chip (a second silicon chip providing signal amplification and correction), or on the same sensor chip. Recent developments have seen values, e.g. for zero and lead correction, stored in digital form in a PROM.

Integrated single-chip sensors with fully electronic calibration are suitable for use as load sensors for electronic-ignition and fuel-injection systems. Due to their extremely compact dimensions, they are suitable for the functionally more favorable installation directly on the intake manifold (earlier designs were mounted either in the relevant ECU or at a convenient location in the engine compartment). Frequently applied are reverse assembly techniques in which the measured pressure is conducted to an electronically passive cavity recessed into the side of the sensor chip. For maximum protection, the – much more sensitive – side of the chip with the printed circuits and contacts is enclosed in a reference-vacuum chamber located between the housing's base and the soldered metal cap.

---

*Thick-film pressure sensor*
*1 Piezoresistive measurement bridge,*
*2 Thick-film diaphragm, 3 Reference-pressure chamber ("bubble"),*
*4 Ceramic substrate. p Pressure.*

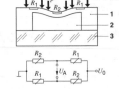

---

*Semiconductor pressure sensor*
*1 Silicon, 2 Vacuum, 3 Glass (Pyrex).*
*p Pressure, $U_0$ Supply voltage,*
*$U_A$ Measurement voltage, strain-gage resistors $R_1$ (expanded) and $R_2$ (deflected) in bridge circuit.*

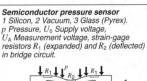

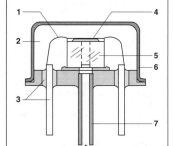

**Integrated silicon intake-manifold pressure sensor**
1 Bonded connections, 2 Reference vacuum, 3 Glass-enclosed electrical connection path, 4 Sensor chip, 5 Glass pedestal, 6 Cap, 7 Pressure connection. p Pressure.

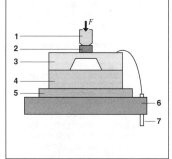

**Integrated silicon combustion-pressure sensor**
1 Force-transfer rod, 2 Si pedestal (force input), 3 Integral Si pressure sensor, 4 Pyrex, 5 Ceramic auxiliary subplate, 6 Steel base plate, 7 Connection pins. F Combustion-chamber pressure force.

These sensors will also be available for application in <u>tire-pressure monitoring systems</u>. Measurement will be continuous and non-contacting (transformer concept). A virtually identical sensor chip can also be used as a <u>combustion-chamber pressure sensor</u>. This is provided that the silicon chip is not directly exposed to high temperatures (max. 600 °C). A metallic insulation diaphragm and a soldered transfer rod of adequate length (several mm) furnish the desired protection. Micromechanical techniques are employed to apply a miniature pedestal in the center of the diaphragm, effectively converting the unit into a force sensor. The rod transmits the compressive forces detected at the front diaphragm through the pedestal and into the sensor chip with a minimum of distortion. This remote installation position means that the chip is only subjected to operating temperatures below 150 °C.

### Recent sensor concepts

#### Piezoelectric sensors
Piezoelectric sensors provide dynamic pressure measurement. On electronically controlled diesel fuel-injection pumps, for determining port opening and port closing (end of delivery and start of delivery re-

spectively), only changes in pump-side pressure are detected by the sensor. A thin intermediate diaphragm is employed for direct or indirect pressure transmission to a cylindrical or rectangular piezoceramic pellet. As extreme precision is not required in this application, deviations resulting from hysteresis, temperature, and aging are not a major consideration. An amplifier featuring a high-resistance input circuit is frequently installed in the sealed housing. This unit decouples the signal locally to prevent shunts from producing measurement errors.

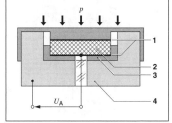

**Piezoelectric pressure sensor**
1 Metallic coating, 2 Piezoelectric disk, 3 Insulation, 4 Housing.
p Pressure, $U_A$ Measurement voltage.

### High-pressure sensors with metal diaphragm

Sensors are also required to monitor extremely high pressures, e.g., in the common rails of diesel injection systems to provide data for closed-loop control. Here, diaphragms made of high-quality spring steel and featuring a strain gage tap furnish much better performance than systems designed to monitor manifold pressure. These units:

- use simple, inexpensive designs to insulate the measured medium.
- differ from silicon as they retain a yield range for enhanced burst resistance.
- are easy to install in metallic housings.

Insulated sputtered (vapor-deposited) metallic thin-film strain gage (K = 2) and also polysilicon strain gage (K = 40) units offer permanently high sensor accuracy. Amplification, calibration, and compensation elements can be combined in a single ASIC, which is then integrated together with the required EMC protection on a small carrier in the sensor housing.

### Force/torque sensors

Applications: Bearing-pin sensors on agricultural tractors in systems for controlling plow force.

### Magnetoelastic bearing-pin sensors

The bearing-pin sensors are based on the magnetoelastic principle. The hollow coupling pin contains a magnetic field coil. Positioned at a 90° angle to this is a sensor coil to which no magnetic flux is applied when no forces are present. However, when the ferromagnetic material in the pin becomes anisotropic under force, a flux proportional to this force permeates the sensor coil, where it induces an electrical voltage. The supply and amplification electronics integrated in a chip are likewise located inside of the pin.

### Recent sensor concepts

- Eddy-current principle: eddy-current torsional-force sensor, radial and axial torsion-measurement spring, radial and axial slotted-disk and coil configuration.
- Measurement with strain-gage resistors (strain-gage principle): pressed-in and welded-in sensors, pressed-in elements.
- Magnetoelastic force sensor.
- Force-measurement ring using thick-film technology: force measurement with orthogonally loaded pressure-sensitive resistors.

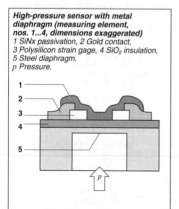

*High-pressure sensor with metal diaphragm (measuring element, nos. 1...4, dimensions exaggerated)*
1 SiNx passivation, 2 Gold contact,
3 Polysilicon strain gage, 4 SiO₂ insulation,
5 Steel diaphragm.
p Pressure.

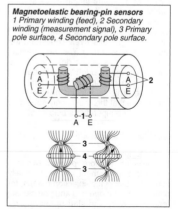

*Magnetoelastic bearing-pin sensors*
1 Primary winding (feed), 2 Secondary winding (measurement signal), 3 Primary pole surface, 4 Secondary pole surface.

- Hydrostatic pressure measurement in plunger-loaded hydrostatic cylinders, generally charged with rubber or gum elastic (no leakage risk).
- Microbending effect: fiber-optic compressive-stress sensor.

Recent applications:
- Measuring coupling forces on commercial vehicles between tractor vehicle and trailer/semitrailer for controlled, force-free braking.
- Measuring damping forces for electronic chassis and suspension-control systems.
- Measuring axle load for electronically controlled braking-force distribution on heavy commercial vehicles.
- Measurement of pedal force on electronically controlled braking systems.
- Measurement of braking force in electrically actuated and electronically controlled braking systems.
- Non-contacting measurement of drive and braking torque.
- Non-contacting measurement of steering/power-steering torque.
- Finger-protection for power-window units and sliding sunroofs.

In the case of the cross-ductor principle used in <u>magnetoelastic tension/compressive-force sensors</u>, no voltage is induced in the secondary transformer coil on account of the right-angled offset in the rest state ($F = 0$). A voltage is only established in the coil when under the application of force the relative permeability of the magnetoelastic sensor material used (special steel) becomes anisotropic. This sensor principle can also be applied for higher operating temperatures (up to 300 °C) (e.g. for installation in proximity to the brakes).

<u>Torque measurement:</u>
There are essentially two different ways of measuring torque: angle- and stress-measuring methods. In contrast to stress-measuring methods (strain gage, magnetoelastic), angle-measuring methods (e.g. eddy current) require a particular length of torsion shaft over which the torsion angle (approx. 0.4...4°) can be tapped. The mechanical stress proportional to the torque $\sigma$ is directed at an angle of under 45° to the shaft axis.

*Basic principles of torque measurement*
1 Torsion bar. $\Phi$ Torsion angle,
$\sigma$ Torsional stress, M Torque, r Radius,
l Rod length.

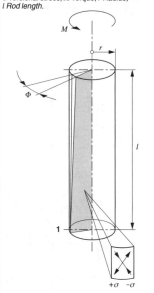

*Magnetoelastic tension/compressive-force sensor according to the cross-ductor principle*
1 Supply coil, 2 Sensor coil, 3 Magnetic yoke,
4 Magnetoelastic force-sensing element,
5 Selective-phase rectifier.
F Force.

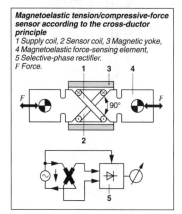

Stress-measuring torque sensor:
The mechanical stress is measured with a strain-gage bridge. The bridge is powered via a transformer and the supply is air-gap-independent due to rectifier and control electronics accommodated on the shaft. Further local electronic components on the shaft enable the measurement signal to be amplified and converted into an air-gap-invariant alternating-current waveform (e.g. analogous to frequency) which is likewise decoupled by a transformer. For larger quantities, the required electronics can be integrated on the shaft in a single chip. The strain-gage resistors can be inexpensively accommodated on a premanufactured round steel plate (e.g. in thin-film technology, P. 97) and then welded with the round plate onto the shaft. High precision levels can be achieved with such a configuration in spite of reasonable manufacturing costs.

Angle-measuring torque sensor:
Concentrically engaged slot sleeves are flanged at each end over a sufficient length of the measurement shaft. The sleeves have two rows of slots which are arranged in such a way that, when the shaft is subjected to torsion, an increasingly larger view of the shaft is exposed in the one row while the view is increasingly blocked off in the other row. Two fixed high-frequency coils (approx. 1 MHz) arranged over each row are thus increasingly or decreasingly damped or varied in terms of their inductance value. In order to achieve sufficient precision, it is essential for the slot sleeves to be manufactured and mounted to exacting standards. The associated electronics are appropriately accommodated very near to the coils.

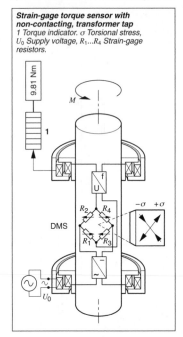

**Strain-gage torque sensor with non-contacting, transformer tap**
1 Torque indicator. $\sigma$ Torsional stress, $U_0$ Supply voltage, $R_1...R_4$ Strain-gage resistors.

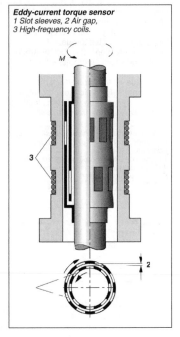

**Eddy-current torque sensor**
1 Slot sleeves, 2 Air gap,
3 High-frequency coils.

### Flow meters

#### Flow quantities in automotive applications

Fuel flow rate, i.e. amount of fuel actually consumed by the engine, is based on the difference between supply and return flow rates. On spark-ignition engines featuring electronically controlled fuel-metering systems using air intake as a primary control parameter, this figure is already available in the form of a calculated metering value; thus, measurement for control of the combustion process is redundant. However, fuel flow-rate measurement is required to determine and display fuel consumption on engines not equipped with electronic control systems.

Air flow in the engine's intake manifold: The mass ratios are the main factors in the chemical process of combustion, thus the actual objective is to measure the mass flow of the intake or charge air, although procedures employing volume and dynamic pressure are also applied. The maximum air-mass flow to be monitored lies within a range of 400...1,000 kg/h, depending on engine output. As a result of the modest idle requirements of modern engines, the ratio between minimum and maximum air flow is 1:90...1:100.

#### Flow measurement

A medium of uniform density $\varrho$ at all points flows through a tube with a constant cross-section $A$ at a velocity which is virtually uniform in the tube cross-section ("turbulent" flow):
- Volume flow rate $Q_V = v \cdot A$
- Mass flow rate $Q_M = \varrho \cdot v \cdot A$

If an orifice plate is then installed in the duct, forming a restriction, this will result in a pressure differential $\Delta p$ in accordance with Bernoulli's Law. This differential is an intermediate quantity between the volume and mass flow rates:

$$\Delta p = const. \cdot \varrho \cdot v^2 = const. \cdot Q_V \cdot Q_M$$

Fixed-position orifice plates can only cover measurement variables within a range of 1:10; variable flaps are able to monitor variations through a substantially greater ratio range.

#### Volume flow sensors

According to the principle of the Karman vortex path whirls and eddies diverge from the air stream at a constant distance behind an obstruction. Their periodicity as measured (e.g. monitoring of pressure or acoustic waves) at their periphery (duct wall) provides an eddy frequency in the form of a signal ratio:
$$f = 1/T = const. \cdot Q_V.$$
Disadvantage: Pulsation in the flow can result in measurement errors.

The ultrasound flow-rate measurement process can be employed to monitor the propagation time $t$ of an acoustic pulse as it travels through the medium measured (e.g. air) at angle $\alpha$ (see figure). One measurement is taken upstream and one downstream using the same measurement path $l$. The resulting transit-time differential is proportional to the volumetric flow rate.

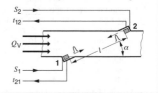

*Ultrasonic flow measurement*
1, 2 Transmitter/receiver 1 and 2.
$l$ Measurement path, S Transmit command,
$t$ Transit period, $Q_V$ Volume flow, $\alpha$ Angle.

#### Pitot-tube air-flow sensors

Pivoting, variable-position sensor plates leave a variable section of the flow cross-section unobstructed, with the size of the free diameter being dependent on the flow rate. A potentiometer monitors the characteristic flap positions for the respective flow rates. The physical and electrical design of the air-flow sensor, e.g. for L-Jetronic (P. 648), is such as to ensure a logarithmic relationship between flow rate and output signal (at very low flow rates the incremental voltage variations referred to the flow-rate variation are substantially greater than at high flow rates). Other types of automotive air-flow sensors are designed for a linear characteristic (KE-Jetronic, P. 646). Measurement errors can occur in cases where the sensor-plate mechanical inertia prevents it from keeping pace with a rapidly pulsating air current (full-load condition at high engine speeds).

### Air-mass meters

Air-mass meters operate according to the hot-wire or hot-film principle; the unit contains no moving mechanical parts. The closed-loop control circuit in the meter's housing maintains a constant temperature differential between a fine platinum wire or thin-film resistor and the passing air stream. The current required for heating provides an extremely precise – albeit nonlinear – index of air-mass flow rate. The system ECU generally converts the signals into linear form and assumes other signal-evaluation tasks. Due to its closed-loop design, this type of air-mass meter can monitor flow rate variations in the millisecond range. However, the sensor's inability to recognize flow direction can produce substantial measuring errors when strong pulsation occurs in the manifold.

The platinum wire in the hot-wire air-mass flow meter functions both as the heater element and as the heater-element temperature sensor. To ensure stable and reliable performance throughout an extended service life, the system must burn-off all accumulated deposits from the hot-wire's surface (at approx. 1,000 °C) after each phase of active operation (when the ignition is switched off).

The hot-film air-mass flow meter combines all measuring elements and the control electronics on a single substrate. In current versions, the heating resistor is located on the back of the base wafer, with the corresponding temperature sensor on the front. This results in somewhat greater response lag than that associated with the hot-wire meter. The temperature-compensation sensor ($R_K$) and the heater element are thermally decoupled by means of a laser cut in the ceramic substrate. More favorable air-flow characteristics make it possible to dispense with the hot-wire meter's burn-off decontamination process.

Extremely compact micromechanical hot-film air-mass flow meters also operate according to thermal principles. Here the heating and measuring resistors are in the form of thin platinum layers sputtered (vapor-deposited) onto the silicon chip acting as substrate. Thermal decoupling from the mounting is obtained by installing the silicon chip in the area of the heating resistor H on a micromechanically thinned section of the substrate (similar to a pressure-sensor diaphragm). The adjacent heater-temperature sensor $S_H$ and the air-temperature sensor $S_L$ (on the thick edge of the silicon chip) maintain the heating resistor H at a constant overtemperature. This method differs from earlier techniques in dispensing with the heating current as an output signal. Instead, the signal is derived from the temperature difference in the

---

**Pitot-tube air-flow sensor**
1 Sensor plate, 2 Compensation flap, 3 Compression volume. Q Flow.

---

**Hot-wire air-mass flow meter**
$Q_M$ Mass flow, $U_m$ Measurement voltage, $R_H$ Hot-wire resistor, $R_K$ Compensation resistor, $R_M$ Measurement resistor, $R_1$, $R_2$ Trimming resistor.

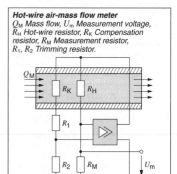

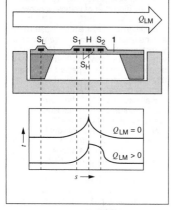

*Micromechanical hot-film air-mass flow meter*
1 Dielectric diaphragm. H Heating resistor,
$S_H$ Heater-temperature sensor,
$S_L$ Air-temperature sensor,
$S_1$, $S_2$ Temperature sensors (upstream and downstream), $Q_{LM}$ Air-mass flow,
s Measurement point, t Temperature.

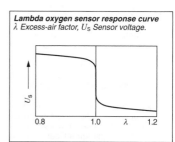

*Lambda oxygen sensor response curve*
$\lambda$ Excess-air factor, $U_S$ Sensor voltage.

medium (air) detected by the two temperature sensors $S_1$ and $S_2$. Temperature sensors are located in the flow path upstream and downstream from the heating resistor H. Although (as with the earlier process) the response pattern remains nonlinear, the fact that the initial value also indicates the flow direction represents an improvement over the former method using the heating current.

**Concentration sensors**
Virtually all chemical concentration sensors run the risk of being poisoned during the necessary direct contact with the measured medium, i.e. irreversibly damaged by harmful foreign substances. For instance, electrolytic oxygen-concentration sensors (lambda oxygen sensors) can be rendered useless by lead that may be present in the fuel or exhaust gas.

<u>Oxygen-concentration sensor (lambda oxygen sensor)</u>
The fuel-metering system employs the exhaust-gas residual-oxygen content as measured by the lambda oxygen sensor to very precisely regulate the air/fuel mixture for combustion to the value $\lambda$ (lambda) = 1 (stoichiometric combustion, P. 605).

The sensor is a solid-state electrolyte made of ZrO ceramic material. At high temperatures, this electrolyte becomes conductive and generates a characteristic galvanic charge at the sensor connections; this voltage is an index of the gas' oxygen content. The maximum variation occurs at $\lambda$ = 1.

Electrically heated sensors are especially well-suited for measurements in the lean range, and already come into operation in the warm-up phase.

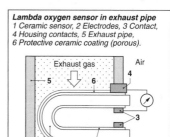

*Lambda oxygen sensor in exhaust pipe*
1 Ceramic sensor, 2 Electrodes, 3 Contact,
4 Housing contacts, 5 Exhaust pipe,
6 Protective ceramic coating (porous).

For the wide lean range, flat and smaller "wafer sensors" of multilayer ceramic design (broadband lambda oxygen sensors) are used; these sensors can also be used in diesel engines. A sensor of this type is essentially a combination of a conventional concentration sensor which acts as a galvanic cell (Nernst sensor) and a limit-current or "pump" cell. A voltage is applied from an external source to the pump cell, which is of the same design as a conventional concentration cell. If the voltage is high enough, a "limit current" sets in which is proportional to the difference in oxygen concentration at both ends of the sensor. Oxygen atoms are transported – depending on the polarity – with the current. An electronic control loop causes the pump cell to supply the concentration sensor permanently through a very narrow diffusion gap with precisely enough oxygen from the exhaust gas to maintain a status of $\lambda = 1$ at the sensor. In other words, oxygen is pumped away in the event of excess air in the exhaust gas (lean range); in the event of a low residual-oxygen content in the exhaust gas (rich range), oxygen is pumped in by reversing the pump voltage. The relevant pump current forms the output signal.

Humidity sensors:
Areas of application:
– Monitoring of air drier for compressed-air brakes
– Monitoring of outside air humidity for slippery-ice warnings
– Calculation of dew point in vehicle interior (air-quality sensing, air conditioning, misting over of vehicle windows)

Capacitive sensors are mostly used to determine relative humidity. A sensor of this type is composed of a thin-film polymer with a metal coating on both sides. The capacitance of this capacitor is considerably but reversibly modified by the adsorption of water. The time constant is typically approx. 30 s. The dew point can also be determined by additionally measuring the air temperature (NTC).

When installed in an air-quality ECU, a Teflon diaphragm protects the sensor against harmful substances. Generally speaking, the air-quality ECU contains above all CO and $NO_x$ sensors, mostly in the form of thick-film resistors ($SnO_x$), which modify their electrical resistance in a wide range (e.g. 1...100 kΩ) by adsorption of the measured media.

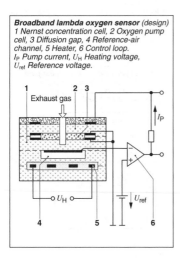

*Broadband lambda oxygen sensor* (design)
1 Nernst concentration cell, 2 Oxygen pump cell, 3 Diffusion gap, 4 Reference-air channel, 5 Heater, 6 Control loop.
$I_P$ Pump current, $U_H$ Heating voltage, $U_{ref}$ Reference voltage.

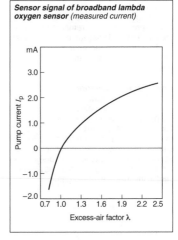

*Sensor signal of broadband lambda oxygen sensor* (measured current)

### Temperature sensors

Temperature measurements in motor vehicles are conducted almost entirely by exploiting the sensitivity to temperature variation found in electrical resistance materials with a positive (PTC) or negative (NTC) temperature coefficient as <u>contact thermometers</u>. Conversion of the resistance variation into analog voltage is performed predominantly with the aid of supplementary temperature-neutral or inversely sensitive resistors as voltage dividers (also providing increased linearity). <u>Non-contacting (pyrometric) temperature sensing</u> has recently come into consideration for passenger safety (passenger observation for airbag activation) and also for passenger comfort (air conditioning, prevention of window misting); this has been made economically viable by the introduction of microsystems technology. The following temperatures occur in motor vehicles:

| Location | Range | °C |
|---|---|---|
| Intake air/charge air | −40... | 170 |
| Outside atmosphere | −40... | 60 |
| Passenger cabin | −20... | 80 |
| Ventilation & heating air | −20... | 60 |
| Evaporator (AC) | −10... | 50 |
| Engine coolant | −40... | 130 |
| Engine oil | −40... | 170 |
| Battery | −40... | 100 |
| Fuel | −40... | 120 |
| Tire air | −40... | 120 |
| Exhaust gas | 100... | 1,000 |
| Disc-brake calipers | −40... | 2,000 |

At many locations, temperature is also measured in order that it can be compensated in cases where temperature variations trigger faults or act as an undesirable influencing variable.

### Sintered-ceramic resistors (NTC)

Sintered-ceramic resistors (NTC resistors, thermistors) made of heavy-metal oxides and oxidized mixed crystals (sintered in pearl or plate-form) are included among those semiconductive materials which display an inverted exponential temperature curve. High thermal sensitivity means that applications are restricted to a "window" of approx. 200 K; however, this range can be defined within a latitude of −40 ... approx. 850 °C.

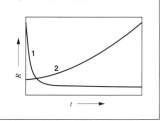

*Temperature sensors (examples)*
1 NTC thermistor, 2 PTC thermistor.
*t* Temperature, *R* Resistance.

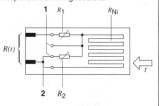

*Metallic-film thermistor*
1 Auxiliary contacts, 2 Bridge.
$R_{Ni}$ Nickel-plated resistor, $R(t)$ Resistance *t* relative to temperature $R_1$, $R_2$ Temperature-independent trimming resistors.

### Thin-film metallic resistors (PTC)

Thin-film metallic resistors, integrated on a single substrate wafer together with two supplementary, temperature-neutral trimming resistors, are characterized by extreme precision, as they can be manufactured and then "trimmed" with lasers to maintain exact response-curve tolerances over long periods of time. The use of layer technology makes it possible to adapt the substrate (ceramic, glass, plastic foil) and the upper layers (plastic molding or paint, sealed foil, glass and ceramic coatings) to the respective application, and thus provide protection against the monitored medium. Although metallic layers are less sensitive to thermal variations than the ceramic-oxide semiconductor sensors, both linearity and reproducibility are better:

| Sensor material | Temperature coefficient TC | Measurement range |
|---|---|---|
| Ni | $5.1 \cdot 10^{-3}$/K | $-60...320\,°C$ |
| Cu | $4.1 \cdot 10^{-3}$/K | $-50...200\,°C$ |
| Pt | $3.5 \cdot 10^{-3}$/K | $-220...850\,°C$ |

Where:
$$TK = [R(100\,°C) - R(0\,°C)] / [R(0\,°C) \cdot 100\,K]$$

### Thick-film resistors (PTC/NTC)

Thick-film pastes with both high resistivity (low surface-area requirement) and positive and negative temperature coefficients are generally employed as temperature sensors for compensation purposes. They have nonlinear response characteristics (without, however, the extreme variations of the massive NTC resistor) and can be laser-trimmed. The measurement effect can be enhanced by using NTC and PTC materials to form voltage-divider circuits.

### Monocrystalline silicon semiconductor resistors (PTC)

When monocrystalline semiconductor materials, such as silicon, are used to manufacture the temperature sensor, it is possible to integrate additional active and passive circuitry on the sensor chip (allowing initial signal conditioning directly at the measuring point).

Due to the closer tolerancing which is possible, these are manufactured according to the spreading-resistance principle. The current flows through the measuring resistor and through a surface-point contact before arriving at the silicon bulk material. It then proceeds, widely distributed, to a counter-electrode covering the base of the sensor chip. As well as the highly reproducible material constants, the high current density after the contact point (high precision achieved through photolithographic manufacture) almost exclusively determines the sensor's resistance value.

The measurement sensitivity is virtually twice that of the Pt resistor (TC = $7.73 \cdot 10^{-3}$/K). However, the temperature-response curve is less linear than that of a metallic sensor.

### Thermopile sensors

For non-contacting measurement of the temperature of a body, the radiation emitted by this body is measured; this radiation is preferably in the infrared (IR) range (wavelength: 5...20 µm). Strictly speaking, the product of the radiated power and the emission coefficient of the body is measured. The latter is material-dependent but mostly close to 1 for materials of technical interest (also for glass). However, for reflective or IR-permeable materials (e.g. air, silicon), it is << 1. The measuring point is reproduced on a radiation-sensitive element, which heats up slightly with respect to its environment (typically 0.01...0.001 °C). This small temperature difference can be effectively measured with thermocouples, many of which are

---

*Si semiconductor resistor (spreading-resistance principle)*
*1 Contacts, 2 Passivation (nitride, oxide), 3 Si substrate, 4 Unconnected counter-electrode.*
*R(t) Temperature-dependent resistor.*

---

*Micromechanical thermopile infrared sensor*
*1 Si chip, 2 Thermocouples connected in series, 3 SiN diaphragm, 4 Thermopile connections, 5 Absorber layer.*

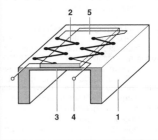

connected in succession to increase the measuring effect (thermopile). It is possible to manufacture a thermopile sensor at low cost using micromechanical processes. All the "hot" points are located on a thermally well insulated, thin diaphragm, while all the cold points are located on the thicker chip edge (temperature sink). The sensor's settling time is typically approx. 20 ms. A "single-pixel sensor" of this type is ideal, e.g. for determining the surface temperature of the windshield so as to prevent it from misting over if the temperature drops below the dew point.

If several pixels are arranged on a chip to form an <u>array</u> (e.g. 4 x 4), rough imaging is thus already possible. However, there should not be too much insensitive surface area between the pixels and the pixels themselves must be thermally well insulated against each other. As all the pixels can optionally respond electrically, the chip has a large number of terminals. For a TO5 housing, the ASIC for instance must be located near the sensor to pre-amplify and serialize the signal. To determine the absolute temperature of the pixels, this ASIC also contains in most cases a reference temperature sensor with which object temperatures can be determined to an accuracy of approx. $\pm 0.5$ K.

In order to reproduce a scene thermally on the sensor array, the array requires an IR optical imaging unit. The highly inexpensive arched mirror must mostly be ruled out for reasons of available space. Glass lenses are impervious to IR light and plastic lenses are only adequate for operating temperatures up to approx. 85 °C. Silicon lenses, however, are very well suited to heat radiation and can be micromechanically manufactured at low cost as diffraction (Fresnel) or refraction lenses with diameters of up to approx. 4 mm. When inserted into the cover of a TO5 housing, they serve at the same time to protect the sensor against direct damage. Although filling the housing with shielding gas increases crosstalk between the pixels somewhat, on the other hand it also reduces their response time.

## Sensors for other applications

### Dirt sensors

The sensor measures the level of contamination on the headlamp lens to furnish the data required for automatic lens cleaning systems.

The sensor's photoelectric reflected-light barrier consists of a light source (LED) and a light receiver (phototransistor). The source is positioned on the inside of the lens, within the cleansed area, but not directly in the headlamp beam path. When the lens is clean, or covered

---

**Micromechanical thermopile array**
1 Si chip, 2 Pixel, 3, 4 Pixel connections.

---

**IR imaging sensor**
1 Si IR lens, 2 TO5 housing, 3 Connection pins, 4 Sensor chip, 5 Evaluation ASIC. $\alpha$ Viewing angle.

with rain droplets, the infrared measurement beam emitted by the unit passes through the lens without being obstructed. Only a minuscule part is reflected back to the light receiver. However, if it encounters dirt particles on the outer surface of the lens, it is reflected back to the receiver at an intensity that is proportional to the degree of contamination and automatically activates the headlamp washer unit once a defined level is reached.

## Rain sensors

The rain sensor recognizes rain droplets on the windshield, so that the windshield wipers can be triggered automatically. The unit thus frees the driver to concentrate on other tasks by making the various control operations used to activate conventional wiper systems redundant. For the time being, the driver can still use the manual controls; if desired, the automatic system must be manually selected when the vehicle is started.

The sensor consists of an optical transmission and reception path (similar to the dirt sensor). In this application, the light is directed toward the windshield at an angle. A dry outer surface reflects (total reflection) it back to the receiver, which is also mounted at an angle. When water droplets are present on the outer surface, a substantial amount of the light is refracted outward, thus weakening the return signal. The windshield wiper also responds to dirt once the activation threshold is exceeded.

## Imaging sensors

With imaging sensors, attempts are now being made to reproduce the superior capability of the human eye and the associated mental recognition faculties (albeit at present only to a very modest extent). It is certain that in the foreseeable future the costs of imaging sensors and the high-power processors needed for interpreting a scene will drop to levels that will be viable for automotive applications. In contrast to the human eye, commercially available imaging sensors are also sensitive in the close IR range (wavelength approx. 1 μm). This means that for all the conceivable applications in an automobile, night-time operation becomes possi-

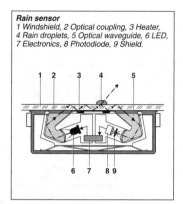

*Rain sensor*
1 Windshield, 2 Optical coupling, 3 Heater,
4 Rain droplets, 5 Optical waveguide, 6 LED,
7 Electronics, 8 Photodiode, 9 Shield.

ble using invisible IR illumination. Imaging sensors could in future find a variety of uses in motor vehicles for monitoring the passenger compartment (seat position, forward displacement in event of a crash etc.) and the vehicle environment (lateral guidance, collision avoidance, parking and back-up assistance, road-sign recognition, etc.).

Imaging sensors are a special instance of "multisensor structures" composed of light-sensitive elements (pixels) which are arranged in line or matrix form, and receive their light from a conventional optical imaging unit. With the silicon imaging sensors available today (CCD Charge-Coupled Devices), the incident light through a transparent electrode generates charge carriers in proportion to the intensity and exposure time. These are then collected in a "potential pot" ($Si$-$SiO_2$ boundary layer). Using further electrodes, these charges are transferred into an opaque zone and further transported in "analog" shift registers (bucket-brigade principle) in lines into an output register which is serially read out at a higher clock-pulse rate.

While CCD sensors are only of restricted use in motor vehicles on account of their limited light/dark dynamic response (50 dB), their readout time and their temperature range (<50 °C), more recent ("smart") imaging sensors based on CMOS technology are appearing which are fully suitable for automotive applications. The logarithmic brightness/signal characteristic curve possible here corresponds to the human eye and has a dynamic response of 120 dB. This dispenses with the need, e.g. for glare control, and delivers constant contrast resolution over the entire brightness range. These sensors permit random access to the individual pixels with simultaneously increased sensitivity (higher readout rate). Even the first signal-preprocessing processes are already possible on the imaging-sensor chip.

Future measurement applications:
- Steering-wheel torque sensing (electromotive power steering, "steer-by-wire" system)
- Drive-torque sensing (misfire detection, load signal)
- Passenger safety: AOS (Automotive Occupancy Sensing, out-of-position sensing)
- Measuring wheel forces and friction-coefficient potential
- Fluid sensors
- Sensors for monitoring the vehicle environment (imaging sensors, etc.) for autonomous driving and detection of an imminent impact

*CCD principle (charge-coupled devices)*
1 Photodiode, 2 Light, 3 Storage electrode, 4 Shift gate, 5 Transfer electrode, 6 Optical cover.

*Imaging-sensor structure*
1 Column cycle $A_1/A_2$, 2 Photosensors, 3 CCD array, 4 Line cycle $B_1/B_2$, 5 Output register, 6 Video output.

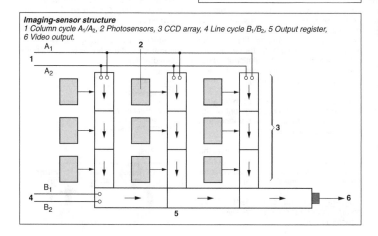

# Actuators

## Quantities and units

| Quantity | | Unit |
|---|---|---|
| $A$ | Pole face; piston surface area | mm² |
| $B$ | Magnetic induction or magnetic flux density | T |
| $F$ | Force | N |
| $I$ | Electric current strength | A |
| $l$ | Length of conductor in field | mm |
| $M$ | Torque | N·m |
| $p$ | Pressure | Pa |
| $Q$ | Volumetric flow rate | l/min |
| $Q_{heat}$ | Heat flow | W |
| $s$ | Distance, piston travel | mm |
| $V$ | Volume | mm³ |
| $V_{th}$ | Displaced volume per revolution | mm³ |
| $\alpha$ | Angle between current flow direction and magnetic lines of force | ° |
| $\delta$ | Air-gap length | mm |
| $\mu_0$ | Permeability constant | |
| $\varphi$ | Rotation angle | ° |

Actuators (final-control elements) form the interface between the electronic signal processor (data processing) and the actual process (mechanical motion). They convert the low-power signals conveying the positioning information in operating signals of an energy level adequate for process control. Signal converters are combined with amplifier elements to exploit the physical transformation principles governing the interrelationships between various forms of energy (electrical – mechanical – fluid – thermal).

Transistor actuator: Element with electronic circuitry for processing control signals. Includes auxiliary energy input and energy output stages.

Servo component: As above, but with the ability to process nonelectrical control signals. Transistor actuator + servo component = final-control element.

Converter: Control component without control-signal processing, receives and transfers energy.

Actuator: Control chain comprising servo component and converter. The term actuator is also employed as a general-purpose designation for servo components without converters on their own.

## Electromechanical actuators

This type of energy conversion represents one option for classifying electromechanical actuators. The energy emanating from the source is transformed into magnetic or electrical field energy, or converted to thermal energy. The individual force-generation principle is determined by these forms of energy, and is bases on either field forces or certain specific material characteristics. Magnetostrictive materials make it possible to design actuators for applications in the micropositioning range. This category also includes piezoelectric actuators, which are built according to a multilayer design similar to ceramic capacitors, and are actuators for high-speed fuel injectors. Thermal actuators depend exclusively on the exploitation of characteristics of specific materials.

Actuators in a motor vehicle are mostly electro-magneto-mechanical converters and, by extension, electrical servomotors (P. 149), translational, and rotational solenoid actuators. An exception is the pyrotechnic airbag system (P. 1034). The solenoid actuators can themselves be the servo element, or they can assume a control function by governing a downstream force-amplification device (e.g. mechanical-hydraulic).

**Actuator chain**
1 Information, 2 Actuator, 3 Converter,
4 Control element, 5 Losses,
6 External electrical energy,
7 External hydraulic energy.

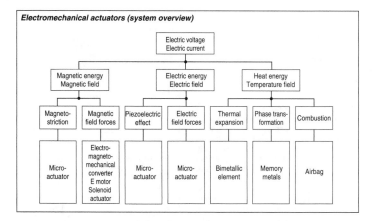

**Electromechanical actuators (system overview)**

**Force generation in the magnetic field**

The distinction between the electrodynamic and the electromagnetic actuator principles stems from the manner in which forces are generated in the magnetic field. Common to both principles is the magnetic circuit with soft-magnetic material and the coil for excitation of the magnetic field. A major difference lies in the force which can be extracted from the unit under technically feasible conditions. Under identical conditions, the force produced by application of the electromagnetic principle is greater by a factor of 40. The electrical time constant for this type of actuator is comparable to the mechanical time constants. Both force-generation principles are applied in linear and rotary drive mechanisms.

Electrodynamic principle

Electrodynamic designs are based on the force exerted on moving charges or charged conductors within a magnetic field (Lorentz force). A field coil or a permanent magnet generates a constant magnetic field. The electrical energy destined for conversion is applied to the moving armature coil (plunger or immersion coil). A high degree of actuator precision is achieved by designing the armature coil with low mass and low inductance. The two energy storage units (one on the fixed and one on the moving component) produce two active force directions via current-direction reversal in the armature and field coils.

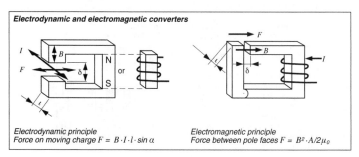

**Electrodynamic and electromagnetic converters**

Electrodynamic principle
Force on moving charge $F = B \cdot I \cdot l \cdot \sin \alpha$

Electromagnetic principle
Force between pole faces $F = B^2 \cdot A / 2\mu_0$

The secondary field produced by the armature current flows in an open magnetic circuit, thereby diminishing the effects of saturation. Approximately speaking, the force (torque) exerted by an electrodynamic actuator over its setting range is proportional to current and independent of travel.

Electromagnetic principle

The electromagnetic principle exploits the mutual attraction displayed by soft ferrous materials in a magnetic field. The electromagnetic actuator is equipped with only one coil, which generates both the field energy and the energy to be transformed. In accordance with the operating principles, the field coil is equipped with an iron core to provide higher inductance. However, as the force is proportional to the square of the density of the magnetic flux, the unit is operative in only a single force-transfer direction. The electromagnetic actuator thus requires a return element (such as a mechanical spring or a magnetic return mechanism).

**Dynamic response**

The dynamic response of an electro-mechanical actuator, i.e. the activation and deactivation operations, is defined by the equation of mechanical motion, the differential equation of electrical circuits and Maxwell's equations of dynamics. The current- and position-dependent force follows from Maxwell's equations.

The most basic electrical circuit consists of an inductance with an ohmic resistor. One means of enhancing the dynamic response is through over-excitation at the instant of activation, while deactivation can be accelerated by a Zener diode. In each case, increasing the dynamic response of the electric circuit involves additional expenditure and increased losses in the actuator's triggering electronics.

Field diffusion is a delay effect which is difficult to influence in actuators with high dynamic response. Rapid switching operations are accompanied by high-frequency field fluctuations in the soft-magnetic material of the actuator's magnetic circuit. These fluctuations, in turn, induce eddy currents, which counteract their

*Switching solenoid*
1 Armature, 2 Coil, 3 Magnetic yoke.

*Switching solenoid (characteristic curves)*
1 Solenoid plunger, 2 Conical armature,
3 Cylindrical armature.

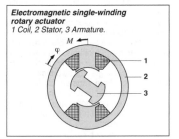

*Electromagnetic single-winding rotary actuator*
1 Coil, 2 Stator, 3 Armature.

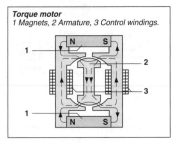

*Torque motor*
1 Magnets, 2 Armature, 3 Control windings.

cause (build-up and decay of the magnetic field). The resultant delay in the build-up or reduction of forces can only be reduced by selecting appropriate materials with low electric conductivity and permeability.

**Design**
Design selection is essentially determined by operating conditions (e.g. installation space, required force/travel curve, and dynamic response).

Electromagnetic actuators
A typical form for translational electromagnetic actuators is the switching solenoid with a force/travel curve which falls as a function of the square of positioning travel. The precise shape of the curve is determined by the type of working air gap (e.g. conical or solenoid plunger).

Rotational electromagnetic actuators are characterized by a defined pole arrangement in stator and rotor. When current is applied to one of the coils, the rotor and stator poles respond with mutual attraction, and in doing so generate a torque.

The single-winding rotary actuator incorporates a pair of poles in each of the two main sections, as well as a coil in the stator. Its maximum adjustment range is approx. 45°.

The torque motor is a bidirectional electromagnetic rotary actuator featuring a stable operating point and without counterforces. The rotor is maintained in a stable position by the excitation field of the permanent magnet in the stator. The magnetic field generated by one or two stator windings produces torque and provides unilateral compensation for the excitation field. This type of layout is suitable for applications in which substantial forces are required over small control angles. The relationship between the applied current and the torque-motor's force is roughly linear. The torque-motor principle is also employed in translational actuators.

Electrodynamic actuators
In a pot magnet (immersion-coil actuator), a cylindrical immersion coil (armature winding) is set in motion in a working air

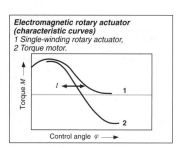

*Electromagnetic rotary actuator (characteristic curves)*
*1 Single-winding rotary actuator,*
*2 Torque motor.*

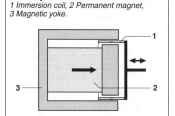

*Electrodynamic immersion-coil actuator*
*1 Immersion coil, 2 Permanent magnet,*
*3 Magnetic yoke.*

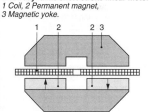

*Electrodynamic short-stroke linear motor*
*1 Coil, 2 Permanent magnet,*
*3 Magnetic yoke.*

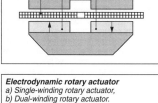

*Electrodynamic rotary actuator*
*a) Single-winding rotary actuator,*
*b) Dual-winding rotary actuator.*
*1 Coil 1, 2 Coil 2, 3 Stator,*
*4 Permanent magnet, 5 Shaft.*

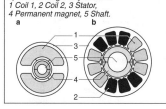

gap. The adjustment range is limited by the axial length of the armature winding and by the air gap.

The <u>short-stroke linear motor</u> is an actuator with a virtually round disk coil.

A distinction is made between single-winding and dual-winding rotary actuators.

Both types include a permanent magnet within the rotor and one or two stator windings. The rotor magnet is magnetized at both ends to produce magnetic flux in the rotary magnet's working air gap, which combines with the armature current to produce a torque. Originating from the position illustrated, the adjustment range is less than ±45°. The positioning range of the <u>single-winding rotary actuator</u> also varies according to both the torque requirement and the angle range in which the necessary flux density can be provided.

The <u>dual-winding rotary actuator</u> can be described as a combination of two single-winding rotary actuators with a 90° peripheral offset and designed to produce opposed torque flows. A stable operating point is achieved at the zero transition point on the resulting torque curve without auxiliary counterforces.

### Applications
Electromechanical actuators are direct-action control elements, and without an intermediate ratio-conversion mechanism, they convert the energy of the electrical control signal into a mechanical positioning factor/work. Typical applications include positioning of flaps, sleeves, and valves. The described actuators are final-control elements without internal return mechanisms, i.e. without a stable operating point. They are only capable of carrying out positioning operations from a stable initial position (operating point) when a counterforce is applied (e.g. return spring and electrical control).

A solenoid plunger provides a stable static operating point when its force/travel curve is superimposed on the characteristic response of a return spring. A variation of the coil current in the solenoid shifts the operating point. Simple posi-

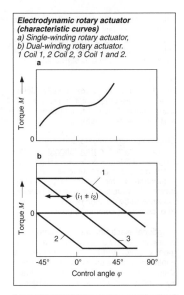

*Electrodynamic rotary actuator (characteristic curves)*
*a) Single-winding rotary actuator,*
*b) Dual-winding rotary actuator.*
*1 Coil 1, 2 Coil 2, 3 Coil 1 and 2.*

a

Torque $M$

0

b

Torque $M$

0

$(i_1 \neq i_2)$

1

2

3

-45°  0°  45°  90°

Control angle $\varphi$

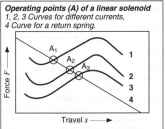

*Operating points (A) of a linear solenoid*
*1, 2, 3 Curves for different currents,*
*4 Curve for a return spring.*

Force $F$

$A_1$

$A_2$

$A_3$

1

2

3

4

Travel $s$

tioning is achieved by controlling the current. However, particular attention must be paid here to the nonlinearity of the force-current characteristic and the positioning system's sensitivity to interference factors (e.g. mechanical friction, pneumatic, and hydraulic forces). The temperature sensitivity of the coil resistance results in positioning errors, making corrective current control necessary. A high-precision positioning system with good dynamic response must incorporate a position sensor and a controller.

| | Hydraulic actuators | Pneumatic actuators |
|---|---|---|
| Medium | – Fluid, mostly oil<br>– Supply from tank, oil sump<br>– Virtually incompressible<br>– Self-lubricating<br>– Viscosity heavily temperature-dependent | – Gas, mostly air<br>– Supply from surrounding air<br>– Compressible<br>– Independent lubrication required<br>– Viscosity fluctuations virtually irrelevant |
| Pressure range | – To approx. 30 MPa (200 MPa for diesel fuel injectors) | – To approx. 1 MPa or greater (approx. 0.05 MPa for vacuum actuators) |
| Line connections | – Supply and return connection (possible leakage connection) | – Pressure connection only, return directly to environment |
| Applications | – Positioning applications with high load rigidity, demanding requirements for synchronization and positioning precision in closed-loop control system | – Actuators with low power requirement, positioning by mechanical stops, in open control loop |

## Fluid-mechanical actuators

Hydraulic and pneumatic actuators utilize similar principles for the conversion and regulation of energy (see "Automotive hydraulics" P. 1170 and "Automotive pneumatics" P. 1186). The table shows the differences in characteristics and applications.

In most applications, fluid-mechanical actuator drives are in the form of hydrostatic energy converters. These operate according to the displacement principle, converting the pressure energy of the fluid medium into mechanical work and vice versa.

In contrast, hydrodynamic transformers operate by converting flow energy (kinetic energy of the moving fluid) into mechanical work (example: hydrodynamic clutch, P. 739).

Losses during energy conversion stem from leakage and friction. Fluid-thermal losses are caused by flow resistance, in which throttle action transforms the hydraulic energy into heat. A portion of this heat is dissipated into the environment, and some of it is absorbed and carried away by the fluid medium.

$$Q_{heat} = Q_1 \cdot p_1 - Q_2 \cdot p_2$$

With incompressible fluids:

$$Q_{heat} = Q_1 \cdot (p_1 - p_2)$$

The flow develops into turbulence at restrictions. The flow rate of the fluid is then largely independent of viscosity. On the other hand, viscosity does play a role in the case of laminar flow in narrow pipes and apertures (see "Automotive hydraulics").

Fluid-mechanical amplifiers control the conversion of energy from fluid to mechanical state. The regulating mechanism must be designed for control with only a very small proportion of the energy required for the ultimate positioning operation.

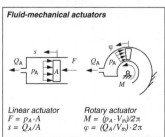

**Fluid-mechanical actuators**

Linear actuator
$F = p_A \cdot A$
$s = Q_A / A$

Rotary actuator
$M = (p_A \cdot V_{th})/2\pi$
$\varphi = (Q_A / V_{th}) \cdot 2\pi$

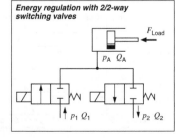

**Energy regulation with 2/2-way switching valves**

Switching valves open and close the orifice governing the flow to and from a fluid-mechanical energy converter. Provided that the control-element opens sufficiently, the throttling losses remain negligible. Pulse-width-modulated opening and closing can be applied to achieve quasi-continuous control of the fluid/mechanical energy conversion process with virtually no losses. In practice, however, pressure fluctuations and mechanical contact between the valve elements result in undesirable vibration and noise.

## Actuator performance data

The table below compares performance data for nine different actuator types.

It contains data based on components with lengths of 50...100 mm and diameters ranging from 20...50 mm.

Comparisons between rotation motors and linear actuators are based on a conversion mechanism consisting of a mechanical spindle with nut (1 mm pitch). Spindle length and motor length are identical.

### Expansion
Expansion is the stroke relative to the length of the inner actuator where energy is generated, e.g. piezoelectric-stack length, coil length, internal length of hydraulic cylinder. The effective stroke (70% of specified spindle length) is assumed as the expansion for rotation motors.

### Mechanical stress
Mechanical stress is the lift force relative to the force-generating area, e.g. cross-sectional area of piezoelectric devices, coil gap surface (end face or lateral surface), inner surface of hydraulic cylinder. The peripheral force at the rotor and the rotor lateral surface are used to calculate the shear stress in electric motors.

### Velocity
The velocity is defined as the control-stroke travel divided by the control time. On rotating motors, it is the peripheral velocity of the rotor.

### Mean control-force density
The mean control-force density is the thermally permissible control force relative to unit volume.

### Performance data

| No. | Actuator type | Expansion % | Mechanical stress N/mm$^2$ | Velocity m/s | Control-force density per stroke W/cm$^3$ | Mean control-force density mW/cm$^3$ | Efficiency % |
|-----|---------------|-------------|----------------------------|--------------|-------------------------------------------|--------------------------------------|--------------|
| 1 | Hydraulic cylinder | 30 | 21 | 0.25 | 9 | 3,020 | 92 |
| 2 | Pneumatic cylinder | 76 | 1 | 1 | 3.5 | 1,180 | 88 |
| 3 | DC motor | 70 | 0.007[2] | 6[3] | 0.8 | 791 | 50 |
| 4 | Ultrasonic-motor | 70 | 0.06[2] | 0.35[3] | 0.13 | 133 | 16 |
| 5 | Piezoeffect actuator | 0.09[5] | 30 | 2[4] | 15.6 | 61 | 7 |
| 6 | Memory wire | 4 | 50 | 0.002 | 0.32 | 53 | 0.3 |
| 7 | Valve linear solenoid[1] | 0.8 | 2.2 | 0.5 | 8 | 44 | 5 |
| 8 | Magnetostrictive actuator | 0.09 | 22 | 1.5 | 1.6 | 5.4 | 5 |
| 9 | Linear solenoid 5% ON | 21 | 0.1 | 0.16 | 0.12 | 4.1 | 5 |

[1] Fuel-cooled. [2] Shear stress in rotor gap/friction gap.
[3] Rotor peripheral velocity. [4] Theoretical limit. [5] New keramites to 0.18%.

### Control-force density per stroke
The control-force density per stroke is the transitional maximum control force for one stroke relative to the unit volume. A spindle (1 mm pitch) with a length equal to the motor length is specified for motors.

### Efficiency
The efficiency is the supplied energy divided by the energy transmitted to the actuator, not including losses associated with electronic or other control assemblies. Options for energy recycling (i.e. with piezoelectric actuators) are not considered.

### Characteristics
Extremely high performance levels in the areas of expansion, mechanical stress and velocity make hydraulic actuators the preferred design for extended heavy-duty applications.

In electric motors, high peripheral velocities compensate for low magnetic-field forces, allowing these motors to provide high levels of force density in continuous operation.

Despite their limited expansion, piezoelectric actuators are capable of generating high force levels and are thus suitable for providing brief bursts of high energy.

Linear solenoids suffer from substantial thermal losses at the coil; with adequate cooling they achieve moderate control-force density ratings, comparable to those of solid-state actuators.

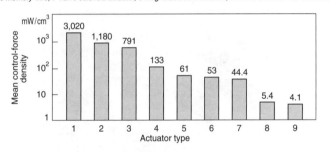

**Mean control-force density of selected actuators**
*1 Hydraulic cylinder, 2 Pneumatic cylinder, 3 DC motor, 4 Ultrasonic motor, 5 Piezoeffect actuator, 6 Memory wire, 7 Valve solenoid actuator, 8 Magnetostrictive actuator, 9 Linear solenoid 5% on-time.*

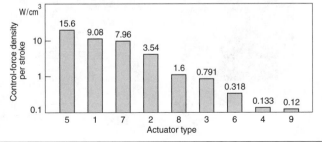

**Control-force density per stroke of selected actuators**
*1 Hydraulic cylinder, 2 Pneumatic cylinder, 3 DC motor, 4 Ultrasonic motor, 5 Piezoeffect actuator, 6 Memory wire, 7 Valve linear solenoid, 8 Magnetostrictive actuator, 9 Linear solenoid 5% on-time.*

## Miniatures

Micromechanics makes it possible to execute sensor functions in the smallest of spaces. Typical mechanical dimensions can extend into the micrometer range. Especially silicon, with its unique properties, has proven to be a suitable material for producing very small, often filigree mechanical structures. Its elasticity, combined with its electrical properties, is virtually ideal for manufacturing sensors. It is possible using modified semiconductor-technology processes to integrate mechanical and electronic sensor functions on a single chip in a different way.

In 1994 an intake-pressure sensor for load sensing in motor vehicles was the first product with a micromechanical measurement cell from Bosch to go into volume production. More recent examples of miniaturization are micromechanical acceleration and yaw-rate sensors in vehicle-safety systems for passenger protection and electronic stability program control. The photos below clearly illustrate the minute size.

## Micromechanical acceleration sensor

Circuit

Bonding wire    Sensor chip

Evaluation circuit

Comb structure compared with an insect

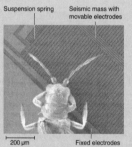

Suspension spring    Seismic mass with movable electrodes

200 µm      Fixed electrodes

## Micromechanical yaw-rate sensors

DRS-MM1 electronic stability program control

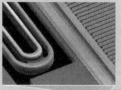

33 mm

DRS-MM2 rollover sensing, navigation

100 µm

# Electrical machines

## Operating concept

Electrical machines are used to convert electrical and mechanical energy. An electric motor converts electrical energy into mechanical energy, and an alternator converts energy in the opposite direction. Electrical machines consist of a stationary component (the stator) and a rotating component (the rotor). There are special designs which depart from this configuration, such as linear machines which produce linear motion. Permanent magnets or several coils (windings) are used to produce magnetic fields in the stator and rotor. This causes torque to develop between the two machine components. Electrical machines have iron stators and rotors in order to control the magnetic fields. As the magnetic fluxes change over time, stators and rotors must consist of stacks of individual laminations which are insulated with respect to one another. The spatial arrangement of the coils and the type of current used (direct current, alternating current, or three-phase current) permit a number of different electrical machine designs. They differ from one another in the way they operate, and therefore have different applications.

## Direct-current machines

The stator of a direct-current machine contains salient poles which are magnetized by the direct-current excitation windings. In the rotor (here also called the armature), the coils are distributed among slots in the laminated stack and connected to a commutator. Carbon brushes in the stator housing wipe against the commutator as it rotates, thereby transferring direct current to the armature coils. The rotation of the commutator causes a reversal in the direction of current flow in the coils. The different rotational speed vs. torque characteristics result from the method selected for connecting the excitation winding and armature:

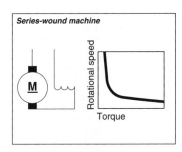

*Series-wound machine*

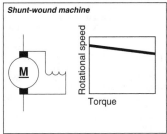

*Shunt-wound machine*

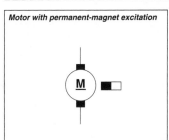

*Motor with permanent-magnet excitation*

**Series connection
(series characteristic)**

Rotational speed is highly dependent on load; high starting torque; "racing" of the machine if the load is suddenly removed, therefore load must be rigidly coupled; direction of rotation changed by reversing the direction of current in the armature or excitation winding; used, among other things, as motor-vehicle drive motor and starter motor for internal-combustion engines.

**Parallel connection
(shunt characteristic)**
Rotational speed remains largely constant regardless of load; direction of rotation is changed by reversing the direction of the current in the armature or excitation winding; used, for instance, as drive motor for machine tools and as direct-current generator. A shunt characteristic can also be obtained by using a separate power supply for the excitation winding (external excitation) or by using permanent-magnet excitation in the stator. Applications for permanent-field motors in motor vehicles: starter, windshield wiper, and small-power motors for various drives. If the motor incorporates both series and shunt excitation windings (compound-wound motor), intermediate levels in the rotational speed/torque characteristic can be obtained; application: e.g. large starters.

All direct-current machines are easily capable of speed control over a wide range. If the machine incorporates a static converter which allows adjustment of the armature voltage, the torque and therefore the rotational speed can be infinitely variable. The rotational speed can be further increased by reducing the excitation current (field weakening) when the rated armature voltage is reached. A disadvantage of direct-current machines is carbon-brush and commutator wear which makes regular maintenance necessary.

## Three-phase machines

A three-phase winding is distributed among the stator slots in a three-phase machine. The three phases of current produce a rotating magnetic field. The speed $n_0$ (in rpm) of this rotating field is calculated as follows:

$$n_0 = 60 \cdot f / p$$

$f$ = frequency (in Hz), $p$ = number of pole pairs. Three-phase machines are either synchronous or asynchronous, depending on rotor design.

**Asynchronous machines**
The laminated rotor contains either a three-phase winding, as in the stator, or a bar winding. The three-phase winding is connected to slip rings which are short-

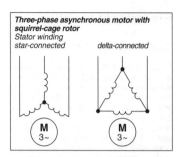

*Three-phase asynchronous motor with squirrel-cage rotor*
Stator winding
star-connected          delta-connected

circuited either directly or via series resistors. In the case of the bar winding, the bars are connected to one another by two short-circuiting rings (squirrel-cage rotor). As long as the rotational speed of the rotor deviates from $n_0$, the rotating stator field induces current in the rotor windings, thereby generating torque. Deviation of the rotational speed of the rotor $n$ from $n_0$ is termed slip $s$:

$$s = (n_0 - n) / n_0$$

Continuous operation is only economical in the vicinity of $n_0$ because losses increase as slip increases (nominal slip ≤ 5%). In this range the asynchronous machine has a shunt characteristic. The machine operates as a motor when $n < n_0$, and as an alternator when $n > n_0$. The direction of rotation is changed by reversing two of the phases.

The asynchronous machine is the most frequently used electric motor in the field of drive engineering. With a squirrel-cage rotor it is easy to operate, and requires little maintenance.

Examples of rotating-field speeds

| No. of poles (2 p) | Frequency | | |
|---|---|---|---|
| | 50 Hz | 150 Hz | 200 Hz |
| | Rotating-field speed in rpm | | |
| 2 | 3,000 | 9,000 | 12,000 |
| 4 | 1,500 | 4,500 | 6,000 |
| 6 | 1,000 | 3,000 | 4,000 |
| 8 | 750 | 2,250 | 3,000 |
| 10 | 600 | 1,800 | 2,400 |
| 12 | 500 | 1,500 | 2,000 |

## Synchronous machines

In the rotor (here, also called the pole wheel), the poles are magnetized by direct-current coils. The magnetizing current is usually transferred via two slip rings to the rotor. The pole wheel can be made of solid steel, because the magnetic flux remains constant over time. Constant torque is generated as long as the rotor rotates at a speed of $n_0$. At other speeds, the torque fluctuates periodically between a positive and a negative maximum value, and excessively high current is produced.

For this reason, a synchronous machine is not self-starting. The synchronous machine also differs from the asynchronous machine in that the reactive power absorption and generation are adjustable. The synchronous machine is most frequently used as a generator in electric power plants. Synchronous motors are used in cases where constant motor speed based on constant line frequency is desired, or where a reactive power demand exists. The automotive three-phase alternator is a special type of synchronous machine.

The rotational speed of all three-phase machines is determined by the stator frequency. Such machines can operate over a wide range of speeds if used in conjunction with static converters which vary the frequency.

## EC motors

The "electronically commutated direct-current" or "EC" motor is becoming increasingly popular. It is essentially a permanent-magnet synchronous machine, and are brushless. The EC motor is equipped with a rotor-position sensor, and is connected to the DC power source through its control and power electronics. The electronic transfer circuit switches the current in the stator winding according to rotor position – the magnets which induce the excitation current are attached to the rotor – to provide the interdependence between rotational speed and torque which is normally associated with a separately excited DC machine. The respective magnetic functions of the stator and rotor are the opposite of what they would be in a classical direct-current machine.

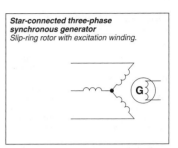

*Star-connected three-phase synchronous generator*
*Slip-ring rotor with excitation winding.*

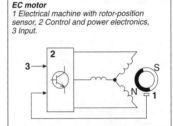

*EC motor*
*1 Electrical machine with rotor-position sensor, 2 Control and power electronics, 3 Input.*

The EC motor's potential applications are a result of the advantages which this drive principle provides: Commutator and carbon brushes are replaced by electronics, dispensing with both brush noise and wear. EC motors are maintenance-free (long service life) and can be constructed to meet high degrees of protection (see below). The electronic control feature makes it easy for drive units with EC motors to incorporate auxiliary functions such as infinitely variable speed governing, direction reversal, soft starts, and antilock protection.

The main areas of automotive application are in the HVAC (Heating/Ventilation/Air-Conditioning) sectors, and for pumps and servo units. In the area of production machinery, EC motors are chiefly employed as precision drive units for feed-control in machine tools. Here the decisive advantages are freedom from maintenance, favorable dynamic properties and consistent torque output with minimal ripple.

## Single-phase alternating-current machines

### Universal motors
The direct-current series-wound motor can be operated on alternating current if a laminated rather than a solid iron stator is used. It is then called a universal motor.

When operated on alternating current, a torque component at twice the frequency of the current is superposed on the constant torque component.

### Single-phase asynchronous motors with squirrel-cage rotor
The simplest design of a single-phase asynchronous motor is a three-phase asynchronous machine in which alternating current is supplied to only two stator phases. Although its operation remains largely the same, the power and the maximum torque are reduced. In addition, the single-phase asynchronous machine is not self-starting.

Machines which are intended only for single-phase operation have only a single-phase main winding in the stator, as well as auxiliary starting circuits. The stator also contains an auxiliary winding connected in parallel with the main winding for this purpose. The necessary phase shift of the auxiliary winding current can be achieved through increased winding resistance (low breakaway torque) or by means of a capacitor connected in series with the auxiliary winding (somewhat greater starting torque).

The auxiliary winding is switched off after the motor starts. The direction of rotation of the motor is changed by reversing the two auxiliary or main winding connections. A motor which has a capacitor in series with the auxiliary winding is called a capacitor motor. Capacitor motors with a starting and running capacitor also operate continuously with capacitor and auxiliary winding. Optimum operation for a specific operating point can be achieved by correct selection of capacitor. An additional capacitor is often used in order to increase the starting torque; this capacitor is then disconnected after the motor starts.

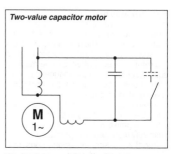

*Two-value capacitor motor*

## Duty-type ratings for electrical machines
(VDE 0530)

### S1: Continuous-running duty
Operation under constant load (rated output) of sufficient duration to reach the continuous-operation temperature.

### S2: Short-time duty
Operation under constant load is so brief that the continuous-operation temperature is not reached. The rest period is so long that the machine is able to cool down to the temperature of the coolant.

Recommended short-time duty periods: 10, 30, 60 and 90 min.

### S3 to S5: Intermittent duty
Continuous alternating sequence of load and idle periods. The continuous-operation temperature is not reached during the load period or during the cooling period of one duty cycle.
S3 Intermittent duty without influence of starting on temperature.
S4 Intermittent duty with influence of starting on temperature.
S5 Intermittent duty with influence of starting and braking on temperature.

### S6: Continuous operation with intermittent loading
Operation with intermittent loading. Continuous alternating sequence of load periods and no-load periods, otherwise as S3.

**S7: Uninterrupted duty**
Operation with starting and braking.

**S8: Uninterrupted duty**
Operation with pole-changing.
For S3 and S6, the duty cycle time is 10 mins unless otherwise agreed; and recommended values for cyclic duration factor are 15, 25, 40 and 60% . For S2, S3 and S6, the operation time or the duty cycle time and the cyclic duration factor are to be specified after the rating; the duty cycle time is only to be specified if it differs from 10 mins. Example: S2 – 60 mins, S3 – 25%.

**Cyclic duration factor**
The cyclic duration factor is the ratio of the loading period, including starting and braking, to the cycle time.

**Winding temperature**
The mean temperature $t_2$ of the windings of an electrical machine can be determined by measuring the resistance ($R_2$) and referring it to an initial resistance $R_1$ at a temperature $t_1$:

$$t_2 = \frac{R_2 - R_1}{R_1} \ (\tau + t_1) + t_1$$

with

$$\tau = \frac{1}{\alpha} - 20 \text{ K}$$

$\alpha$ = Temperature coefficient.

# Degrees of protection for electrical machines
(DIN 40 050)

Examples:

**Degree of protection IP 00**
No protection against accidental contact, no protection against solid bodies, no protection against water.

**Degree of protection IP 11**
Protection against large-area contact by the hand, protection against large solid bodies, protection against dripping water.

**Degree of protection IP 23**
Protection against contact by the fingers, protection against medium-size solid bodies, protection against water sprayed vertically and obliquely up to an angle of 60° to the vertical.

**Degree of protection IP 44**
Protection against contact by tools or the like, protection against small solid bodies, protection against splash water from all directions.

**Degree of protection IP 67**
Total protection against contact, dustproof, protection against entry of dangerous quantities of water when immersed in water under conditions of defined pressure and for a defined period of time.

**Explosion protection Ex**
(VDE 0170/0171)

| Symbol d: | Explosion-containing enclosure; |
| Symbol f: | Auxiliary ventilation; |
| Symbol e: | Increased safety; |
| Symbol s: | Special protection, e.g. for machines operating in flammable liquids. |

# Mathematics

## Mathematical signs and symbols

| ≈ | Approximately equal to |
|---|---|
| ≪ | Much less than |
| ≫ | Much greater than |
| ≙ | Corresponds to |
| . . . | and so forth, to |
| = | Equal to |
| ∓ | Not equal to |
| < | Less than |
| ≤ | Less than or equal to |
| > | Greater than |
| ≥ | Greater than or equal to |
| + | Plus |
| – | Minus |
| · or ★ | Multiplied by |
| or × | |
| – or / | Divided by |
| or : | |
| Σ | Sum of |
| Π | Product of |

| ~ | Proportional to |
|---|---|
| $\sqrt{\ }$ | Square root of ($\sqrt[n]{\ }$ $n$th root of) |
| $n!$ | $n$ factorial (e.g. $3! = 1 \cdot 2 \cdot 3 = 6$) |
| $\lvert x \rvert$ | Absolute value of $x$ |
| → | Approaches |
| ∞ | Infinity |
| i or j | Imaginary unit, $i^2 = -1$ |
| ⊥ | Perpendicular to |
| ‖ | Parallel to |
| ∢ | Angle |
| △ | Triangle |
| lim | Limiting value |
| Δ | Delta (difference between two values) |
| d | Total differential |
| δ | Partial differential |
| ∫ | Integral |
| ln | Logarithm to base e [1] |
| lg | Logarithm to base 10 |

## Useful numbers

| | | | |
|---|---|---|---|
| e | = 2.718282 [1] | $\sqrt{\pi}$ | = 1.77245 |
| $e^2$ | = 7.389056 | $1/\pi$ | = 0.31831 |
| $1/e$ | = 0.367879 | $\pi^2$ | = 9.86960 |
| lg e | = 0.434294 | $180/\pi$ | = 57.29578 |
| $\sqrt{e}$ | = 1.648721 | $\pi/180$ | = 0.017453 |
| $1/\lg e$ | = 2.302585 | $\sqrt{2}$ | = 1.41421 |
| ln 10 | = 2.302585 | $1/\sqrt{2}$ | = 0.70711 |
| $1/\ln 10$ | = 0.434294 | $\sqrt{3}$ | = 1.73205 |
| $\pi$ | = 3.14159 | | |

## Number systems

Number systems are employed to form numerals in cases where the number of digits is to be less than the quantity of individual units being described. This type of notation requires the use of a single symbol (digit) for collective representation of more than one element.

Today's denominational number systems differ from former additive systems by employing groups which increase in uniform increments. The position of the digit within the numeral corresponds to the size of the unit (place value). The number at which the first new unit is formed is equal to the base number of a

denominational number system; it is equal to the maximum number of individual digits which are available. Most frequently used is the decimal system (base 10). In information technology/computer science, the binary system (base 2) using the digits 0 and 1, and the hexadecimal system (base 16) using the digits 0 through 9 and A through F, are also employed. A real number $a$ is represented in the denominational number system by:

$$a = \pm \sum_{i=-\infty}^{\infty} Z_i \cdot B^i$$

i Position, $B$ Base, $Z_i$ Natural number ($0 \le Z_i < B$) at position i. A comma is inserted between the positions i < 0 and i = 0.

| Roman number system (addition system) | Decimal system (base 10) | Binary system (base 2) |
|---|---|---|
| I | 1 | 1 |
| X | 10 | 1010 |
| C | 100 | 1100100 |
| M | 1000 | 1111100110 |
| II | 2 | 10 |
| V | 5 | 101 |
| L | 50 | 110010 |
| D | 500 | 111110010 |
| MIM or MDCCCCLXXXXIX | 1999 | 11111001111 |

(In the Roman system, a smaller numeral is subtracted from a larger subsequent numeral when it directly precedes it.)

[1] e = 1 + 1/1! + 1/2! + 1/3! + ...
(base of natural logarithms).

## Preferred numbers

Preferred numbers are rounded-off terms in geometric series whose increments (the ratio of a term to its predecessor) are as follows:

| Series | R5 | R10 | R20 | R40 |
|---|---|---|---|---|
| Increment | $\sqrt[5]{10}$ | $\sqrt[10]{10}$ | $\sqrt[20]{10}$ | $\sqrt[40]{10}$ |

They are used for selecting preferred size and dimension increments.

In addition to the principal series, DIN 323 also contains the exceptional series R 80 as well as a series of rounded numbers.

Electrical components such as resistors and capacitors are rated in increments in accordance with the E Series:

| Series | E6 | E12 | E24 |
|---|---|---|---|
| Increment | $\sqrt[6]{10}$ | $\sqrt[12]{10}$ | $\sqrt[24]{10}$ |

### Preferred numbers (DIN 323)

| Principal series | | | | Exact values | | E series (DIN 41 426) | | |
|---|---|---|---|---|---|---|---|---|
| R5 | R10 | R20 | R40 | | lg | E6 | E12 | E24 |
| 1.00 | 1.00 | 1.00 | 1.00 | 1.0000 | 0.0 | 1.0 | 1.0 | 1.0 |
| | | | 1.06 | 1.0593 | 0.025 | | | 1.1 |
| | | 1.12 | 1.12 | 1.1220 | 0.05 | | 1.2 | 1.2 |
| | | | 1.18 | 1.1885 | 0.075 | | | 1.3 |
| | 1.25 | 1.25 | 1.25 | 1.2589 | 0.1 | 1.5 | 1.5 | 1.5 |
| | | | 1.32 | 1.3335 | 0.125 | | | 1.6 |
| | | 1.40 | 1.40 | 1.4125 | 0.15 | | 1.8 | 1.8 |
| | | | 1.50 | 1.4962 | 0.175 | | | 2.0 |
| 1.60 | 1.60 | 1.60 | 1.60 | 1.5849 | 0.2 | 2.2 | 2.2 | 2.2 |
| | | | 1.70 | 1.6788 | 0.225 | | | 2.4 |
| | | 1.80 | 1.80 | 1.7783 | 0.25 | | 2.7 | 2.7 |
| | | | 1.90 | 1.8836 | 0.275 | | | 3.0 |
| | 2.00 | 2.00 | 2.00 | 1.9953 | 0.3 | 3.3 | 3.3 | 3.3 |
| | | | 2.12 | 2.1135 | 0.325 | | | 3.6 |
| | | 2.24 | 2.24 | 2.2387 | 0.35 | | 3.9 | 3.9 |
| | | | 2.36 | 2.3714 | 0.375 | | | 4.3 |
| 2.50 | 2.50 | 2.50 | 2.50 | 2.5119 | 0.4 | 4.7 | 4.7 | 4.7 |
| | | | 2.65 | 2.6607 | 0.425 | | | 5.1 |
| | | 2.80 | 2.80 | 2.8184 | 0.45 | | 5.6 | 5.6 |
| | | | 3.00 | 2.9854 | 0.475 | | | 6.2 |
| | 3.15 | 3.15 | 3.15 | 3.1623 | 0.5 | 6.8 | 6.8 | 6.8 |
| | | | 3.35 | 3.3497 | 0.525 | | | 7.5 |
| | | 3.55 | 3.55 | 3.5481 | 0.55 | | 8.2 | 8.2 |
| | | | 3.75 | 3.7584 | 0.575 | | | 9.1 |
| 4.00 | 4.00 | 4.00 | 4.00 | 3.9811 | 0.6 | | | |
| | | | 4.25 | 4.2170 | 0.625 | 10.0 | 10.0 | 10.0 |
| | | 4.50 | 4.50 | 4.4668 | 0.65 | | | |
| | | | 4.75 | 4.7315 | 0.675 | | | |
| | 5.00 | 5.00 | 5.00 | 5.0119 | 0.7 | | | |
| | | | 5.30 | 5.3088 | 0.725 | | | |
| | | 5.60 | 5.60 | 5.6234 | 0.75 | | | |
| | | | 6.00 | 5.9566 | 0.775 | | | |
| 6.30 | 6.30 | 6.30 | 6.30 | 6.3096 | 0.8 | | | |
| | | | 6.70 | 6.6834 | 0.825 | | | |
| | | 7.10 | 7.10 | 7.0795 | 0.85 | | | |
| | | | 7.50 | 7.4989 | 0.875 | | | |
| | 8.00 | 8.00 | 8.00 | 7.9433 | 0.9 | | | |
| | | | 8.50 | 8.4140 | 0.925 | | | |
| | | 9.00 | 9.00 | 8.9125 | 0.95 | | | |
| | | | 9.50 | 9.4409 | 0.975 | | | |
| 10.0 | 10.0 | 10.0 | 10.0 | 10.0000 | 1.0 | | | |

## Trigonometric functions

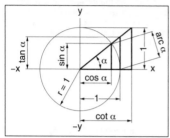

| $\varphi =$ | $\pm \alpha$ | $90 \pm \alpha$ | $180 \pm \alpha$ | $270 \pm \alpha$ |
|---|---|---|---|---|
| $\sin \varphi =$ | $\pm \sin \alpha$ | $\cos \alpha$ | $\mp \sin \alpha$ | $- \cos \alpha$ |
| $\cos \varphi =$ | $\pm \cos \alpha$ | $\mp \sin \alpha$ | $- \cos \alpha$ | $\pm \sin \alpha$ |
| $\tan \varphi =$ | $\pm \tan \alpha$ | $\mp \cot \alpha$ | $\pm \tan \alpha$ | $\mp \cot \alpha$ |
| $\cot \varphi =$ | $\pm \cot \alpha$ | $\mp \tan \alpha$ | $\pm \cot \alpha$ | $\mp \tan \alpha$ |

| | |
|---|---|
| Sine $\alpha$ | opposite side/hypotenuse |
| Cosine $\alpha$ | adjacent side/hypotenuse |
| Tangent $\alpha$ | opposite side/adjacent side |
| Cotangent $\alpha$ | adjacent side/opposite side |
| Arc $\alpha = \widehat{\alpha}$ | radian measure of $\alpha$ in circle of radius 1 |
| inv $\alpha$ | involute function |

$$\sin 0° = \cos 90° = 0$$
$$\cos 0° = \sin 90° = 1$$
$$\tan 0° = \cot 90° = 0$$
$$\cot 0° = \tan 90° = \infty$$
$$\sin 30° = \cos 60° = 0.5$$
$$\cos 30° = \sin 60° = 0.5\sqrt{3}$$
$$\tan 30° = \cot 60° = \sqrt{3}/3$$
$$\cot 30° = \tan 60° = \sqrt{3}$$

$$\widehat{\alpha} = \text{arc } \alpha = \frac{\pi \cdot \alpha}{180°} \text{ rad} = \frac{\alpha}{57.3°}$$

$$\widehat{1}° = \text{arc } 1° = \frac{\pi}{180} = 0.017453$$

$$\text{arc } 57.3° = 1$$

$$\text{inv } \alpha = \tan \alpha - \text{arc } \alpha$$

$$\cos^2 \alpha + \sin^2 \alpha = 1$$

$$\tan \alpha = \frac{\sin \alpha}{\cos \alpha} = \frac{1}{\cot \alpha}$$

$$1 + \tan^2 \alpha = \frac{1}{\cos^2 \alpha}$$

$$1 + \cot^2 \alpha = \frac{1}{\sin^2 \alpha}$$

$$\sin \alpha \approx \widehat{\alpha} - \frac{\widehat{\alpha}^3}{6}$$

Error < 1% at $\alpha < 58°$

$$\sin \alpha \approx \widehat{\alpha}$$
Error < 1% at $\alpha < 14°$

$$\cos \alpha \approx 1 - \frac{\widehat{\alpha}^2}{2}$$
Error < 1% at $\alpha < 37°$

$$\cos \alpha \approx 1$$
Error < 1% at $\alpha < 8°$

$$\sin 2\alpha = 2 \sin \alpha \cdot \cos \alpha$$
$$\cos 2\alpha = \cos^2 \alpha - \sin^2 \alpha$$
$$\tan 2\alpha = 2/(\cot \alpha - \tan \alpha)$$
$$\cot 2\alpha = (\cot \alpha - \tan \alpha)/2$$
$$\sin 3\alpha = 3 \sin \alpha - 4 \sin^3 \alpha$$
$$\cos 3\alpha = 4 \cos^3 \alpha - 3 \cos \alpha$$

$$\sin (\alpha \pm \beta) = \sin \alpha \cdot \cos \beta \pm \cos \alpha \cdot \sin \beta$$
$$\cos (\alpha \pm \beta) = \cos \alpha \cdot \cos \beta \mp \sin \alpha \cdot \sin \beta$$

$$\tan (\alpha \pm \beta) = \frac{\tan \alpha \pm \tan \beta}{1 \mp \tan \alpha \tan \beta}$$

$$\cot (\alpha \pm \beta) = \frac{\cot \alpha \cdot \cot \beta \mp 1}{\cot \beta \pm \cot \alpha}$$

$$\sin \alpha \pm \sin \beta = 2 \sin \frac{\alpha \pm \beta}{2} \cdot \cos \frac{\alpha \mp \beta}{2}$$
$$\cos \alpha + \cos \beta = 2 \cos \frac{\alpha + \beta}{2} \cdot \cos \frac{\alpha - \beta}{2}$$
$$\cos \alpha - \cos \beta = -2 \sin \frac{\alpha + \beta}{2} \cdot \sin \frac{\alpha - \beta}{2}$$
$$\tan \alpha \pm \tan \beta = \frac{\sin (\alpha \pm \beta)}{\cos \alpha \cdot \cos \beta}$$

$$\cot \alpha \pm \cot \beta = \frac{\sin (\beta \pm \alpha)}{\sin \alpha \cdot \sin \beta}$$

**Euler's formula**
(basis of symbolic calculation):

$$e^{\pm ix} = \cos x \pm i \sin x$$

$$\sin x = \frac{e^{ix} - e^{-ix}}{2i}; \cos x = \frac{e^{ix} + e^{-ix}}{2}$$

where $i = \sqrt{-1}$

## Equations for plane and spherical triangles

### Plane triangle

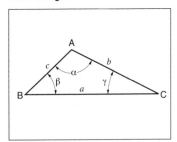

$\alpha + \beta + \gamma = 180°$

**Sine law**
$a : b : c = \sin \alpha : \sin \beta : \sin \gamma$

**Pythagoras' theorem (cosine law)**
$a^2 = b^2 + c^2 - 2bc \cos a$
for right-angle triangle
$a^2 = b^2 + c^2$

### Spherical triangle

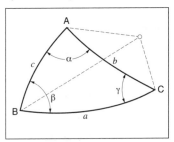

**Sine law**
$\sin a : \sin b : \sin c = \sin \alpha : \sin \beta : \sin \gamma$

**Cosine law** for sides
$\cos a = \cos b \cos c + \sin b \sin c \cos \alpha$

**Cosine law** for angles
$\cos \alpha = -\cos \beta \cos \gamma + \sin \beta \sin \gamma \cos a$

## Equations often used

**Solution of quadratic equation**
$ax^2 + bx + c = 0$

$$x = \frac{-b \pm \sqrt{b^2 - 4ac}}{2a}$$

**Golden section** (continuous division)

$1 : x = x : (1 - x)$, from which $x = 0.618$

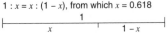

**Conversion of logarithms**

$\lg N = 0.434294 \cdot \ln N$
$\ln N = 2.302585 \cdot \lg N$

**Geometric series**
$a + aq + aq^2 + aq^3 + \dots$

$n$th member $= aq^{n-1}$

for $q > 1$: $\sum_n = a(q^n - 1)/(q - 1)$

for $q < 1$: $\sum_n = a(1 - q^n)/(1 - q)$

for $n \to \infty$ becomes $q^n = 0$
$$\sum_{n \to \infty} = a/(1 - q)$$

**Arithmetic series**

$a + (a + d) + (a + 2d) + (a + 3d) + \dots$
$n$th member $= a + (n - 1)d$

$$\sum_n = \frac{n}{2}[2a + (n - 1)d]$$

## Areas of plane surfaces

| Type of surface | Area $A$ |
|---|---|
| | $\pi \approx 3.1416$ |
| Triangle | $A = \dfrac{a \cdot h}{2}$ |
| Trapezoid | $A = \dfrac{a + b}{2} \, h$ |
| Parallelogram | $A = a \cdot h = a \cdot b \cdot \sin \gamma$ |
| Circle | $A = \dfrac{\pi \cdot d^2}{4} = 0.785 \, d^2$  <br> Circumference $U = \pi \cdot d$ |
| Annulus | $A = \dfrac{\pi}{4} (D^2 - d^2) = \dfrac{\pi}{2} (D + d) \, b$ |
| Sector <br> $\varphi$ in degrees | $A = \dfrac{\pi \cdot r^2 \cdot \varphi}{360°} = 8.73 \cdot 10^{-3} \cdot r^2 \cdot \varphi$ <br> Arc length $l = \dfrac{\pi \cdot r \cdot \varphi}{180°} = 1.75 \cdot 10^{-2} \cdot r \cdot \varphi$ |
| Segment <br> $\varphi$ in degrees | $A = \dfrac{r^2}{2}\left(\dfrac{\pi \cdot \varphi}{180°} - \sin\varphi\right) \approx h \cdot s \left[0.667 + 0.5\left(\dfrac{h}{s}\right)^2\right]$ <br> Chord length $s = 2 \, r \cdot \sin \dfrac{\varphi}{2}$ <br> Arc height $h = r\left(1 - \cos \dfrac{\varphi}{2}\right) = \dfrac{s}{2} \tan \dfrac{\varphi}{4} = 2 \, r \cdot \sin^2 \dfrac{\varphi}{4}$ |
| Hexagon | $A = \dfrac{\sqrt{3}}{2} \, s^2 = 0.866 \, s^2$ <br> Width across corners $e = \dfrac{2s}{\sqrt{3}} = 1.155 \, s$ |
| Ellipse | $A = \pi \cdot D \cdot d / 4 = 0.785 \, D \cdot d$ <br> Circumference $U \approx 0.75 \, \pi \, (D + d) - 0.5 \, \pi \sqrt{D \cdot d}$ |
| Pappus' theorem for surfaces of revolution | The area of a surface or revolution is equal to the length $l$ of the generatrix line multiplied by the distance traveled by the centroid $A = 2\pi \cdot r \cdot l$ |

## Volume and surface area of solids

| Type of solid | Volume $V$, surface $S$, lateral area $M$ $\pi \approx 3.1416$ |
|---|---|
| Regular cylinder | $V = \dfrac{\pi \cdot d^2}{4}\, h = 0.785\, d^2 \cdot h$ <br> $M = \pi \cdot d \cdot h, \ \ S = \pi \cdot d\,(d/2 + h)$ |
| Pyramid    $A$ Area of base <br> $h$ Height | $V = \dfrac{1}{3} A \cdot h$ |
| Circular cone | $V = \dfrac{\pi \cdot d^2 \cdot h}{12} = 0.262\, d^2 \cdot h$ <br> $M = \dfrac{\pi \cdot d \cdot s}{2} = \dfrac{\pi \cdot d}{4} \sqrt{d^2 + 4h^2} = 0.785\, d \cdot \sqrt{d^2 + 4h^2}$ |
| Truncated cone | $V = \dfrac{\pi \cdot h}{12} (D^2 + D \cdot d + d^2) = 0.262\, h\,(D^2 + D \cdot d + d^2)$ <br> $M = \dfrac{\pi\,(D + d)\, s}{2} \quad s = \sqrt{\dfrac{(D - d)^2}{4} + h^2}$ |
| Sphere | $V = \dfrac{\pi \cdot d^3}{6} = 0.524\, d^3$ <br> $S = \pi \cdot d^2$ |
| Spherical segment <br> (spherical cap) | $V = \dfrac{\pi \cdot h}{6} (3\,a^2 + h^2) = \dfrac{\pi \cdot h^2}{3}\,(3r - h)$ <br> $M = 2\,\pi \cdot r \cdot h = \pi\,(a^2 + h^2)$ |
| Spherical sector | $V = \dfrac{2\,\pi \cdot r^2 \cdot h}{3} = 2.094\, r^2 \cdot h$ <br> $S = \pi \cdot r\,(2h + a)$ |
| Spherical segment <br> of two bases <br><br> $r$ Radius of sphere | $V = \dfrac{\pi \cdot h}{6}\,(3\,a^2 + 3b^2 + h^2)$ <br> $M = 2\,\pi \cdot r \cdot h$ |
| Torus <br> ring | $V = \dfrac{\pi^2}{4}\, D \cdot d^2 = 2.467\, D \cdot d^2$ <br> $S = \pi^2 \cdot D \cdot d = 9.870\, D \cdot d$ |
| Ellipsoid    $d_1, d_2, d_3$ Length <br> of axes | $V = \dfrac{\pi}{6}\, d_1 \cdot d_2 \cdot d_3 = 0.524\, d_1 \cdot d_2 \cdot d_3$ |
| Circular cask $D$ Diameter at bung <br> $d$ Diameter at base <br> $h$ Distance between bases | $V \approx \dfrac{\pi \cdot h}{12}\,(2\,D^2 + d^2) \approx 0.26\, h\,(2\,D^2 + d^2)$ |
| Pappus' centroid <br> theorem | The volume of a body of revolution is equal to the generatrix area $A$ multiplied by the distance traveled by the centroid $V = 2\,\pi \cdot r \cdot A$. |

# Strength of materials

## Symbols and units

| Quantity | | Unit |
|---|---|---|
| $A$ | Cross-sectional area | mm² |
| $B$ | Stress (general) | N, N·mm, MPa |
| $C_G$ | Size factor | – |
| $C_L$ | Load factor | – |
| $C_{Lb}$ | Bending load factor | – |
| $C_{Lt}$ | Torsional load factor | – |
| $C_M$ | Mean-stress factor | – |
| $C_O$ | Surface factor | – |
| $C_R$ | Surface factor | – |
| $C_T$ | Temperature factor | – |
| $C_U$ | Ambient factor | – |
| $C_W$ | Material factor | – |
| $d$ | Damage factor | – |
| $D_c$ | Critical damage factor | – |
| $d$ | Diameter | mm |
| $d_{eff}$ | Effective diameter | mm |
| $E$ | Modulus of elasticity | MPa |
| $F$ | Force | N |
| $F_K$ | Critical buckling load | N |
| $F_Q$ | Transverse force | N |
| $G$ | Shear modulus or modulus of elasticity | MPa |
| $H$ | Static area moment of inertia, 1st order | mm³ |
| $Ia$ | Axial area moment of inertia, 2nd order | mm⁴ |
| $I_{min}$ | Minimum area moment of inertia | mm⁴ |
| $I_p$ | Polar area moment of inertia | mm⁴ |
| $I_t$ | Torsional area moment of inertia | mm⁴ |
| $K_f$ | Fatigue-strength reduction factor | – |
| $K_t$ | Stress concentration factor | – |
| $K_{to}$ | Stress concentration factor, direct stress | – |
| $K_{tt}$ | Stress concentration factor, shear stress | – |
| $K_\sigma$ | Characteristic according to direct-stress time history | MPa |
| $K_\tau$ | Characteristic according to shear-stress time history | MPa |
| K | Inclination exponent of fatigue strength for finite life lines | – |
| $k_S$ | Cross-sectional stress concentration factor for shear strain | – |
| $k_R$ | Inclination exponent for cracked components | – |
| $l$ | Bar length | mm |
| $l_K$ | Buckling length (Euler) | mm |
| $M_b$ | Bending moment | N·mm |
| $Mt$ | Torsional moment | N·mm |
| $M_\sigma$ | Mean-stress susceptibility (direct stress) | – |
| $M_\tau$ | Mean-stress susceptibility (shear stress) | – |
| $N$ | Number of vibration cycles | – |
| $N_D$ | Limit vibration-cycle number | – |
| $N_R$ | Reference number of vibration cycles | – |

| Quantity | | Unit |
|---|---|---|
| $N_{90}$ | Number of vibration cycles 90% failure probability | – |
| $n$ | Number of vibration cycles | – |
| $n_\chi$ | Fatigue support factor (dynamic) | – |
| $n_{pl}$ | Fatigue support factor (static) | – |
| $q$ | Ductility parameter for semiductile materials | – |
| $P_A$ | Failure probability | % |
| $P_Ü$ | Survival probability | % |
| $p$ | Internal pressure | bar |
| $R$ | Resistance (general) | N, N·mm, MPa |
| $R$ | Stress ratio | – |
| $Re$ | Yield point (general) | MPa |
| $R_m$ | Tensile strength | MPa |
| $R_{mk}$ | Notch-tensile strength | MPa |
| $R_{p0.01}$ | Technical limit of elasticity | MPa |
| $R_{p0.02}$ | 0.2% yield strength | MPa |
| $R_z$ | Surface roughness | µm |
| $r$ | Ratio, torsion/tension/compression characteristic | – |
| $S$ | Safety factor | – |
| $S_N$ | Safety in lifetime | – |
| $T$ | Temperature | °C |
| $T_N$ | Spread (lifetime) | – |
| $T_S$ | Spread (stresses) | – |
| $W_b$ | Section modulus against bending | mm³ |
| $W_t$ | Section modulus against torsion | mm³ |
| $w$ | Deflection | mm |
| x,y,z | Coordinates | mm |
| $\chi^*$ | Specific strain gradient | rpm |
| $\gamma$ | Shear strain (angular distortion) | |
| $\varepsilon$ | Elongation | |
| $\varepsilon_{max}$ | Maximum elongation (notch root) | |
| $\varphi$ | Angle of rotation | rad |
| $\lambda$ | Slenderness ratio | – |
| $\lambda_G$ | Limit slenderness ratio | – |
| $\mu$ | Poisson's ratio | – |
| $\varrho$ | Notch radius | mm |
| $\sigma$ | Direct stress | MPa |
| $\sigma_a$ | Stress amplitude | MPa |
| $\sigma_A$ | Endurable stress amplitude | MPa |
| $\sigma_{AD}$ | Fatigue-limit amplitude | MPa |
| $\sigma_{AR}$ | Reference amplitude | MPa |
| $\sigma_{Astat}$ | Static limitation of Wöhler curve | MPa |
| $\sigma_b$ | Bending stress | MPa |
| $\sigma_{bW}$ | Fatigue limit under reversed bending stresses | MPa |
| $\sigma_{dP}$ | Compression proportionality limit | MPa |
| $\sigma_{max}$ | Maximum stress (notch root) | MPa |
| $\sigma_m$ | Mean stress | MPa |
| $\sigma_n$ | Nominal stress | MPa |
| $\sigma_{nB}$ | Nominal stress at rupture (notch-tensile strength) | MPa |
| $\sigma_{nk}$ | Nominal stress at notch cross-section | MPa |
| $\sigma_{npl}$ | Nominal stress beyond elastic limit | MPa |

| Quantity | | Unit |
|---|---|---|
| $\sigma_o$ | Maximum stress | MPa |
| $\sigma_{Sch}$ | Fatigue strength under pulsating stresses (compression/tension) (peak-to-peak displacement) | MPa |
| $\sigma_u$ | Minimum stress | MPa |
| $\sigma_v$ | Reduced stress | MPa |
| $\sigma_{zdW}$ | Fatigue strength under reversed alternating stresses (compression/tension) | MPa |
| $\sigma_{H1,H2,H3}$ | Principal stress (unordered) | MPa |
| $\sigma_{1,2,3}$ | Principal stress (algebraically ordered) | MPa |
| $\sigma_{10}$ | Stress amplitude for 10% failure probability | MPa |
| $\sigma_{90}$ | Stress amplitude for 90% failure probability | MPa |
| $\tau$ | Shear stress | MPa |
| $\tau_a$ | Shear-stress amplitude | MPa |
| $\tau_m$ | Mean shear stress | MPa |
| $\tau_n$ | Nominal shear stress | MPa |
| $\tau_t$ | Torsional stress | MPa |
| $\tau_{tB}$ | Shear strength (torsion) | MPa |
| $\tau_{tW}$ | Fatigue limit under reversed torsional stress | MPa |

### References:

Assmann, B.: Technische Mechanik. (Industrial Mechanics) Band 2: Festigkeitslehre. (Vol. 2: Strength mechanics) 14. Auflage, München: Oldenbourg-Verlag, 1999.
FKM-Richtlinie: Rechnerischer Sicherheitsnachweis für Maschinenbauteile. (FKM Guideline: Calculated Proof of Safety for Engineering Components) VDMA-Verlag, Frankfurt: 3. Auflage, 1998.
Holzmann, G., Meyer, H. and Schumpich, G.: Technische Mechanik. (Industrial Mechanics) Teil 3: Festigkeitslehre. (Part 3: Strength Mechanics) 7. Auflage, Stuttgart: Teubner-Verlag, 1990.
Issler, L., Ruoß. H. und Häfele, P.: Festigkeitslehre – Grundlagen. (Strength Mechanics – Basics) 2. Auflage, Berlin Heidelberg New York: Springer-Verlag, 1997.
Leitfaden für eine Betriebsfestigkeitsrechnung, Empfehlung zur Lebensdauerabschätzung von Maschinenbauteilen. (Guideline for Operational Integrity Calculation, Recommendations on Lifetime Estimation for Engineering Components) Verein Deutscher Eisenhüttenleute (VDEh). 4. Auflage, Düsseldorf: Verlag Stahleisen, 2000.
Radaj, D.: Ermüdungsfestigkeit. (Fatigue Strength) Berlin: Springer-Verlag, 1995.
Roark's Formulas for Stress and Strain. Young, W.C. (ed.). 6th Edition, New York: McGraw-Hill, 1989.
Wittenburg, J. and Pestel, E.: Festigkeitslehre. Ein Lehr- und Arbeitsbuch. (Strength Mechanics. Study and Workbook) 3. Auflage, Springer-Verlag: Berlin-Heidelberg, 2001.

## Basic principles of material strength

### Function and basic principle of material strength

Material strength is the technical and scientific field concerned with the optimized shaping, dimensioning, and design of mechanical-engineering components. It helps to quantify and assess the operating safety of components, and thus provides the basic principles for safeguarding the integrity and availability of mechanical engineering systems throughout the design period.

Another important role of material strength is to select suitable materials, machining and quality-assurance procedures, and the inspection and optimization of work processes.

The basic principle for fulfilling these tasks consists of limiting the stress occurring at high-stress points on components (hot spots) in comparison with the limit stress which results in failure. It is also necessary to limit integral and local deformation in order to safeguard the functionality of the component.

### Types of failure

Proper design is intended to prevent components from failing in service with an appropriate margin of safety. Failure here means the loss or imminent loss of functionality. The main types of failure are:
- Unacceptably high elastic or plastic deformation (e.g. yield)
- Instability (exhausting the failure load capability, e.g. collapse, buckling)
- Incipient cracking and fracture (e.g. fatigue fracture)

A considerable impact on failure is exerted by the time history of the stress (static, pulsating, shock), or by ambient conditions such as temperature (e.g. time-fracture failure, creep fatigue), corrosion (e.g. stress corrosion cracking, corrosion fatigue), and radiation (e.g. neutron embrittlement).

The importance of material toughness for failure cannot be overstated, although the characteristic toughness values are usually not directly included in strength analysis. The inherent safety of a tough component is primarily derived from the notch insensitivity associated with toughness (high failure load capability, failure tolerance), deformation preceding fracture (forced elongation, forewarning), the high ultimate resilience (dynamic stress), and the crack-stop capability (leak before fracture).

**Definition of safety**
The safety of a component is essentially derived from comparing stress $B$ occurring in service under normal, test, and failure conditions with resistance $R$ of the material or component. The appropriate choice of safety margin is intended to cover deviations from the mean value caused, for example, by material imperfections, stress fluctuations, and weaknesses in the methods used, but also by human error. As $R$ and $B$ usually involve parameters with a considerable spread, it is necessary to carry out a statistical analysis (see figure).

Recent codes of practice provide a specific safety factor for both stress and resistance (e.g. steel structures, DIN 18800, and Eurocode 3). The FKM Guideline (Rechnerischer Sicherheitsnachweis für Maschinenbauteile) [Calculated Proof of Safety for Engineering Components] (VDMA Verlag, Frankfurt, 3rd Edition, 1998) contains the necessary safety factors, starting with design loads and survival-probability strength factors of 97.5%. Furthermore, this guideline states that the magnitude of the safety factor is dependent on the material group and toughness, the specified quality-assurance measures and inspections in service, and on the possible damage consequences (see table, p. 186).

**Design concepts**
The following concepts, which are derived from the failure types and their cross-sectional progression, are available for up-to-date component design:
– Nominal-stress concept
– Structural-stress concept
– Local (elongation) concept
– Mechanics crushing concept.

In the nominal-stress concept usually used in practice, the nominal stress acting in the component highest-stress cross-section is compared with the nominal stress resulting in failure. The failure stress, which is derived from calculations or component stresses, must be worked out while taking into account all the parameters determining failure.

The structural-stress concept is used primarily for welded constructions. This concept includes the secondary bending stresses (structural stresses) resulting from the geometry.

*Statistical treatment of component safety*

Density distribution $p_A$

$B$ $R$

$B,R \longrightarrow$

Probability of occurrence $P$

$0.99$

$S_{50} = \dfrac{R_{50}}{B_{50}}$

$S_1 = \dfrac{R_1}{B_{99}}$

$B$ $R$

$0.5$

$0.01$

$B_1 \quad B_{50} \quad B_{99} \quad R_1 \; R_{50} \; R_{99}$

$B,R \longrightarrow$

The scientifically more consistent <u>local concept</u> is based on the elastoplastic stress-strain paths occurring in the notch root subjected to the highest stress, and compares these paths with the low cycle fatigue curve (LCF curve) determined from elongation-monitored vibration tests on flat samples.

The <u>mechanics crushing concept</u> starts out from real or hypothetical crack-type defects in the component, and incorporates them in the strength analysis. Linear elastic fracture mechanics is suitable for instances of failure with low deformation (brittle fracture). Yield fracture mechanics (COD concept, J-integral concept) must be applied in instances of failure with greater plastic deformation (stable cracking, ductile fracture). It is important to bear in mind that fracture-mechanics analyses start from an assumption of crack-opening-monitored failure. The threat of ligament-monitored failure (collapse) must therefore also be checked ("two-criteria method").

## Component stressing

### Basic-load cases

The section variables (forces, moments) resulting from external loads and deformations in a component serve as the basis for calculating stress. The figures (pp. 164/165) show the bearing forces, moment characteristics, and bending strains resulting from beam statics for some important load cases.

A bar-shaped component can be stressed basically by three rectilinear and three rotary components (diagram on left). This results in general stress by longitudinal and transverse forces, by torsional and bending moments in the basic-load cases of "tension/compression", "shear", "torsion", and "bending". This figure also shows stress by internal pressure, which causes additional stress in the y direction. Lateral stress of this nature can also be caused by transverse-strain constraints.

### Nominal stresses

Knowledge of the area properties of the cross-section is required in order to calculate the nominal stresses in the cross-section caused by the section loads. This relates to the area moments of inertia of the zero-order $A$ (area content), area moments of inertia of the 1st order $H$ ("static area moments of inertia"), and the axial and polar area moments of inertia of the 2nd order ("inertial torque"). The calculation formulas for area $A$ for important cross-sections are listed in the Mathematics section (p. 158).

The axial area moments of inertia $I_y$ and $I_z$ must be used to calculate the nominal bending stresses at any point of the cross-section and the deformations. The table (p. 166) features the $I$ values for some important technical cross-sections.

The maximum strain at the furthest point from the neutral axis can be determined with the section modulus $W_{by}$ or $W_{bz}$, where the following is defined:

$$W_{by} = \frac{I_y}{z_{max}}, \; W_{bz} = \frac{I_z}{y_{max}}$$

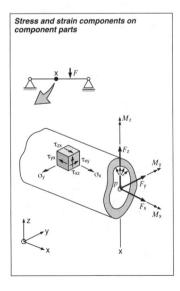

*Stress and strain components on component parts*

**Basic-load cases**
Bending case and moment curve

| Basic-load cases – Bending case and moment curve | Bearing reactions $F_A$ | $F_B$ | Maximum moment $M_{bmax}$ | Elastic line ($\alpha = \frac{x}{l}$) | Deflection | Inclination |
|---|---|---|---|---|---|---|
| **A** | – | $F$ | $F \cdot l$ | $\dfrac{F \cdot l^3}{6 \cdot E \cdot I}\,(2 - 3 \cdot \alpha + \alpha^3)$ | $w_A = \dfrac{F \cdot l^3}{3 \cdot E \cdot I}$ | $\varphi_A = \dfrac{F \cdot l^2}{2 \cdot E \cdot I}$ |
| **B** | – | $0$ | $M_0$ | $\dfrac{M_0 \cdot l^2}{2 \cdot E \cdot I}\,(\alpha - 1)^2$ | $w_A = \dfrac{M_0 \cdot l^2}{2 \cdot E \cdot I}$ | $\varphi_A = \dfrac{M_0 \cdot l}{E \cdot I}$ |
| **C** | – | $q_0 \cdot l$ | $\dfrac{q_0 \cdot l^2}{2}$ | $\dfrac{q_0 \cdot l^4}{24 \cdot E \cdot I}\,(3 - 4 \cdot \alpha + \alpha^4)$ | $w_A = \dfrac{q_0 \cdot l^4}{8 \cdot E \cdot I}$ | $\varphi_A = \dfrac{q_0 \cdot l^3}{6 \cdot E \cdot I}$ |
| **D** $a > b$ | $F \cdot \dfrac{b}{l}$ | $F \cdot \dfrac{a}{l}$ | $F \cdot \dfrac{a \cdot b}{l}$ | $0 \le x_1 \le a:$ $\dfrac{F \cdot l^3}{6 \cdot E \cdot I} \cdot \dfrac{b}{l} \cdot \dfrac{x_1}{l}\left[1 - \left(\dfrac{b}{l}\right)^2 - \left(\dfrac{x_1}{l}\right)^2\right]$ $0 \le x_2 \le b:$ $\dfrac{F \cdot l^3}{6 \cdot E \cdot I} \cdot \dfrac{a}{l} \cdot \dfrac{x_2}{l}\left[1 - \left(\dfrac{a}{l}\right)^2 - \left(\dfrac{x_2}{l}\right)^2\right]$ | $w_C = \dfrac{F \cdot a^2 \cdot b^2}{3 \cdot E \cdot I \cdot l}$ $w_m = \dfrac{F \cdot b \sqrt{(l^2 - b^2)^3}}{9 \cdot \sqrt{3} \cdot E \cdot I \cdot l}$ with $x_m = \sqrt{\dfrac{1}{3}(l^2 - b^2)}$ | $\varphi_A = \dfrac{F \cdot a \cdot b}{6 \cdot E \cdot I \cdot l}\,(l + b)$ $\varphi_B = \dfrac{F \cdot a \cdot b}{6 \cdot E \cdot I \cdot l}\,(l + a)$ $\varphi_C = \dfrac{F \cdot a \cdot b}{3 \cdot E \cdot I \cdot l}\,(a - b)$ |

| | $A$ | $B$ | $M$ | $w(x)$ | $w_{max}$ | $\varphi$ |
|---|---|---|---|---|---|---|
| **E** | $\dfrac{M_0}{l}$ | $-\dfrac{M_0}{l}$ | $a>b:$ $\dfrac{M_0\cdot a}{l}$ <br> $a<b:$ $\dfrac{M_0\cdot b}{l}$ | $0\le x\le a:$ $\dfrac{M_0\cdot l^2}{6\cdot E\cdot I}\cdot\alpha\left(1-3\left(\dfrac{b}{l}\right)^2-\alpha^2\right)$ <br> $a\le x\le l:$ $\dfrac{M_0\cdot l^2}{6\cdot E\cdot I}\cdot(1-\alpha)\left(3\cdot(\alpha)^2-2\cdot+\alpha^2\right)$ | $w_C=\dfrac{M_0\cdot a\cdot b}{3\cdot E\cdot I\cdot l}(a-b)$ <br> $w_m=\dfrac{M_0\cdot z_m^3}{3\cdot E\cdot I\cdot l}$ <br> with $z_m=l\sqrt{\dfrac{1}{3}-\left(\dfrac{b}{l}\right)^2}$ | $\varphi_A=-\dfrac{M_0}{6\cdot E\cdot I\cdot l}(l^2-3\cdot b^2)$ <br> $\varphi_C=+\dfrac{M_0}{3\cdot E\cdot I\cdot l}(l^2-3\cdot a\cdot b)$ <br> $\varphi_B=-\dfrac{M_0}{6\cdot E\cdot I\cdot l}(l^2-3\cdot a^2)$ |
| **F** | $\dfrac{q_0\cdot l}{2}$ | $\dfrac{q_0\cdot l}{2}$ | $\dfrac{q_0\cdot l^2}{8}$ | $\dfrac{q_0\cdot l^4}{24\cdot E\cdot I}\cdot\alpha(1-2\alpha^2+\alpha^3)$ | $w_m=\dfrac{5}{384}\cdot\dfrac{q_0\cdot l^4}{E\cdot I}$ | $\varphi_A=-\varphi_B=\dfrac{q_0\cdot l^3}{24\cdot E\cdot I}$ |
| **G** | $\dfrac{3}{8}\cdot q_0\cdot l$ | $\dfrac{5}{8}q_0\cdot l$ | $M_b=-\dfrac{1}{8}\cdot q_0\cdot l^2$ <br> $M_M=\dfrac{9}{128}q_0\cdot l^2$ <br> with $x_m=\dfrac{3}{8}l$ | $\dfrac{q_0\cdot l^4}{48\cdot E\cdot I}\cdot\alpha(1-3\alpha^2+2\alpha^3)$ | $w_m=\dfrac{q_0\cdot l^4}{185\cdot E\cdot I}$ <br> with $x_m=0.422\cdot l$ | $\varphi_A=-\dfrac{q_0\cdot l^3}{48\cdot E\cdot I}$ |
| **H** | $\dfrac{q_0\cdot l}{2}$ | $\dfrac{q_0\cdot l}{2}$ | $M_A=M_B$ $=-\dfrac{1}{12}\cdot q_0\cdot l^2$ <br> $M_M=\dfrac{1}{24}q_0\cdot l^2$ | $\dfrac{q_0\cdot l^4}{24\cdot E\cdot I}\cdot\alpha^2(1-\alpha)^2$ | $w_m=\dfrac{q_0\cdot l^4}{384\cdot E\cdot I}$ | — |

**Section moduli and 2nd order area moments of inertia**
*NA = neutral axis (line of zero stress)*

| Cross-section | Section modulus $W_b$ under bending $W_t$ under torsion | Area moments of inertia, 2nd order $I_a$ axial, referred to NA $I_p$ polar, referred to centroid |
|---|---|---|
| | $W_b = 0.098\, d^3$ $W_t = 0.196\, d^3$ | $I_a = 0.049\, d^4$ $I_p = 0.098\, d^4$ |
| | $W_b = 0.098\,(d^4 - d_0^4)/d$ $W_t = 0.196\,(d^4 - d_0^4)/d$ | $I_a = 0.049\,(d^4 - d_0^4)$ $I_p = 0.098\,(d^4 - d_0^4)$ |
| | $W_b = 0.098\, a^2 \cdot b$ $W_t = 0.196\, a \cdot b^2$ | $I_a = 0.049\, a^3 \cdot b$ $I_p = 0.196\, \dfrac{a^3 \cdot b^3}{a^2 + b^2}$ |
| | $W_b = 0.098\,(a^3 \cdot b - a_0^3 \cdot b_0)/a$ $W_t = 0.196\,(a \cdot b^3 - a_0 \cdot b_0^3)/b$ | $I_a = 0.049\,(a^3 \cdot b - a_0^3 \cdot b_0)$ $I_p = 0.196\, \dfrac{n^3\,(b^4 - b_0^4)}{n^2 + 1}$ |

for $\dfrac{a}{b} = \dfrac{a_0}{b_0} = n \geq 1$

| Cross-section | Section modulus | Area moments of inertia |
|---|---|---|
| | $W_b = 0.118\, a^3$ $W_t = 0.208\, a^3$ | $I_a = 0.083\, a^4$ $I_p = 0.141\, a^4$ |

| $h:b$ | $x$ | $\eta$ |
|---|---|---|
| 1 | 0.208 | 0.140 |
| 1.5 | 0.231 | 0.196 |
| 2 | 0.246 | 0.229 |
| 3 | 0.267 | 0.263 |
| 4 | 0.282 | 0.281 |
| 10 | 0.312 | 0.312 |
| $\infty$ | 0.333 | 0.333 |

$W_b = 0.167\, b \cdot h^2$
$W_t = x \cdot b^2 \cdot h$

(Originally flat bar cross-sections do not remain flat under torsion.)

$I_a = 0.083 \cdot b \cdot h^3$
$I_p = \eta \cdot b^3 \cdot h$

| Cross-section | Section modulus | Area moments of inertia |
|---|---|---|
| | $W_b = 0.104\, d^3$ $W_t = 0.188\, d^3$ | $I_a = 0.060\, d^4$ $I_p = 0.115\, d^4$ |
| | $W_b = 0.120\, d^3$ $W_t = 0.188\, d^3$ | $I_a = 0.060\, d^4$ $I_p = 0.115\, d^4$ |
| | $W_b = \dfrac{h^2\,(a^2 + 4a \cdot b + b^2)}{12\,(2a + b)}$ | $I_a = \dfrac{h^3\,(a^2 + 4a \cdot b + b^2)}{36\,(a + b)}$ |
| | $W_b = \dfrac{b \cdot h^3 - b_0 \cdot h_0^3}{6\,h}$ | $I_a = \dfrac{b \cdot h^3 - b_0 \cdot h_0^3}{12}$ |
| | $W_b = \dfrac{b \cdot h^3 + b_0 \cdot h_0^3}{6\,h}$ | $I_a = \dfrac{b \cdot h^3 + b_0 \cdot h_0^3}{12}$ |

In the case of areas that are contiguous, it is necessary to revert to the basic relations for area moments of inertia, which contain a parallel shift ("Steiner's principle"), and a rotation of the system of coordinates (see figure).

The nominal stresses in the cross-section result from the load components and the area properties in accordance with the relations entered in the figure (on next page). It is important to note here that the reference axes y and z are principle axes of the cross-section, in which the mixed area moment of inertia $I_{yz}$ disappears. When calculating torsional stresses, it is necessary to distinguish between open and closed thin-walled cross-sections, where an open cross-section is to be avoided if at all possible in components subjected to torsion.

The total direct stress in an area element with the centroid distance y and z is derived from the algebraic addition of the membrane stress and the bending stresses about the y and z axes:

$$\sigma_{x,tot} = \sigma_m + \sigma_{by}(z) + \sigma_{bz}(y)$$

The total shear stress results from the components of shear and torsion that are divided vectorially in the y and z directions, and can be calculated as follows:

$$\tau_{x,tot} = \sqrt{\tau_{xy}^2 + \tau_{xz}^2}$$

---

***Operations with area moments of inertia***

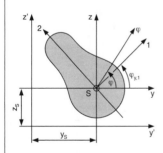

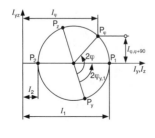

- Parallel shift of coordinate system (Steiner's principle)

$$I_y' = I_y + z_s^2 \cdot A$$
$$I_z' = I_z + y_s^2 \cdot A$$
$$I_{yz}' = I_{yz} + y_s \cdot z_s \cdot A$$

- Rotation of coordinate system

$$I_\varphi = \frac{I_y + I_z}{2} + \frac{I_y - I_z}{2} \cdot \cos 2\varphi - I_{yz} \cdot \sin 2\varphi$$

$$I_{\varphi,\varphi+90} = \frac{I_y - I_z}{2} \cdot \sin 2\varphi + I_{yz} \cdot \cos 2\varphi$$

- Principal area moments of inertia

$$I_{1,2} = \frac{I_y + I_z}{2} \pm \sqrt{\left(\frac{I_y - I_z}{2}\right)^2 + I_{yz}^2}$$

$$\varphi_{y,1} = \frac{1}{2} \arctan\left(\frac{-2\,I_{yz}}{I_y - I_z}\right),$$

for
$I_y \geq I_z$ (otherwise $\varphi_{z,1}$)

*Determination of nominal stress*

| | | Nominal stress | | Strain distribution |
|---|---|---|---|---|
| | | General | Maximum value | |
| $F_x$ | Tension/ compression | $\sigma_{xx} = \dfrac{F_x}{A}$ | $\sigma_{xx} = \dfrac{F_x}{A}$ | |
| $F_y$ | Shear y direction | $\tau_{xy} = \dfrac{F_y}{I_z} \cdot \dfrac{H_z(y)}{b(y)}$ | Centroid axis<br>$\tau_{xy}(O) = \dfrac{F_y}{I_z} \cdot \dfrac{H_z(O)}{b(O)}$ | |
| $F_z$ | Shear z direction ($F_Q$) | $\tau_{xz} = \dfrac{F_z}{I_y} \cdot \dfrac{H_y(z)}{b(z)}$ | $\tau_{xz}(O) = \dfrac{F_z}{I_y} \cdot \dfrac{H_y(O)}{b(O)}$ | |
| $M_x$ | Torsion | Circular:<br>$\tau_t(r) = \dfrac{M_x}{I_p} \cdot r$ | Outer edge:<br>$\tau_t(R) = \dfrac{Mt}{W_t}$ | |
| | | Thin-walled open:<br>$\tau_t(s) = \dfrac{M_x}{I_t} \cdot b$<br>$I_t = \dfrac{\eta}{3} \cdot \Sigma\,(l_i \cdot s_i^3)$ | Middle of widest side ($P_{max}$):<br>$\tau_t(s_{max}) = \dfrac{Mt}{W_t}$<br>$W_t = \dfrac{I_t}{s_{max}} = \dfrac{\eta}{3 \cdot s_{max}} \Sigma\,(l_i \cdot s_i^3)$<br>$\eta \approx 1$ | |
| | | Thin-walled closed:<br>$\tau_t(s) = \dfrac{M_x}{2 \cdot A_{on} \cdot s}$ | Thinnest wall ($P_{min}$):<br>$\tau_t(s_{min}) = \dfrac{M_x}{2 \cdot A_{on} \cdot s_{min}}$ | |
| $M_y$ | Bending y axis | $\sigma_{by}(z) = \dfrac{M_y}{I_y} \cdot z$ | Maximum distance from y axis<br>$\sigma_{by}(z_{max}) = \dfrac{M_y}{I_y} \cdot z_{max}$ | |
| $M_z$ | Bending z axis | $\sigma_{bz}(y) = \dfrac{M_z}{I_z} \cdot y$ | Maximum distance from z axis<br>$\sigma_{bz}(y_{max}) = \dfrac{M_z}{I_z} \cdot y_{max}$ | |

## Deformation variables

Subjecting a component to stress results in elastic or plastic deformation. The axial force causes an elongation (or compression) $\Delta l$. The transverse forces and bending moments cause a deflection $w_s$ and $w_b$ relative to the bearings. Torsion results in twisting of the cross-sections in relation to each other (angle of rotation $\varphi$). The fundamental equations for calculating these variables for linear-elastic behavior are listed in the table below.

Deformation by shearing to be taken into account at high transverse-force stresses must be calculated by integrating the transverse-force characteristic with the aid of the stress concentration factor $k_S$. Bending strain is determined using the differential equation for beam statics, which requires double integration of the bending-moment curve. The integration constants are derived in each case from the bearing boundary conditions.

## General plane strain

Technically speaking, the most important strain state is the biaxial stress state, or plane strain, which occurs on all stress-free surfaces. As the direct and shear stresses equal zero on the surface (z-normal vector), only the direct stresses $\sigma_x$ and $\sigma_y$, and the shear stresses $\tau_{xy} = -\tau_{yx}$ occur (see figure on p. 163).

Direct stress $\sigma(\varphi)$ and shear stress $\tau(\varphi)$ in any direction $\varphi$ to the x axis result from the relations set out in the table on p. 170. The relationship between $\sigma(\varphi)$ and $\tau(\varphi)$ is graphically represented in the form of a circle ("Mohr's circle").

---

*Calculation of elastic deformation*

| Load component | Type of load | Deformation relation | Deformation variable |
|---|---|---|---|
| $F_x$ | Tension/ compression | $\Delta l = \dfrac{F_x}{A \cdot E} \cdot l$ | |
| $F_y$ $F_z$ $(F_Q)$ | Shear | $\dfrac{\mathrm{d}w_s(x)}{\mathrm{d}x} = k_s \cdot \dfrac{F_Q(x)}{G \cdot A}$ $w_s(x) = \dfrac{k_s}{G \cdot A}\int F_Q(x)\cdot \mathrm{d}x$ $= \dfrac{k_s}{G \cdot A} M_b(x) + w_0$ | |
| | | $k_s$ — ● 1.1   ■ 1.2 | |
| $M_x$ $(M_t)$ | Torsion | $\varphi(x) = \dfrac{M_t \cdot x}{G \cdot I_t}$ | |
| $M_y$ $M_z$ $(M_b)$ | Bending | $w_b''(x) = \dfrac{-M_b(x)}{E \cdot I_a}$ | |

*Mohr's circle (biaxial stress state or plane strain)*

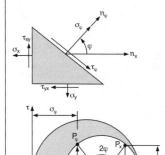

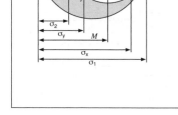

- Section stresses in direction $\varphi$:

$$\sigma_\varphi = \frac{\sigma_x + \sigma_y}{2} + \frac{\sigma_x - \sigma_y}{2} \cdot \cos 2\varphi - \tau_{xy} \cdot \sin 2\varphi$$

$$\tau_\varphi = \frac{\sigma_x - \sigma_y}{2} \cdot \sin 2\varphi + \tau_{xy} \cdot \cos 2\varphi$$

- Center of Mohr's circle:

$$M = \frac{\sigma_x + \sigma_y}{2}$$

- Radius of Mohr's circle:

$$R = \sqrt{\left(\frac{\sigma_x - \sigma_y}{2}\right)^2 + \tau_{xy}^2}$$

- Principal stresses:

$$\sigma_1 = \frac{\sigma_x + \sigma_y}{2} + \sqrt{\left(\frac{\sigma_x - \sigma_y}{2}\right)^2 + \tau_{xy}^2} = M + R$$

$$\sigma_2 = \frac{\sigma_x + \sigma_y}{2} - \sqrt{\left(\frac{\sigma_x - \sigma_y}{2}\right)^2 + \tau_{xy}^2} = M - R$$

$$\sigma_3 = 0$$

- Direction 1 to x:

$$\varphi_{x,1} = \frac{1}{2} \arctan\left(\frac{-2\,\tau_{xy}}{\sigma_x - \sigma_y}\right),$$

when
$\sigma_x > \sigma_y$ (otherwise $\varphi_{y,1}$)

### Principal stresses

Any component subjected to stress contains section directions of primary motion, in which shear stresses disappear and direct stresses assume extreme values simultaneously (see points $P_1$, $P_2$ and $P_3$ in the figure above). These directions are known as principal directions, while the extreme direct stresses acting therein are known as principal stresses.

There are essentially three principal stresses $\sigma_{H1}$, $\sigma_{H2}$, and $\sigma_{H3}$ acting in a given component. The number of principal stresses not equal to zero determines the stress state, which can be uniaxial (two principal stresses equal to zero), biaxial (one principal stress equal to zero), or triaxial (no principal stress equal to zero).

The technically preeminent case is the biaxial stress state, or plane strain, with the stress-free surface as the principal-stress plane not subjected to stress $\sigma_z = \tau_{zx} = \tau_{zy} = 0$). The calculation principles for the principal stresses for plane strain are shown in the figure.

In order to apply the strength hypotheses described below, it is important to place the principal stresses in algebraically ascending order. The result of this categorization can be described as follows:

$$\sigma_1 = \max\{\sigma_{H1}, \sigma_{H2}, \sigma_{H3}\}$$

$$\sigma_3 = \min\{\sigma_{H1}, \sigma_{H2}, \sigma_{H3}\}$$

**Effective or reduced stress**

When calculating the strength of components, it is necessary to compare component stress with any multiaxial stress state with the characteristic material parameters determined (mostly) under uniaxial stress. To solve this problem, there are strength hypotheses which refer the multiaxial stress state in the component to an equivalent uniaxial stress state. This is done with the aid of effective or reduced stress $\sigma_v$.

The disadvantage of defining reduced stress is that it is defined as a scalar parameter. Accordingly, a non-directional, parameter without a sign is formed from signed individual stresses. This involves an unacceptable loss of information, which has a particular impact on multiaxial vibrating stress. The reason for this is that a rotation of the principal-stress framework in the component occurs over time (see direction of greatest principal stress in the figure on p. 170), which prevents the classic strength hypotheses from being applied in unmodified form.

The choice of hypothesis depends primarily on component behavior, whereas a basic distinction must be made between brittleness and ductility.

The direct-stress hypothesis (DSH) is normally used in the case of <u>component brittleness</u>. Failure due to brittle forced rupture occurs when the greatest principal stress $\sigma_1$ reaches the tensile strength of the material $R_m$.

There are basically two strength hypotheses to describe <u>component ductility</u> or failure (yield, ductile fracture):
– Shear-stress theory (SST)
– "Mises" deformation-energy hypothesis (DEH)

Empirically, SST is best suited to describing ductile fracture, while DEH is preferable for yield and fatigue fracture. Applying SST always produces a greater reduced stress (max. 15%) than DEH, which is equivalent to a conservative design when applying SST. The SST-based reduced stress corresponds to the diameter of the largest of the three Mohr circles.

*Reduced stress*

| Component behavior | Brittle | Ductile | |
|---|---|---|---|
| Strength hypothesis | Direct-stress hypothesis (DSH) | Shear-stress theory (SST) | Deformation-energy hypothesis (DEH) |
| Stress state, triaxial $\sigma_1, \sigma_2, \sigma_3$ [1] | $\sigma_1$ [2] | $\sigma_1 - \sigma_3$ [1] | $\dfrac{1}{\sqrt{2}}\sqrt{\left(\sigma_1-\sigma_2\right)^2 + \left(\sigma_2-\sigma_3\right)^2 + \left(\sigma_3-\sigma_1\right)^2}$ |
| Stress state, biaxial (plane strain) $\sigma_x, \sigma_y, \tau_{xy}$ | $\dfrac{\sigma_x+\sigma_y}{2} + \sqrt{\left(\dfrac{\sigma_x-\sigma_y}{2}\right)^2 + \tau_{xy}^2}$ [2] | $\sqrt{\left(\sigma_x-\sigma_y\right)^2 + 4\cdot\tau_{xy}^2}$ when $R$ [3] $\geq M$ [4] $\dfrac{\sigma_x+\sigma_y}{2} + \sqrt{\left(\dfrac{\sigma_x-\sigma_y}{2}\right)^2 + \tau_{xy}^2}$ when $R$ [3] $< M$ [4] | $\sqrt{\sigma_x^2 - \sigma_x\cdot\sigma_y + \sigma_y^2 + 3\,\tau_{xy}^2}$ |
| $\sigma_x, \tau_{xy}$ | $\dfrac{\sigma_x}{2} + \sqrt{\dfrac{\sigma_x^2}{4} + \tau_{xy}^2}$ | $\sqrt{\sigma_x^2 + 4\cdot\tau_{xy}^2}$ | $\sqrt{\sigma_x^2 + 3\cdot\tau_{xy}^2}$ |

[1] $\sigma_1 \geq \sigma_2 \geq \sigma_3$, [2] $\sigma_1 > 0$ (otherwise, check with SST), [3] $R = \sqrt{\left(\dfrac{\sigma_x-\sigma_y}{2}\right)^2 + \tau_{xy}^2}$, [4] $M = \dfrac{\sigma_x+\sigma_y}{2}$

The table on p. 171 contains a summary of the reduced-stress relations for technically important load cases.

Semiductile materials require a continuous transition from DSH to DEH, which is controlled as a function of ductility via the ratio $r$ between shear factor $K_\tau$ and direct-stress factor $K_\sigma$. The FKM Guideline suggests a procedure for calculating reduced stress using the relations given in the diagram below. For ideally ductile materials, $r = 1/\sqrt{3}$ ($q = 0$) produces the DEH and, for brittle materials, $r = 1$ ($q = 1$) produces the DSH.

## Relationship between stress and deformation for linear-elastic behavior

There is a proportionality between stress and deformation in the linear-elastic range. According to Hooke's Law for a uniaxial stress state, the relationship between linear expansion $\varepsilon_x$ and stress $\sigma_x$ is governed by the following:

$$\sigma_x = E \cdot \varepsilon_x$$

Transverse strain $\varepsilon_y$ is derived from the following relation:

$$\varepsilon_y = -\mu \cdot \varepsilon_x$$

These relations contain the modulus of elasticity $E$ and Poisson's ratio $\mu$ as theoretical elasticity constants. Some values for $E$ for important material groups can be found in the "Materials" chapter (p. 250 onwards).

Plane strain (biaxial stress state) ($\sigma_z = 0$) is governed by the relationships between stresses and expansion contained in the table on p. 173.

---

*Ductility-dependent reduced stress*

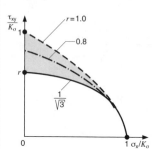

Effective stress:
$$\sigma_v = q \cdot \sigma_{v,DSH} + (1-q) \cdot \sigma_{v,DEH}$$

Ductility parameter:
$$q = \frac{\sqrt{3} - \frac{1}{r}}{\sqrt{3} - 1}$$

| Material | Steel CS | NCI | CP | GCI | Al alloy Wrought | Al alloy Cast |
|---|---|---|---|---|---|---|
| $r = \dfrac{K_\tau}{K_\sigma}$ | 0.58 | 0.65 | 0.75 | 0.85 | 0.58 | 0.75 |

---

*Evaluation 0°-45°-90° strain-gage rosette*
*(biaxial stress state/plane strain)*

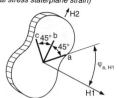

- Strains in strain-gage direction
$$\sigma_a = \frac{E}{1-\mu^2}(\varepsilon_a + \mu \cdot \varepsilon_c), \quad \sigma_c = \frac{E}{1-\mu^2}(\varepsilon_c + \mu \cdot \varepsilon_a)$$

$$\tau_{ac} = \frac{E}{2(1+\mu)}(\varepsilon_a + \varepsilon_c - 2 \cdot \varepsilon_b)$$

- Principal stresses
$$\sigma_{H1, H2} = \frac{\sigma_a + \sigma_c}{2} \pm \sqrt{\left(\frac{\sigma_a - \sigma_c}{2}\right)^2 + \tau_{ac}^2}$$

$$\sigma_{H3} = 0$$

- Direction $\sigma_{H1}$ to a-direction
$$\varphi_{a, H1} = \frac{1}{2}\arctan\left(\frac{-2\,\tau_{ac}}{\sigma_a - \sigma_c}\right),$$
when $\sigma_a \geq \sigma_c$, (otherwise $\varphi_{c, H1}$)

| **Hooke's Law for biaxial stress state (plane strain)** | |
| --- | --- |
| Deformations | Stresses |
| $\varepsilon_x = \frac{1}{E}\left(\sigma_x - \mu \cdot \sigma_y\right)$ | $\sigma_x = \frac{E}{1-\mu^2}\left(\varepsilon_x + \mu \cdot \varepsilon_y\right)$ |
| $\varepsilon_y = \frac{1}{E}\left(\sigma_y - \mu \cdot \sigma_x\right)$ | $\sigma_y = \frac{E}{1-\mu^2}\left(\varepsilon_y + \mu \cdot \varepsilon_x\right)$ |
| $\varepsilon_z = -\frac{\mu}{E}\left(\sigma_x + \sigma_y\right)$ | $\sigma_z = 0$ |
| $\gamma_{xy} = -\gamma_{yx} = \frac{\tau_{xy}}{G}$ | $\tau_{xy} = -\tau_{yx} = G \cdot \gamma_{xy}$ |
| where $G = \frac{E}{2(1+\mu)}$ | |

**Definition of stress concentration factor**

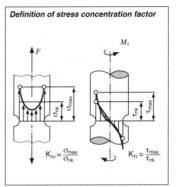

$$K_{t\sigma} = \frac{\sigma_{max}}{\sigma_{nk}} \qquad K_{t\tau} = \frac{\tau_{max}}{\tau_{nk}}$$

A 0°-45°-90° strain-gage rosette applied to the component subjected to load at any angle $\varphi$ to the x direction with strain-gage dimensions a, b, and c (positively rotated mathematically) is governed by the relations derived from Hooke's Law shown in the right diagram on p. 172.

**Notch effect**

Components demonstrate more or less marked imperfections for the internal flow of force. Diverting the flow of force results in a local increase in stress and deformation. In strength analysis, this effect is known as the "notch effect". Such imperfections are, for example, geometric notches (shoulders, grooves, threads), joints (weld seams, rivets, bonds), or fixing points (interference fits). However, surface roughness and flaws (pores, cracks) in components also act as (micro-) notches.

The failure-related points of highest-stress component (hot spots) are often determined by notches, which is why the originating point of cracks and fractures (brittle fracture, fatigue fracture) is usually located in a notch root.

The increased stress caused by a notch is quantified by the stress concentration factor $K_t$ (formerly $\alpha_k$). The stress concentration factor is defined as the ratio of the stress concentration $\sigma_{max}$ or $\tau_{max}$ occurring in the notch root, and the nominal stress $\sigma_{nk}$ or $\tau_{nk}$ referred to the notch cross-section, see figure.

The stress concentration factor is dependent on the notch geometry (notch radius, dimension to bottom of notch) and the type of stress (tension $z$, bending $b$, torsion $t$), where:

$$K_{tt} < K_{tb} < K_{tz}$$

The figure on p. 174 shows examples of stress concentration factor diagrams for notched flat and round bars.

In individual cases, it is also possible to specify closed analytical solutions to calculate the stress concentration factor. However, in the most general case, a finite-element analysis is required (p. 190). The local stress can also be determined experimentally by applying very small strain gages in the notch root.

The transverse-strain constraint in the notch cross-section at the notch root gives rise to a triaxial tensile-stress state which is more pronounced the sharper the notch, and the thicker the component walls are. In the case of very tough materials, this triaxial stress state, compared with uniaxial and biaxial stresses, results in an increase in nominal stress at rupture in the notch cross-section (but never in stability under load!). However, the reduced deformation capability associated with the constraint effect increases the risk of brittle fracture.

*Stress concentration factor diagrams* (flat bars, tube with cross hole, and round bars)

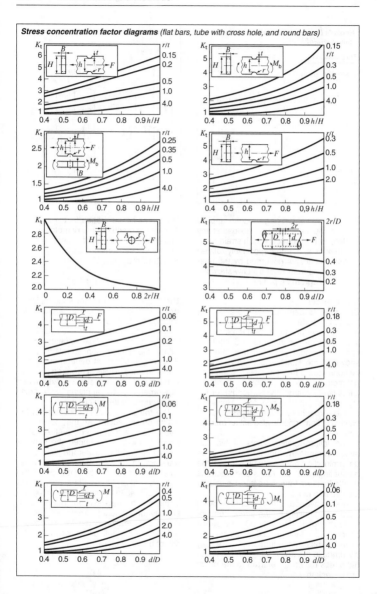

## Determining safety under static stress

### Brittle fracture

Given brittleness in an ideal case, failure due to brittle fracture occurs when the maximum reduced stress in accordance with the direct-stress hypothesis (DSH) $\sigma_{v,max,DSH}$ reaches the tensile strength of the material $R_m$. Accordingly, safety against brittle fracture is:

$$S_B = \frac{R_m}{\sigma_{v,max,DSH}}$$

For a notched bar subjected to tensile stress, the nominal failure stress $\sigma_{nB}$ ("notch-tensile strength" $R_{mk}$) is derived from the stress concentration factor $K_t$:

$$R_{mk} = \sigma_{nB} = \frac{R_m}{K_t}$$

As all the parameters making up stress (secondary bending stresses, stress concentrations, internal stresses) contribute to failure in the case of brittle failure, reduced stress must be formed from all the stress categories. This also means that, under unfavorable conditions, the nominal stress leading to failure $\sigma_{nB}$ is often well below the tensile strength. This may result in the feared and unexpected "fractures of low nominal stress".

The safety factor against brittle fracture must be relatively high, as notch and impact sensitivity, and the lack of forewarning, involve many uncertainties. Standard safety coefficients are between 3 and 5 (in individual cases, up to 10).

### Failure of tough components

The failure of components capable of deformation due to yield, collapse, and ductile fracture is summarized in the diagram below.

#### Start of yield

Start of yield occurs in a deformable component when the maximum reduced stress $\sigma_{v,max}$ in the component reaches the yield point ($R_e$, $R_{p0.01}$). Reduced stress $\sigma_{v,max}$ can be calculated according to the SST or (better still) the DEH.

The safety factor against yield is governed by:

$$S_F = \frac{R_e}{\sigma_{v,max}}$$

For a notched bar, the nominal stress resulting in yield is governed by:

$$\sigma_{nF} = \frac{R_e}{K_t}$$

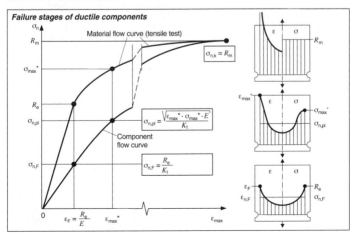

*Failure stages of ductile components*

$$\sigma_{n,pl} = \frac{\sqrt{\varepsilon_{max}^* \cdot \sigma_{max}^* \cdot E}}{K_t}$$

$$\sigma_{n,F} = \frac{R_e}{K_t}$$

$$\sigma_{n,k} = R_m$$

$$\varepsilon_F = \frac{R_e}{E}$$

Start of yield does not have any serious consequences, and yield is limited mostly to narrowly restricted component areas subjected to high stress. Therefore, it is usually sufficient to fix the safety factors against yield to values of between 1.0 and 1.5 (see table), or even to permit limited yield. This makes effective utilization of the material possible by means of its ductility reserves.

Limited plastic deformation

For tough components which are predominantly subjected to static stress, limited plastic deformation in the notch root may be permitted in many areas of application. The relationship between nominal stress in the notch root $\sigma_{n,pl}$, induced maximum elongation in the notch root $\varepsilon_{max}^*$, and maximum stress $\sigma_{max}^*$ is obtainable from the relation derived from Neuber:

$$\sigma_{n,pl} = \frac{\sqrt{\sigma_{max}^* \cdot \varepsilon_{max}^* \cdot E}}{K_t}$$

The correlation between notch-root stress and notch-root strain is provided by the stress-strain diagram obtained in the tensile test (see figure on p. 175).

A permitted total elongation in the notch root $\varepsilon_{max} = 0.5\%$ (for highly ductile materials, e.g. austenitic steels, up to 1%) can serve as the design starting point.

The ratio $\sigma_{n,pl}/\sigma_{nF}$ is known as the fatigue support factor (static) $n_{pl}$.

Collapse (ductile fracture)

When ductile components are subjected to extreme overloading, failure occurs by collapse at the ultimate load, and ultimately due to ductile fracture. The material is no longer in a position to maintain internal equilibrium in the failure cross-section subject to greatest stress by redirecting any additional stress and hardening as the load increases. Collapse is expressed by a horizontal tangent at the maximum-load point in the force-deformation diagram.

Collapse loads can be calculated using the flow-line theory under the assumption of a plane stress state (unconstrained transverse strain) or a level strain state (transverse strain totally constrained).

In the simplest case, and without taking the constraint effect into consideration, it is possible to calculate the nominal stress leading to collapse in the notch cross-section of a notched component subjected to tensile stress in accordance with the following relationship:

$$\sigma_{nk} = R_m$$

The crucial factor is that the increase in stress caused by notches no longer has a load-reducing effect. Furthermore, secondary bending stresses and internal stresses caused by yield are increasingly reduced, and this ultimately accounts for the relevance of ductility in the safety factor.

The required safety factors for ductile fracture in accordance with the FKM Guideline are set out in the adjacent table.

**Buckling of bars**

A further failure criterion, which must be observed in addition to yield and fracture in the case of bars subjected to compressive force and disks subjected to bending load, is failure caused by instability (buckling of slender bars, tilting of narrow bendable bars, denting of thin panels).

A slender bar subjected to compressive force will suddenly yield laterally when a critical compressive force is reached. If the bar is not guided, it will take place along the axis at the lowest 2nd order axial area moment of inertia $I_{min} = I_2$.

**Safety factors** against yield and fracture for ductile ferrous materials (FKM Guideline)

| Material | Destructive test | Probability of occurrence of stress | Damage consequences | Safety factor Yield | Ductile fracture |
|---|---|---|---|---|---|
| Steel | – | High | High | 1.5 | 2.0 |
| | | | Low | 1.3 | 1.75 |
| | | Low | High | 1.35 | 1.8 |
| | | | Low | 1.2 | 1.6 |
| Ductile cast iron CS, NCI (elongation at fracture $A_5 \geq 12.5\%$) | No | High | High | 2.1 | 2.8 |
| | | | Low | 1.8 | 2.45 |
| | | Low | High | 1.9 | 2.55 |
| | | | Low | 1.65 | 2.2 |
| | Yes | High | High | 1.9 | 2.5 |
| | | | Low | 1.65 | 2.2 |
| | | Low | High | 1.7 | 2.25 |
| | | | Low | 1.5 | 2.0 |

In the buckling-stress diagram shown in the figure below, the compressive buckling stress is plotted against the slenderness ratio of a bar. The buckling stress is derived differently for elastic and plastic zones. The limit between elastic and plastic buckling is defined by the slenderness ratio. The slenderness ratio $\lambda$ is derived using the buckling length $l_K$, the 2nd order axial area moment of inertia $I_{min}$, and the cross-sectional area $A$ as:

$$\lambda = \frac{l_K}{\sqrt{\frac{I_{min}}{A}}}$$

The limit between elastic and plastic buckling is described by the limit slenderness ratio $\lambda_G$, which is only dependent on the material parameters E and $\sigma_{dP}$ (compression proportionality limit). Structural steel S235 (St 37), for example, produces a slenderness ratio of roughly 100. Elastic buckling prevails if the slenderness ratio is above the limit slenderness ratio, otherwise plastic buckling prevails.

The buckling condition is crucially dependent on the clamping conditions of the bar. The influence of clamping is taken into account by introducing the buckling length $l_K$ of the bar. The buckling lengths to be used for fixed and articulated mounting are depicted in the diagram below for the four important buckling cases ("Euler's buckling cases"). It must be noted, however, that instances of ideal rigid fixing do not occur in practice, and therefore Euler's calculation may be non-conservative. The same applies to the assumption of an ideal centric stress.

In the elastic zone, the limit load $F_K$ resulting in buckling can be determined by Euler's formulas. The following applies in Euler's buckling stress:

$$F_K = \frac{\pi^2 \cdot E \cdot I_{min}}{l_K{}^2}$$

The relations featured in the diagram below must be used for buckling length.

The decisive boundary conditions for buckling failure cannot be clearly defined in may cases. Furthermore, failure occurs suddenly and usually without forewarning, and the consequences can be catastrophic. It is therefore essential to allow for high safety factors against buckling in a range between 3 and 6.

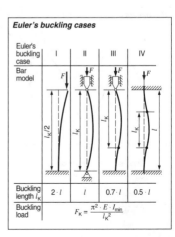

| *Buckling-stress diagram* | *Euler's buckling cases* |

## Proof of safety under vibrating stress

Virtually all technical components are subject to a transient ("vibrating") stress in service. The stress-time characteristic is usually irregularly variable. In the most general case, this requires design with operational integrity methods (next section).

Transient stress can result at the highest-stress points on the component in the failure stages "crack initiation", "cyclic crack propagation" and finally "residual forced rupture".

### Denotation of a load vibration

A load-vibration cycle (as shown in the figure) is defined by the standard parameters of vibration physics. Mean stress $\sigma_m$ and stress amplitude $\sigma_a$ are obtained from the limit values (maximum stress $\sigma_o$ and minimum stress $\sigma_u$).

Another important parameter of vibrational strength is the stress ratio $R$, which defines the relative load intensity. The technically important special cases of vibration curves are governed by:

– $R = -1$: pure alternating stress
– $R = 0$: pure pulsating tensile stress
– $R = -\infty$: pure pulsating compressive stress
– $R = +1$: pure static stress

By transformation, the relationship is obtained between the most important parameters of a vibration:

$$\sigma_m = \frac{1 + R}{1 - R} \cdot \sigma_a$$

The vibration shape and the frequency of a vibration do not play any significant role in metallic materials subjected to stress below the recrystallization temperature and without corrosive influence.

### Wöhler curve

The most important aid to assessing components subjected to load vibration is the Wöhler curve. This can be calculated mathematically (synthetically) or experimentally in fatigue-strength tests under vibrating stresses performed on samples or components.

The Wöhler curve represents the relationship between endurable stress amplitude $\sigma_A$ (or load swing $F_A$) and the fracture vibration-cycle number $N$. As the figure shows schematically, the Wöhler curve can be divided into zones denoted as "static fatigue strength", or "low-cycle fatigue", "fatigue strength of finite life", and "fatigue limit".

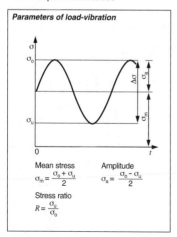

*Parameters of load-vibration*

Mean stress
$$\sigma_m = \frac{\sigma_o + \sigma_u}{2}$$

Amplitude
$$\sigma_a = \frac{\sigma_o - \sigma_u}{2}$$

Stress ratio
$$R = \frac{\sigma_u}{\sigma_o}$$

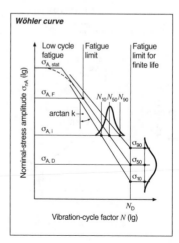

*Wöhler curve*

The static amplitude limitation $\sigma_{A,stat}$ is derived from the condition
maximum stress = (notch) tensile strength:

$$\sigma_{A,stat} \frac{1-R}{2} \cdot R_{mk}$$

The transition between low-cycle fatigue strength and fatigue strength of finite life is floating. However, it can be located approximately within the range of $10^2$ to $10^4$ vibration cycles for purely alternating stresses. This low-cycle fatigue (LCF) causes alternating plastic deformation and is the subject of the local concept, which will not be discussed here.

The limit vibration-cycle number $N_D$, which denotes the transition between fatigue strength for finite life and fatigue limit, likewise cannot be clearly established, as $N_D$ is influenced, for example, by the material, the notch effect and the $R$ ratio. $N_D$ behaves in such a way as to shift to low values for sharp notches and to increase for shallow notches. The limit vibration-cycle number $N_D$ is often simplified to $5 \cdot 10^5 ... 5 \cdot 10^6$ for ferrous metals and $10^7...10^8$ for nonferrous metals. In the case of nonferrous metals, the fatigue-limit range is approximated by a further downward fatigue strength for finite life curve with reduced gradient.

In the case of a vibrating stress in a corrosive environment ("corrosion fatigue"), a loss of lifetime in the fatigue strength for finite life range, and a steady drop in continuous vibrational strength is observed with increasing time in service. Thus, it is not possible to define a definite fatigue limit, but merely a corrosion fatigue strength for finite life. Similar behavior is encountered in the case of vibrational stress at high temperatures ("creep fatigue").

When shown in double-logarithmic form, this usually produces a linear relationship for the fatigue strength for finite life range, which can be formulated as follows:

$$\sigma_A = \sigma_{A,R} \cdot \left(\frac{N}{N_R}\right)^{-\frac{1}{K}}$$

When resolved according to the vibration-cycle number, the following applies:

$$N = N_R \cdot \left(\frac{\sigma_A}{\sigma_{A,R}}\right)^{-k}$$

Here, $N_R$ and $\sigma_{A,R}$ are the coordinates of any reference point $P_R$ on the fatigue strength for finite life lines. $k$ is the inclination exponent of the fatigue strength for finite life curve, which is determined according to the following relation:

$$k = -\frac{lg \frac{N_1}{N_2}}{lg \frac{\sigma_{A1}}{\sigma_{A2}}}$$

The inclination exponent can be used as a reference point for the quality of a component subjected to vibrating stress. For steel components subjected to purely alternating stress, it follows that:

$$k = -\frac{lg \frac{10^6}{10^2}}{lg \frac{\sigma_{AD}}{R_m}} = -\frac{4}{lg \frac{\sigma_{AD}}{R_m}}$$

For an optimized component with a ratio $\sigma_{AD}/R_m = 0.5$, this produces $k = 13$, while for a non-optimized design with $\sigma_{AD}/R_m = 0.05$, the result is an inclination exponent k = 3.

**Experimental determination of Wöhler curve**

For the purpose of determining the Wöhler curve experimentally, load-monitored fatigue-strength tests under vibrating stresses ("Wöhler tests") are carried out on samples or components to the point of fracture (but rarely to the point of cracking). The tests under sinusoidal vibrating stress are conducted with different load swings either at a constant $R$ ratio or (more rarely) at a constant mean stress.

As the test points (lifetime) sometimes show considerable spread, statistical assignment and evaluation are required (see figure on the right on p. 178, cf. also the chapter on "Statistics" on p. 214 onwards). Normal, logit, $\arcsin \sqrt{p}$, and Weibull distribution can be used as the distribution function; however, they differ considerably in the area of low failure probability. The result of evaluation results in Wöhler curves with a constant failure probability $P_A$ or survival probability $P_{\ddot{u}}$. Standard plotting consists of curves for 10%, 50% and 90% failure probability. These curves can be used to determine the spread, which is defined as follows: in vibration-cycle numbers:

$$T_N = \frac{N_{90}}{N_{10}}$$

or in stresses:

$$T_S = \frac{\sigma_{90}}{\sigma_{10}}$$

Typical lifetime spreads range from $T_N = 2$ (e.g. components carefully manufactured in metal-cutting processes) to $T_N = 10$ (e.g. weld joints). A mean value of $T_N = 5$ can be expected. In extremely exceptional cases, the spread may rise to values exceeding of $10^2$ in the case of inhomogeneous and defective components.

**Calculation of fatigue limit**
It is essential to include all the parameters influencing vibrational strength in order to determine fatigue limit by synthetic means. The standard methods correlate endurable fatigue-limit nominal-stress amplitude $\sigma_{nA}$ with tensile strength (occasionally with the yield point). Basically, the following influencing variables impact on vibrational strength and must be taken into account in the calculation by means of appropriate factors:
– material (strength, ductility) $C_W$
– type of stress (tension/compression, bending, torsion) $C_L$
– notch effect $K_f$
– surface (peak-to-valley height) $C_O$
– surface (surface treatment) $C_R$
– component size $C_G$
– environment (temperature, corrosion) $C_U$
– mean stress $C_M$

Combining the individual factors by multiplication results in the following relation for endurable fatigue-limit nominal-stress amplitude:

$$\sigma_{nA} = C_W \cdot C_L \cdot C_O \cdot C_R \cdot C_G \cdot C_U \cdot C_M \cdot \frac{1}{K_f} \cdot R_m$$

This relation explains distinctly why, in the case of non-optimized designs, the vibrational strength of a component is below 10% of the tensile strength under poor circumstances, while the fatigue limit of optimally designed and manufactured components can attain up to 50% of the tensile strength. This equation also provides decisive information on the possibilities of increasing vibrational strength, as a result of polishing, surface hardening and strain hardening, optimizing notch geometry, and corrosion protection.

It must be remembered that an increase in material strength $R_m$ does not necessarily result in an increase in vibrational strength, since (as the following shows) there is a reciprocal effect between individual factors C and tensile strength $R_m$ (see example in the figure on p. 182).

Material influence
The influence of material on vibrational strength is based on the different chemical composition, the manufacturing process, heat treatment, and after treatment. These influencing variables are detected together and in a simplifying way by means of tensile strength $R_m$ and a material-specific correlation factor $C_W$. Reference values for $C_W$ are listed in the table.

*Material and load factors (FKM Guideline)*

| Material group | Steel | Case-hardening steel | Cast steel | Nodular graphite iron | Annealed cast iron | Gray cast iron | Al alloys Wrought | Cast |
|---|---|---|---|---|---|---|---|---|
| $C_W$ | 0.45 | 0.40 | 0.34 | 0.34 | 0.28 | 0.30 | 0.30 | 0.30 |
| $C_{Lb}$ | 1.10 | 1.10 | 1.15 | 1.30 | 1.40 | 1.50 | $\approx 1.1$ | $\approx 1.5$ |
| $C_{Lt}$ | 0.58 | 0.58 | 0.58 | 0.65 | 0.75 | 0.85 | 0.58 | 0.75 |

### Type of stress

The difference between vibrational strength for tensile/compression stress and for bending stress is derived firstly from the support effect of the strain gradient for bending, and secondly from the favorable effect of compressive bending stress (above all, with less ductile materials). The increase in fatigue strength under reversed bending stress $\sigma_{bW}$ compared with fatigue strength under reversed tensile/compression stress $\sigma_{zdW}$ is expressed by the load factor $C_{Lb}$ (see $C_{Lb}$ values in the table on p. 180).

It is always possible to convert the fatigue limit under reversed torsional stress $\tau_{tW}$ from the fatigue limit under reversed tensile/compression stress $\sigma_{zdW}$ using the strength hypotheses, which predict a value of $C_{Lt} = \tau_W/\sigma_{zdW} = 1.0$ for ideal brittleness in accordance with the DSH, and $\tau_W/\sigma_{zdW} = 1/\sqrt{3} = 0.58$ for ideal ductility in accordance with the DEH. The factors for semiductile materials are situated between these limits (see also figure on the left on p. 56). The values used for $C_{Lt}$ can be taken from the table on p. 180.

### Consideration of notch effect

The effect of notches under vibrating stress is taken into consideration by the fatigue-strength reduction factor $K_f$ (formerly $\beta_k$). The fatigue-strength reduction factor is defined as the quotient of the fatigue limit of a flat component $\sigma_{AD,flat}$ to the fatigue limit of the notched component $\sigma_{AD,notched}$:

$$K_f = \frac{\sigma_{AD,flat}}{\sigma_{AD,notched}}$$

$K_f$ depends primarily on notch acuity (stress concentration factor $K_t$), but also on the material and its properties (above all ductility), as well as the strain gradient at the notch root. The limit values of the fatigue-strength reduction factor are:
– $K_f = K_t$: full notch effect
– $K_f = 1$: no notch effect

The difference between $K_t$ and $K_f$ can be explained by the dynamic support effect introduced by Siebel and Neuber, which is dependent on the material (ductility), the size of the process zone, and the strain gradient.

The fatigue-strength reduction factor according to Siebel and Stiehler is calculated using the dynamic fatigue support factor $n_\chi$ by way of the relation:

$$K_f = \frac{K_t}{n_\chi}$$

The dynamic fatigue support factor is determined using the specific strain gradient $\chi^*$, which can be calculated approximatively from the notch radius $\rho$:

$$\chi^* = \frac{2}{\rho} \quad \text{for tension/compression and bending}$$

$$\chi^* = \frac{1}{\rho} \quad \text{for torsion}$$

The diagrams shown in the figure show how to determine the dynamic fatigue support factor $n_\chi$ as a function of the specific strain gradient $\chi^*$ and the material.

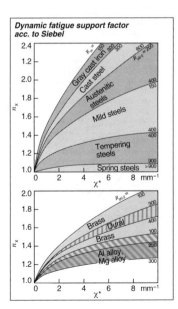

*Dynamic fatigue support factor acc. to Siebel*

Experience shows that the empirical Siebel diagrams, based on test results which are 50 years old, underestimate the actual dynamic support capacity of modern materials (e.g. high-tensile steels and aluminum alloys).

## Surface

A component surface roughened by manufacture, machining, and operation can be interpreted as a micro-notched area. Accordingly, it is observed that vibrational strength decreases as roughness increases. This effect is much more pronounced in high-tensile materials than in low-tensile materials.

Surface roughness $R_z$ usually acts as the measure for identifying peak-to-valley height. The surface factor $C_O$ assumes a value of 1 for polished surfaces. Reference values for surface factors $C_O$ are listed in the diagram as a function of tensile strength and peak-to-valley height.

## Surface

As fatigue fracture starts at the surface, or at least in the area close to the surface, vibrational strength can be decisively influenced negatively or positively by altering the surface. One example of negative influence is surface decarburization. A positive influence is exerted by processes which harden the surface and at the same time introduce compressive internal stresses close to the surface (shot-peening, rolling, nitriding, case hardening). Reference values for surface factors $C_R$ are listed in the table.

## Component size

Vibration tests show that vibrational strength expressed in nominal stresses of large components is set lower than for small components. This size influence can be divided into static, mechanical-strain, and technological effects. The cause for size influence is primarily the fact that the probability of a defect triggering vibrational fatigue failure is greater in

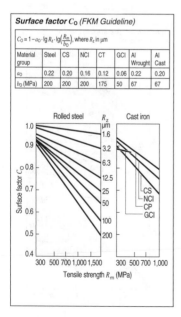

**Surface factor $C_O$ (FKM Guideline)**

$C_O = 1 - a_O \cdot \lg R_z \cdot \lg\left(\frac{R_m}{b_O}\right)$, where $R_z$ in µm

| Material group | Steel | CS | NCI | CT | GCI | Al Wrought | Al Cast |
|---|---|---|---|---|---|---|---|
| $a_O$ | 0.22 | 0.20 | 0.16 | 0.12 | 0.06 | 0.22 | 0.20 |
| $b_O$ (MPa) | 200 | 200 | 200 | 175 | 50 | 67 | 67 |

Rolled steel / Cast iron

Surface factor $C_O$ vs Tensile strength $R_m$ (MPa), with $R_z$ in µm (1.6, 3.2, 6.3, 12.5, 25, 50, 100, 200); CS, NCI, CP, GCI

**Surface factor $C_R$ (FKM Guideline)**

| | Non-notched component | | Notched component | |
|---|---|---|---|---|
| | Ø 8...15 mm | Ø 30...40 mm | Ø 8...15 mm | Ø 30...40 mm |
| **Steels** | | | | |
| Nitriding (700...1,000 HV, 0.1...0.4 mm) | 1.15...1.25 | 1.10...1.15 | 1.90...3.00 | 1.30...2.00 |
| Case hardening (670...750 HV, 0.2...0.9 mm) | 1.20...2.00 | 1.10...1.50 | 1.50...2.50 | 1.20...2.00 |
| Carbonitriding (min. 670 HV, 0.2...0.4 mm) | – | 1.8 | – | – |
| Fixed-rolling Shot-peening | 1.20...1.40 | 1.10...1.25 | 1.50...2.20 | 1.30...1.80 |
| Induction hardening Flame hardening (51...64 HRC, 0.9...1.5 mm) | 1.30...1.60 | 1.20...1.50 | 1.60...2.80 | 1.50...2.50 |
| **Cast iron materials** | | | | |
| Nitriding | 1.15 | 1.10 | 1.9 | 1.3 |
| Case hardening | 1.2 | 1.1 | 1.5 | 1.2 |
| Fixed rolling | 1.2 | 1.1 | 1.5 | 1.3 |
| Shot-peening | 1.1 | 1.1 | 1.4 | 1.1 |
| Induction hardening Flame hardening | 1.3 | 1.2 | 1.6 | 1.5 |

large areas subjected to higher stress than in small volumes. Furthermore, in the case of high strain gradients, there are fewer large component areas below maximum stress. In addition, experience shows that the mechanical and technological properties of a large component are worse than those of a small component (solidification rate, segregation, true strain).

The first two effects are taken into account by the load factor for bending $C_{Lb}$ and reduction of the stress concentration factor $K_t$ to the fatigue-strength reduction factor $K_f$. The remaining technological size influence is corrected by means of the size factor $C_G$. Factors for the technological size influence are featured in the figure below.

### Environmental influence

The most important environmental influences on vibrational strength are high temperatures and a corrosive environment.

The drop in vibrational strength as temperature increases can be explained by decreasing tensile strength and yield point. This drop is very material-specific and cannot be formulated in general terms. In the FKM Guideline, for example, the following applies as the temperature

correction factor for the fatigue strength of steels in the range from room temperature $R_T$ to 500 °C:

$$C_T = 1 - 0.0014\,(T\,[°C] - 100)$$

Above the crystal regeneration temperature, it is important to note the increasing creep tendency of materials, which, in combination with a vibrating stress, results in the complex damage mechanism termed "creep fatigue".

A corrosive attack on components subjected to vibrating stress also results in complex damage which is generally termed "corrosion fatigue". Corrosive attack basically results in a shorter lifetime in the fatigue strength for finite life range, in a continuous extension of the straight fatigue strength for finite life line, and thus to omission of the horizontal fatigue limit in the Wöhler curve.

In the case of creep and corrosion fatigue, not only the vibration-cycle number but also the test duration have an influence on the lifetime, which is why, in these cases, the real frequencies existing in service must be simulated in tests. Time compression is no longer permitted here.

---

### Technological size influence *(FKM Guideline)*

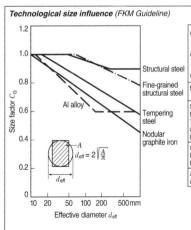

$C_G = 1$ for $d_{eff} < d_{eff,\,0}$

$$C_G = \frac{1 - 0.7686 \cdot a_G \cdot \lg\left(\frac{d_{eff}}{7.5\ \text{mm}}\right)}{1 - 0.7686 \cdot a_G \cdot \lg\left(\frac{d_{eff,\,0}}{7.5\ \text{mm}}\right)} \quad \text{for } d_{eff,\,0} \le d_{eff} \le d_{eff,\,max}$$

$C_G = C_G\,(d_{eff,\,max})$ for $d_{eff} \ge d_{eff,\,max}$

| Material | $a_G$ [mm] | $d_{eff,\,0}$ [mm] |
|---|---|---|
| Structural steel ($d_{eff,\,max} = 250$ mm) | 0.15 | 40 |
| Fine-grained structural steel | 0.20 | 70 |
| Tempering steel | 0.30 | 16 |
| Case-hardening steel | 0.50 | 11 |
| Nitriding steel | 0.20 | 100 |
| Cast steel | 0.15 | 100 |
| Nodular graphite iron | 0.15 | 60 |
| Malleable cast iron | 0.15 | 15 |

Al alloys
$C_G = 1.1\,(d_{eff}/7.5)^{-0.2}$, $12\ \text{mm} \le d \le 150\ \text{mm}$

Size factor $C_G$ (vertical axis, values 0 to 1.2) vs. Effective diameter $d_{eff}$ (horizontal axis: 10, 20, 50, 100, 200, 500 mm). Curves labeled: Structural steel, Fine-grained structural steel, Tempering steel, Nodular graphite iron, Al alloy.

$d_{eff} = 2\sqrt{\dfrac{A}{\pi}}$

## Mean-stress influence

The influence of mean stress under vibrating stress can essentially be expressed in such a way that mean tensile stress on the failure plane reduces the endurable stress amplitude, while mean compression stress increases the endurable amplitude.

The connection between the endurable stress amplitude $\sigma_A$ and the mean stress $\sigma_m$ is shown in the fatigue-limit diagram (FLD). It is customary and recommended here to adopt the Haigh approach of plotting, which involves plotting endurable fatigue-limit amplitude $\sigma_A$ versus mean stress.

The limit curve for tensile/compression and bending stress is usually represented by a straight line (see figure). The straight line represents the fatigue limit under reversed torsional stress $\sigma_W$ as the ordinate intercept, and has a gradient $M_\sigma$. At high $R$ values, the limit curve kinks to adopt a flatter characteristic. $M_\sigma$ is known as mean-stress susceptibility. Experience shows that the mean stress susceptibility of metals increases with material strength (see figure on the right). The mean-stress factor is calculated from the rectilinear limitation of the FLD:

$$C_M = \frac{\sigma_A}{\sigma_w} = 1 - M\sigma \cdot \frac{\sigma_m}{\sigma_w}$$

For torsional and shear stress, the FLD (due to the identity of the positive and negative mean shear stresses) must represent a curve mirrored at the ordinate. This finding, together with the observation that mean torsion stresses (at least within the elastic area) exert relatively little effect on vibrational strength, suggests the formulation of an elliptical FLD limit curve.

## Multiaxial vibrating stress

Treatment of multiaxial vibrating stress refers to the technically important special case of biaxial loading exerted by the direct stress $\sigma_x$ and shear stress $\tau_{xy}$ (e.g. superposition of bending and torsion) (see the figure on p. 186).

Based on the procedure for Bach's strain ratio, a suitable extended formulation is described for both the synchronous vibrating stress subjected to mean stress and the superposition of static and vibrating stress components.

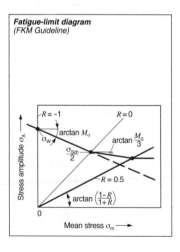

**Fatigue-limit diagram**
(FKM Guideline)

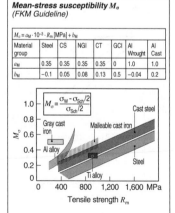

**Mean-stress susceptibility $M_\sigma$**
(FKM Guideline)

$M_\sigma = a_M \cdot 10^{-3} \cdot R_m \,[\text{MPa}] + b_M$

| Material group | Steel | CS | NGI | CT | GCI | Al Wrought | Al Cast |
|---|---|---|---|---|---|---|---|
| $a_M$ | 0.35 | 0.35 | 0.35 | 0.35 | 0 | 1.0 | 1.0 |
| $b_M$ | −0.1 | 0.05 | 0.08 | 0.13 | 0.5 | −0.04 | 0.2 |

The basic idea behind this concept is that failure is described by limit curves which progress in a σ-τ system of coordinates from the characteristic value $K_\sigma$ in accordance with the time history of σ to the characteristic value $K_\tau$ in accordance with the time history of τ. This results in a parabolic limit curve for brittle materials according to DSH, and an elliptical limit curve for ductile materials according to SST/DEH (see figure).

The equation for the limit ellipse is as follows:

$$\tau = K_\tau \sqrt{1 - \left(\frac{\sigma}{K_\sigma}\right)^2}$$

For working point B with coordinates σ and τ, this produces a safety against failure:

$$S_D = \frac{1}{\sqrt{\left(\frac{\sigma}{K_\sigma}\right)^2 + \left(\frac{\tau}{K_\tau}\right)^2}}$$

The variables used in this equation for various load combinations are listed in the table on the next page.

The graphical solution for safety is derived (see diagram on the right) from a comparison of working point B with limit curve G, i.e. from yield ratio:

$$S_D = \frac{\overline{OG}}{\overline{OB}}$$

### Required safety against fatigue fracture

The table at the bottom of p. 186 shows the minimum safety factors suggested in the FKM Guideline for protection against fatigue fracture. These safety factors apply, provided that the design loads are safe and reliable, and the survival probability of the strength measures is $P_Ü = 97.5\%$.

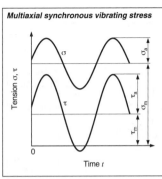

*Multiaxial synchronous vibrating stress*

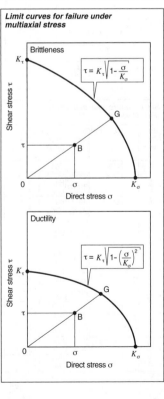

*Limit curves for failure under multiaxial stress*

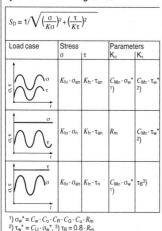

**Strength of materials under multiaxial synchronous vibrating stress**

$$S_D = 1/\sqrt{\left(\frac{\sigma}{K\sigma}\right)^2 + \left(\frac{\tau}{K\tau}\right)^2}$$

| Load case | Stress | | Parameters | |
|---|---|---|---|---|
| | $\sigma$ | $\tau$ | $K_\sigma$ | $K_\tau$ |
| (diagram) | $K_{f\sigma}\cdot\sigma_{an}$ | $K_{ft}\cdot\tau_{an}$ | $C_{M\sigma}\cdot\sigma_w^{*}$ [1] | $C_{Mt}\cdot\tau_w^{*}$ [2] |
| (diagram) | $K_{f\sigma}\cdot\sigma_n$ | $K_{ft}\cdot\tau_{an}$ | $R_m$ | $C_{Mt}\cdot\tau_w^{*}$ [2] |
| (diagram) | $K_{f\sigma}\cdot\sigma_{an}$ | $K_{ft}\cdot\tau_n$ | $C_{M\sigma}\cdot\sigma_w^{*}$ [1] | $\tau_B$ [3] |

[1] $\sigma_w^{*} = C_W \cdot C_O \cdot C_R \cdot C_G \cdot C_u \cdot R_m$
[2] $\tau_w^{*} = C_{Lt}\cdot\sigma_w^{*}$, [3] $\tau_B = 0.8 \cdot R_m$

**Safety factors against fatigue fracture (FKM Guideline)**

| Material group | Component | | Inspections | Damage consequences | Safety factors for fatigue limit $S_D$ |
|---|---|---|---|---|---|
| Rolled steel | Base metal | | Not regular | High | 1.5 |
| | | | | Low | 1.3 |
| | | | Regular | High | 1.35 |
| | | | | Low | 1.2 |
| | Welding | | Not regular | High | 1.9 |
| | | | | Low | 1.6 |
| | | | Regular | High | 1.7 |
| | | | | Low | 1.5 |
| Ductile cast-iron materials ($A_5 \geq 12.5\%$) | Untested castings | Base metal | Not regular | High | 2.1 |
| | | | | Low | 1.8 |
| | | | Regular | High | 1.9 |
| | | | | Low | 1.7 |
| | | Welding | Not regular | High | 2.6 |
| | | | | Low | 2.25 |
| | | | Regular | High | 2.4 |
| | | | | Low | 2.1 |
| | Destructive-tested castings | Base metal | Not regular | High | 1.9 |
| | | | | Low | 1.65 |
| | | | Regular | High | 1.7 |
| | | | | Low | 1.5 |
| | | Welding | Not regular | High | 2.5 |
| | | | | Low | 2.0 |
| | | | Regular | High | 2.1 |
| | | | | Low | 1.9 |

## Introduction to operational integrity calculation

The operational integrity calculation is concerned with determining the lifetime of components under real operating loads. Most engineering components vary stochastically with time. Proof of safety is basically performed on an experimental basis, or on the basis of mathematical calculation through the use of a damage-accumulation hypothesis.

The operational integrity calculation permits the specific shifting of stress to the fatigue strength for finite life range. In turn, this makes it possible to obtain an economical design by means of a lightweight construction.

### Procedure for operational integrity calculation

The procedure for proof of operational integrity on the basis of the nominal-stress concept is clearly shown in the figure at the bottom of p. 187. The stress curve over time is reduced using suitable counting methods to obtain a useful countable quantity in terms of material mechanics for characterizing and classifying the magnitude and number of load vibrations. The nominal-stress population obtained in this way is comparable with the synthetically or experimentally determined Wöhler curve also represented in nominal-stress values.

Using a linear damage-accumulation calculation yields a damage factor which is compared with the critical-damage factor resulting in failure in order to formulate a proposition pertaining to lifetime.

### Counting methods

Different counting methods are used, namely single-parameter methods with one countable quantity as the result (frequently used: level crossing counting procedure, range-pair counting), and two-parameter methods with two resulting countable quantities (usually rainflow counting procedure), see DIN 45 667.

The result of the level-crossing counting procedure is the number of class crossings at the rising edges of the load vibration (see example in the diagram). Counting both sides of the load limits results in plotting a limit curve for maximum and minimum values.

Range-pair counting provides the level-crossing frequency of related peak-to-peak displacements. A range pair consists of one rising edge and one trailing edge of equal size. They must have the same mean value, but can be interrupted by vibration cycles, and be composed of sections.

With the single-parameter methods, the counting result can be portrayed in the form of a load population which represents load swing as a function of frequency (see figure on the right).

Rainflow counting has gained greater acceptance on account of its grounding in material mechanics, and because mean values and amplitudes are recorded. Rainflow counting generates closed stress-strain hysteresis loops and corresponds to range-pair counting with additional recording of mean values.

A clear interpretation of the method is presented in the depiction of rainflow (example in the figure above left), and in the construction of stress-strain hysteresis loops (above centre). The result of rainflow counting is shown in the form of the rainflow matrix, which specifies the start and target classes of the counted hysteresis loops (above right).

Loops that are not fully closed at the end of counting are termed a residuum, and can be included, for example, with the number $n$ = 0.5 in the damage calculation.

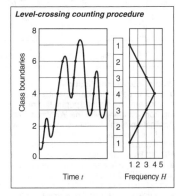

*Level-crossing counting procedure*

Class boundaries — Time $t$ — Frequency $H$

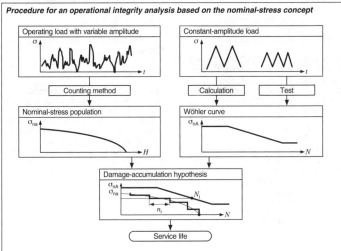

*Procedure for an operational integrity analysis based on the nominal-stress concept*

Operating load with variable amplitude
$\sigma$, $t$

Constant-amplitude load
$\sigma$, $t$

Counting method

Calculation — Test

Nominal-stress population
$\sigma_{na}$, $H$

Wöhler curve
$\sigma_{nA}$, $N$

Damage-accumulation hypothesis
$\sigma_{nA}$
$\sigma_{na}$
$N_i$
$n_i$
$N$

Service life

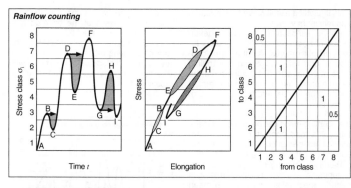

*Rainflow counting*

### Wöhler-curve modifications

In order to determine damage, it is necessary to compare the load population resulting from counting with the Wöhler curve. Application of the Wöhler curve originally used for the damage-accumulation calculation with a pronounced fatigue-limit level MO ("Miner Original") has not gained acceptance, because, in the case of variable amplitudes caused by increasing damage (i.e. decreasing fatigue limit), the load cycles below the fatigue limit also contribute increasingly to failure.

This has resulted over the course of time in various modifications to the Wöhler curve (see figure on p. 189).

#### Miner Elementary (ME) (Corten-Dolan):

The fatigue strength for finite life line of the Wöhler curve is extended to zero stress. Accordingly, the entire counting range is governed by the inclination $k$, and thus the relation:

$$N = N_D \cdot \left( \frac{\sigma_a}{\sigma_{AD}} \right)^{-k}$$

#### Miner Modified (MM) (Miner Haibach):

The fatigue strength for finite life line remains unchanged. The fatigue-limit range is described by a median between the horizontal fatigue-limit curve and the extended fatigue strength for finite life line. For this straight line, the above equation can be used with the exponent $k_{MM}$ instead of $k$:

$$k_{MM} = 2 \cdot k - 1$$

#### Miner Liu/Zenner ML:

A new Wöhler curve is introduced. It starts at the original fatigue strength for life line at the height of the maximum value of the load population $\sigma_{a,max}$, and has the inclination $k_{ML}$. The equation for this straight line is as follows:

$$N = N^* \cdot \left( \frac{\sigma_a}{\sigma_{a,max}} \right)^{-k_{ML}}$$

Value $N^*$ is derived from the original relation for the fatigue strength for finite life line:

$$N^* = N_D \cdot \left( \frac{\sigma_{a,max}}{\sigma_{AD}} \right)^{-k}$$

For the inclination exponent $k_{ML}$, the following applies:

$$k_{ML} = \frac{k + k_R}{2}$$

The inclination exponent for the crack-propagation Wöhler curve lies within a range of 3 and can be set for steels at $k_R = 3.6$.

The fatigue strength for finite life line according to Miner Liu/Zenner ends at the level of half the fatigue limit $\sigma_{AD}/2$, where it is important to bear in mind that vibration cycles below this limit do not contribute to, or contribute only slightly to, damage.

### Damage-accumulation hypothesis

According to the damage-accumulation hypothesis put forward by Palmgren and Miner, each individual load vibration contributes to damage. This share of damage $D_1$ of a vibration of amplitude $\sigma_{ai}$ is calculated from the vibration-cycle factor $N_i$ of the Wöhler curve resulting in fracture:

$$D_1 = \frac{1}{Ni}$$

If at load intensity $i$, a total of $n_i$ vibrations occurs, this produces $i$ damage at this intensity (see figure below):

$$D_i = \frac{n_i}{Ni}$$

Adding the damage factors $D_i$ at all the load intensities m produces the total damage for the counting period:

$$D_{tot} = \sum_{i=1}^{m} D_i = \sum_{i=1}^{m} \frac{n_i}{N_i}$$

The original formulation by Palmgren and Miner started with the assumption that crack initiation results when the damage factor $D_{tot}$ assumes a value of 1.

A whole range of tests has shown, however, that the critical damage factor can be distinctly below 1 (but in individual cases can also reach values of around 10 during failure!). More recent tests show that at least one limitation at $D_c \leq 0.5$ is required.

Individual adaptation of the critical damage factor to intrinsic damage factors, or those familiar from the literature, is known as the Relative Miner rule.

### Lifetime safety

Lifetime safety $S_N$ of a component is obtained using the damage factor $D_{test}$ calculated for the counting period with the vibration cycles $n_{test}$ for the design vibration cycles $n_{EOL}$ with the aid of the damage factor $D_c$ resulting in failure:

$$S_N = \frac{n_{test}}{n_{EOL}} \cdot \frac{D_c}{D_{test}}$$

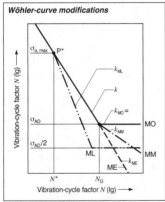

*Wöhler-curve modifications*

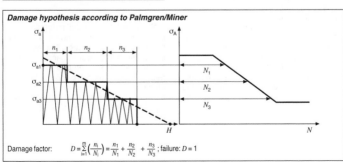

*Damage hypothesis according to Palmgren/Miner*

Damage factor: $D = \sum_{i=1}^{m} \left(\frac{n_i}{N_i}\right) = \frac{n_1}{N_1} + \frac{n_2}{N_2} + \frac{n_3}{N_3}$ ; failure: $D = 1$

# Finite-element method (FEM)

## What is FEM?

The term finite-element method (FEM) was introduced in 1960 by R. W. Clough and has been in general use since the 1970s. Virtually all technical procedures can be simulated on a computer with FEM. However, this involves breaking down any body (gaseous, liquid, or solid) into elements that are simple in shape (line, triangle, square, tetrahedron, pentahedron, or hexahedron), that are as small as possible, and that are permanently connected to each other at their corner points ("nodes"). Small elements are important because the behavior of elements formulated by approximation using linear equations is only applicable to infinitesimal elements. However, the computing time calls for finite elements. The approximation to reality is better, the smaller the elements are.

## Application of FEM

The application of FEM in practice began in the early 1960s in the aviation and aerospace industries and was also to follow very soon in automobile manufacturing. The method is based on work conducted at DaimlerChrysler AG in Stuttgart, Germany. DaimlerChrysler used a proprietary FEM program developed internally called ESEM long before computer-aided design (CAD) came onto the scene at the start of the 1980s. Since then, the method has come to be used in all fields of technology, including weather forecasting, medical science, and for many sectors of the automobile manufacturing ranging from engine and chassis components through to body calculations and crash behavior (for Vehicle bodies, passenger cars, see p. 901; for Operating dynamics for commercial vehicles, see p. 441).

## Problems in application

FEM is an approximation process. The causes of the problems that users encounter are discussed in this article.

Bodies move on paths which are normally higher-order curves. The basic principle of FEM lies in the linearization of all processes (i.e. the behavior of the real structure is described by linear equations), and this motion is limited to a straight path. However, as linear equations describe the behavior of element corners (nodes), they also move on a straight line. Thus, the nodes are only able to realize very small motions correctly (node twists < 3.5°). All nonlinear processes, such as motion along any path or nonlinear material behavior, must be solved linearly step by step.

An element describes only approximatively the behavior of an equivalent real component segment. Only an infinitesimal element delivers correct results. Finite elements, as used in practice, deliver good or bad results, depending on their formulation quality and the fineness of the network.

The linear equation system is formulated and solved with the limited computing accuracy of a computer. Usually, 8 bytes (= 64 bits) are used with a computing accuracy of 13 significant places for the number stored. The 14th digit and every further digit in this number are random numbers. As a result, this rules out the possibility of any rigidity differences in a model. In a body, therefore, the springs must be replaced by rigid bearings.

The great danger lies in the fact that a formal computation model formulated correctly by a beginner will indeed deliver impressively colorful images, but the results shown will center around factors close to reality, and will thus be completely incorrect. If the problems resulting from the above-mentioned limitations are identified by the computing program, the less experienced user will also be able to obtain correct results easily.

### Quality assurance, model error

Model ranges with an excessively coarse network can be identified and shown by an error estimator contained in the program – by stress analysis in the case of static problems, and by flux analysis in the case of potential problems. This creates the problem that an experienced user will model areas subject to low stress with coarse approximation on purpose in order to save computing time. The error estimator must therefore qualify the error by means of maximum stress or maximum flux. It must also be borne in mind that the error is dependent on the load case.

This "model error" is mostly given as a percentage, whereas there are different ways of defining the reference quantity. The relative, i.e. weighted, model error is written to a table containing details of the node or element numbers and, in many cases, as an option to the result file for graphic representation. If there are too many errors, the network in the areas that are modeled with excessive approximation should be refined in the preprocessor and the analysis repeated (this is done automatically in some programs).

### FEM program system

Network creation is mainly performed automatically in the preprocessor mostly on the basis of a CAD geometry. The FEM program calculates the computing model formulated in this way and shows the result found in graphic form in the postprocessor. Thus, an FEM program consists of a preprocessor, a postprocessor, and the actual FEM program.

## Areas of FEM application

In technology terms, physics is generally divided into five areas: mechanics, vibration and oscillation, thermodynamics, electrics, and optics. Owing to the program functions in FEM, a distinction is always made between linear and nonlinear static and dynamic problems and potentially stationary (timefree) and nonstationary (time-dependent) problems (also with nonlinear material) which are solved like nonlinear problems. An important function of an FEM program is to link these different areas, e.g. to calculate a temperature field as a potential problem, and the resulting deformations, stresses and forces in linear statics.

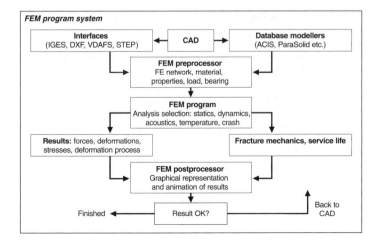

FEM program system

Interfaces (IGES, DXF, VDAFS, STEP) — CAD — Database modellers (ACIS, ParaSolid etc.)

FEM preprocessor
FE network, material, properties, load, bearing

FEM program
Analysis selection: statics, dynamics, acoustics, temperature, crash

Results: forces, deformations, stresses, deformation process

Fracture mechanics, service life

FEM postprocessor
Graphical representation and animation of results

Result OK?

Finished

Back to CAD

**Linear and nonlinear statics**

Mechanics, being the science of forces and motions in gaseous, liquid, and solid bodies, is reflected in linear and nonlinear statics. Linear statics is the problem area in which the stresses in the calculation components occur in the elastic, i.e. the linear field of the law of materials and where local shifts are relatively small, associated with minor node twists.

The second limitation is based on the fact that displacements in the load application points in the element are ignored when formulating the equilibrium conditions at the node. If these preconditions are not satisfied because of elements that are too big, or excessive deformation from rigid body motions on account of elastic bearing arrangements, the results will only be partially usable.

The basic principle of nonlinear statics involves resolution into linear stages by solving the linear equation system. This system consists of the linear elastic rigidity matrix $\underline{K}_K$ of the structure, which describes the elastic behavior of the component, supplemented by the geometric rigidity matrix $\underline{K}_L$. This takes into account the stress state of the previous steps in each case. This is followed by adding the deformations after each step, and (if desired) changing the material in accordance with the specified material curve. This means the step-by-step solution of:

$$\underline{f}_i = [\underline{K}_K + \underline{K}_L]^* \, \underline{v}_i$$

for $i = 1...n$, where
$\underline{f}_i$ vector of node forces (max. three forces $F_x$, $F_y$, $F_z$ and three moments $M_x$, $M_y$, $M_z$) and
$\underline{v}_i$ vector of node deformations (max. three shifts $v_x$, $v_y$, $v_z$ and three twists $d_x$, $d_y$, $d_z$) in step $i$ m referred in each case to the global system of coordinates x, y, z.

The first step where $\underline{K}_L = 0$ thus corresponds to linear statics; for each further step, the preconditions defined in linear statics will apply.

Both nonlinear materials and geometric nonlinearities can be taken into consideration in nonlinear statics. The total stress expressed as force, moment, deformation, or temperature field is applied in stages by load steps. The sum total of all the load steps thus equals the total stress. The steps here do not have to be of equal size. In most programs, there is an automatic breakdown into load increments, together with a step adaptation. Special programs are used for crash calculations.

**Linear and nonlinear dynamics**

Vibration and oscillation, being the science of time-dependent, wave-shape motion of gaseous, liquid, and solid bodies as inert masses, and the special case of sound, are reflected in linear and nonlinear dynamics and acoustics. Nonlinear dynamic problems, such as time-dependent damping, nonlinear material or knock problems (rattling), generally require a special program.

For linear problems, the eigenvalues and eigenvectors (natural frequencies and natural-oscillation forms) of the structure, in conjunction with an associated mass matrix made up of weights and possible additional masses for an undamped, elastic system, are determined using the following equation:

$$\underline{M} \cdot \underline{b} + \, [\underline{K}_K + \underline{K}_L] \cdot \underline{v} = 0$$

where
$\underline{M}$ mass matrix of overall structure
$\underline{b}$ acceleration vector at all nodes
$\underline{K}_K$ linear elastic rigidity matrix of structure
$\underline{K}_L$ geometric rigidity or prestress matrix of structure (with prestress only)
$\underline{v}$ vector of all node motions

The portion of the geometric rigidity matrix contains the initial-stress state of the structure and is therefore only taken into account in the case of prestress.

When solving the general motion equation, it is possible to enact different special cases of the motion equation based on modal analysis performed with damping taken into account. These include harmonic force, base-point excitation and analysis of the response spectra for seismic tests.

$$\underline{M} \cdot \underline{b} + [\underline{K}_\mathrm{K} + \underline{K}_\mathrm{L}] \cdot \underline{v} + \underline{C} \cdot \underline{w} = \underline{f}_\mathrm{r}$$

where
$\underline{C}$ = damping matrix of overall structure in diagonal form
$\underline{w}$ = speed vector at all nodes
$\underline{f}_\mathrm{r}$ = excitation vector (force vector)

**Potential stationary and nonstationary problems**
With regard to potential problems, a distinction is made between stationary and nonstationary problems. In the case of stationary problems, everything is in equilibrium, and thus time plays no role (e.g. constant heat flux). In the case of nonstationary problems, everything is time-dependent (e.g. heating up of a body).

**Analogy of potential problems**
The most common potential problems are (see table):
(a) temperature distribution $T$ from heat flux
(b) steady liquid or gas flow $s$
(c) pressure distribution $p$ (e.g. sound pressure in acoustics)
(d) magnetic field $\Phi$
(e) electric field $U$

When solving nonstationary potential problems, it is necessary to solve the following time-dependent equation:

$$\underline{P} \cdot \underline{T} + \underline{C} \cdot \delta\underline{T}/\delta t + \underline{F} = 0$$

where, in relation to a heat-conduction problem:
$\underline{P}$ potential matrix
$\underline{T}$ vector of node potentials (e.g. temperatures)
$\underline{C}$ capacity matrix
$\delta T/\delta t$ vector of potential changes per time unit
$F$ flux vector (e.g. heat flux, heat sources, sources, and sinks)

A fully implicit time-step procedure serves to solve the equation.
If the capacity matrix $\underline{C}$ and the vector of potential changes per time unit $\delta T/\delta t$ is omitted, the problem is stationary. The equation can then be compared to linear statics. In this case, the potential matrix $\underline{P}$ corresponds to the rigidity matrix $\underline{K}$, the vector of potentials $\underline{T}$ to the node deformation $v$, and the vector of flux quantities $\underline{F}$ to the node forces.
One of the highest-priority applications of this program part lies in solving heat-flux problems. When the heat-flux problem is recognized, it is possible to solve all common potential problems on the basis of the above-mentioned analogy.

---

*Analogy of potential problems*

|  | (a) | (b) | (c) | (d) | (e) |  |
|---|---|---|---|---|---|---|
|  | $\underline{T}$ | $\underline{s}$ | $\underline{p}$ | $\underline{\Phi}$ | $\underline{U}$ | Potential |
|  | grad $\underline{T}$ | grad $\underline{s}$ | – | $\underline{H}$ | $\underline{E}$ | Gradient |
|  | $\underline{\lambda}$ | $\underline{\lambda} = \underline{l}$ | $\underline{\lambda} = \underline{1}$ | $\underline{\mu}$ | $\underline{\varepsilon}$ | Material |
|  | $\underline{a}$ | $\underline{a}$ | $\underline{a}$ | $\underline{B}$ | $\underline{D}$ | Flux quantity |
|  | $\underline{Q}$ | $\underline{Q}$ | $\underline{Q} = 0$ | div $\underline{B} = 0$ | $\underline{Q}$ | Source level |

## Elements of FEM

The properties of the available elements define the most important performance data of an FEM program. The element quality determines the formulation function. Here, a distinction is made between elements with a linear or quadratic formulation along the element edge. The latter can be identified at the intermediate nodes. The quality of a computing model is therefore dependent not just on the fineness of the network used, but quite considerably on the formulation function. The existing elements can be divided into unit elements with two-dimensional projection, volume elements with three-dimensional projection, and bar elements with linear projection (see FEM application examples).

### Unit elements

Unit elements are either triangular or rectangular in shape – ideally an equilateral triangle or a square. If elements without intermediate nodes (linear displacement formulation) have unfavorable height-width ratios, it has been possible to prevent extensively (by max. 30%) the stiffening effect caused by shear (shear locking) so that good results are obtainable even with rectangular elements (see FEM application examples). Rectangular shell elements can often be slightly warped (max. 10° too stiff). For triangular elements, the included angle should not be less than 12° or greater than 156°; for rectangular elements, it should not be less than 24° or greater than 156°. However, these limits established by tests depend on the FEM program used.

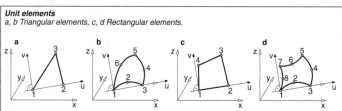

*Unit elements*
a, b Triangular elements, c, d Rectangular elements.

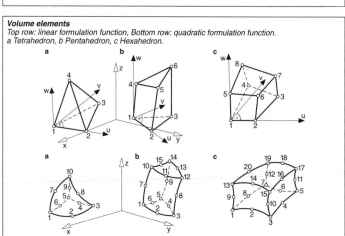

*Volume elements*
Top row: linear formulation function, Bottom row: quadratic formulation function.
a Tetrahedron, b Pentahedron, c Hexahedron.

In the case of unit elements, a distinction is made between the following stresses, regardless of the geometric shape or formulation:

- Only sectional forces in the element plane (disk or membrane), planar stress state, or planar deformation.
- Rotationally symmetrical, three-dimensional stress, and strain as a two-dimensional problem (rotationally symmetrical load) with special case of general force (Fourier element).
- Only sectional moments in the element plane (plate) with or without shear strain originating from a perpendicular transverse force.
- Three-dimensional sectional forces and moments (shell) with or without shear strain.

### Volume elements

Volume elements come mostly in the form of tetrahedrons, pentahedrons, or hexahedrons. Some programs also feature pyramids with rectangular bases. If elements without intermediate nodes (linear displacement formulation) have unfavorable height-width ratios, it has been possible to prevent extensively (max. 30 %) the stiffening effect caused by shear (shear locking) so that good results are obtainable, particularly with hexahedron elements. However, if greater accuracy is called for, elements with a quadratic displacement formulation must be used. This is especially applicable to tetrahedron elements, which are created during automatic volume networking (see application examples).

### Bar elements

As with unit and volume elements, most FEM programs offer two element types here: a straight bar element with linear formulation function and a curved bar element with quadratic formulation function. The length of the bar element is determined by its two connecting nodes. The cross-sections are described by specifying the numerical values for:

- the cross-sectional area ($A$)
- the reduced shear cross-sections $A_{red}$ (shear area)
- the principal moments of inertia ($I_x$, $I_y$)
- the torsional moment of inertia ($I_t$) with the torsional section modulus ($W_t$)
- the sector moment of inertia for warping-force torsion
- the position of the principal axes of inertia ($\alpha$)
- and the maximum four stress points ($S_x$, $S_y$) for stress calculation

These values are entered in the preprocessor under the property definition, or automatically calculated by means of the outline shape (application example 3). As the preprocessor also shows the outline shape in graphic form, this form of input is to be preferred.

In order to define a particular function, it is possible to formulate the general bar element as a tension-compression bar, as a bending bar about the 1st or 2nd principal axis of inertia, or as a torsion bar.

These options can be combined as desired. Special bar-element boundary conditions for the bar element are provided for to define links and joints, for example. Bar elements can be combined with all the remaining element types of the same formulation function.

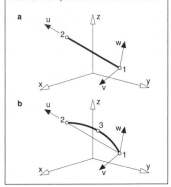

**Bar elements**
*a Straight line with linear formulation function,*
*b Curved with quadratic formulation function.*

## Modeling and evaluation of results

The most important function in using an FEM program is creating the input data with the preprocessor. Here, the user, usually taking CAD geometry as the basis (the unit of length is already defined here), transfers the real component into a computing model irrespective of its area of application in such a way as to achieve the required correspondence with reality, and thus the required accuracy of results (see application examples).

The user should try to achieve this target with as few elements and nodes as possible (a vehicle body has approx. 300,000 to 400,000 nodes) and take account that an approximation method is being used. To do so, the user requires a certain level of experience, but must have an exact knowledge of the quality of the elements used (see application examples 1 and 2). This is different in every FEM program.

The first step in modeling involves choosing the element type, determining the fineness of the network, e.g. by means of the specified middle element-edge length and carefully considering which part of the overall structure to examine. If symmetry exists, only the required part needs to be broken down into elements in order to save time and costs. However, it is customary to create a complete model if model symmetry exists, since flawed considerations are a major factor in increasing costs.

A further step involves determining bearing conditions and stresses (the unit of force and energy is defined in the material data). The crucial factor here is the points where a model is fixed, and where it is subjected to stress. In relation to stress, it is also useful to conduct a breakdown into load cases. This is because an FEM program has no difficulty in calculating a very high number of load cases simultaneously and then superimposing them.

All FEM calculation results are available in list form and/or in postprocessor format, and can therefore be shown in graphic form (as the figures accompanying the application examples show). To this end, the postprocessor offers all the conceivable forms of display, e.g.:
- Deformed and non-deformed structure with shadow effects and isocolors or isolines, also in the form of an animation or video clip (e.g. entire deformation characteristic for nonlinear calculation).
- Stresses, forces and fluxes colored arrow displays.
- XY diagrams.

The images can be exported in all standard formats to prepare an analysis report or a presentation.

## FEM application examples

For all the examples, modeling is performed on the basis of CAD geometry that uses the FEM program WTP 2000, which is available as a CD-ROM with an FEM textbook (for information and the full model inputs in color, log on to: www.IGFgrothTP2000.de).

In reality, all bodies are three-dimensional. However, the aim of simulation is to achieve a maximum in terms of quality of results with a minimum of effort and expenditure. A simple solution is often chosen in order to save time and expense.

It is much easier to realize the automatic networking of a flat surface in unit elements than it is to realize a body in its volume elements. The frequently used tetrahedron network, which nearly every preprocessor now creates for any volume geometry, does not always live up to expectations. The first example, therefore, shows a flat membrane model, followed by the volume-element model, and the mostly used shell model in the second example. This also includes the bar element commonly used in automobile manufacturing with the third example.

### Example 1: Perforated disk with membrane elements

The aim is to use the membrane element for flat, two-dimensional problems (also applies to rotationally symmetrical problems) and to compare different model qualities for four different FEM models (A...D). This makes use of the areas of application of linear statics, linear dynamics, and temperature field with a link to linear statics.

The CAD geometry is a perforated disk with dimensions of 200 x 200 mm and a 100 mm central hole. To save costs and time, only the existing quarter symmetry is used. The computing model is thus only the top left quarter in the figure. The material properties are:

Modulus of elasticity = 210,000 N/mm²
Poisson's ratio = 0.3
Density = 0.00000785 kg/mm³
Thermal conductance = 167 J/mm · sec · °C
Coefficient of linear thermal expansion = 0.00001 mm/°C

The element properties are defined in the properties with the element type "Membrane" and with:
– two node degrees of freedom $v_x$, $v_y$, ($d_z$ omitted in the case of the FEM program used here)
– constant thickness $d = 5$ mm
– linear displacement formulation (without intermediate nodes)

Networking shows the two most important methods – "freemesh" (most used) and (if possible) "mapmesh" (preferred)

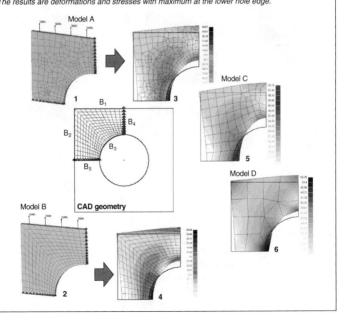

*Perforated disk with membrane elements*
*1 Fine freemesh (model A), 2 Fine mapmesh (model B), 3 Result for 1, 4 Result for 2, 5 Result, coarse freemesh (model C), 6 Result, very coarse freemesh (model D). The results are deformations and stresses with maximum at the lower hole edge.*

Model A: Freemesh with specified number of elements at edges $B_3$, $B_4$, $B_5$ (specification of only one middle edge length is also possible), 20 elements in the 90° quarter circle.

Model B: As the opposing edges are divided in the same way (edges $B_1 + B_2 = B_3$; $B_4 = B_5$), the mapmesh with the better, sought-after element quality at the hole edge is used (equal, qua-

dratic elements if possible). The division of the edges is identical to A.

Model C: Same as A, but only 6 elements instead of 20 at the hole edge for 4 elements in $B_4$ and $B_5$.

Model D: Same as model C, with 3 elements at the hole edge and only 2 elements in $B_4$ and $B_5$.

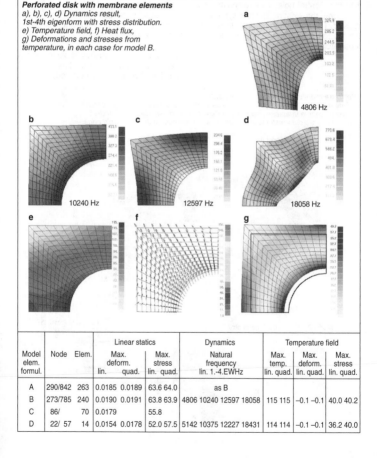

*Perforated disk with membrane elements*
a), b), c), d) Dynamics result,
1st-4th eigenform with stress distribution.
e) Temperature field, f) Heat flux,
g) Deformations and stresses from
temperature, in each case for model B.

a 4806 Hz
b 10240 Hz
c 12597 Hz
d 18058 Hz
e
f
g

| Model elem. formul. | Node | Elem. | Linear statics | | | | Dynamics | Temperature field | | |
|---|---|---|---|---|---|---|---|---|---|---|
| | | | Max. deform. | | Max. stress | | Natural frequency | Max. temp. | Max. deform. | Max. stress |
| | | | lin. | quad. | lin. | quad. | lin. 1.-4.EWHz | lin. quad. | lin. quad. | lin. quad. |
| A | 290/842 | 263 | 0.0185 | 0.0189 | 63.6 | 64.0 | as B | | | |
| B | 273/785 | 240 | 0.0190 | 0.0191 | 63.8 | 63.9 | 4806 10240 12597 18058 | 115 115 | -0.1 -0.1 | 40.0 40.2 |
| C | 86/ | 70 | 0.0179 | | 55.8 | | | | | |
| D | 22/ 57 | 14 | 0.0154 | 0.0178 | 52.0 | 57.5 | 5142 10375 12227 18431 | 114 114 | -0.1 -0.1 | 36.2 40.0 |

All the models are calculated in linear statics with and without intermediate nodes. This is done in the program simply by means of an optional setting.

Bearing conditions:
Symmetry conditions only:
in xz plane $v_y = 0$
in yz plane $v_x = 0$

Stresses:
Linear statics at constant tractive force as linear load where $F = 5,000$ N distributed to 11/9/5 nodes. Here, the two corner nodes, at which only <u>one</u> element arrives, each have half the load.
Dynamics: Only masses from intrinsic weight (0.315 kg).
Temperature field from heat transfer (convection) at hole edge $B_3$ ($T = 250\,°C$, convection constant $= 0.8$ J/mm$^2 \cdot$ sec $\cdot °C$), at left edge $B_2$ (bottom $T = 150\,°C$, top $T = 20\,°C$. Convection constant $= 2.0$ J/mm$^2 \cdot$ sec $\cdot °C$) and at top edge $B_1$ ($T = 20\,°C$, convection constant $= 4.0$ J/mm$^2 \cdot$ sec $\cdot °C$). The heat flux is zero at both planes of symmetry (no additional input required in all programs).

Conclusion:
If the maximum model error is below 15%, the network is fine enough. The type of networking (mapmesh or freemesh) no longer plays a role in this situation. Nothing further can be achieved with intermediate nodes apart from higher computing times (see table, models A and B with linear and quadratic formulation).

Different for a network that is too coarse (D). Here there is a clear improvement in results. A relatively coarse network (C) with only 6 elements at the 90° hole edge delivers, without intermediate nodes:
– the maximum stress with an error of approx. 13%
– the first 4 natural frequencies with 7/1/-3/2% error
– the temperature field and the resulting deformations with only 1% error
– the associated stresses but with 10% error

With intermediate nodes, the results are as in model B.

**Example 2: Cast-steel bracket as shell and volume-element model (linear statics)**
The aim is to compare shell and volume elements in linear statics on a relatively thick-walled cast-steel bracket. In the volume elements, four models A, B, C, and C´ are compared with significantly different result qualities (C´ corresponds to C, but with intermediate nodes). The CAD solid geometry is adopted directly by the preprocessor, and, in addition, the resulting surface model is automatically generated (this is a rare function).

The material properties are:
Modulus of elasticity = 210,000 N/mm$^2$
Poisson's ratio = 0.3
Density = 0.00000785 kg/mm$^3$

The element properties are defined in the properties with the element type "Solid", each with a linear displacement formulation (without intermediate nodes). With three node degrees of freedom $v_x$, $v_y$ and $v_z$ for models A–C´ and "Plate" (as the "Shell" element is called in the preprocessor); with six node degrees of freedom $v_x$, $v_y$, $v_z$ and $d_x$, $d_y$, $d_z$, and constant thickness $d = 3.75$ mm. In model A, the solid networking shows the preferred breakdown into hexahedrons (not fully automatically possible for all geometries), and, in models B and C, the automatic tetrahedron networking. The number of elements in relation to the thickness is specified.

Bearing conditions:
On the rectangular xz plane, $v_y = 0$ applies to all nodes. All the edge nodes on the right, long leg are governed by $v_x = 0$, and those of the lower, short leg are governed by $v_z = 0$.

Stresses:
$\sum F_x = 1,285$ N
$\sum F_y = 2,006$ N
$\sum F_z = -550$ N

All the loads are defined as surface load (pressure) at the small hole at $F_y = 2,006$ N, and at the big hole at $F_x = 985$ N, or as load distributed "manually" to the nodes at the opening $F_x = 300$ N, and at the big hole $F_z = -550$ N.

***Cast-steel bracket as shell and volume-element model A*** *(hexahedron network)*
*1 CAD solid geometry, 2 With fine hexahedron network with bearing conditions,*
*3 Result: deformations and stresses, $\sigma_{max}$ = 175 N/mm² at edge of smaller hole.*

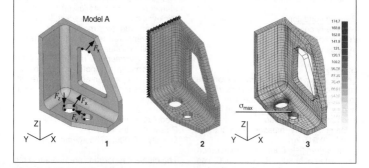

***Cast-steel bracket as shell and volume-element model B*** *(fine tetrahedron network)*
*1 Fine tetrahedron network with three elements in thickness,*
*2 Deformations and stresses for 1, $\sigma_{max}$ = 119 N/mm² at edge of small hole.*

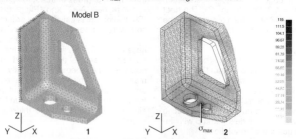

***Cast-steel bracket as shell and volume-element model C*** *(coarse tetrahedron network)*
*1 Coarse tetrahedron network with only two elements in thickness,*
*2 Deformations and stresses for 1, $\sigma_{max}$ = 110 N/mm² at edge of small hole.*

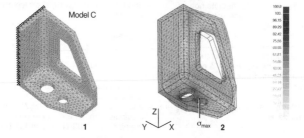

Note: "Isolated" individual loads are only permitted with bar elements.

The results are shown in the table and in the figures in deformed and non-deformed state with stresses represented by isocolors (in the original) or shades of gray.

Conclusion:

Volume elements are very sensitive to incorrectly approximated load distributions (see model C´, intermediate nodes introduced via the option). The loads distributed "manually" to the corner nodes $F_x$ and $F_z$ are now incorrect as the important intermediate nodes remain unloaded. This results in correct deformations but meaningless stress concentrations. Therefore: Volume elements should only ever be subjected to surface loads.

The difference between averaged and maximum node stress should be small. Model A provides good results, the difference being 14%. However, five elements

per thickness are superfluous. An even better result is to be achieved with only 2...3 since the height-width ratio is close to the ideal element of a cube. All model errors are in the area of load initiation. Model B with three tetrahedrons per thickness is 34% too rigid, and the stresses are 30% too low. Model C is even 58% too stiff and has 37% fewer stresses. It can thus hardly be used at all. Model C´ provides with a very high number of nodes and high computing times identical deformations but meaningless stress concentrations (see above). Caution is required with tetrahedron networks.

Model D as a shell model is much too soft (45%, with shear strain even 58%). Shell elements, (mostly defined as thin-walled) with relatively large thicknesses, deliver results which can only partially be used, because even the stresses are 33% too low, particularly in the case of very compact bodies, as here.

---

*Cast-steel bracket as shell model D*
1 Automatically generated surface model from solid (CAD planes),
2 Shell model with bearing conditions and stress,
3 Result: Deformations and stresses for 2, $\sigma_{max} = 123$ N/mm² at edge of big hole.

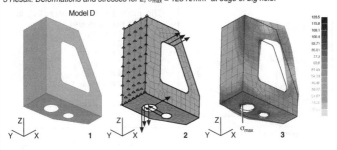

| Model | Type | Results Linear statics | | | | | | | |
|-------|------|------|----------|--------|--------|-------------------|------------------|-------------|-----------------|
| | | Node | Elements | Equil. | Weight | Max. deformation | Max. stress av./max. Diff. | Model error | Computing time |
| A | Hexahedron | 6,228 | 4,735 | 18,000 | 0.119 | 0.029 | 173/203  30 | 34% | 140 sec |
| B | Tetrahedron | 5,407 | 18,385 | 15,500 | 0.119 | 0.019–34% | 119/195  76 | 24% | 100 sec |
| C | Tetrahedron | 2,178 | 6,735 | 6,156 | 0.119 | 0.012 | 110/124  14 | 19% | 20 sec |
| C´ | as C int.n. | 12,500 | 6,735 | 37,767 | 0.119 | 0.029 | 674/795 121 | – | 500 sec |
| D | Shell quad. | 279 | 240 | 1,350 | 0.114 | 0.0421 | 116/123  7 | 21% | 4 sec |

### Example 3: Tubular frame

The aim is to carry out an FEM analysis on a body in the form of a tubular frame (spaceframe) without sheet paneling, including optimized weight and rigidity on the example of a mini-pickup (not a real vehicle). The material properties are:
Modulus of elasticity = 200,000 N/mm²
Poisson's ratio = 0.3
Density = 0.00000785 kg/mm³

Two shapes are used as profile sections. A 90 x 120 x 1.5 mm box-type profile section and a 70 x 2 mm tube profile section, which are defined in the preprocessor in the properties with their shape directly with the element type "Bar" (constant cross-section with linear formulation; different starting and end cross-sections would be "Beam"). This results in the required cross-section values as follows (in mm² or mm⁴ and mm³).

Box:
Cross-sectional area $A = 621$
Reduced shear cross-sections
$A_{redI}$ = shear area = 325
$A_{redII} = 219$
Principal moments of inertia:
$I_I = 1,348,306$
$I_{II} = 869,596$
Torsional moment of inertia $I_t = 1,606,083$
Torsional section modulus $W_t = 7,334$
Position of principal axes of inertia $\alpha = 0°$
Maximum four stress points:
$S_x = $ -45/45/45/-45
$S_y = $ -60/-60/60/60

Tube:
Cross-sectional area $A = 427$
Reduced shear cross-sections:
$A_{redI}$ = shear area = $A_{redII} = 227$
Principal moments of inertia:
$I_I = I_{II} = 247,168$
Torsional moment of inertia $I_t = 494,261$
Torsional section modulus $W_t = 2,177$
Position of principal axes of inertia $\alpha = 0°$
Maximum four stress points:
$S_x = $ 0/35/0/-35
$S_y = $ -35/0/35/0

The main dimensions according to the side and top views are:
$L_1 = 4,114$ mm (max.)
$L_2 = 2,650$ mm
$W_1 = 1,517$ mm (max.)
$W_2 = 1,147$ mm (front)
$W_3 = 1,374$ mm (rear)
$H_1 = 1,402$ mm (max.)
$H_2 = 1,315$ mm
$H_3 = \ \ \ 469$ mm (box)

*Profile sections of tubular frame*
*a) Box-type section, b) Tube section.*

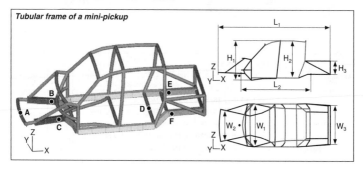

*Tubular frame of a mini-pickup*

Bearing conditions:
*Linear statics, load case – bending:*
A $v_y$ = 0; (A...F see figure),
B, C, E, F $v_z$ = 0; D $v_x$ = 0, $v_y$ = 0.
*Linear statics, load case – torsion:*
A, B, C = free;
E, F $v_z$ = 0;
D $v_x$ = 0, $d_y$ = 0, $d_z$ = 0.
*Free/free dynamics:*
No bearings, body vibrates freely in the springs.

Body design:
The tubular frame consists of 18 components, which are defined as layers 2...19:
2 Side member
3 Pedal cross-member
4 Driver cross-member
5 Cross-member, rear
6 Side reinforcement
7 Cockpit cross-member
8 Side member, front
9 Fender cross-member, front
10 Auxiliary cross-member, front
11 A-pillar
12 B-pillar
13 C-pillar
14 Roof frame, side
15 Roof frame, lateral
16 Rear subframe
17 Side member, load box
18 Cross-member, load box
19 Rear fender cross-member, rear

Stresses:
*Linear statics: load case – bending:*
Per side member 4 x 375 N (4 occupants each weighing 75 kg), per load-box corner 300 N from 120 kg payload, intrinsic weight of structure at 170 kg.
*Linear statics: load case – torsion:*
Torsional moment 300,0000 N·mm as regular unit load on front-axle bearings:
B = –3,593.7 N, C = 3,593.7 N
*Free/free dynamics:*
Only masses from intrinsic weight, no supplementary masses.

Results:
*Linear statics:*
Deformations x, y, z at all nodes, reaction forces, and moments at the bearing nodes, stresses (shear and direct stresses, reduced stresses according to von Mises) at all elements, deformation processes per element and per component (layers 2...19 in %), internal forces, and moments on request.

*Free/free dynamics:*
The body can vibrate freely in its springs, the lower eigenvalues and forms of the undamped, elastic system in ascending order; for free/free beginning with several rigid-body vibration forms (here 1–6) with the natural frequency 0.

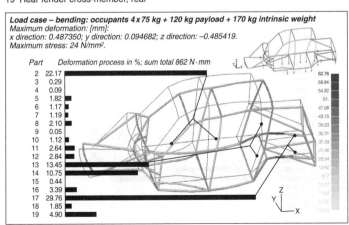

**Load case – bending: occupants 4 x 75 kg + 120 kg payload + 170 kg intrinsic weight**
*Maximum deformation: [mm]:*
*x direction: 0.487350; y direction: 0.094682; z direction: –0.485419.*
*Maximum stress: 24 N/mm².*

| Part | Deformation process in %; sum total 862 N·mm |
|------|------|
| 2 | 22.17 |
| 3 | 0.29 |
| 4 | 0.09 |
| 5 | 1.82 |
| 6 | 1.17 |
| 7 | 1.19 |
| 8 | 2.10 |
| 9 | 0.05 |
| 10 | 1.12 |
| 11 | 2.64 |
| 12 | 2.84 |
| 13 | 13.45 |
| 14 | 10.75 |
| 15 | 0.44 |
| 16 | 3.39 |
| 17 | 29.76 |
| 18 | 1.85 |
| 19 | 4.90 |

62.76
58.84
54.92
51.
47.08
43.15
39.23
35.31
31.39
27.46
23.54
19.62
15.7
11.77
7.85
3.93
0.01

1st eigenvalue = 38 Hz as torsional vibration, 3rd eigenvalue = 48 Hz as flexural vibration; also in each case the normalized deformations x, y, z at all nodes (here normalized to max. 0.1 mm), the normalized stresses (shear and direct stresses, reduced stresses according to von Mises) in all elements, deformation processes per element and per component (layers 2...19

in % as bar chart = force characteristic in the components, internal forces, and moments on request. The distribution of deformations, stresses, forces, etc. are normalized to a selectable maximum node deformation. Absolute values are only obtained in the event of an excitation calculation.

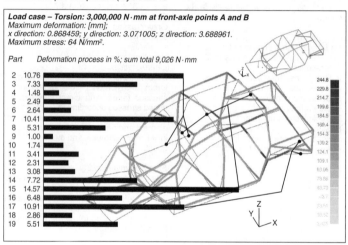

*Load case – Torsion: 3,000,000 N·mm at front-axle points A and B*
Maximum deformation: [mm];
x direction: 0.868459; y direction: 3.071005; z direction: 3.688961.
Maximum stress: 64 N/mm².

Part    Deformation process in %; sum total 9,026 N·mm

| Part | % |
|------|-------|
| 2 | 10.76 |
| 3 | 7.33 |
| 4 | 1.48 |
| 5 | 2.49 |
| 6 | 2.64 |
| 7 | 10.41 |
| 8 | 5.31 |
| 9 | 1.00 |
| 10 | 1.74 |
| 11 | 3.41 |
| 12 | 2.31 |
| 13 | 3.08 |
| 14 | 7.72 |
| 15 | 14.57 |
| 16 | 6.48 |
| 17 | 10.91 |
| 18 | 2.86 |
| 19 | 5.51 |

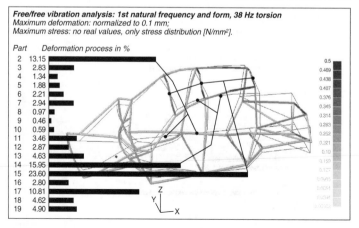

*Free/free vibration analysis: 1st natural frequency and form, 38 Hz torsion*
Maximum deformation: normalized to 0.1 mm;
Maximum stress: no real values, only stress distribution [N/mm²].

Part    Deformation process in %

| Part | % |
|------|-------|
| 2 | 13.15 |
| 3 | 2.83 |
| 4 | 1.34 |
| 5 | 1.88 |
| 6 | 2.21 |
| 7 | 2.94 |
| 8 | 0.97 |
| 9 | 0.46 |
| 10 | 0.59 |
| 11 | 3.46 |
| 12 | 2.87 |
| 13 | 4.63 |
| 14 | 15.95 |
| 15 | 23.60 |
| 16 | 2.80 |
| 17 | 10.81 |
| 18 | 4.62 |
| 19 | 4.90 |

The computation formula for weight/rigidity optimization has been known since the 1960s (error max. 10% for doubled rigidity). It can be used specifically for optimization purposes for the critical load case "Torsion" with consideration of the other load cases (information is also available on the bearing area ratio composed of linear force, torsion, and bending about axles and weight). In this way, the structure can be reinforced using bearing components that take most of the load, and reduce weight via the bearing components that take less of the load.

The following applies:
Rigidity change of overall structure [%] = (rigidity change of component × deformation-process ratio of component)/100

Application of formula:
*1st component* (see figure Load case – torsion).
Load case – torsion, component layer 15 (roof frame, lateral, $G = 11.85$ kg) with 14.57% bearing area ratio:
$(14.57 \times 116)/100 = 16.9\%$ change (i.e. reduction) of torsion between the axles when the rigidity (the planar moment of inertia) of this component is increased by a factor of 2.16 (116%). The weight increase is 3.55 kg. The tube diameter here is increased from 70 to 90 mm.

*2nd component* (see figure Load case – torsion).
Load case – torsion, component layer 6 (linear reinforcement, $G = 11.14$ kg) with 2.64% bearing area ratio:
$(2.64 \times 250)/100 = 6.6\%$ change (i.e. increase) of torsion between the axles when the rigidity (moment of inertia) of this component is reduced by a factor of 3.5 (250%). The weight reduction is 3.34 kg. The tube diameter here is reduced from 70 to 50 mm.

*Result:*
A minimal weight increase of $3.55 - 3.34 = 0.21$ kg increases torsional rigidity by $16.9 - 6.6 = 10.3\%$ (checking with altered profile sections produces 9%, this covers the low error in the computation formula.) A look at the bearing charts of the other load cases shows that this also applies to torsional vibration and is of no importance to bending. It is thus possible with minimal time expenditure to significantly increase the torsional rigidity and flexural strength of this body still further and to safely reduce the total weight by reducing the cross-sections of oversized components.

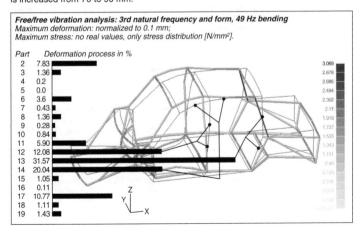

**Free/free vibration analysis: 3rd natural frequency and form, 49 Hz bending**
Maximum deformation: normalized to 0.1 mm;
Maximum stress: no real values, only stress distribution [N/mm²].

| Part | Deformation process in % |
|------|--------------------------|
| 2 | 7.83 |
| 3 | 1.36 |
| 4 | 0.2 |
| 5 | 0.0 |
| 6 | 3.6 |
| 7 | 0.43 |
| 8 | 1.36 |
| 9 | 0.28 |
| 10 | 0.84 |
| 11 | 5.90 |
| 12 | 12.08 |
| 13 | 31.57 |
| 14 | 20.04 |
| 15 | 1.05 |
| 16 | 0.11 |
| 17 | 10.77 |
| 18 | 1.11 |
| 19 | 1.43 |

3.069
2.878
2.686
2.494
2.302
2.11
1.919
1.727
1.535
1.343
1.151
0.96
0.768
0.576
0.384
0.192

# Quality

Quality is defined as the extent to which customer expectations are fulfilled or even exceeded. The desired quality is determined by the customer. With his demands and expectations, he determines what quality is – in both products and services. As competition leads to increased customer expectations, quality remains a dynamic quantity. Quality is defined through product- and service-related factors which are susceptible to quantitative or qualitative analysis. The preconditions for achieving high quality are:

– Quality policy: The company commitment to quality as a top-priority corporate objective.
– Leadership: Employee-motivation measures.
– Quality assurance.

## Quality management (QM)

### Quality system

All elements in a quality system and all quality-assurance measures must be planned systematically. The individual assignments, and the areas of competence and responsibility are to be defined in writing (Quality-Assurance Handbook). Quality systems are also described in international standards, such as DIN ISO 9001 – 9004.

Increased requirements for defect-free products (zero-defect target) and economic considerations (defect prevention instead of sorting and reworking, or scrapping) make it imperative that preventive quality-assurance measures be applied. These serve the following objectives:

– To develop products that are insensitive to production fluctuations.
– To establish production processes to ensure that quality requirements are maintained safely within the specified limits.
– To apply methods which identify the sources of defects preemptively, and which can be applied to rectify the production process in good time.

Three types of "audit" are employed in the regular monitoring of all elements in a quality system:

– System audit: Evaluation of the effectiveness of the quality system regarding its comprehensiveness and the practical application of the individual elements.
– Process audit: Evaluation of the effectiveness of the quality-management (QM) elements, confirmation of quality capability, of adherence to and suitability of particular processes, and the determination of specific measures for improvement.
– Product audit: Evaluation of the effectiveness of the QM elements performed by examining the final products or their components.

### Quality management in development

At the outset, every new product which must fulfill the customer's quality and reliability demands is allocated a project specifications manual.

As early as the definition phase, its contents serve as the basis for the planning of all sample and endurance tests required to verify the new product's serviceability and reliability.

#### Quality assessment

At the conclusion of specific development stages, all the available data regarding quality and reliability are subjected to a quality-assessment procedure, leading to initiation of the required corrective measures. Responsible for the quality assessment are staff members from development, preproduction, and quality assurance; they, in turn, receive support from specialists in specialist departments.

### Failure Mode and Effects Analysis (FMEA)

This cost-reduction and risk-prevention procedure is suitable for investigating the types of defects which can occur in system components and their effects on the system (for details, see "Reliability", p. 212).

### Quality management during procurement

This aspect must extend beyond the incoming inspection; it must comprise an entire system. This system must ensure that the components purchased from suppliers contribute to the reliable fulfill-

Example of Failure Mode and Effects Analysis (FMEA)

| ⊕ **BOSCH** QUALITY ASSURANCE | | | | FMEA Actuator 9 319 150 342 Part 6: Parts production and assembly of bushing holder | | | | | DEPT. FMEA PAGE DATE | | | FVB 75 1289940001 10 10.10.88 | | |
|---|---|---|---|---|---|---|---|---|---|---|---|---|---|---|
| NO. | COMPONENT PROCESS | FUNCTION PURPOSE | DEFECT TYPE | DEFECT EFFECT | DEFECT CAUSES | DEFECT PREVENTION | DEFECT DETECTION | S S | I A | E E | SxE RZ | MEASURES V:/T: |
| 1110 | Assemble bushing holder | Prepare parts for soldering process | Damaged sealing surfaces | Actuator leaking to surroundings → gasoline vapors in engine compartment | Chips in assembly device | Wash before assembly, clean tools regularly | 100% visual inspection of soldering; surface check; 100% visual inspection prior to packing | 10 | 2 | 1 | 20 | |
| 1180 | Solder bushing holder | Hold parts together | Part not soldered | | No solder | Scan solder feed | 100% visual inspection of soldering; 100% visual inspection of surface; 100% leak test | 10 (10 | 2 2 | 2 1 | 40 20) | 100% leak test of bushing-holder assembly V: FVB2 T: 01.89 |
| | | Ensure leak-tightness | Part leaking (bubbles) | | Insufficient solder | Scan solder feed | 100% visual inspection of soldering | 10 (10 | 4 3 | 6 2 | 240 60) | 100% leak test V: FVB2 T: 01.89 + Design improvement at soldering point V: EVA3 T: 03.89 |

S = Severity of fault
V = Department responsible

A = Probability of occurrence
T = Deadline for introduction

E = Probability of detection

Risk number RZ = S x A x E
Copyright 1987 Robert Bosch GmbH Stuttgart

ment of the <u>Technical Specifications</u> defined for the finished product.

It is imperative that suppliers' quality capabilities are supported by modern, preventive quality-assurance techniques (e.g. SPC <u>S</u>tatistical <u>P</u>rocess <u>C</u>ontrol or FMEA). All individual requirements for the product must be specified in a clear and unambiguous manner in order to allow the subcontractor to achieve and competently evaluate comprehensive compliance with the individual quality requirements for the product. These guidelines generally are in the form of drawings, order specifications, standards, formulas, etc.

For example, the actual manufacturer of the supplied product performs the first <u>initial-sample inspection</u>. This inspection must be reproduced by the purchaser when the product is received (with particular emphasis on the interrelationships involving production processes and the finished product), and confirmed by means of an incoming inspection.

The supplier's final or shipping inspection can take place at the premises of the purchaser's incoming inspection in those cases where the manufacturer possesses special knowledge and/or the technical equipment necessary for carrying out specific forms of quality testing. The supplier confirms the relevant quality inspections on the products in <u>quality certificates</u> in accordance with DIN 55 350 or material test certificates in accordance with DIN 50 049. The test results obtained must be forwarded to the purchaser.

**Quality management in preproduction**

The preconditions for supplying assured quality are established in the <u>production-planning</u> phase. Compliance with the following conditions is required:
- Planning of the production process and material flow.
- Planning of resources requirements.
- Selection and procurement of suitable manufacturing methods and production equipment, as well as the requisite test stands (e.g. for SPC).
- Examination of manufacturing methods, production equipment and machines to determine machine and process capability.
- Documentation of the production procedure in the production-sequence plan.
- Determination of the necessary level of employee qualification.
- Preparation of technical drawings and parts lists.

The Process FMEA provides a means of methodically anticipating potential faults in the production process and of assessing their effects on the quality of the attribute or the product. The Process FMEA is employed to discover the sources of defects, and to avoid the defects or minimize their effects. This makes it possible to initiate the necessary production and test-engineering procedures required for defect prevention.

*FMEA working group*

| Area of operation | Product FMEA | Process FMEA | FMEA contribution |
|---|---|---|---|
| FMEA moderator | | ▓▓▓ | Coordination Methods |
| Construction ($\bigvee$ = Responsibility) | $\bigvee$ | ▓▓▓ | Construction |
| Testing | ☐ | ▓▓▓ | Functionality |
| Endurance testing | ☐ | | Durability Climate resistance |
| Technical marketing | ☐ | | Project specifications |
| Customer service | ☐ | | ▓▓▓ Customer service |
| Pre-production ($\bigvee$ = Responsibility) | | $\bigvee$ | Manufacturing verifiability procedures |
| Quality services | ☐ | ☐ | ▓▓▓ Quality and reliability assurance |
| Production | | ☐ | ▓▓▓ Production |
| Materials | | | ▓▓▓ Subcontractor supply |
| Miscellaneous | | | |

Inspection planning comprises the following points:
- Analysis of the functions to be tested.
- Determination of the test criteria.
- Selection of suitable test procedures and measuring and inspection equipment.
- Determination of the extent and frequency of the inspection.
- Documentation of the test procedure in the inspection plan.
- Planning of recording and documentation of quality data (e.g. in quality-control charts for SPC).
- Planning for control of inspection, measuring, and test equipment.
- Possible planning of quality-data documentation.

The specified inspection criteria must always include all essential characteristics of the finished products.

Suitable means for compilation and evaluation of the inspection results are to be specified for assessing the quality of products and their components, and for controlling production processes. Test results are to be processed in such a manner as to be suitable for application in open-loop and closed-loop process-control systems, fault analysis, and fault rectification.

**Machine and process capability**

The evaluation of machine capability is to confirm performance potential in the following two areas:
- The machine under examination must operate with verifiable consistency. If necessary, this consistency must be formulated with the aid of statistical quantities, e.g. as normal distribution with mean value $\bar{x}$ and standard deviation $s$.
- The machine must be able to maintain production within specified tolerances. This can only be confirmed using the quantification of consistency indicated above.

Testing of machine capability is restricted to a limited period, and to the investigation of the equipment-related effects on the production process. However, it should be noted that equipment-related and non-equipment-related factors (e.g. effects of material or procedures) cannot usually be separated completely. Individual tests are designed to determine whether:

- unusual process results are recognized
- mean values and scatter range remain stable within the measurement series (the verification limits of statistical process control are employed for this examination).

If no unusual process results are present, and the mean and the scatter range are stable, the process is considered to be fully controlled; the suitability of the equipment is then described using the familiar statistics $c_m$ and $c_{mk}$. The value for $c_m$ only reflects the scatter range for the machine; it is calculated with the following equation:

$$c_m = (OGW - UGW)/(6 \cdot \hat{\sigma})$$

On the other hand, the value for $c_{mk}$ reflects not only the machine's scatter range, but also the position of the mean within the tolerance range. It is essential that it be calculated for the production equipment on which adjustments are either imprecise or impossible. It is calculated as follows:

$$c_{mk} = (\bar{x} - UGW)/(3 \cdot \hat{\sigma}) \text{ or }$$
$$c_{mk} = (OGW - \bar{x})/(3 \cdot \hat{\sigma}),$$

where the lesser value is valid. The definitions are:
$\bar{x}$   Total mean value
$UGW$   Lower tolerance-range limit
$OGW$   Upper tolerance-range limit
$\hat{\sigma}$   Estimate for process control

Bosch only designates production equipment as capable of ensuring that manufacture will result in the required product attributes if $c_{mk}$ is at least 1.67.

Unusual process results, or an unstable mean or scatter range, indicate that the process is not fully controlled. In this case, nonrandom influences (interference factors) are affecting the process. These must be eliminated or compensated for. The examination of machine capability is then repeated.

If the result of the machine-capability test is positive, it is followed by an examination of the process capability. This is intended to ensure that the production process is capable of consistently meeting the quality requirements placed upon it.

The examination of process capability extends over a longer period of time. All changes to the process (e.g. material changes, tool changes, or method changes) are taken into account when the scope and intervals of sample random testing are determined, and then included in the examination procedure.

Once compiled, the data are subjected to a statistical analysis comparable to that employed for determining machine capability. Particular attention is devoted to ascertaining whether the process mean and process control are stable, i.e. whether the process is fully controlled. If the process is fully controlled, then the process capability is confirmed using known statistics $c_p$ and $c_{pk}$. These statistics are calculated in the same way as those for $c_m$ and $c_{mk}$ where the values $\bar{\bar{x}}$ and $\hat{\sigma}$ from the process examination are used.

If the process is not fully controlled, calculation of $c_p$ and $c_{pk}$ is not permitted. In this case, the causes of instability in the process must be either eliminated or compensated for. The examination of machine capability is then repeated.

Bosch designates a process as capable of ensuring the required product attributes only in cases where $c_{pk}$ is at least 1.33.

Machine- and process-capability analysis are necessary preliminary checks prior to introduction of SPC. However, both investigations are also important for processes which are not controlled by SPC, as the required potential must be confirmed for each type of process.

### Statistical Process Control (SPC)

SPC is a process-control system intended to assist in the prevention of errors and their associated costs. SPC is employed in production, and applied for attributes which are vital to the operation (for details, see "Technical statistics", p. 214).

## Measuring and inspection equipment

The measuring and inspection equipment must be able to demonstrate whether the test criteria of the finished product conform to the prescribed specifications. Measuring and inspection equipment must be monitored, calibrated, and maintained. Uncertainty of measurement is to be considered when using measuring and inspection equipment. It must be minimal relative to the tolerance range for the test criteria. With measuring and inspection equipment, attention must be paid to:
– Defining the measurements to be performed, the required precision, and the suitable measuring and inspection equipment.
– Ensuring that the measuring and inspection equipment meets precision requirements, i.e. uncertainty of measurement is generally not to exceed 10% of the tolerance range.
– All measuring and inspection equipment and measurement systems used for product quality assurance are to be

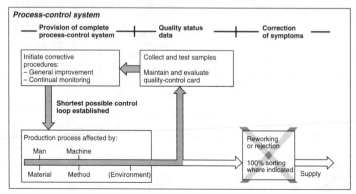

*Process-control system*

Provision of complete process-control system | Quality status data | Correction of symptoms

Initiate corrective procedures:
– General improvement
– Continual monitoring

Collect and test samples

Maintain and evaluate quality-control card

**Shortest possible control loop established**

Production process affected by:
Man  Machine
Material  Method  (Environment)

Reworking or rejection
100% sorting where indicated

Supply

specified in an inspection plan; they must be labeled, and are to be calibrated and adjusted at prescribed intervals.
- Calibration procedures must be specified. These must comprise individual data on the type of unit, its identification, application area and calibration intervals, and are also to include the steps to be taken in case of unsatisfactory results.
- Measuring and inspection equipment must be provided with appropriate identification verifying their calibration status.
- Calibration records (histories) are to be maintained.
- The appropriate ambient conditions for calibrating, testing, and measurement must be maintained.
- Measuring and inspection equipment is to be carefully stored and protected against contamination in order to maintain consistent levels of precision and suitability for use.
- The measuring and inspection equipment and the software are to be protected against any influences which might invalidate their calibration.

### Control of inspection, measuring, and test equipment: type and extent

Satisfactory arrangements for monitoring test and inspection equipment embrace all measuring systems employed in development, production, assembly, and in customer service. This category includes calipers, unit standards, instruments, recording devices, and special test equipment together with its ancillary computer software. In addition, the equipment, mounts, clamps, and instruments employed for process control must also be monitored.

Procedures which extend to include the equipment and the abilities of the operator are employed in evaluating whether a test process is controlled. Measurement errors are compared with the quality specifications. Appropriate corrective action is to be taken when the requirements for precision and functionality in measuring and inspection equipment are no longer satisfied.

### Measuring instruments subject to calibration

German legal requirements on weights and measures stipulate that calibration of measuring instruments which are for use in "business transactions" be officially certified in those cases where the results of their measurements are employed to determine the price of goods or energy. This category includes instruments for measuring length, surface area, volume and mass, and thermal and electrical energy. If these conditions apply, then the calibration of the measuring instruments concerned must be officially certified. Continuing compliance must then be monitored by an official or an officially approved agency.

*Relationship between measurement results, statistical analysis, and process capability*

| Process | ←Tolerance $T$→ | Status | Process capability |
|---|---|---|---|
| Individual values | | Unsure | Not calculated |
| Statistical analysis | $\sigma$ | Result negative due to excessive variance | $C_p = \dfrac{T}{6\sigma} = 0.67$<br>Outside $T$ by 4.6% |
| Minimum requirement | $\sigma$ | Result positive, low variance<br>Mean value maintained | $C_p = 1.33$<br>Outside $T$ by 63 ppm |
| Mean tolerance value displaced | $\sigma$ $D$ | Result negative despite low variance | $C_p = 2.0$ but<br>$C_{pk} = \dfrac{D}{3\sigma} = 0.67$<br>i.e. outside $T$ by 2.3% |

# Reliability

According to DIN 40 041, reliability is the sum total of those characteristics in the unit under investigation which exert an effect on the unit's ability to achieve specified requirements under given conditions during a specified period of time. Reliability is a constituent element of quality ("reliability is quality based on time").

The essential concept here is the word dependability. Dependability comprises the terms reliability, availability, safety, security, and maintainability. Dependability, therefore, equates to the confidence placed in a service which is to be provided by a system. A system is safe when the risk of danger from coming into contact with this system is accepted by society and by the legislative bodies.

Reliability quantifies availability; it is the probability that, at any given time, a system will prove to be fully operational. The failure rate is the conditional probability density of a component failing before time $t+dt$, provided it has survived beyond time $t$. The failure rate has the general shape of a "bathtub curve", which can be described as the superimposition of three Weibull distributions with varying failure steepness components (see the chapter entitled "Technical statistics").

Failure in electronic components is generally spontaneous, with no advance indication of impending defects. This condition is described by a constant failure rate (middle section of the curve). Neither quality control nor preventive maintenance can prevent such failures. Failures caused by incorrect component selection, overstressing, or manufacturing defects show a "burn-in behavior", described by a failure rate that falls with time, while aging of a component is represented by a rising failure rate (left or right section of the curve).

## Reliability analysis and prediction

Mutually supplementary analysis methods are applied to determine the potential failure risk associated with a product, i.e. to discover all possible effects of operational and internal failure, as well as external interference factors (e.g. operator error); these methods are used in different phases during the product lifetime. Mainly FMEA and fault-tree analysis are used in the development of motor vehicles.

### FMEA (DIN 25 448, IEC 812)
FMEA (Failure Mode and Effects Analysis) is a "bottom-up" analysis. Starting from faults at the lowest level of the system hierarchy (generally components in design FMEA, function blocks in system FMEA, work steps in process FMEA), the analysis examines the way in which they spread to higher levels. In this way, all those critical system states caused by individual failures are detected and also evaluated in relation to each other. FMEA can be used in various stages of development and production.

Design FMEA: Under the precondition that parts are manufactured in accordance with their drawings, products/components are examined for conformity between design and specifications in order to avoid system-design errors and to facilitate detection of field risks.

Process FMEA: Under the precondition that the specifications are correct, the process of product manufacture is examined for conformity with the drawings in order to avoid manufacturing defects.

System FMEA: System components are examined for their functional interaction in order to avoid system-design errors and to facilitate detection of field risks.

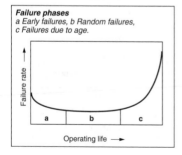

**Failure phases**
a Early failures, b Random failures,
c Failures due to age.

Failure rate ↑

Operating life ⟶

### Fault-tree analysis (DIN 25 424)

Fault-tree analysis (FTA) is a "top-down" analysis procedure, which permits quantitative assessment of probabilities. Starting from the undesirable event (top event), all the conceivable causes are enumerated, even combinations of individual failures. When the occurrence probabilities of individual defects are known, it is possible to calculate the probability of the undesirable event occurring. For this purpose, above all for electrical components, there are collections of empirically determined failure rates such as Mil-Hdbk 217F (which has not been updated in the meantime).

## Reliability enhancement

System reliability can always be improved by fault avoidance or failure tolerances. Preventive measures include, for example, selecting more reliable components with higher permissible stresses, or (for electronic systems) reducing the number of components, and thus connections through increased integration. As a rule of thumb, purely electronic components, such as transistors or integrated circuits, are responsible for 10% of failures, sensors and final controlling elements are responsible for 30% failures, and connections between components and with the outside world are responsible for 60% of failures. If preventive measures do not prove sufficient, then fault-tolerance measures (e.g. multichannel circuitry, self-monitoring) must be implemented in order to mask the effects of a defect.

### Reliability planning

In the case of products to be newly developed, the reliability growth management procedure (RGM, Mil Hdbk 189) provides a planning basis for the extent of testing work required to achieve a reliability target, depending on the reliability initially available.

In the course of product development, its reliability improves due to analysis and elimination, as far as possible, of the causes of observed failures. Strictly speaking, a statistical evaluation of product reliability in its final version can only be started at the end of its development. However, in the case of the lifetimes demanded in the automotive industry, any such evaluation would require so much time that it would delay the series launch. Under certain preconditions, the RGM method allows engineers to assess the reliability of a product at any stage in its development. This assessment is based on the data of earlier product versions and the effectiveness of the failure-correction measures introduced. In this way, this procedure firstly reduces the time to series launch, and secondly, increases the available data volume, and thus the confidence level.

If the current average lifetime MTTF (Mean Time To Failure) is plotted on a log-log scale against the cumulated service time (total test time of all the test specimens), experience shows that, on average, this MTTF value rises in a straight line. Depending on the product and the effort expended, the upgradient of this line will be between 0.35 and 0.5. This empirical relationship between testing effort and achieved reliability can be used for planning.

A comparison between planning and current status can be made at any time. As the RGM program progresses, intermediate reliability targets at specific milestones must also be met. When planning the test program, it is essential to strike an acceptable balance between test time, test effort, and available resources, and also to make a realistic estimate of the possible reliability gains.

# Technical statistics

## Purpose of statistics

### Descriptive statistics
To describe sets of similar units with specific, different characteristic values using statistical characteristics which allow objective comparisons and evaluations.

### Rating statistics
To provide information on the statistical characteristics of larger sets (populations) based on relatively few individual data (samples).

As such statements are based on the laws of chance and the theory of probability, their validity is always subject to a certain confidence level, usually 95% in the field of engineering.

### Examples of populations:
- All products of the same type produced under constant manufacturing conditions.
- Set of all the possible results of a measurement under unchanging conditions.

There are two different types of characteristics:
- Quantitative characteristics, e.g. physical quantities (referred to as "measured values"),
- Attribute characteristics, e.g. "OK" or "Defective" etc. (referred to as "test results" in the following).

Statistical analysis methods provide valuable assistance for ensuring and improving quality standards in industrial products. Today's levels of vehicle reliability would be impossible without it.

## Presentation of measured values

$N$   Population size: the number of all items which form the basis of statistical analysis

$n$   Number of measured values in the sample

$P_A$   Confidence level

$x$   Individual measured value

$R$   Range: $R = x_{max} - x_{min}$

$k$   Number of classes into which $R$ is divided. Recommendation: $k = \sqrt{n}$ ($\geq 5$)

$w$   Class width

$i$   Ordinal number of measured values (as subscript)

$j$   Ordinal number of classes (as subscript)

$x_j$   Midpoint of class no. $j$

$n_j$   Absolute frequency of class no. $j$: number of measured values in class no. $j$

$h_j$   Relative frequency in class no. $j$, $h_j = n_j/n$

$h_j/w$   Frequency density

$G_j$   Cumulative absolute frequency: absolute frequency summed up to a particular class

$$G_j = \sum_{r=1}^{j} n_r$$

$H_j$   Cumulative relative frequency = $G_j/n$

$F(x)$   Distribution function: probability for values $\leq x$

$f(x)$   Frequency-density function d $F(x)$/d $x$

$\mu$   Arithmetic mean of population

$\bar{x}$   Arithmetic mean of a sample

$$\bar{x} = \sum_{i=1}^{n} x_i/n$$

$\bar{\bar{x}}$   Arithmetic mean of several $\bar{x}$ values

$\sigma$   Standard deviation of population

$s$   Standard deviation of sample

$$s = \sqrt{\sum_{i=1}^{n} (x_i - \bar{x})^2 / (n-1)}$$

$V$   Variation coefficient $V = s/\bar{x}$

$u$   Dispersion factor

$X, Y, Z$   Random variable

### Frequency histogram and cumulative frequency curve of an empirical distribution
The simplest way of clearly presenting a larger number of characteristic values is the frequency histogram. In the case of attributes characteristics or variables with few discrete values, bars are drawn over the characteristic values whose height is proportional to the relative frequency of the values, i.e. the frequency $h_j$ of the attribute $j$ in proportion to the total number of all the values $\sum_j h_j$.

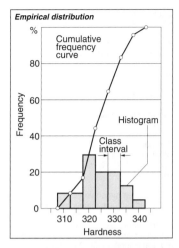

*Empirical distribution*

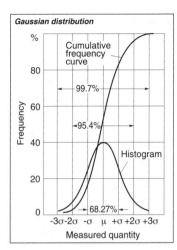

*Gaussian distribution*

In the case of variable attributes with a continuous range of values, the range is divided into $k$ classes and the bars entered over the class midpoints. If the classes are not all the same size, the bars become rectangles whose areas are proportional to the relative frequencies of the classes. Thus, in these cases, the heights of the rectangles are also proportional to the frequency density.

If conclusions are to be drawn from the sample presentation described concerning the population, it is essential to define the classes in such a way that there are at least five values in each class.

Another way of presenting the distribution of attributes is the cumulative frequency curve. The advantage of this curve for variable attributes is that, for each value or each interval, the percentage of measured values below or above can easily be read off (estimate of fraction defectives outside of the tolerance). The cumulative frequency curve can be determined from the frequency histogram by summing the relative frequencies up to the relevant value or interval. For the population, it thus represents the integral for the density function.

**Distributions and statistical parameters**

A random variable $X$ is characterized by its distribution. The distribution function $F(x)$ describes the relationship between the variable value $x$ and the cumulative frequency or probability for values $\leq x$. In empirical distributions, this corresponds to the cumulative frequency curve. The frequency histogram corresponds to the density function $f(x)$.

The most important parameters of a distribution are the arithmetic mean $\mu$ and the standard deviation $\sigma$.

**Gaussian distribution**

Normal, or Gaussian, distribution is the mathematically idealized limit case which always results when many mutually independent random effects are added together. The probability-density function of Gaussian distribution clearly defined by $\mu$ and $\sigma$ forms a symmetrical bell-shaped curve.

The total area under the bell-shaped curve corresponds to 1 = 100%. The standard deviation $\sigma$ and its multiples allow the delimitation of specific areas with the boundaries $\mu \pm u\sigma$ in which $P$% of the values fall (Table 1). The percentages $\alpha = (100 - P)/2$ lie outside these areas on either side.

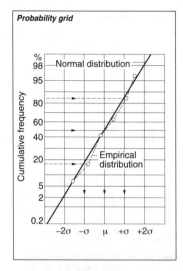

*Probability grid*

**Empirical and Gaussian distribution in probability grid**

In a "probability grid", the ordinate is distorted in such a way that the S-shaped cumulative frequency curve is transformed into a straight line.

Determination of $\mu$ and $\sigma$ from the probability grid:
1. Read off $\mu$ at 50% cumulative frequency.
2. Read off abscissa values at 16% and 84%.

The difference corresponds to $2\sigma$.

**Sums of random variables**

For the mean and standard deviations of a random variable $Z = a \cdot X + b \cdot Y$, created by the linear combination of 2 independently distributed random variables $X$ and $Y$, the following apply:

$$\mu_z = a \cdot \mu_x + b \cdot \mu_y$$
$$\sigma_z^2 = a^2 \cdot \sigma_x^2 + b^2 \cdot \sigma_y^2$$

**Typical applications:**
1. Fits
Hole diameter: $x$
Shaft diameter: $y$
Clearance: $z = x - y$
For $\sigma_x = \sigma_y$ the following applies:
$$\sigma_z^2 = 2 \cdot \sigma_x^2$$

2. Combined dimension
If the individual dimensions are statistically independently distributed about their mean tolerances, the tolerance for the combined dimension can be calculated by quadratic addition (cf. DIN 7186).

# Evaluation of series of measurements

**Random interval for $\bar{x}$ and $s$**
(direct conclusion)
If many samples, each containing $n$ values, are taken from one and the same population with the mean $\mu$, and the standard deviation $\sigma$, the mean values $\bar{x}_1, \bar{x}_2 \ldots$ of the samples are dispersed with the standard deviation:

$$\sigma_{\bar{x}} = \frac{\sigma}{\sqrt{n}} \quad \text{about the true value } \mu.$$

In a similar way, random intervals can be defined for $s$ and $R$.

**Table 1. Value frequency $P$ inside and $\alpha$ outside $\pm u\sigma$**

| $u$ | 1.00 | 1.28 | 1.64 | 1.96 | 2.00 | 2.33 | 2.58 | 3.00 | 3.29 |
|---|---|---|---|---|---|---|---|---|---|
| $P\%$ | 68.27 | 80 | 90 | 95 | 95.4 | 98 | 99 | 99.7 | 99.9 |
| $\alpha\%$ | 15.86 | 10 | 5 | 2.5 | 2.3 | 1 | 0.5 | 0.15 | 0.05 |

| Quantity | Random interval | |
|----------|-----------------|---|
| | Lower limit | Upper limit |
| $\bar{x}$ | $\mu - u\,\dfrac{\sigma}{\sqrt{n}}$ | $\mu + u\,\dfrac{\sigma}{\sqrt{n}}$ |
| $S$ | $D_u \cdot \sigma$ | $D_o \cdot \sigma$ |
| $R$ | $D_u \cdot \sigma \cdot d_n$ | $D_o \cdot \sigma \cdot d_n$ |

$D_u$ and $D_o$ as functions of $n$ and $P$ from Tables 1 and 2.

### Table 2. Auxiliary constants for evaluation of measurement series

| $n$ | $d_n$ | $t$ values for $P =$ | | | $D_u$ | $D_o$ |
|-----|-------|------|------|------|-------|-------|
| | | 90% | 95% | 99% | for $P = 95\%$ | |
| 2 | 1.13 | 6.31 | 12.7 | 63.7 | 0.03 | 2.24 |
| 3 | 1.69 | 2.92 | 4.30 | 9.92 | 0.16 | 1.92 |
| 5 | 2.33 | 2.13 | 2.78 | 4.60 | 0.35 | 1.67 |
| 10 | 3.08 | 1.83 | 2.26 | 3.25 | 0.55 | 1.45 |
| 20 | 3.74 | 1.73 | 2.09 | 2.86 | 0.68 | 1.32 |
| 50 | – | 1.68 | 2.01 | 2.68 | 0.80 | 1.20 |
| ∞ | – | 1.65 | 1.96 | 2.58 | 1.00 | 1.00 |

**Confidence intervals for $\mu$ and $\sigma$**
**(conclusion)**
If only samples with $x$ and $s$ are known, and a statement is to be made on the true mean value $\mu$ resulting from an infinite number of measurements, a so-called confidence interval can be specified which features $\mu$ with a probability of $P_A\%$. The same holds true for $\sigma$.

| Quantity | Confidence interval | |
|----------|---------------------|---|
| | Lower limit | Upper limit |
| $\mu$ | $\bar{x} - t\,\dfrac{s}{\sqrt{n}}$ | $\bar{x} + t\,\dfrac{s}{\sqrt{n}}$ |
| $\sigma$ | $\dfrac{s}{D_o}$ | $\dfrac{s}{D_u}$ |

$t$, $D_o$ and $D_u$ from Table 2.

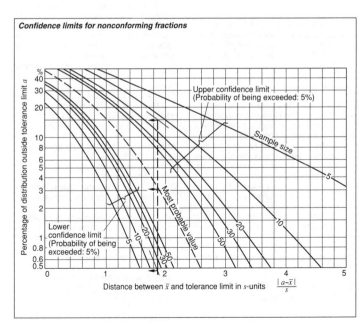

*Confidence limits for nonconforming fractions*

Percentage of distribution outside tolerance limit $a$

Upper confidence limit (Probability of being exceeded: 5%)

Sample size

Most probable value

Lower confidence limit (Probability of being exceeded: 5%)

Distance between $\bar{x}$ and tolerance limit in $s$-units $\dfrac{|a-\bar{x}|}{s}$

**Comparison of mean values**

Two samples with values of $n_1$ and $n_2$ have the same standard deviations $s_1 = s_2$, but different mean values $\bar{x}_1 \neq \bar{x}_2$. The confidence interval for the difference $\mu_1 - \mu_2 = 0$ is:

$$\pm t \cdot s_A \cdot \sqrt{1/n_1 + 1/n_2} \text{ with}$$

$$s_A^2 = \left((n_1 - 1) s_1^2 + (n_2 - 1) s_2^2\right)/(n' - 1)$$

$n' = n_1 + n_2 - 1$ determines $t$ in Table 2.

If the difference $\bar{x}_1 - \bar{x}_2$ is outside of the confidence interval, the two samples come with confidence level $P$ from different populations (e.g. different manufacturing conditions).

**Estimation of nonconforming fractions**

The percentage of parts lying outside of the tolerance limit $a$ is to be estimated based on $\bar{x}$ and $s$ from a sample series.

Calculation procedure:

If $\mu$ and $\sigma$ are known, then the percentage outside of $a$ in Table 1, or in the figure "Confidence limits for nonconforming fractions" ("most probable value" curve) is determined by:

$$u = |a - \mu|/\sigma.$$

A value of $u = 1.65$ would correspond to a percentage of 5%. However, only $\bar{x}$ and $s$ of the sample are known, not the values $\mu$ and $\sigma$ of the population. As these values are random, the nonconforming fraction can only be specified in terms of the confidence interval in which it lies with a particular probability.

In the figure, the confidence limits can be read off as a function of $|a - \bar{x}|/s$ which are exceeded only with a probability of 5%. Separate analyses are required for each of the two tolerance limits.

**Example:**

Prescribed tolerance for ground rollers $14 \, {}^{-0.016}_{-0.043}$ mm.

Tested are 14 parts of 13.961 to 13.983 mm. $\bar{x} = 13.972$ mm; $R = 0.022$ mm.

Estimated value for $s$ from $R$ with $d_n$ from Table 2:

$$s = 0.022/3.5 = 0.0063$$

Upper tolerance limit exceeded:

$$\frac{|a - \bar{x}|}{s} = \frac{13.984 - 13.972}{0.0063} = \frac{0.012}{0.0063} = 1.9$$

Referring to the figure:

| | |
|---|---|
| Upper confidence limit | ≈ 15 % |
| Most probable value | ≈ 3.1% |
| Lowest confidence limit | ≈ 0.5% |

Lower tolerance limit exceeded:

$$\frac{|a - \bar{x}|}{s} = \frac{|13.957 - 13.972|}{0.0063} = \frac{0.015}{0.0063} = 2.38$$

Referring to the figure:

| | |
|---|---|
| Upper confidence limit | ≈ 9 % |
| Most probable value | ≈ 1 % |
| Lowest confidence limit | < 0.5% |

**Statistical Process Control (SPC)**

Quality-control charts are employed to ensure consistent quality in production processes. Small samples are tested at specified intervals; the values $\bar{x}$ and $R$ are entered as test results, while defects are entered for attribute testing.

$T_{lo}$, $T_{up}$ Lower/upper tolerance limits,
$T$ Difference between upper and lower tolerance limits (tolerance range)
$T = T_{lo} - T_{up}$, $T_m = (T_{lo} + T_{up})/2$,
$\bar{x}$, $\bar{R}$ Values from ≥ 20 samples
$\sigma = \bar{R}/d_n$ = Standard deviation
$c_p = T/(6 \times \sigma)$ = Process capability

A process is considered to be "controlled" if
1) $c_p > 1$ (better: $c_p \geq 1.33$);
2) the curve displays no unusual variations (no trends, etc.);
3) $\bar{x}$ and $R$ lie within the "action limits" of the corresponding random intervals.

Table 3 shows the approximate values for action limits as a percentage of $T$. The calculation is based upon the assumptions that values are:
99.7% random intervals and $c_p = 1$.

**Table 3. Action limits as % of $T$**

| $n$ | 3 | 4 | 5 | 6 | 7 | 8 | 10 | 12 | 15 |
|---|---|---|---|---|---|---|---|---|---|
| $R/T < \%$ | 72 | 78 | 82 | 84 | 86 | 88 | 91 | 93 | 95 |
| $(\bar{x} - T_m) < \%$ | 29 | 25 | 22 | 20 | 19 | 18 | 16 | 14 | 13 |

## Weibull distribution of lifetimes

Weibull distribution has gained acceptance as the standard in the investigation of the lifetimes of technical products. Its distribution function (probability for lifetimes $\leq t$) is:

$$F(t) = 1 - e^{-(t/T)^b}$$

Survival probability (reliability)

$$R(t) = 1 - F(t)$$

Failure rate (failures per unit of time referred to remaining products)

$$\lambda(t) = f(t) \, / \, R(t)$$

where:

$T$ Characteristic lifetime, corresponding sum of failures 63.2%.

$b$ Failure steepness (Weibull slope),
    $b < 1$: falling (early failures)
    $b = 1$: constant (random failures)
    $b > 1$: rising (wear)

In the Weibull grid with abscissa $\ln t$ and ordinate $\ln (-\ln R[t])$, $F(t)$ becomes a straight line.

Evaluation of an endurance test involving $n$ test specimens:

The figure shows the evaluation of an endurance test involving $n = 19$ switches, of which $r = 12$ have failed. Against the lifetimes $t$ ordered according to length in cycles, the sum of failures is plotted as

$$H = (i - 0.5)/n$$

The result is:

    $T = 83 \cdot 10^3$ cycles
    $b = 3.2$    (wear).

$T$ and $b$ are random values like $\bar{x}$ and $s$. Approximate confidence intervals ($n \geq 50$) for the "true values" are provided by the formulas:

$$T \pm (u/\sqrt{n}) \cdot (T/b)$$
$$b - 0.5 \cdot (u/\sqrt{n'}) \cdot b \ldots b + (u/\sqrt{n'}) \cdot b$$

$u$ from Table 1.

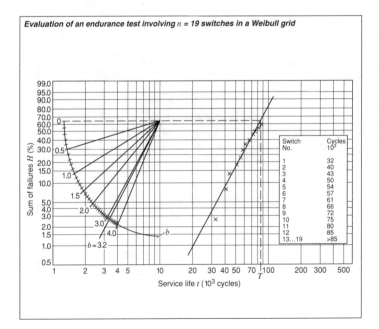

*Evaluation of an endurance test involving $n = 19$ switches in a Weibull grid*

| Switch No. | Cycles $10^3$ |
|---|---|
| 1 | 32 |
| 2 | 40 |
| 3 | 43 |
| 4 | 50 |
| 5 | 54 |
| 6 | 57 |
| 7 | 61 |
| 8 | 66 |
| 9 | 72 |
| 10 | 75 |
| 11 | 80 |
| 12 | 85 |
| 13...19 | >85 |

For incomplete observations ($r < n$):
$$n' \approx r \cdot \left(1 + (r/n)\right)/2$$

$T$, $b$ are therefore less precisely defined by $r$ failures at $r < n$ than at $r = n$. The proportion exceeding a specific lifetime expectancy is estimated in the following section.

## Statistical evaluation of test results

$N$  Population size (batch). An attribute divides the batch into two classes, e.g. "failed" and "OK".

$n$  Number of sample units

$I$  Number of defects in batch

$i$  Number of defects in sample

$p$  Defective fraction in sample
$p = i/n$

$p'$  Defective fraction in batch
$p' = I/N$

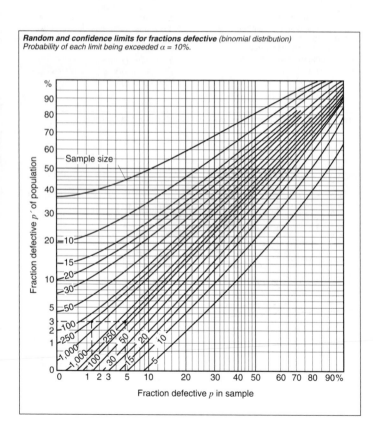

**Random and confidence limits for fractions defective** (binomial distribution)
Probability of each limit being exceeded $\alpha = 10\%$.

## Distribution of defective fraction $p$ in random samples

The number of defectives $i$ within the sample is a random variable. Larger batches ($N > 10 \cdot n$) are characterized by binomial distribution, expected value: $E(i) = n \cdot p'$

Standard deviation:
$$\sigma_i = \sqrt{n \cdot p' \cdot (1 - p')}$$

Random intervals for $p$ ($p'$ known) and confidence intervals for $p'$ ($p$ known) dependent on $n$ are shown in the figure on p. 220 with a nonconforming probability of $\alpha = 10\%$ for each limit.

For the range $p' < 5\%$, frequently encountered in practice, binomial distribution is replaced by Poisson's law of infrequent events, which is exclusively dependent on $n \cdot p'$ with $E(i) = n \cdot p'$, $\sigma_i = \sqrt{n \cdot p'}$.

## Examples:

1. Binomial distribution (see figure on p. 220)

In an endurance test with $n = 20$ units, $i = 2$ units failed after extended use.

What percentage $p'$ of the series will not achieve the corresponding lifetime $T$?

Percentage in random sample $p = 2/20 = 10\%$.

At $p = 10\%$, $n = 20$, the figure provides the following figures:
$$p_u' = 2.8\%, \; p_o' = 24\%.$$
With constant quality, the percentage with a lifetime $< T$ will lie within this range.

2. Poisson distribution (Table 4)

During incoming inspection, a random sample of $n = 500$ parts found $i = 1$ part which exceeded the tolerance.

What is the maximum percentage of defective parts in the batch as expressed with 90% probability?
At $i = 1$, $\alpha = 10\%$, Table 4 indicates:
$$np_o' = 3.89$$
$$p_o' = 3.89/500 = 7.78‰.$$

## Approximation formula for Poisson distribution

The approximate value for $i > 10$ can be derived using:
$$n \cdot p' = i + u \cdot \sqrt{i} + k$$
(see Table 4 for $u$, $k$).

## Example for Poisson approximation

In a preproduction series consisting of $n = 10{,}000$ units, there were $i = 17$ warranty claims. With 97.5% probability, what is the limit for warranty claims which will not be exceeded in normal series production if identical conditions are maintained?

Inserting the values from Table 4 into the approximation formula given above provides the following:
$$np_o' = 17 + 1.96 \cdot \sqrt{17} + 2 = 27.08$$
$$p_o' = 27.08/10\,000 = 2.7‰.$$

## Table 4. Confidence limits for infrequent events

| Obs. no. $i$ | Lower limit $np_u'$ Probability of being exceeded 2.5% | 10% | Upper limit $np_o'$ 10% | 2.5% |
|---|---|---|---|---|
| 0 | — | — | 2.30 | 3.69 |
| 1 | 0.025 | 0.105 | 3.89 | 5.57 |
| 2 | 0.242 | 0.532 | 5.32 | 7.22 |
| 3 | 0.619 | 1.10 | 6.68 | 8.77 |
| 4 | 1.09 | 1.74 | 8.00 | 10.24 |
| 5 | 1.62 | 2.43 | 9.27 | 11.67 |
| 6 | 2.20 | 3.15 | 10.53 | 13.06 |
| 7 | 2.81 | 3.89 | 11.77 | 14.42 |
| 8 | 3.45 | 4.66 | 12.99 | 15.76 |
| 9 | 4.12 | 5.43 | 14.21 | 17.08 |
| 10 | 4.80 | 6.22 | 15.41 | 18.39 |
| $u$ | − 1.96 | − 1.28 | + 1.28 | + 1.96 |
| $k$ | + 1.0 | + 0.2 | + 1.2 | + 2.0 |

## Measurement: basic terms

Measurements can only be used as the basis for responsible decisions if their limits of error are known. Here, statistical terms are used.

**Definition of terms** (as per DIN 1319):

Measured variable
Physical variable which is measured (length, density, etc.).

Measured value
Particular value of the measured variables, e.g. 3 m.

Measurement result
Value calculated from one or more measured values, e.g. mean $\bar{x}$.

Measurement error $F = x_a - x_r$
$x_a$ indicated measured value;
$x_r$ "correct" measured value.
Causes: measured object, measuring instruments, measurement procedure, environment, observer.

Relative measurement error
Normally: $F/x_r$
For the designation of measuring devices $F/x_e$, where $x_e$ = full-scale deflection of measuring instrument.

Systematic measurement errors
Measurement errors which, under the same conditions, have the same magnitude and sign.
   Detectable systematic errors are to be accounted for and corrected by $B = -F$, otherwise the measurement result is incorrect. Systematic errors which cannot be detected are to be estimated ($f$).

Random measurement errors
Measurement errors whose magnitudes and signs are dispersed randomly. Estimated using the standard deviation $s$ of the random errors.

Result of a series of measurements
If $n$ measured values $x_i$ are measured under the same conditions, the following should be specified as the measurement result:
$y = \bar{x}_E \pm u$   Confidence limits for correct measured value, where:
$\bar{x}_E = \bar{x} + B$   Corrected mean value
$u = t \cdot s/\sqrt{n} + |f|$   Measurement uncertainty

Calculation of $s$ p. 196,
for $t$, see Table 2 p. 199.
$f$ Non-detected systematic errors.

Separation of measurement and manufacturing accuracy
On each of $n$ products, an attribute $x_i$ is measured twice with measurement error $f_{ik}$:
$y_{ik} = x_i + f_{ik}$ $(i = 1, \ldots n; k = 1.2)$

The differences between the two measured values on the same product contain two measurement errors:
$$z_i = y_{i1} - y_{i2} = f_{i1} - f_{i2}$$
$$\sigma_z^2 = 2 \, \sigma_f^2$$
$$\sigma_y^2 = \sigma_x^2 + \sigma_f^2$$

The last two relationships can be used to determine the standard deviation $\sigma_f$ of the measurement errors and the corrected standard deviation $\sigma_x$ of the product characteristic $x$.

**Standards**
DIN 55 303 Statistical assessment of data
DIN 53 804 Statistical assessments
DIN 55 350 Quality assurance and statistics terms
DIN 40 080 Regulations and tables for attributive sampling
DIN 7186 Statistical tolerances
DIN/ISO 9000 Quality systems
DGQ-11-04 Quality-assurance terms and formulas (Beuth)

**References**
Graf, Henning, Stange: Formeln und Tabellen der Statistik (Formulas and tables for statistics) Springer-Verlag, Berlin, 1956; Rauhut: Berechnung der Lebensdauerverteilung (Calculation of lifetime distribution) Glückauf-Verlag, Essen, 1982.

# Control engineering

## Terms and definitions (in accordance with DIN 19 226)

| Closed-loop control | Open-loop control |
|---|---|
| **Closed-loop control**<br>Closed-loop control is a process by which a variable, the variable to be controlled (controlled variable $x$), is continuously recorded, compared with another variable, the reference variable $w_1$, and influenced according to the result of this comparison in the sense of an adaptation to the reference variable. The ensuing action takes place in a closed control loop.<br><br>The function of closed-loop control is to adapt the value of the controlled variable to the value specified by the reference variable in spite of disturbances even if the given conditions do not allow for a perfect match. | **Open-loop control**<br>Open-loop control is the process in a system in which one or more variables as input variables influence other variables as output variables on account of the rules characteristic of that system.<br><br>This type of control is characterized by the open action via the individual transfer element or the open control loop.<br><br>The term "control" is often used not only to denote the control process itself but also the entire system in which the control function takes place. |
| **Closed control loop**<br>The closed control loop is formed by all the elements which take part in the closed action of the control operation.<br><br>The control loop is a closed path of action which acts in one direction. The controlled variable $x$ acts in a circular structure in the form of negative feedback on itself.<br><br>**In contrast to open-loop control, closed-loop control takes into account the influence of all the disturbances ($z_1$, $z_2$) in the control loop.**<br><br>The closed control loop is subdivided into controlled system and controlling system. | **Open control loop**<br>An open control loop is an arrangement of elements (systems) which act on each other in a chain structure.<br><br>An open control loop as a whole can be part of a higher-level system and interact in any fashion with other systems.<br><br>An open control loop can only counter the effect of the disturbance which is measured by the control unit (e.g. $z_1$); other disturbances (e.g. $z_2$) are unaffected.<br><br>The open control loop is subdivided into open-loop controlled system and controlling system. |

**Controlling system (open and closed loops)**
The open-loop or closed-loop controlling system is that part of the control loop which acts on the controlled system via the final-controlling element as determined by the control parameters.

**System boundaries**
The open-loop and closed-loop controlling systems include all those devices and elements which act directly to produce the desired condition within the control circuit.

| *Closed control loop* | *Open control loop* |
|---|---|
| 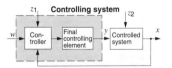 | 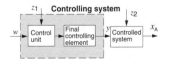 |

| **Input variables and output variable of closed-loop controlling system**<br>The input variables to the controlling system are the controlled variable $x$, the reference variable $w$, and the disturbance(s) $z_1$. The output variable from the controlling system is the manipulated variable $y$. | **Input variables and output variable of open-loop controlling system**<br>The input variables to the controlling system are the reference variable $w$ and the disturbance(s) $z_1$. The output variable from the controlling system is the manipulated variable $y$. |

| Closed-loop control | Open-loop control |
|---|---|

**Controlled system (open and closed loops)**
The open-loop or closed-loop controlled system is that part of the control loop which represents the area of the system to be influenced according to the function.

| **Input variables and output variable of closed-loop controlled system** | **Input variable and output variable of open-loop controlled system** |
|---|---|
| The input variables to the controlled system are the manipulated variable $y$ and the disturbances $z_2$. The output variable from the controlled system is the controlled variable $x$. | The input variable is the manipulated variable $y$. The output variable is the object variable $x_A$ or an output variable which influences the object variable in a predetermined manner. |

**Transfer elements and system elements**
Open- and closed-loop controls can be subdivided into elements along the control loop.
In terms of equipment design and function, these are called system elements and transfer elements, respectively.
In terms of closed- or open-loop control function, only the relationship between the variables and their values, which act upon one another in the system, is described.

**Loop, direction of control action**
Both the open control loop and the closed control loop comprise individual elements (or systems) which are connected together to form a loop.
The loop is that path along which open- or closed-loop control takes place. The direction of control action is the direction in which the control function operates.
The loop and the direction of control action need not necessarily coincide with the path and the direction of corresponding energy and mass flows.

**Final controlling element, control point**
The final controlling element is that element which is located at the upstream end of the controlled system, and which directly affects the flow of mass or energy. The location at which this action takes place is called the control point.

**Disturbance point**
The disturbance point is the location at which a variable not controlled by the system acts on the loop, thereby adversely affecting the condition which the control is designed to maintain.

**Manipulated variable $y$, manipulating range $Y_h$**
The manipulated variable $y$ is both the output variable of the controlling system and the input variable of the controlled system. It transfers the action of the controlling system to the controlled system.
The manipulating range $Y_h$ is the range within which the manipulated variable can be adjusted.

**Reference variable $w$, reference-variable range $W_h$**
The reference variable $w$ of an open- or closed-loop control is a variable which is not acted on directly by the control; it is input to the loop from outside of the control, and is that variable whose value is to be reflected by the output variable in accordance with the control parameters.
The reference-variable range $W_h$ is that range within which the reference variable $w$ of an open- or closed-loop control may lie.

**Disturbances $z$, disturbance range $Z_h$**
Disturbances $z$ in open- and closed-loop controls are all variables acting from outside of the control which adversely affect the action of the control. In many cases, the most important disturbance is the stress or the throughput through the system. The disturbance range $Z_h$ is that range within which the disturbance may lie without adversely affecting the operation of the control.

**Object variable $x_A$, object range $X_{Ah}$**
The object variable $x_A$ of an open- or closed-loop control is that variable which the control is intended to influence.
The object range $X_{Ah}$ of an open- or closed-loop control is that range within which the object variable may lie, with full functional capability of the control.

## Control methods

### Transfer elements
Transfer elements are the basic modules and core elements for the control-engineering analysis and synthesis of dynamic systems. They each contain an illustration specification which allows an output variable to be clearly assigned to each input variable that is permitted for the corresponding transfer element. The general graphical representation of a transfer element is the block diagram (see figure).

The illustration specification $\phi$ is often termed the operator. With the operator $\phi$, the functional relationship between the input and output variables of a transfer element can be described by:

$$y(t) = \phi(u(t), t)$$

A summary of the simplest transfer elements can be found in the accompanying table.

A particular position among the general transfer elements is taken up by linear time-invariant transfer elements. For these elements, the following superposition principle applies:

$$\phi(u_1(t) + u_2(t)) = \phi(u_1(t)) + \phi(u_2(t))$$

together with the condition of time invariance:

$$y(t) = \phi(u(t)) \rightarrow y(t-T) = \phi(u(t-T)), \; T>0$$

With the transfer elements connected to each other by the action lines, it is possible to depict complex dynamic systems such as e.g. a DC motor, hydraulic systems, mechatronic servo-systems, etc.

### Controller design
A series of analytical and synthesizing processes are available for application in control engineering. Control engineers distinguish here between time-range and frequency-range procedures. A classical and effective example of the frequency-range procedure is the design of controllers using Bode diagrams. An efficient time-range procedure is the design of a state controller by means of pole specification or the Riccati controller.

Many of the problems posed by the requirements of control engineering are solved by using certain controller types which are composed as far as possible of the following four transfer elements:

– $P$ element (proportional-action transfer element)
– $I$ element (integral-action transfer element)
– $D$ element (derivative-action transfer element)
– $P\text{-}T_1$ element (1st order time-delay element)

Parallel connection on the input side, addition of the output variables from the three transfer elements $P$, $I$, $D$ and downstream connection of the $P\text{-}T_1$ element can be used to create the controller types $P$, $I$, $PI$, $PP$, $PD$, $PID$, $PPD$. See DIN 19 226 for characteristics and system performance.

### Subdivision of control modes
In control-engineering practice, distinctions are made between the individual control modes according to the following attributes: continuous-time/continuous-value, continuous-time/discrete-value, discrete-time/continuous-value and discrete-time/discrete-value. Of these four attributes, only the instances of continuous-time/continuous-value control and discrete-time/discrete-value control are of significance.

Continuous-time/continuous-value control
In continuous-time/continuous-value control, the controlled variable is recorded in an uninterrupted process and compared with the reference variable. This comparison provides the basis for continuous-time and continuous-value generation of the manipulated variable.

Continuous-time/continuous-value control is also referred to as analog control.

**Table: Summary of some transfer elements**

| Designation | Functional relationship | Transfer function | Course of step response | Symbol |
|---|---|---|---|---|
| $P$ element | $y = Ku$ | $K$ | | |
| $I$ element | $y = K \int_0^t u(\tau)\,d\tau$ | $\dfrac{K}{s}$ | | |
| $D$ element | $y = K\dot{u}$ | $Ks$ | Area = K | |
| $TZ$ element $T_1$ element | $y(t) = Ku(t - T_1)$ | $Ke^{-T_1 s}$ | | |
| $S$ element | $y = u_1 \pm \ldots \pm u_p$ | | | |
| $P\text{-}T_1$ element, $VZ_1$ element | $T\dot{y} + y = Ku$ | $\dfrac{K}{1 + Ts}$ | | |
| $P\text{-}T_2$ element $VZ_2$ element | $T^2\ddot{y} + 2dT\dot{y} + y = Ku$ | $\dfrac{K}{1 + 2dTs + T^2 s^2}$ | Periodic case: $d < 1$<br><br>Aperiodic limit case: $d \geq 1$ | |

<u>Discrete-time/discrete-value control</u>
In discrete-time/discrete-value control, the controlled variable is recorded, quantified, and subtracted from the quantified reference variable only at the sampling instants. The manipulated variable is calculated on the basis of the control difference thus created. For this purpose, an algorithm is generally used which is implemented in the form of a software program on a microcontroller. A/D and D/A converters are used as process interfaces. Discrete-time/discrete-value control is also referred to as digital control.

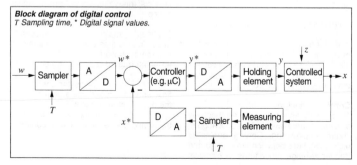

**Block diagram of digital control**
$T$ Sampling time, * Digital signal values.

**Examples of closed-loop control systems in motor vehicles (simplified)**

| Control system | Variables | | | | | Elements | | |
|---|---|---|---|---|---|---|---|---|
| | Object variable ($x_A$) | Controlled variable ($x$) | Reference variable ($w$) | Manipulated variable ($y$) | Disturbances ($z$) | Controlling system | Final controlling element | Controlled system |
| Lambda closed-loop control | Air/fuel ratio ($\lambda$) | $O_2$ content in exhaust gas | $\lambda$ = 1.0 (fixed-command control) | Injected fuel quantity | Inexact pilot control, leaks, crankcase ventilation | Lambda control unit and lambda oxygen sensor | Fuel injectors | Combustion chamber; part of intake system and exhaust-gas system through to $\lambda$ sensor |
| Rotational-speed control in diesel engines | Engine speed | | Setpoint speed (follow-up control) | Injected fuel quantity | Load | Governor | Fuel-injection pump | Mixture-formation area in engine |
| Antilock braking system (ABS control) | Wheel slip | | Slip limit (adaptive) | Braking pressure | Road and driving conditions | Controller in ABS ECU | Pressure-control valve | Tires, road |
| Temperature control (passenger cabin) | Interior temperature | Cabin exhaust-air and ambient-air temperature | Setpoint temperature (follow-up control) | Hot-water flow rate or hot/cold air mixture ratio | Engine temp.; ambient temp.; insolation; driving speed; engine speed | Temperature regulator and temperature sensor | Solenoid heating valve or air flap | Passenger cabin |

**Examples of open-loop control systems in engines**

| Control system | Variables | | | | | Controlling system | Final controlling element | Controlled system |
|---|---|---|---|---|---|---|---|---|
| | Object variable ($x_A$) | Reference variable ($w$) | Input variables of controlling system | Disturbances ($z$) | Manipulated variable ($y$) | | | |
| Jetronic gasoline injection | Air/fuel ratio | Air/fuel ratio (setpoint) | Engine speed, engine temperature, vehicle system voltage, air flow rate, air temperature, throttle-valve position | Fuel temperature, manifold-wall fuel condensation | Injection duration | Jetronic ECU with various measuring elements | Fuel injectors | Mixture formation area |
| Electronic ignition systems | Mixture ignition point | Mixture ignition point (setpoint) | Engine speed, crankshaft position, intake-manifold pressure, throttle-valve position, engine temperature, vehicle system voltage | Condition of spark plugs, air/fuel ratio, fuel grade, mechanical tolerances | Moment of ignition | Ignition control unit | Ignition output stage | Combustion chamber in engine |

# Chemical elements

## Designations

| Element | Symbol | Type[1] | Atomic number | Relative atomic mass | Valence | Year discovered | Discoverer(s) |
|---|---|---|---|---|---|---|---|
| Actinium | Ac | m | 89 | 227 | 3 | 1899 | Debierne |
| Aluminum | Al | m | 13 | 26.9815 | 3 | 1825 | Oersted |
| Americium[2] | Am | m | 95 | 243 | 2; 3; 4; 5; 6 | 1944 | Seaborg et al. |
| Antimony | Sb | m | 51 | 121.760 | 3; 5 | Antiquity | |
| Argon | Ar | g | 18 | 39.948 | 0 | 1894 | Ramsay, Rayleigh |
| Arsenic | As | n | 33 | 74.9216 | 3; 5 | C13 | Magnus |
| Astatine | At | n | 85 | 210 | 1; 3 | 1940 | Corson, MacKenzie, Segré |
| Barium | Ba | m | 56 | 137.327 | 2 | 1808 | Davy |
| Berkelium[2] | Bk | m | 97 | 247 | 3; 4 | 1949 | Seaborg et al. |
| Beryllium | Be | m | 4 | 9.0122 | 2 | 1797 | Vauquelin |
| Bismuth | Bi | m | 83 | 208.9804 | 1; 3; 5 | C15 | Unknown |
| Bohrium[2] | Bh | m[3] | 107 | 262 | −[4] | 1981 | Armbruster, Münzenberg et al. |
| Boron | B | n | 5 | 10.811 | 3 | 1808 | Gay-Lussac, Thénard, Davy |
| Bromine | Br | n | 35 | 79.904 | 1; 3; 4; 5; 7 | 1826 | Balard |
| Cadmium | Cd | m | 48 | 112.411 | 1; 2 | 1817 | Strohmeyer |
| Caesium | Cs | m | 55 | 132.9054 | 1 | 1860 | Bunsen, Kirchhoff |
| Calcium | Ca | m | 20 | 40.078 | 2 | 1808 | Davy |
| Californium[2] | Cf | m | 98 | 251 | 2; 3; 4 | 1950 | Seaborg et al. |
| Carbon | C | n | 6 | 12.011 | 2; 4 | Antiquity | |
| Cer | Ce | m | 58 | 140.116 | 3; 4 | 1803 | Berzelius et al. |
| Chlorine | Cl | g | 17 | 35.4527 | 1; 3; 4; 5; 6; 7 | 1774 | Scheele |
| Chromium | Cr | m | 24 | 51.9961 | 1; 2; 3; 4; 5; 6 | 1780 | Vauquelin |
| Cobalt | Co | m | 27 | 58.9332 | 1; 2; 3; 4; 5 | 1735 | Brandt |
| Copper | Cu | m | 29 | 63.546 | 1; 2; 3 | Antiquity | |
| Curium[2] | Cm | m | 96 | 247 | 2; 3; 4 | 1944 | Seaborg et al. |
| Dubnium[2] | Db | m[3] | 105 | 262 | 5 (?) | 1967/70 | Disputed (Flerov or Ghiorso) |
| Dysprosium | Dy | m | 66 | 162.50 | 2; 3; 4 | 1886 | Lecoq de Boisbaudran |
| Einsteinium[2] | Es | m | 99 | 252 | 3 | 1952 | Ghiorso et al. |
| Erbium | Er | m | 68 | 167.26 | 3 | 1842 | Mosander |
| Europium | Eu | m | 63 | 151.964 | 2; 3 | 1901 | Demarcay |
| Fermium[2] | Fm | m[3] | 100 | 257 | 3 | 1952 | Ghiorso et al. |
| Ferrum | Fe | m | 26 | 55.845 | 2; 3; 6 | Antiquity | |
| Fluorine | F | g | 9 | 18.998 | 1 | 1887 | Moissan |
| Francium | Fr | m | 87 | 223 | 1 | 1939 | Perey |
| Gadolinium | Gd | m | 64 | 157.25 | 2; 3 | 1880 | de Marignac |
| Gallium | Ga | m | 31 | 69.723 | 1; 2; 3 | 1875 | Lecoq de Boisbaudran |
| Germanium | Ge | m | 32 | 72.61 | 2; 4 | 1886 | Winkler |
| Gold | Au | m | 79 | 196.9665 | 1; 3; 5; 7 | Antiquity | |
| Hafnium | Hf | m | 72 | 178.49 | 4 | 1923 | Hevesey, Coster |
| Hassium[2] | Hs | m[3] | 108 | 265 | −[4] | 1984 | Armbruster, Münzenberg et al. |
| Helium | He | g | 2 | 4.003 | 0 | 1895 | Ramsay, Cleve, Langlet |
| Holmium | Ho | m | 67 | 164.9303 | 3 | 1878 | Cleve, Delafontaine, Soret |
| Hydrogen | H | g | 1 | 1.0079 | 1 | 1766 | Cavendish |

[1] m Metal, n Nonmetal, g Gas. [2] Artificially produced; does not occur naturally.
[3] Unknown. The elements are presumably 100...112 metals. [4] Unknown.

| Element | Symbol | Type[1] | Atomic number | Relative atomic mass | Valence | Year discovered | Discoverer(s) |
|---|---|---|---|---|---|---|---|
| Indium | In | m | 49 | 114.818 | 1; 2; 3 | 1863 | Reich, Richter |
| Iodine | I | n | 53 | 126.9045 | 1; 3; 5; 7 | 1811 | Courtois |
| Iridium | Ir | m | 77 | 192.217 | 3; 4 | 1803 | Tennant |
| Krypton | Kr | g | 36 | 83.80 | 0; 2 | 1898 | Ramsay |
| Lanthanum | La | m | 57 | 138.9055 | 3 | 1839 | Mosander |
| Lawrencium[2] | Lr | m[3] | 103 | 262 | 3 | 1961 | Ghiorso et al. |
| Lithium | Li | m | 3 | 6.941 | 1 | 1817 | Arfvedson |
| Lutetium | Lu | m | 71 | 174.967 | 3 | 1907 | Urbain, James |
| Magnesium | Mg | m | 12 | 24.3050 | 2 | 1755 | Black |
| Manganese | Mn | m | 25 | 54.9380 | 2; 3; 4; 6; 7 | 1774 | Grahn |
| Meitnerium | Mt | m[3] | 109 | 266 | −[4] | 1982 | Armbruster, Münzenberg et al. |
| Mendelevium[2] | Md | m[3] | 101 | 258 | 2; 3 | 1955 | Seaborg, Ghiorso et al. |
| Mercury | Hg | m | 80 | 200.59 | 1; 2 | Antiquity | |
| Molybdenum | Mo | m | 42 | 95.94 | 2; 3; 4; 5; 6 | 1781 | Hjelm |
| Sodium | Na | m | 11 | 22.9898 | 1 | 1807 | Davy |
| Neodymium | Nd | m | 60 | 144.24 | 2; 3; 4 | 1885 | Auer von Welsbach |
| Neon | Ne | g | 10 | 20.1797 | 0 | 1898 | Ramsay, Travers |
| Neptunium[2] | Np | m | 93 | 237 | 3; 4; 5; 6 | 1940 | McMillan, Abelson |
| Nickel | Ni | m | 28 | 58.6934 | 2; 3 | 1751 | Cronstedt |
| Niobium | Nb | m | 41 | 92.9064 | 3; 4; 5 | 1801 | Hatchett |
| Nitrogen | N | g | 7 | 14,0067 | 2; 3; 4; 5 | 1772 | Rutherford |
| Nobelium[2] | No | m[3] | 102 | 259 | 2; 3 | 1958 | Ghiorso, Seaborg |
| Osmium | Os | m | 76 | 190.23 | 2; 3; 4; 5; 7; 8 | 1803 | Tennant |
| Oxygen | O | g | 8 | 15.9994 | 1; 2 | 1774 | Priestley, Scheele |
| Palladium | Pd | m | 46 | 106.42 | 2; 4 | 1803 | Wollaston |
| Phosphorus | P | n | 15 | 30.9738 | 3; 5 | 1669 | Brandt |
| Platinum | Pt | m | 78 | 195.078 | 2; 4; 5; 6 | Antiquity | (Mayas) |
| Plutonium[2] | Pu | m | 94 | 244 | 3; 4; 5; 6 | 1940 | Seaborg et al. |
| Polonium | Po | m | 84 | 209 | 2; 4; 6 | 1898 | M. Curie |
| Potassium | K | m | 19 | 39.0983 | 1 | 1807 | Davy |
| Praseodymium | Pr | m | 59 | 140.9076 | 3; 4 | 1885 | Auer von Welsbach |
| Promethium | Pm | m | 61 | 145 | 3 | 1945 | Marinsky et al. |
| Protactinium | Pa | m | 91 | 231.0359 | 4; 5 | 1917 | Hahn, Meitner, Fajans |
| Radium | Ra | m | 88 | 226 | 2 | 1898 | P. & M. Curie |
| Radon | Rn | g | 86 | 222 | 0; 2 | 1900 | Dorn |
| Rhenium | Re | m | 75 | 186.207 | 1; 2; 3; 4; 5; 6; 7 | 1925 | Noddack |
| Rhodium | Rh | m | 45 | 102.9055 | 1; 2; 3; 4; 5; 6 | 1803 | Wollaston |
| Rubidium | Rb | m | 37 | 85.4678 | 1 | 1861 | Bunsen, Kirchhoff |
| Ruthenium | Ru | m | 44 | 101.07 | 1; 2; 3; 4; 5; 6; 7; 8 | 1808 | Klaus |
| Rutherfordium[2] | Rf | m[3] | 104 | 261 | 4 (?) | 1964/69 | Disputed (Flerov or Ghiorso) |

[1] m Metal, n Nonmetal, g Gas.
[2] Artificially produced; does not occur naturally.
[3] Unknown. The elements are presumably 100...112 metals.
[4] Unknown.

| Element | Symbol | Type [1] | Atomic number | Relative atomic mass | Valence | Year discovered | Discoverer(s) |
|---|---|---|---|---|---|---|---|
| Samarium | Sm | m | 62 | 150.36 | 2; 3 | 1879 | Lecoq de Boisbaudran |
| Scandium | Sc | m | 21 | 44.9559 | 3 | 1879 | Nilson |
| Seaborgium [2] | Sg | m [3] | 106 | 263 | − [4] | 1974 | Ghiorso et al. |
| Selenium | Se | n | 34 | 78.96 | 2; 4; 6 | 1817 | Berzelius |
| Silicon | Si | n | 14 | 28.0855 | 2; 4 | 1824 | Berzelius |
| Silver | Ag | m | 47 | 107.8682 | 1; 2 | Antiquity | |
| Sodium | Na | m | 11 | 22.9898 | 1 | 1807 | Davy |
| Strontium | Sr | m | 38 | 87.62 | 2 | 1790 | Crawford |
| Sulfur | S | n | 16 | 32.066 | 1; 2; 3; 4; 5; 6 | Antiquity | |
| Tantalum | Ta | m | 73 | 180.9479 | 1; 3; 4; 5 | 1802 | Eckeberg |
| Technetium | Tc | m | 43 | 98 | 4; 5; 6; 7 | 1937 | Perrier, Segré |
| Tellurium | Te | m | 52 | 127.60 | 2; 4; 6 | 1783 | Müller |
| Terbium | Tb | m | 65 | 158.9253 | 3; 4 | 1843 | Mosander |
| Thallium | Tl | m | 81 | 204.3833 | 1; 3 | 1861 | Crookes |
| Thorium | Th | m | 90 | 232.0381 | 2; 3; 4 | 1829 | Berzelius |
| Thulium | Tm | m | 69 | 168.9342 | 2; 3 | 1879 | Cleve |
| Tin | Sn | m | 50 | 118.710 | 2; 4 | Antiquity | |
| Titanium | Ti | m | 22 | 47.87 | 2; 3; 4 | 1791 | Gregor |
| Tungsten | W | m | 74 | 183.84 | 2; 3; 4; 5; 6 | 1783 | Elhuijar |
| Ununbium [2] [5] | Uub | m [3] | 112 | 277 | − [4] | 1996 | Armbruster, Hofmann |
| Ununnilium [2] [5] | Uun | m [3] | 110 | 270 | − [4] | 1994 | Armbruster, Hofmann |
| Unununium [2] [5] | Uuu | m [3] | 111 | 272 | − [4] | 1994 | Armbruster, Hofmann |
| Uranium | U | m | 92 | 238.0289 | 3; 4; 5; 6 | 1789 | Klaproth |
| Vanadium | V | m | 23 | 50.9415 | 2; 3; 4; 5 | 1801 | del Rio |
| Xenon | Xe | g | 54 | 131.29 | 0; 2; 4; 6; 8 | 1898 | Ramsay, Travers |
| Ytterbium | Yb | m | 70 | 173.04 | 2; 3 | 1878 | de Marignac |
| Yttrium | Y | m | 39 | 88.9059 | 3 | 1794 | Gadolin |
| Zinc | Zn | m | 30 | 65.39 | 2 | Antiquity | |
| Zirconium | Zr | m | 40 | 91.224 | 3; 4 | 1789 | Klaproth |

[1] m Metal, n Nonmetal, g Gas.
[2] Artificially produced; does not occur naturally.
[3] Unknown. The elements are presumably 100...112 metals.
[4] Unknown.
[5] Provisional IUPAC designation.

# Periodic table of elements

| Ia | IIa | IIIb | IVb | Vb | VIb | VIIb | VIIIb | | | Ib | IIb | IIIa | IVa | Va | VIa | VIIa | VIIIa |
|---|---|---|---|---|---|---|---|---|---|---|---|---|---|---|---|---|---|
| 1<br>**H**<br>1.008 | | | | | | | | | | | | | | | | | 2<br>**He**<br>4.003 |
| 3<br>**Li**<br>6.941 | 4<br>**Be**<br>9.012 | | | | | | | | | | | 5<br>**B**<br>10.811 | 6<br>**C**<br>12.011 | 7<br>**N**<br>14.007 | 8<br>**O**<br>15.999 | 9<br>**F**<br>18.998 | 10<br>**Ne**<br>20.180 |
| 11<br>**Na**<br>22.990 | 12<br>**Mg**<br>24.305 | | | | | | | | | | | 13<br>**Al**<br>26.982 | 14<br>**Si**<br>28.086 | 15<br>**P**<br>30.974 | 16<br>**S**<br>32.066 | 17<br>**Cl**<br>35.453 | 18<br>**Ar**<br>39.948 |
| 19<br>**K**<br>39.098 | 20<br>**Ca**<br>40.078 | 21<br>**Sc**<br>44.956 | 22<br>**Ti**<br>47.87 | 23<br>**V**<br>50.942 | 24<br>**Cr**<br>51.996 | 25<br>**Mn**<br>54.938 | 26<br>**Fe**<br>55.845 | 27<br>**Co**<br>58.933 | 28<br>**Ni**<br>58.693 | 29<br>**Cu**<br>63.546 | 30<br>**Zn**<br>65.39 | 31<br>**Ga**<br>69.723 | 32<br>**Ge**<br>72.61 | 33<br>**As**<br>74.922 | 34<br>**Se**<br>78.96 | 35<br>**Br**<br>79.904 | 36<br>**Kr**<br>83.80 |
| 37<br>**Rb**<br>85.468 | 38<br>**Sr**<br>87.62 | 39<br>**Y**<br>88.906 | 40<br>**Zr**<br>91.224 | 41<br>**Nb**<br>92.906 | 42<br>**Mo**<br>95.94 | 43<br>**Tc**<br>(98) | 44<br>**Ru**<br>101.07 | 45<br>**Rh**<br>102.906 | 46<br>**Pd**<br>106.42 | 47<br>**Ag**<br>107.868 | 48<br>**Cd**<br>112.411 | 49<br>**In**<br>114.818 | 50<br>**Sn**<br>118.710 | 51<br>**Sb**<br>121.760 | 52<br>**Te**<br>127.60 | 53<br>**I**<br>126.904 | 54<br>**Xe**<br>131.29 |
| 55<br>**Cs**<br>132.905 | 56<br>**Ba**<br>137.327 | 57<br>**La***<br>138.906 | 72<br>**Hf**<br>178.49 | 73<br>**Ta**<br>180.948 | 74<br>**W**<br>183.84 | 75<br>**Re**<br>186.207 | 76<br>**Os**<br>190.23 | 77<br>**Ir**<br>192.217 | 78<br>**Pt**<br>195.078 | 79<br>**Au**<br>196.967 | 80<br>**Hg**<br>200.59 | 81<br>**Tl**<br>204.383 | 82<br>**Pb**<br>207.2 | 83<br>**Bi**<br>208.980 | 84<br>**Po**<br>(209) | 85<br>**At**<br>(210) | 86<br>**Rn**<br>(222) |
| 87<br>**Fr**<br>(223) | 88<br>**Ra**<br>(226) | 89<br>**Ac****<br>(227) | 104<br>**Rf**<br>(261) | 105<br>**Db**<br>(262) | 106<br>**Sg**<br>(263) | 107<br>**Bh**<br>(262) | 108<br>**Hs**<br>(265) | 109<br>**Mt**<br>(266) | 110<br>**Uun**<br>(269) | 111<br>**Uuu**<br>(272) | 112<br>**Uub**<br>(277) | | | | | | |

| \* | 58<br>**Ce**<br>140.116 | 59<br>**Pr**<br>140.908 | 60<br>**Nd**<br>144.24 | 61<br>**Pm**<br>(145) | 62<br>**Sm**<br>150.36 | 63<br>**Eu**<br>151.964 | 64<br>**Gd**<br>157.25 | 65<br>**Tb**<br>158.925 | 66<br>**Dy**<br>162.50 | 67<br>**Ho**<br>164.930 | 68<br>**Er**<br>167.26 | 69<br>**Tm**<br>168.934 | 70<br>**Yb**<br>173.04 | 71<br>**Lu**<br>174.967 |
|---|---|---|---|---|---|---|---|---|---|---|---|---|---|---|
| \*\* | 90<br>**Th**<br>232.038 | 91<br>**Pa**<br>231.036 | 92<br>**U**<br>238.029 | 93<br>**Np**<br>(237) | 94<br>**Pu**<br>(244) | 95<br>**Am**<br>(243) | 96<br>**Cm**<br>(247) | 97<br>**Bk**<br>(247) | 98<br>**Cf**<br>(251) | 99<br>**Es**<br>(252) | 100<br>**Fm**<br>(257) | 101<br>**Md**<br>(258) | 102<br>**No**<br>(259) | 103<br>**Lr**<br>(262) |

All elements are arranged sequentially according to atomic number (proton number). The horizontal rows represent the periods (or shells), while the various element groups are divided into vertical columns. The relative atomic masses are indicated below the element symbols. The values given in parentheses are the mass numbers (nucleon numbers) of the stablest isotopes of artificially produced radioactive elements.

# Materials

## Material terminology

### State of aggregation
There are three classical states of aggregation depending upon the arrangement of the elementary particles (atoms, molecules, ions): solid, liquid, and gaseous. Plasma (ionized gas which has high electric conductivity) is often considered as a fourth state of aggregation.

### Solution
A solution is a homogeneous mixture of different materials which are distributed at the atomic or molecular level.

### Compound
A compound is the union of two or more chemical elements whose masses are always in the same ratio with respect to one another. Compounds which have metallic characteristics are called intermetallic compounds.

### Dispersion
A dispersion, or disperse system, consists of at least two materials; one material, called the disperse phase, is finely distributed in the other material, called the dispersion medium.

### Suspension
A suspension is a disperse system in which solid particles are distributed in a liquid. Examples: graphite in oil, clay in water.

### Emulsion
An emulsion is a disperse system in which droplets of one liquid are distributed in a second liquid. Examples: drilling oil, butterfat in milk.

### Colloid
A colloid is a disperse system in which the particles of the disperse phase have linear dimensions ranging from roughly $10^{-9}$ to $10^{-6}$ m. Examples: smoke, latex, gold-ruby glass.

## Material parameters

### Density
Density is the ratio of the mass to the volume of a specific amount of substance.

See DIN 1306, 1984 edition, for special density terms.

### Radial crushing strength
Radial crushing strength is a strength parameter which is specified in particular for the sintered metals used for plain bearings. It is determined from the pressure test when a hollow cylinder is crushed.

For additional information see "Technical Conditions of Delivery for PM Parts (Sint. 03)", Aug. 1981 edition.

### 0.2% Yield strength
0.2% yield strength is that tensile stress which causes permanent (plastic) elongation of 0.2% in a solid body; it is determined from the $\sigma$-$\varepsilon$ curve of a tensile test with a defined stress-increase rate.

Cyclic loading of a test specimen by tensile/compressive stresses with increasing amplitude yields the cyclic $\sigma$-$\varepsilon$-curve and from this the cyclic 0.2% yield strength. When compared with the monotonic 0.2% yield strength, this value is a measure of possible softening or hardening brought about by cyclic overloading.

The yield strength ratio is the ratio of the cyclic to the monotonic 0.2% yield strength. $\gamma > 1$ signifies cyclic hardening, $\gamma < 1$ cyclic softening.

### Fracture toughness
Fracture toughness, or $K_{lc}$ factor, is a material parameter of fracture mechanics. The $K_{lc}$ factor is that stress intensity ahead of a crack tip which leads to unstable crack propagation, and therefore to the fracture of the structural part. If the $K_{lc}$ factor of a material is known, the critical fracture load can be determined from crack length, or the critical crack length can be determined from the given external stress value.

## Specific heat capacity
Specific heat capacity (specific heat) is the quantity of heat in J required to raise the temperature of 1 kg of a substance by 1 K. It is dependent on temperature.

In the case of gases, it is necessary to differentiate between specific heat capacity at constant pressure and at constant volume (symbols: $c_p$ and $c_v$, respectively). This difference is usually negligible in the case of solid and liquid substances.

## Specific heat of fusion
The specific heat of fusion of a solid is the quantity of heat in J required to transform 1 kg of a substance at fusion temperature from the solid to the liquid state.

## Specific heat of evaporation
The specific heat of evaporation of a liquid is the quantity of heat in J required to evaporate 1 kg of this liquid at boiling temperature. The specific heat of evaporation is highly dependent on pressure.

## Thermal conductivity
Thermal conductivity is the quantity of heat in J which flows in 1 s through a material sample which has a surface area of 1 m² and a thickness of 1 m if the temperatures of the two end surfaces of the sample differ by 1 K.

In the case of liquids and gases, thermal conductivity is often highly dependent on temperature, whereas temperature is generally not significant in the case of solids.

## Coefficient of thermal expansion
The coefficient of linear expansion indicates the relative change in length of a material caused by a change in temperature of 1 K. For a temperature variation $\Delta T$, the change in length is defined as $\Delta l = l \cdot \alpha \cdot \Delta T$. The cubic or volume coefficient of expansion is defined in the same way. The volume coefficient of expansion for gases is roughly 1/273. For solids, it is roughly three times as large as the coefficient of linear expansion.

## Permeability
Permeability $\mu$ or relative permeability $\mu_r$ describes the dependence of magnetic induction on the applied field:

$$B = \mu_r \cdot \mu_0 \cdot H$$

Depending on the application in which the magnetic material is used, there are roughly 15 types of permeability. These are defined according to modulation range and type of loading (direct-current or alternating-current field loading). Examples:

Initial permeability $\mu_a$
Slope of the virgin curve for $H \rightarrow 0$. In most cases, however, the slope for a specific field strength (in mA/cm) is specified rather than this limit value. Notation: $\mu_4$ is the slope of the virgin curve for $H = 4\,\text{mA/cm}$.

Maximum permeability $\mu_{max}$
Maximum slope of the virgin curve.

Permanent permeability $\mu_p$ or $\mu_{rec}$
Average slope of a retrograde magnetic hysteresis loop whose lowest point usually lies on the demagnetization curve.

$$\mu_p = \Delta B/(\Delta H \cdot \mu_0)$$

## Temperature coefficient of magnetic polarization $TK(J_s)$
This temperature coefficient indicates the relative change in saturation polarization as temperature changes, it is given in % per Kelvin.

## Temperature coefficient of coercive field strength $TK(H_c)$
This temperature coefficient indicates the relative change, in % per Kelvin, of coercive field strength as temperature changes.

## Curie point (Curie temperature) $T_c$
The Curie point is the temperature at which the magnetization of ferromagnetic and ferrimagnetic materials becomes zero and at which they behave like paramagnetic materials (sometimes defined differently, see characteristic values of soft ferrites on P. 265).

## Properties of solids[8]

| Substance | | Density | Melting point[1] | Boiling point[1] | Thermal conductivity[2] | Mean specific heat capacity[3] | Melting enthalpy $\Delta H$[4] | Coefficient of linear expansion[3] |
|---|---|---|---|---|---|---|---|---|
| | | g/cm³ | °C | °C | W/(m · K) | kJ/(kg · K) | kJ/kg | x10⁻⁶/K |
| Aluminum | Al | 2.70 | 660 | 2,467 | 237 | 0.90 | 395 | 23.0 |
| Aluminum alloys | | 2.60...2.85 | 480...655 | – | 70...240 | – | – | 21...24 |
| Amber | | 1.0...1.1 | ≈ 300 | Decomposes | – | – | – | – |
| Antimony | Sb | 6.69 | 630.8 | 1,635 | 24.3 | 0.21 | 172 | 8.5 |
| Arsenic | As | 5.73 | 613[5] | – | 50.0 | 0.34 | 370 | 4.7 |
| Asbestos | | 2.1...2.8 | ≈ 1,300 | – | – | 0.81 | – | – |
| Asphalt | | 1.1...1.4 | 80...100 | ≈ 300 | 0.70 | 0.92 | – | – |
| Barium | Ba | 3.50 | 729 | 1,637 | 18.4 | 0.28 | 55.8 | 18.1...21.0 |
| Barium chloride | | 3.86 | 963 | 1,560 | – | 0.38 | 108 | – |
| Basalt | | 2.6...3.3 | – | – | 1.67 | 0.86 | – | – |
| Beef tallow | | 0.9...0.97 | 40...50 | ≈ 350 | – | 0.87 | – | – |
| Beryllium | Be | 1.85 | 1,278 | 2,970 | 200 | 1.88 | 1,087 | 11.5 |
| Bismuth | Bi | 9.75 | 271 | 1,551 | 8.1 | 0.13 | 59 | 12.1 |
| Bitumen | | 1.05 | ≈ 90 | – | 0.17 | 1.78 | – | – |
| Boiler scale | | ≈ 2.5 | ≈ 1,200 | – | 0.12...2.3 | 0.80 | – | – |
| Borax | | 1.72 | 740 | – | – | 1.00 | – | – |
| Boron | B | 2.34 | 2,027 | 3,802 | 27.0 | 1.30 | 2,053 | 5 |
| Brass CuZn37 | | 8.4 | 900 | 1,110 | 113 | 0.38 | 167 | 18.5 |
| Brickwork | | > 1.9 | – | – | 1.0 | 0.9 | – | – |
| Bronze CuSn 6 | | 8.8 | 910 | 2,300 | 64 | 0.37 | – | 17.5 |
| Cadmium | Cd | 8.65 | 321.1 | 765 | 96.8 | 0.23 | 54.4 | 29.8 |
| Calcium | Ca | 1.54 | 839 | 1492 | 200 | 0.62 | 233 | 22 |
| Calcium chloride | | 2.15 | 782 | >1,600 | – | 0.69 | – | – |
| Cellulose acetate | | 1.3 | – | – | 0.26 | 1.47 | – | 100...160 |
| Cement, set | | 2...2.2 | – | – | 0.9...1.2 | 1.13 | – | – |
| Chalk | | 1.8...2.6 | Decomposes into CaO and CO₂ | | 0.92 | 0.84 | – | – |
| Chamotte (fireclay) | | 1.7...2.4 | ≈ 2,000 | – | 1.4 | 0.80 | – | – |
| Charcoal | | 0.3...0.5 | – | – | 0.084 | 1.0 | – | – |
| Chromium | Cr | 7.19 | 1,875 | 2,482 | 93.7 | 0.45 | 294 | 6.2 |
| Chromium oxide | Cr₂O₃ | 5.21 | 2,435 | 4,000 | 0.42[6] | 0.75 | – | – |
| Clay, dry | | 1.5...1.8 | ≈ 1,600 | – | 0.9...1.3 | 0.88 | – | – |
| Cobalt | Co | 8.9 | 1,495 | 2,956 | 69.1 | 0.44 | 268 | 12.4 |
| Coke | | 1.6...1.9 | – | – | 0.18 | 0.83 | – | – |
| Colophonium (rosin) | | 1.08 | 100...130 | Decomposes | 0.32 | 1.21 | – | – |
| Common salt | | 2.15 | 802 | 1,440 | – | 0.92 | – | – |
| Concrete | | 1.8...2.2 | – | – | ≈ 1.0 | 0.88 | – | – |
| Copper | Cu | 8.96 | 1084.9 | 2,582 | 401 | 0.38 | 205 | – |
| Cork | | 0.1...0.3 | – | – | 0.04...0.06 | 1.7...2.1 | – | – |
| Corundum, fused | | – | – | – | – | – | – | 6.5[7] |
| Cotton wadding | | 0.01 | – | – | 0.04 | – | – | – |
| Diamond | C | 3.5 | 3,820 | – | – | 0.52 | – | 1.1 |
| Foam rubber | | 0.06...0.25 | – | – | 0.04...0.06 | – | – | – |
| Germanium | Ge | 5.32 | 937 | 2,830 | 59.9 | 0.31 | 478 | 5.6 |
| Glass (window) | | 2.4...2.7 | ≈ 700 | – | 0.81 | 0.83 | – | ≈ 8 |
| Glass (quartz) | | – | – | – | – | – | – | 0.5 |
| Gold | Au | 19.32 | 1,064 | 2,967 | 317 | 0.13 | 64.5 | 14.2 |

---

[1] At 1.013 bar. [2] At 20 °C. $\Delta H$ of chemical elements at 27 °C (300 K).
[3] At 0...100 °C, see also P. 233. [4] At the melting point and 1.013 bar.
[5] Sublimed. [6] Powder form. [7] At 20...1,000 °C. [8] Materials, PP. 250...285.

| Substance | | Density g/cm³ | Melting point [1] °C | Boiling point [1] °C | Thermal conductivity [2] W/(m·K) | Mean specific heat capacity [3] kJ/(kg·K) | Melting enthalpy $\Delta H$ [4] kJ/kg | Coefficient of linear expansion [3] x10⁻⁶/K |
|---|---|---|---|---|---|---|---|---|
| Granite | | 2.7 | – | – | 3.49 | 0.83 | – | – |
| Graphite, pure | C | 2.24 | ≈ 3,800 | ≈ 4,200 | 168 | 0.71 | – | 2.7 |
| Gray cast iron | | 7.25 | 1,200 | 2,500 | 58 | 0.50 | 125 | 10.5 |
| Hard coal (anthracite) | | 1,35 | – | – | 0.24 | 1.02 | – | – |
| Hard metal K 20 | | 14,8 | > 2,000 | ≈ 4,000 | 81.4 | 0.80 | – | 5...7 |
| Hard rubber | | 1.2...1.5 | – | – | 0.16 | 1.42 | – | 50...90 [8] |
| Heat-conductor alloy NiCr 8020 | | 8.3 | 1,400 | 2,350 | 14.6 | 0.50 [6] | – | – |
| HR foam, air-filled [5] | | 0.015... ...0.06 | – | – | 0.036... ...0.06 | – | – | – |
| HR foam, freon-filled | | 0.015... ...0.06 | – | – | 0.02... 0.03 | – | – | – |
| Ice (0 °C) | | 0.92 | 0 | 100 | 2.33 [7] | 2.09 [7] | 333 | 51 [8] |
| Indium | In | 7.29 | 156.6 | 2006 | 81.6 | 0.24 | 28.4 | 33 |
| Iodine | I | 4.95 | 113.5 | 184 | 0.45 | 0.22 | 120.3 | – |
| Iridium | Ir | 22.55 | 2,447 | 4,547 | 147 | 0.13 | 137 | 6.4 |
| Iron, pure | Fe | 7.87 | 1,535 | 2,887 | 80.2 | 0.45 | 267 | 12.3 |
| Lead | Pb | 11.3 | 327.5 | 1,749 | 35.5 | 0.13 | 24.7 | 29.1 |
| Lead monoxide | PbO | 9.3 | 880 | 1,480 | – | 0.22 | – | – |
| Leather, dry | | 0.86...1 | – | – | 0.14...0.16 | ≈ 1.5 | – | – |
| Linoleum | | 1.2 | – | – | 0.19 | – | – | – |
| Lithium | Li | 0.534 | 180.5 | 1,317 | 84.7 | 3.3 | 663 | 56 |
| Magnesium | Mg | 1.74 | 648.8 | 1,100 | 156 | 1.02 | 372 | 26.1 |
| Magnesium alloys | | ≈ 1.8 | ≈ 630 | 1,500 | 46...139 | – | – | 24.5 |
| Manganese | Mn | 7.47 | 1,244 | 2,100 | 7.82 | 0.48 | 362 | 22 |
| Marble | CaCO₃ | 2.6...2.8 | Decomposes into CaO and CO₂ | | 2.8 | 0.84 | – | – |
| Mica | | 2.6...2.9 | Decomposes at 700 °C | | 0.35 | 0.87 | – | 3 |
| Molybdenum | Mo | 10.22 | 2,623 | 5,560 | 138 | 0.28 | 288 | 5.4 |
| Monel metal | | 8.8 | 1,240... ...1,330 | – | 19.7 | 0.43 | – | – |
| Mortar, cement | | 1.6...1.8 | – | – | 1.40 | – | – | – |
| Mortar, lime | | 1.6...1.8 | – | – | 0.87 | – | – | – |
| Nickel | Ni | 8.90 | 1,455 | 2,782 | 90.7 | 0.46 | 300 | 13.3 |
| Nickel silver CuNi12Zn24 | | 8.7 | 1,020 | – | 48 | 0.40 | – | 18 |
| Niobium | Nb | 8.58 | 2,477 | 4,540 | 53.7 | 0.26 | 293 | 7.1 |
| Osmium | Os | 22.57 | 3,045 | 5,027 | 87.6 | 0.13 | 154 | 4.3...6.8 |
| Palladium | Pd | 12.0 | 1,554 | 2,927 | 71.8 | 0.24 | 162 | 11.2 |
| Paper | | 0.7...1.2 | – | – | 0,14 | 1.34 | – | – |
| Paraffin | | 0.9 | 52 | 300 | 0.26 | 3.27 | – | – |
| Peat dust, air-dried | | 0.19 | – | – | 0.081 | – | – | – |
| Phosphorus (white) | P | 1.82 | 44.1 | 280.4 | – | 0.79 | 20 | – |
| Pitch | | 1.25 | – | – | 0.13 | – | – | – |
| Plaster | | 2.3 | 1,200 | – | 0.45 | 1.09 | – | – |
| Platinum | Pt | 21.45 | 1,769 | 3,827 | 71.6 | 0.13 | 101 | 9 |
| Plutonium | Pu | 19.8 | 640 | 3,454 | 6.7 | 0.14 | 11 | 55 |
| Polyamide | | 1.1 | – | – | 0.31 | – | – | 70...150 |

[1] At 1.013 bar. [2] At 20 °C. $\Delta H$ of chemical elements at 27 °C (300 K). [3] At 0...100 °C, [4] At melting point and 1.013 bar. [5] HR foam of phenol resin, polystyrene, polyethylene and similar. Values dependent on cell diameter and filler gas. [6] At 0...1,000 °C. [7] At −20...0 °C. [8] At −20...−1 °C.

| Substance | | Density g/cm³ | Melting point [1] °C | Boiling point [1] °C | Thermal conductivity [2] W/(m·K) | Mean specific heat capacity [3] kJ/(kg·K) | Melting enthalpy $\Delta H$ [4] kJ/kg | Coefficient of linear expansion [3] x10⁻⁶/K |
|---|---|---|---|---|---|---|---|---|
| Polycarbonate | | 1.2 | – | – | 0.20 | 1.17 | – | 60...70 |
| Polyethylene | | 0.94 | – | – | 0.41 | 2.1 | – | 200 |
| Polystyrene | | 1.05 | – | – | 0.17 | 1.3 | – | 70 |
| Polyvinyl chloride | | 1.4 | – | – | 0.16 | – | – | 70...150 |
| Porcelain | | 2.3...2.5 | ≈ 1,600 | – | 1.6[5] | 1.2[5] | – | 4...5 |
| Potassium | K | 0.86 | 63.65 | 754 | 102.4 | 0.74 | 61.4 | 83 |
| Quartz | | 2.1...2.5 | 1,480 | 2,230 | 9.9 | 0.80 | | 8[6]/14.6[7] |
| Radium | Ra | 5 | 700 | 1,630 | 18.6 | 0.12 | 32 | 20.2 |
| Red bronze CuSn5ZnPb | | 8.8 | 950 | 2,300 | 38 | 0.67 | – | – |
| Red lead, minium | Pb₃O₄ | 8.6...9.1 | Forms PbO | | 0.70 | 0.092 | – | – |
| Resin bonded fabric, paper | | 1.3...1.4 | – | – | 0.23 | 1.47 | – | 10...25[8] |
| Resistance alloy CuNi 44 | | 8.9 | 1,280 | ≈ 2,400 | 22.6 | 0.41 | – | 15.2 |
| Rhenium | Re | 21.02 | 3,160 | 5,762 | 150 | 0.14 | 178 | 8.4 |
| Roofing felt | | 1.1 | – | – | 0.19 | – | – | – |
| Rubber, raw (caoutchouc) | | 0.92 | 125 | – | 0.15 | – | – | – |
| Rubidium | Rb | 1.53 | 38.9 | 688 | 58 | 0.33 | 26 | 90 |
| Sand, quartz, dry | | 1.5...1.7 | ≈ 1,500 | 2,230 | 0.58 | 0.80 | – | – |
| Sandstone | | 2...2.5 | ≈ 1,500 | – | 2.3 | 0.71 | – | – |
| Selenium | Se | 4.8 | 217 | 684.9 | 2.0 | 0.34 | 64.6 | 37 |
| Silicon | Si | 2.33 | 1,410 | 2,480 | 148 | 0.68 | 1,410 | 4.2 |
| Silicon carbide | | 2.4 | Decomposes above 3,000 °C | | 9[9] | 1.05[9] | – | 4.0 |
| Sillimanite | | 2.4 | 1,820 | – | 1.51 | 1.0 | – | – |
| Silver | Ag | 10.5 | 961.9 | 2,195 | 429 | 0.24 | 104.7 | 19.2 |
| Slag, blast furnace | | 2.5...3 | 1,300......1,400 | – | 0.14 | 0.84 | – | – |
| Sodium | Na | 0.97 | 97.81 | 883 | 141 | 1.24 | 115 | 70.6 |
| Soft rubber | | 1.08 | – | – | 0.14......0.24 | – | – | – |
| Soot | | 1.7...1.8 | – | – | 0.07 | 0.84 | – | – |
| Steatite | | 2.6...2.7 | ≈ 1,520 | – | 1.6[11] | 0.83 | – | 8...9[10] |
| Steel, chromium steel | | – | – | – | – | – | – | 11 |
| Steel, electrical sheet steel | | – | – | – | – | – | – | 12 |
| Steel, high-speed tool steel | | – | – | – | – | – | – | 11.5 |
| Steel, magnet steel AlNiCo12/6 | | – | – | – | – | – | – | 11.5 |
| Steel, nickel steel 36% Ni (invar) | | – | – | – | – | – | – | 1.5 |
| Steel, sintered | | – | – | – | – | – | – | 11.5 |
| Steel, stainless (18Cr, 8Ni) | | 7.9 | 1,450 | – | 14 | 0.51 | – | 16 |
| Steel, tungsten steel (18 W) | | 8.7 | 1,450 | – | 26 | 0.42 | – | – |
| Steel, unalloyed and low-alloy | | 7.9 | 1,460 | 2,500 | 48...58 | 0.49 | 205 | 11.5 |
| Sulfur ($\alpha$) | S | 2.07 | 112.8 | 444.67 | 0.27 | 0.73 | 38 | 74 |
| Sulfur ($\beta$) | S | 1.96 | 119.0 | – | – | – | – | – |
| Tantalum | Ta | 16.65 | 2,996 | 5,487 | 57.5 | 0.14 | 174 | 6.6 |
| Tellurium | Te | 6.24 | 449.5 | 989.8 | 2.3 | 0.20 | 106 | 16.7 |

[1]) At 1.013 bar. [2]) At 20 °C. $\Delta H$ of chemical elements at 27 °C (300 K). [3]) At 0...100 °C. [4]) At melting point and 1.013 bar. [5]) At 0...100 °C. [6]) Parallel to crystal axis. [7]) Perpendicular to crystal axis. [8]) At 20...50 °C. [9]) At 1,000 °C. [10]) At 20...1,000 °C. [11]) At 100...200 °C.

| Substance | | Density | Melting point[1] | Boiling point[1] | Thermal conductivity[2] | Mean specific heat capacity[3] | Melting enthalpy $\Delta H$[4] | Coefficient of linear expansion[3] |
|---|---|---|---|---|---|---|---|---|
| | | g/cm³ | °C | °C | W/(m·K) | kJ/(kg·K) | kJ/kg | x10⁻⁶/K |
| **Thermosets** | | | | | | | | |
| Phenol resin or filler | | 1.3 | – | – | 0.20 | 1.47 | – | 80 |
| Phenol resin w/ asbestos fiber | | 1.8 | – | – | 0.70 | 1.25 | – | 15...30 |
| Phenol resin w/wood dust | | 1.4 | – | – | 0.35 | 1.47 | – | 30...50 |
| Phenol resin w/fabric chips | | 1.4 | – | – | 0.35 | 1.47 | – | 15...30 |
| Melamin resin w/ cellulose fiber | | 1.5 | – | – | 0.35 | – | – | ≈ 60 |
| Thorium | Th | 11.72 | 1,750 | 4,227 | 54 | 0.14 | <83 | 12.5 |
| Tin (white) | Sn | 7.28 | 231.97 | 2,270 | 65.7 | 0.23 | 61 | 21.2 |
| Titanium | Ti | 4.51 | 1,660 | 3,313 | 21.9 | 0.52 | 437 | 8.3 |
| Tombac CuZn 20 | | 8.65 | 1,000 | ≈ 1,300 | 159 | 0.38 | – | – |
| Tungsten | W | 19.25 | 3,422 | 5,727 | 174 | 0.13 | 191 | 4.6 |
| Uranium | U | 18.95 | 1,132.3 | 3,677 | 27.6 | 0.12 | 65 | 12.6 |
| Vanadium | V | 6.11 | 1,890 | 3,000 | 30.7 | 0.50 | 345 | 8.3 |
| Vulcanized fiber | | 1.28 | – | – | 0.21 | 1.26 | – | – |
| Wax | | 0.96 | 60 | – | 0.084 | 3.4 | – | – |
| Wood[5] | Maple | 0.62 | – | – | 0.16 | | – | in fiber direction 3...4, transverse to fiber 22...43 |
| | Balsa | 0.20 | – | – | 0.06 | | – | |
| | Birch | 0.63 | – | – | 0.14 | | – | |
| | Beech | 0.72 | – | – | 0.17 | | – | |
| | Oak | 0.69 | – | – | 0.17 | 2.1...2.9 | – | |
| | Ash | 0.72 | – | – | 0.16 | | – | |
| | Spruce, fir | 0.45 | – | – | 0.14 | | – | |
| | Pine | 0.52 | – | – | 0.14 | | – | |
| | Walnut | 0.65 | – | – | 0.15 | | – | |
| | Poplar | 0.50 | – | – | 0.12 | | – | |
| Wood-wool building slabs | | 0.36...0.57 | – | – | 0.093 | | – | |
| Zinc | Zn | 7.14 | 419.58 | 907 | 116 | 0.38 | 102 | 25.0 |
| Zirconium | Zr | 6.51 | 1,852 | 4,377 | 22.7 | 0.28 | 252 | 5.8 |

[1]) At 1.013 bar. [2]) At 20 °C. $\Delta H$ of chemical elements at 27 °C (300 K). [3]) At 0...100 °C.
[4]) At melting point and 1.013 bar. [5]) Mean values for air-dried wood (humidity approx. 12%).
Thermal conductivity radial; axial approx. twice as high.

## Properties of liquids

| Substance | | Density[2] g/cm³ | Melting point[1] °C | Boiling point[1] °C | Thermal conductivity[2] W/(m·K) | Specific heat capacity[2] kJ/(kg·K) | Melting enthalpy $\Delta H$[3] kJ/kg | Evaporation enthalpy[4] kJ/kg | Coefficient of volume expansion ×10⁻³/K |
|---|---|---|---|---|---|---|---|---|---|
| Acetone | $(CH_3)_2CO$ | 0.79 | -95 | 56 | 0.16 | 2.21 | 98.0 | 523 | – |
| Antifreeze-water mixture | | | | | | | | | |
| 23% by vol. | | 1.03 | -12 | 101 | 0.53 | 3.94 | – | – | – |
| 38% by vol. | | 1.04 | -25 | 103 | 0.45 | 3.68 | – | – | – |
| 54% by vol. | | 1.06 | -46 | 105 | 0.40 | 3.43 | – | – | – |
| Benzene | $C_6H_6$ | 0.88 | +5.5[6] | 80 | 0.15 | 1.70 | 127 | 394 | 1.25 |
| Common-salt solution 20% | | 1.15 | -18 | 109 | 0.58 | 3.43 | – | – | – |
| Diesel fuel | | 0.81...0.85 | -30 | 150...360 | 0.15 | 2.05 | – | – | – |
| Ethanol | $C_2H_5OH$ | 0.79 | -117 | 78.5 | 0.17 | 2.43 | 109 | 904 | 1.1 |
| Ethyl dichloride | $C_2H_5Cl$ | 0.90 | -136 | 12 | 0.11[5] | 1.54[5] | 69.0 | 437 | – |
| Ethyl ether | $(C_2H_5)_2O$ | 0.71 | -116 | 34.5 | 0.13 | 2.28 | 98.1 | 377 | 1.6 |
| Ethylene glycol | $C_2H_4(OH)_2$ | 1.11 | -12 | 198 | 0.25 | 2.40 | – | – | – |
| Fuel oil EL | | ≈ 0.83 | -10 | >175 | 0.14 | 2.07 | – | – | – |
| Gasoline/petrol | | 0.72...0.75 | -50...-30 | 25...210 | 0.13 | 2.02 | – | – | 1.0 |
| Glycerin | $C_3H_5(OH)_3$ | 1.26 | +20 | 290 | 0.29 | 2.37 | 200 | 828 | 0.5 |
| Hydrochloric acid 10% | HCl | 1.05 | -14 | 102 | 0.50 | 3.14 | – | – | – |
| Kerosene | | 0.76...0.86 | -70 | >150 | 0.13 | 2.16 | – | – | 1.0 |
| Linseed oil | | 0.93 | -15 | 316 | 0.17 | 1.88 | – | – | – |
| Lubricating oil | | 0.91 | -20 | >300 | 0.13 | 2.09 | – | – | – |
| Mercury[8] | Hg | 13.55 | -38.84 | 356.6 | 10 | 0.14 | 11.6 | 295 | 0.18 |
| Methanol | $CH_3OH$ | 0.79 | -98 | 65 | 0.20 | 2.51 | 99.2 | 1,109 | – |
| Methyl chloride | $CH_3Cl$ | 0.997[7] | -92 | -24 | 0.16 | 1.38 | – | 406 | – |
| m-xylene | $C_6H_4(CH_3)_2$ | 0.86 | -48 | 139 | – | – | – | 339 | – |
| Nitric acid, conc. | $HNO_3$ | 1.51 | -41 | 84 | 0.26 | 1.72 | – | – | – |

[1] At 1.013 bar. [2] At 20 °C. [3] At melting point and 1.013 bar. [4] At boiling point and 1.013 bar. [5] At 0 °C. [6] Setting point 0 °C. [7] At –24 °C.
[8] For conversion from torr to Pa, use 13.5951 g/cm³ (at 0 °C).

| Substance | | Density[2] g/cm³ | Melting point[1] °C | Boiling point[1] °C | Thermal conductivity[2] W/(m·K) | Specific heat capacity[2] kJ/(kg·K) | Melting enthalpy $\Delta H$[3] kJ/kg | Evaporation enthalpy[4] kJ/kg | Coefficient of volume expansion x10⁻³/K |
|---|---|---|---|---|---|---|---|---|---|
| Paraffin oil | | – | – | – | – | – | – | – | 0.764 |
| Petroleum ether | | 0.66 | –160 | > 40 | 0.14 | 1.76 | – | – | – |
| Rape oil | | 0.91 | ± 0 | 300 | 0.17 | 1.97 | – | – | – |
| Silicone oil | | 0.76...0.98 | – | – | 0.13 | 1.09 | – | – | – |
| Spirit 95%[6] | | 0.81 | –114 | 78 | 0.17 | 2.43 | – | – | – |
| Sulfuric acid, conc. | $H_2SO_4$ | 1.83 | +10.5[5] | 338 | 0.47 | 1.42 | – | – | 0.55 |
| Tar, coke oven | | 1.2 | –15 | 300 | 0.19 | 1.56 | – | – | – |
| Toluene | $C_7H_8$ | 0.87 | –93 | 111 | 0.14 | 1.67 | 74.4 | 364 | – |
| Transformer oil | | 0.88 | –30 | 170 | 0.13 | 1.88 | – | – | – |
| Trichloroethylene | $C_2HCl_3$ | 1.46 | –85 | 87 | 0.12 | 0.93 | – | 265 | 1.19 |
| Turpentine oil | | 0.86 | –10 | 160 | 0.11 | 1.80 | – | 293 | 1.0 |
| Water | | 1.00[7] | ± 0 | 100 | 0.60 | 4.18 | 332 | 2,256 | 0.18[8] |

[1] At 1.013 bar.
[2] At 20 °C.
[3] At melting point and 1.013 bar.
[4] At boiling point and 1.013 bar.
[5] Setting point 0 °C.
[6] Denaturated ethanol.
[7] At 4 °C.
[8] Volume expansion on freezing: 9%.

## Properties of water vapor

| Absolute pressure bar | Boiling point °C | Evaporation enthalpy kJ/kg | Absolute pressure bar | Boiling point °C | Evaporation enthalpy kJ/kg |
|---|---|---|---|---|---|
| 0.1233 | 50 | 2,382 | 25.5 | 225 | 1,837 |
| 0.3855 | 75 | 2,321 | 39.78 | 250 | 1,716 |
| 1.0133 | 100 | 2,256 | 59.49 | 275 | 1,573 |
| 2.3216 | 125 | 2,187 | 85.92 | 300 | 1,403 |
| 4.760 | 150 | 2,113 | 120.5 | 325 | 1,189 |
| 8.925 | 175 | 2,031 | 165.4 | 350 | 892 |
| 15.55 | 200 | 1,941 | 221.1 | 374.2 | 0 |

## Properties of gases

| Substance | | Density[1] kg/m³ | Melting point[2] °C | Boiling point[2] °C | Thermal conductivity[3] W/(m·K) | Specific heat capacity[3] kJ/(kg·K) $c_p$ | $c_v$ | $c_p/c_v$ | Evaporation enthalpy[2] kJ/kg |
|---|---|---|---|---|---|---|---|---|---|
| Acetylene | $C_2H_2$ | 1.17 | −84 | −81 | 0.021 | 1.64 | 1.33 | 1.23 | 751 |
| Air | | 1.293 | −220 | −191 | 0.026 | 1.005 | 0.716 | 1.40 | 209 |
| Ammonia | $NH_3$ | 0.77 | −78 | −33 | 0.024 | 2.06 | 1.56 | 1.32 | 1,369 |
| Argon | Ar | 1.78 | −189 | −186 | 0.018 | 0.52 | 0.31 | 1.67 | 163 |
| Blast-furnace gas | | 1.28 | −210 | −170 | 0.024 | 1.05 | 0.75 | 1.40 | – |
| Carbon dioxide | $CO_2$ | 1.98 | −57[4] | −78 | 0.016 | 0.82 | 0.63 | 1.30 | 368 |
| Carbon disulfide | $CS_2$ | 3.41 | −112 | +46 | 0.0073 | 0.67 | 0.56 | 1.19 | – |
| Carbon monoxide | CO | 1.25 | −199 | −191 | 0.025 | 1.05 | 0.75 | 1.40 | – |
| Chlorine | $Cl_2$ | 3.21 | −101 | −35 | 0.009 | 0.48 | 0.37 | 1.30 | 288 |
| City/town gas | | 0.56...0.61 | −230 | −210 | 0.064 | 2.14 | 1.59 | 1.35 | – |
| Cyanogen (dicyan) | $(CN)_2$ | 2.33 | −34 | −21 | – | 1.72 | 1.35 | 1.27 | – |
| Dichlorodifluoromethane (= Freon F 12) | $CCl_2F_2$ | 5.51 | −140 | −30 | 0.010 | 0.61 | 0.54 | 1.14 | – |
| Ethane | $C_2H_6$ | 1.36 | −183 | −89 | 0.021 | 1.66 | 1.36 | 1.22 | 522 |
| Ethanol vapor | | 2.04 | −114 | +78 | 0.015 | – | – | 1.13 | – |
| Ethylene | $C_2H_4$ | 1.26 | −169 | −104 | 0.020 | 1.47 | 1.18 | 1.24 | 516 |
| Fluorine | $F_2$ | 1.70 | −220 | −188 | 0.025 | 0.82 | 0.61 | 1.35 | 172 |
| Helium | He | 0.18 | −270 | −269 | 0.15 | 5.20 | 3.15 | 1.65 | 20 |
| Hydrogen | $H_2$ | 0.09 | −258 | −253 | 0.181 | 14.39 | 10.10 | 1.42 | 228 |
| Hydrogen chloride | HCl | 1.64 | −114 | −85 | 0.014 | 0.81 | 0.57 | 1.42 | – |
| Hydrogen sulfide | $H_2S$ | 1.54 | −86 | −61 | 0.013[1] | 0.96 | 0.72 | 1.34 | 535 |
| i-butane | $C_4H_{10}$ | 2.67 | −145 | −10.2 | 0.016 | – | – | 1.11 | – |
| Krypton | Kr | 3.73 | −157 | −153 | 0.0095 | 0.25 | 0.15 | 1.67 | 108 |
| Methane | $CH_4$ | 0.72 | −183 | −164 | 0.033 | 2.19 | 1.68 | 1.30 | 557 |
| Methyl chloride | $CH_3Cl$ | 2.31 | −92 | −24 | – | 0.74 | 0.57 | 1.29 | 446 |
| n-butane | $C_4H_{10}$ | 2.70 | −138 | −0.5 | 0.016 | 1.67 | 1.51 | 1.10 | – |
| Neon | Ne | 0.90 | −249 | −246 | 0.049 | 1.03 | 0.62 | 1.67 | 86 |
| Nitrogen | $N_2$ | 1.24 | −210 | −196 | 0.026 | 1.04 | 0.74 | 1.40 | 199 |
| Oxygen | $O_2$ | 1.43 | −218 | −183 | 0.0267 | 0.92 | 0.65 | 1.41 | 213 |
| Ozone | $O_3$ | 2.14 | −251 | −112 | 0.019 | 0.81 | 0.63 | 1.29 | – |
| Propane | $C_3H_8$ | 2.00 | −182 | −42 | 0.018 | 1.70 | 1.50 | 1.13 | – |
| Propylene | $C_3H_6$ | 1.91 | −185 | −47 | 0.017 | 1.47 | 1.28 | 1.15 | 468 |
| Sulfur dioxide | $SO_2$ | 2.93 | −73 | −10 | 0.010 | 0.64 | 0.46 | 1.40 | 402 |
| Sulfur hexafluoride | $SF_6$ | 6.16[3] | −50.8 | −63.9 | 0.011 | 0.66 | – | – | 117[1] |
| Water vapor at 100 °C[5] | | 0.60 | ±0 | +100 | 0.025 | 2.01 | 1.52 | 1.32 | – |
| Xenon | Xe | 5.89 | −112 | −108 | 0.0057 | 0.16 | 0.096 | 1.67 | 96 |

[1]) At 0 °C and 1.013 bar.
[2]) At 1.013 bar.
[3]) At 20 °C and 1.013 bar.
[4]) At 5.3 bar.
[5]) At saturation and 1.013 bar, see also "Properties of liquids" table.

# Materials

## Material groups

The materials in current industrial use can be classified according to one of four categories. Each of these, in turn, includes various subclassifications:
- <u>Metals</u>: wrought, rolled, cast, etc. metals, sintered metals
- <u>Nonmetallic inorganic materials</u>: ceramic materials, glass
- <u>Nonmetallic organic materials</u>: natural materials, plastics
- <u>Composite materials</u>

Magnetic materials form an important material group with special characteristics, and will be described separately.

### Metals

Metals generally exhibit a crystalline structure. Their atoms are arranged in a regular crystal lattice. The valence electrons of the atoms are not bound to a special atom, but are able to move freely within the metal lattice (metallic bond).

This special metal-lattice structure explains the characteristic properties of metals: high electric conductivity which decreases as temperature increases; good thermal conductivity; low light transmittance; high optical reflectivity (metallic luster); ductility; and the resulting high degree of formability. <u>Alloys</u> are metals which consist of two or more components, of which at least one is a metal.

#### Wrought, rolled, cast, etc. metals

Apart from small flaws, such as shrinkholes, and nonmetallic inclusions, these metals contain no voids. Components are produced by casting, either directly (e.g. gray cast iron, diecast aluminum), or from wrought products (machined with or without cutting).

#### Sintered metals

Sintered metals are usually produced by pressing powder or by the injection molding of mixtures composed of metal powder and plastic. Following the removal of parting agents and binders, the parts are then sintered to give them their characteristic properties. Sintering is a type of heat treatment in a range from 800 to 1,300 °C. In addition to its chemical composition, the sintered part's properties and application are to a large extent determined by its degree of porosity. Components with complicated shapes can often be made particularly cheaply from sintered metals, either ready-to-install or requiring only little finishing.

### Nonmetallic inorganic materials

These materials are characterized by ion bonds (e.g. ceramic materials), mixed (heteropolar/homopolar) bonds (e.g. glass), or homopolar bonds (e.g. carbon). These kinds of bonds, in turn, are responsible for several characteristic properties: generally poor thermal and electric conductivity (the latter increases with temperature), poor luminous reflectance, brittleness, and thus almost complete unsuitability for cold forming.

#### Ceramics

Ceramics are at least 30% crystalline in nature; most ceramics also contain amorphous components and pores. Their manufacture is similar to that of sintered metals, however nonmetallic powders or powder mixtures are used; sintering at temperatures generally higher than 1,000 °C gives ceramics their characteristic properties. Ceramic structural parts are sometimes also shaped at high temperatures or even by a melting process, with subsequent crystallization.

#### Glass

Glass is viewed as under-cooled, frozen liquid. Its atoms are only in a short-range order. It is regarded as amorphous. Molten glass turns to solid glass at the transformation temperature $T_g$ ($T_g$ is derived from the former designation "glass formation temperature"). $T_g$ is dependent on a variety of parameters and therefore not clearly determined (better: transformation range).

## Nonmetallic organic materials

These materials consist mainly of compounds of the elements carbon and hydrogen, whereby nitrogen, oxygen and other elements are also often included in the structure. In general, these materials exhibit low thermal and electric conductivity, and are combustible.

### Natural materials

The best-known natural materials are wood, leather, resin, natural rubber, and fibers made of wool, cotton, flax, hemp, and silk. Most natural materials are used in processed or refined form, or serve as raw materials in the manufacture of plastics.

### Plastics

A significant characteristic of plastics is their macromolecular structure. There are three different types of plastics: thermoplastics, thermosets (sometimes also called thermosetting plastics), and elastomers. The transformation temperature $T_E$ for thermoplastics and thermosets lies above the temperature of application; the reverse is true for elastomers. $T_E$ (comparable with the transformation temperature $T_g$ of glass) is understood to mean that temperature below which intrinsic molecular motion ceases. The major importance of thermoplastics and thermosets lies in the fact that they can be shaped and molded without machining.

*Thermoplastics*

Thermoplastics soften and lose their dimensional stability at temperatures above $T_E$. Their physical properties are highly temperature-dependent. The effect of temperature can be somewhat reduced by using mixtures of thermoplastic polymers.

*Thermosets*

Thermosets retain their dimensional stability up to temperatures almost as high as the processing temperature due to closely spaced cross-linking. Their mechanical properties are less temperature-dependent than those of thermoplastics. Fillers are usually added to thermosetting resins to counteract their inherent brittleness.

*Elastomers*

Elastomers are useful in many applications because of their elasticity, which is only present at temperatures above $T_E$. Elastomers are vulcanized (widely spaced cross-linking) in order to stabilize their molecular bonds.

## Composite materials

Composite materials consist of at least two physically or chemically different components. These components must be tightly bonded together at a specific boundary layer. The formation of the boundary layer must have no negative effect on any of the bonded components. Under these two conditions, it is possible to bond many materials together. Composite materials exhibit combinations of properties which none of the components possesses alone. Different classes of composite materials are:

Particle composite materials: e.g. powder-filled resins, hard metals, plastic-bonded magnets, cermets

Laminated composite materials: e.g. composite or sandwich panels, resin-bonded fabric

Fiber composite materials: e.g. with fiber-glass, carbon-fiber, and cotton-fiber-reinforced plastics

## Magnetic materials

Materials which have ferromagnetic or ferrimagnetic properties are called magnetic materials and belong to one of two groups: metals (cast or sintered metals) or nonmetallic inorganic materials. Composite materials are also playing an increasingly important role. They are characterized by their ability to store magnetic energy (permanent magnets), or by their good magnetic flux conductivity (soft magnets). In addition to ferromagnets and ferrimagnets, diamagnetic, paramagnetic, and antiferromagnetic materials also exist. They differ from each other in terms of their permeability $\mu$ (P. 78), or the temperature dependence of their susceptibility $\varkappa$.[1]

$$\mu_r = 1 + \varkappa$$

---

[1] Ratio of the magnetization of a substance to the magnetic field strength or excitation.

<u>Diamagnets</u>: Susceptibility $\varkappa_{Dia}$ is independent of temperature.
See P. 78 for examples.

<u>Paramagnets</u>: Susceptibility $\varkappa_{para}$ drops as temperature increases. Curie's law:
$\varkappa_{para} = C/T$
$C$ Curie constant, $T$ Temperature in K.
See P. 78 for examples.

<u>Ferromagnets and ferrimagnets</u>: Both types exhibit spontaneous magnetization which disappears at the Curie point (Curie temperature $T_c$). At temperatures above the Curie temperature, they behave like paramagnets. For $T > T_c$, the Curie-Weiss law is applicable to susceptibility $\varkappa$:
$\varkappa = C/(T-T_c)$

The saturation induction of ferromagnets is higher than for ferrimagnets because all magnetic moments are aligned in parallel. In the case of ferrimagnets, on the other hand, the magnetic moments of the two sublattices are aligned antiparallel to one another. Nevertheless, these materials are magnetic because the magnetic moments of the two sublattices have different magnitudes.

<u>Antiferromagnets</u>: Examples: MnO, MnS, $FeCl_2$, FeO, NiO, Cr, $V_2O_3$, $V_2O_4$.
As in the case of ferrimagnets, adjacent magnetic moments are aligned antiparallel with respect to one another. As they are of equal magnitude, the effective magnetization of the material is zero.
At temperatures above the Néel point (Néel temperature $T_N$), they behave like paramagnets. For $T > T_N$, the following is applicable to susceptibility: $\varkappa = C/(T+\Theta)$
$\Theta$ Asymptotic Curie temperature

<u>Soft magnetic materials</u>
The following figures are from the applicable DIN Standards. Soft-magnetic metallic materials (DIN-IEC 60 404-8-6).
Many material qualities defined in this standard relate to the materials in DIN 17 405 (DC relays) and DIN-IEC 740-2 (transformers and reactors).

Designation (composition):
Code letter, Number 1 Number 2 – Number 3. The "code letter" indicates the main alloy constituent: "A" pure iron, "C" silicon, "E" nickel, "F" cobalt.

Number 1 indicates the concentration of the main alloy element.
Number 2 defines the different curves: 1: round hysteresis loop; 2: rectangular hysteresis loop.
The significance of the Number 3 following the hyphen varies according to the individual alloy. It indicates the minimum initial permeability $\mu_a/1{,}000$ in nickel alloys; with other alloys, it designates the maximum coercive field strength in A/m. The properties of these materials are strongly geometry-dependent and highly application-specific. The material data quoted in extracts from the standard can therefore provide only a very general overview of the properties of these materials. Refer to P. 260 for material data.

Electrical sheet steel and strip
(formerly in DIN 46 400)
Designation: Code letter 1 Number 1 – Number 2 Code letter 2.
The first code letter is "M" for all varieties (indicates metallic materials). Number 1 is one hundredfold the maximum magnetic reversal loss at 1.5 or 1.7 Tesla and 50 Hz in W/kg. Number 2 is one hundredfold the product's nominal depth in mm.
Code letter 2 provides type data: "A" cold-rolled electric sheets, no granular orientation, finish-annealed (DIN-EN 10 106). Grain-oriented electric sheet, finish-annealed (DIN-EN 10 107): "N" standard magnetic reversal loss, "S" limited magnetic reversal loss, "P" low magnetic reversal loss, "D" cold-rolled electric sheet of unalloyed steel, not finish-annealed (DIN-EN 10 126), "E" cold-rolled steel-alloy electric sheet, not finish-annealed (DIN-EN 10 165). See P. 261 for material properties.

Materials for transformers and reactors (DIN-IEC 740-2).
These materials comprise the alloy classes C21, C22, E11, E31 and E41 from the standard for soft-magnetic materials (DIN-IEC 60 404-8-6).

The standard essentially contains the minimum values for core-sheet permeability for specified core-sheet sections (YEI, YED, YEE, YEL, YUI, and YM). See P. 262 for material properties.

*Materials for DC relays*
(DIN 17 405), see P. 263 for material properties.
Designation comprises a letter and number combination:
a) Code letter "R" (relay material).
b) Code letters for identifying alloy constituents:
Fe = unalloyed, Si = silicon steels, Ni = nickel steels or alloys.
c) Code number for maximum coercive field strength.
d) Code letter for stipulated delivery state: "U" = untreated, "GB" = malleable pre-annealed, "GT" = pre-annealed for deep-drawing, "GF" = final-annealed.
DIN-IEC 60 404-8-10 essentially contains the limit deviations for magnetic relay materials based on iron and steel. The designation code defined in this standard is as follows:
– Code letter "M".
– Permitted maximum value for coercive field strength in A/m.
– Code letter for material composition: "F" = pure iron, "T" = steel alloy, "U" = unalloyed steel.
– Code letter for delivery state: "H" = hot-rolled, "C" = cold-rolled or cold-drawn.
Example: M 80 TH.

*Sintered metals for soft-magnetic components* (DIN-IEC 60 404-8-9)
Designation comprises a letter and number combination:
– Code letter "S": for sintered materials.
– Hyphen, followed by the identifying alloy elements, i.e. Fe plus if necessary P, Si, Ni, or Co.
– The maximum coercive field strength in A/m follows the second hyphen. Refer to P. 264 for material data.

*Soft-magnetic ferrite cores* (DIN 41 280)
Soft-magnetic ferrites are formed parts made of a sintered material with the general formula $MO \cdot Fe_2O_3$ where M is one or more of the bivalent metals Cd, Co, Ca, Mg, Mn, Ni, Zn.

Designation: The various types of soft-magnetic ferrites are classified in groups according to nominal initial permeability, and are designated by capital letters. Additional numbers may be used to further subdivide them into subgroups; these numbers have no bearing on material quality.
The coercive field strength $H_c$ of soft ferrites is usually in the range 4...500 A/m. Based on a field strength of 3,000 A/m, induction $B$ is in the range 350...470 mT. See P. 265 for material properties.

<u>Powder composite materials</u>
Powder composite materials are not yet standardized, but are becoming increasingly more important. They consist of ferromagnetic metal powder (iron or an alloy) and an organic or ceramic grain-boundary phase as "binder". They are manufactured in much the same way as sintered metals. The individual manufacturing stages are:
– Mixing the starting materials (metal powder and binder).
– Shaping by injection-molding, extruding, or pressing.
– Heat treatment below the sinter temperature (< 600 °C).

Depending on the binder type and the amount of binder used, it is possible to optimize the material to achieve high saturation polarization, higher permeability, or high resistivity.
They are used primarily in fields in which all the above-mentioned characteristics are important, and where no excessively high demands are placed on mechanical strength and machinability. These fields currently consist of quick-acting actuators for diesel-injection engineering and high-speed small electric motors for motor vehicles.

The materials currently cover the following spectrum of properties:

| Type | $J_S$ T | $\mu_{max}$ – | $\rho_{el}$ $\mu\Omega$m | $R_{tr}$[1] N/mm² |
|------|------|------|------|------|
| A | 1.6 | 120 | > 500 | 40 |
| B | 1.8 | 400 | > 50 | 60 |
| C | > 2 | > 750 | > 5 | > 100 |

[1] $R_{tr}$ bending strength.

Permanent-magnet materials
(DIN 17 410, replaced by
DIN-IEC 60 404-8-1)
If chemical symbols are used in the abbreviated names of the materials, they refer to the primary alloying constituents of the materials. The numbers before the forward slash denote the $(BH)_{max}$ value in kJ/m³ and those after the slash denote one tenth of the $H_{cJ}$ value in kA/m (rounded values). Permanent magnets with binders are indicated by a final p.

*Designation by abbreviated name
or material number[1])*
DIN: Material number as defined in DIN 17 007, Parts 2 and 4.
IEC: Structure of material numbers Code letters:
R – Metallic permanent-magnet
    materials
S – Ceramic permanent-magnet
    materials
1st number:
    indicates type of material, e.g.:
    1 AlNiCo, 5 RECo
2nd number:
    0: isotropic material
    1: anisotropic material
    2: isotropic material with binder
    3: anisotropic material with binder
3rd number:
    indicates quality level

See P. 266 for material properties.

---

[1]) The designation system for permanent-magnet materials is currently undergoing extensive revision. As discussions were still in progress at the time of going to print, no data or comments are provided.

# EN metallurgy standards

### References
Einführung in die EN-Normen der Metalltechnik (Introduction to EN Metallurgy Standards), 1st Edition 2002,
Karl Manfred Erhardt, Paulernst Seitz,
Holland + Josenhans Verlag.
Order No. 3050.

### Standardization of metals

DIN standards
The oldest steel standards stemming from the 1920s placed the emphasis on the tensile strength guaranteed by the manufacturer.
    Example: St 37.11 where St stands for steel, 37 for minimum tensile strength in kg/mm², and 11 for the steel category.
    From 1943 onwards the standards included details of chemical composition.
    The third version of the steel standard DIN 17 006 in 1949 featured a further subdivision into unalloyed (engineering and carbon steels) and alloyed steels (low- and high-alloy). It was also possible to specify the treatment state and grades.

EC EUROSTANDARDS
With the creation of the European Community (EC), steel grades were classified and designated in 1974 in accordance with EUROSTANDARD 20-74, complete with a classification of chemical composition (coded specification) into alloyed and unalloyed steels, and their application profiles into ordinary low-carbon, high-grade, and special steels. Letters and numbers indicate the mechanical strength properties.

SEW
The steel industry publishes new developments in steel and iron material specification sheets (SEW). They serve as the basis for the industry and for drawing up new standards. DIN EN 10194 was drawn up on the basis of SEW 092.

ISO standards
Since ISO had not drawn up any standards for metals, DIN 17 006 was applicable until the partial introduction of the EUROSTANDARD and/or replacement by EN standards.

### EU EN or DIN EN standards

With the creation of the European Union (EU), the designation system as laid down in DIN EN 10027-1 replaced EUROSTAN-DARD 27-74 in 1989. This system divides steel materials with abbreviated names into two main groups (mechanical or physical properties, and chemical composition). The numbering system according to DIN 17007 was taken over more or less in its entirety in DIN EN 10027-2. Adapted EUROSTANDARDS can be identified by the addition of 10,000 or a multiple (e.g. classification of steels from EU 20 into DIN EN 10020).

### Classification of steels
(as per DIN EN 10020:2000-07)

Steel is defined as an alloy of iron with usually ≤ 2% carbon (ferrous materials with a higher carbon content are usually classified as cast iron). Steel is divided into three categories:

#### 1. Unalloyed steels

These steels, which do not reach any of the defined limit values, are subdivided into:
– unalloyed high-grade steels with generally defined requirements (toughness, malleability, etc.)
– special steels with enhanced properties (high yield point or hardenability, good toughness and/or weldability, high percentage purity, etc.).

#### 2. Stainless steels

Steels containing chromium 0.5% and carbon 1.2%, distinguished according to nickel content < 2.5% or ≥ 2.5%, and with the main properties of corrosion resistance and heat resistance.

#### 3. Other alloyed steels

The following steels, which attain at least one of the specified limit values for differentiation, and which are not classified as stainless steels:
– alloyed high-grade steels with generally defined requirements (toughness, malleability, etc.; usually not intended for quenching and drawing, or surface hardening) and
– alloyed special steels with enhanced properties (alloy, purity, special manufacturing conditions , etc.).

### Designation system for steels with abbreviated names
(as per DIN EN 10027-1)

#### Main symbols

1. Code letter for use or chemical composition.
2. Code number of characteristic properties or composition.

*Abbreviated names of Group 1*

These abbreviated names contain references to use and mechanical or physical properties (the G prefix denotes cast steel):

| | | |
|---|---|---|
| (GS) S | For general structural steel construction |
| (GP) P | For pressure-vessel construction |
| L | For pipeline construction |
| E | Engineering steels |
| B | Concrete reinforcing steels |
| Y | Prestressing steels |
| R | Rail steels |
| H | Cold-rolled flat products made of higher-strength steels for cold-forming |
| D | Flat products made of soft steels for cold-forming |
| T | Black plate and tinplate (packaging) |
| M | Electrical sheet and strip steel |

*Standardization examples, Group 1:*

**S 235 JR**
General for steel construction, 235 MPa yield point, notched-bar impact work 27 J at 20 °C.

**E 335**
Engineering steel, 335 MPa yield point.

**H 240 LA**
Micro-alloyed steel, 240 MPa yield point LA (Low Alloy).

**D C 03 B m**
Flat product, cold-rolled, 34% elongation at fracture, better side as good as flawless, unpolished.

*Abbreviated names of Group 2*
These abbreviated names contain references to the chemical composition:

| | |
|---|---|
| (GC) C | Unalloyed steels, Mn < 1% |
| (G) | Low-alloy and unalloyed steels, Mn ≥ 1% |
| (GX) X | High-alloy steels |
| HS | High-speed tool steel |

*Standardization examples, Group 2:*
**C 15 E**
Unalloyed steel with < 1% manganese, specified upper limit for sulfur.

**X 6 Cr Ni Ti 18 - 10**
High-alloy steel, alloying constituents in whole percentages, the multiplier 100 applies to carbon.

**HS 7 - 4 - 2 - 5**
High-speed tool steel, alloying constituents in whole percentages in the sequence tungsten – molybdenum – vanadium – cobalt.

Supplementary symbols for steels
According to the requirements, it is defined for each steel grade which symbols in Group 1 or 2 apply. The supplementary symbols are sometimes also omitted.

*Supplement to Group 1*
| | |
|---|---|
| A | Precipitation-hardened |
| E | Specified max. S-content |
| M | Thermomechanically rolled |
| N | Normalized or normalization-rolled |
| Q | Quenched and drawn |

*Supplement to Group 2*
| | |
|---|---|
| C | With special cold-formability |
| D | For hot-dip coatings |
| H | Hollow profiles |
| L | For lower temperatures |
| Q | Quenched and drawn |
| W | Weatherproof |

Supplementary symbols for steel products
| | |
|---|---|
| +H | With hardenability |
| +CU | With copper coating |
| +Z | Hot-dip galvanized |
| +ZE | Electrolytically galvanized |
| +A | Soft-annealed |
| +C | Strain-hardened |
| +M | Thermomechanically rolled |
| +Q | Quenched |
| +U | Untreated |

*Standardization example:*
**D X 54 D +Z275**
Flat product for cold-forming, cold- or hot-rolled, extra deep-drawing grade, hot-dip coating, hot-dip galvanized, together on both sides 275 g/m².

**Designation system for steels based on the numbering system**
(as per DIN EN 10027-2)
All steels are also defined together with their abbreviated names by a material number adopted extensively from DIN in accordance with the following structure.

Material main-group number:
0. Pig iron, ferro-alloys; **1.** Steel; 2. Non-ferrous heavy metals; 3 Light alloys; 4...8. Nonmetallic materials; 9. Unassigned for internal use.

Steel-group number (selection):
00 Unalloyed ordinary low-carbon steels; **01**...03 High-grade steels; 08 High-grade steels with special properties; 11, 15 Special steels; 40...49 Chemically stable steels; 20...85 Special steels, etc.

Ordinal number, e.g. **43** for S275J0.

**(xx)** Auxiliary positions currently not used (reserved for more exact details which may be needed later). One alternative permits the attachment of the supplementary symbols for steel products previously only intended for the abbreviated material names (e.g. +Z 275 for galvanizing type and layer thickness).
Example: **1.0143 (xx)**

**Standardization of cast-iron materials**
The structure and form of the carbon (contained as carbide or graphite) and the graphite structure are important to the properties. The following standard sheets record cast iron in four groups:
DIN EN 1561: Lamellar graphite cast iron
DIN EN 1562: Malleable cast iron
DIN EN 1563: Nodular graphite iron
DIN EN 1564: Bainitic cast iron

There are two systems for designating cast iron: in accordance with material numbers or abbreviations.

**Designation system for cast iron with material numbers**
(as per DIN EN 1560:1997-08)
The designation is alphanumeric. The first position is always occupied by EN for European standard. This is followed by J (iron) and then a letter denoting the graphite structure:
L Lamellar graphite
S Nodular graphite
M Temper carbon
N Graphite-free

A further four numbers determine the material.
Main feature (1st digit):
1 Tensile strength
2 Hardness
3 Chemical composition

Material code number (2nd and 3rd digits):
Numbers from 00...99.

Material requirements (4th digit):
0 No special requirements
1 Separately cast sample
2 Cast sample
7 Unfinished casting

*Standardization example:*
**EN-JL1050**
European standard, cast iron, lamellar graphite, tensile strength established as main feature, consecutive counting number (her for 300 N/mm² minimum tensile strength), no special requirements.

**Designation system for cast iron with abbreviations**
(as per DIN EN 1560:1997-08)
The designation is alphanumeric. The letters combination EN-GJ (EN European standard, G Casting, J Iron) is followed in each case by a letter for the graphite structure:
L Lamellar graphite
M Temper carbon
N Graphite-free
S Nodular graphite
V Vermicular graphite
Y Special structure

and if necessary for the micro- or macro-structure:
A Austenite
B Not decarb-annealed
F Ferrite
M Martensite
P Perlite
W Decarb-annealed

Then comes a hyphen followed by numerical values denoting mechanical properties or the chemical composition:
– minimum tensile strength in MPa (1 MPa = 1 N/mm²),
– also minimum elongation at fracture in %,
– type of hardness test (HB, HV, HR) with value,
– test temperature for impact toughness (RT or LT),
– sample manufacture (S, U or C),
– chemical composition (as for steel).

*Standardization example:*
**EN-GJL-300**
European standard, cast iron, lamellar graphite, minimum tensile strength 300 MPa.

**Nonferrous-metal alloys**
As for ferrous materials, the EN also features two ways of denoting nonferrous metals (NF) and their alloys for each material:
– Designation system with aid of chemical symbols (abbreviations) or
– Numerical designation system.

The numerical designation system differs greatly from steel and the earlier designation. For steel, the old designations with five numbers were retained virtually without exception and serve as a good guide for recoding. According to DIN 1700, the first digit determined the main group. The corresponding digit 1 for steel has been retained. However, the 2 for heavy metals, 3 for light alloys, etc., have been dropped. Nonferrous metals are designated according to their own system. Thus, the different properties and requirements of, for example, aluminum, copper or zinc alloys are better taken into account.

Of the nonferrous metals, aluminum and its alloys are the most important. For this reason, the text below only deals with the standardization of aluminum after the basic explanation of the system.

**Designation system of nonferrous metals with abbreviations (chemical symbols in parts)**

The EN standard denotes nonferrous metals (NF metals) according to the following basic system (example):

**EN A W - Al Cu 4 Pb MG Mn T4**

EN European standard

Code letter for metal:
**A** Aluminum
C Copper
M Magnesium

Code letter for processing:
**W** Wrought alloy
C Casting alloy

Designation system with chemical symbols or numeric, here, e.g.:
**Al Cu 4 Pb Mg Mn**

Material condition, here, e.g.: **T4**

The system lists the alloy metals in order of base metal with falling percentages. The notation for aluminum alloys has been standardized in such a way that a blank is inserted after Al. In the case of magnesium alloys, however, the whole designation is written together without a blank and only separated from "EN" by a hyphen.

**Special numerical designation system for aluminum (Al) and aluminum alloys**

For Al wrought products (Al and Al wrought alloys as per DIN EN 573:1994-12), the alloy is determined by four digits (example 1); for Al casting alloys (as per DIN EN 1706:1998-06), by five digits (example 2).

*Standardization example 1:*
**EN AW - 2007**
European standard, AW aluminum wrought alloy, alloy group (series 2 for Al-Cu alloys, 0 original alloy (1.2 changes), 07 designation for the alloy with approx. 4% copper, 1.1% lead, 1% magnesium, and 0.8% manganese.

*Standardization example 2:*
**EN AC - 45 200**
European standard, AC aluminum casting alloy, 45 alloy group AlSi5Cu, 200 number for individual alloy (here Al Si5Cu3Mn).

Code numbers for the alloy groups:
1  Pure Al
2  With copper
3  With manganese
4  With silicon
5  With magnesium
6  With magnesium-silicon
7  With zinc
8  Other

Some aluminum alloys can be precipitation-hardened or aged artificially. This increases the strength of the alloys.

Material condition:
O    Soft-annealed
H    Strain-hardened
H14  Strain-hardened-$1/2$ hard (for sheet)
T    Heat-treated
T6   Solution-annealed and artificially aged

*Standardization examples:*
**EN 1706 AC - Al Si9 Mg S T6**
European standard DIN EN 1706, aluminum casting alloy, aluminum (base metal), 9% silicon, slight quantities of magnesium, sand casting, material condition: solution-annealed and artificially aged.

**EN AW - 5754 [Al Mg3] H16**
European standard, aluminum wrought alloy, alloy group 5 (with magnesium), 754 number for individual alloy, [base metal aluminum, 3% magnesium], material condition: strain-hardened, $3/4$ hard.

# Properties of metallic materials

## Casting and steel materials

### Cast iron and malleable cast iron [6] $E$ [7]) in $10^3$ N/mm²: GG 78...143 [8]); GGG 160...180; GTW and GTS 175...195

| Material | Standard | Abbreviation of selected types | Principal alloy constituents, mean values in % by mass | $R_m$ [1]) N/mm² | $R_e$ [2]) N/mm² | $A_5$ [3]) % | $\sigma_{bW}$ [4]) Ref. value N/mm² | Test bar dia. [5]) mm | Properties, application examples |
|---|---|---|---|---|---|---|---|---|---|
| Cast iron with flake graphite (gray cast iron) | DIN EN 1561 | EN-GJL-200 | Not standardized | 200...300 | – | – | 90 | 30 | Brittle, very good machinability. |
| Nodular graphite iron | DIN EN 1563 | EN-GJS-400-15 | Not standardized | ≥ 400 | ≥ 250 | ≥ 15 | 200 | 25 | More ductile than gray cast iron, good machinability. |
| Malleable cast iron<br>White-heart casting<br>Black-heart casting | DIN EN 1562 | EN-GJMW-400-5<br>EN-GJMB-350-10 | Not standardized | ≥ 400<br>≥ 350 | ≥ 220<br>≥ 200 | ≥ 5 ($A_3$)<br>≥ 10 ($A_3$) | –<br>– | 12<br>12 | Ductility similar to nodular cast iron, good machinability. |
| Cast steel<br>$E$ [7]) as steel | DIN 1681 | GS-45 | Not standardized | ≥ 450 | ≥ 230 | ≥ 22 | 210 | | Heat-treatable. |

### Steel $E$ [7]) in $10^3$ N/mm²: unalloyed and low-alloy steels 212, austenitic steels ≥ 190, high-alloy tool steels ≤ 230

| Material | Standard | Abbreviation of selected types | Principal alloy constituents, mean values in % by mass | $R_m$ [1]) N/mm² | $R_e$ [2]) N/mm² | $A_5$ [3]) % | $\sigma_{bW}$ [4]) Ref. value N/mm² | Test bar dia. [5]) mm | Properties, application examples |
|---|---|---|---|---|---|---|---|---|---|
| Untreated structural steel (dia. 16...40 mm) | DIN EN 10 025 | S 235 JR<br>E 360 | ≤ 0.19 C | 340...510<br>670...830 | ≤ 225<br>≥ 355 | ≥ 26<br>≥ 11 | ≥ 170<br>≥ 330 | –<br>– | Low-stressed parts.<br>Higher-stressed parts. |
| Cold-rolled strip of soft unalloyed steels | DIN EN 10 139 | DC 05 LC | Not standardized | 270...330 | ≤ 180 | ≥ 40 ($A_{80}$) | ≥ 130 | – | Complex deep-drawn parts. |
| Hot-galvanized strip and sheet | DIN EN 10 142 | DX 53 D | Not standardized | ≤ 380 | ≤ 260 | ≥ 30 ($A_{80}$) | ≥ 190 | – | Corrosion-stressed, complex deep-drawn parts. |
| Free-cutting steel (dia. 16...40 mm) | DIN EN 10 087 | 11 SMn30<br>35 S 20 | ≤ 0.14 C; 1.1 Mn; 0.30 S<br>0.35 C; 0.9 Mn; 0.20 S | 380...570<br>520...680 | –<br>– | –<br>– | ≥ 190<br>≥ 260 | –<br>– | Soft free-cutting steel.<br>Free-cutting tempering steel. |

| Material / Material condition | Standard | Abbreviation of selected types | Principal alloy constituents, mean values in % by mass | $R_m$ [1] N/mm² | $R_e$ [2] N/mm² | $A_5$ [3] % | $\sigma_{bW}$ [4] Ref. value N/mm² | Test bar dia. [5] mm | Properties, application examples |
|---|---|---|---|---|---|---|---|---|---|
| Tempering steel, quenched and drawn (⌀ ≤ 16 mm) | DIN EN 10 083 | C 45 E | 0.45 C | 700...850 | ≥ 490 | ≥ 14 | ≈ 280 | – | Increasing hardenability. |
| | | 34 Cr 4 | 0.34 C; 1.1 Cr | 900...1,100 | ≥ 700 | ≥ 12 | ≈ 360 | – | |
| | | 42 CrMo 4 | 0.42 C; 1 Cr; 0.2 Mo | 1,100...1,300 | ≥ 900 | ≥ 10 | ≈ 440 | – | |
| | | 30 CrNiMo 8 | 0.3 C; 2 Cr; 0.4 Mo; 2 Ni | 1,250...1,450 | ≥ 1,050 | ≥ 9 | ≈ 500 | – | |
| | | | | Hardness HV (ref. value) Surface | Core | | | | |
| Case-hardening steel, case-hardened and tempered (⌀ ≤ 11 mm) | DIN EN 10 084 | C 15 E | 0.15 C; | 700...850 | 200...450 | In the case of hard steels – hardened and tempered, case-hardened, nitrided, etc. – the material characteristics measured in the tensile test are unsuitable for dimensioning hard components. | | | High wear resistance, high vibrational strength. |
| | | 16 MnCr 5 | 0.16 C; 1 Cr | 700...850 | 300...450 | | | | |
| | | 17 CrNi 6-6 | 0.17 C; 1.5 Cr; 1.5 Ni | 700...850 | 400...550 | | | | |
| | | 18 CrNiMo 7-6 | 0.18 C; 1.6 Cr; 1.5 Ni; 0.3 Mo | 700...850 | 400...550 | | | | |
| Nitriding steel, quenched, drawn and nitrided | DIN EN 10 085 | 31 CrMoV 9 | 0.31 C; 2.5 Cr; 0.2 Mo; 0.15 V | 700...850 | 250...400 | | | | High wear resistance, high vibrational strength. |
| | | 34 CrAlMo 5 | 0.34 C; 1.0 Al; 1.15 Cr; 0.2 Mo | 850...1,100 | 250...400 | | | | |
| Rolling-bearing steel, hardened and tempered | DIN EN ISO 683-17 | 100 Cr 6 | 1 C; 1.5 Cr | Hardness 60...64 HRC | | | | | High wear resistance. |
| Tool steel Unalloyed cold work steel, hardened and tempered | DIN EN ISO 4957 | C 80 U | 0.8 C | Standard hardness | Standard hardness | | | | Water hardening steel. |
| Alloyed cold work steel, hardened and tempered | DIN EN ISO 4957 | 90 MnCrV 8 | 0.9 C; 2 Mn; 0.3 Cr; 0.1 V | 60...64 HRC | | | | | Water/oil hardening steel. Oil hardening steel. Increasing wear resistance. |
| | | X 153 CrMoV 12 | 1.53 C; 12 Cr; 0.8 Mo; 0.8 V | 60...64 HRC | | | | | |
| | | X 210 Cr 12 | 2.1 C; 12 Cr | 60...64 HRC | | | | | |

| Material Material condition | Standard | Abbreviation of selected types | Principal alloy constituents, mean values in % by mass | $R_m$ [1] N/mm² | $R_e$ [2] N/mm² | $A_5$ [3] % | $\sigma_{bW}$ [4] Ref. value N/mm² | Test bar dia. [5] mm | Properties, application examples |
|---|---|---|---|---|---|---|---|---|---|
| Hot work steel, hardened and tempered | DIN EN ISO 4957 | X 40 CrMoV 5-1 | 0.4 C; 5 Cr; 1.3 Mo; 1 V | 43...45 HRC | | | In the case of hard steels – hardened and tempered, case-hardened, nitrided, etc. – the material characteristics measured in the tensile test are unsuitable for dimensioning of the hard components. | | Wear-resistant at high temperature. |
| High-speed tool steel, hardened and tempered | DIN EN ISO 4957 | HS 6-5-2 | 0.85 C; 6 W; 5 Mo; 2 V; 4 Cr | 61...65 HRC | | | | | |
| Stainless steels -Ferritic steel, annealed | DIN EN 10 088 | X 6 Cr 17 | ≤ 0.08 C; 17 Cr | 450...600 | ≥ 270 | ≥ 20 | 200...315 | | Non-hardenable. |
| -Martensitic steel, hardened and tempered ≤ 200 °C | DIN EN 10 088 | X 20 Cr 13 | 0.20 C; 13 Cr | Hardness approx. 40 HRC | Hardness < 185 HV | | | | Increasing wear resistance. → |
| | | X 46 Cr 13 | 0.46 C; 13 Cr | Hardness approx. 45 HRC | | | | | |
| | | X 90 CrMoV 18 | 0.9 C; 18 Cr; 1.1 Mo; 0.1 V | Hardness ≥ 57 HRC | | | | | |
| | | X 105 CrMo 17 | 1.1 C; 17 Cr; 1.0 Mo | Hardness ≥ 58 HRC | | | | | |
| -Austenitic steel, quenched | DIN EN 10 088 | X 5 CrNi 18-10 | ≤ 0.07 C; 18 Cr; 9 Ni | 500...700 | ≥ 190 | ≥ 45 | – | – | Quenched, nonmagnetic, cold formed, magnetizable, non-hardenable. |
| | | X 8 CrNiS 18-9 | ≤ 0.10 C; 18 Cr; 9 Ni; 0.3 S | 500...700 | ≥ 190 | ≥ 35 | | | |
| Hard metals $E = 440{,}000...550{,}000$ | – | – | W (Ti, Ta) carbide + Co | 800...1,900 HV | | | | | Sintered materials, extremely resistant to pressure and wear, but brittle; machining, cutting, and forming tools. |
| Extremely heavy metals $E = 320{,}000...380{,}000$ | – | – | > 90 W; Ni u. a. | ≥ 650 240...450 HV | ≥ 560 | ≥ 2 | | | Density 17...18.5 g/cm³; governor flyweights, flywheel masses, and counterweights. |

[1] Tensile strength.
[2] Yield point (or $R_{p0.2}$).
[3] Elongation at fracture.
[4] Fatigue strength under reversed bending stress; more precise strength values are to be calculated acc. to FKM Guideline "Mathematical Proof of Fatigue Strength for Engineering Components".
[5] The fatigue limits given apply to the separately cast test bar.
[6] The fatigue limits of all types of cast iron are dependent on the weight and section thickness of the cast pieces.
[7] Modulus of elasticity.
[8] For gray cast iron, $E$ decreases with increasing tensile stress and remains almost constant with increasing compression stress.

## Spring steel

| Material | DIN | Principal alloy constituents, approx. in % by mass; $E$ and $G$ in N/mm² | Diameter mm | $R_m$ [1] min. N/mm² | $Z$ [2] % | $\sigma_b$ [3] N/mm² | $\tau_{th}$ [4] N/mm² | $\tau_{perm}$ [5] N/mm² | Properties, application examples |
|---|---|---|---|---|---|---|---|---|---|
| Spring steel wire D, patented and drawn cold-hammered | 17 223 Sh. 1 | 0.8 C; 0.6 Mn; < 0.35 Si; $E$ = 206,000 $G$ = 81,500 | 1 3 10 | 2,230 1,840 1,350 | 40 40 30 | 1,590 1,280 930 | 380[6] 360[6] 320 | 1,115 920 675 | For high maximum stresses. |
| Stainless spring steel wire | 17 224 | < 0.12 C; 17 Cr; 7.5 Ni; $E$ = 185,000 $G$ = 73,500 | 1 3 | 2,000 1,600 | 40 40 | 1,400 1,130 | – – | 1,000 800 | Stainless springs. |
| Heat-treated valve-spring steel wire | 17 223 Sh. 2 | 0.65 C; 0.7 Mn; ≤ 0.30 Si; $E$ = 206,000 $G$ = 80,000 | 1 3 8 | 1,720 1,480 1,390 | 45 45 38 | 1,200 1,040 930 | 380[7] 380[7] 360[7] | 860 740 690 | For high alternating cyclic stress. |
| Heat-treated, alloyed valve-spring steel wire VD Si Cr | – | 0.55 C; 0.7 Mn; 0.65 Cr; 1.4 Si; $E$ = 200,000 $G$ = 79,000 | 1 3 8 | 2,060 1,920 1,720 | 50 50 40 | – – – | 430[7] 430[7] 380[7] | 1,030 960 860 | For maximum alternating cyclic stress and higher temperatures. |
| Heat-treated, alloyed valve-spring steel wire VD Cr V | – | 0.7 C; 0.7 Mn; 0.5 Cr; 0.15 V; ≤ 0.30 S; $E$ = 200,000 $G$ = 79,000 | 1 3 8 | 1,860 1,670 1,420 | 45 45 40 | – – – | 470[7] 470[7] 400[7] | 930 835 710 | For maximum alternating cyclic stress. |
| Spring steel strip Ck 85 | 17 222 | 0.85 C; 0.55 Mn; 0.25 Si; $E$ = 206,000 | h ≤ 2.5 | 1,470 | – | 1,270 | $\sigma_{bh}$ = 640 | – | Highly stressed leaf springs. |
| Stainless spring steel strip | 17 224 | < 0.12 C; 17 Cr; 7.5 Ni; $E$ = 185,000 | h ≤ 1 | 1,370 | – | 1,230 | $\sigma_{bh}$ = 590 | – | Stainless leaf springs. |

[1] Tensile strength.
[2] Fracture contraction.
[3] Permissible bending stress.
[4] Permissible stress range for number of stress cycles N ≥ 10[7].
[5] Permissible maximum stress for temperatures up to approx. 30 °C and 1...2% relaxation in 10 h; for higher temperatures.
[6] 480 N/mm² for peened springs.
[7] Approx. 40% higher for peened springs.

## Vehicle-body sheet metal

| Material Abbreviated name | Standard Material thickness mm | $R_{p0.2}$ [1] N/mm² | $R_m$ [2] N/mm² | $A_{80}$ [3] % | Properties, applications examples |
|---|---|---|---|---|---|
| St 12 | 0.6...2.5 | ≈ 280 | 270...410 | ≈ 28 | For simple drawn metal parts. |
| St 13 | | ≈ 250 | 270...370 | ≈ 32 | For complex drawn metal parts. |
| St 14 | | ≈ 240 | 270...350 | ≈ 38 | For very complex deep-drawn parts, outer body parts (roof, doors, fenders, etc.; 0.75...1.0 mm); see also DIN 1623. |
| ZE 260 | 0.75...2.0 | 260...340 | ≈ 370 | ≈ 28 | For highly stressed supporting parts whose degree of deformation is not too complex. see EN 10 268. |
| ZE 340 | | 340...420 | ≈ 420 | ≈ 24 | |
| ZE 420 | | 420...500 | ≈ 490 | ≈ 20 | |
| AlMg 0.4 Si 1.2 | 0.8...2.5 | ≈ 140 | ≈ 250 | ≈ 28 | For outer body parts such as front fenders, doors, hood, trunk lid, etc.; mostly 1.25 mm; see DIN 1745. |
| AlMg 4.5 Mn 0.3 | 0.5...3.5 | ≈ 130 | ≈ 270 | ≈ 28 | For inner reinforcements of hinged covers; for parts which are not visible; stress lines toleranced. |
| TRIP (Transformation Induced Plasticity) | | 500...700 | | 20...30 | Structural parts, cross-members |
| DP (Dual Phase) | | 300...700 | | 10...30 | |

[1] Yield point.
[2] Tensile strength.
[3] Elongation at fracture.

## Nonferrous metals, light alloys

| Material Examples | Abbreviated name Examples | Composition, mean values, in % by mass | $E$[1] N/mm² | $R_m$[2] min. N/mm² | $R_{p0.2}$[3] approx. N/mm² | $\sigma_{bW}$[4] approx. N/mm² | Properties, application examples |
|---|---|---|---|---|---|---|---|
| **Wrought copper alloys (DIN EN 1652, 1654, 1758, 12 163…12 168)** | | | | | | | |
| High-conductivity copper | EN CW-Cu-FRTP | 99.90 Cu | $128 \cdot 10^3$ | 200 | 120[5] | 70 | Very good electric conductivity. |
| Brass | EN CW-CuZn 30 R350 EN CW-CuZn 37 R440 EN CW-CuZn 39 Pb3 R430 | 70 Cu; 30 Zn 63 Cu; 37 Zn 58 Cu; 39 Zn; 3 Pb | $114 \cdot 10^3$ $110 \cdot 10^3$ $96 \cdot 10^3$ | 350 440 430 | 200 400 250 | 110 140 150 | Deep-drawing capability. Good cold formability. Machine parts. |
| Nickel silver | EN CW-CuNi 18 Zn 20 R500 | 62 Cu; 20 Zn; 18 Ni | $135 \cdot 10^3$ | 500 | 440 | 175 | Corrosion-resistant. |
| Tin bronze | EN CW-CuSn 6 R420 | 94 Cu; 6 Sn | $118 \cdot 10^3$ | 420 | 290 | 175 | Good antifriction properties; bearing bushings, connectors. |
| **Cast copper alloys (DIN EN 1982)** | | | | | | | |
| Cast tin bronze | CuSn 10-C-GS | 89 Cu; 10 Sn; 1 Ni | $100 \cdot 10^3$ | 250 | 160 | 90 | Corrosion-resistant, wear-resistant; gears, bearings. |
| Red bronze | CuSn 7 Zn 4 Pb 7-C-GZ | 85 Cu; 7 Sn; 4 Zn; 7 Pb | $95 \cdot 10^3$ | 260 | 150 | 80 | |
| **Other alloys** | | | | | | | |
| Tin alloy (DIN ISO 4381) | SnSb 12 Cu 6 Pb | 80 Sn; 12 Sb; 6 Cu; 2 Pb | $30 \cdot 10^3$ | – | 60 | 28 | Plain bearings. |
| Zinc diecastings (DIN EN 12 844) | ZP 0410 | 95 Zn; 4 Al; Cu 1 | $72 \cdot 10^3$ | 330 | 250 | 80 | Dimensionally accurate castings. |
| Heating-conductor alloy (DIN EN 17 470) | NiCr 80 20 NiCr 60 15 | 80 Ni; 20 Cr 60 Ni; 22 Fe; 17 Cr | – | 650 600 | – – | – – | High electrical resistance (P. 272). |
| Resistance alloy (DIN 17 471) | CuNi 44 CuNi 30 Mn | 55 Cu; 44 Ni; 1 Mn 67 Cu; 30 Ni; 3 Mn | – | 420 400 | – – | – – | |

1) Modulus of elasticity, reference values. 2) Tensile strength. 3) 0.2% yield strength. 4) Fatigue strength under reversed bending stress. 5) Maximum.

## Nonferrous metals, light alloys

| Material Examples | Composition, mean values, in % by mass | $R_m$[1] min. N/mm² | $R_{p0.2}$[2] approx. N/mm² | $\sigma_{bW}$[3] approx. N/mm² | Properties, application examples |
|---|---|---|---|---|---|
| **Wrought aluminum alloys** (DIN EN 458, 485, 515, 573, 754 ...), modulus of elasticity $E$ = 65,000...73,000 N/mm² | | | | | |
| ENAW-Al 99.5 O | 99.5 Al | 65 | 20 | 40 | Soft, very good conductor, can be anodized/polished. |
| ENAW-AlMg 2 Mn 0.8 H111 | 97 Al; 2 Mg; 0.8 Mn | 190 | 80 | 90 | Seawater-resistant, can be anodized. |
| ENAW-AlSi 1 MgMn T 6 | 97 Al; 0.9 Mg; 1 Si; 0.7 Mn | 310 | 260 | 90 | Aged artificially, seawater-resistant. |
| ENAW-AlCu 4 MgSi (A) T 4 | 94 Al; 4 Cu; 0.7 Mg; 0.7 Mn; 0.5 Si | 390 | 245 | 120 | Precipitation-hardened, good creep behavior. |
| ENAW-AlZn 5.5 MgCu T 6 | 90 Al; 6 Zn; 2 Mg; 2 Cu; 0.2 Cr | 540 | 485 | 140 | Maximum strength. |
| **Cast aluminum alloys** [5] (DIN EN 1706), modulus of elasticity $E$ = 68,000...80,000 N/mm² | | | | | |
| ENAC-AlSi 7 Mg 0.3 KT 6 | 89 Al; 7 Si; 0.4 Mg; 0.1 Ti | 290 | 210 | 80 | Aged artificially; highly stressed parts with good vibration strength. |
| ENAC-AlSi 6 Cu 4 KF | 89 Al; 6 Si; 4 Cu; 0.3 Mn; 0.3 Mg | 170 | 100 | 60 | Highly versatile, heat-resistant. |
| ENAC-AlCu 4 Ti KT 6 | 95 Al; 5 Cu; 0.2 Ti | 330 | 220 | 90 | Aged artificially; simple parts with maximum strength and toughness. |
| ENAC-AlSi 12 Cu 1 (Fe) DF | 88 Al; 12 Si; 1 Cu; 1 Fe | 240 | 140 | 70 | Thin-walled, vibration-resistant parts. |
| ENAC-AlSi 9 Cu 3 (Fe) DF | 87 Al; 9 Si; 3 Cu; 0.3 Mn; 0.3 Mg | 240 | 140 | 70 [6] | Heat-resistant; complicated diecastings. |
| ENAC-AlMg 9 DF | 90 Al; 9 Mg; 1 Si; 0.4 Mn | 200 | 130 | 60 [6] | Seawater-resistant; medium-stressed parts. |
| **Magnesium alloys** (DIN EN 1753, DIN 9715), modulus of elasticity $E$ = 40,000...45,000 N/mm² | | | | | |
| MgAl 6 Zn F 27 | 93 Mg; 6 Al; 1 Zn; 0.3 Mn | 270 | 195 | – | Parts subject to medium to high stress. |
| EN-MC Mg Al 9 Zn 1(A) DF | 90 Mg; 9 Al; 0.6 Zn; 0.2 Mn | 200 | 140 | 50 | Complex diecastings. Chips are combustible. |
| **Titanium alloys** (DIN 17 850, 17 851, 17 860...17 864), modulus of elasticity $E$ = 110,000 N/mm² | | | | | |
| Ti 1 | 99.7 Ti | 290 | 180 | – | Corrosion-resistant. |
| TiAl 6 V 4 F 89 | 90 Ti; 6 Al; 4 V | 890 | 820 | – | Corrosion-resistant, maximum strength. |

[1] Tensile strength. [2] 0.2% yield strength. [3] Rotating fatigue strength under reversed bending stress. [4] Maximum. [5] Strength values apply to permanent mold castings and diecastings for separately cast test rods. Sand castings have slightly lower values than permanent mold castings. [6] Flat fatigue strength under reversed bending stress.

## Sintered metals
### Sintered metals[1] for plain bearings

| Material | Material code Sint. | Permissible ranges | | | | | Representative examples | | | | | |
|---|---|---|---|---|---|---|---|---|---|---|---|---|
| | | Density $\varrho$ g/cm³ | Porosity $(\Delta V/V)\cdot 100$ % | Chemical composition % by mass % | Radial breaking strength $K^2$) N/mm² | Hardness HB | Density $\varrho$ g/cm³ | Chemical composition % by mass % | Radial breaking strength $K^2$) N/mm² | Compressive yield point $\delta_{m,0.2}$ N/mm² | Hardness HB²) | Thermal conductivity $\lambda$ W/mK |
| Sintered iron | A 00 B 00 C 00 | 5.6…6.0 6.0…6.4 6.4…6.8 | 25 ± 2.5 20 ± 2.5 15 ± 2.5 | <0.3 C; <1.0 Cu; <2 others; rest Fe | >150 >180 >220 | >25 >30 >40 | 5.9 6.3 6.7 | <0.2 others; rest Fe | 160 190 230 | 130 160 180 | 30 40 50 | 37 43 48 |
| Sintered steel containing Cu | A 10 B 10 C 10 | 5.6…6.0 6.0…6.4 6.4…6.8 | 25 ± 2.5* 20 ± 2.5 15 ± 2.5 | <0.3 C; 1…5 Cu; <2 others; rest Fe | >160 >190 >230 | >35 >40 >55 | 5.9 6.3 6.7 | 2.0 Cu; <0.2 others; rest Fe | 170 200 240 | 150 170 200 | 40 50 65 | 36 37 42 |
| Sintered steel containing Cu and C | B 11 | 6.0…6.4 | 20 ± 2.5 | 0.4…1.0 C; 1…5 Cu; <2 others; rest Fe | >270 | >70 | 6.3 | 0.6 C; 2.0 Cu; <0.2 others; rest Fe | 280 | 160 | 80 | 28 |
| Sintered steel containing higher Cu | A 20 B 20 | 5.8…6.2 6.2…6.6 | 25 ± 2.5 20 ± 2.5 | <0.3 C; 15…25 Cu; <2 others; rest Fe | >180 >200 | >30 >45 | 6.0 6.4 | 20 Cu; <0.2 others; rest Fe | 200 220 | 140 160 | 40 50 | 41 47 |
| Sintered steel containing higher Cu and C | A 22 B 22 | 5.5…6.0 6.0…6.5 | 25 ± 2.5 20 ± 2.5 | 0.5…2.0 C; 15…25 Cu; <2 others; rest Fe | >120 >140 | >20 >25 | 5.7 6.1 | 2.0 C³); 20 Cu; <0.2 others; rest Fe | 125 145 | 100 120 | 25 30 | 30 37 |
| Sintered bronze | A 50 B 50 C 50 | 6.4…6.8 6.8…7.2 7.2…7.7 | 25 ± 2.5 20 ± 2.5 15 ± 2.5 | <0.2 C; 9…11 Sn; <2 others; rest Cu | >120 >170 >200 | >25 >30 >35 | 6.6 7.0 7.4 | 10 Sn; <0.2 others; rest Cu | 140 180 210 | 100 130 160 | 30 35 45 | 27 32 37 |
| Sintered bronze containing graphite⁴) | A 51 B 51 C 51 | 6.0…6.5 6.5…7.0 7.0…7.5 | 25 ± 2.5 20 ± 2.5 15 ± 2.5 | 0.5…2.0 C; 9…11 Sn; <2 others; rest Cu | >100 >150 >170 | >20 >25 >30 | 6.3 6.7 7.1 | 1.5 C⁴); 10 Sn; <0.2 others; rest Cu | 120 155 175 | 80 100 120 | 20 30 35 | 20 26 32 |

1) According to "Material Specification Sheets for Sintered Metals". DIN 30 910, Edition 1990. 2) Measured on calibrated bearings 10/16 ∅ · 10.
3) C is mainly present as free graphite. 4) C is present as free graphite.

## Sintered metals¹) for formed parts

| Material | Material code Sint- | Permissible ranges Density ϱ g/cm³ | Porosity (ΔV/V)·100 % | Chemical composition % by mass % | Hardness HB | Representative examples Density ϱ g/cm³ | Chemical composition % by mass % | Tensile strength $R_m$ N/mm² | Yield point $R_{p0.1}$ N/mm² | Elongation at break A % | Hardness HB | Elastic Modulus $E \cdot 10^3$ N/mm² |
|---|---|---|---|---|---|---|---|---|---|---|---|---|
| Sintered iron | C 00 | 6.4...6.8 | 15 ± 2.5 | < 0.3 C; < 1.0 Cu; < 2 others; rest Fe | > 35 | 6.6 | < 0.5 others; rest Fe | 130 | 60 | 4 | 40 | 100 |
|  | D 00 | 6.8...7.2 | 10 ± 2.5 |  | > 45 | 6.9 |  | 190 | 90 | 10 | 50 | 130 |
|  | E 00 | > 7.2 | < 7.5 |  | > 60 | 7.3 |  | 260 | 130 | 18 | 65 | 160 |
| Sintered steel containing C | C 01 | 6.4...6.8 | 15 ± 2.5 | 0.3...0.6 C; < 1.0 Cu; < 2 others; rest Fe | > 70 | 6.6 | 0.5 C; < 0.5 others; rest Fe | 260 | 180 | 3 | 80 | 100 |
|  | D 01 | 6.8...7.2 | 10 ± 2.5 |  | > 90 | 6.9 |  | 320 | 210 | 3 | 100 | 130 |
| Sintered steel containing Cu | C 10 | 6.4...6.8 | 15 ± 2.5 | < 0.3 C; 1...5 Cu; < 2 others; rest Fe | > 40 | 6.6 | 1.5 Cu; < 0.5 others; rest Fe | 230 | 160 | 3 | 55 | 100 |
|  | D 10 | 6.8...7.2 | 10 ± 2.5 |  | > 50 | 6.9 |  | 300 | 210 | 6 | 85 | 130 |
|  | E 10 | > 7.2 | < 7.5 |  | > 80 | 7.3 |  | 400 | 290 | 12 | 120 | 160 |
| Sintered steel containing Cu and C | C 11 | 6.4...6.8 | 15 ± 2.5 | 0.4...1.5 C; 1...5 Cu; < 2 others; rest Fe | > 80 | 6.6 | 0.6 C; 1.5 Cu; < 0.5 others; rest Fe | 460 | 320 | 2 | 125 | 100 |
|  | D 11 | 6.8...7.2 | 10 ± 2.5 |  | > 95 | 6.9 |  | 570 | 400 | 2 | 150 | 130 |
|  | C 21 | 6.4...6.8 | 15 ± 2.5 | 0.4...1.5 C; 5...10 Cu; < 2 others; rest Fe | > 105 | 6.6 | 0.8 C; 6 Cu; < 0.5 others; rest Fe | 530 | 410 | < 1 | 150 | 100 |
| Sintered steel containing Cu, Ni and Mo | C 30 | 6.4...6.8 | 15 ± 2.5 | < 0.3 C; 1...5 Cu; 1...5 Ni; < 0.8 Mo; < 2 others; rest Fe | > 55 | 6.6 | 0.3 C; 1.5 Cu; 4.0 Ni; 0.5 Mo; < 0.5 others; rest Fe | 390 | 310 | 2 | 105 | 100 |
|  | D 30 | 6.8...7.2 | 10 ± 2.5 |  | > 60 | 6.9 |  | 510 | 370 | 3 | 130 | 130 |
|  | E 30 | > 7.2 | < 7.5 |  | > 90 | 7.3 |  | 680 | 440 | 5 | 170 | 160 |
| Sintered steel containing P | C 35 | 6.4...6.8 | 15 ± 2.5 | < 0.3 C; < 1.0 Cu; 0.3...0.6 P; < 2 others; rest Fe | > 70 | 6.6 | 0.45 P; < 0.5 others; rest Fe | 310 | 200 | 11 | 85 | 100 |
|  | D 35 | 6.8...7.2 | 10 ± 2.5 |  | > 80 | 6.9 |  | 330 | 230 | 12 | 90 | 130 |
| Sintered steel containing Cu and P | C 36 | 6.4...6.8 | 15 ± 2.5 | < 0.3 C; 1...5 Cu; 0.3...0.6 P; < 2 others; rest Fe | > 80 | 6.6 | 2.0 Cu; 0.45 P; < 0.5 others; rest Fe | 360 | 290 | 5 | 100 | 100 |
|  | D 36 | 6.8...7.2 | 10 ± 2.5 |  | > 90 | 6.9 |  | 380 | 320 | 6 | 105 | 130 |
| Sintered steel containing Cu, Ni, Mo, | C 39 | 6.4...6.8 | 15 ± 2.5 | 0.3...0.6 C; 1...3 Cu; 1...5 Ni; < 0.8 Mo; < 2 others; rest Fe | > 90 | 6.6 | 0.5 C; 1.5 Cu; 4.0 Ni; 0.5 Mo; < 0.5 others; rest Fe | 520 | 370 | 1 | 150 | 100 |
|  | D 39 | 6.8...7.2 | 10 ± 2.5 |  | > 120 | 6.9 |  | 600 | 420 | 2 | 180 | 130 |

| Material | Material code Sint- | Permissible ranges Density ρ g/cm³ | Porosity $(\Delta V/V) \cdot 100$ % | Chemical composition % by mass % | Hardness HB | Representative examples Density ρ g/cm³ | Chemical composition % by mass % | Tensile strength $R_m$ N/mm² | Yield point $R_{p0.1}$ N/mm² | Elongation at break A % | Hardness HB | Elastic Modulus $E \cdot 10^3$ N/mm² |
|---|---|---|---|---|---|---|---|---|---|---|---|---|
| Stainless sintered steel AISI 316 | C 40 | 6.4...6.8 | 15 ± 2.5 | < 0.08 C; 10...14 Ni; 2...4 Mo; 16...19 Cr; < 2 others; rest Fe | > 95 | 6.6 | 0.06 C; 13 Ni; 2.5 Mo; 18 Cr; < 0.5 others; rest Fe | 330 | 250 | 1 | 110 | 100 |
|  | D 40 | 6.8...7.2 | 10 ± 2.5 |  | > 125 | 6.9 |  | 400 | 320 | 2 | 135 | 130 |
| AISI 430 | C 42 | 6.4...6.8 | 15 ± 2.5 | < 0.08 C; 16...19 Cr; < 2 others; rest Fe | > 140 | 6.6 | 0.06 C; 18 Cr; < 0.5 others; rest Fe | 420 | 330 | 1 | 170 | 100 |
| AISI 410 | C 43 | 6.4...6.8 | 15 ± 2.5 | 0.1...0.3 C; 11...13 Cr; < 2 others; rest Fe | > 165 | 6.6 | 0.2 C; 13 Cr; < 0.5 others; rest Fe | 510 | 370 | 1 | 180 | 100 |
| Sintered bronze | C 50 | 7.2...7.7 | 15 ± 2.5 | 9...11 Sn; < 2 others; rest Cu | > 35 | 7.4 | 10 Sn; < 0.5 others; rest Cu | 150 | 90 | 4 | 40 | 50 |
|  | D 50 | 7.7...8.1 | 10 ± 2.5 |  | > 45 | 7.9 |  | 220 | 120 | 6 | 55 | 70 |
| Sintered aluminum containing Cu | D 73 | 2.45...2.55 | 10 ± 2.5 | 4...6 Cu; < 1 Mg; < 1 Si; < 2 others; rest Al | > 45 | 2.5 | 4.5 Cu; 0.6 Mg; 0.7 Si; < 0.5 others; rest Al | 160 | 130 | 1 | 50 | 50 |
|  | E 73 | 2.55...2.65 | 6 ± 1.5 |  | > 55 | 2.6 |  | 200 | 150 | 2 | 60 | 60 |

[1]) According to "Material Specification Sheets for Sintered Metals": DIN 30 910, 1990 Edition.

# Magnetic materials

## Soft-magnetic metallic materials

| Magnet type | Alloy constituents by mass % | Coercive field strength $H_{c\,max}$ in A/m, Thickness in mm | | Static magnetic properties — Minimum magnetic polarization in tesla (T) at field strength $H$ in A/m | | | | | | | | | AC test data, 50 Hz [1] | | |
|---|---|---|---|---|---|---|---|---|---|---|---|---|---|---|---|
| | | 0.4...1.5 | >1.5 | 20 | 50 | 100 | 300 | 500 | 800 | 1,600 | 4,000 | 8,000 | Measuring point $\hat{H}$ in A/m | Minimum amplitude permeability $\mu_a$, Sheet thickness in mm 0.30...0.38 | 0.15...0.20 |
| A – 240 | 100 Fe | 240 | 240 | | | | 1.15 | 1.30 | | | 1.60 | | Not suitable for AC applications. | | |
| A – 120 | 100 Fe | 120 | 120 | | | | 1.15 | 1.30 | | | 1.60 | | | | |
| A – 60 | 100 Fe | 60 | 60 | | | | 1.25 | 1.35 | | | 1.60 | | | | |
| A – 12 | 100 Fe | 12 | 12 | | | 1.15 | 1.30 | 1.40 | | | 1.60 | | | | |
| C1 – 48 | 0...5 Si (typical 2...4.5) | 48 | 48 | | | 0.60 | 1.10 | 1.20 | | | 1.50 | | | | |
| C1 – 12 | 0...5 Si (typical 2...4.5) | 12 | 12 | | | 1.20 | 1.30 | 1.35 | | | 1.50 | | | | |
| C21 – 09 | 0.4...5 Si (typical 2...4.5) | | | | | | | | | | | | 1.60 | 900 | 750 |
| C22 – 13 | 0.4...5 Si (typical 2...4.5) | | | | | | | | | | | | 1.60 | 1,300 | – |
| E11 – 60 | 72...83 Ni | 2 | 4 | 0.50 | 0.65 | 0.70 | 0.73 | | | | 0.75 | | 0.40 | 40,000 | 40,000 |
| E21 | 54...68 Ni | Not suitable for this thickness | | | | | | | | | | | | On agreement | |
| E31 – 06 | 45...50 Ni | 10 | 10 | 0.50 | 0.90 | 1.10 | 1.35 | | | | 1.45 | | 0.40 | 6,000 | 6,000 |
| E32 | 45...50 Ni | Not suitable for this thickness | | | | | | | | | | | | On agreement | |
| E41 – 03 | 35...40 Ni | 24 | 24 | 0.20 | 0.45 | 0.70 | 1.00 | | | | 1.18 | | 1.60 | 2,900 | 2,900 |
| F11 – 240 | 47...50 Co | 240 | | | | | 1.40 | 1.70 | 1.90 | | 2.06 | 2.15 | As agreed between manufacturer and buyer. | | |
| F11 – 60 | 47...50 Co | 60 | | | | | 1.80 | 2.10 | 2.20 | | 2.25 | 2.25 | | | |
| F21 | 35 Co | 300 | | | | | | 1.50 | 1.60 | | 2.00 | 2.20 | | | |
| F31 | 23...27 Co | 300 | | | | | | | | | 1.85 | 2.00 | | | |

[1] Data apply to laminated rings.

Electrical steel sheet and strip

| Sheet grade Abbreviated name | Material number | Nominal thickness mm | Density ϱ g/cm³ | Max. cyclic magnetization loss (50 Hz) in W/kg under modulation P 1.0 | P 1.5 | P 1.7 | Magnetic polarization in tesla min. at field strength H in A/m (B25) 2,500 | (B50) 5,000 | (B100) 10,000 | Static Coercive field strength H_c in A/m | Permeability μ max. | Properties, application examples |
|---|---|---|---|---|---|---|---|---|---|---|---|---|
| M 270-35A | 1.0801 | 0.35 | 7.60 | 1.10 | 2.70 | – | 1.49 | 1.60 | 1.70 | | | Cyclic magnetization losses. |
| M 330-35A | 1.0804 | 0.35 | 7.65 | 1.30 | 3.30 | – | 1.49 | 1.60 | 1.70 | | | |
| M 330-50A | 1.0809 | 0.50 | 7.60 | 1.35 | 3.30 | – | 1.49 | 1.60 | 1.70 | | | |
| M 530-50A | 1.0813 | 0.50 | 7.70 | 2.30 | 5.30 | – | 1.56 | 1.65 | 1.75 | | | |
| M 800-50A | 1.0816 | 0.50 | 7.80 | 3.60 | 8.00 | – | 1.60 | 1.70 | 1.78 | | | |
| M 400-65A | 1.0821 | 0.65 | 7.65 | 1.70 | 4.00 | – | 1.52 | 1.62 | 1.72 | | | |
| M1000-65A | 1.0829 | 0.65 | 7.80 | 4.40 | 10.00 | – | 1.61 | 1.71 | 1.80 | ≈ 100 | ≈ 5,000 | Manufacture of magnetic circuits with alternating magnetization (e.g. motors). |
| M 800-100A | 1.0895 | 1.00 | 7.70 | 3.60 | 8.00 | – | 1.56 | 1.66 | 1.75 | ...300 | | |
| M1300-100A | 1.0897 | 1.00 | 7.80 | 5.80 | 13.0 | – | 1.60 | 1.70 | 1.78 | | | |
| M 660-50D | 1.0361 | 0.50 | 7.85 | 2.80 | 6.60 | – | 1.62 | 1.70 | 1.79 | | | |
| M1050-50D | 1.0363 | 0.50 | 7.85 | 4.30 | 10.50 | – | 1.57 | 1.65 | 1.77 | | | |
| M 800-65D | 1.0364 | 0.65 | 7.85 | 3.30 | 8.00 | – | 1.62 | 1.70 | 1.79 | | | |
| M1200-65D | 1.0366 | 0.65 | 7.85 | 5.00 | 12.00 | – | 1.57 | 1.65 | 1.77 | | | |
| M 097-30N | 1.0861 | 0.30 | – | – | 0.97 | 1.50 | | at field strength H 800 A/m (BB) 1.75 | | ≈ 1 | ≈ 30,000 | |
| M 140-30S | 1.0862 | 0.30 | – | – | 0.92 | 1.40 | | 1.78 | | | | |
| M 111-30P | 1.0881 | 0.30 | – | – | – | 1.11 | | 1.85 | | | | |
| M 340-50E | 1.0841 | 0.50 | 7.65 | 1.42 | 3.40 | – | 1.54 | 1.62 | 1.72 | ≈ 100 | ≈ 5,000 | |
| M 560-50E | 1.0844 | 0.50 | 7.80 | 2.42 | 5.60 | – | 1.58 | 1.66 | 1.76 | ...300 | | |
| M 390-65E | 1.0846 | 0.65 | 7.65 | 1.62 | 3.90 | – | 1.54 | 1.62 | 1.72 | | | |
| M 630-65E | 1.0849 | 0.65 | 7.80 | 2.72 | 6.30 | – | 1.58 | 1.66 | 1.76 | | | |

Materials for transformers and reactors

Core-sheet permeability for alloy classes C21, C22, E11, E31, and E41 for core-sheet section YEI1.

**Minimum core-sheet permeability $\mu_{lam}$ (min)**

| IEC designation | C21-09 Thickness in mm | | C22-13 Thickness in mm | E11-60 Thickness in mm | | | |
|---|---|---|---|---|---|---|---|
| YEI1 | 0.3...0.38 | 0.15...0.2 | 0.3...0.38 | 0.3...0.38 | 0.15...0.2 | 0.1 | 0.05 |
| -10 | 630 | 630 | 1,000 | 14,000 | 18,000 | 20,000 | 20,000 |
| 13 | 800 | 630 | 1,000 | 18,000 | 20,000 | 22,400 | 20,400 |
| 14 | 800 | 630 | 1,000 | 18,000 | 22,400 | 22,400 | 22,400 |
| 16 | 800 | 630 | 1,000 | 20,000 | 22,400 | 25,000 | 22,400 |
| 18 | 800 | 630 | 1,000 | 22,400 | 25,000 | 25,000 | 22,400 |
| 20 | 800 | 630 | 1,120 | 22,400 | 25,000 | 25,000 | 25,000 |
| 22 | 800 | 630 | 1,120 | | | | |
| 25 | 800 | 630 | 1,120 | | | | |

| IEC designation | E11-100 Thickness in mm | | | | E31-04 Thickness in mm | | | | E31-06 Thickness in mm | | | |
|---|---|---|---|---|---|---|---|---|---|---|---|---|
| YEI1 | 0.3...0.38 | 0.15...0.2 | 0.1 | 0.05 | 0.3...0.38 | 0.15...0.2 | 0.1 | 0.05 | 0.3...0.38 | 0.15...0.2 | 0.1 | 0.05 |
| -10 | 18,000 | 25,000 | 31,500 | 31,500 | 2,800 | 2,800 | 3,150 | 3,150 | 3,550 | 4,000 | 4,500 | 5,000 |
| 13 | 20,000 | 28,000 | 35,500 | 35,500 | 2,800 | 3,150 | 3,150 | 3,550 | 4,000 | 4,500 | 5,000 | 5,000 |
| 14 | 22,400 | 28,000 | 35,500 | 35,500 | 2,800 | 3,150 | 3,150 | 3,550 | 4,000 | 4,500 | 5,000 | 5,000 |
| 16 | 25,000 | 31,500 | 35,500 | 35,500 | 2,800 | 3,150 | 3,150 | 3,550 | 4,000 | 4,500 | 5,000 | 5,000 |
| 18 | 25,000 | 31,500 | 40,000 | 35,500 | 2,800 | 3,150 | 3,550 | 3,550 | 4,500 | 4,500 | 5,000 | 5,000 |
| 20 | 28,000 | 35,500 | 40,000 | 40,000 | 3,150 | 3,150 | 3,550 | 3,550 | 4,500 | 5,000 | 5,000 | 5,000 |

| IEC designation | E31-10 Thickness in mm | | | | E41-02 Thickness in mm | | | | E41-03 Thickness in mm | | | |
|---|---|---|---|---|---|---|---|---|---|---|---|---|
| YEI1 | 0.3...0.38 | 0.15...0.2 | 0.1 | 0.05 | 0.3...0.38 | 0.15...0.2 | 0.1 | 0.05 | 0.3...0.38 | 0.15...0.2 | 0.1 | 0.05 |
| -10 | 5,600 | 6,300 | 5,600 | 6,300 | 1,600 | 1,800 | 1,800 | 2,000 | 2,000 | 2,240 | 2,500 | 2,240 |
| 13 | 6,300 | 7,100 | 6,300 | 6,300 | 1,800 | 1,800 | 2,000 | 2,000 | 2,240 | 2,240 | 2,500 | 2,240 |
| 14 | 6,300 | 7,100 | 6,300 | 7,100 | 1,800 | 1,800 | 2,000 | 2,000 | 2,240 | 2,240 | 2,500 | 2,240 |
| 16 | 6,300 | 7,100 | 6,300 | 7,100 | 1,800 | 1,800 | 2,000 | 2,000 | 2,240 | 2,500 | 2,500 | 2,240 |
| 18 | 7,100 | 7,100 | 6,300 | 7,100 | 1,800 | 1,800 | 2,000 | 2,000 | 2,240 | 2,500 | 2,500 | 2,240 |
| 20 | 7,100 | 7,100 | 6,300 | 7,100 | 1,800 | 2,000 | 2,000 | 2,000 | 2,240 | 2,500 | 2,500 | 2,240 |

## Materials for direct-current relays

| Abbreviated name | Material number | Alloy constituents % by mass | Density $\varrho$ g/cm³ | Hardness[1] HV | Remanence[1] T (tesla) | Permeability[1] $\mu_{max}$ | Specific el. resistance[1] $\Omega \cdot mm^2$/m | Coercive field strength A/m max. | 20 | 50 | 100 | 200 | 300 | 500 | 1,000 | 4,000 | Properties, application examples |
|---|---|---|---|---|---|---|---|---|---|---|---|---|---|---|---|---|---|
| | | | | | | | | | — Magnetic polarization T (tesla) min. at field strength $H$ in A/m | | | | | | | | |
| **Unalloyed steels** | | | | | | | | | | | | | | | | | |
| RFe 160 | 1.1011 | — | 7.85 | max. 150 | — | — | 0.15 | 160 | — | — | — | — | 1.15 | 1.30 | – | 1.60 | Low coercive field strength. |
| RFe 80 | 1.1014 | | | | 1.10 | — | 0.15 | 80 | — | — | — | 1.10 | 1.20 | 1.30 | 1.45 | 1.60 | |
| RFe 60 | 1.1015 | | | | 1.20 | — | 0.12 | 60 | — | — | — | 1.15 | 1.25 | 1.35 | 1.45 | 1.60 | |
| RFe 20 | 1.1017 | | | | 1.20 | ≈ 20,000 | 0.10 | 20 | — | — | 1.15 | 1.25 | 1.30 | 1.40 | 1.45 | 1.60 | |
| RFe 12 | 1.1018 | | | | 1.20 | ≈ 20,000 | 0.10 | 12 | — | — | 1.15 | 1.25 | 1.30 | 1.40 | 1.45 | 1.60 | |
| **Silicon steels** | | | | | | | | | | | | | | | | | Direct-current relays and similar purposes. |
| RSi 48 | 1.3840 | 2.5 Si | 7.55 | 130 | 0.50 | – | 0.42 | 48 | — | — | 0.60 | — | 1.10 | 1.20 | – | 1.50 | |
| RSi 24 | 1.3843 | – | – | – | 1.00 | ≈ 20,000 | – | 24 | — | — | 1.20 | — | 1.30 | 1.35 | – | 1.50 | |
| RSi 12 | 1.3845 | 4 Si | 7.75 | 200 | 1.00 | ≈ 10,000 | 0.60 | 12 | — | — | 1.20 | — | 1.30 | 1.35 | – | 1.50 | |
| **Nickel steels and nickel alloys** | | | | | | | | | | | | | | | | | |
| RNi 24 | 1.3911 | ≈ 36 Ni | 8.2 | 130...180 | 0.45 | ≈ 5,000 | 0.75 | 24 | 0.20 | 0.45 | 0.70 | — | 0.90 | 1.0 | – | 1.18 | |
| RNi 12 | 1.3926 | ≈ 50 Ni | 8.3 | 130...180 | 0.60 | ≈ 30,000 | 0.45 | 12 | 0.50 | 0.90 | 1.10 | — | 1.25 | 1.35 | – | 1.45 | |
| RNi 8 | 1.3927 | ≈ 50 Ni | 8.3 | 130...180 | 0.60 | 30,000...100,000 | 0.45 | 8 | 0.50 | 0.90 | 1.10 | — | 1.25 | 1.35 | – | 1.45 | |
| RNi 5 | 2.4596 | 70 ... 80 Ni small quantities Cu, Cr, Mo | 8.7 | 120...170 | 0.30 | ≈ 40,000 | 0.55 | 5 | 0.50 | 0.65 | 0.70 | — | – | – | – | 0.75 | |
| RNi 2 | 2.4595 | | 8.7 | 120...170 | 0.30 | ≈ 100,000 | 0.55 | 2 | 0.50 | 0.65 | 0.70 | — | – | – | – | 0.75 | |

1) Standard values.

## Sintered metals for soft-magnetic components

| Material Abbreviated name | Characteristic alloy elements (except Fe) % by mass | Sinter density $\varrho_s$ g/cm³ | Porosity $P_s$ % | Maximum Coercive field strength $H_{c(max)}$ A/m | Magnetic polarization in Tesla (T) at field strength $H$ in A/m | | | | Maximum permeability $\mu_{(max)}$ | Vickers hardness HV5 | Specific electrical resistance $\varrho$ μΩm |
|---|---|---|---|---|---|---|---|---|---|---|---|
| | | | | | 500 | 5000 | 15,000 | 80,000 | | | |
| S-Fe-175 | – | 6.6 | 16 | 175 | 0.70 | 1.10 | 1.40 | 1.55 | 2,000 | 50 | 0.15 |
| S-Fe-170 | – | 7.0 | 11 | 170 | 0.90 | 1.25 | 1.45 | 1.65 | 2,600 | 60 | 0.13 |
| S-Fe-165 | – | 7.2 | 9 | 165 | 1.10 | 1.40 | 1.55 | 1.75 | 3,000 | 70 | 0.12 |
| S-FeP-150 | ≈ 0.45 P | 7.0 | 10 | 150 | 1.05 | 1.30 | 1.50 | 1.65 | 3,400 | 95 | 0.20 |
| S-FeP-130 | ≈ 0.45 P | 7.2 | 8 | 130 | 1.20 | 1.45 | 1.60 | 1.75 | 4,000 | 105 | 0.19 |
| S-FeSi-80 | ≈ 3 Si | 7.3 | 4 | 80 | 1.35 | 1.55 | 1.70 | 1.85 | 8,000 | 170 | 0.45 |
| S-FeSi-50 | ≈ 3 Si | 7.5 | 2 | 50 | 1.40 | 1.65 | 1.70 | 1.95 | 9,500 | 180 | 0.45 |
| S-FeNi-20 | ≈ 50 Ni | 7.7 | 7 | 20 | 1.10 | 1.25 | 1.30 | 1.30 | 20,000 | 70 | 0.50 |
| S-FeNi-15 | ≈ 50 Ni | 8.0 | 4 | 15 | 1.30 | 1.50 | 1.55 | 1.55 | 30,000 | 85 | 0.45 |
| S-FeCo-100 | ≈ 50 Co | 7.8 | 3 | 100 | 1.50 | 2.00 | 2.10 | 2.15 | 2,000 | 190 | 0.10 |
| S-FeCo-200 | ≈ 50 Co | 7.8 | 3 | 200 | 1.55 | 2.05 | 2.15 | 2.20 | 3,900 | 240 | 0.35 |

## Soft magnetic ferrites

| Ferrite type | Initial permeability[1] $\mu_i$ ± 25% | Specific loss factor tan $\delta/\mu_i$[2] $10^{-6}$ | MHz | Specific power loss[3] mW/g | Amplitude permeability[4] $\mu_a$ | Curie temperature[5][6] $\Theta_C$ °C | Frequency for $0.8 \cdot \mu_i$[6] MHz | Properties, application examples |
|---|---|---|---|---|---|---|---|---|
| **Materials in largely open magnetic circuits** | | | | | | | | |
| C 1/12 | 12 | 350 | 100 | – | – | > 500 | 400 | Initial permeability. Compared to metallic magnetic materials of high specific resistance ($10^0 ... 10^5$ $\Omega \cdot$ m; Metals $10^{-7} ... 10^{-6}$ $\Omega \cdot$ m), therefore, low eddy-current losses. Telecommunications (coils, transformers). |
| D 1/50 | 50 | 120 | 10 | – | – | > 400 | 90 | |
| F 1/250 | 250 | 100 | 3 | – | – | > 250 | 22 | |
| G 2/600 | 600 | 40 | 1 | – | – | > 170 | 6 | |
| H 1/1200 | 1,200 | 20 | 0.3 | – | – | > 150 | 2 | |
| **Materials in largely closed magnetic circuit** | | | | | | | | |
| E 2 | 60... 160 | 80 | 10 | – | – | > 400 | 50 | |
| G 3 | 400...1,200 | 25 | 1 | – | – | > 180 | 6 | |
| J 4 | 1,600...2,500 | 5 | 0.1 | – | – | > 150 | 1.5 | |
| M 1 | 3,000...5,000 | 5 | 0.03 | – | – | > 125 | 0.4 | |
| P 1 | 5,000...7,000 | 3 | 0.01 | – | – | > 125 | 0.3 | |
| **Materials for power applications** | | | | | | | | |
| W 1 | 1,000...3,000 | – | – | 45 | 1,200 | > 180 | – | |
| W 2 | 1,000...3,000 | – | – | 25 | 1,500 | > 180 | – | |

[1] Nominal values.
[2] tan $\delta/\mu_i$ denotes the frequency-dependent material losses at a low flux density ($B < 0.1$ mT).
[3] Losses at high flux density. Measured preferably at: $f = 25$ kHz, $B = 200$ mT, $\Theta = 100$ °C.
[4] Permeability when subjected to a strong sinusoidal magnetic field. Measured at: $f = 25$ kHz, $B = 320$ mT, $\Theta = 100$ °C.
[5] Curie temperature $\Theta_C$ in this table is the temperature at which initial permeability $\mu_i$ drops to below 10% of its value at 25 °C.
[6] Standard values.

## Permanent-magnet materials

| Material Abbreviated name | Material number DIN | IEC | Chemical composition [1] % by weight Al | Co | Cu | Nb | Ni | Ti | Fe | Density ρ [1] g/cm³ | (BH)max [2] kJ/m³ | Remanence of flux density Br [2] mT | Coercive field strength of flux density HcB kA/m | Coercive field strength of polarization HcJ kA/m | Rel. permanent permeability [1] mp | Curie temp. [1] Tc K | Temp. coeff. of polar. [1][3] TK(Js) %K | Temp. coeff. of coerciv. [1][3] TK(Hc) %K | Manufacture, processing, applications |
|---|---|---|---|---|---|---|---|---|---|---|---|---|---|---|---|---|---|---|---|
| **Metallic magnets** | | | | | | | | | | | | | | | | | | | |
| *Isotropic* | | | | | | | | | | | | | | | | | | | |
| AlNiCo 9/5 | 1.3728 | R 1-0-3 | 11...13 | 0...5 | 2...4 | – | 21...28 | 0...1 | Remainder | 6.8 | 9.0 | 550 | 44 | 47 | 4.0...5.0 | 1,030 | -0.02 | +0.03 | |
| AlNiCo 18/9 | 1.3756 | – | 6...8 | 24...34 | 3...6 | – | 13...19 | 5...9 | mainder | 7.2 | 18.0 | 600 | 80 | 86 | 3.0...4.0 | | | | |
| AlNiCo 7/8p | 1.3715 | R 1-2-3 | 6...8 | 24...34 | 3...6 | – | 13...19 | 5...9 | | 5.5 | 7.0 | 340 | 72 | 84 | 2.0...3.0 | 1,180 | | -0.07 | |
| *Anisotropic* | | | | | | | | | | | | | | | | | | | Manufacture: casting or sintering. For magnets with binders: pressing or injection molding. Processing: grinding. Application: max. 400...500°C. |
| AlNiCo 35/5 | 1.3761 | – | 8...9 | 23...26 | 3...4 | 0...1 | 13...16 | – | Remainder | 7.2 | 35.0 | 1,120 | 47 | 48 | 3.0...4.5 | 1,030 | -0.02 | +0.03 | |
| AlNiCo 44/5 | 1.3757 | R 1-1-2 | 8...9 | 23...26 | 3...4 | 0...1 | 13...16 | – | mainder | 7.2 | 44.0 | 1,250 | 52 | 53 | 2.5...3.0 | | | | |
| AlNiCo 52/6 | 1.3759 | – | 8...9 | 23...26 | 3...4 | 0...1 | 13...15 | 4...6 | | 7.2 | 52.0 | 1,250 | 55 | 56 | 1.5...3.0 | | -0.02 | | |
| AlNiCo 60/11 | 1.3763 | R 1-1-6 | 6...8 | 35...39 | 2...4 | 0...1 | 13...15 | 4...6 | | 7.2 | 60.0 | 900 | 110 | 112 | 1.5...2.5 | | | | |
| AlNiCo 30/14 | 1.3765 | – | 6...8 | 38...42 | 2...4 | 0...1 | 13...15 | 7...9 | | 7.2 | 30.0 | 680 | 136 | 144 | 1.5...2.5 | 1,180 | | -0.07 | |
| | | | Pt | Co | | | | | | | | | | | | | | | |
| PtCo 60/40 | 2.5210 | R2-0-1 | 77...78 | 20...23 | | | | | | 15.5 | 60 | 600 | 350 | 400 | 1.1 | 800 | -0.01 ... -0.02 | -0.35 | |
| | | | V | Co | Cr | Fe | | | | | | | | | | | | | |
| FeCoVCr 11/2 | 2.4570 | R 3-1-3 | 8...15 | 51...54 | 0...4 | Remainder | | | | – | 11.0 | 800 | 24 | 24 | 2.0...8.0 | 1,000 | -0.01 | ≈0 | |
| FeCoVCr 4/1 | 2.4571 | – | 3...15 | 51...54 | 0...6 | der | | | | – | 4.0 | 1,000 | 5 | 5 | 9.0...25.0 | | | | |
| *RECo magnets of type RECo5* | | | | | | | | | | | | | | | | | | | |
| RECo 80/80 | – | R 5-1-1 | Typically MMCo5 (MM = ceramic-metal material) | | | | | | | 8.1 | 80 | 650 | 500 | 800 | 1.05 | 1,000 | -0.05 | -0.3 | |
| RECo 120/96 | – | R 5-1-2 | Typically SmCo5 | | | | | | | 8.1 | 120 | 770 | 590 | 960 | 1.05 | 1,000 | -0.05 | -0.3 | |
| RECo 160/80 | – | R 5-1-3 | Typically (SmPr) Co5 | | | | | | | 8.1 | 160 | 900 | 640 | 800 | 1.05 | 1,000 | -0.05 | -0.3 | |
| *RECo magnets of type RE-Co2,17* | | | | | | | | | | | | | | | | | | | |
| RECo 165/50 | – | R 5-1-11 | | | | | | | | 8.2 | 165 | 950 | 440 | 500 | 1.1 | 1,100 | 0.03 | -0.02 | |
| RECo 180/90 | – | R 5-1-13 | | | | | | | | 8.2 | 180 | 1,000 | 680 | 900 | 1.1 | 1,100 | 0.03 | -0.02 | |
| RECo 190/70 | – | R 5-1-14 | | | | | | | | 8.2 | 190 | 1,050 | 560 | 700 | 1.1 | 1,100 | 0.03 | -0.02 | |
| RECo 48/60p | – | R 5-3-1 | | | | | | | | 5.2 | 48 | 500 | 360 | 600 | 1.05 | 1,000 | -0.05 | -0.3 | |

1) Standard values. 2) Minimum values. 3) In the range of 273...373 K.

| Material | | | Chemical composition [1] % by weight | | | | | | | Density $\varrho$ [1] | $(BH)_{max}$ [2] | Rema-nence $B_r$ [2] | Coercive field strength [2] of flux density $H_{CB}$ | Coercive field strength [2] of polarization $H_{CJ}$ | Rel. per-manent permea-bility [1] $m_p$ | Curie temp. [1] $T_C$ | Temp. coeff. of polar. $TK(J_S)$ [1][3] | Temp. coeff. of coerciv. $TK(H_C)$ [1][3] | Manufacture, processing, applications |
|---|---|---|---|---|---|---|---|---|---|---|---|---|---|---|---|---|---|---|---|
| Abbreviated name | Material number DIN | IEC | Al | Co | Cu | Nb | Ni | Ti | Fe | g/cm³ | kJ/m³ | mT | kA/m | kA/m | $m_p$ | K | % K | % K | |
| CrFeCo 12/4 | – | R 6-0-1 | (no data) | | | | | | | 7.6 | 12 | 800 | 40 | 42 | 5.5..6.5 | 1,125 | -0.03 | -0.04 | |
| CrFeCo 28/5 | – | R 6-1-1 | (no data) | | | | | | | 7.6 | 28 | 1,000 | 45 | 46 | 3..4 | 1,125 | -0.03 | -0.04 | |
| REFe 165/170 | – | R 7-1-1 | (no data) | | | | | | | 7.4 | 165 | 940 | 700 | 1,700 | 1.07 | 583 | -0.1 | -0.8 | |
| REFe 220/140 | – | R 7-1-6 | | | | | | | | 7.4 | 220 | 1,090 | 800 | 1,400 | 1.05 | 583 | -0.1 | -0.8 | |
| REFe 240/110 | – | R 7-1-7 | | | | | | | | 7.4 | 240 | 1,140 | 850 | 1,100 | 1.05 | 583 | -0.1 | -0.8 | |
| REFe 260/80 | – | R 7-1-8 | | | | | | | | 7.4 | 260 | 1,180 | 750 | 800 | 1.05 | 583 | -0.1 | -0.8 | |

| Material | | | Density [1] $\varrho$ | $(BH)_{max}$ [2] | Rema-nence [2] $B_r$ | Coercive field strength [2] of flux density $H_{CB}$ | Coercive field strength [2] of polarization $H_{CJ}$ | Rel. permanent permeability [1] $m_p$ | Curie temp. [1] $T_C$ | Temp. coeff. of polarization [1] $TK(J_S)$ | Temp. coeff. of coerciv. [1] $TK(H_C)$ | Manufacture, processing |
|---|---|---|---|---|---|---|---|---|---|---|---|---|
| Abbr. name | Material number DIN | IEC | g/cm³ | kJ/m³ | mT | kA/m | kA/m | $m_p$ | K | % K | % K | |
| **Ceramic magnets** | | | | | | | | | | | | |
| **Isotropic** | | | | | | | | | | | | |
| Hard ferrite 7/21 | 1.3641 | S 1-0-1 | 4.9 | 6.5 | 190 | 125 | 210 | 1.2 | 723 | -0.2 | 0.2...0.5 | Manufacture: sintering. Plastic-bound magnets produced by pressing, injection molding, rolling, extruding. Processing: grinding. |
| Hard ferrite 3/18p | 1.3614 | S 1-2-2 | 3.9 | 3.2 | 135 | 85 | 175 | 1.1 | | | | |
| **Anisotropic** | | | | | | | | | | | | |
| Hard ferrite 20/19 | 1.3643 | S 1-1-1 | 4.8 | 20.0 | 320 | 170 | 190 | 1.1 | 723 | -0.2 | 0.2...0.5 | |
| Hard ferrite 20/28 | 1.3645 | S 1-1-2 | 4.6 | 20.0 | 320 | 220 | 280 | 1.1 | | | | |
| Hard ferrite 24/23 | 1.3647 | S 1-1-3 | 4.8 | 24.0 | 350 | 215 | 230 | 1.1 | | | | |
| Hard ferrite 25/22 | 1.3651 | S 1-1-5 | 4.8 | 25.0 | 370 | 205 | 220 | 1.1 | | | | |
| Hard ferrite 26/26 | – | S 1-1-8 | 4.7 | 26.0 | 370 | 230 | 260 | 1.1 | | | | |
| Hard ferrite 32/17 | – | S 1-1-10 | 4.9 | 32.0 | 410 | 160 | 165 | 1.1 | | | | |
| Hard ferrite 24/35 | – | S 1-1-14 | 4.8 | 24.0 | 360 | 260 | 350 | 1.1 | | | | |
| Hard ferrite 9/19p | 1.3616 | S 1-3-1 | 3.4 | 9.0 | 220 | 145 | 190 | 1.1 | | | | |
| Hard ferrite 10/22p | – | S 1-3-2 | 3.5 | 10.0 | 230 | 165 | 225 | 1.1 | | | | |

[1] Standard values. [2] Minimum values. [3] In the range of 273...373 K.

## Permanent-magnet materials (continued)

Bosch grades [BTMT] (not standardized)

| Material<br>Abbreviated name | Density [1]<br>$\varrho$<br>g/cm³ | $(BH)_{max}$ [2]<br><br>kJ/m³ | Remanence [2]<br>$B_r$<br>mT | Coercive field strength [2]<br>of flux density<br>$H_{CB}$<br>kA/m | of polarization<br>$H_{CJ}$<br>kA/m |
|---|---|---|---|---|---|
| RBX HC 370 | | 25 | 360 | 270 | 390 |
| RBX HC 380 | | 28 | 380 | 280 | 370 |
| RBX 380K | | 28 | 380 | 280 | 300 |
| RBX 400 | | 30 | 400 | 255 | 260 |
| RBX 400 K | 4.7...4.9 | 31 | 400 | 290 | 300 |
| RBX HC 400 | | 29 | 380 | 285 | 355 |
| RBX 420 | | 34 | 420 | 255 | 270 |
| RBX 410 K | | 33 | 410 | 305 | 330 |
| RBX HC 410 | | 30 | 395 | 290 | 340 |
| RBX 420 S | | 35 | 425 | 260 | 270 |
| RBX HC 400 N | | 28 | 380 | 280 | 390 |

[1]) Standard values. [2]) Minimum values.

## Comparison of permanent and soft magnets

Range of magnetic characteristics of some crystalline materials in widespread use.

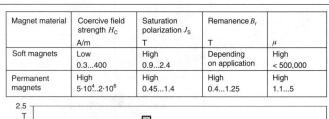

| Magnet material | Coercive field strength $H_C$<br>A/m | Saturation polarization $J_S$<br>T | Remanence $B_r$<br>T | <br>$\mu$ |
|---|---|---|---|---|
| Soft magnets | Low<br>0.3...400 | High<br>0.9...2.4 | Depending on application | High<br>< 500,000 |
| Permanent magnets | High<br>$5 \cdot 10^4 .. 2 \cdot 10^6$ | High<br>0.45...1.4 | High<br>0.4...1.25 | High<br>1.1...5 |

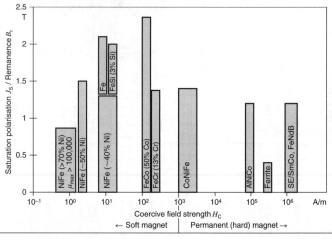

# Solders and filler materials

| Type of alloy | Material code (as per DIN 1707-100 | Principal alloy constituents in % by mass | Melting range of alloy °C | Properties, application examples |
|---|---|---|---|---|
| **Soft solders** (selection from DIN 1707-100 and DIN EN 29 453) | | | | |
| Tin-base, lead-base soft solders | S-Sn 63 Pb 37<br>S-Sn 60 Pb 40 | 62.5-63.5 Sn; rest Pb<br>59.5-60.5 Sn; rest Pb | 183<br>183...190 | Reflow, wave, and iron soldering of printed circuits.<br>Tin plating of copper and copper alloys in the electrical industry. |
| Tin-base, lead-base soft solders with Ag or Cu added | S-Sn 62 Pb 36 Ag 2 | 61.5-62.5 Sn; 1.8-2.2 Ag; rest Pb | 178...190 | Reflow, wave, and iron soldering of printed circuits. |
| | S-Sn 60 Pb 38 Cu 2 | 59.5-60.5 Sn; 1.5-2.0 Cu; rest Pb | 183...190 | Iron soldering of copper and copper alloys in the electrical industry. |
| | S-Sn 60 Pb 40 CuP | 59.5-60.5 Sn; 0.1-0.2 Cu; 0.001-0.004 P; rest Pb | 183...190 | Dip soldering of copper and copper alloys in the electrical industry. |
| Lead-base, tin-base soft solders | S-Pb 92 Sn 8<br>S-Pb 60 Sn 40 | 7.5-8.5 Sn; rest Pb<br>39.5-40.5 Sn; rest Pb | 280...305<br>183...235 | Tin plating; soft soldering of sheet metal parts.<br>Soft soldering of electric motors; radiator construction. |
| | S-Pb 78 Sn 20 Sb 2 | 19.5-20.5 Sn; 0.5-3.0 Sb; rest Pb | 185...270 | Soft soldering in motor-vehicle body construction.<br>Soft soldering of copper in radiator construction. |
| Lead-free soft solders | S-Sn 96 Ag 4 | 3.5-4.0 Ag; rest Sn | 221 | Reflow, wave, and iron soldering of printed circuits. |
| | S-Sn 96 Ag 4 Cu 1 [1] | 3.5-4.0 Ag; 0.5-1.0 Cu: rest Sn | 217...220 | |
| | S-Sn 99 Cu 1 | 0.45-0.90 Cu; rest Sn | 230...240 | Wave soldering of printed circuits. |
| | S-Bi 57 Sn 43 | 42.5-43.5 Sn; rest bi | 138 | Reflow and wave soldering of printed circuits. |
| Special soft solders | S-Sn 95 Sb 5 | 4.5-5.5 Sb; rest Sn | 230...240 | Soft soldering of copper in refrigeration engineering and in the installation of water pipes. |
| | S-Sn 50 In 50 | 49.5-50.5 Sn; rest In | 117...125 | Soft soldering of glass/metal. |
| | S-Bi 57 In 26 Sn 17 [1] | 57 bi; 26 In; rest Sn | 79 | Soft soldering of heat-sensitive components; fuses. |
| | S-Sn 90 Zn 10<br>S-Zn 95 Al 5 | 8.0-15.0 Zn; rest Sn<br>4.0-6.0 Al; rest Zn | 200...250<br>380...390 | Ultrasonic soft soldering of aluminum and copper without flux. |

[1] Not listed in DIN 1707-100 or DIN EN 29 453.

## Filler metals for brazing and high-temperature brazing (selection from DIN 8513 and ISO 3677)

| Type of alloy | Abbreviation | | Principal alloy constituents Mean values in % by mass | Melting range of alloy °C | Properties, application examples |
|---|---|---|---|---|---|
| | Formerly DIN 8513-1 through -5 | Now DIN EN ISO 3677 | | | |
| Aluminum-base filler metals | L-AlSi 12<br>L-AlSi 10<br>L-AlSi 7.5 | B-Al 88 Si-575/585<br>B-Al 90 Si-575/590<br>B-Al 92 Si-575/615 | 12 Si; rest Al<br>10 Si; rest Al<br>7.5 Si; rest Al | 575...590<br>575...595<br>575...615 | Brazing of Al and Al alloys with sufficiently high melting point. |
| Silver-bearing filler metals Ag < 20% | BCu 75AgP 643<br>L-Ag 15 P | B-Cu 75 AgP-645<br>B-Cu 80 AgP-645/800 | 18 Ag; 7.25 P; rest Cu<br>15 Ag; 5 P; rest Cu | 643<br>650...800 | Brazing of Cu/Cu without flux. |
| | L-Ag 5 | B-Cu 55 ZnAg(Si)-820/870 | 5 Ag; 55 Cu; 0.2 Si; rest Zn | 820...870 | Brazing of steel, Cu, Ni, and Ni alloys with flux. |
| Silver-bearing filler metals Ag ≥ 20% | L-Ag55Sn<br>L-Ag44 | B-Ag 55 ZnCuSn-630/660<br>B-Ag 44 CuSn-675/735 | 55 Ag; 22 Cu; 5 Sn; rest Zn<br>44 Ag; 30 Cu; rest Zn | 620...660<br>675...735 | Brazing of steel, Cu, and Cu alloys, Ni and Ni alloys with flux. |
| | L-Ag49 | B-Ag 49 ZnCuMnNi-680/705 | 49 Ag; 16 Cu; 7.5 Mn; 4.5 Ni; rest Zn | 625...705 | Brazing of hard metal, steel, W, Mo, Ta with flux. |
| | BAg 60 CuIn 605-710<br>BAg 60 CuSn 600-700<br>L-Ag 72<br>BCu 58 AgNi 780-900 | B-Ag 60 CuIn-605/710<br>B-Ag 60 CuSn-600/730<br>B-Ag 72 Cu-780<br>B-Cu 58 AgNi-780/900 | 60 Ag; 13 In; rest Cu<br>60 Ag; 10 Sn; rest Cu<br>72 Ag; rest Cu<br>40 Ag; 2 Ni; rest Cu | 605...710<br>600...720<br>780<br>780...900 | Brazing of Cu, Ni, and steel in a vacuum or under shielding gas. |
| | BAg 68 CuPd 807-810<br>BAg 54 PdCu 901-950<br>BAg 95 Pd 970-1010<br>BAg 64 PdMn 1180-1200 | B-Ag 68 CuPd-807/810<br>B-Ag 54 PdCu-901/950<br>B-Ag 95 Pd-970/1010<br>B-Ag 64 PdMn-1180/1200 | 68 Ag; 5 Pd; rest Cu<br>54 Ag; 21 Pd; rest Cu<br>95 Ag; rest Pd;<br>64 Ag; 3 Mn; rest Pd | 807...810<br>901...950<br>970...1,010<br>1,180...1,200 | Brazing of steel, Ni, and Co alloys, Mo, W, Ti in a vacuum or under shielding gas. |
| | L-Ag 56 InNi<br>L-Ag 85 | B-Ag 56 CuInNi-600/710<br>B-Ag 85 Mn-960/970 | 56 Ag; 14 In; 4 Ni; rest Cu<br>85 Ag; rest Mn | 620...730<br>960...970 | Brazing of Cr and Cr/Ni steels in a vacuum or under shielding gas. |
| Copper-base filler metals | BCu 86 SnP 650-700 | B-Cu 86 SnP-650/700 | 6.75 P; 7 Sn; rest Cu | 650...700 | Brazing of Cu and Cu alloys with flux. Not for Fe and Ni alloys or media containing S. |

1) Depending on the process.

| Type of alloy | Abbreviation — Formerly DIN 8513-1 through -5 | Abbreviation — Now DIN EN ISO 3677 | Principal alloy constituents Mean values in % by mass | Melting range of alloy °C | Properties, application examples |
|---|---|---|---|---|---|
| Copper-base filler metals (continued) | L-CuP 8 | B-Cu 92 P-710/770 | 8 P; rest Cu | 710...740 | Brazing of Cu/Cu without flux. Not for Fe and Ni alloys or media containing S. |
| | L-CuZn 40 | B-Cu 60 Zn(Sn)(Si)-875/895 | 60 Cu; 0.2 Si; rest Zn | 890...900 | Brazing of steel, Cu, Ni, and Ni alloys with flux. |
| | L-CuSn 6<br>L-SFCu | B-Cu 94 Sn(P)-910/1040<br>B-Cu 100 (P)-1085 | 6 Sn max; 0.4 P; rest Cu<br>100 Cu | 910...1,083<br>1,040 | Brazing of steel in a vacuum or under shielding gas. |
| | BCu 86 MnNi 970-990<br>BCu 87 MnCo 980-1030<br>BCu 96.9 NiSi 1090-1100 | B-Cu 86 MnNi-970/990<br>B-Cu 87 MnCo-980/1030<br>B-Cu 96.9 NiSi-1090-1100 | 2 Ni; 12 Mn; rest Cu<br>3 Co; 10 Mn; rest Cu<br>0.6 Si; 2.5 Ni; rest Cu | 970...990<br>980...1,030<br>1,090...1,100 | Brazing of hard metal, steel, W, Mo, Ta in a vacuum with shielding-gas partial pressure. |
| Nickel-base filler metals | L-Ni6<br>L-Ni1 | B-Ni 89 P-875<br>B-Ni 73 CrFeSiB(C)-980/1060 | 11 P; rest Ni<br>3 B; 14 Cr; 4.5 Fe; 4.5 Si; rest Ni | 880<br>980...1,040 | Brazing of Ni, Co, and their alloys, unalloyed, low-, and high-alloyed steels in a vacuum or under hydrogen shielding gas. |
| | L-Ni5 | | 19 Cr; 10 Si; rest Ni | 1,080...1,135 | |
| Gold-base filler metals | BAu 80 Cu 910 | B-Au 80 Cu(Fe)-905/910 | 20 Cu; rest Au | 910 | Brazing of Cu, Ni, and steel in a vacuum or under shielding gas. |
| | BAu 82 Ni 950 | B-Au 82 Ni-950 | 18 Ni; rest Au | 950 | Brazing of W, Mo, Co, Ni, and steels in a vacuum or under shielding gas. |
| Active filler metals containing titanium | —<br>—<br>— | | 72.5 Ag; 19.5 Cu; 5 In; rest Ti<br>70.5 Ag; 26.5 Cu; rest Ti<br>96 Ag; rest Ti | 730...760<br>780...805<br>970 | Direct brazing of non-metallized ceramics with each other or combined with steel in a vacuum or under argon shielding gas. |

¹) Depending on the process.

## Electrical properties

### Electrical resistivity at 20 °C
(Resistance of a wire 1 m long with a cross-section of 1 mm$^2$)

Resistivity is highly dependent on the purity of the metal concerned. The mean temperature coefficient $\alpha$ refers to temperatures between 0 and 100 °C whenever possible. Resistivity at a temperature $t$ °C is $\varrho_t = \varrho_{20}\,[1 + \alpha\,(t - 20\,°C)]$. For how to calculate the temperature of a winding based on the increase in resistance, see P. 153.

$$1\ \Omega\ mm^2/m = 1\ \mu\Omega\ m,\ 1\ S\ m/mm^2 = 1\ MS/m\ (S = Siemens)$$

| Material | Electrical resistivity $\varrho$ $\mu\Omega m$ | Electrical conductivity $\gamma = 1/\varrho$ MS/m | Mean temperature coefficient $\alpha$ x 10$^{-3}$ 1/ °C | Maximum operating temperature approx. °C |
|---|---|---|---|---|
| Aluminum, Al 99.5 (soft) | 0.0265 | 35 | 3.8 | – |
| Aluminum alloy E-AlMgSi | < 0.0328 | > 30.5 | 3.8 | – |
| Bismuth | 1.07 | 0.8 | 4.54 | – |
| Brass CuZn 39 Pb 3 | 0.0667 | 15 | 2.33 | – |
| CuZn 20 | 0.0525 | 19 | 1.60 | – |
| Bronze CuBe 0.5, age-hardened | 0.04 ... 0.05 | 20 ... 25 | | 300 |
| Cadmium | 0.068 | 13 | – | – |
| Carbon brushes, unfilled | 10 ... 200 | 0.1 ... 0.05 | – | – |
| metal-filled | 0.05 ... 30 | 20 ... 0.03 | – | – |
| Copper, soft | 0.01754 | 57 | 3.9 | – |
| hard (cold-stretched) | 0.01786 | 56 | 3.9 | – |
| Electrical sheet steel I | 0.21 | 4.76 | – | – |
| Electrical sheet steel IV | 0.56 | 1.79 | – | – |
| Gold (fine gold) | 0.023 | 45 | 4 | – |
| Gold-chromium alloy Cr2.05 | 0.33 | 3.03 | ± 0.001 | – |
| Gray cast iron | 0.6...1.6 | 0.62...1.67 | 1.9 | – |
| Heating-element alloy [1]) CrAl 20 5 | 1.37 | 0.73 | 0.05 | 1,200 |
| NiCr 30 20 | 1.04 | 0.96 | 0.35 | 1,100 |
| NiCr 60 15 | 1.13 | 0.88 | 0.15 | 1,150 |
| NiCr 80 20 | 1.12 | 0.89 | 0.05 | 1,200 |
| Lead Pb 99.94 | 0.206 | 4.8 | 4 | – |
| Mercury | 0.941 | 1.0386 | 0.9 | – |
| Molybdenum | 0.052 | 18.5 | 4.7 | 1,600[3]) |
| Nickel Ni 99.6 | 0.095 | 10.5 | 5.5 | – |
| Nickel silver CuNi 12 Zn 24 | 0.232 | 4.3 | – | – |
| Platinum | 0.106 | 10.2 | 3.923 | – |
| Resistance alloy [2]) CuMn 12 Ni | 0.43 | 2.33 | ± 0.01 | 140 |
| CuNi 30 Mn | 0.40 | 2.50 | 0.14 | 500 |
| CuNi 44 | 0.49 | 2.04 | ± 0.04 | 600 |
| Silver (fine silver) | 0.016 | 66.5 | 4.056 | – |
| Steel C 15 | 0.14 ... 0.16 | 7.15 | – | – |
| Tantalum | 0.124 | 8.06 | 3.82 | – |
| Tin | 0.114 | 8.82 | 4.4 | – |
| Tungsten | 0.056 | 18.2 | 4.82 | – |
| Zinc | 0.06 | 16.67 | 4.17 | – |

[1]) DIN 17 470. [2]) DIN 17 471. [3]) Under shielding gas or in a vacuum.

# Insulating materials

## Electrical properties

The properties of insulating materials are highly dependent on the purity, homogeneity, processing and aging of the material, as well as moisture content and temperature. The following values are given as a guideline for non-aged test specimens at room temperature with average moisture content. 1 min. test voltage at 50 Hz; specimen thickness: 3 mm.
Loss factor $\tan \delta$ = active power/reactive power; in the U.S.: loss factor = $\varepsilon_r \cdot \tan \delta$.

| Insulating material | Relative permittivity at 800 Hz (air = 1) $\varepsilon_r$ | Loss factor $\tan \delta$ at 800 Hz $\times 10^{-3}$ | at $10^6$ Hz $\times 10^{-3}$ | Volume resistivity $10^n$ $\Omega m$ values of $n$ | Dielectric strength $kV_{eff}/mm$ | Tracking resistance acc. to DIN 53480 degree |
|---|---|---|---|---|---|---|
| Cellulose acetates | 4.7...5.8 | 17...24 | 48...66 | 11...13 | 32 | – |
| Epoxy casting resins and molding compounds | 3.2...5 | 2...30 | 2...60 | 10...15 | 6...15 | KA 3 b, KA 3 c |
| Hard porcelain | 5...6.5 | ≈15 | 6...12 | >9 | 30...40 | KA 3 c |
| Mica | 5...8 | 0.1...1 | 0.2 | 13...15 | 60 | KA 3 c |
| Paraffin waxes | 1.9...2.3 | <0.3 | <0.3 | 13...16 | 10...30 | – |
| Phenolic resin molding compounds with inorganic filler | 5...30 | 30...400 | 50...200 | 6...11 | 5...30 | KA 1 |
| Phenolic resin molding compounds with organic filler | 4...9 | 50...500 | 50...200 | 6...10 | 5...20 | KA 1 |
| Polyamides | 8...14 | 20...200 | 20...200 | 6...12 | 10...50 | KA 3 b, KA 3 c |
| Polycarbonates | 3 | 1.0 | 10 | 14...16 | 25 | KA 1 |
| Polyester casting resins and molding compounds | 3...7 | 3...100 | 6...60 | 8...14 | 6...25 | KA 3 c |
| Polyethylene | 2.3 | 0.2...0.6 | 0.2...0.6 | >15 | ≈80 | KA 3 c |
| Polymethyl methacrylate | 3.1...3.4 | 40 | 20 | >13 | 30 | KA 3 b |
| Polypropylene | 2.3 | <0.5 | <0.5 | >15 | – | KA 3 c |
| Polystyrene | 2.5 | 0.1 | 0.1 | 14 | 40 | KA 2, KA 1 |
| Polytetrafluoroethylene | 2 | 0.1...0.5 | 0.1...0.5 | 13...15 | 50 | KA 3 c |
| Polyvinyl chloride | 3.3...6.5 | 15...150 | 10...100 | 10...14 | 15...50 | KA 3 b |
| Quartz glass | 3.5...4.2 | 0.5 | 0.2 | 14...16 | 25...40 | KA 3 c |
| Silicone | 5...8 | ≈4 | ≈4 | 10...14 | 20...60 | KA 3 c |
| Soft rubber | 2...14 | 0.2...100 | – | 2...14 | 15...30 | KA 1...KA 3 |
| Steatite | 5.5...6.5 | 1...3 | 0.3...2 | 10...12 | 20...45 | KA 3 c |
| Titanium ceramic | 12...10,000 | – | 0.05...100 | – | 2...30 | – |
| Transformer oil, dry | 2...2.7 | ≈1 | ≈10 | 11...12 | 5...30 | – |

# Properties of non-metallic materials

## Ceramic materials

| Materials | Composition | $\varrho$[1] g/cm³ | $\sigma_{bB}$[2] MN/m² | $\sigma_{dB}$[3] MN/m² | $E$[4] GN/m² | $\alpha$[5] $10^{-6}$/K | $\lambda$[6] W/mK | $c$[7] kJ/kg·K | $\varrho_D$[8] Ω·cm | $\varepsilon_r$[9] | $\tan\varrho$[10] $10^{-4}$ |
|---|---|---|---|---|---|---|---|---|---|---|---|
| Aluminum nitride | AlN > 97% | 3.3 | 250...350 | 1,100 | 320...350 | 5.1 | 100...220 | 0.8 | > $10^{14}$ | 8.5...9.0 | 3...10 |
| Aluminum oxide | $Al_2O_3$ > 99% | 3.9...4.0 | 300...500 | 3,000...4,000 | 380...400 | 7.2...8.6 | 20...40 | 0.8...0.9 | > $10^{11}$ | 8...10 | 2 |
| Aluminum titanate | $Al_2O_3 \cdot TiO_2$ | 3.0...3.2 | 20...40 | 450...550 | 10...20 | 0.5...1.5 | < 2 | 0.7 | > $10^{11}$ | – | – |
| Beryllium oxide | BeO > 99% | 2.9...3.0 | 250...320 | 1,500 | 300...340 | 8.5...9.0 | 240...280 | 1.0 | > $10^{14}$ | 6.5 | 3...5 |
| Boron carbide | $B_4C$ | 2.5 | 300...500 | 2,800 | 450 | 5.0 | 30...60 | – | $10^{-1}...10^2$ | – | – |
| Cordierite e.g. KER410, 520 | $2MgO \cdot 2Al_2O_3 \cdot 5SiO_2$ | 1.6...2.1 | 40...200 | 300 | 70...100 | 2.0...5.0 | 1.3...2.3 | 0.8 | > $10^{11}$ | 5.0 | 70 |
| Graphite | C > 99.7% | 1.5...1.8 | 5...30 | 20...50 | 5...15 | 1.6...4.0 | 100...180 | – | $10^{-3}$ | – | – |
| Porcelain e.g. KER 110 – 2 (non-glazed) | $Al_2O_3$ 30...35% rest $SiO_2$ + glass phase | 2.2...2.4 | 45...60 | 500...550 | 50 | 4.0...6.5 | 1.2...2.6 | 0.8 | $10^{11}$ | 6 | 120 |
| Silicon carbide hot-pressed HPSiC | SiC > 99% | 3.1...3.2 | 450...650 | > 1,500 | 420 | 4.0...4.5 | 100...120 | 0.8 | $10^3$ | – | – |
| Silicon carbide pressureless-sintered SSiC | SiC > 98% | 3.1...3.2 | 400...450 | > 1,200 | 400 | 4.0...4.5 | 90...120 | 0.8 | $10^3$ | – | – |
| Silicon carbide reaction-sintered SiSiC | SiC > 90% + Si | 3.0...3.1 | 300...400 | > 2,200 | 380 | 4.2...4.3 | 100...140 | 0.8 | 10...100 | – | – |
| Silicon nitride gas-pressure gesintered GPSN | $Si_3N_4$ > 90% | 3.2 | 800...1,400 | > 2,500 | 300 | 3.2...3.5 | 30...40 | 0.7 | $10^{12}$ | – | – |

| Materials | Composition | $\varrho^{1)}$ g/cm³ | $\sigma_{bB}{}^{2)}$ MN/m² | $\sigma_{dB}{}^{3)}$ MN/m² | $E^{4)}$ GN/m² | $\alpha^{5)}$ $10^{-6}$/K | $\lambda^{6)}$ W/mK | $c^{7)}$ kJ/kg · K | $\varrho_D{}^{8)}$ Ω · cm | $\varepsilon_r{}^{9)}$ | $\tan \delta^{10)}$ $10^{-4}$ |
|---|---|---|---|---|---|---|---|---|---|---|---|
| Silicon nitride hot-pressed HPSN | $Si_3N_4$ > 95% | 3.2 | 600...900 | > 3,000 | 310 | 3.2...3.5 | 30...40 | 0.7 | $10^{12}$ | – | – |
| Silicon nitride reaction-sintered RBSN | $Si_3N_4$ > 99% | 2.4...2.6 | 200...300 | < 2,000 | 140...160 | 2.9...3.0 | 15...20 | 0.7 | $10^{14}$ | – | – |
| Steatite e.g. KER 220, 221 | $SiO_2$ 55...65% MgO 25...35% $Al_2O_3$ 2...6% Alk. oxide < 1.5% | 2.6...2.9 | 120...140 | 850...1,000 | 80...100 | 7.0...9.0 | 2.3...2.8 | 0.7...0.9 | > $10^{11}$ | 6 | 10...20 |
| Titanium carbide | TiC | 4.9 | – | – | 320 | 7.4 | 30 | – | $7 \cdot 10^{-5}$ | – | – |
| Titanium nitride | TiN | 5.4 | – | – | 260 | 9.4 | 40 | – | $3 \cdot 10^{-5}$ | – | – |
| Titanium oxide | $TiO_2$ | 3.5...3.9 | 90...120 | 300 | – | 6.0...8.0 | 3...4 | 0.7...0.9 | – | 40...100 | 8 |
| Zirconium dioxide, partially stabilized, PSZ | $ZrO_2$ > 90% rest $Y_2O_3$ | 5.7...6.0 | 500...1,000 | 1,800...2,100 | 200 | 9.0...11.0 | 2...3 | 0.4 | $10^8$ | – | – |
| Standards | | DIN EN 623 Part 2 | DIN EN 843 Part 1 | pr EN 993 Part 5 | DIN EN 843 Part 2 | DIN EN 821 Part 1 | DIN EN 821 Part 2 | DIN EN 821 Part 3 | DIN VDE 0335 Parts 2 and 3 | | |

The characteristic values for each material can vary widely, depending on the raw material, composition, and manufacturing process.
The material data relate to the information provided by various manufacturers.
The designation "KER" corresponds to DIN EN 60 672-1.

1) Density.
2) Bending strength.
3) Cold compressive strength.
4) Modulus of elasticity.
5) Coefficient of thermal expansion RT...1,000 °C.

6) Thermal conductivity at 20 °C.
7) Specific heat.
8) Specific electrical resistivity at 20 °C and 50 Hz.
9) Relative permittivity.
10) Dielectric loss factor at 25 °C and 10 MHz.

## Laminates

| Type | Type of resin | Filler | $\vartheta_G$ [1] °C | $\sigma_{bB}$ [2] min. N/mm² | $a_{cu10}$ [3] min. kJ/m² | CTI [4] min. grade | Properties, application examples |
|---|---|---|---|---|---|---|---|
| **Paper-base laminates** DIN EN ISO 60 893-3-1 | | | | | | | |
| PF CP 201 (Hp 2061) [5] | Phenol resin | Paper web | 120 | 135 | – | CTI 100 | For mechanical loading. |
| PF CP 204 (Hp 2063) [5] | Phenol resin | Paper web | 105 | 75 | – | CTI 100 | For electrical loading; base material FR 2 for PCBs. |
| EP CP 201 (Hp 2361.1) [5] | Epoxy resin | Paper web | 110 | 110 | – | CTI 100 | Good mechanical and electrical properties; flame-resistant; base material FR 3 for PCBs. |
| **Fabric-base laminates** DIN EN ISO 60 893-3-1 | | | | | | | |
| PF GC 201 (Hgw 2072) [5] | Phenol resin | Glass-fiber fabric | 120 | 140 | 25 | CTI 100 | High mechanical, electrical and thermal strength. |
| PF CC 201 (Hgw 2082) [5] | Phenol resin | Fine-weave cotton fabric | 120 | 100 | 8.8 | CTI 100 | Good workability, good sliding and wear behavior; particularly for gears, bearings. |
| PF CC 203 (Hgw 2083) [5] | Phenol resin | Superfine-weave cotton fabric | 120 | 110 | 7 | CTI 100 | |
| EP GC 201 (Hgw 2372) [5] | Epoxy resin | Glass-fiber fabric | 130 | 340 | 33 | CTI 200 | Optimum mechanical and electrical properties |
| EP GC 202 (Hgw 2372.1) [5] | Epoxy resin | Glass-fiber fabric | 155 | 340 | 33 | CTI 200 | Optimum mechanical and electrical properties; base material FR 4 for PCBs. |
| EP GC 203 (Hgw 2372.4) [5] | Epoxy resin | Glass-fiber fabric | 155 | 340 | 33 | CTI 180 | For increased thermal load. |
| SI GC 201 (Hgw 2572) [5] | Silicone resin | Glass-fiber fabric | 180 | 90 | 20 | PTI 450 | For high service temperature. |
| **Glass-mat-base laminates** DIN EN ISO 60 893-3-1 | | | | | | | |
| UP GM 201 (Hm 2472) [5] | Unsaturated polyester resin | Glass-fiber mat | 130 | 130 | 40 | CTI 500 | Good mechanical and electrical properties, particularly resistant to tracking. |

[1] Limit temperature as per VDE 0304, Part 2, for service life of 25,000 h.
[2] Flexural strength as per DIN 53 452.
[3] Impact strength (Charpy) ISO 179 (test procedure IEC 60 893-2).
[4] Tracking resistance according to DIN IEC 112, Comparative Tracking Index (CTI).
[5] Old designation in parentheses.

# Plastic molding compounds

| Chemical name | Material code (ISO 1043/ DIN 7728) | $t_G$ [1] °C | $E$ [2] N/mm² | $a_k \times 10^3$ [3] min. kJ/m² | Resistance at 20° to [4] | | | | | Properties, application examples |
|---|---|---|---|---|---|---|---|---|---|---|
| | | | | | Gasoline | Benzene | Diesel fuel | Alcohol | Mineral oil | |
| **Thermoplastics** (Selection from DIN 7740...7749; DIN 16 771...16 781) | | | | | | | | | | |
| Acrylnitrile-butadien-styrene | ABS | 80 | 2,000 | 5...15 | 0 | – | x | + | + | High gloss, some types transparent; tough housing parts. |
| Fluorinated hydrocarbons | FEP PFA | 250/205 260 | 600 650 | [6] [6] | + + | + + | + + | + + | + + | Extreme reduction in rigidity as temperature increases, resistant to chemicals; coatings, sliding parts, seals. |
| Polyamide 11, 12 | PA 11, 12 | 140/140 | 1,500 | 20...40 | + | + | + | 0 | + | Tough, hard, and resistant to abrasion, low coefficient of friction, good sound absorption, approx. 1...3% water absorption required for good toughness, PA 11/12 have much lower water absorption. |
| Polyamide 6 | PA 6 | 170/140 | 2,500 | 40...90 | + | + | + | x | + | |
| Polyamide 66 | PA 66 | 190/140 | 2,800 | 10...20 | + | + | + | x | + | |
| Polyamide 6 + GF [5] | PA 6-GF | 190/140 | 7,000 | 8...14 | + | + | + | x | + | Impact-resistant machine housings. |
| Polyamide 66 + GF [5] | PA 66-GF | 200/140 | 7,000 | 6...12 | + | + | + | x | + | |
| Polyamide 6T/6I/66 + GF45 | PA 6T/6I/ 66 + GF45 | 285/165 | 14,000 | 8...12 | + | + | + | x | + | Rigid machine housings/components, also at elevated temperatures (engine-compartment components). Lower water absorption than standard PA. |
| Polyamide 6/6T + GF [5] | PA6/6 T-GF | 250/160 | 10,000 | 6...12 | + | + | + | x | + | |
| Polyamide MXD6 + GF50 | PA MXD6 + GF50 | 240/165 | 15,000 | 8...12 | + | + | + | x | + | |
| Polybutylene terephthalate | PBT | 160/140 | 1,700 | 2...4 | + | + | + | + | + | Wear-resistant, chemically resistant, rigidity decreases above 60 °C, hydrolysis above 70 °C in water and fuels. Very good electrical properties. |

[1] Maximum service temperature, short term (1 h)/long-term (5,000 h).
[2] Modulus of elasticity, approx. standard values.
[3] Notched impact strength as per DIN 53 453.
[4] + = good resistance, x = limited resistance, 0 low resistance, – no resistance.
[5] GF Glass fiber (25...35% by weight).
[6] No fracture.
[7] Polyamides, saturated by air humidity at 23 °C and 50% rel. humidity
[7] Polymer mixture of polyphenylene ether and styrene/butadiene.

| Chemical name | Material code (ISO 1043/ DIN 7728) | $t_G$ [1] °C | $E$ [2] N/mm² | $a_{k10}$ [3] min. kJ/m² | Resistance at 20° to [4] | | | | | Properties, application examples |
|---|---|---|---|---|---|---|---|---|---|---|
| | | | | | Gaso-line | Ben-zene | Diesel fuel | Alco-hol | Min-eral oil | |
| Polybutylene terephthalate + GF[5] | PBT-GF | 180/140 | 8,000 | 5...9 | + | + | + | + | + | Higher rigidity than PBT without GF. |
| Polycarbonate | PC | 130/125 | 2,500 | 20...30 | + | − | + | 0 | + | Tough and rigid over wide temperature range, transparent. |
| Polycarbonate + GF[5] | PC-GF | 130 | 5,000 | 6...15 | + | − | + | 0 | + | Very rigid components. |
| Polyethylene | PE | 80 | 1,000 | [6]) | × | 0 | + | + | + | Acid-resistant containers and pipes, films. |
| Polyethylene terephthalate | PET | 180/120 | 2,000 | 2...7 | + | + | + | + | + | Wear-resistant, chemically resistant, rigidity decreases above 60 °C, hydrolysis above 70 °C in water. |
| Cyclo-olefin copolymers | COC | 160 | 3,000 | 1.7...2 | − | − | − | + | − | Highly transparent, weatherproof. |
| Liquid crystal polymers + GF[5] | LCP-GF | 300/240 | 15,000 | 8...16 | + | + | + | + | + | High-temperature shape retention, high impact strength, low bond strength, extremely thin-walled components. Very anisotropic. |
| Polyethersulfon + GF[5] | PES-GF | 220/180 | 9,000 | 6...10 | + | 0 | + | + | + | High continuous service temperature, temperature has no more than a minor influence on properties. Dimensionally stable components. Not resistant to fuel and alcohol at higher temperatures. |
| Polyether ether ketone + GF[5] | PEEK | 320/250 | 9,000 | 6.5...10 | + | + | + | + | + | High-strength components for high temperatures, good antifriction properties, and low wear. Very expensive. |
| Polyethylene terephthalate + GF[5] | PET-GF | 200/120 | 7,000 | 5...12 | + | + | + | + | + | Higher rigidity than PETP without GF. |
| Polymethylmethacrylate | PMMA | 80 | 3,000 | 1.5...2.5 | + | − | × | 0 | + | Transparent in all colors, weatherproof; diffusers, lenses. |
| Polyoxymethylene | POM | 125/120 | 2,000 | 5...7 | + | 0 | + | + | + | Sensitive to acid-induced stress cracking; precision moldings. |
| Polyoxymethylene + GF | POM-GF | 140/120 | 6,000 | 3...5 | + | 0 | + | + | + | |
| Polyphenylene ether + SB [7] | (PPE+S/B) | 120/100 | 2,500 | 4...14 | 0 | − | 0 | 0 | + | Resistant to hot water, flame-resistant. |
| Polyphenylene sulfide + GF 40 | PPS-GF | 270/220 | 13,000 | 4...7 | + | + | + | + | + | High resistance to heat, underhood components, inherently flame-retarding. |

| Chemical name | Material code (ISO 1043/ DIN 7728) | $t_G$ [1] °C | $E$ [2] N/mm² | $a_{K10}$ [3] min. kJ/m² | Resistance at 20° to [4] | | | | | Properties, application examples |
|---|---|---|---|---|---|---|---|---|---|---|
| | | | | | Gaso-line | Ben-zene | Diesel fuel | Alco-hol | Min-eral oil | |
| Polypropylene | PP | 130/110 | 1,500 | 6...10 | x | 0 | + | x | + | Household goods, battery cases, cover hoods. |
| Polypropylene + GF [5] | PP-GF | 130/110 | 4,000 | 4...8 | x | 0 | + | x | + | Fan impellers. |
| Polystyrene | PS | 80 | 2,500 | 2...3 | – | – | 0 | 0 | x | Formed parts, transparent, and coated in all colors. |
| Polyvinyl chloride, plasticized | PVC-P | 80/70 | 200 | [6] | – | – | 0 | 0 | + | Artificial leather, flexible caps, cable insulation, tubing and hosing, seals. |
| Polyvinyl chloride, unplasticized | PVC-U | 70/60 | 3,000 | 2...30 | + | – | + | + | + | Weatherproof exterior parts, pipes, galvanizing equipment. |
| Styrene-acrylonitrile | SAN | 90 | 3,000 | 1.5...2.5 | 0 | – | x | 0 | + | Formed parts, good chemical resistance, also transparent. |
| Styrene-butadiene | S/B | 60 | 1,500 | 4...14 | – | – | – | x | + | Tough housing parts for many applications. |
| Syndiotactic polystyrene | SPS-GF 20 | 180/140 | 5,500 | 6...10 | + | + | + | + | + | Low distortion, brittle, poor crystallization, high tool temperatures required. |
| Non-cross-linked plastics which can be processed only by molding and sintering: | | | | | | | | | | |
| Polyimide | PI | 320/290 | 3,100 | 2 | | | + | + | + | High resistance to heat and radiation, hard. |
| Polytetrafluoroethylene | PTFE | 300/240 | 400 | 13...15 | + | + | + | + | + | Extreme reduction in rigidity as temperature rises, high resistance to heat, aging, and chemicals, low coefficient of friction, sliding parts. |

[1] Maximum service temperature, short term (1 h)/long-term (5,000 h).
[2] Modulus of elasticity, approx. standard values.
[3] Notched impact strength as per DIN 53 453.
[2] + [3] Polyamides, saturated by air humidity at 23 °C and 50% rel. humidity.
[4] + good resistance, x limited resistance, 0 low resistance, – no resistance.
[5] GF Glass fiber (25...35% by weight).
[6] No fracture.
[7] Polymer mixture of polyphenylene ether and styrene/butadiene.

## Thermosets
New standards:
- Pourable phenol molding compounds (PF-PMC) DIN EN ISO 14 526
- Pourable melamine-formaldehyde molding compounds (MF-PMC) DIN EN ISO 14 528
- Pourable melamine/phenol molding compounds (MP-PMC) DIN EN ISO 14 529
- Pourable unsaturated polyester molding compounds (UP-PMC) DIN EN ISO 14 530
- Pourable epoxy-resin molding compounds (EP-PMC) DIN EN ISO 15 252

| Type | Type of resin | Filler | $t_G$[1] °C | $\sigma_{bB}$[2] min. N/mm² | $a_n$[3] min. kJ/m² | CTI[4] min. grade | Properties, application examples |
|---|---|---|---|---|---|---|---|
| (WD30 + MD20) to (WD40 + MD10) (31 and 31.5)[7] | Phenol[8] | Wood flour | 160/140 | 70 | 6 | CTI 125 | For parts subject to high electrical loads. |
| (LF20 + MD25) to (LF30 + MD15) (51)[7] | | Cellulose[5] | 160/140 | 60 | 5 | CTI 150 | For parts with good insulating properties in low-voltage range. Type 74 impact-resistant. |
| *SS40 to SS50 (74)[7] | | Cotton fabric shreds[5] | 160/140 | 60 | 12 | CTI 150 | |
| (LF20 + MD25) to (LF40 + MD05) (83)[7] | | Cotton fibers[6] | 160/140 | 60 | 5 | CTI 150 | Tougher than type 31. |
| – | | Glass fibers, short | 220/180 | 200 | 14 | CTI 125 | High mechanical strength. Very good resistance to automotive fluids, low swelling. |
| – | | Glass fibers, long | 220/180 | 230 | 17 | CTI 175 | |
| (WD30 + MD15) to (WD40 + MD05) (150)[7] | Melamine | Wood flour | 160/140 | 70 | 6 | CTI 600 | Resistant to glow heat, superior electrical properties, high shrinkage factor. |

[1]) Maximum service temperature, short-term (100 h)/continuous (20,000 h).
[2]) Flexural strength.
[3]) Impact strength (Charpy).
[4]) Tracking resistance as per DIN IEC 112 method for determining the Comparative Tracking Index (CTI).
[5]) With or without addition of other organic fillers.
[6]) And/or wood flour.
[7]) Old designation in parentheses.
[8]) Do not use types 13 to 83 (purely organically filled compounds) for new applications (availability no longer guaranteed).

| Type | Type of resin | Filler | $t_G$ [1] °C | $\sigma_{bB}$ [2] min. N/mm² | $a_n$ [3] min. kJ/m² | CTI [4] min. grade | Properties, application examples |
|------|---------------|--------|------|------|------|------|----------|
| **Thermosets** | | | | | | | |
| LD35 to LD45 (181) [7] | Melamine-phenol | Cellulose | 160/140 | 80 | 7 | CTI 250 | For parts subject to electrical and mechanical loads. |
| (GF10 + MD60) to (GF20 + MD50) (802 and 804) [7] | Polyester | Glass fibers, inorganic fillers | 220/170 | 55 | 4.5 | CTI 600 | Types 801, 804: low molding pressure required (large-area parts possible); types 803, 804: glow-heat resistant. |
| MD65 to MD75 | Epoxy | Rock flour | 200/170 | 80 | 5 | CTI 600 | Very good electrical properties. Sheathing sensors and actuators. |
| (GF25 + MD45) to (GF35 + MD35) | | Glass fibers/ mineral | 230/190 | 160 | 10 | CTI 250 | |

[1] Maximum service temperature, short-term (100 h)/continuous (20,000 h).
[2] Flexural strength.
[3] Impact strength (Charpy).
[4] Tracking resistance as per DIN IEC 112 method for determining the Comparative Tracking Index (CTI).
[5] With or without addition of other organic fillers.
[6] And/or wood flour.
[7] Old designation in parentheses.
[8] Do not use types 13 to 83 (purely organically filled compounds) for new applications (availability no longer guaranteed).

### Elastomers

| Material | Material code [7] | Range of application [8] °C | Shore A hardness | Tensile strength [9] N/mm² | Ultimate elongation [9] % | Resistance to [11] | | | | | Flame-retardant hydraulic fluids HF [12] | | | |
|---|---|---|---|---|---|---|---|---|---|---|---|---|---|---|
| | | | | | | Weathering | Ozone | Gasoline | Diesel fuel | Mineral oil | A | B | C | D |
| Acrylate rubber | ACM | -20...+150 | 55...90 | 5...13 | 100...350 | x | + | - | x | + | + | x | x | - |
| Acrylonitrile butadiene rubber | NBR | -30...+120 | 35...100 | 10...25 | 100...700 | x[10] | -[10] | x | x | + | x | x | + | - |
| Butyl rubber | IIR | -40...+125 | 40...85 | 7...17 | 300...600 | x[10] | x[10] | - | - | - | - | - | + | x |
| Chlorinated polyethylene | CM | -30...+140 | 50...95 | 10...20 | 100...700 | + | + | 0 | 0 | x | x | x | + | - |
| Chloroprene rubber | CR | -40...+110 | 20...90 | 7...25 | 100...800 | x | x[10] | x | x | x | 0 | 0 | + | - |
| Chlorosulfonated polyethylene | CSM | -30...+140 | 50...85 | 15...25 | 200...500 | + | + | - | 0 | 0 | x | x | + | - |
| Epichlorohydrin rubber | ECO | -40...+135 | 50...90 | 6...15 | 150...500 | + | + | x | x | + | x | x | + | + |
| Ethylene acrylate rubber | EAM | -40...+185 | 50...75 | 7...14 | 200...500 | + | + | 0 | 0 | 0 | + | x | + | + |
| Ethylene propylene rubber | EPDM | -50...+150 | 20...85 | 7...17 | 150...500 | + | + | - | - | - | - | - | + | + |
| Fluorcarbon rubber | FKM | -25...+250 | 40...90 | 7...17 | 100...350 | + | + | + | + | + | + | + | + | + |
| Fluorsilicon rubber | FVMQ | -60...+200 | 40...70 | 4...9 | 100...400 | + | + | x | + | + | + | + | + | + |
| Hydrogenated nitrile rubber | HNBR | -20...+150 | 45...90 | 15...35 | 100...600 | + | + | x | + | + | + | + | + | - |
| Natural rubber | NR | -55...+90 | 20...100 | 15...30 | 100...800 | 0[10] | -[10] | - | - | - | - | - | + | - |
| Polyurethane rubber | AU EU | -25...+80 | 50...98 | 20...50 | 300...700 | x | x | - | - | 0 | - | - | + | - |
| Silicone rubber | VMQ | -60...+200 | 20...80 | 4...9 | 100...400 | + | + | - | 0 | x | + | + | + | + |
| Styrene butadiene rubber | SBR | -50...+110 | 30...100 | 7...30 | 100...800 | 0[10] | -[10] | - | - | - | - | - | + | - |

[7] DIN ISO 1629.
[8] Not continuous-service temperature.
[9] Depending on composition of compound.
[10] Can be improved by adding protective agents.
[11] + good resistance, x limited resistance, 0 low resistance, - no resistance.
[12] A oil-in-water emulsion; B water-in-oil emulsion; C polyglycol-water solution; D synthetic liquids.

| Material | Material code [7] | Range of application [8] °C | Shore A hardness (D) | Tensile strength [9] N/mm² | Ultimate elongation [9] % | Resistance to [11] Weathering | Ozone | Gasoline | Diesel fuel | Mineral oil |
|---|---|---|---|---|---|---|---|---|---|---|
| **Thermoplastic elastomers** | | | | | | | | | | |
| Blend/olefin with non-linked to fully cross-linked rubber | TPE-O [14] | -40...+100 (120) | 35A...50D | 3...15 | 250...600 | + | + | 0 | 0 | 0 |
| Blend/styrene block polymers | TPE-S [14] | -60...+60 (100) | 30A...90A | 3...12 | 500...900 | + | + | - | - | - |
| Polyester elastomer | TPE-E [14] | -50...+150 | 40D...80D | 9...47 | 240...800 | 0 [10] | x | x | + | + |
| Polyesterurethane | TPE-U [14] | -40...+100 | 55A...70D | 15...55 | 250...600 | 0 [10] | + | 0 | x | + |
| Polyetherblockamide | TPE-A [14] | -40...+80 | 75A...70D | 30...60 | 300...500 | 0 [10] | + | x | + | x |

[7] DIN ISO 1629.
[8] Not continuous-service temperature.
[9] Depending on composition of compound.
[10] Can be improved by adding protective agents.
[11] + good resistance, x limited resistance, 0 low resistance, - no resistance.
[14] No ISO standard to date.

## Plastic codes with chemical names and trade names [3])

| Material code | Chemical name | Trade names |
|---|---|---|
| ABS | Acrylnitrile-butadien-styrene | Cycolac, Novodur, Ronfalin, Terluran |
| ACM | Acrylate rubber | Cyanacryl, Hycar |
| EAM [1]) | Ethylene acrylate rubber | Vamac |
| APE [1]) | Aromatic polyester | Arylef, APEC |
| ASA | Acrylate styrene acrylonitrile | Luran S |
| AU | Polyurethane rubber | Urepan |
| CA | Cellulose acetate | Bergacell, Tenite |
| CAB | Cellulose acetate butyrate | Cellidor, Tenite |
| CM | Chlorinated polyethylene | Bayer CM, CPE |
| CR | Chloroprene rubber | Baypren, Neoprene |
| CSM | Chlorosulfonated polyethylene | Hypalon |
| ECO | Epichlorhydrin rubber | Herclor, Hydrin |
| EP | Epoxy | Araldite, Sumitomo, Shin Etsu, Bakelite EP |
| EPDM | Ethylene propylene rubber | Buna AP, Dutral, Keltan, Nordel, Vistalon |
| EU | Polyurethane rubber | Adiprene C |
| FKM | Fluorcarbon rubber | DAI-EL, Fluorel, Tecnoflon, Viton |
| HNBR [1]) | Hydrogenated NBR | Therban, Zetpol |
| IR | Isoprene rubber | Cariflex IR, Natsyn |
| MF | Melamine-formaldehyde | Bakelite, Resinol, Supraplast, Resopal |
| MPF | Melamine/phenol-formaldehyde | Supraplast, Resiplast |
| MVQ | Silicone rubber | Rhodorsil, Silastic, Silopren |
| NBR | Nitrile butadiene rubber | Buna N, Chemigum, Hycar, Perbunan |
| PA 46 [1]) | Polyamide 46 | Stanyl |
| PA 6-3-T | Amorphous polyamide | Trogamid T |
| PA 6 | Polyamide 6 (polymers of $\varepsilon$-caprolactam) | Akulon, Durethan B, Grilon. Nivionplast, Technyl, Ultramid B, Wellamid, Frianyl B, Schulamid 6 |
| PA 66 | Polyamide 66 (polymers of hexamethyl-ene-diamine and adipic acid) | Akulon, Durethan A, Minlon, Nivionplast, Technyl, Ultramid A, Wellamid, Zytel, Frianyl A, Schulamid 66 |
| PA X [1]) | X = partially aromatic polyamides | Ultramid T [4]), Amodel 1 ... [5]), Amodel 4 ... [6]), Grivory GV [7]), Grivory HTV [8]), Zytel HTN [9]), IXEF [10]), Trogamid |
| PA 11 | Polyamide 11 (polymers of 11-aminoundecanoic acid) | Rilsan B |
| PA 12 | Polyamide 12 (polymers of dodecalactam) | Grilamid, Rilsan A, Vestamid |
| PAI | Polyamide imide | Torlon |
| PAN | Polyacrylonitrile | Dralon, Orlon |
| PBT | Polybutylene terephthalate | Crastin, Pocan, Ultradur, Vestodur, Celanex, Schuladur |
| PC | Polycarbonate | Makrolon, Orgalan, Sinvet, Lexan |
| PA 612 | Polyamide 612 (polymers of hexamethyl-ene-diamine and dodecanoic acid) | Zytel |
| COC [1]) | Cyclo-olefin copolymers | Topas |
| LCP | Liquid crystal polymers | Vectra, Zenite, Xydar |
| PA 6/66 | Copolyamide 6/66 | Ultramid C, Technyl, Grilon TSV |
| SPS [1]) | Syndiotactic polystyrene | Questra, Xarec, Edgetek |
| PK [1]) | Polyketone | Carilon |
| LFT [1]) | Long-fiber reinforced thermoplastic | Celstran (PA, PP, PBT, PPS, ABS base) |

| Material code | Chemical name | Trade names |
|---|---|---|
| (PC + ABS) | Blend of polycarbonate + ABS | Bayblend, Cycoloy |
| (PC + ASA) | Blend of polycarbonate + ASA | Terblend S |
| (PC-PBT) | Blend of polycarbonate + PBT | Xenoy |
| PE | Polyethylene | Hostalen, Lupolen, Stamylan, Vestolen |
| PEEK | Polyether ether ketone | Victrex "PEEK" |
| PEI | Polyether imide | Ultem |
| PES | Polyether sulfone | Victrex "PES", Ultrason E, Rodel |
| PETFE [1] | Polytetrafluoroethylene ethylene copolymer | Hostaflon ET, Tefzel |
| PETP | Polyethylene terephthalate | Arnite, Crastin, Mylar, Rynite, Impet |
| PF | Phenol-formaldehyde | Bakelite, Supraplast, Vyncolit, Sumitomo Durez |
| PFA | Perfluoralkoxy copolymer | Teflon PFA |
| PFEP [1] | Tetrafluoroethylene hexafluoropropylene copolymer | Teflon FEP |
| PI | Polyimide | Kapton, Kerimid, Kinel, Vespel |
| PMMA | Polymethylmethacrylate | Degalan, Diakon, Lucryl, Perspex, Plexiglas, Vedril |
| POM | Polyoxymethylene, polyformaldehyde (a polyacetal) | Delrin, Hostaform, Ultraform |
| PP | Polypropylene | Daplen, Stamylan P, Starpylen, Vestolen, Hostacom |
| (PPE + SB) | Blend of polyphenylene ether + SB | Noryl, Luranyl |
| (PPE + PA) | Blend of polyphenylene ether + PA | Noryl GTX, Ultranyl, Vestoblend |
| PPS | Polyphenylene sulfide | Fortron, Ryton, Tedur |
| PS | Polystyrene | Edistir, Hostyren, Polystyrol, Vestyron |
| PSU | Polysulfone | Udel, Ultrason S |
| PTFE | Polytetrafluoroethylene | Fluon, Hostaflon, Teflon |
| PUR | Polyurethane | Lycra, Vulkollan |
| PVC-P | Polyvinyl chloride, plasticized | Trosiplast, Vestolit, Vinoflex |
| PVC-U | Polyvinyl chloride, unplasticized | Trovidur, Hostalit, Vinidur, Vestolid |
| PVDF | Polyvinylidene fluoride | Dyflor, Kynar, Solef |
| PVF | Polyvinyl fluoride | Tedlar |
| SAN | Styrene-acrylonitrile | Kostil, Luran, Tyril |
| SB | Styrene-butadiene | Hostyren, Lustrex |
| SBR | Styrene butadiene rubber | Buna Hüls, Buna S, Cariflex S |
| TPE-A [1] | Polyetherblockamide | Pebax, Vestamid E |
| TPE-E [1] | TPE[2] polyester base | Arnitel, Hytrel, Riteflex |
| TPE-O [1] | TPE[2] olefin base | Leraflex, Santoprene |
| TPE-S [1] | TPE[2] styrene base | Cariflex, Evoprene, Kraton |
| TPE-11 [1] | Polyesterurethane | Desmopan, Elastollan |
| TPI | Thermoplastic polyimide | Vespel TP |
| UF | Urea-formaldehyde | Bakelite, Pollopas |
| UP | Unsaturated polyester | Keripol, Leguval, Palatal |

[1] Material code not yet standardized.
[2] TPE: Thermoplastic elastomer.
[3] ISO 1043/DIN 7728 (Thermoplastics, Thermosets), ISO 1629 (Elastomers).

[4] PA 6/6T
[5] PA 6T/6I/66
[6] PA 6T/66
[7] PA 66 + PA 6I/6T
[8] PA 6I/6T
[9] PA 6T/MPMDT
[10] PA MXD 6

Material codes [4] – [10] are standardized

# Automotive paints

## Structure of solid-color coatings

| Layer | Layer thickness in mm | Structure | Binders | Composition Solvents | Pigments | Extenders | Additives and SC | Application |
|---|---|---|---|---|---|---|---|---|
| 1 | 20...25 | CD | Epoxy resins Polyurethane | Water, small amounts of water-miscible organic solvents | Inorganic (organic) | Inorganic extenders | Surface-active substances, anti-crater agents, SC 20% | EC |
| 2a | approx. 35 | Extender | Polyester, melamine, urea and, epoxy resins | Aromatic compounds, alcohols | Inorganic and organic | Inorganic extenders | e.g. wetting agents, surface-active substances SC 55...62% | PS ESTA-HR |
| 2b | approx. 35 | Water extender | Water-soluble polyester, polyurethane, melamine resins | Water, small amounts of water-miscible organic solvents | | | SC 43...50% | PS ESTA-HR |
| 2c | approx. 20 | Thin-film water extender | Water-soluble polyurethane, melamine resins | Water, small amounts of water-miscible organic solvents | | Inorganic extenders | e.g. wetting agents, surface-active substances SC 32...45% | PS ESTA-HR |
| 3a | 40...50 | Solid-color top coat | Alkyd and melamine resins | Esters, aromatic compounds, alcohols | | – | e.g. leveling and wetting agents | PS ESTA-HR |
| 3b | 10...35 (color-specific) | Water-borne solid-color base coat | Water-soluble polyester, polyurethane, polyacrylate and melamine resins | Small amounts water-miscible co-solvents | | – | Wetting agents SC 20...40% | PS ESTA-HR |
| 4a | 40...50 | Conventional clear coat | Acrylic and melamine resins | Aromatic compounds, alcohols, esters | – | – | e.g. leveling agents and light stabilizers SC 45% | PS ESTA-HR |
| 4b | 40...50 | 2C-HS | HS acrylate resin polyisocyanates | Esters, aromatic compounds | – | – | e.g. leveling agents and light stabilizers SC 58% | PS ESTA-HR |
| 4c | 40...50 | Powder-slurry clear coat | Urethane-modified epoxy/carboxy system | – | – | – | e.g. light stabilizers SC 38% | PS ESTA-HR |

## Structure of metallic coatings

| Layer | Layer thickness in mm | Structure | Binders | Solvents | Composition | | Additives and SC | Application |
|---|---|---|---|---|---|---|---|---|
| | | | | | Pigments | Extenders | | |
| 1 | 20...25 | CD | Epoxy resins polyurethane | Water, small amounts of water-miscible organic solvents | Inorganic (organic) | Inorganic extenders | Surface-active substances, anti-crater agents, SC 20% | EC |
| 2a | approx. 35 | Extenders melamine, urea, epoxy resins | Polyester, alcohols | Aromatic compounds, alcohols | Inorganic and organic | Inorganic extenders | e.g. wetting agents, surface-active substances SC 55...62% | PS ESTA-HR |
| 2b | approx. 35 | Water extender | Water-soluble polyester, polyurethane, melamine resins | Water, small amounts of water-miscible organic solvents | | | SC 43...50% | PS ESTA-HR |
| 2c | approx. 20 | Thin-film water extender | Water-soluble polyurethane, melamine resins | Water, small amounts of water-miscible organic solvents | | | e.g. wetting agents, surface-active active substances SC 32...45% | PS ESTA-HR |
| 3a | 10...15 | Metallic base coat | CAB, polyester, melamine resins | Esters, aromatic compounds | Aluminum and mica particles | – | SC 15...30% | PS ESTA-HR |
| 3b | 10...15 | Water-soluble metallic base cost | Water-soluble polyester, polyurethane, polyacrylates and melamine resins | Small amounts of water-miscible co-solvents | Aluminum and mica particles organic and inorganic pigments | – | Wetting agent SC 18...25% | PS ESTA-HR |
| 4a | 40...50 | Conventional clear coat | Acrylic and melamine resins | Aromatic compounds alcohols, esters | – | – | e.g. leveling agents and light stabilizers SC 45% | PS ESTA-HR |
| 4b | 40...50 | z2C-HS | HS acrylate resin, polyisocyanates | Esters, aromatic compounds | – | – | e.g. leveling agents and light stabilizers SC 58% | PS ESTA-HR |
| 4c | 40...50 | Powder-slurry clear coat | Urethane-modified epoxy/carboxy system | – | – | – | e.g. light stabilizers SC 38% | PS ESTA-HR |

Acronyms: TFB Thick-film build, ESTA-HR Electrostatic high rotation, EC Electrophoretic coating, SC Solids content, CD Cathodic deposition, PS Pneumatic spray, 2C-HS 2-component high-solid (high levels of non-volatile matter).

# Corrosion and corrosion protection

## Corrosion processes

Corrosion is the attrition of metal as a result of electrochemical reactions with substances in the environment. As it proceeds, metal atoms oxidize to form nonmetallic compounds in a process emanating from the affected material's surface. In thermodynamic terms, the process can be viewed as an entropic transition from an ordered, high-energy state into a less-ordered state of lower energy, and consequently greater stability.

Corrosion processes are always interphase reactions. An example of this type of reaction is metal scaling, i.e. oxidation in hot gases. The following deals exclusively with the corrosion that occurs at the phase boundary between the metal and aqueous phases, generally referred to as electrochemical corrosion.

### Corrosive attack

Two distinct reactions occur in every corrosive attack: in the <u>anodic subprocess</u> – the directly visible corrosive effect – the difference in respective potentials causes the metal to oxidize as described in the reaction equation

$$Me \rightarrow Me^{n+} + ne^-$$

freeing an equivalent number of electrons. The metal ions thus formed can either be dissolved in the electrolyte, or can precipitate out on the metal after reacting with constituents in the attacking medium.

This anodic subprocess can continue only as long as the electrons it produces are consumed in a second process. This second subprocess is a <u>cathodic subreaction</u> in which oxygen is reduced to hydroxyl ions in neutral or alkaline media, in accordance with the reduction equation:

$$O_2 + 2 H_2O + 4 e^- \rightarrow 4 OH^-$$

These hydroxyl ions, in turn, are able to react with the metal ions, whereas, in acidic media, the hydrogen ions are reduced via the formation of free hydrogen, which escapes as a gas according to the following formula:

$$2 H^+ + 2 e^- \rightarrow H_2$$

Each of the individual subreactions corresponds to a partial current/voltage curve. The total current is the sum of the two currents $I_a$ and $I_c$:

$$I_{total} = I_a + I_k$$

The two partial current/voltage curves combine to produce the cumulative current/voltage curve.

If no voltage is supplied externally, i.e. in free corrosion, the system assumes a state in which the anodic and cathodic partial currents are precisely balanced:

$$I_a = -I_k = I_{corr}$$

The anodic current is called the corrosion current $I_{corr}$, while the corresponding potential at which this current compensation occurs is called the "open-circuit potential" $E_{corr}$.

The open-circuit potential is a mixed potential in which there is no equilibrium; matter is converted continuously, as defined in the following general equation:

$$O_2 + 2 H_2O + \frac{4}{n} Me \rightarrow \frac{4}{n} Me^{n+} + 4OH^-$$

The above is essentially applicable for contact corrosion, although the interrelationships are more complicated. In addition to pairs of partial current/voltage curves for each of the two metals and the resulting two cumulative current/voltage

---

*Free corrosion at the metal/corrosive-medium phase boundary*
*In an aggressive medium, oxygen is reduced at the corroding metal, and corrosion products are formed at the same time.*

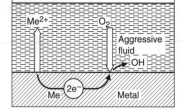

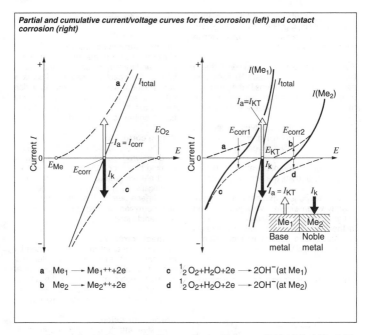

*Partial and cumulative current/voltage curves for free corrosion (left) and contact corrosion (right)*

a   $Me_1 \longrightarrow Me_1^{++}+2e$

b   $Me_2 \longrightarrow Me_2^{++}+2e$

c   $\tfrac{1}{2}O_2+H_2O+2e \longrightarrow 2OH^-$ (at $Me_1$)

d   $\tfrac{1}{2}O_2+H_2O+2e \longrightarrow 2OH^-$ (at $Me_2$)

curves, the resultant total current/voltage curve for the entire system must be considered as a value which can be measured externally.

**Electrochemical series of metals**
Metals are often ranked in "electrochemical series of metals" corresponding to consecutively higher "standard potentials." Here, the term "standard potential" indicates that the specified values apply to standard conditions, especially to the activities (in the electrochemically active part of the concentration) of the dissolved metal ions and hydrogen in a concentration of 1 mol/l at a hydrogen pressure of 1 bar at 25 °C. Such conditions are seldom found in practice; in fact, most solutions are virtually free of ions from the metal in question.

It should be emphasized that the table ("Standard electric potentials of metals") is limited to thermodynamic values, and does not reflect the effects of corrosion kinetics, for example as encountered in the formation of protective layers. For instance, lead is shown as a base metal; as such it should dissolve in sulfuric acid. Although the "practical" and "technical" electrochemical series of metals do not have this disadvantage, their practical application range remains restricted. In contrast, electrochemical corrosion measurements provide unambiguous data.

For general reference purposes, the following relationships between electrical potential and corrosion susceptibility can be specified for metals with no application of external voltages provided that the metal's response is not affected by secondary reactions such as complexing reactions or the formation of protective layers:

Very base metals (potential less than 0.4 V), e.g. Na, Mg, Be, Al, Ti, and Fe, corrode in neutral aqueous solutions, even in the absence of oxygen.

Base metals (potential between 0.5 and 0 V), e.g. Cd, Co, Ni, Sn, and Pb, corrode in neutral aqueous solutions in the presence of oxygen, and corrode in acids to produce hydrogen even in the absence of oxygen.

Semi-noble metals (potential between 0 and +0.7 V), e.g. Cu, Hg, and Ag, corrode in all solutions only if oxygen is present.

Noble metals (potentials above +0.7 V), e.g. Pd, Pt, and Au, are generally stable.

These response patterns can vary sharply when external voltage is applied to the metals. The variations are exploited in the field of electrochemical corrosion protection (see section headed "Corrosion protection").

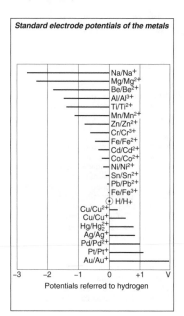

*Standard electrode potentials of the metals*

Na/Na$^+$
Mg/Mg$^{2+}$
Be/Be$^{2+}$
Al/Al$^{3+}$
Ti/Ti$^{2+}$
Mn/Mn$^{2+}$
Zn/Zn$^{2+}$
Cr/Cr$^{3+}$
Fe/Fe$^{2+}$
Cd/Cd$^{2+}$
Co/Co$^{2+}$
Ni/Ni$^{2+}$
Sn/Sn$^{2+}$
Pb/Pb$^{2+}$
Fe/Fe$^{3+}$
H/H$^+$
Cu/Cu$^{2+}$
Cu/Cu$^+$
Hg/Hg$_2^{2+}$
Ag/Ag$^+$
Pd/Pd$^{2+}$
Pt/Pt$^+$
Au/Au$^+$

−3    −2    −1    0    +1    V
Potentials referred to hydrogen

## Types of corrosion

### General surface corrosion
Uniform attrition of material over the entire boundary surface between the material and the attacking medium. This is a very frequent type of corrosion in which the material penetration rate (removal depth) can be calculated per unit of time based on the corrosion current.

### Pitting corrosion
Limited localized attack by a corrosive medium which penetrates the material by forming holes, or pits, whose depth is almost always greater than their diameter. Practically no material is removed from the surface outside the pitted areas. Pitting corrosion is frequently caused by halogenide ions.

### Contact corrosion
When two different metals moistened by the same medium are in mutual electrical contact, a cathodic subprocess occurs at the more noble metal, while the anodic subprocess progresses at the baser material. This is called contact corrosion.

### Crevice corrosion
Corrosive attack primarily occurring in narrow crevices, caused by concentration differences in the corrosive medium, e.g. as a result of long oxygen diffusion paths. This type of corrosion generates potential differences between the crevice extremities, leading to intensified corrosion in more poorly ventilated areas.

### Stress corrosion cracking
Corrosion stemming from the simultaneous concerted action of a corrosive medium and mechanical tensile stress (which can also be present as internal stress in the object itself). Intergranular or transgranular fissures form, in many cases without the appearance of visible corrosion products.

### Vibration corrosion cracking
Corrosion caused by the simultaneous effects of a corrosive medium and mechanical fatigue stress, e.g. caused by vibrations. Transgranular fissures are formed, frequently without visible deformation.

### Intergranular and transgranular corrosion
Types of corrosion characterized by selective formation along the grain boundaries or roughly parallel to the deformation plane in the grain interior.

### Dezincification
Selective dissolution of zinc from brass, leaving behind a porous copper structure. Denickelification and dealuminification are analogous processes.

## Corrosion testing

### Electrochemical corrosion-testing procedures
Corrosion currents are the main parameters measured in electrochemical testing procedures, in addition to determining the relationship between potentials and object materials during the corrosion reaction. In the case of uniform surface corrosion, the corrosion-current parameters are then used for the precise definition of the attrition mass and removal depth per unit of time. The relevant conversion factors are listed in Table 2.

These electrochemical processes thus represent a valuable supplement to non-electrochemical methods.

### Polarization-resistance measurement
The rate of free corrosion is defined based on the polarization resistance (slope of the cumulative current/voltage curve). Testing entails subjecting the metal to minimal, alternating anodic and cathodic pulses.

### Impedance spectroscopy
Electrochemical Impedance Spectroscopy (EIS) is employed to examine corrosion mechanisms. This alternating-current technique determines the AC resistance (impedance) and the phase angle of an electrochemical test object as a function of frequency. A low-amplitude sinusoidal alternating voltage is superimposed on the working electrode's potential, and the current response is measured. After measurement, the system is approximated in the form of an equivalent network. By way of example, the figure headed "Evaluation of EIS data" shows the equivalent network for the metal/coating/medium system.

The parameter-fit method is used to fit the equivalent networks to the experimental data. The impedance elements (resistances, capacitances, inductances) are assigned physical properties. Direct conclusions can then be drawn about various characteristics, such as the effectiveness of corrosion-protection measures, porosity, thickness, a coating's water-absorption ability, the effectiveness of inhibitors, the corrosion rate of the base metal, and so on.

### SRET
The Scanning Reference Electrode Technique (SRET) is used for detecting corrosion in its early stages and for examining local corrosion processes.

Pit, gap, and intergranular corrosion are examples of local processes that can significantly impair mechanical properties and even result in failure in extreme cases. A high local rate of corrosion and a change in local potential are typical of these processes.

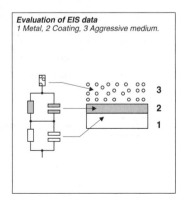

*Evaluation of EIS data*
1 Metal, 2 Coating, 3 Aggressive medium.

### Table 1. Overview of selected standardized non-electrochemical corrosion-testing procedures

| Standard | Type of corrosion-testing procedure |
|---|---|
| DIN EN ISO 196 (supersedes DIN 50 911) | Testing of wrought copper and copper alloys; mercury nitrate test |
| DIN EN ISO 3651-1 & 2 (supersedes DIN 50 914) | Determination of resistance to intergranular corrosion of stainless steels |
| DIN EN ISO 4628-3 (draft) 6, 7 & 8 | Paints and varnishes – Evaluation of degradation of coatings, Part 3: Assessment of degree of rusting |
| DIN 53 210 | Designation of quantity and size of defects, and of intensity of uniform changes in appearance (to be superseded by DIN EN ISO 4628-3) |
| DIN EN ISO 8565 (sup. DIN 50 917-1) | Metals and alloys – Atmospheric corrosion testing |
| DIN EN ISO 11 306 (sup. DIN 50 917-2) | Corrosion of metals and alloys. Guidelines for exposing and evaluating metals and alloys in sea water |
| DIN 50 016 | Method of test in damp, alternating atmosphere |
| DIN 50 017 | Condensation water test atmospheres |
| DIN 50 018 | Testing in a saturated atmosphere in the presence of sulfur dioxide |
| DIN 50 021 | Spray tests with different sodium chloride solutions |
| DIN 50 900-2 | Corrosion of metals – Terms – Part 3 – Electrochemical terms |
| DIN 50 905-1...4 | Corrosion of metals; corrosion testing; principles, corrosion characteristics under uniform surface corrosion attack, corrosion characteristics under nonuniform and localized corrosion attack without mechanical stress |
| DIN 50 915 | Testing the resistance of unalloyed and low-alloy steels to intergranular stress corrosion cracking by attack of nitrate medium |
| DIN 50 919 | Investigations of galvanic corrosion in electrolytic solutions |
| DIN 50 920-1 | Corrosion testing in flowing liquids |
| DIN 50 922 | Testing the resistance of metallic materials to stress corrosion cracking |
| DIN 50 928 | Testing and assessment of the corrosion protection of coated metallic materials in contact with aqueous corrosive agents |
| DIN EN 10 244-2 | Testing of nonferrous metallic coatings on steel wire (tin, zinc alloy) |
| N42AP 206 | Climatic tests; testing in constant condensate climate |
| N42AP 209 | Climatic tests; cyclic humidity tests |
| N42AP 213 | Climatic tests; industrial-climate tests |

The figure headed "SRET principle" is a schematic diagram of the equipotential lines at a local, active corrosion point. A sensor consisting of two offset platinum tips measuring the micropotential changes above a rotating probe is used to pick up the signal.

Data is recorded automatically on a PC using the appropriate software for analysis and presentation in the form of 2D graphics. SRET is used to examine pitting corrosion, activation and repassivation, to detect defects in organic coatings and at welds, and to trace delamination, etc.

### Electrochemical noise
Electrochemical noise, which can be potential and/or current noise, results from micro-electrochemical actions on the corroding metal surface. Small, stochastic fluctuations around the corresponding mean values serve as the evaluation criterion. This allows changes in the system state to be identified at a very early stage. The particular advantage of noise diagnostics is that there is no external intervention into the corroding system.

Areas of application are basic examinations of local corrosion processes, inhibition of corrosion processes and corrosion monitoring.

### Contact-corrosion current measurement
To measure <u>contact corrosion</u>, the current which flows between the two affected metals is measured directly with both immersed in the same corrosive medium.

The attrition rates determined through electrochemical measurements closely reflect those obtained in field testing. In addition to the small amount of corrosive medium required, another advantage of electrochemical procedures over non-electrochemical methods is that they provide quantitative data on attrition rates.

### Non-electrochemical corrosion-testing procedures
Non-electrochemical test procedures rely on determining the weight loss by weighing, or defining the rust level. DIN EN ISO 4628-3 (formerly DIN 53210) defines 5 different rust categories according to rust coverage or surface perforation (Table 3).

The corrosion tests have been defined to reflect actual field requirements. In addition to the standard DIN corrosion-testing procedures (Table 1), processes have evolved to reflect specific requirements, e.g. motor-vehicle testing. These tests provide reliable indices of projected service life under normal operating conditions by using short-term exposure in extremely harsh conditions to simulate long-term stresses in the real world. (These tests include operating the vehicle under exposure to climatic factors, splashwater tests of air/fuel mixture systems).

**Table 2. Attrition mass and removal depth due to surface corrosion of various metals with a corrosion current density of 1 $\mu A/cm^2$**

| Metals | Relative atomic mass | Density $g/cm^3$ | Attrition mass mg/ $(cm^2 \cdot year)$ | Removal depth $\mu m/year$ |
|---|---|---|---|---|
| Fe | 55.8 | 7.87 | 9.13 | 11.6 |
| Cu | 63.5 | 8.93 | 10.40 | 11.6 |
| Cd | 112.4 | 8.64 | 18.40 | 21.0 |
| Ni | 58.7 | 8.90 | 9.59 | 10.8 |
| Zn | 65.4 | 7.14 | 10.70 | 15.0 |
| Al | 27.0 | 2.70 | 2.94 | 10.9 |
| Sn | 118.7 | 7.28 | 19.40 | 26.6 |
| Pb | 207.2 | 11.30 | 33.90 | 30.0 |

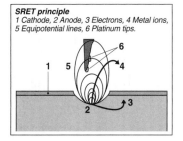

**SRET principle**
1 Cathode, 2 Anode, 3 Electrons, 4 Metal ions, 5 Equipotential lines, 6 Platinum tips.

**Table 3. Rust level and proportion of rust penetrations and visible sub-rusting at the surface to DIN EN ISO 4628-3**

| Rust level | Rust surface in % |
|------------|-------------------|
| $R_i0$ | 0 |
| $R_i1$ | 0.05 |
| $R_i2$ | 0.5 |
| $R_i3$ | 1 |
| $R_i4$ | 8 |
| $R_i5$ | 40...50 |

# Corrosion protection

The manifestations and mechanisms of corrosion are many and varied, so widely differing methods can be adopted to protect metals against corrosion attack. Corrosion protection means intervening in the corrosive process with the object of reducing the rate of corrosion in order to prolong the service life of the components.

Corrosion protection can be achieved by applying four basic principles:

– Measures in planning and design: the choice of suitable materials and the suitable structural design of components.
– Measures that intervene in the corrosive process by electrochemical means.
– Measures that separate the metal from the corrosive medium by protective layers or coatings.
– Measures that influence the corrosive medium, for example, the addition of inhibitors to the medium.

## Corrosion protection by means of suitable structural design

Selecting suitable materials which feature optimum resistance to corrosion under the expected conditions can be of considerable assistance in avoiding corrosion damage. When the costs that would otherwise be incurred for upkeep and repair are factored into the long-term cost of ownership equation, a more expensive material can often be the more cost-effective alternative.

Design measures, too, are of major importance. A great deal of skill and expertise goes into design, particularly regarding the connections between parts that are made of the same material or different materials.

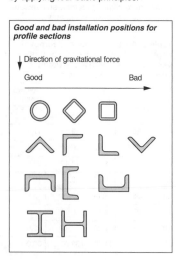

*Good and bad installation positions for profile sections*

↓ Direction of gravitational force

Good                    Bad

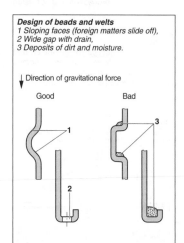

*Design of beads and welts*
*1 Sloping faces (foreign matters slide off),*
*2 Wide gap with drain,*
*3 Deposits of dirt and moisture.*

↓ Direction of gravitational force

Good                    Bad

Corners and edges of sections are difficult to protect, and this is where corrosion can easily attack. A favorable installation position can avoid corrosion.

Beads and welts can trap dirt and moisture. Suitable surfaces and drain openings can help avoid this problem.

Welds, which generally modify the microstructure for the worse, are another weak point. In order to avoid crevice corrosion, welds have to be smooth and free of gaps.

Contact corrosion can be avoided by joining same or similar metals, or by installing washers, spacers, or sleeves to ensure that both metals are electrically insulated.

### Electrochemical processes

The schematic current/voltage curves for a metal suitable for passivation coating show how these processes work. The current-density values arranged in ascending order on the y-axis represent anodic currents corresponding to the corrosion reaction defined in the equation

$$Me \rightarrow Me^{n+} + ne^-$$

In contrast, the descending current-density values represent cathodic currents with the reaction equation progressing from right to left. The schematic indicates that external voltage can be applied to suppress corrosion. There are two basic ways of doing this:

*Design-related crevices in welds and how they can be avoided*

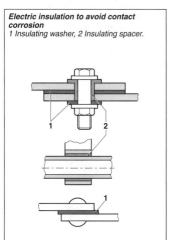

*Electric insulation to avoid contact corrosion*
*1 Insulating washer, 2 Insulating spacer.*

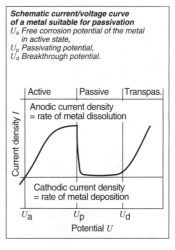

*Schematic current/voltage curve of a metal suitable for passivation*
$U_a$ *Free corrosion potential of the metal in active state,*
$U_p$ *Passivating potential,*
$U_d$ *Breakthrough potential.*

For <u>cathodic protection</u> the potential is shifted so far toward the left that no anodic currents flow, leading to $U < U_a$. As an alternative to applying voltage from an external source, it is also possible to shift the potential by using a base metal to act as a "sacrificial" reactive anode.

Another option is to shift the potential of the threatened electrode into the passive range, i.e. into the potential range between $U_p$ and $U_d$. This is called <u>anodic protection</u>. The anodic currents, which flow in the passive range, are less than those in the active range by exponential powers of between 3 and 6, depending on the type of metal and the corrosive medium. The result is excellent protection for the metal.

However, the potential should not exceed $U_d$, as oxygen would be produced in this transpassive range, potentially leading to higher rates of oxidation. Both of these effects would cause the current to increase.

## Coatings

Coatings inhibit corrosion by forming protective films applied directly to the metal to be protected, where they resist attack by the corrosive medium. These protective coatings should be neither porous nor electrically conductive and must be of sufficient thickness (for further coatings, see P. 297).

## Inhibitors

Inhibitors are substances added to the corrosive medium in low concentrations (up to a maximum of several hundred ppm) for absorption at the surface of the protected metal. Inhibitors drastically reduce the rate of corrosion by blocking either the anodic or the cathodic subprocess (frequently blocking both subprocesses simultaneously). Organic amines and amides of organic acids are the most frequent inhibitors. In automotive applications, for example, inhibitors are used in fuel additives; they are also added to antifreeze in order to inhibit corrosion damage in the coolant circuit.

<u>Vapor-phase inhibitors</u> provide only temporary protection for metallic products during storage and shipping. They must be easy to apply and remove.

The drawback of vapor-phase inhibitors is that they are potentially injurious to health.

<u>V</u>apor-<u>p</u>hase <u>i</u>nhibitors (VPI), or <u>v</u>olatile <u>c</u>orrosion <u>i</u>nhibitors (VCI), are organic substances of moderate vapor pressure. They are frequently enclosed in special-purpose packing materials or as solvents in liquids or emulsions with oil. The inhibitors evaporate or sublimate over the course of time, and are adsorbed as monomolecules on the metal, where they inhibit either anodic or cathodic corrosion subreactions, or both at once. Dicyclohexylamin nitrite is a typical example.

For optimal effectiveness, the inhibitor should form a sealed coating extending over the largest possible surface area. This is why they are generally enclosed in packing materials such as special paper or polyethylene foil. An airtight edge seal is not required; the packing can be opened briefly for inspection of contents. The duration of the packing's effectiveness depends on the tightness of the seal and the temperature (normally approx. 2 years, but less in environments substantially hotter than room temperature).

Standard commercial vapor-phase inhibitors are generally a combination of numerous components capable of providing simultaneous protection for several metals or alloys. Exceptions: cadmium, lead, tungsten and magnesium.

# Coating systems

Coating systems are used to adapt the surface properties of components to particular requirements ("surface engineering"). It is thus possible, for example, for a component to be made from a tough, low-cost material which still has a hard and wear-resistant surface. The mains uses for coatings are:
– Corrosion protection (as well as functional retention, often for decorative reasons).
– Wear protection.
– Joining and bonding techniques (plug-in, welded, soldered, bonded, and crimped contacts).

In coating systems, distinctions are made between the following types of coating:
– Coatings in which one layer is applied.
– Conversion coatings, in which the functional coating is produced by chemical/electrochemical conversion of the base material.
– Diffusion coatings, in which the functional coating is produced by diffusion of atoms or ions into the base material.

## Coatings

### Electroplated liners
Electroplated liners are deposited using an external power source. Before coating, the workpieces are immersed into an electrolyte. The progression and distribution of the field lines influence the layer-thickness distribution. A uniform layer thickness can be achieved by means of an optimized configuration of anodes and screens.

Electroplated liners are widely used as corrosion-protection coatings, wear-protection coatings, and coatings for electrical contacts. Some important coating systems are described below.

#### Zinc and zinc alloys
Electrolytically deposited zinc coatings are widely used as corrosion-protection coatings for steel components and are a cathodically effective means of corrosion protection (sacrificial effect). Zinc coatings are passivated to increase the corrosion-protection effect. Zinc alloys, such as zinc-nickel with approx. 15% Ni, offer a significantly higher degree of corrosion protection.

*Production of electroplated liners*
*a) Progression and distribution of electrical field lines between anode and cathode as caused by nonuniform liner-thickness distribution.*
*b) Comparison of liner-thickness distribution during electroplating without auxiliary agent, with auxiliary anodes and with screens (schematic representation).*
*1 Anode, 2 Cathode, 3 Auxiliary anode, 4 Screen.*

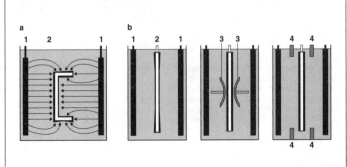

## Table 1. Areas of application for coatings

| Coating system | Coating material | Main application |
|---|---|---|
| Electroplated liner | Zn, ZnNi<br>Cr<br>Sn, Ag, Au | Corrosion protection<br>Wear protection<br>Electrical contacts |
| Chemical coatings | NiP, NiP dispersions<br>Cu, Sn, Pd, Au | Wear and corrosion protection<br>Electronic applications |
| Hot-immersion coatings | Zn, Al<br>Sn | Corrosion protection<br>Electrical contacts |
| Paints<br>(wet and powder-based paints) | Organic polymers<br>Pigments (color particles) | (Decorative) corrosion protection<br>Wear reduction<br>Electrical insulation |
| PVD/CVD coatings<br>(plasma technology) | TiN, TiCN, TiAlN<br>DLC: diamond-like carbon<br>i-C(WC), a-C:H | Wear protection of tools<br>Reducing friction and<br>wear on components |

### Nickel
Electrolytically deposited nickel coatings offer limited corrosion protection with an attractive visual appearance. One area of automotive engineering in which this is chiefly used is the nickel-plating of spark-plug shells.

### Chrome
In the case of chrome coatings, a distinction is made between hard chrome and bright chrome. Bright chrome is used as a protective top coating approx. 0.3 µm thick with a nickel or copper/nickel intermediate layer. In the past, fenders and molding strips were coated with bright chrome. However, this coating system has experienced a noticeable decline in automotive engineering.

Hard-chrome coatings are chrome coatings with a thickness >2 µm. Owing to the high level of hardness of the electrolytically deposited chrome coating, it is ideally suited for use as a wear-protection coating. In the past, hard-chrome coatings were often applied in strong thicknesses and then mechanically reworked. Due to further developments in plant engineering, components today are increasingly custom-coated with coating thicknesses ranging from 5 to 10 µm, and then used without reworking (e.g. components for fuel injectors).

### Tin
Electrolytically deposited tin coatings are mainly used as contact surfaces for plug-in and switch contacts, and as solder contact surfaces. A coating thickness of 2...3 µm is ideal for plug-in contacts. Greater coating thicknesses are required for solder applications in order to ensure solderability even after extended storage periods.

### Gold
Gold coatings are normally used for contacts subject to stringent requirements. They are characterized by good conductivity, low contact resistance, and good resistance to corrosion and pollutant gases. This ensures contact stability. Hard-gold coatings (with approx. 0.5% alloy constituents) are harder and more abrasion-resistant than pure-gold coatings and are suitable for contacts subject to mechanical load.

### Chemically deposited coatings (no external current)

In contrast to electroplated liners, chemically deposited coatings are characterized by a more uniform coating-thickness distribution on the component, since deposition does not occur under the influence of an external electric field. Owing to the slow deposition rate and the costly chemicals in the coating bath, they are more expensive than electroplated liners. The following have become widespread in industry:

– <u>Chemical nickel</u> (nickel/phosphorus) as a corrosion- and wear-protection coating.
– <u>Chemical copper</u> and <u>chemical tin</u> in pcb technology.

### Hot-immersion coatings

Hot-immersion coatings are deposited by immersing the substrates in a molten metal bath.

Cathodically effective hot-immersion coatings are used to protect low-alloyed steels against corrosion. Zinc, zinc/aluminum and aluminum are used. Coating start material such as sheet and strip is a cheap and widely used practice. However, free punch edges must be accepted here.

Tin and tin-alloy coatings deposited in hot-immersion priming are primarily used as surfaces for plug connectors and as soldering surfaces.

### Zinc-lamella coatings

Zinc-lamella structures are coatings based on zinc and aluminum lamellas and an inorganic binder. They are applied by immersion centrifuging or electrostatic spraying and thermal hardening. Zinc-lamella coatings are low-coast corrosion-protection coatings for mass-produced steel parts (e.g. screws).

### Paint coatings

Paints have a wide variation range because of their broad chemical bases and numerous means of application, such as brushing, spraying, and immersing, even with the use of current (CD: <u>c</u>athodic deposition).

Paint coatings can also fulfill a multitude of different functions. In motor vehicles, the primary function fulfilled by paint coatings is corrosion protection accompanied by a decorative effect, but other functions include wear protection, sound-proofing, or electrical insulation.

The body of a passenger car is protected and improved by a complex layered structure. The assemblies in the engine compartment, on the other hand, are usually only given one or two coats of paint. Less importance is placed here on decorative properties.

Low-solvent systems, above all water-based paints, are almost always used in automotive engineering. Powder-based paints and UV-hardening paints are even entirely solvent-free (P. 286 onwards).

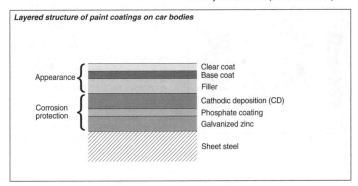

*Layered structure of paint coatings on car bodies*

Appearance
{
Clear coat
Base coat
Filler
}

Corrosion protection
{
Cathodic deposition (CD)
Phosphate coating
Galvanized zinc
}

Sheet steel

## PVD/CVD coatings

PVD/CVD coating systems are generally deposited in a vacuum supported by plasma or heat treatment on components and tools. There are two different procedures, depending on whether the coating-forming material is obtained from the solid (PVD: physical vapor deposition) or gaseous (CVD: chemical vapor deposition) phase. Most modern procedures combine both categories in "reactive" processes.

### Hard-material coatings

Tools are coated with hard material to increase their service life and their performance. A typical example of the tool coatings widely introduced onto the market is the gold-colored titanium nitride (TiN), which is produced, for example, by the cathodic sputtering or arc evaporation of titanium in a reaction with nitrogen. More recent coating systems, such as TiCN or TiAlN, can be used for high-speed cutting and sometimes also for material machining using low-volume lubricooling or when dry.

Superhard materials, such as diamond, are increasingly used to coat carbide tools.

### DLC coatings

Protecting components against wear is subject to special conditions. Here, the coating should establish a low coefficient of friction for the components that come into contact with each other and minimize the wear for the entire layout. DLC (diamond-like carbon) coatings protect not only the coated component against wear, but also the uncoated opposed body. They have a very low coefficient of friction of 0.1...0.2, both in a dry friction pairing against steel and under media. DLC layers are media-resistant and have a corrosion-inhibiting effect. Due to these advantages, DLC coatings have become the most important in the field of coating components. However, it must be noted that coatings containing hydrogen will degrade in an oxidizing atmosphere at a local temperature of 350 °C and higher. Hard-material coatings, such as TiN, can withstand considerably higher temperatures and are also used in component coating.

Different coating compositions and processes allow materials to be adapted to different wear loads or combinations of abrasive, vibration, sliding, seizure, and adhesive wear. As there is no standardization for DLC coatings, it is necessary to carefully check the coating properties in wear tests before replacing a coating with a diamond-like coating made by a different manufacturer. Plasma-assisted PVD and CVD processes are conducted in such a way that the temperature of the component does not exceed 250 °C during coating. This avoids impairing the hardness of the steel base material.

Low-friction carbon coatings containing metal carbide i-C(WC) are electrically conductive and have a microhardness of approx. 1,800 HV at a modulus of elasticity of 150 to 200 GPa.

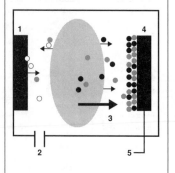

**Schematic of plasma-assisted PVD/CVD coating in vacuum chamber**
1 Unbalanced magnetron cathode with sputter target, 2 Gas inlet,
3 Intensive ion bombardment,
4 Substrate, 5 Substrate tension.

○ Argon,
● Metal/carbon,
● Nitrogen/hydrogen.

In comparison, metal-free carbon coatings (a-C:H) offer increased hardness of approx. 3,500 HV and significantly improved wear resistance, but this is accompanied by an increase in brittleness. They are electrically insulating.

With thicknesses of 2 to 4 µm, diamond-like carbon coatings offer very good wear protection and are especially suitable for precision components subject to high mechanical loads. There is no rework needed after coating. In high-pressure pumps for diesel and gasoline injection, the piston is sealed against the cylinder only by way of a particularly close-toleranced gap of a few micrometers. Here, DLC coatings on the piston ensure reliable operation throughout its service life.

# Diffusion coatings

Surface treatment can be selectively combined with surface hardening by using the diffusion process to thermochemically carburize, carbonitride, or chromate the metal, or treat it with boron or vanadium (see P. 386 onwards.). The metal can also be oxidized, nitrided, or sulfided without hardening.

# Conversion coatings

Conversion coatings are formed not by the application of a material, but by the chemical/electrochemical conversion of the base material.

### Browning coatings
Browning coatings consist of thin iron-oxide layers (predominantly $Fe_3O_4$) which are formed by the oxidation of the steel in an alkaline, aqueous solution containing nitrite at temperatures >100 °C. With subsequent oiling, they offer temporary corrosion protection.

### Phosphating coatings
Phosphating coatings are formed on steel, galvanized steel, and aluminum in solutions containing phosphoric acid by immersion or spraying. Zinc-phosphate coatings are predominantly used as a wash primer for paint coatings. Manganese phosphate serves as a wear-protection coating with anti-seizure properties, and as a wash primer for other coatings to improve component antifriction properties.

### Anodized coatings
Anodized coatings are formed by the electrochemical conversion of metal into metal oxide in aqueous electrolytes. Aluminum, magnesium, and titanium can be anodized. Anodized coatings on aluminum materials are widely used for corrosion and wear protection.

## Patent system

New ideas and inventions need not only be thought out, they also must be protected against imitators. In the case of inventions whose imitation cannot be proven (e.g. manufacturing methods), the competitive advantage derived from an invention can be protected by secrecy. However, this is not always possible or sensible. Patent law provides a better means of protection.

### What is a patent?
A patent is a legal title conferring on the patent holder (e.g. person, company, institution) the sole right over a specific area (e.g. domestically and in other countries) for a limited time (maximum 20 years) to prevent others from manufacturing, selling, or using the patented invention.

### What can be patented?
Patents are only granted to inventions which are new, are based on an inventive activity, and are commercially utilizable. An invention is deemed to be new if, prior to the day of the patent application, i.e. the "priority date", it was not known to the public in any form, i.e. it did not belong to state-of-the-art technology. It is deemed to be based on an inventive activity if, to the expert, it is not obviously derived from state-of-the-art technology. The following are patentable:
- Objects (e.g. spark plug)
- Processes/procedures (e.g. a specific manufacturing process)
- Chemical substances/materials (e.g. medicines)
- Computer programs, provided they make a technical contribution to state-of-the-art technology (e.g. ABS software)

A patent is a form of industrial property right. In addition, there are utility-model patents which are used to protect commodities. Further possibilities of protection are derived from the design law, copyright, trademark law, and the recent semiconductor-protection law.

### Registering an invention
The patent engineer of a company checks whether the possibility exists to protect an invention application submitted by an employee, and whether the application for an industrial property right appears advisable from an economic point of view. If the prerequisites are in place, the application for an industrial property right is submitted to the relevant patent offices, both at home and in other countries. However, not every patent application will result in a patent. Roughly 50% of applications are rejected because they are familiar from state-of-the-art technology (e.g. earlier patent applications).

The number of new patent applications is an indicator of the creativity of the patent applicant and its employees. Bosch, for example, registered more than 2,400 patents in the year 2000.

### Publication
Patent applications and granted patents are published. Not only are they useful instruments for market observation, they also provide an insight into innovative developments in all fields of technology. They are, therefore, an effective means of avoiding parallel developments and double research.

### Benefits of patents
Patents are important aids for technology transfer to promote innovation potential:
- The exclusive right to a commercially utilizable invention simplifies the financing of corporate research and development costs.
- Patents, in their capacity as an exclusive right, strengthen the market position of companies.
- Patented inventions prompt research into alternative solutions.
- Licenses for patents encourage the spread of new technologies.

# Tribology

## Purpose and goals

Tribology is defined as "The study of the phenomena and mechanisms of friction, lubrication, and wear of surfaces in relative motion". Industrial application is directed toward gathering information for use in extending the service lives of products and maximizing utilization of resources. The specific activities are as follows:

- Analysis of friction and wear
- Analysis and evaluation of tribological damage
- Provision of technical recommendations on materials, lubricants, and design (for damage control and in the design of new components and products)
- Quality assurance
- Assistance in providing optimum performance
- Service-life assessment
- Development and selection of new materials and lubricants

The complexity of the task renders a synergetic approach essential. The disciplines involved include materials science, physics, chemistry, and mechanical engineering.

## Definitions

**Friction** (GfT Worksheet No. 7)
Friction is physical resistance to relative motion at two or more surfaces in a state of mutual contact. The most significant physical parameters for describing friction are:
Friction force: The amount of force with which a motion is resisted.
Coefficient of friction (or friction factor): Friction force relative to normal force.
Friction power: Friction force x sliding speed.
Classification of friction:
1. According to condition of friction (type of contact)
2. According to type of motion

Condition of friction (type of contact)
Gas friction: A gas layer completely separates the base object and the opposed body from one another, thereby assuming the entire load.

Fluid friction (hydrodynamic and hydrostatic friction): A fluid layer completely separates the base object and opposed body from one another, thereby assuming the entire load.
Combination friction: The base object and the opposed body are in mutual contact at surface peaks. The load is shared by the fluid/lubricating film and by the objects in contact.
Dry or boundary friction: The lubricating film no longer performs any support function, but residue from previously absorbed lubricants continues to exercise a tribological effect.
Solid-body friction: Direct contact between the opposed surfaces.

Types of motion
Possible types of motion contact include sliding friction, rolling friction, and combinations of the two.

In many cases, the effects which friction produces in machine components are undesirable, as there are negative consequences for energy consumption and/or associated temperature increases and/or changes to the material. In other cases, friction can make a necessary contribution to proper operation. This is the case with self-locking transmission devices, where the lubricant must furnish a specific coefficient of friction, and in some types of clutches, in which defined levels of friction are also required.

**Tribological concepts**
(GfT Worksheet No. 7)
Tribology embraces the science and associated technology devoted to the interaction of surfaces in mutually opposed states of motion. It focuses on the entire range of friction, wear, and lubrication, and also includes the effects at the contact surfaces of solids as well as those between solids and gases.

Tribotechnology (GfT Worksheet No. 7)
This branch is devoted to the actual technical application of tribology.

Tribological stress
(GfT Worksheet No. 7)
The stress which results at a solid body from contact with, and the relative motion of, an opposed body in solid, fluid, or gaseous form.

Tribological damage
Damage resulting from tribological stress. This contrasts with the concepts of wear and wear damage as defined in GfT Worksheet No. 7, which always include material erosion. Here, the term "tribological damage" extends to embrace both numerous tribologically induced changes to the material's surface, as well as reductions in operational efficacy which according to DIN are not regarded as wear.

**Wear**
(GfT Worksheet No. 7)
Progressive loss of material from the surface of a solid body, caused by tribological stress. Wear is characterized by the presence of abraded particles, as well as changes in both the material and structure of the surface which is exposed to tribological stress. This type of wear is generally undesirable, and impairs functionality (exception: "running-in" processes). Thus any such procedures which enhance the object's operational value are not considered as wear.

## Tribological system

Wear can be regarded as a system characteristic. There exists no specific material value for "wear-resistance" as such, corresponding to, say, tensile strength in materials science. The tribological system for the contact surfaces which are the focus of the present discussion consists of:
– The material "A elements": base object, opposed body, intermediate material and surrounding medium (see figure)
– The properties P of the elements A
– The reciprocal influence R between the elements A

The element properties and their reciprocal effects form the <u>structure of the tribological system</u>. As the composite stress factor (comprising forces, motion, temperature) acts on this structure, it is transformed into useful quantities and loss quantities. The latter include friction and wear.

As tribological stresses are surface stresses, the previously mentioned P properties must also be viewed as surface characteristics. In technical applications, there is frequently a substantial discrepancy between the material values measured for the base material and those actually found on examination of the surfaces. Manufacturing procedures, cleaning processes, and the operating environment can all cause changes in the surface layer, provoking variations in the tribological response of the material.

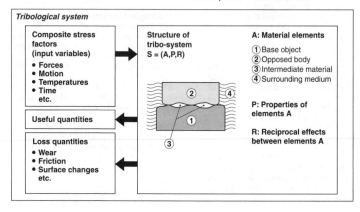

*Tribological system*

## Types of wear

Wear processes can be classified according to the type of stress and the materials involved (system structure), a classification from which the following types of wear emerge (GfT Worksheet No. 7):

**System structure**
**Solid body/solid body:**
Sliding → Sliding wear
Rolling → Rolling wear
Oscillation → Vibration wear

**System structure**
**Solid body/liquid:**
Flow/oscillation → cavitation erosion

## Manifestations of wear

The manifestations of wear as defined by GfT Worksheet No. 7 apply to the surface changes resulting from abrasion, as well as to the type and shape of the resulting particles.

## Wear mechanisms

### Adhesion
Formation and separation of (atomic) surface bonds. There is a transfer of material when the separation deviates from the original boundary between the base object and the opposed body.

The adhesion process starts at the molecular level, but can expand until damage on a massive scale occurs (seizing).

### Abrasion
Scraping stress and microscopic scraping action, performed by the base object, the opposed body, reaction products, or solid particles in the intermediate medium.

### Surface fatigue
Alternating tribological loads (e.g. impact, rolling, sliding stress, cavitation) cause mechanical stresses. The resulting fissures lead to material separation (separation of wear particles).

### Tribo-chemical reactions
Reaction of the base and/or opposed object with the intermediate material (and surrounding medium), caused by tribological stress.

## Wear quantities

Rates of wear are defined by the so-called wear quantities. These provide direct or indirect indices of the variations in the shape or in the mass of a body which are traceable to wear (definitions based on GfT Worksheet No. 7).

### Coefficient of wear
The quantities by which wear is defined can only be indicated as system-specific quantities.

The wear coefficient $k$ facilitates comparison of wear rates at varying surface pressures and speeds:

$$k = W_v/(F \cdot s) \text{ in mm}^3/(\text{N} \cdot \text{m})$$

$F$     Force
$W_v$     Volumetric wear
$s$     Sliding distance

## Tribological damage analysis

In cases where operation of a component results in damage or changes of a kind which could be expected to affect the component's functional integrity, GfT indicates that all stresses and characteristics occurring at the points of tribological contact should be investigated (GfT Worksheet No. 7).

The topographical and material analysis of tribological contact (base object, opposed body, intermediate material) provides information on the mechanisms causing the damage and/or wear (adhesion, abrasion, surface fatigue, tribochemical reaction). These investigations also provide data on accompanying phenomena and on changes in the lubricant.

The analysis must be based on the following information:
– surface structure
– material composition of the surface
– microstructure
– microhardness
– intrinsic tension
– material composition and chemical/physical changes in the lubricant

## Tribological test procedures

GfT Worksheet No. 7 divides wear testing into 6 categories:
Category I: Operational testing.
Category II: Test-stand procedure with complete machine.
Category III: Test-stand procedure with assembly or entire unit.
Category IV: Testing with unmodified component or reduced assembly.
Category V: Simulated operational stress with test specimens.
Category VI: Model test with simple test specimens.

The original production assembly is employed for testing according to Categories I through III, while the structure of the system is modified substantially from Category IV onward. It is highly advisable to integrate the tribological examinations of essential and safety-related products into a tribological test sequence:
– Model testing (e.g. pin and sphere, plate for sliding and vibration wear)
– Component testing
– Product testing

Model tests (with simple test specimens), although frequently employed in basic research, are no longer used for examining complex tribological systems. Of the various elements in the sequence of tribological tests, it is examination of the actual product itself that provides the most reliable information. Modern research procedures (such as radio-nuclide testing) make it possible to garner precise data on wear as a function of composite stress.

For Radio-nuclide testing (RNT) the parts to be examined are marked radioactively. The abraded particles can then be detected "on-line" by gamma-ray measurement.

## Inhibiting wear

Variations in design, materials and lubricants can all be employed to improve tribological properties.

**Design**
The design options include:
– Improving the surface topography
– Reduction of surface pressures by raising the contact-surface ratio
– Surface reinforcement
– Improving lubrication efficiency

**Material**
The materials options include:
– Skin-layer hardening
– Skin-layer remelting
– Surface-layer remelt alloying
– Thermochemical processes
– Electrical and chemical plating
– Resurface welding
– Thermal spraying
– Metal plating
– PVD/CVD layers (physical/chemical vapor deposition, e.g. TiN, TiC)
– Ion-beam treatment (e.g. ion implantation, ion-beam mixing, transition-layer mixing, and ion-beam supported coating)
– Diamond-like carbon coatings (metallic)
– Anti-friction paints
– Penetration coatings (soft metals prevent high local surface pressures)

*Material layers subject to tribological stress at surface*

There exist a multiplicity of surface treatment and coating processes. The process parameters can frequently be adjusted to focus on specific kinds of wear. The result is a wide potential field of options for applying tribology to assist products in meeting numerous requirements.

### Lubricants

In many cases, selection of the appropriate lubricant (P. 266) and optimal lubrication-system design will exercise a dramatic effect on the tribological properties – the potential is frequently greater than that represented by a change in materials. The choice of lubricant is the initial response when dealing with unsatisfactory operating characteristics.

### Lubricity

Lubricity testing is based on specially defined wear parameters. The test results provide a relative index of the efficiency of fluids as separating media in defined tribological systems. In evaluations under otherwise identical conditions, a fluid displays a higher lubricity than another when it produces relative reductions in wear between the opposed elements in the tribological system and/or lower generation of friction energy (DIN/ISO 12156).

It is important to distinguish between lubricity and viscosity.

Descriptions and specific numerical data on lubricity are derived from product, component and model wear testing with specifically defined stress and load parameters. The results are indicated in specific test data for wear.

The results of this type of testing are valid only for the object tribological system.

In many products, the separating element in the tribological system is also a flow medium, as in hydraulic and fuel-injection systems.

The lubricity level of such a fluid must suffice to ensure reliable operation and a long service life.

Special additives can be employed to enhance lubricity.

## References:

Source of the often quoted Worksheet No. 7 (50 pages):
Gesellschaft für Tribologie e. V. (German Tribology Society) (GfT)
Ernststrasse 12, D-47443 Moers.
www.gftev.de

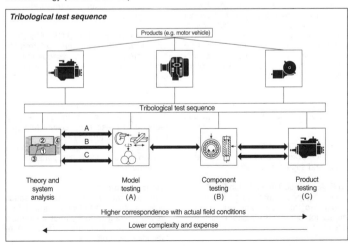

**Tribological test sequence**

Products (e.g. motor vehicle)

Tribological test sequence

A
B
C

Theory and system analysis

Model testing (A)

Component testing (B)

Product testing (C)

Higher correspondence with actual field conditions

Lower complexity and expense

# Lubricants

## Terms and definitions

Lubricants provide mutual insulation for components in a state of relative motion. The lubricant's function is to prevent direct contact between these components, thereby reducing wear and minimizing, or optimizing, friction. Lubricants serve as coolants, friction-surface sealants, and corrosion inhibitors, and can also reduce running noise. Lubricants may be solid, consistent, liquid, or gaseous in form. Specific lubricants are selected with reference to design characteristics, materials combinations, the ambient conditions, and the stress factors encountered at the friction surface.

### Additives

Additives are substances mixed into the lubricant in order to improve specific properties. These substances modify either the lubricant's physical characteristics (e.g. viscosity index improvers, pour-point depressors) or its chemical properties (e.g. oxidation inhibitors, corrosion inhibitors). In addition, the properties of the friction surfaces themselves can be modified by additives which change the friction characteristics (friction modifiers), protect against wear (anti-wear agents), or provide protection against scoring and seizure (extreme-pressure additives). Great care must be exercised in order to ensure that the additives are correctly matched with each other and with the base lubricant.

### AFC (Anti-Friction Coating)

Solid lubricant combinations which a binding agent holds in place on the friction surfaces.

### Ash (DIN 51 575, 51 803)

The mineral residue which remains after oxide and sulfate incineration.

### ATF (Automatic Transmission Fluid)

Special-purpose lubricants specifically formulated to meet stringent requirements for operation in automatic transmissions.

### Bingham bodies

Materials whose flow characteristics differ from those of Newtonian liquids.

### Bleeding (Oil separation, DIN 51 817)

Separation of the base oil and the thickener in a lubricating grease.

### Cloud point (DIN ISO 3015)

The temperature at which mineral oil becomes opaque due to the formation of paraffin crystals or precipitation of other solids.

### Consistency (DIN ISO 2137)

A measure of the ease with which lubricating greases and pastes can be deformed.

### Doped lubricants

Lubricants containing additives for improving specific properties (e.g. aging stability, wear protection, corrosion protection, viscosity-temperature characteristics).

### Dropping point (DIN ISO 2176)

Temperature at which a lubricating grease attains a specified viscosity under specified test conditions.

### EP lubricants (Extreme Pressure)

See high-pressure lubricants.

### Fire point/flash point (DIN ISO 2592)

The lowest temperature (referred to 1,013 hPa) at which a gaseous mineral product initially flashes (flash point), or continues to burn for at least 5 secs (burning point).

### Flow pressure (DIN 51 805)

According to Kesternich, the gas pressure required to press a consistent lubricant through a standardized test nozzle. The flow pressure is an index of a lubricant's starting flow characteristics, particularly at low temperatures.

### Friction modifiers

Polar lubricant additives which reduce friction in the mixed-friction range and increase bearing capacity after adsorption on the surface of the metal. They also inhibit stick-slip behavior.

### Gel-type greases
Lubricants with inorganic gelling agents (e.g. Bentonites, silica gels).

### Graphite
Solid lubricant with layer-lattice structure. Graphite provides excellent lubrication when combined with water (e.g. high atmospheric humidity) and in carbon-dioxide atmospheres or when combined with oils. It does not inhibit friction in a vacuum.

### High-pressure lubricants
Contain additives to enhance load-bearing capacity, to reduce wear, and to reduce scoring (generally provide good performance in steel-to-steel and steel-to-ceramic applications).

### Hydro-crack oils
Refined mineral oils with increased VI (130 to 140).

### Induction period
The period which elapses before substantial changes occur in a lubricant (e.g. aging of an oil containing an oxidation inhibitor).

### Inhibitors
Lubricant protection additives (e.g. oxidation and corrosion inhibitors).

### Longlife engine oils
Oils for significantly extended oil-change intervals.

### Low-temperature sludge
Products of oil degradation which form in the engine crankcase due to incomplete combustion and condensate at low engine load. Low-temperature sludge increases wear and can cause engine damage. Modern high-quality engine oils inhibit its formation.

### Metal soaps
Reaction products from metals or from their compounds with fatty acids. They are used as thickeners for grease and as friction modifiers.

### Mineral oils
Mineral oils are distillates or raffinates produced from petroleum or coal. They consist of numerous hydrocarbons in various chemical compositions. Classification is according to the predominant component: paraffin-based oils (chain-shaped saturated hydrocarbons), naphthene-based oils (closed-chain saturated hydrocarbons, generally with 5 or 6 carbon atoms per ring) or aromatic oils (e.g. alkylbenzene). These substances are distinguished by major variations in their respective chemical and physical properties.

### Molybdenum disulfide ($MoS_2$)
A solid lubricant with layer-lattice structure. Only low cohesive forces are present between the individual layers, so their mutual displacement is characterized by relatively low shear forces. A reduction in friction is only obtained when $MoS_2$ is applied in suitable form to the surface of the metal (e.g. in combination with a binder such as ($MoS_2$ anti-friction coating).

### Multigrade oils
Engine and transmission lubricants with good resistance to viscosity-temperature change (high viscosity index VI). These oils are formulated for year-round use in motor vehicles; their viscosity ratings extend through several SAE grades.

### Penetration (DIN ISO 2137)
Depth (in $10^{-1}$ mm) to which a standardized cone penetrates into a consistent lubricant within a defined period and at a specified temperature. The larger the number, the softer the lubricant.

### Polar substances
Dipolar molecules are easily adsorbed onto metal surfaces. They enhance adhesion and bearing capacity, thus reducing friction and wear. This category includes, for example, esters, ethers, polyglycols, and fatty acids.

### Pour point (DIN ISO 3016)
The lowest temperature at which an oil continues to flow when cooled under defined conditions.

**PTFE** (<u>p</u>oly<u>t</u>e<u>t</u>ra<u>f</u>luor <u>e</u>thylene, Teflon®,)
Thermoplastic with outstanding properties as a solid lubricant, particularly at very low sliding velocities (< 0.1 m/s). PTFE only becomes brittle below approx. 270 °C. The upper service temperature for use is approx. 260 °C. Above this level, it decomposes with toxic cleavage products.

## Rheology

Science dealing with the flow characteristics of materials. These are generally represented in the shape of flow curves. Coordinate plotting:

Shear stress $\tau = F/A$ (N/m² = Pa)

$F$ force, $A$ surface area vs. shear rate $D = v/y$ (s⁻¹)
(linear shear rate)
$v$ velocity, $y$ thickness of lubricating film.

### Dynamic viscosity

$\eta = \tau/D$ (Pa · s)
The former unit "centiPoise" (cP) is equal to the unit (mPa · s).

### Kinematic viscosity

$\nu = \eta/\varrho$ (mm²/s)
$\varrho$ density (kg/m³).
The former unit "centiStokes" (cSt) is equal to the unit (mm²/s).

### Newtonian fluids

They display a linear relationship between $\tau$ and $D$ in the shape of a straight line through zero, with the slope increasing as a function of viscosity.

All materials not characterized by this kind of flow behavior are classified as non-Newtonian fluids.

### Intrinsically viscous flow behavior

Decrease in viscosity with increasing shear rate (e.g. liquid grease, multigrade oil with VI improvers).

### Dilatant flow behavior

Increase in viscosity with increasing shear rate.

### Plastic flow behavior

Formability of an intrinsically viscous fluid supplemented by yield point (e.g. lubricating greases).

### Thixotropy

A characteristic of those non-Newtonian fluids that display an increase in viscosity proportional to shear time, and only gradually recover their original viscosity once shearing ceases.

### Rheopexy

A characteristic of those non-Newtonian fluids that display an increase in viscosity proportional to shear time, and only gradually recover their original viscosity once shearing ceases.

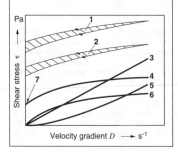

*Flow curves*
*1 Rheopex, 2 Thixotropic, 3 Newtonian,*
*4 Plastic, 5 Dilatant, 6 Intrinsically viscous,*
*7 Yield point.*

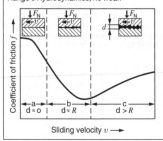

*Stribeck curve*
*R Surface roughness, $F_N$ Normal force,*
*d Distance between basic and opposed body,*
*Range a Solid-body friction, high wear,*
*Range b Mixed friction, moderate wear,*
*Range c Hydrodynamics, no wear.*

## Stribeck curve
Portrays friction levels between two liquid- or grease-lubricated tribological systems separated by a narrowing gap (e.g. lubricated plain or roller bearings) as a function of sliding speed.

### Solid-body friction
The height of the lubricant layer is lower than that of the roughness protrusions in the material's surface.

### Mixed friction
The height of the lubricant layer is approximately equal to that of the roughness protrusions.

### Hydrodynamics
Complete separation between primary and opposed body (virtually wear-free condition).

## Table 1. Viscosity grades for industrial lubricating oils to ISO 3448 (DIN 51 519).

| ISO viscosity grade | Medium viscosity at 40 °C mm²/s | Kinematic viscosity limits at 40 °C mm²/s min. | max. |
|---|---|---|---|
| ISO VG 2 | 2.2 | 1.98 | 2.42 |
| ISO VG 3 | 3.2 | 2.88 | 3.52 |
| ISO VG 5 | 4.6 | 4.14 | 5.06 |
| ISO VG 7 | 6.8 | 6.12 | 7.48 |
| ISO VG 10 | 10 | 9.00 | 11.0 |
| ISO VG 15 | 15 | 13.5 | 16.5 |
| ISO VG 22 | 22 | 19.8 | 24.2 |
| ISO VG 32 | 32 | 28.8 | 35.2 |
| ISO VG 46 | 46 | 41.4 | 50.6 |
| ISO VG 68 | 68 | 61.2 | 74.8 |
| ISO VG 100 | 100 | 90.0 | 110 |
| ISO VG 150 | 150 | 135 | 165 |
| ISO VG 220 | 220 | 198 | 242 |
| ISO VG 320 | 320 | 288 | 352 |
| ISO VG 460 | 460 | 414 | 506 |
| ISO VG 680 | 680 | 612 | 748 |
| ISO VG 1000 | 1,000 | 900 | 1,100 |
| ISO VG 1500 | 1,500 | 1,350 | 1,650 |

## Viscosity (DIN 1342, DIN EN ISO 3104)
Defines the internal friction of substances. It indicates the degree of resistance (internal friction) with which the substance's molecules oppose displacement forces (see Rheology).

## Viscosity grades
Classification of oils in specific viscosity ranges. ISO viscosity grades (DIN 51 519, see Table 1).
SAE viscosity grades (ISO/DIS 10 369, SAE J300, DIN 51 512, SAE J306c, see Tables 2 and 3).

## Viscosity index (VI) (DIN ISO 2909)
The viscosity index VI is a mathematically-derived number expressing the change in a mineral-oil product's viscosity relative to its temperature. The greater the VI, the lower the effect of temperature on the viscosity.

## Worked penetration (DIN ISO 2137)
Penetration of a grease sample after it is warmed to 25 °C and processed in a grease kneader.

## Yield point (DIN 13 342)
The minimum shear stress at which a substance begins to flow. Above the yield point, the rheological characteristics of plastic substances are the same as those of liquids.

## Table 2. SAE viscosity grades for transmission lubricants (SAE J306c).

| SAE viscosity grade | Maximum temperature °C for dynamic viscosity at 150,000 mPa·s (ASTM D 2983) | Kinematic viscosity mm²/s at 100 °C (ASTM D 445) min. | max. |
|---|---|---|---|
| 70 W | -55 | 4.1 | – |
| 75 W | -40 | 4.1 | – |
| 80 W | -26 | 7.0 | – |
| 85 W | -12 | 11.0 | – |
| 90 | – | 13.5 | 24.0 |
| 140 | – | 24.0 | 41.0 |
| 250 | – | 41.0 | – |

**Table 3. SAE viscosity grades for engine oils/transmission lubricants (SAE J300, April 1997)**

| SAE viscosity grade | Viscosity (ASTM D 5293) mPa·s at °C max. | Limit pumping viscosity (ASTM D 4684) with no yield point mPa·s at °C max. | Kinematic viscosity (ASTM D 445) mm²/s at 100 °C min. | max. | Viscosity under high shear (ASTM D 4683, CEC L-36-A-90, ASTM D 4741) mPa·s at 150 °C and 10⁶ s⁻¹ min. |
|---|---|---|---|---|---|
| 0 W | 3,250 at −30 | 60,000 at −40 | 3.8 | − | − |
| 5 W | 3,500 at −25 | 60,000 at −35 | 3.8 | − | − |
| 10 W | 3,500 at −20 | 60,000 at −30 | 4.1 | − | − |
| 15 W | 3,500 at −15 | 60,000 at −25 | 5.6 | − | − |
| 20 W | 4,500 at −10 | 60,000 at −20 | 5.6 | − | − |
| 25 W | 6,000 at −5 | 60,000 at −15 | 9.3 | − | − |
| 20 | − | − | 5.6 | <9.3 | 2.6 |
| 30 | − | − | 9.3 | <12.5 | 2.9 |
| 40 | − | − | 12.5 | <16.3 | 2.9 (0W−40, 5W−40, 10W−40) |
| 40 | − | − | 12.5 | <16.3 | 3.7 (15W−40, 20W−40, 25W−40, 40) |
| 50 | − | − | 16.3 | <21.9 | 3.7 |
| 60 | − | − | 21.9 | <26.1 | 3.7 |
| 5W-50 | 3,500 at −30 | 30,000 at −40 | 16.5 | 20.0 | 5.0 |

## Engine oils

Engine oils are employed primarily to lubricate contiguous components in relative motion within the internal-combustion engine. The oil also removes heat generated by friction, carries abraded particles away from the friction surface, washes out contaminants, holds them in suspension, and protects metals against corrosion. The most common engine oils are mineral oils treated with additives (HD oils: <u>H</u>eavy <u>D</u>uty for extreme operating conditions). Higher stress-resistance requirements combined with extended oil-change intervals have led to widespread application of semi and semi-synthetic oils (e.g. hydro-crack oils). The quality of an engine oil is determined by its origin, the refining processes used on the mineral oil (except in the case of synthetic oils) and the additive composition.

Additives are classified according to their respective functions:
– Viscosity-index (VI) improvers
– Pour-point improvers
– Oxidation and corrosion inhibitors
– Detergent and dispersant additives
– Extreme-pressure (EP) additives
– Friction modifiers
– Anti-foaming agents

Oil is subjected to considerable thermal and mechanical stresses in the IC engine. The data on the physical properties of engine oils provide information on their application limits, but are not indicative of their other performance characteristics.

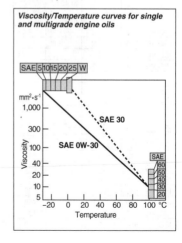

*Viscosity/Temperature curves for single and multigrade engine oils*

Therefore, there are several different test procedures for evaluating engine oils (see comparison of engine-oil performance categories):
– ACEA (Association des Constructeurs Européens de l'Automobile) standards, replaced the CCMC standards (Comité des Constructeurs d'Automobiles du Marché Commun) at the beginning of 1996
– API Classification (American Petroleum Institute)
– MIL Specifications (Military)
– Manufacturer's specifications

The approval criteria include the following:
– Sulfate-ash content
– Zinc content
– Engine type (diesel or spark-ignition engines, naturally aspirated or forced-induction engines)
– Load on power-transmission components and bearings
– Wear-protection properties
– Oil operating temperature (in oil pan)
– Combustion residue and chemical stress exerted on the oil by acidic combustion products
– The oil's detergent and residue-scavenging properties
– Its suitability for use with gasket and sealing materials

## ACEA (CCMC) Specifications

### Engine oils for gasoline engines
A1: Special high-lubricity oils with reduced viscosity at high temperatures and high shear.
A2: Conventional and high-lubricity engine oils without any restriction on viscosity grades. Higher requirements than CCMC G4 and API SH.
A3: Oils of this category meet higher requirements than A2 and CCMC G4 and G5.
A5: Improved "fuel economy" properties compared with A3 occasioned by lower viscosity incl. improved additive composition. Caution: Only for use in engines which have been designed for this purpose.

### Engine oils for passenger-car diesel engines
B1: Corresponding to A1 for low friction losses and, consequently, reduced fuel consumption.

B2: Conventional and high-lubricity engine oils compliant with the current minimum requirements (higher than those of CCMC PD2).
B3: Exceeds B2.
B4: Corresponds to B2, particularly suitable for VW TDI engines.
B5: Oils surpass B3 and B4, improved "fuel economy" properties, also satisfies VW 50600 and 50601. Caution: Only for use in engines which have been designed for this purpose.

### Engine oils for commercial-vehicle diesel engines
E1: Oils for naturally aspirated and turbocharged engines with normal intervals between oil changes.
E2: Derived from MB Specification Sheet 228.1. Primarily for engine designs predating the Euro-II standard.
E3: For Euro-II engines, derived from MB Specification Sheet 228.3. In comparison with the predecessor category CCMC D5, these evince a significant improvement in soot dispersion capability and a much reduced tendency to thicken.
E4: Currently the highest quality category for diesel engines compliant with the Euro-I and Euro-II standards and with high requirements, particularly for extended intervals between oil changes (according to manufacturer's specification). Based to a large extent on MB 228.5.

## API classification grades
S Grades (Service) for gasoline engines.
C Grades (Commercial) for diesel engines.
SF: For engines produced in the 1980s.
SG: Applicable since 1988, with more stringent sludge test, improved oxidation stability and wear protection.
SH: Since mid-1993, corresponds to API SG quality level, but with more stringent process requirements for oil grade testing.
SJ: Since October 1996, more tests than API SH.
SL: Since 2001, lower oil consumption compared with SJ, lower volatility, improved engine cleanness, greater resistance to aging.

CC: Engine oils for non-turbocharged diesel engines with low stress factors.

CD: Engine oils for non-turbocharged and turbocharged diesel engines, replaced by API CF in 1994.

CD-2: API CD requirements, plus additional requirements relevant to 2-stroke diesel engines.

CF-2: Oils with special 2-stroke properties (since 1994).

CE: Oils with CD performance characteristics, with supplementary test operation in U.S. Mack and Cummins engines.

CF: Replaced API CD in 1994. Specially for indirect injection, even if the sulfur content of the fuel is > 0.5%.

CF-4: As API CE, but with more stringent test procedure in single-cylinder Caterpillar turbo-diesel engines.

CG-4: For diesel engines operating under very stringent conditions. Exceeds API CD and CE. Fuel sulfur content < 0.5%. Required for engines compliant with post-1994 emission-control legislation.

CH4: Modern commercial-vehicle engine oil since 1998. Surpasses CG-4 in standards of wear, soot and viscosity. Longer oil-change intervals.

### ILSAC GF-3

Joint standard by General Motors, DaimlerChrysler, the Japanese automobile-manufacturers association, and U.S. engine-manufacturers association. In addition to API-SL, the standard requires a fuel-economy test.

### SAE viscosity grades

(ISO/DIS 10 369, SAE J 300, DIN 51 512, SAE J 306c)

The SAE (Society of Automotive Engineers) grades are the internationally accepted standard for defining viscosity. The standard provides no information on the quality of the oil. A distinction is drawn between single-grade and multigrade oils. Multigrade oils are the type in widespread use today.

Two series are employed for the designation (see Tables 2 and 3) where the letter "W" (Winter) is used to define specific cold-flow properties. The viscosity grades including the letter "W" are rated according to maximum cold viscosity, maximum

viscosity pumping temperature and the minimum viscosity at 100 °C; viscosity grades without the "W" are rated only according to viscosity at 100 °C.

### Multigrade oils

Multigrade oils are characterized by a less pronounced proportional relationship between temperature and viscosity. They reduce friction and wear, can be used all year round, and provide rapid lubrication for all engine components in cold starts.

### High-lubricity oils

Lubricating oils with multigrade properties, low cold viscosity, and special anti-friction additives. Extremely low engine friction under all operating conditions reduces fuel consumption.

## Transmission lubricants

Specifications for transmission oils are defined by the type of transmission and the stresses to which it is subjected throughout the entire range of operating conditions. The requirements (high pressure resistance, high viscosity stability relative to temperature, high resistance to aging, good anti-foaming properties, compatibility with gaskets and seals) can only be satisfied by lubricants treated with special additives. In contrast to engine oils, transmission oils contain no, or only minimal, "detergent" additives, considerably fewer basic constituents, and mostly no VI improvers (most of them would be sheared and thus become inactive). The use of unsuitable and qualitatively inferior oils results typically in damage to bearings and gear-tooth flanks.

The viscosity must also suit the specific application. Viscosity grades for vehicular transmissions are defined in DIN 51 512 and SAE J 306 (see Table 3).

Synthesized oils are being increasingly used to meet special requirements (e.g. poly-$a$-olefines). Advantages over standard mineral oils include superior temperature-viscosity properties and increased aging resistance.

**API Classification grades for transmission oils**

GL-1-GL-3: Outdated, no longer of practical significance.

GL-4: Transmission lubricants for moderate-stressed hypoid-gear transmissions, and for transmissions which operate at extreme speeds and impact loads, high rotational speeds and low torques, or low rotational speeds and high torques.

GL-5: Transmission lubricants for high-stressed hypoid-gear transmissions in passenger cars and in other vehicles where they are exposed to impact loads at high rotational speeds, and at high rotational speeds and low torques, or low rotational speeds and high torques.

GL-6: Oils for hypoid-gear transmissions with high axle offset and high loads.

MT-1: Non-synchromesh manual transmissions in U.S. trucks.

Many truck and component manufacturers have drawn up their own specifications and no longer rely on API.

**Lubricants for automatic transmissions**

(ATF: Automatic Transmission Fluid)
Automatic transmissions differ from their manual-shifted counterparts in the way they transfer torque; non-positive mechanical and hydrodynamic force transfer is supplemented by friction coupling arrangements. Thus, the friction response of automatic-transmission fluids is extremely important. Applications are basically classified according to the friction characteristics:

General Motors: Superseded grades: Type A, Suffix A, DEXRON®, DEXRON®B, DEXRON®II C, DEXRON® II D.
DEXRON® II E (valid through 1994).
DEXRON® III F/G. Valid since January 1 1994. Features more stringent requirements for oxidation stability and consistency in frictional coefficient.
Ford: MERCON® (valid since 1987).
Other manufacturers: In accordance with operating instructions.

## Lubricating oils

Lubricating oils comprise the components of basic oil and additive. The additives improve the properties of the basic oils, e.g. with regard to oxidation stability, corrosion protection, protection against scoring and seizure, or viscosity-temperature characteristics. In addition, system properties such as (static) friction and wear are optimized in the desired direction.

There are a wide range of designations in the form of letters and numbers (e.g. DIN 51 502) for the most varied applications (e.g. hydraulic fluids:

HL: Mineral-oil-based hydraulic fluid with additives for improving corrosion protection and resistance to aging.

HLP: Like HL, but with extra additives against scoring and seizure, HVLP: like HLP with extra VI improver).

**Table 4. Composition of lubricating greases**

| Base oils | Thickeners | Additives |
|---|---|---|
| Mineral oils | Metal soaps | Oxidation inhibitors |
| – Paraffinic | (Li,Na,Ca,Ba,Al) | Fe, Cu ions, sequestering agents |
| – Naphthenic | Normal | Corrosion inhibitors |
| – Aromatic | Hydroxi- | Extreme-pressure additives |
| | Complex | (EP additives) |
| Poly-$\alpha$-olefines | | Wear-protection additives |
| Alkyl aromatics | Polyureas | (anti-wear additives) |
| Esterols | | Friction reducers |
| Polyalcohols | PTFE | (friction modifiers) |
| Silicones | PE | Adhesion improvers |
| Phenyletherols | Bentonites | Detergents, dispersants |
| Perfluorpolyethers | Silica gels | VI improvers |
| | | Solid lubricants |

Whatever the friction pairing, the large number of lubricant components can be used to develop a high-performance lubricant.

## Lubricating greases

Lubricating greases are thickened lubricating oils. A great advantage that greases enjoy over oil is that they do not drain from the friction surfaces. Complicated measures designed to seal them in place are therefore unnecessary (e.g. application in wheel bearings and moving systems such as ABS, alternators, ignition distributors, windshield-wiper motors, servo motors). Table 4 provides a general overview of the components in a consistent lubricating grease as blended from three basic components – base oil, thickener, and additive.

Mineral oils are usually employed as the basic oil component, although full-synthetic oils have recently become more common as a replacement (e.g. due to more stringent requirements for aging stability, cold-flow properties, viscosity-temperature characteristics).

Thickeners are used as a binder for the base oil component; metal soaps being generally employed. They bind the oil in a sponge-like soap structure (micelle) by means of inclusions and Van der Waals forces. The higher the proportion of thickener in the grease (depends on the type of thickener), the less the penetration (depth of penetration of a test cone into the grease sample) and the higher the NLGI grades (see Table 5).

The additives serve to modify physical and chemical properties of the lubricating grease to achieve specific objectives (such as improvement of anti-oxidation properties, increased protection against scoring and seizure (EP additives), and reduction of friction and wear).

Solid lubricants (e.g. $MoS_2$) are also added to lubricating greases (for instance for lubricating constant-velocity joints in motor vehicles).

Specific lubricating greases are selected with reference to their physical characteristics and their effects on the friction surface, and to minimize interaction between the grease and the contact materials.

Example:
Mutually antagonistic effects with polymers:
– Formation of stress cracks
– Consistency changes
– Polymer degradation
– Swelling, shrinkage, brittleness

Thus, for example, mineral-oil greases and greases based on synthetic hydrocarbons should not come in contact with elastomers used together with brake fluid (polyglycol base) (e.g. substantial swelling of EPDM elastomers).

In addition, lubricating greases with varying compositions should not be mixed (changes in physical properties, grease liquefaction due to drop-point reduction).

Thermal and mechanical stresses result in chemical and/or physical changes which may have a detrimental effect on the function of the entire tribological system. Oxidation, for example, results in acidification, which can trigger corrosion on metal surfaces or stress cracking on some plastics. In the event of excessive thermal load, polymerization can cause the lubricant to solidify.

Every chemical change automatically causes a change in physical properties. These include the rheological properties as well as changes in the viscosity-temperature characteristics or the dropping point. A marked lowering of the dropping point would result in the lubricant flowing away from the friction surface, even at moderate heat.

It is particularly important to remember that metals such as iron or copper (or metals containing copper such as bronze

### Table 5. Consistency grades for lubricating greases (DIN 51818)

| NLGI grade | Worked penetration as per DIN ISO 2137 in units (0.1 mm) |
|---|---|
| 000 | 445...475 |
| 00 | 400...430 |
| 0 | 355...385 |
| 1 | 310...340 |
| 2 | 265...295 |
| 3 | 220...250 |
| 4 | 175...205 |
| 5 | 130...160 |
| 6 | 85...150 |

or brass) catalyze the oxidation of a lubricant, i.e. oxidation occurs much more quickly than without catalyst contact. Oxidation quickly renders the lubricity of grease insufficient. Often the soap structure decomposes, the grease then becomes oily, flows away from the friction surface, or polymerizes.

By correctly matching the lubricating grease and tribological system while taking into account the load and interaction, it is possible to enhance the performance potential of products substantially with sliding-contact opposed parts (e.g. transmission, friction and roller bearings, actuator and control systems).

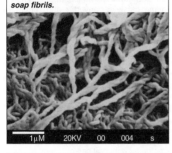

*Photo of lithium soap taken by a scanning electron microscope.*
*The oil is retained between the twisted soap fibrils.*

1μM  20KV  00  004  s

*Stress cracks on a gearwheel made of POM, caused by PAO*

2 mm

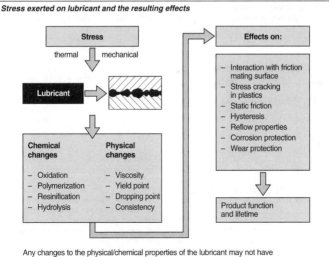

*Stress exerted on lubricant and the resulting effects*

**Stress**

thermal — mechanical

**Lubricant**

**Chemical changes**
- Oxidation
- Polymerization
- Resinification
- Hydrolysis

**Physical changes**
- Viscosity
- Yield point
- Dropping point
- Consistency

**Effects on:**
- Interaction with friction mating surface
- Stress cracking in plastics
- Static friction
- Hysteresis
- Reflow properties
- Corrosion protection
- Wear protection

Product function and lifetime

Any changes to the physical/chemical properties of the lubricant may not have any negative impact on product quality and lifetime.

# Fuels

## Characteristics

### Net and gross calorific values
The specific values for the net (formerly: low) and gross (formerly: high, or combustion heat) calorific values, or $H_u$ and $H_o$ respectively, provide an index for the energy content of fuels. Only the net calorific value $H_u$ (combustion vapor) is significant in dealing with fuels with which water is produced as a byproduct of combustion.

Oxygenates, fuel constituents which contain oxygen, such as alcohols, ether, and fatty-acid methyl ester, have a lower calorific value than pure hydrocarbons because the oxygen bonded in them does not contribute to the combustion process. Power comparable to that achievable with oxygenate-free fuels can only be attained at the cost of higher fuel-consumption rates.

### Calorific value of air/fuel mixture
The calorific value of the combustible air/fuel mixture determines the engine's output. Assuming a constant stoichiometric ratio, this figure remains roughly the same for all liquid fuels and liquefied gases (approx. 3.5...3.7 MJ/m³).

## Fuels for spark-ignition engines (gasoline/petrol)

### General requirements
European Standard EN 228 defines the requirements for unleaded fuel for use in spark-ignition engines. Further country-specific characteristic values are set down in the national appendices.

In the U.S.A., fuels for spark-ignition engines are defined in ASTM D4814 (American Society for Testing and Materials). Mineral-oil-based fuels for spark-ignition engines are hydrocarbon compounds, to which oxygenous organic components or other additives may be added to improve performance.

A distinction is made between regular, premium (super-grade), and "Super Plus" gasolines. Premium gasolines have higher antiknock qualities and are formulated for use in high-compression engines. Volatility ratings vary according to region, and whether the fuel is intended for summer or winter use.

Unleaded fuel is indispensable for vehicles equipped with catalytic converters for treating exhaust gases, as lead would damage the noble metals (e.g. platinum) in the catalytic converter and render it inoperative. It would also destroy the lambda oxygen sensors employed to monitor exhaust-gas composition in closed-loop emissions control system.

Leaded gasoline is prohibited in Europe. Leaded fuel is still available in some countries, although their number is steadily decreasing.

Unleaded fuels are a special mixture of high-grade, high-octane components (e.g. platformates, alkylates, and isomerisates). Ether (e.g. MTBE: methyl tertiary butyl ether, 3...15%) and alcohols (methanol, ethanol) can be added to good effect as metal-free supplements to increase the antiknock quality. The following, for example, are permitted: E5 in Europe E5 (max. 5% ethanol), E10 in the U.S., and E20...E26 in Brazil.

### Density
European Standard EN 228 limits the fuel-density range to 720...775 kg/m³. As premium fuels generally include a higher proportion of aromatic compounds, they are denser than regular gasoline, and thus also have a slightly higher calorific value.

### Antiknock quality (octane rating)
The octane rating defines the gasoline's antiknock quality (resistance to pre-ignition). The higher the octane rating, the greater the resistance to engine knock. Two different procedures are in international use for determining the octane rating; these are the Research Method and the Motor Method.

**Table 1. Essential data for unleaded gasoline, Draft European Standard prEN 228 (draft 2002)**

| Requirements | | Unit | Specification |
|---|---|---|---|
| Antiknock quality | | | |
| Premium, min. | | RON/MON | 95/85 |
| Regular, min. [1]) | | RON/MON | 91/82.5 |
| Super Plus [1]) | | RON/MON | 98/88 |
| Density | | kg/m³ | 720...775 |
| Sulfur, max. | up to 12.31.2004 | mg/kg | 150 |
| | 2005 to 2008 | mg/kg | 50 (low-sulfur) |
| | from 2009 [2]) | mg/kg | 10 (sulfur-free) |
| Benzene, max. | | % volume | 1 |
| Lead, max. | | mg/l | 5 |
| Volatility | | | |
| Vapor pressure, summer, min./max. | | kPa | 45/60 |
| Vapor pressure, winter, min./max. | | kPa | 60/90 [1]) |
| Evaporated vol. at 70 °C, summer, min./max. | | % volume | 20/48 |
| Evaporated vol. at 70 °C, winter, min./max. | | % volume | 22/50 |
| Evaporated vol. at 100 °C, min./max. | | % volume | 46/71 |
| Evaporated vol. at 150 °C, min./max. | | % volume | 75/– |
| Final boiling point, max. | | °C | 210 |
| VLI transitional period [3]), max. [4]) | | | 1150 [1]) |

[1]) National values for Germany, [2]) EU proposal, [3]) VLI: Vapor Lock Index, [4]) Spring and Fall.

RON, MON
The number determined in testing using the Research Method is the Research Octane Number, or RON. It serves as the essential index of acceleration knock.

The Motor Octane Number, or MON, is derived from testing according to the Motor Method. The MON basically provides an indication of the tendency to knock at high speeds.

The Motor Method differs from the Research Method by using preheated mixtures, higher engine speeds, and variable ignition timing, thereby placing more stringent thermal demands on the fuel under test. MON figures are lower than those for RON.

Octane numbers indicate the volumetric content in percent of $C_8H_{18}$ iso-octane (trimethyl pentane) contained in a mixture with $C_7H_{16}$ n-heptane, at the point where the mixture's knock-resistance in a test engine is identical to that of the fuel under test. Iso-octane, which is extremely knock-resistant, is assigned the octane number 100 (100 RON and MON), while n-heptane, with low-resistance to pre-ignition, is assigned the number 0.

Increasing the antiknock quality
Normal (untreated) straight-run gasoline displays a low antiknock quality. Various knock-resistant refinery components must be added to obtain high-octane fuels which are suitable for modern engines. The highest-possible octane level must also be maintained throughout the entire boiling range. Cyclic hydrocarbons (aromatics) and branched chains (iso-paraffins) provide greater knock resistance than straight-chain molecules (n-paraffins).

Additives based on oxygenous components (methanol, ethanol, methyl tertiary butyl ether) have a positive effect on the octane number, but can lead to difficulties in other areas (alcohols raise the volatility level and can affect the materials used in fuel-injection equipment, such as elastomer swelling and corrosion).

**Volatility**
Gasolines must satisfy stringent volatility requirements to ensure satisfactory operation. The fuel must contain a large enough proportion of highly volatile components to ensure good cold starting, but the volatility must not be so high as to im-

pair operation and starting when the engine is hot (vapor lock). In addition, environmental considerations demand that evaporative losses be kept low. Volatility is defined in various ways.

EN 228 defines 10 different volatility classes (A...F, C1...F1), distinguished by various levels of vapor pressure, boiling curve, and VLI (Vapor Lock Index). To meet special requirements stemming from variations in climatic conditions, countries can incorporate specific individual classes in their own national appendix.

### Boiling curve

Individual ranges on the boiling curve exercise a particularly pronounced effect on operating behavior. EN 228 therefore defines limit values for volumetric fuel evaporation at 70 °C, 100 °C and 150 °C. The percentage of vaporized fuel up to 70 °C must be a minimum amount to ensure good cold starting (previously important for carburetor engines), but no so large as to promote the formation of vapor bubbles. The percentage of vaporized fuel at 100 °C determines the engine's warm-up qualities, as well as its acceleration and response characteristics once it has reached normal operating temperature. The vaporized volume up to 150 °C should be high enough to minimize dilution of the engine's lubricating oil, especially with the engine cold.

### Vapor pressure

Fuel vapor pressure as measured at 37.8 °C (100 °F) in accordance with EN 13016-1 is primarily an index of the safety with which the fuel can be pumped in and out of the vehicle's fuel tank. All specifications place upper and lower limits on this vapor pressure: In Germany, for example, it is max. 60 kPa in summer and max. 90 kPa in winter. To be able to design a modern fuel-injection system, it is important to know the vapor pressure at higher temperatures (80 °C, 100 °C). A rise in vapor pressure by adding alcohol only becomes apparent at higher temperatures, for example.

### Vapor/liquid ratio

This specification provides an index of a fuel's tendency to form vapor bubbles. It is defined as the volume of vapor generated by a specific quantity of fuel at a set temperature. A drop in pressure (e.g. when driving over a mountain pass), and/or an increase in temperature, will raise the vapor/liquid ratio and with it the possibility of operating problems. ASTM D4814, for example, specifies a vapor/liquid ratio requirement of max. 20 for different volatility classes.

### Vapor-Lock Index (VLI)

This parameter is the sum of tenfold the vapor pressure (in kPa at 37.8 °C) and sevenfold the proportion of fuel that vaporizes up to 70 °C. The VLI provides more useful information on the fuel's influence on starting and operating a hot engine than that supplied by the vapor-pressure and boiling data alone.

### Sulfur

For the purpose of reducing $SO_2$ emissions, and on account of the required catalytic converters for exhaust-gas treatment for gasoline direct-injection systems, the sulfur content of gasoline will be restricted to 10 mg/kg throughout Europe starting in 2009. This sulfur-free product has already been launched in Germany in response to the introduction in 2003 of a penalty tax on fuels containing sulfur.

### Additives

Additives can be used to improve fuel grade so as to avoid impairing vehicle performance and exhaust-gas composition while driving. The packages generally used combine individual components with various attributes.

Extreme care and precision are required both when testing additives and in determining their optimum concentrations. Undesirable side-effects must be avoided. They are usually added on a brand-specific basis when the tankers are filled at the refinery (end-point metering). Vehicle operators should refrain from adding supplementary additives to the fuel tank as this will invalidate any warranty claims against the vehicle manufacturer.

Anti-aging additives
Anti-aging agent (antioxidants) are added to fuels to increase their stability in storage. They prevent oxidation due to atmospheric oxygen. Metal deactivators inhibit the catalytic effect of metal ions on fuel aging.

Intake-system contamination inhibitors
The entire intake system (injectors, intake valves) must be kept free of contamination and deposits for several reasons. A clean intake tract is essential for maintaining the factory-defined A/F ratios, as well as for troublefree operation and minimum exhaust emissions. To achieve this end, effective detergent agents should be added to the fuel.

Corrosion protection
Penetration by water can cause corrosion in the fuel-injection system. An extremely effective remedy is adding corrosion inhibitors, which form a thin protective film on the metal surface.

**Reformulated gasoline**
Environmental authorities and legislative bodies are imposing increasingly stringent regulations for fuels to ensure low evaporation and pollutant emissions ("reformulated gasoline"). As defined in the regulations, the main characteristics of these fuels include reduced vapor pressure, lower levels of aromatic components and benzene, and a lower final boiling point. In the U.S., additives designed to prevent deposit formation in the intake tract are also mandatory.

# Diesel fuels

Diesel fuels contain a whole range of individual hydrocarbons with boiling points ranging from roughly 180 °C to 370 °C. They are the product of graduated distillation of crude oil. The refineries are adding increasing amounts of conversion products to diesel fuel; these "cracked components" are derived from heavy oil by breaking up (cracking) large molecules. European Standard EN 590 applies to diesel fuels throughout Europe. The most important specifications in this standard are listed in Table 2.

**Ignition quality, cetane number, cetane index**
As the diesel engine dispenses with an externally supplied ignition spark, the fuel must ignite spontaneously (auto-ignition) and with minimum delay (ignition lag) when injected into the hot, compressed air in the combustion chamber. Ignition quality is an expression of the fuel's suitability for spontaneous auto-ignition in a diesel engine. The cetane number (CN) expresses the ignition quality. The higher the cetane number, the greater the fuel's tendency to ignite. The cetane number 100 is assigned to n-hexadecane (cetane), which ignites very easily, while slow-burning methyl naphthalene is allocated the cetane number 0. The cetane number is determined using a test engine. A cetane number in excess of 50 is desirable for optimum operation in modern engines (smooth running, low exhaust emissions). High-quality diesel fuels contain a high proportion of paraffins with high CN ratings. Conversely, aromatic compounds have a detrimental effect on ignition quality.

Yet another indication of ignition quality is provided by the cetane index, which is calculated on the basis of density and various points on the boiling curve. This purely mathematical quantity naturally does not take into account the influence of cetane improvers on ignition quality. In order to limit the adjustment of the cetane number by means of cetane improvers, both the cetane number and the cetane index have been included in the list of requirements in EN 590.

## Cold-flow properties, filtration

Precipitation of paraffin crystals at low temperatures can result in fuel-filter blockage, ultimately leading to interruption of the fuel flow. In worst-case conditions, paraffin particles can start to form at temperatures of 0 °C or even higher. Special selection and manufacturing procedures are thus necessary for winter diesel fuels in order to ensure troublefree operation during the cold season of the year. Normally, flow improvers are added to the fuel at the refinery. Although they do not actually prevent paraffin precipitation, they severely limit crystal growth, which remain small enough to pass through the pores in the filter material. Other additives can be used to maintain the crystals in a state of suspension, extending the filtration limit downward even further.

Suitability for cold-weather operation is defined with reference to a standardized procedure for determining the "limit of filtration". This is known as the CFPP, or Cold Filter Plugging Point. European Standard EN 590 defines the CFPP for various classes, and can be determined by the individual countries depending on the prevailing geographical and climatic conditions.

Formerly, owners sometimes added regular gasoline to their vehicle fuel tanks to improve the cold response of diesel fuel. This practice is no longer necessary now that fuels conform to standards, and this would in any case invalidate any warranty claims if damage occurs.

## Flash point

The flash point is the temperature at which the quantities of vapor which a combustible fluid emits to the atmosphere are sufficient to allow a spark to ignite the vapor-air mixture above the fluid. Safety considerations (transport, storage) dictate that diesel fuels must meet the requirements for Class A III (flash point > 55 °C). Less than 3% gasoline in the diesel fuel is sufficient to lower the flash point to such an extent that ignition becomes possible at room temperature.

## Boiling range

The boiling range affects several parameters of major importance in determining the diesel fuel's operating characteristics. Extending the boiling range downward to embrace lower temperatures improves the fuel's cold-operation properties, but at the price of a reduction in the cetane number. Particularly critical is the negative effect on the fuel's lubrication properties, with the related increase in the risk of wear to injection-system components. In contrast, raising the final temperature at the upper end of the boiling range, although desirable from the standpoint of efficient utilization of petroleum resources, also results in higher soot emissions as well as carbon deposits (combustion residue) in the nozzles.

## Density

There is a reasonably constant correspondence between a diesel fuel's calorific value and its density; higher densities have a higher calorific value. Assuming constant fuel-injection-pump settings (and thus constant injection volume), the use of fuels with widely different densities in a given system will be accompanied by variations in mixture ratios stemming from fluctuations in calorific value. Higher densities provoke increased particulate emissions, while lower densities lead to reductions in engine output.

## Viscosity

Leakage losses in the fuel-injection pump result if viscosity is too low, and this in turn results in lower power. Significantly higher viscosity results in an increased peak injection pressure at high temperatures in non-pressure-regulated systems (e.g. unit injector systems). This is the case, for example, when FAME (bio-diesel) is used. Mineral-oil diesel may not then be applied to the maximum permitted primary pressure. High viscosity also changes the spray pattern due to the formation of larger droplets.

**Lubricity**

The hydrodynamic lubricity of diesel fuels is not as important as that in the mixed-friction range. The introduction of environment-compatible, hydrogenation-desulfurized fuels resulted in huge wear problems with distributor injection pumps in the field. Lubricity enhancers have to be added to the fuel to avoid these problems. Lubricity is tested using a high-frequency reciprocating rig (HFRR). Minimum lubricity is defined in EN 590.

**Sulfur**

Diesel fuels contain chemically bonded sulfur, and the actual quantities depend on the quality of the crude petroleum and the components which are added at the refinery. Cracked components are generally characterized by high sulfur contents, but these can be reduced by treatment with hydrogen (hydrogenation) at the refinery. Starting 2005 all regular gasolines and diesel fuels will be subject to a minimum low-sulfur requirement (sulfur content < 50 mg/kg) throughout Europe. Starting 2009 only sulfur-free fuels (sulfur content < 10 mg/kg) will be allowed.

In Germany, a penalty tax has been levied on fuels containing sulfur since 2003. For this reason, only sulfur-free diesel fuels are available on the German market. This results in less $SO_2$ during combustion, which, in turn, further reduces both direct $SO_2$ emissions and the emitted particulate mass (sulfate in the soot). This also makes it possible to use particulate filters and denitrification catalysts.

**Carbon-deposit index** (carbon residue)

The carbon-deposit index describes the fuel's tendency to form carbon residue on the nozzles. The mechanisms of deposit formation are complex and not easy to describe.

Above all, components which the diesel fuel contains at the final boiling point (particularly cracking constituents) influence carbon-deposit formation (coking).

**Additives**

Additives, long a standard feature in gasolines, have attained increasing significance as quality improvers in diesel fuels. The various agents are generally combined in additive packages to achieve a variety of objectives. As the total concentration of the additives generally lies < 0.1%, the fuel's physical characteristics – such as density, viscosity, and boiling curve – remain unchanged.

Lubricity enhancers

It is possible to improve the lubricity of diesel fuels with poor lubrication properties by adding fatty acids, fatty-acid esters, or glycerins. Bio-diesel is also a fatty-acid ester. Therefore, blends of diesel containing up to 5% bio-diesel (B5), which are approved in accordance with EN 590, are not given any further additives.

Cetane improvers

Cetane improvers are alcohol-derived esters of nitric acid, which shorten the ignition lag with positive effects on noise and particulate emissions.

Flow improvers

Flow improvers are polymers whose application is generally restricted to winter (see Cold-flow properties).

Detergent additives

Detergent additives help to clean the air-intake system to ensure efficient mixture formation. They can also inhibit the formation of deposits and reduce the buildup of carbon deposits on the nozzles.

Corrosion inhibitors

These additives prevent metallic components from corroding if water enters the fuel-injection system.

Antifoaming agents (defoamants)

Adding defoamants helps to avoid excessive foaming when the vehicle is refueled quickly.

# Properties of liquid fuels and hydrocarbons

| Substance | Density kg/l | Main constituents % by weight | Boiling temperature °C | Latent heat of evaporation kJ/kg[1] | Specific calorific value MJ/kg[1] | Ignition temperature °C | Air requirement, theoretical kg/kg | Ignition limit Lower | Upper |
|---|---|---|---|---|---|---|---|---|---|
| | | | | | | | | % by vol. of gas in air | |
| Spark-ignition engine fuel, | | | | | | | | | |
| Regular | 0.720...0.775 | 86 C, 14 H | 25..210 | 380...500 | 42.7 | ≈ 300 | 14.8 | ≈ 0.6 | ≈ 8 |
| Premium | 0.720...0.775 | 86 C, 14 H | 25..210 | – | 43.5 | ≈ 400 | 14.7 | – | – |
| Aviation fuel | 0.720 | 85 C, 15 H | 40..180 | – | 43.5 | ≈ 500 | – | ≈ 0.7 | ≈ 8 |
| Kerosene | 0.77...0.83 | 87 C, 13 H | 170..260 | – | 43 | ≈ 250 | 14.5 | ≈ 0.6 | ≈ 7.5 |
| Diesel fuel | 0.820...0.845 | 86 C, 13 H | 180..360 | ≈ 250 | 42.5 | ≈ 250 | 14.5 | ≈ 0.6 | ≈ 7.5 |
| Crude oil | 0.70...1.0 | 80...83 C, 10...14 H | 25..360 | 222...352 | 39.8...46.1 | ≈ 220 | – | ≈ 0.6 | ≈ 6.5 |
| Lignite tar oil | 0.850...0.90 | 84 C, 11 H | 200...360 | – | 40.2...41.9 | – | 13.5 | – | – |
| Bituminous coal oil | 1.0...1.10 | 89 C, 7 H | 170...330 | – | 36.4...38.5 | – | – | – | – |
| Pentane $C_5H_{12}$ | 0.63 | 83 C, 17 H | 36 | 352 | 45.4 | 285 | 15.4 | 1.4 | 7.8 |
| Hexane $C_6H_{14}$ | 0.66 | 84 C, 16 H | 69 | 331 | 44.7 | 240 | 15.2 | 1.2 | 7.4 |
| n-Heptane $C_7H_{16}$ | 0.68 | 84 C, 16 H | 98 | 310 | 44.4 | 220 | 15.2 | 1.1 | 6.7 |
| Iso-octane $C_8H_{18}$ | 0.69 | 84 C, 16 H | 99 | 297 | 44.6 | 410 | 15.2 | 1 | 6 |
| Benzene $C_6H_6$ | 0.88 | 92 C, 8 H | 80 | 394 | 40.2 | 550 | 13.3 | 1.2 | 8 |
| Toluene $C_7H_8$ | 0.87 | 91 C, 9 H | 110 | 364 | 40.6 | 530 | 13.4 | 1.2 | 7 |
| Xylene $C_8H_{11}$ | 0.88 | 91 C, 9 H | 144 | 339 | 40.6 | 460 | 13.7 | 1 | 7.6 |
| Ether $(C_2H_5)_2O$ | 0.72 | 64 C, 14 H, 22 O | 35 | 377 | 34.3 | 170 | 7.7 | 1.7 | 36 |
| Acetone $(CH_3)_2CO$ | 0.79 | 62 C, 10 C, 28 O | 56 | 523 | 28.5 | 540 | 9.4 | 2.5 | 13 |
| Ethanol $C_2H_5OH$ | 0.79 | 52 C, 13 H, 35 O | 78 | 904 | 26.8 | 420 | 9 | 3.5 | 15 |
| Methanol $CH_3OH$ | 0.79 | 38 C, 12 H, 50 O | 65 | 1,110 | 19.7 | 450 | 6.4 | 5.5 | 26 |

**Viscosity** at 20 °C in mm²/s (= cSt, P. 37); gasoline ≈ 0.6; ethanol ≈ 1.5; methanol ≈ 0.75.

[1] Values per l = values per kg x density in kg/l.

## Properties of gaseous fuels and hydrocarbons

| Substance | Density at 0 °C and 1,013 mbar kg/m³ | Main constituents % by weight | Boiling temp. at 1,013 mbar °C | Specific calorific value Fuel MJ/kg[1] | Air-fuel mixture MJ/m³[1] | Ignition temperature °C | Air requirement, theoretical kg/kg | Ignition limit Lower % by vol. of gas in air | Upper % by vol. of gas in air |
|---|---|---|---|---|---|---|---|---|---|
| Liquefied gas (natural gas) / Municipal gas | 2.25[2] / 0.56...0.61 | $C_3H_8$, $C_4H_{10}$ / 50 H, 8 CO, 30 $CH_4$ | −30 / −210 | 46.1 / ≈30 | 3.39 / ≈3.25 | ≈400 / ≈560 | 15.5 / 10 | 1.5 / 4 | 15 / 40 |
| Natural gas H (North Sea) | 0.83 | 87 $CH_4$, 8 $C_2H_6$, 2 $C_3H_8$, 2 $CO_2$, 1 $N_2$ | −162 ($CH_4$) | 46.7 | – | 584 | 16.1 | 4.0 | 15.8 |
| Natural gas H (Russia) | 0.73 | 98 $CH_4$, 1 $C_2H_6$, 1 $N_2$ | −162 ($CH_4$) | 49.1 | 3.4 | 619 | 16.9 | 4.3 | 16.2 |
| Natural gas L | 0.83 | 83 $CH_4$, 4 $C_2H_6$, 1 $C_3H_8$, 2 $CO_2$, 10 $N_2$ | −162 ($CH_4$) | 40.3 | 3.3 | ≈600 | 14.0 | 4.6 | 16.0 |
| Water gas / Blast-furnace gas / Sewage gas[3] | 0.71 / 1.28 / – | 50 H, 38 CO / 28 CO, 59 N, 12 $CO_2$ / 46 $CH_4$, 54 $CO_2$ | – / −170 / – | 15.1 / 3.20 / 27.2[3] | 3.10 / 1.88 / 3.22 | ≈600 / ≈600 / – | 4.3 / 0.75 / – | 6 / ≈30 / – | 72 / ≈75 / – |
| Hydrogen $H_2$ / Carbon monoxide CO / Methane $CH_4$ | 0.090 / 1.25 / 0.72 | 100 H / 100 CO / 75 C, 25 H | −253 / −191 / −162 | 120.0 / 10.05 / 50.0 | 2.97 / 3.48 / 3.22 | 560 / 605 / 650 | 34 / 2.5 / 17.2 | 4 / 12.5 / 5 | 77 / 75 / 15 |
| Acetylene $C_2H_2$ / Ethane $C_2H_6$ / Ethene $C_2H_4$ | 1.17 / 1.36 / 1.26 | 93 C, 7 H / 80 C, 20 H / 86 C, 14 H | −81 / −88 / −102 | 48.1 / 47.5 / 47.1 | 4.38 / – / – | 305 / 515 / 425 | 13.25 / 17.3 / 14.7 | 1.5 / 3 / 2.75 | 80 / 14 / 34 |
| Propane $C_3H_8$ / Propene $C_3H_6$ / Butane $C_4H_{10}$ / Butene $C_4H_8$ / Dimethylether $C_2H_6O$ | 2.0[2] / 1.92 / 2.7[2] / 2.5 / 2.05[5] | 82 C, 18 H / 86 C, 14 H / 83 C, 17 H / 86 C, 14 H / 52 C, 13 H, 35 O | −43 / −47 / −10; +1[4] / −5; +1[4] / −25 | 46.3 / 45.8 / 45.6 / 45.2 / 28.8 | 3.35 / – / 3.39 / – / 3.43 | 470 / 450 / 365 / – / 235 | 15.6 / 14.7 / 15.4 / 14.8 / 9.0 | 1.9 / 2 / 1.5 / 1.7 / 3.4 | 9.5 / 11 / 8.5 / 9 / 18.6 |

[1] Values per m³ = values per kg × density in kg/m³.
[2] Density of liquefied gas 0.54 kg/l, density of liquefied propane 0.51 kg/l, density of liquefied butane 0.58 kg/l.
[3] Purified sewage gas contains 95% $CH_4$ (methane) and has a calorific value of 37.7 MJ/kg.
[4] First value for isobutane, second value for n-butane or n-butene.
[5] Density of liquefied dimethylether 0.667 kg/l.

## Table 2. Essential data for diesel fuels, prEN 590 (draft 2002)

| Requirements | | Unit | Specification |
|---|---|---|---|
| Flash point, min. | | °C | >55 |
| Water, max. | | mg/kg | 200 |
| Sulfur content, max. | up to 12.31.2004 | mg/kg | 350 |
| | 2005 to 2008 | mg/kg | 50 (low-sulfur) |
| | from 2009 [1] | mg/kg | 10 (sulfur-free) |
| Lubricity, "wear scar diameter" max. | | µm | 460 |
| FAME content, max. | | % by vol. | 5 |
| **For temperate climates:** | | | |
| Density (at 15 °C), min./max. | | kg/m$^3$ | 820/845 |
| Viscosity (at 40 °C), min./max. | | mm$^2$/s | 2/4.5 |
| Cetane number, min. | | – | 51 |
| Cetane index, min. | | – | 46 |
| at 250 °C collected quantity, max. | | % by vol. | <65 |
| at 350 °C collected quantity, min. | | % by vol. | 85 |
| Distillation temperature at which 95% is evaporated ($T_{95}$), max. | | °C | 360 |
| CFPP [2] in 6 classes A ... F, max. | | °C | +5 ... –20 |
| **For arctic climates (in 5 classes 0 ... 4):** | | | |
| Density (at 15 °C), min./max. | | kg/m$^3$ | 800/845 ... 800/840 |
| Viscosity (at 40 °C), min./max. | | mm$^2$/s | 1.5/4 ... 1.2/4 |
| Cetane number, min. | | – | 49 ... 47 |
| Cetane index, min. | | – | 46 ... 43 |
| up to 180 °C, distilled, max. | | % volume | 10 |
| up to 340 °C distilled, min. | | % volume | 95 |
| CFPP [2], max. | | °C | –20 ... –44 |

[1] EU proposal, [2] Filtration limit.

# Alternative fuels

## Alcohol fuels

Specially adapted spark-ignition engines can also run on methanol (M100) or ethanol (E100, Brazil). For the most part, however, these alcohols are used as fuel components to increase the octane number (e.g. E24 in Brazil, and E10, E85, M85 in the U.S.). Even the methyl (MTBE) or ethyl tertiary butyl ethers (ETBE), which can be produced from alcohols with isobutylene, are also important octane-number improvers. Ethanol is extremely important on account of its biogenous origin (fermentation of sugar cane in Brazil and cereals in the U.S.). Methanol can be derived from the plentiful hydrocarbon reserves represented by coal, natural gas, and heavy oil, etc.

Compared with mineral-oil-based gasoline, alcohols have different material values (calorific value, vapor pressure, material resistance, corrosiveness, etc.), which must be taken into account in design engineering. Engines which can burn regular gasoline and alcohol in any combination without intervention by the driver are used in "flexible fuel" vehicles.

## CNG (Compressed Natural Gas)

This usually assumes the form of compressed methane, and is suitable for obtaining ultra-low emissions from combustion engines. Due to its higher H/C ratio of 4:1 compared with 2:1 for gasoline, CNG also produces less $CO_2$ during combustion. CNG requires four times the volume of gasoline for the same energy content. CNG can also be liquefied at $-162\,°C$ into LNG (Liquefied Natural Gas). However, the storage capacity of LNG, which is threefold greater than CNG, comes at the expense of high energy requirements. For this reason, it is almost exclusively CNG which is currently used in passenger-car applications.

CNG is mainly used in spark-ignition engines (ON ≈ 130), but is undergoing trials in diesel engines. Soot production is virtually zero when this fuel is combusted in the diesel cycle. The vehicles must be specially adapted to run on CNG.

There is as yet no European standard for CNG.

## Liquefied Petroleum Gas (LPG)

The two major components of LPG (Liquefied Petroleum Gas) are butane and propane. It is in limited use as a fuel for motor vehicles. LPG is a byproduct of the crude-oil refining process, and can be liquefied under pressure. The demands placed on LPG for its use in motor vehicles are laid down in a European standard (prEN 589, draft 2002). The octane number is > 89 MON.

## Fatty-acid methyl ester (FAME)

Fatty-acid methyl ester (FAME) – known colloquially as "bio-diesel" – is the generic term applied to vegetable or animal oils and greases which have been transesterified with methanol. FAME can be produced from various raw materials. The most common are rapeseed (RME, Europe) and soya methyl esters (SME, U.S.A.). There are also sunflower and palm esters, UFOME (Used Frying Oil Methyl Esters), and TME (Tallow Methyl Esters), but these are mostly used in conjunction with other FAMEs. Ethanol can also be used instead of methanol. Thus, soya ethyl ester (SEE) is produced in Brazil. Pure, unesterified vegetable oils, however, are hardly used any more in direct-injection diesel engines. They give rise to considerable problems, mainly due to their high viscosity and severe tendency to cause nozzle coking.

FAME can be used in pure form (B100) or up to max. 5% as additives in diesel fuel (B5). Even the use of FAME can be accompanied by malfunctions. Therefore, the demands placed on FAME are comprehensively regulated (prEN 14214, draft March 2003).

It is essential in particular to ensure good aging stability (oxidation stability) and to eliminate contamination caused by the process. FAME must satisfy Standard prEN 14214, regardless of whether FAME is used directly as B100 or as an additive in diesel fuel. The B5 blend created by FAME additives must also comply with the requirements for pure diesel fuel (prEN 590, 2002).

The production of FAME is uneconomical in comparison with mineral-oil-based diesel fuels and must be heavily subsidized (exemption from mineral-oil tax).

**Table 3. Essential data for fatty-acid methyl esters (FAME) prEN 14 214 (draft March 2003)**

| Requirements | Unit | Specification |
|---|---|---|
| Flash point, min. | °C | >120 |
| Water, max. | mg/kg | 500 |
| Sulfur content, max. | mg/kg | 10 |
| Oxidation stability (at 110°C), min. | h (hours) | 6 |
| Density (at 15°C), min./max. | kg/m³ | 860/900 |
| Viscosity (at 40°C), min./max. | mm²/s | 3.5/5.0 |
| Cetane number, min. | – | 51 |
| For temperate climates: CFPP[1]) in 6 classes A … F, max. | °C | +5 … −20 |
| For arctic climates: CFPP[1]) in 5 classes 0…4, max. | °C | −20 … −44 |

[1]) Filtration limit.

## Emulsions (diesel fuels)

Emulsions of water and ethanol in diesel fuels are undergoing trials at a number of different institutes. Water and alcohols are difficult to dissolve in diesel. Effective emulsifiers are required to keep the mixture stable and prevent it from demulsification. Wear- and corrosion-inhibiting measures are also necessary. Soot and nitrogen-oxide emissions can be reduced by these emulsions, but to date their use has been restricted to fleets which for the most parts are equipped with in-line fuel-injection pumps.

## Dimethylether (DME)

This is a synthetic product with a high cetane number CN ≈ 55, producing little soot and reduced nitrogen oxide when combusted in diesel engines. Its calorific value is low on account of its low density and high oxygen content. It is a gas-phase fuel, so the fuel-injection equipment has to be modified. Other ethers (dimethoxymethane, di-n-pentylether, and others) are also undergoing trials.

## Synfuels® and Sunfuels®

The terms Synfuel and Sunfuel refer to fuels which are produced from synthesis gas ($H_2$ and CO) using the Fischer-Tropsch process. The end product is known as Synfuel when coal, coke, or natural gas is used to produce the synthesis gas, and as Sunfuel when biomass is used. In the Fischer-Tropsch process, synthesis gas is catalytically converted to produce hydrocarbons. Diesel fuels are produced by preference. This results in high-quality, sulfur- and aromatic-free diesel fuels which are mainly used to improve the quality of conventional diesel fuels. Depending on the catalysts used, it is also possible to produce gasoline. The byproducts are liquefied gas and paraffins.

Due to the high costs involved, the production of synthetic fuels has been and is restricted to special markets (oil embargo in South Africa in the 1970s, surplus natural gas in Malaysia, research laboratories).

# Antifreeze and brake fluid

## Brake fluids

Brake fluid is the hydraulic medium employed to transmit actuation forces within the braking system. Compliance with stringent requirements is essential to ensure reliable brake-system operation. These requirements are defined in various standards of similar content (SAE J 1703, FMVSS 116, ISO 4925). The performance data contained in FMVSS 116 (<u>F</u>ederal <u>M</u>otor <u>V</u>ehicle <u>S</u>afety <u>S</u>tandard), mandatory in the U.S., also serve as an international reference. The U.S. <u>D</u>epartment of <u>T</u>ransportation (DOT) has defined specific ratings for salient characteristics (Table 1).

### Requirements

#### Equilibrium boiling point
The equilibrium boiling point provides an index of the brake fluid's resistance to thermal stress. The heat encountered in the wheel-brake cylinders (which are subjected the highest temperatures in the entire braking system) can be especially critical. Vapor bubbles can form at temperatures above the brake fluid's instantaneous boiling point, resulting in brake failure.

#### Wet boiling point
The wet boiling point is the fluid's equilibrium boiling point subsequent to moisture absorption under specified conditions (approx. 3.5%). Hygroscopic (glycol-based) fluids respond with an especially pronounced drop in boiling point.

The wet boiling point is tested to quantify the response characteristics of used brake fluid. Brake fluid absorbs moisture, mostly by diffusion through brake-system hoses. This is the main reason why it should be replaced every 1...2 years. The

figure shows the drops in boiling point that result from moisture absorption in two different brake fluids.

#### Viscosity
To ensure consistent reliability throughout the braking system's extended operating range (–40 °C ... +100 °C), viscosity should remain as constant as possible, with minimum sensitivity to temperature variations. Maintaining the lowest possible cold viscosity at very low temperatures is especially important in ABS/TCS/ESP systems.

#### Compressibility
The fluid should maintain a consistently low level of compressibility with minimum sensitivity to temperature fluctuations.

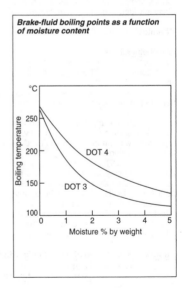

*Brake-fluid boiling points as a function of moisture content*

## Table 1. Brake fluids

| Reference standard for testing | FMVSS 116 | | |
|---|---|---|---|
| Requirements/Date | DOT3 | DOT4 | DOT5 |
| Dry boiling point min. °C | 205 | 230 | 260 |
| Wet boiling point min. °C | 140 | 155 | 180 |
| Cold viscosity at −40 °C in mm²/s | < 1,500 | < 1,800 | < 900 |

## Corrosion protection

FMVSS 116 stipulates that brake fluids shall exercise no corrosive effect on those metals generally employed in braking systems. The required corrosion protection can be achieved only by using additives.

## Elastomer swelling

The elastomers employed in a particular brake system must be able to adapt to the type of brake fluid in use. Although a small amount of swelling is desirable, it may not exceed approximately 10% under any circumstances. Otherwise, it has a negative effect on the strength of the elastomer components. Even minute levels of mineral-oil contamination (such as mineral-oil-based brake fluid, solvents) in glycol-based brake fluid can lead to destruction of rubber components (such as seals) and ultimately lead to brake-system failure.

## Chemical composition

### Glycol-ether fluids

Most brake fluids are based on glycol-ether compounds. These generally consist of monoethers of low polyethylene glycols. Although these components can be used to produce a brake fluid which conforms to DOT3 requirements, their undesirable hygroscopic properties cause this fluid to absorb moisture at a relatively rapid rate, with an attendant swift reduction in the boiling point.

If the free OH (hydroxyl) groups are partially esterified with boric acid, the result is a superior DOT4 (or "DOT4+", "Super DOT4", "DOT5.1") brake fluid capable of reacting with moisture to neutralize its effects. As the DOT4 brake fluid's boiling point drops much more slowly than that of a DOT3 fluid, its service life is longer.

### Mineral-oil fluids (ISO 7308)

The great advantage of mineral-oil-based fluids is the fact that they are not hygroscopic, so the boiling point does not drop due to moisture absorption. The mineral and synthetic oils for this fluid must be selected with utmost care. Viscosity-index improvers are generally added to achieve the desired relationship between viscosity and temperature.

The petroleum industry can also supply a range of further additives to improve other brake-fluid properties. It should be noted that mineral-oil-based fluids should never be added to braking systems designed for glycol ether (or vice versa), as this destroys the elastomers.

### Silicone fluids (SAE J1705)

As silicone fluids – in the same way as mineral oils – do not absorb moisture, they formerly saw occasional use as brake fluids. The disadvantages of these products include considerably higher compressibility and inferior lubrication, both of which reduce their suitability for use as hydraulic fluid in many systems. A critical factor with brake fluids based on silicone or mineral oils is the absorption of free water in a fluid state, as the water forms vapor bubbles when it heats up to more than 100 °C and freezes when it cools to less than 0 °C.

The less used brake fluids based on silicone oil or mineral oil usually correspond to DOT5 requirements.

**Table 2. Classification of brake fluids with different chemical bases**

| Parameter / Classification | DOT3 Glycol ether | DOT4 Glycol ether | DOT5 | | |
|---|---|---|---|---|---|
| | | | DOT5.1 Glycol ether | DOT5 SB Silicone | Mineral oil |
| Boiling point [°C] | 205 | 230 | 260 | | |
| Wet boiling point [°C] | 140 | 155 | 180 | | |
| Viscosity at −40 °C [mm²/s] | < 1,500 | < 1,800 | < 900 | | |
| Difference in color | Colorless to amber | | | Purple | Green |

## Coolants

### Requirements

The cooling system must dissipate that part of the engine's combustion heat that is not converted into mechanical energy. A fluid-filled cooling circuit transfers the heat absorbed in the cylinder head to a heat exchanger (radiator) for dispersal into the air (see P. 512 onwards). The fluid in this circuit is exposed to extreme thermal loads; it must also be formulated to ensure that it does not attack the materials within the cooling system (corrosion).

Owing to its high specific heat and its correspondingly substantial thermal-absorption capacity, water is a very good cooling medium. Its disadvantages include its corrosive properties and limited suitability for application in cold conditions (freezing).

This is why additives must be mixed with the water for satisfactory performance.

### Antifreeze

It is possible to lower the coolant's freezing point by adding ethylene glycol. When glycol is added to form a mixture with water, the resulting coolant no longer freezes at a given temperature. Instead, ice crystals are precipitated in the fluid once the temperature drops to the ice flaking point. At this temperature, the fluid medium can still be pumped through the cooling circuit. Glycol also raises the coolant's boiling point (Table 3).

In car owner's manuals, automobile manufacturers usually specify various optional antifreeze mixture ratios for different levels of low-temperature frost protection.

### Table 3. Ice flaking and boiling points for water-glycol mixtures.

| Glycol % by vol. | Ice flaking point °C | Boiling point °C |
|---|---|---|
| 10 | −4 | 101 |
| 20 | −9 | 102 |
| 30 | −17 | 104 |
| 40 | −26 | 106 |
| 50 | −39 | 108 |

### Additives

Coolants must include effective additives to protect the glycol against oxidation (which forms extremely corrosive by-products) and to protect metallic cooling-system components against corrosion.

Common additives include:
- Corrosion inhibitors: silicates, nitrates, nitrites, metal salts of organic acids, benzthiazole derivates.
- Buffers: borates.
- Antifoaming agents: silicones.

Many of these additives are subject to aging deterioration, leading to a gradual reduction in coolant performance. Automobile manufacturers have responded to this fact by granting official approval exclusively for coolants of proven long-term stability.

# Names of chemicals

Hazard codes: E = explosive, O = oxidizing, F = readily flammable, F+ = highly flammable, C = caustic, Xn = slightly toxic, Xi = irritant, T = toxic, T+ = highly toxic.

| Commercial name English (hazard code) | German | French | Chemical name | Chemical formula |
|---|---|---|---|---|
| (Glacial) acetic acid (C) | Eisessig (Essigessenz) | Acide acétique glacial | Acetic acid | $CH_3COOH$ |
| Acetic ether; vinegar naphtha (F) | Essigester (Essigäther) | Ether acétique | Ethyl acetate | $CH_3COOC_2H_5$ |
| Aerosil (fumed silica) | Aérosil® | Aérosil | Silicon dioxide in extremely fine particles | $SiO_2$ |
| Ammonia liquor (Xi, C) | Salmiakgeist | Ammoniaque hydroxide | Aqueous solution of ammonium hydroxide | $NH_4OH$ in $H_2O$ |
| Anon; pimelic ketone (Xn) | Anon | Anone | Cyclohexanone | $C_6H_{10}O$ |
| Aqua fortis (C) | Scheidewasser | Eau forte | Nitric acid (50% aqueous solution) | $HNO_3$ in $H_2O$ |
| Aqua regia (C, T+) | Königswasser | Eau régale | Mixture of nitric and hydrochloric acids | $HNO_3 + HCl$ (1 + 3) |
| Bitter almond oil (T) | Bittermandelöl | Essence d'amandes amères | Benzaldehyde | $C_6H_5CHO$ |
| Bleach, Chlorid of Lime (C) | Chlorkalk | Chlorure de chaux | Calcium chloride hypochlorite | $Ca(OCl)Cl$ |
| Blue vitriol | Kupfervitriol | Vitriol bleu | Copper sulfate | $CuSO_4 \cdot 5H_2O$ |
| Borax (tincal) | Borax (Tinkal) | Borax (tincal) | Sodium tetraborate | $Na_2B_4O_7 \cdot 10H_2O$ |
| Butoxyl | Butoxyl® | Butoxyl | (3-methoxybutyl) acetate | $CH_3COO(CH_2)_2CH(OCH_3)CH_3$ |
| Butter of tin (C) | Zinnbutter | Beurre d'étain | Tin tetrachloride | $SnCl_4 \cdot 5H_2O$ |
| Calcium carbide (F) | Karbid | Carbure de calcium | Calcium carbide | $CaC_2$ |
| Calomel (Xn) | Kalomel | Calomel | Mercury (I) chloride | $Hg_2Cl_2$ |
| Carbitol acetate™ [1]) | Carbitolacetat® | Diethylene glycol ethylether acetate | Diethylene glycol ethylether acetate | $CH_3COOCH_2CH_2OCH_2CH_2OC_2H_5$ |

| | | | | |
|---|---|---|---|---|
| Carbitol™ (solvent) ¹⁾ | Carbitol®, Dioxitol® | Carbitol | Diethylene glycol monoethylether | $HOCH_2CH_2OCH_2CH_2OC_2H_5$ |
| Carbolic acid (T) | Karbolsäure | Acide carbolique | Phenol | $C_6H_5OH$ |
| Caustic potash (C) | Atzkali | Potasse caustique | Potassium hydroxide | $KOH$ |
| Caustic soda (C) | Atznatron | Soude caustique | Sodium hydroxide | $NaOH$ |
| Cellosolve™ (solvent) ¹⁾ | Cellosolve®, Oxitol® | | Ethylene glycol monoethylether | $HOCH_2CH_2OC_2H_5$ |
| Cellosolve™ acetate ¹⁾ | Cellosolveacetat® | | Ethylene glycol ethylether acetate | $CH_3COOCH_2CH_2OC_2H_5$ |
| Chalk | Kreide | Craie | Calcium carbonate | $CaCO_3$ |
| Chloramine-T (X_n) | Chloramin T | Chloramine | Sodium salt of the p-toluene sulfonic acid chloramide | $Na[CH_3C_6H_4SO_2NCl] \cdot 3H_2O$ |
| Chloroprene (F, X_n) | Chloropren | Chloroprène | 2-chloro 1.3-butadiene | $CH_2=CClCH=CH_2$ |
| Chlorothene™ (X_n) "Methylchloroform" | Chlorothene®, ("1.1.1"); "Methylchloroform" | Chlorothène | 1.1.1-trichloroethane | $Cl_3CCH_3$ |
| Chromic anhydride (C, O, X_t) | Chromsäure | Anhydride chromique | Chromium trioxide (chromic acid anhydride) | $CrO_3$ |
| Cinnabar | Zinnober | Vermillon; cinabre | Mercury (II) sulfide | $HgS$ |
| Colophony; rosin | Kolophonium | Colophane | Naturally occurring abietic acid | $C_{19}H_{29}COOH$ |
| Corrosive sublimate (T) | Sublimat | Sublimé corrosif | Mercury (II) chloride | $HgCl_2$ |
| Cryolite (X_n) | Kryolith | Cryolite | Sodium hexafluoroaluminate | $Na_3[AlF_6]$ |
| Decalin | Dekalin | Décaline | Decahydro naphthalene | $C_{10}H_{18}$ |
| Diane, Sisphénol A | Bisphenol A; Diphenylol propan | Sisphénol A | Dihydroxyphenyl propane-2.2 | $(CH_3)_2C(C_6H_4(OH)-4)_2$ |
| Diisobutylene (F) | Diisobutylen | Diisobutylene | 2.4.4-trimethyl pentenes 1 and 2 | $(CH_3)_3CCH_2C(CH_3)=CH_2$ and $(CH_3)_3C-CH=C(CH_3)_2$ |
| DMF (X_n) | DMF (Xn) | DMF | N.N-dimethyl formamide | $HCON(CH_3)_2$ |

¹) methyl-, propyl-, i-propyl-, butyl-c.: names for analogous ethers containing the above mentioned groups instead of ethyl-.

| Commercial name English (hazard code) | German | French | Chemical name | Chemical formula |
|---|---|---|---|---|
| DMSO | DMSO | DMSO | Dimethyl sulfoxide | $(CH_3)_2SO$ |
| Dry ice | Trockeneis | Carboglace | | $CO_2$ |
| English red | Polierrot | Rouge d'Angleterre | Iron (III) oxide | $Fe_2O_3$ |
| Epsomite, bitter salt | Bittersalz (Magnesiumvitriol) | Epsomite | Magnesium sulfate | $MgSO_4 \cdot 7H_2O$ |
| Fixing salt; (hypo) | Fixiersalz ("Antichlor") | Sel fixatif | Sodium thiosulfate | $Na_2S_2O_3 \cdot 5H_2O$ |
| Fluorspar; fluorite | Flussspat; Fluorit | Spath fluoré; fluorine | Calcium fluoride | $CaF_2$ |
| Formalin (T) | Formalin® | Formol | Aqueous solution of formaldehyde | $H_2CO$ in $H_2O$ |
| Freon™(es) | Freon®(e); Frigen®(e) | Fréon(s); frigène(s) | Compounds of C, H, F, Cl, (Br) | Numerical designation [2] |
| GB-Ester; Polysolvan O | GB-Ester; Polysolvan O® | Polysolvan O | Glycol acid butyl ester (hydroxyacetic acid butyl ester) | $HOCH_2COOC_4H_{10}$ |
| Glauber's salt; mirabilite | Glaubersalz | Sel de Glauber | Sodium sulfate | $Na_2SO_4 \cdot 10H_2O$ |
| Glycol ($X_f$) | Glysantin® ; Glykol | Glycol | 1.2-ethandiol | $HOCH_2CH_2OH$ |
| Golden antimony sulphide | Goldschwefel | Sulfure doré d'antimoine | Antimony (V) sulfide | $Sb_2S_5$ |
| Green vitriol | Eisenvitriol | Vitriol vert; couperose verte | Iron (II) sulfate | $FeSO_4 \cdot 7H_2O$ |
| Halone(s) | Halon(e) | Halon(s) | Compounds of C, F, Cl, Br | Numerical designation [3] |
| Halon™ | Halon® | | Tetrafluoroethylene polymer | $(C_2F_4)n$ |
| Halothane | Halothan | | 2-bromine 2-chlorine 1.1.1-trifluoroethane | $F_3CCHClBr$ |
| Hartshorn salt | Hirschhornsalz | Sel volatil d'Angleterre | Ammonium hydrogen carbonate + ammonium carbonate | $(NH_4)HCO_3 + (NH_4)_2CO_3$ |
| Hexalin | Hexalin® | Hexaline | Cyclohexanol (also: hexahydronaphthalene) | $C_6H_{11}OH$ $(C_{10}H_{14})$ |
| Hexone (F) | Hexon; MIBK | | 4-methylpentanone 2 (methyl isobutyl ketone) | $(CH_3)_2CHCH_2COCH_3$ |

| | | | | |
|---|---|---|---|---|
| Hydrochloric acid (C) | Salzsäure | Esprit de sel | Aqueous solution of hydrogen chloride | $HCl$ in $H_2O$ |
| Hydrofluoric acid (T, C) | Flusssäure | Acide fluorhydrique | Aqueous solution of hydrogen fluoride | $HF$ in $H_2O$ |
| Hydrogen peroxide | Perhydrol® | Eau oxygénée | Hydrogen dioxide | $H_2O_2$ |
| Laughing gas (O) | Lachgas ("Stickoxydul") | Gaz hilarant | Nitrous oxide | $N_2O$ |
| Lead sugar ($X_n$) | Bleizucker | Sel de Saturne | Lead acetate | $Pb(CH_3COO)_2 \cdot 3H_2O$ |
| Lead vinegar ($X_n$) | Bleiessig | Vinaigre de plomb; eau blanche | Aqueous solution of lead acetate and lead hydroxide | $Pb(CH_3COO)_2 \cdot Pb(OH)_2$ |
| Libavius' fuming spirit (C) | Spiritus fumans Libavii | | Tin (IV) chloride | $SnCl_4$ |
| Lime saltpeter | Salpeter, Kalk-; Norge- | Salpêtre de Norvège | Calcium nitrate | $Ca(NO_3)_2 \cdot 4H_2O$ |
| Liquid gas (F) | Flüssiggas | Gaz liquéfié | Propane, n- and i-butane | $C_3H_8 + C_4H_{10}$ |
| Lunar caustic (C) | Höllenstein; "lapis infernalis" | Pierre infernale | Silver nitrate | $AgNO_3$ |
| Marble | Marmor | Marbre | Calcium carbonate | $CaCO_3$ |
| Microcosmic salt | Phosphorsalz | | Sodium ammonium hydrogen phosphate | $NH_4NaHPO_4 \cdot 4H_2O$ |
| Mine gas (F) | Grubengas; Sumpfgas | Grisou; gaz des marais | Methane | $CH_4$ |

[2] Numerical codes for freons (fluorine-chlorine derivatives of methane and ethane, $CH_4$ and $C_2H_6$):
Number in hundreds column = number of carbon atoms −1
Number in tens column = number of hydrogen atoms +1
Number in ones column = number of fluorine atoms
The missing atoms for valence saturation are chlorine atoms. Examples: F 113 = $C_2F_3Cl_3$; F 21 = $CHFCl_2$

[3] Numerical codes for halones (fully halogenated hydrocarbons):
Number in thousands column = number of C atoms
Number in hundreds column = number of F atoms
Number in tens column = number of Cl atoms
Number in ones column = number of Br atoms
Examples: halone 1211 = $CF_2ClBr$; halone 2402 = $C_2F_4Br_2$

| Commercial name English (hazard code) | German | French | Chemical name | Chemical formula |
|---|---|---|---|---|
| Minium | Mennige | Minium | Lead (II) orthoplumbate | $Pb_3O_4$ ($Pb_2PbO_4$) |
| Mohr's salt | Mohr'sches Salz | Sel de Mohr | Iron (II) ammonium sulfate | $(NH_4)_2[Fe(SO_4)_2] \cdot 6H_2O$ |
| Mordant salt [4] | Tonerde, essigsaure | Mordant rouge | Basic aluminum acetate | $(CH_3COO)_2AlOH$ |
| Mota ($X_n$) | Meta® | Alcool solidifié | Tetramethyl tetroxacyclooctane (metaldehyde) | $(CHCH_3)_4O_4$ |
| Muthmann's liquid | Muthmann's Flüssigkeit | | 1.1.2.2-tetrabromethane | $Br_2CHCHBr_2$ |
| Nitroglycerin (E, F) | Nitroglycerin | Nitroglycérine | Glycerol trinitrate | $CHONO_2(CH_2ONO_2)_2$ |
| Nitrolim; lime nitrogen | Kalkstickstoff | Chaux azotée | Calcium cyanamide | $CaCN_2$ |
| Norway saltpeter | Salpeter, Ammon- | Nitrate d'ammonium | Ammonium nitrate | $NH_4NO_3$ |
| Oleum (C) | Oleum ("Vitriolöl") | Oléum | Sulfuric acid + disulfuric acid | $H_2SO_4 + H_2S_2O_7$ |
| Oxalic acid ($X_n$) | Kleesäure | Acide oxalique | Oxalic acid | $(COOH)_2 \cdot 2H_2O$ |
| Phosgene (T) | Phosgen | Phosgène | Carbonic acid dichloride | $COCl_2$ |
| Phosphine ($T_+$) | Phosphin | Phosphine (sel de phosphore) | Hydrogen phosphide | $PH_3$ |
| Picric acid (T, E) | Pikrinsäure | Acide picrique | 2.4.6-trinitrophenol | $C_6H_2(NO_2)_3OH$ |
| Potash | Pottasche | Potasse | Potassium carbonate | $K_2CO_3$ |
| Potash alum | Alaun, Kali- | Alun de potassium | Potassium aluminum sulfate | $KAl(SO_4)_2 \cdot 12H_2O$ |
| Potassium chlorate (O, $X_n$) | Knallsalz | Sel de Berthollet | Potassium chlorate | $KClO_3$ |
| Potassium metabisulphite | Kaliummetabisulfit | Métabisulfite de potassium | Potassium disulfite | $K_2S_2O_5$ |
| Pyrolusite ($X_n$) | Braunstein | Pyrolusite | Manganese dioxide | $MnO_2$ |
| Quicklime; burnt lime; caustic lime | Kalk, gebrannter | Chaux vive | Calcium oxide | $CaO$ |
| Rochelle salt; salt of Seignette | Seignettesalz (Natronweinstein) | Sel de Seignette | Potassium sodium tartrate | $(CHOH)_2COOKCOONa$ |

| Red prussiate of potash | Blutlaugensalz, rotes; Kaliumferricyanid | Prussiate rouge | Potassium hexacyanoferrate (III) | $K_3[Fe(CN)_6]$ |
|---|---|---|---|---|
| Sal ammoniac ($X_n$) | Salmiak (Salmiaksalz) | Salmiac | Ammonium chloride | $NH_4Cl$ |
| Saltpeter | Salpeter, Kali- | Salpêtre (sel de pierre) | Potassium nitrate | $KNO_3$ |
| Silica gel with indicator | Blaugel (Silicagel) | Gel bleu (gel de silice) | Porous silicon dioxide with humidity indicator | $SiO_2$ with cobalt compound |
| Slaked lime | Kalk, gelöschter | Chaux éteinte | Calcium hydroxide | $Ca(OH)_2$ |
| Soda crystals | Soda (Kristall-) | Soude (cristaux de) | Sodium carbonate | $Na_2CO_3 \cdot 10H_2O$ |
| Soda niter; Chile saltpeter | Salpeter, Chile; Natronsalpeter | Salpêtre du Chili | Sodium nitrate | $NaNO_3$ |
| Sorrel salt; potassium binoxalate | Kleesalz | Sel d'oseille | Potassium tetraoxalate | $(HOOCCOOK) \cdot (COOH)_2 \cdot 2H_2O$ |
| Sulphuric ether (F) | Schwefeläther | Éther sulfurique | Diethyl ether | $C_2H_5OC_2H_5$ |
| Tetrachloroethylene ($X_n$) | Per | Tétrachloroéthylène | Tetrachloroethylene (perchloroethylene) | $Cl_2C=CCl_2$ |
| Tetrachloromethane (T) | Tetra ("Tetraform") | Tétrachlorométhane | Tétrachloromethane | $CCl_4$ |
| Tetralin (O, C) | Tetralin | Tétraline | 1.2.3.4-tetrahydronaphthalene | $C_{10}H_{12}$ |
| Tin foil | Stanniol | Papier d'étain | Foil tin | Sn |
| Tin salt | Zinnsalz | Sel d'étain | Tin (II) chloride | $SnCl_2 \cdot 2H_2O$ |
| TNT; trotyl (E) | TNT | TNT; tolite | 2.4.6-trinitro toluene | $C_6H_2(NO_2)_3CH_3$ |
| Trichlorethylene ($X_n$) | Tri | Trichloréthylène | Trichloroethylene | $Cl_2C=CHCl$ |
| Urea | Harnstoff | Urée | Carbonic acid diamide | $CO(NH_2)_2$ |
| Urotropine | Urotropin | Urotropine | 1.3.5.7-tetra acadamantane | $(CH_2)_6N_4$ |
| Vichy salt; baking soda | Bullrichsalz; Natron (Natriumbicarbonat) | Sel de Vichy | Sodium hydrogen carbonate | $NaHCO_3$ |
| Waterglass | Wasserglas (Kali- bzw. Natron-) | Verre soluble | Aqueous solution of potassium or sodium silicates | $M_2SiO_3 + M_2Si_2O_5$ (M = K or Na) |
| Yellow prussiate of potash | Blutlaugensalz, gelbes; Kaliumferrocyanid | Prussiate jaune | Potassium hexacyanoferrate (II) | $K_4[Fe(CN)_6]$ |

4) Mordanting agent, for instance, for dying textiles red. Cf. e.g. Hawley's Condensed Chemical Dictionary, 11th ed. 1987 under "Aluminum acetate".

# Frictional joints

| Quantity | | Unit |
|---|---|---|
| $C$ | Taper ratio | – |
| $D$ | Diameter | mm |
| $E$ | Modulus of elasticity | N/mm² |
| $F$ | Force | N |
| $F_a$ | Axial force | N |
| $F_N$ | Normal force | N |
| $F_R$ | Frictional force | N |
| $K_A$ | Application factor (service factor) | – |
| $M_t$ | Torque | Nm |
| $M_{t,nominal}$ | Nominal load torque | Nm |
| $Q$ | Diameter ratio | – |
| $R_z$ | Surface roughness | mm |
| $S_B$ | Factor of safety against rupture | – |
| $S_F$ | Factor of safety against yield | – |
| $U$ | Tolerance | mm |
| $Z$ | Allowance | mm |
| $b$ | Hub width | mm |
| $d$ | Diameter | mm |
| $l$ | Taper or lever length | mm |
| $n$ | Number of bolts | – |
| $p$ | Surface pressure | N/mm² |
| $t$ | Temperature | °C |
| $\alpha$ | Cone angle | ° |
| $\alpha_A$ | Coefficient of linear expansion, outer part | 10⁻⁶/K |
| $\alpha_I$ | Coefficient of linear expansion, inner part | 10⁻⁶/K |
| $\mu$ | Coefficient of friction | – |
| $\nu$ | Poisson ratio | – |
| $\xi$ | Specific allowance | mm³/N |

## References

DIN 7190: Press fits. Calculation and design rules,
Beuth-Verlag 2001.
Haberhauer/Bodenstein:
Maschinenelemente (Machine parts),
12th edition,
Springer-Verlag 2003.
Kollmann: Welle-Nabe-Verbindungen (Shaft-hub connections),
Springer-Verlag 1984.

## Basic principles

For frictional joints, press fits are produced in the joints (friction surfaces = effective areas) in which the parts to be assembled are in direct contact. The surface pressure $p$ can be generated by bolt forces, keys, elastic separators, or the elasticity of the components themselves. The resulting normal force $F_N = p \cdot A$ (where $A$ = friction surface) induces a frictional force $F_R$, which opposes a movement caused by external forces.

## Press fit (cylindrical interference fit)

For a press fit, the required surface pressure is produced by the elastic deformation of the shaft and hub, resulting from an interference fit. "Interference fit" is the pairing of cylindrical fitting parts, which have an interference before assembly.

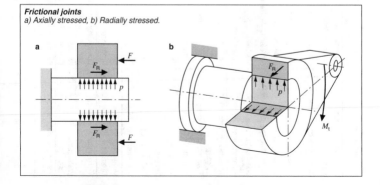

*Frictional joints*
*a) Axially stressed, b) Radially stressed.*

They are often used because they are easy to produce, and can transfer even jerky and variable torques and linear forces.

### Elastic design of simple press-fit assemblies

A press fit must be designed so that:
- At least a minimum surface pressure $p_{min}$ is present, in order to ensure the transfer of the greatest occurring stress.
- A maximum surface pressure $p_{max}$ is not exceeded, so that the components are not overstressed.

In principle, two calculation aims are possible:
1. To define the required fit for a given stress (Table 1).

2. To determine the permissible stress for a given fit (Table 2, next page).

The diameter ratios:
$Q_A = D_F / D_{Aa}$
$Q_I = D_{Ii} / D_F$
and the specific allowance

$$\xi = D_F \cdot \left[ \frac{1}{E_I} \left( \frac{1 + Q_I^2}{1 - Q_I^2} - \nu_I \right) + \frac{1}{E_A} \left( \frac{1 + Q_A^2}{1 - Q_A^2} + \nu_A \right) \right]$$

can be used to design press fits with reference to their function and the required component safety.

The maximum tensions occur at the internal diameters of hollow shaft and hub.

Solid shafts are noncritical, and do not usually have to be calculated.

### Table 1. Defining fits.

| Stress $M_t$ and/or $F_a$ given | $\sigma_{perm} = R_e / S_F$ or $\sigma_{perm} = R_m / S_B$ given |
|---|---|
| Required fit:<br><br>$p_{min} = \dfrac{\sqrt{F_a^2 + \dfrac{4 \cdot M_{t,nominal}^2}{D_F^2}}}{\mu \cdot \pi \cdot D_F \cdot b} \cdot K_A$ | Permissible fit in hub:<br>$p_{max} = (1 - Q_A^2) \cdot \sigma_{perm} / \sqrt{3}$<br><br>permissible pressure in hollow shaft:<br>$p_{max} = (1 - Q_I^2) \cdot \sigma_{perm} / \sqrt{3}$ |
| Required allowance:<br>$Z_{min} = p_{min} \cdot \xi$ | Permissible allowance:<br>$Z_{max} = p_{max} \cdot \xi$ |
| Required tolerance:<br>$U_{min} = Z_{min} + 0.8 \cdot (R_{zI} + R_{zA})$ | Permissible tolerance:<br>$U_{max} = Z_{max} + 0.8 \cdot (R_{zI} + R_{zA})$ |
| Select ISO fit with $U_k \geq U_{min}$ and $U_g \leq U_{max}$ | |

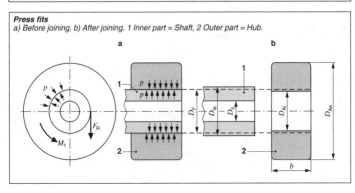

**Press fits**
*a) Before joining, b) After joining. 1 Inner part = Shaft, 2 Outer part = Hub.*

**Table 2. Calculating stress**

| Tolerance $U_k$ given | Tolerance $U_g$ given |
|---|---|
| Minimum allowance:<br>$Z_k = U_k + 0.8 \cdot (R_{zl} + R_{zA})$ | Maximum allowance:<br>$Z_g = U_g + 0.8 \cdot (R_{zl} + R_{zA})$ |
| Minimum surface pressure:<br><br>$p_k = \dfrac{Z_k}{\xi}$ | Maximum surface pressure:<br><br>$p_g = \dfrac{Z_g}{\xi}$ |
| Permissible stress:<br>$M_t = 0.5 \cdot p_k \cdot \mu \cdot \pi \cdot D_F^2 \cdot b$    (only $M_t$)<br>$F_a = p_k \cdot \mu \cdot \pi \cdot D_F \cdot b$    (only $F_a$)<br><br>$M_t = \dfrac{D_F}{2} \cdot \sqrt{(p_k \cdot \mu \cdot \pi \cdot D_F \cdot b)^2 - F_a^2}$  (given $F_a$)<br><br>$F_a = \sqrt{(p_k \cdot \mu \cdot \pi \cdot D_F \cdot b)^2 - \dfrac{4 \cdot M_t^2}{D_F^2}}$  ($M_t$ given) | Hub safety factor:<br><br>$S_F = \dfrac{1 - Q_A^2}{\sqrt{3} \cdot p_g} \cdot R_e$   or   $S_B = \dfrac{1 - Q_A^2}{\sqrt{3} \cdot p_g} \cdot R_m$<br><br>Hollow shaft safety factor:<br><br>$S_F = \dfrac{1 - Q_I^2}{\sqrt{3} \cdot p_g} \cdot R_e$   or   $S_B = \dfrac{1 - Q_I^2}{\sqrt{3} \cdot p_g} \cdot R_m$ |

## Assembly

There are two types of press fit depending on the assembly method: linear and transverse. Linear press fits are produced by "cold" assembly at room temperature. The large press-fit forces required are usually applied by hydrostatic presses. The press-fit velocity should not exceed 2 mm·s⁻¹. For the press-fit force:

$$F_e = \frac{\left[ U_g - 0.8 \cdot (R_{zl} + R_{zA}) \right] \cdot \mu \cdot \pi \cdot D_F \cdot b}{\xi}$$

Before transverse press-fits are made, either the outer part is expanded by heating, or the diameter of the inner part is reduced by supercooling, so that the parts can be assembled stress-free. If the outer part is heated, it shrinks onto the inner part as it cools (shrink fit). If the inner part is cooled so that expands when it is heated to room temperature, this is an expansion fit. To make force-free assembly possible, a joint clearance of $\Delta D = 0.001 \cdot D_F$ must be provided (Table 3).

Assembly temperature for shrink fit:
$$t_A = t_U + (U_g + \Delta D) / (\alpha_A \cdot D_F)$$

Assembly temperature for expansion fit:
$$t_A = t_U - (U_g + \Delta D) / (|\alpha_i| \cdot D_F)$$

**Table 3. Poisson ratio, modulus of elasticity, and linear coefficient of thermal expansion for metallic materials**

| Material | Poisson ratio | Modulus of elasticity $E$ N/mm² | Coefficient of linear expansion $\alpha$ $10^{-6}$/K Heating | Cooling |
|---|---|---|---|---|
| Gray cast iron | 0.24 | 100,000 | 10 | −8 |
| Malleable cast iron | 0.25 | 90,000...100,000 | | |
| Steel | 0.3 | 200,000...235,000 | 11 | −8.5 |
| Bronze | 0.35 | 110,000...125,000 | 16 | −14 |
| Gunmetal | 0.35...0.36 | 110,000...125,000 | 17 | −15 |
| CuZn | 0.36 | 80,000...125,000 | 18 | −16 |
| Mg Al 8 Zn<br>AlMgSi | 0.3<br>0.34 | 65,000...75,000 | 23 | −18 |

## Tapered connection (tapered interference fit)

### Applications
A tapered connection is suitable for transferring dynamic forces and torques. It is mainly used for fixing parts to shaft ends. It has the following advantages:
– Can be re-tensioned.
– Easily detachable.
– Does not weaken the shaft.
– Very good centering (no imbalance).
The disadvantages are:
– High production costs.
– Not adjustable in the axial direction.

The following taper ratios are specified as guidelines:
$C = 1{:}5$  Connection is easily detachable.
$C = 1{:}10$  Connection is detachable only with difficulty.
$C = 1{:}20$  Tool holder for twist drill.

Taper ratio:  $C = (d_1 - d_2)/l$

Cone angle:  $\tan \alpha/2 = (d_1 - d_2) / 2\,l$

### Operation
The effective area pair of a tapered connection takes the form of a truncated cone (frustum). The required surface pressure $p$ is usually applied by an axial bolt force $F_a$. The relationship between the axial press-fit force $F_a$ and the transferable torque $M_t$ is expressed by the following equation:

$$F_a \geq \frac{2 \cdot K_A \cdot M_{t,\text{nominal}}}{\mu_U \cdot d_m} \cdot \left( \sin\frac{\alpha}{2} + \mu_a \cdot \cos\frac{\alpha}{2} \right)$$

This takes account of the possible difference between the coefficients of friction in the circumferential direction $\mu_U$ and in the axial direction $\mu_a$. Self-locking exists if an expulsion force is required to detach the connection. This means that a torque can be transferred even if the bolt is removed after the parts are axially stressed. By contrast, with a non-self-locking tapered connection, there is no pressure between the effective areas after the axial application force is released. Condition for self-locking:

$\alpha/2 \leq \arctan \mu_a$

### Component safety
The critical component is the hub. It is calculated as an open, thick-walled hollow cylinder. If $Q = d_m/D_a$, the following applies to the safety of the hub, with elastic design, depending on the modified maximum shear stress theory:

$$S_F = \frac{1 - Q^2}{\sqrt{3}} \cdot \frac{\left( \sin\frac{\alpha}{2} + \mu_a \cdot \cos\frac{\alpha}{2} \right) \cdot \pi \cdot d_m \cdot l}{F_{a,\text{max}}}$$

## Taper-lock joints

The required surface pressure in the effective areas can also be applied by elastic separators. The great advantages of these taper-lock joints is that they can be used to fix hubs, gears, couplings, etc. securely to smooth, cylindrical shafts. They can also be freely adjusted axially and tangentially. Their disadvantages include the space required and the high costs. They are usually designed as specified by the manufacturer (see product catalogs or Table 4, next page).

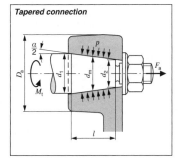

**Tapered connection**

**Table 4. Taper-lock joints**

| Name | Illustration | Features |
|------|--------------|----------|
| Clamping sleeve (SPIETH) | | Axial distortion is applied to enlarge the external diameter of the clamping sleeve and reduce the internal diameter. The danger of loosening under dynamic loads is reduced by using long bolts. |
| Hydraulic hollow jacket spring collet (LENZE) | | Axial distortion is applied to generate a pressure in a thin-walled hollow cylinder. The spring collet is self-centering because of even pressure distribution, and thus has true-running properties. At higher temperatures, the thermal expansion of the pressure fluid must be taken into account. |
| Tolerance ring (OECHSLE) | | Tolerance rings are slotted made from thin wave-shaped sheet metal. The required initial force is provided by forced deformation of the elastic connecting member. They can bridge relatively large machining tolerances, compensate for thermal expansion, and transfer torques. |
| Star washers (RINGSPANN) | | Star washers are thin-walled, very flat conical shells with radial slots. The axial initial force is translated by forced deformation into a fivefold to tenfold radial force. Star washers do not center. |
| Taper lock ring (RINGFEDER) | 1 Precentering | Taper lock rings consist of two coaxially arranged conical rings. Radial prestressing is achieved by axially distorting the rings. Taper lock rings do not center. They are not self-locking and thus can easily be detached. |
| Taper lock set (BIKON) | | Axial distortion is applied by means of the bolts belonging to the taper lock set. Taper lock sets are very true-running and can transfer very large torques, particularly with multiple pairs of effective areas. |

## Clamp joints

In the case of clamp joints, external forces apply the required surface pressure to the joint, mostly by means of bolts. The joints with a sectional or slotted hub are preferably used for low torques which have little fluctuation. Their advantage is that the hub position is easily adjustable in the axial and tangential directions. They provide a very easy means of fixing wheels or levers to smooth shafts. However, there are also self-locking clamp joints. Here, the tilting force $F_K$ generates edge pressures in A and B to prevent axial movement (Table 5).

## Keyed joints

### Longitudinal keyed joints
A one-sided radial distortion is achieved by driving in a standardized key (taper 1:100) between the shaft and hub. However, because of their imprecise assembly (hammer assembly) and the resulting eccentricities, keys are only of secondary importance.

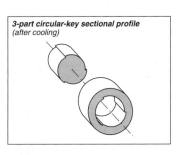

**3-part circular-key sectional profile** (after cooling)

### Circular keyed joints
A new type of keyed joint is the 3-part circular-key sectional profile. Three circular keys are arranged circumferentially on the cylindrical surface of a shaft (inner part). The hub (outer part) contains an appropriate number of corresponding keys in a cylindrical hole. Twisting results in radial distortion and this can transfer large axial and tangential forces in any direction. As opposed to press fits, circular keyed joints are detachable. Application examples: shaft-hub connections, camshaft, hinges in vehicle construction.

### Table 5. Clamp joints

| Name | Illustration | Calculation |
|---|---|---|
| Clamp joint with separated hub | | Transferable torque:<br><br>$M_t = n \cdot F_S \cdot \mu \cdot (\pi/2) \cdot D_F$<br><br>($n$ number of bolts) |
| Clamp joint with slotted hub | | Transferable torque:<br><br>$M_t = n \cdot F_S \cdot \mu \cdot (\pi/2) \cdot D_F \cdot (l_S / l_N)$<br><br>($n$ number of bolts) |
| Self-locking Clamp joint | | Condition for self-locking:<br><br>$l / b = 1 / (2 \mu)$ |

# Positive or form-closed joints

| Quantity | | Unit |
|---|---|---|
| $D$ | Diameter | mm |
| $F$ | Force | N |
| $K_A$ | Application factor (service factor) | – |
| $M_t$ | Torque | Nm |
| $b$ | Width | mm |
| $d$ | Diameter | mm |
| $h$ | Height | mm |
| $i$ | Number of shear surfaces | – |
| $l$ | Length | mm |
| $l_{tr}$ | Supporting feather key length | mm |
| $n$ | Number of drivers | – |
| $p$ | Surface pressure | N/mm² |
| $t_1$ | Groove depth (shaft) | mm |
| $t_2$ | Groove depth (hub) | mm |
| $\sigma_b$ | Bending stress | N/mm² |
| $\tau_s$ | Shear stress | N/mm² |
| $\varphi$ | Contact-surface ratio | – |

## References

DIN 6892:
Feather keys Calculation and design, Beuth-Verlag 1998.
Haberhauer/Bodenstein:
Maschinenelemente (Machine parts), 12th edition, Springer-Verlag 2003.
Kollmann:
Welle-Nabe-Verbindungen (Shaft-hub connections), Springer-Verlag 1984.

## Basic principles

Positive or form-closed joints have the task of transfering forces, which themselves maintain contact via mating surfaces, by means of their geometrical shape. The forces are always transferred perpendicularly to the mating surfaces, resulting mainly in compressive and shear stress.

Form closure generally produces easily detachable connections. Depending on the choice of press fit, relative axial movements may occur during operation. If necessary, they must be prevented by suitable locking devices (e.g. locking ring according to DIN 471).

## Feather-key and woodruff-key couplings

Feather-key couplings are used for the torsion-resistant connection of belt pulleys, gears, coupling hubs, etc. to shafts. Feather keys are sometimes used to secure frictional joints or to fix a specified position in the circumferential direction.

The cheaper woodruff key, the round side of which fits into the shaft, is mainly used for this purpose in automotive construction and to transfer smaller torques.

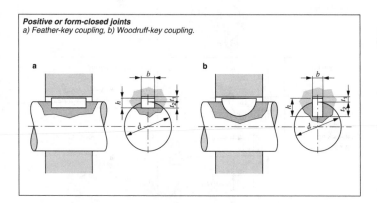

**Positive or form-closed joints**
*a) Feather-key coupling, b) Woodruff-key coupling.*

In the case of feather-key couplings, the groove faces lie against the feather-key faces. In contrast to keyed joints, there is clearance (backlash) between the rear of the feather key and the base of the groove. This means that the forces are transferred exclusively via the flanks of the feather key.

For feather key width, the tolerance zone $h\,9$ (key steel to DIN 6880) is provided. For groove widths $b$, the following tolerance zones apply:

| Groove fit | Fixed fit | Easy fit | Sliding fit |
|---|---|---|---|
| in hub | $P\,9$ | $N\,9$ | $H\,8$ |
| in shaft | $P\,9$ | $J\,9$ | $D\,10$ |

A sliding seat must be used if a hub must move on the shaft in the longitudinal direction (e.g. gear in manual-shift transmission). Usually, the sliding spring is firmly bolted into the shaft groove. Round (Shape A) and angular (Shape B) feather keys are manufactured. DIN 6885 defines the standard in terms of their shape and dimensions, depending on the shaft diameter (Table 1 and Figure).

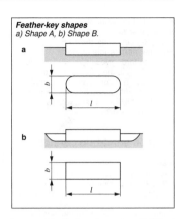

**Feather-key shapes**
a) Shape A, b) Shape B.

In practice, feather keys are designed only for surface pressure. If $p \leq p_{perm}$, the required supporting feather key length is:

$$l_b = \frac{2 \cdot K_A \cdot M_t}{d \cdot (h - t_1) \cdot n \cdot \varphi \cdot p_{perm}}$$

**Table 1. Feather-key dimensions according to DIN 6885.**

| Shaft diameter $d$ over mm | up to mm | Width x height $b$ x $h$ mm | Groove depths $t_1$ mm | $t_2$ mm | Length $l$ mm |
|---|---|---|---|---|---|
| 6 | 8 | 2 x 2 | 1.2 | 1.0 | 6...20 |
| 8 | 10 | 3 x 3 | 1.8 | 1.4 | 6...36 |
| 10 | 12 | 4 x 4 | 2.5 | 1.8 | 8...45 |
| 12 | 17 | 5 x 5 | 3.0 | 2.3 | 10...56 |
| 17 | 22 | 6 x 6 | 3.5 | 2.8 | 14...70 |
| 22 | 30 | 8 x 7 | 4.0 | 3.3 | 18...90 |
| 30 | 38 | 10 x 8 | 5.0 | 3.3 | 22...110 |
| 38 | 44 | 12 x 8 | 5.0 | 3.3 | 28...140 |
| 44 | 50 | 14 x 9 | 5.5 | 3.8 | 36...160 |
| 50 | 58 | 16 x 10 | 6.0 | 4.3 | 45...180 |
| 58 | 65 | 18 x 11 | 7.0 | 4.4 | 50...200 |
| 65 | 75 | 20 x 12 | 7.5 | 4.9 | 56...220 |
| 75 | 85 | 22 x 14 | 9.0 | 5.4 | 63...250 |
| 85 | 95 | 25 x 14 | 9.0 | 5.4 | 70...280 |
| 95 | 110 | 28 x 16 | 10.0 | 6.4 | 80...320 |
| Feather-key lengths in mm: | | 6, 8, 10, 12, 14, 16, 18, 20, 22, 25, 28, 32, 36, 40, 45, 50, 56, 63, 70, 80, 90, 100, 110, 125, 140, 160, 180, 200, 220, 250, 280, 320 | | | |

For round-faced feather keys (Form A), the feather key length is $l = l_{tr} + b$. For straight-faced ones (Form B), it is $l = l_{tr}$. For the permissible surface pressures, the standard gives $p_{perm} = 0.9 \cdot R_{e,min}$, where $R_{e,min}$ is the minimum yield point of the shaft, hub or feather-key material. With one feather key ($n = 1$), the contact-surface ratio is $\varphi = 1$, and with two feather keys, it is $\varphi = 0.75$.

## Profiled shaft-hub connections

Instead of inserting multiple feather keys into shaft grooves, the shaft cross-section can also be shaped directly in the form of a polygonal profile, and the mating hub cross-section has a corresponding shape. The profiled shaft-hub connection has the advantage that it does not require any additional separator (feather key) to transfer torque. The hub is centered either via a cylinder jacket surface (smallest diameter of shaft) or via the flanks of the drivers. Very smooth running can be achieved with internal centering (Table 2).

Flank centering insures very low circumferential backlash. It is therefore very suitable for alternating and jerky torques. As with the feather key, a rough design is drawn up based on surface pressure.

## Bolt and pin connections

Bolt and pin connections provide a simple and inexpensive means of connecting two or more components. These are among the oldest and most widely used types of connection.

### Bolt connections
Bolt connections are mainly used for joining linkages, shackles, chain links, and connecting rods, as well as axles for bearing impeller rings, rollers, levers, etc. Since relative movements occur in these connections, at least one part must be movable. The main prevailing stresses are surface pressure and shear. Bending stress is negligible in most cases. It only occurs to a significant extent in the case of bolt connections which are relatively long in relation to their diameter.

### Pin connections
Pins are suitable for the permanent connection of hubs, levers, and set collars on shafts or axles. They also secure the precise position of two machine parts, and as guide pins to fix springs, etc. Since they are forced into holes as press fits with tolerances, all parts are permanent.

**Table 2. Profiled shaft-hub connections**

| Name | Standard | Illustration | Driver | Centering | Contact-surface ratio |
|------|----------|--------------|--------|-----------|----------------------|
| Spline | ISO 14 DIN 5464 | | Prismatic driver | Inner | $\varphi = 0.75$ |
| | | | | Flanks | $\varphi = 0.9$ |
| Cog shaft with grooved toothing | DIN 5481 | | Grooved toothing | Flanks | $\varphi = 0.5$ |
| Cog shaft with involute teeth | DIN 5480 DIN 5482 | | Involute teeth | Flanks | $\varphi = 0.75$ |

**Table 3. Bolt and pin connections**

| Name | Illustration | Calculation |
|---|---|---|
| Articulated joint | 1 Clearance fit | Surface pressure in fork: $p_G = \dfrac{F}{2 \cdot b_1 \cdot d} \le p_{perm}$ |
| | | Surface pressure in rod: $p_S = \dfrac{F}{b \cdot d} \le p_{perm}$ |
| | | Surface pressure in pin: $\tau_S = \dfrac{4 \cdot F}{i \cdot \pi \cdot d^2} \le \tau_{S,perm}$ |
| Transverse pin joint | | Surface pressure in shaft: $p_{W,max} = \dfrac{6 \cdot M_t}{d \cdot D_W^2} \le p_{perm}$ |
| | | Surface pressure in hub: $p_N = \dfrac{4 \cdot M_t}{d \cdot (D_N^2 - D_W^2)} \le p_{perm}$ |
| | | Surface pressure in pin: $\tau_S = \dfrac{4 \cdot M_t}{D_W \cdot \pi \cdot d^2} \le \tau_{S,perm}$ |
| Guide pin | | Maximum Pressure: $p_{max} = p_b + p_d = \dfrac{F}{d \cdot s}\left(1 + 6 \cdot \dfrac{h + s/2}{s}\right) \le p_{perm}$ |
| | | Bending stress at clamping point: $\sigma_b = \dfrac{32 \cdot F \cdot h}{\pi \cdot d^3} \le \sigma_{b,perm}$ |
| | | Shear stress in clamping point: $\tau_S = \dfrac{4 \cdot F}{\pi \cdot d^2} \le \tau_{S,perm}$ |

**Table 4. Permissible mean surface pressure for bolt and pin connections.**

| Permanent fits | | | Sliding fits | |
|---|---|---|---|---|
| Material | Mean surface pressure static | swelling | Material pairing | Mean surface pressure |
| | $p_{perm}$ N/mm² | $p_{perm}$ N/mm² | | $p_{perm}$ N/mm² |
| Gray cast iron | 70 | 50 | Steel/Gray cast iron | 5 |
| S 235 (St 37) | 85 | 65 | St/CS | 7 |
| S 295 (St 50) | 120 | 90 | St/Bz | 8 |
| S 335 (St 60) | 150 | 105 | St hard./Bz | 10 |
| S 369 (St 70) | 180 | 120 | St hard./St hard. | 15 |

# Threaded fasteners

## Symbols and units

| Quantity | | Unit |
|---|---|---|
| $A$ | Cross-sectional area | mm² |
| $A_S$ | Stress area | mm² |
| $D_{Km}$ | Effective diameter for friction torque in fastener-head or nut bearing surface | mm |
| $E$ | Modulus of elasticity | N/mm² |
| $F_A$ | Axial operating force | N |
| $F_K$ | Clamping force | N |
| $F_M$ | Assembly preload | N |
| $F_N$ | Normal force | N |
| $F'_N$ | Normal force component in plane force polygon | N |
| $F_{PA}$ | Additional plate force | N |
| $F_Q$ | Transverse force, operating forceapplied perpendicular to fastener axis | N |
| $F_S$ | Fastener force | N |
| $F_{SA}$ | Additional fastener force | N |
| $F_V$ | Preload | N |
| $F_z$ | Loss of preload due to settling | N |
| $M_A$ | Tightening torque | Nm |
| $M_G$ | Effective tightening torque component in thread | Nm |
| $M_{KR}$ | Head friction torque | Nm |
| $M_L$ | Release torque | Nm |
| $P$ | Thread pitch | mm |
| $R_e$ | Yield point | N/mm² |
| $R_{p0.2}$ | 0.2% yield strength | N/mm² |
| $R_P$ | Spring rate of stressed parts | N/mm |
| $R_S$ | Spring rate of fastener | N/mm |
| $R_z$ | Surface roughness | µm |
| $W_t$ | Section modulus against torsion | mm³ |
| $d$ | Nominal thread diameter | mm |
| $d_2$ | Thread flank diameter | mm |
| $d_3$ | Thread root diameter | mm |
| $d_h$ | Hole diameter of stressed parts | mm |
| $d_w$ | External diameter of flat fastener-head or nut bearing surface | mm |
| $f_A$ | Elastic linear expansion by $F_A$ | mm |
| $f_{PV}$ | Elastic linear expansion of stressed parts by $F_V$ | mm |
| $f_{SV}$ | Elastic linear expansion of fastener by $F_V$ | mm |
| $f_z$ | Contact stress | mm |
| $i$ | Friction surface pairs | – |
| $l$ | Length | mm |
| $m$ | Nut height or thread reach | mm |
| $n$ | Force application factor | – |
| $n_S$ | Number of fasteners | – |
| $\alpha$ | Flank angle of thread | ° |

| Quantity | | Unit |
|---|---|---|
| $\alpha_A$ | Tightening factor | – |
| $\mu_G$ | Coefficient of friction in thread | – |
| $\mu_K$ | Coefficient of friction in head bearing surface | – |
| $\mu_T$ | Coefficient of friction in parting line | – |
| $\mu'_G$ | Apparent coefficient of friction in thread | – |
| $\varrho'_G$ | Angle of friction to $\mu'_G$ | – |
| $\sigma_a$ | Alternating stress on fastener | N/mm² |
| $\sigma_A$ | Permissible variable stress | N/mm² |
| $\sigma_{red,B}$ | Reduced stress in Operating state | N/mm² |
| $\sigma_{red,M}$ | Reduced stress in Fitted state | N/mm² |
| $\sigma_{z,M}$ | Max. tensile stress in Fitted state | N/mm² |
| $\sigma_z$ | Max. tensile stress in Operating state | N/mm² |
| $\tau_t$ | Max. torsional stress in thread | N/mm² |
| $\varphi$ | Pitch | ° |
| $\Phi$ | Force ratio | – |
| $\Phi_n$ | Force ratio at $n < 1$ | – |

## References

DIN-Taschenbuch 10: Mechanische Verbindungselemente – Schrauben (Mechanical threaded fasteners – screws and bolts), Beuth-Verlag 2001.
DIN-Taschenbuch 45: Gewindenormen (Thread standards), Beuth-Verlag 2000.
DIN-Taschenbuch 140: Mechanische Verbindungselemente – Muttern, Zubehörteile für Schraubenverbindungen (Mechanical threaded fasteners – Nuts, accessories for threaded fasteners), Beuth-Verlag 2001.
Haberhauer/Bodenstein: Machinenelemente (Machine parts), 12th edition, Springer-Verlag 2003.
VDI Directive 2230: Systematische Berechnung hochbeanspruchter Schraubenverbindungen (Systematic calculation of high-stress threaded fasteners), VDI-Verlag, 2003.
Wiegand/Kloos/Thomala: Schraubenverbindungen (Threaded fasteners), Springer-Verlag 1988.

## Basics

Threaded fasteners include "screws and bolts". They are used to make secure joints that are detachable any number of times. The purpose of screws and bolts is to stress the mating parts so that the static or dynamic operating forces acting on the joint do not cause any relative movement between the parts.

The prevailing basis for calculating high-stress threaded fasteners is VDI Directive 2230. It can be used as a simple, sufficiently precise calculation for a cylindrical single-threaded fastener, which can be considered as a section of a highly rigid multiple-threaded fastener. This means that, in many cases, even complex multiple-threaded fasteners can be considered as single-threaded fasteners. The precondition for this is that the fastener axes are parallel to each other and perpendicular to the parting planes. The components must also be elastic. Another important factor here is that only centrally preloaded and centrally stressed fasteners are considered. For large, eccentric stresses, which may cause the parting line to gape open, please refer to VDI 2230 (see figure).

## Threads

When a fastener is tightened or loosened, a screwing motion takes place. In one full rotation of the fastener, an axial shift corresponding to the pitch $P$ occurs. If a fastener line is uncoiled on a cylinder that has a flank diameter $d_2$, it will produce a straight line with a pitch angle $\varphi = \arctan[P/(\pi \cdot d_2)]$.

In general, fasteners are right-threaded (the straight line rises to the right). Special applications may require left-threaded bolts.

For normal fixing bolts or screws, metric thread profiles (DIN 13, ISO 965) are used. For pipes, fittings, threaded flanges, etc., pipe threads to DIN ISO 228-1 or DIN 2999 are used (PP. 356, 357).

## Property classes

According to DIN EN 20898, the properties of a fastener are identified by <u>two</u> numbers separated by a decimal point. The first number equals 1/100th of the minimum tensile strength; the second is a number that is 10 times the ratio of the yield point in relation to the tensile strength. Multiplying the two numbers gives 1/10 of the minimum yield point (example: $8.8 \rightarrow R_e = R_{p0.2} = 640$ MPa).

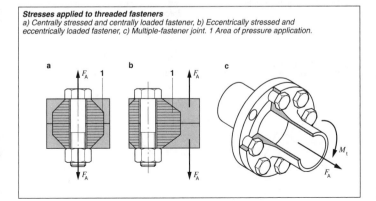

*Stresses applied to threaded fasteners*
*a) Centrally stressed and centrally loaded fastener, b) Eccentrically stressed and eccentrically loaded fastener, c) Multiple-fastener joint. 1 Area of pressure application.*

The property class of a standard nut is identified by <u>one number</u>. This number corresponds to 1/100 of the minimum tensile strength of a bolt of the same property class. To optimize material exploitation, therefore, bolts and nuts of equal property classes should always be paired (e.g. bolt 10.9 with nut 10).

## Tightening threaded fasteners

### Preload
Threaded fasteners are preloaded joints in which the fastener is expanded by $f_{SV}$ by being tightened, and the parts or plates to be tightened are pressed together by $f_{PV}$. The deformation depends on the dimensions (cross-section and length) and on the materials (moduli of elasticity). According to Hooke's Law, in the elastic range, these are proportional to the prevailing linear force. The ratio of force $F$ to change in length $f$ is the spring rate

$$R = \frac{F}{f} = \frac{E \cdot A}{l} .$$

If the rigidities of fasteners and stressed parts are known (they can be calculated according to VDI 2230), the pre-loaded threaded fastener can be represented by a load-extension diagram. After assembly, an equilibrium of forces arises so that the preload in the bolt and the stressed parts are of identical size (see figure).

### Operating forces
In the case of transversely stressed threaded fasteners (operating force $F_Q$ perpendicular to fastener axis), the forces are transferred in the parting plane by friction. Provided that the frictional forces, which are generated by the fastener preload, are greater than the operating forces to be transferred, the assembly load-extension diagram does not change. This means fastener "notices" nothing about the external stress.

At a coefficient of friction $\mu_T$ in the parting line, $n_S$ number of fasteners, $i$ number of friction surface pairs, and $S_R$ factor of safety against sliding, the minimum required clamping force is calculated as follows:

$$F_{K,min} = F_V \geq \frac{S_R \cdot F_Q}{\mu_T \cdot n_S \cdot i} .$$

If an external operating force $F_A$ acts in the direction of the fastener axis, the bolt is extended by $f_A$. At the same time the compression of the stressed parts is reduced by the same amount. The bolt is thus subjected to an additional stress of $F_{SA}$, whereas the stressed parts are relieved by $F_{PA}$. The additional fastener force $F_{SA}$ thus depends on the rigidity and yield of the fastener.

The "softer" the fastener (tensile bolt: long and thin), the smaller the additional bolt stress caused by an external axial operating force $F_A$. This must be the objective, particularly with dynamic operating forces (e.g. cylinder-head bolts).

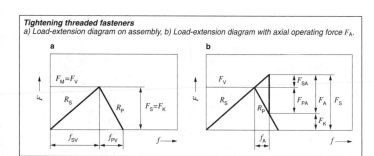

**Tightening threaded fasteners**
*a) Load-extension diagram on assembly, b) Load-extension diagram with axial operating force $F_A$.*

### Force application

The rigidities of the fastener and the stressed parts also depend on force application. If the external operating force $F_A$ is not applied directly to the fastener head or the nut bearing surface, only part of the stressed parts is relieved. This hardens the spring rate $R_P$ of the stressed parts, since grip is reduced. The stressed parts of the plates are hammered onto the fastener, which then becomes apparently longer and therefore softer. Small $n$ values therefore result in small additional fastener forces. This has a good impact of the fastener safety factor. However, the clamping force is reduced at the same time, and this is not good for the joint function.

There is no simple method of calculating the force application factor $n$, which defines the point of force application. Either $n$ ($0 \leq n \leq 1$) is estimated, or an approximate calculation is made according to VDI 2230 (as figure and Table 1).

## Fastener forces and torques

### Calculation model

The simplest way to represent force ratios in a threaded fastener is by concentrating the surface pressure distributed to all thread turns on a single nut element. During tightening and loosening, the nut element moves along the bolt thread, which, if unwound, represents a slanting plane or a wedge.

### Tightening a threaded fastener

When tightened, the nut element is pushed up the wedge by the peripheral force $F_U$. The resulting normal force $F_N$ causes a frictional force $F_R$ which acts in the opposite direction and includes the angle of friction $\varrho$. However, since all standardized thread profiles have inclined flanks, only the component $F'_N = F_N \cdot \cos \alpha/2$ appears in the plane force polygon.

**Table 1. Fastener forces** (depending on force application)

| Forces | Force application on fastener head $n = 1$ | Force application any $0 < n < 1$ | Force application in parting line $n = 0$ |
|---|---|---|---|
| Max. fastener force | $F_S = F_V + \Phi \cdot F_A$ | $F_S = F_V + \Phi_n \cdot F_A$ | $F_S = F_V$ |
| Clamping force | $F_K = F_V - (1 - \Phi) \cdot F_A$ | $F_K = F_V - (1 - \Phi_n) \cdot F_A$ | $F_K = F_S - F_A$ |
| Additional fastener force | $F_{SA} = \Phi \cdot F_A$ | $F_{SA} = \Phi_n \cdot F_A$ | $F_{SA} = 0$ |
| Additional plate force | $F_{PA} = (1 - \Phi) \cdot F_A$ | $F_{PA} = (1 - \Phi_n) \cdot F_A$ | $F_{PA} = F_A$ |

Where $\Phi = R_S/(R_P + R_S)$ and $\Phi_n = n \cdot \Phi$

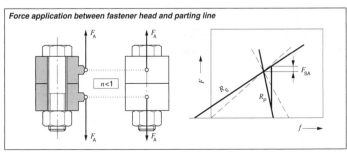

*Force application between fastener head and parting line*

The frictional force can then be calculated as follows:

$$F_R = F_N \cdot \mu_G = F'_N \cdot \mu'_G.$$

In order to calculate the force polygon in a plane parallel to the fastener axis, an apparent coefficient of friction is introduced:

$$\mu'_G = \frac{\mu_G}{\cos \alpha/2} = \tan \varrho'$$

When the peripheral force acts on the flank diameter $d_2$, the thread torque becomes:

$$M_G = F_V \cdot \frac{d_2}{2} \cdot \tan (\varphi + \varrho').$$

To tighten a bolt to preload $F_V$, a head friction torque $M_{KR}$ is required to overcome the friction between the head and nut bearing surfaces, in addition to the thread torque $M_G$. At a coefficient of friction $\mu_K$ and a mean head friction diameter $D_{Km}$, the head friction torque is calculated as follows:

$$M_{KR} = F_V \cdot \mu_K \cdot \frac{D_{Km}}{2} \,.$$

The bolt tightening torque applied during assembly is then (see also figures):

$$M_A = M_G + M_{KR} = F_V \cdot \left[ \frac{d_2}{2} \cdot \tan (\varphi + \varrho') + \mu_K \cdot \frac{D_{Km}}{2} \right]$$

**Loosening a threaded fastener**

When a threaded fastener is loosened, the frictional force changes in the opposite direction to the tightening action. The bolt loosening torque is calculated as follows:

$$M_L = F_V \cdot \left[ \frac{d_2}{2} \cdot \tan (\varphi - \varrho') - \mu_K \cdot \frac{D_{Km}}{2} \right]$$

In the case of self-locking threads ($\varphi < \varrho'$), the loosening torque becomes negative. This means that a torque must be applied in the opposite direction to the tightening action.

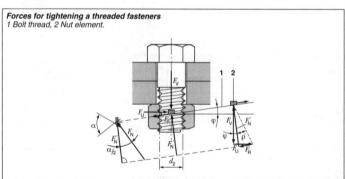

**Forces for tightening a threaded fasteners**
1 Bolt thread, 2 Nut element.

**Effective diameter $D_{Km}$ for head friction torque**
a) For Allen screw ($d_w$ = head diameter),
b) For hexagonal bolt/nut ($d_w$ = width across flats).

$$D_{Km} = (d_w + d_h)/2$$

# Design of threaded fasteners

## Overstressing
If the minimum thread reach $m = (1.0...1.5) \cdot d$ is maintained, a threaded fastener fails if overstressed, not because the thread turns are stripped, but because the cylindrical screw bolt ruptures.

## Assembly stress
When the fastener is tightened to preload $F_V$, it is stressed up to tensile stress. Due to the thread torque $M_G$, it is also stressed to torsion. As the friction in the thread prevents the bolt from turning back, the torsional stress also acts after tightening. According to the theory shape modification energy, the reduced stress in the bolt is:

$$\sigma_{red,M} = \sqrt{\sigma_{z,M}^2 + 3 \cdot \tau_t^2} \leq \nu \cdot R_{p0.2}$$

at tensile stress:

$$\sigma_{z,M} = \frac{F_{V,max}}{A_S} = \frac{\alpha_A \cdot F_V}{A_S}$$

and torsional stress:

$$\tau_t = \frac{M_{G,max}}{W_t} = \frac{16 \cdot \alpha_A \cdot F_V \cdot d_2 \cdot \tan(\varphi + \varrho')}{2 \cdot \pi \cdot d_3^3}$$

The tightening factor $\alpha_A$ takes account of the imprecision that is unavoidable during assembly.

For torque-controlled tightening (torque wrench), it is $\alpha_A = 1.4...1.6$; for pulse-controlled tightening (impact wrench), it is $\alpha_A = 2.5...4.0$.

To ensure high functional security, it is necessary to aim for the highest possible material exploitation. This is taken into account by efficiency $\nu$. Table 2 shows the permissible preload and tightening torques during assembly for different coefficients of friction at 90% efficiency ($\nu = 0.9$) of the standardized minimum yield point.

**Table 2.**
**Permissible preload and tightening torques for regular bolts** (to DIN 2230)

| Thread | Assembly preload $F_V$ for different coefficients of friction μ in thread | | | | | | Tightening torque $M_A$ with thread friction μ = 0.12 | | | | | |
| | $F_V$ in $10^3 \cdot$ N where μ = 0.1 | | | $F_V$ in $10^3 \cdot$ N where μ = 0.2 | | | $M_A$ in Nm where $μ_K = 0.1$ | | | $M_A$ in Nm where $μ_K = 0.2$ | | |
| | 8.8 | 10.9 | 12.9 | 8.8 | 10.9 | 12.9 | 8.8 | 10.9 | 12.9 | 8.8 | 10.9 | 12.9 |
|---|---|---|---|---|---|---|---|---|---|---|---|---|
| M4 | 4.5 | 6.7 | 7.8 | 3.9 | 5.7 | 6.7 | 2.6 | 3.9 | 4.5 | 4.1 | 6.0 | 7.0 |
| M5 | 7.4 | 10.8 | 12.7 | 6.4 | 9.4 | 11.0 | 5.2 | 7.6 | 8.9 | 8.1 | 11.9 | 14.0 |
| M6 | 10.4 | 15.3 | 17.9 | 9.0 | 13.2 | 15.5 | 9.0 | 13.2 | 15.4 | 14.1 | 20.7 | 24.2 |
| M8 | 19.1 | 28.0 | 32.8 | 16.5 | 24.3 | 28.4 | 21.6 | 31.8 | 37.2 | 34.3 | 50.3 | 58.9 |
| M10 | 30.3 | 44.5 | 52.1 | 26.3 | 38.6 | 45.2 | 43 | 63 | 73 | 68 | 100 | 116 |
| M12 | 44.1 | 64.8 | 75.9 | 38.3 | 56.3 | 65.8 | 73 | 108 | 126 | 117 | 172 | 201 |
| M14 | 60.6 | 88.9 | 104.1 | 52.6 | 77.2 | 90.4 | 117 | 172 | 201 | 187 | 274 | 321 |
| M16 | 82.9 | 121.7 | 142.4 | 72.2 | 106.1 | 124.1 | 180 | 264 | 309 | 291 | 428 | 501 |
| M18 | 104 | 149 | 174 | 91.0 | 129 | 151 | 259 | 369 | 432 | 415 | 592 | 692 |
| M20 | 134 | 190 | 223 | 116 | 166 | 194 | 363 | 517 | 605 | 588 | 838 | 980 |
| M22 | 166 | 237 | 277 | 145 | 207 | 242 | 495 | 704 | 824 | 808 | 1,151 | 1,347 |
| M24 | 192 | 274 | 320 | 168 | 239 | 279 | 625 | 890 | 1,041 | 1,011 | 1,440 | 1,685 |
| M27 | 252 | 359 | 420 | 220 | 314 | 367 | 915 | 1,304 | 1,526 | 1,498 | 2,134 | 2,497 |
| M30 | 307 | 437 | 511 | 268 | 382 | 447 | 1,246 | 1,775 | 2,077 | 2,931 | 2,893 | 3,386 |

## Static stress

An axial operating force $F_A$ increases tensile stress in the bolt. Since, in the operating state, the effect of torsional stress is less than in the fitted state, VDI 2230 applies to reduced stress

$$\sigma_{red,B} = \sqrt{\sigma_z^2 + 3(0.5 \cdot \tau_t)^2} < R_{p0,2}$$

at tensile stress:

$$\sigma_z = \frac{F_{S,max}}{A_S} = \frac{a_A \cdot F_V + F_{SA}}{A_S}$$

## Vibrational stress

At a dynamic operating force $F_A$, the variable stress component $\sigma_a$ must not exceed the permissible variable stress $\sigma_A$

$$\sigma_a = \frac{F_{S,max} - F_{S,min}}{2 \cdot A_S} \leq \sigma_A$$

The permissible variable stress $\sigma_A$ does not depend on the property class, but on the nominal diameter only (Table 3).

## Surface pressure between head and nut bearing surface

In the case of a large preload, the surface pressure on the head and nut bearing surfaces must be checked. Excessive surface pressures can cause plastic deformation and loss of preload. This can result in threaded fasteners coming loose.

The surface pressure $p$ resulting from the maximum fastener force must not exceed the permissible surface pressure limit $p_G$ (guideline values for $p_G$, see Table 4):

$$p = \frac{4 \cdot F_{S,max}}{\pi \cdot (d_w^2 - d_h^2)} \leq p_G$$

**Table 3.**
**Permissible variable stress $\sigma_A$**

| Diameter range | M6...M8 | M10...M18 | M20...M30 |
|---|---|---|---|
| Permissible variable stress $\sigma_A$ in N/mm² | 60 | 50 | 40 |

**Table 4.**
**Standard values for surface pressure limit $p_G$ as per VDI 2230**

| Material | Surface pressure limit $p_G$ in N/mm² |
|---|---|
| GD-AlSi 9 Cu 3 | 290 |
| S 235 J | 490 |
| E 295 | 710 |
| EN-GJL-250 | 850 |
| 34 CrNiMo 6 | 1,080 |

# Threaded fastener locking devices

The spontaneous loosening of a threaded fastener is caused by complete or partial loss of preload, which in turn is caused by settling events (loosening) or relative movements in the parting line (unscrewing).

## Loosening

Contact stress $f_z$ caused by plastic deformation results in loss of preload

$$F_z = \frac{R_P \cdot R_S}{R_P + R_S} \cdot f_z$$

Contact stress $f_z$ in µm depends on the surface properties and the number of parting lines (Table 5).

Total contact stress equals the sum of individual component parts. However, contact stress determined in this way is only valid if the surface pressure limits are not exceeded. Otherwise, significantly greater settling will arise. Locking devices are intended to reduce or compensate for settling.

The following measures provide reliable protection against loosening
– High preload
– Elastic threaded fasteners
– Low surface pressures due to large bearing surfaces and sufficient thread reach
– Low number of parting lines
– No plastic or quasi-elastic elements (e.g. seals) with stress

## Unscrewing

Dynamic stresses, particularly perpendicular to the fastener axis, may cause threaded fasteners to come loose despite sufficient preload. If transverse movements can occur, locking devices to prevent unscrewing insure that the joint retains its function.

Suitable measures include:
– Avoid transverse movements by positive locking in the parting line.
– Elastic bolts.
– Large grip lengths.
– High preload.
– Suitable locking devices (locking or bonding elements).

Locking devices (examples)
a) Flat-headed self-locking screw,
b) Flat-headed self-locking nut,
c) Locking washer pair.

**Table 5.**
**Contact stress $f_z$ depending on surface properties and number of parting lines**

| Surface | Load | Contact stress $f_z$ in µm in thread | per head or nut bearing surface | per parting line |
|---|---|---|---|---|
| $R_z < 10$ | Tension/pressure | 3.0 | 2.5 | 1.5 |
| | shear | 3.0 | 3.0 | 2.0 |
| $10 \leq R_z < 40$ | Tension/pressure | 3.0 | 3.0 | 2.0 |
| | shear | 3.0 | 4.5 | 2.5 |
| $40 \leq R_z < 160$ | Tension/pressure | 3.0 | 3.0 | 4.0 |
| | shear | 3.0 | 6.5 | 3.5 |

# Thread selection

**ISO metric screw threads**
(DIN 13, ISO 965); Nominal dimensions

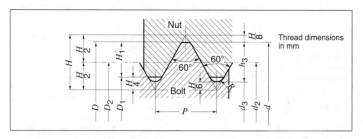

Nut

60° 60°

Bolt

Thread dimensions in mm

Metric standard thread
Example designation: M8 (nominal thread diameter: 8 mm)

| Nominal thread diam. | Pitch | Pitch diam. | Minor diam. | | Thread depth | | Stress area |
|---|---|---|---|---|---|---|---|
| $d = D$ | $P$ | $d_2 = D_2$ | $d_3$ | $D_1$ | $h_3$ | $H_1$ | $A_s$ in mm² |
| 3 | 0.5 | 2.675 | 2.387 | 2.459 | 0.307 | 0.271 | 5.03 |
| 4 | 0.7 | 3.545 | 3.141 | 3.242 | 0.429 | 0.379 | 8.78 |
| 5 | 0.8 | 4.480 | 4.019 | 4.134 | 0.491 | 0.433 | 14.2 |
| 6 | 1 | 5.350 | 4.773 | 4.917 | 0.613 | 0.541 | 20.1 |
| 8 | 1.25 | 7.188 | 6.466 | 6.647 | 0.767 | 0.677 | 36.6 |
| 10 | 1.5 | 9.026 | 8.160 | 8.376 | 0.920 | 0.812 | 58.0 |
| 12 | 1.75 | 10.863 | 9.853 | 10.106 | 1.074 | 0.947 | 84.3 |
| 14 | 2 | 12.701 | 11.546 | 11.835 | 1.227 | 1.083 | 115 |
| 16 | 2 | 14.701 | 13.546 | 13.835 | 1.227 | 1.083 | 157 |
| 20 | 2.5 | 18.376 | 16.933 | 17.294 | 1.534 | 1.353 | 245 |
| 24 | 3 | 22.051 | 20.319 | 20.752 | 1.840 | 1.624 | 353 |

Metric fine thread
Example designation: M8 x 1 (Nominal thread diameter: 8 mm; pitch 1 mm)

| Nominal thread diam. | Pitch | Pitch diam. | Minor diam. | | Thread depth | | Stress area |
|---|---|---|---|---|---|---|---|
| $d = D$ | $P$ | $d_2 = D_2$ | $d_3$ | $D_1$ | $h_3$ | $H_1$ | $A_s$ in mm² |
| 8 | 1 | 7.350 | 6.773 | 6.917 | 0.613 | 0.541 | 39.2 |
| 10 | 1.25 | 9.188 | 8.466 | 8.647 | 0.767 | 0.677 | 61.2 |
| 10 | 1 | 9.350 | 8.773 | 8.917 | 0.613 | 0.541 | 64.5 |
| 12 | 1.5 | 11.026 | 10.160 | 10.376 | 0.920 | 0.812 | 88.1 |
| 12 | 1.25 | 11.188 | 10.466 | 10.647 | 0.767 | 0.677 | 92.1 |
| 16 | 1.5 | 15.026 | 14.160 | 14.376 | 0.920 | 0.812 | 167 |
| 18 | 1.5 | 17.026 | 16.160 | 16.376 | 0.920 | 0.812 | 216 |
| 20 | 2 | 18.701 | 17.546 | 17.835 | 1.227 | 1.083 | 258 |
| 20 | 1.5 | 19.026 | 18.160 | 18.376 | 0.920 | 0.812 | 272 |
| 22 | 1.5 | 21.026 | 20.160 | 20.376 | 0.920 | 0.812 | 333 |
| 24 | 2 | 22.701 | 21.546 | 21.835 | 1.227 | 1.083 | 384 |
| 24 | 1.5 | 23.026 | 22.160 | 22.376 | 0.920 | 0.812 | 401 |

## Pipe threads for non self-sealing joints

(DIN ISO 228-1); Parallel internal threads and external threads; nominal dimensions

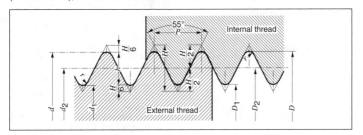

Example of designation: G 1/2 (nominal thread size 1/2 inch)

| Nominal thread size | Number of threads per inch | Pitch $P$ mm | Thread depth $h$ mm | Major diameter $d = D$ mm | Pitch diameter $d_2 = D_2$ mm | Minor diameter $d_1 = D_1$ mm |
|---|---|---|---|---|---|---|
| 1/4 | 19 | 1.337 | 0.856 | 13.157 | 12.301 | 11.445 |
| 3/8 | 19 | 1.337 | 0.856 | 16.662 | 15.806 | 14.950 |
| 1/2 | 14 | 1.814 | 1.162 | 20.955 | 19.793 | 18.631 |
| 3/4 | 14 | 1.814 | 1.162 | 26.441 | 25.279 | 24.117 |
| 1 | 11 | 2.309 | 1.479 | 33.249 | 31.770 | 30.291 |

## Whitworth pipe threads for threaded pipes and fittings

(DIN 2999); Parallel internal threads and tapered external threads; nominal dimensions (mm)

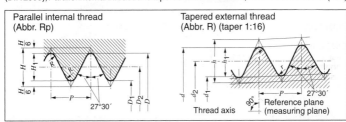

| Abbreviation | | Major diameter $d = D$ | Pitch diameter $d_2 = D_2$ | Minor diameter $d_1 = D_1$ | Pitch $P$ | Number of threads per inch $Z$ |
|---|---|---|---|---|---|---|
| External thread | Internal thread | | | | | |
| R 1/4 | Rp 1/4 | 13.157 | 12.301 | 11.445 | 1.337 | 19 |
| R 3/8 | Rp 3/8 | 16.662 | 15.806 | 14.950 | 1.337 | 19 |
| R 1/2 | Rp 1/2 | 20.955 | 19.793 | 18.631 | 1.814 | 14 |
| R 3/4 | Rp 3/4 | 26.441 | 25.279 | 24.117 | 1.814 | 14 |
| R 1 | Rp 1 | 33.249 | 31.770 | 30.291 | 2.309 | 11 |

Areas of application: For joining parallel internal threads to valves and fittings, threaded flanges, etc. with tapered external threads.

# Springs

## Symbols and units

| Quantity | | Unit |
|---|---|---|
| $b$ | Width of spring leaf | mm |
| $d$ | Wire diameter | mm |
| $D$ | Mean coil diameter | mm |
| $E$ | Modulus of elasticity | MPa |
| $F$ | Spring force | N |
| $G$ | Shear modulus | MPa |
| $h$ | Height of spring leaf | mm |
| $h_0$ | Spring deflection (disc spring) | mm |
| $i$ | Number of leaves (leaf spring) | – |
| $i'$ | Number of leaves, which continue to ends | – |
| $k$ | Stress coefficient | – |
| $L_c$ | Block length (solid length) | mm |
| $l_t$ | Active length | mm |
| $M_b$ | Bending moment | N·m |
| $M_t$ | Torsional moment | N·m |
| $n$ | Number of active coils | – |
| $n_t$ | Total number of coils | – |
| $R$ | Spring rate (spring constant) | N/mm |
| $R_t$ | Torsional spring rate | N·m/rad |
| $s$ | Spring deflection | mm |
| $S_a$ | Total of minimum distances | mm |
| $t$ | Thickness (disc spring) | mm |
| $W$ | Spring duty | J |
| $W_R$ | Frictional work | J |
| $\alpha$ | Twist angle | rad |
| $\sigma_b$ | Bending stress | MPa |
| $\tau_t$ | Torsional stress | MPa |
| $\psi$ | Damping | – |

## References

DIN-Taschenbuch 29:
Federn (Springs). Beuth-Verlag 2003.
Haberhauer/Bodenstein:
Maschinenelemente (Machine parts).
12th edition, Springer-Verlag 2003.
Fischer/Vondracek:
Warm geformte Federn
(Hot-formed springs).
Hoesch Hohenlimburg AG 1987.
Meissner/Schorcht:
Metallfedern (Metal springs).
Springer-Verlag 1997.

## Functions

All elastic components to which forces are applied are spring elements. However, springs in the narrower sense mean only those elastic elements that can absorb, store, and release work over a relatively long distance. The stored energy can also be used to maintain a force.

The most important applications of industrial springs are:
– Absorbing and damping shocks (shock absorbers)
– Storing potential energy (spring motors)
– Applying a force (coupling springs)
– Vibrating systems (vibrating table)
– Force measurement (spring balance).

## Characteristic, work and damping

### Spring characteristic

The spring characteristic shows the behavior of a spring or spring system. This means the dependency of spring force or spring torque on deformation. Metal springs have linear characteristics (Hooke's Law), rubber springs have progressive characteristics, and disc springs have degressive characteristics. The gradient of the characteristic is called the spring rate.

For translational motion:

$$R = \frac{dF}{ds}$$

For rotational motion:

$$R_t = \frac{dM_t}{d\alpha}$$

### Spring duty

For frictionless springs under stress, the area under the characteristic represents the absorbed or released work:

$$W = \int F \cdot ds$$

### Spring damping

If friction occurs, the prevailing force when the spring is loaded is greater than when the load is removed. The area enclosed by the two characteristics represents frictional work $W_R$, and is thus a measure of the damping rate:

$$\psi = \frac{W_R}{W}$$

Damping due to internal friction can be very high with rubber springs ($0.5 < \psi < 3$). With metal springs, however, it is rather low ($0 < \psi < 0.4$). This means that metal springs have a notable damping rate that is only achievable by means of external friction, e.g. that occurs in layers of leaf and disc springs.

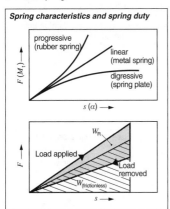

*Spring characteristics and spring duty*

## Spring combinations

A very wide variety of spring characteristics can be achieved by combining several springs. In principle, springs can be combined in parallel or in series. A combination of parallel and series springs is also possible.

### Parallel combinations

If springs are arranged in parallel, the external load is distributed proportionally between the individual springs. However, the spring deflection ($s$) is equal for all springs. The spring rate of the spring system is the sum of individual spring rates:

$$R_{tot} = R_1 + R_2 + R_3 + \dots + R_n$$

Accordingly, spring systems comprising parallel springs are harder than individual springs.

### Series combinations

With series springs, the total external load acts on each individual spring. However, spring travel for each spring is different depending on the individual spring rates, and are added. The following applies to the resulting spring rate of the overall system:

$$\frac{1}{R_{tot}} = \frac{1}{R_1} + \frac{1}{R_2} + \dots + \frac{1}{R_n}$$

Spring systems consisting of series springs are softer than the softest individual springs.

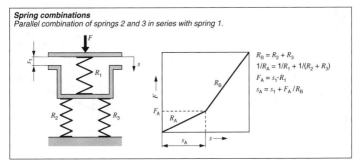

*Spring combinations*
*Parallel combination of springs 2 and 3 in series with spring 1.*

$$R_B = R_2 + R_3$$
$$1/R_A = 1/R_1 + 1/(R_2 + R_3)$$
$$F_A = s_1 \cdot R_1$$
$$s_A = s_1 + F_A / R_B$$

## Metal springs

Normally, metal springs are classified according to their stresses:

| Stress | Construction |
|---|---|
| Tensile, compression stress | Tensile test bar, ring spring |
| Bending stress | Leaf spring, coil spring, spiral spring, disc spring |
| Torsional stress | Torsion bar, helical spring |

It should be noted that the tendency of the springs to relax increases as working temperature rises. At 120 °C, relaxation is no longer negligible. However, with unalloyed spring steels, settling may begin to occur at 40 °C. At higher working temperatures, springs can only be properly evaluated using relaxation-tension diagrams.

### Springs subjected to tensile and compression stress
Due to their high spring rate, metal tensile and compression test bars are suitable only for very few special applications.

### Springs subjected to bending stress
Leaf springs
A simple leaf spring is used as a compression or guide spring. Layered leaf springs are used for suspension and wheel control in vehicles. They are usually made of spring steel to DIN 17221 and 17222. The draft design may assume the following permissible bending stresses:

| Steel bands to DIN 17222 | Static stress $\sigma_{b,perm}$ | Dynamic stress $\sigma_{b,perm} = \sigma_m + \sigma_{A,perm}$ |
|---|---|---|
| cold rolled, hardened and draw-tempered | 1,000 MPa | |
| individual leaves ground | | 500 ± 320 MPa |
| individual leaves with rolling skin | | 500 ± 100 MPa |
| layered leaves with rolling skin | | 500 ± 80 MPa |

Torsion and spiral springs
In the case of deflection of torsion and spiral springs, recoil torques are generated about the axis of rotation. Due to the clamping conditions, the bending stresses in the angle are almost uniform. The same equations are used for calculating torsion and spiral springs.

*Permissible bending stresses*
*For coil springs made of spring steel wire according to DIN 17223. With static and quasi-static stress, and if excessive stress caused by wire curvature is neglected, these $\sigma_b$ values can be used for design calculation purposes.*

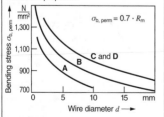

$\sigma_{b,\,perm} = 0.7 \cdot R_m$

*Disc springs according to DIN 2093*
*a) Without contact bearing surfaces,*
*b) With contact bearing surfaces,*
*c) Calculated spring characteristic of a disc spring to DIN 2092.*

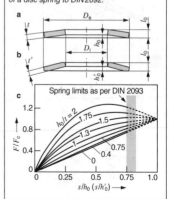

## Disc springs

The cone-bowl shaped disc springs are primarily subjected to bending stresses. A wide variety of applications results from the large number of possible of parallel and series combinations. Disc springs are mainly used where spring force and travel must be absorbed within confined spaces.

At $h_0/t > 0.4$, the nonlinearities of the springs are no longer negligible. Spring forces, spring travel, and spring rates can be calculated with sufficient precision according to DIN 2092, or they can be taken from the manufacturer's data.

For disc springs subjected to static stress ($< 10^4$ stress reversals), fatigue strength calculation is not required if the maximum spring force at $s = 0.75 \cdot h_0$ is not exceeded.

| Type | Spring force, spring torque | Deflection |
|---|---|---|
| **Simple straight leaf spring** (constant cross-section) | $F_{max} = \dfrac{b \cdot h^2}{6 \cdot l} \, \sigma_{b,perm}$ | $s = \dfrac{4 \cdot F \cdot l^3}{E \cdot b \cdot h^3}$ |
| | **Spring rate** | **Spring duty** |
| | $R = \dfrac{F}{s} = \dfrac{E \cdot b \cdot h^3}{4 \cdot l^3}$ | $W_{max} = \dfrac{\sigma_{b,perm}^2}{18 \cdot E} \cdot b \cdot h \cdot l$ |
| **Layered leaf spring** | **Spring force, spring torque** | **Deflection** |
| | $F_{max} = \dfrac{i \cdot b \cdot h^2}{6 \cdot l} \cdot \sigma_{b,perm}$ | $s = \dfrac{12 \cdot F \cdot l^3}{(2 \cdot i + i') \cdot E \cdot b \cdot h^3}$ |
| | **Spring rate** | **Spring duty** |
| | $R = \dfrac{(2i + i') \cdot E \cdot h^3 \cdot b}{12 \cdot l^3}$ | $W_{max} = \dfrac{\sigma_{b,perm}^2}{3 \cdot E} \cdot \dfrac{i^2}{(2i + i')} \cdot b \cdot h \cdot l$ |

| Type | | Spring force, spring torque | Deflection |
|---|---|---|---|
| **Coil spring** $l_f = \pi \cdot D \cdot n$ | Circular cross-section | $M_{t,max} = \dfrac{\pi \cdot d^3}{32} \cdot \sigma_{b,perm}$ | $\widehat{\alpha} = \dfrac{64 \cdot M_t \cdot l}{E \cdot \pi \cdot d^4}$ |
| | | **Spring rate** | **Spring duty** |
| | | $R = \dfrac{M_t}{\alpha} = \dfrac{E \cdot \pi \cdot d^4}{64 \cdot l}$ | $W_{max} = \dfrac{\sigma_{b,perm}^2}{32 \cdot E} \cdot \pi \cdot d^2 \cdot l$ |
| **Spiral spring** $l_f = 2 \cdot \pi \cdot n \cdot [r_0 + 0.5 \cdot n \cdot (h + \delta_t)]$ | Rectangular section | **Spring force, spring torque** | **Deflection** |
| | | $M_{t,max} = \dfrac{b \cdot h^2}{6} \cdot \sigma_{b,perm}$ | $\widehat{\alpha} = \dfrac{12 \cdot M_t \cdot l}{E \cdot b \cdot h^3}$ |
| | | **Spring rate** | **Spring duty** |
| | | $R = \dfrac{M_t}{\alpha} = \dfrac{E \cdot b \cdot h^3}{12 \cdot l}$ | $W_{max} = \dfrac{\sigma_{b,perm}^2}{6 \cdot E} \cdot b \cdot h \cdot l$ |

**Springs subjected to torsional stress**

Torsion bars

Circular cross-sections are usually selected for torsion bars. They have a very high volume utilization factor, which means that that they can absorb a lot of energy, but they occupy little space.

Helical springs

Cylindrical helical springs are manufactured as compression and extension springs. The calculation equations are identical for both types. Compression springs in conical form can optimize the use of space if the individual coils can be pushed into each other.

Force eccentricity can be minimized on compression springs by coiling the spring so that the wire end at each end of the spring touches the adjoining coil. Each end of the spring is then ground flat, perpendicular to the axis of the spring. To avoid overloading the spring, a minimum distance between the active coils must be maintained. For static stresses, the following applies:

| | Total number of coils | Block length | Sum of minimum distances |
|---|---|---|---|
| cold-formed | $n_t = n + 2$ | $L_c \leq n_t \cdot d$ | $S_a = (0.0015 \cdot D^2/d + 0.1 \cdot d) \cdot n$ |
| hot-formed | $n_t = n + 1.5$ | $L_c = (n_t - 0.3) \cdot d$ | $S_a = 0.02 \cdot (D + d) \cdot n$ |

| Type | Spring force, spring torque | Deflection |
|---|---|---|
| **Torsion bar** with circular cross-section (DIN 2091) | $M_{t,max} = \dfrac{\pi \cdot d^3}{16} \cdot \tau_{t,perm}$ | $\hat{a} = \dfrac{32 \cdot M_t \cdot l_t}{G \cdot \pi \cdot d^4}$ |
| | **Spring rate** | **Spring duty** |
| | $R = \dfrac{M_t}{\hat{a}} = \dfrac{G \cdot \pi \cdot d^4}{32 \cdot l_t}$ | $W_{max} = \dfrac{\tau_{t,perm}^2}{16 \cdot G} \cdot \pi \cdot d^2 \cdot l_t$ |
| **Cylindrical helical springs** with circular cross-section (DIN 2089) Compression spring    Extension spring | **Spring force, spring torque** | **Deflection** |
| | $F_{max} = \dfrac{\pi \cdot d^3}{8 \cdot k \cdot D} \cdot \tau_{t,perm}$ | $s = \dfrac{8 \cdot D^3 \cdot n}{G \cdot d^4} \cdot F$ |
| | **Spring rate** | **Spring duty** |
| | $R = \dfrac{G \cdot d^4}{8 \cdot D^3 \cdot n}$ | $W_{max} = \dfrac{\tau_{t,perm}^2}{16 \cdot G} \cdot d^2 \cdot D \cdot \pi^2 \cdot n$ |
| **Tapered helical springs** with circular cross-section | **Spring force, spring torque** | **Deflection** |
| | $F_{max} = \dfrac{\pi \cdot d^3}{16 \cdot k \cdot r_2} \cdot \tau_{t,perm}$ | $s = \dfrac{16 \cdot (r_1 + r_2) \cdot (r_1^2 + r_2^2) \cdot n \cdot F}{G \cdot d^4}$ |
| | **Spring rate** | **Spring duty** |
| | $R = \dfrac{G \cdot d^4}{16 \cdot (r_1 + r_2) \cdot (r_1^2 + r_2^2) \cdot n}$ | $W_{max} = \dfrac{\tau_{t,perm}^2}{32 \cdot G}$ $\cdot \dfrac{d^2 (r_1 + r_2) \cdot (r_1^2 + r_2^2) \cdot \pi^2 \cdot n}{r_2^2}$ |

For dynamic stress, $S_a$ must be doubled. Additionally, the spring ends are arranged at 180° to each other. The total number of coils is then always a multiple of a half coil (e.g. $n_t = 7.5$).

The effect of the wire curvature is taken into account by the stress coefficient $k$:

| $D/d$ | 3 | 4 | 6 | 8 | 10 | 14 | 20 |
|---|---|---|---|---|---|---|---|
| $k$ | 1.55 | 1.38 | 1.24 | 1.17 | 1.13 | 1.10 | 1.07 |

In the case of static stress, this effect can be neglected, i.e. $k$ is then set $= 1$. The following applies to the stress range prevailing in the case of dynamic stress:

$$\tau_{kh} = k\frac{8 \cdot D}{\pi \cdot d^3} \cdot (F_2 - F_1) \leq \tau_{kH}$$

### Extension springs

Extension springs are formed either with loops or with rolled-in or screwed-in end pieces. Since service life is determined primarily by the loops, it is impossible to give general fatigue limit values. Cold-formed extension springs hardened and tempered after drawing can be manufactured with an internal preload. This allows significantly higher stresses.

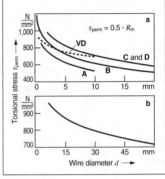

*Permissible torsional stresses for helical springs with static stress*
*a) Cold-formed from patented drawn spring-steel wires (A, B, C, and D) and valve spring-steel wires to DIN 17223.*
*b) Hot-formed from spring steels to DIN 17221.*

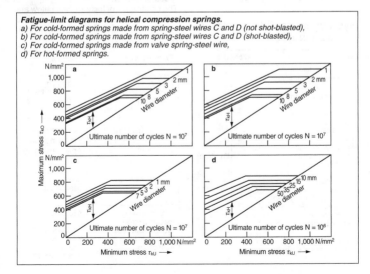

*Fatigue-limit diagrams for helical compression springs.*
*a) For cold-formed springs made from spring-steel wires C and D (not shot-blasted),*
*b) For cold-formed springs made from spring-steel wires C and D (shot-blasted),*
*c) For cold-formed springs made from valve spring-steel wire,*
*d) For hot-formed springs.*

# Fluid-film bearings and rolling-contact bearings

## Characteristics

Different types of fluid-film bearings (also termed plain bearings or sliding bearings) range from bearings with usually complete separation of the sliding surfaces by a lubrication film (fluid friction), through self-lubricating bearings, most of which are characterized by mixed friction, i.e. some of the bearing forces are absorbed by solid contact between the sliding surfaces, to sliding-contact bearings which are subjected to solid-body friction (i.e. without any effective fluid lubricating film), but which nevertheless have an adequate service life.

Most of the hydrodynamic sliding-bearing types used in automotive applications are circular cylindrical radial-sleeve bearings (often with oval clearance) for holding crankshafts, camshafts, and turbocharger bearings. Thrust bearings are usually used only as axial locators, and are not subjected to large forces.

## Hydrodynamic sliding bearings
### Symbols (DIN 31 652)

| Name | Symbol | Unit |
|---|---|---|
| Axial bearing length | $B$ | m |
| Inside bearing diameter (nominal diameter) | $D$ | m |
| Shaft diameter (nominal diameter) | $d$ | m |
| Eccentricity (displacement between shaft and bearing centers) | $e$ | m |
| Load | $F$ | N |
| Min. film thickness | $h_0$ | m |
| Local film pressure | $p$ | Pa = N/m² |
| Specific bearing load $\bar{p} = F/(B \cdot D)$ | $\bar{p}$ | Pa |
| Bearing clearance $s = (D - d)$ | $s$ | m |
| Sommerfeld number | $So$ | – |
| Relative eccentricity $2\,e/s$ | $\varepsilon$ | – |
| Effective dynamic viscosity of film | $\eta_{eff}$ | Pa · s |
| Relative bearing clearance $\psi = s/D$ | $\psi$ | – |
| Displacement angle | $\beta$ | ° |
| Hydrodynamically effective angular velocity | $\omega_{eff}$ | s⁻¹ |

A hydrodynamic sliding bearing is reliable in service if it remains sufficiently unaffected by the following:
– <u>Wear</u> (sufficient separation of the contact surfaces by the film)
– <u>Mechanical stress</u> (bearing material of sufficient strength)
– <u>Thermal loading</u> (observance of thermal stability of bearing material and viscosity/temperature behavior of film)

The dimensionless Sommerfeld number $So$ is used when determining load capacity, i.e. when assessing the formation of the lubricating film:

$$So = F \cdot \psi^2 / (D \cdot B \cdot \eta_{eff} \cdot \omega_{eff})$$

As the Sommerfeld number $So$ increases, so does the relative eccentricity $\varepsilon$ and the minimum lubrication film thickness $h_0$:

$$h_0 = (D - d)/2 - e = 0.5\,D \cdot \psi \cdot (1 - \varepsilon)$$

Relative eccentricity
$$\varepsilon = 2e/(D - d)$$

### Table 1. Orders of magnitude of the coefficients of friction for different types of friction
The coefficients of friction given below are approximate values, and are intended solely for comparison of the different types of friction.

| Type of friction | Coefficient of friction $f$ |
|---|---|
| Dry friction | 0.1 to > 1 |
| Mixed friction | 0.01 to 0.1 |
| Fluid friction | 0.01 |
| Friction in rolling bearings | 0.001 |

### Table 2. Empirical values for maximum approved specific bearing load
(maximum values only apply for very low sliding velocities)

| Bearing materials | Maximum specif. bearing load $\bar{p}_{lim}$ |
|---|---|
| Pb and Sn alloys (babbitt metals) | 5 to 15 N/mm² |
| Bronze, lead base | 7 to 20 N/mm² |
| Bronze, tin base | 7 to 25 N/mm² |
| AlSn alloys | 7 to 18 N/mm² |
| AlZn alloys | 7 to 20 N/mm² |

The Sommerfeld number is also used to determine the coefficient of friction in the bearing, and to calculate friction loss and thermal loading (cf. DIN 31 652, VDI Directive 2204).

As hydrodynamic bearings also operate with mixed friction some of the time, they must be able to withstand a certain amount of contamination without loss of function, and they are also subjected to high dynamic and thermal stress (particularly in piston engines), the bearing material must meet a number of requirements, some of which are mutually exclusive.
– <u>Conformability</u> (compensation of misalignment by plastic deformation without shortening service life)
– <u>Wettability</u> by fluid film
– <u>Embeddability</u> (ability of the bearing surface to absorb particles of dirt without increasing bearing or shaft wear)
– <u>Wear resistance</u> (in the case of mixed friction)
– <u>Seizure resistance</u> (bearing material must not weld to shaft material, even under high compressive load and high sliding velocity)
– <u>Anti-seizure performance</u> (resistance to welding)
– <u>Run-in performance</u> (a combination of conformability, resistance to wear, and embeddability)
– <u>Mechanical loadability</u>

– <u>Fatigue strength</u> (under fatigue loading, particularly at high thermal stress)

If a bearing (e.g. piston-pin bushing) is simultaneously subjected to high loads and low sliding velocities, high fatigue strength and wear resistance should take precedence over resistance to seizing. Bearing materials used in such cases are hard bronzes, e.g. leaded tin bronzes (Table 3). To protect the environment, lead must be avoided in future applications.

Since they are subjected to high dynamic loads with high sliding velocities, connecting-rod and crankshaft bearings in internal-combustion engines must fulfill a number of different requirements. In these applications, <u>multilayer bearings</u>, above all trimetal bearings, have proved themselves in practice.

The service life of crankshaft bearings can be further increased through the use of <u>grooved sliding bearings</u>. In these bearings, fine grooves have been machined into the running surface in the sliding direction, and filled with a liner made of soft material (an electroplated liner similar to that found in trimetal bearings). The contact areas are separated from one another by a harder light-alloy metal.

These bearings feature low rates of wear and high fatigue strength with good embeddability regarding film impurities.

---

**Multilayer bearing**
*(Design of a trimetal bearing)*
*1 Steel backing shell, 2 Cast lead-bronze (0.4 mm), 3 Nickel barrier between lead-bronze and babbitt metal (1 to 2 µm), 4 Electroplated babbitt metal (overlay, e.g. 20 µm).*

Detail X

1 2 3 4

---

**Section through a grooved sliding bearing**
*(MIBA patent)*
*Running surface with very fine grooves in the running direction; $V_G$.*
*1 Wear-resistant light metal, 2 Soft liner, 3 Nickel barrier.*

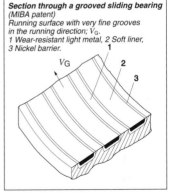

## Table 3. Selection of materials for hydrodynamic sliding bearings

| Material | Alloy designation | Composition in % | HB hardness 20°C | HB hardness 100°C | Remarks Application examples |
|----------|-------------------|------------------|------------------|-------------------|------------------------------|
| Tin-base babbitt metal | LgPbSn 80 (WM 80) | 80 Sn; 12 Sb; 6 Cu; 2 Pb | 27 | 10 | Very soft, good conformance of contact surfaces to off-axis operation, excellent anti-seizure performance. |
| Lead-base bab-bitt metal | LgPbSn 10 (WM 10) | 73 Pb; 16 Sb; 10 Sn; 1 Cu | 23 | 9 | Reinforcement necessary, e.g. as composite steel casting or with inter-mediate nickel layer on lead bronze. |
| Lead-base bronze | G-CuPb 25 | 74 Cu; 25 Pb; 1 Sn | 50 | 47 | Very soft, excellent anti-seizure performance, less resistant to wear. |
| | G-CuPb 22 | 70 Cu; 22 Pb; 6 Sn; 3 Ni | 86 | 79 | |
| Lead-tin base bronze | G-CuPb 10 Sn | 80 Cu; 10 Pb; 10 Sn | 75 | 67 | Improved anti-seizure performance by alloying with Pb. More resistant to off-axis operation than pure tin bronzes, therefore high-load Pb-Sn bronzes preferable for use as crank-shaft bearings. Composite bearings in internal-combustion engine manufacture, piston-pin bushings. $\bar{p}$ to 100 N/mm². |
| | G-CuPb 23 Sn | 76 Cu; 23 Pb; 1 Sn | 55 | 53 | Composite casting for low-load bearings (70 N/mm²). Also thick-wall bearing shells. Very good anti-seizure performance. Crankshaft bearings, camshafts, connecting-rod bearings. |
| Tin-base bronze | G-CuSn 10 Zn | 88 Cu; 10 Sn; 2 Zn | 85 | | Hard material. friction-bearing shells can be subjected to moderate loads at low sliding velocities. Worm gears. |
| | CuSn 8 | 92 Cu; 8 Sn | 80...220 | | High-grade wrought alloy. Good performance under high loads and in the absence of sufficient lubrica-tion. Steering-knuckle bearings. Particularly well suited for use as thin-walled sliding bearing bushings. |
| Red brass | G-CuSn7 ZnPb | 83 Cu; 6 Pb; 7 Sn; 4 Zn | 75 | 65 | Tin partially replaced by zinc and lead. Can be used instead of tin bronze, but only for moderate loads (40 N/mm²). General sliding bear-ings for machinery. Piston pins, bushings, crankshaft bearings, and knuckle-joint bearings. |

| Material | Alloy designation | Composition in % | HB hardness 20°C 100°C | Remarks Application examples |
|---|---|---|---|---|
| Brass | CuZn 31 Si | 68 Cu; 31 Zn; 1 Si | 90... 200 | Zn content is unfavorable at high bearing temperatures. Can be used instead of tin bronze; low loads. |
| Aluminum bronze | CuAl 9 Mn | 88 Cu; 9 Al; 3 Mn | 110... 190 | Thermal expansion comparable to that of light alloys. Suitable for use as interference-fit bearings in light-alloy housings. Better wear resistance than tin bronze, but higher friction. |
| Aluminum alloy | AlSi 12 Cu NiMn | 1 Cu; 85 Al; 12 Si; 1 Ni; 1 Mn | 110    100 | Piston alloy for low sliding velocities. |
| Rolled aluminum cladding | AlSn 6 | 1 Cu; 6 Sn; 90 Al; 3 Si | 40    30 | Liquated tin stretched by rolling, therefore high loadability, good antifriction properties. Improved by electroplated liner. |
| Electro-plated liners | PbSn 10 Cu | 2 Cu; 88 Pb; 10 Sn | 50... 60 | Used in modern trimetal bearings, 10 to 30 µm thick, electroplated, very fine grain. Intermediate nickel layer on bearing metal. |

For materials, see also DIN 1703, 1705, 1716, 17660, 17662, 17665, 1494, 1725, 1743. ISO 4381, 4382, 4383.

**Table 4. Materials for sintered-metal bearings.**
Sint-B indicates 20% P (porosity) (Sint-A: 25% P; Sint-C: 15% P).

| Material groups | Designation Sintered ... | Composition | Remarks |
|---|---|---|---|
| Sintered iron | B 00 | Fe | Standard material which meets moderate load and noise requirements. |
| Sintered steel, containing Cu | B 10 | < 0.3 C 1 to 5 Cu Rest Fe | Good resistance to wear, can be subjected to higher loads than pure Fe bearing. |
| Sintered steel, higher Cu content | B 20 | 20 Cu Rest Fe | Low-priced than sintered bronze, good noise behavior and $p \cdot v$ values. |
| Sintered bronze | B 50 | < 0.2 C 9 to 10 Sn Rest Cu | Standard Cu-Sn based material, good noise behavior. |

## Sintered-metal sliding bearings

Sintered-metal sliding bearings consist of sintered metals which are porous and impregnated with liquid lubricants. For many small motors in motor automotive applications, this type of bearing is a good compromise in terms of precision, installation, freedom from maintenance, service life, and cost. They are used primarily in motors with shaft diameters from 1.5 to 12 mm. Sintered-iron bearings and sintered-steel bearings (inexpensive, less likely to interact with the lubricant) are preferable to sintered-bronze bearings for use in motor vehicles (Table 4). The advantages of sintered-bronze bearings are greater loadability, lower noise, and lower friction coefficients (this type of bearing is used in record-players, office equipment, data systems, and cameras).

The performance of sintered bearings over long periods of service is closely related to the use of optimum lubricants.
Mineral oils: Inadequate cold-flow properties, moderate resistance to aging.
Synthetic oils: (e.g. esters, poly-$\alpha$ olefins): Good cold-flow properties, high resistance to thermal stresses, low evaporation tendency.
Synthetic greases: (oils which include metal soaps): Low starting friction, low wear.

## Dry sliding-contact bearings

(see Table 5, P. 370)

### Solid polymer bearings made of thermoplastics

Advantages: Low-priced, no danger of seizure with metals.
Disadvantages: Low thermal conductivity, relatively low operating temperatures, possible swelling due to humidity, low loadability, high coefficient of thermal expansion.

The most frequently used polymer materials are polyoxymethylene (POM, POM-C), polyamide (PA), polyethylene and polybutylene terephthalate (PET, PBT), and polyetheretherketone (PEEK).

The tribological and mechanical properties can be varied over a wide range by incorporating lubricants and reinforcements in the thermoplastic base material.
Lubrication additives: polytetrafluoroethylene (PTFE), graphite (C), silicone oil, and other liquid lubricants, recently also enclosed in microcapsules.
Reinforcement additives: glass fibers (GF), carbon fibers (CF).
Application examples: windshield wiper bearings (PA and fiberglass), idle actuators (PEEK + carbon fiber, PTFE and other additives).

### Polymer bearings made of duroplastics and elastomers

These materials, with their high levels of intrinsic friction, are seldom used as bearing materials in motor vehicles. Duroplastics include: phenol resins (high friction, e.g. Resitex), epoxy resins (require the addition of PTFE or C in order to reduce their high intrinsic brittleness, reinforcement necessary usually by fibers), polyimides (high thermal and mechanical loadability).
Application examples: polyimide axial stop in wiper motor.

### Metal-backed composite bearings

Composite bearings are combinations of polymer materials, fibers, and metals. Depending on the bearing structure, they provide advantages over pure or filled polymer plain bearings in terms of loadability, bearing clearance, thermal conductivity, and installation (suitable for use with oscillating motion).
Example of bearing structure: tinplated or copper-clad steel backing (several millimeters thick), onto which a layer of porous bronze is sintered 0.2 to 0.35 mm thick with a porosity of 30 to 40%. A low-friction polymer material is rolled into this bronze layer as a liner. Liner made of a) acetal resin, either impregnated with oil or containing lubricating recesses, or b) PTFE + Pb or $MoS_2$ additive.

Metal-backed composite bearings are available in a number of different shapes and compositions. Metal-backed composite bearings with woven PTFE fiber inserts have unusually high loadability and are suitable for use in ball-and-socket joints.

Examples of motor-vehicle applications for this type of bearing include shock-absorber piston bearings for spring struts, release-lever bearings for clutch pressure plates, brake-shoe bearings in drum brakes, ball-and-socket bearings, door-hinge bearings, bearings for seat-belt winding shafts, steering-knuckle bearings, gear-pump bearings.

**Carbon-graphite bearings**
Carbon-graphite bearings are members of the ceramic bearing family due to their method of manufacture and material properties. The base materials are powdered hydrocarbons; tar or synthetic resins are used as binders.
<u>Advantages</u>: Heat-resistant up to 350 °C (hard-burnt carbon) or 500 °C (electro-graphite), good antifriction properties, good corrosion resistance, good thermal conductivity, good thermal shock resistance. They are highly brittle, however.

Examples of carbon-graphite bearing applications: fuel-pump bearings, bearings in drying ovens, adjustable blades in turbochargers.

**Metal-ceramic bearings**
Metal-ceramic bearings consist of material manufactured by powder metallurgy processes; in addition to the metallic matrix, the bearing material also contains finely distributed solid lubricant particles.
<u>Matrix</u>: e.g. bronze, iron, nickel.
<u>Lubricant</u>: e.g. graphite, $MoS_2$.

These materials are suitable for use under extremely high loads, and are at the same time self-lubricating.

Application example: steering-knuckle bearings.

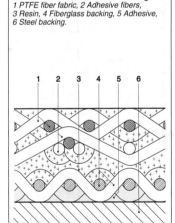

*Cutaway view of a self-lubricating composite bearing*
1 Polymer liner, 2 Porous bronze layer, 3 Copper layer, 4 Steel backing, 5 Tin layer.

*Section through composite bearing with fabric insert made of PTFE and fiberglass*
1 PTFE fiber fabric, 2 Adhesive fibers, 3 Resin, 4 Fiberglass backing, 5 Adhesive, 6 Steel backing.

**Table 5. Properties of maintenance-free, self-lubricating bearings**

| | Sintered bearings oil-impregnated | | Polymer bearings | | Composite bearings Liner | | Synthetic carbons |
|---|---|---|---|---|---|---|---|
| | Sintered iron | Sintered bronze | Thermoplastic polyamide | Duroplastic polyamide | PTFE + additive | Acetal resin | |
| Compression strength N/mm² | 80 to 180 | | 70 | 110 | 250 | 250 | 100 to 200 |
| Max. sliding velocity m/s | 10 | 20 | 2 | 8 | 2 | 3 | 10 |
| Typical load N/mm² | 1 to 4 (10) | | 15 | 50 (at 50 °C) 10 (at 200 °C) | 20 to 50 | 20 to 50 | 50 |
| Permissible operating temperature Short-term °C | − 60 to 180 (depends on oil) 200 | | − 130 to 100 120 | − 100 to 250 300 | − 200 to 280 | − 40 to 100 130 | − 200 to 350 500 |
| Coefficient of friction without lubrication | with lubrication 0.04 to 0.2 | | 0.2 to 0.4 (100 °C) 0.4 to 0.6 (25 °C) | 0.2 to 0.5 (unfilled) 0.1 to 0.4 (filled) | 0.04 to 0.2 | 0.07¹) to 0.2 ¹) PTFE filled | 0.1 to 0.35 |
| Thermal conductivity W/(m · K) | 20 to 40 | | 0.3 | 0.4 to 1 | 46 | 2 | 10 to 65 |
| Corrosion resistance | poor | good | very good | | good | good | very good |
| Chemical resistance | none | | very good | | conditional | conditional | good |
| Max. $p \cdot v$ (N/mm²) · (m/s) | 20 | | 0.05 | 0.2 | 1.5 to 2 | | 0.4 to 1.8 |
| Embeddability of dirt and abraded material | less good | | good | good | less good | good | less good |

# Rolling bearings

## Characteristics

In rolling bearings, forces are transferred by rolling elements (balls or rollers). Here, rolling is a form of movement comprising rolling and sliding. In rolling bearings, a microslip (i.e. sliding) nearly always occurs in addition to the pure rolling movement. In the case of mixed friction, this sliding movement leads to increased wear.

### Advantages

Low static coefficient of friction (0.001...0.002), therefore particularly well suited to applications in which starting occurs frequently.
Low maintenance.
Suited to permanent lubrication.
Low lubricant consumption.
Small bearing width.
High precision.

### Disadvantages

Sensitive to impact loads, sensitive to dirt.
Bearing noise is too high for some applications.
Standard bearings are only 1-piece bearings.

## Parameters

### Bearing materials

Bearing races and rolling elements consist mainly of chrome-alloy special steels ($100\ Cr_6H$), with a high degree of purity and hardness in the range of 58...65 HRC.

Depending on the application, the bearing cages are made of stamped sheet steel or brass. Cages made of polymer materials have come into recent use due to their ease of manufacture, improved adaptability to bearing geometry and other tribological advantages (e.g. antifriction properties). Polymer materials made of fiberglass-reinforced polyamide 66 can withstand continuous operating temperatures of up to 120°C, and can be operated for brief periods at temperatures up to 140°C.

### Static loadability (ISO 76-1987)

The static load rating $Co$ is used as a measure of the loadability of very slow-moving or static rolling bearings. $Co$ is the load at which total permanent deformation of rolling elements and races at contact points subjected to the highest loads amounts to 0.0001 of the diameter of the rolling element. A load equal to this load rating $Co$ generates a maximum compressive stress of 4,000 N/mm² in the center of the rolling element subjected to the highest load.

### Dynamic loadability

The dynamic load rating $C$ is used for calculating the service life of a rotating rolling bearing. $C$ indicates the bearing load for a nominal bearing service life of 1 million revolutions. In accordance with ISO 281:

Service life equation $L_{10} = \left(\dfrac{C}{P}\right)^p$

$L_{10}$ Nominal service life in millions of revolutions achieved or exceeded by 90% of a large batch of identical bearings.
$C$  Dynamic load rating in N (determined empirically).
$P$  Equivalent dynamic bearing load in N.
$p$  Empirical exponent of the service life equation: for rolling bearings, $p = 3$, for roller bearings, $p = 10/3$

### Modified nominal service life

$$L_{na} = a_1 \cdot a_2 \cdot a_3 \cdot \left(\frac{C}{P}\right)^p$$

$L_{na}$ Modified nominal service life in millions of revolutions.
$a_1$  Factor for survival probability, e.g. 90%: $a_1 = 1$; 95%: $a_1 = 0.62$.
$a_2$  Material coefficient of friction.
$a_3$  Coefficient of friction for operating conditions (bearing lubrication).

As the frictional coefficients $a_2$ and $a_3$ are not mutually independent, the combined coefficient $a_{23}$ is employed.

Rolling bearings are subject to fatigue stress. It is included, along with other influencing parameters such as contamination, in the calculation of service life (see catalogs issued by rolling-bearing manufacturers).

# Gears and tooth systems

(with involute flanks)

## Quantities and units (DIN 3960)

| Quantity | | Unit |
|---|---|---|
| $a$ | Center distance | mm |
| $b$ | Face width | mm |
| $c$ | Bottom clearance | mm |
| $d$ | Reference diameter | mm |
| $d_a$ | Outside diameter | mm |
| $d_b$ | Base diameter | mm |
| $d_f$ | Root diameter | mm |
| $d_w$ | Pitch diameter | mm |
| $h_a$ | Addendum $= m \cdot h_{aP}^*$ | mm |
| $h_f$ | Dedendum $= m \cdot h_{fP}^*$ | mm |
| $i$ | Transmission ratio $= z_2/z_1$ | – |
| $j_n$ | Normal backlash | mm |
| $m$ | Module $m = d/z$ | mm |
| $n$ | Rotational speed | rpm⁻ |
| $p$ | Pitch $p = \pi \cdot m$ | mm |
| $s$ | Tooth thickness (circular) | mm |
| $W$ | Span measurement | mm |
| $x$ | Addendum-modification coefficient | – |
| $z$ | Number of teeth | – |

| Quantity | | Unit |
|---|---|---|
| $\alpha$ | Pressure angle | ° |
| $\beta$ | Helix angle | ° |
| $\varepsilon$ | Contact ratio | ° |
| $*$ | Specific value, multiplied by $m$ | |
| | | |
| Superscripts and subscripts | | |
| 1 | referred to gear 1 | |
| 2 | referred to gear 2 | |
| a | referred to tooth tip | |
| b | referred to base circle | |
| f | referred to root | |
| n | referred to normal profile | |
| t | referred to transverse profile | |
| w | referred to operating pitch circle | |
| F | referred to root-tooth load | |
| P | referred to basic rack | |
| W | referred to contact pressure | |

Gear type and shape are determined by the position of the shafts which are joined by the gears in order to transfer forces or movements.

Cycloidal teeth: Cycloidal teeth are used primarily in the watch and clock industry. They permit small numbers of teeth without cutter interference (undercut). They are characterized by low contact pressure, but are sensitive to variations in the distance between centers.

Involute teeth: Involute teeth, on the other hand, are not sensitive to variations in the distance between centers. They can be produced with relatively simple tools using the generating method. The automobile industry uses involute teeth almost exclusively, therefore the following information is limited to this type of gear system.

All spur gears with the same module (and the same pressure angle) can be produced using the same generating tool,

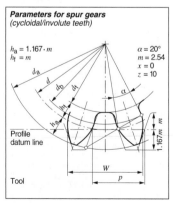

**Parameters for spur gears**
(cycloidal/involute teeth)

$h_a = 1.167 \cdot m$
$h_f = m$

$\alpha = 20°$
$m = 2.54$
$x = 0$
$z = 10$

Profile datum line

Tool

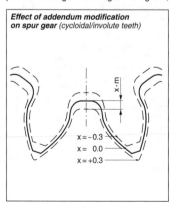

**Effect of addendum modification on spur gear** (cycloidal/involute teeth)

$x \cdot m$

$x = -0.3$
$x = 0.0$
$x = +0.3$

## Definitions

### Table 1. Gear types

| Position of shafts | Gear type | Properties | Application examples in automotive engineering |
|---|---|---|---|
| Parallel | External or internal spur gear pair with straight or helical teeth | Helical teeth, run more smoothly but are subject to axial thrust | Manual transmissions |
| Intersecting | Bevel-gear pair with straight, helical, or curved teeth | Sensitive to fluctuations in angular and axial clearance | Differentials |
| Intersecting | Offset bevel-gear pair with helical or curved teeth | | Rear-axle drives |
| | Crossed helical-gear pair | For small loads | Distributor drives |
| | Worm-gear pair | High-ratio, single-stage transmission | Windshield wiper drives |
| Coaxial | Toothed shaft and hub | Sliding shaft coupling | Starters (Bendix shaft and pinion) |

regardless of the number of teeth and addendum modification. A number of modules have been standardized in order to limit the number of such tools and the number of master gears required for gear testing:

Module for spur and bevel gears: DIN 780 (see table on P. 375); module for worms and worm gears: DIN 780, module for toothed shafts and hubs: DIN 5480. The module in the normal profile for crossed helical gears is also selected in conformance with DIN 780 in most cases. A series of modules suited to the manufacturing process is generally used for curve-toothed bevel gears.

### Tooth shape

Basic rack for spur gears: DIN 867, DIN 58 400; basic rack for bevel gears: DIN 3971; basic rack for worms and worm gears: DIN 3975; basic rack for toothed shafts and hubs: DIN 5480.

The tooth shape for crossed helical gears can also be designed in conformance with the basic rack as per DIN 867. In addition to the standardized pressure angles (20° for running gears and 30° for toothed shafts and hubs), pressure angles of 12°, 14°30', 15°, 17°30', 22°30' and 25° are used.

### Table 2. List of standards

| Standard | Title |
|---|---|
| DIN 3960 | Definitions, parameters and equations for involute spur gears and spur-gear pairs |
| DIN 3961...4 | Tolerances for cylindrical gear teeth |
| DIN 3990/1...5 | Calculation of load capacity of spur gears |
| DIN 58 405/1...4 | Spur-gear drives for precision engineering |
| DIN 3971 | Definitions and parameters for bevel gears and bevel-gear pairs |
| DIN 5480 | Involute spline joints |
| DIN 3975 | Terms and definitions for cylindrical worm gears with 90° shaft angle |

### Addendum modification

Addendum modification (see figure) is used to avoid undercut when the number of teeth is small, to increase root strength, and to achieve a specific distance between centers.

## Table 3. Basic equations for spur gears

| Designation | Straight gear ($\beta = 0$) | Helical gear ($\beta \neq 0$) |
|---|---|---|
| Reference diameter | $d = z \cdot m$     Module $m$ see P. 372 <br> The neg. value of $z$ is to be used for internal teeth; distance between centers $a$ becomes neg. | $d = \dfrac{z \cdot m_n}{\cos \beta}$    Module $m_n$ see P. 372 |
| Base diameter | $d_b = d \cdot \cos \alpha_n$ | $d_b = d \cdot \cos \alpha_t$    $\alpha_t$ from $\tan \alpha_t = \dfrac{\tan \alpha_n}{\cos \beta}$ |
| Distance between centers, no backlash; if normal backlash $j_n = 0$ | $a = m \dfrac{z_1 + z_2}{2} \cdot \dfrac{\cos \alpha}{\cos \alpha_w} = \dfrac{d_{b1} + d_{b2}}{2 \cdot \cos \alpha_w}$ <br> acc. to DIN 867, $\alpha = 20°$ <br> $\alpha_w$ from: <br> $\mathrm{inv}\,\alpha_w = \dfrac{2(x_1 + x_2)\sin\alpha + j_n/m}{(z_1 + z_2)\cos\alpha} + \mathrm{inv}\,\alpha$ | $a = m_t \dfrac{z_1 + z_2}{2} \cdot \dfrac{\cos \alpha_t}{\cos \alpha_{wt}} = \dfrac{d_{b1} + d_{b2}}{2 \cdot \cos \alpha_{wt}}$ <br> $m_t = \dfrac{m_n}{\cos \beta}$    $\cos \beta_b = \dfrac{\sin \alpha_n}{\sin \alpha_t}$ <br> $\mathrm{inv}\,\alpha_{wt} = \dfrac{m_n \cdot 2(x_1 + x_2)\sin\alpha_n + j_n/\cos\beta_b}{m_t(z_1 + z_2)\cos\alpha_t} + \mathrm{inv}\,\alpha_t$ |
| Involute | $\mathrm{inv}\,\alpha = \tan\alpha - \mathrm{arc}\,\alpha$    P. 156. | for $\alpha = 20°$, $\mathrm{inv}\,\alpha = 0.014904$ |
| Pitch diameter | $d_w = d_b/\cos \alpha_w$ | $d_w = d_b/\cos \alpha_{wt}$ |
| Root diameter | $d_f = d + 2xm - 2h_{fP}^* \cdot m$ <br> with dedendum $h_{fP}^* \cdot m$ ($h_{fP}^* = 1.167$ or $1.25$ as per DIN 3972) | $d_f = d_b + 2xm_n - 2h_{fP}^* \cdot m_n$ |
| Tip-circle diameter | $d_a = d + 2xm + 2h_{aP}^* \cdot m$ <br> with addendum $h_{aP}^* \cdot m$   ($h_{aP}^* = 1.0$ to DIN 867) | $d_a = d \cdot 2xm_n + 2h_{aP}^* \cdot m_n$ |
| Bottom clearance | $c_1 = a_{min} - d_{a1}/2 - d_{f2}/2$;   $c_2 = a_{min} - d_{a2}/2 - d_{f1}/2$ | $c \geq 0.15\, m_n$ |
| Tooth thickness in reference circle (circular) | $s = m\,(\pi/2 + 2 \cdot x \cdot \tan\alpha)$ | Normal profile <br> $s_n = m_n(\pi/2 + 2 \cdot x \cdot \tan\alpha_n)$ <br> Transverse profile <br> $s_t = s_n/\cos\beta = m_t\,(\pi/2 + 2 \cdot x \cdot \tan\alpha_n)$ |
| Ideal number of teeth | $z_i = z$ | $z_i = z\,\dfrac{\mathrm{inv}\,\alpha_t}{\mathrm{inv}\,\alpha_n}$ |
| Number of teeth spanned | $k \approx z_i \dfrac{\alpha_{nx}}{180} + 0.5$ <br> for $k$, take the next whole number | $\alpha_{nx}$ from $\cos\alpha_{nx} \approx \dfrac{z_i}{z_i + 2x}\cos\alpha_n$ |
| Base tangent length over $k$ teeth | $W_k = \{[(k' - 0.5)\,\pi + z_i\,\mathrm{inv}\,\alpha_n]\cos\alpha_n + 2x \cdot \sin\alpha_n\}\,m_n$ | |
| Back-reckoning of $x$ from base tangent length | $x = \dfrac{(W/m_n) - [(k - 0.5)\cdot\pi + z_i\cdot\mathrm{inv}\,\alpha_n]\cdot\cos\alpha_n}{2\cdot\sin\alpha_n}$ | |
| Transverse contact ratio for gears without allowance for undercut | $\varepsilon_\alpha = \dfrac{\sqrt{d_{a1}^2 - d_{b1}^2} + \dfrac{z_2}{|z_2|}\sqrt{d_{a2}^2 - d_{b2}^2} - (d_{b1} + d_{b2})\tan\alpha_w}{\qquad}$ (straight teeth) <br><br> $\varepsilon_\alpha = \dfrac{\sqrt{d_{a1}^2 - d_{b1}^2} + \dfrac{z_2}{|z_2|}\sqrt{d_{a2}^2 - d_{b2}^2} - (d_{b1} + d_{b2})\tan\alpha_{wt}}{2\cdot\pi\cdot m_t\cdot\cos\alpha}$ (helical teeth) | |
| Overlap ratio | – | $\varepsilon_\beta = \dfrac{b\cdot\sin|\beta|}{m_n\cdot\pi}$ |
| Total contact ratio | $\varepsilon_\gamma = \varepsilon_\alpha$ | $\varepsilon_\gamma = \varepsilon_\alpha + \varepsilon_\beta$ |
| | Apply only if: $\varepsilon_\gamma > 1$ for $d_{a\,min}$ and $a_{max}$ | |

### Gear pair with reference center distance

With a gear pair at reference center distance, the addendum modifications to the gear and pinion are equal but opposite, so the distance between centers does not change. This design is preferred for crossed helical- and bevel-gear pairs.

### Gear pair with modified center distance

The addendum modifications to the gear and pinion do not cancel each other out, so the distance between centers changes.

### Terms and errors

Terms and errors are explained in detail in the following standards: DIN 3960, DIN 58 405 (spur gears), DIN 3971 (bevel gears), and DIN 3975 (worms and worm gears).

Inserting $j_n = 0$ in the preceding formulas results in gearing with zero backlash. The tooth thickness and span measurement deviations required to produce backlash can be specified in accordance with DIN 3967 and DIN 58 405, taking into consideration the quality of the gears. It is necessary to ensure that the minimum backlash is great enough to compensate for tooth error (such as total composite error, alignment deviation, center-to-center distance error, etc.) without reducing backlash to zero, and without leading to gear jamming. Other parameters for which the tolerances must be determined (with reference to the tooth errors given above in parentheses) are those for (two-flank) total composite error and (two-flank) tooth-to-tooth composite error (DIN 3963, DIN 58 405), alignment deviation (DIN 3962 T2, DIN 3967, DIN 58 405), and distance between centers (DIN 3964, DIN 58 405).

## DIN gear qualities (DIN 3961 to DIN 3964)

### Table 4. Manufacture and applications

| Quality | Application examples | Manufacture |
|---|---|---|
| 2 | Primary-standard master gears | Form grinding (50...60% scrap rate) |
| 3 | Master gears for the inspection department | |
| 4 | Master gears for the workshop, measuring mechanisms | |
| 5 | Transmissions for machine tools, turbines, measuring equipment | Form grinding and generative grinding |
| 6 | As 5, also highest gears of passenger-cars and bus transmissions | |
| 7 | Motor-vehicle transmissions (highest gears), machine tools, rail vehicles, hoisting and handling equipment, turbines, office machines | Non-hardened gears (with sufficient care) by hobbing, generative shaping, and planing (subsequent shaving is desirable); additional grinding is required for hardened gears |
| 8 and 9 | Motor-vehicle transmissions (middle and lower gears), rail vehicles, machine tools, and office machines | Hobbing, generative shaping, and planing (non-ground but hardened gears) |
| 10 | Transmissions for agricultural tractors, agricultural machinery, subordinate gear units in general machine equipment, hoisting equipment | All of the usual processes apply, including extrusion and sintering, and injection molding for plastic gears |
| 11 and 12 | General agricultural machinery | |

**Module series for spur and bevel gears**
in mm (extract from DIN 780)

| | | | | |
|------|-------|-----|----|----|
| 0.3 | 1 | 3 | 10 | 32 |
| 0.35 | 1.125 | 3.5 | 11 | 36 |
| **0.4** | **1.25** | 4 | 12 | 40 |
| 0.45 | 1.375 | 4.5 | 14 | 45 |
| **0.5** | **1.5** | 5 | 16 | 50 |
| 0.55 | 1.75 | 5.5 | 18 | 55 |
| **0.6** | 2 | 6 | 20 | 60 |
| 0.65 | 2.25 | 7 | 22 | 70 |
| 0.7 | **2.5** | 8 | 25 | |
| 0.75 | 2.75 | 9 | 28 | |
| **0.8** | | | | |
| 0.85 | | | | |
| 0.9 | | | | |
| 0.95 | | | | |

Modules in bold type are preferred.

## Addendum-modification coefficient $x$

**Table 5. Addendum-modification coefficient $x$ for straight-tooth gearing,** $\alpha = 20°$,
Basic rack I, DIN 3972 ($h_{fP} = 1.167 \cdot m$)

| 1 | 2 | 3 | 4 |
|---|---|---|---|
| Number of teeth $z$, for helical undercut, teeth $z_i$ | Tooth free from if $x \geq$ | Top-land width $0.2 \cdot m$, if $x \approx$ | Tooth pointed if $x \geq$ |
| 7 | + 0.47 | – | + 0.49 |
| 8 | + 0.45 | – | + 0.56 |
| 9 | + 0.4 | + 0.4 | + 0.63 |
| 10 | + 0.35 | + 0.45 | + 0.70 |
| 11 | + 0.3 | + 0.5 | + 0.76 |
| 12 | + 0.25 | + 0.56 | + 0.82 |
| 13 | + 0.2 | + 0.62 | + 0.87 |
| 14 | + 0.15 | + 0.68 | + 0.93 |
| 15 | + 0.1 | + 0.72 | + 0.98 |
| 16 | 0 | + 0.76 | + 1.03 |

If the number of teeth is greater than $z = 16$, $x$ should not be less than $x = (16 - z)/17$, for helical teeth $x = (16 - z_i)/17$.

## Starter-tooth design

The "Standard distance between centers" is a system of tolerances for gears customary in mechanical engineering and is specified in DIN 3961. This system, in which the required backlash is produced by negative tooth thickness tolerances, cannot be used in starter-tooth designs. Starter gear teeth require far more backlash than constant-mesh gears due to the starter engagement process. Such backlash is best achieved by increasing the distance between centers.

The high torque required for starting necessitates a high transmission ratio ($i = 10$ to $20$). For this reason, the starter pinion has a small number of teeth ($z = 8$ to $12$). The pinion generally has positive addendum modification. In the case of pitch gears, this addendum modification is expressed using the following notation outside Germany: number of teeth, for instance = 9/10.

This means that only 9 teeth are cut on a gear blank with a diameter for 10 teeth; this corresponds to an addendum-modification coefficient of + 0.5. Slight deviations of $x = + 0.5$ are quite common and do not affect the above-mentioned notation method: number of teeth = 9/10. (This notation should not be confused with the $P$ 8/10 notation, see below and next page.)

**Table 6. Customary starter gearing**

| Module $m$ mm | Diametral pitch $P$ 1/inch | Pressure angle of basic rack | American standard | European standard |
|---|---|---|---|---|
| 2.1167 | 12 | 12° | SAE J 543 c | ISO 8123    1991 E |
| 2.5 | – | 15° | | ISO 9457–1 1991 E |
| 2.54 | 10 | 20° | SAE J 543 c | ISO 8123    1991 E |
| 3 | – | 15° | | ISO 9457–1 1991 E |
| 3.175 | 8 | 20° | SAE J 543 c | ISO 8123    1991 E |
| 3.5 | – | 15° | | ISO 9457–1 1991 E |
| 4.233 | 6 | 20° | SAE J 543 c | ISO 8123    1991 E |

## American gear standards

Instead of the module, the standard is based on the number of teeth on a pitch diameter of 1 inch = diametral pitch ($P$).

$$P = z/d$$

The conversion is as follows:
Module $m = 25.4$ mm/$P$

The tooth spacing in the pitch circle is called circular pitch ($CP$):

$$CP = \frac{1 \text{ inch}}{P} \cdot \pi$$

Pitch $t = 25.4$ mm $\cdot CP = \pi \cdot m$

### Full-depth teeth

Full-depth teeth have an addendum $h_a = m$ in German standards, however the dedendum is frequently somewhat different.

### Stub teeth

The formulas are the same as for full-depth teeth, but calculation of the addendum is based on a different module from the other dimensions. Notation (example):

P 5/7 —— $P$ 7 to calculate the addendum

—— $P$ 5 to calculate all other dimensions

### Notation and conversions:

Outside diameter:
$OD = d_a$
$d_a$ Outside diameter

Pitch diameter:
$PD = z/P = d$ in inches
$d$ Reference diameter

Root diameter:
$RD = d_f$
$d_f$ Root diameter

Layout diameter:
$LD = (z + 2x)/P$ in inches
$LD = (z + 2x) \cdot m$ in mm
$LD \approx d_w$
$d_w$ Pitch diameter

Measurement over $D_M$ pins:
$M_d$ = measurement over $D_M$ pins

## Table 7. Diametral pitches $P$ and modules derived from them

| Diametral pitch $P$ 1/inch | Corresponds to module $m$ mm | Diametral pitch $P$ 1/inch | Corresponds to module $m$ mm | Diametral pitch $P$ 1/inch | Corresponds to module $m$ mm |
|---|---|---|---|---|---|
| 20 | 1.27000 | 6 | 4.23333 | 2 | 12.70000 |
| 18 | 1.41111 | 5.5 | 4.61818 | 1.75 | 14.51429 |
| 16 | 1.58750 | 5 | 5.08000 | 1.5 | 16.93333 |
| 14 | 1.81429 | 4.5 | 5.64444 | 1.25 | 20.32000 |
| 12 | 2 11667 | 4 | 6.35000 | 1 | 25.40000 |
| 11 | 2.30909 | 3.5 | 7.25714 | 0.875 | 29.02857 |
| 10 | 2.54000 | 3 | 8.46667 | 0.75 | 33.86667 |
| 9 | 2.82222 | 2.75 | 9.23636 | 0.625 | 40.64000 |
| 8 | 3.17500 | 2.5 | 10.16000 | 0.5 | 50.80000 |
| 7 | 3.62857 | 2.25 | 11.28889 | | |

## Calculation of load-bearing capacity

The following can be employed for rough estimations as an alternative to DIN 3990 "Calculation of load-bearing capacity of spur bevel gears". It applies to 2-gear pairs in a stationary transmission unit.

The quantities that appear in the following formulas must be entered in the units given below:

| Term | | Unit | | Term | | Unit |
|------|------|------|------|------|------|------|
| $P$ | Power | kW | | $\varphi$ | Life factor | – |
| $P_{PS}$ | Metric horsepower | HP | | HB | Brinell hardness | |
| $M$ | Torque | $N \cdot m$ | | HRC | Rockwell hardness | |
| $n$ | Rotational speed | rpm | | $b_N$ | Effective flank width | mm |
| $F$ | Peripheral force | N | | $k$ | Contact pressure | $N/mm^2$ |
| $u$ | Gear ratio | – | | $L_h$ | Service life | h |

### Table 8. Calculating load-bearing capacity of spur gears

| | |
|------|------|
| Power | $P = 0.736 \cdot P_{PS}$ <br> $P = M \cdot n/9{,}549$ <br> $P = F_t \cdot d \cdot n/(19.1 \cdot 10^6)$ |
| Peripheral force in pitch circle | $F_{tw} = 2{,}000 \cdot M/d_w = 19.1 \cdot 10^6 \, P/(d_w \cdot n)$ |
| in reference circle | $F_t = 2{,}000 \cdot M/d = 19.1 \cdot 10^6 \, P/(d \cdot n)$ |
| Gear ratio | $u = z_2/z_1 = n_1/n_2$    for pairs of internal gears $u < -1$ |
| Life factor | $\varphi = \sqrt[6]{5{,}000/L_h}$    or from the table on P. 379 |
| Contact pressure for the small gear | $k_{perm} = \dfrac{(HB)^2}{2{,}560 \cdot \sqrt[6]{n}} = \dfrac{(HRC)^2}{23.1 \cdot \sqrt[6]{n}}$    or from the table on P. 379 |
| Straight teeth | $k_{ACT} = \dfrac{F_{tw}}{b_N \cdot d_{w1}} \cdot \dfrac{4\,(u+1)}{u \cdot \sin^2 \alpha_w}$ |
| Helical teeth | $k_{ACT} = \dfrac{F_{tw}}{b_N \cdot d_{w1}} \cdot \dfrac{4\,(u+1) \cdot \cos^2 \beta}{u \, \sin^2 \alpha_{wt}}$    $\cos^2 \beta$ only with full contact, otherwise = 1 |
| Resistance to pitting | $S_w = \varphi \cdot k_{perm}/ k_{ACT} \geq 1$ |

Resistance to pitting and wear due to excessive contact pressure is provided if the equations for $S_w$ for the smaller gear (gear 1) yield a value equal to or greater than 1. In the case of gear pairs where $z_1 < 20$, select $S_w \geq 1.2...1.5$ on account of the greater contact pressure at the inside single engagement point. As the contact pressure $k$ is equal in magnitude for <u>both</u> gears of the pair, for $k_{perm}$ a material can be selected for gear 2 from the table. It should have at least the same contact pressure as for gear 1 at rotational speed $n_2$.

The $k_{perm}$ values in the table below apply when both gears are made of steel. For cast iron on steel, or bronze on steel, the values should be roughly 1.5 times higher; for cast iron on cast iron, or bronze on bronze, they should be approximately 1.8 times higher. For the gear with non-hardened surfaces, 20% higher $k_{perm}$ values are permissible if the other gear in the pair hardened tooth flanks. The values in the table apply to a service life of 5,000 hours. A different service life is allowed for in the equation for resistance to pitting $S_w$ by means of the life factor $\varphi$.

**Table 9. Permissible contact pressure $k_{perm}$ in N/mm² for a service life $L_h$ = 5,000 hours**

| Hardness of teeth HB | HRC | Rotational speed in rpm (with 1 load change per revolution) | | | | | | | | | | | |
|---|---|---|---|---|---|---|---|---|---|---|---|---|---|
| | | 10 | 25 | 50 | 100 | 250 | 500 | 750 | 1,000 | 1,500 | 2,500 | 5,000 | 10,000 |
| 90 | | 2.2 | 1.9 | 1.7 | 1.5 | 1.3 | 1.1 | 1.05 | 1.0 | 0.94 | 0.86 | 0.77 | 0.68 |
| 100 | | 2.7 | 2.3 | 2.0 | 1.8 | 1.6 | 1.4 | 1.3 | 1.2 | 1.15 | 1.06 | 0.94 | 0.84 |
| 120 | | 3.8 | 3.3 | 2.9 | 2.6 | 2.2 | 2.0 | 1.9 | 1.8 | 1.66 | 1.53 | 1.36 | 1.21 |
| 140 | | 5.2 | 4.5 | 4.0 | 3.6 | 3.0 | 2.7 | 2.5 | 2.4 | 2.26 | 2.08 | 1.85 | 1.65 |
| 170 | | 7.7 | 6.6 | 5.9 | 5.2 | 4.5 | 4.0 | 3.75 | 3.6 | 3.34 | 3.06 | 2.73 | 2.43 |
| 200 | | 10.7 | 9.1 | 8.1 | 7.3 | 6.2 | 5.6 | 5.2 | 4.9 | 4.6 | 4.24 | 3.78 | 3.37 |
| 230 | | 14.1 | 12.1 | 10.8 | 9.6 | 8.2 | 7.3 | 6.9 | 6.5 | 6.1 | 5.61 | 5.0 | 4.45 |
| 260 | | 18.0 | 15.4 | 13.8 | 12.2 | 10.5 | 9.4 | 8.8 | 8.4 | 7.8 | 7.17 | 6.39 | 5.69 |
| 280 | | 20.9 | 17.9 | 16.0 | 14.2 | 12.2 | 10.9 | 10.2 | 9.7 | 9.0 | 8.31 | 7.41 | 6.6 |
| 300 | | 24.0 | 20.6 | 18.3 | 16.3 | 14.0 | 12.5 | 11.7 | 11.1 | 10.4 | 9.54 | 8.5 | 7.6 |
| 330 | | 29.0 | 24.9 | 22.2 | 19.8 | 17.0 | 15.1 | 14.1 | 13.5 | 12.6 | 11.6 | 10.3 | 9.2 |
| 400 | | 42.6 | 36.6 | 32.6 | 29.0 | 24.9 | 22.2 | 20.7 | 19.8 | 18.5 | 17.0 | 15.1 | 13.5 |
| | 57 | 96.0 | 82.3 | 73.3 | 65.3 | 56.0 | 49.9 | 46.7 | 44.5 | 41.6 | 38.2 | 34.0 | 30.3 |
| | ≥ 62 | 112 | 96.5 | 86.0 | 76.6 | 65.8 | 58.6 | 54.8 | 52.2 | 48.8 | 44.8 | 39.9 | 35.6 |

Corresponding materials are given in the table "Material parameters" on P. 381.

**Table 10. Life factor $\varphi$.**
The life factor is used to convert the values in the table (referred to a service life of 5,000 hours) to values which correspond to a different service life period.

| Service life in operating hours $L_h$ | 10 | 50 | 150 | 312 | 625 | 1,200 | 2,500 | 5,000 | 10,000 | 40,000 | 80,000 | 150,000 |
|---|---|---|---|---|---|---|---|---|---|---|---|---|
| Life factor $\varphi$ | 2.82 | 2.15 | 1.79 | 1.59 | 1.41 | 1.27 | 1.12 | 1 | 0.89 | 0.71 | 0.83 | 0.57 |

Guidelines for selection of service life: Drives in continuous operation at full load: 40,000 to 150,000 hours of operation; drives run intermittently or only intermittently at full load: 50 to 5,000 hours of operation.

## Teeth calculations for bending and tooth fracture

### Table 11. Formulas for calculating the strength of spur gears

| | | |
|---|---|---|
| Peripheral velocity $v_1 = v_2$    m/s | $v_1 = \dfrac{\pi \cdot d_1 \cdot n_1}{60{,}000}$    $d_1$ in mm, $n_1$ in rpm | |
| Velocity factor $f_v$ | Take from table below or calculate. | |
| Permissible root stress $\sigma_{F\,perm}$    N/mm² | Take $\sigma_{F\,lim}$ and $Y_{NT}$ from table on P. 381, estimate intermediate values. $\sigma_{F\,perm} = \sigma_{F\,lim} \cdot Y_{NT} \cdot Y_L$    $Y_L = 1$ for pulsating loads $Y_L = 0.7$ for alternating loads. | |
| Tooth-profile factor $Y_{Fa}$ | Take from graph below. | |
| Root stress of tooth $\sigma_{F\,actual}$    N/mm² | For straight teeth $\sigma_{F\,ACT} = \dfrac{F_t}{b \cdot m} \cdot \dfrac{Y_{Fa}}{f_v \cdot \varepsilon_\alpha}$ $\varepsilon_\alpha$, see P. 374 $m$, $m_n$, $b$ in mm, $F_t$ in N see P. 378 | For helical teeth $\sigma_{F\,ACT} = \dfrac{F_t}{b \cdot m_n} \cdot \dfrac{Y_{Fa}}{f_v \cdot \varepsilon_\alpha}\left(1\,\dfrac{\varepsilon_\beta \cdot \beta}{120°}\right)$ where $(1 - \varepsilon_\beta \cdot \beta /120°) \geq$ must be 0.75. $\varepsilon_\beta$ see P. 374, $\beta$ in ° |
| Resistance to tooth fracture $S_F$ | $S_F = \sigma_{F\,perm}/\sigma_{F\,ACT} \geq 1$ | |

Resistance to tooth fracture exists if the equations for $S_F$ for the smaller gear (gear 1) yield a value greater than or equal to 1.

If a better material is selected for gear 1 than for gear 2, the calculation for bending must also be made for gear 2.

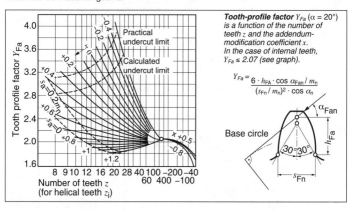

**Tooth-profile factor** $Y_{Fa}$ ($\alpha = 20°$) is a function of the number of teeth $z$ and the addendum-modification coefficient $x$. In the case of internal teeth, $Y_{Fa} \leq 2.07$ (see graph).

$$Y_{Fa} = \frac{6 \cdot h_{FA} \cdot \cos \alpha_{Fan} / m_n}{(s_{Fn} / m_n)^2 \cdot \cos \alpha_n}$$

### Table 12. Velocity factor $f_v$

| Materials | Peripheral velocity $v$ m/s | | | | | | | Base equation |
|---|---|---|---|---|---|---|---|---|
| | 0.25 | 0.5 | 1 | 2 | 3 | 5 | 10 | |
| Steel and other metals | Velocity factor $f_v$ | | | | | | | $f_v = \dfrac{A}{A + v}$ [1)] |
| | 0.96 | 0.93 | 0.86 | 0.75 | 0.67 | 0.55 | 0.38 | |
| Fabric-based laminates and other non-metals | 0.85 | 0.75 | 0.62 | 0.5 | 0.44 | 0.37 | 0.32 | $f_v = \dfrac{0.75}{1 + v} + 0.25$ |

# Gear materials

**Table 13. Material parameters**

| Material | | Condition | Tensile strength $R_m$ N/mm² min. | Fatigue strength for reversed bending stress $\sigma_{bw}$ N/mm² min. | Hardness HB or HRC min. | Permissible root stress[2] $\sigma_{F\,lim}$ N/mm² | Life factor $Y_{NT}$[3] at number of load changes $N_L = L_h \cdot 60 \cdot n$ | | | | |
|---|---|---|---|---|---|---|---|---|---|---|---|
| | | | | | | | $\geq 3 \cdot 10^6$ | $10^6$ | $10^5$ | $10^4$ | $10^3$ |
| Tempering steel | St 60-2, C 45 | annealed | 590 | 255 | 170 HB | 160 | | | | | |
| | | heat-treat. | 685 | 295 | 200 HB | 185 | | | | | |
| | | heat-treat. | 980 | 410 | 280 HB | 245 | | | | | |
| | St 70-2, C 60 | annealed | 685 | 295 | 200 HB | 185 | | | | | |
| | | heat-treat. | 785 | 335 | 230 HB | 209 | | | | | |
| | | heat-treat. | 980 | 410 | 280 HB | 245 | 1 | 1.25 | 1.75 | 2.5 | 2.5 |
| | 50 Cr V 4 | annealed | 685 | 335 | 200 HB | 185 | | | | | |
| | | heat-treat. | 1,130 | 550 | 330 HB | 294 | | | | | |
| | | heat-treat. | 1,370 | 665 | 400 HB | 344 | | | | | |
| | 37 Mn Si 5 | annealed | 590 | 285 | 170 HB | 160 | | | | | |
| | | heat-treat. | 785 | 355 | 230 HB | 200 | | | | | |
| | | heat-treat. | 1,030 | 490 | 300 HB | 270 | | | | | |
| Case-hardening steel | RSt 34-2, C 15 | annealed | 335 | 175 | 100 HB | 110 | 1 | 1.25 | 1.75 | 2.5 | 2.5 |
| | | surf.-hard.[4] | 590 | 255 | 57 HRC | 160 | 1 | 1.2 | 1.5 | 1.9 | 2.5 |
| | 16 Mn Cr 5 | annealed | 800 | – | 150 HB | – | – | – | – | – | – |
| | | surf.-hard.[4] | 1,100 | – | 57 HRC | 300 | 1 | 1.2 | 1.5 | 1.9 | 2.5 |
| | 20 Mn Cr 5 | annealed | 590 | 275 | 170 HB | 172 | – | – | – | – | – |
| | | surf.-hard.[4] | 1,180 | 590 | 57 HRC | 330 | 1 | 1.2 | 1.5 | 1.9 | 2.5 |
| | 18 Cr Ni 8 | annealed | 640 | 315 | 190 HB | 200 | – | – | – | – | – |
| | | surf.-hard.[4] | 1,370 | 590 | 57 HRC | 370 | 1 | 1.2 | 1.5 | 1.9 | 2.5 |
| Gray iron | GG-18 | – | | 175 | 200 HB | 50 | 1 | 1.1 | 1.25 | 1.4 | 1.6 |
| | GS-52.1 | – | | 510 | 140 HB | 110 | 1 | 1.25 | 1.75 | 2.5 | 2.5 |
| | G-SnBz 14 | | | 195 | 90 HB | 100 | 1 | 1.25 | 1.75 | 2.5 | 2.5 |
| Polyamide PA 66 Pa 66 + 30% GF | | at 60 °C | – 140 | 40 43 | – – | 27 29 | 1 | 1.2 | 1.75 | – | – |
| Fabric-base fine laminates | fine | | – | – | – | 75 | 1 | 1.15 | 1.4 | 1.65 | 2.0 |
| | coarse | | – | – | – | 50 | 1 | 1.2 | 1.6 | 2.1 | 2.8 |

For tempering (heat-treatable) steels, two values are given in each case for the heat-treated condition. For smaller gears up to roughly module 3, the larger of the two values can be specified. With very large gears, however, only the smaller value can be achieved with certainty.

[1] Values are valid for $A = 6$ (average tooth quality). With cast gears and high-precision gears, $A = 3$ and 10 respectively.
[2] For pulsating loads with a material fatigue strength $N_L \geq 3 \cdot 10^6$. In the case of alternating loads (idler gears), take into account the alternating load factor $Y_L$.
[3] Within fatigue strength of finite life, root bending stress is multiplied by the factor $Y_{NT}$, depending on the number of load changes $N_L = L_h \cdot 60 \cdot n$.
[4] Surface-hardened.

# Belt drives

## Friction belt drives

### Quantities and units

| Quantity | | Unit |
|---|---|---|
| $A$ | Belt cross-section | mm² |
| $F$ | Contact force | N |
| $F_1$ | Belt force on load side | N |
| $F_2$ | Belt force on slack side | N |
| $F_F$ | Centrifugal force of belt | N |
| $F_f$ | Centrifugal force per side | N |
| $F_R$ | Frictional force | N |
| $F_u$ | Peripheral force | N |
| $F_v$ | Pretensioning force | N |
| $F_w$ | Tensioning force of shaft | N |
| $P$ | Required power transmission | kW |
| $k_1$ | Pretension factor, with reference to operating conditions and wrap angle | – |
| $k_2$ | Centrifugal force factor | – |
| $v$ | Belt speed | m/s |
| $z$ | Number of belts (V-belt drives) or ribs (V-ribbed belts) | – |
| $\alpha$ | Groove angle | ° |
| $\beta$ | Wrap angle | ° |
| $\mu$ | Coefficient of friction | |
| $\mu'$ | Wedge coefficient of friction | |
| $\varrho$ | Mean density of belt material | g/cm³ |

### Transmission of force

The general equation for friction:

$$F_R = \mu \cdot F$$

yields the following equation for V-belt pulleys (see figure)

$$F_R = \mu \cdot 2 \cdot F'$$

or $F_R = \mu' \cdot F$

where $\mu' = \mu/\sin(\alpha/2)$

The Eytelwein equation describes the transition from static friction to sliding friction as:

$$F_1/F_2 = e^{\mu'\beta}$$

where $\mu' \approx 0.5 \pm 0.15$

according to the specifications of V-belt manufacturers with the incorporation of various safety factors.

As long as the ratio of forces on the two belt sides is:

$$F_1/F_2 \leq e^{\mu'\beta}$$

the belt will not slip during transmission of the peripheral force:

$$F_u = F_1 - F_2 = P \cdot 1{,}020/v$$

A pretensioning force $F_v$ is required in order to transmit the peripheral force $F_u$; at high rotational speeds, the centrifugal force constituent $F_F$ of the belt must be taken into consideration. The pretensioning force is:

$$F_v = F_w \cdot F_F$$

where $F_w = F_u \cdot [(e^{\mu'\beta} + 1)/(e^{\mu'\beta} - 1)] \cdot \sin(\beta/2)$

$$F_F = 2 \cdot z \cdot F_f \cdot \sin(\beta/2)$$

$$F_f = \varrho \cdot A \cdot v^2 \cdot 10^{-3}$$

or in simplified form:

$$F_F = 2 \cdot z \cdot k_2 \cdot v^2 \cdot \sin(\beta/2)$$

In practice, the following approximation process is frequently sufficient for calculating the pretensioning force (according to Continental):

$$F_v = (k_1 \cdot F_u + 2 \cdot z \cdot k_2 \cdot v^2) \cdot \sin(\beta/2)$$

The following rule of thumb can often be used for drives with 2 pulleys:

$$F_v = (1.5...2) \cdot F_u$$

In order to check belt pretensioning, the static force applied to each side of each belt:

$$F_s = F_v/[2z \cdot \sin(\beta/2)]$$

is compared with the value obtained by measuring belt deflection.

Belt drive calculations are performed in accordance with DIN 2218, or in accordance with the specifications supplied by the belt manufacturers. The performance values of the V-belts are based on a theoretical service life of 25,000 hours. Computer programs are used to perform service-life calculations. In properly designed drives, belt creep is less than 1% and V-belt efficiency is 94% to 97%.

Belt service life is shortened if the maximum permissible belt speed and bending frequency are exceeded, if the belt pulleys are smaller than the minimum permissible pulley diameter or, in the case of V-belts, belt tensioners are used to apply force to the back of the belt.

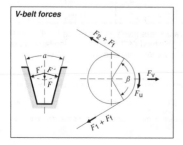

**V-belt forces**

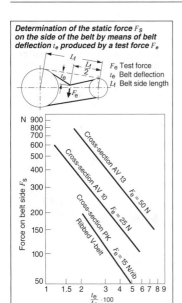

***Determination of the static force $F_s$ on the side of the belt by means of belt deflection $t_e$ produced by a test force $F_e$***

$F_e$ Test force
$t_e$ Belt deflection
$L_f$ Belt side length

| Pretension factor $k_1$ | | | | |
|---|---|---|---|---|
| Belt | $\beta$ | Drive | | |
| | | Light constant loads | Moderate loads | Heavy shock |
| V-belts | 180° | 1.5 | 1.7 | 1.9 |
| | 90° | 2.6 | 2.8 | 3.0 |
| V-ribbed belts | 180° | 1.8 | 2.0 | 2.2 |
| | 90° | 3.3 | 3.5 | 3.7 |

Intermediate values for other wrap angles may be interpolated.

| Belt factor $k_2$ | Cross-section | Centrifugal force |
|---|---|---|
| V-belt | SPZ | 0.07 |
| | SPA | 0.12 |
| V-ribbed belt | K | 0.02 |

Belt velocities up to 30 m/s and bending frequencies up to 40 s⁻¹ are permissible. See DIN 2217 for corresponding pulley dimensions.

### Narrow V-belts

In accordance with DIN 7753, Part 1; machine construction, motor vehicles built in the 1960s and 1970s. Ratio of top width to height: 1.2:1. The narrow V-belt is a modified version of the standard V-belt in which the central section, which in any case transmits only limited forces, is omitted. Higher capacity than standard V-belts of equal width. Toothed version exhibits less creep when bending around small pulleys. Belt velocities up to 42 m/s and bending frequencies up to 100 s⁻¹ are permissible (see DIN 2211 for corresponding pulley dimensions).

### Raw-edge V-belts

Raw-edge standard V-belts in accordance with DIN 2215, and raw-edge narrow V-belts for motor vehicles in accordance with DIN 7753, Part 3 (draft). Sub-surface belt fibers perpendicular to the direction of belt motion provide a high degree of flexibility while at the same time giving extreme transverse stiffness and high wear resistance. They also provide excellent support for the specially treated tension member. Particularly with small-diameter pulleys, this design increases

### Standard V-belts

(classical V-belts)
In accordance with DIN 2215, for household appliances, agricultural machinery, heavy machinery. Ratio of top width to height: 1.6:1. Belt designs which use corded cable and bundled fibers as the tension members transmit considerably less power than equally wide narrow V-belts. Due to their high tensile strength and transverse stiffness, they are suitable for use under rough operating conditions with sudden load changes.

***V-belt types***
1 Wrapped standard V-belt,
2 Wrapped narrow V-belt,
3 Raw-edge narrow V-belt.

1          2          3

belt capacity and provides a longer service life than wrapped narrow V-belts.

### Further developments
The latest development are V-belts with tension members made of Kevlar. Kevlar has very high tensile strength with a very small degree of elongation, and has greater temperature resistance.

### V-ribbed belts (poly-grooved belts)
In accordance with DIN 7867. Very flexible; the back of the belt may also be used to transmit power. This capability makes it possible for one such belt to be used to drive several vehicle accessories simultaneously (alternator, fan, water pump, air-conditioner compressor, power-steering pump, etc.) if the wrap angle around each driven pulley is sufficiently large. Optional cross-sections include the PH, PJ, PK, PL,

and PM, of which the PK cross-section has been widely used in motor vehicles in recent years. This allows use of narrower pulley diameters ($d_{b\,min} \approx 45$ mm) than those possible with narrow V-belts (cross-section: AVX 10). A pretension with a 20% increase compared with narrow V-belts is recommended to provide the same force-transmission capabilities with the same belt width. With a width of more than 6 ribs, a tenfold force may be required for power transmission in order to steady the belt.

*V-ribbed belts* (poly-grooved belts)

---

*Narrow V-belts for motor vehicles* in accordance with DIN 7753 Part 3
Example of designation: narrow V-belt DIN 7753 AVX 10 × 750 La.
Raw-edge, toothed with belt cross-section code AVX 10 $L_a$ = 750 mm.

| Narrow V-belt | | Wrapped | | Raw-edge | | | |
|---|---|---|---|---|---|---|---|
| | | | | Solid cross-section | | Toothed | |
| Belt cross-section | Code | 9.5 | 12.5 | AVP10 | AVP13 | AVX10 | AVX13 |
| | ISO code | AV 10 | AV 13 | AV 10 | AV 13 | AV 10 | AV 13 |
| Top width | $b_0 \approx$ | 10 | 13 | 10 | 13 | 10 | 13 |
| Belt height | $h \approx$ | 8 | 10 | 7.5 | 8.5 | 8 | 9 |
| Eff. line differential | $h_b$ | 1.8 | 2.6 | 0.9 | | | |
| Belt runout | $h_{a\,max}$ | – | | 2.4 | | | |
| Effective length | $L_a$ | 500 to 2,550: in increments of 25 mm | | | | | |

Dimensions in mm

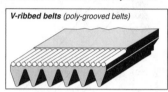

Active zone

| Groove cross-section code | | AV 10 | | AV 13 | |
|---|---|---|---|---|---|
| Effective diameter | $d_b$ | < 57 | ≥ 57 | < 70 | ≥ 70 |
| Groove angle | $\alpha \pm 0.5°$ | 34° | 36° | 34° | 36° |
| Effective width | $b_b$ | 9.7 | | 12.7 | |
| Groove depth | $t_{min}$ | 11 | | 14 | |
| Radius of curvature | $r$ | 0.8 | | | |
| Distance bet. grooves | $e_{min}$ | 12.6 | | 16 | |

## Positive belt drives

### Synchronous drive belts (toothed belts)
in accordance with DIN/ISO 5296

Toothed belts are used in motor vehicles for camshaft drives, and in some cases as distributor drives.

Synchronous drive belts with trapezoidal or rounded teeth combine the advantages of a belt drive (any desired distance between pulley centers, low-noise running, low maintenance) with the advantages of a positive transmission (synchronous operation, low bearing stress due to low shaft load).

Synchronous drive belts must be guided on both sides to prevent them from running off. This is accomplished by using either a toothed pulley with two flanges or two toothed pulleys with one flange each on opposite sides.

See DIN/ISO 5294 for corresponding toothed-pulley dimensions.

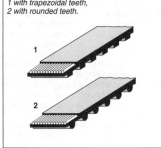

*Synchronous drive belts (toothed belts)*
1 with trapezoidal teeth,
2 with rounded teeth.

---

*V-ribbed belts and pulleys* as per DIN 7867

Designation for a 6-ribbed V-belt,
cross-section code PK and
effective length 800 mm:
V-ribbed belt DIN 7867-6 PK 800.

Designation for the
corresponding V-belt pulley
with 90 mm effective diameter:
V-ribbed belt pulley DIN 7867-6 Kx 90.

| Dimensions in mm | Belt | Groove profile |
|---|---|---|
| Cross-section code | PK | K |
| Rib or groove spacing $s$ or $e$ | 3.56 | 3.56 |
| Perm. deviation tolerance for $s$ or $e$ | ± 0.2 | ± 0.05 |
| Sum of deviation tolerances $s$ or $e$ | ± 0.4 | ± 0.30 |
| Groove angle $\alpha$ | | 40° ± 0.5° |
| $r_k$ at rib / $r_a$ at groove head | 0.50 | 0.25 |
| $r_g$ at rib / $r_i$ at groove seat | 0.25 | 0.50 |
| Belt height $h$ | 6 | |
| Nominal diam. of test pin $d_s$ | | 2.50 |
| $2 \cdot h_s$ nominal dimension | | 0.99 |
| $2 \cdot \delta$ (see figure) | | 2.06 |
| $f$ (see figure) | | 2.5 |

Belt cross-section

Groove cross-section

Determining
effective diameter

1 Position of tension member

Belt width $b = n \cdot s$
with number of ribs = $n$

Effective diameter
for K cross-section

$d_w = d_b + 2 h_b$
$h_b = 1.6$ mm

# Heat treatment of metallic materials

Heat treatment is employed to endow metallic tools and components with the specific qualities required either for subsequent manufacturing processes or for actual operation. The heat-treating process includes one or several time and temperature cycles. First, the parts to be treated are heated to the required temperature, where they are maintained for a specific period before being cooled back down to room temperature (or below in some processes) at a rate calculated to achieve the desired results.

The process modifies the microstructure to achieve the hardness, strength, ductility, wear resistance, etc. required to withstand the stresses associated with static and dynamic loads. The most significant industrial processes are summarized in Table 1 (see DIN EN 10 052 for terminology).

## Hardening

Hardening procedures produce a martensitic microstructure of extreme hardness and strength in ferrous materials such as steel and cast iron.

The parts being treated are heated to the austenitizing, or hardening temperature, at which they are maintained until an austenitic structure emerges, and until an

**Table 2. Standard austenitizing temperatures**

| Type of steel | Quality specification | Austenitizing temperature °C |
|---|---|---|
| Unalloyed and low-alloy steels | DIN EN 10 083-1 DIN 17 211 DIN 17 212 | 780...950 |
| < 0.8% by mass of C | | |
| ≥ 0.8% by mass of C | – | 780...820 |
| Cold- and hot-working tool steels | DIN 17 350 | 950...1,100 |
| High-speed tool steels | | 1,150...1,230 |
| Cast iron | – | 850...900 |

adequate quantity of carbon (released in the decay of carbides, such as graphite in cast iron) is dissolved in the treated material. The material is then quenched or otherwise cooled back to room temperature as quickly as possible in order to obtain a maximum degree of conversion to a martensitic microstructure (the time-temperature transformation chart for the specific steel in question contains the reference figures for the necessary cooling rate).

The austenitizing temperature varies according to the composition of the material in question (for specific data, consult the DIN Technical Requirements for Steels). Table 2 above furnishes reference data. See DIN 17 022, Parts 1 and 2, for practical information on hardening procedures for tools and components.

**Table 1. Summary of heat-treatment processes**

| Hardening | Austempering | Draw tempering | Thermo-chemical treatment | Annealing | Precipitation hardening |
|---|---|---|---|---|---|
| Through hardening | Isothermic transformation in the bainite stage | Tempering of hardened parts | Carburizing | Stress-relief | Solution treatment and aging |
| Surface hardening | | | Carbo-nitriding | Recrystallization annealing | |
| Hardening of carburized parts (case-hardening) | | Hardening and tempering above 550°C | Nitriding | Soft annealing, spheroidization | |
| | | | Nitro-carburizing | Normalizing | |
| | | | Boron treatment | Homogenizing | |
| | | | Chromating | | |

Not all types of steel and cast iron are suitable for hardening. The following equation describes the hardening potential for alloyed and unalloyed steels with mass carbon contents of between 0.15 and 0.60%, and can be applied to estimate the hardness levels achievable with a completely martensitic microstructure:

Max. hardness = 35 + 50 · (%C) ± 2 HRC

If the microstructure does not consist entirely of martensite, then the maximum hardness will not be reached.

When the carbon content exceeds 0.6% by mass, it may be assumed that the material's structure contains untransformed austenite (residual austenite) in addition to the martensite. This condition prevents the maximum hardness from being achieved, and the wear resistance will be lower. In addition, residual austenite is metastable, i.e. there exists a potential for subsequent transformation to martensite at temperatures below room temperature or under stress, with changes in specific volume and internal stress as the possible results. Low-temperature follow-up procedures or draw-tempering operations at over 230°C can be useful in cases where residual austenite is an unavoidable product of the hardening procedure.

The surface and core hardnesses remain virtually identical in components with material thicknesses up to approx. 10 mm. With greater cross-sections, core hardness is lower. There is a hardness progression or gradient. The rate of the progression depends upon the hardening response (testing described in DIN 50 191), which is a function of the material's composition (Mo, Mn, Cr). This factor requires particular attention with parts which do not cool well (large cross-sections and/or slow or graduated cooling processes designed to minimize the risk of cracks and/or distortion).

DIN 50 150 defines the method for using hardness as the basis for estimating tensile strength $R_m$. This method can only be applied in cases where the surface and core hardnesses are virtually identical:

$R_m \approx (34...37.7) ·$ Rockwell C hardness number in N/mm$^2$ or
$R_m \approx (3.2...3.35) ·$ Vickers hardness number in N/mm$^2$.

The specific volume of the martensitic microstructure is approximately 1.0% greater than that of the original material. In addition, stresses result from the rearrangement of the microstructure and from contraction during cooling. As the latter phenomenon does not take place at a uniform rate in all sections of the part, it produces variations in shape and dimensions. Tensile stresses near the surface and pressure tension at the core are the common result.

**Surface hardening**

The process is especially suited for integration within large-scale manufacturing operations, and can be adapted to fit the rhythm of the production line.

Heating and hardening are restricted to the surface, thereby minimizing alterations in shape and dimensions. Heating is generally provided by high- or medium-frequency alternating current (inductive hardening) or by a gas burner (flame hardening). Friction (friction hardening) and high-energy beams (e.g. electron or laser beams) can also provide the heat required for austenitizing. Table 3 provides an overview of the specific heat energies for the individual procedures.

These methods can be used to treat both linear and flat surfaces, meaning that the parts can be heated either while stationary or in motion. The heat source itself can also be moved. Rotation is the best way of dealing with radially symmetrical parts, as it ensures concentric hardening.

**Table 3. Comparison of power densities when heating with different sources**

| Energy source | Normal power density W/cm$^2$ |
|---|---|
| Laser beam | $10^3...10^4$ |
| Electron beam | $10^3...10^4$ |
| Induction (MF, HF, HF pulse) | $10^3...10^4$ |
| Flame heating | $10^3...6·10^3$ |
| Plasma beam | $10^4$ |
| Molten saline solution (convection) | 20 |
| Air/gas (convection) | 0.5 |

Either immersion or spraying arrangements can be applied for quenching.

Heat rise is rapid, so the temperatures must be 50...100 °C higher than those used in furnace heating so as to compensate for the shorter dwell period. The procedure is generally employed with low-alloy or unalloyed steels with mass carbon contents of 0.35...0.60% (consult DIN 17212 for list of suitable steels). However, surface hardening processes can also be applied with alloyed steels, cast iron and rolling-bearing steels. The parts can be heat-treated to provide a combination of improved base strength and high surface hardness, making them suitable for high-stress applications (recessed edges, bearing surfaces, cross-sectional transitions).

Surface hardening generally results in internal compression stresses along the edge. This leads to increased fatigue resistance, especially when notched parts are exposed to inconstant vibration stress (see figure).

The relationship defined above can be employed to estimate the potential surface hardness. There is a substantial reduction in hardness between the surface and the unhardened core region. The hardening depth $R_{ht}$ – the depth at which 80% of the Vickers surface hardness is found – can be derived from the hardness progression curve (see DIN 50190, Part 2).

## Austempering

The object of this process is to achieve a bainite microstructure. This microstructure is not as hard as martensite, but does display greater ductility as well as smaller changes in specific volume.

After austenitizing (see hardening), the parts for austempering are first cooled to a temperature of 200...350 °C (depending upon the exact composition of the material) at the required rate. The parts are then held at this temperature until the microstructure's transformation into bainite has been completed. The parts can then be cooled to room temperature (no special procedure required).

Austempering is an excellent alternative for parts whose geometrical configuration makes them sensitive to distortion and/or

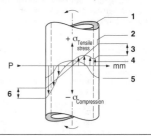

*Cyclically alternating stress according to surface-layer hardening*
$+\sigma$ *Tensile stress,* $-\sigma$ *Compression.*
*1 Case layer, 2 Bending stress, 3 Reduction of tensile stress, 4 Resulting tension, 5 Internal stress, 6 Increase in compressive stress.*

cracks, or in which high ductility is required together with substantial hardness, or which should combine hardness with a low level of residual austenite.

## Draw tempering

Parts emerge from the hardening process in a brittle state. They must be tempered to increase their ductility in order to reduce the risk of damage associated with excessive internal stress, such as delayed cracking after hardening or splintering during grinding. This tempering process is based on the elimination of carbides, a phenomenon accompanied by an increase in ductility, albeit at the price of reductions in hardness.

The parts are heated in the draw to a temperature of between 180 and 650 °C. They are then held there for at least one hour before being allowed to cool to room temperature. Depending upon the specific composition of the material, tempering at temperatures in excess of 230 °C may result in any residual austenite being transformed into bainite and/or martensite.

Tempering at temperatures as low as 180 °C is enough to reduce the hardness of unalloyed and low-alloy steels by approx. 1...5 HRC. The individual materials respond to higher temperatures with specific characteristic hardness loss. The graph on the right shows a characteristic tempering curve for typical types of steel.

The graph illustrates the fact that the hardness of high-alloy steels remains constant until the temperature exceeds 550 °C, after which it drops.

The mutual relationships between tempering temperature on the one side, and hardness, strength, yield point, fracture contraction and elongation at fracture on the other, can be taken from the tempering diagrams for the various steels (see DIN EN 10083).

Tempering of hardened parts is accompanied by a reduction in specific volume. In some cases, tempering can also induce changes in the progressive variation in internal stress at different depths in the parts.

It must be remembered that steels alloyed with manganese, chromium, manganese and chromium, chrome-vanadium, and chromium and nickel should not be tempered at temperatures of 350...500 °C, as brittleness could result. When these types of materials are cooled from higher tempering temperatures, the transition through this critical range should also be effected as rapidly as possible (see DIN 17 022, Parts 1 and 2 for additional information).

## Quench and draw

This type of quench and draw process combines hardening and tempering at temperatures above 500 °C. This procedure is designed to achieve an optimal relationship between strength and ductility. It is applied in cases where extreme ductility or malleability is required.

Particular care must be devoted to avoiding brittleness in the quench and draw operation (see above).

## Thermochemical treatment

In thermochemical treatment, the parts are annealed in agents which emit specific elements. These diffuse into the surface layer of the parts being treated and modify their composition. This results in very specific properties. Of particular importance for this process are the elements carbon, nitrogen and boron.

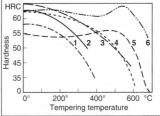

*Tempering response of various types of steel*
*1 Unalloyed tempering steel (C45), 2 Unalloyed cold-working tool steel (C80W2), 3 Low-alloyed cold-working tool steel (105WCr6), 4 Alloyed cold-working tool steel (X165CrV12), 5 Hot-working tool steel (X40CrMoV51), 6 High-speed tool steel (S6-5-2).*

## Carburizing, carbonitriding, case hardening

Carburizing increases the carbon content in the surface layer, while carbonitriding supplements the carbon enrichment with nitrogen. This process takes place at temperatures ranging from 850...1,050 °C in gases which give off carbon or nitrogen of their disintegration by heat or excited in the plasma. The actual hardening is performed subsequently, either by quenching directly from the carburizing/carbonitriding temperature (direct hardening), or by allowing the parts to cool to room temperature (single hardening), or by allowing them to cool to a suitable intermediate temperature (e.g. 620 °C) prior to reheating (hardening after isothermic conversion). This process produces a martensitic surface layer, while the degree of martensite at the core is a function of hardening temperature, hardenability and part thickness.

Specific temperatures can be selected for either surface hardening in the upper layers with higher carbon content (case refining), or for the non-carburized core (core refining) (see DIN 17 022, Part 3). Carburizing and carbonitriding produce a characteristic carbon declivity, with levels dropping as the distance from the surface increases (carbon curve). The distance between the surface and the point at which the mass carbon content is still 0.35% is normally defined as the carburization depth $At_{0.35}$.

The length of the carburizing or carbonitriding process depends upon the required carburization depth, the temperature and the atmosphere's carbon-diffusion properties. A reasonable approximation is possible:

$$At = K \cdot \sqrt{t} - D/\beta \text{ in mm}$$

Depending on temperature and carbon levels, $K$ lies between 0.3 and 0.6 during carburization in a gas atmosphere, for example; the correction factor $D/\beta$ is generally 0.1...0.3 mm; the time $t$ in h must be inserted.

Generally, the objective is to achieve a carbon gradient with a concentration of at least 0.60% mass carbon content, the ultimate goal being a surface hardness of 750 HV (corresponding to 65 HRC). Higher concentrations of carbon can lead to residual austenite and/or carbide diffusion, which could have negative effects on the performance of case-hardened parts in actual use. Control of the atmosphere's carbon level, and thus the part's ultimate carbon content, is thus extremely important.

The gradient defining the relationship between hardness and depth corresponds to the carbon concentration curve. The case-hardening depth is used to define the case depth $Eht$. DIN 50 190, Part 1 defines this as the maximum distance from the surface before the hardness drops below 550 HV.

The case-hardened part generally exhibits compression tension at the surface, and tensile stresses at the core. As with surface-hardened materials, this distribution pattern provides enhanced resistance to vibration loads.

In carbonitriding, nitrogen is also absorbed; it serves to improve the material's tempering properties, increase its durability and enhance its wear resistance. The positive effects are especially pronounced with unalloyed steels. For additional, more detailed information on case-hardening procedures consult DIN 17 022, Part 3, and Information Sheet 452 of the Steel Information Center, Düsseldorf.

**Nitriding and nitrocarburizing**

Nitriding is a thermal treatment process (temperature range: 400...600 °C) which can be used to enrich the surface layer of virtually any ferrous material with nitrogen. In nitrocarburizing, a certain amount of carbon is diffused into the material to form nitrogen at the same time.

Nitrogen enrichment is accompanied by precipitation hardening. This strengthens the surface layer, enhancing the material's resistance to wear, corrosion and alternating cyclic stress.

As the process employs relatively low temperatures, there are no volumetric changes of the kind associated with transformations in the microstructure, so that changes in dimensions and shape are minute.

The nitrided region consists of an outer layer, several millimeters in depth, and a transitional white layer, the hardness of which may be anywhere from 700 to over 1,200 HV, depending upon the composition of the material. Still deeper is a softer diffusion coating extending several tenths of a millimeter. The thickness of the individual layers is determined by the temperature and duration of the treatment process. The process produces a hardness gradient (similar to that which results from surface and case-hardening); this gradient furnishes the basis for determining the nitriding depth $Nht$. DIN 50 190, Part 3 defines this as the depth from the surface at which the hardness is still 50 HV above the core hardness.

The material's resistance to wear and corrosion is essentially determined by the white layer, which contains up to 10 mass components of nitrogen in %. The nitriding depth and the surface hardness determine the material's resistance to alternating cyclic stress (for additional details, see DIN 17 022, Part 4, and Information Sheet 447 from the Steel Information Center, Düsseldorf).

**Boron treatment**

This is a thermochemical treatment method which employs boron to enrich the surface layer of ferrous materials. Depending upon duration and temperature (normally 850...1,000 °C), an iron-boron white layer of 30 μm...0.2 mm in depth and with a hardness of 2,000...2,500 HV is produced. It consists of iron-boron.

Boron treatment is particularly effective as a means of protecting against abrasive wear. However, the comparatively high process temperature leads to relatively large changes in shape and dimensions, meaning that this treatment is only suitable for applications in which large tolerances can be accepted.

## Annealing

Annealing can be applied to optimize certain operational or processing characteristics of parts. With this method, the parts are heated to the required temperature and maintained there for an adequate period before being cooled to room temperature. Table 1 lists the various processes used in specific individual applications.

### Stress-relief

Depending upon the precise composition of the parts, this operation is carried out at temperatures ranging from 450 to 650 °C. The object is to achieve the maximum possible reduction in internal stress in components, tools and castings by inducing plastic deformation.

After an oven time of 0.5...1 h, the parts are cooled back to room temperature; this cooling should be as gradual as possible to prevent new stresses from forming.

### Recrystallization annealing

Recrystallization annealing is applied with parts that have been formed using non-cutting procedures. The goal is to restructure the grain pattern in order to prevent increased hardening, thereby facilitating subsequent machining work.

The temperature requirement depends upon the composition of the material and the degree of deformation: it lies between 550 and 730 °C for steel.

### Soft annealing, spheroidization

Soft annealing is intended to facilitate the machining and/or shaping of workpieces which have hardened owing to deformation processes or other heat-treatment processes.

The temperature requirement is determined by the material's composition. It is in a range of 650...720 °C for steel, and lower for nonferrous materials.

Spheroidizing of cementite is applied when a microstructure with a granular carbide pattern is desired. If the initial structure is martensite or bainite, the result will be an especially homogeneous carbide distribution.

### Normalizing

Normalizing is carried out by heating the parts to austenitizing temperature and then allowing them to gradually cool to room temperature. In low-alloy and unalloyed steels, the result is a structure consisting of ferrite and perlite. This process is essentially employed to reduce grain size, reduce the formation of coarse grain patterns in parts with limited reshaping, and to provide maximum homogeneity in the distribution of ferrite and perlite.

### Precipitation hardening treatment

This process combines solution treatment with aging at ambient temperature. The parts are heated and then maintained at temperature to bring precipitated structural constituents into a solid solution, and quenched at room temperature to form a supersaturated solution. The aging process comprises one or several cycles in which the material is heated and held at above-ambient temperatures (hot aging). In this process, one or several phases, i.e. metallic bonds between certain base alloys, are formed and precipitated in the matrix.

The precipitated particles enhance the hardness and strength of the base microstructure. The actual characteristics are determined by the temperature and duration of the aging process (option of mutual substitution). Exceeding a certain maximum will usually reduce the strength and hardness of the final product.

Precipitation hardening is mostly applied for nonferrous alloys, but some hardenable steels (maraging steels) can also be processed.

# Hardness

## Hardness testing

Hardness is the property of solid materials that defines their resistance to deformation. In metallic materials the hardness is used to assess mechanical properties such as strength, machinability, malleability, and resistance to wear. DIN 50 150 defines guidelines for converting hardness to tensile strength. Measurement processes are practically nondestructive.

The test data are generally derived from the size or depth of the deformation produced when a specified indentor is applied at a defined pressure.

A distinction is made between static and dynamic testing. Static testing is based on measurement of the permanent impression left by the indentor. Conventional hardness tests include the Rockwell, Vickers and Brinell procedures. Dynamic testing monitors the rebound height of a test tool accelerated against the surface of the test specimen.

Another option for obtaining an index of surface hardness is to scratch the surface with a harder test tool and then measure the groove width. The table (next page) compares the standard application ranges for the Rockwell, Vickers and Brinell hardness tests.

## Test procedure

### Rockwell hardness (DIN EN 10 109)

This method is particularly suitable for large-scale testing of metallic workpieces. A steel or diamond test tool is positioned vertically against the surface of the test specimen and a minor load applied prior to application of the full test pressure (major load) for a period of at least 30 s. The Rockwell hardness is the resulting penetration depth $e$ in mm (see Table 1).

The test surface should be smooth (depending on hardness range, $R_{max} \leq$ 1.2...3.4 μm) and as flat as possible. If the specimen's radius of curvature is less than 20 mm then the results must be scaled using the correction factor for the individual resistance level.

Selection of the individual test procedures enumerated in Table 1 is based upon either the test specimen's thickness or the case depth of the hardened surface layer (refer to Figs. A.1...A.3 in DIN EN 10 109). The abbreviation for the selected test method should be appended to the numerical data when specifying hardness, e.g., 65 HRC, 76 HR 45 N. The Rockwell C procedure's error range is approx. ± 1 HRC.

Advantages of the Rockwell test method include minimal specimen preparation and rapid measurement. This test process can also be fully automated.

**Table 1. Rockwell test methods**

| Abbreviation force | Indentor | Minor load N | Total test N | Hardness number ($e$ indentor penetration depth) | |
|---|---|---|---|---|---|
| HRC | Diamond cone | 98 ± 2 | 1,471 ± 9 | 100 − $e$ / 0.002 | 20...70 |
| HRA | Diamond cone | 98 ± 2 | 588 ± 5 | 100 − $e$ / 0.002 | 60...881 |
| HRB | Steel ball | 98 ± 2 | 980 ± 6.5 | 130 − $e$ / 0.002 | 35...100 |
| HRF | Steel ball | 98 ± 2 | 588 ± 5 | 130 − $e$ / 0.002 | 60...100 |
| HR15N HR30N HR45N | Diamond cone | 29.4 ± 0.6 | 147 ± 1 294 ± 2 441 ± 3 | 100 − $e$ / 0.001 | 66...92 39...84 17...75 |
| HR15T HR30T HR45T | Steel ball | 3 ± 0.06 | 15 ± 0.1 30 ± 0.2 45 ± 0.3 | 100 − $e$ / 0.001 | 50...94 10...84 0...75 |

Any tester vibration, or shifting and movement of either the test probe or the test specimen itself can lead to testing errors, as can an uneven support surface or a damaged indentor.

### Brinell hardness (DIN EN 10 003)

This procedure is used for metallic materials of low to medium hardness. The test tool (indentor) is a hard-metal or hardened-steel ball. It is applied to the surface of the specimen at an individually specified force $F$ for at least 15 s[1]. Microscopic examination of the resulting deformation diameter $d$ provides the basis for calculating the Brinell hardness. These data can be correlated with standard charts or calculated as follows:

$$\text{Brinell hardness} = \frac{0.204 \cdot F}{\pi \cdot D \cdot (D - \sqrt{D^2 - d^2})} \text{ HB}$$

$F$  Force in N
$D$  Ball diameter in mm
$d$  Indentation diameter in mm

Test pressures range from 9.81 to 29,420 N. Results obtained using spheres of different diameters are only conditionally comparable, and any comparisons should be based on testing at identical force levels.

[1] At least 30 s for lead, zinc, etc.

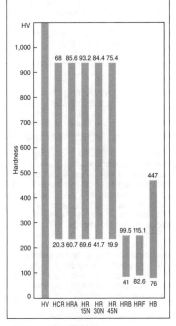

*Comparison of hardness ranges for different test methods*
The figures at the range extremities indicate the hardness data for the respective methods.

### Table 2. Application of the Brinell hardness test

| Material | Brinell hardness | Load factor 0.102 $F/D^2$ |
|---|---|---|
| Steel; nickel and titanium alloys | | 30 |
| Cast iron[1] | < 140 | 10 |
| | ≥ 140 | 30 |
| Copper and copper alloys | < 35 | 5 |
| | 35 to 200 | 10 |
| | < 200 | 30 |
| Light metals and their alloys | < 35 | 2.5 |
| | 35 to 80 | 5 |
| | | 10 |
| | | 15 |
| | > 80 | 10 |
| | | 15 |
| Lead and tin | | 1 |
| Sintered metals | see EN 24 498-1 | |

[1] Ball nominal diameters of 2.5, 5 or 10 mm are specified for testing cast iron.

Testing should always be performed using the largest possible spherical sphere, while load factors should be selected to obtain an indentation diameter of between $0.24 \cdot D$ and $0.6 \cdot D$. Table 2 lists the recommended load factors and ball diameters for a variety of materials as laid down in DIN EN 10003.

In the Brinell hardness designation the numeric data are accompanied by the procedure code, the material of the ball (W for hard metal, S for steel) and the ball diameter. The final element is the test force (in N) multiplied by a factor of 0.102. Example: 250 HBW 2.5/187.5.

To prevent test errors stemming from deformation of the ball itself, testing at hardness factors in excess of 450 HB is to be carried out exclusively with a hard-metal ball.

High test pressures producing deformations extending over a relatively wide surface area can be employed to gather data on materials with inconsistent structures. An advantage of the Brinell method is the relatively high degree of correlation between the Brinell hardness factor and the steel's tensile strength.

The range of application for the Brinell test method is limited by specifications for the thickness of the test specimen (cf. DIN EN 10003) and by the ball material. The required preparations and ensuing test procedures are more complex than those used for Rockwell testing. Potential error sources are the test's reliance on visual evaluation of the diagonal of impression and the possibility of inconsistencies in the impression itself.

**Vickers hardness** (DIN 50 133)
This test method can be used for all metallic materials, regardless of hardness. It is especially suitable for testing minute and thin specimens, while the potential application range extends to include surface and case-hardened parts as well as nitrided workpieces and parts carburized in nitrogen-based atmospheres.

The test tool is a square-based diamond pyramid with an apical angle of 136°. This is applied to the surface of the test specimen at the specified force $F$.

The diagonal $d$ of the rhomboidal cavity remaining after removing the indentor is measured using a magnifying glass to obtain the basis for calculating the Vickers hardness, which can be read from tables or calculated as follows:

Vickers hardness = $0.189 \cdot F/d^2$ HV

$F$ Applied force in N
$d$ Diagonal of impression in mm

Table 3 gives an overview of the graduated force levels defined in DIN 50 133.

In the formula for Vickers hardness data, the actual test figure is accompanied by the abbreviation HV, the force in N (multiplied by a factor of 0.102) and, following a slash, the force application period (if other than the standard 15 s) in seconds, e.g.: 750 HV 10/25.

The test specimen's surface should be smooth ($R_{max} \leq 0.005 \cdot d$) and flat. DIN 50 133 stipulates that correction factors be used to compensate for any error stemming from surface curvature. Test pressure levels are selected with reference to either the thickness of the test specimen itself or of its hardened outer layer (cf. Fig. 2 in DIN 50 133). Practical experience indicates an error range of approximately ± 25 HV. Although the geometrical configurations are similar, hardness data vary as a function of applied-force levels.

A major advantage of this test method is that there are virtually no limitations on using it to assess thin parts or layers. It allows the use of extremely small force levels to determine the hardness of individual structural sections. The Brinell and Vickers numbers correlate up to approximately 350 HV.

However, a certain minimal degree of surface consistency is necessary to en-

**Table 3. Vickers hardness force increment**

| Abbreviation | HV0.2 | HV0.3 | HV0.5 | HV1 | HV2 | HV3 | HV5 | HV10 | HV20 | HV30 | HV50 | HV100 |
|---|---|---|---|---|---|---|---|---|---|---|---|---|
| Applied force N | 1.96 | 2.94 | 4.9 | 9.8 | 19.6 | 29.4 | 49 | 98 | 196 | 294 | 490 | 980 |

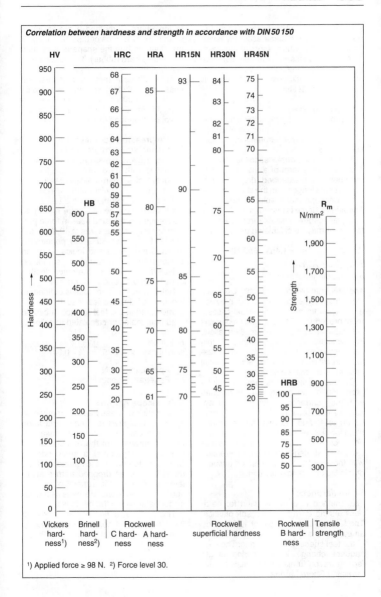

*Correlation between hardness and strength in accordance with DIN 50 150*

1) Applied force ≥ 98 N.  2) Force level 30.

sure accurate results. Vickers testing furnishes roughly the same accuracy levels as the Brinell method, although the measurement process is extremely sensitive to movement of the test setup. The indentors are more expensive than the balls used in Brinell testing.

## Knoop hardness

This process closely resembles the Vickers procedure. It is the method of choice for testing thin-layer hardness in English-speaking countries.

The test tool is designed to leave an impression in the form of a thin, elongated rhombus. The extended diagonal $d$ is seven times longer than the short one and is the only one that is actually measured. The applied force is less than 9.8 N. Hardness ratings are available from standard tables, or may be calculated as follows:

Knoop hardness = $1.451 \cdot F/d^2$ HK

$F$ Applied load in N
$d$ Long diagonal in mm

The diagonal, which is roughly 2.8 times longer than in the Vickers method, provides more accurate results with visual assessment procedures. The penetration depth is 1/3 less than in the Vickers method, allowing evaluation of surface hardness in thin parts and layers. By making Knoop impressions in different directions, even material anisotropies can be detected.

Disadvantages of this method include pronounced sensitivity to misaligned specimen surfaces, which must be absolutely perpendicular to the force-application axis, and the fact that the maximum force is restricted to 9.8 N. There are no special German standards for this procedure. Test results cannot be correlated with those of the Vickers test, on account of this lack of standardization.

## Shore hardness

This method is primarily used for hardness testing on rubber and soft plastics. The test tool is a steel pin of 1.25 mm diameter; this is forced against the surface of the test specimen by a spring. The subsequent change in the spring length (spring travel) furnishes the basis for determining Shore hardness.

In the Shore D method a pretensioned spring exerts a force of 0.55 N. The tip of the steel pin has the shape of a frustum (for testing hard rubber). The spring rate $c$ is 4 N/mm.

In the Shore A method, measurement uses a conical steel pin with a rounded tip and no pretension. The spring rate $c$ is 17.8 N/mm. Each 0.025 mm of spring travel corresponds to 100 Shore units.

## Ball impression hardness (DIN 53 456)

This is the standard test for determining hardness levels in plastomers, and is also employed with hard rubber substances. The test tool is a hardened steel ball 5 mm in diameter. It is applied with a minor load of 9.81 N to the surface of the test specimen which must be at least 4 mm thick. Subsequent graduated rises in force provide application pressures of 49, 132, 358 and 961 N. After 30 s the penetration depth is measured and indicated on an analog display. The test load $F$ should be selected to provide a penetration depth $h$ of between 0.15 and 0.35 mm.

Ball impression hardness is defined as the ratio of the applied load to the deformed area in the test surface. It can be read from tables or calculated as follows:

$$\text{Ball impression hardness} = \frac{0.21 \cdot F}{1.25 \cdot \pi \cdot (h - 0.04)} \text{ N/mm}^2$$

$F$ Applied load in N
$h$ Penetration depth in mm

## Scleroscope hardness

This dynamic measurement method is specially designed for heavy and large metal pieces. This process is based on the measurement of the rebound height (energy of impact) of a steel indentor (hammer) featuring a diamond or hard metal tip. This is dropped from a stipulated height onto the surface of the test specimen. The rebound serves as the basis for determining the hardness.

The method is not standardized and there is no direct correlative relationship with any other hardness testing method.

# Tolerances

## Correlations

In the absence of special supplementary definitions, envelope analysis is mandatory for all individual form elements in prints based on standardized DIN definitions for tolerances and fits (e.g. Independence Principle from ISO 8015). The envelope concept is based on the Taylor gage test, which specifies that maximum intolerance material mass shall not penetrate the geometric envelope at any point.

As it is not possible to produce geometrically ideal workpieces, dimension limits (dimensional tolerances) are defined for production.

DIN 7167 includes all form tolerances, including tolerances of parallelism, position and planar regularity as well as dimensional tolerances. The geometrical tolerance may lie anywhere within the dimensional tolerance (see diagram).

For the following tolerances of position, the envelope dimension at maximum material dimension is not defined:

tolerances of perpendicularity, slope, symmetry, coaxiality, and concentricity. For these tolerances of position, either direct specifications on the drawing or the general tolerances are necessary.

No generally applicable correlative data are defined for the relationship between dimensional tolerance and peak-to-valley height (general formula: $R_z \leq 0.5 \cdot T$).

---

ISO International Organization for Standardization.

---

**Tolerance zone**
1 Actual form.
a Form tolerance, b Dimensional tolerance.

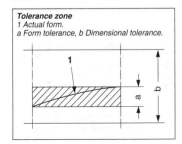

## ISO system for limits and fits

ISO tolerance classes are indicated by letters (for basic allowances) and numbers (for basic tolerance grades). The definitions are:
– The **letters** A to Z indicate the position of the tolerance zone relative to the base line; lower-case letters for shafts; upper-case letters for bores.
– The **numbers** 01 to 18 indicate the magnitude of the tolerance grade.

The ISO tolerance zones for shafts and bores can be combined as desired to give fits; the standard bore and standard shaft systems of fits are preferred.
**Standard bore:** The basic allowances for all holes are identical, and different fits are obtained by selecting the appropriate shaft sizes.
**Standard shaft:** The basic allowances for all shafts are identical, and different fits are obtained by selecting the corresponding bore dimensions.

Most common clearance, transition and interference fits can be defined using the following selection of ISO tolerances from ISO 286.

Example of tolerance class:   H 7
Basic allowance ⌐
Tolerance grade ⌐

## Tolerances of form and position

Tolerances of form and position should be specified only where required (e.g. in response to functional requirements, interchangeability and possible production conditions).

An element's geometrical and positional tolerances define the zone within which it must be located (surface, axis or generating line).

Within the tolerance zone, the toleranced element may have any desired form or directional orientation. The tolerance applies to the entire length or surface of the toleranced element.

Symbols are employed when entering the tolerances in prints (see table on next page).

## Symbols for toleranced properties.

| Properties | | Symbols |
|---|---|---|
| Straightness | 1) | — |
| Flatness | | $\square$ |
| Roundness (circularity) | | $\bigcirc$ |
| Cylindricity | | $\oslash$ |
| Profile of any line | | $\frown$ |
| Profile of any surface | | $\triangle$ |
| Parallelism | 2) | $//$ |
| Perpendicularity | | $\perp$ |
| Slope | | $\angle$ |
| Position | 3) | $\bigoplus$ |
| Concentricity, coaxiality | | $\bigodot$ |
| Symmetry | | $=$ |
| Path | 4) | $\nearrow$ |
| Overall path | | $\nearrow\!\!\nearrow$ |

1) Tolerances of form, 2) Tolerances of direction,
3) Tolerances of location, 4) Running tolerances.

## Supplementary symbols.

| Description | | Symbols |
|---|---|---|
| Identification of the toleranced element | direct | |
| | with letter | $A$ |
| Identification of the reference | direct | |
| | with letter | $\boxed{A}$ $\boxed{A}$ |
| Reference point | | $\frac{\varnothing 2}{A1}$ |
| Theoretically precise dimension | | $\boxed{50}$ |
| Projected tolerance zone | | $\textcircled{P}$ |
| Maximum material condition | | $\textcircled{M}$ |

## Geometrical deviations

The term "geometrical deviation" refers to all disparities between the actual surface and its ideal geometrical configuration.

Critical considerations may be restricted to dimensional deviations, surface irregularities or undulations, or may encompass the entire potential deviation range, depending upon the specified application. To help distinguish between the different types of geometrical deviation DIN 4760 defines a classification system including examples of deviation types and their possible sources:

### 1st order geometrical deviations

Formal deviations are first-order geometrical irregularities which can be detected when an entire surface area is examined. Usually, the general relationship between formal deviation intervals and depth is > 1,000 : 1.

### 2nd to 5th-order geometrical deviations

Undulations, or waviness, are geometrical irregularities of the 2nd order. These essentially periodic irregularities are defined using a representative section of the actual surface area on the geometrical element under investigation.

Roughness consists of geometrical irregularities of orders 3 through 5. It is characterized by periodic or irregular formal deviations in which the deviation intervals are a relatively low multiple of their depth.

## Surface parameters

Stylus instruments are employed to record sectioning planes of surface profiles, registering vertically, horizontally, and as a function of the two components in combination. The characteristics are derived from the unfiltered primary profile (P profile), the filtered roughness profile (R profile), and the filtered waviness profile (W profile). Roughness and waviness are differentiated by means of profile filters.

**Profile height** $P_t$, $R_t$, $W_t$

Maximum excursion above the centerline $Z_p$ plus the maximum excursion below the centerline $Z_v$ within the traversing length $l_n$.

The <u>traversing length</u> $l_n$ can consist of one or more sampling lengths $l_r$. The value of a parameter is computed from the measured data for its sampling length. As a rule, five sampling lengths are required for computing the roughness and waviness parameters. The standardized measuring conditions are based on the maximum roughness peak-to-valley height and include, for example, limit wave length $\lambda_c$, sampling length $l_r$, traversing length $l_n$, profile length $l_t$, stylus-tip radius $r_{SP\,max}$ and digitizing cutoff $\Delta x_{max}$. For industrial purposes, the parameters generally employed in describing surfaces are as follows:

**Arithmetic roughness average** $R_a$

Arithmetic average of the absolute values of the ordinates of the roughness profile.

**Maximum peak-to-valley height** $R_z$

Maximum excursion above the centerline $R_p$ plus the maximum excursion below the centerline $R_v$ within a sampling length. As the vertical distance between the highest peak and the lowest valley, $R_z$ is a measure of scatter of the roughness ordinates.

**Material content of the roughness profile** $R_{mr(c)}$

The material-content curve reflects the material content as a function of section height $c$. The characteristic is formed by a percentage relationship between the sum of the material lengths $MI(c)$ of the profile elements in a specified section height $c$ and traversing length $l_n$.

**Parameters of the material-content curve** $R_k$, $R_{pk}$, $R_{vk}$, $M_{r1}$, $M_{r2}$

The material-content curve derived from the filtered roughness profile is divided into three sections characterized by parameters (core peak-to-valley height $R_k$, reduced peak height $R_{pk}$ and reduced score depth $R_{vk}$). The parameters $M_{r1}$ and $M_{r2}$ reflect the material content at the limits of the roughness core profile.

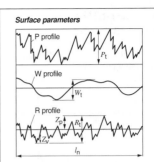

*Surface parameters*

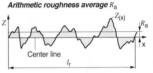

*Arithmetic roughness average* $R_a$

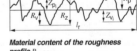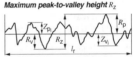

*Maximum peak-to-valley height* $R_z$

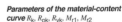

*Material content of the roughness profile* $R_{mr(c)}$

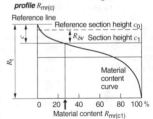

*Parameters of the material-content curve* $R_k$, $R_{pk}$, $R_{vk}$, $M_{r1}$, $M_{r2}$

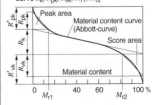

# Sheet-metal processing

## Deep-drawing technology

### Quantities and units

| Symbols | | Units |
|---|---|---|
| $D$ | Section diameter | mm |
| $d_B$ | Support diameter of hold-down device | mm |
| $d_1$ | Punch diameter, 1st draw | mm |
| $d_2$ | Punch diameter, 2nd draw | mm |
| $F$ | Total deep-drawing force | kN |
| $F_B$ | Sheet retention force | kN |
| $F_Z$ | Deep-drawing force | kN |
| $p$ | Pressure of hold-down device | N/mm² |
| $R_m$ | Tensile strength | N/mm² |
| $s$ | Sheet thickness | mm |
| $\beta_1, \beta_2$ | Individual drawing ratio | |
| $\beta_{max}$ | Maximum possible drawing ratio | |

### Deep-drawing methods

The drawing procedure employs a drawing die, punch and sheet-metal retaining device to reshape flat sections, blanks and round plates.

The variables exercising an influence on the deep-drawing of three-dimensional bodywork components are exceedingly complex; rough calculations thus do not provide a suitable basis for their definition. The finite-element method (FEM), in which powerful computers employ numerical procedures from continuum mechanics, is used to calculate deep-drawing processes. Software development has reflected the significance of specific parameters affecting the deep-drawing process, including the influence of friction, of bilateral contact, of material values which vary according to rolling direction, and additional factors.

Deep-draw simulation is of major assistance in designing deep-drawing tools, helping to optimize production times for this equipment.

### Deep-drawing process

The drawing process reshapes a flat blank into a concave section. A punch, surrounded by a retaining mechanism (holding-down clamp, blank holder), pulls the sheet metal into the matrix. The clamp applies the defined force to the sheet, prevents creases from forming, and permits application of tensile force.

The maximum possible drawing ratio is determined by various factors:
– material strength
– tool dimensions and sheet thickness
– retention force
– friction
– lubrication
– material and surface of the workpiece

### Drawing on single-action presses

This category includes all crank presses in which the ram represents the only moving component.

*Deep drawing*
*a) With single-action press, b) With double-action press; 1 Ram, 2 Air cushion, 3 Hold-down device, 4 Matrix, 5 Punch, 6 Air pins, 7 Matrix insert, 8 Hold-down ram.*

Applications: for deep-drawing flat work-pieces in simple reshaping operations to produce trimmers, arches, supports.

### Drawing on double-action presses

Double-action drawing presses employ separate rams to retain the metal and to pull it. The hold-down ram is actuated mechanically via disk or toggle, or hydraulically.

Applications: for deep-drawn components of complex geometry, including fenders, wheel arches, hatchbacks.

### Calculations for the drawing process

$$F_Z = \pi \cdot (d_1 + s) \cdot s \cdot R_m$$
$$F_B = \frac{\pi}{4} \cdot (D^2 - d_B{}^2) \cdot p$$
$$F = F_Z + F_B$$
$$\beta_1 = D/d_1; \quad \beta_2 = d_1/d_2.$$

<u>Example</u>
$D = 210$ mm; $d_B = 160$ mm; $d_1 = 140$ mm; $p = 2.5$ N/mm²; $R_m = 380$ N/mm²; $s = 1$ mm; $\beta_{max} = 1.9$.
<u>Result</u>
Drawing ratio $\beta_1 = 1.5$; Deep-drawing force $F_Z = 112.2$ kN; Sheet retention force $F_B = 36.3$ kN; Total deep-drawing force $F = 148.5$ kN.

The diagram shows the motions of the drawing ram and the hold-down ram in the course of one cycle. The rams have differing strokes. The drawing ram, with its longer stroke, is set in motion first,

| Material | $\beta_1$ max. | $\beta_2$ max. | Pressure of hold-down device $p$ N/mm² |
|---|---|---|---|
| St 12 | 1.8 | 1.2 | 2.5 |
| St 13 | 1.9 | 1.25 | |
| St 14 | 2.0 | 1.3 | |
| Copper | 2.1 | 1.3 | |
| CuZn 37 w | 2.1 | 1.4 | 2.0...2.4 |
| CuZn 37 h | 1.9 | 1.2 | |
| CuSn 6 w | 1.5 | – | |
| Al 99.5 w | 2.1 | 1.6 | |
| AlMg 1 w | 1.85 | 1.3 | 1.2...1.5 |
| AlCuMg 1 pl w | 2.0 | 1.5 | |
| AlCuMg 1 pl ka | 1.8 | 1.3 | |

[1] Valid up to $d_1/s = 300$; specified for $d_1 = 100$ mm, $s = 1$ mm. Different sheet thicknesses and punch diameters result in minor deviations from the figures given. Basic qualities are also used with galvanized surfaces. The figures can vary slightly.

while the shorter-stroke hold-down ram starts second, but is first to achieve contact.

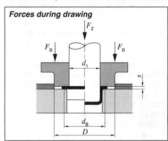

***Forces during drawing***

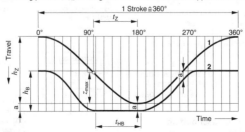

***Time-distance diagram for a double-action drawing press***
*1 Curve for drawing ram, 2 Curve for hold-down ram.*
*$h_Z$ Stroke of drawing ram, $h_B$ Stroke of hold-down ram, $z_{max}$ Max. drawing depth,*
*$t_Z$ Duration of drawing process, $t_{HB}$ Holding time of hold-down ram, $a$ Approach of drawing ram.*

## Laser technology

Deviation mirrors are used to deflect the coherent light beam generated by the laser (see P. 53) for concentration in a focusing device. At the focal point the laser beam has a diameter of approx. 0.3...0.5 mm, allowing intensities in excess of $10^6...10^8$ W/cm$^2$ to be achieved. The workpiece melts and vaporizes in milliseconds if the focal point is in its immediate vicinity, an effect which can be exploited in laser-based processing operations. According to the physical condition of the active medium, the device is classified as a solid-state, gas, semiconductor or liquid laser. The following are applied in industrial metal processing:

### Solid-state laser (Nd:YAG)

Neodynium (Nd) is an element of the rare-earth group, while YAG stands for yttrium-aluminum-garnet ($Y_5Al_5O_{12}$).

The Nd:YAG laser emits light in the infrared band of the spectrum, with a wavelength of 1.06 µm. The essential advantage of the Nd:YAG laser lies in the fact that the generated beam can be transmitted through optical fibers, making it possible to dispense with complicated beam-relaying systems. Present laser power ratings are in the range of 400...4,200 W. pulse-mode operation is generally employed. The foremost application for solid-state lasers is in welding parts with high requirements for precision, e.g. in precision mechanics. Welding depths depend on power and welding speed, and are in the range of tenths of a millimeter.

### Gas-laser (CO₂)

The CO₂ laser is among the most important gas-laser devices. Molecular gas serves as the active medium. Radiation emissions are in the medium infrared band, with wavelengths spread across a number of spectral ranges between 9.2 and 10.9 µm; the mean is 10.6 µm. This type of laser is generally used in continuous operation, with standard laser power ratings of between 2 and 5 kW. Laboratory units with up to 20 kW have already been installed.

### Characteristics of laser cutting

– Clean, burr-free edges

– High dimensional/manufacturing precision (no subsequent processing necessary)
– Minimal thermal and mechanical stresses on the workpiece during the cutting process
– Uncomplicated clamping devices
– Sheet metal of up to 10 mm can be cut (1 kW), rapid cutting (10 m/min with metal 1 mm thick)

### Characteristics of laser welding

– High depth/width ratio (e.g. approx. 1 mm seam width at 5 mm seam depth)
– Minimal base-material thermal stress results in narrow heat-affected zone (HAZ)
– Minimal distortion
– Welding in protective-gas atmosphere
– Joint gaps must be virtually zero
– Welding with filler metals is possible (for bridging gaps and achieving specific effects at the weld)
– Specialized clamping and equipment technology is required

### Applications in machine tool and automotive engineering

– Welding, soldering and cutting bodywork sheet metal
– Welding (joining) blanks of various thicknesses
– Welding (joining) of rotationally symmetrical parts (transmission components, tappets, automotive components)
– Boring and perforation
– Surface hardening, e.g. in treating valve seats, etc.
– Providing surfaces with upgraded finishes, e.g. structural transformation around cylinder liners

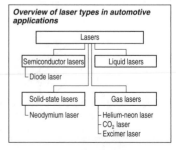

*Overview of laser types in automotive applications*

Lasers
- Semiconductor lasers
  - Diode laser
- Liquid lasers
- Solid-state lasers
  - Neodymium laser
- Gas lasers
  - Helium-neon laser
  - CO₂ laser
  - Excimer laser

# Joining and bonding techniques

## Welding

Automotive components and subassemblies are joined using a wide and highly varied range of welding and bonding techniques. Resistance-pressure and fusion welding are among the most commonly applied welding methods. This overview concentrates on the resistance-welding procedures in standard production use (processes and symbols based on DIN 1910, Part 5).

### Resistance welding

#### Resistance spot welding

In resistance spot welding, locally applied electrical current is used to melt the contact surfaces of the parts to be joined into a soft or fluid state. The parts are then joined together under pressure. The spot-welding electrodes which conduct the welding current also convey the electrode force to the parts. The amount of heat required to form the welding joint is determined according to $Q = I^2 \cdot R \cdot t$ (Joule's Law).

The precise amount of heat required is a function of current, resistance and time. The following factors should be coordinated in order to achieve a good weld and adequate spot diameter $d_1$:
– welding current $I$
– electrode force $F$, and
– welding time $t$

According to the manner in which the current is conducted, a distinction is drawn between:
– bilateral direct resistance spot welding, and
– unilateral indirect resistance spot welding

The electrode for a specific spot welding operation is selected with reference to shape, outside diameter and point diameter. Before welding, the parts must always be completely free of scaling, oxides,

paint, grease and oil. They therefore receive appropriate surface treatment prior to welding (where indicated).

#### Projection welding

Projection welding is a process in which electrodes with a large surface area are employed to conduct the welding current and the electrode force to the workpiece. The projections, which are generally incorporated into the thicker of the workpieces, cause the current to concentrate at the contact surfaces. The electrode force compresses the projections partially or completely during the welding process. A permanent, inseparable joint is produced at the contact points along the welding seam. One or more than one projection can be welded simultaneously, depending on the type of projection (round or annular) and the power available from the welding unit.

Depending on the number of spots welded, a distinction is drawn between:
– single-projection welding, and
– multiple-projection welding

This technique requires high welding currents applied for short periods of time.

Applications:
– Welding parts of different thicknesses
– Welding multiple projections in a single operation

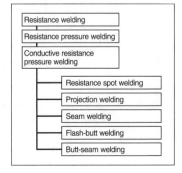

#### Seam welding

In this process, roller electrodes replace the spot-welding electrodes used in resistance spot welding. Contact between the roller set and the workpiece is limited to an extremely small surface area. The roller electrodes conduct the welding current and apply the electrode force. Their rotation is coordinated with the movement of the part.

Applications:

Production of sealed welds or seam spot welds (e.g. fuel tanks).

#### Flash-butt welding

In flash-butt welding, the butt ends of the workpieces are joined under moderate pressure while the flow of current at the contact surfaces produces localized heat and melting (high current density). The metal's vapor pressure drives molten material from the contact patches (burn-off) while force is applied to form an upset butt weld. The butt ends should be parallel to each other and at right angles to the direction in which the force is applied (or virtually so). Smooth surfaces are not required. A certain amount of extra length must be factored in to compensate for the losses incurred in the flash-butt welding process.

Result:

A weld with the characteristic projecting seam (burr).

#### Butt-seam welding

This process employs copper jaws to conduct the welding current to the workpieces being joined. When the welding temperature is reached, the current switches off. Constant pressure is maintained and the workpieces then weld together (requirement: properly machined butting faces). The result is a burr-free seam. The process does not completely displace contamination that may be present at the butt ends.

**Welding techniques**
*a) Bilateral resistance spot welding, b) Unilateral resistance spot welding,
c) Projection welding, d) Seam welding, e) Flash-butt welding, f) Butt-seam welding.*

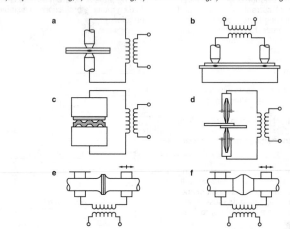

## Fusion welding

The term "fusion welding" describes a process employing limited local application of heat to melt and join the parts. No pressure is applied.

Shielded (inert gas) arc welding is a type of fusion welding. The electrical arc extending between the electrode and the workpiece serves as the heat source. Meanwhile, a layer of inert gas shields the arc and the melted area from the atmosphere. The type of electrode is the factor which distinguishes between various techniques:

Tungsten inert-gas welding
In this process, an arc is maintained between the workpiece and a stable, nonmelting tungsten electrode. The shielding (inert) gas is argon or helium. Weld material is supplied from the side (as in gas fusion welding).

Gas-shielded metal-arc welding
In this process, an arc is maintained between the melting end of the wire electrode (material feed) and the workpiece. The welding current flows to the wire electrode via sliding contacts in the torch holder. Insert-gas metal-arc welding uses inert gases (slowly reacting and noble gases such as argon, helium, or combinations of the two) as protective gas. Active-gas metal-arc welding, on the other hand, employs reactive gases such as $CO_2$ and mixed gases containing $CO_2$, argon and sometimes oxygen, and is frequently referred to as $CO_2$ welding.

This process is employed for welding unalloyed and low-alloy steels.

In addition, the following welding techniques are employed in the automobile industry:
– electron-beam welding
– friction welding
– arc pressure welding (stud welding)
– stored-energy welding (pulsed-current arc welding)

# Soldering

In soldering, a supplementary material (solder) is melted onto two or more parts of similar or varying metallic composition in order to produce a permanent connection between them. Flux and/or protective gas may also be used. The melting temperature of the solder is below that of the parts being joined. The solder is distributed along the join to produce the connection without the parts themselves being melted.

Soldering processes are classified by working temperature. This is defined as the lowest surface temperature at the connection between the workpieces to be joined at which the solder can be melted and distributed to form a bond.

## Soft soldering

Soft soldering is employed to form permanent solder joints at melting temperatures below 450 °C (as with soldering tin). Soft solders which melt at temperatures of 200 °C and below are also known as quick solders.

## Hard soldering

Hard soldering (brazing) is used to form permanent joins at melting temperatures above 450°C (as with copper/zinc, combined copper/zinc and silver alloys, e.g. silver brazing filler). Further data on soldering materials is contained in DIN Sheets 1707, 8512, 8513 and 8516.

Fluxes (non-metallic substances) are applied to remove any film (oxidation) remaining on the surface of the parts after cleaning and to prevent a new film from forming: this makes it possible to apply a consistent coat of solder to the joint surfaces. Data on fluxes can be found in DIN 8511.

The strength of a soldered joint can be equal to that of the base material itself. This phenomenon is due to the fact that the more rigid adjoining materials limit the solder's deformation potential.

The method used for heating provides yet another criterion for the classification of soldering processes. The two standard types are: open-flame soldering and iron soldering.

**Flame soldering**
A hand-held burner or a gas-fired unit provides the heat. Depending on the specific soldering operation, either oxyacetylene burners (familiar from gas welding) or soldering lamps are employed.

**Iron soldering**
A hand-held or mechanically guided soldering iron provides the heat. Irons can also be used to solder pretinned surfaces.

Other processes include: oven, salt-bath, immersion, resistance, and induction soldering, as well as MIG, plasma, and laser soldering.

# Adhesive technologies

Organic or anorganic adhesives are employed to form permanent rigid connections between two metallic or non-metallic materials. The adhesive bonds under pressure, either at room temperature or with moderate heat. The bond is adhesive, in other words physical and chemical bonding forces operate at the molecular level to bond the surfaces. A distinction is drawn between single-component and two-component adhesives, referring to their as-delivered condition.

**Single-component adhesives**
These are components which contain all the constituents necessary to form a bond.

**Two-component adhesives**
The second component in an adhesive of this type is a hardener that initiates the cross-linking process. An accelerator may be added to the hardener. Metal adhesives are generally of the two-component type. The hardening (cross-linking) process is polymerization, polycondensation or polyaddition under the influence of temperature and/or time. Spatially interlinked macromolecules are the result. Depending on the hardening temperature, a distinction is drawn between cold adhesives (harden at room temperature, relatively easy to apply, and hot adhesives harden at 100...200 °C).

Adhesive connections should be designed to ensure that the bond is subjected exclusively to tensile shear loads. Overlapping joints are virtually the only application for adhesives. Butt joints subjected to tensile or sliding forces should be avoided.

Metal adhesives can be employed in conjunction with spot welding. The adhesive prevents premature swelling of the sheets between the resistance-welded spots. This method is also suitable for reducing stress peaks at the edges of the weld spots and limited the number of spots required. Constructions of this nature evince enhanced structural integrity, rigidity, and damping when subjected to dynamic loads. Welding is carried out when the adhesive is still soft; otherwise the adhesive would act as an insulator.

The most significant metal adhesives include: epoxy, polyester and acrylic resins, vinyl acetate, and metal cement.

**Automotive applications**
Adhesive joining has become a standard technique in automotive engineering. The individual areas of application can be classified as follows:
– Body shell: raised-seam and brace bonding for attached components.
– Painting line: attachment of stiffeners.
– Assembly line: attachment of insulating material, appliqués, moldings, mirror-support bracket to windshield.
– Component production: bonding brake pads, laminated safety glass (LSG), rubber-to-metal connections to absorb vibration.

# Riveting

Riveting is used to produce a permanent fixed connection between two or more components made of identical or dissimilar materials. Depending on the method and application, riveted connections are divided into the following categories:
- Permanent rigid connections (interference fits, for example in mechanical and plant engineering),
- Permanent, sealed connections (for example in boilers and pressure vessels), and
- Extremely tight seals (for example in pipes, vacuum equipment, etc.).

In some areas, such as mechanical engineering in general and in tank manufacture, riveting has largely been displaced by welding. A distinction is drawn between cold and hot riveting, depending on the temperature used. Cold riveting is employed for rivet joints up to 10 mm in diameter in steel, copper, copper alloys, aluminum, etc. Rivets with diameters in excess of 10 mm are installed hot.

The most common types of rivet are mushroom head, countersunk, tallowdrop, hollow and tubular. There are also standardized rivets for specialized applications, for example explosive rivets and pop rivets. Pop rivets are hollow and are expanded by a drift or punch. The types of rivet and the corresponding materials are defined in DIN sheets; structural integrity and chemical composition are specified in DIN 17 111. In order to avoid the danger of electrochemical corrosion, the rivet material and the material of the parts being joined should be similar, if possible.

## Advantages/disadvantages compared to other joining techniques
- Unlike welding, riveting exerts no effects such as hardening or molecular alteration on the material.
- No distortion of the components.
- Suitable for joining dissimilar materials.
- Riveting weakens the components.
- Butt joints cannot be riveted, and
- Riveting is generally more expensive than welding when performed outside the factory.

## Automotive applications
- Riveting joint pins (power-window units, windshield-wiper linkages),
- Riveting reinforcement plates (in the course of repairs).

# Punch riveting

The punch riveting technique joins solid materials employing stamping and riveting elements (solid or semi-hollow rivets) in a combined cutting and joining operation.

The parts to be joined do not have to be predrilled and stamped, as is the case with other riveting techniques.

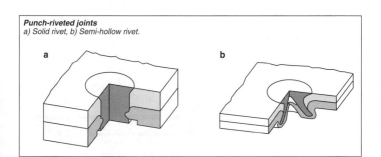

**Punch-riveted joints**
a) Solid rivet, b) Semi-hollow rivet.

### Punch riveting with solid rivets

The first stage in punch riveting with solid rivets is to position the work on the die plate.

The top section of the rivet unit, including the blank holder, descends and the rivet die presses the rivet through the parts to be joined in a single stamping operation.

### Punch riveting with semi-hollow rivets

The first stage in punch riveting with semi-hollow rivets is to position the work on the (bottom) die plate. The rivet die descends and presses the semi-hollow rivet through the upper sheet into the lower sheet in a single stamping operation. The rivet deforms and the bottom spreads to form a securing element, usually without fully penetrating the lower sheet.

### Equipment

Highly rigid hydraulic tools are used in punch riveting. Rivets can be singled from a batch feed or carried in belts with individual holders to the riveting tool.

### Materials

The rivets must be harder than the materials to be joined. The most common materials are steel, stainless steel, copper and aluminum with various coatings.

### Characteristics

- Used to join similar and dissimilar materials (e.g. steel, plastic or aluminum), parts of various thicknesses and strengths, and painted sheets.
- No preliminary stamping or drilling, no electrical current or vacuum extraction required.
- Approved overall material thicknesses: steel 6.5 mm; aluminum 11 mm.
- Low-heat, low-noise joining process.
- Tools have a long service life (approx. 300,000 rivet applications) with consistent quality.
- Process dependability with monitored process parameters.
- High forces have to be applied.
- Restricted jaw reach.

### Applications

Punch riveting with solid rivets: joining metal sheets in automotive engineering, e.g. power-window drives in passenger cars.

Punch riveting with semi-hollow rivets: joining materials at the body-in-white stage in automotive engineering, household appliances, joining metals to composites (heat shields).

*Punch force/punch travel curve*
A Combined indentation and melding.
B Upsetting and expansion.
C Filling upper contour of mold.
D Filling annular canal.
E Cup extrusion.

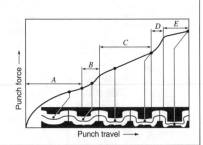

# Bonding and joining (pressurized clinching)

Pressurized clinching is a mechanical process for penetration assembly of layered materials. It combines cutting, penetration and cold upsetting in a single continuous joining operation without the application of additional heat. The basic principle is one of joining through reshaping. DIN 8593, Part 5, issued in September 1985, contains the first reference to this process as a means of joining sheetmetal panels by deformation.

The past few years have marked the advent of tox clinching as yet another joining process. It resembles penetration clinching, but does not include a cutting process. The tools employed for tox clinching are relatively small. The diameter can be varied to suit specific applications. At present, pressurized clinching can be used to join panels up to 3 mm thick, whereby the total thickness of the two sheets should not exceed 5 mm. The panels being joined can be of the same material (e.g. steel/steel) or dissimilar materials (e.g. steel/nonferrous metal. In addition, pressurized clinching can be used to join coated sheets and painted parts, as well as components to which adhesives have been applied. Multiple clinching can be used to produce numerous pressure-assembly elements (up to 50) in a single process (one stroke of the press,

for example). The typical curve for punch force relative to punch travel can be divided into five characteristic phases (A...E).

## Advantages/disadvantages of pressurized clinching
– No need for noise encapsulation.
– Tox clinching does not impair corrosion protection.
– When combined with a cutting operation there is a partial loss of corrosion protection.
– No heat distortion.
– Painted, protected (oil, wax) and glued sheets can be clinched.
– Different materials can be joined (e.g. steel/plastic).
– Energy savings, no power supply required for welding and no cooling water.
– One side of the workpiece evinces a projection similar to that produced by a rivet head, while the other side has a corresponding depression.

## Automotive applications
– Windshield wiper brackets
– Fastening interior door panels
– Positioning individual components

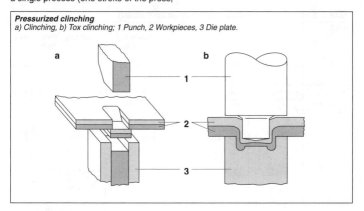

**Pressurized clinching**
a) Clinching, b) Tox clinching; 1 Punch, 2 Workpieces, 3 Die plate.

# Snap-on connections on plastic components

## Characteristics

Snap-on connections are a cheap and efficient way of fitting plastic components. They are used to connect housing halves, on plug connectors, and to secure mounting parts in plastic housings. They exploit the high expansibility of the plastics with relatively low rigidity.

All snap-on connections are characterized by the brief excursion of a resilient element in the joining process before it snaps into place behind a locating lug. Depending on the configuration of the joining angles at the snap-on elements, it is possible to produce nondestructively detachable and nondetachable connections (see figure).

The basic shapes of snap-on connections are (Table 1, below):
- Resilient snap-on hooks (bending springs fixed on one side),
- Resilient clips,
- Ring-shaped snap-on connections, also segmented (slotted lengthways),
- Spherical snap-on connections, also segmented, and
- Torsion snap-on hooks

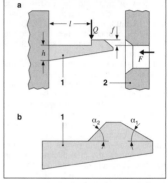

*Snap-on connection* (principle)
a) Decisive variables, b) Joining and release angles (detachable connection: $\alpha_2 < 90°$, nondetachable connection: $\alpha_2 \geq 90°$).
1 Spring element, 2 Locating lug.
$f$ Spring travel (rear section), $l$ Length,
$h$ Thickness at fixation cross-section,
$F$ Joining force, $Q$ Excursion force,
$\alpha_1$ Joining angle, $\alpha_2$ Release angle.

## Design guidelines and layout

The spring elements are designed to accommodate the permitted elongation of the plastic in the joining process. The least favorable material condition must be taken into account here (e.g. dry polyamide).

**Table 1. Basic shapes and types of snap-on connection**

| Shape | Hook shape | | | Ring shape | | |
|---|---|---|---|---|---|---|
| | | | | Annular ring/ ring groove | Annular ring, segmented/ ring groove | Hollow-sphere section |
| Spring element | Bending spring | Torsion spring (+ bending spring) | Catch spring | Annular spring | Annular spring, segmented | Annular spring |
| Designation | (Bending) snap-on hook | Torsion snap-on hook | Resilient clip | Ring snap-on element | Ring snap-on connection | Spherical snap-on element |
| Type | | | | | | |

The elongation-dependent secant modulus $E_s = \sigma_1/\varepsilon_1$ is used as the modulus of elasticity (see diagram).

The modulus values of the different plastics can be called up from the Bosch MATIS materials database or from the CAMPUS database offered by the raw-material manufacturers (http://www.campusplastics.com).

In order to achieve a uniform distribution of strain and optimum material utilization in the bending range of the spring elements, the thickness from the root to the free end should decrease by half. As an alternative, the width to the end of the hook can be reduced to one quarter.

Radii at the point of connection of the spring element to the component can help to eliminate concentrations of strain.

When joined, the spring element must be fully returned to its initial state in order to prevent creeping under load and thus permanent deformation.

Tensile stress in the snap-on element as a result of operational forces is permitted.

**Permitted spring travel (excursion)**
Table 2 (P. 364) contains the formulas for some basic shapes of snap-on hook. The permitted excursion (spring travel) $f$ in joining is dependent on the geometry of the snap-on hook and the permitted elongation $\varepsilon$ of the plastic, see Table 3.
Formulas for other cross-sectional shapes can be taken from the relevant technical literature or are provided by special calculation programs (see section headed "Calculation programs").

**Excursion force**
Included in the calculation of the excursion force $Q$ are the rigidity of the plastic as the secant modulus $E_s$ and the geometry as the bending moment/section modulus $W$.

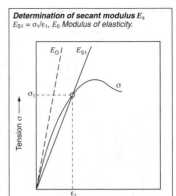

*Determination of secant modulus $E_s$*
$E_{S1} = \sigma_1/\varepsilon_1$, $E_0$ Modulus of elasticity.

**Joining force**
The joining force $F$ is calculated from the excursion force $Q$, the joining angle $\alpha_1$ (usually 30°) and the coefficient of friction $\mu$ (Table 4, P. 325d) between the joining components to be joined according to the formula

$$F = \frac{Q \cdot (\mu + \tan\alpha_1)}{(1 - \mu \cdot \tan\alpha_1)}$$

**Release force**
The release force of a snap-on connection is calculated according to the same formula as the joining force, where the release angle $\alpha_2$ of the snap-on hook (usually 60°) is to be used.
In the case of a nondetachable connection ($\alpha_2 \geq 90°$), the thrust capacity of the snap-on arms limits the strength.

**Calculation programs**
Various plastics manufacturers offer as a service to their customers easy-to-use calculation programs (e.g. "Snaps" from BASF, "FEAsnap" from Bayer, and "Fitcalc" from Ticona). Most of the material data for manufacturers' product ranges are integrated in these programs.

**Table 2. Geometry and calculation of snap-on hooks (selection)**

| Cross-sectional shape ▶ <br><br> ▼ Type | | **A:** Rectangle <br> | **B:** Trapezoid <br> |
|---|---|---|---|
| (Permitted) excursion | **1** $h_1 : h_0 = 1 : 1$ <br> $b_1 : b_0 = 1 : 1$ | $f = 0.67 \dfrac{\varepsilon \cdot l^2}{h_0}$ | $f = \dfrac{a + b^1)}{2a + b} \cdot \dfrac{\varepsilon \cdot l^2}{h_0}$ |
| | **2** $h_1 : h_0 = 1 : 2.5$ <br> $b_1 : b_0 = 1 : 1.0$ | $f = 1.20 \dfrac{\varepsilon \cdot l^2}{h_0}$ | $f = 1.79 \dfrac{a + b^1)}{2a + b} \cdot \dfrac{\varepsilon \cdot l^2}{h_0}$ |
| | **3** $h_1 : h_0 = 1 : 1$ <br> $b_1 : b_0 = 1 : 4$ | $f = 0.82 \dfrac{\varepsilon \cdot l^2}{h_0}$ | $f = 1.22 \dfrac{a + b^1)}{2a + b} \cdot \dfrac{\varepsilon \cdot l^2}{h}$ |
| Excursion force | **1** <br> **2** <br> **3** | $Q = \dfrac{\overset{W^1)}{\overbrace{\dfrac{b \cdot h_0^2}{6}}}}{} \cdot \dfrac{E_s \cdot \varepsilon}{l}$ | $Q = \dfrac{\overset{W^1)}{\overbrace{\dfrac{h_0^2}{12} \cdot \dfrac{a^2 + 4ab + b^2}{2a + b}}}}{} \cdot \dfrac{E_s \cdot \varepsilon}{l}$ |

**Resilient snap-on hooks**
*(application example: connection
of pneumatic modules)*
*1 Snap-on hook, 2 Pneumatic module.*

**Table 3. Reference values for permitted elongation ε for snap-on connections** (short-term for one-off joining, frequent activation approx. 60% there of)

| Material | ε |
|---|---|
| Thermoplastics, semi-crystalline, unfilled | |
| PE | 0.080 |
| PP | 0.060 |
| PA conditioned | 0.060 |
| PA dry | 0.040 |
| POM | 0.060 |
| PBT | 0.050 |
| Thermoplastics, amorphous, unfilled | |
| PC | 0.030 |
| ABS/SB | 0.025 |
| CAB | 0.025 |
| PVC | 0.020 |
| PS | 0.018 |
| Thermoplastics, glass-fiber-filled | |
| 30% GF-PA conditioned | 0.020 |
| 30% GF-PA dry | 0.015 |
| 30% GF-PC | 0.018 |
| 30% GF-PBT | 0.015 |
| 30% GF-ABS | 0.012 |

*Key to Table 2:*

$a,b$ Widths at fixation cross-section
$e$  Surface-zone spacing from neutral surface zone (center of gravity)
$f$  Permitted excursion (spring travel)
$h$  Thickness at fixation cross-section
$l$  Arm length
$E_S$ Secant modulus
$Q$  Permitted excursion force
$W$  Axial section modulus ($W = I/e$)
$\varepsilon$  Permitted elongation in surface zone of fixation point (as absolute value, see Table 3)

[1]) *The formulas apply to the situation where width $b$ is on the pulling side of the bending element. If width $a$ is on the pulling side, $a$ and $b$ must be switched round in the respective formula.*

**Table 4. Reference values for coefficient of friction μ**

| Material | Pairing plastic/ steel μ | Pairing plastic/ plastic factor |
|---|---|---|
| PTFE | 0.12...0.22 | |
| PE-hard | 0.20...0.25 | (x2) |
| PP | 0.25...0.30 | (x1.5) |
| POM | 0.20...0.35 | (x1.5) |
| PA | 0.30...0.40 | (x1.5) |
| PBT | 0.35...0.40 | |
| PS | 0.40...0.50 | (x1.2) |
| SAN | 0.45...0.55 | |
| PC | 0.45...0.55 | (x1.2) |
| PMMA | 0.50...0.60 | (x1.2) |
| ABS | 0.50...0.65 | (x1.2) |
| PE-soft | 0.55...0.60 | (x1.2) |
| PVC | 0.55...0.60 | (x1.0) |

# Road-going vehicle requirements

## Drivability
The vehicle must be capable of effecting the transition from a stationary to a mobile state. Once in motion, it must be able to ascend gradients and accelerate to the desired cruising speed with a reasonable degree of alacrity. With a given power $P$, ideal correspondence with these requirements is achieved when force $M$ and the engine speed $n$ can be varied according to the formula $P = M \cdot n$. Under these conditions, the limits on the potential field of operation are defined by $P_{nominal}$, resulting in an inverse relationship between available force and vehicle speed (limit curve defined by tractive-force hyperbola).

## Power density and storage density
Both the power density (W/kg) and the energy-storage density (W·h/kg) of the combined engine/energy-storage system must be high if the size of the vehicle – and with it the mass to be accelerated – are to be maintained at a modest level. Low density factors for power and energy storage would increase vehicle size and mass, with attendant escalations in the power and energy consumption which would be needed to achieve the desired performance (acceleration, speed).

## Discharge or operating time of the energy-storage device
The vehicle's operating time – and thus the operating range which can be covered before the energy-storage device must be replenished (renewed/refilled/recharged) – is a function of the energy-storage density, the power requirement, and the vehicle weight; the latter, in turn, is influenced by the power-to-weight ratio of the drive system.

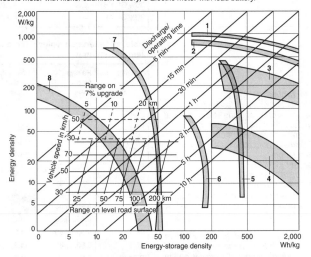

**Power and energy-storage densities for various propulsion concepts**
(engine/motor and storage unit)[1]
1 Gas turbine, 2 Internal-combustion engine, 3 External-combustion engine, 4 Electric motor with fuel cell, 5 Electric motor with lithium-chloride battery, 6 Electric motor with zinc-air battery, 7 Electric motor with nickel-cadmium battery, 8 Electric motor with lead battery.

[1] From "The Automobile and Air Pollution", U.S. Dep. of Commerce (Morsebericht); Mahle "Kolben-Handbuch" (Piston Handbook).

The drive and energy-storage configuration employed for a specific application determines the relationship between power density/energy-storage density and operating time; it also exerts a decisive influence on the shape of the torque curve. Favorable power-to-weight ratios combine with high energy-storage densities (period of operation per tank of fuel) to make internal-combustion engines particularly suitable for vehicular applications. However, the torque curves provided by the standard piston powerplants (diesel and spark-ignition engines) are less satisfactory. They thus need some form of transmission unit for both the transfer and the conversion of torque. The unit must be capable of transmitting torque in the slip range (for starting off) while incorporating various torque-conversion ratios (for ascending gradients and selecting different speed ranges). Electric and steam-driven powerplants also need a

transmission due to the limitations imposed by the respective maxima for current and steam pressure.

In addition to fulfilling the basic requirements enumerated above, the powerplant and energy-storage system must also meet the following demands:

Economic efficiency, characterized by minimal fuel consumption, low manufacturing and maintenance costs, long service life;

Environmental compatibility, with low emissions levels for both pollutants and noise, sparing use of raw materials;

Flexibility in operation, including good starting from −30 °C to +50 °C, operation unaffected by climate and altitude, good driveoff, acceleration and braking characteristics.

Internal-combustion (IC) engines are thus the most favorable option for independent self-contained vehicles, whereby the priority assigned to the individual factors in the above list will vary according to application.

Passenger cars: High power density, low exhaust and noise emissions, low manufacturing costs;

Trucks and buses: Maximum economy, long service life, and conformity with all emissions requirements.

Special drive systems, such as those relying exclusively on electric motors, or hybrids (dual-system buses, etc.) can represent the best, or indeed only, option for special applications and/or under certain operating conditions.

### Basic requirements for fuels

Engines featuring external combustion place the least exacting demands on fuel quality, as their combustion and working gases are not identical and remain isolated from each other. In contrast, the fuel used in internal-combustion engines must burn rapidly and virtually without residue. Moreover, modern exhaust gas treatment systems require fuels and lubricants that are free of sulfur.

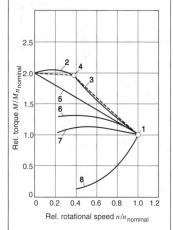

**Relative torques for various power units**
1 Reference point: Gas-turbine base point, Piston engine $n_{max}$, 2 Steam engine, 3 Electric motor, 4 Limit curve for max. pressure/max. current, 5 Dual-shaft gas turbine, 6 Gasoline (SI) engine, 7 Diesel engine, 8 Single-shaft gas turbine.

Rel. torque $M/M_{n\,nominal}$

Rel. rotational speed $n/n_{nominal}$

# Fuel consumption

## Determining fuel consumption

Test cycles are run for the purpose of determining fuel consumption (see P. 566 onwards).

The New European Driving Cycle (NEDC, 93/116/EEC), for instance, is a cycle run on a dynamometer to ascertain fuel consumption. It consists of four similarly weighted urban cycles each lasting 195 s and an extra-urban cycle lasting 400 s (P. 568). The exhaust gas is collected in a sample bag and its components subsequently analyzed. CO, HC and $CO_2$ are factored into the calculations in accordance with the carbon analysis.

The $CO_2$ content of the exhaust gas is proportional to the fuel consumption. It can therefore be used as an indicator to gauge the vehicle's fuel consumption (diesel or gasoline, as appropriate).

The test mass specified for the vehicle equals the vehicle's empty mass plus a payload of 100 kg. The vehicle mass has to be simulated by finite balanced inertia masses on the dynamometer, so an inertia-mass class is assigned to the vehicle test mass.

According to current legislation (EU 3), testing commences when the engine is started. The previously permitted lead-in time of 40 s before testing commences is no longer allowed.

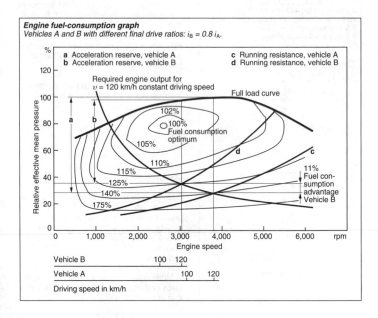

**Engine fuel-consumption graph**
Vehicles A and B with different final drive ratios: $i_B = 0.8 \, i_A$.

a Acceleration reserve, vehicle A
b Acceleration reserve, vehicle B
c Running resistance, vehicle A
d Running resistance, vehicle B

## Effect of vehicle design on fuel consumption

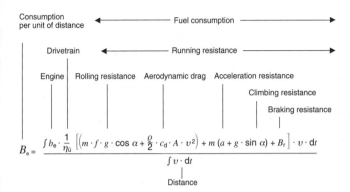

| Quantity | | Unit |
|---|---|---|
| $B_e$ | Consumption per unit of distance | g/m |
| $\eta_\ddot{u}$ | Transmission efficiency of drivetrain | – |
| $m$ | Vehicle mass | kg |
| $f$ | Coefficient of rolling resistance | – |
| $g$ | Gravitational acceleration | m/s² |
| $\alpha$ | Angle of ascent | ° |
| $\varrho$ | Air density | kg/m³ |
| $c_d$ | Drag coefficient | – |
| $A$ | Frontal area | m² |
| $v$ | Vehicle speed | m/s |
| $a$ | Acceleration | m/s² |
| $B_r$ | Braking resistance | N |
| $t$ | Time | s |
| $b_e$ | Specific fuel consumption | g/kWh |

The consumption equation distinguishes between three distinct groups of factors:
– Engine,
– Transmission and
– External resistance factors.

### Transmission (gearbox)
The influence of the gearbox is determined by both the power-transmission losses and the transmission (gear) ratios selected for the application. The former should be kept as low as possible; the latter determine the correspondence between vehicle speed and specific points on the engine's fuel-consumption curve.

"Long (wide-ratio)" gearing will generally move a specific operating state onto a point on the curve corresponding to lower fuel consumption (see illustration), albeit at the expense of reduced acceleration.

### External resistance factors
Outside resistance to motion can be counteracted by measures such as weight reduction, improved aerodynamics and lower rolling resistance.

On an average production vehicle, 10% reductions in weight, drag and rolling resistance result in fuel-economy improvements of roughly 6%, 3%, and 2%, respectively.

The cited formula distinguishes between acceleration resistance and braking resistance, thereby illustrating with particular clarity the fact that the increased fuel consumption associated with acceleration largely stems from subsequent application of the brakes. If the brakes are not applied, then the vehicle's kinetic energy is exploited to impel it forward (retardation = negative acceleration), with attendant reductions in overall fuel consumption.

# Motor-vehicle dynamics

## Dynamics of linear motion

| Quantity | | Unit |
|---|---|---|
| $A$ | Largest cross-section of vehicle [1]) | m² |
| $a$ | Acceleration, braking (deceleration) | m/s² |
| $c_d$ | Drag coefficient | – |
| $F$ | Motive force | N |
| $F_{cf}$ | Centrifugal force | N |
| $F_L$ | Aerodynamic drag | N |
| $F_{Ro}$ | Rolling resistance | N |
| $F_{St}$ | Climbing resistance | N |
| $F_W$ | Running resistance | N |
| $f$ | Coefficient of rolling resistance | – |
| $G$ | Weight = $m \cdot g$ | N |
| $G_B$ | Sum of wheel forces on driven or braked wheels | N |
| $g$ | Gravitational acceleration = 9.81 m/s² ≈ 10 m/s² | m/s² |

| Quantity | | Unit |
|---|---|---|
| $i$ | Gear or transmission ratio between engine and drive wheels | – |
| $M$ | Engine torque | N · m |
| $m$ | Vehicle mass (weight) | kg |
| $n$ | Engine speed | rpm |
| $P$ | Power | W |
| $P_w$ | Motive power | W |
| $p$ | Gradient (= 100 · tan $\alpha$) | % |
| $r$ | Dynamic radius of tire | m |
| $s$ | Distance traveled | m |
| $t$ | Time | s |
| $v$ | Vehicle speed | m/s |
| $v_0$ | Headwind speed | m/s |
| $W$ | Work | J |
| $\alpha$ | Gradient angle | ° |
| $\mu_r$ | Coefficient of static friction | – |

Additional symbols and units in text.

### Total running resistance
The <u>running resistance</u> is calculated as:

$$F_W = F_{Ro} + F_L + F_{St}$$

<u>Running-resistance power</u>
The power which must be transmitted through the drive wheels to overcome running resistance is:

$$P_W = F_W \cdot v$$

or

$$P_W = \frac{F_W \cdot v}{3,600}$$

with $P_W$ in kW, $F_W$ in N, $v$ in km/h.

---

[1]) On passenger cars $A \approx 0.9 \times$ Track $\times$ Height.

### Rolling resistance
The <u>rolling resistance</u> $F_{Ro}$ is the product of deformation processes which occur at the contact patch between tire and road surface.

$$F_{Ro} = f \cdot G \cdot \cos \alpha = f \cdot m \cdot g \cdot \cos \alpha$$

An approximate calculation of the rolling resistance can be made using the coefficients provided in the following table and in the diagram on P. 379.

The increase in the coefficient of rolling resistance $f$ is directly proportional to the level of deformation, and inversely proportional to the radius of the tire. The coefficient will thus increase in response to

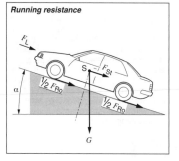

**Running resistance**

| Road surface | Coefficient of rolling resistance $f$ |
|---|---|
| Pneumatic car tires on | |
|     Large sett pavement | 0.013 |
|     Small sett pavement | 0.013 |
|     Concrete, asphalt | 0.011 |
|     Rolled gravel | 0.02 |
|     Tarmacadam | 0.025 |
|     Unpaved road | 0.05 |
|     Field | 0.1...0.35 |
| Pneumatic truck tires on concrete, asphalt | 0.006...0.01 |
| Strake wheels in field | 0.14...0.24 |
| Track-type tractor in field | 0.07...0.12 |
| Wheel on rail | 0.001...0.002 |

greater loads, higher speeds and lower tire pressure.

In turns, the rolling resistance is augmented by the

Cornering resistance

$$F_K = f_K \cdot G$$

The coefficient of cornering resistance $f_K$ is a function of vehicle speed, curve radius, suspension geometry, tires, tire pressure, and the vehicle's response under lateral acceleration.

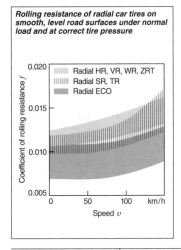

*Rolling resistance of radial car tires on smooth, level road surfaces under normal load and at correct tire pressure*

Legend:
- Radial HR, VR, WR, ZRT
- Radial SR, TR
- Radial ECO

Y-axis: Coefficient of rolling resistance $f$ — 0.005, 0.010, 0.015, 0.020
X-axis: Speed $v$ — 0, 50, 100 km/h

**Aerodynamic drag**

Aerodynamic drag is calculated as:

$$F_L = 0.5 \cdot \varrho \cdot c_d \cdot A \, (v + v_0)^2$$

With $v$ in km/h, $F_L$ in N, $\varrho$ in kg/m³, $A$ in m²:

$$F_L = 0.0386 \cdot \varrho \cdot c_d \cdot A \cdot (v + v_0)^2$$

Air density $\varrho$
(at 200 m altitude: $\varrho = 1.202$ kg/m³),
Drag coefficient $c_d$ P. 420.

Aerodynamic drag in kW

$$P_L = F_L \cdot v = 0.5 \cdot \varrho \cdot c_d \cdot A \cdot v \cdot (v + v_0)^2$$

or

$$P_L = 12.9 \cdot 10^{-6} \cdot c_d \cdot A \cdot v \cdot (v + v_0)^2$$

with $P_L$ in kW, $F_L$ in N, $v$ and $v_0$ in km/h, $A$ in m², $\varrho = 1.202$ kg/m³.

**Empirical determination of coefficients for aerodynamic drag and rolling resistance**

Allow vehicle to coast down in neutral under windless conditions on a level road surface. The time that elapses while the vehicle coasts down by a specific increment of speed is measured from two initial velocities, $v_1$ (high speed) and $v_2$ (low speed). This information is used to calculate the mean deceleration rates $a_1$ and $a_2$. See following table for formulas and example.

The example is based on a vehicle weighing $m = 1{,}450$ kg with a cross-section $A = 2.2$ m².

The method is suitable for application at vehicle speeds of less than 100 km/h.

| | 1st Trial (high speed) | 2nd Trial (low speed) |
|---|---|---|
| Initial velocity<br>Terminal velocity<br>Interval between $v_a$ and $v_b$ | $v_{a1} = 60$ km/h<br>$v_{b1} = 55$ km/h<br>$t_1 = 7.8$ s | $v_{a2} = 15$ km/h<br>$v_{b2} = 10$ km/h<br>$t_2 = 12.2$ s |
| Mean velocity | $v_1 = \dfrac{v_{a1} + v_{b1}}{2} = 57.5$ km/h | $v_2 = \dfrac{v_{a2} + v_{b2}}{2} = 12.5$ km/h |
| Mean deceleration | $a_1 = \dfrac{v_{a1} - v_{b1}}{t_1} = 0.64 \dfrac{\text{km/h}}{\text{s}}$ | $a_2 = \dfrac{v_{a2} - v_{b2}}{t_2} = 0.41 \dfrac{\text{km/h}}{\text{s}}$ |
| Drag coefficient | $c_d = \dfrac{6 \, m \cdot (a_1 - a_2)}{A \cdot (v_1^2 - v_2^2)} = 0.29$ | |
| Coefficient of rolling resistance | $f = \dfrac{28.2 \, (a_2 \cdot v_1^2 - a_1 \cdot v_2^2)}{10^3 \cdot (v_1^2 - v_2^2)} = 0.011$ | |

## Drag coefficient and associated power requirements for various body configurations

| | | Drag coefficient $c_d$ | Aerodynamic drag in kW, average values for $A = 2$ m² at various speeds [1] | | | |
|---|---|---|---|---|---|---|
| | | | 40 km/h | 80 km/h | 120 km/h | 160 km/h |
| | Open convertible | 0.33...0.50 | 0.70 | 5.3 | 18 | 42 |
| | Offroad vehicle | 0.35...0.50 | 0.71 | 5.5 | 19 | 44 |
| | Notchback sedan (conventional form) | 0.26...0.35 | 0.50 | 3.8 | 13 | 31 |
| | Station wagon | 0.30...0.34 | 0.52 | 4.1 | 14 | 33 |
| | Wedge shape, headlamps and fenders integrated in body, wheels covered, underbody paneling, optimized flow of cooling air | 0.3...0.4 | 0.58 | 4.6 | 16 | 37 |
| | Headlamps and all wheels enclosed within body, underbody paneled | 0.2...0.25 | 0.37 | 3.0 | 10 | 24 |
| | Reversed wedge shape (minimal cross-section at tail) | 0.23 | 0.38 | 3.0 | 10 | 24 |
| | Optimum streamlining | 0.15...0.20 | 0.29 | 2.3 | 7.8 | 18 |
| Trucks, truck-trailer combinations | | 0.8...1.5 | – | – | – | – |
| Motorcycles | | 0.6...0.7 | – | – | – | – |
| Buses | | 0.6...0.7 | – | – | – | – |
| Streamlined buses | | 0.3...0.4 | – | – | – | – |

[1] No headwind ($v_0 = 0$).

**Climbing resistance and downgrade force**

Climbing resistance ($F_{St}$ with positive sign) and downgrade force ($F_{St}$ with negative sign) are calculated as:

$$F_{St} = G \cdot \sin \alpha$$
$$= m \cdot g \cdot \sin \alpha$$

or, for a working approximation:

$$F_{St} \approx 0.01 \cdot m \cdot g \cdot p$$

valid for gradients up to $p \le 20\%$, as $\sin \alpha \approx \tan \alpha$ at small angles (less than 2% error).

Climbing power is calculated as:

$$P_{St} = F_{St} \cdot v$$

With $P_{St}$ in kW, $F_{St}$ in N, $v$ in km/h:

$$P_{St} = \frac{F_{St} \cdot v}{3{,}600} = \frac{m \cdot g \cdot v \cdot \sin \alpha}{3{,}600}$$

or, for a working approximation:

$$P_{St} \approx \frac{m \cdot g \cdot p \cdot v}{360{,}000}$$

The gradient is:
$p = (h/l) \cdot 100\%$ or
$p = (\tan \alpha) \cdot 100\%$,

with $h$ as the height of the projected distance $l$. In English-speaking countries, the *gradient* is calculated as follows:
Conversion:

*Gradient* $1$ in $100/p$

Example: 1 in 2.

| Gradient angle $\alpha$ | Incline $p$ % | Gradient | Climbing resistance at $m$ = 1,000 kg N |
|---|---|---|---|

(Nomogram scale)

Gradient angle: 45°, 40°, 35°, 30°, 25°, 20°, 15°, 10°, 5°, 0°

$p$ %: 100, 90, 80, 70, 60, 50, 40, 30, 20, 10, 0

Gradient: 1 in 1, 1 in 1.5, 1 in 2, 1 in 2.5, 1 in 3, 1 in 4, 1 in 5, 1 in 10, 1 in 20, 1 in 50, 1 in 100

Climbing resistance: 6,500, 6,000, 5,500, 5,000, 4,500, 4,000, 3,500, 3,000, 2,500, 2,000, 1,500, 1,000, 500, 0

Values at $m$ = 1,000 kg

| Climbing resistance $F_{St}$ N | Climbing power $P_{St}$ in kW at various speeds | | | | |
|---|---|---|---|---|---|
| | 20 km/h | 30 km/h | 40 km/h | 50 km/h | 60 km/h |
| 6,500 | 36 | 54 | 72 | – | – |
| 6,000 | 33 | 50 | 67 | – | – |
| 5,500 | 31 | 46 | 61 | – | – |
| 5,000 | 28 | 42 | 56 | 69 | – |
| 4,500 | 25 | 37 | 50 | 62 | – |
| 4,000 | 22 | 33 | 44 | 56 | 67 |
| 3,500 | 19 | 29 | 39 | 49 | 58 |
| 3,000 | 17 | 25 | 33 | 42 | 50 |
| 2,500 | 14 | 21 | 28 | 35 | 42 |
| 2,000 | 11 | 17 | 22 | 28 | 33 |
| 1,500 | 8.3 | 12 | 17 | 21 | 25 |
| 1,000 | 5.6 | 8.3 | 11 | 14 | 17 |
| 500 | 2.3 | 4.2 | 5.6 | 6.9 | 8.3 |
| 0 | 0 | 0 | 0 | 0 | 0 |

Example: To climb a hill with a gradient of $p = 18\%$, a vehicle weighing 1,500 kg will require approximately $1.5 \cdot 1{,}700$ N = 2,550 N motive force and, at $v = 40$ km/h, roughly $1.5 \cdot 19$ kW = 28.5 kW climbing power.

**Motive force**

The higher the engine torque $M$ and overall transmission ratio $i$ between engine and driven wheels, and the lower the power-transmission losses, the higher is the <u>motive force</u> $F$ available at the drive wheels.

$$F = \frac{M \cdot i}{r} \cdot \eta \quad \text{or} \quad F = \frac{P \cdot \eta}{v}$$

$\eta$ Drivetrain efficiency level
(inline engine $\eta \approx 0.88...0.92$)
(transverse engine $\eta \approx 0.91...0.95$)

The motive force $F$ is partially consumed in overcoming the running resistance $F_W$. Numerically higher transmission ratios are applied to deal with the substantially increased running resistance encountered on gradients (gearbox).

**Vehicle and engine speeds**

$$n = \frac{60 \cdot v \cdot i}{2 \cdot \pi \cdot r}$$

or with $v$ in km/h:

$$n = \frac{1,000 \cdot v \cdot i}{2 \cdot \pi \cdot 60 \cdot r}$$

**Acceleration**

The surplus force $F - F_W$ accelerates the vehicle (or retards it when $F_W$ exceeds $F$).

$$a = \frac{F - F_W}{k_m \cdot m} \quad \text{or} \quad a = \frac{P \cdot \eta - P_W}{v \cdot k_m \cdot m}$$

The rotational inertia coefficient $k_m$, compensates for the apparent increase in vehicle mass due to the rotating masses (wheels, flywheel, crankshaft, etc.).

**Motive force and road speed on vehicles with automatic transmissions**

When the formula for motive force is applied to automatic transmissions with hydrodynamic torque converters or hydrodynamic clutches, the engine torque $M$ is replaced by the torque at the converter turbine, while the rotational speed of the converter turbine is used in the formula for engine speed.

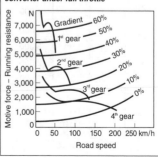

*Hydrodynamic converter*
1 Input shaft, 2 Turbine, 3 Pump, 4 Stator,
5 One-way clutch, 6 Driven shaft.

The relationship between $M_{Turb} = f\ (n_{Turb})$ and the engine characteristic $M_{Mot} = f\ (n_{Mot})$ is determined using the characteristics of the hydrodynamic converter (P. 739).

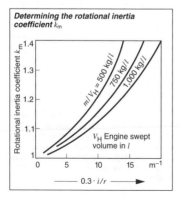

*Determining the rotational inertia coefficient $k_m$*

$m/V_H = 500$ kg/l, 750 kg/l, 1,000 kg/l

$V_H$ Engine swept volume in $l$

$0.3 \cdot i/r$

*Running diagram for car with automatic transmission and hydrodynamic Trilok converter under full throttle*

Motive force – Running resistance

Gradient 60%, 50%, 40%, 30%, 20%, 10%, 0%

1st gear, 2nd gear, 3rd gear, 4th gear

Road speed

## Adhesion to road surface

**Coefficients of static friction for pneumatic tires on various surfaces**

| Vehicle speed km/h | Tire condition | Road condition | | | | |
|---|---|---|---|---|---|---|
| | | Dry | Wet Water approx. 0.2 mm | Heavy rainfall Water approx. 1 mm | Puddles Water approx. 2 mm | Iced (black ice) |
| | | Coefficient of static friction $\mu_r$ | | | | |
| 50 | new | 0.85 | 0.65 | 0.55 | 0.5 | 0.1 and less |
| | worn [1] | 1 | 0.5 | 0.4 | 0.25 | |
| 90 | new | 0.8 | 0.6 | 0.3 | 0.05 | |
| | worn [1] | 0.95 | 0.2 | 0.1 | 0.05 | |
| 130 | new | 0.75 | 0.55 | 0.2 | 0 | |
| | worn [1] | 0.9 | 0.2 | 0.1 | 0 | |

The coefficient of static friction (between the tires and the road surface), also known as the tire-road-interface friction coefficient, is determined by the vehicle's speed, the condition of the tires and the state of the road surface (see table above). The figures cited apply for concrete and tarmacadam road surfaces in good condition. The coefficients of sliding friction (with wheel locked) are usually lower than the coefficients of static friction.

Special rubber compounds providing friction coefficients of up to 1.8 are employed in racing tires.

The maxima for acceleration and uphill driving, and for deceleration and downhill braking, are provided on P. 425.

### Aquaplaning
Aquaplaning, has a particularly dramatic influence on the contact between tire and road surface. It describes the state in which a layer of water separates the tire and the (wet) road surface. The phenomenon occurs when a wedge of water forces its way underneath the tire's contact patch and lifts it from the road. The tendency to aquaplane is dependent upon

such factors as the depth of the water on the road surface, the vehicle's speed, the tread pattern, the tread wear, and the load pressing the tire against the road surface. Wide tires are particularly susceptible to aquaplaning. It is not possible to steer or brake an aquaplaning vehicle, as its front wheels have ceased to rotate, meaning that neither steering inputs nor braking forces can be transmitted to the road surface.

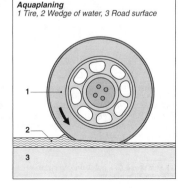

***Aquaplaning***
*1 Tire, 2 Wedge of water, 3 Road surface*

[1] Worn to tread depth of $\geq$ 1.6 mm (legal minimum in Germany, as per Para. 36.2, StVZO (FMVSS/CUR)).

## Accelerating and braking

The vehicle is regarded as accelerating or braking (decelerating) at a constant rate when $a$ remains constant. The following equations apply to an initial or final speed of 0:

|  | Equations for $v$ in m/s | Equations for $v$ in km/h |
|---|---|---|
| Acceleration or braking (deceleration) in m/s² | $a = \dfrac{v^2}{2 \cdot s} = \dfrac{v}{t} = \dfrac{2 \cdot s}{t^2}$ | $a = \dfrac{v^2}{26 \cdot s} = \dfrac{v}{3.6 \cdot t} = \dfrac{2 \cdot s}{t^2}$ |
| Accelerating or braking time in s | $t = \dfrac{v}{a} = \dfrac{2 \cdot s}{v} = \sqrt{\dfrac{2 \cdot s}{a}}$ | $t = \dfrac{v}{3.6 \cdot a} = \dfrac{7.2 \cdot s}{v} = \sqrt{\dfrac{2 \cdot s}{a}}$ |
| Accelerating or braking distance [1] in m | $s = \dfrac{v^2}{2 \cdot a} = \dfrac{v \cdot t}{2} = \dfrac{a \cdot t^2}{2}$ | $s = \dfrac{v^2}{26 \cdot a} = \dfrac{v \cdot t}{7,2} = \dfrac{a \cdot t^2}{2}$ |

Stopping distance, P. 427.
Symbols and units, P. 25.

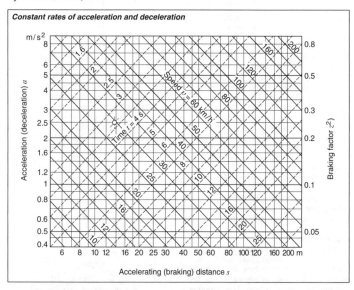

*Constant rates of acceleration and deceleration*

*Each point on the graph represents a particular relationship between $v$, $a$ or $z$[2]), $s$ and $t$. Two values must be given for all values to be determined.*
*Given: Vehicle speed $v = 30$ km/h, braking distance $s = 13.5$ m.*
*Determined: Mean deceleration $a = 2.5$ m/s², retardation $z = 0.25$,*
*Braking time $t = 3.3$ s.*

---

[1] If final speed $v_2$ is not 0, braking distance $s = v_1 \cdot t - at^2/2$ at $v_1$ in m/s.
[2] Deceleration rate relative to 1 g.

## Maxima for acceleration and braking (deceleration)

When the motive or braking forces exerted at the vehicle's wheels reach such a magnitude that the tires are just still within their limit of adhesion (maximum adhesion is still present), the relationships between the gradient angle $\alpha$, coefficient of static friction $\mu_r$[1]) and maximum acceleration or deceleration are defined as follows. The real-world figures are always somewhat lower, as all the vehicle's tires do not simultaneously exploit their maximum adhesion during each acceleration (deceleration). Electronic traction control and antilock braking systems (TCS, ABS, ESP)[2]) maintain the traction level in the vicinity of the coefficient of static friction.

$k$ = Ratio between the load on driven or braked wheels and the total weight. All wheels driven or braked: $k = 1$. At 50% weight distribution $k = 0.5$.

Example:
$k = 0.5$; $g = 10$ m/s²;
$\mu_r = 0.6$; $p = 15\%$;
$a_{max} = 10 \cdot (0.5 \cdot 0.6 \pm 0.15)$ m/s²
  Upgrade braking (+): $a_{max} = 4.5$ m/s²,
  Downgrade braking (–): $a_{max} = 1.5$ m/s²

## Work and power

The power required to maintain a consistent rate of acceleration (deceleration) varies according to vehicle speed. Power available for acceleration:

$$P_a = P \cdot \eta - P_W$$

where
$P$ = engine output,
$\eta$ = efficiency, and
$P_W$ = motive power.

### Acceleration and braking (deceleration)

|  | Level road surface | Inclined road surface $\alpha°$; $p = 100 \cdot \tan \alpha \%$ |  |
|---|---|---|---|
| Limit acceleration or deceleration $a_{max}$ in m/s² | $a_{max} = k \cdot g \cdot \mu_r$ | $a_{max} = g\,(k \cdot \mu_r \cdot \cos \alpha \pm \sin \alpha)$ approximation[3]): $a_{max} \approx g\,(k \cdot \mu_r \pm 0.01p)$ | + Upgrade braking or downgrade acceleration − Upgrade acceleration or downgrade braking |

### Achievable acceleration $a_e$ ($P_a$ in kW, $v$ in km/h, $m$ in kg)

| Level road surface | Inclined road surface |  |
|---|---|---|
| $a_e = \dfrac{3{,}600 \cdot P_a}{k \cdot m \cdot v}$ | $a_e = \dfrac{3{,}600 \cdot P_a}{k \cdot m \cdot v} \pm g \cdot \sin \alpha$ | + Downgrade acceleration − Upgrade acceleration for $g \cdot \sin \alpha$ the approximation[3]) $g \cdot p/100$ |

### Work and power

|  | Level road surface | Inclined road surface $\alpha°$; $p = 100 \cdot \tan \alpha \%$ |  |
|---|---|---|---|
| Acceleration or braking work $W$ in J[4]) | $W = k \cdot m \cdot a \cdot s$ | $W = m \cdot s\,(k \cdot a \pm g \cdot \sin \alpha)$ approximation[3]): $W = m \cdot s\,(k \cdot a \pm g \cdot p/100)$ | + Downgrade braking or upgrade acceleration − Downgrade acceleration or upgrade braking |
| Acceleration or braking power $P_a$ at velocity $v$ in W | $P_a = k \cdot m \cdot a \cdot v$ | $P_a = m \cdot v\,(k \cdot a \pm g \cdot \sin \alpha)$ approximation[3]): $P_a = m \cdot v\,(k \cdot a \pm g \cdot p/100)$ | $v$ in m/s. For $v$ in km/h, use $v/3.6$. |

---

1) See P. 423 for numerical values.
2) ABS: antilock braking system;
   P. 809 onwards, P. 858 onwards.
   TCS: traction control system;
   P. 817 onwards, P. 862 onwards.

ESP: electronic stability program;
P. 802 onwards, P. 864 onwards.
3) Valid to approx. $p = 20\%$ (under 2% error).
4) J = N · m = W · s; conversions, P. 26.

## Actions: Reaction, braking and stopping

(in accordance with ÖNORM V5050)

### Hazard recognition time

The hazard recognition time, also known as the danger reaction time, is the period of time that elapses between perceiving a visible obstacle and/or its movement and the time required to recognize it as a hazard. If, as part of this danger recognition and response process, it is necessary for the driver to turn his eyes towards the hazardous situation, the hazard recognition and danger reaction time will extend by roughly 0.4 s.

### Prebraking time ($t_{VZ}$)

The prebraking time is the period of time that elapses between the moment the hazard is recognized and the start of braking, defined by way of calculation. Based on the following formula, the prebraking time is in the range from approx. 0.8 to 1.0 s:

$$t_{VZ} = t_R + t_U + t_A + t_S/2$$

Reaction time ($t_R$): This is the period of time that elapses between the moment a defined incitement to action occurs and the start of the first specifically targeted action.

Instinctive hazard recognition triggers an inherent, automatic reaction (spontaneous reaction), enabling the vehicle driver to determine both the point of the reaction as well as the position of the reason for the reaction, delayed by the distance covered during the prebraking time. Human beings require about 0.2 s for the spontaneous reaction; however, the reaction time will be at least 0.3 s if the driver needs to make a decision to perform a preventative or evasive action in response to conscious hazard recognition (choice reaction).

Transfer time ($t_U$): This is the period of time the driver requires to transfer the foot from the gas pedal to the brake pedal. The transfer time is in the range of about 0.2 s.

Response time ($t_A$): This is the period of time it takes to transmit the pressure applied at the brake pedal via the brake system through to the point when the braking action becomes effective (complete build-up of the application force and incipient increase in vehicle deceleration).

Pressure build-up time ($t_S$): The pressure build-up time is the period of time that elapses between the braking action taking effect and reaching fully effective braking deceleration. Alternatively, half the pressure build-up time ($t_S/2$) may be assumed as the start of braking, determined by way of calculation.

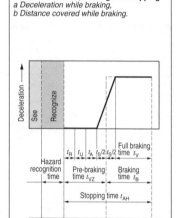

*Actions: Reaction, braking and stopping*
*a Deceleration while braking,*
*b Distance covered while braking.*

|  | Equations for $v$ in m/s | Equations for $v$ in km/h |
|---|---|---|
| Stopping time $t_{AH}$ in s | $t_{AH} = t_{VZ} + \dfrac{v}{a}$ | $t_{AH} = t_{VZ} + \dfrac{v}{3.6 \cdot a}$ |
| Stopping distance $s_{AH}$ in m | $s_{AH} = v \cdot t_{VZ} + \dfrac{v^2}{2 \cdot a}$ | $s_{AH} = \dfrac{v}{3.6} t_{VZ} + \dfrac{v^2}{25.92 \cdot a}$ |

In accordance with the EU Council of Ministers Directive EEC 71/320 Addendum 3/2.4, the sum of the response time and pressure build-up time may not exceed 0.6 s. A poorly maintained braking system will lengthen the response and pressure build-up time.

### Braking time ($t_B$)

The braking time ($t_B$) is the period of time that elapses between the mathematically calculated start of braking and the moment the vehicle comes to a complete stop. This period of time comprises half the pressure build-up time ($t_S/2$) (calculation assumption: only half the pressure build-up time but complete braking deceleration) as well as the full braking time ($t_V$), during which maximum braking deceleration is actually effective.

$$t_B = t_S/2 + t_V$$

### Stopping time ($t_{AH}$) and Stopping distance ($s_{AH}$)

The stopping time ($t_{AH}$) is the sum of the prebraking time ($t_{VZ}$) and braking time ($t_B$).

$$t_{AH} = t_{VZ} + t_B$$

The stopping distance ($s_{AH}$) can be calculated by way of integration.

### References:

Sacher in Fucik/Hartl/Schlosser/Wielke Verkehrsunfall II (Traffic accidents II) (1998), MANZ'sche Verlags- und Universitätsbuchhandlung AG.
ISBN 3-214-12894-9.

| Deceleration $a$ in m/s² | Vehicle speed prior to braking in km/h | | | | | | | | | | | | |
|---|---|---|---|---|---|---|---|---|---|---|---|---|---|
|  | 10 | 30 | 50 | 60 | 70 | 80 | 90 | 100 | 120 | 140 | 160 | 180 | 200 |
|  | Distance during prebraking time (delay) of 1 s in m | | | | | | | | | | | | |
|  | 2.8 | 8.3 | 14 | 17 | 19 | 22 | 25 | 28 | 33 | 39 | 44 | 50 | 56 |
|  | Stopping distance in m | | | | | | | | | | | | |
| 4.4 | 3.7 | 16 | 36 | 48 | 62 | 78 | 96 | 115 | 160 | 210 | 270 | 335 | 405 |
| 5 | 3.5 | 15 | 33 | 44 | 57 | 71 | 87 | 105 | 145 | 190 | 240 | 300 | 365 |
| 5.8 | 3.4 | 14 | 30 | 40 | 52 | 65 | 79 | 94 | 130 | 170 | 215 | 265 | 320 |
| 7 | 3.3 | 13 | 28 | 36 | 46 | 57 | 70 | 83 | 110 | 145 | 185 | 230 | 275 |
| 8 | 3.3 | 13 | 26 | 34 | 43 | 53 | 64 | 76 | 105 | 135 | 170 | 205 | 250 |
| 9 | 3.2 | 12 | 25 | 32 | 40 | 50 | 60 | 71 | 95 | 125 | 155 | 190 | 225 |

## Passing (overtaking)

| Symbol | | Unit |
|---|---|---|
| $a$ | Acceleration | m/s² |
| $l_1, l_2$ | Vehicle length | m |
| $s_1, s_2$ | Safety margin | m |
| $s_H$ | Relative distance traveled by passing vehicle | m |
| $s_L$ | Distance traveled by vehicle being passed | m |
| $s_u$ | Passing distance | m |
| $t_u$ | Passing time | s |
| $v_L$ | Speed of slower vehicle | km/h |
| $v_H$ | Speed of faster vehicle | km/h |

The complete passing maneuver involves pulling out of the lane, overtaking the other vehicle, and returning to the original lane. Passing can take place under a wide variety of highly differing circumstances and conditions, so precise calculations are difficult. For this reason, the following calculations, graphs, and illustrations will confine themselves to an examination of two extreme conditions: passing at a constant velocity and passing at a constant rate of acceleration.

We can simplify graphic representation by treating the passing distance $s_u$ as the sum of two (straight-ahead) components, while disregarding the extra travel involved by pulling out of the lane and back in again.

### Passing distance

$$s_U = s_H + s_L$$

The distance $s_H$ which the more rapid vehicle must cover compared to the slower vehicle (considered as being stationary) is the sum of the vehicle lengths $l_1$ and $l_2$ and the safety margins $s_1$ and $s_2$.

$$s_H = s_1 + s_2 + l_1 + l_2$$

During the passing time $t_u$, the slower vehicle covers the distance $s_L$; this is the distance that the overtaking vehicle must also travel in order to maintain the safety margin.

$$s_L = t_u \cdot v_L / 3.6 \text{ (for } v \text{ in km/h)}$$

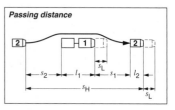

*Passing distance*

### Safety margin

The minimum safety margin corresponds to the distance covered during the pre-braking time $t_{VZ}$ (P. 426). The figure for a prebraking time of $t_{VZ} = 1.08$ s (velocity in km/h) is $(0.3 \cdot v)$ meters. However, a minimum of $0.5 \cdot v$ is advisable outside of built-up areas.

### Passing at constant speed

On highways with more than two lanes, the overtaking vehicle will frequently be traveling at a speed adequate for passing before the actual process begins. The passing time (from initial lane change until return to the original lane has been completed) is then:

$$t_u = \frac{3.6 \cdot s_H}{v_H - v_L}$$

The passing distance

$$s_u = \frac{t_u \cdot v_H}{3.6} = \frac{s_H \cdot v_H}{v_H - v_L}$$

$t$ in s,
$s$ in m,
$v$ in km/h

### Passing with constant acceleration

On narrow roads, the vehicle will usually have to slow down to the speed of the preceding car or truck before accelerating to pass. The attainable acceleration figures depend upon engine output, vehicle weight, speed and running resistance (P. 425). These generally lie within the range of 0.4...0.8 m/s², with up to 1.4 m/s² available in lower gears for further reductions in passing time. The distance required to complete the passing maneuver should never exceed half the visible stretch of road.

Operating on the assumption that a constant rate of acceleration can be maintained for the duration of the passing maneuver, the passing time will be:

$$t_u = \sqrt{2 \cdot s_H / a}$$

The distance which the slower vehicle covers within this period is defined as $s_L = t_u \cdot v_L / 3.6$. This gives a passing distance of:

$$s_u = s_H + t_u \cdot v_L / 3.6 \qquad \begin{array}{l} t \text{ in s,} \\ s \text{ in m,} \\ v \text{ in km/h.} \end{array}$$

The left side of the graph below shows the relative distances $s_H$ for speed differentials $v_H - v_L$ and acceleration rates $a$, while the right side shows the distances $s_L$ covered by the vehicle being passed at various speeds $v_L$. The passing distance $s_u$ is the sum of $s_H$ and $s_L$.

First, determine the distance $s_H$ to be traveled by the passing vehicle. Enter this distance on the left side of the graph between the Y axis and the applicable line for ($v_H - v_L$) or acceleration. Then extrapolate the line to the right, over to the speed line $v_L$.

Example (represented by dash-dot lines in the graph):

$v_L = v_H = 50$ km/h,
$a = 0.4$ m/s²,
$l_1 = 10$ m, $l_2 = 5$ m,
$s_1 = s_2 = 0.3 \cdot v_L = 0.3 \cdot v_H = 15$ m.

Solution: Enter intersection of $a = 0.4$ m/s² and $s_H = 15 + 15 + 10 + 5 = 45$ m in the left side of the graph. Indication $t_u = 15$ s, $s_L = 210$ m. Thus $s_u = s_H + s_L = 255$ m.

**Visual range**

For safe passing on narrow roads, the visibility must be at least the sum of the passing distance plus the distance which would be traveled by an oncoming vehicle while the passing maneuver is in progress. This distance is approximately 400 m if the vehicles approaching each other are traveling at speeds of 90 km/h, and the vehicle being overtaken at 60 km/h.

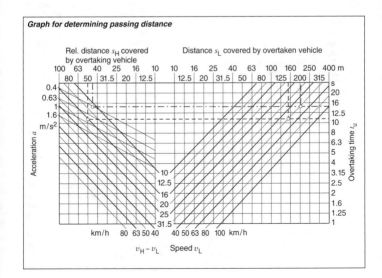

*Graph for determining passing distance*

## Dynamics of lateral motion

### Quantities and units

| Quantity | | Unit |
|---|---|---|
| $\delta$ | Axle steering angle | rad |
| $\delta_H$ | Steering-wheel angle | rad |
| $\alpha_V$ | Slip angle of front axle | rad |
| $\alpha_H$ | Slip angle of rear axle | rad |
| $\beta$ | Float angle | rad |
| $\psi$ | Yaw angle | rad |
| $l$ | Wheelbase | m |
| $l_v$ | Distance between front axle and center of gravity | m |
| $l_h$ | Distance between rear axle and center of gravity | m |
| $v$ | Longitudinal velocity | m/s |
| $v_r$ | Resulting wind impact velocity | m/s |
| $C_v$ | Front cornering stiffness | N/rad |
| $C_h$ | Rear cornering stiffness | N/rad |
| $m$ | Total mass (weight) | kg |
| $i_l$ | Steering ratio | – |
| $F_{SV}$ | Lateral force on front axle | N |
| $F_{SH}$ | Lateral force on rear axle | N |
| $a_y$ | Lateral acceleration | m/s² |
| $\theta$ | Yaw moment of inertia | Nms² |
| $\varrho$ | Air density | kg/m³ |
| $A$ | Frontal area | m² |
| $\tau$ | Angle of impact | rad |
| $F_S$ | Crosswind force | N |
| $M_Z$ | Crosswind yaw moment | Nm |

### References:

Willumeit, H.-P.: Modelle und Modellierungs-verfahren in der Fahrzeugdynamik; (Models and Modeling Methods in Motor Vehicle Dynamics); Teubner-Verlag Stuttgart, 1998.
Mitschke, M.: Dynamik der Kraftfahrzeuge, Band C Fahrverhalten; (Motor Vehicle Dynamics, Volume C, Drivability); Vogel-Buchverlag Würzburg, 1987.
Zomotor, A.: Fahrwerktechnik: Fahrverhalten; (Chassis and Suspension Control System: Drivability); Vogel-Buchverlag Würzburg, 1987.

### Ranges of lateral acceleration

Today passenger vehicles can reach lateral acceleration levels of up to 10 m/s². Lateral acceleration is subdivided into the following ranges:

– The range from 0...0.5 m/s² is known as the <u>small-signal range</u>. The phenomenon to be considered in this range is the straight-running behavior, triggered by excitation sources in the road such as ruts and crosswind. Crosswind excitation is induced by blustery, gusty wind or by driving into and out of wind shadow areas.

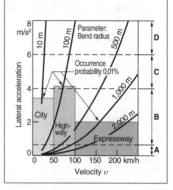

*Lateral acceleration ranges*
*A Small-signal range, B "Linear" range (relevant to normal car driver), C Transition range, D Limit range (emphasis on stability, relevant to press and experts).*
*For the average car driver, the probability of lateral acceleration occurring decreases exponentially with lateral acceleration.*

– The range from 0.5...4 m/s² is known as the <u>linear range</u>, as the vehicle behavior that occurs in this range can be described with the aid of the linear single-track model. Typical maneuvers involving dynamics of lateral motion include sudden steering input, changing driving lanes as well as combinations of maneuvers involving dynamics of both lateral and longitudinal motion, such as load change reactions in turns.

– In the lateral acceleration range from 4...6 m/s², depending on their design features, passenger vehicles are categorized as either still linear or already nonlinear. This range is therefore considered to be a <u>transition range</u>. In this range, vehicles with maximum lateral acceleration of 6...7 m/s² (e.g. true off-road vehicles) already feature nonlinear characteristics, while vehicles that achieve higher levels of lateral acceleration (e.g. sports cars) still behave in line with linear characteristics.

– The lateral acceleration range above 6 m/s² is reached only in extreme situations and is therefore referred to as the <u>limit range</u>. In this range, the vehicle characteristics are predominantly non-linear, with the main emphasis shifted to vehicle stability. This range is reached on racing circuits or in situations leading up to accidents in normal road traffic.

The average driver generally drives in the range up to 4 m/s². This means both the small signal range as well as the linear range are relevant to the car driver when subjectively assessing the situation (see illustration). Important deductions relating to the dynamic characteristics of lateral motion can be gained from the linear single-track model.

### Single-track model

The single-track model combines the lateral dynamic properties of one axle and its wheels to form one effective wheel. In the simplest version, as illustrated here, the characteristics under consideration are positioned in the linear range, which explains why this type of model is referred to as a <u>linear single-track model</u>. The main assumptions in the model encompass:

- Kinematics and elastokinematics of the axle are considered only in linear form.
- The lateral force structure of the tire is linear and the aligning or return torque of the tire is ignored.
- The center of gravity is at the level of the road surface. This means the vehicle executes only the yaw motion as a rotational degree of freedom. Roll, pitch and lift are not taken into consideration

(see illustration on P. 436 for a definition of the angles; lift is the translational movement in z-axis).

### Steady-state skidpad

The illustration below represents the single-track model in connection with the fast and slow skidpad. This representation results in the following interrelationships describing the kinematics of slip angles:

$$\alpha_v = \delta - \beta - \frac{\dot{\psi} \cdot l_v}{v}$$

$$\alpha_h = -\beta + \frac{\dot{\psi} \cdot l_h}{v}$$

The slip angle is the angle that is formed between the longitudinal axis and the velocity vector of the tire. Analogously, the float angle $\beta$ is the angle that occurs between the velocity vector at the center of gravity and longitudinal axis of the vehicle.

Together with the torque balance, it is possible to calculate the change in the steering-wheel angle in connection with increasing lateral acceleration for the skidpad maneuver at a constant radius. This results in the definition of the self-steering gradient EG:

$$EG = \frac{d\delta}{da_y} = \frac{m}{l} \cdot \left( \frac{l_h}{C_v} - \frac{l_v}{C_h} \right)$$

All passenger vehicles are designed so that they understeer in the linear lateral acceleration range. The EG value for passenger vehicles is in the range of about 0.30 degrees · s²/m.

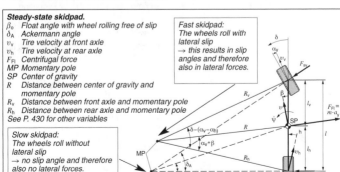

**Steady-state skidpad.**
$\beta_o$   Float angle with wheel rolling free of slip
$\delta_A$   Ackermann angle
$v_v$   Tire velocity at front axle
$v_h$   Tire velocity at rear axle
$F_{Fl}$   Centrifugal force
MP   Momentary pole
SP   Center of gravity
$R$   Distance between center of gravity and momentary pole
$R_v$   Distance between front axle and momentary pole
$R_h$   Distance between rear axle and momentary pole
See P. 430 for other variables

Fast skidpad:
The wheels roll with lateral slip
→ this results in slip angles and therefore also in lateral forces.

Slow skidpad:
The wheels roll without lateral slip
→ no slip angle and therefore also no lateral forces.

In terms of the dynamics of lateral motion, the self-steering gradient characterizes the stability and damping of the vehicle. In addition, the significance of the self-steering gradient for the average car driver becomes apparent in that the steering angle requirement increases the faster the cornering speed. This draws the driver's attention to the increasing lateral acceleration.

The float angle gradient SG can be calculated from the same illustration. The float angle gradient should be as low as possible in order to increase the stability of the vehicle.

$$SG = \frac{d\beta}{da_y} = \frac{m \cdot l_v}{C_h \cdot l}$$

**Yaw gain**

The yaw gain defines the degree of yaw response that a vehicle executes in response to a steering angle in the quasi-steady-state range. The yaw gain factor can be determined by conducting the following test procedure: When driving at a constant speed, the steering wheel is turned with sinusoidal motion at a frequency of less than 0.2 Hz. The steering angle amplitude is selected in order to achieve a maximum lateral acceleration of about 3 m/s². Starting at a speed of 20 km/h, the maneuver is repeated at a speed that is increased by 10 km/h each time. Providing no aerodynamic influences occur at high

speeds (lift or upthrust forces at the front and rear axles), the test will produce yaw gain curves that essentially agree with the following equation, derived from the linear single-track model:

$$\left(\frac{\dot{\psi}}{\delta}\right)_{\text{stat.}} = \frac{v}{l + \text{EG} \cdot v^2}$$

The illustration shows the yaw gain for a vehicle that tends to oversteer (EG < 0), that has neutral steering (EG = 0), and that understeers (EG > 0).

Only the vehicle that understeers is acceptable at high speeds and therefore has the right vehicle dynamics even when driving in a straight line. The speed at which a vehicle that tends to understeer has the greatest yaw response is known as the "characteristic speed" $v_{\text{char}}$. In the linear single-track model, this speed is expressed as:

$$v_{\text{char}} = \sqrt{\frac{l}{\text{EG}}}$$

**Damping factor**

The following equilibrium of forces in the lateral direction is derived for the linear single-track model:

$$m \cdot a_y = F_{sv} \cdot \cos(\delta) + F_{sh}$$

and the following torque balance:

$$\theta \cdot \ddot{\psi} = F_{sv} \cdot \cos(\delta) \cdot l_v + F_{sh} \cdot l_h$$

The damping factor $D$ for excitation in terms of the dynamics of linear motion can be derived from the two equations:

$$D = \frac{1}{\omega_e} \cdot \left( \frac{C_v + C_h}{m \cdot v} + \frac{C_v \cdot l_v^2 + C_h \cdot l_h^2}{\theta \cdot v} \right)$$

The following equation expresses the undamped natural frequency:

$$\omega_e = \sqrt{\left( \frac{C_h \cdot l_h - C_v \cdot l_v}{\theta} + \frac{C_v \cdot C_h \cdot l^2}{\theta \cdot m \cdot v^2} \right)}$$

The damping factor of a vehicle can be identified from the yaw response of sudden steering or step input. The vehicle is designed to ensure that damping is as high as possible.

The illustration shows the damping factor and yaw gain for various self-steering gradients. This results in the following conflict of objectives:

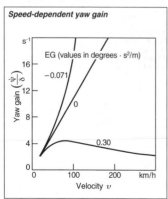

*Speed-dependent yaw gain*

EG (values in degrees · s²/m)

−0.071

0

0.30

Yaw gain $\left(\frac{\dot{\psi}}{\delta}\right)$ — s⁻¹

16

12

8

4

0

0    100    200    km/h

Velocity $v$

– A high self-steering gradient is required if the vehicle is to have good straight-running characteristics.
– The self-steering gradient must be as low as possible to facilitate a high damping factor, particularly at high speeds.

**Steering ratio**

A further important variable governing vehicle balance is the total steering ratio $i_l$. The steering-wheel angle, together with the total steering ratio $i_l$, is calculated from the axle steering angle:

$$\delta_H = i_l \cdot \delta$$

This results in the following equation for maximum yaw gain:

$$\left(\frac{\dot\psi}{\delta_H}\right)_{max} = \frac{1}{2 \cdot i_l \cdot \sqrt{l \cdot EG}}$$

This maximum is plotted in the "lateral agility diagram" as a function of the steering ratio. The diagram additionally shows the EG-isolines. The self-steering gradient is constant along these curves. The desired target ranges for the yaw gain and steering ratio can be plotted in this diagram for the purpose of defining the necessary self-steering gradients.

If only the steering ratio is changed in a vehicle, the maximum yaw gain can be determined in the lateral agility diagram by shifting the baseline along the EG-isolines. The shift will be along the vertical axis if the axis characteristics are varied.

**Dynamics of lateral motion caused by crosswind**

Wind can induce lateral dynamics in motor vehicles. The vehicle responds to this external influence by drifting off course, lateral acceleration, and a change in yaw angle and roll angle. The driver then attempts to take corrective action to counteract this discrepancy. Consequently, the response capabilities of the driver as well as the correctability of the vehicle are taken into consideration in a second stage.

According to current findings, the direct response of the vehicle to crosswind is the principal variable for subjectively assessing overall vehicle stability in crosswinds. This offers the advantage that the interaction of crosswind and vehicle response

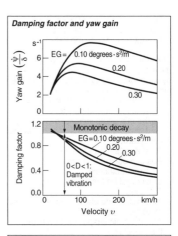

*Damping factor and yaw gain*

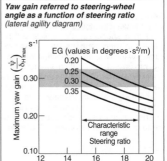

*Yaw gain referred to steering-wheel angle as a function of steering ratio (lateral agility diagram)*

can be effectively observed by analysis. The entire vehicle – driver – environment closed-loop control circuit (see illustration on P. 436) is currently still the subject of extensive research and is therefore not dealt with in further detail here.

Characteristically, the average car driver perceives two states induced by wind excitation:
– Natural crosswind, which can vary in terms of direction and wind velocity while driving.

– Driving into or out of wind shadow areas where forces of greatly varying strength can act on the vehicle.

The automotive industry strives to minimize the effects of excitations triggered by wind forces by taking the following vehicle factors into consideration:
– "Cornering stiffness" of the tires, i.e. to what extent the lateral force changes as the slip angle increases. The wheel load of the tire remains constant in this consideration.
– Total weight rating of the vehicle
– Position of center of gravity
– Axle characteristics
– Equilateral and reciprocal suspension
– Damping
– Kinematics and elastokinematics of the axles
– Aerodynamic shape and frontal area of the vehicle

**Aerodynamic forces and moments**

When a vehicle moves at velocity $v$ in a wind at a speed $v_w$, the vehicle will be subject to wind impact applied at the resulting velocity $v_r$. In connection with natural crosswind, the angle of impact $\tau$ generally differs from 0 degrees and therefore generates a lateral force $F_S$ and a yaw moment $M_Z$ that acts on the vehicle.

In aerodynamics, it is standard practice to specify dimensionless coefficients instead of forces and moments. Therefore:

$$F_s = C_s \cdot \frac{\varrho}{2} \cdot v_r^2 \cdot A$$

$$M_Z = c_M \cdot \frac{\varrho}{2} \cdot v_r^2 \cdot A \cdot l$$

The moment $M_Z$ and the lateral force $F_S$, which is defined at the mid-point of the wheelbase, can be represented by a single lateral force $F_S$ when the point of impact is located at the center of the pressure point $d$. The distance $d$ from the mid-point of the wheelbase is calculated as follows:

$$d = \frac{M_Z}{F_S} = \frac{c_M \cdot l}{c_S}$$

To keep aerodynamic influences as low as possible, appropriate steps should be taken to ensure that the center of the pressure point is as close to the vehicle's center of gravity as possible. This consequently reduces the effective impact of the moment.

The illustration represents the aerodynamic coefficients for the two most typical structural shapes of vehicles, i.e. the station wagon and sedan, as a function of the angle of impact $\tau$. The resulting pressure point is considerably lower for station wagons than for sedans (see illustration). For vehicles with the center of gravity located at the mid-point of the wheelbase, the station wagon structure is therefore less sensitive to crosswind than the sedan structure.

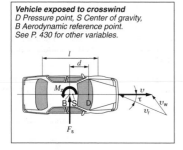

**Vehicle exposed to crosswind**
D Pressure point, S Center of gravity,
B Aerodynamic reference point.
See P. 430 for other variables.

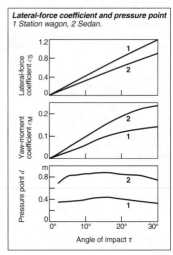

**Lateral-force coefficient and pressure point**
1 Station wagon, 2 Sedan.

# Cornering behavior

## Centrifugal force in turns

$$F_{cf} = \frac{m \cdot v^2}{r_K} \quad \text{(P. 40)}$$

## Body roll in turns
### Roll axis
In turns, the centrifugal force which concentrates around the center of gravity causes the vehicle to tilt away from the path of travel. The magnitude of this rolling motion depends upon the rates of the springs and their response to alternating compression, and upon the lever arm of the centrifugal force (distance between the roll axis and the center of gravity). The roll axis is the body's instantaneous axis of rotation relative to the road surface. Like all rigid bodies, the vehicle body consistently executes a screwing or rotating motion; this motion is supplemented by a lateral displacement along the instantaneous axis.

The higher the roll axis, i.e. the closer it is to a parallel axis through the center of gravity, the greater will be the transverse stability and the less the roll in turns. However, this generally implies a corresponding upward displacement of the instantaneous axes of the wheels, resulting in a change in track width (with negative effects on driving safety). For this reason, designs seek to combine a high instantaneous roll center with minimal track change. The goal therefore is to place the instantaneous axes of the wheels as high as possible relative to the body, while simultaneously keeping them as far from the body as possible.

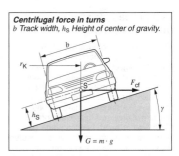

*Centrifugal force in turns*
$b$ Track width, $h_S$ Height of center of gravity.

### Determining the roll axis
A frequently applied means for finding the approximate roll axis is based on determining the centers of rotation of an equivalent body motion. This body motion takes place in those two planes through the front and rear axles which are vertical relative to the road. The centers of rotation are those (hypothetical) points in the body which remain stationary during the rotation. The roll axis, in turn, is the line which connects these centers (instantaneous roll centers). Graphic portrayals of instantaneous roll centers are based on a rule according to which the instantaneous poles of rotation of three systems in a state of relative motion lie along a common pole line.

The complexity of the operations required for a more precise definition of the spatial relationships involved in wheel motion make it advisable to employ general, three-dimensional simulation models.

## Critical speeds (numerical value equations)

| | Flat curve | Banked curve |
|---|---|---|
| Speed at which the vehicle exceeds the limit of adhesion (skid) | $v \leq 11.28 \sqrt{\mu_r \cdot r_K}$ km/h | $v \leq 11.28 \sqrt{\dfrac{(\mu_r + \tan \gamma)\, r_K}{1 - \mu_r \cdot \tan \gamma}}$ km/h |
| Speed at which the vehicle tips | $v \geq 11.28 \sqrt{\dfrac{b \cdot r_K}{2 \cdot h_S}}$ km/h | $v \geq 11.28 \sqrt{\dfrac{\left(\dfrac{b}{2 \cdot h_S} + \tan \gamma\right) \cdot r_K}{1 - \dfrac{b}{2 \cdot h_S} \cdot \tan \gamma}}$ km/h |

$h_S$ Height of center of gravity (in m), $\mu_r$ Max. coefficient of friction, $b$ Track width (in m), $r_K$ Curve radius (in m), $\gamma$ Curve camber.

# ISO procedures for evaluating vehicle handling

The science devoted to studying the dynamics of vehicle handling generally defines its subject as the overall behavior of the entire system represented by "driver + vehicle + environment". As the first link in the chain, the driver makes judgements on the vehicle's handling qualities based on the sum of diverse subjective impressions. On the other hand, handling data derived from specific driving maneuvers executed without driver input (open-loop operation) provide an objective description of the vehicle's handling qualities. The driver, who up to the present day still cannot be defined accurately in terms of behavior, is replaced in these tests by a specific, objectively quantifiable interference factor. The resulting vehicular response can then be analyzed and discussed.

Standardized versions of the driving maneuvers in the list (performed on a dry road surface) below have either already been defined by ISO or are under consideration; they serve as recognized standard procedures for vehicular evaluation [1], [2]:
– Steady-state skidpad [3]
– Transient response [4], [5], [6]
– Braking in turns [7]
– Crosswind sensitivity
– Straight-running stability, and
– Reaction to throttle change on the skidpad

*"Driver-vehicle-environment" synergism represented as a closed-loop control system*

To date, it has still not been possible to arrive at comprehensive objective definitions for the dynamic characteristics associated with closed-loop operation, as adequate data on the precise control characteristics of the human element are still unavailable.

### Test quantities
The main criteria employed in evaluating vehicle dynamics are:
– Steering-wheel angle
– Lateral acceleration
– Longitudinal acceleration and deceleration

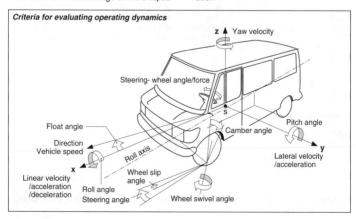

*Criteria for evaluating operating dynamics*

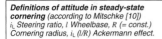

***Definitions of attitude in steady-state cornering*** *(according to Mitschke [10])*
$i_L$ Steering ratio, $l$ Wheelbase, $R$ (= const.)
Cornering radius, $i_L$ $(l/R)$ Ackermann effect.

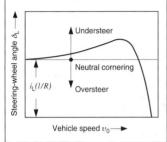

*Steering-wheel angle $\delta_L$*

▲ Understeer

● Neutral cornering

$i_L(l/R)$

Oversteer

Vehicle speed $v_0$ ⟶

– Yaw velocity
– Float and roll angles

Additional data are employed to verify and confirm the previously derived information on specific points of vehicle handling:
– Linear and lateral velocities
– Steering angles at front and rear wheels
– Slip angles at all wheels
– Camber and pitch angles
– Steering-wheel force

**Steady-state skidpad**
Besides the maximum attainable lateral acceleration, the most important data obtained in steady-state skidpad testing are the changes that occur in individual dynamic parameters as a factor of lateral acceleration until the maximum value is reached. This information is employed in evaluating the vehicle's self-steering response [2], [3]. Compliance in both the steering system and the suspension is represented in the current standard definition of steering response, which employs the terms "oversteer", "understeer" and "neutral steering". Several dynamic factors and their derivatives are considered in conjunction with lateral acceleration in describing vehicle handling, examples being steering-wheel angle, roll angle and float angle. Other significant vehicle parameters are steering angle and slip angle.

In the following, a light utility van (similar to a passenger car) and a heavy truck are used to provide examples of the results gathered on a dry surface.

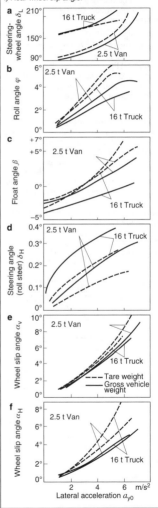

*Steady-state skidpad (42 m radius)*
*a) Steering-wheel angle, b) Roll angle,*
*c) Float angle, d) Rear-axle steering angle (roll steer), e) Front-wheel slip angle,*
*f) Rear-wheel slip angle.*

### Steering-wheel angle

As light utility vehicles are fitted with tires similar to those used in passenger cars, and are also equipped with relatively high-power engines, they achieve high rates of lateral acceleration. Both vehicle types understeer.

### Roll angle

The degree of self-steering which prevails at the axles is largely determined by the roll angle. Higher loads result in more pronounced roll angles due to the greater vehicle mass and the attendant increase in effective centrifugal force.

### Float angle

The float angle encountered at high rates of lateral acceleration is regarded as an index of controllability, in other words the vehicle's response to driver input. High absolute figures or fluctuations in float angle are regarded as particularly undesirable [8].

At low rates of lateral acceleration, the float angle is a function of the radius of the driven circle, and the vehicle's center of gravity which varies along with changes in vehicle load.

### Rear-axle roll steer

The relationship between the steering angle at the rear axle (roll-steer angle) and lateral acceleration illustrates how the roll-steer angle at the rear axle decreases in response to higher vehicle loads.

### Slip angle

The wheel slip angles at the individual wheels provide information on the vehicle's self-steering characteristics. The wheel slip angles increase in response to higher vehicle loads, a consequence of the tires requiring greater slip angles as their loading increases [2], [9].

**Transient response**

In addition to self-steering in steady-state testing, another significant factor is the vehicle's response during directional changes (e.g. for rapid evasive maneuvers) [2]. Two test methods have become accepted internationally. These are defined according to the type of input stimulus, and illustrate both the time and frequency ranges of the vehicle's response:

***Step input*** *(unloaded, $v_0 = 60$ km/h)*
*a) Steering-wheel angle $\delta_L$, b) Roll angle $\varphi$,*
*c) Lateral acceleration $a_{y0}$, d) Yaw velocity $\dot{\psi}$.*

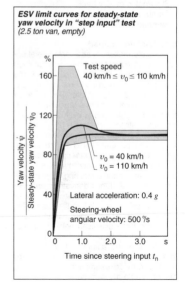

***ESV limit curves for steady-state yaw velocity in "step input" test***
*(2.5 ton van, empty)*

Yaw velocity $\dot{\psi}$ / Steady-state yaw velocity $\dot{\psi}_0$

Test speed
40 km/h $\leq v_0 \leq$ 110 km/h

$v_0 = 40$ km/h
$v_0 = 110$ km/h

Lateral acceleration: 0.4 $g$

Steering-wheel angular velocity: 500 °/s

Time since steering input $t_n$

– Step-input (sharp change in steering angle)
– Sinusoidal input (sinusoidal step input)

<u>Step input (time response)</u>
Starting with the vehicle traveling in a straight line, the steering wheel is abruptly "pulled" to a specified angle; the vehicle's response serves as the basis for evaluation. The most important quantities to be measured are [5]:
– Steering-wheel angle
– Yaw velocity
– Vehicle speed, and
– Lateral acceleration

A light utility van responds to step input with a more rapid change in lateral acceleration – and thus in yaw – than a heavy truck.

U.S. authorities have defined a transient yaw requirement for Experimental Safety Vehicles (ESV) [11]. Vehicles which are classified as being similar to passenger cars may exhibit relatively pronounced overswing in the initial input phase (this effect must cease after a certain period).

<u>Sinusoidal step input (frequency response)</u>
Permanent sinusoidal steering inputs at the steering wheel are also used to measure frequency-response characteristics. This provides yet another basis for evaluating a vehicle's transitional handling response, the intensity and phase of which varies according to the steering frequency. The most important factors for this evaluation are [6]:
– Steering-wheel angle
– Lateral acceleration
– Yaw velocity, and
– Roll angle

**Braking in turns**
Of all the maneuvers encountered in everyday driving situations, one of the most critical – and thus one of the most important with regard to vehicle design – is braking in turns. The vehicle's concept must be optimized so that its reaction to this maneuver is characterized by the best possible compromise between steerability, stability and retardation [2], [7]. Testing starts from a specified initial rate of lateral

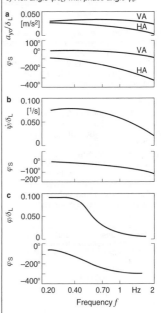

***Sinusoidal step input***
*(16-ton truck, $v_0 = 60$ km/h, $\delta_L = 60°$)*
*Relative to steering-wheel angle:*
*a) Lateral acceleration $a_{y0}/\delta_L$*
*b) Yaw velocity $\dot{\psi}/\delta_L$ and*
*c) Roll angle $\varphi/\delta_L$; with phase angle $\varphi_s$.*

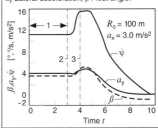

***Time curves for braking in turns***
*(7.5 ton truck, loaded)*
*1 Steady-state skidpad, 2 Initial braking,*
*3 Evaluation point. $\dot{\psi}$ Yaw velocity,*
*$a_y$ Lateral acceleration, $\beta$ Float angle.*

acceleration, and focuses upon float angle and yaw velocity relative to lateral deceleration as the significant factors.

The vehicle, initially in steady-state circulation at a stipulated lateral acceleration, is braked with the rate of deceleration being increased incrementally. In every test, using the time functions, the measurements are taken "1 s after start of braking" for vehicles with hydraulic brakes (a delay of 1.5...2 s after initial braking is applied for heavy-duty commercial vehicles with compressed-air brake systems, Item c in the illustration).

### Float angle

Due to the weight transfer away from the rear axle and the tires' response to this phenomenon, higher rates of retardation result in greater float angles (Item a in the illustration). At high rates of deceleration, in the vicinity of the traction limit, the distribution of brake force is the decisive factor for the float angle. The decisive factor for the stability of the vehicle is the remaining cornering grip of the rear wheels.

### Yaw velocity

The yaw velocity serves as a reference in determining whether braking performance in turns is stable or unstable. In the illustration, Item b, both vehicles' yaw-speed curves move towards zero as the vehicles progress to phases of increasing deceleration. This indicates acceptable braking response: The vehicle remains stable.

### References

[1] Rönitz, R.; Braess, H. H.; Zomotor, A. Verfahren und Kriterien des Fahrverhaltens von Personenwagen. (Testing procedure and evaluation of passenger-car drivability). AI 322, 1972, Volume 1.
[2] von Glasner, E.C.: Einbeziehung von Prüfstandsergebnissen in die Simulation des Fahrverhaltens von Nutzfahrzeugen (Including test-bench results in the simulation of commercial-vehicle handling). Habilitation, Universität Stuttgart, 1987.
[3] ISO. Road Vehicles – Steady-State Circular Test Procedure. ISO, 1982, No.4138.
[4] ISO. Road Vehicles – Double Lane Change. ISO, 1975, TR 3888.
[5] ISO. Draft Proposal for an International Standard, Road Vehicles – Transient Response Test Procedure (Step/Ramp Input). ISO/TC 22/SC 9/N 185.
[6] ISO. Draft Proposal for an International Standard, Road Vehicles – Transient Response Test Procedure (Sinusoidal Input). ISO/TC 22/SC 9/N 219.
[7] ISO. Road Vehicles – Braking in a Turn. Open-Loop Test Procedure. ISO/DIS 7975.
[8] Zomotor, A.; Braess, H. H.; Rönitz, R. Doppelter Fahrspurwechsel, eine Möglichkeit zur Beurteilung des Fahrverhaltens von Kfz? (Double Lane Change, a Method for Evaluating a Vehicle's Drivability?) ATZ 76, 1974, Volume 8.
[9] Mitschke, M. Dynamik der Kraftfahrzeuge. (Dynamics of the Motor Vehicle), Springer Verlag, 1st Edition 1972, 2nd Edition 1982 and 1984, and subsequent editions.
[10] Mitschke, M. Fahrtrichtungshaltung – Analyse der Theorien. (Maintaining Direction of Travel – Analysis of Theories). ATZ 70, 1968, Volume 5.
[11] Mischke, A.; Göhring, E.; Wolsdorf, P.; von Glasner, E.C. Contribution to the Development of a Concept of Driving Mechanics for Commercial Vehicles. SAE 83 0643.

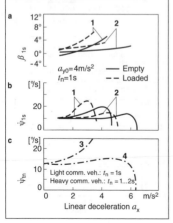

*Typical responses when braking in turns*
a) Float angle $\beta_{1s}$ and b) Yaw velocity $\dot\psi_{1s}$ 1s after initial braking ($t_n$), c) Yaw velocity $\dot\psi$ at moment $t_n$.
1: 16-ton truck, 2: 2.5-ton van, 3: Vehicle starts to skid, 4: Vehicle remains stable.

a

$a_{y0} = 4\,\text{m/s}^2$ —— Empty
$t_n = 1\,\text{s}$ – – Loaded

b [°/s]

c [°/s]

Light comm. veh.: $t_n = 1\,\text{s}$
Heavy comm. veh.: $t_n = 1...2\,\text{s}$

Linear deceleration $a_x$

# Special operating dynamics for commercial vehicles

Quantities and units

| | | |
|---|---|---|
| $G_V$ | N | Front-axle load |
| $G_H$ | N | Rear-axle load |
| $G_G$ | N | Total weight |
| $G_F$ | N | Sprung weight |
| $U_V$ | N | Unsprung weight, front |
| $U_H$ | N | Unsprung weight, rear |
| $C_{DSt}$ | N · m/wheel | Torsional spring rate for all stabilizers |
| $C_{FV,H}$ | N/m | Spring rates for axle springs |
| $C_{RV,H}$ | N/m | Spring rates for tires |
| $S_{FV,H}$ | m | Spring track |
| $S_{RV,H}$ | m | Tire track |
| $m_{V,H}$ | m | Instantaneous center height |
| $h_F$ | m | Height of center of gravity, sprung weight |
| $h_G$ | m | Height of center of gravity, total vehicle |
| $C_{QV,H}$ | N/m | Lateral stiffness rate of tires |
| $r$ | m | Turn radius |

## Self-steering properties

In the development phase in which the parameters affecting a vehicle's self-steering properties are determined, empirical and test-stand measurements and computer simulations are employed in an optimization process. The major determinants are the geometry and compliance rates of the steering system, the frame and the suspension.

The objects of analysis are the interference factors influencing straight-running stability and cornering behavior which can be traced to the interaction between

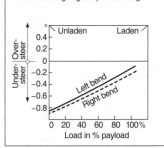

*Self-steering angle of an 18-ton truck cornering at 3 m/s² lateral acceleration*
The self-steering angle is plotted along Y.

steering and suspension, and which do not stem from driver inputs. The self-steering effect is examined at both the front and rear axles, in steady-state skid-pad testing, during braking and under unilateral spring compression.

When the springs are compressed on one side, a solid axle supported on leaf springs will tend to rotate about the vehicle's vertical axis. The degree of spring tilt exercises a major impact on this type of roll-steer phenomenon. Neutral behavior or mild understeer, desirable from the safety point of view, are enhanced by tilting the front spring up at the front and down at the rear, while the rear spring is mounted in the opposite direction, i.e. down at the front and up at the rear.

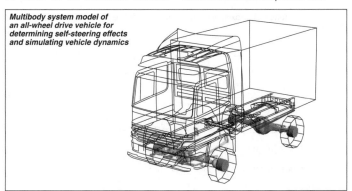

*Multibody system model of an all-wheel drive vehicle for determining self-steering effects and simulating vehicle dynamics*

Heavy-duty commercial vehicles with air suspension are normally equipped with solid or rigid axles controlled with suspension arms and links. Such axles are generally designed to ensure that the proportion of self-steering properties in axle control is virtually constant for all laden states since there is no difference in level between the "unladen" and "laden" states. To date, axle control concepts involving independent wheel control have only been implemented on light commercial vans and buses.

Wheel loads at the truck's rear axle vary dramatically, depending on whether the truck is unladen or laden. This leads to the vehicle responding to reductions in load with more pronounced understeer.

On three-axle 6 x 4 vehicles, the non-steered tandem-axle assembly represents a constraining force around the vehicle's vertical axis, thus enhancing straight-line stability. For low speeds, the additional cornering force required at the front and rear axles is determined as follows:

Cornering forces resulting from constraint
$F_{S1} = F_{S2} - F_{S3}$ where
$F_{S2} = c_{p2} \cdot n_2 \cdot \alpha_2$
$F_{S3} = c_{p3} \cdot n_3 \cdot \alpha_3$

Slip angle
$$\alpha_2 = \frac{1}{r} \cdot \frac{c_{p3} \cdot n_3 \cdot b \cdot (a+b)}{c_{p3} \cdot n_3 \cdot (a+b) + c_{p2} \cdot n_2 \cdot a}$$
$$\alpha_3 = (b/r) - \alpha_2$$

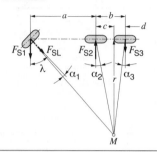

*Cornering forces $F_s$ and slip angle $\alpha$ on a 3-axle vehicle with non-steered tandem axle*

$c_p$ Coefficient of cornering stability from tire performance curve, $n$ Number of tires per axle, other designations as in illustration.

**Tipping resistance**

As the vehicle's total height increases, the vehicle will also have an increasing tendency to tip to the side in a turn before it starts to slide. In the same way as the overall dynamic behavior, the tipping limits of vehicles are determined by means of multibody system simulations. The simulations investigate various (quasi-) stationary and non-stationary maneuvers (steady-state skidpad, steering pull, VDA swerve, or evasion test, etc.).

---

**Tipping resistance.** Approximation equation for critical velocities $v_{tip}$ on a 2-axle truck (in km/h):

$$v_{tip} = 7.98 \cdot \sqrt{\frac{r \cdot (G_V \cdot S_{RV} + G_H \cdot S_{RH})}{G_G \cdot h_G + \frac{G_V^2}{C_{QV}} + \frac{G_H^2}{C_{QH}} + \frac{G_F^2 \cdot h_m^2}{C_D - G_F \cdot h_m}}}$$

with $C_D = \dfrac{C_{DF} \cdot C_{DR} \cdot i^2}{C_{DF} + C_{DR} \cdot i^2}$; $\quad i = \dfrac{h_m}{h_m + m}$;

$h_m = h_F - m$; $\quad m = \dfrac{(G_V - U_V) \cdot m_v + (G_H - U_H) m_H}{G_F}$

$C_{DF} = 1/2 \cdot (C_{FV} \cdot S_{FV} + C_{FH} \cdot S_{FH}^2) + C_{DSt}$

$C_{DR} = 1/2 \cdot (C_{RV} \cdot S_{RV}^2 + C_{RH} \cdot S_{RH}^2)$

Achievable rates of lateral acceleration at the tipping limit:

Van             $b = 6...8 \; \text{m} \cdot \text{s}^{-2}$
Truck           $b = 4...6 \; \text{m} \cdot \text{s}^{-2}$
Double-decker bus  $b = 3 \; \text{m} \cdot \text{s}^{-2}$

The increasing use of ESP systems also on commercial vehicles (see P. 864 onwards) can largely reduce the risk of tipping by estimating/determining the load status and load distribution.

### Width requirement

The width requirement of motor vehicles and truck-trailer combinations is greater during cornering than when the vehicle moves in a straight line. With respect to selected driving maneuvers, it is necessary to determine the radius described by the vehicle's outer extremities during cornering, both in order to ascertain its suitability for certain applications (e.g. narrow transit routes through constricted areas) and to confirm compliance with legal regulations. Evaluation is conducted with reference to the tractrix principle using electronic programs.

### Handling characteristics

Objective analyses of vehicle handling are based on various maneuvers such as steady-state skidpad testing, sudden steering inputs, wag/frequency response, and braking in a turn.

The dynamic lateral response of truck-trailer combinations generally differs from that of rigid vehicles. Particularly significant are the distribution of loads between truck and trailer, and the design and geometry of the mechanical coupling device within a given combination.

Oscillation, with the vehicle's masses turning against the stiffness of tires about the vertical axis, impairs straight-running stability. This phenomenon is induced by
- rapid steering corrections associated with evasive maneuvers
- crosswinds, and
- uneven road, obstacles on one side, ruts in the road surface, and cambers.

Oscillations associated with this pendulum motion must subside rapidly if vehicle stability is to be maintained. The oscillations associated with pendulum motion can be assessed based on the yaw-velocity frequency responses.

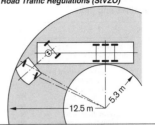

*Tractor-semitrailer combination in the circular area as stipulated by the German Road Traffic Regulations (StVZO)*

5.3 m
12.5 m

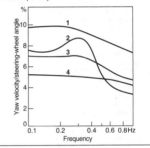

*Yaw-velocity frequency responses*
*1 Semitrailer unit (laden), 2 Truck-trailer unit (unladen/laden), 3 Truck-trailer unit (laden), 4 Truck (laden).*

Below is a graphic depiction of the yaw-velocity frequency responses for various types of truck-trailer combination. The worst case is represented by a combination, in which the towing vehicle is unladen, while the center-axle trailer is laden. Here, the curve indicates an excessive increase in resonance. This type of combination demands a high degree of driver skill and defensive driving style.

With semitrailer units, braking maneuvers undertaken under extreme conditions can induce jackknifing.

This process is initiated when, on a slippery road surface (μ-low), loss of lateral-force is induced by excess braking force applied to the tractor's rear axle, or due to excess yaw moment under μ-split conditions. Installation of an electronic stability program (ESP) represents the most effective means of preventing jackknifing.

## Requirements for agricultural tractors

### Quantities and units

| Symbol | | Unit |
|---|---|---|
| $F$ | Weight (wheel load) of a wheel | N |
| $F_R$ | Rolling resistance | N |
| $F_{Rh}$ | Rolling resistance, rear axle | N |
| $F_{Rv}$ | Rolling resistance, front axle | N |
| $F_{St}$ | Climbing resistance | N |
| $F_T$ | Traction (motive) force at wheel circumference | N |
| $F_{Th}$ | Traction (motive), rear | N |
| $F_{Tv}$ | Traction (motive), front | N |
| $F_w$ | Soil (ground) resistance | N |
| $F_Z$ | Drawbar pull of tractor | N |
| $F_{Zerf.}$ | Drawbar-pull requirement of implement | N |
| $P_e$ | Net engine power | kW |
| $P_{trans.}$ | Transmission power losses | kW |
| $P_N$ | Rated engine power | kW |
| $P_R$ | Automotive power requirement | kW |
| $P_S$ | Slip power losses | kW |
| $P_{St}$ | Hill-climbing power requirement | kW |
| $P_Z$ | Drawbar power | kW |
| $v$ | Vehicle speed | km/h |
| $v_0$ | Circumferential speed of a driving wheel | km/h |
| $\eta_{trans.}$ | Transmission/gearbox efficiency | – |
| $\eta_L$ | Tractive efficiency at tractor wheels | – |
| $\eta_T$ | Tractive efficiency of a single wheel | – |
| $\eta_Z$ | Tractive efficiency of an agricultural tractor | – |
| $\lambda$ | Engine utilization ratio | – |
| $\varkappa$ | Coefficient of traction force | – |
| $\varrho$ | Coefficient of rolling resistance | – |
| $\sigma$ | Wheel slip | % |

### Applications

Agricultural tractors are employed for field work and for general transport and farmyard duties. Depending upon the type of unit, power from the engine can be transmitted through an auxiliary PTO shaft and hydraulic lines, as well as via the drive wheels. The engine outputs for farm tractors used in the Federal Republic of Germany range up to approximately 250 kW, with weights of over 120 kN.

Higher engine outputs exaggerate the problems associated with supporting the weight at the ground on large-volume tires of adequate capacity, as well as the difficulties encountered in transforming the engine's power into tractive power at acceptable tractor speeds.

### Essential requirements of a tractor

- High drawbar pull, high tractive efficiency.
- The engine must combine high torque increase and low specific fuel consumption with as constant a power characteristic as possible.
- Depending upon application and the distances involved, vehicle speeds (rated speeds) up to 25, 32, 40, 50 km/h, with > 60 km/h for special-purpose tractors; multiple conversion ratios with appropriate gear spacing (especially important up to 12 km/h), suitable for shifting under load if possible.
- Power take-off (PTO) shaft and hydraulic connections for powering auxiliary equipment. Option of installing and/or powering equipment at the front of the tractor.
- Facilities for monitoring and operating auxiliary equipment from the driver's seat, e.g. with hydraulic control levers (P. 1179).
- Clear and logical layout of control levers in ergonomically correct arrangement.
- Measures to protect and preserve ground (wide tires, reduced tire inflation pressure).
- Driver protection against vibration, dust, noise, climatic influences and accident.
- Universal applicability.

### Drawbar pull and drawbar power of a tractor in field work

The effective drawbar pull is essentially determined by the tractor's weight, the type of drive (rear-wheel or 4-wheel drive) and the operating characteristics of its tires. The operational response of the tractor's drive tires is determined by such factors as type of soil and ground conditions (moisture and porosity), tire dimensions, carcass and tread design, and tire pressure. Due to these particular operating characteristics, the farm tractor in field work develops its maximum drawbar pull only when tire slip is high, whereas the maximum drawbar power is achieved at relatively low levels of slip and drawbar pull. With the engine developing 90% of its maximum output, the drawbar pull of an AWD tractor will not exceed 60% of the rated engine power, even under extremely favorable conditions.

The effective engine output is:
$$P_e = P_Z + P_R + P_S + P_{trans.}$$
$$(+ P_{St} \text{ on gradients})$$

The drawbar power is calculated as:
$$P_Z = F_Z \cdot v$$

With rear-wheel drive, the power required to propel the tractor itself is:
$$P_R = F_{Rv} \cdot v + F_{Rh} \cdot v_o$$

The slip power losses are defined as:
$$P_S = F_T \cdot (v_o - v) = F_T \cdot \sigma \cdot v_o$$

The power losses in the transmission unit are determined with the equation:
$$P_{trans.} = P_e \cdot (1 - \eta_{trans.})$$

Efficiency levels:
With rear-wheel drive:
$$\eta_L = \frac{F_{Th} - F_{Rv}}{F_{Th} + F_{Rh}} \cdot (1 - \sigma)$$

With all-wheel drive (AWD):
$$\eta_L = \frac{F_{Th} + F_{Tv}}{F_{Th} + F_{Tv} + F_{Rh} + F_{Rv}} \cdot (1 - \sigma)$$

For single wheel:
$$\eta_T = \frac{F_T}{F_T + F_R} \cdot (1 - \sigma) = \frac{\varkappa}{\varkappa + \varrho} (1 - \sigma)$$

For the tractor:
$$\eta_Z = \eta_{trans.} \cdot \eta_L = P_Z/P_e$$

The coefficients are calculated as follows:
$$\varkappa = F_T/F$$
$$\varrho = F_R/F$$
$$\lambda = P_e/P_N$$
$$\sigma = (v_o - v)/v_o$$

## Drawbar-pull requirements of auxiliary equipment and trailers

At a constant speed on a flat surface, the drawbar-pull requirement depends either on the rolling resistance $F_R$ (e.g. farm equipment) or on soil resistance $F_W$ (e.g. the force needed to move a tool through the soil) or on both at the same time (e.g. beet lifter). Rolling resistance is calcu-

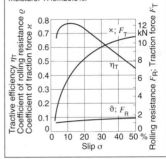

***Operating characteristics of a tractor drive wheel***
Tire: 6.9/14-30 AS; Wheel load: 1582 daN; Tire pressure 1.1 bar; Ground: loamy clay, wheat stubble, treated with disk harrow, moisture: 17.3...20.8%.

lated using the coefficient of rolling resistance and the sum of the weights supported by the wheels, giving:
$$F_R = \varrho \cdot \Sigma F$$

For pneumatic tires on asphalt: $\varrho \leq 0.03$
For pneumatic tires on field:
$$\varrho = 0.04...0.35$$

Soil resistance is determined by the type and condition of the soil, number and type of implements, working depth and vehicle speed. General reference figures for plowing would be a specific ground resistance of 400...600 N/dm² on moderate soils, with 600...1,000 N/dm² on hard (clay) soils. On moderate ground at speeds of between 6 and 9 km/h, the soil resistance per meter of working width of a cultivator is 5,500...7,800 N for a working depth of 13...15 cm, and 11,000...12,500 N for a depth of 22...25 cm.

**Table 1. Examples of the power required by PTO-driven agricultural equipment working a 1 meter swath on moderate ground.**

| Implement | Required engine power kW | Working depth cm | Vehicle speed km/h |
|---|---|---|---|
| Tiller on loose soil | 10.5...25 | 8 | 3...7 |
| Vibrating harrow | 8...22 | 8 | 3.5...6.5 |
| Circular harrow | 0...15 | 8 | 3.5...6.5 |

# Environmental stresses on automotive equipment

## Climatic factors

Climatic stress factors acting upon automotive components encompass the effects of the natural environment, i.e. the macroclimate, and influences stemming from the vehicle itself (such as fuel vapor) and the microclimate within a component (such as the heat generated in electrical devices).

### Temperature and temperature variations
The range extends from extremely low temperatures (storage, transport) all the way to the high temperatures associated with operation of the internal-combustion engine.

### Atmospheric humidity and variations
This range embraces everything from arid desert climates to tropical environments, and can even extend beyond these under certain conditions (as occur for instance when water is sprayed against a hot engine block). Humid heat (high temperatures combined with high atmospheric humidity) is especially demanding. Alternating humidity results in surface condensation, which causes atmospheric corrosion.

### Corrosive atmospheres
Salt spray encountered when the vehicle is operated on salt-treated roads and in coastal areas promotes electrochemical and atmospheric corrosion. Industrial atmospheres in concentrated manufacturing regions lead to acid corrosion on metallic surfaces. When they are present in sufficient concentrations, today's increasing amounts of atmospheric pollutants ($SO_2$, $H_2S$, $Cl_2$ and $NO_x$) promote the formation of contaminant layers on contact surfaces, with the result that resistance increases.

### Water
Stresses of varying intensities result from rain, spray, splash, and hose water as encountered when driving in rain, during car and engine washes, and – in exceptional cases – during submersion.

### Aggressive chemical fluids
The product in question must be able to resist the chemical fluids encountered in the course of normal operation and maintenance at its particular operating location. Within the engine compartment, such chemicals include fuel (and fuel vapor), engine oil and engine detergents. Certain components are confronted by additional substances, for example, brake-system components and the brake fluid used to operate them.

### Sand and dust
Malfunctions result from the friction due to sand and dust on adjacent moving surfaces. In addition, under the influence of moisture, certain types of dust layers can cause current tracking in electrical circuits.

### Solar radiation
The sun's rays cause plastics and elastomers to age (a factor to be taken into account in the design of external, exposed components).

### Atmospheric pressure
Fluctuations in atmospheric pressure affect the operation and reliability of differential-pressure components, such as diaphragms, etc.

## Laboratory simulation of stress

Climatic and environmental conditions are simulated both according to standardized test procedures (DIN IEC 68 – Environmental testing procedures for electronic components and equipment) and in special field-testing programs designed specifically for individual cases. The goal is to achieve the greatest possible approximation of the stresses encountered in actual practice ("test tailoring").

### Temperature, temperature variation and atmospheric humidity
Simulation is carried out in temperature and climate chambers as well as in climate-controlled rooms which afford access to test personnel.

The dry heat test allows evaluation of a component's suitability for storage and operation at high temperatures. Testing is not restricted to ascertaining the effects of heat upon operation; it also monitors influences on material characteristics. Depending upon the particular application (component mounted on body, engine, or exhaust system), the degree of heat can cover an extremely wide range. The stress time can be up to several hundred hours.

Testing the product's operation under <u>cold conditions</u> devotes particular attention to starting behavior and changes in materials characteristics at low temperatures. The testing range extends down to – 40 °C for operation, and to – 55 °C for storage. At less than 100 h, the actual testing times are shorter than those employed for dry heat.

A further test simulates <u>temperature fluctuation</u> between the extremes encountered in actual operation; the temperature gradient and the dwell time also contribute to determining the degree of stress. The dwell time must be at least long enough to ensure that the sample achieves thermal equilibrium. The different levels of thermal expansion mean that the temperature variations induce both material aging and mechanical stresses within the component. The selection of appropriate test parameters makes it possible to achieve substantial time-compression factors.

<u>Atmospheric humidity</u> testing under steady-state damp heat (e.g. + 40 °C/93% relative humidity) is employed in the evaluation of a product's suitability for operation and storage at relatively high humidity levels (tropical climates).

### Corrosive atmospheres

<u>Salt fog</u> is produced by diffusing a 5% NaCl solution at a room temperature of 35°C. Depending upon the intended installation location, the test times can extend to several hundred hours. <u>Cyclic salt fog</u> is a combination test comprising the following: "salt fog, dry heat and damp heat". It yields a closer correlation with field results. The <u>industrial-climate</u> test comprises up to 6 cyclical alternations between an 8-hour dwell period at 40 °C/100% relative humidity at 0.67% $SO_2$ and 16 hours at room temperature. The <u>pollutant</u> test with $SO_2$, $H_2S$, $NO_x$ and $Cl_2$ is performed either for single gases or as a multisubstance test. Testing is carried out at 25 °C/75% relative humidity with concentrations in the ppm and ppb ranges, and lasts up to 21 days.

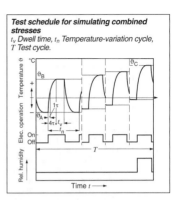

*Test schedule for simulating combined stresses*
$t_v$ Dwell time, $t_n$ Temperature-variation cycle, $T$ Test cycle.

### Water spray

A pivoting sprayer is used to simulate water spray. Water pressure, spray angle and the pivot angle can all be adjusted for different stress severity levels. The water-spray test employs high-pressure jets and standard steam-cleaners of the type used for cleaning engines.

### Aggressive chemical fluids

The sample is wetted with the fluid in question for a defined period. This is followed by 24-hour storage at elevated temperature. This test can be repeated numerous times, according to the particular application.

### Sand and dust

Dust simulation is carried using a device which maintains a dust density of 5 g per m³ in moving air. A mixture of lime and fly ash is one of the substances employed.

### Combined tests

Combined temperature, temperature variation and humidity tests on an operating electrical product ensure a high degree of convergence with the aging effects to be anticipated under extreme operating conditions. The advantage of this test is its high level of conformity with actual practice. The disadvantage is the test duration, which is generally well in excess of that required for the corresponding individual investigations.

# Internal-combustion engines

## Operating concepts and classifications

The internal-combustion (IC) engine is the most frequently employed power source for motor vehicles. Internal-combustion engines generate power by converting chemical energy bound in the fuel into heat, and the heat thus produced into mechanical work. The conversion of chemical energy into heat is accomplished through combustion, while the subsequent conversion of this thermal energy into mechanical work is performed by allowing the heat energy to increase the pressure within a medium which then performs work as it expands.

Liquids, which supply an increase in working pressure via a phase transformation (vaporization), or gases, whose working pressure can be increased through compression, are used as working media.

The fuels – largely hydrocarbons – require oxygen in order to burn; the required oxygen is usually supplied as a constituent of the intake air. If fuel combustion occurs in the cylinder itself, the process is called internal combustion. Here the combustion gas itself is used as the working medium. If combustion takes place outside of the cylinder, the process is called external combustion.

Continuous mechanical work is possible only in a cyclic process (piston engine) or a continuous process (gas turbine) of heat absorption, expansion (production of work) and return of the working medium to its initial condition (combustion cycle).

If the working medium is altered if it absorbs heat, e.g. when a portion of its constituents serve as an oxidant, restoration of its initial condition is possible only through replacement.

This is called an open cycle, and is characterized by cyclic gas exchange (expulsion of the combustion gases and induction of the fresh charge). Internal combustion therefore always requires an open cycle.

In external combustion, the actual working medium remains chemically unchanged, and can thus be returned to its initial condition by suitable measures (cooling, condensation). This enables the use of a closed process.

**Table 1. Classification of the internal-combustion engine**

| Type of process | Open process | | | Closed process | | |
|---|---|---|---|---|---|---|
| | Internal combustion | | | External combustion | | |
| | Combustion gas △ working medium | | | Combustion gas ≠ working medium | | |
| | | | | Phase transformation in working medium | | |
| | | | | No | | Yes |
| Type of combustion | Cyclic combustion | | | Continuous combustion | | |
| Type of ignition | Auto-ignition | Externally supplied ignition | | | | |
| Type of machine — Engine △ machine enclosing a working chamber | Diesel | Hybrid | Spark ignition | Rohs | Stirling | Steam |
| Type of machine — Turbine △ gas turbine | – | – | – | Gas | Hot steam | Steam |
| Type of mixture | Heterogeneous (in the combustion chamber) | Homogenous | Heterogeneous (in a continuous flame) | | | |

In addition to the main process characteristics (open/closed) and the type of combustion (cyclic/continuous), the various combustion processes for internal-combustion engines can also be defined according to their air/fuel mixture formation and ignition arrangements.

In external air/fuel mixture formation, the mixture is formed <u>outside of the combustion chamber</u>. In this type of mixture formation, a largely homogenous air/fuel mixture is present when combustion is initiated, so it is also referred to as homogenous mixture formation.

In <u>internal air/fuel mixture formation</u>, the fuel is introduced directly into the combustion chamber. The later the internal mixture formation occurs, the more heterogeneous the air/fuel mixture will be at the time combustion is initiated. Internal mixture formation is therefore also called heterogeneous mixture formation. External ignition designs rely on an electric spark or a glow plug to initiate <u>combustion</u>. In <u>autoignition</u>, the mixture ignites as it warms to or beyond its ignition temperature during compression, or when fuel is injected into air whose boundary conditions permit evaporation and ignition.

## Cycles

### The $p$-$V$ diagram

A basic precondition for continuous conversion of thermal energy into kinetic energy is a modification in the condition of the working medium. It is also desirable that as much of the working medium as possible be returned to its initial condition.

For technical applications, the focus can rest on changes in pressure and the corresponding volumetric variations which can be plotted on a pressure vs. volume work diagram, or $p$-$V$ diagram for short.

As the figure shows, the addition of heat and the change in condition of the working medium that accompany the progress of the process in the 1→2 phase must consume less energy than that required for the 2→1 phase. Once this condition is satisfied, the result is an area corresponding to the process work potential: $L = \oint V \mathrm{d}p$.

### The $T$-$S$ diagram

The temperature entropy, or $T$-$S$ diagram, is used to provide a similar graphic representation of the bidirectional thermal energy transfers in this cyclic process.

In the $T$-$S$ diagram, heat quantities can be represented as areas in the same manner that work is represented as an area in the $p$-$V$ diagram. With known specific working-medium heats, the $T$-$S$ diagram can be transformed into the H-$S$ diagram, known as the enthalpy-entropy diagram, in accordance with the equation $\mathrm{d}H = c_p \cdot \mathrm{d}T$.

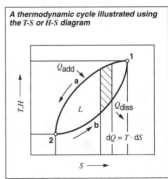

**A thermodynamic cycle illustrated using the $p$-$V$ diagram**

**A thermodynamic cycle illustrated using the $T$-$S$ or H-$S$ diagram**

The cycle illustrated in the $p$-$V$ diagram on P. 449 shows the amount of heat added along "a":

$$Q_{add} = \int_2^1 T_a \, dS$$

and the amount of heat dissipated along "b":

$$Q_{diss} = \int_2^1 T_b \, dS, \text{ where}$$

$$Q_{add} - Q_{diss} = L = \oint V dp$$

(difference between the amount of heat supplied and the amount of heat discharged) which corresponds to the available amount of mechanical work. The diagram also shows that a thermal efficiency $\eta_{th} = (Q_{add} - Q_{diss})/Q_{add}$ can be defined based on the equality of mechanical work and the difference between the heat quantities. It also illustrates the theoretical cycle providing the maximum amount of technical work, as found in the area between two specified temperatures for the working medium (Efficiency definition P. 453).

---

[1] Isothermal change in condition: temperature does not change.
[2] Isentropic change in condition: adiabatic (heat is neither added nor dissipated) and frictionless (reversible).
[3] Isochoric change in condition: volume does not change; see P. 451.

## The Carnot cycle

This cycle, described in 1824 by Carnot, consists of two isothermal[1] and two isentropic[2]) changes in condition, which yield the maximum area in the $T$-$S$ diagram between $T_{max}$ and $T_{min}$. As the Carnot cycle represents maximum process efficiency between the defined temperature limits, it is the theoretical optimum for converting heat into work:

$$\eta_{thCarnot} = (T_{max} - T_{min})/T_{max}$$

## Real combustion processes

Internal-combustion engines operate according to different cycles, however, because isothermal compression, i.e. a pressure increase in the working medium without an increase in temperature, and isothermal expansion are not technically feasible.

Theoretical treatment today involves the following ideal combustion cycles:
– the constant-volume cycle for all piston engines with periodic combustion and generation of work, and
– the constant-pressure cycle for all turbine engines with continuous combustion and generation of work

Both cycles will be dealt with in more detail in the discussion of the corresponding machines.

---

**The Carnot cycle in the $p$-$V$ and $T$-$S$ diagrams**

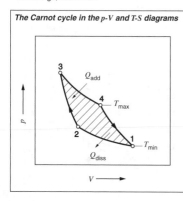
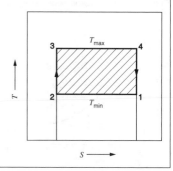

# Reciprocating-piston engines with internal combustion

## Operating concept

All reciprocating-piston engines operate by compressing air or an air/fuel mixture in the working cylinder prior to igniting the mixture, or by injecting fuel into the hot compressed air to initiate combustion. The crankshaft assembly converts the work generated in this process into torque available at the end of the crankshaft.

The $p$-$V$ diagram reflects the actual power-generation process in the engine as a function of piston travel. It shows the mean effective pressures $p_{mi}$ within the cylinder during a complete working cycle. Easier to produce are other diagrams such as the pressure vs. time $(p$-$t)$ and the pressure vs. crankshaft angle $(p$-$\alpha)$ diagrams. The surfaces defined in these two diagrams do not directly indicate the amount of work generated, but they do provide a clear picture of essential data such as ignition point and peak injection pressure.

The product of the mean effective pressure in the cylinder and the piston displacement yields the piston work, and the number of working cycles per unit of time indicates the piston power or the internal power (power index) for the engine. Here it will be noted that the power generated

by a reciprocating-piston internal-combustion engine increases as engine speed rises (see equations on P. 498 to P. 505).

### Ideal combustion cycle for piston engines with internal combustion

For reciprocating-piston engines with internal combustion, the ideal thermodynamic combustion process is the "constant-volume process" (see figure on P. 452). This process consists of isentropic[2] (see footnote on P. 450) compression (1–2), isochoric[3] heat supply (2–3, isentropic expansion (3–4) and isochoric reversion of the ideal working gas to its initial condition (4–1). This cycle is only possible if the following conditions are met:

– No heat or gas losses, no residual exhaust gas
– Ideal gas with constant specific heats $c_p$, $c_v$, and $\varkappa = c_p/c_v = 1.4$
– Infinitely rapid heat supply and discharge
– No flow losses

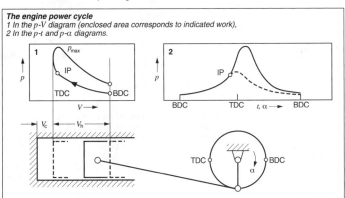

*The engine power cycle*
*1 In the $p$-$V$ diagram (enclosed area corresponds to indicated work),*
*2 In the $p$-$t$ and $p$-$\alpha$ diagrams.*

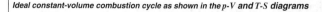

*Ideal constant-volume combustion cycle as shown in the p-V and T-S diagrams*

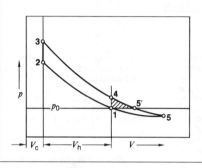
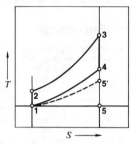

As the crankshaft assembly restricts expansion to finite levels, the 4–5–1 surface in the diagrams is not directly available for use. Section 4–5′–1, lying above the atmospheric pressure line, becomes available when an exhaust-gas turbine is connected downstream.

The efficiency of the ideal constant-volume combustion cycle is calculated in the same manner as all thermal efficiencies:

$$\eta_{th} = \eta_v = (Q_{add} - Q_{diss})/Q_{add}$$

where $Q_{add} = Q_{23} = m \cdot c_v \cdot (T_3 - T_2)$ and $Q_{diss} = Q_{41} = m \cdot c_v \cdot (T_4 - T_1)$.

Using the same $\varkappa$ for compression and expansion:

$$\eta_{th} = 1 - Q_{diss}/Q_{add} = 1 - \frac{T_4 - T_1}{T_3 - T_2} = 1 - T_1/T_2$$

Where $T_1/T_2 = \varepsilon^{\varkappa-1}$ then

$$\eta_{th} = 1 - \varepsilon^{1-\varkappa},$$

where the compression ratio is defined as $\varepsilon = (V_c + V_h)/V_c$ with a piston displacement of $V_h$ and a compression volume of $V_c$.

Real internal-combustion engines do not operate according to ideal cycles, but rather with real gas, and are therefore subject to fluid, thermodynamic and mechanical losses.

**Efficiency sequence** (DIN 1940)

The overall efficiency $\eta_e$ includes the sum of all losses, and can thus be defined as the ratio of effective mechanical work to the mechanical work equivalent of the supplied fuel:

$$\eta_e = W_e/W_B \text{ where}$$

$W_e$ is the effective work available at the clutch, and

$W_B$ is the work equivalent of the supplied fuel.

In order to better distinguish among the different losses, a further distinction can be made:

the fuel conversion factor $\eta_B$ provides an index of combustion quality:

$$\eta_B = (W_B - W_{Bo})/W_B \text{ where}$$

$W_B$ is the work equivalent of the supplied fuel,

$W_{Bo}$ is the work equivalent of the unburned fuel.

There are no operating conditions in which complete combustion takes place. A portion of the supplied fuel does not burn (hydrocarbon constituents in the exhaust gas), or fails to combust completely (CO in exhaust).

$\eta_B$ is often defined as "1" for small diesel engines at operating temperature and for comparisons.

**Table 2. Graphic representations and definitions of the individual and overall efficiencies of the reciprocating-piston engine.**

| Pressure vs. volume diagram | Designation | Conditions | Definition | Efficiencies | | |
|---|---|---|---|---|---|---|
| | Theoretical reference constant-volume cycle | Ideal gas, constant specific heat, infinitely rapid heat addition and -dissipation, etc. | $\eta_{th} = 1 - \varepsilon^{1-\varkappa}$ Theoretical or thermal efficiency | $\eta_{th}$ | | |
| | Real high pressure working cycle | Wall heat losses, real gas, finitely rapid head addition and dissipation, variable specific heat | $\eta_{gHD}$ Efficiency factor of the high-pressure cycle | $\eta_g$ | $\eta_i$ | $\eta_e$ |
| | Real charge cycle (4-stroke) | Flow losses, heating of the mixture or the air, etc. | $\eta_{gLW}$ Charge exchange efficiency | | | |
| Mechanical losses | Losses due to friction, cooling, auxiliary units | Real engine | $\eta_m$ | $\eta_m$ | $\eta_m$ | |

The <u>efficiency index</u> $\eta_i$ is the ratio of indicated high-pressure work to the calorific content of the supplied fuel $\eta_i = W_i/W_B$.

The <u>efficiency of cycle factor</u> $\eta_g$ includes all internal losses occurring in both high-pressure and low-pressure processes. These stem from:
– Real working gas
– Residual exhaust gas
– Wall heat losses
– Gas losses, and
– Charge cycle losses

For this reason, $\eta_g$ is more appropriately broken down into $\eta_{gHD}$ for the high-pressure portion and $\eta_{gLW}$ for gas-exchange processes. The efficiency of the cycle factor therefore indicates how closely engine performance approaches the theoretical ideal combustion cycle:

$$\eta_g = \eta_{gHD} \cdot \eta_{gLW} = W_i/W_{th} \text{ where}$$

$W_i$ is the indicated work, and

$W_{th}$ is the work generated in the ideal combustion cycle.

The <u>mechanical efficiency</u> defines the relationship between the effective work available at the clutch $W_e$ and the indicated work $W_i$. The difference between the indicated work and the effective available work is attributed to the mechanical losses, comprising in particular the friction losses in the powertrain and gas-exchange control systems, drive losses in the oil, water and fuel-supply pumps as well as in the alternator.

$$\eta_m = W_e/W_i \text{ where}$$

$W_e$ is the effective work available at the clutch, and

$W_i$ is the work index

The efficiency chain therefore appears as follows:

$$\eta_e = \eta_{th} \cdot \eta_{gHD} \cdot \eta_{gLW} \cdot \eta_m$$

(See Table 2.)

## Engine types

### Single-piston power unit
The working chamber is formed by the cylinder head, cylinder liner, and piston.

#### In-line engine (1)
The cylinders are arranged consecutively in a single plane.

#### V-engine (2)
The cylinders are arranged in two planes in a V configuration.

#### Radial engine (3)
The cylinders are arranged radially in one or more planes.

#### Opposed-cylinder (boxer) engine (4)
The cylinders are horizontally opposed.

### Multi-piston power unit
More than one (usually two) working pistons share a common combustion chamber.

#### U-engine (5)
The pistons move in the same direction.

#### Opposed-piston engine (6)
The pistons move in opposite directions.

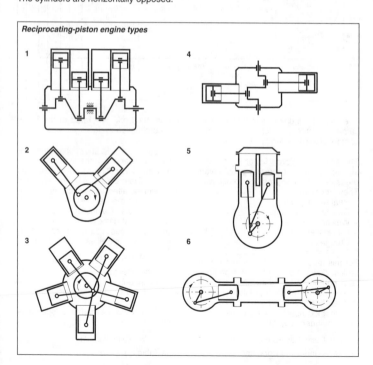

*Reciprocating-piston engine types*

## Definitions

### Direction of rotation (DIN 73 021) [1]
Clockwise rotation: as viewed looking at the end of the engine opposite the power-output end. Abbreviation: cw.

Counterclockwise rotation: as viewed looking at the end of the engine opposite the power-output end. Abbreviation: ccw.

### Numbering the cylinders (DIN 73 021) [1]
The cylinders are numbered consecutively 1, 2, 3, etc. in the order in which they would be intersected by an imaginary reference plane, as viewed looking at the end of the engine opposite the power-output end.

This plane is located horizontally to the left when numbering begins; the numerical assignments then proceed clockwise about the longitudinal axis of the engine (see figures below). If there is more than one cylinder in a reference plane, the cylinder nearest the observer is assigned the number 1, with consecutive numbers being assigned to the following cylinders. Cylinder 1 is to be identified by the number 1.

### Firing sequence
The firing sequence is the sequence in which combustion is initiated in the cylinders. Engine design configuration, uniformity in ignition intervals, ease of crankshaft manufacture, optimal crankshaft load patterns, etc. all play a role in defining the firing sequence.

| Design | | Number of cylinders | Normal firing sequence (examples) |
|---|---|---|---|
| | Power output | 4<br>5<br>6<br><br><br><br>8 | 1 3 4 2 or 1 2 4 3<br>1 2 4 5 3<br>1 5 3 6 2 4 or<br>1 2 4 6 5 3 or<br>1 4 2 6 3 5 or<br>1 4 5 6 3 2<br>1 6 2 5 8 3 7 4 or<br>1 3 6 8 4 2 7 5 or<br>1 4 7 3 8 5 2 6 or<br>1 3 2 5 8 6 7 4 |
| | Power output | 4<br>6<br><br>8 | 1 3 2 4<br>1 2 5 6 4 3 or<br>1 4 5 6 2 3<br>1 6 3 5 4 7 2 8 or<br>1 5 4 8 6 3 7 2 or<br>1 8 3 6 4 5 2 7 |
| | Power output | 4 | 1 4 3 2 |

## Crankshaft-assembly operation and dynamic properties

The purpose of the piston, connecting rod and crankshaft assembly in the recipro-cating-piston engine is to transform the gas forces generated during combustion within the working cylinder into a piston stroke, which the crankshaft then con-verts into useful torque available at the power-output end of the engine. The cyclic principle of operation leads to un-equal gas forces, and the acceleration and deceleration of the reciprocating power-transfer components generate in-ertial forces. It is usual to distinguish be-tween internal and external effects of the gas-pressure and inertial forces.

The external effects, consisting of free forces or moments, impart movement to the engine. This is then transmitted to the engine supports in the form of vibration.

In this context, the <u>smooth running</u> of an engine is understood to mean freedom from low-frequency vibration, while <u>quiet running</u> means freedom from high-frequency, audible vibration.

The internal forces induce periodically variable loads in the engine block, piston, connecting rod, crankshaft assembly and force-transfer components. These factors must be included in calculations for defin-ing their dimensions and fatigue limit.

### Crankshaft assembly and gas force

The crankshaft assembly of a single-cylinder powerplant comprises the piston, connecting rod (conrod), and crankshaft. These components react to gas forces by generating mass inertial forces of their own.

The gas force $F_G$ which acts on the piston can be subdivided into the side forces $F_N$ applied by the piston to the cylinder wall and supported by it, and the connecting-rod force $F_S$. The connecting-rod force, in turn, causes the tangential force $F_T$ to be applied at the crankshaft journal offset. This force together with the crank radius generates the shaft torque and the radial force $F_R$.

These forces can be calculated as a function of the gas force using the crank-shaft angle $\alpha$, the pivoting angle of connecting rod $\beta$, and the stroke/connect-ing rod ratio $\lambda$:

Connecting-rod force: $F_S = F_G/\cos \beta$
Piston side force: $F_N = F_G \cdot \tan \beta$
Radial force: $F_R = F_G \cdot \cos (\alpha + \beta)/\cos \beta$
Tangential force: $F_T = F_G \cdot \sin (\alpha + \beta)/\cos \beta$
where $\lambda = r/l$; $\sin \beta = \lambda \cdot \sin \alpha$;

$$\cos \beta = \sqrt{1 - \lambda^2 \cdot \sin^2 \alpha}$$

All of these relationships can be repre-sented in the form of a Fourier series, which can be useful in vibration calculations.

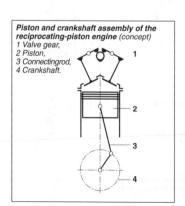

*Piston and crankshaft assembly of the reciprocating-piston engine* (concept)
1 Valve gear,
2 Piston,
3 Connectingrod,
4 Crankshaft.

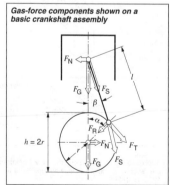

*Gas-force components shown on a basic crankshaft assembly*

**Inertial forces and -moments of inertia**

The mass inertial properties of the piston, connecting rod and crankshaft assembly are a composite of the forces of the rotating masses of the crankshaft about their axis ($x$-axis) and the reciprocating masses in the cylinder direction ($z$-axis for in-line engines). With multiple-cylinder machines, free moments of inertia occur owing to different points of application for gas and inertial forces. The inertial properties of a single-cylinder engine can be determined using the piston mass $m_K$ (exclusively oscillating mass), the crankshaft mass $m_W$ (exclusively rotating mass) and the corresponding connecting-rod mass components (usually assumed to consist of oscillating and rotating rod masses amounting to $1/3$ and $2/3$ of the total mass, respectively):

Oscillating mass

$$m_o = m_{Pl}/3 + m_K$$

Rotating mass

$$m_r = 2\,m_{Pl}/3 + m_W$$

The rotating inertial force acting on the crankshaft is as follows:

$$F_r = m_r \cdot r \cdot \omega^2$$

Oscillating inertial force:

$$F_o = m_o \cdot r \cdot \omega^2 \cdot (\underbrace{\cos\alpha}_{\text{1st Order}} + \underbrace{\lambda \cdot \cos2\alpha}_{\text{2nd Order}} + ...)$$

The following approximations also apply:

$$F_y = r \cdot \omega^2 \cdot m_r \cdot \sin\alpha$$
$$F_z = r \cdot \omega^2 \cdot [m_r \cdot \cos\alpha +$$
$$m_o \cdot (\cos\alpha + \lambda \cdot \cos2\alpha)]$$

where $\lambda = r/l$

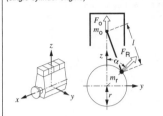

*Reference coordinates and inertial forces* (single-cylinder engine)

The inertial-force components are designated as inertial forces of the 1st, 2nd or 4th order, depending upon their rotational frequencies relative to engine speed.

In general, only the 1st- and 2nd-order components are significant. Higher orders can be disregarded.

In the case of multiple-cylinder engines, free moments of inertia are present when all of the complete crankshaft assembly's inertial forces combine to produce a force couple at the crankshaft. The crankshaft assembly must therefore be regarded as a three-dimensional configuration when determining the free moments of inertia, while the inertial forces can be determined using a two-dimensional system.

*Moments of inertia of a crankshaft with three throws* (example)

Practical configuration

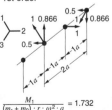

Moments of inertia, 1st order

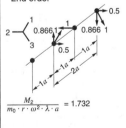

Moments of inertia, 2nd order

$$\frac{M_1}{(m_r + m_o) \cdot r \cdot \omega^2 \cdot a} = 1.732$$

$$\vec{M}\updownarrow = 0.866 \cdot (-1 + 3) = 1.732$$

$$\overleftrightarrow{M} = 0.5 \cdot 1 - 1 \cdot 2 + 0.5 \cdot 3 = 0$$

$$\frac{M_2}{m_o \cdot r \cdot \omega^2 \cdot \lambda \cdot a} = 1.732$$

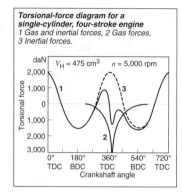

*Torsional-force diagram for a single-cylinder, four-stroke engine*
1 Gas and inertial forces, 2 Gas forces, 3 Inertial forces.

tion. It is one of the most important characteristic curves in assessing dynamic engine behavior.

With multiple-cylinder engines, the tangential-pressure curves for the individual cylinders are superimposed with a phase shift dependent on the number of cylinders, their configuration, crankshaft design and the firing sequence. The resulting composite curve is characteristic for the engine design, and covers a full working cycle (i.e. 2 crankshaft rotations for 4-stroke engines). It is also called a torsional-force diagram.

Harmonic analysis can be employed to replace the torsional-force diagram with a series of sinusoidal oscillations featuring whole-number multiples of the basic frequencies, and to obtain the "torsional harmonics". When defined according to engine speed, these multiples are also called orders. When applied to a four-stroke engine, this procedure generates half orders, e.g. the 0.5th order.

The cyclical fluctuations in torsional force encountered in all reciprocating-piston engines lead to variations in the crankshaft's rotation speed, the so-called coefficient of cyclic variation.

$$\delta_s = (\omega_{max} - \omega_{min})/\omega_{min},$$

An energy storage device (the flywheel) provides adequate compensation for these variations in rotation rate in normal applications.

## Torsional-force diagram for the reciprocating-piston engine

If the periodic gas force acting on the piston and the periodic mass inertial forces acting on the piston, connecting rod and crankshaft assembly are grouped together, they generate a sum of tangential force components at the crankshaft journal. When multiplied by the crank radius, this produces a periodically variable torque value. If this torque value is referred to the piston surface and the crank radius, the result is a value valid for any engine size: tangential pressure. The torsional-force diagram shows the curve for this pressure as a function of crankshaft position. It is one of the most important charac-

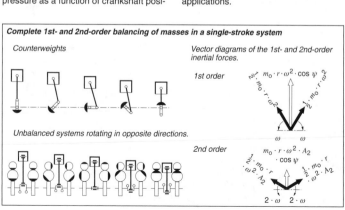

*Complete 1st- and 2nd-order balancing of masses in a single-stroke system*

Counterweights

Unbalanced systems rotating in opposite directions.

Vector diagrams of the 1st- and 2nd-order inertial forces.

1st order

$$m_o \cdot r \cdot \omega^2 \cdot \cos \psi$$

2nd order

$$m_o \cdot r \cdot \omega^2 \cdot A_2$$
$$\cdot \cos \psi$$

# Balancing of masses in the reciprocating-piston engine

Mass balancing encompasses a wide array of measures employed to obtain partial or complete compensation for the inertial forces and moments of inertia emanating from the crankshaft assembly. All masses are externally balanced when no free inertial forces or moments of inertia are transmitted through the block to the outside. However, the remaining internal forces and moments subject the engine mounts and block to various loads as well as deformative and vibratory stresses. The basic loads imposed by gas-based and inertial forces are shown in Table 3.

## Balancing of inertial forces in the single-stroke powerplant

The simplest way to balance rotating masses is to use counterweights to generate an equal force to oppose the centrifugal force. Oscillating masses generate periodic forces. The 1st-order forces are propagated at crankshaft speed, while the periodicity of the 2nd-order forces is twice the crankshaft's rotational

**Table 3. Forces and moments applied to the piston, connecting rod and crankshaft assembly**

| Forces and moments at the engine | | | | |
|---|---|---|---|---|
| Designation | Oscillating torque, transverse tilting moment, reaction torque | Free inertial forces | Free inertial moment, longitudinal tilting moment about the $y$-axis (transverse axis) ("pitching" moment) about the $z$-axis (vertical axis) ("rolling" moment) | Internal bending moment (flex forces) |
| Cause | Tangential gas forces as well as tangential inertial forces for the ordinals 1, 2, 3 and 4 | Unbalanced oscillating inertial forces 1st order in 1- and 2-cylinders; 2nd order in 1-, 2-, 4-cylinders | Unbalanced oscillating inertial forces as a composite of 1st- and 2nd-order forces | Rotating and oscillating inertial forces |
| Design factors | Number of cylinders, ignition intervals, displacement, $p_i$, $\varepsilon$, $p_z$, $m_0$, $r$, $\omega$, $\lambda$ | Number of cylinders, crank configuration $m_0$, $r$, $\omega$, $\lambda$ | Number of cylinders, crank configuration, cylinder spacing, counter-weight size influences inertial torque components about the $y$- and $z$-axes $m_0$, $r$, $\omega$, $\lambda$, $a$ | Number of throws, crank configuration, engine length, engine block rigidity |
| Remedy | Can only be compensated for in exceptional cases | Free mass effects can be eliminated with rotating balancing systems, however this process is complex and therefore rare; crank sequences with limited or no mass effects are preferable | | Counterweights, rigid engine block |
| | Shielding of the environment through flexible engine mounts (in particular for orders ≥ 2) | | | |

**Table 4.**
**Residual 1st-order inertial forces with differing balancing rates**

| | | Balancing rate | | |
|---|---|---|---|---|
| | | 0% | 50% | 100% |
| Size of counter-weight | $m_G \triangleq$ | $m_r$ | $m_r + 0.5\, m_0$ | $m_r + m_0$ |
| Residual inertial force ($z$) 1st order | $F_{1z} =$ | $m_0 \cdot r \cdot \omega^2$ | $0.5 \cdot m_0 \cdot r \cdot \omega^2$ | 0 |
| Residual inertial force ($y$) 1st order | $F_{1y} =$ | 0 | $0.5 \cdot m_0 \cdot r \cdot \omega^2$ | $m_0 \cdot r \cdot \omega^2$ |

rate. Compensation for these forces is available in the form of a counterweight balance system designed for opposed rotation at a rate equal to or twice that of the crankshaft. The balance forces' magnitudes must equal those of the rotating inertial-force vectors while acting in the opposite direction.

**Balancing rate**
The forces exerted by the counterweights used to balance the rotating masses can be increased by a certain percentage of the oscillating mass in order to reduce the oscillating forces acting in the direction of the cylinders ($z$). The percentage of this inertial force which is counteracted then appears in the $y$-axis. The ratio of the compensated inertial-force component in

**Table 5.**
**Star diagram of the 1st and 2nd orders for three- to six-cylinder, in-line engines**

| | 3-cylinder | 4-cylinder | 5-cylinder | 6-cylinder |
|---|---|---|---|---|
| Crank sequence | | | | |
| Star diagram 1st order | | | | |
| Star diagram 2nd order | | | | |

the $z$-axis relative to the initial value for the 1st-order inertial force is termed the balancing rate (Table 4).

## Balancing of inertial forces in the multiple-cylinder engine

In multiple-cylinder engines, the mutual counteractions of the various components in the crankshaft assembly are one of the essential factors determining the selection of the crankshaft's configuration, and with it the design of the engine itself. The inertial forces are balanced if the common center of gravity for all moving crankshaft-assembly components lies at the crankshaft's midpoint, i.e. if the crankshaft is symmetrical (as viewed from the front). The crankshaft's symmetry level can be defined using geometrical representations of 1st- and 2nd-order forces (star diagrams). The 2nd-order star diagram for the four-cylinder in-line engine is asymmetrical, meaning that this order is characterized by substantial free inertial forces. These forces can be balanced using two countershafts rotating in opposite directions at double the rate of the crankshaft (Lanchester system).

## Balancing of inertial and gas forces

The tangential gas forces produce yet another periodic torque. This can be detected as reaction torque in the engine block. The composite forces generated in a four-cylinder in-line engine include free inertial forces of the 2nd order as well as oscillating torque forces from the 2nd-order inertial and gas forces. Balancing of 2nd-order forces, along with a reduction in the intensity of the 2nd-order force transitions, is available from two offset countershafts.

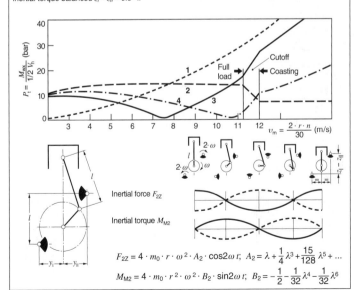

*Balancing 2nd-order inertial and oscillating forces in a four-cylinder, in-line engine with two offset countershafts*
*1 Inertial torque only, 2 Gas torque only or complete balancing of inertial torque $z_I - z_{II} = -2\,B_2/A_2 \cdot r$, 3 Gas and inertial torque without force compensation, 4 Gas and inertial torque with half of the inertial torque balanced $z_I - z_{II} \approx 0.5 \cdot l$.*

Inertial force $F_{2Z}$

Inertial torque $M_{M2}$

$$F_{2Z} = 4 \cdot m_0 \cdot r \cdot \omega^2 \cdot A_2 \cdot \cos 2\omega\,t; \quad A_2 = \lambda + \frac{1}{4}\lambda^3 + \frac{15}{128}\lambda^5 + \dots$$

$$M_{M2} = 4 \cdot m_0 \cdot r^2 \cdot \omega^2 \cdot B_2 \cdot \sin 2\omega\,t; \quad B_2 = -\frac{1}{2} - \frac{1}{32}\lambda^4 - \frac{1}{32}\lambda^6$$

## Table 6. Free forces and moments of the 1st and 2nd order, and ignition intervals of the most common engine designs

$$F_r = m_r \cdot r \cdot \omega^2 \qquad F_1 = m_0 \cdot r \cdot \omega^2 \cdot \cos\alpha \qquad F_2 = m_0 \cdot r \cdot \omega^2 \cdot \lambda \cdot \cos 2\alpha$$

| Cylinder arrangement | Free forces of 1st order[1] | Free forces of 2nd order | Free moments of 1st order[1] | Free moments of 2nd order | Ignition intervals |
|---|---|---|---|---|---|
| **3-cylinder** | | | | | |
| In-line, 3 throws | 0 | 0 | $\sqrt{3} \cdot F_1 \cdot a$ | $\sqrt{3} \cdot F_2 \cdot a$ | 240°/240° |
| **4-cylinder** | | | | | |
| In-line, 4 throws | 0 | $4 \cdot F_2$ | 0 | 0 | 180°/180° |
| Opposed-cylinder (boxer), 4 throws | 0 | 0 | 0 | $2 \cdot F_2 \cdot b$ | 180°/180° |
| **5-cylinder** | | | | | |
| In-line, 5 throws | 0 | 0 | $0.449 \cdot F_1 \cdot a$ | $4.98 \cdot F_2 \cdot a$ | 144°/144° |
| **6-cylinder** | | | | | |
| In-line, 6 throws | 0 | 0 | 0 | 0 | 120°/120° |

[1] Without counterweights

| Cylinder arrangement | Free forces of 1st order[1] | Free forces of 2nd order | Free moments of 1st order[1] | Free moments of 2nd order | Ignition intervals |
|---|---|---|---|---|---|
| **6-cylinder (continued)** | | | | | |
| V 90°, 3 throws | 0 | 0 | $\sqrt{3} \cdot F_1 \cdot a$ [2] | $\sqrt{6} \cdot F_2 \cdot a$ | 150°/90° 150°/90° |
| Normal balance V 90°, 3 throws, 30° crank offset | 0 | 0 | $0.4483 \cdot F_1 \cdot a$ | $(0.966 \pm 0.256) \cdot \sqrt{3} \cdot F_2 \cdot a$ | 120°/120° |
| Opposed-cylinder, 6 throws | 0 | 0 | 0 | 0 | 120°/120° |
| V 60°, 6 throws | 0 | 0 | $3 \cdot F_1 \cdot a/2$ | $3 \cdot F_2 \cdot a/2$ | 120°/120° |
| **8-cylinder** | | | | | |
| V 90°, 4 throws in two planes | 0 | 0 | $\sqrt{10} \cdot F_1 \cdot a$ [2] | 0 | 90°/90° |
| **12-cylinder** | | | | | |
| V 60°, 6 throws | 0 | 0 | 0 | 0 | 60°/60° |

[1] Without counterweights, [2] Can be completely balanced by using counterweights.

## Main components of reciprocating-piston engine

### Piston

Pistons in today's motor-vehicle engines must perform a wide range of functions:
- They transmit the force generated by the combustion gas to the connecting rods.
- They serve as crosstails to define the connecting rods' travel paths within the cylinders.
- They support the normal force applied against the cylinder walls while the cylinder pressure is conveyed to the connecting rod.
- Together with their sealing elements, they seal the combustion chamber from the crankcase.
- They absorb heat for subsequent transfer to the cooling system.

Both the piston's design and the wristpin configuration employed to transfer the combustion gas forces to the connecting rod are largely determined by the combustion chamber's shape, including the geometry of the piston crown, while other variables include the selected combustion process and the associated pressure maxima. The priority is to produce the lightest possible piston in a unit capable of withstanding intense forces during operation in an environment with temperatures that can approach the physical limits of the materials used in its manufac-

*Piston shapes in various engine designs*
*a) Commercial-vehicle aluminum diesel engine piston with ring carrier and cooling channel,*
*b) Commercial-vehicle forged steel piston,*
*c) Passenger-vehicle aluminum diesel engine piston with ring carrier and cooling channel,*
*d) Passenger-vehicle aluminum diesel engine piston with cooled ring carrier, e) Passenger-vehicle aluminum piston for MPI spark-ignition engine (Multi-Point Injection), f) Passenger-vehicle aluminum piston for GDI spark-ignition engine.*

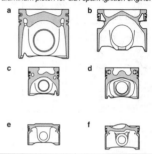

ture. Precise definition of the dimensions for the piston, wristpin and wristpin bushings are essential for achieving this goal.

The most frequently used materials for cylinder liners and pistons are gray cast iron and aluminum. Variations in piston clearance within the cylinder must be minimized to reduce noise (piston slap) and improve sealing, despite the fact that piston and cylinder liner have different coef-

*Piston operating temperatures in motor-vehicle engines at WOT (schematic, values in °C)*
*a) Passenger-vehicle diesel engine piston 16 MPa ignition pressure, 58 kW/l,*
*b) Passenger-vehicle spark-ignition engine piston 7.3 MPa ignition pressure, 53 kW/l.*

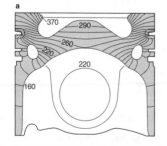
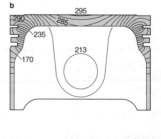

---

### Piston-ring shapes and configurations

**Diesel engine:**
1 Keystone ring, 2 Taper-face compression ring with crowned, inner bevel, 3 Stepped compression ring, 4 Double-beveled ventilated oil control ring with spiral-type expander.

**Spark-ignition engine:**
5 Plain compression ring, 6 Taper-face compression ring, 7 Stepped ring, 8 Double-beveled ring, 9 Multipart steel oil ring.

---

### Passenger-car engine connecting rod

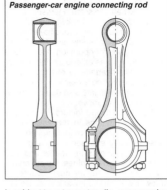

---

ficients of expansion. To this end, steel strips or similar elements are sometimes cast into the piston to limit its expansion.

Piston rings form the sealing element between the combustion chamber and the crankcase. The upper two – the compression rings – serve as gas seals. At least on additional ring (oil control ring or scraper ring, generally of a different design) ensures correct lubrication of the piston and the seals. Owing to the rings' extreme initial forces that they exert against the cylinder walls, they are a major source of friction loss within the reciprocating-piston engine.

#### Connecting rod
The connecting rod (conrod) is the joining element between piston and crankshaft. It

---

### Crankshaft throw
Primary stresses and deformations due to gas pressure and inertial forces.

Gas pressure

Inertial forces

---

is subject to extreme tensile, compression and bending stresses, while it also houses the wristpin bushings and crankshaft bearings. Connecting-rod length is determined by the piston stroke and the counterweight radius; whereby the engine height can also be an important factor (usually the case in vehicle engines).

#### Crankshaft
The crankshaft with its rod extensions, or throws, converts the reciprocating motion of the pistons – conveyed to it by the connecting rods – into rotary motion, making effective torque available at the crankshaft's end. The forces acting on the crankshaft are characterized by highly variable periodicities and vary greatly according to location. These torques and bending moments, and the secondary vibrations which they generate, all represent intense and highly complex stress factors for the crankshaft itself. As a result, its structural properties and vibrational response patterns rely upon precise calculations and carefully defined dimensions. Calculations and dimensioning though are further complicated by the fact that too many multiple journal bearings are practically always installed as a precautionary measure.

The number of crankshaft bearings is primarily determined by the overall load factor and maximum engine speed. To accommodate their intense operating pressures, all diesel-engine crankshafts incorporate a main bearing journal between each crankshaft throw and at each end of the crankshaft. This arrangement is also found in high-speed spark-ignition (SI) engines designed for high specific outputs.

Crankshafts in some smaller SI engines designed for operation at lower load factors sometimes extend the interval between main bearings to every 2 crankshaft throws for cost reasons. The number of counterweights also depends upon the criteria cited above.

Stresses and load factors are also primary considerations in the selection of both materials and manufacturing processes. Highly stressed crankshafts are usually drop-forged. In smaller and less highly stressed engines, cast crankshafts, incorporating the dual advantages of lower weight and lower costs, are becoming increasingly popular.

### Crankshaft vibrations

Flexural vibration is significant only on engines with a small number of cylinders, because the crankshaft and the neces-

*Cast crankshaft*

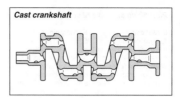

sary large flywheel form an oscillatory system with a low natural frequency. Flexural vibration is not a critical factor on engines of 3 cylinders or more. By logical extension, this also applies to the longitudinal crankshaft vibrations induced by flexural vibrations.

At the same time, the rotational oscillations of the vibrating system formed by crankshaft, connecting rods and pistons become increasingly critical with higher numbers of cylinders. This system, in which the mass moments of inertia for connecting rods and pistons vary according to crankshaft angle,

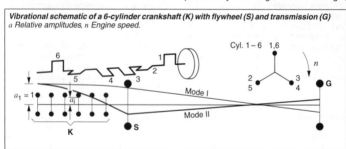

*Vibrational schematic of a 6-cylinder crankshaft (K) with flywheel (S) and transmission (G)*
$a$ Relative amplitudes, $n$ Engine speed.

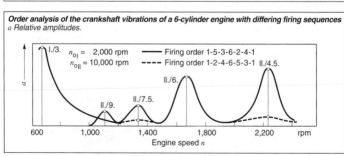

*Order analysis of the crankshaft vibrations of a 6-cylinder engine with differing firing sequences*
$a$ Relative amplitudes.

can be calculated by reducing it to a smooth, flexible shaft free of inertia with equivalent masses mounted on it. The oscillation reduction model makes it possible to determine both the system's natural frequency and the intensity of the vibration forces. The oscillations emanate from the tangential forces generated by a combination of gas forces and oscillating inertial forces at the crank pin. Vibration dampers are required to reduce the crankshaft's torsional vibrations to acceptable levels (e.g. bonded rubber vibration dampers or viscous vibration dampers).

### Engine block and crankcase

The block and crankcase unit supports the force-transfer mechanism between cylinder head and crankshaft assembly. It bears the crankshaft assembly's support bearings, and incorporates (or holds) the cylinder sleeves. Also included in the block are a separate water jacket and sealed oil chambers and galleries. The block also serves as a mounting and support surface for most of the engine's ancillary units.

A cast block and crankcase unit is the standard configuration for automotive applications. The cylinder-head bolts oppose the gas forces to facilitate a force transfer of maximum linearity and minimal flexural tendency through transverse support walls and to the main bearings. For greater strength, the crankcase is frequently extended to below the crankshaft's center axis. The pistons in spark-ignition engines almost always run in integral cylinders machined from the block casting. In diesel engines, separate dry or wet liners made of special wear-resistant materials are usually used.

Whereas, virtually all blocks for truck engines continue to be manufactured in gray cast iron, aluminum passenger-car blocks are becoming increasingly popular owing to their weight-saving potential.

### Cylinder head

The cylinder head seals off the upper end of the block and cylinder(s). It houses the gas-exchange valves as well as the spark plugs and/or fuel injectors. Together with the piston, it also provides the desired combustion-chamber shape. In the vast majority of passenger-car engines, the

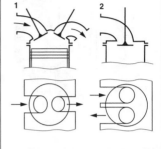

*Cylinder-head designs according to intake and exhaust tract location*
1 Crossflow design,
2 Counterflow design.

entire valve gear is also mounted in the cylinder head.

Based on the gas-exchange concepts, a distinction is made between two basic design configurations:

<u>Counterflow cylinder head</u>: Intake and exhaust passages open onto the same side of the cylinder head. This limits the space available for the intake and exhaust-gas passages, but due to the short flow tracts, this represents a substantial advantage in supercharged applications. This design, with the gas supply and discharge tracts on a single side, also provides practical advantages in transverse-mounted engines.

<u>Crossflow cylinder head</u>: Intake and exhaust passages are located on opposite sides of the engine, providing a diagonal flow pattern for the intake and exhaust gases. This layout's advantages include more freedom in intake and exhaust-tract design as well as less complicated sealing arrangements.

In truck and large industrial engines, individual cylinder heads are often used on each cylinder for better sealing-force distribution and easier maintenance and repair. Separate cylinder heads are also specified for improved cooling efficiency on air-cooled engines.

In passenger-car and low-power engines, one cylinder head is usually em-

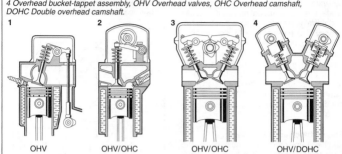

*Valve-gear designs (source: Hütten "Motoren")*
*1 Push-rod assembly, 2 Single rocker-arm assembly, 3 Twin rocker-arm assembly,*
*4 Overhead bucket-tappet assembly, OHV Overhead valves, OHC Overhead camshaft,*
*DOHC Double overhead camshaft.*

1        2        3        4

OHV     OHV/OHC     OHV/OHC     OHV/DOHC

ployed for all cylinders together. The cylinder heads on water-cooled diesel truck engines are usually made of gray cast iron. The substantial increase in cylinder pressures has give rise to the increased use of vermicular castings.

Superior heat dissipation and lower weight have combined to make aluminum the material of choice in the construction of cylinder heads for air-cooled engines as well as on virtually all spark-ignition and diesel engines for passenger cars.

### Valve gear

It is the function of the valve-gear assembly in a 4-stroke engine to permit and to control the exchange of gases in the IC engine (see P. 470). The valve gear includes the intake and exhaust valves, the springs which close them, the camshaft drive assembly and the various force-transfer devices.

### Valve-timing concepts

In the following widely-used designs, the camshaft is located in the cylinder head:

Overhead bucket-tappet assembly, in which a "bucket" moving back and forth in the cylinder head absorbs the cam lobe's lateral force, while transferring its linear actuating pressure to the valve stem.

Cam follower or single rocker-arm assembly actuated by an overhead cam, in which the cam lobe's lateral and linear forces are absorbed and relayed by a cylinder-head mounted lever rocking

back and forth between the cam lobe and the valve. In addition to transferring forces and absorbing lateral forces, the intermediate rocker arm can also be designed to magnify the cam pitch effect.

Twin rocker-arm assembly actuated by overhead cam, in which the rocker arm's tilt axis is located between the camshaft and the valve. Here, too, the rocker arm is usually designed as a cam pitch multiplier to produce the desired valve travel.

When the camshaft is installed within the block, the camshaft lobe acts against an intermediate lifter and pushrod assembly instead of directly against the valve.

### Valve arrangements

The valve control arrangement and the design of the combustion chamber are closely interrelated. Today, nearly all valve assemblies are overhead units mounted in the cylinder head. In diesels and simpler spark-ignition engines, the valves are parallel to the cylinder axis, and are usually actuated by twin rocker arms, bucket tappets or single rocker arms. With increasing frequency, current spark-ignition engines designed for higher specific outputs tend to feature intake and exhaust valves which are inclined towards each other. This configuration allows larger valve diameters for a given cylinder bore, while also providing greater freedom for optimizing intake and exhaust passage design. Twin rocker-arm assemblies actuated by overhead cams

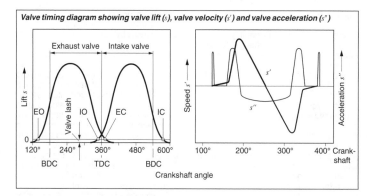

*Valve timing diagram showing valve lift ($s$), valve velocity ($s'$) and valve acceleration ($s''$)*

are used most often here. High-performance and racing engines are increasingly using four valves per cylinder and overhead bucket-tappet valve assemblies.

An engine's valve-timing diagram shows the opening and closing times of the valves, the valve-lift curve with maximum lift, and the valve's velocities and acceleration rates.

Typical valve acceleration rates for passenger-car OHC (overhead camshaft) valve assemblies:
$s'' = 60...65$ mm $(b/\omega^2) \triangleq 6,400$ m/s² at 6,000 rpm for single and twin rocker-arm assemblies,
$s'' = 70...80$ mm $(b/\omega^2) \triangleq 7,900$ m/s² at 6,000 rpm for overhead bucket-tappet assemblies. For heavy-duty commercial-vehicle engines with block-mounted camshafts:
$s'' = 100...120$ mm $(b/\omega^2) \triangleq 2,000$ m/s² at 2,400 rpm.

### Valve, valve guide and valve seat

The materials employed in manufacturing valves are heat and scale-resistant. The valve seat's contact surface is frequently hardened. A proven method for improving the thermal conductivity characteristics of exhaust valves is to fill their stems with sodium. To extend service life and improve sealing, valve-rotating systems (rotocaps) are now in common use.

The valve guides in high-performance engines must feature high thermal conductivity and good antifriction properties.

They are usually pressed into the cylinder head and are often supplemented by valve-stem seals at their cold ends for reducing oil consumption.

Valve-seat wear is generally reduced by making the valve seats of cast or sintered materials and shrink-fitting them into the cylinder head.

### Lobe design and timing dynamics

The cam lobe must be able to open (and close) the valve as far, as fast and as smoothly as possible. The closing force for the valves is applied by the valve springs, which are also responsible for maintaining contact between the cam lobe and the valve. Dynamic forces impose limits on cam and valve lift.

The entire valve-gear assembly can be viewed as a spring/mass system in which the conversion from stored to free energy causes forced vibration. Valve-gear assemblies with overhead camshafts can be represented with sufficient accuracy by a single-mass system (consisting of the propelled mass, valve-gear assembly rigidity, and the corresponding damping effects).

Dual-mass systems are becoming increasingly popular for use with block-mounted camshafts and pushrods.

The maximum permissible surface pressure, usually regarded as the decisive parameter limiting cam-lobe radius and the rate of opening on the flank, currently lies between 600 and 750 N/mm², depending upon the employed material pairings.

# Gas exchange

In combustion engines employing open processes, the gas-exchange (exhaust and refill) system must serve two decisive functions:
1. Replacement is employed to return the gas medium to its initial (start of cycle) condition, and
2. The oxygen required to burn the fuel is provided in the form of fresh air.

The parameters defined in DIN 1940 can be used to evaluate the gas-exchange process. For overall <u>air flow</u> (air expenditure $\lambda_a = m_g/m_{th}$) the entire charge transferred during the work cycle $m_g$ is defined with reference to the theoretical maximum for specific displacement. In contrast, the <u>volumetric efficiency</u> $\lambda_{a1} = m_z/m_{th}$ is based exclusively on the fresh charge $m_z$ actually present or remaining in the cylinder. The difference between $m_z$ and the total charge transfer $m_g$ consists of the proportion of gas that flows directly into the exhaust tract in the overlap phase, making it unavailable for subsequent combustion.

The <u>retention rate</u> $\lambda_a = m_z/m_g$ is an index of the residual charge in the cylinder.

The <u>scavenge efficiency</u> $\lambda_S = m_z/(m_z+m_r)$ indicates the volume of the fresh charge $m_z$ relative to the existing total charge, consisting of the fresh charge and the residual gas $m_r$. Here, the parameter $m_r$ indicates the amount of residual gas from earlier working cycles remaining in the cylinder after the exhaust process.

In a 2-stroke cycle, the gas is exchanged with every rotation of the crankshaft at the end of the expansion in the area around bottom dead center. In a 4-stroke cycle, separate intake and exhaust strokes provide a supplementary gas-exchange cycle.

## 4-stroke process

Valve timing – and thus gas exchange – are regulated by a control shaft (camshaft) rotating at half the frequency of the crankshaft by which it is driven. The camshaft opens the gas-exchange valves by depressing them against the valve springs to discharge the exhaust gas and to draw in the fresh gas (exhaust and intake valves respectively). Just before piston bottom dead center (BDC), the exhaust valve opens and approx. 50% of the combustion gases leave the combustion chamber under a supercritical pressure ratio during this predischarge phase. As it moves upward during the exhaust stroke, the piston sweeps nearly all of the combustion gases from the combustion chamber.

Shortly ahead of piston top dead center (TDC) and before the exhaust valve has closed, the intake valve opens. This crankshaft top dead center position is called the gas-exchange TDC or overlap TDC (because the intake and exhaust processes overlap at this point) in order to distinguish it from the ignition TDC. Shortly after gas-exchange TDC, the exhaust valve closes and, with the intake valve still open, the piston draws in fresh air on its downward stroke. This second stroke of the gas-exchange process, the intake stroke, continues until shortly after BDC. The subsequent two strokes in the

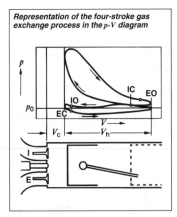

*Representation of the four-stroke gas exchange process in the p-V diagram*

4-stroke process are compression and combustion (expansion).

On throttle-controlled gasoline engines during the valve overlap period, exhaust gases flow directly from the combustion chamber into the intake passage, or from the exhaust passage back into the combustion chamber and from there into the intake passage. This tendency is especially pronounced at low throttle openings with high manifold vacuum. This "internal" exhaust-gas recirculation can have negative effects on idle quality, but it is impossible to avoid entirely, as a compromise has to be found between adequate high-speed valve lift and a satisfactory idle.

Early exhaust-valve timing allows a high degree of blowdown, and thus guarantees low residual-gas compression as the piston sweeps through its upward stroke, although at the price of a reduction in the work index for the combustion gases.

The "intake valve closes" (IC) timing exercises a decisive effect on the relationship between air expenditure and engine speed. When the intake valve closes early (IC), the maximum charge efficiency occurs at low engine speeds, while late closing shifts the efficiency peak toward the upper end of the engine speed spectrum.

Obviously, fixed valve timing will always represent a compromise between two different design objectives: maximum brake mean effective pressure – and thus torque – at the most desirable points on the curve, and the highest possible peak output. The higher the engine speed at which maximum power occurs, and the wider the range of engine operating speeds, the less satisfactory will be the ultimate compromise. Large variations in the valves' effective flow opening relative to stroke (i.e. in designs featuring more than two valves) will intensify this tendency.

**4-stroke gas-exchange process**

E       Exhaust,
EO      Exhaust opens,
EC      Exhaust closes,
I       Intake,
IO      Intake opens,
IC      Intake closes,
TDC     Top dead center,
OTDC    Overlap TDC,
ITDC    Ignition TDC,
BDC     Bottom dead center,
IP      Ignition point.

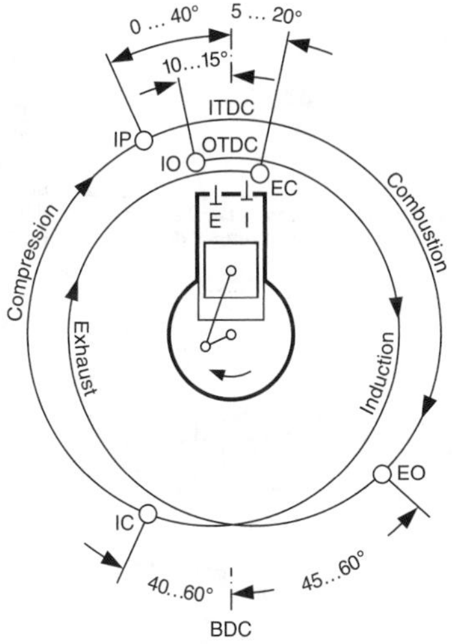

At the same time, the demands for minimum exhaust emissions and maximum fuel economy mean that low idle speeds and high low-end torque (despite and along with high specific outputs for reasons of power-unit weight) are becoming increasingly important. These imperatives have lead to the application of variable valve timing (see P. 474 onwards).

Advantages of the 4-stroke process
– Very good volumetric efficiency over the entire engine-speed range.
– Low sensitivity to pressure losses in the exhaust-gas system, and
– Relatively good control of the charging-efficiency curve through selection of appropriate valve timing and intake system designs.

Disadvantages of the 4-stroke process
– Valve control is highly complex.
– The power density is reduced because only every second shaft rotation is used to generate work.

## 2-stroke process

To maintain gas exchange without an additional crankshaft rotation, the gases are exchanged in the two-stroke process at the end of expansion and at the beginning of the compression stroke. The intake and exhaust timing are usually controlled by the piston as it sweeps past the intake and exhaust ports in the cylinder housing near BDC. This configuration, however, requires symmetrical control times and involves the problem of short-circuit scavenging. In addition, 15...25% of the piston stroke cannot produce work because only charge volume $V_f$ and not displacement volume $V_h$ can be exploited for power generation. As the two-stroke process lacks separate intake and exhaust strokes, the cylinder must be filled and scavenged using positive pressure, necessitating the use of scavenging pumps. In an especially simple and very frequently-used design, the bottom surface of the piston works in conjunction with a crankcase featuring a minimal dead volume to form a scavenging pump. The figures show a 2-stroke engine with crankcase scavenging or crankcase pre-compression along with the associated control processes. The processes which take place on the scavenging pump side are shown in the inner circle, while those occurring on the cylinder side are shown in the outer circle. Satisfactory cylinder scavenging is achievable by using cross-flow scavenging, loop scavenging and uniflow scavenging.

Advantages of the 2-stroke process
– Simple engine design
– Low weight
– Low manufacturing costs
– Better torsional force pattern

Disadvantages of the 2-stroke process
– Higher fuel consumption, and
– Higher HC emissions (cylinder scavenging is problematic)
– Lower mean effective pressures (poorer volumetric efficiency)
– Higher thermal loads (no gas-exchange stroke)
– Poor idle (high percentage of residual gas)

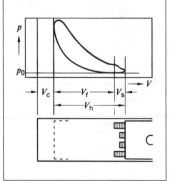

*Graphical representation of the 2-stroke gas-exchange process in the $p$-$V$ diagram*

### 2-stroke gas-exchange process with crankcase compression

E  Exhaust,
EO  Exhaust opens,
EC  Exhaust closes,
I  Intake,
IO  Intake opens,
IC  Intake closes,
T  Transfer passage closes,
TO  Transfer passage,
TC  Transfer passage opens,
TDC  Top dead center,
BDC  Bottom dead center,
IP  Ignition point.

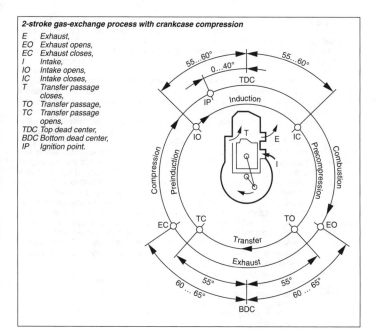

### 2-stroke scavenging
1 Crossflow scavenging, 2 Loop scavenging, 3 and 4 Uniflow scavenging.

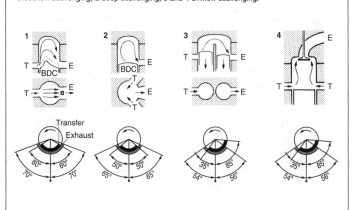

## Variable valve timing

### Camshaft phase adjustment

Engines equipped with variable valve timing provide the option of adjusting the phase of the camshafts with respect to the crankshaft without affecting the valve opening period and valve lift (see figure). Electrically or electrohydraulically operated actuators permit camshaft adjustment as a function of engine speed. Simple control systems permit adjustment only to two defined positions, while more intricate control systems facilitate infinitely variable adjustment within a defined crankshaft angle range.

The camshaft is set to "retarded intake close" at idle speed and in the upper engine speed range. The reduced valve overlap results in decreased internal exhaust-gas recirculation, while providing more stable idle characteristics with the possibility of lowering the idle speed. Boost effects attributed to the dynamic property of gases at high engine speeds result in an increase in engine output.

These gas-dynamic effects decrease in the medium engine speed range. The intake valve closing earlier prevents the air already drawn in from being expelled, thus increasing the output.

Systems that also permit adjustment of the exhaust camshaft provide the additional option of varying internal exhaust-gas recirculation (measure used to reduce nitrogen-oxide emissions).

### Camshaft-lobe control

Selective camshaft-lobe control makes it possible to alternate between two separate camshaft lobes featuring two different lift profiles for the purpose of varying the valve timing as well as the valve lift (see figure). The first lobe features a profile tailored for optimum intake and exhaust timing and valve lift in the lower and middle engine-speed ranges. The second cam lobe provides greater valve lift and extended opening times for high engine speeds.

Such systems can involve, for example, a rocker arm which pivots freely at low speeds and which is coupled to the standard rocker arm. This rocker arm rides on the second cam lobe. A further control option is provided by overhead bucket tappets.

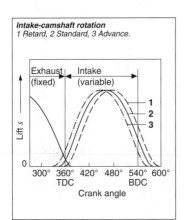

*Intake-camshaft rotation*
1 Retard, 2 Standard, 3 Advance.

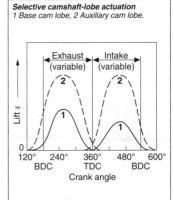

*Selective camshaft-lobe actuation*
1 Base cam lobe, 2 Auxiliary cam lobe.

## Fully variable valve timing with camshaft

A valve timing system that permits variation of both valve lift as well as valve timing is known as a fully variable valve timing or control system. Cam lobes with a curved three-dimensional profile and lateral cam shift permit substantial degrees of freedom in engine operation (see figure). This type of camshaft control system facilitates infinitely variable adjustment of both valve lift (on the intake side only),

and therefore the opening angle of the valves, as well as the phase position between the camshaft and crankshaft.

By closing the intake valve earlier, this fully variable camshaft control makes it possible to control the load in such a way as to essentially dispense with the need for a throttling facility in the intake manifold This has the added advantage of having a positive effect on efficiency.

## Fully variable valve timing without camshaft

Systems that permit valve timing without involving the camshaft offer the greatest degree of freedom with respect to valve timing and the greatest potential for reducing fuel consumption. In such systems, the valves are operated by means of electromagnetic (solenoid) or electrohydraulic actuators. The aim of this fully variable valve timing gear without involving the camshaft is to largely achieve de-throttling of the intake manifold with very low charge cycle losses, and to facilitate flexible exhaust-gas recirculation levels to reduce nitrogen-oxide emissions.

*Example of a system with infinitely variable valve timing and valve lift*
*a) Minimum lift,*
*b) Maximum lift.*

## Supercharging processes

The power of an engine is proportional to the air-mass flow $m_z$. As this air throughput, in turn, is proportional to air density, the power of an engine, given a specific displacement and engine speed, can be increased by precompressing the air before it enters the cylinders, i.e. by supercharging.

The supercharging ratio indicates the density rise as compared to a naturally-aspirated engine. One determining factor is the system used (potential pressure ratio). The maximum ratio for a given pressure increase is obtained when the temperature of the compressed air (boost air) is not increased or is returned to its initial level by intercooling.

In the spark-ignition engine, the supercharging ratio is restricted by the pre-ignition threshold. In the diesel engine maximum permissible peak pressures are the limiting factor. In order to avoid these problems, supercharged engines usually have lower compression ratios than their naturally aspirated counterparts.

### Dynamic supercharging

Besides the valve timing, the geometry of the intake air and exhaust-gas lines has an influence on the charge cycles. Induced by the induction work of the piston, as the intake valve opens it initiates a propagating pressure wave that reflects off the open end of the intake manifold and returns to the intake valve. The resulting pressure pulsation can be utilized to increase the air mass intake. In addition to the geometry in the intake manifold, this supercharging effect based on gas dynamics also depends on the engine speed.

### Ram-pipe supercharging

In connection with ram-pipe supercharging, each cylinder features a separate individual intake runner of a specific length, usually connected to a common plenum chamber. The pressure waves are able to propagate independent of each other in these intake runners (see figure). The supercharging effect depends on the geometry of the intake manifold and the engine speed. The lengths of the individual intake runners are adapted to the valve timing in such a way that a pressure wave reflected at the end of the intake runner passes through the open intake valve.

While the length of the runners must be adapted to the engine speed range, it is necessary to match the diameters of the runners to the cylinder displacement. Long runners produce a high supercharging effect in the lower engine speed range while shorter runners provide the same in the upper engine speed range.

In the case of the ram-effect supercharging system shown in the figure, a distinction can be made between two different types of intake runners. The changeover valve or flap closes in the lower engine speed range to allow the air intake to flow through the long intake runner to the cylinders. The air takes the route through the short intake runner at high engine speeds when the changeover valve open.

### Tuned-intake-tube charging

At a certain engine speed, the gas oscillations in the intake manifold induced by the periodical piston movement resonate, thus producing an additional supercharg-

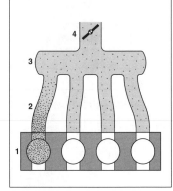

***Ram-pipe supercharging*** (principle)
1 Cylinder,
2 Individual runner,
3 Common plenum chamber,
4 Throttle valve (butterfly valve).

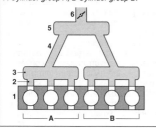

**Tuned-intake-tube charging**
1 Cylinder, 2 Short intake manifold,
3 Common plenum chamber, 4 Resonance
tube (tuned tube), 5 Common plenum.
chamber, 6 Throttle valve (butterfly valve).
A Cylinder group A, B Cylinder group B.

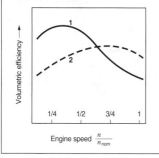

**Increase of volumetric efficiency through dynamic supercharging**
1 System with dynamic supercharging,
2 System with standard intake manifold.

ing effect. In tuned-intake charging systems (see figure), short ducts connect groups of cylinders with the same ignition intervals to assigned resonance chambers. These resonance chambers are connected to a common plenum chamber by tuned tubes, and act as Helmholtz resonators. The length and size of the tuned tubes are determined by the engine speed range at which the supercharging effect induced by the resonance is to occur.

Variable-geometry intake manifold systems
Since the effect of dynamic supercharging depends on the operating point of the engine (see figure), variable intake manifold geometry makes for a virtually ideal torque curve. Variable systems can be implemented by:
– Adjusting the length of the intake runners.
– Alternating between various lengths of the intake runners, or
– Different diameters of the intake runners.
– Alternately disabling one individual runner per cylinder in multiple intake runner systems, or
– Switching to different intake volumes.

Switch-over in variable-configuration intake systems is achieved by electrically or electropneumatically operated flaps or valves.

**Oscillatory intake system**
a) Intake duct geometry with changeover valve closed,
b) Intake duct geometry with changeover valve open.
1 Changeover valve,
2 Common plenum chamber,
3 Long, thin oscillatory intake passage with changeover valve closed,
4 Short, wide oscillatory intake passage with changeover valve opened.

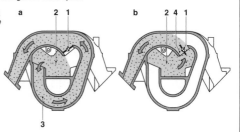

**Mechanical supercharging**

In mechanical supercharging, a compressor is powered directly by the internal combustion engine. Mechanically-driven compressors take the form of:
- Various types of positive-displacement superchargers (compressors) (e.g. roots superchargers, sliding-vane superchargers, spiral-type superchargers, screw-type superchargers), or
- Hydrokinetic flow compressors (e.g. radial compressors).

The engine and charger usually feature a fixed transmission ratio. Mechanical or electromagnetic clutches are used to control supercharger activation.

For a description of supercharging devices, see P. 528 onwards.

<u>Advantages of mechanical supercharging</u>
- Relatively simple superchargers on cold side of engine.
- Engine exhaust gas is not involved, and
- The supercharger responds almost immediately to load changes.

<u>Disadvantages of mechanical supercharging</u>
- The supercharger must be driven by the effective power of the engine.
- This results in increased fuel consumption.

**Exhaust-gas turbocharging**

In exhaust-gas turbocharging, the energy for the turbocharger is extracted from the engine's exhaust gases. Although the process exploits energy that remains unused (owing to crankshaft assembly expansion limits) by naturally-aspirated engines, exhaust backpressure increases as the gases furnish the power required to turn the compressor.

Current turbocharged engines employ an exhaust-driven turbine to convert the energy in the exhaust gas into mechanical energy, making it possible for the turbocharger to compress the induction gas.

The exhaust-gas turbocharger is a combined exhaust-driven turbine and flow compressor (see P. 532 onwards).

Exhaust-gas turbochargers are usually designed to generate a high boost pressure even at low engine speeds. Conversely, however, boost pressure at the high end of the engine speed range can increase to levels that could place excessive load on the engine. Engines with wide speed ranges in particular therefore

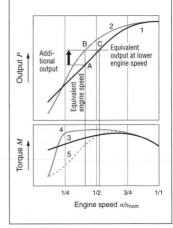

***Power and torque curves***
*1, 3 Naturally aspirated engine for stationary application, 2, 4 Supercharged engine for stationary operation, 5 Torque curve of supercharged engine for non-stationary (dynamic) operation.*

require a wastegate bypassing the turbine, although this means a loss of exhaust-gas energy. Much more satisfactory results can be achieved with a compromise between high charge pressure in the low engine speed range and avoidance of engine overload at the high end of engine speed range by employing Variable Turbine Geometry (VTG). The blading of a VTG turbine adjusts to suit the flow cross-section and thus the gas pressure at the turbine by variation of the turbine geometry.

Advantages of exhaust-gas turbocharging
– Considerable increase in power output per liter from a given configuration.
– Improved torque curve within the effective engine-speed range.
– Significant improvement in fuel consumption figures relative to naturally-aspirated engines with the same output power.
– Improvement in exhaust-gas emissions.

Disadvantages of exhaust-gas turbocharging
– Installation of the turbocharger in the hot exhaust-gas tract requiring materials resistant to high temperatures.
– Complexity and space requirements for turbocharger and intercooler.
– Low basic torque at low engine speeds.
– Throttle response is extremely sensitive to the efficient matching of the turbocharger to the engine.

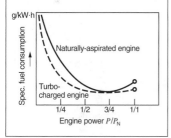

*Specific part-load fuel consumption curves for atmospheric-induction and turbocharged engines of the same power*

**Electrically assisted exhaust-gas turbocharging (EUATL)**
In electrically-assisted exhaust-gas turbocharging systems, an integrated electric motor maintains the turbocharger at a high speed in the lower engine speed range in order to immediately make available the charge air necessary as the load increased (see P. 538 onwards).

Advantage
– Avoidance of delayed startup characteristics (turbo lag).

Disadvantages
– High power intake of the electric motor renders necessary an increase in the system voltage.
– Complexity.

**Pressure-wave supercharging**
The pressure-wave supercharger uses direct energy exchange between exhaust gas and the intake air to increase the latter's density. This is accomplished by utilizing the differing speeds of the gas particles and pressure waves on the one side, and the reflection properties of these pressure waves on the other (see P. 530).

The pressure-wave supercharger consists of a cell rotor with an air casing on one side and an exhaust casing on the other. These incorporate specific timing edges and gas-pocket configurations.

Advantages of pressure-wave supercharging
– Rapid throttle response because energy exchange between exhaust gas and boost air takes place at the speed of sound.
– High compression at low enginespeeds.

Disadvantages of pressure-wave supercharging
– Restrictions on installation flexibility owing to the belt drive and gas lines.
– Increased quantities of exhaust gas and scavenge air.
– Loud operation.
– Extremely sensitive to increased resistance on the low-pressure side.

**Volumetric flow-rate map**

A clear illustration of the relationship between the engine and the supercharger is provided by the diagram for pressure vs. volumetric flow rate, in which the pressure ratio is plotted against volumetric flow rate $V$.

The curves for unthrottled 4-stroke engines (diesel) are particularly descriptive because they contain sloped straight lines (engine mass flow characteristics) which represent increasing engine air-throughput values as the pressure ratio $n_c = p_2/p_1$ increases at constant engine speed.

The diagram shows pressure ratios which result at corresponding constant supercharger speeds for a positive-displacement supercharger and a hydrokinetic compressor.

Only superchargers whose delivery rates vary linearly with their rotational speeds are suitable for vehicle engines. These are positive-displacement superchargers of piston or rotating-vane design or Roots blowers (see P. 528 f). Hydrokinetic flow compressors are not suitable.

## Evaluating gas-exchange components

The intake and exhaust tracts can be evaluated using stationary flow testing with flow numbers or passage efficiency levels. It is useful to evaluate the exhaust valves in the lower lift range with reference to supercritical pressures of the kind occurring in the blowdown phase.

Besides assessment of the flow number, analysis of in-cylinder flow is becoming increasingly significant. These studies can also be based on stationary flow testing and the derived parameters for swirl and tumble. Increasing use is being made of 3D computer models which, unlike the available measuring techniques, can furnish local information about flow conditions. Highly developed engine models are widely used today in the theoretical assessment of the overall gas cycle.

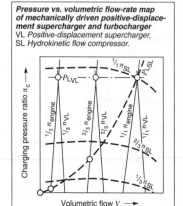

*Pressure vs. volumetric flow-rate map of mechanically driven positive-displacement supercharger and turbocharger*
VL *Positive-displacement supercharger,*
SL *Hydrokinetic flow compressor.*

Charging pressure ratio $\pi_c$

Volumetric flow $V$ —→

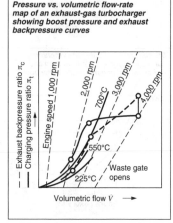

*Pressure vs. volumetric flow-rate map of an exhaust-gas turbocharger showing boost pressure and exhaust backpressure curves*

Exhaust backpressure ratio $\pi_c$
Charging pressure ratio $\pi_t$

-- -- Exhaust backpressure ratio $\pi_c$
—— Charging pressure ratio $\pi_t$

Engine speed 1,000 rpm, 2,000 rpm, 3,000 rpm, 4,000 rpm
700°C
550°C
225°C
Waste gate opens

Volumetric flow $V$ —→

# Cooling

In order to avoid thermal overload, combustion of the lubricating oil on the piston's sliding surface, and uncontrolled combustion due to excessive component temperatures, the components surrounding the hot combustion chamber (cylinder liner, cylinder head, valves and in some cases the pistons themselves) must be intensively cooled. Refer to P. 512 onwards for a description of the necessary cooling systems.

## Direct cooling

Direct air cooling removes heat directly from the components. The underlying principle is based on intensive air flow, usually through a finned surface. Although primarily used in motorcycle and aircraft engines, this form of cooling is also employed for some passenger-car and commercial-vehicle diesel and spark-ignition engines. Its main advantage is its high reliability and freedom from maintenance. On the negative side, the design measures required to ensure efficient heat dissipation to the cooling air increase the cost of the components.

## Indirect cooling

As water has a high specific heat capacity and provides efficient thermal transition between the materials, most contemporary vehicle engines are water-cooled. The air/water recirculation cooling system is the most prevalent system. It comprises a closed circuit allowing the use of anti-corrosion and antifreeze additives. The coolant is pumped through the engine and through an air/water radiator. The cooling air flows through the radiator in response to vehicle movement and/or is forced through it by a fan. The coolant temperature is regulated by a thermostatic valve which bypasses the radiator as required.

# Lubrication

The internal-combustion engine employs oil to lubricate and cool all of the power-transmission components. This oil is also used to remove dirt and neutralize chemically active combustion products, as well as for transmitting forces and damping vibration. The oil can only fulfill all these requirements if it is transported in adequate quantities to the engine's critical points, and if its properties are adapted to the specific requirements by appropriate measures taken during manufacture (e.g. inclusion of additives).

In total-loss lubrication (fresh-oil lubrication), a metering system supplies oil to the lubrication points, where it is subsequently consumed. A special case of this type of lubrication is mixture lubrication in which oil is either added to the fuel in a ratio ranging from 1:20 to 1:100, or metered to the engine (this process is used primarily in small two-stroke engines).

In most motor-vehicle engines, force-feed lubrication systems are used in combination with splash and oil mist lubrication (see P. 522 onwards).

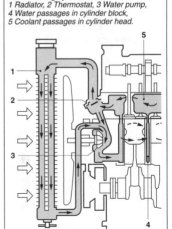

*Water cooling system with coolant circuit*
1 Radiator, 2 Thermostat, 3 Water pump,
4 Water passages in cylinder block,
5 Coolant passages in cylinder head.

# The spark-ignition (Otto) engine

The spark-ignition engine (or SI engine) is a piston engine with external or internal air/fuel mixture formation. External mixture formation generally produces homogeneous mixtures, whereas an internally formed mixture is largely heterogeneous at the instant of ignition. The time of mixture formation and fuel distribution in the combustion chamber are major factors in influencing the degree of homogenization achievable by internal mixture formation.

In both cases, the mixture is compressed to approximately 20...30 bar ($\varepsilon$ = 8...12) on the compression stroke, to generate a final compression temperature of 400...500 °C. This is still below the auto-ignition threshold of the mixture, which then has to be ignited by a spark shortly before the piston reaches TDC.

Since reliable ignition of homogeneous air/fuel mixtures is only possible within a narrowly defined window of the air/fuel ratio (excess-air factor $\lambda$ = 0.6...1.6), and flame velocity drops steeply as the excess-air factor $\lambda$ increases, SI engines with homogeneous mixture formation have to operate in a range $\lambda$ = 0.8...1.4 (best overall efficiency is achieved at $\lambda$ = 1.2...1.3). The $\lambda$ range is further restricted to 0.98...1.02 for engines with three-way catalytic converters.

On account of this narrow $\lambda$ range, load has to be controlled by the quantity of mixture entering the cylinders (quantity control). This is achieved by throttling the amount of air/fuel mixture entering the cylinders under part-load operating conditions (throttle control).

Optimization of the overall efficiency of SI engines has given rise to increasing development effort directed at engines with internal heterogeneous mixture formation. The improved efficiency is a result of the higher compression and lower throttling losses.

Homogenous and heterogeneous mixture formation are alike in that economic efficiency and untreated emissions depend on the combustion process which takes place after ignition. Combustion, in turn, can be influenced to a very large extent by the flows and turbulence that can be produced in the combustion chamber by the geometry of the intake duct and the combustion chamber.

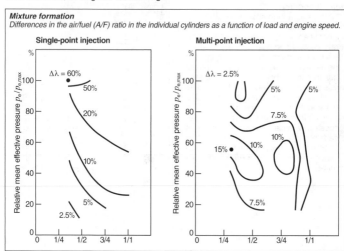

*Mixture formation*
Differences in the air/fuel (A/F) ratio in the individual cylinders as a function of load and engine speed.

## Mixture formation

### Homogenous mixture formation

The homogenous mixtures present at the time when ignition commences cause the fuel to vaporize fully, because only gas or gas/vapor mixtures can achieve homogeneity.

If some factor (such as low temperature during a cold start) inhibits complete vaporization of the fuel, sufficient additional fuel must be provided to ensure that the volatile, vaporizable constituent can produce an adequately rich – and therefore combustible – air/fuel ratio (cold-start enrichment).

In addition to mixture homogenization, the mixture-formation system is also responsible for load control (throttle control) and for ensuring the minimization of deviations in the A/F ratio from cylinder to cylinder and from working cycle to working cycle.

### Heterogeneous mixture formation

The aim pursued in heterogeneous internal mixture formation is that of operating the engine without throttle control across the entire operating map. Internal cooling is a side-effect of direct injection, so engines of this type can operate at higher compression ratios. The conjunction of these two factors, no throttle control and higher compression, means that the degree of efficiency is higher than that attainable with a homogenous mixture. Load is controlled by means of the mass of injected fuel.

Development in mixture-formation systems gave fresh impetus to the "hybrid" or "stratified-charge" techniques that were the subject of much research from about 1970 onwards. The definitive breakthrough came with the electromagnetic fuel injectors that allowed flexibility in start of injection and could achieve the high injection pressures required.

GDI (Gasoline Direct Injection) was the generic term applied to worldwide development in "jet-directed", "wall-directed" or "air-directed" mixture-formation systems (see figure on P. 612 onwards). The positions of spark plug and injector have a major influence on mixture formation, but flows in the combustion chamber are an-

other, supporting factor. Swirl (induced by spiral or tangential channels) is primarily rotation about an axis in parallel with that of the cylinder, whereas the axis of tumble, which is induced by fill channels, is normal to the cylinder's axis.

Precision positioning of the spark plug and the jet from the fuel injector is essential for jet-directed spray injection. The spark plug is under severe strain because it is struck directly by the jet of liquid fuel. Wall-directed and air-directed configurations direct the mixture to the spark plug by means of the motion of the charge, so requirements in this respect are not as high.

Heterogeneous mixture formation works with excess air (unthrottled operation), lean-burn catalytic converters have to be used in order to reduce nitrogen-oxide emissions.

## Ignition

The ignition system must reliably ignite the compressed mixture at a precisely defined instant, even under dynamic operating conditions with the attendant substantial fluctuations in mixture flow patterns and air/fuel ratios. Reliable ignition can be promoted by selecting spark-plug locations with good mixture access in combination with efficient mixture swirl patterns. These are especially important considerations for lean operation and at very low throttle apertures. Similar improvements can also be achieved by positioning the spark plug in small auxiliary "ignition chambers".

Ignition-energy requirements depend on the mixture's air/fuel (A/F) ratio. An ignition energy of 0.2 mJ is required for gasoline/air mixtures in the stoichiometric range, while up to 3 mJ may be required to ignite richer or leaner mixtures.

The ignition voltage required increases with the gas pressure at the instant of ignition. Increasing the electrode gap is one way of improving ignition reliability, but at the expense of higher ignition voltage and accelerated electrode wear.

The energy content of the mixture ignited by the spark must be sufficient to ignite the adjacent mixture. This defines the leanest possible mixture and the earliest possible instant of ignition. In engines with a compression ratio of $\varepsilon = 8...12$, this range is approximately 40...50 °crankshaft before TDC.

**Combustion process**
The initial thermal reaction which occurs between provision of ignition energy by the spark and the exothermic reaction of the air/fuel mixture is the ignition phase. This phase is roughly constant over time, with mixture composition as the only influencing factor. As a result, increasing engine speeds are accompanied by proportionately greater ignition lag – as a function of piston travel (°crankshaft) – which change together with excess-air factor (lambda).

The moment of ignition, therefore, has to be advanced as engine speed increases and excess-air factor $\lambda$ rises. Ignition advance, however, is limited by the drop in the mixture's energy density in the vicinity of the electrodes (see above). When this physical limit is reached, designers can resort to twin spark-plug configurations or ignition chambers to improve the situation.

The heat-release transient is determined by the rate of combustion, which in turn is defined by the flame velocity and the area of the flame front. Flame velocity depends on diffusion processes at the flame front and reaches a peak of approximately 20...40 m·s⁻¹ in gasoline-air mixtures with approx. 10% air deficiency ($\lambda = 0.9$). It is influenced by the excess-air factor $\lambda$ and the temperature of the mixture.

The area of the flame front can be influenced by the geometry of the combustion chamber and the position of the spark plug. Folding of the flame front due to turbulence and induced flows (such as swirl and tumble) is a significant factor in this respect. The flows induced primarily by the induction process and to a lesser extent by combustion-chamber geometry in conjunction with the compression squish fold the flame front and thus accelerate the process of energy conversion. Tum-

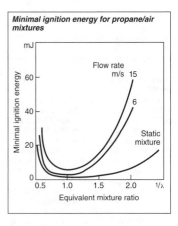

*Minimal ignition energy for propane/air mixtures*

ble, swirl and squish increase with engine speed and consequently, folding of the flame front also becomes more pronounced. This explains why the rate of heat release increases with speed despite the fact that by definition, flame velocity must remain constant.

Although it can factor in ultra-low-turbulence processes or in tests in low-flow pressure chambers, the turbulence created by flame propagation itself is of no significance in the combustion process as it takes place in modern SI engines.

The rising pressure due to local flame propagation causes an increase in temperature throughout the mixture, including that not yet reached by the flame and known as the "end gas". On account of local heat radiation and heat conduction, however, the temperature in the flame front is higher than in the rest of the mixture. This ensures regular flame propagation. The anomaly known as combustion knock or pre-ignition, due to simultaneous combustion of the end gas, occurs when the increase in pressure causes the temperature of the end gas to exceed its ignition limits.

Low fuel consumption and high efficiency are promoted by high combustion rates (brief duration), combined with the optimal heat release pattern relative to piston travel. Maximum heat release should occur shortly (approx. 5...10 °crankshaft) after top dead center. If most of the heat is released too early, wall heat losses and mechanical losses (high peak injection pressure) are increased. Late heat release leads to sacrifices in thermal efficiency (efficiency of cycle factor) and high exhaust-gas temperatures.

The ignition point must be selected for optimum heat release curves, while taking into consideration the following aspects:

– Air/fuel mixture ratio $(\lambda, T)$.
– Effects of engine parameters (particularly load and speed) on combustion-chamber turbulence.
– Constant-duration ignition and flame propagation processes, meaning that variations in ignition lag are required as engine speed increases.

**Problems and limits of combustion**

In actual practice, reliable flame initiation and propagation in engines with external mixture formation and spark ignition prohibit the use of mixtures leaner than $\lambda > 1.3$, although these would be desirable for improving the levels of theoretical (polytropic exponent) and gas-exchange (low throttling losses) efficiency, along with useful reductions in wall-heat and dissociation losses (reduction in combustion temperature). GDI engines (Gasoline Direct Injection) offer additional improvement potential.

Although higher compression ratios provide enhanced part-load efficiency, they also increase the risk of combustion knock at wide-open throttle (WOT). Combustion knock occurs when the entire charge of end gas reaches ignition temperature and burns within an extremely short space of time without regular flame propagation. The end gas is highly compressed and its energy density is therefore very high, so combustion knock releases very large amounts of heat within a very short space of time. The high local temperatures caused in this way place extreme loads on the engine components and can also damage them. The high-energy cycles also result in extreme pressure peaks. Within the combustion chamber these pressure peaks propagate at the velocity of sound and can cause damage to the piston, cylinder head, and cylinder-head gasket at critical points.

The risk of combustion knock can be reduced by using fuel additives or by richer mixtures (additional internal cooling).

The current expedient of avoiding combustion knock by retarding the moment of ignition raises problems of its own, especially when used on high-compression engines. As the ignition curve (mean pressure relative to ignition point) becomes gradually steeper as compression increases, the resulting sacrifices in mean effective pressure are accompanied by extreme exhaust-gas temperatures. Reliable detection and avoidance of combustion knock are thus vitally important at compression ratios of $\varepsilon = 11...13$.

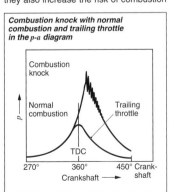

*Combustion knock with normal combustion and trailing throttle in the p-α diagram*

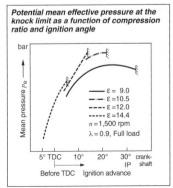

*Potential mean effective pressure at the knock limit as a function of compression ratio and ignition angle*

## Load control

In unthrottled GDI engines with heterogeneous mixture, load is controlled by means of the quantity of fuel injected. Spark-ignition engines with homogenous mixture formation, on the other hand, afford little freedom of operation with lean mixtures, so load control has to be implemented by adjusting the mass flow of the mixture. In carburetor engines, which have lost virtually all their significance in automotive engineering, this can be achieved by throttling the mixture mass flow. In engines with intake-manifold injection, throttle control to reduce the density of the intake air is the conventional approach. This arrangement, however, increases charge-cycle losses, so development is concentrating on alternative methods of load control. Mass flow can be influenced, for example, by prematurely closing the intake valves and thus shortening the effective intake periods. This complicated means of load control, however, requires fully variable valve timing and can cause fuel condensation as the result of expansion when the intake valves are closed. This drawback can be countered with "feedback control", an arrangement in which the intake valves are not closed until the requisite mass of mixture has just had time to fill the cylinder.

Another way of reducing or even eliminating throttling losses is exhaust-gas recirculation with the intake valves open. Load can be varied across a wide range by modulating the exhaust-gas recirculation rate.

Regulating charge-air pressure is a method of accomplishing load control over wide regions of the characteristic map with supercharged spark-ignition engines.

## Power output and economy

The efficiency index for engines with external mixture formation and spark ignition falls primarily in the lower portion of the map. This is owing to cycle-factor inefficiency (insufficient turbulence, inadequate charge density) along with an inefficient gas-exchange process.

Effective efficiency is further reduced by the low mechanical efficiency characteristic of this region of the map.

All measures for avoiding these lower sections of the map therefore contribute to improving the engine's overall efficiency.

Selective interruption of the fuel supply to individual cylinders allows the remaining cylinders to operate at higher cycle-factor efficiency levels with improved combustion and gas exchange. Valve deactivation provides further reductions in power loss by allowing the intake and exhaust valves for the deactivated cylinders to remain closed. Cylinder shutoff entails immobilizing the mechanical power-transmission components of the idle cylinders for further increases in mechanical efficiency.

The measures cited above vary in terms of sophistication, but engine speed reduction also enhances general cycle-factor efficiency while promoting effective gas exchange. Simultaneous reductions in mean frictional pressure also improve mechanical efficiency.

# The diesel engine

A diesel engine is a reciprocating-piston engine with internal (and thus heterogeneous) mixture formation and auto-ignition. During the compression stroke, intake air is compressed to 30...55 bar in naturally aspirated engines, or 80...110 bar in supercharged engines, so that its temperature increases to 700...900 °C. This temperature is sufficient to induce auto-ignition in the fuel injected into the cylinders shortly before the end of the compression stroke, as the piston approaches TDC. In heterogeneous processes the mixture formation is decisive in determining the quality of the combustion which then follows, and the efficiency with which the inducted combustion air is utilized, and thus in defining the available mean effective pressure levels.

## Mixture formation

In heterogeneous mixtures, the air/fuel ratio $\lambda$ extends from pure air ($\lambda = \infty$) in the spray periphery to pure fuel ($\lambda = 0$) in the spray core.

The figure provides a schematic illustration of the $\lambda$ distribution and the associated flame zone for a single static droplet. As this zone always occurs for every drop of injected jet, load control with heterogeneous mixture formation can be performed by regulating the fuel supply. This is termed mixture-quality control.

As with homogenous mixtures, combustion takes place in the relatively narrow range between $0.3 < \lambda < 1.5$. The mass transport necessary for generating these combustible mixtures relies on diffusion and turbulence. These are produced by the mixture formation energy sources described below as well as by the combustion process itself.

### Kinetic energy of the fuel spray
The spray's kinetic energy varies according to the pressure differential at the nozzle orifice. Along with the spray pattern (as determined by the nozzle geometry) and the fuel's exit velocity, it determines the configuration of the space in which the air and fuel interact as well as the range of droplet sizes in the chamber. The spray energy is influenced by the delivery rate of the fuel-injection pump and the dimensions of the metering orifice in the injector nozzle.

### Thermal energy
Thermal energy stored in the combustion-chamber walls and the compressed air vaporize the injected fuel (as a film layer on the walls and as droplets).

### Combustion-chamber shape
The shape of the combustion chamber and the action of the piston can be utilized to create turbulence (squish), or to distribute liquid fuel or the air/fuel vapor jet.

### Controlled air patterns (swirling action)
If the direction of fuel flow is roughly perpendicular to the direction of the vortex and droplet vaporization is taking place, a movement imparted to the combustion air inside the combustion chamber, usually in the form of solid-particle rotating flow, promotes the flow of air toward the fuel stream, and removes the combusted gases from the stream.

As the wall film evaporates, the air's swirling motion absorbs the vapor layer and provides thermal insulation between the combusted and fresh gases, while the microturbulence patterns superimposed upon the solid-particle vortex ensure rapid mixture of air and fuel. The air's controlled solid-particle swirl can be induced

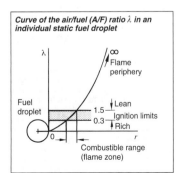

*Curve of the air/fuel (A/F) ratio $\lambda$ in an individual static fuel droplet*

$\lambda$

$\infty$
Flame periphery

Fuel droplet

Lean
1.5
Ignition limits
0.3
Rich

0

$r$

Combustible range (flame zone)

using special induction tract geometries or by shifting a portion of the cylinder charge into a rotationally symmetric prechamber (by transporting it through a side passage).

**Partial combustion in a prechamber**
When fuel is partially combusted in a prechamber, its pressure rises above that in the main combustion chamber. This increase then propels the partially oxidized combustion gases and vaporized fuel through one or more passages into the main combustion chamber, where they are thoroughly mixed with the remaining combustion air.

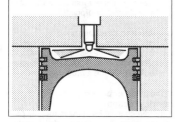

*Combustion-chamber shape and nozzle location for the static-charge spray-injection process without air swirl*

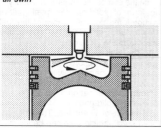

*Combustion-chamber shape and nozzle location for the multiple-orifice process with air swirl*

# Diesel combustion process

The diesel combustion process makes use of at least one (but usually an appropriate combination) of these mixture formation methods.

**Direct injection process**
This term refers to all combustion processes that do not rely on division of the combustion chamber. In such systems, the mixture is formed by the air movement and turbulence produced by the intake duct (swirl) and piston movement (squish) as well as the injection jet. With the advent of ever higher injection pressures, the influence of jet-controlled mixture formation is increasing in line with the decrease in the significance of swirl-based systems.

<u>Low-swirl combustion process</u>
Injection pressures of up to 2,000 bar make it possible to increase the number of orifices in multihole nozzles to 8...9 while retaining the necessary spray propagation pattern in the area of the walls of the piston recess. This makes it possible to reduce air swirl while at the same time utilizing the positive effect on the design of the intake ducts and gas-exchange efficiency. Modern combustion processes for commercial-vehicle diesel engines are therefore characterized by very low swirl values. Shallow and wide piston recesses as well as nozzles with holes producing large cone angles are used to improve the air utilization rate.

On account of the extended speed range and the small combustion chambers, direct-injection engines used in passenger vehicles cannot fully dispense with swirl.

<u>Swirl-assisted combustion process</u>
The mixture-forming energy of the injection jets alone is not enough for sufficiently uniform and rapid mixture preparation in high-revving diesels with wide operating-speed ranges and small swept volumes (in other words, the engines most frequently found in passenger cars and light commercial vehicles). Supportive motion of the air inside the combustion chamber is required especially as the

small cylinder diameters render it unavoidable that liquid fuel hits the wall of the combustion chamber.

These distinctly narrower piston recesses are deeper and constricted at the top edge in order to create highly turbulent squish from the piston gap on the one hand, and to accelerate the swirl of the air charge induced by the design of the intake ducts on the other. The total swirl velocity of the in-cylinder air mass achieved in this way is selected to ensure the sectors located between the injection jets are covered during the injection time. If the air/fuel mixture fails to completely fill the combustion-chamber segment, both air utilization and power output will suffer. On the other hand, if there is an overlap and the A/F mixture extends beyond the space between individual injection events, the resulting local fuel over-enrichment will lead to increased soot production.

M system

The MAN wall-distribution combustion process (M System) was developed in the early stages of direct injection in connection with commercial-vehicle engines for the purpose of controlling the originally harsh combustion noise produced by direct-injection engines. The fuel sprayed against the combustion chamber wall by means of a single-orifice nozzle evaporates at a substantially slower rate than the "air-distributive" method, so that less fuel is prepared during the ignition lag phase. It is specifically this proportion of fuel that largely influences the combustion noise, making the M system comparatively quieter.

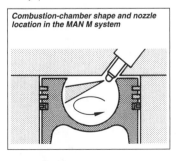

*Combustion-chamber shape and nozzle location in the MAN M system*

With the increased use of supercharging and thanks to the advances made in fuel-injection technology, other methods can now be used to limit combustion noise, thus contributing to the dwindling significance of this system.

**Divided-chamber process**

The time required for the fuel injected directly into the combustion chamber to evaporate depends to a great extent on the droplet surface area, i.e. on the number of fuel droplets produced and therefore on injection pressure. If injection pressure is limited, the speed range and control-force density of the engine will also be limited over the associated vaporization time of the fuel.

Divided-chamber processes promote fuel vaporization and mixture formation in the main combustion chamber. For this purpose, part of the fuel injected into the chamber is also burned in this chamber. The resulting pressure drop between the prechamber and main combustion chamber produces a gas flow from the chamber and intensive mixture formation in the main combustion chamber. Consequently, mixture formation and combustion are protracted compared to the direct-injection diesel engine. This results in increased wall heat losses and therefore distinctly higher fuel consumption.

With the advent of modern fuel-injection systems that produce pressures up to 2,000 bar, the significance of divided-chamber processes has diminished, initially in the commercial-vehicle sector, but recently also for passenger vehicles.

Whirl-chamber system

This process features an almost spherical prechamber, comprising approx. 50% of the total compression volume, located at the edge of the main combustion chamber. The prechamber is connected to the main chamber by a passage which enters the main chamber at an angle directed toward the center of the piston. The whirl chamber houses the injector and the glow plug (start-assist measure). The compression stroke generates an intense air vortex in the whirl chamber. As in the M System, fuel is injected eccentrically to converge with the swirl pattern and strike against the chamber wall. Critical factors are the design of the whirl chamber (for instance, with additional mixture vaporization surfaces where the injection jet strikes the wall), and the locations of the injector and the glow plug. These factors define the quality of the combustion process. This process combines very high engine speeds (> 5,000 rpm), with good air utilization and low particulate emissions.

Prechamber system
The prechamber system features an auxiliary chamber (prechamber) which is centrally located relative to the main combustion chamber, with 35...40% of the compression volume. Here too, the injection nozzle and glow plug (start-assist measure) are located in the prechamber. It communicates with the main combustion chamber through several orifices to allow combustion gases to mix as completely as possible with the main combustion air. One optimized prechamber concept utilizes the baffle surface ("spherical pins")

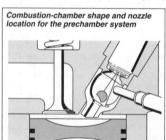

*Combustion-chamber shape and nozzle location for the prechamber system*

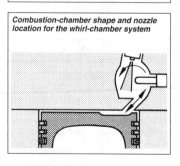

*Combustion-chamber shape and nozzle location for the whirl-chamber system*

below the injector nozzle to simultaneously induce rapid mixture formation and a controlled turbulence pattern (on some designs) in the prechamber. The turbulent flow meets the injection jet, which is also aimed into the swirl at an angle. The entire system, including the downstream glow plug, provides combustion with very low emissions and major reductions in particulates. The process is distinguished by a high air-utilization factor, and is also suitable for high engine speeds.

**Homogeneous diesel combustion**
The term Homogeneous Charge Compression Ignition (HCCI) refers to combustion processes that facilitate homogeneous operation also in diesel engines. In these systems, fuel is injected into the combustion chamber during an earlier phase of the compression stroke so as to produce a homogeneous mixture with the combustion air at the start of combustion with the aim of reducing particulate and nitrogen-oxide emissions.

Problems are encountered in the control of the ignition timing (avoidance of advanced ignition) and in the thermal-release pattern. For this reason, the compression ratio is reduced to $\varepsilon = 12...14$ in connection with the increased use of exhaust-gas recirculation. Variable valve timing and variable compression are further options that may be employed to control the ignition timing and the combustion process.

Development of this combustion process is still in its infancy.

# Combustion process

The start of injection (and thus the start of mixture formation) and the initiation of the exothermic reaction (start of ignition) are separated by a certain period of time, called ignition lag. The actual delay is defined by:
- the ignition quality of the fuel (cetane number)
- the compression end pressure (compression ratio, boost factor)
- the compression end temperature (compression ratio, component temperatures, intercooling), and
- the fuel-management system

The combustion process, which begins with the start of ignition, can be subdivided into three phases. In the "premixed flame" phase, the fuel injected prior to the start of ignition and mixed with the air combusts. The fuel injected once ignition has started combusts in a "diffusion flame". That portion of the combusted fuel which burns as a very rapid premixed flame is primarily responsible for the pressure rise, and thus is the primary cause of both combustion noise and oxides of nitrogen. The slower-burning diffusion flame is the main source of particulates and unburned hydrocarbons.

The third, end-of-injection, phase is when the soot formed primarily during the second phase is oxidized. This phase is becoming increasingly significant in modern combustion processes.

The heat release of a diesel engine depends on the combustion process itself, but also to a very large extent on the start of injection, the injection rate, and the maximum injection pressure. In direct-injection diesel engines, the number of injection orifices in the nozzle is another crucial factor. The fuel-injection system, moreover, requires a pre-injection capability (pilot injection) in order to reduce combustion noise and ensure that injection for the main injection phase commences as early as possible. This reduces fuel consumption for given levels of nitrogen-oxide emissions.

The diagram illustrates the thermal-release patterns which are characteristic of the various fuel-injection methods. The dual-stage combustion available with the divided-chamber process provides yet another means of influencing the combustion process by allowing selection of different diameters for the passage between the prechamber and the main combustion chamber.

### Problems and limits of combustion
As the fuel injected into diesel engines must ignite through auto-ignition, the fuel must have a high ignition quality (cetane number CN ≈ 45...50). Since, at low starting speeds, compression does not begin until after intake-valve closure (that is, significantly after BDC), the effective compression ratio, and with it the compression temperature, are greatly reduced. This means that despite high compression ratios, ignition problems can occur on starting, particularly when the engine is cold.

In addition, cold engine components tend to absorb thermal energy from the compressed air (polytropic exponent n = 1.1...1.2). The equation $T_1 = T_0 \cdot \varepsilon^{n-1}$ indicates that a reduction in the effective compression or the polytropic exponent causes a reduction in the final compres-

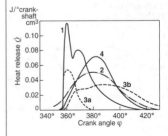

***Thermal-release curves.***
*1 Air-distributed direct fuel injection (naturally aspirated engine tuned for maximum economy), 2 Wall-distribution direct injection (designed for minimal noise), 3 Divided-chamber process in prechamber (3a) and main combustion chamber (3b), 4 Minimum emissions static-charge spray injection (intercooled turbocharged engines).*

J/°crankshaft cm³

Heat release $\dot{Q}$

0.10
0.08
0.06
0.04
0.02
0

340°  360°  380°  400°  420°
Crank angle φ

sion temperature. At the same time, mixture formation is unsatisfactory at low engine speeds (low injection pressure, large fuel droplets) and air movement is inadequate. Extended vaporization times (injection begins sooner) and an increase in the injected-fuel quantity – to significantly higher levels than full-load delivery (providing more low-boiling fuel) can only partially solve the starting problem, because the higher-boiling fuel constituents leave the engine in the form of white or blue smoke. Thus start-assist measures designed to increase temperature, such as glow plugs or flame-starting systems, are essential, especially in small engines.

As a significant portion of the mixture-formation process occurs during combustion in heterogeneous processes, it is important to avoid local concentrations of over-rich mixture in the diffusion flame, as the result would be an increase in soot emissions, even if there is a very large quantity of excess air. The air/fuel ratio limits at the legally required tolerance level for the smoke limit provide an indication of air-utilization efficiency. Divided-chamber engines reach the smoke limit with excess air of 5...15%, while the comparable figure is 10...80% for direct-injection diesels. It should be noted that large-volume diesel engines must also be run with significant levels of excess air owing to thermal component load.

Soot is an inevitable byproduct of heterogeneous combustion, so a sootless diesel engine must inevitably remain a conditional development and will require significant improvement in soot oxidation.

It has, however, proven possible to reduce particulate emissions from modern diesel engines to below the visibility threshold using a variety of measures. These include raising injection pressures at the nozzle, and the transition to optimized spray injection processes featuring larger combustion recesses in the piston, multiple injector orifices, exhaust-gas turbocharging, and charge-air cooling. The planned limits for particulates, however, dictate the need for the development of particulate filters employing the requisite regenerative systems (see P. 716 onwards).

Due to the abrupt combustion in that portion of the fuel that vaporizes and mixes with air during the ignition-lag period, the auto-ignition process may be characterized by "hard", loud combustion during operation under those conditions where this fuel comprises a large proportion of the total. These conditions include idle, low part-throttle on turbocharged engines, and high-load operation on high-speed naturally aspirated powerplants.

The situation can be improved by decreasing the ignition lag (preheating the intake air, supercharging or increasing compression) and/or by reducing the injected-fuel quantity during the ignition-lag period. On direct-injection engines, this reduction is usually obtained by applying pilot injection, whereas on divided-chamber engines a special injector configuration is employed (throttling pintle nozzle).

Not to be confused with the "hard" combustion inherent to the design is the "knock" to which divided-chamber processes with pintle nozzles are particularly susceptible, and which occurs primarily in the medium- and low-load areas of the diesel's operating curve. This phenomenon is traceable to inadequacies in the mixture-formation system (poor injector "chatter" or soot at the nozzles), and is characterized by a pulsating metallic sound.

The diesel engine must be designed for operation at peak injection pressures, and its materials and their dimensions must be selected accordingly. The reasons include:
– High compression ratios required for reliable starting and noise reductions
– Combustion process with maximum ignition propagation for fuel economy, and
– Increasingly frequent use of supercharging featuring higher charge-air pressures

Owing to the fact that diesel engines must also operate with excess air (lean) at wide-open throttle, they generally have lower control-force densities than their spark-ignition counterparts.

# Hybrid engines

Hybrid engines share characteristics with both diesel and spark-ignition engines (internal mixture formation with externally supplied ignition).

## Charge stratification

In stratified-charge SI engines, the mixture directly adjacent to the spark plug is enriched to ensure reliable ignition, while the rest of the combustion process proceeds in an extremely lean mixture. The objective is to combine the part-throttle economy comparable to that of a diesel with (especially important) low $NO_x$ and CO emissions.

### Open-chamber combustion

Research on open-chamber combustion systems with many characteristics similar to those of diesel systems (mixture quality control, high-pressure fuel injection, etc.) is focusing on employing internal mixture formation (Texaco TCCS, Ford PROCO, Ricardo, MAN-FM, KHD-AD) to generate an ignitable mixture at the spark plug while using progressively leaner mixtures (down to pure air) in the remainder of the combustion chamber (see gasoline direct injection).

Processes which use internal mixture formation have an air-utilization factor comparable to that of diesel engines.

### Divided-chamber combustion systems

Divided-chamber combustion systems tend to resemble spark-ignition engines in their basic layout (throttle control, mixture induction, etc.). The spark plug is located within a small prechamber – the ignition chamber – corresponding to roughly 5...25% of total compression volume. One or several passages connect this primary ignition chamber with the main combustion chamber.

The prechamber features an additional injector which injects a portion of the fuel directly (VW, Porsche-SKS), or a supplementary valve to supply air/fuel mixture to the ignition chamber (Honda-CVCC).

A disadvantage of these processes is their more complex design and the higher HC emissions stemming from lower exhaust-gas temperatures and the attendant reductions in secondary combustion activity in the exhaust tract.

Systems developed between 1970 and 1980 were abandoned due to their lack of impact in terms of fuel consumption and their high HC emissions.

## Multifuel engines

In multifuel engines, the ignition quality and knock resistance of the fuel can be relatively insignificant. These engines must be able to burn fuels of varying qualities without sustaining damage.

As fuels used with multifuel engines can have a very low knock-resistance rating, external mixture formation would be accompanied by the danger of combustion knock or advanced ignition. For this reason, multifuel engines always use internal mixture formation and retarded start of injection (similar to the diesel engine).

As the low ignition quality of the fuels makes auto-ignition difficult or even impossible, multifuel engines operate with extremely high compression ratios (Mercedes-Benz, MTU: $\varepsilon = 25:1$). As an alternative, they may be equipped with an auxiliary ignition source such as spark plugs or glow plugs (MAN-FM). At $\varepsilon = 14...15$, the compression ratio in these engines with externally supplied ignition lies between that of spark-ignition and diesel engines.

Multifuel engines have become less and less viable as they cannot comply with today's stringent emission limits.

# Empirical values and data for calculation

## Comparisons

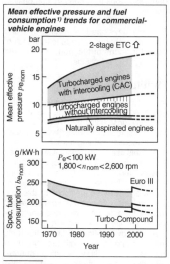

Mean effective pressure and fuel consumption [1] trends for commercial-vehicle engines

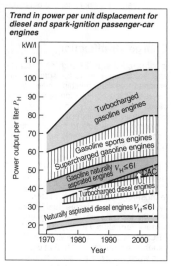

Trend in power per unit displacement for diesel and spark-ignition passenger-car engines

[1] See P. 417 for on-vehicle measures influencing fuel consumption.
ETC Exhaust-gas turbocharger, CAC Intercooling, TC Turbocompound.

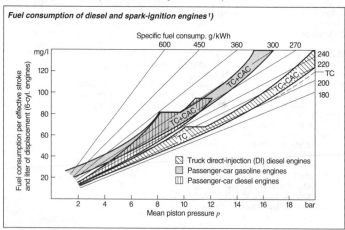

Fuel consumption of diesel and spark-ignition engines [1]

## Comparative data

| Engine type/ Application | | | Engine speed $n_{nominal}$ rpm | Compression ratio $\varepsilon$ | Max. mean pressure $p_e$ bar | Power per liter kW/$l$ | Weight-to-power ratio kg/kW | Specific fuel consumption g/kW · h | Torque increase % |
|---|---|---|---|---|---|---|---|---|---|
| Spark-ignition engines | Motorcycles | 2-stroke | 4,500–14,000 | 7–11 | 5–12 | 40–160 | 2.0–0.4 | 500–380 | 5–10 |
| | | 4-stroke | 5,000–13,000 | 9–12 | 9–13 | 50...150 | 2.5–0.5 | 400–320 | 10–15 |
| | Pass. cars | SM | 5,000–8,000 | 9–11 | 11–14 | 40–80 | 2.0–0.8 | 350–300 | 15–20 |
| | | CAC/ AM | 5,000–7,500 | 8–10 | 15–22 | 60–110 | 1.5–0.5 | 340–280 | 20–40 |
| | Com. veh. | SM | 2,000–3,500 | 8–9 | 8–10 | 20–35 | 5.0–3.0 | 360–240 | 15–20 |
| Diesel engines | Pass. cars/ Light comm. veh. | SM | 3,500–4,500 | 19–24 | 7–9 | 20–35 | 4.0–2.0 | 300–240 | 5–10 |
| | | AM/ CAC | 3,500–4,500 | 18–22 | 12–20 | 35–55 | 3.0–1.3 | 280–230 | 20–40 |
| | Medium-duty Com. veh. | SM | 2,000–4,000 | 16–19 | 7–10 | 15–25 | 6.0–3.0 | 250–220 | 10–15 |
| | | AM/ CAC | 1,800–2,600 | 15–18 | 18–24 | 25–40 | 4.0–2.5 | 225–200 | 20–40 |
| | | TC | 1,800–2,400 | 15–18 | 20–24 | 30–45 | 4.0–3.0 | 210–190 | 20–40 |

SM ≙ Naturally aspirated engine; AM ≙ Supercharged engine; CAC = Intercooling; TC = Turbocompound ≙ AM + CAC + Turbine

*Power and torque curves*

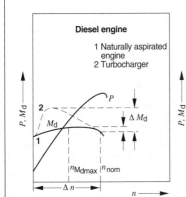

**Diesel engine**

1 Naturally aspirated engine
2 Turbocharger

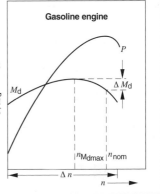

**Gasoline engine**

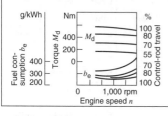

*Performance curves (part-load behavior) for a specific control-rack travel or specific accelerator-pedal position*

Diesel engine with constant control-rack travel $M_d$ remains roughly constant at $n$.

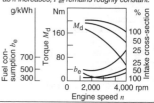

Single-point mixture formation (four-stroke) with constant throttle-valve position. $M_d$ drops rapidly as $n$ increases, $P_{eff}$ remains roughly constant.

## Torque position

The position on the engine-speed curve (relative to rpm for max. output) at which maximum torque is developed, specified in % ($n_{Mdmax}/n_{nominal} \cdot 100$).

## Useful speed range
(minimum full-load speed/nominal speed)

| Engine type | | Useful speed range $\Delta n_N$ | Torque position % |
|---|---|---|---|
| Diesel engine | Pass. cars | 3.5...5 | 15...40 |
| | Trucks | 1.8...3.2 | 10...60 |
| Spark-ignition engine | | 4...7 | 25...35 |

## Torque increase

| Engine type | | Torque increase $M_d$ in % |
|---|---|---|
| Diesel engine Pass.cars | Nat. asp. engine | 15...20 |
| | SC[1] | 20...30 |
| | SC[1] + CAC[2] | 25...35 |
| Diesel engine Trucks | Nat. asp. engine | 10...15 |
| | SC[1] | 15...30 |
| | SC[1] + CAC[2] | 25...40 |
| Spark-ignition engine | Nat. asp. engine | 25...30 |
| | SC[1] + CAC[2] | 30...35 |

[1] With supercharging, [2] With intercooling.

## Engine output, atmospheric conditions

The torque and thus the power output of an internal-combustion engine are essentially determined by the heat content of the cylinder charge. The flow rate of air (or, more precisely, of oxygen) in the cylinder charge provides a direct indication of heat content. The change which the engine will display at full power can be calculated as a function of variations in the condition of the ambient air (temperature, barometric pressure, humidity), provided that engine speed, air/fuel (A/F) ratio, volumetric efficiency, combustion efficiency, and total engine power loss remain constant. The A/F mixture responds to lower atmospheric density by becoming richer. The volumetric efficiency (pressure in cylinder at BDC relative to pressure in ambient air) only remains constant for all atmospheric conditions at maximum throttle-valve aperture (WOT). Combustion efficiency drops in cold thin air as vaporization rate, turbulence, and combustion speed all fall. Engine power loss (friction losses + gas-exchange work + boost power drain) reduces the indicated power.

### Effect of atmospheric conditions

The quantity of air which an engine draws in, or is inputted to the engine by supercharging, depends upon ambient-air density; colder, heavier, denser air increases engine output. Rule of thumb: Engine power drops by approximately 1% for each 100 m rise in elevation. Depending upon engine design, the cold intake air is normally heated to some degree while traversing the intake passages, thereby reducing its density and thus the engine's ultimate output. Humid air contains less oxygen than dry air and therefore produces lower engine power outputs. The decrease is generally modest to the point of insignificance. The warm humidity of air in tropical regions can result in a noticeable engine power loss.

## Definitions of power

The effective power is the engine's power as measured at the crankshaft or ancillary mechanism (such as the transmission) at the specified engine speed. When measurements are made downstream from the transmission, the transmission losses

must be factored into the equation. Rated power is the maximum effective power of the engine at full throttle. Net power corresponds to effective power.

Conversion formulas are used to convert the results of dynamometer testing to reflect standard conditions, thereby negating the influences of such factors as time of day and year while simultaneously allowing the various manufacturers to provide mutually comparable data. The procedure converts air density – and thus the effective volume of air in the engine – to defined "standard conditions" for air mass.

The cross-references in the following table show the most important standards used in power correction.

**Power correction standards (comparison)**

| Standard (Date of publication) | EEC 80/1269 (4/81) | ISO 1585 (5/82) | JIS D 1001 (10/82) | SAE J 1349 (5/85) | DIN 70020 (11/76) |
|---|---|---|---|---|---|
| **Barometric pressure during testing (*vapor pressure subtracted!)** | | | | | |
| Dry $p_{PT}$*    kPa | 99 | 99 | 99 | 99 | – |
| Absolute $p_{PF}$  kPa | – | – | – | – | 101.3 |
| **Temperature during testing** | | | | | |
| Absolute $T_p$   K | 298 | 298 | 298 | 298 | 293 |
| **Engines with spark ignition, naturally aspirated and supercharged** | | | | | |
| Correction factor   $\alpha_A$ | $\alpha_a = A^{1.2} \cdot B^{0.5}$ $A = 99/p_{PT}$ $B = T_p/298$ | | | | $\alpha_a = A \cdot B^{0.5}$ $A = 101.3/p_{PF}$ $B = T/293$ |
| Corrected power: $P_0 = \alpha_a \cdot P\,(\text{kW})$ ($P$ measured power) | | | | | |
| **Diesel engines, naturally aspirated and supercharged** | | | | | |
| Atmospheric correction factor   $f_a$ | $f_a = A \cdot B^{0.7}$ ($A = 99/p_{PT}$; $B = T_p/293$) (naturally aspirated and mechanically supercharged engines) | | | | as $\alpha_a$ for SI engines |
| | $f_a = A^{0.7} \cdot B^{1.5}$ ($A = 99/p_{PT}$; $B = T_p/293$) (turbocharged engines with/without intercooling) | | | | |
| Engine correction factor   $f_m$ | $40 \le q/r \le 65$: $\quad f_m = 0.036 \cdot (q/r) - 1.14$ $q/r < 40$: $\quad\quad\quad f_m = 0.3$ $q/r > 65$: $\quad\quad\quad f_m = 1.2$ | | | | $f_m = 1$ |
| $r = p_L/p_E$ Charge-air pressure response at $p_L$ absolute charge-air pressure, $p_E$ absolute pressure upstream of compressor, $q$ spec. fuel consumption (SAE J 1349). 4-stroke engines: $q = 120,000\ F/DN$, 2-stroke engines: $q = 60,000\ F/DN$, with $F$ fuel flow (mg/s); $D$ Displacement ($l$); $N$ Engine speed (rpm) | | | | | |
| Corrected power: $P_0 = P \cdot f_a{}^{fm}\,(\text{kW})$ ($P$ measured power) | | | | | |
| **Mandatory accessories** | | | | | |
| Fan | Yes, with electric/viscous-drive fan at max. slip | | | | ⎫ Not |
| Emissions control system | Yes | | | | ⎬ defined |
| Alternator | Yes, loaded with engine-current draw | | | | Yes |
| Servo-pumps | No | | | | No |
| Air conditioner | No | | | | No |

## Calculation

| Quantity | | Unit |
|---|---|---|
| $a_K$ | Piston acceleration | $m/s^2$ |
| $B$ | Fuel consumption | kg/h; $dm^3$/h |
| $b_e$ | Spec. fuel consumption | g/kWh |
| $D$ | Cylinder diameter $2 \cdot r$ | mm |
| $d_v$ | Valve diameter | mm |
| $F$ | Force | N |
| $F_G$ | Gas force in the cylinder | N |
| $F_N$ | Piston side thrust | N |
| $F_o$ | Oscillating inertial force | N |
| $F_r$ | Rotating inertial force | N |
| $F_s$ | Connecting-rod force | N |
| $F_T$ | Tangential force | N |
| $M$ | Torque | $N \cdot m$ |
| $M_o$ | Oscillating moments | $N \cdot m$ |
| $M_r$ | Rotating moments | $N \cdot m$ |
| $M_d$ | Engine torque | $N \cdot m$ |
| $m_p$ | Power-to-weight ratio | kg/kW |
| $n$ | Engine speed | rpm |
| $n_p$ | Fuel-injection pump speed | rpm |
| $P$ | Power | kW |
| $P_{eff}$ | Effective power[1] | kW |
| $P_H$ | Power output per liter | $kW/dm^3$ |
| $p$ | Pressure | bar |
| $p_c$ | Final compression | bar |
| $p_e$ | Mean piston pressure (Mean pressure, mean working pressure) | bar |
| $p_L$ | Charge-air pressure | bar |
| $p_{max}$ | Peak injection pressure | bar |
| $r$ | Crankshaft radius | mm |
| $s_d$ | Injection cross-section of the nozzle | $mm^2$ |
| $S, s$ | Stroke, general | mm |
| $s$ | Piston stroke | mm |
| $s_f$ | Induction stroke of a cylinder (2-stroke) | mm |
| $s_F$ | Induction stroke, 2-stroke engine | mm |
| $S_k$ | Piston clearance from TDC | mm |
| $S_s$ | Slot height, 2-stroke engine | mm |
| $T$ | Temperature | °C, K |
| $T_c$ | Final compression temperature | K |
| $T_L$ | Charge-air temperature | K |
| $T_{max}$ | Peak temperature in combustion chamber | K |
| $t$ | Time | s |
| $V$ | Volume | $m^3$ |

| Quantity | | Unit |
|---|---|---|
| $V_c$ | Compression volume of a cylinder | $dm^3$ |
| $V_E$ | Injected fuel quantity per pump stroke | $mm^3$ |
| $V_f$ | Charge volume of a cylinder (2-stroke) | $dm^3$ |
| $V_F$ | Charge volume of a 2-stroke engine | $dm^3$ |
| $V_h$ | Displacement of a cylinder | $dm^3$ |
| $V_H$ | Displacement of the engine | $dm^3$ |
| $\upsilon$ | Velocity | m/s |
| $\upsilon_d$ | Mean velocity of the injection jet | m/s |
| $\upsilon_g$ | Gas velocity | m/s |
| $\upsilon_m$ | Mean piston velocity | m/s |
| $\upsilon_{max}$ | Max. piston velocity | m/s |
| $z$ | Number of cylinders | – |
| $\alpha_d$ | Injection time (in °crankshaft at fuel-injection pump) | ° |
| $\beta$ | Pivoting angle of connecting rod | ° |
| $\varepsilon$ | Compression ratio | – |
| $\eta$ | Efficiency | – |
| $\eta_e$ | Net efficiency | – |
| $\eta_{th}$ | Thermal efficiency | – |
| $v, v_1$ | Polytropic exponent of real gases | – |
| $\varrho$ | Density | $kg/m^3$ |
| $\varphi, \alpha$ | Crankshaft angle ($\varphi_0$ = top dead center) | ° |
| $\omega$ | Angular velocity | rad/s |
| $\lambda$ | = $r/l$ Stroke/connecting-rod ratio | – |
| $\lambda$ | Excess-air factor | – |
| $\varkappa$ | = $c_p/c_v$ Adiabatic exponent of ideal gases | – |

### Superscripts and subscripts

| | |
|---|---|
| 0, 1, 2, 3, 4, 5 | Cycle values/main values |
| o | Oscillating |
| r | Rotating |
| 1st, 2nd | 1st, 2nd order |
| A | Constant |
| ', " | Subdivision of main values, derivations |

[1] Effective power $P_{eff}$ is the effective horsepower delivered by the internal-combustion engine, with it driving the auxiliary equipment necessary for operation (e.g., ignition equipment, fuel-injection pump, scavenging-air and cooling-air fan, water pump and fan, supercharger) (DIN 1940). This power is called net engine power in DIN 70020 (see P. 497).

**Conversion of units**
(See PP. 29...38)

| | |
|---|---|
| 1 g/hp · h | = 1.36 g/kW · h |
| 1 g/kW · h | = 0.735 g/hp · h |
| 1 kp · m | = 9.81 N · m ≈ 10 N · m |
| 1 N · m | = 0.102 kp · m ≈ 0.1 kp · m |
| 1 hp | = 0.735 kW |
| 1 kW | = 1.36 hp |
| 1 at | = 0.981 bar ≈ 1 bar |
| 1 bar | = 1.02 at ≈ 1 at |

**Calculation equations**

| **Mathematical relationship between quantities** | **Numerical relationship between quantities** |
|---|---|

**Piston displacement**
Displacement of a cylinder

$$V_h = \frac{\pi \cdot d^2 \cdot s}{4}; \quad V_f = \frac{\pi \cdot d^2 \cdot s_f}{4} \text{ (2-stroke)}$$

$V_H = 0.785 \cdot 10^{-6} \, d^2 \cdot s$
$V_h$ in dm³, $d$ in mm, $s$ in mm

Displacement of an engine
$V_H = V_h \cdot z; \quad V_F = V_f \cdot z$ (2-stroke)

$V_H = 0.785 \cdot 10^{-6} \, d^2 \cdot s \cdot z$
$V_h$ in dm³, $d$ in mm, $s$ in mm

**Compression**
Compression ratio

$$\varepsilon = \frac{V_h + V_c}{V_c} \text{ (see P. 502 for diagram)}$$

Final compression pressure

$p_c = p_0 \cdot \varepsilon^{\nu}$

Final compression temperature

$T_c = T_0 \cdot \varepsilon^{\nu-1}$

**Piston movement** (see P. 503 for diagram)
Piston clearance from top dead center

$$S_k = r\left[1 + \frac{l}{r} - \cos\varphi - \sqrt{\left(\frac{l}{r}\right)^2 - \sin^2\varphi}\right]$$

*4-stroke engine*    *2-stroke engine*

Crankshaft angle

$\varphi = 2 \cdot \pi \cdot n \cdot t$ ($\varphi$ in rad)

Piston velocity (approximation)

$v \approx 2 \cdot \pi \cdot n \cdot r\left(\sin\varphi + \frac{r}{2l}\sin 2\varphi\right)$

$\varphi = 6 \cdot n \cdot t$
$\varphi$ in °, $n$ in rpm, $t$ in s

$v \approx \dfrac{n \cdot s}{19,100}\left(\sin\varphi + \dfrac{r}{2l}\sin 2\varphi\right)$

$v$ in m/s, $n$ in rpm, $l$, $r$ and $s$ in mm

Mean piston velocity

$v_m = 2 \cdot n \cdot s$

$v_m = \dfrac{n \cdot s}{30,000}$ (see P. 504 for diagram)

Maximum piston velocity (approximate, if connecting rod is on a tangent with the big-end trajectory; $a_k = 0$)

$v_m$ in m/s, $n$ in rpm, $s$ in mm

| $l/r$ | 3.5 | 4 | 4.5 |
|---|---|---|---|
| $v_{max}$ | $1.63 \cdot v_m$ | $1.62 \cdot v_m$ | $1.61 \cdot v_m$ |

(see P. 504 for diagram)

**Piston acceleration** (approximation)

$$a_k \approx 2 \cdot \pi^2 \cdot n^2 \cdot s \left(\cos\varphi + \frac{r}{l}\cos 2\varphi\right)$$

$a \approx \dfrac{n^2 \cdot s}{182,400}\left(\cos\varphi + \dfrac{r}{l}\cos 2\varphi\right)$

$a_k$ in m/s², $n$ in rpm, $l$, $r$ and $s$ in mm

---

[1] The variables can be entered in the equations in any units. The unit of the quantity to be calculated is obtained from the units chosen for the terms of the equation. The numerical equations apply only with the units of measure specified under the equation.

**Calculation equations** (continued)

| Mathematical relationship between quantities | Numerical relationship between quantities |
|---|---|
| **Gas velocity** Mean gas velocity in the valve section $$v_g = \frac{d^2}{d_v^2} \cdot v_m$$ | $$v_g = \frac{d^2}{d_v^2} \cdot \frac{n \cdot s}{30{,}000}$$ $v_g$ in m/s, $d$, $d_v$, and $s$ in mm, $n$ in rpm |
| **Fuel delivery** Injected fuel quantity per fuel-injection pump stroke $$V_E = \frac{P_{eff} \cdot b_e}{\varrho \cdot n_p \cdot z}$$ | $$V_E = \frac{1{,}000 \cdot P_{eff} \cdot b_e}{60 \cdot \varrho \cdot n_p \cdot z}$$ $V_E$ in mm³, $P_{eff}$ in kW, $b_e$ in g/kW · h (or also $P_{eff}$ in hp, $b_e$ in g/hp · h), $n_p$ in rpm, $\varrho$ in kg/dm³ (for fuels $\varrho \approx 0.85$ kg/dm³) |
| Mean velocity of injection jet $$v_d = \frac{2 \cdot \pi \cdot n_p \cdot V_E}{S_d \cdot \alpha_d} \quad (\alpha_d \text{ in rad})$$ | $$v_d = \frac{6 \, n_p \cdot V_E}{1{,}000 \cdot S_d \cdot \alpha_d}$$ $v_d$ in = in m/s, $n_p$ in rpm, $V_E$ in mm³, $S_d$ in mm², $\alpha_d$ in ° |
| **Engine power** $$P = M \cdot \omega = 2 \cdot \pi \cdot M \cdot n$$ $$P_{eff} = V_H \cdot p_e \cdot n/K$$ $K = 1$ for 2-stroke engine $K = 2$ for 4-stroke engine | $$P = M \cdot n/9{,}549$$ $P$ in kW, $M$ in N · m (= W · s), $$P_{eff} = \frac{V_H \cdot p_e \cdot n}{K \cdot 600} = \frac{M_d \cdot n}{9{,}549}$$ $P_{eff}$ in kW, $p_e$ in bar, $n$ in rpm. $M_d$ in N · m |
| Power per unit displacement (power output per liter) $$P_H = \frac{P_{eff}}{V_H}$$ | $$P = M \cdot n/716.2$$ $P$ in hp, $M$ in kp · m, $n$ in rpm |
| Power-to-weight ratio $$m_p = \frac{m}{P_{eff}}$$ | |

**Calculation equations** (continued)

| Mathematical relationship between quantities | Numerical relationship between quantities |
|---|---|

**Mean piston pressure** (mean pressure, mean working pressure)

| 4-stroke engine | 2-stroke engine | 4-stroke engine | 2-stroke engine |
|---|---|---|---|
| $p = \dfrac{2 \cdot P}{V_H \cdot n}$ | $p = \dfrac{P}{V_H \cdot n}$ | $p = 1{,}200\,\dfrac{P}{V_H \cdot n}$ | $p = 600\,\dfrac{P}{V_H \cdot n}$ |

$p$ in bar, $P$ in kW, $V_H$ in dm³, $n$ in rpm

| | | $p = 833\,\dfrac{P}{V_H \cdot n}$ | $p = 441\,\dfrac{P}{V_H \cdot n}$ |
|---|---|---|---|

$p$ in bar, $P$ in PS, $V_H$ in dm³, $n$ in rpm

| $p = \dfrac{4 \cdot \pi \cdot M}{V_H}$ | $p = \dfrac{2 \cdot \pi \cdot M}{V_H}$ | $p = 0.1257\,\dfrac{M}{V_H}$ | $p = 0.0628\,\dfrac{M}{V_H}$ |
|---|---|---|---|

$p$ in bar, $M$ in N · m, $V_H$ in dm³

**Engine torque**

| $M_d = \dfrac{V_H \cdot p_e}{4\,\pi}$ | $M_d = \dfrac{V_H \cdot p_e}{2\,\pi}$ | $M_d = \dfrac{V_H \cdot p_e}{0.12566}$    $M_d = \dfrac{V_H \cdot p_e}{0.06284}$ |
|---|---|---|

$M_d$ in N · m, $V_H$ in dm³, $p_e$ in bar
$M_d = 9{,}549 \cdot P_{eff}/n$
$M_d$ in N · m, $P_{eff}$ in kW, $n$ in rpm

**Fuel consumption** [1]

$B$ = Measured values in kg/h
$b_e = B/P_{eff}$
$b_e = 1/(H_u \cdot \eta_e)$

$B$ in dm³/h or kg/h

$V_B$ = Measured volume on test dynamometer

$t_B$ = Elapsed time for measured volume consumption

$b_e = \dfrac{V_b \cdot \varrho_B \cdot 3{,}600}{t_B \cdot P_{eff}}$

$\varrho_B$ = Fuel density in g/cm³, $t_B$ in s, $V_B$ in cm³, $P_{eff}$ in kW.

**Efficiency**

$\eta_{th} = 1 - \varepsilon^{1-v}$
$\eta_e = P_{eff}/(B \cdot H_u)$

$\eta_e = 86/b_e$
where $H_u$ = specific calorific value 42,000 kJ/kg
$b_e$ in g/(kW · h)

---

[1] See P. 417 for on-vehicle measures influencing fuel consumption.

**Displacement and compression area**                    See P. 499 for diagram and equation.

The diagram below applies to the displacement $V_h$ and compression space $V_c$ of the individual cylinder, and to the total displacement $V_H$ and total compression space $V_C$.

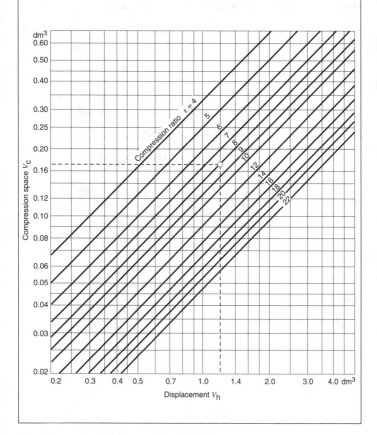

Example:
An engine with a displacement of 1.2 dm³ and a compression ratio $\varepsilon = 8$ has a compression area of 0.17 dm³.

**Piston clearance from top dead center**    *See P. 499 for equation.*

*Conversion of degrees of crankshaft angle to mm piston travel.*

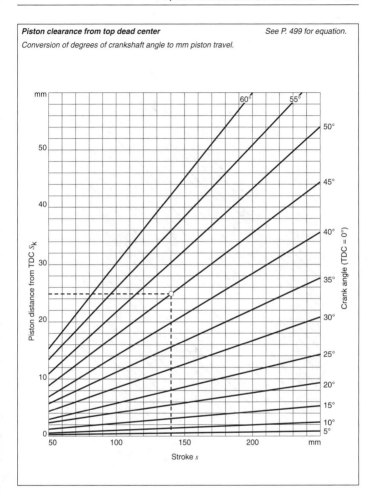

Example:
The piston clearance from top dead center is 25 mm for a stroke of 140 mm at 45°
crankshaft.

The diagram is based on a crank ratio $l/r = 4$ ($l$ connecting-rod length, $r$ one half of the
stroke length). However, it also applies with very good approximation (error less than
2%) for all ratios $l/r$ between 3.5 and 4.5.

**Piston velocity** *See P. 499 for equation.*

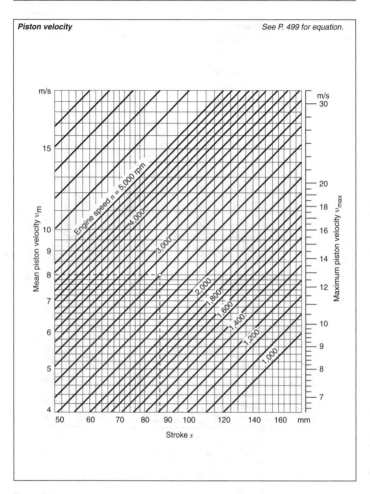

Stroke $s$

Example:
Mean piston velocity $v_m$ = 8 m/s and maximum piston velocity $v_{max}$ = 13 m/s for stroke $s$ = 86 mm and at an engine speed of $n$ = 2,800 rpm

The diagram is based on $v_{max}$ = 1.62 $v_m$ (see P. 499).

### Density increase of combustion air in cylinder on turbo/supercharging

*Increase in density on supercharging as a function of the pressure ratio in the compressor, the compressor efficiency and the intercooling rate for charge-air cooling (CAC)*

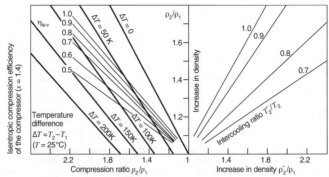

$p_2/p_1 = \pi_c$ = Pressure ratio during precompression,
$\varrho_2/\varrho_1$ = Increase in density, $\varrho_1$ = Density upstream of compressor,
$\varrho_2$ = Density downstream of compressor in kg/m³
$T_2'/T_2$ = Intercooling rate, $T_2$ = Temperature before CAC, $T_2'$ = Temperature after CAC in K
$\eta_{is-v}$ = Isentropic compressor efficiency

### Final compression pressure and temperature

*Final compression temperature as a function of the compression ratio and the intake temperature.*

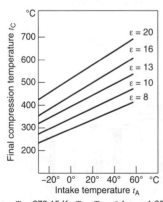

$t_C = T_C - 273.15$ K, $T_C = T_A \cdot \varepsilon^{n-1}$, $n = 1.35$

*Final compression pressure as a function of the compression ratio and boost pressure.*

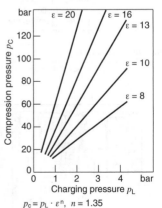

$p_C = p_L \cdot \varepsilon^n$, $n = 1.35$

# Reciprocating-piston engine with external combustion (Stirling engine)

## Operating concept and efficiency

Cycle sequence: In phase I, the power piston (bottom), or working piston, is at its lowest position and the displacer (top piston) is at its highest. All of the working gas is expanded in the "cold" area between the two pistons. During the transition from phase I to phase II, the power piston compresses the working medium in the cold chamber. The displacer remains in its top position. During the transition from phase II to phase III, the displacer moves down to push the compressed working medium through the heat exchanger and into the regenerator (where it absorbs the stored heat), and from there into the heater (where it is heated to maximum working temperature). As the power piston remains in its lowest position, the volume does not change.

After treatment, the gas enters the "hot" area above the displacer. During the transition from phase III to phase IV, the hot gas expands. The power piston and displacer are pushed into their lowest positions and power is produced. The cycle is completed with the transition from phase IV back to phase I, where the displacer's upward motion again propels the gas through the heater and into the regenerator, radiating substantial heat in the process. The residual heat is extracted at the heat exchanger before the gas re-enters the cold area.

Thus the theoretical cycle largely corresponds to isothermal compression (the working gas is cooled back down to its initial temperature in the heat exchanger after adiabatic compression), isochoric heat addition via the regenerator and heater, quasi-isothermal expansion (the working gas is reheated to its initial condition in the heater after adiabatic expansion), and isochoric heat dissipation via the regenerator and heat exchanger.

The ideal cycle shown in the $p$-$V$ and $T$-$S$ diagrams could only be achieved if – as described – the movement of the power and displacer systems were discontinuous.

If both pistons are connected to a shaft, i.e., via a rhombic drive, they carry out phase-shifted sinusoidal movements leading to a rounded work diagram with the same cycle efficiency – similar to the efficiency of the Carnot cycle – but with trade-offs in power and net efficiency.

---

**The Stirling engine cycle**
*Four states of discontinuous power-piston and displacer movement.*
*1 Power piston, 2 Displacer, 3 Cold space, 4 Hot space, 5 Heat exchanger, 6 Regenerator, 7 Heater.*

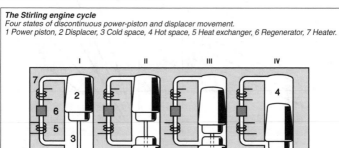

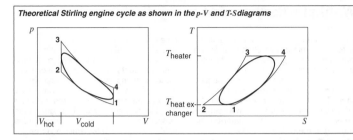

**Theoretical Stirling engine cycle as shown in the p-V and T-S diagrams**

## Design and operating characteristics

Modern Stirling engines are double-acting engines with (for instance) 4 cylinders operating with a defined phase shift. Each cylinder has only one piston whose top surface acts as a power piston, and whose bottom surface acts as a displacer for the following cylinder. The heat exchanger, regenerator and heater are located between the cylinders.

In order to maintain an acceptable power output per unit of engine capacity, the engines run at high pressures of 50 to 200 bar, variable for purposes of load control. Gases with low flow losses and high specific heats (usually hydrogen) must be used as working fluids. As the heat exchanger must transfer all of the heat which is to be extracted from the process to the ambient air, Stirling engines require considerably larger heat exchangers than IC engines.

Advantages of the Stirling engine: very low concentrations of all the pollutants which are subject to legislation (HC, CO and $NO_x$); quiet operation without combustion noise; burns a wide variety of different fuels (multifuel capability); fuel consumption (in program map) roughly equivalent to that of a direct-injection diesel engine at comparable speeds.

Disadvantages: high manufacturing costs due to complicated design; very high operating pressures with only moderate power output relative to the unit's volume and weight; expensive load-control system required; large cooling surface and/or ventilation power required.

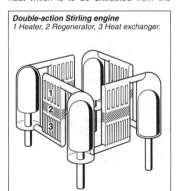

**Double-action Stirling engine**
1 Heater, 2 Regenerator, 3 Heat exchanger.

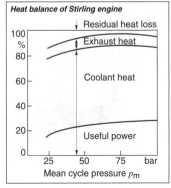

**Heat balance of Stirling engine**

# Wankel rotary engine

The rotary engine is an unconventional piston powerplant in which the crankshaft mechanism is replaced by an eccentric drive unit operated by a rotary piston.

The piston forms the combustion chambers as it proceeds through its trochoidal rotation pattern. Viewed from the side, the rotor is a triangle with convex sides. Located within the water-cooled housing is the oval – or more precisely: hourglass shaped – piston chamber (epitrochoid). As the rotor turns, its three apexes follow the wall of the housing to form three mutually sealed, variable-displacement chambers (A, B and C) spaced at 120° intervals. Each of these chambers hosts a complete four-stroke-combustion cycle during each full rotation of the rotor, i.e. after one full rotation of the triangular rotor, the engine has completed the four-stroke cycle three times and the eccentric shaft has completed an equal number of rotations.

The rotor is equipped with both face and apex seals. It incorporates a concentric internal ring gear and the bearings for the engine shaft's eccentric. The rotary piston's internal ring gear turns against a housing-mounted gear: This gear runs concentrically relative to the eccentric shaft. This gear set transmits no force. Instead, it maintains the rotary piston in the trochoidal orbit pattern required to synchronize piston and eccentric shaft.

The teeth of the gear set act in accordance with a 3:2 conversion ratio. The rotor turns at two thirds of the shaft's angular velocity and in the opposite direction. This arrangement produces a relative rotor velocity that is only one third of the shaft's angular velocity relative to the housing.

*Design and operating concept of the Wankel rotary engine*
1 Rotor, 2 Internal gearing in rotor, 3 Spark plug, 4 Fixed pinion, 5 Running surface of eccentric.
a) Cell **A** takes in air-fuel mixture, cell **B** compresses the mixture, and the combustion gases are exhausted from cell **C**. (Depressions in the rotor flanks allow gas to pass by the trochoidal restriction.)
b) Cell **A** is filled with fresh gas, the combustion gases expand in cell **B**, thereby turning the eccentric shaft via the rotor, combustion gases continue to be exhausted from cell **C**. The next phase of combustion is again that shown in figure a), whereby cell **C** has taken the place of cell **A**. Thus the rotor, by turning through 120° of one rotation, has carried out the complete four-stroke process at its three flanks. During this process, the eccentric shaft has made one complete rotation.

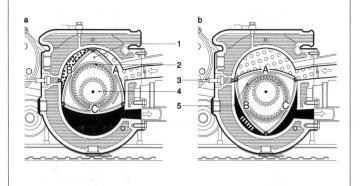

Gas exchange is regulated by the piston itself as it moves past slots in the housing. An alternative to this arrangement – with peripheral intake ports located along the trochoidal patha of the apexes – is represented by intake ducts in the side of the block (side ports).

Considerably higher gas velocities and engine speeds are made possible by the lack of restrictive gas passages and the absence of reciprocating masses. Every rotary engine can be completely balanced mechanically. The only remaining irregularity is the uneven torque flow, a characteristic of all internal-combustion engines. However, the torsional force curve of a single-rotor engine is considerably smoother than that of a conventional single-cylinder engine, due to the fact that the power strokes occur over 270° of the eccentric shaft's rotation. Power-flow consistency and operating smoothness can both be enhanced by joining several rotary pistons on a single shaft. In this context, a three-rotor Wankel corresponds to an eight-cylinder, reciprocating-piston engine. The torque curve can be made to assume the characteristics of a throttled engine or a racing engine by changing the timing (location) and the intake cross-section.

Advantages of the rotary engine: complete balancing of masses; favorable torsional force curve; compact design; no valve-gear assembly; excellent tractability.

Disadvantages: less than optimal combustion-chamber shape with long flame paths, high HC emissions, increased fuel and oil consumption, higher manufacturing costs, diesel operation not possible, high location of output shaft.

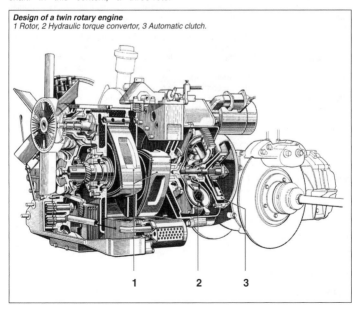

*Design of a twin rotary engine*
*1 Rotor, 2 Hydraulic torque convertor, 3 Automatic clutch.*

**1**    **2**    **3**

# Gas turbine

In the gas turbine, the individual changes of state during the cycle take place in spatially separate components (compressors, burners and turbines), which communicate with one another via flow-conducting components (diffusers, spirals and the like). These changes of state therefore occur continuously.

## Operating concept, comparative cycle and efficiency

In automotive gas turbines, the intake air is drawn in continuously through filters and mufflers prior to condensation in a radial compressor and subsequent warming in a heat exchanger. The heat exchanger in current automotive units is usually designed as a rotating regenerator.

The compressed and preheated air then flows into the burner where it is directly heated through injection and combustion of gaseous, liquid or emulsified fuels. Energy from the compressed and heated gases is then transmitted to one, two or three turbine stages on one to three shaft assemblies. The radial or axial-flow turbines initially drive compressors and auxiliary assemblies, which then relay the remaining power to the propshaft via a power turbine, reduction gear and transmission.

The turbine usually incorporates adjustable blades (AGV turbine) designed to reduce fuel consumption at idle and in part-load operation whilst simultaneously enhancing tractability during acceleration. In single-shaft machines, this necessitates an adjustment mechanism for the transmission.

After partial cooling in the expansion phase the gases flow through the gas section of the heat exchanger, where most of their residual heat is discharged into the air. The gases themselves are then expelled through the exhaust passage, whereby they can also supply heat for the vehicle's heating system.

The thermal efficiency and with it the fuel consumption of the gas turbine are largely determined by the maximum possible operating temperature (burner exit temperature). The temperatures that can be achieved using highly heat-resistant cobalt- or nickel-based alloys do not allow fuel consumption that is comparable with present-day piston engines. It will need the changeover to ceramic materials before similar or even better fuel efficiency can be achieved.

The comparative thermodynamic cycle for the gas turbine is the constant-pressure or Joule cycle. It consists of isentropic compression (process 1→2), isobaric heat addition (process 2→3), isentropic expansion (process 3→4) and isobaric heat dissipation (process 4→1). High levels of thermal efficiency are only available when the temperature increase from $T_2$ to $T_{2'}$, supplied by the heat exchanger, is coupled with a thermal discharge (4→4'). If heat is completely ex-

**Characteristic operating temperatures (orders of magnitude) at various positions in metallic and ceramic automotive gas turbines at WOT.**

| Measuring point | Metal turbine | Ceramic turbine |
|---|---|---|
| Compressor exit | 230 °C | 250 °C |
| Heat-exchanger exit (air side) | 700 °C | 950 °C |
| Burner exit | 1,000 °C...1,100 °C | 1,250 °C...1,350 °C |
| Heat-exchanger inlet (gas side) | 750 °C | 1,000 °C |
| Heat-exchanger exit | 270 °C | 300 °C |

***Thermodynamic comparative cycle as shown in the p-V and T-S diagrams***

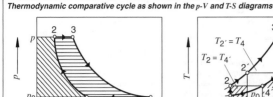
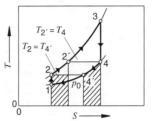

changed, the quantity of heat to be added per unit of gas is reduced to

$$q_{add} = c_p \cdot (T_3 - T_{2'}) = c_p \cdot (T_3 - T_4)$$

and the quantity of heat to be removed is

$$q_{rem} = c_p \cdot (T_{4'} - T_1) = c_p \cdot (T_2 - T_1)$$

The maximum thermal efficiency for the gas turbine with heat exchanger is:

$$\eta_{th} = 1 - Q_{rem}/Q_{add} = 1 - (T_2 - T_1)/(T_3 - T_4)$$

Where $p_2/p_1 = (T_2/T_1)^{\frac{\chi}{\chi-1}} = (T_3/T_4)^{\frac{\chi}{\chi-1}}$ and $T_4 = T_3 \cdot (T_1/T_2)$ it follows that

$$\eta_{th} = 1 - (T_2/T_3)$$

Current gas-turbine powerplants achieve thermal efficiencies of up to 35%.

<u>Advantages of the gas turbine</u>: clean exhaust without supplementary emission-control devices; extremely smooth running; multifuel capability; good static torque curve; extended maintenance intervals.

<u>Disadvantages</u>: manufacturing costs still high, poor transitional response, higher fuel consumption, less suitable for low-power applications.

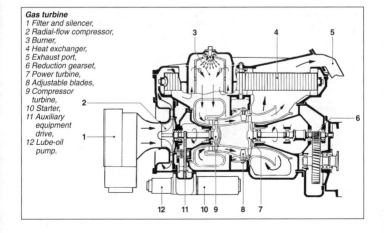

*Gas turbine*
1 Filter and silencer,
2 Radial-flow compressor,
3 Burner,
4 Heat exchanger,
5 Exhaust port,
6 Reduction gearset,
7 Power turbine,
8 Adjustable blades,
9 Compressor turbine,
10 Starter,
11 Auxiliary equipment drive,
12 Lube-oil pump.

# Engine cooling

## Air cooling

Cooling air is routed by dynamic pressure and/or a fan around the finned external walls of the cylinder casing. Facilities designed to restrict the flow of cooling air and control the fan speed can be employed to regulate the volumetric flow rate. Power consumption is 3...4% of total engine output.

Heat absorbed by the engine oil is dispersed by an air-cooled oil cooler mounted at a suitable position in the air stream.

The noise emission level and the inefficiency in maintaining consistent engine temperatures are considered to be disadvantages compared to liquid-cooled engines. Today, air cooling is mainly used for motorcycle engines and in special applications.

## Water cooling

Water cooling has become the standard in both passenger cars and heavy-duty vehicles.

Instead of pure water, coolants are now a mixture of water (drinking quality), antifreeze (generally ethylene glycol), and various corrosion inhibitors selected for the specific application. An antifreeze concentration of 30...50% raises the coolant-mixture boiling point to allow operating temperatures of up to 120 °C at a pressure of 1.4 bar in passenger cars.

### Radiator designs and materials

The cores of the coolant radiators in modern passenger cars are almost exclusively made of aluminum. Aluminum radiators are also being used to an ever-increasing extent in a wide range of commercial vehicles and trucks throughout the world. There are two basic assembly variants:
– Brazed radiators, and
– Mechanically joined or assembled radiators

For cooling high-performance engines, or when space is limited, the best solution is a brazed flat-tube and corrugated-fin radiator layout with minimized aerodynamic resistance on the air-intake side.

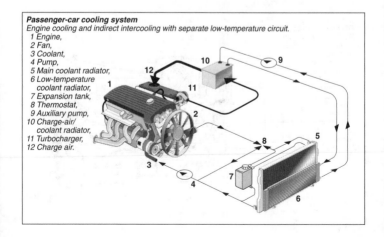

*Passenger-car cooling system*
*Engine cooling and indirect intercooling with separate low-temperature circuit.*
1 Engine,
2 Fan,
3 Coolant,
4 Pump,
5 Main coolant radiator,
6 Low-temperature
  coolant radiator,
7 Expansion tank,
8 Thermostat,
9 Auxiliary pump,
10 Charge-air/
  coolant radiator,
11 Turbocharger,
12 Charge air.

The less expensive, mechanically assembled finned-tube system is generally employed for applications with less powerful engines or when more space is available.

When the radiator is assembled mechanically, the cooling grid is formed by mounting stamped fins around round, oval or flat-oval tubes. The fins are corrugated and/or slotted at right angles to the direction of air flow.

Gills and corrugations are integrated in the cooling fins on the cooling-air side to enhance thermal transfer. Further measures to increase cooling efficiency include the use of tubes with the lowest possible width and wall thickness, and turbulators on the coolant side, provided the attendant pressure losses remain within acceptable limits.

The radiator tank ensures that the coolant is distributed throughout the block. These tanks are made of fiberglass-reinforced polyamides, and are injection-molded with all connections and mountings in a single unit. They are flange-mounted to the radiator core and sealed by an integrated elastomer sealing element.

New developments encompass all-aluminum radiators with a radiator tank which is also made of aluminum and brazed to the radiator core in one operation.

**Radiator design**

Regardless of operating and environmental conditions, the radiator must continue to provide reliable thermal transfer by dissipating engine heat to the surrounding air. The size and therefore the cooling capacity of a specific radiator can be determined by calculation, based on correlation equations derived from tests relating to thermal transfer and flow-pressure loss.

The mass of air that flows through the radiator in the vehicle is a decisive factor and depends on:
- the driving speed
- the resistance to flow in the engine compartment
- the resistance to flow of the radiator, and
- the efficiency of the fan

The primary objective of radiator design is to maintain the coolant temperature at the engine outlet below a maximum permissible value under given operating conditions. At low air-mass flow rates, large and high-output radiators are required to achieve this objective, while a high air-mass flow rate facilitates the use of smaller radiators. However, a more powerful fan with high energy consumption is often required to achieve higher air-mass flow rates.

The task of determining the most favorable solution in terms of technical feasibility and economic efficiency is a matter of optimization that is best solved by the application of simulation tools. The most suitable and effective simulation tools describe all components that have an influence on air-mass flow and depict the radiator as an integral heat transfer medium or heat exchanger. The simulation results are verified by on-vehicle tests conducted in wind tunnels.

**Regulation of coolant temperature**

A motor vehicle's engine operates in a very wide range of climatic conditions and with major fluctuations in engine load. The temperature of the coolant – and also the engine – must be regulated if they are to remain constant within a narrow range.

Expansion-element regulated thermostat
An efficient way to compensate for varying conditions is to install a temperature-sensitive thermostat incorporating an expansion element to regulate temperature independent of pressure variations in the cooling system. The expansion element employed in this type of thermostat operates a double-acting disk valve, which – until the operating temperature is reached – closes the connection to the radiator while simultaneously releasing coolant flow from the engine outlet to the bypass line, allowing the coolant to flow uncooled back into the engine ("secondary circuit").

Both sides of the double valve are partially opened within the control range of the thermostat. This allows a mixture of cooled and uncooled coolant to flow to the engine at such a rate as to maintain a constant operating temperature.

The opening to the radiator is completely opened and the bypass line closed off at wide-open throttle ("primary circuit").

Electronic map-controlled thermostat
Further possibilities are permitted when a
program-map thermostat is used. An electronically controlled thermostat differs from
purely expansion-element regulated ther-
mostats in that the opening temperature
can be controlled. A map-controlled thermostat features a heating resistor that is
used to heat the expansion element additionally for the purpose of enlarging the
opening of the double valve to the radiator,
thereby reducing the coolant temperature.
The heating resistor is controlled by the engine management system in order to ensure that the engine operating temperature
is optimally adapted to the operating conditions. The information necessary for this
purpose is stored in the form of program
maps in the engine management system.

Raising the operating temperature in
the part-load range and reducing the operating temperature at wide-open throttle
provide the following benefits:

- Lower fuel consumption
- Low-pollutant exhaust-gas composition
- Reduced wear, and
- Improved heating efficiency of the
  vehicle interior

**Coolant expansion tank**
The expansion tank provides a reliable
escape channel for pressurized gases,
preventing cavitation of the kind that
tends to occur on the intake side of the
water pump. The expansion tank's air volume must be large enough to absorb the
coolant's thermal expansion during rapid
pressure buildup, and prevent the coolant
from boiling over when the hot engine is
shut off.

Expansion tanks are injection-molded
in plastic (generally polypropylene), although simple designs can also be blow-
molded to shape. A system of hoses is
normally used to connect the expansion
tank to the cooling system. The expansion tank is mounted in the engine compartment at the location representing the
highest point in the cooling system to ensure air is expelled effectively. In some
cases, the expansion tank can form a single unit with the radiator tank, or the two
can be joined by means of a flange or plug
connection.

---

*Map-controlled thermostat*
*1 Connector, 2 Connection to radiator,*
*3 Housing of working element, 4 Elastomer*
*insert, 5 Piston, 6 Bypass spring, 7 Bypass*
*valve, 8 Housing, 9 Heating resistor,*
*10 Main valve, 11 Main spring,*
*12 Connection from engine, 13 Tie bar,*
*14 Connection to engine (bypass).*

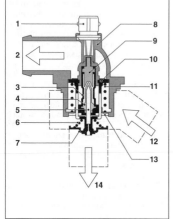

---

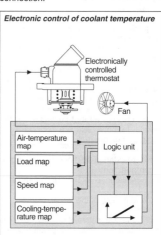

*Electronic control of coolant temperature*

The position and shape of the filler opening can be used to limit capacity, thus preventing overfilling. An electronic level sensor can be fitted to monitor the level of the coolant. The coolant level can also be monitored by manufacturing the expansion tank completely or partially in natural-color, transparent plastic with molded level markers. However, colorless polypropylene is sensitive to ultraviolet rays. For this reason, the transparent part of the expansion tank should not be exposed to direct sunlight.

## Cooling-air fan

### Design
Since motor vehicles also require substantial cooling capacity at low speeds, force-air ventilation is required for the radiator. Single-piece injection-molded plastic fans are generally employed in passenger cars; likewise, injection-molded fans with drive-power ratings extending up to 30 kW are now also used in commercial vehicles.

Fans with more modest power ratings are mostly driven electrically by DC motors or brushless DC motors (up to 850 W). Although blade design and arrangement can be selected to provide relatively quiet running, these fans have considerable noise levels at high rotation speeds.

In some passenger-car applications, in particular those involving very high engine power outputs and equipment options for operation in hot climates or equipment variants for diesel engines and air-conditioning systems, the capacity of the electric drive is no longer sufficient to provide the volume of air necessary to ensure effective cooling. In such cases, the fan is powered directly by the engine driven by V-belts. As a rule, fans on commercial vehicles and heavy-duty trucks are driven via the belt drive. In some rare applications, the fan may also be mounted directly on the crankshaft.

### Fan control
The fan-control arrangement requires particular attention. Depending upon vehicle and operating conditions, the unassisted air stream can provide sufficient cooling up to 95% of the time. It is thus possible to economize on energy that

would otherwise have to provide the power to drive the fan. For this purpose, electric fans use a multistage or continuous control system that specifically adapts the operating periods and speed of the fan to the required cooling capacity. A multistage control system may consist of relays and series resistors, while continuous variable control necessitates the use of power electronics. Electric thermostatic switches or the engine control unit supply the input signals for the control system.

### Drive layout
The fluid-friction or viscous-drive fan (VISCO® clutch) is a mechanical-drive arrangement of proven effectiveness for application in both passenger cars and commercial vehicles. It essentially consists of three assemblies (see figure on P. 516):
– the driven primary disk
– the driven secondary section, comprising the basic body and cover, and
– the control facility

An intermediate disk divides the secondary section in a supply chamber and a working chamber through which the fluid circulates. The primary disk rotates freely in the working chamber. Torque is transmitted by the internal friction of the highly-viscous fluid and its adhesion to the inner surfaces. There is a degree of slippage between input and output.

The viscous working fluid is a silicone oil. The amount of silicone oil located in the working chamber determines the output power transmitted by the clutch and therefore the speed of the fan. A valve located between the supply chamber and working chamber controls the amount of silicone oil in the working chamber.

A distinction can be made between two operating modes of the fluid-friction or viscous-drive fan clutch based on the type of valve operation:
– Firstly, the temperature-dependent, self-governing clutch which varies its speed infinitely by means of a bimetallic element, an operating pin and a valve lever. The controlled variable is the temperature of the air leaving the

radiator, and thus indirectly the temperature of the coolant.

– Secondly, the electrically activated clutch; this clutch is electronically controlled and electromagnetically actuated. Instead of just one controlled variable, a wide range of input variables is used for control purposes. These are usually the temperature limits of the various cooling media.

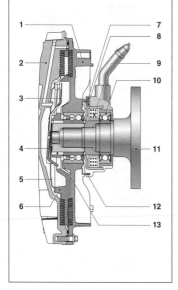

**Electronically controlled Visco clutch**
*1 Basic body, 2 Cover, 3 Valve-lever spring,
4 Solenoid armature, 5 Intermediate disk,
6 Primary disk, 7 Hall-effect sensor,
8 Permanent magnet, 9 Solenoid coil,
10 Magnet bearing, 11 Flanged shaft,
12 Speed pulse ring, 13 Magnetic flux
control ring.*

# Intercooling (charge-air cooling)

Trends in engine development show a constant increase in specific engine output power. This development goes hand in hand with the current transition from naturally aspirated engines to supercharged engines and ultimately to supercharged, intercooled engines. The need for intercooling (charge-air cooling) is attributed to the higher air density levels associated with supercharging systems and therefore the amount of oxygen available in the combustion air. Intercooling also reduces exhaust-gas emissions from supercharged diesel engines. If intercooling (charge-air cooling) were not employed on supercharged spark-ignition engines, appropriate steps would need to be taken to prevent engine knocking attributed to mixture enrichment and/or retarded ignition timing. Consequently, intercooling indirectly serves to reduce fuel consumption and pollutant emissions.

### Design variations

Basically speaking, both the ambient air and the engine coolant can be employed to cool the charge air. With only few exceptions, air-cooled intercoolers are now used both on passenger cars and commercial vehicles.

Air-cooled intercoolers can be mounted in front of or next to the engine radiator, or even at a completely different location above the cooling module. A remotely located intercooler can utilize either the unassisted vehicle air stream or its own fan. With the intercooler located in front of the engine radiator, the cooling-air fan ensures sufficient air flow even at low vehicle speeds. However, a drawback of this arrangement is that the cooling air is itself heated in the process. To compensate for this effect, the capacity of the engine radiator must be increased accordingly.

Coolant-cooled intercoolers can be installed in virtually any location in the engine compartment, as there are no technical. difficulties to supply the system with coolant. In addition, thanks to its modest dimensions, this type of intercooler requires substantially less space than the air-cooled intercooler. Coolant-cooled intercoolers have a high power density. However, coolant at a very low temperature must be available in order to effectively cool the charge air. This requirement is of particular significance in commercial vehicles and heavy-duty trucks as, in this case, it is necessary to heat the charge air to a level of 15 K above the ambient temperature. It therefore may be necessary to install a low-temperature radiator in the cooling module to ensure coolant is available at the required temperature level. Without a low-temperature radiator, the charge air can be cooled only down to levels in the vicinity of the engine coolant temperature.

The system of corrugated aluminum fins and tubes employed for the intercooler core is similar to the design of the engine coolant radiator. Wide tubes with internal fins provide superior performance and structural integrity in actual practice. The fin density on the cooling-air side is relatively low and corresponds approximately to the density of the inner fins in order to achieve a good distribution of thermal-transfer resistance.

The diffusion rate $\Phi$ is a particularly important intercooler property. It defines the relationship between charge-air cooling efficiency and the charge-air/cooling-air temperature differential:

$$\Phi = (t_{1E} - t_{1A}) / (t_{1E} - t_{2E})$$

The equation's elements are:

| | |
|---|---|
| $\Phi$ | Diffusion rate |
| $t_{1E}$ | Charge-air inlet temperature |
| $t_{1A}$ | Charge-air outlet temperature |
| $t_{2E}$ | Cooling-air inlet temperature |

For passenger cars: $\Phi = 0.4...0.7$;
For commercial vehicles: $\Phi = 0.9...0.95$.

Wherever possible, the plenum chamber is injection-molded in fiberglass-reinforced polyamide as a single casting incorporating all connections and mounts. Plenum chambers which are subject to increased stresses, e.g. the charge-air inlet system, are injection-molded from highly heat-resistant PPA or PPS. They are flange-mounted to the radiator core and sealed by an integrated elastomer sealing element. Plenum chambers which feature undercut shapes or are intended for high-temperature applications are cast in aluminum, and welded to the core.

## Oil and fuel cooling

Oil coolers are often needed in motor vehicles to cool both the engine oil and transmission oil. They are used when the heat losses from the engine or transmission can no longer be dissipated via the surface of the oil pan or the transmission with the result that the permitted oil temperatures are exceeded.

Oil coolers are designed as air-cooled or coolant-cooled units. They can be installed either in the cooling module or in any other position in the engine compartment. Suitable measures must be employed to supply cooling air to oil-to-air coolers located separately outside the cooling module, e.g. situated in the unassisted flow of air.

### Oil-to-air coolers

Oil-to-air coolers are predominantly made of aluminum. In most cases, they consist of a system of flat tubes and corrugated fins characterized by a high power density. Mechanically assembled systems with round tubes and fins are less commonly used. Turbulence inserts are brazed in the flat-tube system to increase cooling capacity and strength (to resist high internal pressures).

### Oil-to-coolant coolers

Aluminum stack designs employed in oil-to-coolant coolers have largely replaced stainless steel disk coolers and aluminum forked-tube coolers.

Disk coolers are mounted between the engine block and the oil filter. They have a separate casing and a central channel for the oil to pass through. The oil flowing back from the oil filter is routed through a labyrinth of perforated disks separated by turbulence inserts. This labyrinth is cooled by coolant flowing through the casing.

Forked-tube coolers are made of finned forked tubes through which the coolant flows. On the oil side, they have no casing and must therefore be integrated in the oil-filter housing or in the oil pan.

Disk-stack oil coolers are made of individual disks with turbulence inserts inserted between the disks. The upright edges of the disks fit together in a casing. Passages connect the channels formed by the disks in such a way that coolant and oil flow through alternate channels.

If only a modest cooling output is required (e.g. to cool transmission fluid in automatic transmissions) oil coolers can be used for passenger cars and commercial vehicles. They have no casing on the coolant side and are integrated in the outlet water tank of the coolant radiator. The oil coolers most suitable for this purpose are nonferrous metal double-tube coolers and aluminum flat-tube coolers. Double-tube oil coolers consist of two concentric tubes with turbulence inserts installed between them. Flat-tube oil coolers are made up of a brazed system of flat tubes and turbulence plates on the coolant side. The flat tubes are interconnected by openings at their ends. Turbulence inserts are brazed in the flat tubes to increase cooling capacity and strength.

An oil-to-air cooler is used to cool transmission oil in heavy-duty commercial vehicles. The unit is mounted in front of the engine radiator in order to ensure good ventilation.

The engine oil in commercial vehicles is generally cooled by stainless-steel disk coolers or aluminum flat-tube coolers without a casing on the coolant side. They are accommodated in an extended coolant duct in the engine block.

**Fuel coolers**

Fuel coolers are installed in modern diesel engines in order to cool excess diesel fuel down to permissible levels. This excess diesel fuel heats up during the injection process as the result of compression in the high-pressure pump, before it is routed back via the return line to the fuel tank. The fuel can be cooled by means of an air-cooling or coolant-cooling system. As a result, various types of oil-to-air or disk-stack oil coolers are used for this purpose.

## Cooling-module technology

Cooling modules are structural units which consist of various cooling and air-conditioning components for a passenger vehicle, and include a fan unit complete with drive, e.g. an electric motor and/or a Visco® clutch.

Cooling-module technology encompasses the design of the components, taking into consideration their interactions, the dimensioning of the components with respect to the package space in the vehicle, and the procedure for dealing with interfaces. The problems to be considered in relation to interfaces include:
– the mounting methods
– cooling-air ducts, and
– seals on the cooling air side
– fluid connections of the components, and
– electrical connectors

In principle, module technology features a whole range of technical and economic advantages:
– Simplified logistics by combining components to form one structural unit
– Reduced number of interfaces
– Simplified mounting and assembly
– Optimum component design by using matched components
– Modular systems, encompassing various engine and equipment variants

Simulation and test methods are employed for the purpose of achieving optimized component design and layout in the cooling module. Assuming exact knowledge of the fan characteristics, the fan drive and the heat exchangers, simulation programs are created to replicate both the cooling-air side as well as the fluid side. By integrating the individual components in the simulation models, it is possible to examine the interactions of the individual components under various operating conditions. Ever greater significance is being attached to this type of virtual analysis, which is characterized by the use of computer-aided development tools. In line with this development, all geometric data are entered and processed in a CAD system (Computer-Aided Design). CFD analyses (Computational Fluid Dynamics) are conducted to examine the flow of cooling air in the engine compartment, while FEM analyses (Finite-Element Method) provide statements concerning the strength and stability of the design layout. The design analysis phase concludes with verification tests that may also be performed in a wind tunnel and on vibration test rigs.

## Cooling-system technology

While the cooling module comprises a structural unit of components with defined functions, the cooling system encompasses all components that are associated with the functions of the cooling system, even if they do not form complete structural units. This includes components that are not part of the cooling module, e.g. lines, pumps, expansion tanks, and control elements.

Cooling-system technology offers a whole range of technical and economic advantages:
– Reduced parasitic losses through appropriate hydraulic design matching
– Consideration of control systems and dynamics
– Consideration of the passenger-compartment heating system
– Larger scope of intervention options for the purpose of optimizing the design
– Standardized assembly concept for all cooling-system components
– Reduced development expenditure by cutting the number of development interfaces

## Intelligent thermomanagement

Future trends are heading toward the system-optimized regulation of various heat and substance flows.

Thermomanagement goes beyond cooling-system technology in that it takes into consideration all material and heat flow systems in the vehicle, i.e. in addition to the flow structures of the cooling system, it also deals with those of the air-conditioning system. The optimization objectives include:
– reducing fuel consumption and pollutant emissions
– increasing air-conditioning comfort
– extending the service life of the components, and
– improving cooling capacity in the part-load states

One of the basic principles of thermomanagement concerns itself with the fact that auxiliary energy employed to operate the cooling system always represents a loss for the vehicle energy balance, and component efficiency cannot be increased arbitrarily at a constant supply of auxiliary energy. To achieve the optimization objectives, the cooling system is therefore equipped with "intelligence", installed in familiar and new types of actuators as well as in microprocessor-controlled control systems that operate these actuators. For instance, radiator shutters to control cooling air and controllable fan drives can be employed to ensure that cooling-air throughput is kept to the minimum necessary under all operating conditions (demand-triggered regulation). In addition to improving the vehicle's drag coefficient $c_d$), this measure also ensures that all media achieve their operating temperature more effectively during the warm-up phase after a cold start, and that the passenger compartment is heated more efficiently. Cutting back the use of auxiliary energy in this way means that auxiliary energy can be diverted for use in operating states that are critical to the cooling output, while still achieving the optimization objectives.

Another important basic principle is to maintain a constant temperature in the components to be cooled as far as possible, irrespective of the operating state and the ambient conditions. An example of this temperature control principle is to use coolant to regulate the transmission oil temperature. Heating the transmission oil during the warm-up phase and employing an efficient cooling system to prevent the transmission oil from overheating reduce friction losses in the transmission, increase the service life of the transmission, and extend the service intervals for the transmission oil.

Ultimately, considering the cooling and air-conditioning systems in their entirety opens up the option of utilizing "thermal integration". Heat flow from one of the systems can be utilized or dissipated by another system without the need for any major additional input in auxiliary energy. An example of this is the utilization of waste heat from the exhaust-gas cooling system to heat up the vehicle interior.

Thermomanagement measures related to engine cooling include:

– Transmission oil temperature equalization
– Program-map thermostat
– Electrically controlled Visco® clutch
– Controllable, electric coolant pump
– Cooling-air control, e.g. radiator shutter
– Exhaust-gas cooling, and
– Coolant-cooled charge-air cooling (intercooling)

The fuel saving potential based on the sum of all measures is in the range of 5% (for passenger vehicles). On top of this, there is a range of further advantages corresponding to the above-mentioned optimization objectives. The extent to which engine management utilizes the cooling system control options is of decisive significance in leveraging this potential.

In the meantime, individual measures have been implemented to achieve system-optimized temperature equalization in motor vehicles. Nevertheless, thermomanagement as an all-encompassing optimization principle remains the reserve of future vehicle generations.

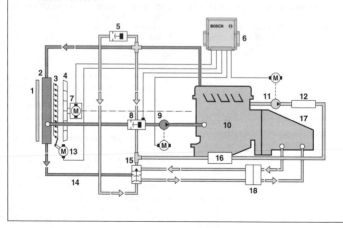

***Controlled cooling system***
*Example architecture with heat exchangers and actuators.*
*1 Condenser, 2 Coolant radiator, 3 Shutter, 4 Fan, 5 Thermostat, 6 Control unit,*
*7 Electric motor (fan drive), 8 Electronically controlled thermostat, 9 Electric motor with pump,*
*10 Internal-combustion engine, 11 Electric motor with pump, 12 Heater core, 13 Stepper motor,*
*14 Low-temperature circuit, 15 Low-temperature regulator, 16 Oil cooler, 17 Transmission,*
*18 Transmission oil cooler.*

## Exhaust-gas cooling

Due to the introduction of new, stricter emission-control legislation for diesel engines, new technologies for reducing emissions have become the focus of engineering attention. One such technology is cooled exhaust-gas recirculation (EGR). The EGR system is accommodated in the high-pressure area of the engine. The recirculated exhaust gas is extracted from the main flow between the cylinder and turbine of the exhaust-gas turbocharger. It is cooled by the engine coolant and then reintroduced to the fresh air downstream of the intercooler. The EGR system consists of a valve which regulates the amount of recirculated exhaust gas, the exhaust pipes, and the exhaust-gas cooler.

Due to its location in the high-pressure area, the exhaust-gas cooler is subject to extreme operating conditions. For instance, the exhaust-gas temperature can reach up to 450°C in passenger cars and up to 700°C in commercial vehicles, a fact which makes it imperative to use heat-resistant materials.

Added to this, the material must be resistant to corrosion and have high mechanical strength properties. Special stainless steels are therefore used for this purpose.

The design of exhaust-gas coolers must allow for a very low pressure drop on the exhaust-gas side to achieve the necessary recirculation rates. Steps must also be taken to ensure low susceptibility to soiling. The design of exhaust-gas coolers is therefore based on the tubular bundle design, utilizing smooth or structured tubes. The exhaust gas flows through the tubes, while the coolant is routed through the jacketing.

One application for exhaust-gas coolers on spark-ignition engines is for exhaust-gas precooling. Precooling is required in connection with exhaust-gas treatment systems with accumulator-type catalytic converters to maintain the exhaust-gas temperature within the working range of the catalytic converter.

*Cooled exhaust-gas recirculation* (schematic)
1 Engine, 2 Exhaust-gas heat exchanger, 3 Water connection, 4 Intercooler, 5 EGR valve, 6 Turbine, 7 Compressor.

# Engine lubrication

## Force-feed lubrication system

The force-feed lubrication system in combination with splash and oil mist lubrication is the most commonly used system for lubricating motor-vehicle engines. An oil pump (usually a gear pump) conveys pressurized oil to all bearing surfaces in the engine while the sliding parts are lubricated by splash lubrication systems and oil mist.

After flowing through the bearing surfaces and sliding parts, the oil collects below the power plant in the oil pan. The oil pan is a reservoir where the oil cools, and the foam dissipates and settles. Engines subject to high stresses are fitted additionally with an oil cooler.

Engine service life can be prolonged drastically by keeping the oil clean.

## Components

### Oil filters
Task
Oil filters remove and reduce particulates (combustion residues, metal abrasion, dust, etc.) from the engine oil which otherwise could cause damage or wear in the lubrication circuit. Since the engine oil is constantly circulating in the lubricating oil system, inadequate filtration, could cause particulates to accumulate and this would accelerate the rate of wear. The oil filter does not filter out liquid or soluble constituents such as water, additives or decay products attributed to the effects of oil aging.

In terms of wear, the significance of particulates in the oil circuit depends on the quantity and size of the particles. The typical size of particles in engine oil ranges from 0.5 to 500 µm. The fineness of the oil filter is therefore specifically adapted to the requirements of a particular engine.

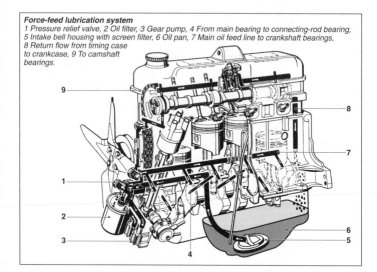

**Force-feed lubrication system**
1 Pressure relief valve, 2 Oil filter, 3 Gear pump, 4 From main bearing to connecting-rod bearing, 5 Intake bell housing with screen filter, 6 Oil pan, 7 Main oil feed line to crankshaft bearings, 8 Return flow from timing case to crankcase, 9 To camshaft bearings.

### Different types and designs
In principle, oil filters are based on two specific designs: easy-change filters and housing filters. In <u>easy-change filters</u>, the filter element is located in a housing that cannot be opened and which is secured by means of a threaded stud to the engine block. The complete easy-change filter unit is replaced as part of the oil service.

The <u>housing filter</u> is made up of a housing that is permanently connected to the engine block and can be opened to access the replaceable filter element. During the oil service, only the filter element is replaced, the housing is a permanent component. The filter element used on recent engines is based on a metal-free design. This means that the filter element can be completely incinerated.

Besides the filter element, the two filter designs normally feature a filter bypass valve, which opens at high differential pressures to ensure effective lubrication at the necessary points in the engine. Typical opening pressures range from 0.8 to 2.5 bar. Elevated differential pressures can occur in connection with high oil viscosities or when the filter element is heavily contaminated.

Depending on the specific engine requirements, the two filter designs may also feature a non-return or backflow check valve on the filtered or unfiltered oil side (contaminated oil side). These valves prevent the oil filter housing from draining empty after the engine is turned off.

Currently, the oil and oil filter change intervals for passenger-car engines are between 15,000 and 50,000 km, and between 60,000 and 120,000 km for commercial vehicles and trucks.

### Filter media
Various types of deep-bed filter media are employed in oil filtration. They mainly consist of fiber-pile structures that are arranged in various configurations. The filter material most commonly used is a flat media which, in the majority of cases, is pleated, but in some applications is also wound or used in the form of fiber packings, especially in bypass filters. The material generally used for the fibers is cellulose. Additional quantities of plastic or glass fiber in virtually any proportions may be added to the cellulose. These filter media are impregnated with resin to enhance their resistance to oil. However, filter me-

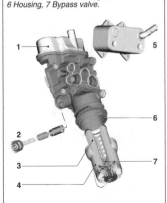

**Housing oil filter**
1 Oil mist separator, 2 Control valve,
3 Filter element, 4 Plastic cover,
5 Oil-to-water heat exchanger,
6 Housing, 7 Bypass valve.

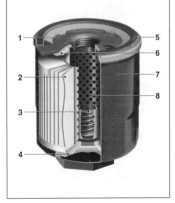

**Replaceable oil filter**
1 Threaded cover, 2 Filter element,
3 Bypass valve, 4 Spring, 5 Seal,
6 Non-return diaphragm, 7 Housing,
8 Center tube.

dia made of purely synthetic fibers are being used to an ever greater extent, as they have a much enhanced resistance to chemicals that allows longer service intervals. They also provide better options for structuring the three-dimensional fiber matrix to optimize filtration and increase particulate retention efficiency.

### Full-flow filters

All recent motor vehicles are equipped with full-flow filters. Based on this filtration principle, the entire volumetric flow of oil that is pumped to the lubricating points in the engine is routed through the filter. Consequently, all particles which could cause damage and wear due to their size are trapped the first time they pass through the filter.

The decisive factors governing the filter area are oil volumetric flow and particulate retention capacity.

### Bypass filters

Bypass filters, designed as deep-bed filters or as centrifuges, are used for superfine or microfiltration of the engine oil. These filters remove much finer particles from the oil than is possible using full-flow filters. They can remove minute abrasive particles to enhance wear protection. Soot particles are also filtered out to reduce any increase in oil viscosity. The maximum permissible soot concentration is roughly 3...5%. Oil viscosity increases substantially at higher soot concentrations, resulting in a drop in the operational effective-

ness of the oil. For this reason, bypass filters are used mainly on diesel engines. Only part of the oil flow (8...10%) from the engine is routed via the bypass filter.

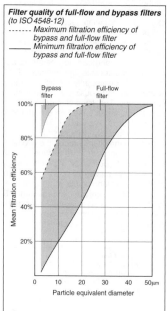

**Filter quality of full-flow and bypass filters**
(to ISO 4548-12)
------ Maximum filtration efficiency of bypass and full-flow filter
——— Minimum filtration efficiency of bypass and full-flow filter

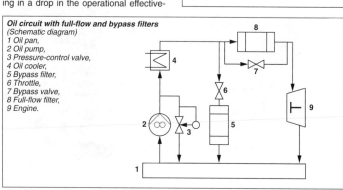

**Oil circuit with full-flow and bypass filters**
(Schematic diagram)
1 Oil pan,
2 Oil pump,
3 Pressure-control valve,
4 Oil cooler,
5 Bypass filter,
6 Throttle,
7 Bypass valve,
8 Full-flow filter,
9 Engine.

# Air filtration

## Air impurities

Engine intake-air filters, also referred to as air cleaners, reduce the particles contained in the intake air. Typical impurities in the intake air include oil mist, aerosols, diesel soot, industrial exhaust gases, pollen, and dust. These particles vary greatly in terms of size (see figure on P. 959). Typically, the dust particles drawn in by the engine together with the air have a diameter from 0.01 µm (predominantly soot particles) and 2 mm (grains of sand). Approximately 75% of the particles (referred to the mass (weight)) are in the size range between 5 µm and 100 µm.

The mass concentration in the intake air greatly depends on the environment in which the vehicle is operated (e.g. highway or sand track). In extreme cases, over a period of ten years, the mass concentration accumulated in a passenger car can range between a few grams through to several kilograms of dust.

## Air filters (air cleaners)

### Task

The air filter prevents mineral dust and particles from being drawn into the engine and contaminating the engine oil. It therefore serves to reduce wear, e.g. in the bearings, at the piston rings, and on the cylinder walls.

### Filter medium and design

Air filters are mostly designed as deep-bed filters which, in contrast to surface filters, retain the particles in the structure of the filter medium. Deep-bed filters with a high dust absorption capacity are always used to advantage wherever an economic solution is required to filter large volumetric flow rates with low particulate concentrations.

In terms of mass, state-of-the-art air filters achieve levels of total filtration efficiency of up to 99.8% (passenger cars) and 99.95% (trucks). It is necessary to maintain these values under all prevailing conditions, i.e. also under dynamic conditions as found in the engine's intake system (pulsation). Poor-quality filters will exhibit an increased rate of dust breakdown or rupture.

Filter elements are designed to meet the requirements of each individual type of engine. This ensures that pressure losses remain minimal and that high levels of filtration efficiency are not dependent on air throughput. The filter medium that makes up the filter elements in flat or cylindrical filters is installed in folded or pleated layers in order to achieve a maximum filter surface area in the smallest possible space. These media, mostly consisting of cellulose fibers, go through a special embossing and impregnation process to achieve the necessary mechanical strength, sufficient water stability, and resistance to chemicals.

The elements are replaced at the service intervals defined by motor vehicle manufacturers (for passenger cars, from two to four or sometimes every six years, i.e. after 40,000 km, 60,000 km or 90,000 km respectively, or when a backpressure of 20 mbar is reached).

The demands for compact, high-performance filter elements (due to reduced package space) as well as longer service intervals are the driving force behind the development of new, innovative air filter media. New air filter media consisting of synthetic fibers with much improved performance data have already been phased into series production. The figure shows a photographic image of a synthetic, high-performance filter medium (fleece). It has continuously increasing density and re-

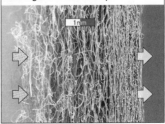

*Photographic image of an air filter medium consisting of synthetic fibers, taken with a scanning electron microscope*

duced fiber diameter across the entire cross-section from the intake side to the filtered air or clean air side.

Better values than with pure cellulose medium are also achieved with "composite grades" (e.g. paper with meltblown coating), and special nanofiber filter media. Here, ultra-thin fibers with a diameter of only 30...40 nm are applied on a relatively large support layer made of cellulose.

New folding or pleating structures with the channels alternately closed off similar to diesel soot filters will soon be launched on the market.

Conical, oval, stepped, as well as trapezoidal geometries complement the standard structures with the aim of optimizing the use of package space that is becoming very scarce and confined in the engine compartment.

### Mufflers (intake-noise damping)

In the past, air filter casings were almost exclusively designed as intake-noise damping or sound-absorbing filters. The large volume in connection with these casings is intended for acoustic purposes. In the meantime, there has been an increasing trend to consider the functions of "filtration" and "acoustics/engine noise reduction" separately and to optimize individual resonators. Consequently, it has been possible to reduce the dimensions of the filter casing or housing, resulting in extremely flat filters that can be integrated, for example, in the design covers of the engines, while locating the resonators in less accessible positions in the engine compartment.

### Passenger-car air filters

In addition to the casing with the cylindrical air filter element, the passenger-car air-intake module comprises the entire system of air supply lines and the intake manifold. Arranged between them are the Helmholtz resonators and the quarter-wave pipes for the acoustics (refer to Exhaust system mufflers on P. 547 onwards). Optimizing the complete system in this way allows more effective design matching of individual components and provides the requirements for complying with the gradually stricter regulations governing noise emission levels.

There is a great demand for water-separation components to be integrated in the air-intake system. Their main purpose is to protect the air-mass sensor or air-mass meter (HFM) that measures the air-mass flow. If the intake fitting is in the wrong location, water droplets sucked in under

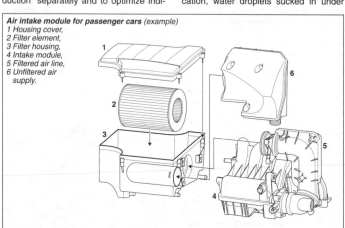

*Air intake module for passenger cars* (example)
1 Housing cover,
2 Filter element,
3 Filter housing,
4 Intake module,
5 Filtered air line,
6 Unfiltered air
   supply.

heavy rain, splash water (e.g. offroad vehicles) or snowfall may reach the sensor and cause problems in sensing the cylinder charge.

Built-in baffles or cyclone-like structures are fitted in the intake line to separate the water droplets. The shorter the distance from the air intake to the filter element, the less effective the water separation system will be, as this layout allows for only very low flow pressure losses. However, a special structure of the filter elements can be designed to collect (coalesce) the water droplets and direct the water film to the outside ahead of the actual particulate filter element. The entire system is accommodated in a casing specifically designed to promote this function. This layout can also be used successfully to separate water in connection with very short unfiltered air lines.

Another new component that will probably become a standard feature in all passenger-car air intake systems in the near future is the "HC trap" (HydroCarbon) for separating (adsorbing) hydrocarbons (primarily fuel) that can diffuse from the intake manifold/engine inlet and the crankcase ventilation system (crankcase breather) in the direction of the unfiltered air inlet after the engine is turned off. This development has been driven by the demands stipulated by extremely strict Californian legislation, e.g. for SULEV (Super Ultra Low Emission Vehicles). Over a defined period of time, these vehicles may emit only an extremely small amount of hydrocarbons to the environment. The intake system that is open to the outside represents a source of such emissions. No specific design has really gained acceptance. Integration in the air filter casing immediately downstream of the particulate filter element is just as feasible as installing it in the filtered or clean air line upstream or downstream of the air mass meter. For the most part, the systems feature components which are coated with activated carbon and which have very low pressure losses over a relatively large surface area. As dictated by current legislation, these HC traps must remain directly in the air flow, i.e. they must not be activated while the engine is turned off. As soon as the engine is running again, the air flow induces desorption of the hydrocarbons, resulting in regeneration or reactivation of the separator.

### Commercial-vehicle air filters

The figure opposite shows a maintenance-friendly and weight-optimized plastic air filter for commercial vehicles and trucks. In addition to high filtration efficiency, the matching filter elements are dimensioned such as to facilitate service intervals of more than 100,000 km. These intervals are therefore much longer than those for passenger vehicles.

A preliminary filter is mounted upstream of the filter element on vehicles used in countries with very dusty climates. However, this layout is also employed on construction and agricultural machinery. This preliminary filter or separator removes the coarse, heavy dust fraction. This drastically increases the service life of the fine filter element. In its simplest form, this separator is designed as a ring of baffle plates or blades that cause the incoming air to rotate. The resulting centrifugal force separates the coarse dust particles. However, the full potential of centrifugal separators in heavy-duty truck air filters can only be entirely employed by installing upstream mini-cyclone batteries optimally matched to the downstream filter element.

***Paper air filter for commercial vehicles*** *(example)*
*1 Air outlet, 2 Air inlet, 3 Filter element, 4 Support tube, 5 Housing, 6 Dust bowl.*

# Turbochargers and superchargers for internal-combustion engines

By compressing the air inducted for combusting fuel in the internal-combustion (IC) engine, and thereby increasing its air throughput, turbochargers and superchargers increase the output obtained for a given displacement at a given engine speed. There are of generally three basic types of "compressor" used in IC engines: the mechanically driven supercharger, the exhaust-gas turbocharger and the pressure-wave supercharger.

Mechanical superchargers compress the air using power supplied by the engine crankshaft (mechanical coupling between engine and supercharger), while the turbocharger is powered by the engine's exhaust gases (fluid coupling between engine and turbocharger).

Although the pressure-wave supercharger also derives its compression force from the exhaust gases, it requires a supplementary mechanical drive (combination of mechanical and fluid coupling).

## Superchargers (mechanically driven)

These fall into two categories: mechanical centrifugal superchargers (MKL) and mechanical positive-displacement superchargers (MVL).

### Mechanical centrifugal supercharger

The MKL compressor corresponds to the configuration of the exhaust-gas turbocharger. This type of device is very efficient, providing the best ratio between unit dimensions and volumetric flow. However, the extreme peripheral velocities required to generate the pressure mean that drive speeds must be very high. As the secondary drive pulley (2:1 conversion ratio relative to primary pulley) does not rotate fast enough to drive a centrifugal supercharger, a single-stage planetary gear with a 15:1 speed-increasing ratio is employed to achieve the required peripheral velocities. In addition, a transmission unit must be included to vary the rotational speeds if the pressure is to be maintained at a reasonably constant level over a wide range of volumetric flow rates (~ engine speed).

The necessity of using extreme rotational speeds, and the technical limits imposed on the transmission of drive power, mean that the centrifugal supercharger's range of potential applications is limited to medium- and large-displacement diesel and gasoline passenger-car engines. This design has not been extensively employed for mechanical superchargers.

### Positive-displacement superchargers

Positive-displacement superchargers (MVL) operate both with and without internal compression. Internal-compression superchargers include the reciprocating-piston, the screw-type, the rotary-piston and the sliding-vane compressor. The Roots supercharger is an example of a unit without internal compression. All of these positive-displacement superchargers share certain characteristics as shown in the figure of a Roots supercharger.

– The curves for the constant rotational speed $n_{LAD}$ = const in the program map of $p_2/p_1$ against $\dot{V}$ are extremely steep, indicating that increases in the pressure

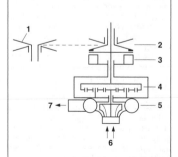

*Mechanical centrifugal supercharger (MKL)*
(schematic)
1 Variable-speed primary pulley, 2 Variable-speed secondary pulley, 3 Solenoid clutch, 4 Step-up planetary-gear set, 5 Compressor, 6 Air intake, 7 Air outlet.

ratio $p_2/p_1$ are accompanied by only slight reductions in the volumetric flow $\dot{V}$. The precise extent of the drop in flow volume is basically determined by the efficiency of the gap seal (backflow losses). It is a function of the pressure ratio $p_2/p_1$ and of time, and is not influenced by rotational speed.

– The pressure ratio $p_2/p_1$ does not depend upon the rotational speed. In other words, high pressure ratios can also be generated at low volumetric flow rates.

– Volumetric flow $\dot{V}$ remains independent of the pressure ratio, and is, roughly formulated directly proportional to rotational speed.

– The unit retains stability throughout its operating range. The positive-displacement compressor operates at all points of the $p_2/p_1$-$\dot{V}$ program map as determined by supercharger dimensions.

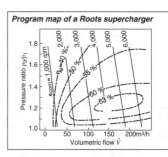

*Program map of a Roots supercharger*

Roots supercharger
The two twin-bladed rotary pistons of the Roots supercharger operate without directly contacting each other or the housing. The size of the sealing gap thus created is determined by the design, the choice of materials and the manufacturing tolerances. An external gear set synchronizes the motion of the two rotary pistons.

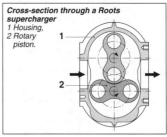

*Cross-section through a Roots supercharger*
1 Housing,
2 Rotary piston.

Sliding-vane supercharger
In the sliding-vane supercharger, an eccentrically mounted rotor drives the three centrally mounted sliding vanes; the eccentric motion provides the internal compression. The extent of this internal compression can be varied for any given eccentricity by altering the position of the outlet edge A in the housing.

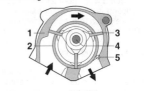

*Cross-section through a sliding-vane supercharger*
1 Housing, 2 Rotor, 3 Vanes, 4 Shaft, 5 Outlet edge A.

Spiral-type supercharger
The spiral-type supercharger employs an eccentrically mounted displacer element which is designed to respond to rotation of the input shaft by turning in a double-eccentric oscillating pattern. In sequence, the working chambers open for charging, close for transport and open once again for discharge at the hub. The spirals can be extended beyond the length shown in the figure to provide internal compression.

*Cross-section through a spiral-type supercharger*
1 Air intake into second working chamber,
2 Drive shaft,
3 Displacer element,
4 Air intake into primary working chamber,
5 Housing,
6 Displacer element.

The displacer element is driven by a belt-driven, grease-lubricated auxiliary shaft, while the input shaft is lubricated by the engine's oil circuit. Radial sealing is via gaps, while lateral sealing strips provide the axial seal.

### Rotary-piston supercharger

The rotary-piston supercharger incorporates a rotary piston moving about an internal axis. The driven inner rotor (rotary piston) turns through an eccentric pattern in the cylindrical outer rotor. The rotor ratios for rotary-piston superchargers are either 2:3 or 3:4. The rotors turn in opposing directions about fixed axes without contacting each other or the housing. The eccentric motion makes it possible for the unit to ingest the maximum possible volume (chamber I) for compression and discharge (chamber III). The internal compression is determined by the position of the outlet edge A.

A ring and pinion gear with sealed grease lubrication synchronizes the motion of the inner and outer rotors. Permanent lubrication is also employed for the roller bearings. Inner and outer rotors use gap seals, and usually have some form of coating. Piston rings provide the seal between working chamber and gear case.

Superchargers on IC engines are usually belt-driven (toothed or V-belt). The coupling is either direct (continuous duty) or via clutch (e.g. solenoid-operated coupling, actuation as required). The turns ratio may be constant, or it may vary according to engine speed.

Mechanical positive-displacement superchargers (MVL) must be substantially larger than centrifugal superchargers (MKL) in order to produce a given volumetric flow. The mechanical positive-displacement supercharger is generally applied to small- and medium-displacement engines, where the ratio between charge volume and space requirements is still acceptable.

## Pressure-wave superchargers

The pressure-wave supercharger exploits the dynamic properties of gases, using pressure waves to convey energy from the exhaust gas to the intake air. The energy exchange takes place within the cells of the rotor (known as the cell rotor or cell wheel), which also depends upon an engine-driven belt for synchronization and maintenance of the pressure-wave exchange process.

Inside the cell rotor, the actual energy-exchange process proceeds at the velocity of sound. This depends upon exhaust-gas temperature, meaning that it is essentially a function of engine torque, and not engine speed. Thus the pressure-wave process is optimally tailored to only a single operating point if a constant turns ratio is employed between engine and supercharger. To get around this disadvantage, appropriately designed "pockets" can be incorporated in the forward part of the housings. These achieve high efficiency levels extending through a relatively wide range of engine operating conditions and provide a good overall boost curve.

The exchange of energy occurring within the rotor at the velocity of sound ensures that the pressure-wave supercharger responds rapidly to changes in engine demand, with the actual response times being determined by the charging processes in the air and exhaust pipes.

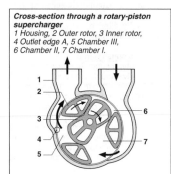

*Cross-section through a rotary-piston supercharger*
1 Housing, 2 Outer rotor, 3 Inner rotor,
4 Outlet edge A, 5 Chamber III,
6 Chamber II, 7 Chamber I.

The pressure-wave supercharger's cell rotor is driven by the engine's crankshaft via a belt assembly. The cell walls of the rotor are irregularly spaced in order to reduce noise. The cell rotor turns within a cylindrical housing, with the fresh air and exhaust-gas pipes feeding into the housing's respective ends. On one side are low-pressure air intake and pressurized air, while the high-pressure exhaust and low-pressure exhaust-gas outlet are located on the other side. The accompanying gas-flow and state diagrams illustrate the pressure-wave process in a basic "Comprex" at WOT and moderate engine speed. Developing (or unrolling) rotor and housing converts the rotation to a translation. The state diagram contains the boundary curves for the four housing openings in accordance with local conditions. The diagrams for the ideal no-loss process have been drafted with the assistance of the intrinsic characteristic process.

The pressure-wave supercharger's rotor is over-mounted and is provided with permanent grease lubrication, with the bearing located on the unit's air side. The air housing is made of aluminum, whereas the gas housing is made of NiResist materials. The rotor with its axial cells is cast using the lost-wax method. An integral

governing mechanism in the supercharger regulates charge-air pressure according to demand.

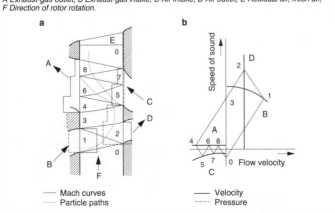

*Pressure-wave supercharger*
1 Engine, 2 Rotor, 3 Belt drive, 4 High-pressure exhaust gas, 5 High-pressure air, 6 Low-pressure air inlet, 7 Low-pressure gas outlet.

*Gas-flow diagram (a) and state diagram (b) for pressure-wave supercharger*
A Exhaust-gas outlet, B Exhaust-gas intake, C Air intake, D Air outlet, E Residual air, fresh air, F Direction of rotor rotation.

a

b

—— Mach curves
······ Particle paths

—— Velocity
- - - Pressure

# Exhaust-gas turbochargers

## Operating principle

The exhaust-gas turbocharger (ATL) consists of two turbo elements: a turbine and a compressor installed on a single shaft. The turbine uses the energy of the exhaust gas to drive the compressor. The compressor, in turn, draws in fresh air which it supplies to the cylinders in compressed form. In terms of energy, the air and the mass flow of the exhaust gases represent the only coupling between the exhaust-gas turbocharger and engine. Turbocharger speed does not depend upon engine speed, but is rather a function of the balance of drive energy between the turbine and the compressor.

Supercharging generally increases the efficiency of internal-combustion engines.

## Applications

Exhaust-gas turbochargers are traditionally used for the purpose of supercharging diesel engines. Originally, however, they were mainly used on heavy-duty engines for truck, marine and locomotive power plants as well as for agricultural and construction machinery applications. The mid-1970s saw the advent of the first production turbocharged diesel engines

in passenger cars. In the meantime, virtually all diesel engines manufactured in Europe are now equipped with an exhaust-gas turbocharger and intercooling (charge-air cooling).

For technical reasons, supercharging of spark-ignition engines was originally the reserve of only high-output sports engines and was rarely found on the mass market. In the meantime, gasoline-engine supercharging has become an integral part of engine development, predominantly in connection with small to medium-sized engines. In addition to the improvement in efficiency, one of the main objectives of supercharging is to avoid the increases in the number of engine cylinders, thus positively influencing package space and fuel consumption.

In contrast to the diesel engine, mechanical supercharging is also employed on spark-ignition engines in addition to turbocharging, predominantly with the aim of improving the transient buildup in boost pressure. In this context, the extensive volumetric flow range of the spark-ignition engine (approx. 1:75 from idle to WOT point) has a negative effect on the behavior of the exhaust-gas turbocharger. With the introduction of spark-ignition engines with direct fuel injection,

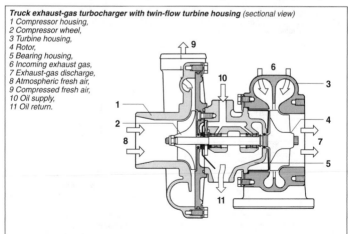

*Truck exhaust-gas turbocharger with twin-flow turbine housing* (sectional view)
1 Compressor housing,
2 Compressor wheel,
3 Turbine housing,
4 Rotor,
5 Bearing housing,
6 Incoming exhaust gas,
7 Exhaust-gas discharge,
8 Atmospheric fresh air,
9 Compressed fresh air,
10 Oil supply,
11 Oil return.

turbocharging will again become a more interesting prospect compared with other supercharging processes.

**Turbocharger design**
The exhaust-gas turbocharger consists of four basic components:
– the bearing housing
– the compressor
– the turbine, and
– the boost-pressure control facility

Bearing housing
The bearing housing accommodates the bearings and sealing elements. State-of-the-art exhaust-gas turbochargers usually feature a specially developed plain bearing both in the radial as well as the axial (thrust) bearing assembly. The radial bearings are designed either as rotating double plain bushings or as stationary plain-bearing bushings. The requirements relating to stability, power loss and noise-emission characteristics govern what type of bearing system is used. The thrust bearing is made up of a multiple-spline surface bushing that is subject to load from both sides and which is lubricated either centrally or individually for each spline surface. The lubricating oil is supplied by connecting the turbocharger to the engine's oil circuit. The oil outlet is connected directly to the oil pan in the crankcase. Today this type of bearing assembly is used to control rotational speeds of up to 300,000 rpm reliably

The shaft is equipped with piston rings at the casing openings to seal off the oil chamber to the exterior and to minimize the entry of charge air or exhaust gas to the charger interior. In some special applications, the sealing effect can be enhanced by implementing additional measures such as providing an air seal or slide ring seals on the cold compressor side. With the aim of completely avoiding any oil overflow in order to reduce overall emission levels, intensive development is currently being conducted on creating alternative bearing assemblies such as air or magnet bearings. On account of the extremely high speeds involved, roller bearings are ruled out for small turbochargers.

No additional cooling measures are necessary to maintain efficient operation of the bearing assemblies under standard operating conditions, i.e. at exhaust-gas temperatures up to approx. 800 °C. The relevant temperatures can be maintained below critical levels using devices such as a heat shield, and by thermally isolating the hot turbine housing, supplemented by incorporating suitable design elements in the bearing housing itself. Water-cooled bearing housings are employed for higher exhaust-gas temperatures, for example, on spark-ignition engines operating at up to 1,000 °C.

Compressor
Generally, the compressor units consists of a radial-flow impeller made of a cast aluminum alloy and a compressor housing also made of cast aluminum. The performance characteristics of a compressor are determined by its program map. This helps to determine the required size of the turbocharger based on the air-mass flow required by the engine and the necessary boost pressure curve. By implementing appropriate measures, the effective range as well as the speed and efficiency characteristics of the compressor can be adapted to the required boost pressure curve. The effective range of the com-

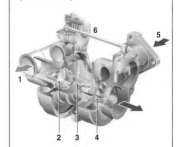

*Exhaust-gas turbocharger with wastegate*
1 Compressed air outlet,
2 Compressor wheel,
3 Shaft,
4 Exhaust-gas turbine,
5 Exhaust gas mass flow intake,
6 Wastegate with linkage and flap (in turbine inlet).

pressor is determined by the surge limit on the "left" side (minimum throughput) and by the choke limit on the "right" side (maximum throughput). The surge limit is defined as the transition from the stable to the unstable operating range. Unstable means that, triggered by a severance in flow at the inlet of the compressor wheel, the air-mass flow is alternately interrupted and re-established to produce a pumping effect. Among other factors, the extent of the surge limit is also governed by the design of the intake line. The choke limit, identifiable by the range of steeply descending speed curves, is determined based on the free inlet cross-section of the compressor wheel and therefore across the wheel diameter.

In view of the proportionality of the engine speed and volumetric air flow of the compressor, it is easy to deduce that compressors must have a substantially larger effective map width for engines with a large rotational speed spread (spark-ignition engines) than is the case for large diesel engines, for instance. The dimensionless compressor program maps in the figure show the characteristic air requirements along the WOT for passenger cars, commercial vehicles and large heavy-duty engines.

Measures such as variable pilot control adjustment, characteristic curve stabilization devices or specific adaptation of the blade inlet angle are successfully employed to extend the effective range. This effectively amounts to a shift towards the lower throughput rates. A special feature in spark-ignition engine applications is the use of a "bypass valve". It has the task of preventing pumping on the compressor side when load is abruptly removed from the engine (throttle valve closes). This is achieved by creating a short-circuit between the outlet and inlet of the compressor with the effect that delivery no longer takes place.

Turbine

The turbine wheel for standard applications is designed as a centripetal or inward-flow turbine. Axial turbines are only used in large heavy-duty turbine applications (engine output > 2,000 kW/turbocharger). Turbine housing design differs substantially according to intended use. Turbine housings for commercial vehicle/truck applications are mostly designed as double-flow housings (see figure, P. 532) in which the two streams join just before reaching the impeller. This turbine housing configuration is employed to achieve pulse turbocharging with the effect that kinetic energy as well as exhaust-gas pressure energy are used to generate power at the turbine. This effect can be particularly well utilized at low engine speeds where pressure surges can develop effectively due to the long time interval from one outlet pulse to the other. For this reason, pulse turbocharging is mainly used on medium- and slow-speed engines.

Constant-pressure supercharging is used on high-speed engines such as the diesel engines in passenger vehicles. This system facilitates the use of single-flow turbine housings. Single-flow turbine housings are also used in applications where a nozzle ring is mounted ahead of the turbine wheel – an arrangement frequently used on large engines to improve turbine throughput, which is finely graduated.

The turbine wheels made of a material containing high levels of nickel are manufactured using the lost-wax process. They are joined to the steel rotor shaft by means of friction welding or electron-beam welding. The turbine housing made of high-alloy spheroidal or spherulitic cast iron, depending on the specific application, are produced in an open sand-casting process. Al-

---

*Compression graph with typical engine operation curves valid for all displacements*

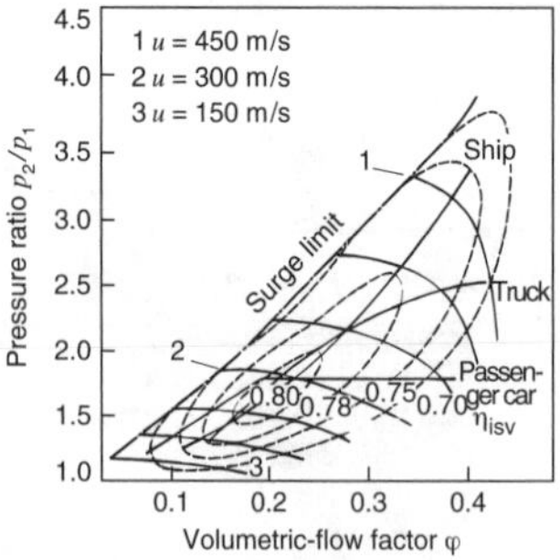

$1 u = 450$ m/s
$2 u = 300$ m/s
$3 u = 150$ m/s

Pressure ratio $p_2/p_1$

Volumetric-flow factor $\varphi$

Surge limit

Ship

Truck

Passenger car

$\eta_{isv}$

0.80  0.78  0.75  0.70

loyed cast steels, normally cast using the lost-wax process, are used in high-temperature applications (up to 1,050°C).

Intensive research is currently being conducted with the aim of developing sheet-metal turbine housings specifically for use on spark-ignition engines. This development is focused on reducing the heat-sink effect during the cold-start phase by decreasing the size of the mass to be heated. The catalytic converter then reaches the minimum temperature of approx. 250°C, as required for the conversion process, at a faster rate.

**Boost-pressure control**
In view of the large rotational speed spread of passenger-car engines, a boost-pressure control facility is indispensable to maintain the maximum permissible charge-air pressure if the design torque is to remain acceptable. Standard practice presently favors turbine output control on the exhaust-gas side.

Bypass control
A simple method still in widespread use is bypass control, which involves a flap mechanism to tap off part of the exhaust gas and route it around the turbine (wastegate). This controls the turbine output. To simplify matters, air is used as the actuating energy. The actuators can be controlled both with overpressure directly from the supercharger as well as with negative pressure from the vehicle's vacuum system. In most cases, the control pressures are regulated by using clocked-pulse valves. More recent developments are clearly heading towards the use of electric actuators that can adjust the control characteristics faster and with greater precision.

With appropriate microelectronic assistance, the boost-pressure characteristics of the turbocharger can be adapted not only to the WOT range, but also to the entire engine program map, irrespective of the type of actuating energy.

Variable turbine geometry
Compared to bypass control, variable turbine geometry (VTG) offers by far the best options for adapting the supercharger within the overall program map. With variable turbine geometry, the entire mass exhaust-gas flow is routed via the turbine, providing specific benefits in exploiting the available energy. By varying the turbine cross-sections, the turbine's resistance to flow is adjusted corresponding to the required boost pressure level.

*Boost-pressure regulation via exhaust-side boost-pressure control valve* (wastegate)
1 Engine, 2 Exhaust-gas turbocharger, 3 Wastegate.

*Variable turbine geometry*
(schematic diagram)
1 Turbine housing, 2 Adjusting ring, 3 Control cams, 4 Adjusting blades, 5 Adjusting blades with control lever, 6 Air intake.

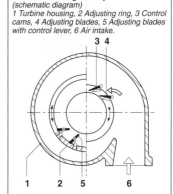

Of all the potential designs, adjustable blades have achieved general acceptance, as they combine a wide control range with high efficiency levels. The blade angle can be easily adjusted by turning it. The blades, in turn, are set to the required position using adjusting cams, or directly via control levers attached to the individual blades. Consequently, all blades engage in an adjusting ring which, in turn, is connected to the actuator. The actuator is driven as described above.

This type of variable turbine geometry is state-of-the-art in diesel engine applications. Development work is in full swing on VTG systems for spark-ignition engines. Here, the specific design challenge is to achieve complete functional reliability and thermodynamics despite the very high exhaust-gas temperatures.

### VST supercharger

Besides the variable turbine with adjustable blades, the variable sleeve turbine (VST) is suitable for small-displacement car engines. The mode of operation of the VST provides that, similar to the fixed turbine, only one duct of the double-flow turbine housing initially determines ram performance (sleeve position 1).

When maximum charge-air pressure is reached, the sleeve opens continuously in the axial direction and exposes the second duct (sleeve position 2). Both ducts together are configured in such a way that by far the largest part of the exhaust-gas mass flow is routed through the turbine. The remaining volume is routed past the impeller by further displacement of the control sleeve (sleeve position 3).

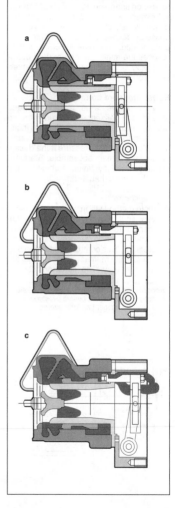

*Operation of variable sleeve supercharger (VST)*
*a) Sleeve position 1 (only left duct open),*
*b) Sleeve position 2 (both ducts open),*
*c) Sleeve position 3 (both ducts and bypass open).*

## Multistage supercharging

Multistage supercharging is an improvement on single-stage supercharging in that the power limits can be significantly extended. The objective here is to improve the air supply on both a stationary and a non-stationary basis and at the same time to improve the specific consumption of the engine. Two supercharging processes have proven successful in this respect.

### Sequential supercharging

Due to the extensive charger switching equipment, sequential supercharging is predominantly used in ship propulsion systems or generator drives. In this case, as engine load and speed increases, one or more turbochargers are cut in to the basic supercharging process. Thus, in comparison with a large supercharger which is geared to the rated output, two or more supercharging optima are achieved.

### Dual-stage controlled supercharging

This supercharging process is used in motor-vehicle applications on account of its simple control response. Dual-stage controlled supercharging involves the serial connection of two turbochargers of different sizes with a bypass control system and ideally a second intercooler.

The exhaust-gas mass flow from the cylinders initially passes into the exhaust manifold. From this point, there is the possibility of either expanding the exhaust-gas mass flow through the high-pressure turbine (HP) or diverting a partial mass flow through the bypass line. The entire exhaust-gas mass flow is then used again by the downstream low-pressure turbine (LP).

The entire fresh-air mass flow is initially precompressed by the low-pressure stage and ideally intercooled. The flow is then further compressed and intercooled in the high-pressure stage. As a result of precompression, the relatively small HP compressor works at a higher pressure level so it is able to generate the required air-mass flow.

At low engine speeds, i.e. small exhaust-gas mass flow rates, the bypass remains fully closed and the entire exhaust-gas mass flow expands through the HP turbine. This results in a very rapid and high buildup of boost pressure. As engine speed increases, the expansion work is continuously switched to the LP turbine whereby the bypass cross-section is enlarged accordingly.

Dual-stage controlled supercharging thus enables infinitely variable adaptation on the turbine and compressor sides to the requirements of engine operation.

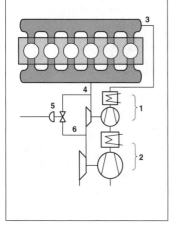

*Schematic structure of dual-stage controlled supercharging*
1 HP stage (high pressure),
2 LP stage (low pressure),
3 Intake manifold,
4 Exhaust manifold,
5 Bypass valve,
6 Bypass line.

## Acceleration aids

Since the introduction of exhaust-gas turbocharging, particularly in passenger-car applications, there has been an ongoing conflict in terms of design matching between optimization with respect to the stationary target values of the engine and the dynamic behavior of the turbocharger during a load change cycle. In the case of single-stage supercharging and in connection with a charger dimensioned for a specific application, the transient behavior can be influenced either by controlling turbine output (variable turbine geometry or wastegate) or by design measures implemented on the charger itself. Reducing the moved masses is a typical example, since it promoted the development objective of further increasing the thermodynamic power density of the turbocharger, with the result that distinctly smaller turbochargers can now be used for a specific application than was the case in the early 1980s. A second development objective was to reduce the polar moment of inertia of the rotor by employing low-density materials, thus improving the startup characteristics

of the charger. Pursuing these aims, intense development was conducted in the field of industrial ceramics as a substitute material for the turbine, as well as magnesium and plastics for the compressor. In view of the required high specific performance ratings of the components in addition to reliability and cost requirements, the solutions have not gained acceptance in large-scale projects.

A further option is to assist the charger with externally applied auxiliary energy whenever insufficient exhaust-gas energy is available. Basically, two different versions are of fundamental interest. The first proposed that a type of Pelton turbine wheel be installed on the rotor between the bearings and connected to the engine's oil circuit for its pressurized oil feed. As part of the second solution, the Pelton wheel was replaced by an electric motor, powered via a power electronics stage from the vehicle electrical system. In both cases, the auxiliary energy was applied only in charger acceleration mode. In quasi-stationary mode, the units were only carried along and thus incurred losses. In terms of utilizing the total avail-

---

*eBooster supercharging systems*
a) Schematic representation of electrically assisted exhaust-gas turbocharger (ATL),
b) Schematic representation of series connection of eBooster and exhaust-gas turbocharger.
1 Internal-combustion engine, 2 Intercooler, 3 Bypass valve for ATL, 4 Turbine of ATL,
5 Compressor of ATL, 6 Electric motor, 7 Triggering electronics for electric motor,
8 Bypass valve for eBooster, 9 eBooster compressor, 10 Exhaust gas, 11 Intake air.

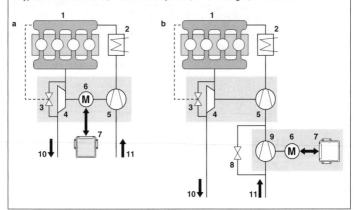

able energy and from the point of view of reliability, these methods were ruled out relatively quickly for reasons relating to serial production.

A more effective method is to separate the two functions, i.e. to retain the advantages of exhaust-gas turbocharging in quasi-stationary mode and to use a separate booster to compensate for startup weaknesses in the low-load range. The solution employs a hydrokinetic flow compressor, also known as a centrifugal turbocompressor, specifically developed for the low pressure range. Together with an electric motor to provide the drive, the compressor forms a separate unit and is known under its market name of "eBooster".

The "eBooster" is connected in series with the turbocharger, thus utilizing the advantage of multiplying the pressure ratios of both compressors to the effect that even a low graduated pressure delivers a large total pressure ratio. The unit can be positioned both ahead of as well as in the air feed downstream of the turbocharger. When the "eBooster" is not in operation, a valve opens a bypass line to allow the entire air flow, or a proportion of it, to bypass the acceleration compressor. The boost quality depends on the availability of electrical energy taken from the vehicle electrical system. Consequently, an operating voltage of 42 V offers the best conditions for the use of an eBooster system. Current development, however, is geared to 12 V as it does not appear that the 42 V electrical system will be introduced in the near future.

The eBooster is a compact unit that essentially consists of the hydrokinetic flow compressor, electric motor, carrier housing, and bearing assembly. In terms of design, the hydrokinetic flow compressor essentially corresponds to the turbocharger. The electric motor is an asynchronous motor, permitting speeds of up to approx. 100,000 rpm – speeds that roughly correspond to a graduated pressure factor of about 1.5 for a 50-mm compressor. In connection with service life requirements, this speed facilitates the use of lifetime grease-lubricated hybrid bearings, thus rendering an external lubricant feed unnecessary. With ambient thermal conditions permitting, the electronic power stage may also be integrated in the eBooster.

### References

Mayer, M.: Abgasturbolader – sinnvolle Nutzung der Abgasenergie (Practical use of exhaust-gas energy). 5. Auflage, Verlag Moderne Industrie, 2003. ISBN 3-478-93120-7.

Zinner, K.: Aufladung von Verbrennungsmotoren (Supercharging of internal combustion engines). 3. Auflage, Springer-Verlag, 1985. ISBN 3-540-07300-0.

Hiereth, H., and Prenninger, P.: Aufladung der Verbrennungskraftmaschine (Supercharging of external combustion engines). Springer-Verlag, 2003. ISBN 3-211-83747-7.

Hack, G., and Langkabel, G.-I.: Turbo- und Kompressormotoren – Entwicklung und Technik (Turbochargers and compressor engines – development and engineering). 1. Auflage, Motorbuchverlag, 1999.

*Sectional view of eBooster supercharger*
*1 Compressor housing, 2 Compressor wheel, 3 Carrier housing, 4 Electric motor, 5 Bearing.*

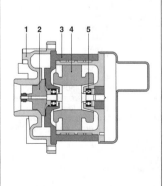

# Emission reduction systems

## Exhaust-gas recirculation system

External exhaust-gas recirculation can be utilized to control the cylinder charge and therefore the combustion process (refer to Internal Exhaust-Gas Recirculation Through Valve Overlap, P. 474). The exhaust gas recirculated to the intake manifold increases the proportion of inert gas in the fresh gas filling. This results in a reduction in the peak combustion temperature and, in turn, a drop in temperature-dependent untreated $NO_X$ emission.

There is a connection between the exhaust pipe and the intake manifold. Due to the pressure differential, the intake manifold can draw in exhaust gas via this connection. Together with the electrically operated exhaust-gas recirculation valve, the engine control unit adjusts the opening cross-section (aperture) and therefore controls the partial flow tapped from the main exhaust-gas flow.

Exhaust-gas recirculation plays an important part in reducing pollutant emissions both on diesel as well as spark-ignition engines (see PP. 659 and 716). As part of efforts to further reduce $NO_X$ emissions, increasing importance is being attached to

systems designed to cool the recirculated exhaust gas with the aid of an EGR cooler (see page 521).

## Secondary-air injection

Additionally injecting air into the exhaust pipe triggers an exothermic reaction. This leads to the combustion of HC and CO components that prevail particularly during the warm-up phase. This oxidation process additionally releases heat. Consequently, the exhaust gas becomes hotter, causing the catalytic converter to heat up at a faster rate as the hot exhaust gas passes through it. For spark-ignition engine vehicles, secondary-air injection is an effective means of reducing HC and CO emissions after starting the engine and to rapidly heat up the catalytic converter. This ensures that the conversion of $NO_X$ emissions commences earlier.

The electrically operated secondary-air pump draws in air and conveys it – controlled via the secondary-air valve – into the exhaust system. The valve prevents exhaust gas from flowing back to the pump. It must therefore be closed when the pump is switched off.

The electrically operated control valve switches the secondary-air valve pneumatically. For this purpose, intake-manifold pressure (the secondary-air valve opens) or atmospheric pressure (the valve closes) is applied via the control valve to the secondary-air valve. The engine control unit actuates the pump and control valve, ensuring that secondary air can be injected at a defined point in time.

The secondary air must be injected as close to the outlet valve as possible in order to exploit the high temperatures to utilize the exothermic reaction effectively. However, to avoid thermal stress, the secondary-air valve should not be arranged too close to the manifold. On the other hand, appropriate measures should be implemented to ensure that the "dead tube" between the valve and the inlet point does not cause any resonance (whistling effect).

*Principle of exhaust-gas recirculation*
*1 Inducted fresh air, 2 Throttle valve,*
*3 Recirculated exhaust gas, 4 Engine control unit, 5 Exhaust gas recirculation valve (EGR valve), 6 Exhaust gas.*

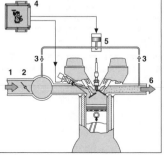

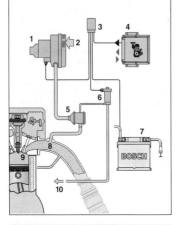

*Secondary-air system*
*1 Secondary-air pump, 2 Inducted air,*
*3 Relay, 4 Engine control unit, 5 Secondary-air valve, 6 Control valve, 7 Battery, 8 Inflow point in exhaust pipe, 9 Exhaust valve, 10 To intake manifold connection.*

# Evaporative-emissions control system

An evaporative-emissions control system is required for vehicles equipped with a spark-ignition engine. Its purpose is to intercept and collect fuel vapors from the fuel tank and to comply with the legal stipulations governing emission limits for evaporative loss. In view of the high boiling temperature of diesel fuel (see P. 324), evaporative-emissions control systems are not necessary on diesel-engine vehicles.

Fuel evaporates from the fuel tank at an increasing rate when:
– the temperature of the fuel in the fuel tank rises, either due to higher ambient temperatures or due to power loss of the fuel pump and – depending on the fuel tank system – due to the return of fuel heated in the engine and no longer required for the combustion process (see P. 596)
– the ambient pressure drops, for example, when driving uphill

The evaporative-emissions control system consists of a carbon canister, into which the vent line from the fuel tank projects, as well as a canister-purge valve that is connected both to the carbon canister as well as to the intake manifold.

The activated carbon absorbs the fuel contained in the fuel vapor and allows only air to escape to the atmosphere. Due to the vacuum prevailing in the intake manifold, fresh air is drawn through the activated carbon when the canister-purge valve frees up the line between the carbon canister and the intake manifold. The fresh air picks up the absorbed fuel and feeds it to the combustion process (carbon-canister purge).

The engine control unit (Motronic) controls the purge-gas volume depending on the engine operating point. Purging or regeneration must be performed regularly to ensure that the carbon canister is always ready to accept and absorb fuel vapor (see P. 661).

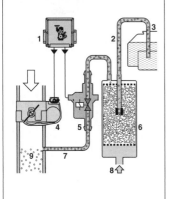

*Evaporative-emissions control system*
*1 Engine control unit, 2 Fuel tank vent line, 3 Fuel tank, 4 Throttle valve, 5 Canister-purge valve, 6 Carbon canister, 7 Line to intake manifold, 8 Fresh air, 9 Intake manifold.*

# Crankcase ventilation

## Ventilation system

### Blowby gas
Crankcase ventilation gas (blowby gas) is produced as a result of the combustion processes in an internal-combustion engine. Gas flows out of the combustion chamber and into the crankcase through design-related gaps between the cylinder walls and pistons, pistons and piston rings, through the ring gaps of the piston rings, and through valve seals. In addition to products arising from complete and incomplete combustion, water (vapor), soot and carbon residue, this gas also contains engine oil in the form of minute droplets. In the closed-circuit system, the untreated gas flow from the crankcase is routed through a ventilation system comprising additional components (e.g. pressure control devices, non-return valves) to the combustion-air intake. In open-loop ventilation systems, the treated gas is given off directly to the atmosphere. However, legislation now restricts the use of open systems to only a few exceptional cases.

Particularly in connection with turbocharged diesel engines and spark-ignition engines with direct fuel injection, engine oil and soot contained in the blowby gas can cause deposits which form on turbochargers, in the intercooler, on valves, and in the downstream soot or particulate filter (ash deposits from inorganic additives in the engine oil). Consequently, this may impair operation. An additional important aspect, however, is to reduce oil consumption resulting from engine oil migrating through the crankcase ventilation system.

### Composition of oil in blowby gas
The engine oil contained in the gas originates from the splash oil generated by moving engine parts, from the lubricant film on the cylinder walls, and engine oil evaporated from condensate as part of piston crown cooling. The average droplet size and the proportion in the total spectrum differ depending on the origin of the engine oil. The proportion of the relatively coarse splash oil can be influenced to a considerable extent by suitably selecting the tapping point or by implementing simple measures in the engine. The mainly very fine droplets from the lubricant film, and especially from the condensate, are extracted in large volumes out of the engine compartment. Their share in the total spectrum essentially depends on operating conditions (load and engine speed). The droplet size distribution of the oil in the gas as depicted in the figure shows that the mass-based mean droplet diameter is between 0.5 and 2 μm irrespective of engine type. The droplet diameters become ever smaller as the mean pressure in the combustion chamber increases and the oil temperature rises. The minimum droplet diameters mostly occur in the load range about the maximum engine torque.

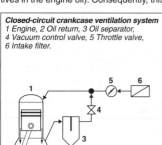

***Closed-circuit crankcase ventilation system***
*1 Engine, 2 Oil return, 3 Oil separator,*
*4 Vacuum control valve, 5 Throttle valve,*
*6 Intake filter.*

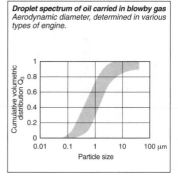

***Droplet spectrum of oil carried in blowby gas***
*Aerodynamic diameter, determined in various types of engine.*

## Oil separators

Various separation methods may be used to remove the oil contained in the blowby gas.

Labyrinth separators are simple, relatively large-volume inertial separators. They feature obstructions located in the direction of flow designed to eliminate the droplets. They are predominantly used for the purpose of separating large oil drops and large quantities of oil. In practical terms, it is not possible to separate small droplets ≤ 1...2 μm with this system.

Cyclone separators are also designed as inertial separators. They employ a rotating flow field to expel the drops out of the gas flow. To increase separation efficiency, several small cyclones are preferably connected in parallel. With a corresponding design, such systems can still effectively eliminate droplets in the range about 1.5 μm. Cyclone separators require a precise definition of the operating point since the separating efficiency is closely linked to pressure loss and therefore the volumetric flow rate.

Labyrinth and cyclone separators are designed as lifetime components.

Fiber separators are predominantly diffusion separators and depend on the selection of fiber material (small fiber diameters). This means they can separate droplets down to a size of ≤ 1 μm. In the majority of cases, these fine-fiber fleece materials must be designed as service components as the pores in these materials tend to clog when exposed to high levels of soot.

Centrifuges are rapidly rotating components in which the drops are eliminated from the gas flow in an imposed centrifugal field. Due to the external drive, pressure loss can be decoupled from separation efficiency to allow maximum filtration efficiency. Disk separators offer the greatest potential as they allow maximum separation efficiency in a small package space and at acceptable speeds.

Electrical separators utilize the forces acting on charged droplets in an electric field to achieve the separation process. These centrifuges therefore permit maximum separation efficiency and low pressure losses. The high voltage necessary for efficient separation is in the range of approx. 5...15 kV. Problems frequently occur as the result of engine-oil and blowby-gas deposits forming on the electrodes.

*Duocyclone oil separator*

**Table 1. Comparison of various oil separator systems**

|  | Labyrinth | Cyclone | Fiber separators | Centrifuges | Electrostatic separator |
|---|---|---|---|---|---|
| Separation efficiency | – to 0 | 0 to + | 0 to ++ | ++ | ++ |
| Pressure loss | + to ++ | 0 to – | + to – | ++ | ++ |
| Package space | 0 to + | ++ | + | + | 0 |
| Volumetric flow sensitivity | 0 | – to 0 | 0 | + | + |
| Lifetime component | Yes | Yes | No | Yes | Yes |
| Auxiliary energy | No | No | No | Yes | Yes |

# Exhaust-gas systems

## Design and purpose

In compliance with legal requirements, the exhaust-gas system reduces the pollutants in the exhaust gas that are generated by an internal combustion engine (see P. 554 onwards). The exhaust-gas system also helps to muffle exhaust-gas noise and to discharge the exhaust gas at a convenient point on the vehicle. Engine power should be reduced as little as possible during the process.

## Components

A passenger-car exhaust-gas system consists of:
– manifold
– components for exhaust-gas treatment
– components for sound absorption
– and the system of pipes connecting these components

Components for treating the exhaust gas are not always included in exhaust-gas systems for commercial vehicles and trucks. When the European EU 4 emissions control standard comes into force for commercial vehicles (see P. 564), it will be necessary for all commercial vehicle exhaust-gas systems to include emissions-control facilities.

Depending on engine displacement and the type of muffler used, the exhaust-gas system weighs between 8 and 40 kg. The components are generally made of high-alloy steels on account of the extreme stresses that occur in exhaust-gas systems.

## Emissions control

Components used for treating the exhaust gas include:
– the catalytic converter to break down the gaseous pollutants in the exhaust gas, and
– the particulate filter (or soot filter) to filter out the fine, solid particles in the exhaust gas (especially on diesel engines).

Catalytic converters are installed in the exhaust-gas system as close as possible to the engine so that they can quickly reach their operating temperature and therefore be effective in urban driving. Diesel particulate filters are also installed in the front area of the exhaust-gas system to ensure that the soot particles they have retained are burnt off more effectively at the higher exhaust-gas temperatures. Both components also assume a sound-absorbing function, especially the higher frequency components of exhaust-gas noise.

## Sound absorption

Mufflers dampen or absorb the noise produced by exhaust gas. In principle, they can be installed at any position in the exhaust-gas system. However, they are mostly located in the middle and rear sections of the exhaust-gas system.

Depending on the number of cylinders and engine output, generally 1 to 3 mufflers are used in an exhaust-gas system. In V-engines, the left and right cylinder banks are often run separately, each being fitted with its own catalytic converters and mufflers.

The noise emission limit for the complete vehicle is defined by legislation (see P. 58). The noise produced by the exhaust-

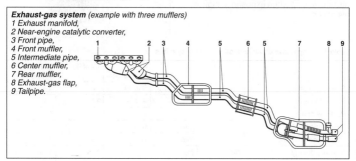

*Exhaust-gas system* (example with three mufflers)
1 Exhaust manifold,
2 Near-engine catalytic converter,
3 Front pipe,
4 Front muffler,
5 Intermediate pipe,
6 Center muffler,
7 Rear muffler,
8 Exhaust-gas flap,
9 Tailpipe.

gas system represents a substantial source of noise emission in a vehicle. This fact makes it necessary to devote particular attention and resources to the development of mufflers. Although the aim is to reduce noise in compliance with the legislation, they can also create the sound specific to the type of vehicle (see P. 1130).

## Manifold

The manifold is an important component in the exhaust-gas system. It routes the exhaust gas out of the cylinder outlet ports into the exhaust-gas system. The geometric design of the manifold (i.e. length and cross-section of the individual pipes) has an impact on the performance characteristics, the acoustic behavior of the exhaust-gas system, and the exhaust-gas temperature. In some cases, the manifold is insulated with an air gap to achieve high exhaust-gas temperatures faster and to shorten the time taken by the catalytic converter to reach its operating temperature.

*Manifold with near-engine catalytic converter*
1 Manifold, 2 Lambda oxygen sensor, 3 Metal monolith, 4 Insulating shell, 5 Lambda oxygen sensor.

## Catalytic converters

A catalytic converter consists of an inflow and outflow funnel, and a monolith. The monolith is made up of a large number of very fine, parallel channels covered with an active catalytic coating. The number of channels ranges from 400 to 1,200 cpsi (cells per square inch). The functional principle of the active layer in the catalytic converter is described in the section entitled "Catalytic exhaust treatment" on P. 662.

The monolith can be made of metal or ceramic material.

### Metal monolith
The metal monolith is made of finely corrugated, 0.05 mm thick metal foil, wound and brazed in a high-temperature process. Due to the very thin walls between the channels, the metal monolith offers an extremely low resistance to the exhaust gas. It is therefore frequently installed on high-performance vehicles.

The metal monolith can be welded directly to the funnels.

### Ceramic monolith
The ceramic monolith is made of cordierite. Depending on the cell density, the wall thickness between the channels ranges from 0.05 mm (at 1,200 cpsi) to 0.16 mm (at 400 cpsi).

Ceramic monoliths have an extremely high stability to temperature and thermal shock. However, they cannot be installed directly in the metal housing and require a special mounting. This mounting is necessary in order to compensate for the differ-

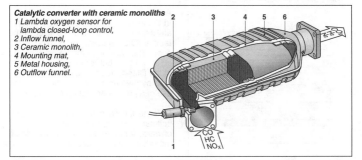

*Catalytic converter with ceramic monoliths*
1 Lambda oxygen sensor for lambda closed-loop control,
2 Inflow funnel,
3 Ceramic monolith,
4 Mounting mat,
5 Metal housing,
6 Outflow funnel.

ence between the thermal-expansion coefficients of steel and ceramics, and to protect the sensitive monolith against shocks. Extreme care and attention is required in the mounting and production process, particularly for thin-walled monoliths (< 0.08 mm). The monolith is mounted on a mat located between the metal housing and the ceramic monolith. The mounting mat is made up of ceramic fibers. It is extremely flexible to ensure that to minimize the pressure load exerted on the monoliths. It also serves as a heat insulator.

For operational reasons, several differently coated monoliths are often used in one catalytic converter. Particular attention must be paid to the shape of the inflow funnel to ensure that the exhaust gas is distributed evenly over the monoliths. The external shape of the ceramic monolith depends on the package space available, and may be triangular, oval or round.

*Ceramic particulate filter*
*1 Exhaust-gas inlet, 2 Ceramic plug,*
*3 Cell partition, 4 Exhaust-gas outlet.*

## Particulate filter

As with catalytic converter monoliths, there are metallic and ceramic filter systems. So far, however, only ceramic filters have been used in passenger-car applications. The method of installing and mounting ceramic particulate filters in the metal housing is the same as the process used for catalytic converters.

In the same way as the ceramic monolith for the catalytic converter, the ceramic particulate filter is made up of a large number of parallel channels. However, these channels are alternately open and closed. Consequently, the exhaust gas is forced to flow through the porous walls of the honeycomb structure. The solid particles are deposited in the pores. Depending on the porosity of the ceramic body, the filtration efficiency of these filters can attain up to 97%.

The soot deposits in the particulate filter induce a steady rise in flow resistance. For this reason, the particulate filter must be regenerated at certain intervals in two different processes.

### Passive process
In the passive process, the soot is burnt off by a catalytic reaction. For this purpose, additives in the diesel fuel reduce the flammability of the soot particles to normal exhaust-gas temperatures.

Other passive regeneration options include catalytic-coated filter particles or the CRT™ process (Continuous Regeneration Trap).

### Active process
In the active process, external measures are implemented to heat the filter to the temperature necessary for burning off the soot. This rise in temperature can be achieved by a burner mounted upstream of the filter or by secondary injection initiated by the engine management and the use of a preliminary catalytic converter.

Refer to the section entitled "Minimizing pollutants from diesel engines" on P. 716 onwards for more detailed information on the regeneration processes.

# Mufflers

Mufflers (or silencers) are intended to smooth out exhaust-gas pulsations and make them as inaudible as possible. There are basically two physical principles involved:
– reflection, and
– absorption

Mufflers also differ according to these principles. However, they mostly comprise a combination of reflection and absorption.

As mufflers and the exhaust-gas system pipes together form an oscillating system with its own natural resonance, the position of the mufflers is highly significant for the quality of sound-damping. The objective is to tune the exhaust-gas systems as low as possible, so that their natural frequencies do not excite bodywork resonances. To avoid structure-borne noise and to provide heat insulation for the vehicle underbody, mufflers often have double walls and an insulating layer.

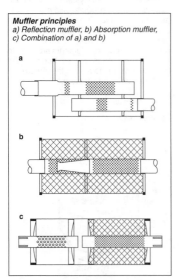

**Muffler principles**
*a) Reflection muffler, b) Absorption muffler, c) Combination of a) and b)*

a

b

c

## Reflection mufflers

Reflection mufflers consist of chambers of varying lengths interconnected by pipes. The differences in the cross-sections of the pipes and the chambers, the diversion of the exhaust gases, and the resonators formed by the connecting pipes and the chambers produce a muffling effect which is particularly efficient at low frequencies. The more such chambers are used, the more efficient is the muffler.

Reflection mufflers cause a higher exhaust-gas backpressure. As a rule, they are therefore associated with greater power loss.

## Absorption mufflers

Absorption mufflers are designed with one chamber, through which a perforated pipe passes. The chamber is filled with absorption material. The sound enters the absorption material through the perforated pipe and is converted into heat by friction.

The absorption material usually consists of long-fiber mineral wool with a bulk density of 100...150 g/$l$. The level of muffling depends on the bulk density, the sound-absorption grade of the material, and on the length and coating thickness of the chamber. Damping takes place across a very broad frequency band, but only begins at higher frequencies.

The shape of the perforations, and the fact that the pipe passes through the wool, ensures that the material is not blown out by exhaust-gas pulses. Sometimes the mineral wool is protected by a layer of stainless-steel wool around the perforated pipe.

## Muffler design

Depending on the space available under the vehicle, mufflers are produced either as spiral-wound casing or from half-shells.

To produce the jacket for a <u>spiral-wound muffler</u>, one or several metal sheet blanks are shaped over a round mandril and joined together either by the longitudinal folds or by laser welding. The completely assembled and welded core is then installed in the jacket casing. It consists of internal tubes, baffles, and intermediate layers. The outer layers are then connected to the jacket in a folding or laser-welding process.

It is often not possible to effectively accommodate a spiral-wound muffler in view of the complicated space conditions in the floor assembly. In such cases, a <u>shell-type muffler</u> made of deep-drawn half-shells is used as it can assume virtually any required shape.

The total volume of the mufflers in a passenger-car exhaust-gas system corresponds to approximately eight to twelve times the engine displacement.

## Connecting elements

Pipes are used to connect the catalytic converters and mufflers together. Arrangements where the catalytic converter and muffler are integrated in a single housing may also be used on very small engines and vehicles.

The pipes, the catalytic converter and muffler are connected to form an integrated system by means of plug-in connections and flanges. Many original-equipment systems are fully welded for faster mounting.

The entire exhaust-gas system is connected to the vehicle underbody via elastic <u>mountings</u>. The fixing points must be carefully selected, otherwise vibration may be transmitted to the bodywork and generate noise in the passenger compartment. The wrong fixing points may also create strength and therefore durability problems. In some cases, these problems are counteracted by the use of vibration absorbers. These components oscillate at the critical frequency in precisely the opposite direction of the exhaust-gas system, thereby eliminating vibration energy in the system.

The exhaust-gas system noise at the exhaust-emission point (tailpipe) as well as sound radiation from the mufflers can also cause bodywork resonance. Depending on the intensity of the engine vibrations, <u>decoupling elements</u> are used to insulate the exhaust-gas system from the engine block and to relieve the stress load on the exhaust-gas system.

*Muffler with integrated catalytic converter*
*1 Inlet pipe, 2 Mounting mat,*
*3 Ceramic monolith, 4 Tailpipe.*

*Mounting element*
*1 Rubber mount, 2 Metal bracket,*
*3 Muffler shell.*

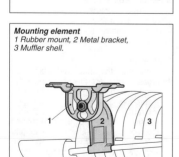

*Decoupling element*
*1 Liner, 2 Corrugated sheathing,*
*3 Wire braiding.*

Ultimately, the mounting arrangement of an exhaust-gas system is tuned so that it is rigid enough to withstand vibrations reliably on the one hand, and it exhibits sufficient flexibility and damping properties to reduce the transfer of forces to the bodywork effectively on the other.

---

**Helmholtz resonator**
1 Helmholtz volume,
2 Gas-carrying exhaust pipe,
3 Helmholtz pipe,
4 Muffler shell.

---

**Exhaust-gas flap, controlled by external vacuum**
1 Vacuum unit, 2 Butterfly valve,
3 Tailpipes.

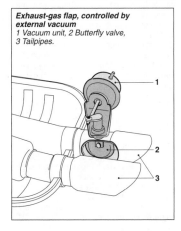

## Acoustic tuning devices

A number of different components can be used to eliminate disturbing frequencies in the noise emitted from the tailpipe.

### Helmholtz resonator
The Helmholtz resonator consists of a pipe arranged along the side of the exhaust-gas train and a defined volume connected to it. The gas volume acts as a spring, while the gas in the pipe section acts as a mass. At its resonant frequency, this spring-mass system provides a very high degree of sound absorption but in a narrow frequency band. The resonant frequency $f$ depends on the size of the volume $V$ as well as the length $L$ and cross-sectional area $A$ of the pipe:

$$f = c \cdot \sqrt{A/(L \cdot V)} \, / 2\pi$$

The value $c$ is the speed of sound.

### Quarter-wave resonators
Quarter-wave resonators consist of a pipe branching off from the exhaust-gas system. The resonant frequency $f$ of these resonators is derived from the length $L$ of the pipe branch. It is expressed as $f = c /(4 \cdot L)$. These resonators also feature a very narrowband damping range about their resonant frequency.

### Exhaust-gas flaps
Exhaust-gas flaps are most commonly found in rear mufflers. Depending on the engine speed or exhaust-gas throughput, they close off a bypass pipe in the muffler or a second tailpipe. As a result, exhaust-gas noise can be substantially damped at lower engine speeds without the need to trade off power losses at high engine speeds.

Exhaust-gas flaps can be either self-controlling based on pressure and flow, or they can be controlled externally. An interface to the engine management system must be provided for externally controlled flaps. This makes them more complex than self-controlled flaps. However, their application range is also more flexible.

# Exhaust emissions

Exhaust gases are produced in gasoline and diesel engines when fuel burns. These gases contain different combustion products, some of which are categorized as pollutants.

## Combustion products

### Complete combustion

When combustion of pure fuel is complete and ideal, i.e. complete combustion of fuel with oxygen and without any unwanted secondary reactions, only the following would be produced:
- Water ($H_2O$), and
- Carbon dioxide ($CO_2$)

### Incomplete combustion

In addition to the main combustion products of water and carbon dioxide, some unwanted minor components are produced because the combustion conditions are not ideal, (e.g. non-vaporized fuel droplets or a liquid fuel film on the combustion chamber wall ). This is also caused by the fuel composition:
- Unburned hydrocarbons:
  $C_nH_m$ (paraffins, olefins, aromatic hydrocarbons)
- Partially burned hydrocarbons:
  e.g. $C_nH_m \cdot CHO$ (aldehydes)
  $C_nH_m \cdot CO$ (ketones)
  $C_nH_m \cdot COOH$ (carboxylic acids)
  $CO$ (carbon monoxide)
- Thermal crack products and derivatives:
  e.g. $C_2H_2$ (acetylene)
  $C_2H_4$ (ethylene)
  $H_2$ (hydrogen)
  $C$ (soot), and
  polycyclic hydrocarbons

### Combustion byproducts

A small amount of the nitrogen ($N_2$) contained in the intake air reacts with oxygen ($O_2$) at high combustion temperatures to form nitrogen monoxide ($NO$) and nitrogen dioxide ($NO_2$), which are also referred to together as nitrogen oxides ($NO_x$). Further byproducts are produced in the form of sulfur oxides as a result of the sulfur content in the fuel.

## Properties of exhaust-gas components

### Major components

Exhaust gas comprises primarily the non-toxic major components:
- Nitrogen (component of the intake air)
- Water vapor
- Carbon dioxide
- Oxygen, in diesel engines and gasoline engines with lean-burn operation

Carbon dioxide is present in the air as a natural component and is not categorized as a pollutant in respect of exhaust-gas emissions for motor vehicles. However, it is considered to be one of the causes of the greenhouse effect and the associated global climate change. Since 1920 the $CO_2$ content in the atmosphere has increased by approx. 20% to over 360 ppm in 1995.

The amount of released carbon dioxide is directly proportional to fuel consumption. Measures taken to reduce fuel consumption are therefore becoming increasingly significant.

### Minor components

The quantity of minor components produced during combustion is very dependent on the engine operating status. For the gasoline engine, the quantity of untreated exhaust gas (exhaust gas after combustion and before exhaust-gas treatment) amounts to approximately 1% of the total amount of the exhaust gas for an engine at normal operating temperature and with a stoichiometric mixture composition ($\lambda = 1$). The composition of diesel exhaust gases is very much dependent on excess air (the diesel engine is always operated at $\lambda > 1$).

Table 1 shows typical values for the composition of exhaust gases from diesel engines.

#### Carbon monoxide (CO)

Carbon monoxide is a colorless, odorless, and tasteless gas. It reduces a human being's capacity to absorb oxygen in the blood and therefore results in poisoning. Inhaling air with a volumetric concentration of 0.3% carbon monoxide can result in death within 30 minutes.

### Hydrocarbons (HC)

Hydrocarbons are present in exhaust gases in a variety of forms. Aliphatic hydrocarbons (alkanes, alkenes, alkines as well as their cyclic derivatives) are very nearly odorless. Cyclic aromatic hydrocarbons do exude an odor, (e.g. benzene, toluene, polycyclic hydrocarbons).

Some hydrocarbons are considered to be carcinogenic under constant exposure. Partially oxidized hydrocarbons have an unpleasant odor, (e.g. aldehydes, ketones), and they form derivatives in sunlight that are also considered to be carcinogenic under constant exposure in certain concentrations.

### Nitrogen oxides (NO$_x$)

Nitrogen monoxide (NO) is a colorless, odorless, and tasteless gas that slowly changes to nitrogen dioxide (NO$_2$) in the atmosphere. Pure NO$_2$ is a poisonous, reddish-brown gas with a penetrating odor. When it is highly concentrated, NO$_2$ can irritate the mucous membranes.

Nitrogen oxides are part of the cause of damage to forests (acid rain) and it forms smog when combined with hydrocarbons.

### Oxidants

When exposed to sunlight, the emitted hydrocarbons and nitrogen oxides produce oxidants of:
- Organic peroxides
- Ozone
- Peroxy-acetylnitrates

Ozone, not to be confused with oxygen, is a toxic, oxidizing gas. It has a penetrating odor and in high concentrations it causes irritation of the throat and respiratory tract as well as burning to the eyes. It is a contributory factor to smog formation.

### Particulates

Particulates in exhaust gas are primarily produced by the diesel engine. Particulate emissions are negligibly small from the combustion process (intake-manifold injection) in the conventional gasoline engine.

Particulates in the form of particulate matter is formed if combustion is not complete. These particulates consist mainly of chained carbon particles (soot) with a very large specific surface, dependent on the combustion system and engine operating status. Unburned or partially burned hydrocarbons, as well as aldehydes with a penetrant odor, accumulate on the soot. Fuel and grease aerosols (solids or liquid materials dispersed in gases) as well as sulfates bind themselves to the soot.

Particulates are suspected of being carcinogenic.

**Table 1: Composition of diesel exhaust gas** (typical values).

| Exhaust-gas component | at idle | at maximum output |
|---|---|---|
| Nitrogen oxides (NO$_x$) | 50...200 ppm | 600...2,500 ppm |
| Hydrocarbons (HC) | 50...500 ppm | < 50 |
| Carbon monoxide (CO) | 100...450 ppm | 350...2,000 |
| Carbon dioxide (CO$_2$) | ...3.5 Vol.% | 12...16 Vol.% |
| Water vapor (H$_2$O) | 2...4 Vol.% | ...11 Vol.% |
| Oxygen (O$_2$) | 18 Vol.% | 2...11 Vol.% |
| Nitrogen (N$_2$) etc. | Rest | Rest |
| Smoke number, passenger cars | SN = < 0.5 | SN = 2...3 |
| Exhaust-gas temperature downstream of exhaust valve | 100...200°C | 550...800°C |

# Emission-control legislation

The constantly growing volume of traffic combined with the subsequent enlarged environmental impact, particularly due to the city traffic, has become an ever bigger problem in the past. Exhaust-gas emissions from motor vehicles therefore had to be limited. Legislators define permissible emission limits and testing procedures. Every new registered vehicle type has to satisfy these legal requirements.

## Overview

The U.S. State of California was a forerunner in the attempt to apply legal limits to exhaust emissions caused by motor vehicles. The reason for this is that the geographic location of large cities, such as Los Angeles, means that exhaust gases are not blown away by the wind, but gather over the cities in the form of haze. The resulting smog formation does more than merely impact the health of city inhabitants, it also causes massive line-of-sight obstructions.

Since the first emission-control legislation for gasoline engines came into effect in California in the mid-1960s, the permissible emission limits for the different pollutant components have been reduced even further. In the meantime all industrial nations have introduced emission-control laws that specify the permissible emission limits for gasoline and diesel engines in addition to the test procedures. In some countries, regulations governing exhaust-gas emissions are supplemented by limits placed on evaporative losses from the fuel system.

The primary emission-control legislation include:
- CARB legislation (California Air Resources Board)
- EPA legislation (Environmental Protection Agency)
- EU legislation (European Union)
- Japanese legislation

### Test procedures

Following the lead taken by the U.S.A., the EU states and Japan have developed their own test procedures for emission-control certification of motor vehicles. Other nations have adopted these procedures in the same or modified form. Three test procedures have been specified by legislators for different vehicle categories and test goals:
- type approval for attaining General Certification,
- serial testing for the inspection agency to carry out random testing of current serial production, and
- in-field monitoring for checking specific exhaust-gas constituents from vehicles in use.

Type approval requires the greatest test outlay. Simplified procedures are used for in-field monitoring.

### Classification

Vehicles are categorized into different classes in those nations that have vehicle emission-control legislation (see P. 884):
- Passenger cars: Testing is performed on a vehicle chassis dynamometer.
- Light commercial vehicles: The upper limit for the permissible total weight lies at 3.5...3.8 t depending on national legislation. Testing is performed on a vehicle chassis dynamometer (as for passenger cars).
- Heavy commercial vehicles: Permissible total weight over 3.5...3.8 t. Testing is performed on an engine test bed and vehicle measurement is not facilitated.
- Off-highway, (e.g. construction vehicles, agricultural and forestry machinery): Testing on an engine test bed as for heavy-duty commercial vehicles.

### Type approval

A condition for granting the General Certification for a vehicle and engine model are exhaust-gas tests in which test cycles must be driven under specific operating conditions and emission limits must be complied with. The test cycles and emission limits are specified individually by each nation.

## Test cycles

Different dynamic test cycles are prescribed by each country for passenger cars and light commercial vehicles. They are categorized into two different types dependent on the method in which they are performed:
- test cycles derived from recordings made in actual on-road trips (e.g. FTP Test Cycle in the U.S.A.), and
- test cycles (synthetically generated) made up of road sections with constant acceleration and speed (e.g. MNEDC in Europe).

To determine the amount of pollutant masses emitted, the vehicle is driven at precisely fixed speeds along a test cycle. The exhaust gases are collected for analysis of the pollutant masses at the end of the driving schedule. For heavy commercial vehicles, stationary exhaust-gas tests (e.g. 13-stage test in the EU), or dynamic tests (e.g. transient cycle in the U.S.A.) are conducted on the engine test bench.

## Serial testing

Manufacturers normally perform serial testing themselves during production as part of quality control. The approval agency may request rechecks as often as it deems necessary. The EU Regulations and ECE Directives (Economic Commission of Europe) incorporate production scatter by performing random tests on three to a maximum of 32 vehicles. The strictest requirements are applied in the U.S.A. where, particularly in California, very nearly 100% quality monitoring is required.

## On-board diagnosis

Emission-control legislation also specifies how compliance with emission limits is monitored. The engine control unit contains diagnosis functions (software algorithms) that detect system faults associated with the exhaust gas. The OBD diagnosis functions (on-board diagnosis) check all components that cause an increase in exhaust emissions if they fail. Each country defines their own limits for exhaust-gas emissions. The fault indicator lamp notifies drivers of a defect when emission limits are exceeded.

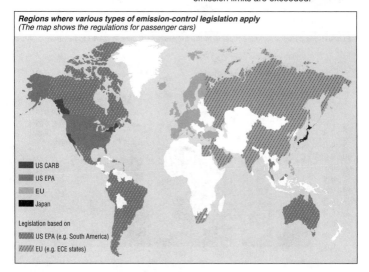

*Regions where various types of emission-control legislation apply*
*(The map shows the regulations for passenger cars)*

US CARB
US EPA
EU
Japan

Legislation based on
US EPA (e.g. South America)
EU (e.g. ECE states)

## CARB legislation (passenger cars/light-duty trucks)

Emission limits in the Californian CARB (California Air Resources Board) emission-control legislation for passenger cars and light-duty trucks (LDT) are specified in the emission-control standards:
– LEV I, and
– LEV II.

Standard LEV I applies to passenger cars and light-duty trucks with a permissible total weight of up to 6,000 lbs for model years 1994 to 2003. On January 1 2004 the LEV II standard comes into force and is binding for all new vehicles up to a permissible total weight of 8,500 lbs (3.85 t) commencing with model year 2004.

### Emission limits

The CARB legislation specifies emission limits for:
– carbon monoxide (CO),
– nitrogen oxides ($NO_x$),
– NMOG (Non-Methane Organic Gases),
– formaldehyde (only LEV II), and
– particulates (diesel: LEV I and LEV II; gasoline: planned for LEV II).

Exhaust emissions are measured in the FTP 75 driving schedule (Federal Test Procedure). The emission limits are correlated with the route driven during the test and are expressed in grams per mile. During the period 2001 to 2004 the SFTP standard (Supplement Federal Test Procedure) was introduced and included further test cycles. They include additional emission limits in addition to the FTP emission limits.

### Exhaust-gas categories

Automobile manufacturers may use different vehicle designs that are subdivided into the exhaust-gas categories below according to the vehicle emission values for NMOG, CO, $NO_x$ and particulate emissions:
– Tier 1,
– TLEV (Transitional Low-Emission Vehicle),
– LEV (Low-Emission Vehicle, i.e. vehicles with low exhaust gas and evaporative emissions),
– ULEV (Ultra-Low-Emission Vehicle),
– SULEV (Super Ultra-Low-Emission Vehicle),

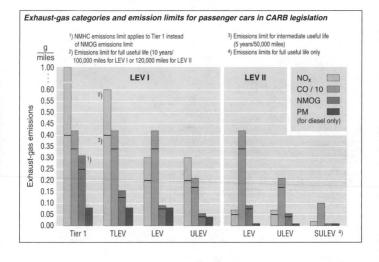

*Exhaust-gas categories and emission limits for passenger cars in CARB legislation*

- ZEV (Zero-Emission Vehicle, i.e. vehicles without exhaust-gas and evaporative emissions), and
- PZEV (Partial ZEV, generally equates to the SULEV, however with higher requirements for evaporative emissions and durability).

The categories Tier 1, TLEV, LEV and ULEV are decisive for LEV I. Emission-control standard LEV II applies from 2004 onwards. The Tier 1 and TLEV categories will no longer apply and SULEV will come into force with significantly lower emission limits. The LEV and ULEV categories will remain. The CO and NMOG emission limits from LEV I will remain unchanged, but the NO, and particulate emission limits will be significantly lower for LEV II. Additional formaldehyde emission limits will be introduced with the LEV II standard.

### Durability
In order to gain approval for vehicle types, manufacturers must certify that the exhaust emissions limited in emission-control legislation do not exceed the emission limits of:
- 50,000 miles or 5 years ("intermediate useful life"), or
- 100,000 miles (LEV I) or 120,000 miles (LEV II) or 10 years ("full useful life")
150,000 miles or 15 years apply to vehicles in the PZEV exhaust-gas category.

Optionally, a vehicle manufacturer may certify its vehicles for a mileage of 150,000 miles with the same emission limits that apply for 120,000 miles. The auto manufacturer will then receive a bonus when the NMOG fleet average is calculated.

The manufacturer must supply two vehicle fleets from its production line for this durability test:
- One fleet in which each vehicle must have driven 4,000 miles before the test.
- One fleet for the endurance test; it will be used to measure the deterioration factors of individual components in a continuous-duty test.

The vehicles are subjected to a specific driving schedule of 50,000 or 100,000 miles for the endurance test. The exhaust-gas emissions are measured at intervals of 5,000 miles. Servicing and maintenance tasks may only be performed at the specified intervals.

Users of the U.S. test cycles also permit the prescribed deterioration factors to be applied for the purposes of simplification, (e.g. Switzerland).

### Phase-in
At least 25% of newly registered vehicles must satisfy the LEV II standard after it becomes effective in 2004. The phase-in ruling also stipulates that an additional 25% of vehicles must comply with the LEV II standard each year. With effect from 2007 all vehicles must be certified in accordance with the LEV II standard.

### Fleet average (NMOG)
Each vehicle manufacturer must ensure that its vehicles do not exceed an average specific emission limit for exhaust-gas emissions. The NMOG emissions are used as the criteria in this regard. The fleet average is produced from the mean value of the NMOG emission limit for all vehicles produced by a vehicle manufacturer. The emission limits for the fleet average are different for passenger cars and light-duty trucks.

The emission limits for the NMOG fleet average are reduced every year. This means that vehicle manufacturers must increasingly produce vehicles in the better or cleaner exhaust-gas categories in order to comply with the lower emission limit. The phase-in ruling does not impact on the fleet average.

### Fleet fuel consumption
US lawmakers specify mandatory requirements on automobile manufacturers with regard to the mean fuel consumption of vehicle fleets, or the number of miles driven per gallon. The CAFE value (Corporate Average Fuel Economy) currently lies at 27.5 miles/gallon for passenger cars. This equates to a fuel consumption of 8.55 $l$/100 km. The figure for LDT is 20.3 miles/gallon or 11.6 $l$/100 km. There are no regulations for heavy commercial vehicles.

The mean fuel economy of sold vehicles is calculated for each automobile manufacturer at the end of a year. A $5.50 penalty per vehicle must be paid to the state for each 0.1 mile/gallon that undercuts the consumption limit. Purchasers pay a penalty tax for vehicles that have a high fuel consumption (gas-guzzlers). The consumption limit lies at 22.5 miles/gallon (equates to 10.45 l/100 km).

These measures have the purpose of promoting the development of vehicles with a low fuel consumption.

Fuel consumption is measured by completing the highway cycle in addition to the FTP 75 test cycle.

## On-board diagnosis

The introduction of OBD II (1994) makes it mandatory for all new registered passenger cars and light-duty trucks with a permissible total weight up to 3.85 t and up to 12 seats to have a diagnosis system to detect faults impacting on vehicle exhaust-gas characteristics.

Exhaust-gas emissions may not exceed 1.5 times the prevailing emission limit for the vehicle exhaust-gas category. Otherwise, the fault indicator lamp must light up to indicate a fault after the second driving schedule at the latest. The fault indicator lamp can switch off after three trips with no fault detected.

## In-field monitoring

### Non-routine inspection

An exhaust-gas emission test in accordance with the FTP 75 test method as well as an evaporation test are carried out on in-use vehicles on a random-test basis. Only vehicles with a mileage of less than 50,000 or 75,000 miles are selected (depending on the type of certification procedure for the vehicles concerned).

### Vehicle monitoring by the manufacturer

Since model year 1990 vehicle manufacturers have been obliged to produce reports with regard to complaints or damage to specific emission components or systems. This obligation to produce reports lasts for 5 or 10 years or 50,000 or 100,000 miles depending on the warranty period of the component or assembly. The reporting method is split into the three reporting levels:
- Emissions Warranty Information Report (EWIR),
- Field Information Report (FIR), and
- Emission Information Report (EIR)

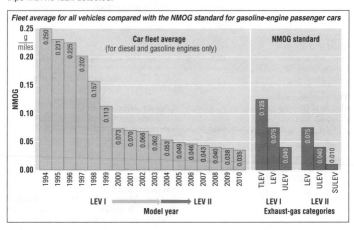

Fleet average for all vehicles compared with the NMOG standard for gasoline-engine passenger cars

Each level has an increasing requirement to supply detailed information. The environment agency is notified of information with regard to:
– complaints,
– fault quotas,
– fault analysis, and
– impacts on emissions.

The agency uses the FIR as the basis to decide whether to enforce a recall action on the vehicle manufacturer.

### Emission-free vehicles

With effect from 2003 in California, 10% of new registered vehicles must be manufactured to the ZEV (Zero-Emission Vehicle) exhaust-gas category. These vehicles may not release any emissions when they are in operation. These are primarily electric cars.

Vehicles in the PZEV (Partial Zero Emission Vehicles) exhaust-gas category are not zero-emission, however they must emit very low levels of pollutants. The figure of 10% of ZEV-category vehicles registered after 2003 may also be covered by PZEV. The vehicles are weighted with a factor of 0.2...1 depending on their emissions reduction. The following requirements must be satisfied for the minimum factor of 0.2:
– SULEV certification for a durability of 150,000 miles or 15 years,
– warranty period of 150,000 miles or 15 years on all emission-related parts,
– no evaporative emissions from the fuel system (0-EVAP, zero evaporation) This is achieved by complex encapsulation of the tank system.

Special provisions apply to hybrid vehicles equipped with a gasoline engine and electric motor. These vehicles may also contribute to the 10% quota.

## EPA legislation (passenger cars/light-duty trucks)

EPA legislation (Environment Protection Agency) applies principally in the federal states of the U.S., excluding California, where CARB legislation prevails. The EPA laws for passenger cars and light-duty trucks (LDT) are less strict than CARB laws. However, U.S. federal states are free to apply CARB legislation. Some states have taken up this option, such as Maine, Massachusetts and New York.

This legislation is based on the Clean Air Act, a law that specifies many measures to protect the environment. It sets global targets but does not stipulate any emission limits.

The Tier 1 standard currently applies for the EPA legislation. The next level, Tier 2, will come into force in 2004.

NLEV (National Low Emission Vehicle) is a voluntary program carried out by the U.S. federal states (excluding California) to reduce emission limits. Vehicles are categorized in four emission categories: Tier 1, TLEV, LEV and ULEV. As in California, these are used together with NMOG emissions to calculate the fleet average.

The NLEV program will lapse when the Tier 2 emission-control standard is introduced.

### Emission limits

EPA legislation specifies emission limits for the pollutants:
– Carbon monoxide (CO),
– Nitrogen oxides ($NO_x$),
– Non-Methane Organic Gases (NMOG),
– Formaldehyde (HCHO), and
– Solid matter (particulates).

Exhaust emissions are measured in the FTP 75 driving schedule. The emission limits are correlated with the route driven during the test and are expressed in grams per mile.

The SFTP standard (Supplemental Federal Test Procedure) with further test cycles has been in force since 2002. Prevailing emission limits apply must be satisfied in addition to FTP emission limits.

The same emission limits will apply to vehicles with gasoline and diesel engines when the Tier 2 emission-control standard comes into force.

### Exhaust-gas categories

In the Tier 1 standard, an emission limit applies to each pollutant that is subject to legislation. In Tier 2, the emission limits are divided into 10 (passenger cars) or 11 (HLDT, heavy LDT) emissions standards (Bin). Bin 10 and Bin 9 are interim bins that will cease to apply after 2007.

The following changes will apply after switchover to Tier 2:
- A fleet average will be introduced for $NO_x$.
- Formaldehydes (HCHO) will be subject to legislation as pollutants in their own right.
- Passenger cars and light duty trucks up to 6,000 lbs (2.72 t) will be combined to form a single vehicle category.
- There will be an additional vehicle category: MDPV (Medium Duty Passenger Vehicle, previously assigned to HDV).
- Full useful life will be increased to 120,000 miles (192,000 km).

### Phase-in

After introduction of Tier 2 in 2004, at least 25% of new registered passenger cars and LLDTs (light LDT) must be certified in compliance with the final Tier 2 standard (Tier 2, final). The remaining 75% may still be certified in compliance with an interim standard (Tier 2, interim). The phase-in ruling also stipulates that an additional 25% of vehicles must comply with the final Tier 2 standard each year. The Tier 2 standard for passenger cars and LLDT will be applicable in full from 2007. The phase-in for HLDT/MDPV will terminate in 2009.

### Fleet average ($NO_x$)

$NO_x$ emissions will be used as the criteria for a vehicle manufacturer's fleet average with respect to EPA legislation. This is different to the calculations for CARB specifications that use NMOG emissions for the fleet average.

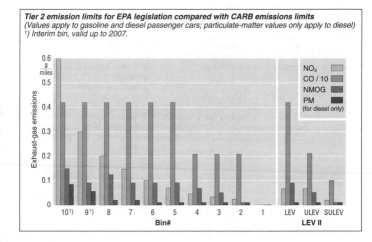

**Tier 2 emission limits for EPA legislation compared with CARB emissions limits**
*(Values apply to gasoline and diesel passenger cars; particulate-matter values only apply to diesel)*
[1] Interim bin, valid up to 2007.

## Fleet fuel consumption

The same regulations as in California apply to determine fleet fuel consumption for new vehicles registered in the U.S. Above an emission limit of 27.5 miles/gallon (8.55 $l$/100 km) for passenger cars, the vehicle manufacturer must pay a penalty tax. The purchaser must also pay a penalty tax if the new car has an emission limit of over 22.5 miles/gallon.

## OBD

On-board diagnosis traces faults in the exhaust-gas system. EPA legislation is generally equivalent to CARB requirements.

### In-field monitoring

Non-routine inspection

EPA legislation, just like CARB legislation, provides for an exhaust-gas emission test in accordance with the FTP 75 test method to be carried out on in-use vehicles on a random-test basis. Vehicles with a low mileage (10,000 miles, approx. one year old) and a high mileage (50,000 miles, but at least one vehicle per test group with 75,000/90,000 miles, approx. four years old) are tested. The number of vehicles is dependent on the number sold. At least one vehicle with a gasoline engine per test group is also tested for evaporation losses.

Vehicle monitoring by the manufacturer

Since model year 1972 manufacturers have been obliged to produce reports of damage to specific emission components or systems. This obligation to produce a report exists if at least 25 emission-related parts of a similar type have experienced a defect in a model year. It ceases five years after the end of the model year. In addition to listing the relevant components by name, the report form also includes a description of the damage, the impact on exhaust-gas emissions, and details of remedial action taken by the manufacturer. The environmental agency uses the report agency as the basis to decide whether to enforce a recall action on the vehicle manufacturer.

## EU legislation (passenger cars/light-duty trucks)

The EU Commission issues directives for European emission-control legislation. Emission limits for passenger cars and light commercial vehicles (LDT, Light-Duty Trucks) are contained in the emission-control standards:
- EU 1 (from July 1, 1992)
- EU 2 (from January 1, 1996)
- EU 3 (from January 1, 2000), and
- EU 4 (from January 1, 2005)

A new emission-control standard is normally brought into force in two stages. In the first stage, new vehicle type approvals must comply with the new specified emission limits (TA, Type Approval). In the second stage – normally one year later – each new registered vehicle must comply with the new emission limits (FR, First Registration). Legislators can inspect production vehicles for compliance with emission limits (COP, Conformity Of Production).

Individual EU member states have adopted the directives in national law for the EU Level 1 and EU Level 2. Germany created the D Level 3 and D Level 4 for this purpose. Emission limits for the D 3 standard were stricter than the EU 2 limits. Germany is therefore leading the way in the EU.

Since the EU Level 3 came into force on January 1, 2000, the EU standards take precedence over the national laws of the member states of the European Union. The EU Level 4 will come into force on January 1, 2005.

In Germany, there are different rates motor-vehicle taxation dependent on the emission-control standard. The EU directives permit tax incentives if emission limits are satisfied before they become compulsory.

## Emission limits

The EU standards specify emission limits for the following pollutants:
- Carbon monoxide (CO)
- Hydrocarbons (HC)
- Nitrogen oxides ($NO_x$), and
- Particulates, although only for diesel-engined vehicles for the time being

Permissible emission limits are based on the distance covered and are expressed in grams per kilometer (g/km). Exhaust-gas measurements are made on the vehicle chassis dynamometer, and the MNEDC (Modified New European Driving Cycle) has been in force since EU 3.

The values for hydrocarbons and nitrogen oxides are combined to form a total (HC+NO$_x$) for the EU Level 1 and EU Level 2. Separate emission limits have applied to these pollutants and for carbon monoxide since EU 3.

The CO emission limit for gasoline engines is slightly higher for EU 3 than for EU 2. This "deterioration" of the emission limit is the result of the fact that, when EU 3 came into force, the exhaust gases were measured in the exhaust-gas test during the engine-start procedure. The start was not previously included in the test, and measurement commenced only after a lead-in time of 40 seconds. However, CO emissions are very high in this phase in particular. As a result, the CO emission limits for EU 2 and EU 3 are not comparable.

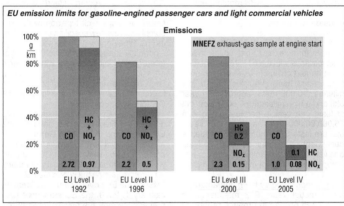

*EU emission limits for gasoline-engined passenger cars and light commercial vehicles*

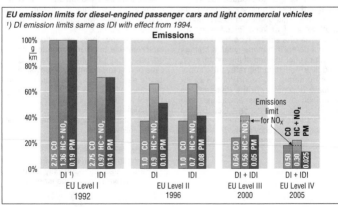

*EU emission limits for diesel-engined passenger cars and light commercial vehicles*
¹) DI emission limits same as IDI with effect from 1994.

The emission limits are different for vehicles with gasoline and diesel engines. In future, however, they will be harmonized.

There is no standard solution for emission limits for LDTs. LDTs are categorized into three classes (1...3) dependent on the vehicle-reference weight (tare weight + 100 kg). The emission limits for Class 1 are identical to those of passenger cars.

## Type approval

Type approval is performed similar to the method in the U.S.A. but with the following differences: Measurements are made of pollutants HC, CO, $NO_x$, and of particulates and exhaust-gas opacity for diesel-engined vehicles. The run-in distance of the test vehicle prior to the start of the test is 3,000 km. The deterioration factors applied to the test result for each pollutant component are specified by law; alternatively, vehicle manufacturers may document smaller factors as part of a specified continuous test running over 80,000 km (from EU 4: 100,000 km).

Compliance with the specified emission limits must last for a distance of 80,000 km (EU 3) or 100,000 km (EU 4) or 5 years. This requirement is part of the certification test.

## Directives

Directive 70/220/EC dates from 1970 and forms the basis for emission-control legislation for passenger cars and light-duty trucks. This directive was the first to specify emission limits for exhaust-gas emissions. Since its appearance, it has been updated several times.

## Type tests

Six different tests are specified in this directive:

Exhaust emissions are measured after cold start in the Type I test. In addition, the opacity of the exhaust gas is recorded for diesel-engined vehicles. New registered vehicles must currently satisfy the requirements of EU 3, but many vehicles already satisfy the emission limits for EU 4 (binding from 2005).

In the Type IV test (only for vehicles with a gasoline engine), the evaporative emissions of the vehicle are measured with the engine switched off. This primarily concerns fuel vapor that evaporates from the fuel tank.

The Type VI test (only for vehicles with a gasoline engine) records hydrocarbon and carbon-monoxide emissions after a cold start at −7°C. The first section (city section) of the MNEDC is driven for this test. This test has been binding since 2002.

## $CO_2$ emissions

$CO_2$ emissions must be expressed in grams per kilometer for new vehicles registered in the EU states. There is no legislation that specify limits for these emissions or fuel consumption, although European vehicle manufacturers have imposed voluntary limits (ACEA, Association des Constructeurs Européens d'Automobiles). In 2003 the $CO_2$ emission for vehicles in Class M1 was 165...170 g/km. This equates to a fuel consumption of 6.8...7.0 l/100 km. A $CO_2$ emission of 140 g/km (5.8 l/100 km) must be achieved by 2008.

In Germany, a tax incentive currently applies to vehicles with very low $CO_2$ emissions.

## On-board diagnosis

EOBD (European On-Board Diagnosis) was introduced for gasoline engines when the EU 3 emission-control standard came into force. Accordingly, all new registered passenger cars and light-duty trucks with a permissible total weight up to 3.5 t and up to 9 seats must be equipped with a diagnosis system to detect faults in the vehicle impacting on the vehicle's exhaust-gas characteristics. EOBD has applied to vehicles with a diesel engine since January 1, 2003.

The absolute emission limits below are specified as fault thresholds for pollutant components:

- Carbon monoxide (CO): 3.2 g/km,
- Hydrocarbons (HC): 0.4 g/km,
- Nitrogen oxides (NOx): 0.6 g/km (gasoline) or 2 g/km (diesel), and
- Particulates: 0.18 g/km (diesel).

The fault indicator lamp lights up after the third driving schedule at the latest if the system diagnoses faults that cause these emission limits to be exceeded. The route driven since the fault display is stored in the control unit. The fault indicator lamp can be switched off after three trips without a fault detected.

### In-field monitoring

In the Type I test, EU legislation specifies an inspection of conformity for vehicles in use. The minimum number of vehicles to be inspected is three, the maximum number is dependent on the test procedure. The vehicles inspected must satisfy certain criteria (e.g. vehicle age, mileage, documentation of inspections performed).

If a vehicle attracts attention as its emission levels exceed the required norm by a considerable margin, the cause must be determined. If more than one vehicle from the sample has excessive emissions for the same cause, the sample is awarded a negative result. If the causes are different, the sample is increased by one vehicle as long as the maximum sample size has not yet been reached.

If the type approval agency is convinced that a vehicle type does not satisfy the requirements, it will request the vehicle manufacturer to produce a plan of action for rectifying the defects. The measures must relate to all vehicles that are presumed to have the same defect. Vehicle recall may be part of the planned remedial action.

### German emissions testing (AU)

Exhaust-gas in-field inspections in the Federal Republic of Germany are regulated by the Road Traffic Licensing Regulations (StVZO). In accordance with Section 47a or Annex XI a, each passenger car must undergo emissions testing three years after its first registration, and then every two years. The primary focus is on CO measurement for vehicles with a gasoline engine and on opacity measurement for diesel-engined vehicles (see P. 575 onwards and P. 1164).

## Japanese legislation (passenger cars/light-duty vehicles)

In Japan, the previous emission limits were replaced by stricter limits at the end of 2002. More stringent emission limits are planned for 2005.

Besides passenger cars (seating up to 10 persons), Japan has the vehicle categories LDV (Light-Duty Vehicle) up to 1.7 t and MDV (Medium-Duty Vehicle) up to 2.5 t permissible total weight. MDV has slightly higher emission limits for $NO_x$ and particulates than the other two vehicle categories.

### Emission limits

Japanese legislation specifies emission limits for the following pollutants:
– Carbon monoxide (CO),
– Nitrogen oxides ($NO_x$),
– Hydrocarbons (HC),
– Particulates (only diesel-engined vehicles), and
– Smoke (only diesel-engined vehicles).

Exhaust emissions are measured in the 10·15-mode test, and also in the 11-mode test for gasoline engines. A discussion is taking place as to whether a modified 10·15-mode test with a cold start will be introduced in 2005.

### OBD

Since October 2000 all new passenger car models have had to be equipped with an on-board diagnosis system, and all new passenger cars since September 2002. The required functions in the Japanese OBD include monitoring the fuel system, exhaust-gas recirculation, and the fuel-injection system.

### Fleet fuel consumption

Japan plans to introduce measures to reduce the $CO_2$ emissions from passenger cars. One proposal envisages specifying a mean fuel consumption of 33.5 miles/gallon for the whole passenger car fleet by the year 2010. Another proposal bases this value on vehicle weight.

## U.S. legislation (commercial vehicles)

EPA legislation defines heavy commercial vehicles as vehicles with a permissible total weight over 8,500 lbs (equivalent to 3,850 kg). When Tier 2 is introduced (in 2004), vehicles between 8,500 and 10,000 lbs for passenger transport (MDPV, Medium Duty Passenger Vehicle) will be categorized as light-duty trucks. Consequently, they will be certified on a chassis dynamometer. In California, all vehicles over 14,000 lbs (equivalent to 6,350 kg) are classified as heavy commercial vehicles. To a great extent, Californian legislation is identical to parts of EPA legislation. However, there is an additional program for city buses.

### Emission limits
U.S. standards specify emission limits for diesel engines for:
– Hydrocarbons (HC),
– Some NMHC,
– Carbon monoxide (CO),
– Nitrogen oxides (NO$_x$),
– Particulates, and
– Exhaust-gas opacity.

The permissible emissions limits are based on engine performance and are expressed in g/kW · h. In the dynamic test cycle, emissions are measured on the engine test bench at cold start (HDTC,

Heavy-Duty Transient Cycle). Exhaust-gas opacity is subject to the Federal Smoke Test.

Emission limits for the 1998 model year are prescribed through to 2003. Over the same period, there will be a voluntary program (Clean Fuel Fleet Program) which will attract tax reliefs if a vehicle achieves lower emission standards. The next emission-limit level with significantly reduced limits for NO$_x$ will come into force starting with the 2006 model year. Nonmethane hydrocarbons and nitrogen oxides are combined to form a composite limit (HC+NO$_x$). The CO and particulate emission limits will remain at the 1998 level.

A further and very drastic reduction of limits will take effect starting with the 2007 model year. The new particulate emission limits are lower than previous limits by a factor of 10. NO$_x$ and NMHC emission limits will be phased-in between model years 2007 and 2010. The maximum permissible sulfur content in diesel fuel will be reduced from mid-2006 from the present 500 ppm to 15 ppm enforce compliance with the strict emission regulations.

As opposed to passenger cars and LDTs, no emission limits have been specified for average fleet emissions or fleet fuel consumption for heavy commercial vehicles.

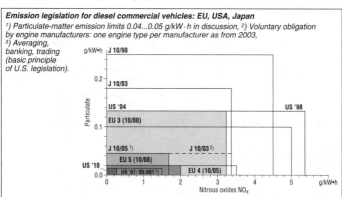

***Emission legislation for diesel commercial vehicles: EU, USA, Japan***
[1]) Particulate-matter emission limits 0.04...0.05 g/kW · h in discussion, [2]) Voluntary obligation by engine manufacturers: one engine type per manufacturer as from 2003,
[3]) Averaging, banking, trading (basic principle of U.S. legislation).

## Consent decree

In 1998 a court settlement was reached between EPA, CARB and several engine manufacturers. It included penalties for the manufacturer if impermissible engine modifications are performed in order to optimize fuel consumption in the highway cycle that would cause a rise in $NO_x$ emission. The major highlights of the "Consent Decree" include:

– The engine manufacturers concerned must satisfy the emission limits starting with model year 2004 and preferably with effect from October 2002.

– In addition to the dynamic test cycle, the emission limits must also undercut the stationary European 13-stage test (ESC). Furthermore, emissions within a specific engine speed or torque zone ("Not-to-Exceed" Zone) must be only 25% above the emission limits specified for model year 2004 in any driving style. These additional tests are mandatory for all diesel commercial vehicles starting with model year 2007.

## Durability

Compliance with emission limits must be certified over a specified route or a specific time period in which a distinction is drawn between three weight classes, each with increasing durability requirements:

– Light commercial vehicles from 8,500 (EPA) or 14,000 (CARB) up to 19,500 lbs,
– Medium-heavy commercial vehicles from 19,500 to 33,000 lbs,
– Heavy commercial vehicles over 33,000 lbs.

At present, an emission durability of 8 years or 290,000 miles must be documented for heavy commercial vehicles. Starting with model year 2004, the requirement will increase to 13 years or 435,000 miles.

# EU legislation (commercial vehicles)

In Europe, heavy commercial vehicles include all vehicles with a permissible total weight over 3,500 kg and designed to transport more than nine people. The emission regulations are contained in Directive 88/77/EEC, which is continuously updated.

As for passenger cars and light commercial vehicles, new emission-limit levels for heavy commercial vehicles are introduced in two stages. In order to receive type approval (TA), new engine type must first comply with the new emission limits. One year later compliance with the new emission limits is a prerequisite for registering a new vehicle. The legislator can inspect conformity of production (COP) by taking engines out of serial production and testing them for compliance with the new emission limits.

## Emission limits

EU standards specify emission limits for hydrocarbons (HC), some NMHCs, carbon monoxide (CO), nitrogen oxides ($NO_x$), particulates and exhaust-gas opacity for diesel commercial-vehicle engines.

The Euro Level 3 emission limits have become valid for the type approvals of all new engines since October 2000, and for all production vehicles since October 2001. Emissions are measured in the stationary 13-stage test (ESC, European Steady-State Cycle). Exhaust-gas opacity is subject to the opacity test (ELR, European Load Response). Diesel engines that are fitted with "advanced systems" for exhaust-gas treatment (e.g. $NO_x$ catalytic converter or particulate filter) must also be tested in the dynamic ETC (European Transient Cycle). The European test cy-

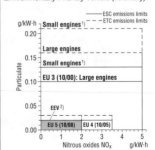

***EU emission limits for diesel commercial vehicles***
[1] $V_{cyl} \leq 0.75\ l$, $n_{rated\ speed} \geq 3,000\ rpm$, [2] Enhanced Environmentally-Friendly Vehicle (voluntary).

cles are started with the engine running at normal operating temperature.

Somewhat higher particulate emissions are permitted for small engines, i.e. engines with a piston displacement under 0.75 *l* per cylinder and a rated speed over 3,000 rpm than for large engines. Separate emission limits apply to ETC, e.g. particulate emission limits due to anticipated soot peaks in dynamic operation. They are approximately 50% higher than ESC emission limits.

Starting October 2005, the Euro Level 4 emission limits will come into force initially for new type approvals, and for serial production one year later. All emission limits are significantly reduced from Euro 3, in particular the particulate emission limits which are lower by approx. 80%. The following changes will also apply after introduction of Euro 4:

– In addition to ESC and ELR, the dynamic exhaust-gas test (ETC) will be binding for all diesel engines.
– All new vehicle types must be fitted with an on-board diagnosis system (OBD).
– The operation of emission-related components must be documented during the service life of the vehicle.

Starting October 2008, the Euro Level 5 emission limits will come into force initially for new engine type approvals, and for series production one year later. Only the NO$_x$ emission limits reduced as compared to Euro 4. NO$_x$ emission limits will then be reduced by a total of approx. 80% compared with the Euro 3 standard.

**Enhanced environmentally friendly vehicles**
The EU directives permit tax incentives for EEV vehicles (Enhanced Environmentally Friendly Vehicle) and if emission limits are met before an emission limit level becomes legally binding. The EEV category includes specifications for voluntary emissions limits for ESC, ETC and ELR exhaust-gas tests. The NO$_x$ and particulate emission limits are identical to Euro 5 ESC emission limits. The standards for HC, NMHC, CO and exhaust-gas opacity are stricter.

## Japanese legislation (commercial vehicles)

In Japan, all heavy commercial vehicles are those which have a permissible total weight over 2,500 kg and are capable of transporting more than ten people.

**Emission limits**
The emission limit level currently valid in Japan was introduced between 1997 and 1999. It stipulates emission limits for HC, NO$_x$, CO, particulates and exhaust-gas opacity. Emissions are measured in the stationary Japanese 13-stage test (hot test). Exhaust-gas opacity is subject to the Japanese smoke test. The durability of the emissions must be documented over a distance of 45,000 km.

The new emission limit level (New Short-Term Regulation) with reduced emission levels and increased requirements for the durability of emissions (80,000...650,000 km, dependent on the permissible total weight) applies with effect from October 2003. In accordance with a voluntary obligation undertaken by Japanese engine manufacturers, one engine type per manufacturer should already meet the particulate emission level of the next emission limit level.

The New Long-Term Regulation will probably come into force in October 2005. The regulations have not yet been approved. In general, Japan intends to halve emissions compared with 2003, and even strive for a 75% reduction in particulate levels. In addition, there is an ongoing discussion on introducing a dynamic Japanese test cycle.

**Regional programs**
In addition to national regulations that apply to new vehicles, there are regional vehicle-fleet regulations. The objective is to reduce in-field emissions by replacing or retrofitting old diesel-engined vehicles (e.g. "Vehicle NO$_x$ Law" or particulate legislation by the Tokyo City Council).

## U.S.A. test cycles
## for passenger cars
## and light-duty trucks

### FTP 75 test cycle
The FTP 75 test cycle (Federal Test Procedure), which consists of three test sections, represents actual speeds measured in the U.S. on the streets of Los Angeles during morning commuter traffic.

### Conditioning
The vehicle under test is first conditioned (allowed to stand with the engine off for 12 hours at a room temperature of 20...30 °C). It is then started and run through the prescribed test cycle.

### Collection of pollutants
The emitted pollutants are collected separately during the different phases.

*ct phase:*
Collection of diluted exhaust gas in sample bag 1 of the test equipment for the CVS test during the cold transition phase.

*s phase:*
Changeover to sample bag 2 at the start of the stabilized phase (after 505 seconds) without any interruption in the driving schedule. The engine is switched off for 600 seconds at the end of the s phase after a total of 1,365 seconds.

*ht phase:*
The engine is restarted for the hot test. The speeds used in this phase correspond directly to those in the cold transition phase (phase ct). Exhaust gases are collected in a third sample bag.

### Evaluation
The bag samples from the previous phases are analyzed during the pause before the hot test, as the samples should not remain in the bags for longer than 20 minutes.

The exhaust-gas sample in the third sample bag is analyzed at the end of the driving schedule. The individual results of the three phases are weighted by factors of 0.43 (ct phase), 1 (s phase), and 0.57 (ht phase) for the overall result. The weighted sums of the pollutant masses (HC, CO and $NO_x$) from all three bags are correlated with the distance covered during the test and then expressed as pollutant emission per mile.

This test cycle is applied in the U.S. including California, and in other countries (e.g. South America).

### SFTP schedules
The tests according to the SFTP standard will be gradually phased-in from 2001 to 2004. They comprise the following driving schedules:
– FTP 75,
– SC03, and
– US06.

The extended tests are intended to examine the following additional driving conditions:
– Aggressive driving,
– Major changes in driving speed,
– Starting the engine and starting-off,
– Frequent minor changes in driving speed,
– Time taken for switching off the engine, and
– Running the engine with the air conditioner on.

In the SC03 and US06 schedules, the ct phase of the FTP 75 test cycle is applied after preconditioning with no collection of exhaust gases. However, other conditioning procedures are also possible.

The SC03 schedule is carried out at a temperature of 35°C and a relative humidity of 40% (only vehicles with air conditioner). The individual driving schedules are weighted as follows:
– Vehicles with air conditioner:
  35% FTP 75 + 37% SC03 + 28% US06.
– Vehicles without air conditioner:
  72% FTP 75 + 28% US06.

The vehicle must pass the each of the SFTP and FTP 75 test schedules separately.

Cold-start enrichment, which is necessary when a vehicle engine is started at low temperatures, produces particularly high emissions. These cannot be measured in current exhaust-gas testing, which is conducted at ambient temperatures of 20...30 °C. An additional exhaust-gas test is performed at −7 °C on vehicles with a gasoline engine in order to limit these pollutants. However, this test only prescribes a limit for carbon monoxide.

## Test cycles for determining fleet fuel consumption

Every vehicle manufacturer must determine the fuel consumption of its vehicle fleet. If a manufacturer exceeds certain limits, they are liable to a fine. The carmaker is awarded a bonus if consumption is below certain limits.

Fuel consumption is determined from the exhaust emissions produced during two test cycles: the FTP 75 test cycle (55%) and the highway test cycle (45%). The highway test cycle is conducted once after preconditioning (vehicle allowed to stand with the engine off for 12 hours at 20...30 °C) without measurement. The ex-

---

### USA test cycles for passenger cars and light commercial vehicles

| | a | b | c | d |
|---|---|---|---|---|
| **Test cycle** | **FTP 75** | **SC03** | **US06** | **Highway** |
| Cycle distance: | 17.87 km | 5.76 km | 12.87 km | 16.44 km |
| Cycle duration: | 1877 s + 600 s pause | 594 s | 600 s | 765 s |
| Average cycle speed: | 34.1 km/h | 34.9 km/h | 77.3 km/h | 77.4 km/h |
| Maximum cycle speed: | 91.2 km/h | 88.2 km/h | 129.2 km/h | 96.4 km/h |

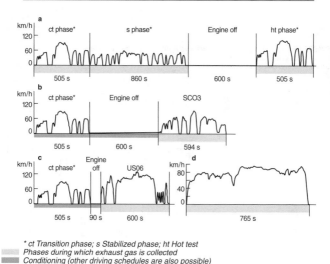

* ct Transition phase; s Stabilized phase; ht Hot test
Phases during which exhaust gas is collected
Conditioning (other driving schedules are also possible)

haust emissions from a second test run are then collected. Fuel consumption is extrapolated based on the emissions.

### Further test cycles
#### FTP 72 test
The FTP 72 test – also referred to as the UDDS (Urban Dynamometer Driving Schedule) – is equivalent to the FTP 75 test but excludes the *ht* test section (hot test). This cycle is driven during the running-loss test for vehicles with a gasoline engine.

#### New York City Cycle (NYCC)
This cycle is also an element in the running-loss test (for vehicles with a gasoline engine).

# European test cycle for passenger cars and light-duty trucks

The EU/ECE test cycle (Economic Commission of Europe) – also referred to as the European driving schedule – is driven with a test cycle that is calculated to provide a reasonable approximation of driving behavior in city traffic (UDC, Urban Driving Cycle). In 1993 the cycle was supplemented by highway section with speeds up to 120 km/h (EUDC, Extra-Urban Driving Cycle). The test cycle produced from combining these cycles is referred to as the NEDC (New European Driving Cycle).

The lead-in time of 40 seconds before starting to measure the exhaust gas (MNEDC, modified NEDC) is omitted in the EU 3 (2000) stage. This means that the cold start is also included in measurement.

### Conditioning
For the exhaust-gas test, the vehicle must be at a specific temperature for at least six hours with the engine switched off. The temperature at present lies at 20...30 °C. Since 2002 the starting temperature for the Type VI test has been lowered to –7 °C for vehicles with a gasoline engine.

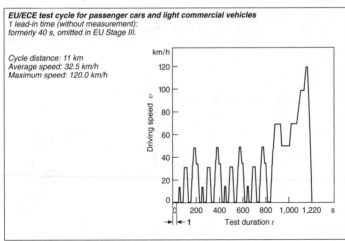

*EU/ECE test cycle for passenger cars and light commercial vehicles*
*1 lead-in time (without measurement):*
*formerly 40 s, omitted in EU Stage III.*

*Cycle distance: 11 km*
*Average speed: 32.5 km/h*
*Maximum speed: 120.0 km/h*

### City driving cycle
The city driving cycle comprises four identical sections each lasting 195 seconds and driven without a break. The route driven measures 4.052 km. This results in an average speed of 18.7 km/h at a maximum speed of 50 km/h.

### Highway driving cycle
Directly after the city driving cycle, a trip is made at speeds up to 120 km/h. This section lasts for 400 seconds and the route driven measures 6.955 km.

### Evaluation
During measurement, exhaust gas is collected in a sample bag using the CVS method. The pollutant masses determined by analyzing the bag contents are converted to the driven distance.

## Japanese test cycle for passenger cars and light-duty trucks

Two test cycles with differing synthetically generated test cycles are combined to provide the complete test for vehicles with a gasoline engine. After a cold start, the 11-mode cycle (only for vehicles with a gasoline engine) is run four times, with evaluation of all four cycles. The 10 · 15-mode test (for gasoline and diesel engines) as a hot test is run through once. This test cycle simulates the characteristic drivability in Tokyo and has been extended to include a high-speed component. However, the maximum speed is lower than for the European test cycle, as the driving speed in Japan is normally lower due to higher traffic density.

Preconditioning for the hot test also includes the stipulated idle emissions test and is conducted as follows: After warming up the vehicle at 60 km/h for approx. 15 minutes, the HC, CO and $CO_2$ concentrations in the exhaust pipe are measured. After a second warm-up period of 5 minutes at 60 km/h, the 10 · 15-mode hot test is then started. In the 11-mode test as well as in the 10 · 15-mode test, analysis is performed using a CVS system. The diluted exhaust gas is collected in a bag in each case. In the cold test, the pollutants are specified in terms of g/test. In the hot test, they are correlated with the distance driven, i.e. they are converted to g/km.

Emission-control legislation in Japan includes limits on evaporative emissions which are measured using the SHED method.

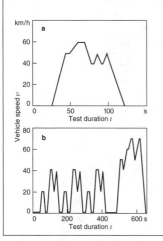

**Japanese test cycles for passenger cars and light commercial vehicles**
a) 11-mode cycle (cold test)

| | |
|---|---|
| Cycle distance: | 1.021 km |
| Cycles per test: | 4 |
| Average speed: | 30.6 km/h |
| Maximum speed: | 60 km/h |

b) 10 · 15-mode cycle (hot test)

| | |
|---|---|
| Cycle distance: | 4.16 km |
| Cycles per test: | 1 |
| Average speed: | 22.7 km/h |
| Maximum speed: | 70 km/h |

## Test cycles for commercial vehicles

All test cycles for commercial vehicles are performed on the engine test bench. In the transient test cycles, the emissions are collected and evaluated according to the CVS principle. The untreated emissions came in the stationary test cycles. The emissions are based on the engine performance and are expressed in g/kW·h.

### Europe

In Europe until the year 2000, vehicles with a permissible total weight of over 3.5 tons and more than 9 seats were required to meet the stipulations of the 13-stage test in accordance with EEC R49. The new 13-stage test ESC (European Steady-State Cycle) with changed operating points came into force with the introduction of the EU 3 stage (October 2000). The operating points are determined from the engine full-load curve. The test sequence stipulates a series of 13 different steady-state operating modes. Factors are used to weight the measured gaseous emissions and particulates as well as the power output at each operating point. The test result expressed in g/kW·h is derived from the total of the weighted emissions

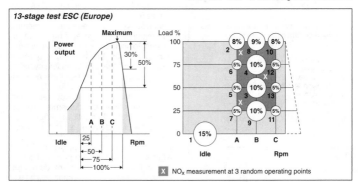

*13-stage test ESC (Europe)*

X NO$_x$ measurement at 3 random operating points

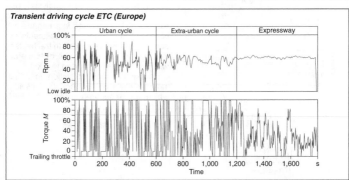

*Transient driving cycle ETC (Europe)*

divided by the total weighted power output. An additional three $NO_x$ test may be performed in the test range when certification is performed. The $NO_x$ emissions may only differ by a small amount from those at the adjacent operating points. The additional measuring has the goal of preventing engine modifications performed specially for the test.

In addition to the ESC, the ETC (European Transient Cycle) for measuring gaseous emissions and particulates as well as the ELR (European Load Response) for determining exhaust-gas opacity were also introduced in EU 3.

The ETC applies only to commercial vehicles with "advanced" exhaust-gas treatment ($NO_x$ catalytic converter, particulate filter) in the EU 3 stage. With effect from EU 4 (10/2005), it will be binding for all vehicles. The test cycle is derived from real on-road trips and is divided into three sections – a city section, a highway section and an expressway section. The test lasts for 30 minutes. Nominal values are specified for engine speed and torque in steps of one second.

All European test cycles start with a hot engine.

**Japan**

Exhaust emissions are measured using the Japanese 13-stage steady-state test (hot test). However, the operating points, their order and their relative weighting differ from those of the European 13-stage test. Compared with the ESC, the test focuses on lower engine speeds and loads, a consequence of the high traffic density in Japan.

There is also discussion on the introduction of a dynamic Japanese test cycle for the emission limit level to take effect in 2005.

**U.S.A.**

Since 1987 engines for heavy commercial vehicles have been tested from a cold start on an engine test bench in a transient driving schedule. The test cycle is based on highway operation under real-world conditions. It has significantly more idle times than the ETC.

Exhaust-gas opacity is monitored in a further test (Federal Smoke Cycle) under transient and quasi-steady-state operating conditions.

Starting with model year 2007 (and from as early as October 2002 for signatories of the Consent Decree ), the U.S. emission limits must also be met in the European 13-stage test (ESC).

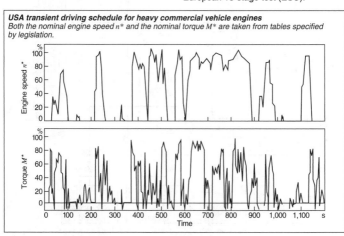

*USA transient driving schedule for heavy commercial vehicle engines*
*Both the nominal engine speed $n^*$ and the nominal torque $M^*$ are taken from tables specified by legislation.*

# Exhaust-gas measuring techniques

## Emissions testing on chassis dynamometers

### Requirements

Exhaust-gas tests on chassis dynamometers are used for the type approval to attain General Certification as well as to develop engine or other components. It differs from exhaust-gas tests as such since workshop measuring devices are used for in-field monitoring. In addition, exhaust-gas tests are carried out on engine test benches, for instance for the type approval of heavy commercial vehicles.

The exhaust-gas test on chassis dynamometers is performed on the vehicle. The methods used are defined to simulate actual vehicle operation on the road as far as possible. Measurement on a chassis dynamometer offers the following advantages here:

- Highly reproducible results, as environmental conditions can be kept constant.
- Good comparability of tests, as a defined speed-time profile can be driven independently of traffic flow, and
- The necessary measuring techniques can be set up in a stationary environment.

*Exhaust-gas test on the chassis dynamometer*
*1 Roller with dynamometer, 2 Primary catalytic converter, 3 Main catalytic converter, 4 Filter,*
*5 Particulate filter, 6 Dilution tunnel, 7 Mix-T, 8 Valve, 9 Dilution air conditioner, 10 Dilution air,*
*11 Exhaust air, 12 Blower, 13 CVS system, 14 Dilution-air sample bag, 15 Exhaust-gas sample*
*bag (Mix-T), 16 Exhaust-gas sample bag (tunnel).*
*① Path for exhaust-gas measurement, gasoline engine, ② Path for exhaust- gas measurement,*
*diesel engine.*

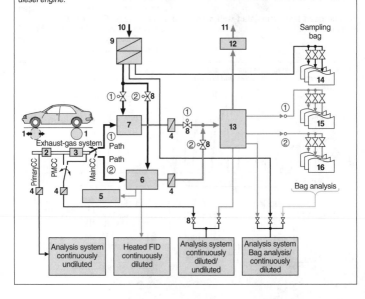

## Test setup
### General setup

The driven wheels of the vehicle under test are placed on rotating rollers. This means that the forces acting on the vehicle, i.e. the vehicle's moments of inertia, rolling resistance and aerodynamic drag, must be simulated so that the trip on the test bench reproduces emissions comparable to those obtained during an on-road trip. For this purpose, asynchronous machines, direct-current machines, or even electrodynamic retarders on older test benches, generate a suitable speed-dependent load that acts on the rollers for the vehicle to overcome. More modern machines use electric flywheel simulation to reproduce this inertia. Older test benches use real flywheels of different sizes attached by rapid couplings to the rollers to simulate the vehicle mass. A blower mounted a short distance in front of the vehicle provides the necessary engine cooling.

The exhaust pipe of the vehicle under test is generally a gas-tight attachment to the exhaust-gas collection system – the dilution system described below. A proportion of the exhaust gas is collected there. At the end of the driving test, the gas is analyzed for emission-limit components (hydrocarbons, nitrogen oxides and carbon monoxide) and carbon dioxide (to determine fuel consumption).

In addition, and for development purposes, part of the exhaust gas flow can be extracted continuously from sampling points along the vehicle's exhaust-gas system or dilution system to analyze the pollutant concentrations.

The test cycle is repeated by a driver in the vehicle. The required and current vehicle speeds are displayed on a driver control-station monitor. In some cases, an automated driving system replaces the driver to increase the reproducibility of test results.

### Test setup for diesel-engined vehicles

The pollutant emission of diesel-engined vehicles is measured in a similar way to the method for vehicles with gasoline-engines, although some changes must be made to the test-bed setup and the measuring techniques used. The complete sample-taking system including the exhaust-gas measuring device for hydrocarbons must be heated to 190 °C. This is to prevent condensation of hydrocarbons, which have high boiling points, and to evaporate the hydrocarbons that have already condensed in the diesel exhaust gas. In addition, a "dilution tunnel" is used with a high internal flow turbulence (Reynolds number > 40,000). Particulate filters are also used to calculate particulate emission based on load.

Legislators tend to apply the same emission limits for vehicles powered by gasoline and diesel engines. The design of test benches for vehicles with gasoline and diesel engines will therefore become increasingly similar in the future. Mixed operation is possible in principle. However, testing vehicles with very different emission levels (e.g. vehicles on SULEV level and vehicles complying with the EU 3 standard) on a <u>single</u> test bench requires extremely complex control instrumentation (e.g. separate sample-taking systems, special purge procedures).

## Dilution system

The most commonly used method of collected the exhaust gases emitted from an engine is the CVS dilution procedure (<u>C</u>onstant <u>V</u>olume <u>S</u>ampling). It was introduced for the first time in the U.S.A. in 1972 for passenger cars and light-duty trucks. In the meantime it has been improved in several stages. The CVS method is used in other countries such as Japan. It has also been used in Europe since 1982. It is therefore an exhaust-gas collection that is recognized throughout the world.

Objectives
In the CVS method, the exhaust gas is only analyzed at the end of the test. The following requirements must be fulfilled:
– Water vapor must be prevented from condensing, otherwise there will be a loss of nitrogen oxides.
– Secondary reactions must be prevented from occurring in the collected exhaust gas.

Principle of the CVS method
The CVS method operates on the following principle. The exhaust gases emitted by the test vehicle are diluted with ambient air at a mean ratio of 1:5...1:10, and extracted using a special system of pumps in such a way that the total volumetric flow composed of exhaust gas and dilution air is constant. The admixture of dilution air is therefore dependent on the momentary exhaust-gas volume. A representative sample is continuously extracted from the diluted exhaust-gas flow and is collected in one or more (exhaust-gas) sample bags. The volumetric flow during sampling remains constant within a bag-filling phase. Therefore, the pollutant concentration in a sample bag at the end of the filling process is identical to the mean value of the concentration in the diluted exhaust gas during the bag-filling process.

At the same time as the exhaust-gas sample bags are being filled, a sample of the dilution air is taken and collected in one or more (air) sample bags in order to measure the pollutant concentration in the dilution air.

Filling of sample bags generally corresponds with the phases or partial cycles in which the test cycles are split (e.g. ht phase in the FTP 75-test cycle, see P. 567).

The pollutant mass emitted during the test is calculated from the total volume of the diluted exhaust gas and the pollutant concentrations in the exhaust-gas and air-sample bags.

Dilution systems
Two alternative methods exist to achieve the constant volumetric flow in the diluted exhaust gas:
– PDP method (Positive Displacement Pump): A rotary-piston blower (Roots blower) is used.

– CFV method (Critical Flow Venturi): A venturi tube and a standard blower are used in the critical state.

Advances in the CVS method
Diluting the exhaust gas causes a reduction in pollutant concentrations as a factor of the dilution. The concentrations of some pollutants (especially hydrocarbon compounds) in the diluted exhaust gas are comparable to the concentrations in the dilution air (or lower) in certain test phases, since pollutant emissions have been significantly reduced in recent years as emission limits have become more stringent. This poses a problem from the measuring-process aspect as the difference in the two values is crucial for the exhaust emissions. A further challenge is presented by the precision of the measuring devices used to analyze the pollutants.

The measures below have been generally implemented on chassis dynamometers that have more modern CVS dilution systems in order to counter the problems described above:
– Lowering the dilution; the required precautions to prevent water from condensing, e.g. by heating sections of the dilution systems, or drying or warming dilution air on vehicles with a gasoline engine.
– Reducing and stabilizing pollutant concentrations in the dilution air, e.g. by using active-charcoal filters.
– Optimizing the measuring devices (including dilution systems), e.g. by selecting or pretreating the materials used and system setups; using modified electronic components.
– Optimizing processes, e.g. by applying special purge procedures.

Bag Mini Diluter
As an alternative to the improvements in CVS technology described above, a new type of dilution system was developed in the U.S.A.: the Bag Mini Diluter (BMD). Here, part of the exhaust gas flow is diluted at a constant ratio with a dried, heated zero gas (e.g. cleaned air). During the test, part of this diluted exhaust-gas flow that is proportional to the exhaust-gas volumetric flow is filled in (exhaust-gas)

sample bags and analyzed at the end of the driving test.

In this procedure, dilution is performed with a pollutant-free zero gas free of pollutants and not with air containing pollutants. This has the purpose of avoiding the air-sample bag analysis and the subsequent differential formation of exhaust-gas and air-sample bag concentrations. However, a more complex procedure is required than for the CVS method, e.g. one requirement is to determine the (undiluted) exhaust-gas volumetric flow and the proportional sample-bag filling.

**Table 1: Test procedure**

| Components | Procedure |
| --- | --- |
| CO, $CO_2$ | Non-Dispersive Infrared Analyzer (NDIR) |
| Nitrogen oxides $NO_x$ | Chemiluminescence detector (CLD). Note: $NO_x$ is generally interpreted as the total of NO and $NO_2$ |
| Total hydrocarbon (THC) | Flame ionization detector (FID) |
| $CH_4$ | Combined design of gas chromatographic procedure and flame ionization detector (GC FID) |
| $CH_3OH$, $CH_2O$ | Combined design of impinger or cartridge process and chromatographic analysis techniques; mandatory in the U.S.A. when certain fuels are used |
| Particulate | gravimetric procedure (weighing particulate filters before and after the test), in Europe and Japan only mandatory at present for diesel-engined vehicles |

# Exhaust-gas measuring devices

### Exhaust-gas measuring devices for taking measurements on gasoline- and diesel-engined vehicles

Emission-control legislation defines worldwide standard test procedures for pollutants under control in order to measure the concentrations in exhaust-gas and air-sample bags (see Table 1).

For development purposes, many test benches also include the continuous measurement of pollutant concentrations in the vehicle exhaust-gas system or the dilution system. The reason is to capture data for the components under control as well as for other components not subject to legislation. Other test procedures than listed in Table 1 are required for this, e.g.:
– Paramagnetic method (to measure $O_2$ concentration).
– Cutter FID: a combination of flame-ionization detector and absorber for non-methane hydrocarbons (to measure the $CH_4$ concentration).
– Mass spectroscopy (multi-component analyzer).
– FTIR (**F**ourier-**T**ransform **I**nfra**r**ed) spectroscopy (multi-component analyzer).
– IR laser spectroscopy (multi-component analyzer).

A description of the main measuring devices is given below.

### NDIR analyzer
The NDIR (Non-Dispersive Infrared) analyzer utilizes the property of certain gases to absorb infrared radiation in a narrow wavelength range. Absorbed radiation is converted to vibration or rotation energy by the absorbing molecules. In turn, this energy can be measured as heat The phenomenon described occurs in molecules that are formed from atoms of at least two different elements, e.g. CO, $CO_2$, $C_6H_{14}$ or $SO_2$.

There are a number of variants of NDIR analyzers; the main component parts are a source of infrared light, an absorption cell (cuvette) through which the test gas is routed, a reference cell generally positioned in parallel (filled with inert gas, e.g. $N_2$), a rotating chopper and a detector. The detector comprises two chambers connected by a membrane and containing samples of the gas components under analysis. Radiation from the reference cell is absorbed in one chamber and radiation from the cuvette in the other. This may have already been reduced by absorption in the test gas. The difference in radiant energy causes a flow movement that is measured by a flow sensor or a pressure sensor. The rotating chopper interrupts the infrared radiation in cycles, causing the flow movement to change direction and therefore a modulation of the sensor signal.

NDIR analyzers possess strong cross sensitivity to water vapor in the test gas since $H_2O$ molecules absorb a wide range of infrared radiation wavelengths. This is the reason why, when NDIR analyzers are used to make measurements on undiluted exhaust gas, they are positioned downstream from a test-gas treatment device (e.g. a gas cooler) to dry the exhaust gas.

Chemiluminescence Detector (CLD)

In a reaction chamber, the test gas is mixed with ozone that is produced from oxygen in a high-voltage discharge. The nitrogen monoxide content in the test gas oxidizes to nitrogen dioxide in this environment; some of the molecules produced are in a state of excitation. When these molecules return to their basic state, energy is released in the form of light (chemiluminescence). A detector, e.g. a photomultiplier, measures the emitted luminous energy; under specific conditions, it is proportional to the nitrogen-monoxide concentration in the test gas.

It is a requirement to measure the NO and $NO_2$ molecules as the legislation regularizes the emission of the total nitrogen oxides. However, since the test principle of the CLD is limited to measuring the NO concentration, the test gas is channeled through a converter that reduces the nitrogen dioxide to nitrogen monoxide.

*Test chamber for the NDIR method*
*1 Gas outlet, 2 Absorption cell, 3 Test gas inlet, 4 Optical filter, 5 Infrared light source, 6 Infrared radiation, 7 Reference cell, 8 Rotating chopper, 9 Detector.*

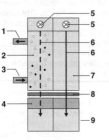

*Design of the chemiluminescence detector*
*1 Reaction chamber, 2 Ozone inlet, 3 Test gas inlet, 4 Gas outlet, 5 Filter, 6 Detector.*

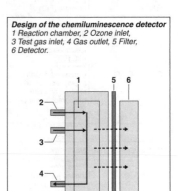

### Flame Ionization Detector (FID)
The test gas is burned in a hydrogen flame where carbon radicals are formed and some of these radicals are temporarily ionized. The radicals are discharged at a collector electrode; the current produced is measured and is proportional to the number of carbon atoms in the test gas.

### GC FID and Cutter FID
There are two generally common methods to measure the methane concentration in the test gas. Each method consists of the combination of a $CH_4$-separating element and a flame ionization detector. In these methods, either a gas-chromatography column (GC FID) or a heated catalytic converter oxidizes the non-$CH_4$ hydrocarbons (cutter FID) in order to separate the methane.

Unlike the cutter FID, the GC FID can only determine the $CH_4$ concentration discontinuously (typical interval between two measurements: 30...45 seconds).

### Paramagnetic Detector (PMD)
There are different constructions of paramagnetic detectors (dependent on the manufacturer). The constructions are based on the phenomenon that forces with paramagnetic properties (such as oxygen) act on molecules in inhomogeneous magnetic fields. These forces cause the molecules to move. The movement is sensed by a special detector and is proportional to the concentration of molecules in the test gas.

## Exhaust-gas measuring devices for measurements on diesel-engined vehicles
Essentially, the same devices are used to measure the concentrations of gaseous pollutants in the exhaust gas of gasoline-engined vehicles as for diesel-engined vehicles.

### Test system for measuring HC
However, there is a difference when it comes to measuring hydrocarbon emissions (HC): It is not performed in the exhaust-gas sample bag but by continuous analysis of part of the diluted exhaust-gas flow. The concentration measured throughout the driving test is then added. The reason for this is that the hydrocarbons (which have a high boiling point) condense in the (non-heated) exhaust-gas sample bag.

### Measuring particulate emission
In addition to gaseous pollutants, (solid) particulates are also measured for diesel-engined vehicles as they are also pollutants subject to legislation. The gravimetric process is the process specified by law to measure particulate emissions.

#### *Gravimetric process*
*(particulate filter process)*
Part of the diluted exhaust gas is sampled from the dilution tunnel during the driving test and then channeled through particulate filters. The particulate loading is calculated from the weight of the particulate filters before and after the test. The particulate emission during the driving test is then calculated from the load, the total volume of the diluted exhaust gas, and the partial volume channeled through the particulate filters.

The gravimetric process has the following disadvantages:

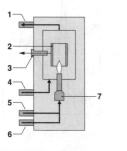

*Design of the flame ionization detector*
1 Gas outlet, 2 Collector electrode,
3 Amplifier, 4 Combustion air,
5 Test gas input, 6 Combustion gas ($H_2$/He),
7 Burner.

- Relatively high detection limit, only reducible to a limited extent by using complex instrumentation (e.g. to optimize the tunnel geometry).
- Not possible to measure particulate emissions continuously.
- Complex process as particulate filters have to be conditioned in order to minimize environmental influences.
- No selection with regard to the chemical composition of particulates or particulate size.

The disadvantages stated above and the significant reduction in emission limits for particulate emissions expected in the future have caused legislators to consider phasing out the gravimetric process. However, an alternative process has not yet been found.

*Continuous process for particulate-emissions testing*
The gravimetric process does not permit continuous measurement of emissions throughout the driving test. It is only possible to make an integral measurement throughout the whole test, or individual test phases, or partial cycles. Therefore, for development purposes, further measuring devices are used with the primary goal to measure the particulate emission continuously throughout the test. The turbidity meter (opacimeter) is an example of this.

These devices are used, for instance, during the diesel smoke emission test that is legally prescribed in some countries (description of the devices, see P. 579 onwards).

*Further developments*
There is increasing interest on acquiring knowledge of the size distribution of particulates in the exhaust gas of a diesel-engined vehicle. Examples of devices that supply this information are:
- "Scanning Mobility Particle Sizer" (SMPS),
- "Electrical Low Pressure Impactor" (ELPI), and
- "Photo-acoustic Soot Sensor" (PASS).

**Testing commercial vehicles**
The transient-test method for emission test of diesel engines in heavy commercial vehicles over 8,500 lbs (U.S.A.) or over 3.5 t (Europe) was prescribed in the U.S.A. starting model year 1986 and is planned for introduction in Europe from 2000/2005. This test is performed on dynamic engine test benches and also uses the CVS testing method. Due to engine size, however, a test system with a considerably higher throughput capacity is required in order to comply with the same dilution conditions that apply to the CVS testing method for passenger cars and light-duty trucks. Double dilution (through a secondary tunnel) approved by legislators helps t limit the increased complexity of instrumentation.

The diluted exhaust-gas volumetric flow can either be measured with a calibrated Roots blower or a venturi tube in the critical state.

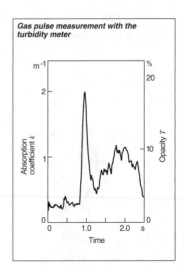

*Gas pulse measurement with the turbidity meter*

## Diesel smoke emission test (opacity measurement)

### Method

Separate legislation for testing the smoke emissions of diesel-engined vehicles came into force long before the introduction of legislation for testing gaseous pollutants, and they are still applicable today in their original form. Test methods are not standardized in the countries that have a legal requirement for diesel smoke emission testing. All existing smoke tests are coupled closely to the measuring devices used. The smoke number is one measurement for the smoke (carbon-particulate emission, particulates). Two methods are essentially customary for measuring this value.

– In the <u>absorption method</u> (opacity measurement), the opacity of the exhaust gas is indicated by the degree to which it blocks the passage of a beam of light shining through it.

– In the <u>filter method</u> (measurement of reflected light), a specified quantity of exhaust gas is routed through a filter element. The degree of filter discoloration provides an indication of the amount of soot contained in the exhaust gas.

Measurement of diesel-engined smoke emissions is relevant only if the engine is under load, since it is only when the engine is operated under load that emission of significant levels of particulates occur. Here, as well, two different test procedures are in common use:

– Measurement under full load, e.g. on a chassis dynamometer or over a specified test course, against the vehicle brakes.

– Measurements made under conditions of unhindered acceleration with a defined amount of accelerator pedal depression and load applied by the flywheel mass of the accelerating engine.

As the results of testing for diesel smoke emissions vary according to both test procedure and type of load, they are not generally suitable for direct mutual comparisons.

### Turbidity meter (absorption method)

During unhindered acceleration, some of the exhaust gas is routed from the vehicle exhaust pipe via an exhaust-sample probe and sampling hose to the measuring chamber (without vacuum assistance). In particular, since temperature and pressure

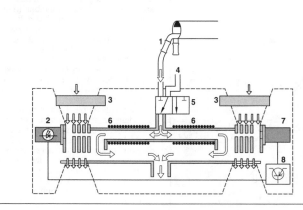

*Turbidity meter* (absorption method)
1 Exhaust-sample probe, 2 Green LED, 3 Fan, 4 Purge air for calibration,
5 Calibrating valve, 6 Heater, 7 Receiver, 8 Electronic analyzer and display.
⇨ Exhaust-gas path

are controlled, this method prevents the test results from being affected by exhaust-gas backpressure and its fluctuations.

Inside the measuring chamber, the diesel exhaust gas is penetrated by a beam of light. The attenuation of the light is measured photoelectrically, and is indicated as % opacity $T$ or as a coefficient of absorption $k$. A high degree of accuracy and reproducibility of the test results requires that the length of the measuring chamber be precisely defined, and that the optical windows be kept free of soot (by air curtains, i.e. tangential purge air flows).

During testing under load, measurement and display are a continuous process. In the case of unhindered acceleration. the entire test curve can be digitally stored. The tester automatically determines the maximum value and calculates the mean from several gas pulses.

**Smoke tester (filter method)**

The smoke tester extracts a specified quantity (e.g. 0.1 or 1$l$) of diesel exhaust gas through a strip of filter paper. Consistent, mutually comparable test results are achieved by recording the volume of gas processed in each test step; the device converts the results to a setpoint value. The system also takes into account the effect of pressure and temperature, as well as the dead volume between the exhaust-sample probe and the filter paper.

The darkened filter paper is analyzed optoelectronically using a reflective photometer. The results are usually displayed as a Bosch smoke number or as a mass concentration (mg/m³).

## Evaporative-emissions test

Independently of the combustion pollutants produced in the engine, a gasoline-engined motor vehicle emits additional quantities of hydrocarbons (HC) through evaporation of fuel from the fuel tank and fuel system. The quantities evaporated are dependent on the design of the vehicle and the fuel temperature. Some countries (e.g. the U.S.A. and Europe) have regulations which limit these evaporative losses.

### Test procedure

These evaporative emissions are normally measured in a gas-tight climate chamber known as the SHED chamber (Sealed House for Evaporation Determination). There, the HC concentration is measured at the beginning and end of a test and then determined by the difference in the evaporative losses.

The evaporative losses must – depending on the country – be measured in some or all of the operating statuses below and satisfy emission limits:
– Evaporation from the fuel system due to temperature fluctuations throughout the course of the day: "tank-breathing test" or "diurnal test" (EU and U.S.A.).
– Evaporation from the fuel system after parking the vehicle and switching off the engine at normal operating temperature: hot soak (EU and U.S.A.).
– Evaporation in use: running-loss test (U.S.A.).

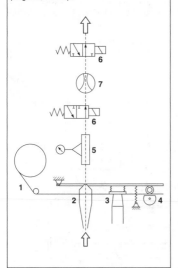

**Smoke tester** (filter method)
1 Filter paper, 2 Gas passage, 3 Reflective photometer, 4 Paper transport, 5 Volume measurement, 6 Changeover valve for purge air, 7 Pump.

Evaporations are measured in several phases during a detailed prescribed test procedure. The test is performed after the vehicle has been preconditioned including preparation of the active-charcoal filter, and filling the fuel tank to a specific level (40%).

**Test procedures**

1st test: hot-soak losses

To measure the evaporative emissions in this test phase, the vehicle is heated up before the test by running through the test cycle valid for the country concerned. The engine is then turned off when the vehicle is in the SHED chamber. The increase in HC concentration is measured for a period of one hour as the vehicle cools.

The vehicle's windows and trunk lid must remain open during the test. This allows evaporative losses from the vehicle interior to be included in measurements.

2nd test: tank-breathing losses

In this test, the temperature profile of a hot summer day (maximum temperature for EU: 35 °C; EPA: 35.5 °C; CARB: 40.6 °C) is simulated in a hermetically sealed climate chamber, and the hydrocarbons released from the vehicle in this process are collected.

In the U.S.A., both a 2-day diurnal test (48 hours) and a 3-day diurnal test (72 hours) must be carried out. EU legislation provides for a 24-hours test.

Running-loss test

In the running-loss test, which precedes the hot-soak test, hydrocarbon emissions are measured in prescribed test cycles (once FTP 72, twice NYCC, once FTP 72; see "U.S. test cycles" section, P. 566) while the vehicle is driven.

**Emission limits**

EU legislation

The total of the measurement results from the first and second tests produces the evaporative losses. This total must lie below the current limit value of 2 gm of evaporated hydrocarbons for all the measurements.

U.S.A.

In the U.S.A. (CARB and EPA Tier 1), the evaporative losses during the running-loss test must be lower than 0.05 g/mile. Additional emission limits are:
- 2-day diurnal: 2.5 g (total from the first and second tests)
- 3-day diurnal: 2.0 g (total from the first and second tests),

These emission limits must be maintained over 100,000 miles.

EPA has decided to make emission limits even more stringent in the Tier 2 legislation:
- 2-day diurnal: 1.2 g (total from the first and second tests)
- 3-day diurnal: 0.95 g (total from the first and second tests)

These emission limits must be maintained over 120,000 miles. They will be introduced in stages starting with model year 2004 and will apply in full starting with model year 2007.

**Additional tests**

Refueling test

In the refueling test, HC emissions are measured during refueling in order to monitor the evaporation of hydrocarbon vapors that are dispelled during refueling (emission limit: 0.053 g HC per liter of fuel filled).

In the U.S.A., this test applies to both CARB as well as EPA.

Spitback test

In the spitback test, the quantity of fuel splashed out during each refueling operation is measured. The fuel tank must be filled to at least 85% capacity.

This test is only performed if the refueling test was not successfully completed (emission limit: 1 g HC per test).

# Diagnostics

## Introduction

The dominant role being assumed by electronics in the motor vehicle makes it necessary to devote increased attention to the problems associated with service. In addition, because essential vehicle functions are becoming increasingly dependent upon electronics, these systems must satisfy stringent reliability requirements, while emergency default programs are required to deal with system errors that occur.

The solution is to incorporate electronic-system self-diagnosis. This relies on the electronic "intelligence" already in place in the vehicle to continuously monitor the system, detect faults, store fault data, and perform diagnostics. Supervisory algorithms check input and output signals during operation. Furthermore, the overall system is checked for malfunctions and defects. Faults detected during this diagnosis are stored in the ECU. When the vehicle is serviced in the dealer's workshop, the stored information is exported over a serial interface. This allows troubleshooting and repairs to be carried out quickly and reliably.

To date, system function is manufacturer-specific. As exhaust-gas limits have become more severe and the requirement for continuous monitoring has been added, legislation has also recognized that self-diagnosis is an aid for monitoring exhaust gas and have created standardization that is independent of the manufacturer. This additional system is called the OBD System (On Board Diagnosis System).

## Self-diagnosis

The diagnostics integrated in the ECU is a basic feature of electronic engine management systems. In addition to the self-check in the ECU, input and output signals, and ECU intercommunication are also monitored.

### Monitoring input signals

The sensors, connectors and connecting lines (signal path) to the ECU are monitored by using the evaluated input signals. In addition to sensor faults, these checks can also detect short-circuits to the steady-state voltage $V_{batt}$, and to the equipment ground, as well as line interruptions. The following procedures are used for this purpose:

– Monitoring the supply voltage to the sensor (if installed).
– Examining measurements recorded for permissible value ranges (e.g. 0.5...4.5 V).
– If additional information is available, a plausibility check is performed by using the recorded value (e.g. comparison of crankshaft and camshaft rotary speeds).
– Particularly important sensors are designed to be redundant (e.g. pedal-travel sensor). This allows a direct comparison of their signals.

### Monitoring output signals

In addition to monitoring connections to the ECU, the actuators are monitored by means of these functions. The checks implemented are capable of detecting line interruptions and short-circuits as well as actuator faults. The following procedures are used for this purpose:

– Using the output stage to monitor the electric circuit of an output stage. The electric circuit is monitored for short-circuits to the steady-state voltage $V_{batt}$, to equipment ground, or for interruptions.

– System impacts on actuators are checked for plausibility. For instance, in the exhaust-gas recirculation of the gasoline system, a check is made whether the intake-manifold pressure lies within specific limits and whether it reacts sufficiently to actuator control. Actuators in the diesel system are monitored indirectly via the closed control loops (e.g. permanent governor deviation) and some also by means of position sensors (e.g. the position of the turbine geometry in the turbocharger).

## Monitoring internal ECU functions

Monitoring functions are installed in the ECU hardware (e.g. "intelligent" output stage modules) and software to ensure that the ECU operates correctly at all times. The monitoring functions check the individual ECU components (e.g. microcontroller, Flash EPROM, RAM). Many tests are performed immediately after switch-on. Further monitoring functions are repeated at regular intervals during normal operation so that component failure can also be detected during operation. Test procedures that require a high amount of computing capacity, or which cannot be performed during vehicle operation for other reasons, are carried out in the after-run after "engine off". This avoids impacting the other functions. During the run-up to speed or after-run in the common-rail diesel engine, the injector shutoff paths are tested.

## Monitoring ECU communication

Communication with the other control units normally takes place over the CAN bus. Control mechanisms for error detection are incorporated in the CAN protocol so that transmission errors can be detected in the CAN chip. Additionally, further tests are performed in the ECU. As the control units send the majority of CAN messages at regular intervals, a CAN controller failure in a control unit can be detected by checking the time intervals (see CAN, P. 1072). If redundant information is stored in the ECU, all input signals are checked against this information.

## Responding to errors

### Fault detection

A signal path is categorized as totally defective if a fault occurs over a specific length of time. The system will continue to use the last valid value until the defect is categorized. After defect categorization, a substitute function is normally initiated (e.g. engine-temperature substitute value $T = 90\,°C$).

An "intact-again signal" is available for the majority of faults. The signal path must be detected as intact for a specific period of time for this purpose.

### Fault storage

All faults are stored as an error code in the non-volatile area of the data memory. Additional information is stored for each fault entry, such as operating and environmental conditions (freeze frame) that were present when the fault occurred (e.g. engine speed, engine temperature). Further information is also stored, such as the failure mode (e.g. short-circuit, line interruption) and in some cases the fault status (e.g. fault present in a static state, fault occurs sporadically).

### Limp-home function

Limp-home measures (e.g. limitation of the engine performance or rpm) may be initiated in addition to alternative values when a fault is detected. The measures are used to:
– maintain driving safety,
– prevent consequential damage (e.g. catalytic converter overheating), or
– minimize exhaust-gas emissions.

**Workshop diagnosis**

Fault read-out

Fault entries can be read out with the aid of a special workshop tester produced by the vehicle manufacturer or a system tester (e.g. Bosch small tester series 650). After the fault memory has been read out in the workshop and the fault has been rectified, the tester can then be used to delete the fault storage. A suitable interface must be defined for communication between the ECU and tester.

Diagnosis interface

Depending on their scope of application, different communication protocols are used throughout the world:
– ISO 9141-2 for European passenger cars,
– SAE J1850 for American passenger cars,
– ISO 14230-4 (KWP 2000) for European passenger cars and commercial vehicles, and
– SAE J1708 for U.S. commercial vehicles.

These serial interfaces work at a bit rate (baud rate) of 5 to 10 Kbaud. They are designed as a single-wire interface with a common transmit and receive wire, or as a two-wire interface with a separate "data line" (K-line) and "initiate line" (L-line). Several electronic control units (such as Motronic and ESP or EDC and transmission-shift control, etc.) can be routed together to one diagnostic plug.

Communication between the tester and control unit is set up in three phases:
– Initiate the electronic control unit,
– Detect and generate the baud rate,
– Read the key bytes used to identify the transmission protocol.

This is followed by evaluation using the following functions generally available: identify ECU, read fault storage, delete fault storage, read actual values, trigger actuators.

In the future, communication between ECUs and the tester will take place over the CAN bus (ISO 15765-4).

# On-Board Diagnosis (OBD)

The engine system and components must be continuously monitored so that compliance with the emission limits required by law can be achieved in everyday use. Therefore, starting in California, regulations were adopted to monitor exhaust-gas related systems and components. This has had the effect of standardizing and extending the self-diagnosis procedures which were previously manufacturer-specific in most cases.

**OBD I**

In 1988 the first stage of CARB legislation (California Air Resources Board) came into force in California with OBD I. This first OBD stage requires the following:
– Monitor exhaust-gas related electrical components (short-circuits, line interruptions) and store faults in the ECU fault storage.
– A fault indicator lamp (MIL: Malfunction Indicator Lamp) to display detected faults to the driver.
– "On-board means" (e.g. blink code on a diagnosis lamp) to provide a readout of which component has malfunctioned.

**OBD II**

In 1994 the second stage of diagnosis legislation was introduced in California with OBD II. In addition to the stipulations contained in OBD I, system functionality is now monitored (e.g. sensor signals are tested for plausibility).

OBD II requires that all exhaust-gas systems and components should be monitored if a malfunction in one of these systems or components causes a significant increase in noxious exhaust-gas emissions (OBD emission limits). In addition, all components used to monitor emission-related components or which affect the diagnosis result must be monitored.

The diagnostic functions for all components and systems inspected must normally run at least once in the exhaust-gas test cycle (e.g. FTP 75). An additional requirement is that all diagnostic functions must operate a sufficient number of times in normal everyday vehicle operation. From model year 2005 onwards, a specific monitoring frequency (In-Use Monitor

Performance Ratio) is required for many monitoring functions in normal everyday vehicle operation.

The OBD II legislation prescribes standardization of the fault-memory information and access to the information (connector, communication) compliant with ISO 15031 and the corresponding SAE standards (Society of Automotive Engineers). This permits a fault-storage readout over standardized, commercially available testers (scan tools).

The law has been revised several times (updates) since OBD II was introduced. The last update became valid from model year 2004.

OBD II legislation is also in force in four other U.S. Federal states.

## EPA

Laws enforced by the EPA (Environmental Protection Agency) have been in force in the remaining Federal states since 1994. The requirements of these diagnostics are essentially equivalent to the CARB legislation (OBD II). However, the requirements have less severe in some points.

## EOBD

OBD adapted to European conditions is known as European On-Board Diagnosis (EOBD) and has been in force for gasoline-engined passenger cars since 2000. It is based on the EPA OBD.

The regulation applies to diesel-engined passenger cars starting in 2003, and, together with introduction of the EU 4 emission-control standard for heavy commercial vehicles with effect from 2005.

## Other countries

Some other countries have already adopted EU or U.S. OBD or plan to introduce it.

## On-board diagnosis requirements

The ECU must use suitable measures to monitor all the systems and components in the motor vehicle if a malfunction in one of these systems or components causes a significant deterioration in emission test values. A malfunction must be displayed to the driver by means of the MIL if a fault results in an excess in OBD emission limits.

### Validity

CARB and EPA OBD regulations apply to all passenger cars up to 12 seats and small commercial vehicles up to 6.35 t. Regulations for heavy commercial vehicles is expected in 2007.

EOBD has been in force since January 2000 for all passenger cars and light-duty trucks with gasoline engines up to 3.5 t and up to 9 seats. Since January 2003 the EOBD has also affected passenger cars and light-duty trucks with diesel engines.

OBD will be required for commercial vehicles and buses over > 3.5 t from October 2005.

### Emission limits

The U.S. OBD II (CARB and EPA) prescribes thresholds that are defined based on emission limits. Accordingly, there are different OBD emission limits for various exhaust-gas categories that are applied when certifying vehicles (e.g. TIER, LEV, ULEV, see P. 554). Absolute emission limits are binding in the EOBD that applies under European legislation (see Table 1 on the next page).

### Functional requirements

Just as for self-diagnosis, all ECU input and output signals must be monitored as well as the components themselves.

EOBD legislation primarily requires electrical monitoring (short-circuit, line interruption). CARB legislation, on the other hand, also requires a plausibility check for sensors and functional monitoring for actuators.

The pollutant concentration expected if a component fails (empirical values) determines the type of diagnostics. A simple functional test (black-white test) only checks operability of the system or components (e.g. secondary-air valve opens and closes). The qualitative functional test

**Table 1. OBD emission limits**

| | Gasoline passenger cars | | Diesel passenger cars | | Diesel commercial vehicles |
|---|---|---|---|---|---|
| CARB | – Relative emission limits<br>– Mostly 1.5x the emission limit of the exhaust-gas categories | | – Relative emission limits<br>– Mostly 1.5x the emission limit of the exhaust-gas categories | | – |
| EPA (U.S. Federal) | – Relative emission limits<br>– Mostly 1.5x the emission limit of the exhaust-gas categories | | – Relative emission limits<br>– Mostly 1.5x the emission limit of the exhaust-gas categories | | – |
| EOBD | 2000<br><br>CO: 3.2 g/km<br>HC: 0.4 g/km<br>$NO_x$: 0.6 g/km | 2005 (proposed)<br>CO: 1.9 g/km<br>HC: 0.3 g/km<br>$NO_x$: 0.53 g/km | 2003<br><br>CO: 3.2 g/km<br>HC: 0.4 g/km<br>$NO_x$: 1.2 g/km<br>PM: 0.18 g/km | 2005 (proposed)<br>CO: 3.2 g/km<br>HC: 0.4 g/km<br>$NO_x$: 1.2 g/km<br>PM: 0.18 g/km | 2005 (proposed)<br>NOx: 7.0 g/kWh<br>PM: 0.1 g/kWh |

provides more detailed information on system operability. Therefore, for instance, when the catalytic converter is tested, the values measured are used to calculate the extent of catalytic converter aging (in gasoline systems). This value can be read out over the diagnosis interface.

The complexity of diagnostic systems has developed in pace with emission-control legislation.

Malfunction indicator lamp (MIL)

The MIL (Malfunction Indicator Lamp) informs the driver that a component has malfunctioned. When a fault is detected in an area where CARB and EPA apply, the MIL must light up no later than after two driving schedules with the fault present. In the area where EOBD applies, the MIL must light up no later than the third driving schedule after the fault was detected.

If a fault disappears (e.g. loose contact), the fault remains in the fault storage for 40 trips (warm-up cycles). The MIL goes out after three fault-free driving schedules. The MIL flashes for faults in the gasoline system if such a fault could cause damage to the catalytic converter (combustion misses).

Communication with scan tool

The protocols for passenger cars stated in the "Diagnosis interface" section (see P. 584) are also permissible today for OBD diagnostics. However, diagnostics will only be permitted over CAN (ISO 15765) in 2008.

Vehicle repair

Any workshop can use the scan tool to read out emission-related fault information from the ECU. This permits even non-franchised workshops to carry out repairs.

Manufacturers are obliged to provide the required tools and information (repair manual on the web), against a suitable fee, to ensure that repairs can be carried out with the correct degree of expertise.

Switch-on conditions

Diagnostic functions are only started if the switch-on conditions are fulfilled. These include:
– torque thresholds,
– engine temperature thresholds, and
– engine-speed thresholds or limits.

### Inhibit conditions

Diagnostic functions and engine functions cannot always operate simultaneously. Inhibit conditions prohibit certain functions from starting. For instance, tank ventilation (evaporative-emissions control system) in the gasoline system cannot function while the catalytic converter diagnosis is in operation. In the diesel system, the hot-film air-mass meter (HFM) can only be monitored satisfactorily if the exhaust-gas recirculation valve is closed.

### Temporary disabling of diagnostic functions

Diagnostic functions may only be disabled under certain conditions in order to prevent faults from being detected incorrectly. Examples of such conditions are:
- elevation too high,
- low ambient temperature at engine switch-on, or
- low steady-state voltage.

### Readiness codes

When the fault storage is checked, it is important to know that the diagnostic functions have run at least once. This can be checked by reading out the readiness codes over the diagnosis interface. These readiness codes are set for each component that is monitored on completion of the diagnoses required by law.

### Vehicle recall

If vehicles do not fulfill the legal OBD requirements, the legislation may require a vehicle recall at the expense of the vehicle manufacturer.

### Diagnostic System Management (DSM)

The diagnostic functions for all components and systems under review must normally run at least once in the exhaust-gas test cycle (e.g. FTP 75, NEDC). Similarly, diagnostic functions must operate during normal vehicle operation. The Diagnostic System Management (DSM) can dynamically change the sequence for running the diagnostic functions depending on the driving condition. The objective here is to run the diagnostic functions frequently in everyday vehicle operation.

The DSM comprises the following three components:

#### Diagnosis Fault Path Management (DFPM)

The primary role of DFPM is to store the fault states that are detected in the system. Other information is stored, such as environmental conditions (freeze frame).

#### Diagnostic Function Schedule (DSCHED)

The DSCHED is responsible for coordinating the assigned engine and diagnostic functions, and obtains information from DVAL and DFPM to carry this out. Functions that require release by the DSCHED report their readiness to start. The present system state and function activation are then checked.

#### Diagnosis Validator (DVAL)

The DVAL (only installed in gasoline systems to date) uses current fault-memory entries and additional stored information to make a decision whether each detected fault is the actual cause or a consequence of the fault. As a result, validation provides stored information for the diagnostic tester used for fault storage readout.

Diagnostic functions can therefore be released in any sequence. All released diagnoses and their results are evaluated retroactively.

## OBD functions

Whereas EOBD and EPA OBD only prescribe few explicit emission reduction systems and provide detailed monitoring regulations, the specific requirements of the CARB OBD II are much more detailed. A further review was made for the model years from 2004 (OBD I update). The list below shows the current state of the CARB requirements (from model year 2004) for gasoline-engined and diesel-engined passenger cars. (E) identifies the requirements that also apply to EOBD.

- Catalytic converter (E), heated catalytic converter,
- Combustion (misfire) misses (E; diesel system: not for EOBD),
- Evaporation reduction system (tank-leak diagnosis, only for gasoline system),
- Secondary-air injection,
- Fuel system,
- Oxygen (lambda) sensors (E),
- Exhaust-gas recirculation,
- Crankcase ventilation,
- Cooling system,
- Cold-start emission reduction system,
- Air conditioner (components),
- Variable valve timing (at present only for gasoline systems),
- Direct ozone reduction system,
- Particulate filter (soot filter, only for diesel system) (E),
- "Comprehensive components" (E),
- "Other emission-related components" (E).

Some of the components listed here are categorized as "comprehensive components" or "other emission-related components" with EOBD and EPA. These categories have the following meaning:
- Other components or subsystems of the emission reduction system, or
- Emission-relevant components connected to a computer, or
- Drivetrain subsystems, which, if they malfunction or become defective, may result in exhaust-gas emissions exceeding the OBD emission limits or the disabling of other diagnostic functions.

## Catalytic converter diagnosis

### Gasoline system

This diagnostic function monitors the conversion efficiency of the three-way catalytic converter. This is measured by the catalytic converter's oxygen retention capability. Monitoring is performed by observing the signals from the Lambda oxygen sensors in reaction to a specific alteration of the setpoint value of the lambda closed-loop control.

Additionally, the $NO_x$ accumulation capacity (catalytic-converter quality factor) must be assessed for the $NO_x$ accumulator-type catalytic converter. For this purpose, the actual $NO_x$ accumulator content resulting from consumption of the reduction agent during regeneration of the catalytic converter is compared with an expected value.

### Diesel system

In the diesel system, carbon monoxide (CO) and unburned hydrocarbons (HC) are oxidized in the oxidation-type catalytic converter (to minimize pollutants, see P. 716). There is ongoing development on diagnostic functions to monitor the operation of the oxidation-type catalytic converter based on temperature and differential pressure.

At the same time, work is underway on developing monitoring functions for the accumulation and regeneration capabilities of the $NO_x$ accumulator-type catalytic converter that will also be installed in the diesel system in the future.

## Combustion-miss detection

A misfire or combustion miss results in an increase in HC and CO emissions. The misfire detector evaluates the time expired (segment time) from one combustion to the next for each cylinder. This time is derived using the speed-sensor signal. A segment time that is longer compared to the other cylinders indicates a misfire.

Fuel injection is disabled at the cylinder concerned if the misfire rates exceed permissible levels (gasoline system).

In the diesel system, diagnosis of combustion misses is only required and performed when the engine is at idle.

Tank-leak diagnosis
*Gasoline system*
Tank-leak diagnosis detects evaporation from the fuel system that may cause an increase in HC values, in particular. EOBD is limited to simply testing the electrical control circuit of the tank-pressure sensor and the canister-purge valve (evaporative-emissions control system, see P. 541). In the U.S., on the other hand, it must be possible to detect leaks in the fuel system. There are two different methods of doing this.

The low-pressure method observes the tank pressure and first tests its operability by deliberately actuating the tank ventilation and carbon-canister check valves. A conclusion can then be drawn on the leak size using the time curve of the tank pressure – again by deliberately actuating the valves.

The overpressure method uses a diagnosis module with an integrated electrically powered vane pump that can be used to pump up the tank system. The flow from the pump is high when the tank is hermetically sealed. A conclusion can then be drawn on leak size by evaluating the flow from the pump.

Secondary-air injection diagnosis
*Gasoline system*
This diagnosis is a functional test for testing whether the secondary-air pump is functioning, or whether there are defects in the supply line to the exhaust-gas tract (secondary-air injection, see P. 540). The diagnosis is based on calculating the injected secondary-air mass. This valued can be derived from the Lambda closed-loop control, or directly from evaluating the Lambda oxygen sensor signals.

Fuel system diagnosis
*Gasoline system*
Faults in the fuel system may prevent optimized mixture formation. Measured values (e.g. air mass, throttle-valve position) as well as information on the operating status are processed to diagnose the fuel system. The measured values are then compared with model calculations.

*Diesel system*
In the common-rail system, diagnosis of the fuel system includes electrical monitoring of the injectors and the rail-pressure regulator (high-pressure regulator). Special functions of the fuel-injection system that increase the injected-fuel quantity precision are also monitored. Examples of this include zero fuel-quantity calibration, quantity mean-value adaptation and the AS MOD observer function (air-system observer). The two functions last named use information from the Lambda oxygen sensor as input signals and calculate deviations between setpoint and actual quantities using the input signals and models.

Lambda oxygen sensors diagnosis
The two-step Lambda oxygen sensors are tested for plausibility (output voltage) and dynamics (signal-increase speed when changing from rich to lean and from lean to rich, as well as period duration).

Broadband O sensors require a different diagnosis method than two-stage sensors, as their settings may differ by $\lambda = 1$. They are monitored electrically (short-circuit, line interruption) and for plausibility. The heater element of the sensor heater is tested electrically and for permanent governor deviation.

Exhaust-gas recirculation system diagnosis
*Gasoline system*
There are two methods for diagnosing the exhaust-gas recirculation system (exhaust-gas recirculation, see P. 540). One method tests the closing operation of the exhaust-gas recirculation valve. The change in intake-manifold pressure is observed when the valve is closed briefly and this is then compared with a computer model. The other method observes the expected increase in uneven running when the engine is at idle speed and the exhaust-gas recirculation valve is open.

*Diesel system*

In the exhaust-gas recirculation system, the air-mass regulator and position controller of the exhaust-gas recirculation valve are monitored for long-term governor deviation. Consequently, this is a functional test of the exhaust-gas recirculation valve, which is also monitored electrically.

## Crankcase ventilation diagnosis

The blowby gas flows from the crankcase to the intake manifold through the PCV valve (Positive Crankcase Ventilation) (crankcase ventilation, see P. 542). One possible diagnostic principle for this system is based on measuring the idle speed, which should display a specific computer-model response when the PCV valve is opened. Faults in the crankcase ventilation can also be detected by the air-mass sensor, depending on the system. The legislation does not require any monitoring if the crankcase ventilation has a "rugged" design.

## Cooling system diagnosis

The cooling system comprises a thermostat and a coolant-temperature sensor. If the thermostat is defective, for instance, the engine temperature can only rise slowly and this increases the exhaust emission rates. The diagnostic functions for the thermostat uses the coolant-termperature sensor to check that a nominal temperature has been reached. A temperature model is used for monitoring.

The coolant-termperature sensor is monitored to ensure that a minimum temperature has been reached. In addition, electrical faults are monitored by means of a dynamic plausibility function. Dynamic plausibility is performed as the engine cools down. These functions can monitor the sensor for "sticking" in both low- and high-temperature ranges.

## Emission-reduction system diagnosis at cold start

Emission-reduction strategies at cold start, e.g. rapid heating of the catalytic converter, must be monitored from engine start in order to ensure that emissions are low in everyday operation. Rapid heating can be checked by monitoring and evaluating certain parameters such as ignition angle, rpm or fresh-air mass. At the same time specific diagnostics are performed on vital heater components (e.g. camshaft position).

## Air-conditioner diagnosis

*Gasoline system*

The engine can be operated at a different operating point under the given requirements in order to cover the air-conditioner's electrical load requirements. The diagnosis monitors that the engine is operated in this operating point when the air conditioner is switched on.

## Variable Valve Timing (VVT) diagnosis

Diagnosis is currently performed by a setpoint/actual comparison of the camshaft position. More stringent requirements will be introduced starting in model year 2006.

## Direct ozone-reduction system

A special feature of Californian emission-control legislation is the requirement to reduce the concentration of ozone (an airborne pollutant) in addition to reducing exhaust gases and evaporative emissions. This is achieved with a catalytic coating that is applied to the vehicle's radiator (Direct Ozone Reduction, DOR). A credit is awarded dependent on ozone reduction, and this is incorporated in the overall calculation of the reduction in exhaust gas and evaporative emissions achieved. This means that it is an emission-reducing component, and it must therefore be monitored by the OBD system starting in model year 2006.

Discussions on several testing procedures are taking place.

## Particulate filter diagnosis
### Diesel system
The particulate filter is presently monitored for destruction, removal and blockage. A differential-pressure sensor is used to measure the pressure differential (exhaust-gas backpressure downstream and upstream of the filter) at a specific volumetric flow. The measured value can be used to verify whether the filter is defective.

## Comprehensive components
On-board diagnosis requires that all sensors (e.g. air-mass sensor, speed sensor, temperature sensors) and actuators (e.g. throttle valve, high-pressure pump, glow plugs) must be monitored if they have either an impact on emissions or if they are used to monitor other components or systems (and consequently, may disable other diagnoses).

Sensors monitor the following errors:
- Electrical faults, i.e. short-circuits and line interruptions.
- Range faults (range check), i.e. undercutting or exceeding voltage limits set by the sensors' physical measurement range.
- Plausibility faults (rationality checks); these are faults that lie in the components themselves (e.g. drift) or which may be caused by line connections. Monitoring is carried out by a plausibility check on the sensor signals, either by using a model or directly by other sensors.

Actuators must be monitored for electrical faults and – if technically possible – also for function. Functional monitoring means that, when a control command (setpoint value) is given, it is monitored by observing or measuring (e.g. by a position sensor) system response (actual value) in a suitable manner by using system information.

The actuators monitored include:
- all output stages,
- the throttle valve,
- the exhaust-gas recirculation valve,
- the variable turbine geometry of the exhaust-gas turbocharger,
- the swirl valve,
- the glow plug (diesel system),
- the tank-ventilation system (gasoline system), and
- the active-charcoal check valve (gasoline system).

## OBD functions for heavy commercial vehicles
OBD monitoring as planned in the U.S. (2007) will be very similar to passenger-car legislation, although no details have been revealed yet.

European legislation (2005) requires monitoring of the following functions:
- the fuel-injection system for a closed electric circuit and total failure,
- emission-related engine components or systems for compliance with OBD emission limits (these functions are performed similar to "comprehensive components" for passenger cars), and
- the exhaust-gas treatment system for major functional faults (e.g. damaged catalytic converter, urea deficit in the SCR system).

Stage 2 of the EOBD (2008), which has already been announced, has the purpose of monitoring the emission limits of the exhaust-gas treatment system. This means that it will not be possible to avoid using exhaust-gas sensors (e.g., $NO_x$).

# Description of the engine management system

Engine management ensures that driver commands, e.g. to accelerate, are translated into appropriate SI engine performance. It regulates all engine functions in such a way that the engine delivers the required level of torque, but fuel consumption and emissions are kept low.

The power output from a spark-ignition (SI) engine is determined by the available clutch torque and the engine speed. The clutch torque is produced from the torque generated by the combustion process, reduced by friction torque (friction losses in the engine), charge-cycle losses, and the torque required for operating the auxiliary systems.

Combustion torque is generated in the power cycle and is mainly determined by the following variables:
– The air mass that is available for combustion when the intake valves close.
– The fuel mass available in the cylinder.
– The point at which combustion occurs.

There are also other variables which have less influence, e.g. mixture composition (residual gas) and the combustion process.

The primary function of engine management is to coordinate the various subsystems in order to adjust the torque generated by the engine and at the same time meet the exacting demands placed on:
– Exhaust-gas emissions
– Fuel consumption
– Power output
– Convenience
– Safety

The engine-management system also performs diagnoses on the subsystems.

## Cylinder-charge control

In engine-management systems with electronic throttle control (ETC), the "cylinder-charge control" subsystem calculates the required cylinder charge with air and electronically actuates the throttle valve accordingly. Other influencing variables are the intake and exhaust valve timing and exhaust-gas recirculation.

On conventional systems, the driver controls the opening of the throttle valve (and thus charging the cylinder with fresh air) directly via the accelerator pedal.

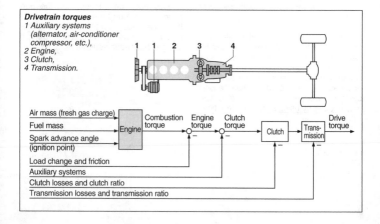

*Drivetrain torques*
*1 Auxiliary systems*
*(alternator, air-conditioner*
*compressor, etc.),*
*2 Engine,*
*3 Clutch,*
*4 Transmission.*

### Fuel supply

The function of the "fuel supply" subsystem is to continuously supply the engine with the required fuel mass at the required fuel pressure in all operating conditions. As far as the required pressure level is concerned, a fundamental distinction is made between systems with internal (gasoline direct injection) and external (intake-manifold injection) mixture formation.

### Mixture formation

In the "mixture formation" subsystem, the associated fuel mass is calculated and from this, the necessary injection time and the optimum injection point are determined. With gasoline direct injection, the current operating mode (e.g. stratified-charge operation) also has to be taken into consideration.

### Ignition

The "ignition" subsystem determines the crankshaft angle at which the ignition spark ignites the A/F mixture at the correct time.

# Cylinder charge

## Component parts

The gas mixture located in the cylinder after the intake valves have closed is termed the cylinder charge. It consists of the supplied fresh A/F mixture and the residual exhaust gas.

### Fresh A/F mixture

The component parts of the fresh mixture drawn in are fresh air and – on systems with external mixture formation – the fuel suspended in it. Most of the fresh air flows through the throttle valve; additional fresh A/F mixture can be drawn in through the evaporative-emissions control system (if fitted). The air mass present in the cylinder after the intake valves have closed is the decisive factor in the work performed above the piston during combustion, and ultimately in the torque delivered by the engine. Therefore, measures for increasing maximum torque and maximum engine power almost always require an increase in the maximum possible cylinder charge. The theoretical maximum charge is predetermined by the piston displacement and, in the case of turbocharged engines, by the achievable charge-air pressure, as well.

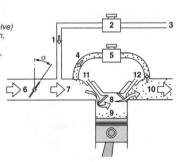

*Cylinder charge in the SI engine*
1 Air and fuel vapor,
2 Canister-purge valve,
3 Connection to evaporative-emissions control system,
4 Exhaust gas,
5 Exhaust-gas recirculation valve (EGR valve) with variable valve-opening cross-section,
6 Air-mass flow (ambient pressure),
7 Air-mass flow (intake-manifold pressure),
8 Fresh gas filling (combustion-chamber pressure),
9 Residual exhaust-gas charge (combustion-chamber pressure),
10 Exhaust gas (exhaust-gas backpressure),
11 Intake valve,
12 Exhaust valve.
$\alpha$ Throttle-valve angle.

**Residual exhaust gas**

The residual exhaust gas in the charge is formed by:
- The exhaust-gas mass which remains in the cylinder and is not discharged when the exhaust valve is open.
- The mass of recirculated exhaust gas in systems with exhaust-gas recirculation (EGR).

The amount of residual exhaust gas is determined by the charge cycle. It does not contribute directly to the combustion process, but does influence ignition and the combustion process as a whole. At wide-open throttle, the amount of residual exhaust gas generally needs to be as small as possible in order to maximize the fresh-air mass and also the power output of the engine.

At part load, however, the amount of residual exhaust gas is desirable in order to reduce fuel consumption. This is achieved by a more favorable cycle, resulting from a change in mixture composition, and also to a reduction in pump losses during the charge cycle, as a higher intake-manifold pressure is required for the same air charge. A specifically introduced amount of residual exhaust gas can likewise reduce the emission of nitrogen oxides ($NO_x$) and unburned hydrocarbons (HC).

## Controlling the air charge

On spark-ignition engines with external mixture formation, and on systems with internal mixture formation and homogeneous cylinder charge, the torque delivered by the engine is determined by the air charge. By contrast, on systems with internal mixture formation and excess air, the engine torque can also be controlled directly by varying the injected fuel mass (stratified-charge operation, P. 612).

**Throttle valve**

The critical adjustment mechanism for controlling air-mass flow is the throttle valve. When the throttle valve is not fully open, the air flow drawn in by the engine is throttled, thus reducing maximum engine torque. This throttling effect is dependent on the position, and thus the opening cross-section of the throttle valve, as well as on engine speed. The maximum engine torque is achieved when the throttle valve is fully open (see figure).

On systems with electronic throttle control (ETC), the required air charge is calculated from the desired engine torque (accelerator-pedal position), and the throttle valve is opened accordingly.

On conventional systems, the driver directly controls the opening of the throttle valve by pressing the accelerator pedal.

**Charge cycle**

The charge cycle of fresh A/F mixture and residual exhaust gas is controlled by the opening and closing of the intake and exhaust valves. The opening and closing times of the valves (control times) and the valve lift curve are critical factors.

The valve overlap, i.e. the overlapping of the opening times of the intake and exhaust valves, has a decisive impact on the residual exhaust-gas mass in the cylinder. The quantities of fresh A/F mixture and residual exhaust gas in the cylinder can be controlled by changing the valve-lift time curves.

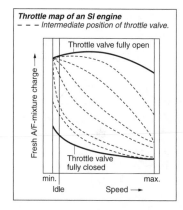

*Throttle map of an SI engine*
*– – – Intermediate position of throttle valve.*

Throttle valve fully open

Fresh A/F-mixture charge →

Throttle valve fully closed

min.    max.
Idle    Speed →

By varying the valve timing accordingly, it is possible to control the air-mass flow, and thus engine performance, without having to use the throttle valve. The amount of residual exhaust gas can also be adjusted by means of valve timing.

On today's systems, the valves are actuated mechanically via the camshaft. Actuation can be varied to a certain extent by additional measures (e.g. variable-valve timing or camshaft-lobe control, P. 474). However, these mechanical systems cannot dispense with the throttle valve completely.

### Exhaust-gas recirculation (EGR)

As described in the "Charge cycle" section, the mass of residual exhaust gas can be controlled by means of the intake and exhaust valve control times. This situation involves "interior exhaust-gas recirculation". The mass of residual exhaust gas in the cylinder can also be increased by "exterior exhaust-gas recirculation" (EGR). In this case, an additional EGR valve connects the intake manifold and exhaust pipe (P. 540). When the valve is open, the engine draws in a combination of fresh A/F mixture and exhaust gas. The engine control unit calculates the level of EGR for a specific operating state, and the EGR valve is activated accordingly.

### Supercharging

The torque obtainable is proportional to the charge of fresh gas filling. It is therefore possible to increase maximum torque by compressing the air in the cylinder by dynamic supercharging, mechanical supercharging, or exhaust-gas turbocharging (P. 476 onwards, P. 528 onwards).

## Air-system components

The main components responsible for controlling air charge are shown in the figure on page 593. The throttle valve is the most important component on modern systems.

### Electronic-throttle control (ETC) components

The electronic throttle control system consists of the accelerator-pedal module, the engine control unit, and the throttle device. The throttle device mainly consists of the throttle valve, the electric throttle-valve drive element, and the throttle-valve position sensor. The drive element is a DC motor, which acts on the throttle-valve shaft via a gear unit. The throttle-valve position sensor, designed as a redundant unit, detects the position of the throttle valve.

The driver command is detected by a redundant sensor system in the accelerator-pedal module, and the signal is sent to the engine control unit. This calculates the required cylinder charge, based on the current engine operating point, and regulates the opening angle of the throttle valve by means of the throttle-valve drive element and the throttle-valve position sensor.

The redundancy incorporated in the accelerator-pedal module and the throttle device is part of the ETC monitoring concept for avoiding malfunctions.

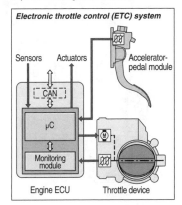

*Electronic throttle control (ETC) system*

Sensors  Actuators  Accelerator-pedal module

CAN

µC

Monitoring module

Engine ECU    Throttle device

# Fuel supply

## Fuel supply and delivery with intake-manifold injection

### Standard system

An electric fuel pump (P. 599 onwards) supplies the fuel and generates the injection pressure. The fuel is drawn out of the fuel tank and pressed through paper filters (fuel filters, see P. 604) into a high-pressure line, from where it flows to the fuel rail and injectors mounted on the engine. The pressure regulator is installed on the fuel rail. It keeps the differential pressure constant at the fuel-metering orifice, regardless of engine load (intake-manifold pressure).

After flowing through the fuel rail, the excess amount of fuel not required by the engine flows through the return line connected to the pressure regulator back to the fuel tank. The returning fuel heats up on its way back from the engine to the fuel tank. The fuel temperature in the tank rises as a result. Fuel vapor is generated as a function of fuel temperature. For environmental purposes, the vapor is routed through the tank ventilation system for intermediate storage in a carbon canister until it is returned via the intake manifold to the intake air and the engine (P. 541).

### Returnless system

In a returnless fuel supply system, the fuel in the fuel tank does not heat up as much as in a standard system. This makes it easier to comply with the legal requirements governing vehicular evaporative emissions.

The pressure regulator is located either in the fuel tank or in its immediate vicinity, which means that the return line from the engine to the fuel tank is no longer required. Only the quantity of fuel required by the injectors is applied to the fuel rail (with no return flow). The additional fuel conveyed by the electric fuel pump returns directly to the tank without having to move to the engine compartment and back again. Assuming equivalent operating conditions, and depending on the specific vehicle application, this system can reduce in-tank fuel temperatures by approx. 10 K, thus cutting vaporization by roughly one third.

### Control demand system

In-tank fuel temperatures can be further reduced, and fuel consumption cut at the same time, by using a control demand system. In this system, the fuel pump only supplies the quantity of fuel actually required by the engine and to adjust the pressure. This dispenses with the mechanical pressure regulator. Pressure is controlled by means of a closed control loop in the engine control unit, and pres-

---

*Fuel supply and delivery with intake-manifold injection*
*a) Standard system,*
*b) Returnless system.*
*1 Fuel tank 2 Electric fuel pump, 3 Fuel filter,*
*4 High-pressure line, 5 Pressure regulator,*
*6 Injectors, 7 Fuel rail (continuous flow),*
*8 Return line, 9 Fuel rail (no return flow).*

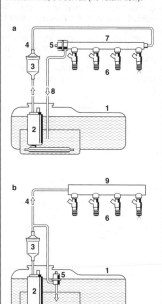

sure is detected by a low-pressure sensor. To adjust the fuel pump's delivery quantity, the pump's operating voltage is changed by means of a timing module activated by the engine control unit. A pressure relief valve completes the system (to prevent excessive fuel pressure as a result of the fuel heating up in overrun fuel cutoff and pump shutoff modes).

In addition to further reducing fuel temperature and fuel consumption by up to 0.1 $l$/100 km, variable pressure adjustment can also be used to increase fuel pressure in hot-start conditions or to extend the fuel-metering range of the injectors in turbocharger applications. In addition, fuel-system diagnostics have been considerably improved compared with previous systems. Another advantage is that fuel pressure is taken into account in the injection timing calculation in the engine control unit. This is of special importance for pressure rise when cold-starting the engine.

# Fuel supply and delivery with gasoline direct injection

When a gasoline direct-injection engine is operating in stratified-charge mode, fuel must be injected at higher pressures than for intake-manifold injection. In addition, the time window available for fuel injection is smaller. Fuel systems for gasoline direct injection therefore require a higher fuel pressure. The fuel system comprises the following components:
– The low-pressure system
– The high-pressure system

### Low-pressure system
The gasoline direct injection low-pressure system principally utilizes the same fuel systems and components used for intake-manifold injection. As the present high-pressure pumps generally require a higher admission pressure in hot-start and hot-running conditions to prevent the formation of vapor bubbles, it can be an advantage to vary the low pressure. This is ideally done using a control-demand low-pressure system. Returnless systems with switchable admission pressure – controlled by a shutoff valve – are also used as well as systems with a constantly high admission pressure.

### High-pressure system
The high-pressure system consists of:
– The high-pressure pump
– The fuel rail (high-pressure accumulator)
– The high-pressure sensor
 and, depending on the system:
– The pressure-control valve or
– The pressure limiter

A distinction is made between continuous supply and control demand systems.

Depending on the operating point, a high-pressure regulation system in the engine control unit sets a primary pressure of between 5 and 12 MPa. The high-pressure injectors are connected to the rail and inject the fuel directly into the engine's combustion chamber.

*Fuel supply and delivery with intake-manifold injection*
Control demand system.
1 Electric fuel pump with fuel filter (alternatively, fuel filter can also be outside the tank), 2 Pressure relief valve and pressure sensor, 3 Timing module, 4 Injectors, 5 Fuel rail (no return flow).

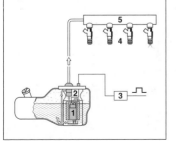

Continuous-supply system

A pump driven by the engine camshaft, e.g. the HDP1 triple-plunger radial-piston pump (P. 602), delivers the fuel to the rail against primary pressure. The pump delivery quantity cannot be adjusted. The pressure of the excess fuel not required for injection or maintaining pressure is reduced by the pressure-control valve, and the excess fuel is then returned to the low-pressure system. The pressure-control valve is activated by the engine control unit in such a way that the desired pressure is set depending on the operating point. The pressure-control valve also serves as a mechanical pressure-relief valve.

In continuous-supply systems, more fuel is compressed to primary pressure than the engine requires for most operating points. This requires additional power, and the excess fuel quantity, whose pressure is reduced by the pressure-control valve, contributes to the rise in fuel temperature. This is where the control demand system can offer advantages.

Control demand system

A pump, e.g. the HDP2 single-plunger radial-piston pump (P. 603) will only supply the rail with the amount of fuel that is actually required for injection or to maintain the pressure. This occurs against primary pressure and with an adjustable delivery quantity. The pump is driven by the engine camshaft. The control system in the engine control unit actuates the pump in such a way that the desired primary pressure can be adjusted in the rail depending on the operating point. A mechanical pressure-relief valve is required in the rail.

Due to the discrete delivery of the single-plunger radial-piston pump, this system requires a greater rail volume than the continuous-supply system and is therefore fitted with a triple-plunger radial piston pump. This is so that the pressure drops caused by fuel-injection processes can be maintained at a constant level.

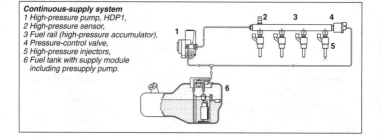

*Continuous-supply system*
1 High-pressure pump, HDP1,
2 High-pressure sensor,
3 Fuel rail (high-pressure accumulator),
4 Pressure-control valve,
5 High-pressure injectors,
6 Fuel tank with supply module including presupply pump.

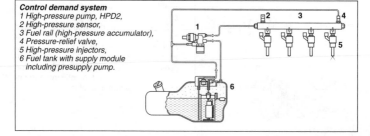

*Control demand system*
1 High-pressure pump, HPD2,
2 High-pressure sensor,
3 Fuel rail (high-pressure accumulator),
4 Pressure-relief valve,
5 High-pressure injectors,
6 Fuel tank with supply module including presupply pump.

# Fuel supply and delivery components

## Electric fuel pump

### Function

The electric fuel pump must deliver sufficient quantities of fuel to the engine and maintain the pressure required for efficient fuel injection in all operating states. Essential requirements include:

- Maintaining delivery quantities of between 60 and 250 $l$/h at nominal voltage.
- Maintaining fuel-system pressures of between 300 and 650 kPa.
- Generating primary pressure when operating at and above 50% to 60% of nominal voltage (important for cold-start response).

### Design and operating concepts

The electric fuel pump consists of:

- The end cover including the electrical connections, non-return valve (to maintain fuel-system pressure), and the hydraulic discharge fitting. Most end covers also include the carbon brushes for the drive-motor commutator and interference-suppression elements (inductance coils, with capacitors in some applications).
- Electric motor with armature and permanent magnets (standard design is a copper commutator, carbon commutators are used for special applications and diesel systems).
- A positive-displacement or flow-type pump.

*Positive-displacement pump*

As the pump element of the positive-displacement unit rotates, it draws in volumes of fuel on the suction side to a sealed chamber (except for leakages), and routes the fuel to the high-pressure side of the pump. The <u>roller-cell pump</u>, the <u>internal-gear pump</u>, and the <u>screw pump</u> are used as the electric fuel pump. Positive-displacement pumps perform well at high primary pressures (450 kPa and above). They also perform well at low supply voltages, i.e. the flow-rate curve remains relatively "flat" and constant throughout a wide range of operating voltages. Efficiency ratings may be as high as

25%. The unavoidable pressure pulses may cause noise; the extent of this problem varies according to the pump's design configuration and mounting location.

While the flow-type pump has, to a large extent, replaced the positive-displacement pump in electronic gasoline injection systems for performing the classic function of the electric fuel pump, a new field of application has opened up for the positive-displacement pump, i.e. presupplying fuel for direct-injection (DI) systems (gasoline and diesel) to cover much higher pressures and viscosity range.

*Flow-type pumps*

Flow-type pumps are commonly used for gasoline applications up to 500 kPa. An impeller ring equipped with numerous peripheral vanes rotates within a chamber consisting of two fixed housing sections. Each of these sections features a passage along the path of the impeller blades, with openings at one end of the passage starting at the suction openings. From there, they extend to the point

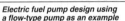

**Electric fuel pump design using a flow-type pump as an example**
1 Electrical connection,
2 Hydraulic connection (fuel outlet),
3 Non-return valve,
4 Carbon brushes,
5 Motor armature with permanent magnet,
6 Impeller ring of flow-type pump,
7 Hydraulic connection (fuel inlet).

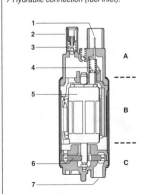

where the fuel exits the pump at primary pressure. A small gas-discharge orifice, located at a specified angular distance from the suction opening, improves performance when pumping hot fuel; this orifice facilitates the discharge of any gas bubbles that may have formed (with minimal leakage).

The pulses reflected between the impeller blades and the fluid molecules result in pressurization along the length of

*Electric fuel pump designs*
a) Roller-cell pump,
b) Internal-gear pump,
c) Flow-type pump.

A Suction opening,
B Outlet.
1 Slotted washer (eccentric), 2 Roller,
3 Inner driving wheel, 4 Rotor (eccentric),
5 Impeller ring, 6 Impeller blades,
7 Passage (peripheral).

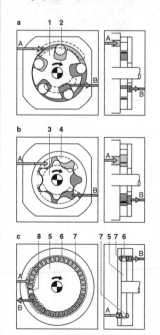

the passage, inducing a spiral rotation of the fluid volume in the impeller ring and in the passages.

As pressure buildup is continuous and virtually pulse-free, flow-type pumps are quiet in operation. Pump design is also much less complex than the positive-displacement unit. Single-stage pumps generate primary pressures ranging up to 500 kPa. These pumps have an efficiency of up to 22%.

**Fuel delivery module**
Whereas the first electronic gasoline-injection systems always featured electric fuel pumps located outside the tank (inline systems), the majority of today's designs house the electric fuel pump inside the tank (in-tank systems). The electric fuel pump has become part of a fuel delivery module, which may also contain other components:
– A fuel-baffle chamber to maintain fuel delivery during cornering (usually with its own "active" supply from a suction jet pump, or a "passive" supply from a system of flaps, a changeover valve, or similar).
– A fuel-level sensor.
– A pressure regulator (see P. 601) for returnless systems (RLFS).
– An intake filter to protect the pump.
– A pressure-side fine-mesh fuel filter, which will not need replacing for the entire life of the vehicle (see P. 604).
– Electrical and hydraulic connections.
– Tank pressure sensors (for diagnosing tank leaks), fuel-pressure sensors (for control demand systems), and valves may also be incorporated.

Outlook
Some modern vehicles already use control-demand fuel supply and delivery systems (see P. 596). In these systems, an electronic module operates the pump as a function of the required pressure, which is checked by a fuel-pressure sensor. The advantages of these systems are:
– Lower power consumption
– Less heat introduced by the electric motor
– Reduced pump noise
– Facilities to set variable fuel-system pressures

On future systems, pure pump control functions will be supplemented by other functions. For example:
– Tank leak diagnosis and evaluation function for the fuel-level sensor signal will be moved out of the engine control unit.
– Valve activation, e.g. for fuel-vapor management.

In order to meet increasing pressure and service-life requirements and cope with the various fuel grades encountered throughout the world, non-contacting motors with electronic commutation are likely to play a more significant role in the future.

**Fuel-pressure regulator**
The fuel-pressure regulator maintains specific pressure ratios in the fuel system. The regulator is a diaphragm-controlled overflow pressure regulator. A rubber-weave diaphragm divides the regulator into a fuel chamber and a pressure chamber. The valve spring incorporated in the diaphragm helps the diaphragm to push a moving valve plate onto a valve seat. When the force exerted on the diaphragm

by fuel pressure exceeds the spring force, the valve opens and allows exactly the right amount of fuel to flow off in order to establish a force equilibrium at the diaphragm.

On fuel systems with a return circuit, the upper connection of the pressure regulator is connected to the intake manifold. As a result, the pressure ratio at the diaphragm is the same as at the fuel injectors. The pressure differential across the injectors is therefore only dependent on the spring force and the surface area of the diaphragm.

On returnless fuel systems, the pressure regulator is located in the delivery module. There is no pneumatic connection to the intake manifold. The fuel pressure in the fuel rail is kept constant with respect to ambient pressure. The variable pressure differential with respect to intake-manifold pressure must be taken into account in the injection time calculation.

The same pressure regulators are used to regulate pressure in the low-pressure system on gasoline direct-injection systems.

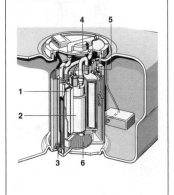

*Delivery module*
1 Fuel filter, 2 Electric fuel pump,
3 Suction-jet pump (regulated),
4 Pressure regulator,
5 Fuel-level sensor, 6 Prefilter.

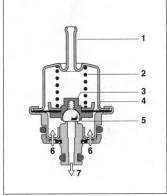

*Fuel-pressure regulator (DR2)*
1 Connection (intake manifold or ambient pressure), 2 Spring, 3 Valve holder,
4 Diaphragm, 5 Valve, 6 Fuel inlet,
7 Fuel-return line.

**High-pressure pump**

The function of the high-pressure pump is to compress the fuel to a pressure of 5...12 MPa, which is the level required for high-pressure fuel injection (gasoline direct injection). The fuel is supplied to the inlet by the electric fuel pump in sufficient quantities at an admission pressure of 0.3...0.5 MPa.

When the engine starts up, the fuel is initially injected at admission pressure. As the engine runs up to speed, the high pressure builds up.

In operation, the high-pressure pump is lubricated and cooled only by the fuel.

Triple-plunger pumps and demand-controlled single-plunger pumps are used.

Triple-plunger pump HDP1

The unit is basically a radial-piston pump with three plungers arranged at an offset angle of 120° to each other. The figures show longitudinal and cross-sectional views of the design.

The drive shaft, driven by the engine camshaft, turns with the eccentric element, which is responsible for lifting the pump plunger in the pump barrel. When the plunger moves down, fuel flows out of the fuel supply line at an admission pressure of 0.3...0.5 MPa through a hollow pump plunger and intake valve into the delivery chamber. When the plunger moves up, the fluid volume is compressed and, when the rail pressure is exceeded, flows via the outlet valve to the high-pressure connection.

The selected plunger layout means delivery overlaps; this reduces delivery flow pulses, thus reducing pressure pulses in the rail. The delivery quantity itself is proportional to the rotational speed.

To ensure that the primary pressure can still be varied quickly enough to meet the engine's fuel requirements, even at maximum injected fuel quantity, the maximum delivery quantity of the high-pressure pump is designed to be larger by a specific amount. When the pump operates at constant rail pressure or at part load, the pressure of the excess fuel is re-

*Triple-plunger pump (HDP1)*
*a Longitudinal section, b Cross-section.*
*1 Eccentric element, 2 Slipper, 3 Pump barrel, 4 Pump plunger (hollow plunger, fuel inlet),*
*5 Closure ball, 6 Outlet valve, 7 Inlet valve, 8 High-pressure connection to rail,*
*9 Fuel inlet (low pressure), 10 Cam ring, 11 Axial seal (slide ring seal),*
*12 Static seal, 13 Drive shaft.*

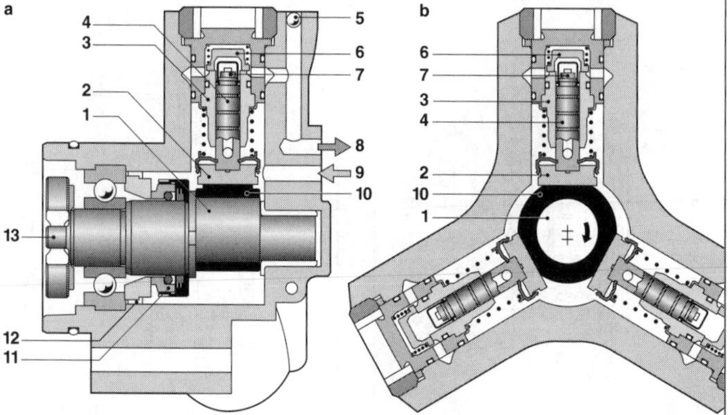

duced to admission pressure level by the pressure-control valve and returned to the intake side of the high-pressure pump.

### Single-plunger pump HDP2

The HDP2 single-plunger pump is a plug-in pump driven directly by the camshaft. A bucket tappet incorporated directly into the barrel head is responsible for transferring the lift movement to the pump plunger.

The figure shows the principle design of the unit. In addition to the inlet and outlet valves, the delivery chamber now houses an electrically switchable delivery-quantity control valve with a return line to the supply system. When de-energized, the valve is open and there is no high-pressure delivery because the entire delivery quantity flows back to the supply system. When activated, the valve closes when the pump plunger is at bottom dead center and opens to terminate delivery when the specified rail pressure is reached. The fuel that continues to be delivered until top dead center is reached flows back to the supply system. This type of control ensures that only as much fuel is deliv-

ered as the engine requires; this in turn reduces the pump's power consumption and thus fuel consumption.

To attenuate pressure pulses caused by delivery operations of the single-plunger pump, a fuel-pressure attenuator is installed in the supply system directly upstream of the inlet valve. The operating principle used here is the diaphragm spring accumulator, familiar from intake-manifold injection.

Another important component is the plunger seal. It is located in the pump barrel and acts as an interface to separate the fuel and engine-oil sections. To increase operating safety, the seal is connected to the leakage line running to the tank to relieve pressure there.

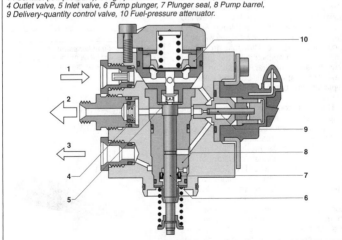

**Single-plunger pump (HDP2)**
*1 Fuel inlet (low pressure), 2 High-pressure connection to rail, 3 Leak return, 4 Outlet valve, 5 Inlet valve, 6 Pump plunger, 7 Plunger seal, 8 Pump barrel, 9 Delivery-quantity control valve, 10 Fuel-pressure attenuator.*

## Fuel filters

Fuel-injection systems for spark-ignition and diesel engines are sensitive to the smallest impurities in the fuel. Damage can be caused above all by particulate erosion and water corrosion. The service life of the fuel-injection system can only be guaranteed if the fuel supplied to the components at risk from wear meets a specific minimum purity.

The fuel filter has the task of reducing particulate impurities. The fuel-injection system determines the required filter fineness. As well as guaranteeing wear protection, the fuel filter must have a sufficient particulate retention capacity. Filters with insufficient particulate retention capacity are liable to become clogged before the end of the change interval. This will result in a reduction in fuel delivery quantity and thus a drop in engine performance. It is therefore essential to install a fuel filter that is customized to the fuel-injection system. Using the wrong filters has at best, unpleasant, and at worst, very costly consequences (replacement of components up to and including the entire fuel-injection system).

### Fuel filters for gasoline injection systems

Fuel filters for spark-ignition engines are always located on the pressure side downstream of the fuel pump. As new HC emission regulations are introduced, the preferred option for new vehicles will be to incorporate the fuel filter into an in-tank unit. For these applications, the fuel filter must be a lifetime filter. In addition, external in-line filters will still be used, either as replacement parts or lifetime components.

The more complex fuel-injection technology used in direct-injection spark-ignition engines requires greater wear protection and, as a result, finer filters must be used. The once-through filtration efficiency for a particulate fraction of between 3 and 5 μm (ISO/TR 13353: 1994) must be 25% to 45% for engines with intake-manifold injection, and 45% to 85% for gasoline direct-injection engines. To comply with these more stringent requirements, spiral vee-shaped filter mediums are used. They are made from a mixture of extremely fine cellulose and polyester fibers and, increasingly, multilayered composite filter mediums with layers of fine all-synthetic fibers.

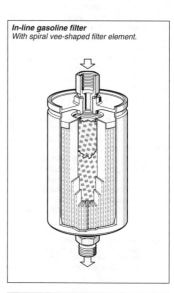

*In-line gasoline filter*
*With spiral vee-shaped filter element.*

*Lifetime gasoline filter element*
*With pleated filter medium and non-cylindrical geometry for optimum space utilization in in-tank units.*

# A/F mixture formation

## Basic principles

### Air/fuel (A/F) mixture

To be able to operate, a spark-ignition engine requires a specific air/fuel ratio. Ideal theoretical complete combustion is available at a mass ratio of 14.7:1. This is also termed the stoichiometric ratio, i.e. 14.7 kg of air are required to burn 1 kg of fuel. Or, expressed as a volume: 1 $l$ fuel burns completely in roughly 9,500 $l$ air.

The specific fuel consumption of a spark-ignition engine is essentially dependent on the mixture ratio of the A/F mixture. Excess air is required in order to ensure genuine complete combustion, and thus as low a fuel consumption as possible. However, limits are imposed due to the flammability of the mixture and the available combustion time.

The A/F mixture also has a decisive impact on the efficiency of exhaust-gas treatment systems. State-of-the-art technology is represented by the three-way catalytic converter. However, it needs a specific stoichiometric A/F ratio in order to operate at maximum efficiency. This type of catalytic converter helps to reduce harmful exhaust-gas constituents by more than 98%. The engines available today are therefore operated with a stoichiometric mixture as soon as their operating status allows this.

Certain engine operating statuses require mixture adaptation. Specific adaptation of the mixture composition is necessary, e.g. when the engine is cold. The mixture-formation (carburation) system must therefore be in a position to satisfy variable requirements.

### Excess-air factor $\lambda$

The excess-air factor or lambda $\lambda$ has been chosen to designate the extent to which the actual air/fuel mixture differs from the theoretically necessary mass ratio (14.7:1):

$\lambda$ Indicates the ratio of supplied air mass to air requirement with stoichiometric combustion.

$\lambda = 1$: The supplied air mass corresponds to the theoretically necessary air mass.

$\lambda < 1$: There is an air deficiency and thus a rich A/F mixture. Maximum power output at $\lambda = 0.85...0.95$.

$\lambda > 1$: There is an excess of air or a lean mixture in this range. This excess-air factor is characterized by reduced fuel consumption, but also by reduced power output. The maximum achievable value for $\lambda$, known as the "lean-misfire limit", is very heavily dependent on the design of the engine and the mixture-formation system used. The mixture is no longer ignitable at the lean-misfire limit. Combustion misses occur, and this is accompanied by a marked increase in uneven running.

At constant engine performance, fuel consumption in spark-ignition engines with intake-manifold injection is at its lowest when there is excess air of 20% to 50% ($\lambda = 1.2$ to 1.5), depending on the engine.

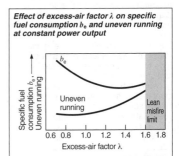

*Effect of excess-air factor $\lambda$ on specific fuel consumption $b_e$ and uneven running at constant power output*

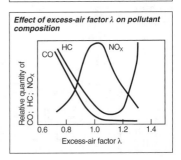

*Effect of excess-air factor $\lambda$ on pollutant composition*

The graphs (P. 605) show the dependence of specific fuel consumption, uneven running, and pollutant buildup on the excess-air factor for a typical engine with intake-manifold injection at constant engine performance. It can be deduced from these graphs that there is no ideal excess-air factor at which all the factors assume the most favorable value. For engines with intake-manifold injection, excess-air factors of $\lambda = 0.9$ to $1.1$ have proven effective in realizing "optimum" consumption at "optimum" power output.

Engines with direct injection and charge stratification involve different combustion conditions so that the lean-misfire limit occurs at significantly higher lambda values. These engines can therefore be operated in the part-load range at significantly higher excess-air factors (up to $\lambda = 4$).

For catalytic exhaust-gas treatment using a three-way catalytic converter, it is absolutely essential to adhere exactly to $\lambda = 1$ with the engine at normal operating temperature. To achieve this, the air mass drawn in must be precisely recorded and an exactly metered fuel mass added to it.

For optimum combustion in engines with intake-manifold injection that are common today, not only is a precise injected fuel quantity necessary, but also a homogeneous A/F mixture. This requires efficient fuel atomization. If this precondition is not satisfied, large fuel droplets will precipitate on the intake manifold or the combustion-chamber walls. These large droplets cannot fully combust and will result in increased hydrocarbon emissions.

## Mixture-formation systems

It is the job of fuel-injection systems, or carburetors, to provide an A/F mixture which is adapted as well as possible to the relevant engine operating status. Fuel-injection systems, especially electronic systems, are better designed to maintaining narrowly defined limits for A/F mixture composition. This helps to improve fuel consumption, drivability, and power output. Increasingly stringent emission-control legislation has meant that, in the automotive sector, fuel-injection systems have completed superseded the carburetor.

Until now, the automotive industry has almost exclusively used systems in which A/F mixture formation takes place outside the combustion chamber. Systems with internal A/F mixture formation, i.e. where the fuel is injected directly into the combustion chamber, are designed to reduce fuel consumption even further and are therefore becoming increasingly important.

---

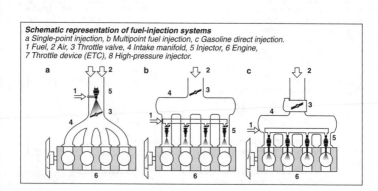

*Schematic representation of fuel-injection systems*
a Single-point injection, b Multipoint fuel injection, c Gasoline direct injection.
1 Fuel, 2 Air, 3 Throttle valve, 4 Intake manifold, 5 Injector, 6 Engine,
7 Throttle device (ETC), 8 High-pressure injector.

# Carburetors

## Carburetor system
Fuel is transported from the fuel tank to the carburetor by a fuel-supply pump (usually a diaphragm pump) driven by the camshaft or distributor shaft. The system is designed to limit the maximum delivery pressure. A fine-mesh fuel filter can be installed upstream or downstream of the pump as required.

## Design and operating concept
The driver uses the accelerator pedal to vary the throttle-valve aperture so that the air flow rate into the engine is varied and with it the engine power output. The carburetor varies the amount of fuel metered to the engine to reflect the current air flow rate. Together with the needle valve, the float regulates the fuel flow to the carburetor while maintaining a constant fuel level in the float chamber.

The air flow rate is monitored by an air funnel designed to induce a venturi effect. The progressively narrower cross-section increases the air velocity, producing a corresponding vacuum at the narrowest point. The resulting pressure differential relative to the float chamber helps to supply and deliver the fuel. Metering systems adapt fuel delivery to air flow rate.

### Fuel-metering systems
#### Main system
The fuel is metered by the main jet. Correction air is added as a delivery aid to the fuel through orifices in the side of the venturi tube.

#### Idle and progression systems
At idle, the vacuum, which the air flow produces at the fuel outlet, is not sufficient to withdraw fuel from the main system. For this reason, there is a separate idle system with an outlet located downstream from the throttle valve at the point of maximum vacuum. The emulsion required for idling emerges from the idle system after initial processing by the idle fuel and air-correction jets.

During transitions to the main metering system, the throttle valve controls a series of orifices (or a slit), drawing fuel from the idle system.

#### Other systems
The basic systems are supplemented by a range of additional systems. They are designed to adapt carburetor performance to the program map of a hot engine (part-load control, full-load enrichment), to compensate for fuel accumulation within the intake manifold during acceleration (accelerator pump), and to

*Schematic of a carburetor system*
*1 Fuel tank, 2 Fuel supply pump, 3 Fuel fine filter, 4 Carburetor, 5 Intake manifold.*

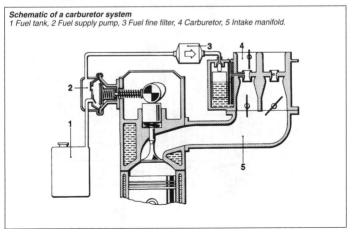

meet the special engine requirements encountered during starting and in the warm-up phase. Other examples include adding correction air via solenoid valves to the lambda closed-loop control and devices to activate overrun fuel cutoff.

## Carburetor types
### Downdraft carburetors
Downdraft carburetors are the most common type. Designs featuring optimized float chamber and metering-jet configurations result in efficient units. These designs work in conjunction with the corresponding intake-manifold layouts for optimum mixture formation and distribution.

### Horizontal-draft carburetors
Horizontal-draft carburetors (familiar as fixed-venturi and constant-depression units) are useful for minimizing engine height.

Constant-depression carburetors feature venturi cross-sections which vary in size during operation to maintain essentially constant vacuum levels at the fuel outlet.

The variation in intake cross-section is provided by a pneumatically actuated plunger; attached to the plunger is a needle which regulates fuel quantity.

### Venturi configurations
The single-throat carburetor with one venturi is the least expensive design. The two-stage carburetor featuring two venturis provides convenient tuning for individual applications and has become the standard in 4-cylinder applications. The first barrel controls part-load operation, while the throttle valve of the second venturi only opens when full power is reached.

The double-barrel carburetor features two carburetor sections sharing a single float chamber and operating in parallel, making it ideal for use on 6-cylinder engines. The two-stage four-barrel carburetor has four venturis fed from a single float chamber.

---

*Schematic of a two-stage carburetor*
*a) Primary stage, b) Secondary stage.*
*1 Idle cutoff valve, 2 Accelerator pump, 3 Idle switch, 4 Choke, 5 Boost venturi,*
*6 Main systems with venturi tubes, 7 Full-load enrichment, 8 Float,*
*9 Fuel inlet, 10 Needle valve, 11 Bypass plug, 12 Idle mixture screw,*
*13 Throttle valves, 14 Air funnel, 15 Part-load control valve, 16 Venturi.*

### Electronically controlled carburetor system (ECOTRONIC)

#### Basic carburetor
The basic carburetor is restricted to the throttle valve, float system, idle and transition systems, main system, and choke. An idle-air control system with a choke-activated needle jet is also provided.

#### Additional components and actuators
The throttle-valve actuator is an electropneumatic servo device for cylinder-charge control. The actuator plunger moves the throttle valve via a lever attached to the carburetor throttle-valve shaft.

The choke actuator is a final-control element designed to adapt the mixture ratio in response to variations in engine operating conditions. This unit closes the choke valve to enrich the mixture by raising the pressure differential (vacuum) at the main jets while simultaneously increasing flow rates from the idle system.

#### Sensors
The throttle-valve potentiometer monitors the throttle-valve position and travel. One temperature sensor monitors the engine operating temperature, while a second sensor can be installed if necessary to monitor the temperature within the intake manifold.

The idle system helps to detect overrun; it can be replaced by appropriate software in the electronic control unit (ECU).

#### Electronic control unit (ECU)
The ECU input circuit converts incoming analog signals into digital form. The processor performs further operations with the input variables in order to calculate output values with reference to the program map. The output signals control several functions, including regulation of the servo elements that operate the choke valve and main throttle valve.

#### Basic functions
The basic carburetor determines the primary functions of the system. The idle, transition and full-throttle systems all contribute to matching performance to the engine map. The base calibrations can be intentionally "lean", as choke-valve control can provide a corrective enrichment.

#### Electronic functions
Electronic open- and closed-loop control circuits regulate a number of secondary operations within the ECU. Several of these are illustrated in the figure below. Further functions may include ignition control, transmission-shift control, fuel consumption displays, and diagnostic functions.

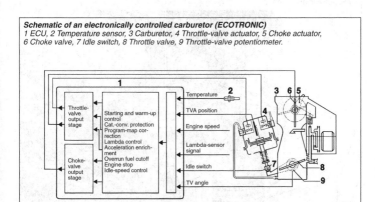

*Schematic of an electronically controlled carburetor (ECOTRONIC)*
*1 ECU, 2 Temperature sensor, 3 Carburetor, 4 Throttle-valve actuator, 5 Choke actuator, 6 Choke valve, 7 Idle switch, 8 Throttle valve, 9 Throttle-valve potentiometer.*

## Intake-manifold injection (external A/F mixture formation)

Gasoline injection systems for external A/F mixture formation are characterized by the fact that the air/fuel mixture is created outside of the combustion chamber (in the intake manifold). Although carburetor engines also utilize external A/F mixture formation, they have been almost completely superseded by spark-ignition engines with intake-manifold injection because they feature better fuel metering and fuel management. Electronic intake-manifold injection systems are currently the state of the art. They inject fuel intermittently, i.e. at intervals, immediately upstream of the intake valves for each individual cylinder.

Systems based on continuous mechanical injection or single-point injection located upstream of the throttle valve are no longer an option for new developments (see the section headed "Development of fuel-injection systems", P. 642 onwards).

The high requirements for engine smooth running and exhaust emissions make high demands on the A/F mixture composition in each power cycle. Precise injection timing is vital as well as precise metering of the injected fuel mass as a factor of the engine intake air. In electronic multipoint fuel-injection systems, therefore, not only is each engine cylinder assigned an electromagnetic fuel injector, but this fuel injector is also activated individually for each cylinder. The control unit has the task of calculating both the required fuel mass for each cylinder and the correct start of injection for the fuel mass drawn in and the current engine operating status. The injection time required to inject the calculated fuel mass is a function of the opening cross-section of the fuel injector and the pressure differential between the intake manifold and the fuel supply system.

In intake-manifold injection systems, fuel is sent via the electric fuel pump, fuel supply lines, and filters at primary pressure to the fuel rail, which ensures that the fuel is evenly distributed to the injectors. How the fuel is prepared by the injectors is extremely important for the quality of the air/fuel mixture. It is essential that the fuel is atomized into the very fine droplets. The spray shape and spray dispersal

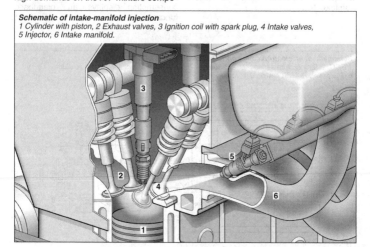

*Schematic of intake-manifold injection*
*1 Cylinder with piston, 2 Exhaust valves, 3 Ignition coil with spark plug, 4 Intake valves,*
*5 Injector, 6 Intake manifold.*

angle of the fuel injectors (P. 614) are adapted to the geometric shape of the intake manifold or cylinder head.

If the precisely metered fuel mass is injected directly upstream of the cylinder intake valve(s), most of the finely atomized fuel may evaporate. The required air/fuel mixture can therefore be formed at the right time using the air flowing in via the throttle valve. The amount of time available for A/F mixture formation can be increased by injecting the fuel into the intake valves that are still closed.

A proportion of the fuel precipitates onto the wall near the intake valves and forms a film; the thickness of this film essentially depends on the pressure in the intake manifold, and thus on the engine load condition. In transient or dynamic engine operating conditions, this coating can cause the lambda value to temporarily deviate from the desired value ($\lambda = 1$). It is therefore important to minimize the fuel mass stored in the wall film as much as possible. Wall coating effects in the intake duct, particularly in cold start conditions, cannot be neglected either: As fuel does not evaporate sufficiently, more fuel is required initially in the starting phase in order to create an ignitable A/F mixture.

When the intake-manifold pressure then drops, parts of the previously formed wall film will vaporize. This may result in increased HC emissions if the catalytic converter is not running at operating temperature. Irregular fuel injection may also result in the formation of wall films in the combustion chamber, and may in turn become critical emission sources. Defining the geometric alignment of fuel sprays ("spray targeting") will allow the selection of suitable injectors which will control or minimize manifold-wall fuel condensation in the area of the intake duct and the intake valves.

Compared with carburetor engines and single-point injection systems, manifold-wall fuel condensation in multipoint injection systems is reduced significantly. At the same time the intake manifolds used can be optimally adapted to the combustion air flow and the dynamic gas requirements of the engine.

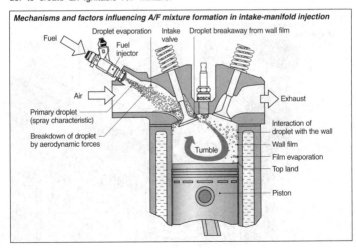

*Mechanisms and factors influencing A/F mixture formation in intake-manifold injection*

Fuel

Droplet evaporation

Intake valve

Droplet breakaway from wall film

Fuel injector

Air

Exhaust

Primary droplet (spray characteristic)

Breakdown of droplet by aerodynamic forces

Interaction of droplet with the wall

Wall film

Film evaporation

Top land

Tumble

Piston

BOSCH

## Gasoline direct injection (internal A/F mixture formation)

In gasoline direct injection, unlike intake-manifold injection, pure air flows through the intake valves into the combustion chamber. Only then is the fuel injected into the air via an injector located directly in the cylinder head. There are basically two main operating modes. Fuel injection in the induction stroke is called homogeneous operation, while fuel injection during compression is called stratified-charge operation. There are also various special modes, which are either a mixture of the two main operating modes or a slight variation of them.

### Homogeneous operation

In homogeneous operation, mixture formation is similar to intake-manifold injection. When formed, the A/F mixture has a stoichiometric ratio ($\lambda = 1$). However, from a mixture formation point of view, there are some differences. For instance, there is no flow process around the intake valve to promote mixture formation, and there is much less time available for the mixture formation process itself. Whereas with in-

take-manifold injection, fuel injection can take place over the entire 720° crankshaft-angle (CA) range of the four power cycles (stored and synchronous with induction), gasoline direct injection only has an injection window of 180 °CA. Fuel injection is only permitted in the induction stroke. This is because, prior to this, the exhaust valves are open and unburned fuel would otherwise escape into the exhaust-gas train. This would cause high HC emissions and catalytic converter problems. In order to deliver a sufficient quantity of fuel in this shortened period, the fuel flow through the injector must be increased for gasoline direct injection. This is achieved mainly by increasing fuel pressure. The increase in pressure brings with it an additional advantage as it increases turbulence in the combustion chamber, which in turn promotes mixture formation. The fuel and air can therefore be completely mixed, even though the fuel/air interaction time is shorter compared with intake-manifold injection.

### Stratified-charge operation

In stratified-charge operation, a distinction is made between several combustion strategies. All strategies have one thing in common, namely they all attempt to

---

*Schematic of gasoline direct injection*
*1 Piston, 2 Intake valve, 3 Ignition coil with spark plug, 4 Exhaust valve,*
*5 High-pressure injector, 6 Rail.*

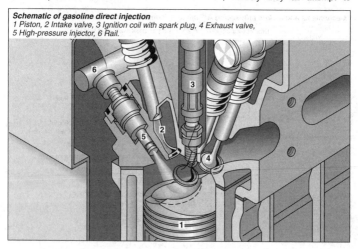

achieve charge stratification. This means that, instead of supplying the corresponding stoichiometric air flow rate to the fuel quantity required for a specific load point by adjusting the throttle valve, the full air flow rate is supplied to the combustion chamber, and only a portion of it interacts with the fuel before it is conveyed to the spark plug. The rest of the fresh air surrounds the stratified charge. In addition to having a cooling effect, which reduces knock tendency and makes it possible to increase compression, the dethrottling action also offers considerable fuel-saving potential.

### Wall-directed combustion system

In a wall-directed combustion system, fuel is injected into the combustion chamber from the side. A recess in the piston crown deflects the fuel spray in the direction of the spark plug. Mixture formation takes place on the path from the injector tip to the spark plug. As the mixture formation time is even shorter, the fuel pressure for this system must usually be even higher than for homogeneous operation. The increased fuel pressure shortens the injection time and increases interaction with the air because pulse reflection is greater.

The disadvantage of the wall-directed combustion system is that fuel condenses on the wall, which increases HC emissions. As mixture formation time is short, the charge cloud usually contains rich mixture zones at higher loads, and this increases the risk of soot production. At low loads, the fuel pulse, which is used as a means of transporting the stratified charge cloud to the spark plug, is low. As a result, the flow must usually be restricted here so that the fuel meets with a lower density of air.

### Air-directed combustion system

In principle, an air-directed combustion system works in exactly the same way as a wall-directed system. The main difference is that the fuel cloud does not interact directly with the piston recess. Instead, the charge cloud moves on a cushion of air. This solves the problem of fuel condensing on the piston recess. How-

*A/F mixture-formation systems for gasoline direct injection*
(assisted by swirl or tumble in each case)
a) Wall-directed,
b) Air-directed,
c) Jet-directed.
1 Injector,
2 Spark plug.

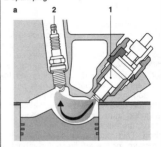

a

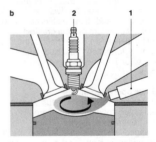

b

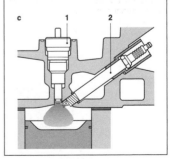

c

ever, air-directed combustion systems are not as stable as wall-directed ones, as it is difficult to reproduce the air flows fully.

Often, the actual combustion processes are a mixture of wall-directed and air-directed processes, depending on the operating point in each case.

<u>Jet-directed combustion process</u>
The jet-directed combustion process is visually different from the other two processes in that the injector is installed at a different location. It is located at top center and injects vertically down into the combustion chamber. The spark plug is located immediately next to the injector. The fuel spray is not deflected; instead, it is ignited immediately after injection. As a result, the mixture formation time is very short. This requires an even higher fuel pressure for the jet-directed combustion process. This combustion process can eliminate the disadvantages of fuel condensing on the manifold walls, air-flow dependency, and flow restriction at low loads. It therefore has the greatest potential for fuel saving. Nevertheless, the short mixture formation time is a huge challenge for fuel-injection and ignition systems.

**Other operating modes**
In addition to homogeneous and stratified-charge operation, there are also special operating modes. They include changeover between operating modes (homogeneous-stratified mode), catalytic converter heating, and knock protection (homogeneous-split mode), and homogeneous-lean mode.

## A/F mixture formation components

Essentially, A/F mixture formation components must ensure that the air/fuel mixture is formed properly for a particular system. In intake-manifold injection, this is mainly the task of the fuel injector, while in gasoline direct injection, the high-pressure fuel injector can be assisted by a turbulence flap.

**Intake manifold fuel injector**
<u>Design and operation</u>
Fuel injectors essentially consist of:
– A valve housing with solenoid coil and electrical connection
– A valve seat with spray-orifice disk
– A moving valve needle with solenoid armature

*Fuel injector EV6* (example)
*1 O-rings, 2 Filter strainer, 3 Valve housing with electrical connection, 4 Current coil, 5 Spring, 6 Valve needle with solenoid armature, 7 Valve seat with spray-orifice disk.*

A filter strainer in the fuel inlet protects the injector against contamination. Two O-rings seal the injector from the fuel-distribution pipe and the intake manifold. When the coil is de-energized, the spring and the force resulting from the fuel pressure press the valve needle against the valve seat to seal the fuel-supply system from the intake manifold (see figure).

When the injector is energized, the coil generates a magnetic field which pulls in the armature and lifts the valve needle off of its seat to allow fuel to flow through the injector.

The injected fuel quantity per unit of time is determined mainly by primary pressure and the free cross-section of the injection orifices in the spray-orifice disk. The valve needle closes again when the excitation current is switched off.

Spray formation and direction
The spray formation functions performed by the fuel injectors, i.e. spray shape, spray dispersal angle, and droplet size, influences the formation of the A/F mixture. Individual geometries of intake manifold and cylinder head make it necessary to have different types of spray formation. To meet these requirements, there are various types of spray formation.

*Tapered spray*
Individual fuel sprays emerge through the openings in the spray-orifice disk. These fuel sprays combine to form a tapered spray. Tapered sprays can also be obtained by means of a pintle projecting through the injector needle tip.

Tapered-spray injectors are typically used in engines with one intake valve per cylinder. The tapered spray is directed into the opening between the intake-valve disk and the intake-manifold wall.

*Dual spray*
Dual-spray formation is used in engines with two intake valves per cylinder. The openings in the spray-orifice disk are arranged in such a way that two fuel sprays emerge from the injector. Each of these sprays supplies an intake valve.

*Air-shrouding*
In the case of an air-shrouded injector, the pressure drop between intake-manifold and ambient pressure is used to improve mixture formation. Air is routed through an air-shrouding attachment into the outlet area of the spray-orifice disk. In the narrow air gap, the air is accelerated to a very high speed, and the fuel is finely atomized when it mixes with it.

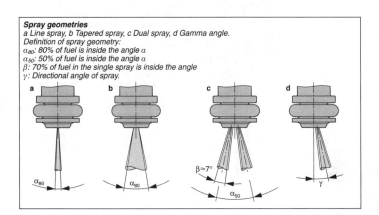

**Spray geometries**
a Line spray, b Tapered spray, c Dual spray, d Gamma angle.
Definition of spray geometry:
$\alpha_{80}$: 80% of fuel is inside the angle $\alpha$
$\alpha_{50}$: 50% of fuel is inside the angle $\alpha$
$\beta$: 70% of fuel in the single spray is inside the angle
$\gamma$: Directional angle of spray.

### High-pressure injector

The higher fuel pressure required for gasoline direct injection means that the fuel injector components have to meet additional requirements. As a result, special high-pressure injectors have been developed for gasoline direct injection.

#### Design and operation

The function of the high-pressure injector is to meter and atomize the fuel. Atomization ensures that the fuel is quickly mixed with the air in the combustion chamber. In the process, the air/fuel mixture is formed within a physically restricted area. Here, a distinction is made between whether the air/fuel mixture is concentrated in the area around the spark plug (stratified-charge operation), or distributed uniformly throughout the entire combustion chamber (homogeneous operation). In both cases, an ignitable A/F mixture should be present at the spark plug.

The high-pressure injector consists of the following individual components:
– Housing
– Valve seat
– Nozzle needle with solenoid armature
– Spring
– Coil

When an electric current flows through it, the coil generates a magnetic field. The magnetic field lifts the valve needle away from the valve seat against spring pressure and releases the valve outlet opening. As the fuel pressure is considerably higher than the combustion-chamber pressure, the fuel is injected into the combustion chamber. To improve atomization, the fuel spray can be swirled.

When the current is switched off, the valve needle is pushed back into the seat by the spring, and this stops the injection process.

With needle valves that open inward, the pressure in the rail helps the closing process. On opening, therefore, it acts in the opposite direction to the opening direction. As a result, a stronger magnetic field is required than with conventional intake manifold fuel injectors.

#### Spray formation

Reproducible fuel quantities can be metered by defining the opening and keeping the opening cross-section constant with the needle fully raised. Here, the fuel quantity is dependent on the pressure in the fuel rail, the backpressure reaction in the combustion chamber, and the valve opening time. The fuel atomization process is supported by an appropriate valve-seat geometry and a flow guide to create swirl.

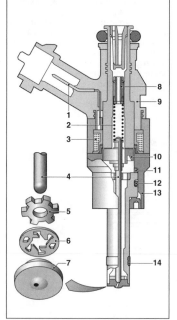

***High-pressure injector***
*1 Electrical connection, 2 Spring, 3 Coil, 4 Nozzle needle, 5 Guide washer, 6 Swirl plate, 7 Seat washer, 8 Adjusting nozzle, 9 Housing cover, 10 Solenoid armature, 11 Shim, 12 O-ring, 13 Valve housing, 14 Teflon ring.*

*Signal curves for activating the high-pressure injector*
a Triggering signal calculated by the ECU,
b Current curve in the fuel injector,
c Needle lift,
d Injected fuel quantity.

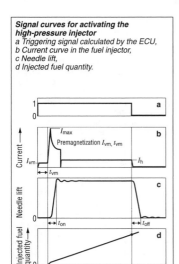

*Turbulence flap*
1 Intake manifold, 2 Throttle valve,
3 Turbulence flap, 4 Partition, 5 Intake valve.

## Activating the high-pressure injector

To ensure a defined and reproducible injection process, the high-pressure injector has to be activated by a complex current curve. The engine control unit delivers a digital signal for this purpose. A special module uses this signal to generate the triggering signal, which the driver stage in the high-pressure injector will use to activate the injector.

A booster capacitor generates an activation voltage of 50 to 90 V. This voltage creates a high current at the beginning of the activation process, thus ensuring that the valve needle is raised quickly. When the injector is open (maximum valve-needle lift), a lower control current is sufficient to keep the valve-needle lift constant. A constant valve-needle lift produces an injected fuel quantity that is proportional to the injection time.

The pre-magnetizing time when the injector has not yet opened is taken into consideration in the injection calculation.

## Turbulence flap

The available mixture formation time is much shorter with gasoline direct injection than with intake-manifold injection. In order to guarantee sufficiently good mixture formation in this shortened period, gasoline direct injection systems often use a turbulence flap. It is located in front of the intake valves and can be aligned horizontally (tumble flap) or vertically (swirl flap). Its alignment depends on the combustion process. A tumble flap generates turbulence, which helps to mix the air and fuel in the combustion chamber; it also influences the direction of air flow in the combustion chamber. The flap can thus support moving the charge in a specific direction.

There are two different types of turbulence flaps: two-point designs and continuously operating systems.

# Ignition

## Basic principles

On a spark-ignition engine, the combustion process is initiated by an externally supplied ignition. The ignition is responsible for igniting the compressed air/fuel mixture at the right time. This is done by producing an electric spark between the electrodes of a spark plug in the combustion chamber.

Consistent, reliable ignition under all conditions is essential to ensure fault-free engine operation. Misfiring leads to:
- Combustion misses
- Damage or destruction of the catalytic converter
- Poorer emission values
- Higher fuel consumption
- Lower engine performance

### Ignition spark

An electric spark can only occur at the spark plug if the necessary ignition voltage is exceeded. The ignition voltage is dependent on the spark-plug electrode gap and the density of the air/fuel mixture at the moment of ignition. After flashover, the voltage at the spark plug drops to the firing voltage. The firing voltage depends on the length of the spark plasma (electrode gap and excursion by the A/F mixture flow). During the ignition-spark combustion time (spark duration), the ignition-system energy is converted into the igni-

tion spark. After the spark has broken away, the voltage is damped and drops to zero.

### Mixture ignition and ignition energy

The electric spark between the spark-plug electrodes generates a high-temperature plasma. If mixture conditions at the spark plug are suitable and sufficient energy has been supplied by the ignition system, the resulting arc develops into a flame front that propagates of its own accord.

The ignition must guarantee this process under all engine operating conditions. In order for an electric spark to ignite an air/fuel mixture in ideal conditions (e.g. in a "combustion bomb"), an energy of about 0.2 mJ is required for each individual ignition event, provided the mixture composition is static, homogeneous, and stoichiometric. In real engine operation, however, much higher energy levels are required. Some of the spark energy is converted at flashover, and the rest in the spark combustion phase.

Larger electrode gaps generate a larger arc, but require higher ignition voltages. Lean A/F mixtures or turbocharged engines need higher ignition voltages. At a given level of energy, the spark duration shortens as the ignition voltage increases. A longer spark duration generally stabilizes combustion; a longer spark duration can also compensate for mixture inhomogeneity around the spark plug at the moment of ignition. Turbulence in the A/F mixture, which occurs in stratified-charge operation on gasoline direct injection systems, for example, can deflect the ignition spark until it breaks away. Follow-up sparks are then required to ignite the A/F mixture again.

The need for higher ignition voltages, longer spark durations, and the provision of follow-up sparks have resulted in the design of ignition systems with higher ignition energy. If not enough ignition energy is produced, ignition will not occur, resulting in combustion misses. The system must therefore deliver enough ignition energy to ensure reliable ignition of the air/fuel mixture under all operating conditions.

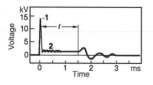

*Spark-plug voltage characteristic with static or semi-static A/F mixture*
1 Ignition voltage, 2 Spark voltage.
*t* Spark duration.

Efficient fuel atomization and good access of the A/F mixture to the ignition sparks enhance ignitability, extend spark duration and spark length, and lengthen the electrode gap. The dimensions of the spark plug determine the position and length of the spark; spark duration depends on the type and design of the ignition system, as well as on the instantaneous ignition conditions in the combustion chamber. Depending on the engine's requirements (intake-manifold injection, gasoline direct injection, or turbocharger), the spark energy of ignition systems is in the range of approx. 30...100 mJ.

## Moment of ignition

The start of combustion in an SI engine can be controlled by selecting the moment of ignition. The moment of ignition is always referred to the top dead center of the SI-engine power cycle. If the moment of ignition is advanced, it is before top dead center; if it is retarded, it is after. The earliest possible moment of ignition is determined by the knock limit, and the latest possible moment of ignition by the combustion limit or the maximum permissible exhaust-gas temperature. The moment of ignition influences:
– Torque output
– Exhaust-gas emissions
– Fuel consumption

### Basic ignition point
The speed at which the flame front propagates in the combustion chamber increases with higher cylinder charge and higher rotational speed. To deliver maximum engine torque, maximum combustion, and thus maximum combustion pressure, should occur shortly after top dead center. Ignition must therefore occur before top dead center, and the moment of ignition must be advanced as rotational speed increases or charge decreases.

Likewise, the moment of ignition must also be advanced in the case of lean A/F mixtures, because the flame front propagates more slowly. Ignition timing adjustment, therefore, essentially depends on rotational speed, charge, and the excess-air factor. The moments of ignition are determined on the engine test bench and are stored in program maps in the case of electronic engine-management systems (see the figure on P. 620).

### Ignition timing corrections and operation-dependent moments of ignition
Electronic engine-management systems can take other effects on the moment of ignition into consideration in addition to rotational speed and charge. The basic ignition point can be modified either by adding corrective parameters, or it can be replaced for specific operating points or ranges by special ignition angles or ignition maps. Examples of ignition timing

*Combustion-chamber pressure characteristic for various moments of ignition*
1 Correct ignition advance ($Z_a$),
2 Excessive ignition advance ($Z_b$),
3 Excessive ignition retard ($Z_c$).

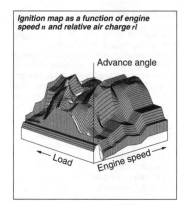

*Ignition map as a function of engine speed n and relative air charge rl*

Advance angle

Load

Engine speed

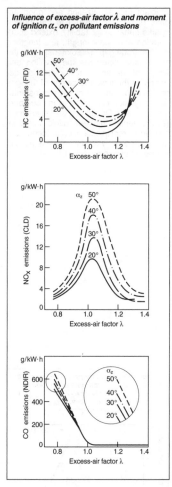

*Influence of excess-air factor λ and moment of ignition $\alpha_z$ on pollutant emissions*

corrections are knock control, the correction angle for the gasoline direct injection homogeneous-lean operation, and warm-up. Examples of special ignition angles or ignition maps are gasoline direct injection stratified-charge operation, and starting operation. Final implementation depends on the prevailing electronic control unit concept.

**Exhaust gas and fuel consumption**

The moment of ignition has a considerable impact on exhaust gas because it can be used to control the various untreated exhaust-gas constituents directly. However, the various optimization criteria, such as exhaust gas, fuel economy, drivability, etc., may not always be compatible, so it is not always possible to derive the ideal moment of ignition from them.

Shifts in the moment of ignition induce mutually inverse response patterns in fuel consumption and exhaust-gas emissions. Whereas more spark advance increases power and reduces fuel consumption, it also raises HC and, in particular, nitrogen-oxide emissions. Excessive spark advance can cause engine knock that may damage the engine. Retarded ignition results in higher exhaust-gas temperatures, which can also harm the engine.

Electronic engine-management systems featuring programmed ignition curves are designed to adapt the moment of ignition in response to variations in factors such as rotational speed, load, temperature, etc. They can thus be employed to achieve the optimum compromise between these mutually antagonistic objectives.

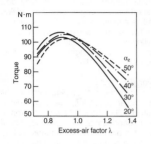

*Influence of excess-air factor λ and moment of ignition $\alpha_z$ on fuel consumption and torque*

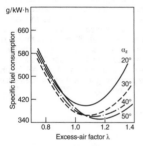

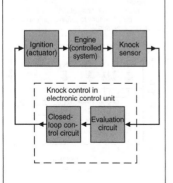

*Schematic of knock-control system*

### Knock control
#### Basic principles
Electronic control of the moment of ignition offers the possibility of accurate control of the ignition angle as a function of rotational speed, load, temperature, etc. Nevertheless, if there is no knock control, there must still be some means to define a clear safety margin to the knock limit.

This margin is necessary to ensure that, even in the most knock-sensitive case with regard to engine tolerances, engine aging, environmental conditions, and fuel quality, no cylinder can reach or exceed the knock limit. The resulting engine design leads to lower compression, retarded moments of ignition, and thus worsening of fuel consumption and torque.

These disadvantages can be avoided through the use of knock control. Experience shows that knock control increases engine compression and significantly improves fuel consumption and torque. However, the precontrol ignition angle no longer needs to be determined for the most knock-sensitive conditions, but rather for the most insensitive conditions (e.g. engine compression at lower tolerance limit, best possible fuel grade, most knock-insensitive cylinder). Each individual engine cylinder can now be operated throughout its service life in virtually all operating ranges at its knock limit, and thus at optimum efficiency.

For this type of ignition angle adjustment, a reliable method of knock detection is essential. It should detect knock for each cylinder throughout the engine's operating range starting from a specified knock intensity.

#### Knock-control system
A knock-control system consists of:
- Knock sensor
- Signal evaluation system
- Knock detection system
- Ignition-angle control system with adaptation facility

### Knock sensor

A typical symptom of combustion knock is high-frequency vibrations which are superimposed on the low-pressure curve in the combustion chamber. These vibrations are best detected directly in the combustion chamber by means of pressure sensors. Since it is relatively complex and costly to install these pressure sensors in the cylinder head for each cylinder, the vibrations are usually detected by knock sensors located externally on the engine. The piezoelectric acceleration sensors detect the characteristic vibrations of combustion knock and convert them into electrical signals.

There are two types of knock sensor. A broadband sensor, with a typical frequency band of 5 to 20 kHz, and a resonance sensor, which preferably transmits only one knock-signal resonant frequency. When combined with the flexible signal-evaluation system in the ECU, it is possible to evaluate different or several resonant frequencies from one broadband knock sensor. This improves knock detection performance, which is why the broadband knock sensor is increasingly replacing the resonance sensor.

To ensure sufficient knock detection in all cylinders and across all operating ranges, the number and location of the required knock sensors must be carefully determined for each engine type. Four-cylinder in-line engines are usually fitted with one or two knock sensors, while 5- and 6-cylinder engines are fitted with two, and 8- and 12-cylinder engines with four knock sensors.

### Signal evaluation

For the duration of a timing range in which knock can occur, a special signal evaluation circuit in the ECU evaluates from the broadband signal(s) with the best knock information and generates a representative variable for each combustion process. This extremely flexible signal-evaluation system using a broadband sensor produces considerably better knock-detection results than a resonance knock sensor. This is because the resonance knock sensor transmits just one resonant frequency for analysis for all cylinders assigned to it and across the entire engine map.

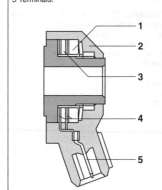

*Knock sensor*
1 Seismic mass, 2 Sealing compound,
3 Piezoceramic element, 4 Contacts,
5 Terminals.

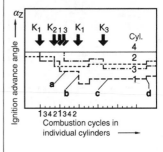

*Knock control*
Control algorithm for ignition adjustment on a 4-cylinder engine.
$K_{1...3}$ Knock in cylinders 1...3, cylinder 4, no knock;
a Delay prior to ignition retard, b Drop height, c Delay before return to original ignition point, d Ignition advance.

## Knock detection

The variable produced by the signal-evaluation circuit is classified in a knock-detection algorithm as "knock" or "no knock" for each cylinder and for each combustion process. This is done by comparing the variable for the current combustion process with a variable which represents combustion without knock.

## Ignition-angle control system with adaptation facility

If combustion knock is detected in a cylinder, the moment of ignition for that cylinder is retarded. When knock stops, the moment of ignition is advanced again in stages up to the precontrol value. The knock-detection and knock-control algorithms are matched in such a way as to eliminate any knock that is audible and damaging to the engine, even though each cylinder is operated at knock limit within the optimum efficiency range.

Real engine operation produces different knock limits, and thus different moments of ignition for individual cylinders. In order to adapt precontrol values for the moment of ignition to a particular knock limit, the ignition retard values are stored for each cylinder dependent on the operating point. They are stored in non-volatile program maps in the permanently powered RAM for load and engine speed. In this way, the engine can be operated at optimum efficiency at each operating point and without audible combustion knocks, even if there are rapid load and engine-speed changes.

This adaptation even allows the use of fuels with lower antiknock qualities (e.g. regular instead of super gasoline).

# Ignition systems

On modern vehicles, the ignition systems are almost always incorporated as subsystems of the engine-management system. Separate ignition systems are only used in special applications (e.g. low-power engines). Coil ignition (inductive ignition) with one dedicated ignition circuit per cylinder (static HT distribution system with single spark coils) is the usual choice for vehicle ignition systems. Also used, but to a lesser extent, are high-voltage capacitor ignition systems (capacitive ignition), or other special designs, such as solenoid ignition for low-power engines. The next section will focus on coil ignition alone.

## Coil ignition (inductive ignition)

### Principle of coil ignition

The ignition circuit of a coil-ignition system consists of:
- An ignition coil with a primary and secondary winding.
- An ignition driver stage to control current in the primary winding (incorporated in the engine control unit or the ignition coil).
- A spark plug, which is connected to the high-voltage connection of the secondary winding.

*Structure of an ignition circuit with single spark coils*
1 Ignition driver stage, 2 Ignition coil,
3 Activation arc diode (suppression of activation spark), 4 Spark plug.
15, 1, 4, 4a Terminal designations,
⊓ Triggering signal.

Before the desired moment of ignition, the ignition driver stage switches a current from the vehicle electrical system through to the primary winding of the ignition coil. While the primary current circuit is closed (dwell period), a magnetic field builds up in the primary winding.

At the moment of ignition, the current through the primary winding is interrupted again, and the magnetic-field energy is discharged, mainly via the magnetic-coupled secondary winding (induction). In the process, a high voltage is produced in the secondary winding, which in turn generates the spark at the spark plug. The ignition voltage required at the spark plug (ignition voltage demand) must always be less than the maximum possible ignition voltage in the ignition system (ignition voltage supply).

After flashover, the remaining energy is converted at the spark plug while the spark is present.

Functions of an ignition system
with coil ignition
The basic functions of an inductive ignition system are:
– To determine the moment of ignition.
– To determine the dwell period.
– To release the ignition energy.

*Determining the moment of ignition*
The instantaneous moment of ignition is determined from program maps as a function of the operating point (see P. 620), and the ignition energy is then released.

*Determining the dwell period*
The required ignition energy is made available at the moment of ignition. The amount of ignition energy is dependent on the amount of primary current at the moment of ignition (cutoff current) and the inductance of the primary winding. The amount of cutoff current is mainly dependent on the operating point (dwell period) and on the battery voltage at the ignition coil. The dwell periods required to achieve the desired cutoff current are contained in characteristic curves or program maps as a function of the steady-state voltage. The change in dwell period with temperature can also be compensated for.

*Ignition release*
Ignition release ensures that the ignition spark occurs at the right cylinder at the right time and with the required level of ignition energy. On electronic-controlled systems, a trigger wheel with a fixed-angle reference mark (typically 60-2 teeth) located on the crankshaft is usually scanned by an induction-type pulse generator (sensor system). From this, the ECU can calculate the crankshaft angle and the momentary rotational speed. The ignition coil can be switched on and off at any required crankshaft angle. An additional phase signal from the camshaft is required for the unambiguous identification of the cylinder.

For each combustion process, the ECU calculates the switch-on point from the desired moment of ignition, the required dwell period, and the current rotational speed, and switches on the driver stage accordingly. The moment of ignition, or the switchoff point for the driver stage, can be triggered either when the dwell period expires or when the desired angle is reached.

*Ignition system with single spark coils*
1 Ignition lock, 2 Ignition coil, 3 Spark plug,
4 ECU, 5 Battery.

## Ignition components

### Ignition output stage

Function
The ignition output stage is responsible for switching the current in the ignition coil.

Design and operating concept
The ignition output stages are usually three-stage power transistors in BIP technology (Bosch Integrated Power, bipolar technology). The "primary-voltage limitation" and "primary-current limitation" functions are monolithically integrated onto the ignition output stage and protect the ignition components from overloading.

The ignition output stage and ignition coil heat up when operating. To ensure that the permissible operating temperatures are not exceeded, suitable measures must be in place to dissipate the resulting heat losses into the environment, even when operating at high temperatures. To avoid high heat losses in the ignition output stage, the primary-current limitation function is only responsible for limiting current in the event of a fault (e.g. short-circuit) (current safety wire).

---

**Risk of accidents**
All electronic ignition systems are high-voltage systems. To avoid any risks, always switch off the ignition, or disconnect the power supply when working on the ignition system. Such work includes, for example:
- Replacing parts such as spark plugs, ignition coils, or ignition transformers, ignition distributors, high-tension ignition cables, etc.
- Connecting engine analyzers, such as stroboscopic lamps, dwell angle/ rotational speed testers, ignition oscilloscopes, etc.

When testing the ignition system with the ignition switched on, dangerous voltages will occur throughout the entire system. Therefore, test work should only be carried out by trained specialists.

---

In the future, three-stage circuit breakers will be superseded by the new IGBTs (Insulated Gate Bipolar Transistor, a combination of a field-effect and bipolar transistor), which have also been developed for ignition-system applications. IGBTs have certain advantages over BIPs:
- Virtually no power required for activation (voltage-controlled instead of current-controlled).
- Lower saturation voltage.
- Higher load current.
- Low switching times.
- Higher terminal voltage possible.
- Higher continuous operating temperature.
- Protection against polarity reversal in the 12-V vehicle electrical system.

Design variations
Ignition output stages are divided into internal and external driver stages. The internal driver stages are incorporated on the printed-circuit board of the engine ECU. The external driver stages are located in a separate housing outside of the engine ECU. For cost reasons, external driver stages will no longer be used on new products.

Another increasingly popular option is to integrate the driver stages into the ignition coil. This solution avoids having to have cables in the wiring harness, which carry high currents and are subjected to high voltages. Likewise, the power loss in the Motronic ECU is correspondingly lower.

Ignition output stages integrated in the ignition coil are being subjected to increasing requirements in terms of activation, diagnostics capability, and temperature loads.

## Ignition coil

### Function

The ignition coil is principally an energy-charged high-voltage source similar in structure to a transformer. Energy is supplied by the vehicle electrical system during the dwell period or charging time. At the moment of ignition, which also marks the end of the charging time, the energy is released at the required high voltage and spark energy levels to the spark plug (inductive ignition system, P. 623).

### Design

The ignition coil consists of two windings coupled magnetically by means of an iron core. This iron core may contain a permanent magnet for energy optimization. Compared with the secondary winding, the primary winding has significantly fewer coils. The turns ratio $\ddot{u}$ is in the range of $\ddot{u} = 80...100$.

The windings must have good electrical insulation to prevent electrical discharge and/or flashovers either to the inside or to the outside. For this purpose, the windings are usually cast in epoxy resin in the ignition coil housing.

The iron core usually consists of a number of stacked ferromagnetic discs to minimize eddy-current losses.

Alternatively, the ignition output stage can be incorporated in the ignition coil instead of in the engine control unit. Interference-suppression elements may also be incorporated in the ignition coil along together with the activation arc diode. An interference-suppression resistor is commonly used on the high-voltage output to the spark plug.

### Operation

The ignition output stage switches the primary current in the ignition coil. The current rises with a delay, in accordance with the inductance. A magnetic field is created in the ignition coil in the process, and energy is stored in the coil. The dwell period is calculated in such a way that a specific cutoff current, and thus a specific level of energy, will be reached by the end of the dwell period.

The current is cut off by the driver stage, which causes voltage induction in the ignition coil. On the primary side, this may be several hundred volts. Due to the large turns ratio between the primary and secondary windings, voltages in the order of 30,000 volts occur on the secondary side.

When the ignition-coil voltage supply equals the voltage demand at the spark-plug electrodes, the voltage drops to a spark voltage of about 1,000 V. A spark current then flows and decreases as spark duration increases, until the spark

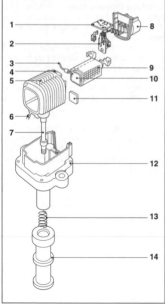

*Design of the compact ignition coil*
*1 Printed-circuit board, 2 Driver stage, 3 Activation arc diode, 4 Secondary winding housing, 5 Secondary winding, 6 Contact plate, 7 High-voltage pin (connection to the contact spring), 8 Primary connector, 9 Primary winding, 10 I-core, 11 Permanent magnet, 12 O-core, 13 Spring (spark-plug contact), 14 Silicone sleeve (high-voltage insulation).*

is finally extinguished. At this point, the energy stored during the charging process has now been fully converted.

As the current changes over time when the primary current is cut off, an induction voltage occurs at the ignition coil output, similar to the start of charging time. However, this voltage is much smaller and its polarity is inverse to that of the voltage at the moment of ignition. To prevent this "transient voltage" causing unwanted ignition, it is usually suppressed by means of a high-voltage diode in the secondary circuit (activation arc diode).

The design of an ignition coil can determine its electrical characteristics. In this respect, the requirements in terms of installation space and the two specified interfaces are decisive, namely:
– The ECU and driver stage (e.g. cutoff current)
– The spark plug or engine (e.g., ignition voltage, spark data)

Design variations
There are several types of ignition coil that are distinguishable by their various features.

In addition to the individual coils, which normally sit directly on the spark plug, several ignition coils can be grouped together in a single housing as a module or rail. They are then mounted directly on the spark plugs, or they may be located a short distance away, in which case the high voltage must be supplied via appropriate cables.

In addition to ignition coils with just one high-voltage output (single-spark ignition coil), there are also coils that use both ends of the secondary winding as an output (dual-spark ignition coil). The electric circuit must always be closed by both spark gaps to prevent discharge on the secondary side. One feasible application for this design is dual ignition, i.e. two spark plugs per cylinder supplied by one ignition coil. Another application involves splitting up the two high-voltage outputs between two spark plugs on different cylinders. In this case, one of the two spark plugs will always be in the ignition stroke. As a result, the voltage and energy requirements of the "passive spark"

(backup spark) are reduced substantially. Above all, this variant offers cost advantages; however, it must be matched to the overall system to prevent damage from unwanted ignition events caused by backup sparks.

Ignition coils are also distinguishable by their basic design. For example, there is the conventional compact ignition coil, that features an equal-sided coil body and an O/I core or C/I core magnetic circuit. The coil body sits in the engine above the spark-plug well.

Another type is the pencil coil whose coil body projects into the spark-plug well. Here, too, the windings are located on an I or pencil core, with a plate (yoke plate) arranged concentrically around the windings serving as a magnetic yoke.

Outlook
Future design challenges for ignition coils will focus on developing even smaller units, while continuing to meet extremely high insulation and temperature requirements. In addition, they will incorporate electronic circuits. The beginnings of this have already been seen with the ignition output stage. The reason for integrating electronics is to take the strain off the ECU and to accommodate New functions, e.g.:
– Protective functions (e.g. overheat cutoff)
– Diagnostic functions (e.g. charging-time checks)
– Ionic-current measurement (combustion diagnosis)
– Multispark ignition (spark control)

### Spark plug

#### Function
The spark plug introduces the ignition energy generated by the ignition coil into the combustion chamber. The high voltage applied creates an electric spark between the spark-plug electrodes, which ignites the compressed A/F mixture. As this function must also be guaranteed under extreme conditions (cold start, wide-open throttle), the spark plug plays a decisive role in the optimized performance and reliable operation of a spark-ignition engine. These requirements remain the same over the entire service life of the spark plug.

#### Requirements
The spark plug must satisfy a variety of extreme performance demands: It is exposed to the varying periodic processes within the combustion chamber, as well as external climatic conditions.

When spark plugs are used with electronic ignition systems, ignition voltages of up to 30,000 V can occur; these high voltages may not cause ceramic or head flashovers. This insulation capability must be maintained for the entire service life and must be guaranteed even at high temperatures (up to approx. 1,000 °C).

Mechanically, the spark plug is subjected to the pressures (up to 100 bar) occurring periodically in the combustion chamber; however, gas tightness may not be impaired. In addition, the spark-plug electrode materials exhibit extreme resistance to thermal loads and continuous vibratory stress. The shell must be able to absorb tightening forces without any lasting deformation.

At the same time, the section of the spark plug that protrudes into the combustion chamber is exposed to high-temperature chemical processes, making resistance to aggressive combustion deposits essential. As it is subjected to rapid variations between the heat of combustion gases and the cool A/F mixture, the spark-plug insulator must feature high resistance to thermal stresses (thermal shock). The electrodes and the insulator at the cylinder head must have good heat dissipation properties – essential for reliable spark-plug performance.

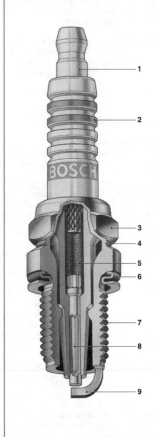

*Spark-plug design*
1 *Terminal stud with terminal nut,*
2 *Al$_2$O$_3$ ceramic insulator,*
3 *Housing,*
4 *Heat-shrinkage zone,*
5 *Conductive glass,*
6 *Captive gasket (seal seat),*
7 *Thread,*
8 *Compound center electrode (Ni/Cu),*
9 *Ground electrode (here Ni/Cu compound electrode).*

## Design

In a special high-grade ceramic insulator, an electrically conductive glass seal forms the connection between the center electrode and terminal stud. This conductive glass seal acts as a mechanical support for the components, while providing a gas seal against the high combustion pressure. It can also incorporate resistor elements for interference suppression and burn-off.

At the connection end, the insulator has a lead-free glaze to repel moisture and dirt. This avoid insulator flashovers to a great extent.

The connection between the insulator and the nickel-plated steel shell must also be gas-tight.

The ground electrode(s), like the center electrode, is (are) usually manufactured from nickel-based alloys to cope with the high thermal stresses, and welded to the shell. Compound electrodes with a jacket material made of a nickel alloy and a copper core are used to improve heat dissipation for both center and ground electrodes. Silver and platinum, or platinum alloys, are employed as electrode material for special applications.

The spark plugs have either an M4 or a standard SAE thread, depending on the type of high-voltage connection. Spark plugs with metal shields are available for watertight systems and for maximum interference suppression.

## Heat range

When the engine is operating, the spark plug is heated by combustion heat. Some of the heat absorbed by the spark plug is diverted to the fresh A/F mixture. Most of the heat is transmitted to the spark-plug shell via the center electrode and the insulator, and is diverted to the cylinder head. The operating temperature represents a balance between heat absorption from the engine and heat dissipation to the cylinder head. The aim is for the insulator nose to reach a self-cleaning temperature of approx. 500 °C even at low engine performance.

If the temperature drops below this level, there is the danger that soot and oil residue from incomplete combustion will settle on the cold areas of the spark plugs (particularly when the engine is not at normal operating temperature, at low outside temperatures and during repeated starts). This can create a conductive connection (shunt) between the center electrodes and the spark-plug shell. This will cause ignition energy to leak away in the form of short-circuit current (risk of misfiring). At higher temperatures, the residue containing carbons burn on the insulator nose; the spark plug thus "cleans" itself.

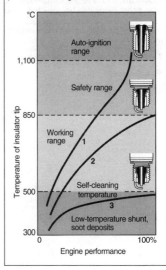

***Spark-plug temperature response***
*1 Spark plug with excessively high heat-range code number (hot spark plug),*
*2 Spark plug with suitable heat-range code number,*
*3 Spark plug with excessively low heat-range code number (cold spark plug).*
*The working range temperature should be from 500 °C to 900 °C for different engine performance ratings.*

An upper temperature limit of approx. 900 °C should be observed since, in this range, spark-plug electrode wear increases drastically (due to oxidation and hot-gas corrosion). If this limit is exceeded by a significant extent, it increases the risk of auto-ignition (ignition of the air/fuel mixture on hot surfaces). Auto-ignition subjects the engine to extreme loads, and may result in engine destruction within a short period of time. The spark plug must therefore be adapted to the engine type in terms of its heat-absorbing property.

The identifying feature of a spark plug's thermal loading capacity is its heat range, which is defined by a code number and determined in comparison measurements with a reference standard source.

The Bosch ionic-current measurement procedure uses combustion characteristics to determine the engine's heat range requirements. The ionizing effect of flames is used to assess how combustion develops over time; this is done by measuring conductivity in the spark gap. Characteristic changes in the combustion process due to increased thermal loading of the spark plugs can be detected using ionic current and used in the assessment of the auto-ignition process. The spark plug must be adapted in such a way as to prevent thermal ignition (particularly pre-ignition) before the actual moment of ignition.

The use of materials with a higher thermal conductivity (silver or nickel alloys with copper core) for center electrodes makes it possible to extend the insulator nose length substantially without changing the heat-range code number. This extends the spark-plug operating range down to a lower thermal-load range and reduces the probability of soot formation. These advantages are inherent in all Bosch Super (thermoelastic) spark plugs.

Reducing the likelihood of combustion misses and misfiring – with their attendant massive increases in hydrocarbon emissions – provides benefits in exhaust emissions and fuel consumption in part-throttle operation at low load factors.

### Electrode gap and ignition voltage

The electrode gap is the shortest gap between center and ground electrodes, and determines, amongst other things, the ignition-spark length. The electrode gap should be, on the one hand, as large as possible so that the ignition spark activates a large volume element, and thus results in reliable ignition of the air/fuel mixture by developing a stable flame core. On the other hand, the smaller the electrode gap, the lower the voltage required to generate a spark. If the electrode gap is too small, however, only a small flame core will be created around the electrode. Energy will be drawn from the flame core via the contact areas with the electrodes (quenching), and the flame core will propagate very slowly. In extreme cases, so much energy may be drawn off that ignition misses will occur.

Although ignition conditions improve as the electrode gap increases (e.g. due to electrode wear), the amount of ignition voltage required will increase. As the ignition coil's voltage supply is a fixed amount, the voltage reserves are reduced and the risk of misfiring increases.

---

*Diagram of the ionic-current measurement procedure*
*1 High voltage from the ignition coil,*
*2 Ionic-current adapter, 2a Trigger diode,*
*3 Spark plug, 4 Ionic-current device,*
*5 Oscilloscope.*

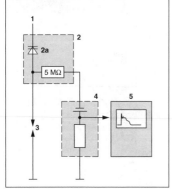

The required ignition voltage is influenced not only by the size of the electrode gap, but also by electrode shape and temperature, and the electrode material. Parameters specific to the combustion chamber, such as mixture composition (lambda value), flow velocity, turbulence, and density of the ignitable gas, also play an important role.

On modern high-compression engines, which frequently feature high charge turbulence, electrode gaps must be carefully defined in order to guarantee reliable ignition, and thus misfire-free operation throughout the required service life.

## Spark position

The position of the spark gap relative to the combustion chamber wall defines the spark position. On modern engines (and particularly with gasoline direct-injection engines), the spark position has a considerable influence on combustion. A perceptible improvement in ignition response is observed when the spark position projects deeper into the combustion chamber. Combustion can be characterized by smooth-running or uneven-running engine performance, either derived directly from engine speed fluctuations, or described indirectly by means of a static analysis of the mean induced pressure.

However, because the ground electrodes are longer, higher temperatures are achieved. This, in turn, has an effect on electrode wear and electrode durability. It is possible to achieve the required service life by implementing design measures (extending the spark-plug shell beyond the combustion chamber wall), or by using compound electrodes, or high temperature-resistant materials.

## Spark-plug concepts

The spark-plug type is determined by the relative location of the electrodes to each other and the position of the ground electrodes with respect to the insulator.

*Spark air gap concepts (a)*
In spark air gap concepts, the ground electrode is positioned with respect to the center electrode in such a way that the ignition spark jumps directly between the electrodes, igniting the air/fuel mixture between the electrodes.

*Surface gap concepts (b)*
As a result of defining the position of the ground electrodes with respect to the ceramic element, the spark first travels from the center electrode over the surface of the insulator nose before arcing across a

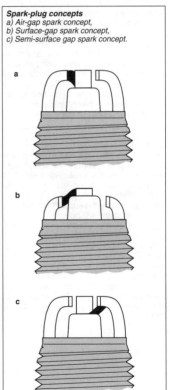

**Spark-plug concepts**
a) Air-gap spark concept,
b) Surface-gap spark concept,
c) Semi-surface gap spark concept.

gas-filled gap to the ground electrode. As less ignition voltage is required for discharging across the surface than for discharging across an air gap of the same size, the surface-gap spark can bridge bigger electrode gaps than the air gap spark given the same ignition voltage. The resulting larger flame core improves ignition properties considerably.

These spark-plug concepts also have much better repeat cold-starting performance because the surface-gap spark cleans the insulator end-face, or prevents soot from settling there.

*Semi-surface gap concepts (c)*
In these spark-plug concepts, the ground electrodes are positioned at a specific distance from the center electrode and the end face of the ceramic insulator. Two alternative spark gaps are created as a result, thus allowing both forms of discharge with different ignition voltage requirements. Depending on operating conditions, the spark behaves either as an air-gap spark or a surface-gap spark.

Spark-plug operating performance
*Changes in operation*
As the spark plug operates in an aggressive atmosphere, sometimes at high temperatures, the electrodes will wear, thus increasing the ignition voltage requirement. When this requirement can no longer be met by the supply from the ignition coil, misfiring will occur.

Dirt and changes in the engine caused by aging (e.g. higher oil consumption) can also affect operation of the spark plug. Deposits on the spark plug can result in shunts, and thus in misfiring,. This, in turn, may cause a considerable rise in pollutant emissions, and even damage the catalytic converter. The spark plugs must therefore be replaced at regular intervals.

*Electrode wear*
Electrode wear is the erosion of electrode material. As a result, the electrode gap grows, the longer the spark plug is in service. There are essentially two mechanisms that are responsible for this:
– Spark erosion
– Corrosion in the combustion chamber

Materials with a high thermal resistance (e.g. platinum and platinum alloys) are used to minimize electrode wear. Material wear can also be reduced for the same period of use, by appropriate selection of electrode geometry and spark-plug concept (surface-gap spark plugs).

The resistor in the conductive glass seal reduces burn-off, and thus helps to reduce wear.

Abnormal operating conditions
Abnormal operating conditions (auto-ignition, combustion knock, etc.) can damage the engine and spark plugs beyond repair.

The engine and the spark plugs my sustain damage due to incorrectly set ignition systems, the use of spark plugs whose heat range is unsuitable for the engine, or the use of unsuitable fuels.

*Auto-ignition*
Auto-ignition is an uncontrolled ignition process where the temperature in one spot in the combustion chamber (e.g. at the spark-plug insulator nose, at the exhaust valve, or at the cylinder-head gaskets) may rise to such an extent that serious damage is caused to the engine and spark plug.

*Combustion knock*
Knock is uncontrolled combustion with a very steep pressure rise (see P. 619). The combustion process is considerably faster than normal combustion. Due to high pressure gradients, the components (cylinder head, valves, pistons, and spark plugs) are subjected to high temperature loads. This may result in damage to one or several of the components (see knock control, P. 621).

### Designation codes for Bosch spark plugs.

*Individual spark-plug specifications are contained in the designation code. This code includes all vital spark-plug characteristics except the electrode gap, which is indicated on the package. Spark-plug specifications for individual engine applications are defined by Bosch and the engine manufacturers.*

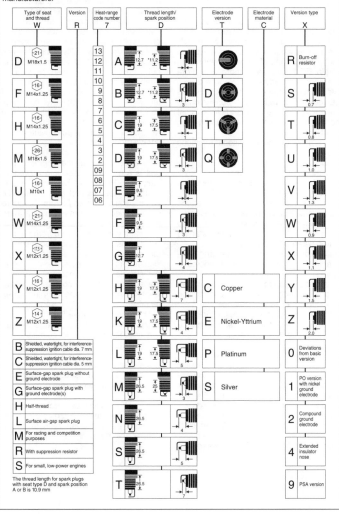

# Motronic engine-management system

## Function

Motronic is the name given to Bosch systems for the open- and closed-loop control of SI engines. Originally, Motronic's function essentially combined electronic fuel injection and electronic ignition in a single ECU. Gradually, more and more functions were added in response to legislative requirements to reduce exhaust-gas emissions, reduce fuel consumption, and meet increased demands in terms of performance, driving comfort, and driving safety.

Examples of these additional functions are:
- Idle-speed control
- Lambda closed-loop control
- Control of the evaporative-emissions control system
- Exhaust-gas recirculation to reduce $NO_x$ emissions and fuel consumption
- Control of the secondary-air system to reduce HC emissions in the starting and warm-up phases
- Control of the turbocharger and variable-tract intake manifold to increase engine performance
- Camshaft control to reduce exhaust-gas emissions and fuel consumption and to increase performance
- Component protection (e.g. knock control, engine-speed limitation, exhaust-gas temperature control)

Another important function of Motronic is the monitoring of the operational ability of the entire system, using On-Board-Diagnosis (OBD). Legal requirements (for diagnostics legislation see P. 584 onwards) have placed extra demands on Motronic, with the result that about half of Motronic system capacity (in terms of computing-power and memory requirements) is dedicated to diagnostics-related tasks.

## System overview

The Motronic system comprises all the sensors for detecting ongoing operating from the engine, vehicle, and all the actuators that perform the required adjustments to the SI engine. The ECU uses data from the sensors to scan the status of the vehicle and engine at very short intervals (every few milliseconds to meet the system's real-time requirements). Input circuits suppress sensor-signal interference and convert the signals to a single uniform voltage scale. An analog/digital converter then transforms the conditioned signals into digital values. Other signals are received via digital interfaces (e.g. CAN bus) or via pulse-width-modulated (PWM) interfaces.

The nerve center of the engine control unit is a microcontroller with a program memory (EPROM or flash), which stores all the process control algorithms – i.e. arithmetical processes performed according to a specific pattern – and data (parameters, characteristics, program maps). The input variables derived from the sensor signals influence the calculations in the algorithms, and thus the triggering signals for the actuators. From these input signals, the microcontroller detects the sort of vehicle response the driver wants and calculates the following, for example:
- The required torque
- The resulting cylinder charge with the associated injected fuel quantity
- The correct ignition timing
- The triggering signals for the actuators, e.g. the evaporative-emissions control system, the exhaust-gas turbocharger, the secondary-air system

The low-level signal data from the microcontroller outputs are adapted by the driver stages to the levels required by the various actuators.

## Versions of Motronic

The Motronic engine-management system has undergone substantial development since its introduction in 1979. In addition to systems with electronic multipoint fuel injection, the following simpler and, at that time, cost-effective systems were also developed to allow Motronic to be used in mid-range and compact vehicles:

- KE-Motronic, based on KE-Jetronic continuous gasoline injection (P. 646)
- Mono-Motronic, based on Mono-Jetronic intermittent single-point injection (P. 642)

Now, only multipoint fuel-injection systems are used for new vehicles. They include:

- M-Motronic for controlling ignition and fuel injection on intake-manifold injection systems (see P. 610) However, this Motronic system is becoming an increasingly less popular choice.
- ME-Motronic electronic throttle control (ETC) for controlling gasoline injection, ignition, <u>and</u> fresh-air charge on intake-manifold injection systems

- DI-Motronic (formerly called MED-Motronic), with additional open- and closed-loop control functions for the high-pressure fuel circuit on gasoline direct-injection systems and to implement the various operating modes of this engine type (P. 612)

### M-Motronic

M-Motronic covers all the components required to control an engine with intake-manifold injection and a conventional throttle valve.

The driver adjusts the air-mass flow, and thus the torque, directly via the accelerator pedal and the throttle valve. At low engine temperatures, for example, or to control idle speed, M-Motronic adapts the air requirements using the bypass air actuator. The M-Motronic then calculates the required fuel mass and the optimum ignition angle for the set operating point from the air-mass flow drawn in, the amount of which is calculated with the aid of load sensors (e.g. air-mass meter, intake-manifold pressure sensor). Optimized engine operation is achieved by activating the injectors and ignition coils at the right time.

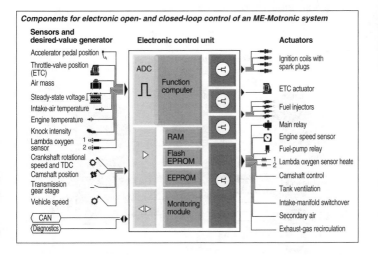

*Components for electronic open- and closed-loop control of an ME-Motronic system*

**Sensors and desired-value generator**
- Accelerator pedal position
- Throttle-valve position (ETC)
- Air mass
- Steady-state voltage
- Intake-air temperature
- Engine temperature
- Knock intensity
- Lambda oxygen sensor 1 / 2
- Crankshaft rotational speed and TDC
- Camshaft position
- Transmission gear stage
- Vehicle speed
- CAN
- Diagnostics

**Electronic control unit**
- ADC
- Function computer
- RAM
- Flash EPROM
- EEPROM
- Monitoring module

**Actuators**
- Ignition coils with spark plugs
- ETC actuator
- Fuel injectors
- Main relay
- Engine speed sensor
- Fuel-pump relay
- Lambda oxygen sensor heater 1 / 2
- Camshaft control
- Tank ventilation
- Intake-manifold switchover
- Secondary air
- Exhaust-gas recirculation

## ME-Motronic

The ME-Motronic comprises all the components required to control an engine with intake-manifold injection and electrically adjustable throttle valve (ETC, electronic throttle control) (see system diagram). It is based on the M-Motronic. The main difference between the two systems is that, on ME-Motronic, the throttle valve is activated electrically, and there is no bypass air actuator.

### Setting the torque

To set the operating status required by the driver, the accelerator pedal position, detected by the pedal-travel sensor, is converted into an engine torque setpoint value by the microcontroller. Taking into consideration the mass of real-time operating data available to the ME-Motronic, the setpoint value is converted into the variables that determine engine torque:
– Charging the cylinders with fresh air
– The mass of the injected fuel
– The ignition angle

These variables are set by means of:
– The electrically activated throttle valve (ETC)
– The fuel-injection system (correctly timed injector activation)
– The ignition system (correctly timed ignition coil activation)

### Torque guidance

The ME-Motronic saw the introduction of torque structure. The aim of torque guidance is to sort the many, sometimes very different, functions that require a torque.

Most additional open- and closed-loop control functions also affect engine torque (e.g. transmission-shift control, ASR or ESP, idle-speed control, catalytic converter heating). Each of these functions requires a separate engine torque. In a torque-guided control system, these functions are prioritized with the driver command. The torque-guided ME-Motronic uses torque coordination to sort often contradictory torque requirements, and then to implement the most important requirement.

### Exhaust-gas treatment and catalytic-converter control

Voltage-jump sensors (2-point sensors), and optionally continuous broadband O sensors, are used upstream of the three-way catalytic converter to control the air/fuel mixture. The sensors downstream of the catalytic converter are always voltage-jump sensors (see Lambda closed-loop control, P. 665 onwards).

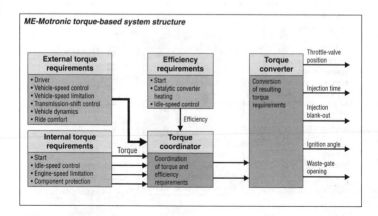

**ME-Motronic torque-based system structure**

| External torque requirements |
|---|
| • Driver |
| • Vehicle-speed control |
| • Vehicle-speed limitation |
| • Transmission-shift control |
| • Vehicle dynamics |
| • Ride comfort |

| Efficiency requirements |
|---|
| • Start |
| • Catalytic converter heating |
| • Idle-speed control |

*Efficiency*

| Internal torque requirements |
|---|
| • Start |
| • Idle-speed control |
| • Engine-speed limitation |
| • Component protection |

*Torque*

| Torque coordinator |
|---|
| Coordination of torque and efficiency requirements |

| Torque converter |
|---|
| Conversion of resulting torque requirements |

Throttle-valve position

Injection time

Injection blank-out

Ignition angle

Waste-gate opening

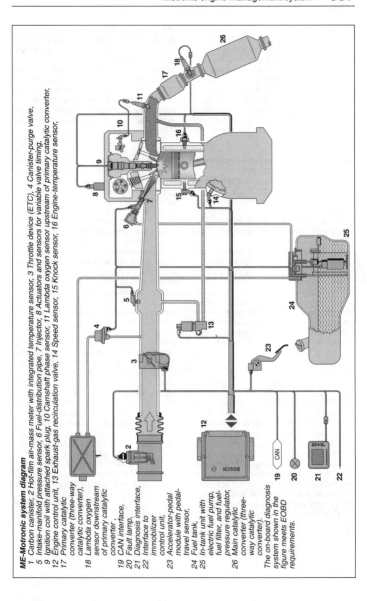

**ME-Motronic system diagram**

1 Carbon canister, 2 Hot-film air-mass meter with integrated temperature sensor, 3 Throttle device (ETC), 4 Canister-purge valve, 5 Intake-manifold pressure sensor, 6 Fuel-distribution pipe, 7 Injector, 8 Actuators and sensors for variable valve timing, 9 Ignition coil with attached spark plug, 10 Camshaft phase sensor, 11 Lambda oxygen sensor upstream of primary catalytic converter, 12 Engine control unit, 13 Exhaust-gas recirculation valve, 14 Speed sensor, 15 Knock sensor, 16 Engine-temperature sensor, 17 Primary catalytic converter (three-way catalytic converter), 18 Lambda oxygen sensor downstream of primary catalytic converter, 19 CAN interface, 20 Fault lamp, 21 Diagnosis interface, 22 Interface to immobilizer control unit, 23 Accelerator-pedal module with pedal-travel sensor, 24 Fuel tank, 25 In-tank unit with electric fuel pump, fuel filter, and fuel-pressure regulator, 26 Main catalytic converter (three-way catalytic converter).

The on-board diagnosis system shown in the figure meets EOBD requirements.

**DI-Motronic**

The DI-Motronic (Direct Injection) comprises all the components required to control an engine with gasoline direct injection (see P. 612) and electrically adjustable throttle valve (ETC, electronic throttle control) (see system diagram). It is based on the ME-Motronic. The main difference between these two systems is that DI-Motronic has an additional high-pressure circuit for the fuel system.

Requirements

The DI-Motronic engine-management system is essentially required to:
- Set the necessary cylinder charge for the required engine torque (ETC).
- Generate the necessary injection pressure.
- Define the correct start of injection.
- Precisely meter the required fuel quantity.
- Introduce the fuel directly and precisely into the engine combustion chambers.
- Set the ignition angle calculated for the purpose.

It must also coordinate the various torque demands on the engine in order then to make the required adjustments on the engine. This is the task of torque guidance, already familiar from the ME-Motronic.

Fuel system

As with intake-manifold injection, the high-pressure direct-injection system is designed as an accumulator injection system. The pressurized fuel stored in the accumulator (rail) can therefore be injected directly into the cylinder at any time via the electromagnetic high-pressure injectors. The DI-Motronic sets the rail pressure as a function of the operating point.

Compared with the basic ME-Motronic ECU, the gasoline direct-injection variant also features a driver stage for activating the pressure-control valve and the delivery-quantity control valve incorporated in the ECU (see P. 602), and special driver stages for the high-pressure injectors.

Operating modes

A complex engine-management system is required for the gasoline direct-injection system to be exploited to the full in terms of low fuel consumption and high engine power output. Although it is only possible to operate the engine with homogeneous mixture distribution on systems with intake-manifold injection, gasoline direct injection can run on other operating modes besides homogeneous operation.

At lower engine speed and torque range, the engine runs with a heavily stratified cylinder charge and a high level of excess air in order to achieve the lowest possible fuel consumption (stratified-charge operation). The ideal state is to achieve two zones in the combustion chamber by retarding fuel injection just before the moment of ignition. In one zone, the combustible air/fuel mixture cloud is situated at the spark plug, and an insulating layer of air and residual exhaust gas is embedded in a second zone. A turbulence flap assists A/F mixture formation. In this way, the engine can run to a large degree without throttling losses. In addition, thermodynamic efficiency increases by avoiding heat losses at the combustion-chamber walls.

As engine torque and also injected fuel quantity increase, the stratified charge cloud becomes increasingly richer. This would result in a deterioration in exhaust emissions, particularly with regard to soot. Therefore, the engine is operated with a homogeneous cylinder charge in this higher torque range (homogeneous operation). Fuel is injected during the intake stroke in order to ensure that fuel and air are thoroughly mixed. This operating mode must also be used at high engine speeds ($>3,000$ rpm), as it is no longer possible to maintain charge stratification and the proper conveyance of the A/F mixture to the spark plug. This is because turbulence is too high and there is not enough time to inject the required quantity of fuel.

**DI-Motronic system diagram.**

1 Carbon canister, 2 Canister-purge valve, 3 High-pressure pump (HDP2) with integrated delivery-quantity control valve, 4 Actuators and sensors for variable valve timing, 5 Ignition coil with attached spark plug, 6 Hot-film air-mass meter with integrated temperature sensor, 7 Throttle device (electronic throttle control (ETC) with position sensor), 8 Intake-manifold pressure sensor, 9 Fuel-pressure sensor, 10 High-pressure fuel rail (fuel-distribution pipe), 11 Camshaft phase sensor, 12 Lambda oxygen sensor upstream of primary catalytic converter, 13 Exhaust-gas recirculation valve, 14 High-pressure injector, 15 Knock sensor, 16 Engine-temperature sensor, 17 Primary catalytic converter (three-way catalytic converter),

18 Lambda oxygen sensor upstream of primary catalytic converter (optional),
19 Engine-speed sensor,
20 Engine control unit,
21 CAN interface,
22 Fault lamp,
23 Diagnosis interface,
24 Interface to immobilizer control unit,
25 Accelerator-pedal module with pedal-travel sensor,
26 Fuel tank,
27 In-tank unit with electric fuel pump, fuel filter, and fuel-pressure regulator,
28 Exhaust-gas temperature sensor,
29 Main catalytic converter (NO$_x$ accumulator-type catalytic converter plus three-way catalytic converter),
30 Lambda oxygen sensor downstream of main catalytic converter.

In the transitional zone between stratified and homogeneous operation, the engine can be operated with a homogeneous lean mixture ($\lambda > 1$). In this homogeneous lean-burn operation, the fuel consumption is lower than in homogeneous operation, as throttling losses are fewer.

In homogeneous-stratified operation, the entire combustion chamber is filled with a homogeneous lean basic mixture. This A/F mixture is obtained by injecting a small amount of fuel in the induction stroke. A second injection operation in the compression cycle generates a richer zone in the area around the spark plug. This stratified charge is easily ignited, and the flame can then ignite the homogeneous lean mixture in the rest of the combustion chamber. This operating mode is activated for some cycles in the transition between stratified and homogeneous operation. As a result, the engine-management system is able to adjust torque better during the transition.

Homogeneous knock protection operation prevents engine knock at wide-open throttle by means of charge stratification. This means there is no need to retard the ignition – the usual practice on intake-manifold injection systems. Engine efficiency and torque are improved.

Another form of double fuel injection, stratified catalytic-converter heating, allows the catalytic converter to heat up quickly. Retarded fuel injection in the compression cycle heats up the exhaust gas.

In the event of a changeover between homogeneous and stratified-charge operation, it is crucial to control injected fuel quantity, air charge, and ignition angle in such a way that the torque delivered to the transmission by the engine remains constant. Torque structure means that, here too, the main functions for controlling the electronic throttle valve have been transferred directly from the ME-Motronic and enhanced. The throttle valve must be closed before the actual transition from stratified-charge to homogeneous operation.

Operating-mode coordination

DI-Motronic can inject fuel as required to set the desired operating mode. The functions serving as input variables for operating-mode coordination include, e.g.:
– Component protection
– Catalytic converter heating
– $NO_x$ and $SO_x$ regeneration of the accumulator-type catalytic converter
– Start and warm-up
– Operating mode map (engine speed/torque range)

The operating-mode coordinator in DI-Motronic evaluates any deviating operating-mode requirements using a priority list, and calculates the desired operating mode. However, before making the switch to the new operating mode for fuel injection and ignition, the control functions for exhaust-gas recirculation, tank ventilation, turbulence flap, and throttle valve setting are requested if necessary, and the system then waits for acknowledgment from these functions.

Exhaust-gas system

An important consideration with gasoline direct injection is that, in stratified-charge operation, the high $NO_x$ content in the very lean exhaust gas cannot be reduced by a three-way catalytic converter. Exhaust-gas recirculation with a high exhaust-gas recirculation rate helps to reduce the $NO_x$ content in the exhaust gas significantly. To meet emission-control legislation, treatment of $NO_x$ emissions with a $NO_x$ accumulator-type catalytic converter is vital (see P. 663).

A mixture check is performed by universal lambda oxygen sensors, LSF (voltage jump) and LSU (broadband), in the exhaust-gas flow upstream and downstream of the catalytic converter. They help to control $\lambda = 1$ operation, lean-burn operation, and – if no $NO_x$ sensor is present – they are also responsible for precise control of $NO_x$ regeneration in the catalytic converter. It is important to set the exhaust-gas recirculation rate exactly, particularly in dynamic operation.

## Motronic system structure

The Motronic system can be divided into various subsystems. In addition to the main functions (software), some of these subsystems contain hardware components (e.g. throttle device, injectors, lambda oxygen sensors).

The <u>torque demand</u> subsystem detects all torque requirements (e.g. driver command, air-conditioner requirements, vehicle-speed controller).

The <u>torque structure</u> subsystem coordinates all the torque requirements and converts them into a setpoint torque value. The setpoint torque is divided up into portions for the air, fuel, and ignition systems.

The <u>air system</u> contains the throttle device (on ETC systems), sensors to detect the charge, and equipment for valve timing, intake-manifold control, exhaust-gas recirculation, and supercharging.

The <u>fuel system</u> contains the components for the fuel supply and delivery system (e.g. fuel pump) and for fuel injection (injectors).

The <u>ignition system</u> contains the ignition coils, spark plugs, and knock sensors.

The lambda oxygen sensors, the catalytic converters, and, optionally, the exhaust-gas temperature sensor are part of the <u>exhaust system</u>.

The <u>operating data</u> subsystem uses sensors to detect all the operating parameters essential for engine operation.

<u>Accessory control</u> contains components such as the engine fan or air-conditioner compressor.

The <u>communication</u> subsystem provides a connection to other systems in the vehicle (e.g. transmission ECU) via the CAN bus, communicates with the immobilizer ECU, and provides the connection to the diagnostic testers for reading out the OBD fault storage (see P. 584).

The <u>monitoring</u> system monitors all Motronic elements that determine torque and engine speed, thus preventing impermissible engine operating statuses.

The <u>diagnostic system</u> is responsible for coordinating component and system diagnoses, which are carried out in the main functions of the subsystems.

The main functions communicate via specific interfaces. This ensures that a Motronic system can be developed using modular design. To a large extent, each main function can be developed independently of the entire system, although external interfaces must be taken into consideration.

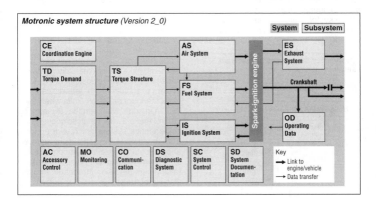

*Motronic system structure* (Version 2_0)

# History of fuel-injection systems

## Overview

Single-point injection is an electronically controlled fuel-injection system in which an electromagnetic fuel injector injects fuel intermittently into the intake manifold at a central point upstream of the throttle valve. They differ from multipoint injection systems in that most systems operate at low pressure (0.7...1 bar). This allows the use of an inexpensive, hydrodynamic electric fuel pump, generally in the form of an in-tank pump. The injector is flushed continuously by fuel flowing through it in order to inhibit the formation of vapor bubbles. This arrangement is an absolute necessity in such a low-pressure system.

The designation "Single-Point Injection (SPI)" corresponds to the terms Central Fuel Injection (CFI), Throttle Body Injection (TBI) and Mono-Jetronic (Bosch).

Multipoint injection creates the ideal conditions to satisfy the demands placed on an A/F mixture-formation system. In multipoint injection systems, each cylinder is assigned a fuel injector, which injects fuel directly upstream of the cylinder intake valve. A distinction is made between mechanical, mechanical-electronic, and electronic fuel-injection systems. The difference between them is the way in which the fuel quantity is calculated or metered. These systems are called K-Jetronic, KE-Jetronic, and L-Jetronic (and variants thereof).

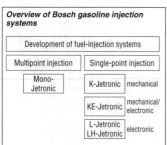

***Overview of Bosch gasoline injection systems***

| Development of fuel-injection systems | | |
|---|---|---|
| Multipoint injection | Single-point injection | |
| Mono-Jetronic | K-Jetronic | mechanical |
| | KE-Jetronic | mechanical/electronic |
| | L-Jetronic LH-Jetronic | electronic |

## Mono-Jetronic

Mono-Jetronic is an electronically controlled, low-pressure single-point injection system for 4-cylinder engines, and features a centrally located solenoid-controlled fuel injector. At the heart of the system is the central injection unit, which uses the throttle valve to meter the intake air while injecting the fuel intermittently above the throttle valve. The intake manifold then distributes the fuel to the individual cylinders. Various sensors monitor all important engine operating data, which are then are used to calculate the triggering signals for the injectors and other system actuators.

### Central injection unit

The injector is located above the throttle valve in the intake-air path in order to ensure homogeneous mixture formation and consistent mixture distribution. The fuel jet is shaped so that the fuel is directed into the sickle-shaped orifice between the housing and throttle valve, avoiding fuel condensation on the manifold walls to a great extent. There, the high pressure differential promotes optimized mixture formation. The injector operates at a primary pressure of 1 bar (referred to atmospheric pressure). Efficient fuel atomization ensures consistently good mixture distribution, even in the critical wide-open throttle range. Injector triggering is synchronized with the ignition pulses.

### System control

In addition to the engine speed $n$, the main actuating variables for the fuel-injection system can include the air flow rate/air mass, the absolute manifold pressure, and the throttle-valve position $\alpha$. The ($\alpha/n$) system used with Mono-Jetronic can also meet stringent emission limits when used in conjunction with lambda closed-loop control and a 3-way catalytic converter. A self-adaptive system employs the signal from the lambda oxygen sensor as reference to compensate for component tolerances and engine changes, thus maintaining high precision throughout the service life of the system.

**Schematic of a Mono-Jetronic system**
*1 Fuel tank, 2 Electric fuel pump, 3 Fuel filter, 4 Pressure regulator, 5 Injector, 6 Air-temperature sensor, 7 ECU, 8 Throttle-valve actuator, 9 Throttle-valve potentiometer, 10 Canister-purge valve, 11 Carbon canister, 12 Lambda oxygen sensor, 13 Engine-temperature sensor, 14 Ignition distributor, 15 Battery, 16 Ignition switch, 17 Relay, 18 Diagnosis connection, 19 Central injection unit.*

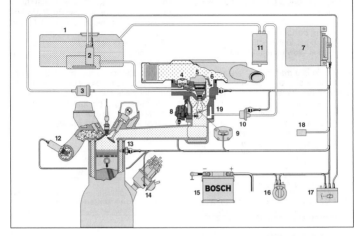

## Adaptation functions

The injection time is extended to provide additional fuel for cold starts, and during post-start and warm-up phases. When the engine is cold, the throttle-valve actuator adjusts the throttle valve to supply more air to the engine, thus maintaining idle speed and exhaust emission rates at a constant level. The throttle-valve potentiometer recognizes the change in throttle-valve position, and initiates an increase in fuel quantity in the ECU. The system regulates enrichment quantity for acceleration and wide-open throttle in the same way. The overrun fuel cutoff provides reductions in fuel consumption and in exhaust emissions during overrun operation. Adaptive idle-speed control lowers the idle speed and stabilizes it. For this purpose, the ECU issues a signal to the servomotor to adapt the throttle-valve position as a function of engine speed and temperature.

**Mono-Jetronic central injection unit**
*1 Pressure regulator, 2 Air-temperature sensor, 3 Injector, 4 Upper part (hydraulics), 5 Fuel inlet, 6 Fuel return, 7 Insulator plate, 8 Throttle valve, 9 Lower part.*

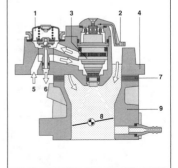

## K-Jetronic

The K-Jetronic system operates without a drive and injects fuel continuously. The injected fuel mass is not determined by the fuel injector, but is preset by the fuel distributor.

### Operating concept
– Continuous fuel injection
– Direct air-flow measurement

K-Jetronic is a mechanical system which does not require an engine-driven fuel-injection pump. It meters a continuous supply of fuel proportional to the air flow rate in the engine intake duct.

Owing to direct air-flow measurement, K-Jetronic also takes into account changes caused by the engine, and permits the use of emission-control equipment, for which precise intake-air monitoring is an essential requirement.

### Operating concept
The intake air flows through the air filter, the air-flow sensor, and the throttle valve, before entering the intake manifold and continuing to the individual cylinders.

The fuel is delivered from the fuel tank by an electric (roller-cell) fuel pump. It then flows through the fuel accumulator and fuel filter to the fuel distributor. A primary-pressure regulator in the fuel distributor maintains the fuel at a constant primary pressure. The fuel flows from the fuel distributor to the injectors. Excess fuel not required by the engine is returned to the fuel tank.

*Schematic of a K-Jetronic system*
*1 Fuel tank, 2 Electric fuel pump, 3 Fuel accumulator, 4 Fuel filter, 5 Warm-up regulator, 6 Injector, 7 Intake manifold, 8 Electric cold-start valve, 9 Fuel distributor, 10 Air-flow sensor, 11 Pulse valve, 12 Lambda oxygen sensor, 13 Thermo-time switch, 14 Ignition distributor, 15 Auxiliary-air valve, 16 Throttle-valve switch, 17 ECU, 18 Ignition switch, 19 Battery.*

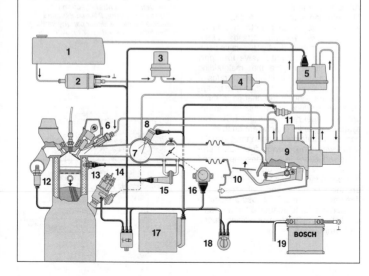

## Components
### Mixture-control unit
The mixture-control unit consists of the air-flow sensor and the fuel distributor.

### Air-flow sensor
The air-flow sensor consists of an air funnel and a pivoting air-flow sensor plate. A counterweight compensates for the weight of the sensor plate and pivot assembly. The sensor plate is displaced by the air flow, while the control plunger in the fuel distributor exerts hydraulic counterpressure to maintain the system in a balanced state. The position of the air-flow sensor plate provides an index of intake air flow rate, and is transmitted to the fuel-distributor control plunger by a lever.

### Fuel distributor
Fuel metering to the individual cylinders is regulated by varying the aperture of the fuel-metering slits in the fuel distributor. The number of rectangular-shaped metering slits in the barrel corresponds to the

number of engine cylinders. The specific size of the fuel-metering slit aperture depends on the control-plunger position. In order to ensure a constant pressure drop across the slits for various flow rates, a differential-pressure valve is located downstream of each fuel-metering slit.

### Fuel Injector
The injector opens automatically at a gage pressure of approximately 3.8 bar, and has no metering function. It provides efficient mixture formation by opening and closing at a frequency of approx. 1,500 Hz ("chatter").

It is held in place by a rubber molding. It is pressed, not screwed, into position. The hexagon serves to brace the injector when the fuel-supply line is screwed on.

### Warm-up regulator
The warm-up regulator is controlled by an electrically heated bimetallic element; it enriches the A/F mixture in the warm-up phase by reducing the backpressure (control pressure) exerted against the control plunger. A reduction in this control pressure means that the stroke of the air-flow sensor plate for a given air flow rate increases (reflected by a correspondingly larger metering-slit aperture). The result is a richer mixture during warm-up.

Where desired, the warm-up regulator can be expanded to incorporate the following functions:
– Full-load enrichment
– Acceleration enrichment
– Altitude compensation

### Auxiliary-air valve
The auxiliary-air valve, controlled by either a bimetallic spring or an expansion element, supplies the engine with additional air (metered by the air-flow sensor, but bypassing the throttle valve) during the warm-up phase. This additional air compensates for the higher friction losses in the cold engine; it either maintains the idle speed constant, or increases it in order to heat the engine and exhaust gas more quickly.

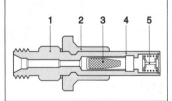

***Fuel injector***
1 Hexagon, 2 Rubber molding, 3 Fine-mesh strainer, 4 Valve body, 5 Valve needle.

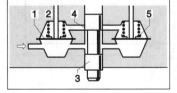

***Fuel distributor in mixture-control unit***
1 Diaphragm, 2 To injector, 3 Control plunger, 4 Fuel-metering slit, 5 Differential-pressure valve.

Electric cold-start valve,
Thermo-time switch

The thermo-time switch activates the electric cold-start valve as a function of engine temperature and elapsed time. During low-temperature starts, the cold-start valve injects additional fuel into the intake manifold (cold-start enrichment).

**Lambda closed-loop control**

Open-loop control systems do not regulate the air/fuel ratio with enough accuracy to allow compliance with emission limits.

Lambda closed-loop control is required to operate the 3-way catalytic converter. When it is installed, the K-Jetronic system must include an electronic control unit which uses the lambda oxygen sensor's signal as its main input variable.

A solenoid pulse valve regulates the A/F ratio by controlling the differential pressure across the metering slots. This principle can no longer be used to meet today's more stringent emission limits.

## KE-Jetronic

KE-Jetronic is based on the basic mechanical system of K-Jetronic. Due to the extended operating-data acquisition, this system permits additional electronic control functions in order to adapt the injected fuel quantity more exactly to the various engine operating states. KE-Jetronic is therefore an advanced version of the K-Jetronic system. KE-Jetronic includes an ECU for increased flexibility and additional functions. Additional components include:

- a sensor for the intake air flow rate
- a pressure actuator to adjust the mixture composition
- a pressure regulator to maintain primary pressure at a constant level and provide a fuel-cutoff function when the engine is switched off

**Operating concept**

An electric fuel pump generates the primary pressure. Fuel flows through the fuel distributor, while a diaphragm governor maintains the primary pressure at a

---

*Schematic of a KE-Jetronic system*
*1 Fuel tank, 2 Electric fuel pump, 3 Fuel accumulator, 4 Fuel filter, 5 Fuel-pressure regulator,*
*6 Injector, 7 Intake manifold, 8 Electric cold-start valve, 9 Fuel distributor, 10 Air-flow sensor,*
*11 Electrohydraulic pressure actuator, 12 Lambda oxygen sensor, 13 Thermo-time switch,*
*14 Engine-temperature sensor, 15 Ignition distributor, 16 Auxiliary-air valve,*
*17 Throttle-valve switch, 18 ECU, 19 Ignition switch, 20 Battery.*

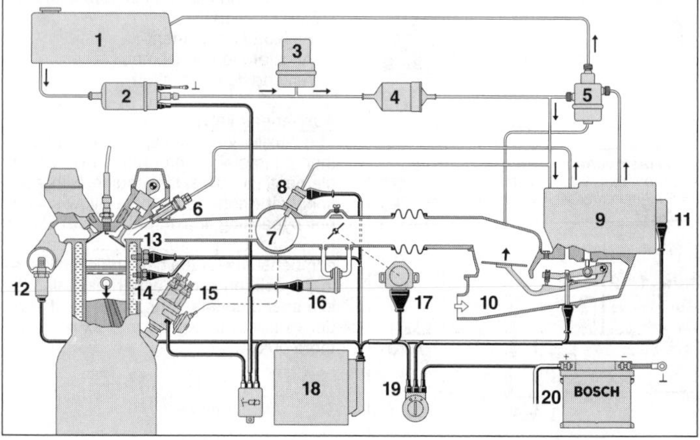

constant level. With K-Jetronic, the control circuit performs mixture adaptation via the warm-up regulator. In contrast, the primary pressure and the pressure exerted on the control plunger in the KE-Jetronic are equal. The A/F mixture is adapted by adjusting the pressure differential in all fuel-distributor chambers simultaneously.

The primary pressure is present upstream of the fuel-metering slits in the fuel distributor, and applies a backpressure to the control plunger. As with K-Jetronic, the control plunger is moved by an air-flow sensor plate. A damping throttle prevents vibrations that could be induced by forces generated at the sensor plate. From the control plunger, the fuel flows through the pressure actuator, the lower chambers of the differential-pressure valve, a fixed flow restrictor, and the pressure regulator, before returning to the fuel tank. Together with the flow restrictor, the actuator forms a pressure divider in which the pressure can be adjusted electrodynamically. This pressure is present in the lower chambers of the differential-pressure valves.

A pressure drop corresponding to the actuator current occurs between the two connections of the actuator. This causes variations in differential pressure at the fuel-metering slits, and alters the amount of fuel injected. The current can also be reversed to shut down the fuel supply completely. This feature can be employed for such functions as overrun fuel cutoff and engine-speed limitation.

## Components

### Electrohydraulic pressure actuator
This electrohydraulic actuator is flange-mounted on the fuel distributor. It is an electrically controlled pressure regulator which operates using the nozzle/baffle-plate system. Mixture enrichment is directly proportional to current flow.

### Electronic control unit (ECU)
The ECU processes signals from the ignition (engine speed), temperature sensor (engine temperature), throttle-valve potentiometer (intake air flow rate), throttle-valve switch (idle and overrun, WOT), starter switch, lambda oxygen sensor, pressure sensor, and other sensors. Its most important functions are the control of:
– Start and post-start enrichment
– Warm-up enrichment
– Acceleration enrichment
– Full-load enrichment
– Overrun fuel cutoff
– Engine-speed limitation
– Idle-speed control
– Altitude compensation
– Lambda closed-loop control

A coding switch (trim plug) makes it possible to select between operation with lambda closed-loop control (with catalytic converter) and without it.

### Lambda closed-loop control
The signal from the lambda oxygen sensor is processed in the KE-Jetronic ECU. The pressure actuator carries out the necessary adjustments.

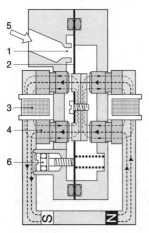

*Electrohydraulic pressure actuator*
*1 Nozzle, 2 Valve plate, 3 Coil, 4 Magnetic pole, 5 Fuel inlet, 6 Adjusting screw.*

## L-Jetronic

Electronic-control fuel-injection systems inject fuel intermittently with electromagnetically actuated fuel injectors. The injected fuel mass is determined by the injector opening time (for a given pressure drop across the injector).

### Operating concept
– Air-flow measurement
– Main controlled variables: air flow rate and engine speed
– Intermittent fuel injection

L-Jetronic combines the advantages of direct air-flow measurement with the unique possibilities afforded by electronics. It is similar to K-Jetronic in that it recognizes all changes in engine condition (due to wear, combustion-chamber deposits, changes in valve setting). This ensures consistently good exhaust-gas composition.

L3-Jetronic incorporates functions extending beyond those provided by L-Jetronic analog technology. Contrary to the L-Jetronic, the L3 system ECU employs digital technology to adjust the A/F ratio based on a load/engine-speed program map. The ECU is installed in the engine compartment, directly on the air-flow sensor, where the two components form a single measuring and control unit.

### Operating concept
Fuel is injected through the engine solenoid-operated injectors. A solenoid valve assigned to each cylinder is triggered once per crankshaft revolution. All the injectors are wired in parallel to reduce the complexity of the electrical circuit. The differential pressure between fuel and intake-manifold pressures is maintained at a constant level of 2.5 or 3 bar so that the injected fuel quantity is only dependent on the opening time of the valves. For this purpose, the ECU delivers control pulses whose duration is dependent on the intake air flow rate, the engine speed, and other influencing variables. These are monitored by sensors and processed in the ECU.

---

*Schematic of an L-Jetronic system*
1 Fuel tank, 2 Electric fuel pump, 3 Fuel filter, 4 ECU, 5 Injector, 6 Fuel-pressure regulator,
7 Intake manifold, 8 Electric cold-start valve, 9 Throttle-valve switch, 10 Air-flow sensor,
11 Lambda oxygen sensor, 12 Thermo-time switch, 13 Engine-temperature sensor,
14 Ignition distributor, 15 Auxiliary-air valve, 16 Battery, 17 Ignition switch.

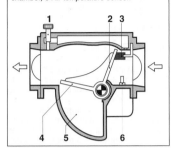

***Air-flow sensor***
*1 Idle-mixture adjustment screw, 2 Sensor flap, 3 Stop, 4 Compensation flap, 5 Damping chamber, 6 Air-temperature sensor.*

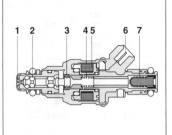

***Fuel injector***
*1 Pintle, 2 Valve needle, 3 Armature, 4 Spring, 5 Solenoid winding, 6 Electrical terminals, 7 Fuel strainer.*

## Fuel supply
An electric fuel pump supplies the fuel and generates the injection pressure. L-Jetronic primarily uses standard systems with fuel return, though returnless fuel supply systems have also been used (see P. 596).

## Components
### Air-flow sensor
The intake air flow deflects a sensor plate against the constant return force of a spring to a specific angular position, which is converted by a potentiometer into an electrical voltage ratio. This voltage ratio determines the switching time of a timing element in the ECU. A temperature sensor in the air-flow sensor indicates changes in air density caused by temperature variations.

### Fuel injectors
Fuel injectors serve to meter and atomize the fuel. When the solenoid winding is energized, the nozzle needle is lifted by a mere 0.05 mm from its seat.

### Throttle-valve switch
This transmits a control signal to the ECU when the throttle valve is either completely closed (idle) or fully opened (WOT).

### Engine-temperature sensor
The engine-temperature sensor is designed as a temperature-sensitive resistor (thermistor) and controls warm-up enrichment.

### Auxiliary-air valve, electric start-valve, thermo-time switch
Design and function are similar to those of the corresponding K-Jetronic components.

### Electronic control unit (ECU)
This ECU converts the engine influencing variables into electrical pulses. The point of application for these pulses is correlated with the moment of ignition, while their duration is basically a function of engine speed and intake air flow rate. Since all injectors are activated simultaneously, only a single driver stage is required. The temperature sensors respond to lower engine and air temperatures by increasing the injection time. The throttle-valve switch signals allow mixture adaptation for idle and wide-open throttle.

## Lambda closed-loop control
The ECU compares the signal from the lambda oxygen sensor with a setpoint value before activating a two-state controller. The control adjustment is then performed, as are all corrections, by modifying the injector opening time.

## LH-Jetronic

LH-Jetronic is closely related to L-Jetronic.
The difference lies in the method of intake
air-flow measurement, where LH-Jetronic
uses a hot-wire air-mass meter to measure the mass of the intake air. It measures
the air mass drawn in by the engine. Thus,
the results no longer depend on air density, which varies with temperature and
pressure.

The other LH-Jetronic components and
the basic system concept are the same as
those in L-Jetronic to a large extent.

### Operating-data processing in the ECU

LH-Jetronic is equipped with a digital
ECU and, in contrast to the L-Jetronic,
uses a load/engine-speed program map
to adjust the air/fuel ratio. It is programmed for minimum fuel consumption
and low exhaust-gas emissions. The ECU
processes the sensor signals when calculating the injection time that determines
the injected fuel quantity. The ECU includes a microcomputer, a program, a
data memory, and an A/D converter. The
microcomputer is provided with a suitable
power supply and with a stable clock rate
for data processing. The clock rate is supplied by a quartz oscillator.

### Air-mass meter

Hot-wire air-mass flow meter

The stream of intake air is conducted past
a heated wire (hot wire). The wire forms
part of an electrical bridge circuit. The
flow of current through the wire helps to
maintain it at a constant temperature
above that of the intake air. This principle
makes it possible to employ the current
requirement as a factor of the air mass
drawn into the engine. A resistor converts
the heating current into a voltage signal,
which the ECU then processes along with
engine speed as a main input variable. A
temperature sensor is mounted in the hot-
wire air-mass flow meter to ensure that its
output signal is not influenced by the temperature of the intake air. The A/F ratio at
idle can be adjusted with a potentiometer.
As contamination on the surface of the

*Schematic of an LH-Jetronic system*
*1 Fuel tank, 2 Electric fuel pump, 3 Fuel filter, 4 ECU, 5 Injector, 6 Fuel rail, 7 Fuel-pressure
regulator, 8 Intake manifold, 9 Throttle-valve switch, 10 Hot-wire air-mass flow meter,
11 Lambda oxygen sensor, 12 Engine-temperature sensor, 13 Ignition distributor,
14 Rotary idle actuator, 15 Battery, 16 Ignition switch.*

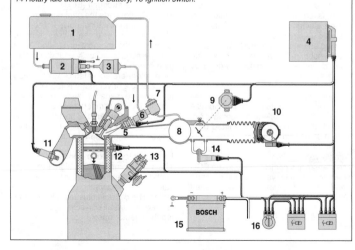

hot wire could affect the output signal, the wire is electrically heated for one second to burn off any contamination each time the engine is shut down. The hot-wire air-mass flow meter has no moving parts, and its flow resistance within the intake port is negligible.

## Hot-film air-mass flow meter

The operating principle of the hot-film air-mass flow meter is the same as that of the hot-wire sensor. However, in the interests of simplified design, a substantial portion of the electrical bridge circuit is installed on a ceramic substrate, in the form of thin-film resistors. In addition, there is no need to burn contaminants from the air-mass flow meter. The contamination problem is solved by placing the sensor-element areas that are decisive for thermal transmission at a position further downstream. This prevents them from the inevitable deposit accumulation on the sensor-element leading edge.

## Kármán vortex volumetric flow meter

Yet another option for measuring intake air is provided by a sensor which uses the Kármán vortex principle to measure the volumetric flow rate. This meter monitors vortices generated as the intake air flows past vortex generators. The frequency of these vortices is a measure of the volumetric flow rate. This frequency is measured by emitting ultrasonic waves perpendicular to the direction of the intake-air flow. The propagation velocity of these waves as modified by the vortices is detected by an ultrasonic receiver and the resulting signals are evaluated in the ECU.

**Hot-film air-mass flow meter**
*a Housing, b Hot-film sensor*
*(installed in center of housing).*
*1 Heat sink, 2 Spacer, 3 Driver stage,*
*4 Hybrid, 5 Sensor element (metallic film).*

a

b

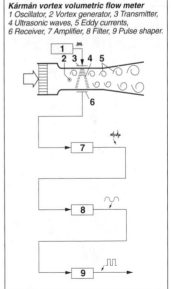

**Kármán vortex volumetric flow meter**
*1 Oscillator, 2 Vortex generator, 3 Transmitter,*
*4 Ultrasonic waves, 5 Eddy currents,*
*6 Receiver, 7 Amplifier, 8 Filter, 9 Pulse shaper.*

# History of coil-ignition systems

The purely mechanical functions of ignition systems, such as ignition triggering, spark retard, and ignition distribution have been replaced by electrical and electronic functions over the course of development. However, the principle of high-voltage generation by means of an ignition coil has been retained on modern-day systems. An overview is given in the following table.

***Overview of the various coil-ignition systems***

| Inductive ignition systems | Control coil current | Ignition timing adjustment | Voltage distribution |
|---|---|---|---|
| Conventional coil ignition CI | mechanical | mechanical | mechanical |
| Transistorized ignition TI | electronic | mechanical | mechanical |
| Electronic ignition EI | electronic | electronic | mechanical |
| Distributorless ignition DLI | electronic | electronic | electronic |

mechanical / electronic

# Conventional coil ignition (CI)

### Design and operating concept

Older vehicles are still equipped with a conventional coil-ignition system. Here, all the engine cylinders are supplied with a high voltage by one ignition coil. The high voltage is distributed to the individual cylinders at the right time by means of a mechanical system that utilizes an ignition distributor. The ignition distributor also features a mechanical switch (distributor contact points), which is controlled by a circulating cam and switches the current through the ignition coil.

While the switch is closed (dwell period), a magnetic field builds up in the ignition coil. At the moment of ignition, the distributor contact points open the electric circuit, and the coil's magnetic field discharges via the secondary winding of the ignition coil into the ignition spark.

The ignition distributor also has a facility for adjusting the moment of ignition as a function of engine speed (centrifugal advance mechanism) and load (vacuum adjustment mechanism).

The ignition distributor is driven by the ignition-distributor shaft and runs at half the speed of the crankshaft. The cam on the ignition-distributor shaft closes the distributor contact points for a specific angle range (dwell angle). The operating time decreases with increasing engine

***Conventional coil-ignition system (CI);*** *components on left, circuit diagram on right*
*1 Battery, 2 Ignition switch, 3 Ignition coil, 4 Ignition distributor, 5 Ignition capacitor,*
*6 Contact breaker, 7 Spark plugs.* $R_V$ *Ballast resistor for starting-voltage increase (optional).*

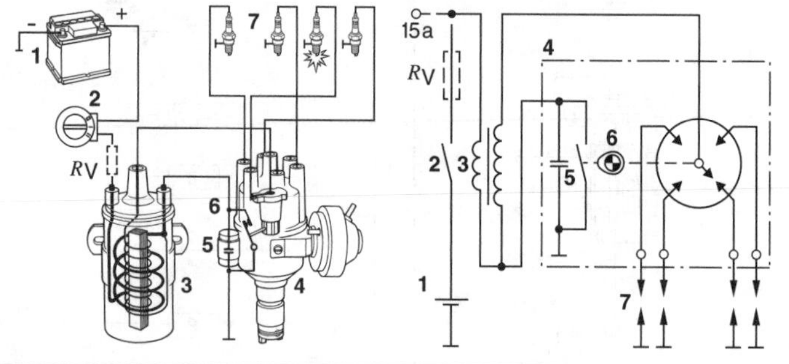

speed and the current through the ignition coil drops. As a result, the ignition-system high-voltage supply decreases with engine speed.

## Components
### Ignition coil
Conventional coil ignition uses asphalt- or oil-filled ignition coils enclosed in a casing. The coils were designed for low currents and are resistant to continuous current loads. Resistors were connected upstream of some ignition coils; they were bypassed when the engine was started with reduced battery voltage (starting enrichment).

### Ignition distributor
The ignition distributor is a separate, self-contained component within the ignition system. It has the following functions:
- It distributes the ignition voltage pulses to the engine spark plugs in a specific sequence (rotating high-voltage distribution).
- It triggers the ignition pulse using the primary current breaker.
- It adjusts the moment of ignition using the spark-advance mechanism.

The ignition contact breaker and the spark-advance mechanism perform separate functions from those of the ignition distributor proper. They are combined with it in a single unit because they require a synchronized drive.

The ignition pulse passes through the center connection, and the carbon brush or the center-tower spark gap to the distributor rotor. The ignition pulse then distributes the ignition energy by arcing it to fixed electrodes impressed in the periphery of the distributor cap. It then travels through the high-tension ignition cables to the spark plugs. A dust cover is sometimes installed to separate this high-voltage section from the rest of the unit.

### Ignition contact breaker
The ignition contact breaker has a cam-operated contact, which switches on the ignition-coil primary current before the moment of ignition and interrupts it at the moment of ignition. The number of lobes on the distributor cam is equal to the number of cylinders in the engine. The portion of the ignition-distributor shaft rotation during which the points remain closed is the dwell angle.

The ignition contact breaker wears during operation and the ignition system adjusts itself. Contact erosion stems from the contact-breaking sparks (residual arcing) induced by induction voltage when the primary current is interrupted. The ignition capacitor is designed to suppress this type of arcing, but contact-breaking sparks continue to occur. Although contact erosion and rubbing-block wear are mutually counteractive, the effects of the latter are generally more pronounced, resulting in a tendency for the moment of ignition to drift toward "retard" at a later ignition point.

### Spark-advance mechanism
Ignition distributors normally have two spark-advance mechanisms:
- The rotational-speed dependent, centrifugal force-controlled advance mechanism (centrifugal advance mechanism)
- The load-sensitive, intake-manifold controlled advance mechanism (vacuum adjustment mechanism)

The centrifugal advance mechanism adjusts the moment of ignition in response to changes in engine speed. The support plate on which the flyweights are mounted rotates with the ignition-distributor shaft, The flyweights move outward as engine speed increases, thus turning the driver

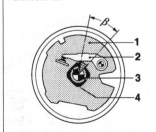

**Contact breaker**
1 Moving breaker-plate assembly,
2 Breaker lever, 3 Ignition-distributor shaft,
4 Distributor cam.

over the contact path to the ignition-distributor shaft in the direction of rotation. In this way, the distributor cam also turns toward the ignition-distributor shaft by the ignition advance angle $\alpha$. The moment of ignition is advanced by this angle.

The <u>vacuum adjustment mechanism</u> adapts the moment of ignition to changes in engine performance and load factor. An indication of spark advance is the intake-manifold vacuum in the vicinity of the throttle valve. The vacuum acts on two aneroid capsules.

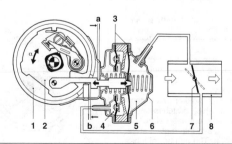

*Centrifugal advance mechanism, at rest (above), in operation (below)*
*1 Support plate, 2 Distributor cam,*
*3 Contact path, 4 Advance flyweight,*
*5 Ignition-distributor shaft, 6 Driver.*

## Transistorized ignition (TI)

The switching capacity of the distributor contact points is limited. The need for more powerful ignition systems and the availability of electronic high-power switches resulted in the development of transistorized ignitions and the first electronic ignition trigger boxes.

### Breaker-triggered transistorized ignition

At first, the current was switched through the ignition coil by a power transistor. All the distributor contact points did was trigger the ignition via an ignition trigger box and there was much less wear as a result (breaker-triggered transistorized coil ignition).

### Breakerless transistorized ignition

In a second stage, the distributor contact points were replaced by breakerless, and therefore wear-free, triggering systems. In breakerless transistorized coil ignition, the cam-actuated ignition contact breaker is replaced by a "pulse generator", which activates an ignition trigger box with a power transistor. The pulse generator is installed in the ignition distributor.

These triggering devices operate according to various operating concepts:

*Vacuum adjustment mechanism with ignition advance and retard units*
*a Advance adjustment up to stop, b Retard adjustment up to stop.*
*1 Ignition distributor, 2 Breaker-plate assembly, 3 Diaphragm, 4 Retard unit,*
*5 Advance unit, 6 Vacuum unit, 7 Throttle valve, 8 Intake manifold.*

### Induction-type pulse generators (TI-I)

The induction-type pulse generator is a permanently excited AC generator consisting of stator and rotor. The number of teeth or arms corresponds to the number of cylinders in the engine. The frequency and amplitude of the alternating voltage generated by the unit vary according to engine speed. The ignition trigger box processes this AC voltage and uses it for ignition control.

### Hall-effect pulse generators

This type of ignition-pulse generator utilizes the Hall effect. A speed-sensitive magnetic field produces voltage pulses in an electrically charged semiconductor layer to control activation of the ECU's primary current in the ignition trigger box.

### Ignition trigger boxes

Ignition trigger boxes contain the triggering electronics and the driver stages with primary-voltage and primary-current limitation for protection. Dwell-angle control ensures that the desired primary current is achieved as close to the moment of ignition as possible across a wide speed range. This minimizes power losses in the ignition trigger box as a result. In addition, dwell-angle control compensates for battery-voltage fluctuations and the temperature effects of the ignition coil.

Depending on system design, dwell-angle control is effective up to mid-range engine speeds. At high engine speeds, the dwell angle is determined by the break time required to achieve adequate arcing durations.

Breakerless transistorized ignition systems either do not have closed-circuit current or have closed-circuit current deactivation.

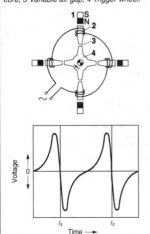

**Ignition distributor with induction-type pulse generator**
1 Permanent magnet, 2 Induction coil with core, 3 Variable air gap, 4 Trigger wheel.

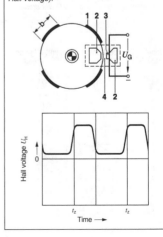

**Ignition distributor with Hall generator**
1 Vane of width b, 2 Soft-magnetic conductive elements, 3 Hall IC, 4 Air gap. $U_G$ Pulse-generator voltage (transformed Hall voltage).

Sparkless closed-circuit current deactivation switches off the primary current with the ignition on and the engine off to ensure that the secondary voltage does not cause sparks at the spark plug.

### Ignition coils

The ignition coils for transistorized ignition systems have been designed for considerably higher primary currents than the ignition coils for contact breaker systems. The ignition coils are not resistant to continuous current loads.

### Spark retard

Like conventional coil ignition systems, spark retard as a function of engine speed and load is adjusted using flyweights and a vacuum advance mechanism in the ignition distributor.

# Electronic ignition (EI and DLI)

In electronic ignition, the centrifugal-force and vacuum-adjustment lines in the ignition distributor are replaced by ignition maps (see P. 620) in the ECU software. The engine operating conditions are detected by the ECU and the associated ignition angle is calculated. After other input signals have been processed, the ignition coil is then activated at the correct time.

The ignition driver stages are either installed in the ECU or a separate ignition trigger box or are attached to the ignition coil. Electronic ignition can be usefully combined with knock control.

### Electronic ignition (EI) with rotating high-voltage distribution

Ignition triggering can either be performed by a sensor system in the ignition distributor or a sensor system on the crankshaft. Ignition triggering using a crankshaft sensor system can achieve a more accurate ignition angle as there are no distributor-shaft drive tolerances to deal with. The high voltage is still distributed mechanically by an ignition distributor (P. 653).

### Distributorless ignition with stationary high-voltage distribution

On this system, the ignition distributor is replaced by a stationary distribution system. This requires an ignition coil for each cylinder. In certain conditions, one ignition coil for every two cylinders is sufficient. As there is no ignition distributor, the ignition must be triggered by a sensor system on the crankshaft.

### Stationary voltage distribution with single-spark ignition coil

Each cylinder is assigned a separate ignition driver stage and ignition coil. The ignition control unit switches the firing sequence of the ignition output stages accordingly.

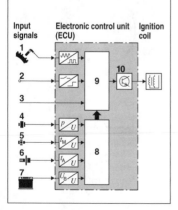

***Electronic ignition, signal processing***
1 Engine speed, 2 Switch signals, 3 CAN (serial bus), 4 Intake-manifold pressure, 5 Engine temperature, 6 Intake-air temperature, 7 Battery voltage, 8 Microcomputer, 9 Analog/digital converter, 10 Driver stage.

| Input signals | Electronic control unit (ECU) | Ignition coil |
|---|---|---|

This system, suitable for engines with any number of cylinders, provides the greatest latitude for adjustment, as there is only one spark per cycle.

Synchronization with the camshaft position (phase sensor) is necessary. On engines with an even number of cylinders, the system reverts to crankshaft triggering in the event of camshaft-sensor failure, although two coils are then always activated simultaneously (one of the sparks is discharged during the exhaust stroke).

Stationary voltage distribution
with dual-spark ignition coil

Two cylinders share one ignition coil. Activation can be simply via the crankshaft. The high-voltage end of each ignition coil is connected to the spark plugs for two cylinders, whose operating cycles are 360° out of phase with each other. At the moment of ignition, a spark is present simultaneously at both spark plugs.

As a backup spark occurs in the cylinder with valve overlap between the exhaust and the induction stroke, it is important to ensure that any ignitable residual mixture or intake fresh A/F mixture is not ignited. As a result, the possible spark-retard range is restricted. Furthermore, the dual-spark ignition coil is only suited for use with even numbers of cylinders. As a cheaper alternative to the single-spark ignition coil, the use of dual-spark ignition coil systems was widespread.

The distributorless ignition system marked the end of development of independent ignition systems. Since then, the functions of distributorless ignition have been incorporated into the Motronic engine-management system.

## Capacitor-discharge ignition (CDI)

The operating concept behind capacitor-discharge ignition (CDI), or "thyristor ignition", as it is also known, differs from that of the ignition systems described above. CDI was developed for use with high-speed, high-output multi-cylinder reciprocating IC engines in high-performance and competition applications, and for rotary-piston engines.

The salient characteristic of the CDI system is that it stores ignition energy in the electric field of a capacitor. The capacitance and charge voltage of the capacitor determine the amount of energy stored. The ignition transformer converts the primary voltage discharged from the capacitor to the required high voltage.

Capacitor-discharge ignition is available in both breaker-triggered and breakerless versions.

The major advantage of CDI is that it generally remains impervious to electrical shunts in the high-voltage ignition circuit, especially those stemming from spark-plug contamination. For many applications, the spark duration of 0.1...0.3 ms is too brief to ensure that the air/fuel mixture will ignite reliably. Thus, CDI is only designed for specific types of engine, and today its use is restricted to a limited application range, as transistorized ignition systems now provide virtually the same performance. CDI is not suited for after-market installations.

Stationary, i.e. distributorless, high-voltage distribution can also be employed for CDI by using one ignition transformer per cylinder. Energy distribution takes place at the medium voltage level.

# Minimizing pollutants in the spark-ignition engine

Measures for controlling the exhaust-gas composition in spark-ignition engines can be divided into "engine-design measures", "reduction of engine external interference", and "exhaust-gas treatment". The strict emission limits in force in most industrial countries usually require a combination of these strategies.

## Engine-design measures

### Mixture formation

#### General
The fuel used in spark-ignition (SI) engines is more volatile than diesel fuel, while the air/fuel mixture up to start of combustion usually extends over a longer period than in a diesel engine. The result is that spark-ignition engines operate on a more homogeneous A/F mixture than their diesel counterparts.

Where A/F mixture formation is concerned, a distinction must be made between spark-ignition engines with direct and indirect injection. Apart from a few operating points, the indirect-injection spark-ignition engine is operated with a stoichiometric A/F mixture ($\lambda = 1$). The direct-injection spark-engine engine also uses a stoichiometric mixture when working in homogeneous operation. In this mode, fuel is injected directly into the combustion chamber during the induction stroke. Then, during the compression phase, most of the A/F mixture is homogenized.

Another operating mode for the direct-injection engine is stratified-charge operation. Here, like on a diesel engine, fuel is not injected until the compression stroke, creating a generally lean A/F mixture.

### Setting the A/F ratio
On spark-ignition engines, the A/F ratio is set essentially by calculating the cylinder air charge and the resulting injected fuel quantity as accurately as possible.

The excess-air factor $\lambda$ (see P. 605) of the A/F mixture supplied to the engine has a major impact on exhaust-gas composition. The engine produces its maximum torque at approximately $\lambda = 0.9$. In many cases, enriching the mixture at wide-open throttle is necessary to reduce the exhaust-gas temperature in order to prevent thermal damage to the exhaust valves, exhaust manifold, and catalytic converter.

A certain level of excess air is required for low fuel consumption. Low CO (carbon monoxide) and HC (hydrocarbons) values are also obtained with this setting. However, $NO_x$ (nitrogen oxides) emissions are at their highest here.

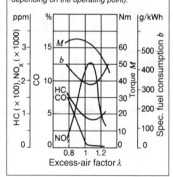

*The excess-air factor $\lambda$ influences:*
*Exhaust-gas composition (CO, $NO_x$, HC), torque (M), and specific fuel consumption (b). The values apply to the part-load range of a spark-ignition engine operating at a constant moderate speed and cylinder charge ($\lambda$ values implemented in the vehicle engine range from approx. 0.85...1.15, depending on the operating point).*

An excessively lean mixture results in the engine reaching or exceeding its lean misfire limit (LML), and as the mixture becomes progressively leaner, combustion misses cause a rapid increase in HC emissions. In overrun mode, fuel supply is completely shut off above idle speed (overrun fuel cutoff).

Electronic fuel-injection systems (Motronic systems) allow precise adjustment of the A/F ratio.

## A/F mixture formation

Mixture formation covers not only the setting of the A/F ratio, but also the quality of the A/F mixture which actually enters the combustion chamber, or is present at the moment of ignition. Fuel homogeneity, its stratification patterns, and its temperature at the moment of ignition are all essential factors in determining flammability and combustion characteristics, with consequent effects on exhaust-gas composition. Homogeneous A/F mixture formation and controlled stratification (rich mixture at the spark plug, lean mixture in the vicinity of the combustion-chamber walls) are examples of two different development objectives.

The homogeneity of the air/fuel mixture is optimized by "spray targeting". Fuel pressure, spray pattern, and spray direction are defined at the design stage as a function of engine geometry (see section on "Intake-manifold injection", P. 610).

To improve A/F mixture formation, turbulence flaps can also be fitted in the intake manifold. Depending on their position, these flaps shut off sections of the intake port, thus influencing airflow behavior and speeds.

In the engine starting phase, A/F mixture-formation conditions are much poorer due to the prevailing low temperatures. As a result, manifold-wall fuel condensation increases. This causes much higher concentrations of pollutants in the exhaust gas during the starting and post-start phases.

## Uniform mixture distribution

Maximum engine efficiency can only be achieved if every cylinder is operated with the same excess-air factor. This necessitates a system which ensures that both air and fuel are distributed evenly among the individual cylinders. However, it should be noted that charge fluctuations at constant lambda cause unavoidable fluctuations in torque, and should not be compensated for by cylinder matching utilizing the fuel quantity. In these conditions, smooth-running control, which permits uneven lambda, is an advantage (see P. 667).

## Exhaust-gas recirculation (EGR)

Exhaust gas can be conducted back to the combustion chamber to reduce peak combustion temperatures. Higher combustion temperatures induce an over-proportional increase in $NO_x$ formation, and as exhaust-gas recirculation (EGR) reduces combustion temperatures, it represents a particularly effective means of controlling $NO_x$ emissions.

As the EGR rate increases intake-manifold pressure, the throttle valve must be opened wider to maintain the fresh gas filling. Additional dethrottling reduces fuel consumption considerably.

EGR can be implemented in either of two ways:
- Internal exhaust-gas recirculation by appropriate valve overlap (see P. 474)
- External exhaust-gas recirculation by controlling the exhaust-gas recirculation valves (see P. 540)

With external exhaust-gas recirculation, the EGR valve is activated electrically, depending on the engine operating point, to feed a proportion of exhaust gas to the fresh A/F mixture.

Exhaust-gas recirculation is also used on gasoline direct-injection engines to reduce fuel consumption and $NO_x$ emissions. This aspect is more significant here. It is the main way to minimize untreated $NO_x$ emissions, and thus prolong the duration of lean-burn operation, which is limited by the $NO_x$ accumulator-type catalytic converter.

To allow exhaust gas to be drawn in via the EGR valve, there must be a pressure differential between the intake manifold and the exhaust-gas duct. As direct-injection engines operate virtually unthrottled, even in the part load range, and since a not insignificant amount of oxygen returns via the EGR valve in lean-burn modes, gasoline direct injection systems require a control strategy that coordinates both the throttle valve and the EGR valve.

### Valve timing

Large valve overlaps (early opening of the intake valve) increase internal exhaust-gas recirculation, and can therefore help to reduce $NO_x$ emissions. However, since recirculated exhaust gas displaces fresh A/F mixture, opening the intake valve early also leads to a reduction in the maximum torque. In addition, excessively high exhaust-gas recirculation, particularly at idle, can lead to combustion misses which, in turn, cause an increase in HC emissions. The optimized solution is achievable with variable valve timing (see P. 475), where valve timing is varied as a function of the operating point.

### Engine geometry

#### Compression ratio

It has long been recognized that the enhanced thermal efficiency associated with high compression ratios represents an effective means of improving fuel economy. However, the increase in peak combustion temperature also results in higher $NO_x$ emissions.

#### Combustion-chamber design

Low HC emissions are best achieved with a compact combustion chamber featuring a minimal surface area and no recesses. A centrally located spark plug with short flame travel produces rapid and relatively complete combustion of the A/F mixture, resulting in low HC emissions and reduced fuel consumption. Induced combustion-chamber turbulence also provides rapid combustion. Combustion chambers optimized in this way feature favorable HC emissions at $\lambda = 1$, and improve the engine's lean-mixture operation.

A thoroughly optimized combustion-chamber design, coupled with external measures (such as intake swirl or tumble) produce a lean-burn engine capable of running with excess-air factors in the range of $\lambda \approx 1.4...1.6$. Although the lean-burn engine features low exhaust-gas emissions and excellent fuel economy, it does require catalytic exhaust-gas treatment in order to meet the most stringent emissions limits for CO, HC, and $NO_x$. Particularly due to the fact that developments in the aftertreatment of $NO_x$ in lean exhaust gas are still in their infancy, the lean-burn engine has so far only been successful in Europe and Japan, and only in a few models using lean/mix concepts, which compromised between emissions and fuel consumption.

A new way of substantially improving the lean-running behavior of the spark-ignition engine is to inject fuel directly into the combustion chamber with stratified charge. Here, systems using a combination of three-way and accumulator-type catalytic converters are favored for exhaust-gas treatment.

The lean-running characteristics achieved by combustion-chamber design and induced turbulence can also be applied to implement high EGR rates for designs with $\lambda = 1$. As a result, fuel consumption can be reduced to an extent comparable with lean-burn engines, with external A/F mixture formation, and without increasing the amount of exhaust-gas treatment work required.

### Ignition system and combustion process

The design of the spark plug, its position in the combustion chamber, together with spark energy and spark duration, all exert a major impact on ignition, and therefore on exhaust-gas emissions as a result of the combustion process. This becomes even more significant the further into the lean-burn range ($\lambda > 1.1$) the engine is operated.

The combustion process defines combustion as a function of time, and applies the ratio of the already combusted fuel to the fuel awaiting combustion. The point at which 50% of the energy is converted has a particular effect on efficiency and combustion temperature, and thus on fuel consumption and $NO_x$ formation.

On spark-ignition engines, combustion is initiated by the moment of ignition. Using the moment of ignition for optimized fuel economy as a baseline, timing can be retarded so that the exhaust valve opens before the combustion process is completed, or at the very least, very high exhaust-gas temperatures predominate. This causes a thermal post-reaction of unburned hydrocarbons to occur in the exhaust-gas system, and allows the catalytic converter to heat up to operating temperature more effectively (see P. 664). Owing to the low combustion-chamber temperatures, $NO_x$ emissions are low, but fuel consumption increases.

Fuel consumption and $NO_x$ and HC emissions increase when the moment of ignition is advanced, compared with the optimum.

# Reducing engine external interference

### Crankcase ventilation (blowby)

The concentration of hydrocarbons in the crankcase may be many times that found in the engine's exhaust gases. Control systems conduct these gases to a suitable point in the engine's air-intake system, from where they are drawn into the combustion chamber for burning (see P. 542).

Originally, these gases were allowed to escape untreated directly to the atmosphere; today crankcase emission-control systems are a standard legal requirement.

### Evaporative-emissions control system

Evaporated fuel from the fuel tank is stored by the evaporative-emissions control system in a carbon canister, and then fed to the engine for combustion (see figure on P. 541). To do this, the engine-management system selectively activates the canister-purge valve. This valve is located between the carbon canister and the intake manifold. When the valve is open, air flows into the carbon canister due to the pressure differential, and takes the fuel vapors stored in the canister with it to the intake manifold.

The canister-purge valve is activated by a PWM signal. The engine-management system is able to adjust the valve-opening cross-section, and thus the regeneration flow (scavenging flow), as a function of the engine operating status.

On gasoline direct-injection systems, regeneration of the carbon canister is limited in stratified-charge operation because of the lower intake-manifold pressure (caused by extensive dethrottling), and because of incomplete combustion of the homogeneously distributed regeneration gas. The regeneration-gas flow is therefore reduced, compared with homogeneous operation. If this is not sufficient, as a lot of fuel has evaporated, for example, the engine must operate in homogeneous operation until the initially high concentration of fuel in the regeneration-gas flow has dropped.

## Catalytic exhaust-gas treatment

While diesel engine development aims at minimizing the production of pollutants in the combustion process itself, exhaust-gas treatment is the preferred method for spark-ignition engines. Catalytic converters convert the pollutants produced during combustion into harmless components.

### Catalytic converters

Three-way catalytic converter
*Function*
The state-of-the-art for engines operating with a stoichiometric air/fuel mixture is the three-way catalytic converter. Its task is to convert pollutant components HC (hydrocarbons), CO (carbon monoxide), and NOₓ (nitrogen oxides), which arise during the combustion process, into harmless components. The end products are $H_2O$ (water vapor), $CO_2$ (carbon dioxide), and $N_2$ (nitrogen).

---

**Catalytic converter efficiency as a function of the excess-air factor λ**
a) Exhaust-gas emissions upstream of the three-way catalytic converter, b) Exhaust emissions downstream of the 3-way catalytic converter, c) Electrical signal from lambda oxygen sensor. $U_\lambda$ Sensor voltage.

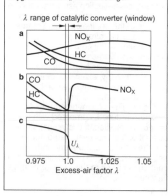

---

*Design and operating concept*
The catalytic converter consists of a sheet-metal housing, a substrate, and an active catalytic noble-metal coating (see P. 545 onwards). The substrate is usually a ceramic monolith, though metallic monoliths are used for special applications. On the monolith is a substrate layer, which enlarges the effective area of the catalytic converter by a factor of 7,000. The catalytic layer on top of this contains noble metals such as platinum and/or palladium, and rhodium. Platinum and palladium accelerate the oxidation of HC and CO, while rhodium is responsible for reducing NOₓ. The oxygen required for the oxidation process is either present in the exhaust gas as exhaust-gas oxygen (resulting from incomplete combustion), or it is taken from the NOₓ, which is reduced at the same time.

The concentrations of pollutants in the untreated exhaust gas (upstream of the catalytic converter) depend on the excess-air factor λ. To allow the three-way catalytic converter to convert as much of all three pollutant components as possible, the pollutants must be present in chemical equilibrium. This requires a mixture composition with a stoichiometric ratio of λ = 1. The "window" (lambda control range), in which the mean time value of λ must lie, is very small. Mixture formation must therefore be corrected in a lambda closed-control loop (see P. 665 onwards).

*Oxygen-type catalytic converter*
Here, the oxygen storage capacity of three-way catalytic converters plays a crucial role. In dynamic operation, λ accuracy is typically 5%, i.e. fluctuations of this order about λ = 1 are unavoidable. These deviations cause no problems, however, because the catalytic converter stores excess oxygen in the lean phase for use in the following rich phase.

The task of the engine-management system is, therefore, clear. The mean time value of the resulting lambda upstream of the catalytic converter must be very accurate (to a few thousandths). The integral mean value deviations, converted to oxygen input and output, must not overtax the available oxygen retained in the catalytic converter. Typical oxygen storage values are in the range of 100 mg...1 g. All conventional methods of diagnosing catalytic converters are based on the direct or indirect determination of this oxygen storage capacity (osc, oxygen storage capacity).

This allows conversion rates of >99% to be achieved for the limited pollutants when the catalytic converter is operating at operating temperature.

## $NO_x$ accumulator-type catalytic converter
### Function, design and operating concept

On gasoline direct-injection engines, the oxygen required to oxidize HC and CO is not taken from $NO_x$. Instead, it is taken from the high proportion of oxygen remaining in the exhaust gas. As a result, a three-way catalytic converter alone is not sufficient.

The catalytic layer of the $NO_x$ accumulator-type catalytic converter also contains substances which can store $NO_x$ (e.g. barium oxide). All conventional $NO_x$ accumulator coatings also have the properties of a three-way catalytic converter, with the result that the $NO_x$ accumulator-type catalytic converter operates like a three-way catalytic converter at $\lambda = 1$.

In lean stratified-charge operation, $NO_x$ is converted in three stages. In the storage phase, $NO_x$ is first oxidized to $NO_2$, which then reacts with the additives in the coating to become nitrates (e.g. barium nitrate).

As the quantity of stored $NO_x$ (load) increases, the ability to continue binding $NO_x$ decreases. At a predefined laden state, the $NO_x$ accumulator must be regenerated, i.e. the nitrogen oxides stored in it must be removed (released) and converted. For this purpose, the engine switches briefly to rich homogeneous operation ($\lambda < 0.8$) to reduce NO to N, without emitting CO and HC in the process.

The ends of the storage and output phases are either calculated using models or measured with a $NO_x$ sensor, or lambda oxygen sensor downstream of the catalytic converter.

### Desulfating

The sulfur contained in the fuel also reacts with the accumulator material in the catalytic layer. This creates sulfates (e.g. barium sulfate) which are very temperature-resistant. Special measures (e.g. switching to stratified-catalytic converter heating mode or other chemical heating methods) must be used to heat the catalytic converter up to >650 °C before exposing it alternately to rich ($\lambda = 0.95$) and lean ($\lambda = 1.05$) exhaust gas for a few minutes. This process reduces the sulfates still further.

The various methods to heat up the $NO_x$ accumulator-type catalytic converter located in the underfloor region must be careful not to overheat the primary catalytic converter.

### Catalytic-converter operating temperature

Catalytic converters do not start significant conversion until they have reached a specific operating temperature (light-off temperature). On a three-way catalytic converter, this is 300 °C. Ideal conditions for a high conversion rate are achieved at 400...800 °C. With an accumulator-type catalytic converter, this temperature range is 200...500 °C, and is therefore much lower than on a three-way catalytic converter.

Operating temperatures of 800...1,000 °C result in thermal aging of the catalytic converter. This is caused by sintering of the noble metals and the substrate layer, which reduces the active surface. At temperatures above 1,000 °C, thermal aging increases considerably until the catalytic converter has no effect at all.

*Typical catalytic-converter configurations*
*a) Primary catalytic and main catalytic converters: two-step lambda closed-loop control with sensors upstream and downstream of the primary catalytic converter.*
*b) Primary catalytic and main catalytic converter: two-step lambda closed-loop control with sensors upstream of the primary catalytic converter and downstream of the main catalytic converter.*
*c) Main catalytic converter: two-step lambda closed-loop control with sensors upstream and downstream of the main catalytic converter.*
*d) y configuration for gasoline direct injection with two primary catalytic converters and one NO$_x$ accumulator-type catalytic converter: two-step lambda closed-loop control with sensors upstream and downstream of the primary catalytic converter. NO$_x$ sensor for controlling the accumulator-type catalytic converter.*

*1 Primary catalytic converter, 2 Main catalytic converter, 3 Two-step sensor (LSF) or broadband sensor (LSU), 4 Two-step sensor (LSF), 5 NO$_x$ sensor.*

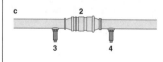

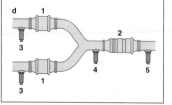

## Catalytic converter configurations

Various concepts are used, depending on requirements. In principle, there are two types of catalytic converter and they differ mainly in their size:
– Primary catalytic converters, usually installed next to the engine
– Main catalytic converters, which, for size reasons, are usually located in the underfloor area (underfloor catalytic converters) instead of near the engine

Primary and main catalytic converters can be combined in a number of ways. Engines with two cylinder banks (usually those with six or more cylinders) have two primary and main catalytic-converter combinations.

One special case is the "y configuration", used mainly on gasoline direct-injection engines with NO$_x$ accumulator-type catalytic converters. On these engines, each exhaust-gas tract has a primary catalytic converter. The shared main catalytic converter is located after the point where the two tracts join.

## Exhaust-gas treatment at $\lambda = 1$

### Cold engine

Combustion of the air/fuel mixture is never complete. Unburned fuel is fed into the exhaust-gas system during the exhaust cycle and creates HC and CO emissions. These emissions are particularly high when the engine is cold, as fuel condenses onto the cold cylinder walls and then leaves the combustion chamber unburned.

Adding to the problem is the fact that the catalytic converter must have reached a minimum temperature before it can convert pollutants. It is therefore important to minimize untreated emissions during the warm-up phase before the catalytic converter lights off. This is achieved by:
– Optimized start (injection time, ignition)
– A lean warm-up phase (engine must be capable of lean-burn operation)
– Secondary-air injection (see P. 540)

Measures are also required to bring the catalytic converter up to operating temperature quickly. This is achieved by:
– Locating catalytic converters near to the engine
– Retarding the ignition angle and increasing the mass gas flow to increase exhaust-gas temperatures
– Secondary-air injection

Motronic uses torque coordination to ensure that the catalytic converter reaches its operating temperature as quickly as possible.

Electric-heated catalytic converters are also used for special applications (EHC: electric heated catalyst). The use of a fuel-powered burner to heat up the catalyst is also under consideration.

Hot engine
The stoichiometric air/fuel mixture can be set when smooth-running performance and temperature conditions permit operation at $\lambda = 1$. The three-way catalytic converter achieves its highest conversion rate for the pollutants HC, CO, and $NO_x$ at this excess-air factor. However, the air/fuel ratio is only permitted to fluctuate within a range of $\lambda = 1 \pm 0.005$ to maintain the high conversion rate. This accuracy means that closed-loop mixture control (lambda closed-loop control) is required.

**Exhaust-gas treatment for lean-burn operation**
On gasoline direct injection engines, the $NO_x$ storage effect can also be used, to a limited degree, in homogeneous lean-burn operation. Typical lambda limits are $\lambda = 1.5...1.6$. Lean-burn limits are generally determined by the smooth running of the engine, whereas rich mixture limits are dictated by the need to minimize $NO_x$ emissions. It is therefore essential to observe these limits as closely as possible. Continuous lambda closed-loop control can be used for closed-loop control of lean-burn setpoint values.

**Lambda closed-loop control**
Lambda closed-loop control evaluates the signals from the lambda oxygen sensors (see P. 133 onwards). These sensors measure the oxygen content in the exhaust gas, and thus provide information about mixture composition. All current lambda closed-loop control strategies for spark-ignition engines use the injected fuel quantity as the manipulated variable and, strictly speaking, can only compensate for fuel errors (e.g. injector faults, fuel pressure faults, etc.). Here, the pilot control accuracy, based on charge calculation (dynamic charge as well) determines the amount of actuator adjustments required.

Two-step control
The two-step lambda oxygen sensor with its voltage-jump characteristic at $\lambda = 1$ is suitable for two-step controls. A manipulated variable, composed of the voltage jump and the ramp, changes its direction of control for each voltage jump. This indicates a change from rich/lean or lean/rich (see the figure on the next page). The typical amplitude of this manipulated variable has been set in the range of 2% to 3%. The result is a limited controller dynamic, which is predominantly determined by the sum of the response times (pre-storage of fuel in the intake manifold, four-stroke principle of the spark-ignition engine, and gas travel time).

The typical "false measurement" of this sensor, caused by variations in exhaust-gas composition, can be compensated by selective control. Here, the preferred method is to hold the ramp value at the voltage jump for a controlled dwell time $t_v$ after the sensor is subjected to a voltage jump.

Continuous lambda closed-loop control
The defined dynamic response of a two-step control can only be improved if the deviation from $\lambda = 1$ can actually be measured. The broadband sensor can be used to achieve continuous-action control at $\lambda = 1$ with a stationary, very low amplitude in conjunction with high dynamic response. The control parameters are calculated and adapted as a function of the engine's operating points. Above all, with this type of lambda closed-loop control,

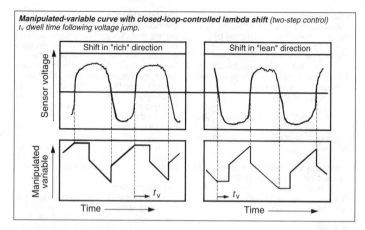

*Manipulated-variable curve with closed-loop-controlled lambda shift (two-step control)*
$t_v$ *dwell time following voltage jump.*

compensation for the unavoidable offset of the stationary and non-stationary pilot control is far quicker.

If demanded by certain engine operating conditions (e.g. warm-up), further optimization of exhaust-gas emissions lies in the potential inherent in the control setpoints $\lambda \neq 1$, for instance, in the lean range. An expansion to a lean-mixture control system, with the advantages and disadvantages described above, requires merely a definition of different control setpoints.

### Lambda closed-loop control with reference sensor downstream of the catalytic converter

Protective layer systems in the lambda oxygen sensor have helped minimize interference both with an accuracy of $\lambda = 1$ at the voltage-jump point of a two-step sensor, and with the characteristics of a broadband sensor. Nevertheless, aging and environmental influences (poisoning) still have an effect. A sensor downstream of the catalytic converter is subjected to these influences to a much lesser extent. The principle of two-step control is based on the fact that the controlled rich or lean shift, or the setpoint value of a continuous closed-loop control are changed by a "slow" control loop, which adds corrections. The long-term constant perfor-

mance achieved with this system is required for current emissions legislation.

### Three-step control

The use of a third sensor downstream of the main catalytic converter is required on SULEVs (Super Ultra-Low-Emission Vehicle, see P. 554) for catalytic-converter diagnosis as well as for exhaust-gas constancy. The two-step control system (single cascade) has been supplemented by an extremely slow closed-loop control system using a third sensor located downstream of the main (underfloor) catalytic converter.

### Single-cylinder closed-loop control

With primary catalytic converters located near the engine, there is no guarantee that the exhaust gases in the individual cylinders will be adequately mixed before flowing through the catalytic converter. The conversion performance of segments of the catalytic converter exposed to straggling exhaust-gas flow is poorer, depending on the extent to which the cylinder deviates from $\lambda = 1$. Lambda matching for the individual cylinders can considerably improve exhaust-gas performance in these conditions. In order to obtain individual-cylinder lambda values from one measured lambda signal, the lambda oxygen sensor must be extremely dynamic.

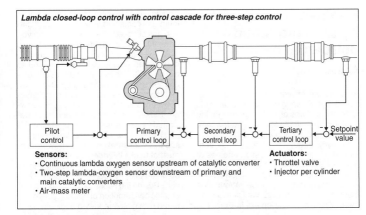

**Lambda closed-loop control with control cascade for three-step control**

**Sensors:**
- Continuous lambda oxygen sensor upstream of catalytic converter
- Two-step lambda-oxygen senosr downstream of primary and main catalytic converters
- Air-mass meter

**Actuators:**
- Throttel valve
- Injector per cylinder

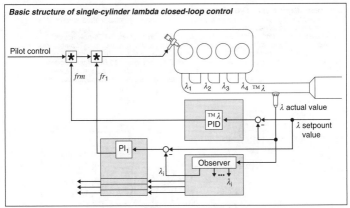

**Basic structure of single-cylinder lambda closed-loop control**

#### Torque equalization

Lambda matching only results in torque equalization if no charge errors are present. If necessary, it must be replaced by torque equalization, which, particularly in the lean-burn range, compensates for cylinder-charging errors by measuring the engine's smooth-running performance, and thus any fluctuations in torque.

# Engines fueled by LPG (liquefied petroleum gas)

## Applications

As a mixture of propane and butane, liquefied petroleum gas assumes a liquid state at pressures of 2...20 bar, depending on the propane/butane ratio and the temperature (see Section on "Fuels", P. 327).

In early 2000, LPG was being consumed by internal-combustion engines at a rate of approximately 14.4 million metric tonnes annually, of which 3 million tonnes were consumed in Europe. Worldwide there are 7 million LPG vehicles on the road, of which 1.5 million are in Europe.

Should efforts to utilize the liquefied petroleum gas contained in petroleum and natural gas succeed, then the production volume of LPG could increase exponentially.

Any vehicle equipped with an internal-combustion engine can be converted to run on LPG. For the most part, spark-ignition (SI) engines are re-equipped for dual-fuel operation (system can be switched between gasoline and LPG). LPG-powered taxis and buses are generally designed for single-fuel or monovalent (LPG only) operation, while regulations stipulate this configuration on gas-powered industrial trucks intended for indoor use.

When engines are converted, it should be noted that, at equivalent efficiency levels, LPG fueling causes an increase in volumetric consumption of approx. 25% compared with gasoline-fueled engines.

---

*Schematic diagram of an LPG system (injection principle)*
*The figure shows a system for monovalent operation. Bi-fuel systems feature additional components for gasoline operation.*
*1 Gas shutoff valve (low pressure), 2 Evaporator pressure regulator, 3 Throttle device,*
*4 Intake-manifold pressure sensor, 5 Injector, 6 Ignition coil with spark plug, 7 Lambda oxygen sensor, 8 ECU, 9 Speed sensor, 10 Engine-temperature sensor, 11 Primary catalytic converter,*
*12 Lambda oxygen sensor, 13 CAN interface, 14 Diagnosis lamp, 15 Diagnosis interface,*
*16 Ventilation line for tank fittings, 17 LPG tank, 18 Housing with tank fittings, 19 External filler valve designed to stop refueling at 80% of container capacity, 20 Main catalytic converter.*

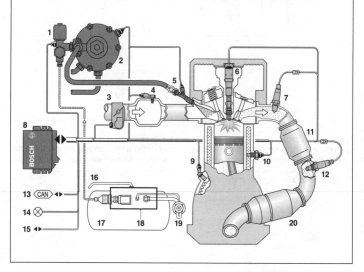

## LPG systems

### Storage of LPG

LPG is stored in a liquid state under pressure. Additional storage space is required on bivalent vehicles for the purpose of accommodating the cylindrical LPG tanks.

The new development of polymorphic composite tanks in combination with a smaller gasoline tank makes it possible for vehicles to cover ranges comparable with those of pure gasoline-operated vehicles without trading off cargo space.

All tanks are subject to stringent European safety regulations (ECE Regulation R 67-01) for new vehicles as well as national regulations for converted vehicles. Safety measures include:
– a non-return valve
– a fill restriction facility, designed to ensure the fill volume does not exceed 80% of the maximum tank volume (the remaining 20% is required to allow the liquid gas to expand at higher temperatures)

– a 27-bar blow-off valve
– a 120 °C temperature safety valve, and
– a gas take-off valve with flow limiter

Presently there are still three different types of tank coupling used throughout the world. Since 2002 new vehicles in Europe are equipped with standardized couplings. All LPG vehicles in Europe will be equipped with this coupling system as from 2008.

### Mixture formation

In most systems, LPG is injected in the intake manifold in the same way as in conventional multipoint gasoline-injection systems. A common fuel rail and the connected injector valves inject the LPG in the intake manifold either continuously at variable pressure or intermittently. The engine management calculates the required injection quantity. The system includes lambda closed-loop control to facilitate exhaust-gas treatment using a three-way catalytic converter.

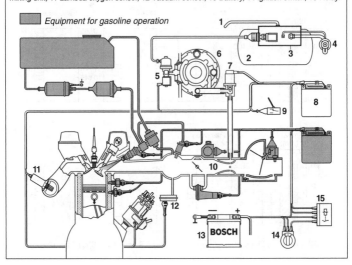

*Schematic diagram of an LPG system (carburetor principle)*
*1 Ventilation line for tank fittings, 2 LPG tank, 3 Housing with tank fittings, 4 External filler valve designed to stop refueling at 80% of tank capacity, 5 Gas shutoff valve, 6 Pressure regulator for evaporator, 7 Servomotor for gas control, 8 ECU, 9 Gas/gasoline changeover switch, 10 Venturi mixing unit, 11 Lambda oxygen sensor, 12 Vacuum sensor, 13 Battery, 14 Ignition switch, 15 Relay.*

Equipment for gasoline operation

In most cases, LPG is injected in gaseous form after evaporation in a pressure regulator. However, there are also systems in use which inject the LPG in liquid form. A fuel pump produces a specific pressure above the tank pressure. These systems comply with the current European emissions standard EURO 4 (applicable as from 2005).

Systems with a venturi mixing unit (carburetor principle) upstream of the throttle valve (with or without lambda closed-loop control) meet requirements adequately in countries with less stringent emission-control legislation.

Compared to the gasoline engine, the LPG engine develops an equivalent or a maximum of 5% less power output depending on the type of mixture formation system used.

**Exhaust emissions**

Compared to gasoline, the combustion of LPG produces approximately 10% less $CO_2$ emissions. In many countries, including Germany, a lower rate of mineral oil tax is levied on LPG-operated vehicles.

The limited emissions of LPG engines are only marginally lower than those of modern EURO 4 gasoline engines equipped with 3-way closed-loop catalytic converters. The advantages come from the non-limited pollutants that are in part carcinogenic or contribute to smog and acid formation. Compared to diesel engines, the formation of particulate is lower by several orders of magnitude (see diagram).

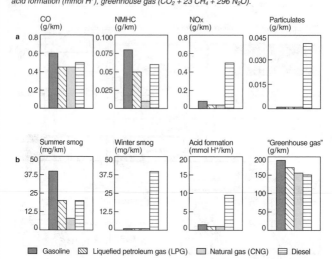

**Exhaust emissions and effects from fueling with gasoline, LPG, natural gas and diesel (direct injection)**
*Emission values for new mid-sized vehicle registrations with spark-ignition and diesel engine in the EU in 2002.*
*a) Pollutant emissions: CO, non-methane HC, $NO_X$, particulates,*
*b) Pollutant effect: summer smog (ethylene equivalent), winter smog (particulates), acid formation (mmol $H^+$), greenhouse gas ($CO_2 + 23\ CH_4 + 296\ N_2O$).*

■ Gasoline   ▨ Liquefied petroleum gas (LPG)   ▢ Natural gas (CNG)   ▤ Diesel

# Engines fueled by natural gas

## Applications

Against the backdrop of worldwide efforts to reduce $CO_2$ emissions and to comply with ever more stringent emission limits, natural gas is becoming increasingly important as an alternative fuel. The extended use of natural gas also serves to increase supply reliability, while reducing the dependence on crude-oil or petroleum imports.

In early 2002 there were worldwide 2 million natural-gas-operated vehicles, of which 15,000 were in operation in Germany. In its Directive KOM(2001)-547, the EU Commission proposes to replace 10% of total fuel consumption by natural gas by the year 2020. This would then correspond to a total of 25 million natural-gas operated vehicles in Europe.

## Natural-gas systems

### Storage of natural gas

The main component of natural gas is methane ($CH_4$), making up 80...99% depending on its origin. The remainder consists of inert gases such as carbon dioxide, nitrogen and other low-order hydrocarbons. A differentiation is made between L-gas (80...90% methane) and H-gas (> 90%), depending on the gas quality.

Natural gas can be stored both in liquid form at −162 °C as LNG (Liquefied Natural Gas) or in compressed form at a pressure of 200 bar as CNG (Compressed Natural Gas). In view of the great expense involved in storing the gas in liquid form, natural gas is used in compressed form in virtually all applications. The low-energy density of natural gas is a particular disadvantage. Based on the same energy content, CNG requires a storage tank with 4 times the volume compared to gasoline.

The ISO standard (International Organization for Standardization) uniformly governs the worldwide requirements relating to gas-carrying components and their installation in the vehicle. The mandatory ECE (Economic Commission for Europe) Directive 110 applies to all new vehicle registrations.

### Mixture formation

In most systems, gas is injected in the intake manifold in the same way as in conventional multipoint gasoline-injection systems. A low-pressure common rail supplies the injector valves that inject natural gas at intermittent intervals in the intake manifold. Mixture formation is improved by the completely gaseous supply of fuel, as natural gas does not condense on the intake-manifold walls and does not deposit a film there. This has a positive effect on emissions, particularly during the warm-up phase.

Both bi-fuel as well as mono-fuel vehicles are available on the market. Bi-fuel vehicles can operate both on natural gas as well as on gasoline, comparatively however, the engine output is approximately 10–15% lower in natural-gas-fueled engines. This is due to the lower volumetric efficiency attributed to displacement caused by the injected natural gas.

Monovalent vehicles can be optimized specifically for fueling by natural gas.

The extremely high antiknock quality of natural gas (up to 130 RON) enables very high engine compression of approx. 13:1 (gasoline engine approx. 9...11:1). As a result, the natural-gas engine is ideally suited for supercharging. Combined with reduced piston displacement (downsizing concept), efficiency increases due to additional dethrottling and reduced friction.

### Exhaust emissions

Compared to gasoline engines, natural-gas vehicles are characterized by approx. 20–30% lower $CO_2$ emissions due to the better hydrogen/carbon ratio (H/C ratio) of almost 4:1 (gasoline approx. 2:1) and the resulting shift in the main combustion products from $CO_2$ to $H_2O$. For this reason, many countries have reduced the mineral oil tax levied on natural gas.

Apart from the virtually particle-free combustion, in conjunction with a three-way closed-loop catalytic converter, only very low levels of the pollutants $NO_X$, CO and NMHC ("non-methane hydrocarbons": the sum of all hydrocarbons minus methane) are produced. Methane is classified as nontoxic and, in contrast to Europe, is therefore not considered to be a pollutant by American emissions-control legislation. Natural-gas vehicles comply with the current European emission-control legislation EURO 4 (valid as from 2005) while natural-gas operated buses conform to the stringent EEV emissions limits ("Enhanced Environmentally friendly Vehicle").

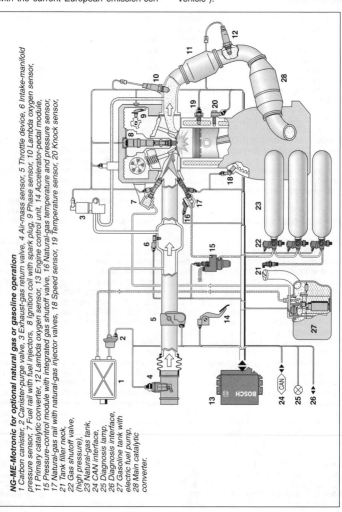

**NG-ME-Motronic for optional natural gas or gasoline operation**

1 Carbon canister, 2 Canister-purge valve, 3 Exhaust-gas return valve, 4 Air-mass sensor, 5 Throttle device, 6 Intake-manifold pressure sensor, 7 Fuel rail with fuel injectors, 8 Ignition coil with spark plug, 9 Phase sensor, 10 Lambda oxygen sensor, 11 Primary catalytic converter, 12 Lambda oxygen sensor, 13 Engine control unit, 14 Accelerator-pedal module, 15 Pressure-control module with integrated gas shutoff valve, 16 Natural-gas temperature and pressure sensor, 17 Natural-gas rail with natural-gas injector valves, 18 Speed sensor, 19 Temperature sensor, 20 Knock sensor, 21 Tank filler neck, 22 Gas shutoff valve, (high pressure), 23 Natural-gas tank, 24 CAN interface, 25 Diagnosis lamp, 26 Diagnosis interface, 27 Gasoline tank with electric fuel pump, 28 Main catalytic converter.

The natural-gas engine offers distinct advantages compared to gasoline and diesel engines, particularly with regard to the non-limited pollutant emissions that are in part carcinogenic or contribute to smog and acid formation (see diagram on P. 670).

### Natural-gas engine applications

In view of their limited range and the poor filling-station infrastructure (there are only about 300 filling stations in Germany in early 2003), natural-gas engines have so far been mainly in use in local public transportation fleets (e.g. buses and taxis). One thousand new natural-gas filling stations are planned by 2006.

Bi-fuel systems, which can be easily changed over from natural gas to gasoline operation, are used primarily in passenger cars.

### Engine management for natural-gas vehicles

The air drawn in by the engine is routed via the air-mass sensor and the electronic throttle valve to the intake manifold. From there, it enters the combustion chamber through the intake valves (see figure). The natural gas stored in the gas tank at a pressure of 200 bar flows via a high-pressure shutoff valve to the gas-pressure regulator that reduces the gas pressure to a constant system pressure of approximately 8 bar. The gas then flows through a low-pressure shutoff valve to a common gas-distributor rail, supplying one injector valve per cylinder. The mixture is prepared by intermittent injection of the natural gas in the intake manifold.

The spark plug ignites the gas mixture in the combustion chamber. Controlled by ignition output stages in the engine management, single-spark ignition coils provide the ignition energy in a distributorless system. Speed and phase sensors ensure correct synchronization. A knock sensor detects the possible occurrence of combustion knock.

The exhaust gas is forced past the exhaust valves to the exhaust-gas system. This comprises a methane-selective catalytic converter and a lambda oxygen sensor arranged upstream and downstream of the catalytic converter, similar to the arrangement used on the gasoline engine.

# Engines fueled by alcohol

## Applications

The alcohol fuels methanol and ethanol can be produced in a regenerative process from biomass (plants, wood, etc.) and can therefore contribute to reducing global carbon-dioxide emissions. The limited availability of fossil fuels and the increasing dependence on oil-producing countries has lead to an increased effort to develop engines and fuel-injection systems capable of using alcohols as alternative fuels (see "Alternative Fuels", P. 327). Due to its scarce availability, virtually the only places where ethanol is used are Brazil and the U.S.A. Spark-ignition engines running on alcohol generate lower emissions: reduced $CO_2$ output along with reduced ozone and smog formation. Added to this, alcohol fuels are completely free of sulfur.

## System

In the absence of full-coverage alcohol-distribution networks to ensure universal availability, engines and engine control systems must be designed for flexible dual-fuel operation, i.e. they must be capable of operating with variable proportions of methanol or ethanol. The mixed ethanol-gasoline fuel offered at filling stations predominantly in Brazil and the U.S.A. is also referred to as "Flex-Fuel" (e.g. E15 = 15% ethanol + 85% gasoline or E85 = 85% ethanol + 15% gasoline). Alcohol fuels place particularly high demands on engines and fuel-delivery components. Moisture, acids and gums contained in the fuel pose a hazard to metals, plastics and rubber seals. Compared to methanol, ethanol has the advantage of a lower toxicity level.

The higher antiknock quality of methanol and ethanol compared to gasoline permits higher engine compression, making the engines more efficient. On the other hand, methanol's lower calorific value means that volumetric fuel consumption is almost doubled and about 1.5 times higher using ethanol compared to gasoline. This requires larger tank volumes and adaptation of the fuel injectors. Special lubricants are able to maintain long-term stability despite the aggressiveness of alcohol and its combustion products.

The exhaust gas is treated by a three-way closed-loop catalytic converter. Exact pilot control of the fuel mixture requires a fuel sensor which sends a signal to the ECU, reflecting the proportion of methanol or ethanol in the fuel.

The engine management system calculates the necessary mixture and ignition corrections applicable to a particular set of engine operating characteristics.

# Engines fueled by hydrogen

## Applications

Increasing significance is being attached to hydrogen as an alternative fuel in view of its $CO_2$-free combustion properties, and the fact that it can be produced from renewable energy sources. The production of hydrogen, the required infrastructure, refueling technology, and the on-board storage pose complex issues that have no technically or economically feasible solutions that been proved to be satisfactory so far. Producing hydrogen by means of electrolysis requires large quantities of electrical power, e.g. from regenerative power sources such as solar energy, wind power or nuclear power. Today hydrogen is produced from natural gas almost exclusively on a large scale through steam reforming – however this process involves the release of $CO_2$.

*Hydrogen-powered passenger car with spark-ignition engine (BMW 735i)*
$LH_2$ *Liquid hydrogen,* $GH_2$ *Gaseous hydrogen. 1 Valve block for* $LH_2$ *fueling and* $GH_2$ *supply (vacuum-insulated), 2 Hydrogen lines, vacuum-insulated, 3* $LH_2$ *Evaporator, 4 Metering valve for regulating power with electronic control, 5 Hydrogen injectors, 6 Overcurrent and safety valves, 7 Liquid-hydrogen tank with vacuum super-insulation, 8 Hydrogen sensors for automatic leak monitoring, 9 Throttle valve for gasoline operation with electronic control, 10 Variable-speed centrifugal supercharger.*

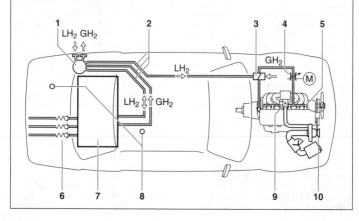

## Hydrogen system

### Storing hydrogen in the vehicle

Gaseous storage (pressurized tanks)

In view of the low volumetric energy density of hydrogen, extremely high pressures are required for its storage in gaseous form (350 to 700 bar). These pressures place special demands on the properties of the materials used. At a pressure of 700 bar, the storage volume is 7 times that of a gasoline tank with equivalent energy content.

Liquid storage (cryogenic tank)

Liquid storage currently represents the most feasible alternative with regard to both weight and energy density (approx. 4 times the storage volume compared to gasoline). The extremely low temperature required (–253 °C) places substantial demands on thermal insulation. Residual heat input causes evaporation loss when the vehicle is parked for longer periods (longer than 3...12 days). This poses a problem for the use of hydrogen in motor vehicles, as hydrogen is consumed even when the engine is turned off. An electric evaporator maintains the tank pressure during operation to a setpoint value.

A further disadvantage of this type of storage is the high energy required for the liquefaction, amounting to roughly 30% of the source energy.

Other forms of storage

Other storage options include chemical storage, e.g. the storage of hydrogen in metal hydrides, methylcyclohexane, sodium boronate or liquid organic hydrides. Carbon-based nanostructures are still at the research stage.

None of these methods has yet gained widespread acceptance. This means that pressure and liquid storage methods are currently used almost exclusively for the purpose of storing hydrogen.

### Mixture formation

Regardless of storage mode, gaseous hydrogen is injected in the intake manifold in all systems. Due to the low density of hydrogen, a large proportion of the air drawn in during injection is displaced by the hydrogen. This results in a reduction of the air delivery rate and therefore a reduction in the engine output compared to gasoline.

Although there are a number of advantages in injecting hydrogen directly in the combustion chamber (improved charge for higher output, mixture cooling for low $NO_x$ emissions, no danger of backfiring) the high demands place on the injector valves means this can only be implemented with great difficulty.

External mixture-formation concepts rely on a continuous-injection system in which a common electromechanical metering valve and a distributor feed gaseous hydrogen to the individual intake tracts. Backfiring into the intake passage is prevented by lean mixtures or supplementary water injection. A supercharging device can be used to compensate for a portion of the power loss associated with lean operation.

As is the case with natural gas, intermittent sequential injection systems are being used to an ever greater extent to inject hydrogen in the intake ports of the engine. This method's unlimited range of options for injection timing allows it to inhibit backfiring almost completely, even with rich mixtures.

Compared to gasoline, the use of hydrogen places more stringent demands on the injector valve with regard to its sealing properties and the necessary high volumetric flow resulting from the low density of hydrogen.

### Exhaust emissions

During combustion, pure hydrogen oxidizes with the oxygen contained in air to form water. Provided no fossil fuels are used in its production, hydrogen is thus the only fuel which can be used to avoid all $CO_2$ emissions. Nitrogen oxides ($NO_x$ emissions) produced during the combustion process can be effectively reduced by extremely lean mixtures or catalytic exhaust-gas treatment.

# Fuel supply (low-pressure stage)

The function of the fuel-supply system is to store and filter the required fuel and to make fuel available to the fuel-injection installation at a specific supply pressure under all operating conditions. The return fuel is also cooled in some applications.

The fuel-supply system comprises the following essential components (see figures):
– fuel tank
– preliminary filter (not for passenger-car UIS)
– ECU cooler (optional)
– presupply pump (optional, also in-tank pump for passenger cars)
– fuel filter
– fuel-supply pump (low pressure)
– pressure-control valve (overflow valve)
– fuel cooler (optional)
– low-pressure fuel lines

Individual components can be combined to form assemblies (e.g. fuel-supply pump with pressure limiter). In axial- and radial-piston distributor pumps and partially in the common-rail system, the fuel-supply pump is integrated in the high-pressure pump.

## Diesel fuel-injection system

As the following figures for passenger-car UIS, radial-piston distributor pump and common rail show, the fuel supply differs markedly, depending on the fuel-injection system used.

### Fuel tank
The fuel tank stores the fuel. It must be corrosion-resistant and leakproof to pressures which are double the operating pressure, but at least to a gage pressure of 0.3 bar. Gage pressure that occurs must escape automatically through suitable openings or safety valves. When the vehicle is cornering, is at an inclined position, or is subject to jolts or impacts, no fuel is permitted to emerge from the filler plug or the pressure-compensation devices. The fuel tank must be mounted separately from the engine in such a way as to prevent the fuel from igniting, even in the event of an accident.

### Fuel lines
In addition to metal tubes, flexible, flame-retardant tubes braced with steel braiding can be used for the low-pressure stage. They must be arranged in such a way as to avoid mechanical damage and to prevent dripping or vaporizing fuel from collecting or igniting. The function of the fuel lines must not be impaired in any way in the event of torsional movement in the ve-

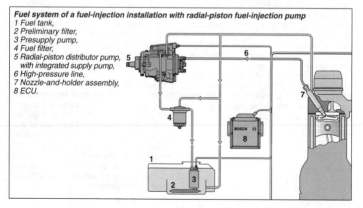

*Fuel system of a fuel-injection installation with radial-piston fuel-injection pump*
1 Fuel tank,
2 Preliminary filter,
3 Presupply pump,
4 Fuel filter,
5 Radial-piston distributor pump, with integrated supply pump,
6 High-pressure line,
7 Nozzle-and-holder assembly,
8 ECU.

hicle frame, engine movement or the like. All fuel-carrying parts must be protected against the operation-impairing influence of heat. In buses, fuel lines must not be located in the passenger compartment or the driver's position, and fuel must not be delivered by the force of gravity.

**Diesel filter**
The function of this filter is prevent the fuel from being contaminated by particulates and so ensure a minimum level of fuel purity upstream of components subject to wear (see P. 681).

Design variations
The right choice of filter is dependent on the fuel-injection system used and on the operating conditions.

Preliminary filter for presupply pumps: The preliminary filter is usually a strainer with a mesh size of 300 µm and is used in addition to the actual fuel filter.

Main filter: Easy-change filters with spiral vee-shape or wound filter elements are widely used (see P. 681). They are bolted to a filter mounting bracket. It is also possible to mount two filters in parallel (greater storage capacity) or in series (multistage filter for increasing the filtration efficiency or fine filter with adapted preliminary filter). Housing filters, in which only the filter element is changed, are increasingly being used.

Water separator: Prevents water from entering the fuel-injection equipment in emulsified or free form (see P. 682).

Fuel preheater: Prevents the filter pores from being clogged by paraffin crystals during winter operation. The components mostly integrated in the filter heat the fuel electrically by means of cooling water or return fuel.

Hand pumps: Help to fill and vent the system after a filter has been changed. They are usually integrated in the filter cover.

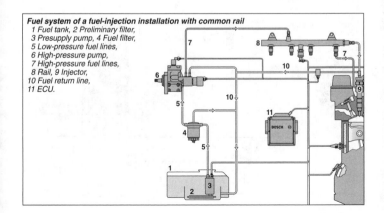

*Fuel system of a fuel-injection installation with common rail*
1 Fuel tank, 2 Preliminary filter,
3 Presupply pump, 4 Fuel filter,
5 Low-pressure fuel lines,
6 High-pressure pump,
7 High-pressure fuel lines,
8 Rail, 9 Injector,
10 Fuel return line,
11 ECU.

**Presupply pump**
The presupply pump – an electric fuel pump or a remotely driven gear fuel-supply pump – draws in fuel from the fuel tank and delivers it continuously to the high-pressure pump (see following section).

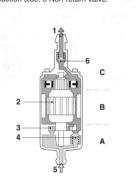

*Single-stage electric fuel pump*
A Pump element, B Electric motor,
C Connecting cover.
1 Pressure side, 2 Motor armature,
3 Pump element, 4 Pressure limiter,
5 Suction side, 6 Non-return valve.

# Diesel fuel-supply components

### Fuel-supply pump
The function of the fuel-supply pump in the low-pressure stage (presupply pump) is to supply the high-pressure components with sufficient fuel
– in every operating state,
– with a low level of noise,
– at the required pressure, and
– over the entire service life of the vehicle

Different types are used, depending on the field of application.

<u>Electric fuel pump</u>
Application:
– Optional for distributor injection pumps (only in event of long fuel lines or great difference in height between fuel tank and fuel-injection pump).
– For unit injector system (passenger cars).
– For common-rail system (passenger cars).

The electric fuel pump corresponds to the design variations of the pumps used with spark-ignition engines (see P. 599 onwards). Roller-cell pumps are usually used for diesel applications.

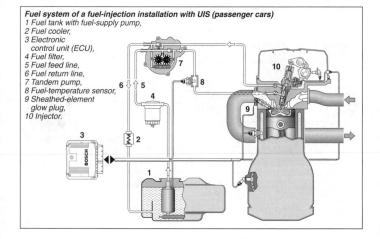

*Fuel system of a fuel-injection installation with UIS (passenger cars)*
1 Fuel tank with fuel-supply pump,
2 Fuel cooler,
3 Electronic control unit (ECU),
4 Fuel filter,
5 Fuel feed line,
6 Fuel return line,
7 Tandem pump,
8 Fuel-temperature sensor,
9 Sheathed-element glow plug,
10 Injector.

Gear pump
Application:
– For single-cylinder pump systems for commercial vehicles (unit injector and unit pump system, individual injection pump (PF)).
– Partially for common-rail system (commercial vehicles, passenger cars and offroad vehicles).

The gear pump is mounted directly on the engine or, in the case of a common rail, it is integrated in the high-pressure pump. It is driven mechanically by way of a clutch, or a gear wheel, or toothed belt.

The primary components are two intermeshing, counter-rotating gear wheels which deliver the fuel into the tooth spaces from the suction side to the pressure side. The line of contact of the gear wheels provides the seal between the suction and pressure sides and prevents fuel from flowing back.

The delivery quantity is roughly proportional to the engine speed. Fuel delivery is therefore controlled either by means of restrictors on the suction side or by an overflow valve on the pressure side.

Vane-type supply pump
Application: Presupply pump integrated in distributor injection pumps.

The vane-type supply pump is mounted on the drive shaft in the distributor injection pump. The impeller is centered on the drive shaft and supported by a Woodruff key. An eccentric ring mounted in bearings in the housing surrounds the impeller.

The centrifugal force generated by the motion of rotation presses the four vanes of the impeller outwards against the eccentric ring. The fuel between the underside of the vanes and the impeller supports this outward movement of the vanes.

The fuel passes through the inlet passage and a kidney-shaped recess into the space created by the impeller, the vane and the eccentric ring. The rotary motion forces the fuel located between the vanes into the upper kidney-shaped recess and through a bore to the outlet.

*Gear fuel pump (diagram)*
*1 Suction side, 2 Drive gear, 3 Pressure side.*

*Rotary vane pump*
*1 Inner pump chamber, 2 Eccentric ring,*
*3 Sickle-shaped cell, 4 Fuel inlet,*
*5 Pump housing, 6 Fuel outlet,*
*7 Woodruff key, 8 Drive shaft,*
*9 Vane, 10 Impeller.*

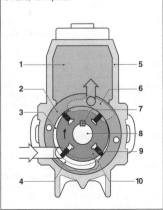

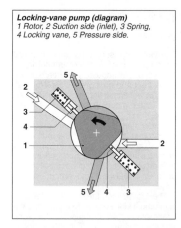

*Locking-vane pump (diagram)*
*1 Rotor, 2 Suction side (inlet), 3 Spring,*
*4 Locking vane, 5 Pressure side.*

Locking-vane pump

Application: Unit injector system for passenger cars.

In a locking-vane pump, springs press two locking vanes against a rotor. As the rotor turns, the volume is increased on the suction side and fuel is drawn into two chambers. The volume is reduced on the pressure side and fuel is delivered from the two chambers.

The locking-vane pump delivers fuels at very low speeds.

Tandem fuel pump

Application: Unit injector system for passenger cars.

This pump is an assembly consisting of a fuel-supply pump (locking-vane or gear pump) and a vacuum pump for the brake booster. It is integrated in the engine cylinder head and driven by the engine camshaft.

**Low-pressure control valve**
The pressure-control valve (also known as the overflow restrictor) is installed in the fuel-return line. It provides an adequate operating pressure in the low-pressure stage of the UIS and UPS multipoint fuel-injection systems under all operating conditions and ensures that the pumps are filled uniformly.

The valve accumulator plunger opens at a pressure of 300...350 kPa (3...3.5 bar). A compression spring compensates for minor pressure variations in accumulator volume. At an opening pressure of 4...4.5 bar, an edge seal opens and produces a noticeable increase in flow rate.

There are two screws with different spring-force settings for presetting the opening pressure.

**Fuel cooler**
The high pressure in the injector of the UIS for passenger cars and some common-rail systems heats up the fuel to such an extent that it has to be cooled before it flows back. The fuel returning from the injector flows through the fuel cooler (heat exchanger) and dissipates thermal energy to the coolant in the fuel-cooling circuit. This is separate from the engine-cooling circuit because the coolant temperature of an engine running at operating temperature is too high to cool the fuel. The fuel-cooling circuit is connected to the engine-cooling circuit at the compensating reservoir. This helps to keep the fuel-cooling circuit filled and compensates for any changes in volume caused by temperature fluctuations.

*Fuel-cooling circuit*
*1 Fuel-supply pump, 2 Fuel-temperature sensor, 3 Fuel cooler, 4 Fuel tank,*
*5 Compensating reservoir, 6 Engine-cooling circuit, 7 Coolant pump, 8 Auxiliary cooler.*

## Fuel filter

As in spark-ignition engines, it is essential in a diesel engine to ensure that the fuel system is protected against contamination. The function of the fuel filter is to reduce contamination from particulates (for general requirements, see P. 604).

<u>Fuel filters for diesel fuel-injection systems</u>
Compared with gasoline-injection systems, diesel fuel-injection systems require increased wear protection and finer filters to cater for the much higher injection pressures. Diesel fuel is also more heavily contaminated than gasoline. Diesel filters are therefore designed as easy-change filters. Bolt-on easy-change filters, in-line filters and nonmetal filter elements are widely used as replacement parts in aluminum, plastic or sheet-steel filter cases (to comply with increased requirements in crashes). Spiral vee-shape filter elements are the preferred choice. The diesel filter is usually located in the low-pressure system between the electric fuel pump and the high-pressure pump.

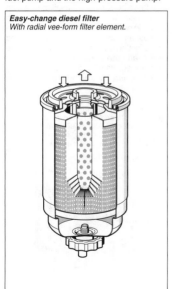

***Easy-change diesel filter***
*With radial vee-form filter element.*

In the last few years the requirements for filter fineness have become more stringent owing to the introduction of second-generation common-rail systems and advanced unit injector systems for passenger cars and commercial vehicles. Depending on the application (fuel contamination, periods of engine standstill), the new systems require a filtration efficiency of between 85% and 98.6% (single pass, particulate interval 3 and 5 µm, ISO/TR 13353: 1994). The fuel filters fitted to the latest generation of automobiles must be capable of storing larger volumes of particulates due to the longer service intervals, and of separating superfine particulates efficiently. This can only be achieved by using special filter mediums, e.g. consisting of multiple layers made of synthetic microfiber. These filter mediums exploit the effects of a fine prefilter, and guarantee maximum particulate-retention capability by separating particulates inside each filter layer. The new superfine filter generation allows engines to run on fatty-acid methyl esthers (biodiesel). However, the servicing philosophy must provide for a shorter filter service life due to the higher concentration of organic particulates.

A second essential function of the diesel filter is to separate emulsified and free water in order to prevent corrosion damage. An effective water separation of more than 93% at rated flow (ISO 4020) is particularly important for distributor injection pumps and common-rail systems. Water separation takes place by coalescence on the filter medium (formation of droplets due to the different surface tensions of water and fuel). The separated water collects in the water chamber in the bottom of the filter case. Conductivity sensors are partly used to monitor the water level. The water is drained off manually via a water drain plug or a push-button switch. Fully automatic water-disposal systems are under development.

For extra heavy-duty requirements, an additional preliminary filter/water separator, with a filter fineness adapted to the fine filter, is fitted on the suction or pressure side. Preliminary filters of this type are mostly used for commercial vehicles in countries where diesel quality is poor.

New-generation diesel filters integrate additional modular functions such as:
– Fuel preheating (electric; fuel return) to prevent paraffin clogging during winter operation.
– Fuel cooling.
– Maintenance indication by way of a differential-pressure measurement, and
– Filling and venting devices.

# Diesel fuel-injection systems

## Overview

In the diesel combustion process, the fuel is always injected directly into the combustion chamber at a nozzle pressure ranging from 200 to > 2,000 bar. Depending on the combustion process, fuel is injected into a prechamber in indirect-injection engines (at a relatively low pressure of < 350 bar). In the meantime, direct injection has become the most common process, in which fuel is injected (at high pressure up to > 2,000 bar) into the nondivided combustion chamber.

For more details on diesel fuel-injection systems, refer to the bibliography on P. 711.

### Diesel-engine management
#### Requirements
The power output $P$ from a diesel engine is determined by the available clutch torque and the engine speed. The clutch torque is produced from the torque generated by the combustion process, reduced by the friction torque and the charge-cycle losses, and the torque required for operating the auxiliary systems driven directly by the engine. The combustion torque is generated in the power cycle and is de-

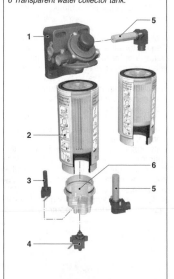

*Diesel filter with water drain*
1 Filter head with filler pump, 2 Easy-change filter element, 3 Water sensor, 4 Automatic water discharge valve, 5 PTC heater in filter head and in collector tank (optional), 6 Transparent water collector tank.

*Modular diesel housing filter for passenger cars with additional functions*
1 Fuel cooler, 2 Thermostat-controlled return line, 3 Electric PTC heater, 4 Water sensor, 5 Two nonmetal superfilter elements.

termined by the following variables if the excess air is sufficient:
- the supplied fuel mass,
- the start of combustion determined by the start of injection,
- the injection/combustion process.

In addition, the maximum speed-dependent torque is limited by:
- smoke emissions,
- the cylinder pressure,
- the temperature load of different components, and
- the mechanical load of the complete drivetrain.

Primary function of engine management
The primary function of engine management is to adjust the torque generated by the engine or, in some applications, to adjust a specific engine speed within the permitted operating range (e.g. idling).

In a diesel engine, exhaust-gas treatment and noise suppression are performed to a great extent inside the engine, i.e. by controlling the combustion process. This, in turn, is performed by engine management by changing the following variables:
- cylinder charge,
- tempering of the cylinder charge during the induction stroke,
- composition of the cylinder charge (exhaust-gas recirculation),
- charge motion (intake swirl),
- start of injection,
- injection pressure, and
- rate-of-discharge curve control (e.g. pilot injection, divided fuel injection, etc.).

Until the 1980s fuel injection in vehicle engines, i.e. injected fuel quantity and start of ignition, was governed exclusively by mechanical means. Here, the injected fuel quantity is varied via a helix on the plunger or via sleeves as a function of load and speed. In the case of mechanical injection, the start of injection/delivery is adjusted by flyweight governors (speed-dependent), or hydraulically by pressure control as a function of speed and load. This is discussed in more detail in the sections headed "In-line injection pump" and "Distributor injection pump".

Emission-control legislation calls for highly precise control of the injected fuel quantity and start of injection as a function of variables such as temperature, speed, load, height, etc. This can only be provided effectively by electronic control. This form of control has become widespread not just in the automotive field. This is the only form of control that permits continuous monitoring of the emission-related function of the fuel-injection system. Legislation also requires onboard diagnosis in some applications.

Control of injected fuel quantity and start of injection is performed in EDC (Electronic Diesel Control) systems by means of low- or high-pressure solenoid valves or other electrical actuators. Control of the rate of discharge, i.e. the quantity provided per crankshaft degree, can be performed indirectly by means of servo valves and needle-lift control.

**Details**
A fuel-injection system comprises a low-pressure stage and a high-pressure stage. The low-pressure delivery circuit has already been discussed in the chapter headed "Fuel supply". The system-specific differences will be explained for the different fuel-injection systems in the relevant sections.

Mechanical and electronic (EDC) control systems will be described in general first.

Mechanical control is used exclusively for discrete fuel-injection (PF) pumps, in-line fuel-injection and axial-piston distributor pumps. There are a multitude of governors and add-on modules which are required for in-line fuel-injection and distributor injection pumps, depending on the application. Mechanical control is always a compromise when compared with electronic control, as the latter is more precise, permits a whole range of influencing variables to be taken into consideration, and allows ongoing adaptation of manipulated variables in the closed-control loop. The advantages are:

- Lower fuel consumption, reduced emissions, higher power output and torque through improved fuel-delivery control and more precise start of injection.
- Low, constant idle speed and adaptation of idle speed to additional components (e.g. air conditioners).
- Improved comfort and convenience functions such as surge damping control, smooth-running control or cruise control.
- Improved diagnostic options.
- Additional control functions such as boost-pressure control, preheating time (glow-plug), exhaust-gas recirculation (EGR), exhaust-gas treatment, electronic vehicle immobilizer.
- Data communication with other electronic systems, such as traction control (TCS), electronic transmission-shift control, and integration in the overall vehicle system.

Electronic fuel-delivery control is known as "drive by wire", i.e. there is no longer any direct connection between the accelerator pedal and the fuel-injection pump, for example.

The following fuel-injection systems are used in motor-vehicle diesel engines:

In-line fuel-injection pump with mechanical or electronic control: The in-line fuel-injection pump is used mainly in commercial-vehicle engines. A number of plunger-and-barrel assemblies corresponding to the number of engine cylinders are accommodated in a common housing and driven by a camshaft situated in the housing (pump with internal drive, PE).

In in-line fuel-injection pumps, timing is performed by means of an upper helix on top of the assembly or an external centrifugal timing device. Only the control-sleeve pump has an integrated timing device. Two electric actuators control injected fuel quantity and start of delivery.

Distributor injection pump with mechanical or electronic governor and integrated timing device: The axial-piston distributor pump is used in particular in high-speed IDI diesel engines and in DI diesel engines for passenger cars and light com-

mercial vehicles. In this type of pump, a central plunger driven by a cam plate generates pressure and distributes the fuel to the individual cylinders. A control sleeve or solenoid valve meters the injected fuel quantity.

The radial-piston distributor pump is primarily used on modern high-speed DI diesel engines for passenger cars and light commercial vehicles. Pressure is generated and the fuel is delivered by two to four plungers in a radial configuration driven by a cam ring. A solenoid valve controls the injected fuel quantity and start of delivery.

In addition to the in-line fuel-injection and distributor injection pumps, there are also individual injection pumps, also called plug-in pumps (PF: pumps with external drive). These are mostly used on large marine engines, construction machinery and low-power engines.

Another modern fuel-injection system is the UIS (Unit Injector System), in which the fuel-injection pump and fuel injector form a single unit. One unit injector per cylinder is installed in the cylinder head. The unit is driven by the engine camshaft, either directly via a push rod, or indirectly via a rocker-arm assembly.

The UPS (Unit Pump System) operates according to the same principle as the Unit Injector System. However, in this type of pump, a short high-pressure delivery line is connected between the pump and nozzle. This permits more freedom of design, as the camshaft can be located either in the engine block or the cylinder head.

Common to all of these systems is the fact that the required injection pressure is generated at the moment each injection occurs. In the case of electronically controlled systems, however, the rate-of-discharge curve can be influenced by the cam contour as well as by solenoid valve actuation. Nevertheless, the maximum possible pressure depends directly on engine speed and injected fuel quantity.

The injection pressure can be set virtually independently of engine speed and load using an accumulator injection system. In this so-called <u>Common Rail System</u> (CRS), pressure generation and fuel injection are decoupled from time or location. Injection pressure is generated by a separate high-pressure pump. This pump need not necessarily be driven synchronously with fuel injection. The pressure can be set independently of the engine speed and load in accordance with an applied pressure map and electrically operated injectors are used instead of pressure-controlled fuel injectors. The time and duration of injector actuation determine the start of injection and the injected fuel quantity. This system also offers a great deal of freedom with regard to the design of multiple or divided injection.

All the systems must demonstrate minimum scatter from lift to lift and from cylinder to cylinder for the purpose of precise open- and closed-loop control of injected fuel quantity and start of injection. To guarantee this over a long service life, it is imperative that all system components be manufactured from high-precision, close-tolerance individual parts.

## In-line fuel-injection pump

(PE = pump with internal drive, i.e. separate camshaft).

Depending on the application purpose, there are in-line fuel-injection pumps for different quantity and pressure levels. The various in-line pump generations are distinguished according to their designations:

– <u>Size M</u> for small engines including passenger cars with indirect injection ($p_{Ppe} < 350$ bar).
– <u>Size A</u> for mid-sized engines with direct injection and low pressure requirement ($p < 650$ bar).
– <u>Size MW</u> for mid-sized DI vehicle engines with displacements up to approx. 1 l/cylinder and pressures up to approx. 850 bar.
– <u>Size P</u> with different versions for big DI vehicle engines up to ≥ 2 l/cylinder displacement and pump-side pressures up to approx. 1,150 bar.
– <u>Size ZW</u> has been developed for marine and off-highway engines with high specific power outputs of > 60 kW/cylinder.

*Fuel-injection system with mechanical in-line fuel-injection pump*
*1 Fuel tank, 2 Governor, 3 Fuel-supply pump, 4 Fuel-injection pump, 5 Timing device, 6 Drive from engine, 7 Fuel filter, 8 Vent, 9 Nozzle-and-holder assembly, 10 Fuel return line, 11 Overflow line.*

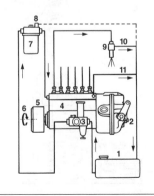

*Applications for various types of in-line fuel-injection pump*

Pump pressure $p$ (bar) vs Output per cylinder $P$ (kW/cyl.)

As the figure on P. 685 shows, the in-line fuel-injection pump system consists of:
– Fuel tank,
– Fuel-supply pump,
– Filter,
– Fuel-injection pump with governor,
– High-pressure lines, and
– Nozzle-and-holder assemblies

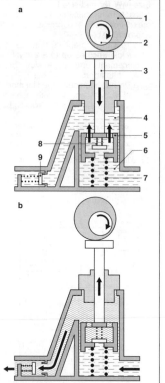

*Single-acting presupply pump (operating principle)*
*a) Cam stroke, b) Spring stroke.*
*1 Drive eccentric, 2 Fuel-injection pump camshaft, 3 Tappet, 4 Working chamber, 5 Pump plunger, 6 Fuel gallery, 7 Compression spring, 8 Suction valve, 9 Delivery valve.*

a

b

### Fuel-supply pump

A piston pump delivers the fuel to the fuel-injection pump fuel gallery at a gage pressure of 1...2.5 bar. The cam-driven supply-pump plunger travels to TDC on every stroke. It is not rigidly connected to the drive element; instead, a spring supplies the return pressure. The plunger spring responds to increases in line pressure by reducing the plunger's return travel to a portion of the full stroke. The greater the pressure in the delivery line, the lower the delivery quantity.

### High-pressure pump

Every in-line fuel-injection pump has a plunger-and-barrel assembly (<u>pumping element</u>) for each engine cylinder. An engine-driven camshaft moves the plunger in

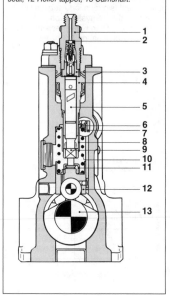

*Size P in-line fuel-injection pump*
*1 Delivery-valve holder, 2 Spring seat, 3 Delivery valve, 4 Pump barrel, 5 Pump plunger, 6 Lever arm with ball head, 7 Control rack, 8 Control sleeve, 9 Plunger control arm, 10 Plunger return spring, 11 Spring seat, 12 Roller tappet, 13 Camshaft.*

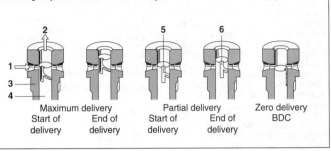

**Fuel-delivery control in the in-line fuel-injection pump**
1 From fuel gallery, 2 To nozzle, 3 Barrel, 4 Plunger, 5 Lower helix, 6 Vertical (stop) groove.

| Maximum delivery | | Partial delivery | | Zero delivery |
| Start of delivery | End of delivery | Start of delivery | End of delivery | BDC |

the delivery direction, and a spring presses it back to its initial position. Although the plunger has no seal, it is fitted with such precision (clearance 3...5 μm) that its operation is virtually leak-free, even at high pressures and low engine speeds.

The plunger's actual stroke is constant. The delivery quantity is changed by altering the plunger's effective stroke. Inclined helices have been machined into the plunger for this purpose, so that the plunger's effective stroke changes when it rotates. Active pumping starts when the upper edge of the plunger closes the intake port. The high-pressure chamber above the plunger is connected by a vertical groove to the chamber below the helix. Delivery ceases when the helix uncovers the intake port.

Various helix designs are employed in the plunger. On plunger-and-barrel assemblies with a lower helix only, delivery always starts with the same plunger lift. However, the plunger advances or is retarded at the end of delivery depending on its rotation position. An upper helix can be employed to vary the start of delivery. There are also plunger-and-barrel assemblies on the market which combine upper and lower helices in a single unit.

In order of their suitability for use at high injection pressures, the major types of delivery valve currently in use are:
− Constant-volume valve,
− Constant-volume valve with return-flow restriction,
− Constant-pressure valve.

The pressure-control valves and pressure-relief characteristics must be specially designed for the specific application. Units incorporating a return-flow restriction or constant-pressure valve have an additional throttle element to dampen the pressure waves reflected back from

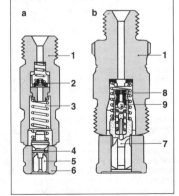

**Delivery-valve holder with delivery valve**
a) With constant-volume valve and return-flow restriction,
b) With constant-pressure valve.
1 Delivery-valve holder, 2 Return-flow restriction, 3 Dead volume, 4 Retraction piston, 5 Valve ball, 6 Valve holder, 7 Foward-delivery valve, 8 Calibrated restriction, 9 Pressure-holding valve.

a                                    b

the nozzle, thus preventing it from opening again. The constant-pressure valve is generally employed to maintain stable hydraulic characteristics in high-pressure fuel-injection systems, e.g. on small, high-speed direct-injection engines.

In fuel-injection pumps which generate moderate pressures of up to 600 bar (e.g. Size A), the plunger-and-barrel assembly is installed in the pump housing in a fixed position, where it is held in place by the delivery valve and the delivery-valve holder.

In pumps which generate injection pressures greater than approx. 600 bar, the plunger-and-barrel assembly, delivery valve and delivery-valve holder are screwed together to form a single unit, which means that the high sealing forces need no longer be absorbed by the pump housing (e.g. Sizes MW, P).

The in-line fuel-injection pump and the attached governor are connected to the engine lube-oil system.

## Speed governing

The main function of the governor is to limit the high idle speed. In other words, it must ensure that the diesel engine does not exceed the high idle speed specified by the manufacturer. Depending upon type, the governor's functions may include maintaining specific, constant engine speeds independently of load, such as idle, or other speeds in the range between idle and high-idle speed. The governor can also be used, for example, to adjust full-load delivery in accordance with engine speed (adaptation), charge-air or atmospheric pressure, and it can be used to meter the extra fuel required for starting. For these functions, the governor moves the control rack accordingly. The control rack then turns the plunger helices to the desired position, thus adapting the delivery quantity.

## Mechanical (flyweight) governors

The mechanical governor (also known as a flyweight or centrifugal governor) is driven by the fuel-injection pump camshaft, and provides the performance curves described below. The flyweights, which act against the force of the governor springs, are connected to the control rack by a

*Governor characteristic curves*
a Positive torque control in upper speed range, b Uncontrolled range, c Negative torque control.
1 Idle-speed adjustment point, 2 Full-load curve, 3 Full-load curve turbocharged engine, 4 Full-load curve naturally aspirated engine, 5 Full-load curve naturally aspirated engine with altitude compensation, 6 Intermediate engine-speed control, 7 Temperature-dependent excess-fuel quantity.

*Variable-speed governor*

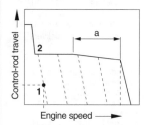

*Minimum-maximum-speed governor*

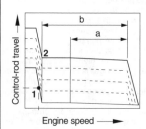

*Complex governor with additional control functions*

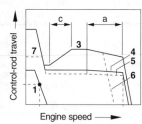

system of levers. During steady-state operation, centrifugal and spring forces are in a state of equilibrium, and the control rack assumes a position for fuel delivery corresponding to engine power output at that operating point. A drop in engine speed – for instance, due to increased load – results in a corresponding reduction in centrifugal force, and the governor springs move the flyweights, and with them the control rack, in the direction for increased fuel delivery until equilibrium is restored.

Various functions are combined to produce the following types of governor:

### Governor types
#### Variable-speed governors
The variable-speed governor maintains a virtually constant engine speed in accordance with the position of the control lever.

Applications: Preferably for commercial vehicles with auxiliary power take-offs, for construction machinery, agricultural tractors, in ships and in stationary installations.

#### Minimum-maximum-speed governors
From the program map for the minimum-maximum-speed governor, it can be seen that this type of governor is effective only at idle and when the engine reaches high idle speed. The torque in the range between these two extremes is determined exclusively by the position of the accelerator pedal.

Applications: For road vehicles.

#### Combination governors
Combination governors are a synthesis of the two governor types described above. Depending upon the specific application, active control can be in the upper or lower engine-speed range.

### Governor types
In the RQ and RQV governors, the flyweights act directly on the governor springs, and control-lever movements vary the transfer ratio at the variable-fulcrum lever.

In the RSV and RSF governors, the governor spring is outside of the flyweights; the transfer ratio at the fulcrum lever remains essentially constant.

### Speed droop
The governor's performance characteristics are essentially a function of the slope of the control curve, defined as speed droop:

$$\delta = \frac{n_{LO} - n_{VO}}{n_{VO}} \cdot 100\%$$

---

**RSV Variable-speed governor**
*1 Pump plunger, 2 Control rack, 3 High-idle-speed stop, 4 Control lever, 5 Starting spring, 6 Stop or low-idle stop, 7 Governor spring, 8 Auxiliary idle-speed spring, 9 Fuel-injection pump camshaft, 10 Flyweight, 11 Sliding bolt, 12 Torque-control spring, 13 Full-load stop.*

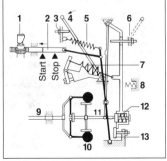

---

**RQ Minimum-maximum-speed governor**
*1 Pump plunger, 2 Control rack, 3 Full-load stop, 4 Control lever, 5 Fuel-injection pump camshaft, 6 Flyweight, 7 Governor spring, 8 Sliding bolt.*

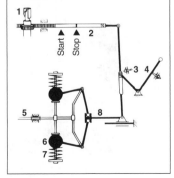

The smaller the difference between the upper no-load speed ($n_{LO}$) and the upper WOT speed ($n_{VO}$), the lower the speed droop, i.e. the greater the precision with which the governor maintains a specific engine speed. Variable-speed governors in small high-speed engines generally achieve a full-load speed regulation (top-end breakaway consistency) of 6...10%.

### Mechanical add-on equipment
Torque control

An auxiliary spring (torque-control spring) is installed at a suitable position in the

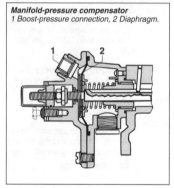

**Manifold-pressure compensator**
1 Boost-pressure connection, 2 Diaphragm.

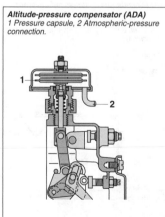

**Altitude-pressure compensator (ADA)**
1 Pressure capsule, 2 Atmospheric-pressure connection.

governor mechanism. The spring precisely adapts the governor's output curve to the diesel engine's full-load fuel requirements by lowering it slightly. When a given engine speed is reached, the spring compresses and causes the control rack to move in the direction for reduced fuel-delivery quantity (positive torque control). Negative torque control, which responds to increased engine speed by augmenting the fuel-delivery quantity, is also possible, albeit at the price of far more components and more complicated adjustment procedures.

Manifold-pressure compensator (LDA)

Due to the larger air mass, turbocharged engines are capable of converting a greater amount of fuel into torque as the charge-air pressure increases. The manifold-pressure compensator is used to make a corresponding correction in the full-load fuel-delivery quantity. Increasing charge-air pressure acts on the spring-loaded diaphragm, which is connected to the control rack in such a way that the injected fuel quantity increases as the charge-air pressure increases.

Altitude-pressure compensator (ADA)

The altitude-pressure compensator is similar to the LDA. It reduces the full-load delivery in response to the low atmospheric pressure (and low air density) encountered at high elevations. The unit includes a barometric capsule which displaces the control rack in the direction for lower delivery quantity once atmospheric pressure drops by a specific increment.

Temperature-compensating start-quantity stop (TAS)

A cold engine requires a certain amount of additional fuel (enrichment) in order to start. This enrichment is not necessary on a hot engine and could otherwise lead to the emission of smoke clouds.

The solution is TAS, which features a control-rod stop, employing an expansion element to prevent enrichment during hot starts.

Control-rack travel sensor (RWG)

The RWG monitors the control-rack position inductively.

After processing in an evaluation circuit, the signal can be used for tasks such as control of hydraulic or mechanical transmissions, for measuring fuel consumption, for exhaust-gas recirculation, and for diagnostics.

### Port-closing sensor (FBG)

The FBG is an inductive unit which, with the engine running, monitors the point at which pump delivery starts (port closing). It can also check the timing device.

In addition, fuel-injection pumps equipped with this device can be supplied with the camshaft locked in the port-closing position. This setting facilitates simple and precise pump installation on the engine.

### Timing devices

Centrifugally controlled timing devices are positioned in the drivetrain between the engine and the fuel-injection pump. The flyweights respond to increasing engine speed by turning the fuel-injection pump's camshaft, with respect to the drive shaft, in the "delivery advance" direction.

Front-mounted clutch-driven units and gear-driven in-pump devices, with a setting range of 3°...10° on the pump shaft are available.

### Pump shutoff

A mechanical (stop lever), electric or pneumatic shutoff device is employed to shut down the diesel engine by interrupting the fuel supply.

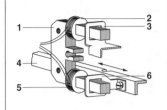
**Rack-travel sensor (RWG)**
1 Iron core, 2 Reference coil, 3 Fixed short-circuiting ring, 4 Control rack, 5 Measuring coil, 6 Moving short-circuiting ring.

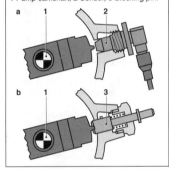
**Port-closing sensor (FBG)**
a) Measurement with sensor,
b) Blocking position.
1 Pump camshaft, 2 Sensor, 3 Blocking pin.

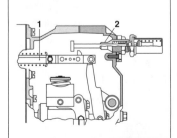
**Temperature-dependent starting device**
1 Control rack, 2 Start-quantity stop with expansion element.

**Timing device**
Off position.

**Electronic governor**

Instead of a mechanical governor, the electronic governor for the in-line fuel-injection pump uses a solenoid actuator with a non-contacting inductive position sensor to position the control rack (control-rack travel sensor). The solenoid actuator is triggered by an ECU.

The ECU microprocessor compares accelerator-pedal position, rpm, and a number of additional correction factors with the program maps stored in its memory in order to determine the correct injected fuel quantity, i.e. the control-rack setpoint position.

An electronic controller compares the monitored control-rack position with the specified setpoint in order to determine the required excitation-current input to the solenoid, which operates against a return spring. When deviations are detected, the excitation current is regulated to shift the control rack to precisely the specified position.

An inductive speed sensor monitors a camshaft-mounted sensor ring; the ECU uses the pulse intervals to calculate engine speed.

As it can monitor a number of engine and vehicle parameters and combine them to calculate the injected fuel quantity, an electronic governor has a number of additional functions, thus giving it an advantage over a mechanical unit:

– Engine can be switched on and off with key.
– Complete freedom in determining the full-load curve.
– Maximum injected fuel quantity can be precisely coordinated with the charge-air pressure in order to remain below the smoke limit.
– Corrections for air and fuel temperatures.
– Temperature-dependent excess-fuel quantity.
– Engine-speed control for auxiliary power take-offs.
– Cruise control.
– Maximum-speed limiter.
– Constant, low idle speed.
– Surge damping control.
– Smooth-running control.
– Option for intervention in traction control (TCS)/automatic transmission.
– Signal outputs for display of fuel consumption and engine speed.
– Service support through integral error diagnosis.

*Electronic diesel control (EDC) for in-line fuel-injection pumps*
1 Control rack, 2 Actuator, 3 Camshaft, 4 Engine-speed sensor, 5 ECU Input/output quantities:
a Redundant shutoff, b Boost pressure, c Vehicle speed, d Temperature (water, air, fuel),
e Fuel-quantity command, f Engine speed, g Control-rack travel, h Solenoid position,
i Fuel-consumption and engine-speed display, k Diagnostics, l Accelerator position,
m Speed preset, n Clutch, brakes, engine brake.

## In-line control-sleeve fuel-injection pump

The in-line control-sleeve fuel-injection pump makes it possible to provide electronically controlled adjustment of port closing (start of pump delivery). It is, therefore, an in-line fuel-injection pump with integrated timing device. A control-sleeve pump is only available for size P. The spill port, which on conventional in-line pumps is fixed in the housing, is incorporated in the control sleeve which is a movable component in each plunger-and-barrel assembly. A setting shaft, with control-sleeve levers which engage the sleeves, changes the positions of all sleeves at the same time.

Depending on the position of the control sleeve (up or down), the start of delivery is advanced or retarded relative to the position of the camshaft lobe. An electromagnetic actuator mechanism similar to that used for fuel-delivery control in the distributor injection pump turns the setting shaft, but without position feedback.

A needle-motion sensor monitors the start of injection directly at the nozzle. It transmits a signal to the ECU, which compares it with the setpoint value as a function of rpm, injected fuel quantity, etc. in order to adjust the solenoid-excitation current to achieve congruence between the actual and setpoint values for start of injection.

The engine-speed sensor obtains precise information on the start of injection relative to TDC by monitoring pulses from reference marks on the crankshaft flywheel.

*In-line control-sleeve fuel-injection pump*
1 Pump plunger, 2 Control sleeve,
3 Control-sleeve shaft, 4 Control rack.

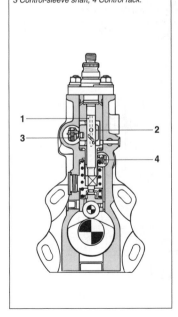

*Plunger-and-barrel assembly with control sleeve*
a) Start of delivery, b) End of delivery.
1 Helix, 2 Control sleeve, 3 Spill port,
4 Control groove, 5 Pump plunger.

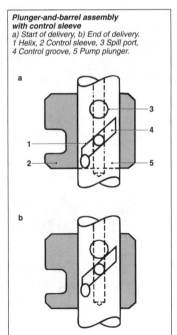

## Distributor injection pump

Distributor injection pumps are used in 3-, 4-, 5- and 6-cylinder diesel engines in passenger cars, tractors and light- and medium-duty commercial vehicles. They generate up to 50 kW per cylinder, depending on engine speed and combustion system. Distributor injection pumps for direct-injection (DI) engines achieve a peak injection pressure of up to 1,950 bar in the nozzle at engine speeds up to 2,400 rpm.

A distinction is made between distributor injection pumps with mechanical control, and those with an electronic governor available in versions with a rotary-magnet actuator and with solenoid-valve open-loop control.

### Mechanically controlled axial-piston distributor pumps (VE)

These mechanically controlled axial-piston distributor pumps comprise the following major assemblies:

#### Fuel-supply pump

If no presupply pump is fitted, this integral vane-type supply pump draws fuel from the tank and, together with a pressure-control valve, generates an internal pump pressure which increases with engine speed.

#### High-pressure pump

The VE axial-piston distributor pump incorporates only one pump element for all cylinders. The plunger displaces the fuel during its stroke and rotates at the same time to distribute the fuel to the individual outlets.

*VE Distributor-type fuel-injection pump (basic version)*
*1 Vane-type supply pump, 2 Governor drive, 3 Timing device, 4 Cam plate, 5 Control collar, 6 Distributor plunger, 7 Delivery valve, 8 Solenoid-actuated shutoff, 9 Governor lever mechanism, 10 Overflow restriction, 11 Mechanical shutoff device, 12 Governor spring, 13 Speed-control lever, 14 Control sleeve, 15 Flyweight, 16 Pressure-control valve.*
*a Fuel inlet, b Return to fuel tank, c To nozzle.*

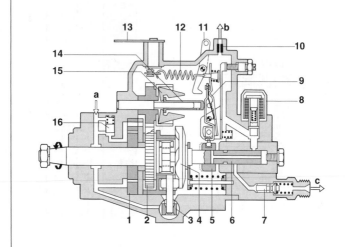

During each rotation of the drive shaft, the plunger completes a number of strokes equal to the number of engine cylinders to be supplied. Via the yoke, the distributor pump's drive shaft turns the cam plate and the pump plunger fixed to it. The cam lifts on the underside of the cam plate turn against the rollers of the roller ring, causing the cam plate and plunger to make a stroke movement in addition to their rotary movement (distribution and delivery).

The pump delivers fuel for as long as the spill port in the plunger remains closed off during the working stroke. Delivery ends when the spill port is uncovered by the control collar. The position of the control collar thus determines the effective stroke and the injected fuel quantity. The governor determines the position of the sliding control collar on the plunger.

Mechanical (flyweight) governor
A ball head connects the control collar to the governor levers. The governor springs and the centrifugal force generated by the flyweights then act on the governor levers. Idling, transition ranges and maximum engine speed can be adapted to meet engine requirements.

Speed droop, governor types: The description of speed droop and governor types (variable-speed governors, minimum-maximum-speed governors) for in-line fuel-injection pumps also applies to governors used with distributor injection pumps.

Load signal: On fuel-injection pumps equipped with minimum-maximum-speed governors, the position of the outer control lever can be monitored via microswitches or potentiometers to provide information on load. This is required, for example, for controlled exhaust-gas recirculation.

Add-on equipment
A number of add-on modules are available to process additional operating parameters for regulation of delivery quantity (such as manifold-pressure compensator (LDA), start quantity, hydraulic and mechanical full-load torque control) and for adjustment of the start of delivery – (e.g. cold-start accelerator, load-dependent start of delivery).

Hydromechanically controlled timing device
The speed-dependent supply-pump pressure (5...10 bar) acts on the front end of the spring-loaded timing-device plunger via a throttle bore. The plunger rotates the roller ring counter to the direction of rotation of the pump as a function of engine speed, thereby advancing the start of delivery.

Pump shutoff
A solenoid-operated shutoff device (solenoid valve) shuts off the diesel engine by interrupting the fuel supply.

**Electronic Diesel Control (EDC): distributor injection pump with rotary-magnet actuator**
In contrast to the mechanically controlled distributor injection pump, the EDC pump with rotary-magnet actuator has an electronic governor and an electronically controlled timing device.

Electronic governor (EDC)
An eccentrically mounted ball head provides the connection between the VE pump control collar and the solenoid rotary actuator. The actuator's rotary setting determines the position of the control collar, and with it the effective stroke of the pump. A non-contacting position sensor is connected to the rotary actuator.

The ECU's microcomputer receives various signals from the sensors: accelerator-pedal position; engine speed; air, coolant and fuel temperature; charge-air pressure; atmospheric pressure; etc. It uses these input variables to determine the correct injected fuel quantity, which is then converted to a specific control-rack position with the aid of program maps stored in the unit's memory. The ECU varies the excitation current to the rotary actuator until it receives a signal indicating convergence between the setpoint and actual values for control-rack position.

### Electronically controlled timing device

In this device, the signal from a sensor in the nozzle-holder assembly, which indicates when the nozzle begins to open, is compared with a programmed setpoint value. A clocked solenoid valve connected to the working chamber of the plunger in the timing device varies the pressure above the plunger and thus the position of the timing device. The actuation clock ratio of the solenoid valve is varied until the setpoint and actual values agree.

Advantages of electronic versus mechanical control:
- Improved fuel-delivery control (fuel consumption, engine power, emissions).
- Improved control of engine speed (low idle speed, adjustment for air conditioner, etc.).
- Enhanced comfort (surge-damping control, smooth-running control).
- More precise start of injection (fuel consumption, emissions).
- Improved service possibilities (diagnostics).

The application options extend to features such as open-loop and closed-loop control of exhaust-gas recirculation, boost-pressure control, glow-plug control, and interconnection with other on-board electrical systems.

## Electronic Diesel Control (EDC): solenoid-valve-controlled distributor injection pumps

In the case of solenoid-valve-controlled VE distributor pumps, the fuel is metered by a high-pressure solenoid valve which directly closes off the pump's element chamber. This permits even greater flexibility in fuel metering and for varying the start of injection (see figure for operating principle). Furthermore, the pressure potential of the solenoid-valve-controlled axial-piston distributor pump is greater on account of the reduced dead volumes.

The main assemblies of this generation of VE distributor pumps are:
- the high-pressure solenoid valve,
- the ECU, and
- the incremental angle/time system for angle/time control of the solenoid valve using an angle-of-rotation sensor integrated in the pump.

The solenoid valve closes to define the start of delivery, which then continues until the valve opens. The injected fuel quantity is determined by the length of time the valve remains closed. Solenoid-valve control permits rapid opening and closing of the element chamber irrespective of engine speed. In contrast to mechanically governed pumps and EDC pumps with a rotary-magnet actuator, di-

---

*Electronic diesel control (EDC) for distributor-type fuel-injection pumps*
1 Supply pump, 2 Solenoid valve, 3 Timing device, 4 Control collar, 5 Rotary actuator with sensor, 6 ECU Inputs/outputs: a Speed, b Start of injection, c Temperature, d Charge-air pressure, e Accelerator-pedal position, f Fuel return, g To injection nozzle.

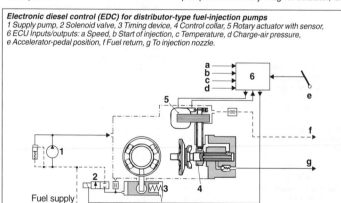

rect triggering by means of solenoid valves results in lower dead volumes, improved high-pressure sealing, and therefore greater efficiency.

The fuel-injection pump is equipped with its own, integral ECU for precise start-of-delivery control and fuel metering. Individual pump program maps and example-specific calibration data are stored in this ECU.

The engine ECU determines the start of injection and delivery on the basis of engine operating parameters, and sends this data to the pump ECU via the data bus. The system can control both the start of injection and the start of delivery.

The pump ECU also receives the injected fuel quantity signal via the data bus. This signal is generated by the engine ECU according to the accelerator-pedal signal and other parameters for required fuel quantity. In the pump ECU, the injected fuel quantity signal and the pump speed for a given start of delivery are taken as the input variables for the pump map on which the corresponding actuation period is stored as degrees of cam rotation.

And finally, the actuation of the high-pressure solenoid valve and the desired period of actuation are determined on the basis of the angle-of-rotation sensor integrated in the VE distributor pump.

The angle-of-rotation sensor in the pump is used for angle/time control. It consists of a magnetoresistive sensor and a reluctor ring divided into 3° increments interrupted by a reference mark for each cylinder. The sensor determines the precise angle of cam rotation at which the solenoid valve opens and closes. This requires the pump ECU to convert timing data to angular position data and vice versa.

The low fuel-delivery rates at the start of injection, which result from the design of the VE distributor pump, are further reduced by the use of a two-spring nozzle holder. With a hot engine, these low delivery rates permit low basic noise levels.

*Solenoid-valve-controlled axial-piston pump*
*1 Angle-of-rotation sensor, 2 Pump drive, 3 Pump ECU, 4 High-pressure solenoid valve, 5 Delivery valve, 6 Timing-device solenoid valve.*

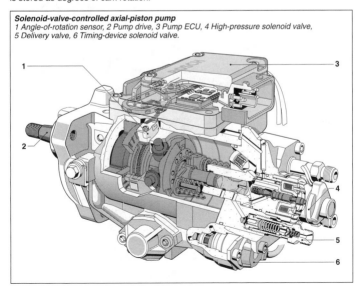

### Pilot injection

Pilot injection allows the combustion noise to be further reduced without sacrificing the objects of the system's design which aim at generating maximum power output at the rated-power operating point. Pilot injection does not require additional hardware. Within a matter of milliseconds, the ECU actuates the solenoid valve twice in rapid succession. The solenoid valve controls the injected fuel quantity with a high degree of precision and dynamic response (typical pilot-injection fuel quantity: 1.5 mm³).

Solenoid-valve-controlled axial-piston distributor pumps use the same principle of pressure generation as EDC pumps with rotary-magnet actuators. The injection pressure at the nozzle can be as high as 1,500 bar, depending on the application.

By shifting the point at which delivery begins from the bottom dead center position of the pump plunger to a point within the plunger stroke, the pressure at low speeds can be increased and maximum pump torque can be substantially reduced at high speeds. For special applications, the variable start of delivery permits the start of injection to be advanced even at cranking speed.

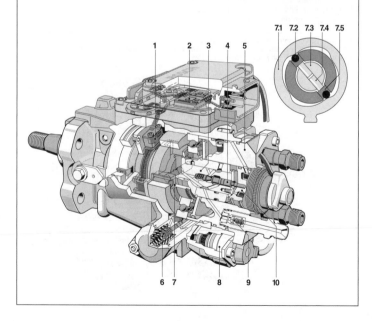

*Solenoid-controlled radial-piston distributor pump*
*1 Sensor (position/timing), 2 ECU, 3 Distributor shaft, 4 Solenoid valve needle,*
*5 Distributor head, 6 Timing device, 7 Radial-piston pump, 7.1 Cam ring, 7.2 Roller,*
*7.3 Distributor shaft, 7.4 Delivery plunger, 7.5 Roller support, 8 Timing-device pulse valve,*
*9 Return-flow throttle valve, 10 Pushing electromagnet.*

## Solenoid-valve-controlled radial-piston distributor pumps

Radial-piston distributor pumps (see figure on left page) for high-performance direct-injection engines achieve element-chamber pressures of up to 1,100 bar and nozzle pressures as high as 1,950 bar.

As the cam-drive design employs a direct, positive link, flexibility and compliance remain minimal, so the performance potential is greater. Fuel delivery is shared between at least two radial plungers. The small forces involved mean that steep (fast) cam profiles are possible. The fuel-delivery rate can be further increased by increasing the number of plungers. These systems are used in high-speed passenger cars and in commercial vehicles up to 50 kW/cylinder.

<u>Version with full electronic circuitry on fuel-injection pump</u>

The latest generation of distributor injection pumps are compact, self-contained systems incorporating an ECU to control both the pump and the engine-management functions. As a separate engine ECU is no longer required, the fuel-injection system requires fewer connectors and the wiring harness is less complex, thus making installation simpler.

The engine and complete fuel-injection system can be installed and tested as a self-contained system independent of vehicle type.

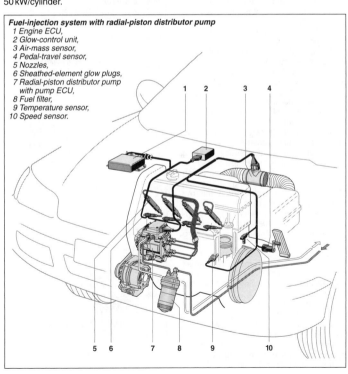

**Fuel-injection system with radial-piston distributor pump**
1 Engine ECU,
2 Glow-control unit,
3 Air-mass sensor,
4 Pedal-travel sensor,
5 Nozzles,
6 Sheathed-element glow plugs,
7 Radial-piston distributor pump
   with pump ECU,
8 Fuel filter,
9 Temperature sensor,
10 Speed sensor.

## Time-controlled single-cylinder pump system

The time-controlled, modular single-cylinder pumps systems include the electronically controlled "Unit Injector System" (UIS), which is used in passenger cars and commercial vehicles with direct-injection engines, and the "Unit Pump System" (UPS), which is used in commercial-vehicle engines.

### Unit injector system (UIS) for commercial vehicles

The electronically controlled unit injector is a single-cylinder fuel-injection module with integral high-pressure pump, nozzle and solenoid valve. It is installed directly in the cylinder head of the diesel engine. Each engine cylinder is allocated a separate unit injector which is operated by a rocker arm driven by an injection cam on the engine camshaft.

The start of injection and the injected fuel quantity are controlled by the high-speed solenoid valve. The values for these variables can be selected as desired from those stored in the program map. When de-energized, the solenoid valve is open. This means that fuel can flow freely from the fuel inlet of the low-pressure system through the pump and back into the low-pressure system in the engine cylinder head, thereby allowing the pump chamber to be filled during the pump plunger's intake stroke. Energizing the solenoid valve during the pump plunger's delivery stroke closes this bypass, causing pressure to build up in the high-pressure system and fuel to be injected into the combustion chamber of the engine once the nozzle-opening pressure is exceeded.

The compact design of the unit means that high-pressure volume is very small and hydraulic rigidity very high. As a result, injection pressures of 2,000 bar can be achieved.

Such high injection pressures combined with electronic map-based control allow emission levels to be substantially reduced while simultaneously keeping fuel consumption low. The unit injector system is capable of meeting both present and future emission limits.

Electronic control enables this fuel-injection system to perform additional functions which are primarily intended to considerably improve driving smoothness.

By using adaptive cylinder equalization, the complete drivetrain's rotational irregularity up to rated speed can be reduced. This ensures that the complete drivetrain runs much more smoothly. At the same time this function can equalize the injected fuel quantity from the engine's individual injectors.

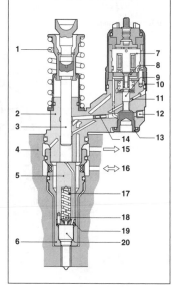

*Unit Injector (UI)*
*1 Return spring, 2 Pump body, 3 Pump plunger, 4 Cylinder head, 5 Spring retainer, 6 Tension nut, 7 Stator, 8 Armature plate, 9 Solenoid-valve needle, 10 Solenoid-valve tension nut, 11 High-pressure plug, 12 Low-pressure plug, 13 Solenoid travel stop, 14 Restriction, 15 Fuel return, 16 Fuel supply, 17 Injector spring, 18 Pressure pin, 19 Shim, 20 Injector.*

Electrically controlled pilot injection (double triggering of the solenoid valve) can significantly reduce combustion noise and improve cold-starting characteristics.

In addition, the system permits the shut-off of individual cylinders. For instance, when the engine is running in the part-load range.

### Unit pump system (UPS) for commercial vehicles

The unit pump system is also a modular, time-controlled single-cylinder high-pressure pump system, and is closely related to the UIS. Each of the engine's cylinders is supplied by a separate module with the following components:

– high-pressure single-cylinder pump with integral high-speed solenoid valve,
– short high-pressure delivery line,
– nozzle-and-holder assembly

The unit pump is integrated into the diesel-engine cylinder block and operated directly by an injection cam on the engine's camshaft via a roller tappet.

The method of solenoid valve actuation is the same as that of the UIS.

When the solenoid valve is open, the fuel can be drawn into the pump barrel during the pump plunger's intake stroke, and return during the delivery stroke. Only when the solenoid valve is energized, and thus closed, can pressure build up in the high-pressure system between the pump plunger and the nozzle during the pump plunger delivery stroke. Fuel is injected into the combustion chamber of the engine once the nozzle-opening pressure is exceeded.

*Unit Pump (UP)*
*1 Solenoid-valve needle-travel stop,*
*2 Engine block, 3 Pump body,*
*4 Pump plunger, 5 Return spring,*
*6 Roller tappet, 7 Armature plate,*
*8 Stator, 9 Solenoid-valve needle,*
*10 Filter, 11 Fuel supply, 12 Fuel return,*
*13 Retainer, 14 Locating groove.*

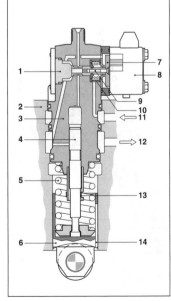

*Unit Pump System (UPS)*
*1 Injector holder, 2 Engine, 3 Nozzle,*
*4 Solenoid valve, 5 Supply,*
*6 High-pressure pump, 7 Cam.*

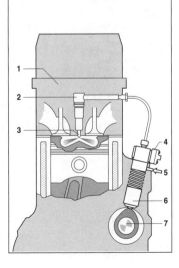

Solenoid-valve closure thus defines the start of injection, and valve opening determines the injected fuel quantity.

The unit pump system allows injection pressures as high as 2,000 bar. As is the case with the UIS, these high injection pressures combined with electronic map-based control enable this fuel-injection system to meet both present and future emission limits, while at the same time providing for low fuel consumption. This fuel-injection system also allows implementation of additional functions such as adaptive cylinder equalization, and shut-off of individual cylinders.

## Unit injector system (UIS) for passenger cars

The unit injector system for passenger cars (see figure) is designed to meet the demands of modern direct-injection diesel engines with high levels of power density. It is characterized by its compact design, high injection pressures of up to 2,000 bar, and mechanical-hydraulic pilot injection throughout the entire program-map range to substantially reduce combustion noise.

The unit injector system for passenger cars is also a single-pump fuel-injection system, i.e. there is a separate unit injector (consisting of a high-pressure pump, nozzle and solenoid valve) for each engine cylinder. The unit injector is installed in the cylinder head between the valves, with the nozzle protruding into the com-

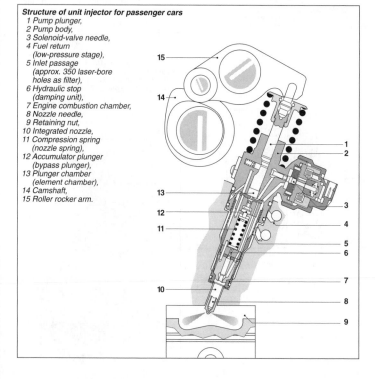

*Structure of unit injector for passenger cars*
1 Pump plunger,
2 Pump body,
3 Solenoid-valve needle,
4 Fuel return
  (low-pressure stage),
5 Inlet passage
  (approx. 350 laser-bore
  holes as filter),
6 Hydraulic stop
  (damping unit),
7 Engine combustion chamber,
8 Nozzle needle,
9 Retaining nut,
10 Integrated nozzle,
11 Compression spring
  (nozzle spring),
12 Accumulator plunger
  (bypass plunger),
13 Plunger chamber
  (element chamber),
14 Camshaft,
15 Roller rocker arm.

bustion chamber. The unit injectors are operated by rocker arms driven by an overhead valve camshaft. The transverse mounting of the solenoid valve makes the unit more compact and achieves minimal high-pressure volume with correspondingly high hydraulic efficiency.

The fuel-injection system is filled during the pump-plunger intake stroke, while the solenoid valve is de-energized and thus open.

The injection period begins when the solenoid valve is energized (closed) during the pump-plunger delivery stroke. Pilot injection begins when pressure builds up in the high-pressure system and the nozzle-opening pressure is reached. Pilot injection ends when a mechanical valve (bypass plunger) opens and abruptly reduces the pressure in the plunger chamber so that the nozzle closes. The stroke and shaft diameter of the bypass plunger determine the length of the interval, the so-called injection interval, between the end of pilot injection and the start of main injection. The movement of the bypass plunger also tensions the nozzle spring, which rapidly closes the nozzle at the end of pilot injection. Due to the strong hydraulic damping produced by a damper located between the nozzle needle and the nozzle spring, the opening stroke of the nozzle needle remains very short during pilot injection. Main injection begins when the nozzle opening pressure is reached. However, due to the additional force applied by the pretensioned nozzle spring, this pressure is twice as high as at the start of pilot injection. Injection ends when the solenoid valve is de-energized, and thus open. The time interval between re-opening of the nozzle and opening of the solenoid valve therefore determines the quantity of fuel injected during the main-injection phase.

Electronic control allows the values for the start of injection and the injected fuel quantity to be selected as desired from those stored in the program map. This feature, together with the high injection pressures, makes it possible to achieve very high power densities combined with very low emission levels and exceptionally low fuel consumption.

The further reduction in size of the unit injectors will allow them to be used on 4-valve-per-cylinder engines in the future, thereby making it possible to reduce emissions even more. Its ability to further reduce emissions, coupled with further optimization of injection characteristics, makes the unit injector system capable of meeting future emission limits.

### Electronic control unit (ECU)

The solenoid valves on the unit injector and unit pump are triggered by an ECU. The ECU analyzes all of the relevant status parameters in the system relative to the engine and its environment, and defines the exact start of injection and injected fuel quantity for the operating state of the engine at any given time, thereby enabling nonpolluting and economical engine operation. The start of injection is also controlled by a BIP signal (begin of injection period) in order to balance out the tolerances in the overall system. Start of injection is synchronized with engine piston position by precise analysis of the signals from an incremental trigger wheel.

In addition to the basic fuel-injection functions, there are a variety of additional functions for improving driving smoothness such as surge dampers, idle-speed governors, and adaptive cylinder equalization. In order to meet strict safety requirements, the ECU automatically corrects and compensates for any faults and deviations that may occur in the system components and, when required, enables precise diagnosis of the fuel-injection system and the engine. The ECU communicates with other electronic systems on the vehicle via the high-speed CAN data bus, such as the antilock braking system (ABS), the traction control system (TCS), and the transmission-shift control system.

## Common-rail system (CRS)

Common-rail (accumulator) fuel-injection systems make it possible to integrate the fuel-injection system together with a number of its extended functions in the diesel engine, and thus increase the degree of freedom available for defining the combustion process.

The common-rail system's principal feature is that injection pressure is independent of engine speed and injected fuel quantity. This is only the case with the common-rail system and not with all the cam-driven systems described previously.

### System design

The functions of pressure generation and fuel injection are separated by an accumulator volume. This volume, which is essential to the correct operation of the system, is made up of the common fuel rail, the fuel lines and the injectors themselves (see figure).

The pressure is generated by a high-pressure plunger pump. This pump is partly designed as an in-line fuel-injection pump for commercial vehicles and otherwise as a radial-piston pump. The pump operates at low maximum torques and thus substantially reduces drive-power requirements. In high-pressure pumps for passenger cars, the desired rail pressure is regulated by a pressure-control valve mounted on the high-pressure side of the pump or the rail. High-pressure pumps for commercial vehicles and the second generation for passenger cars have an injected-fuel quantity control system on the intake side. This reduces the temperature of the fuel within the system.

The system pressure generated by the high-pressure pump and regulated by a pressure-control circuit is applied to the injector. This injector serves as the core of this concept by ensuring correct fuel delivery into the combustion chamber. At a precisely defined instant the ECU transmits an activation signal to the injector so-

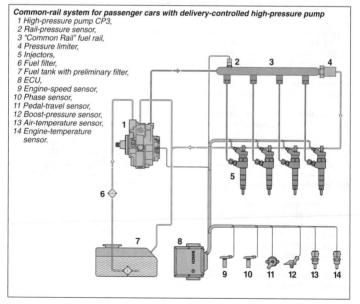

*Common-rail system for passenger cars with delivery-controlled high-pressure pump*
1 High-pressure pump CP3,
2 Rail-pressure sensor,
3 "Common Rail" fuel rail,
4 Pressure limiter,
5 Injectors,
6 Fuel filter,
7 Fuel tank with preliminary filter,
8 ECU,
9 Engine-speed sensor,
10 Phase sensor,
11 Pedal-travel sensor,
12 Boost-pressure sensor,
13 Air-temperature sensor,
14 Engine-temperature sensor.

lenoid to initiate fuel delivery. The injected fuel quantity is defined by the injector opening time and the system pressure.

The ECU, sensors and most of the other system functions in the common-rail system are basically the same as in other time-controlled single-cylinder pump systems.

## Hydraulic performance potential

This system enhances the latitude for defining combustion-process patterns by separating the pressurization and injection functions. Injection pressure can basically be selected from any point on the program map. The pressures currently used are 1,600 bar for passenger-car systems and 1,400 bar for commercial-vehicle systems.

Pilot injection and multiple injection can be used to further reduce exhaust-gas and particularly noise emissions.

In the common-rail system, the movement of the nozzle needle, and thus the rate-of-discharge curve, can be controlled within a defined range. Multiple injections, i.e. up to 5 injections per injection cycle, can be generated by repeated activation of the extremely fast solenoid valve. Hydraulic pressure is used to augment nozzle-needle closing, ensuring rapid termination of the injection process.

## System application engineering on the engine

No major modifications are required to adapt the diesel engine for operation with the common-rail system. A high-pressure pump replaces the fuel-injection pump, while the injector is integrated in the cylinder head in the same manner as a conventional nozzle-and-holder assembly. Today, common rail is the most frequently used fuel-injection system in modern high-speed passenger-car DI engines.

## High-pressure pump

The high-pressure pump used in passenger cars is designed as a radial-piston pump (three pistons arranged at 120° to each other) (cf. HDP1 for gasoline direct injection, P. 602). The mode of operation of these pumps is the same for spark-ignition and diesel engines, but, when compared with gasoline direct injection, the high-pressure pump for common rail

is designed for significantly higher pressures (as high as 1,600 bar).

As the high-pressure pump is designed for high delivery quantities, there is (in the 1st CRS generation) an excess of compressed fuel in idle and part-load operation. This excess fuel is returned to the fuel tank via the pressure-control valve flanged to the pump or to the rail. In this way, pressure in the rail can be set as a function of the engine load condition. As the compressed fuel expands here, the energy introduced by compression is lost.

A partial remedy lies in adapting the delivery rate to the fuel demand by deactivating a plunger-and-barrel assembly. In these high-pressure pumps with assembly deactivation, the suction valve of a plunger-and-barrel assembly is held permanently open with the aid of a solenoid valve. Thus, pressure can now build up in the element chamber and the fuel drawn in flows back into the low-pressure passage.

The 2nd generation saw the introduction of low-pressure-side control, which ensures that only as much fuel as is injected is actually compressed. This significantly improves hydraulic efficiency and lowers the fuel-temperature level.

## Solenoid-valve injector

Start of injection and injected fuel quantity are set with the electrically activated injector. The injection point is set by the angle/time system of electronic diesel control (EDC).

The fuel is routed from the high-pressure port via an inlet passage to the nozzle and via the inlet restrictor into the valve control chamber. The valve control chamber is connected by the outlet restrictor, which can be opened by a solenoid valve, to the fuel return.

When closed, the outlet restrictor overcomes the hydraulic force acting on the valve plunger opposing the force acting on the pressure shoulder of the nozzle needle. As a result, the nozzle needle is pressed into its seat and seals off the high-pressure passage to the engine chamber tight. The nozzle spring closes the injector when the engine is not running and there is no pressure in the rail.

The outlet restrictor is opened when the solenoid valve is activated. The inlet restrictor prevents a complete pressure compensation in such a way that the pressure in the valve control chamber and thus the hydraulic force acting on the valve control plunger decrease. The nozzle needle opens as soon as the hydraulic force drops below that acting on the pressure shoulder of the nozzle needle. Fuel is now admitted through the injection orifices into the engine combustion chamber.

When the solenoid valve is no longer activated, the armature is forced downwards by the force of the valve spring. The valve ball closes off the outlet restrictor. In this way, there is a renewed buildup of pressure in the valve control chamber and in the rail caused by fuel flowing in from the inlet restrictor. This buildup of

pressure exerts an increased force on the control plunger in such a way that the nozzle needle closes again. The through-flow from the inlet restrictor determines the speed with which the nozzle needle closes.

This indirect activation of the nozzle needle via a hydraulic force-boost system is used because the forces needed to open the nozzle needle quickly cannot be generated by the solenoid valve. The control quantity required in addition to the injected fuel quantity passes through the control-chamber restrictors into the fuel return.

*Solenoid-valve injector*
*1 Fuel return, 2 Solenoid coil,*
*3 Solenoid armature, 4 Valve ball,*
*5 Valve control chamber, 6 Nozzle-needle*
*pressure shoulder, 7 Injection orifice,*
*8 Outlet restrictor, 9 High-pressure port,*
*10 Inlet restrictor, 11 Valve plunger.*

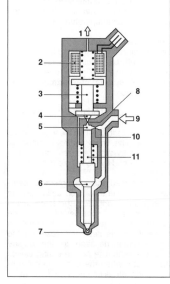

*Piezo-injector*
*1 Fuel return, 2 High-pressure port,*
*3 Piezo-actuator module, 4 Hydraulic*
*booster, 5 Valve, 6 Nozzle needle,*
*7 Injection orifice.*

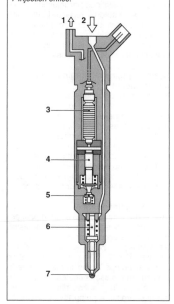

### Piezo-injector

The latest injector development in the 3rd CRS generation works with a piezo-actuator instead of with a solenoid valve. The piezo-actuator is significantly faster than the solenoid valves used previously. However, this requires a modification of the design in order to be able to utilize the advantages of the piezo-feature to full effect. This has been achieved for the first time by the design shown in the figure.

The nozzle needle is directly controlled hydraulically by the actuator so that there is no mechanical connection between actuator and nozzle needle. This approach eliminates all friction as well as any elastic deformation of the connection elements.

As the nozzle needle in the piezo-injector is now much lighter and the leak-fuel quantity at the actuator has been dramatically reduced, the piezo-injector offers a further series of advantages:

- The structural space is significantly smaller, i.e. more compact.
- The weight is reduced by almost half.
- Several injections per injection cycle can be effected, e.g. two pilot injections, one main injection and two post-injections.
- The injected fuel quantities of the pilot injection can again be significantly reduced.
- The intervals between injections can be shortened still further.

For the engine application, there are thus further degrees of freedom which can be utilized either:

- to reduce engine noise,
- to reduce emissions by up to 20%,
- to increase engine power output,
- or to lower fuel consumption.

Smaller high-pressure pumps can be used on account of the lower leak-fuel quantities.

These are all positive advantages which have been achieved with this completely new concept.

## Injection-system components

### Nozzles and nozzle holders
Functions

In the overall system of a diesel engine, the nozzles connect the fuel-injection system to the engine. Their functions are to:
- Assist in metering the fuel.
- Process the fuel.
- Define the rate-of-discharge curve.
- Seal off the combustion chamber.

In systems with separate fuel-injection pumps (in-line, distributor and plug-in pumps), the nozzles are integrated in the nozzle holders. In unit injector systems (UIS) and common-rail systems (CRS), the nozzles are integral parts of the injectors.

Diesel fuel is injected at high pressure. Peak injection pressure can range as high as 2,000 bar, a figure which will become even higher in the future. Under these conditions, the diesel fuel ceases to behave as a solid, incompressible fluid, and becomes compressible. During the brief delivery period (in the order of 1 ms), the fuel-injection system is locally "inflated". For a given pressure and injection time, the nozzle cross-section determines the quantity of fuel injected into the engine's combustion chamber.

The length and diameter of the nozzle spray hole (or orifice), the direction of the fuel jet and (to a certain extent) the shape of the spray hole affect mixture formation, and thus the engine power output, fuel consumption, and emission levels.

Within certain limits, it is possible to achieve the required rate-of-discharge curve through optimal control of the flow cross-section from the nozzle (defined by the needle lift) and by regulating the needle response. Finally, the nozzle must be capable of sealing the fuel-injection system against the hot, highly-compressed combustion gases with temperatures up to approx. 1,000 °C. To prevent blowback of the combustion gases when the nozzle is open, the pressure in the nozzle pressure chamber must always be higher than the combustion pressure. This requirement becomes particularly relevant toward the end of the injection sequence (when a stark reduction in injection pressure is accompanied by massive increases in combustion pressure), where it can only be ensured by careful matching.

### Designs

Diesel engines with divided or two-section combustion chambers (prechamber and whirl-chamber engines) require nozzle designs differing from those used in single-section chambers (direct-injection engines).

In prechamber and whirl-chamber engines with divided combustion chambers, throttling-pintle nozzles are used which feature a coaxial spray pattern and which are generally equipped with nozzle needles which retract to open.

Direct-injection engines with single-section combustion chambers generally require hole-type nozzles.

### Throttling-pintle nozzles

One nozzle (Type DN..SD..) and one nozzle holder (Type KCA for threaded socket installation) represent the standard combination for use with prechamber and whirl-chamber engines (see figure). DN O SD.. nozzles with a needle diameter of 6 mm and a spray aperture angle of 0° are usually used; less common are nozzles with a defined spray dispersal angle (for example 12° in the DN 12 SD.. nozzles).

As a distinctive feature, throttling-pintle nozzles vary the outlet cross-section – and thus the flow rate – as a function of needle lift. The hole-type nozzle displays an immediate, sharp rise in cross-section when the nozzle needle opens; in contrast, the throttling-pintle nozzle is characterized by an extremely flat cross-section progression at moderate needle lifts. Within this stroke range, the pintle (an extension at the end of the needle) remains in the injection orifice. The flow opening consists only of the small annular gap between the larger injection orifice and the throttling pintle. As needle lift increases, the pintle completely opens the injection orifice, with an attendant substantial increase in the size of the flow cross-section.

This stroke-sensitive cross-sectional regulation can be employed to exert a certain amount of control on the rate-of-discharge curve (quantity of fuel injected into the engine within a specific unit of time). At the start of injection, only a limited amount of fuel emerges from the nozzle, while a substantial quantity is discharged at the end of the cycle. This rate-of-discharge curve has a particularly positive effect on combustion noise.

It must be remembered that excessively small cross-sections, i.e. excessively short needle lifts, cause the fuel-injection pump to more strongly push the nozzle needle in the "open" direction, thereby causing the needle to quickly emerge from the throttling stroke area. The injected fuel quantity per unit of time increases dramatically, and combustion noise rises accordingly.

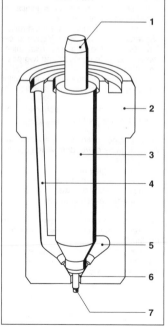

*Throttling-pintle nozzle*
1 Pressure pin, 2 Nozzle body, 3 Needle,
4 Inlet passage, 5 Pressure chamber,
6 Injection orifice, 7 Pintle.

Similarly, negative effects result from excessively small openings at the end of the injection cycle: The volume displaced by the closing nozzle needle is restricted by the narrow cross-section. The result is an undesirable extension of the end of injection. Thus, cross-section configurations must accurately reflect both the fuel-injection pump's delivery rate and the specific combustion conditions.

Carbon deposits sometimes appear in the annular orifice during operation due to the fact that the throttling pintle and injection orifice are situated behind the nozzle-needle seat.

Fewer and more even deposits are found on flatted pintle nozzles, a special form of the throttling pintle nozzle, in which the annular orifice size between the injection orifice and the throttling pintle is almost zero. Here, the throttling pintle utilizes a machined surface to open the flow cross-section. The machined surface is frequently parallel to the needle axis. Additional inclination can be employed to produce a more pronounced rise in the flat part of the flow curve, allowing a smoother transition to full nozzle opening. This expedient has a positive effect on part-load noise emissions and on operating characteristics.

Temperatures above 220 °C also promote deposit formation on nozzles. Thermal-protection plates are available to transfer the heat from the combustion chamber back to the cylinder head.

#### Hole-type nozzles

A wide range of nozzle-and-holder assemblies (DHK) is available for hole-type nozzles. In contrast to throttling pintle nozzles, hole-type nozzles must generally be installed in a specific position to ensure correct alignment between the injection orifices (which are at different angles in the nozzle body) and the engine combustion chamber. For this reason, lugs or hollow screws are usually employed to attach the nozzle-and-holder assemblies to the cylinder head while a locating device ensures the proper orientation.

Hole-type nozzles are available with needle diameters of 6 and 5 mm (Size S) and 4 mm (Size P), with sac-less (vco) nozzles available in the latter size only.

The compression springs must be suitable for use with the particular needle diameters and the normally extreme opening pressures (> 180 bar). At the end of the injection sequence, there is a pronounced danger of the combustion gases being blown back into the nozzle. This is a phenomenon that would, in the course of time, result in destruction of the nozzle and hydraulic instability. The nozzle-needle diameter and the compression spring are carefully matched to one another to ensure a good seal.

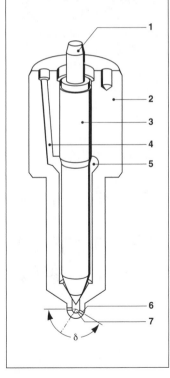

*Hole-type nozzle*
1 Pressure pin, 2 Nozzle body,
3 Nozzle needle, 4 Inlet passage,
5 Pressure chamber, 6 Injection orifice,
7 Blind hole, δ Spray-hole cone angle.

There are three different ways in which the injection orifices are arranged in the cone of the hole-type nozzle. These three designs differ in the amount of fuel which can freely evaporate into the combustion chamber – also known as the dead volume. The designs with a cylindrical blind hole, conical blind hole, as well as the sac-less (vco) nozzle, have successively smaller dead volumes in that order. The engine hydrocarbon emissions decrease in the same order as there is less unburned fuel available for evaporation.

The length of the injection orifice is limited by the nozzle cone's mechanical integrity. At present, the minimum injection-orifice length is 0.6...0.8 mm for cylindrical

and conical blind holes. The minimum injection-orifice length is 1 mm for sac-less (vco) nozzles

The tendency is toward shorter holes, as these generally allow better control of smoke emissions. Fuel flow tolerances of around ± 3.5% can be achieved in drilled hole-type nozzles. Additional hydro-erosion rounding of the inflow edges of the injection orifices can refine these tolerances to ± 2%.

Particularly for use in low-emission direct-injection diesel engines for cars, further refinement has been carried out on the nozzle. By optimizing the dead-volume space in the nozzle body and modifying the injection-orifice geometry, it has been possible to achieve maximum pressure at the injection orifice outlet in order to produce optimum mixture formation. An improvement in even spray distribution in nozzles without blind holes is achieved by using a double needle guide.

The high-temperature strength of the material used in hole-type nozzles limits peak temperatures to approx. 300 °C. Thermal-protection sleeves are available for operation in especially difficult conditions, and there are even cooled nozzles for large-displacement engines.

### Standard nozzle holders

A nozzle-and-holder assembly comprises the holder and the nozzle. The nozzle consists of two sections: the body and the needle. The nozzle needle moves freely within the body's guide bore. while at the same time providing a positive seal against high injection pressures.

The opening pressure of a nozzle-and-holder assembly (approx. 110...140 bar for a throttling pintle nozzle and 150...250 bar for a hole-type nozzle) is adjusted by placing shims under the compression spring.

Closing pressures are then defined by the nozzle's geometry (ratio of needle-guide diameter to needle-seat diameter).

---

*Nozzle shapes*
*1 Throttling-pintle nozzle,*
*2 Throttling-pintle nozzle with flat-cut pintle,*
*2a Side view, 2b Front view,*
*3 Hole-type nozzle with conical blind hole,*
*4 Hole-type nozzle with cylindrical blind hole,*
*5 Sac-less (vco) nozzle.*

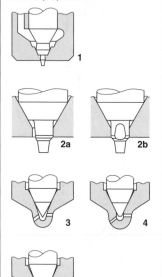

Dual-spring nozzle holders

These nozzle holders are used primarily in direct-injection engines, where rate-of-discharge curve control is an important factor in reducing combustion noise. The use of a dual-spring nozzle holder achieves this desired effect and is created by adjusting and matching:

– opening pressure 1,
– opening pressure 2,
– plunger lift to port closing (prestroke), and
– overall stroke

*Nozzle-holder assembly*
with throttling-pintle nozzle
1 Inlet, 2 Nozzle-holder body, 3 Nozzle-retaining nut, 4 Shim, 5 Nozzle, 6 Union nut with high-pressure line, 7 Edge filter, 8 Leak-fuel port, 9 Pressure-adjusting shims, 10 Pressure passage, 11 Compression spring, 12 Pressure pin.

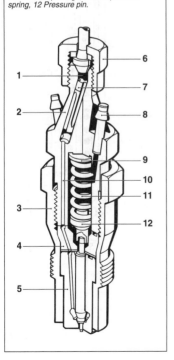

(See figure on next page.) Opening pressure 1 is set and tested as with the single-spring nozzle holder. Opening pressure 2 is the sum of the pretension figures for spring 1 and auxiliary spring 2. Spring 2 is supported on a stop sleeve into which has been machined to the dimension of the prestroke. During injection, opening of the nozzle needle is initially restricted to the prestroke range. Common prestroke figures are 0.03...0.06 mm. As the pressure in the nozzle holder rises, the stop sleeve lifts, allowing the nozzle needle to move to the end of its stroke.

There are also dual-spring holders available for prechamber and whirl-chamber engines. The setpoints are adapted to a particular fuel-injection system.

### References for diesel fuel-injection systems:
Bosch Yellow Jackets, Expert Know-How on Automotive Engineering:
Diesel In-Line Fuel-Injection Pumps, ISBN 3-934584-68-3.
Distributor-Type Diesel Fuel-Injection Pumps, ISBN 3-934584-65-9.
Diesel Accumulator Fuel-Injection System Common Rail, ISBN 3-934584-40-3.
Diesel Fuel-Injection Systems
Unit Injector System/Unit Pump System, ISBN 3-934584-41-1.

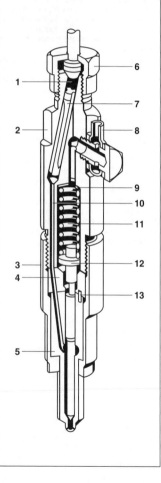

*Nozzle-holder assembly*
with hole-type nozzle
1 Inlet, 2 Nozzle-holder body, 3 Nozzle-retaining nut, 4 Intermediate disk, 5 Nozzle, 6 Union nut with high-pressure line, 7 Edge filter, 8 Leak-fuel port, 9 Pressure-adjusting shims, 10 Pressure passage, 11 Compression spring, 12 Pressure pin, 13 Locating pins.

*KBEL..P... Dual-spring nozzle holder*
$H_1$ Prestroke, $H_2$ Main stroke, $H_{tot} = H_1 + H_2$ Total stroke
1 Holder body, 2 Shim, 3 Compression spring 1, 4 Pressure pin, 5 Guide washer, 6 Compression spring 2, 7 Pressure pin, 8 Spring seat, 9 Shim, 10 Stop sleeve, 11 Spacer, 12 Nozzle-retaining nut.

## Start-assist systems

The colder the diesel engine, the more reluctant it is to start. Higher levels of internal friction combine with blowby and thermal losses to reduce compression pressures and temperatures to such a degree as to render starting impossible without the assistance of auxiliary start-assist devices. The individual temperature threshold also depends upon the specific engine design. Direct-injection engines are subject to lower thermal losses than prechamber or whirl-chamber engines and therefore start more readily. On DI engines with prechambers and whirl chambers, the glow element projects into the combustion chamber.

On large-displacement DI engines, a flame glow plug or a heating flange is employed to preheat the air in the intake tract.

### Sheathed-element glow plugs
#### Design and characteristics

The main component in the sheathed-element glow plug is the tubular heating element. Firm, gas-tight installation in the glow-plug shell ensures that it can resist both corrosion and hot gases. The element contains a spiral filament embedded in magnesium-oxide powder. This spiral filament consists of several elements. The two resistor elements are installed in series. The tip-mounted heater coil maintains virtually constant electrical resistance regardless of temperature, while the control coil consists of a material with a positive temperature coefficient.

Circuit continuity is provided by welding the ground side of the heater coil to the inner tip of the glow tube, and by connecting the control coil to the terminal screw. The terminal screw, in turn, connects the glow plug to the vehicle's electrical system.

#### Operation

The glow plug responds to the initial application of voltage by converting most of the electrical energy into heat within the heater coil, producing a radical increase in the tip's temperature. The temperature of the control coil increases with a delay, and thus also the resistance. The resulting delayed rise in resistance reduces current draw and overall heat generation within the glow plug as it approaches its continuous-operation temperature. Individual heating patterns are defined by component dimensions.

*Position of glow plug in the whirl chamber*
1 Nozzle, 2 Glow plug, 3 Whirl chamber.

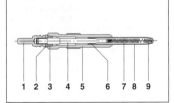

*GSK2 sheathed-element glow plug*
1 Terminal, 2 Insulator shim, 3 Double seal,
4 Terminal pin, 5 Casing, 6 Element seal,
7 Heater and control coils, 8 Glow tube,
9 Filling powder.

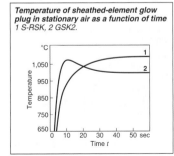

*Temperature of sheathed-element glow plug in stationary air as a function of time*
1 S-RSK, 2 GSK2.

Start phase: Here, the glow plug must heat to starting temperature (approx. 850 °C) as rapidly as possible. Plug locations within the combustion chamber are selected to ensure access to an ignitable mixture. Modern glow plugs heat to the required temperature in roughly 2 seconds.

Post-start phase: The glow plugs continue to operate briefly after the engine has started, improving initial engine operation while reducing blue-smoke emissions and combustion noise. This post-start phase is ≤ 180 s.

### Design variations
GSK2 sheathed-element glow plugs
Nickel control coils are used in conventional S-RSK sheathed-element glow plugs, while second-generation GSK2 glow plugs feature coils in CoFe alloy (see figure on P. 713). These plugs reach ignition temperature more quickly and have a lower steady-state temperature. As a result, the preheating time prior to starting is shorter and the post-start phase becomes possible.

Rapiterm ceramic sheathed-element glow plug
The new low-voltage sheathed-element glow plugs from Bosch feature glow elements made from a new kind of highly heat-resistant ceramic composite material with outstanding properties. This latest glow-plug generation offers the following advantages:
– Immediate starting thanks to fastest preheating rates (1,000 °C/s) even in the event of a dip in the vehicle system voltage,

– Maximum heating temperatures of 1,300 °C,
– High continuous-operation temperature up to 1,150 °C,
– Long service life (like the engine),
– Extended post-start and intermediate-glow times lasting several minutes,
– Low power consumption.

### Internal engine temperatures
The temperature at the glow plug changes according to the engine's operating mode. In direct-injection engines, the maximum temperatures occur at low revolutions and high load (low air throughput resulting in less efficient cooling of the glow plug). By contrast, the highest temperatures in prechamber/whirl-chamber engines occur during operation at high loads and high revolutions per minute.

### Glow-control unit
The complete glow-plug system incorporates not only the glow plugs themselves but also a switching element for the high electrical currents and a unit for controlling this switch. In addition, the system features an indicator lamp (also controlled by the control unit) for signaling when the system is ready for engine start.

In the past, simple bimetallic switches were used, but nowadays glow-plug systems have electronic control units. On more basic vehicles, independent glow-plug control units which handle all control and display functions are used. On modern vehicles, these functions are controlled by the central engine management system. Such units also perform safety and monitoring functions.

Design
The glow-control unit essentially consists of a power relay to regulate the glow-plug current, a printed-circuit board with the electronic circuitry to control glow duration and trigger the ready-to-start indicator, and the elements for the protective functions. The later generations of control units increasingly use semiconductor switches (power MOSFET) instead of an electro-mechanical relay. The unit is enclosed in a plastic housing for protection against dust and water (this applies especially when it is installed in the engine compartment).

*Rapiterm ceramic sheathed-element glow plug*
*1 Pin terminal, 2 Insulating washer, 3 Sealing ring, 4 Terminal stud, 5 Glow-plug shell, 6 Contact element, 7 Sealing ring, 8 Insulating layer, 9 Semiconducting layer, 10 Hot spot.*

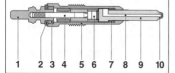

1  2 3 4  5 6  7 8 9  10

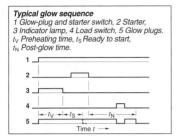

**Typical glow sequence**
1 Glow-plug and starter switch, 2 Starter,
3 Indicator lamp, 4 Load switch, 5 Glow plugs.
$t_V$ Preheating time, $t_S$ Ready to start,
$t_N$ Post-glow time.

### Operation
The preheating and starting sequence is initiated by the glow-plug and starter switch in a similar manner to starting a gasoline engine. The preheating phase begins when the key is turned to "Ignition On".

*Independent glow control units*
On basic units, a temperature sensor in the glow control unit controls the preheating period. This is designed to suit the specific requirements of the particular combination of engine and glow-plug so that the glow plug can reach the temperature necessary for efficient starting. At the end of the glow period, the start-indicator lamp goes out to signal that the engine can be started. The glow process continues for as long as the starter remains in operation, or until the safety override comes into effect (this limits the loads on battery and glow plugs). A strip fuse provides protection against short-circuits.

With more sophisticated independent control units, an engine-temperature sensor (coolant NTC sensor) determines the heating periods more precisely. The glow control unit takes account of differences in battery voltage by adjusting the preheating period accordingly. Current continues to flow through the glow plugs once the engine has started. An engine-load monitor is used to interrupt or switch off the glow process. Protection against overvoltage and short-circuits is provided by an electronic override circuit. A monitoring circuit detects glow-plug failure and relay errors. These are then displayed using the start-indicator lamp.

*EDC-controlled glow control units*
This type of unit receives information on when glow-plug operation is required, and when not, directly from the engine's central ECU. That unit provides (statically or by means of a serial data protocol) the information relating to the engine operating status (coolant temperature, engine speed and load) that is required for optimum control of the glow plugs. Similarly, the glow control unit also signals any faults it detects to the engine ECU via a diagnosis cable or the serial interface. There, they are stored for servicing purposes or displayed if necessary for compliance with OBD requirements.

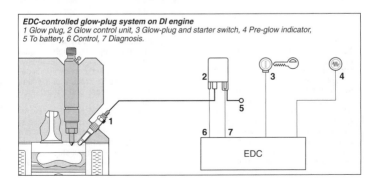

**EDC-controlled glow-plug system on DI engine**
1 Glow plug, 2 Glow control unit, 3 Glow-plug and starter switch, 4 Pre-glow indicator,
5 To battery, 6 Control, 7 Diagnosis.

# Minimizing pollutants in diesel engines

## Engine-design measures

A diesel engine's efficiency is closely linked to the pollutants created during the engine's combustion process. During the diesel combustion process, fuel is introduced within a short period of time into the combustion chamber. Rapid combustion close to TDC in conjunction with a leaner-than-stoichiometric excess-air factor gives rise to good diesel-engine efficiency. However, rapid fuel combustion is also associated with high local peak combustion temperatures, which for their part result in the formation of nitrogen oxides (NO and $NO_2$, usually referred to jointly as $NO_x$). The engine's minimal tendency to knock permits a high compression ratio. This provides good efficiency but also contributes to high combustion temperatures.

Rapid combustion close to TDC is made possible by direct injection of the fuel into the combustion chamber. A certain proportion of the injected fuel burns after the ignition lag in premixed form, while the greater proportion of the fuel burns as a diffusion flame. A local oxygen deficiency is unavoidable here. The fuel does not burn completely and this results in the creation of soot, the second major pollutant component of exhaust gas from a diesel engine.

Increasing the injection pressure improves mixture formation. By utilizing this approach, it has been possible in the last few years to reduce drastically the amount of soot in diesel-engine exhaust gas. Exhaust-gas recirculation lowers the peak combustion temperature through the higher amount of inert gas and through the slower rate of combustion, thereby reducing the amount of nitrogen oxides created. Diesel engines are therefore characterized by low untreated emissions (pollutant concentration in the exhaust gas prior to exhaust-gas aftertreatment) combined with good efficiency. However, in view of the ever more stringent emission standards (Euro IV, ULEV,

etc.), measures for active exhaust-gas treatment will also be essential in diesel engines in the future.

## Exhaust-gas treatment

Different processes are currently under development to remove the major components $NO_x$ and soot from the exhaust gas. This involves converting $NO_x$ and soot in separate processes into the nontoxic, unlimited components $N_2$ and $CO_2$. Technology, such as a three-way catalytic converter as used in spark-ignition engines, can be ruled out for diesel engines since it is virtually impossible to reduce $NO_x$ in the presence of $O_2$ (the diesel engine is run on excess air).

Common processes for reducing soot and $NO_x$ are described separately in the following.

### Oxidation-type catalytic converter

Already used in series production, diesel oxidation catalytic converters (DOC) remove the partially oxidized carbon (CO) and unburned hydrocarbons (HC) efficiently from the exhaust gas. The ejected particulate mass is also reduced by oxidizing the high-boiling-point hydrocarbons that are condensed out of the soot particles.

Oxidation catalytic converters are positioned as close to the engine as possible in order to obtain the temperature required as quickly as possible to ensure their efficient operation (light-off temperature).

### Particulate filters

The particulates emitted by a diesel engine are made up of roughly equal amounts of carbon, ash and unburned hydrocarbons. The exact composition is dependent on the sulfur content of the fuel, the combustion process and the exhaust-gas temperature.

The particulates can be efficiently removed from the exhaust gas by filters. Filters composed of porous ceramics are the favored options at present. Cordierite and silicon carbide are suitable ceramic materials. Particulate filters are usually designed in the same way as ceramic catalytic converters and feature a large number of parallel square channels. The channel walls are typically 300...400 μm thick. The size of the channels is usually given by specifying the cell density per square inch (cpsi) (typical value: 100...300 cpsi).

In particulate filters, adjoining channels are sealed off at the opposing ends by ceramic plugs. Exhaust gas flows through the porous ceramic walls. The soot particles are conveyed by diffusion to the pore walls, and there they adhere to the walls (deep-bed filtration). As the filter is subjected to increasing soot loads, a layer of soot forms on the channel walls.

Wall-flow filters accumulate the particulates on the surface (surface filtration). Particulate filters are characterized by a particle retention rate of more than 90% over the entire relevant size spectrum (10...1,000 nm).

The main problem associated with particulate-filter technology is not the retention of the particulates in the filter, but rather the subsequent burn-off of the soot that has collected in the filter. This process is also known as regeneration. The rising soot contamination of the filter is accompanied by a continuous increase in exhaust-gas backpressure, which in turn has a negative effect on engine economy and drivability.

The carbon levels in the particulates can be oxidized at temperatures above approx. 600°C into nontoxic $CO_2$ with the oxygen constantly present in the exhaust gas. Temperatures of this magnitude are not obtained in normal driving operation, with the result that special measures have to be adopted.

### CRT system

The CRT principle (Continuously Regenerating Trap), which is being tested in the first fleet trials, is a means of regenerating the particulate filter in commercial vehicles. This principle has the effect that soot containing $NO_2$ can already be oxidized at temperatures of 250...350 °C based on the reaction:

$$2NO_2 + C \rightarrow CO_2 + 2NO$$

This process is also known as passive regeneration since it does not require any active intervention in engine operation. To use this process, an oxidation catalytic converter, which oxidizes NO into $NO_2$, is located upstream of the particulate filter. These catalytic converters are dependent on the use of fuel with a low sulfur content. The process works reliably at temperatures above those specified if the $NO_2$/soot mass ratio is greater than 8:1. These conditions are more often than not obtained with commercial vehicles.

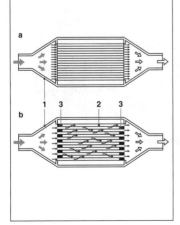

*Exhaust-gas treatment with different methods*
a Oxidation catalytic converter (noble-metal-coated), b Particulate filter.
1 Housing, 2 Extruded honeycomb ceramic, 3 Ceramic plug.

## Additive system

With the serial introduction of particulate filters in passenger cars, the diesel fuel is sometimes given an additive which lowers the soot oxidation temperature with $O_2$ from 600 °C to approx. 450 °C (additive concentration: approx. 10...20 ppm). Even this exhaust-gas temperature is not achieved in normal operation, with the result that the soot does not burn continuously. The filter load factor is calculated on measuring the pressure drop across the particulate filter using a differential-pressure sensor and with the aid of a soot-mass simulation. Above a specific soot (load) factor, soot burn-off is initiated by active measures (active regeneration). Here, the engine is operated in terms of its combustion performance so that significantly higher exhaust-gas temperatures occur than would be the case in normal operation. This can be achieved, for example, by a significantly greater retardation of the start of injection, if necessary by afterburning the unburned fuel content in a catalytic converter.

Once the soot has reached its ignition temperature, the filter continues to heat up automatically due to the heat released as the soot is burned. The rising temperatures further accelerate soot burn-off and further increase the introduction of heat into the filter and the exhaust gas.

The peak temperatures that occur during regeneration of a particulate filter (1,000 °C and higher) soul even destroy the filter. As the soot (load) factor increases, so does the risk of unacceptably high temperatures. Regeneration, therefore, has to be initiated before this critical load condition is reached. Depending on the filter material, a filter volume of 5...10 g soot per liter is specified as the critical load quantity.

The additive given to the fuel (usually cerium or iron compounds) forms an ash which is deposited in the filter and cannot be burned. This ash, like the ash from engine-oil or fuel residue, gradually clogs the filter and also increases the exhaust-gas backpressure. It is assumed that the filter will have to be removed and cleaned

---

*Exhaust-gas treatment: particulate filter with additive system*
*1 Additive ECU, 2 Engine ECU, 3 Additive pump, 4 Level sensor, 5 Additive reservoir,*
*6 Additive nozzle, 7 Fuel tank, 8 Diesel engine, 9 Oxidation catalytic converter,*
*10 Particulate filter, 11 Temperature sensor, 12 Differential-pressure sensor.*

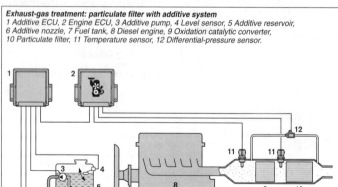

by mechanical means roughly every 120,000 km. For this reason, engineers are looking for processes which will permit a safe and intermittent regeneration of the particulate filter without the use of an additive. A promising approach is the catalytic coating of the filter, which can likewise bring about a lowering of the ignition temperature, but is generally less than when an additive is used.

Catalytic burners

Catalytic burners are suitable for raising the exhaust-gas temperature up to the soot ignition temperature. In this case, fuel is introduced directly into the exhaust-gas system. The fuel burns in an oxidation catalytic converter and thus brings about the desired increase in temperature.

External burners or partial-flow burners, as are used in construction machinery, for example, or the electrical heating of particulate filters, are only of secondary importance in motor-vehicle applications.

## Selective catalytic reduction of nitrogen oxides

Selective catalytic reduction (SCR) is about to be introduced for the reduction of nitrogen oxides. For several years this technology has been a proven means of removing nitrogen from exhaust gases in industrial furnaces. It is based on the principle that selected reducing agents selectively reduce the nitrogen oxides in the presence of oxygen. Selective in this case means that the oxidation of the reducing agent takes place by preference (selectively) with the oxygen from the nitrogen oxides and not with the significantly more abundant molecular oxygen present in the exhaust gas. Ammonia ($NH_3$) has proven itself to be the reducing agent with the greatest selectivity in this respect.

As ammonia is a toxic substance, the actual reducing agent used in motor-vehicle applications is obtained from the non-toxic catalyst carrier carbamide. Carbamide [$(NH_2)_2CO$] is manufactured commercially as fertilizer and feed, and is both groundwater-compatible and chemically stable under environmental conditions. Carbamide demonstrates very good solu-

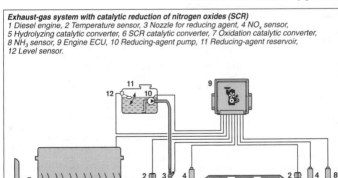

**Exhaust-gas system with catalytic reduction of nitrogen oxides (SCR)**
1 Diesel engine, 2 Temperature sensor, 3 Nozzle for reducing agent, 4 $NO_x$ sensor,
5 Hydrolyzing catalytic converter, 6 SCR catalytic converter, 7 Oxidation catalytic converter,
8 $NH_3$ sensor, 9 Engine ECU, 10 Reducing-agent pump, 11 Reducing-agent reservoir,
12 Level sensor.

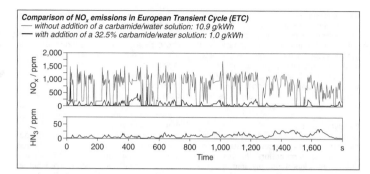

**Comparison of NO$_x$ emissions in European Transient Cycle (ETC)**
— without addition of a carbamide/water solution: 10.9 g/kWh
— with addition of a 32.5% carbamide/water solution: 1.0 g/kWh

bility properties in water, which is why a carbamide/water solution is added to the exhaust gas for reasons of simple dosability. Here, a 32.5% (weight percentage) solution is used because it has the lowest freezing point (eutectic at −11 °C).

In many applications, a hydrolyzing catalytic converter is located in the exhaust-gas system upstream of the actual SCR catalytic converter. Here, one carbamide molecule and one water molecule decompose in two stages into two ammonia molecules and one $CO_2$ molecule:

$$(NH_2)_2CO \rightarrow NH_3 + HNCO \text{ (thermolysis)}$$
$$HNCO + H_2O \rightarrow NH_3 + CO_2 \text{ (hydrolysis)}$$

The ammonia created by thermohydrolysis primarily reacts in the SCR catalytic converter according to the following equations:

$$4NO + 4NH_3 + O_2 \rightarrow 4N_2 + 6H_2O$$
$$NO + NO_2 + 2NH_3 \rightarrow 2N_2 + 3H_2O$$

Modern SCR catalytic converters can incorporate the function of the hydrolyzing catalyst so that there is frequently no need to use a hydrolyzing catalyst.

An oxidation catalytic converter, which oxidizes NO into $NO_2$, brings about an improvement in the conversion with an $NO_2$ share of the NO$_x$ of up to 50%. This enables the SCR catalytic converter to work at optimum efficiency, especially at low exhaust-gas temperatures (< 250 °C).

Owing to the toxicity of $NH_3$, it is important when operating an SCR system to limit ammonia leakage, i.e. the permeation of $NH_3$ through the catalytic-converter system. This can be achieved by integrating an additional oxidation catalytic converter downstream of the SCR catalytic converter. This check catalytic converter oxidizes the ammonia that may occur into $N_2$ and $H_2O$. Alternatively, a careful application of the carbamide/water-solution dose is essential.

A parameter important to this application is the feed ratio $\alpha$, defined as the molar ratio of NO$_x$ present in the exhaust gas and added $NH_3$. Under ideal operating conditions (no $NH_3$ leakage, no secondary reactions, no $NH_3$ oxidation), $\alpha$ is directly proportional to the NO$_x$ reduction rate. Where $\alpha = 1$, a complete NO$_x$ reduction achieved in theory. In practice, with an $NH_3$ leakage of less than 20 ppm, a NO$_x$ reduction of up to 90% can be achieved in stationary and non-stationary operation. The quantity of carbamide/water solution required corresponds to roughly 5% of the amount of diesel fuel used.

With current SCR catalytic converters, a NO$_x$ conversion rate of > 50% can only be achieved at temperatures in excess of approx. 200 °C. Optimum conversion rates are obtained in a temperature window of 250...450 °C. Increasing the temperature operating range, in particular improving low-temperature activity, is now the object of catalytic-converter research.

## NOₓ accumulator-type catalytic converter

The $NO_x$ accumulator-type catalytic converter has already been launched on the market in engines with gasoline direct injection (see P. 663). Like diesel engines, these engines are operated with excess air for fuel-economy reasons. In lean-burn operation, the nitrogen oxides are not reduce in a conventional three-way catalytic converter, which is why this type of catalytic converter cannot be used. In diesel passenger cars, the $NO_x$ accumulator-type catalytic converter is favored over other nitrogen-removal technologies, since an additional operating agent (e.g. carbamide/water solution in SCR technology) is not wanted.

There are two different operating modes in relation to the $NO_x$ accumulator-type catalytic converter. In normal lean-burn operation ($\lambda > 1$), NO is first oxidized into $NO_2$ and then adheres in the form of a nitrate ($NO_3$) to a basic metal oxide (e.g. barium oxide) in the catalytic converter. Storage is only optimum in a material-dependent exhaust-gas temperature range between 250 and 450 °C. Below this, the oxidation of NO into $NO_2$ is very slow; above this, the $NO_2$ is unstable.

As with the particulate filter, the real challenge associated with the $NO_x$ accumulator-type catalytic converter is posed by regeneration, i.e. emptying the accumulator at regular intervals. In order to regenerate the accumulator, it is essential for rich conditions ($\lambda < 1$) to prevail in the exhaust gas. Under these operating conditions, there are so many reducing agents in the exhaust gas (CO, $H_2$ and various hydrocarbons) that the nitrate compound is abruptly dissolved and the released $NO_2$ is reduced to $N_2$ directly in the noble-metal catalytic converter. The load phase lasts between 30 and 300 s, depending on the operating point; regeneration takes place within 2...10 s.

In engines with gasoline direct injection, rich operating conditions can be created simply by switching from lean-burn stratified-charge operation to rich homogeneous operation. In diesel engines, $\lambda < 1$ is obtained through retarded injection and intake-air throttling, among other things. It is important when switching from lean- to rich-burn operation to maintain unrestricted drivability, as well as constant torque, response and noise.

One problem associated with $NO_x$ accumulator-type catalytic converters is their sulfur sensitivity, since $SO_2$ is also stored in the catalytic converter on account of its chemical similarity to $NO_2$. The sulfate ($SO_4$) compound formed is not dissolved during normal regeneration of the accumulator, with the result that the amount of stored $SO_2$ increases gradually during the period of use. In this way, there is less room for $NO_x$ storage and $NO_x$ conversion diminishes. During operation with 10 ppm sulfur in the fuel, sulfur regeneration is necessary on account of the reduced $NO_x$ storage capability after approx. 10,000 km. A period of more than 5 minutes at temperatures in excess of 600 °C and $\lambda < 1$ is required for this purpose.

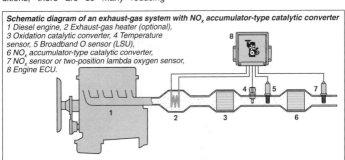

*Schematic diagram of an exhaust-gas system with $NO_x$ accumulator-type catalytic converter*
1 Diesel engine, 2 Exhaust-gas heater (optional),
3 Oxidation catalytic converter, 4 Temperature sensor, 5 Broadband O sensor (LSU),
6 $NO_x$ accumulator-type catalytic converter,
7 $NO_x$ sensor or two-position lambda oxygen sensor,
8 Engine ECU.

# Electric drives

The electric drive is quiet, produces no exhaust emissions and is very efficient. Whereas in purely electrically powered vehicles the electric drive alone powers the wheels, hybrid vehicles have at least two different sources of drive energy, one of which is usually an electric drive.

In contrast to internal-combustion engine vehicles, on electric-only vehicles the energy accumulator generally determines the vehicle's performance. The capacity of the electric motor is matched to the maximum output of the energy accumulator. The energy accumulator may take the form of an electrochemical battery or a fuel cell (P. 732) and its associated fuel tank.

Depending on the intended application, battery-powered electric vehicles can be classified as either road vehicles or industrial trucks. Industrial trucks are used for transporting goods on company premises, and are generally not licensed for use on public roads. Their top speed is below 50 km/h. Due to the low energy density of the batteries, the range of battery-powered on-road vehicles is significantly less than that of vehicles powered by internal-combustion engines. The maximum speed of such vehicles is also normally limited to around 130 km/h. Whereas more than half of all new industrial trucks are electrically powered, the percentage of electrically powered on-road vehicles is very low.

## Power supply

There is no shortage of power for electric vehicles that are recharged by plugging them into a wall socket. If electric vehicles in Germany were largely recharged at night, existing power plants could provide enough energy to charge more than 10 million vehicles. That number of electric vehicles would require less than 5% of Germany's total electricity output.

Any household power outlet can be used to charge the batteries. However, these outlets can provide only 3.7 kW of electrical power, which means that an hour of charging would provide enough power to drive a distance of no more than about 20 km. Shorter recharging times can be achieved by using a three-phase AC power source (as for industrial trucks). Compared to the refueling times for diesel vehicles in particular, the recharging times required by comparable electric vehicles in order to cover the same distances are roughly 100 times longer, even in the case of very high charging capacity.

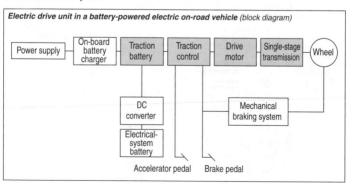

*Electric drive unit in a battery-powered electric on-road vehicle (block diagram)*

# Batteries

Whereas cost considerations dictate that the lead-acid battery is the most frequent power source used in industrial trucks, in electric cars it is increasingly being replaced by nickel and lithium battery systems.

## Lead-acid battery

Although the basic design of the lead-acid battery is the same as that of the starter battery (P. 967), the combination of materials and the cell design are specially adapted to the particular requirements of traction operation. The batteries commonly used in industrial trucks are generally combinations of individual cells, whereas a modular design with 3 or 6 cells per module is used in most electric on-road vehicles due to the higher energy density.

Industrial trucks generally use lead-acid batteries with a liquid electrolyte which must be topped up with water on a regular basis. In the case of electric on-road vehicles, this level of maintenance is not acceptable for the vehicle's user. Consequently, maintenance-free batteries with a solid electrolyte (gel) have become standard in these applications. Under real-world conditions, vehicles equipped with lead-acid batteries have a range of 50...70 km per battery charge in city driving. The daily range of an electric vehicle can be increased through intermediate charging of the batteries when the vehicle is parked.

The capability of lead-acid batteries to store energy decreases as temperature drops. This means a battery heating system is required at temperatures below 0 °C in order to fully charge the battery within an acceptable period of time. The energy required for this purpose is normally taken together with the charging energy from the power supply network. The amount of power and energy that can be drawn from a lead-acid battery also decreases as temperature drops, resulting in more sluggish acceleration and reduced range.

As the electrolyte takes part in the chemical reaction inside a lead-acid battery, the available capacity varies as a function of load current. Driving at constant full load therefore equates to a 20% or more reduction in range.

Batteries in industrial-truck applications can achieve service lives of 7...8 years with 1,200...1,500 cycles. Fleet experiences with electric passenger cars indicate that lead-acid batteries can be expected to last for around 5 years and roughly 700 cycles. The shorter service life in electric on-road vehicle applications is primarily a result of

## Battery systems

| Properties | Lead-acid system open/sealed | Nickel systems Nickel-cadmium (Ni/Cd) Nickel-metal hydride (NiMH) | Lithium systems Lithium-ion Lithium-polymer |
|---|---|---|---|
| Cell voltage | 2 V | 1.2 V | 3...4 V |
| Energy density | 25...30 Wh/kg | 35...80 Wh/kg | 60...150 Wh/kg |
| Energy efficiency without hating/cooling | 75...80% | 60...85% | 85...90% |
| Power density | 100...200 W/kg | 100...1,000 W/kg | 300...1,500 W/kg |
| Service life in cycles | 600...900 | > 2,000 | > 1,000 projected |
| Operating temperature | 10...55 °C | −20...55 °C | −10...50 or 60 °C |
| Maintenance-free | Depending on design | Depending on design | yes |

## Commercially available vehicles (examples)

| Vehicle type | Type of battery | Engine power | Acceleration 0...50 km/h | Typical speed | Typical range per charge | Typical line-power consumption |
|---|---|---|---|---|---|---|
| Passenger car | Ni/Cd | 21 kW | 9 s | 90 km/h | 80 km | 18 kWh/100 km |
| Passenger car | NiMH | 49 kW | 7 s | 130 km/h | 200 km | 26 kWh/100 km |
| Passenger car | Lithium-ion | 62 kW | 6 s | 120 km/h | 200 km | 23 kWh/100 km |
| Van | Lead-acid | 80 kW | 7 s | 120 km/h | 90 km | 35 kWh/100 km |

the much greater battery load. In these vehicles, the battery is discharged in an average of 2 hours or less, whereas discharge times in industrial trucks are generally in the 7...8 hour range.

### Nickel-based batteries

Nickel-cadmium batteries and, increasingly, nickel-metal hydride batteries with an alkaline electrolyte are used in many electrical appliances. As cadmium is harmful to the environment, it is likely that the nickel-cadmium battery will be replaced by the nickel-metal hydride system in the foreseeable future. Whereas electrical appliances normally use sealed batteries, in traction applications open nickel-cadmium cells are often used. These cells, like open lead-acid batteries, must be refilled with water at regular intervals. Nickel-metal hydride batteries must be sealed due to the inherent characteristics of the system. The low cell voltage of only 1.2 V means that a higher number of cells is required (e.g. for a 6 V module) than in a lead-acid battery. A battery service life of up to 10 years or 2,000 cycles has been demonstrated in a number of applications. The higher costs resulting from the use of relatively expensive materials and the complex manufacturing process are partially offset by a much longer service life than that of lead-acid batteries.

Nickel-cadmium and nickel-metal hydride batteries are cooled when used in electric on-road vehicles; heating is required only at temperatures below −20 °C. Available capacity is virtually independent of discharge time. The alkaline battery's higher energy density can be exploited both to increase payload and to extend the vehicle's radius of action. Electric cars have a typical range of approx. 80...100 km using nickel-cadmium batteries.

In the nickel-metal hydride system, cadmium is replaced by a metal alloy that is able to store hydrogen. The nickel-metal hydride battery has a higher energy density and a somewhat longer service life than the nickel-cadmium battery. Nickel-based batteries generally feature a higher power density, making them particularly interesting for use in hybrid vehicles.

### Lithium battery systems

Lithium systems allow energy densities of over 100 Wh/kg and power densities of over 300 W/kg in vehicle traction batteries. They can be operated at ambient temperature or slightly higher temperatures, and are characterized by high cell voltages of over 4 V. In the demanding electrical-appliance battery market (for products such as laptops and video recorders), the lithium-ion system has already become successfully established.

Lithium systems do not show any memory effect as do nickel-cadmium systems. A disadvantage of the lithium batteries is that they require a relatively complex battery protection system. For example, each individual cell must be monitored because they are not protected against overcharging. To protect the environment, these batteries must also be specially protected against short-circuits.

#### Lithium-ion battery

A lithium-ion battery stores lithium ions in electrically reversible form on the negative electrode in a graphite lattice. The positive electrode of commercially available batteries contains cobalt oxide as the main constituent, making the system rather expensive. Attempts are therefore ongoing to use more economical materials such as manganese or nickel oxides. Organic material is used as the electrolyte; aqueous electrolytes cannot be used because lithium reacts strongly with water.

#### Lithium-polymer battery

Another very promising lithium system is the lithium polymer battery. It consists of a thin lithium film, a polymer electrolyte and a positive film electrode made primarily of vanadium oxide. Individual cells are formed by rolling or folding this film, which has an overall thickness of approx. 0.1 mm. The operating temperature is approx. 60 °C. Further developments in connection with lithium-ion batteries involve replacing the organic liquid electrolyte by a polymer electrolyte.

# Drivetrains

The drivetrain in an electric vehicle generally consists of the power controller, the motor, and the transmission. The power controller translates the position of the accelerator pedal into the appropriate motor current and voltage. In most cases, the drive torque is a function of the accelerator pedal position, as in the case of IC engines.

The cost of the motor depends largely on the required maximum torque; the ideal solution is to use the highest possible reduction gear ratio between the engine and the drive wheels. The reduction gearing may consist of one or two stages, depending on the desired hill-climbing ability and the vehicle's maximum speed for the given maximum torque and variable speed range of the drive train. Today's electric cars feature single-stage reduction gears.

A difference between electric drive units and combustion engines is the necessary distinction between short-term and extended-duty performance. Short-term performance is usually limited by the maximum setting of the power controller. The maximum power available over longer periods is defined by the half-hourly output in the case of on-road electric vehicles, which is generally limited by the permissible motor temperature. This distinction also applies to most battery systems. Depending on the type of drive, short-term and extended-duty ratings vary by a factor of 1 to 3. Maximum drive power must therefore be monitored and adjusted, if necessary, in accordance with the characteristic thermal limits of the power controller, motor or batteries.

This distinction between short-term and half-hourly operation has also lead to the adoption of two maximum-speed ratings for electric on-road vehicles: maximum speed over a distance of 2 x 1 kilometer and maximum speed over a period of 30 minutes.

## Series-wound direct-current drive

This type of drive unit has the simplest type of power controller. The motor voltage is set in accordance with the desired current by applying the battery voltage to the motor in a variable on/off ratio and/or chopper frequency by means of a circuit breaker (thyristor or transistor(s)).

For the recovery of braking energy, the power controller must operate as a step-up chopper, which means that additional components are needed. As the field and armature of the motor are in series, drive torque drops in proportion to the square of the motor speed with the full battery voltage applied.

Although its efficiency is relatively low, this type of drive is still used in most industrial trucks today because of its simple design and low cost. The low top speeds of these vehicles make it possible to use single-stage reduction gears.

## Separately excited direct-current drive

In this type of drive unit, the motor's magnetic excitation is provided by its own controller (field rheostat). Depending on the size of the motor, the field can be weakened at a ratio of up to approx. 1:4. Field strength starts to diminish at a nominal motor speed obtained with full motor voltage at the armature and maximum field current. During initial acceleration with maximum field current, an electronic armature-control device limits the motor current until the motor reaches its nominal speed, with the full motor voltage applied to the armature. In the reduced field-strength range, consistent armature currents produce relatively constant power outputs. As commutation becomes more difficult with a decrease in field current, the armature current must usually be reduced before the maximum speed is reached.

Since commutating poles are required, this design is somewhat more complex than that of a series-wound motor. The mechanical commutator limits rotational speed to roughly 7,000 rpm.

*Torque and power as a function of rotational speed for various types of drive*
a) Series-wound DC drive,
b) Separately excited DC drive,
c) Asynchronous drive,
d) Permanently excited synchronous drive.
$M_{max}$ Maximum torque,
$P_{max}$ Maximum power.

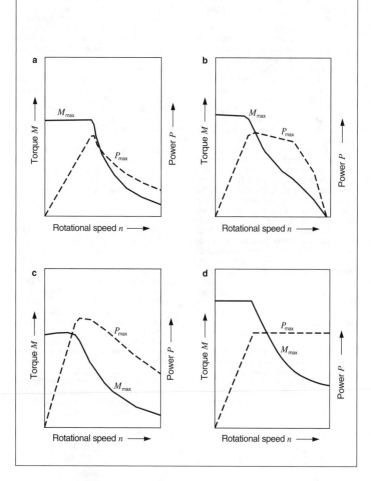

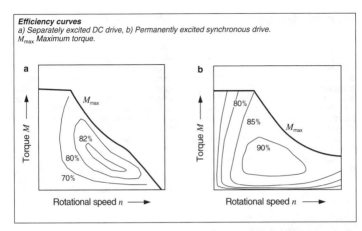

**Efficiency curves**
a) Separately excited DC drive, b) Permanently excited synchronous drive.
$M_{max}$ Maximum torque.

This type of drive unit can be used with a multistage transmission to reduce motor cost and weight. Efficient energy recovery during braking is possible without requiring additional components. However, very few electric cars today are being equipped with direct-current drive units. Three-phase AC asynchronous or synchronous drives are now the norm, due in part to their low maintenance requirements. The carbon brushes in DC motors must be regularly replaced, although at relatively long intervals.

## Asynchronous drive

The motor in an asynchronous drive unit is the simplest and most economical in design, and is also considerably smaller in size and weight than a direct-current motor. In principle, however, the controller in a three-phase drive unit is more complex than that used in DC drives. As with the separately excited DC drive, operation with reduced field current is possible. Since these motors have no mechanical commutator, they can operate at speeds of up to 20,000 rpm if appropriately designed. This means that single-stage transmissions can be used, even in on-road vehicles. These drives are more efficient than direct-current drives, but not quite as efficient as synchronous drives with permanent magnets. Braking energy can also be recovered with a high degree of efficiency.

## Permanently excited synchronous drive

This type of drive is characterized by very high efficiencies, also in the part-load range, because it uses permanent magnets to generate the excitation field. Rare-earth magnets (high energy density) allow very compact dimensions combined with high torque. However, rare-earth magnets make the motor more expensive than asynchronous designs, for example. This type of motor is not capable of operating with reduced field current. Nevertheless, quasi reduced-field-current operation can be implemented by increasing the longitudinal component of the stator current by way of reducing the torque-generating component. Motors with "buried" magnets are currently available which, due to their pronounced asymmetry, achieve reduced-field current factors of up to 1:3. Alternatively, windings featuring particularly high inductance levels are capable of achieving considerably higher reduced-field current factors. Since virtually constant-output operation is possible, a single-stage reduction gear is generally sufficient in this case, too.

# Hybrid drives

In the broadest sense, the term "hybrid drives" is used to denote vehicle drives with more than one drive source. Hybrid drives can incorporate several similar or dissimilar types of energy accumulator and/or power converter. The goal of hybrid-drive development is to combine different drive components. The advantages of each component are utilized under varying operating conditions so that the overall advantages outweigh the higher technical outlay associated with hybrid drives.

## Drive configurations

### Hybrid drives with internal-combustion engines

In terms of available performance and range, the IC engine as a drive source is superior to all other drive systems. Its disadvantages – drop in efficiency at part load, and the generation of toxic emissions – have lead to the development of hybrid drives which incorporate the IC engine. IC engines in some hybrid drives are therefore designed for use over the medium-power range, whereby the differences between generated power and the power required at any given time are made up by the additional mechanical or electrical energy accumulator.

*Hybrid drive configurations*
1 Series hybrid, 2 Mixed drive, 3 Parallel hybrid.
VM *IC engine*, EL *Electric drive (M operated as a motor or G alternator/generator)*,
BA *Battery or external power supply*,
SG *Manually shifted transmission.*

**Table 1. Hybrid drive configurations.**

|  | Series hybrid (1) | Mixed drive (2) |  | Parallel hybrid (3) |
|---|---|---|---|---|
| + | IC engine mechanically decoupled from drive unit | Permits compensation of the advantages and drawbacks of series parallel hybrids | + | Output power of IC engine and electric drive are superimposed |
| + | Output of IC engine independent of current drive power |  | + | Design of both drive machines adaptable to specific application requirements |
| + | Operating point of IC engine adaptable to "emission", "fuel consumption", "noise" criteria |  | + | Permits synchronization of mechanical transmission |
| – | Complete drive power delivered by traction engine |  | – | Design restrictions posed by mechanical connection of both drive machines |
| – | Efficiency reduced by multiple energy conversion |  |  |  |
|  | **Series hybrid is a drive concept for reducing emissions** |  |  | **Parallel hybrid is a drive concept for reducing fuel consumption** |

Mechanical energy accumulator systems generally involve the use of pressure accumulators or rotating flywheel masses. Although pressure accumulators normally exhibit higher gravimetric energy densities than mechanical storage systems, they rely on the conversion between mechanical energy and pressure energy for the energy exchange process. The "flywheel" as a mechanical energy accumulator requires no energy conversion for the energy exchange process. The storage characteristics, however, require an infinitely variable conversion ratio for the energy exchange process. The flywheel speed and vehicle speed are inversely proportional (opposing). This means the driving speed increases and the flywheel speed decreases when the vehicle is accelerated. Energy can be transmitted only if a transmission with an infinitely variable transmission ratio is able to compensate for this opposing disposition. Hydraulic or electric power delivery is generally used for these transmissions (possibly with splitter transmission). However, the media change process in this configuration is subject to the deterioration in transmission efficiency characteristic of series hybrids.

### Hybrid drives without internal-combustion engines

Hybrid drives which have no IC engines and use only electrical drive components are designed to avoid the disadvantages of the purely battery-powered electric drive. The useful energy stored in the battery allows only a limited driving range. The energy is further reduced disproportionately as power demand increases.

Combining a mechanical energy accumulator with the battery protects it from power peaks, so contributing to more efficient utilization of the battery energy. A hybrid system which uses a combination of two different electrochemical energy sources (battery and fuel cell) separates the energy sources so that one source has a high power, and the other has good energy-storage capability. In the case of hybrid electric drives with an external supply of energy (trolley systems), the vehicle's own energy accumulator is used as a short-time storage medium for short distances of travel without overhead power supply. This confi-

guration reduces the high costs associated with overhead contact wires and increases versatility in traffic.

## Hybrid drive designs

### Drive configurations

Hybrid drives which combine an internal-combustion (IC) engine and an electric drive are the only hybrid drives which have warranted serious attention to date. The electric drive component of such drives is powered either by an on-board battery or via an overhead contact wire and current-collector system. The figure below shows the various basic drive configurations. The battery indicated in each configuration can be replaced by the external power supply.

The main difference among the various configurations is the serial, parallel or mixed interconnection of the power sources. In the serial configuration, the individual drive components are connected in series, whereas in the parallel configuration, the drive power of both drive sources is added mechanically. The letters M and G indicate whether the electric drive is operating in "motor" or "generator" mode.

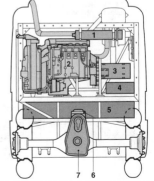

*Series hybrid drive in rear of bus*
1 Braking resistor, 2 Diesel engine,
3 Alternator, 4 Converter, 5 Batteries,
6 Traction motor, 7 Reduction gear.

### Series hybrid

As the diesel engine in the serial configuration is mechanically decoupled from the vehicle drive, the diesel engine can be operated at constant speed, i.e. at its optimum operating point in terms of efficiency and emissions. Despite the advantages of the serial configuration, its disadvantage is that energy must be converted several times. Including battery storage efficiency, the mechanical efficiency between the diesel engine and the powered axle is hardly greater than 55%.

A series hybrid configuration is therefore advantageous as a bus drive system because all drive components can be accommodated in the rear of the low-platform bus.

### Parallel hybrid

The parallel hybrid configuration has the advantage that, when operated in the mode which incorporates an IC engine, it is just as efficient as a conventional vehicle. In the illustrated drive configuration, the gearbox required by the diesel-engine drive is also part of the electric drive branch. In this configuration, the electric drive also profits from the torque conversion by the downstream transmission, as a result of which the electric motor must only be dimensioned for low drive torque. This leads to an equivalent reduction in electric motor mass which is roughly proportional to motor torque.

A parallel hybrid configuration is particularly suitable for delivery vehicles that are used to cover short distances in pedestrian zones or warehouses and are totally emission-free. The figure shows the drive components necessary for a parallel hybrid drive configuration. It also indicates the extent of the driven ancillaries: The auxiliary drives normally driven by the diesel engine are provided in a dual arrangement to facilitate operation in pure electric drive mode when the diesel engine is stationary. The structure of the parallel hybrid configuration clearly reflects the close relationship of this arrangement with the integrated starter generator (ISG). The starter generator is normally coupled directly to the internal-combustion engine while, in the parallel hybrid configuration, the connection between the electric motor and combustion engine can be interrupted by the standard clutch.

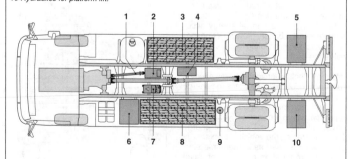

*Parallel hybrid drive in truck*
*1 Propshaft electric motor, 2 Electric motor, 3 Lead-acid battery, 4 Battery charger,*
*5 Compressor with converter, 6 Fuse box and converter (power-steering pump),*
*7 Converter for electric motor, 8 Lead-acid battery, 9 Coolant reservoir (drive system),*
*10 Hydraulics for platform lift.*

## Operating modes

Besides the pure diesel or electric drive (Nos. 1 and 2 in the figure depicting operating modes), the various operating modes also permit <u>simultaneous operation</u> of both drive units and appear to offer the greatest potential in connection with parallel hybrid drives. In this configuration, the electric motor can be operated either as a motor to increase the drive power output or as a generator/alternator to charge the battery while driving (Nos. 3 and 4). A further distinction can be made in the second case as to whether the mechanical energy to feed the alternator is produced by the vehicle in connection with regenerative braking or by the diesel engine when the vehicle is stationary (Nos. 5 and 6). Considered on its own, operating mode No. 6 may be of interest as an efficient source of electrical energy separate from the standard power supply system.

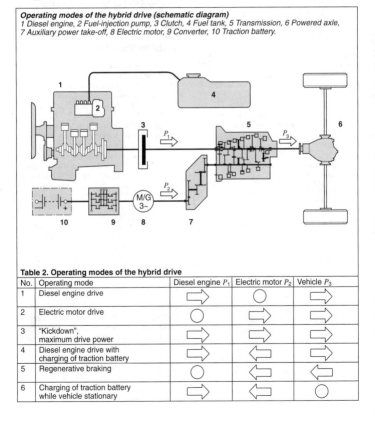

***Operating modes of the hybrid drive (schematic diagram)***
*1 Diesel engine, 2 Fuel-injection pump, 3 Clutch, 4 Fuel tank, 5 Transmission, 6 Powered axle, 7 Auxiliary power take-off, 8 Electric motor, 9 Converter, 10 Traction battery.*

**Table 2. Operating modes of the hybrid drive**

| No. | Operating mode | Diesel engine $P_1$ | Electric motor $P_2$ | Vehicle $P_3$ |
|---|---|---|---|---|
| 1 | Diesel engine drive | ⇨ | ◯ | ⇨ |
| 2 | Electric motor drive | ◯ | ⇨ | ⇨ |
| 3 | "Kickdown", maximum drive power | ⇨ | ⇨ | ⇨ |
| 4 | Diesel engine drive with charging of traction battery | ⇨ | ⇦ | ⇨ |
| 5 | Regenerative braking | ◯ | ⇦ | ⇦ |
| 6 | Charging of traction battery while vehicle stationary | ⇨ | ⇦ | ◯ |

# Fuel cells

Fuel cells are electrochemical cells in which the chemical energy of a suitable fuel is continuously converted into electrical energy using atmospheric oxygen ($O_2$). The most common fuels which lend themselves to such applications are hydrogen ($H_2$), methanol ($CH_3OH$) and, to a more limited degree, methane (at very high temperatures). As conventional fuels cannot be used directly, they must be converted into $H_2$ in a chemical gas-reforming reaction. Fuel-cell operation is very efficient, and produces low levels of pollutant emissions. They are modular in design, and can therefore be used over a wide power range from a few watts to several megawatts.

Due to these characteristics and promising new developments in the field of low-temperature fuel cells, many carmakers now see the fuel-cell drive as a serious alternative to the internal-combustion engine for automotive applications. For this reason, the major vehicle manufacturers in particular are working intensively on the development of fuel cells suitable for automotive use.

*Polymer electrolyte fuel cell*
(principle of operation)
1 Hydrogen, 2 Electrical load, 3 Air (oxygen),
4 Catalyst, 5 Electrolyte, 6 Bipolar plate,
7 Water vapor and residual air.

Source: DaimlerChrysler

However, a realistic assessment of the fuel-cell drive in terms of its environmental and customer benefit is only possible by looking at the whole picture. As far as emissions are concerned, not only must the direct emissions from the vehicle be taken into account, but also those produced in the fuel-cell manufacturing process. The same applies to the system's efficiency, which can only be compared with other types of drive if the overall efficiency of the entire process from the primary energy source to the driving wheels is considered.

The most important application for fuel cells to date has been as a means of generating electrical energy in spacecraft and submarines.

## Design variations

In contrast to combustion engines, fuel-cell operation does not require a specific (high) temperature; some fuel cells operate at room temperature, while others are designed for temperatures of up to approximately 1,000 °C (Table 1). The various designs differ from one another above all in the type of electrolyte used, which depends on the temperature. Up to around 90 °C the electrolyte is aqueous or contains water. For mid-range temperatures (500...700 °C) molten alkaline carbonate electrolytes have become the standard, while for high temperatures (800... 1,000 °C), only ceramic-based solid electrolytes (e.g. zirconium dioxide) can be used. Apart from the differences in the type of electrolyte used, fuel cells also differ according to their electrode materials.

Fuel cells are often referred to by the acronyms shown in Table 1.

## Fuel conditioning

Although attempts have long been made to operate fuel cells directly using various fuels, the fuel cells available today must use $H_2$ as their energy source. At present, $H_2$ is generally obtained from natural gas or other fossil fuels by means of a chemical gas-reforming reaction. For mobile applications, $H_2$ must either be stored in the vehicle or derived from another on-board fuel.

**Hydrogen storage medium**

For automotive applications, $H_2$ can be stored and transported in gaseous form in cylinders at pressures of up 300 bar or in liquid form in cryotanks at $-253\,°C$. For low-power applications or in submarines, hydrogen is stored in metal hydrides or even in special modified carbon compounds. If $H_2$ is stored as a gas under pressure or as a liquid, it must be remembered that a considerable portion of the primary energy is required simply to compress or liquefy the $H_2$. Furthermore, the energy density of an $H_2$ storage medium is less than that of a conventional fuel tank.

**Methanol reforming**

$CH_3OH$ is produced from natural gas with an efficiency of approx. 65%. Its advantage over $H_2$ is that it can be dispensed in liquid form similar to conventional vehicle fuels. However, a separate infrastructure must be made available to handle $CH_3OH$; it cannot be stored in existing fuel tanks because it is considerably more corrosive than gasoline or diesel fuel. $CH_3OH$ can be converted into $H_2$, $CO_2$ and CO in a catalytic reforming process using water vapor at temperatures of $250...450\,°C$. The CO combines with water to produce $H_2$ and $CO_2$ in a subsequent catalytic conversion stage. The residual CO must be removed in a gas purifier because it chemically inhibits the fuel-cell electrodes.

**Gasoline reforming**

The advantages of gasoline are its high energy density and widespread availability through an already existing infrastructure. However, it is considerably more difficult to reform gasoline into $H_2$ than it is to reform $CH_3OH$, for example. Conversion involves partial oxidation in the presence of air and water at temperatures of $800...900\,°C$, producing $H_2$, $CO_2$ and CO. The CO is converted in two subsequent catalytic stages using $H_2O$ into $H_2$ and $CO_2$. The residual CO must be separated out in a gas purifier in this case as well, because it inhibits the fuel-cell electrodes. The problems associated with gasoline reformation concern primarily the complex system which must be controlled at high temperatures, and the inhibition of the catalysts by the formation of coke.

# Thermodynamics and kinetics

The electrochemical reactions which take place in fuel cells are essentially the same as those in galvanic cells (e.g. batteries). However, in fuel cells, only gaseous or liquid fuels are used. The oxidizing agent is generally $O_2$ or atmospheric oxygen. For this reason, fuel cells require special porous electrode structures.

Table 2 gives the reaction equations and the calculated fuel-cell data (theoretical cell voltage $E_0$ and thermodynamic efficiency $h_{th}$) for the two fuels of interest, $H_2$ and $CH_3OH$, at different temperatures. The first reaction equation describes the

**Table 1. Types of fuel cells**

| Fuel cell designation | | Electrolyte | Temperature °C | Cell efficiency (load – partial load) % | Application |
|---|---|---|---|---|---|
| Alkaline Fuel Cell | AFC | Aqueous KOH | 60...90 | 50...60 | Mobile, stationary |
| Polymer Electrolyte Fuel Cell | PEFC | Polymer electrolyte | 50...80 | 50...60 | Mobile, stationary |
| Direct Methanol Fuel Cell | DMFC | Membrane | 110...130 | 30...40 | Mobile |
| Phosphoric Acid Fuel Cell | PAFC | $H_3PO_4$ | 160...220 | 55 | Stationary |
| Molten Carbonate Fuel Cell | MCFC | Alkaline carbonates | 620...660 | 60...65 | Stationary |
| Solid Oxide Fuel Cell | SOFC | $ZrO_2$ | 800...1,000 | 55...65 | Stationary |

familiar electrolytic gas reaction, which in fuel cells is a controlled process ("cold combustion") rather than an explosive one. This reaction takes place in a controlled manner in fuel cells because the important subreactions ($H_2$ oxidation and $O_2$ reduction) occur at physically separate electrodes and at a relatively low temperature (Figure and Table 1). It is therefore possible in fuel cells to directly and completely convert the chemical energy, which corresponds to the decrease in free enthalpy $\Delta G_R$ of the reaction, into electrical work $A_e$ in accordance with Equation 1:

$$A_e = -\Delta G_R = n \cdot F \cdot E_0 \qquad \text{(Equation 1)}$$

(where $n$ is the number of electrons converted per fuel molecule, $F$ Faraday constant).

Since the customary indirect path via the generation of heat is avoided in this type of energy conversion, fuel-cell efficiency is not limited by the relatively poor efficiency of the Carnot cycle.

As shown in Table 2, the cell voltages $E_0$ for the two fuels are close to one another (approx. 1.2 V) and the thermodynamic efficiency $\eta_{th}$ calculated according to Equation 2 is also < 1 for $CH_3OH$ if liquid water is formed as the reaction product:

$$\eta_{th} = \Delta G_R / \Delta H_R \qquad \text{(Equation 2)}$$

At temperatures above 100 °C (if $CH_3OH$ and $H_2O$ are present in gaseous form), the $CH_3OH/O_2$ fuel cell shows that in principle fuel cells can also attain a thermodynamic efficiency of > 1.

In practice the theoretical fuel-cell figures are not reached with any of the fuels, even at high temperatures. The reasons for this are primarily to be found in the kinetic inhibition at the two electrodes (e.g. charge penetration and material transfer) as well as in the mixed potential formation at the positive electrode and the electrolyte impedance. The resulting polarization can be reduced but not completely eliminated by using noble metals (platinum, ruthenium) as catalysts, specially structured porous electrodes and small electrode gaps. This applies even in the absence of current flow when a steady-state voltage of only approx. 1 V is measured at an $H_2/O_2$ PEFC (see Table 1) instead of the expected 1.23 V. When a load is applied, fuel-cell voltage and efficiency drop by varying degrees, depending on the fuel, as current increases due to increasing polarization (see graph). Other variables which have a significant effect on the shape of the current/voltage characteristic of a fuel cell are temperature, gas pressure (1.5...3 bar) and the noble-metal electrode coating, which is now as little as 0.1...0.5 mg Pt/cm².

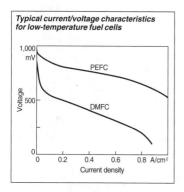

*Typical current/voltage characteristics for low-temperature fuel cells*

**Table 2. Reaction equations and calculated data for hydrogen ($H_2$) and methanol ($CH_3OH$) as energy sources for fuel cells.**

| Reaction equations | State of $H_2O/CH_3OH$ | Temperature °C | $E_0$    V | $\eta_{th}$    % |
|---|---|---|---|---|
| $H_2 + \frac{1}{2}O_2 \rightarrow H_2O$ | Liquid | 25 | 1.23 | 83 |
| | Liquid | 127 | 1.15 | 81 |
| | Gaseous | 127 | 1.16 | 92 |
| | Gaseous | 227 | 1.11 | 87 |
| $CH_3OH + \frac{3}{2}O_2 \rightarrow$ $CO_2 + 2\,H_2O$ | Liquid/liquid | 25 | 1.21 | 97 |
| | Liquid/liquid | 127 | 1.20 | 99 |
| | Gaseous/gaseous | 127 | 1.20 | 103 |
| | Gaseous/gaseous | 227 | 1.21 | 104 |

The typical working voltage of an $H_2$/air PEFC at rated continuous output (0.4...0.5 W/cm² of electrode surface area) is around 0.75...0.70 V (see graph) which, according to Equation 2, results in an efficiency of 51...48%. With $CH_3OH$ as the PEFC energy source, despite the higher temperature (110...130 °C), lower power density (0.1...0.2 W/cm²) and greater amount of Pt on the electrodes, a lower voltage (0.50...0.35 V) and a correspondingly lower thermodynamic efficiency (41...30%) is produced than in the case of an $H_2$/air PEFC. However, this does not take into account the fact that, in the case of $CH_3OH$, its permeation through the electrolyte membrane results in a loss to the anode due to which the efficiency of a direct methanol fuel cell is even further reduced.

## Fuel cells in motor vehicles

As clean, high-efficiency energy converters, from the point of view of environmental protection and conservation of resources, fuel cells represent an interesting alternative to the traditional methods of generating electrical power. Of the types of fuel cells described here, PEFCs in particular show the most promise in both fixed and mobile applications by virtue of their low operating temperature and compact and robust design. In the area of mobile applications, driven by the increasingly stringent emission-control legislation in the U.S.A. and Europe, fuel-cell power units are clearly at the forefront of development efforts. In addition, however, the possibility of using PEFCs as the electrical power source in vehicles with conventional engines is also being investigated, and initial experiments have been carried out. A vehicle electrical system with a power supply independent of the engine which provides the motive power would enable implementation of desirable timer-controlled or remotely controlled auxiliary functions (e.g. preheating of the engine/catalytic converter, air-conditioner operation without the engine running).

All of the automobile manufacturers engaged in comprehensive fuel-cell development work have focused on two key problems, which in principle affect all fuel-cell applications: the high cost of PEFCs and the availability of pure $H_2$, which is essential for the operation of PEFCs and for which there is no infrastructure at present which could be used to supply vehicles powered by such fuel cells. An additional disadvantage of $H_2$ as a fuel for fuel-cell powered vehicles is the fact that its energy density is satisfactory only if it is stored in pressurized or liquefied form. For reasons of safety alone, there are serious concerns regarding the storage of $H_2$ in those forms in private passenger cars.

When using fuel cells as automotive drives, efficiency drops to around 30% from the $H_2$ storage tank to the wheels. This loss is attributable in part to the auxiliary systems required for monitoring and operation of the fuel cells (e.g. air compressor, coolant pumps, fan cooler, control equipment and, where applicable, gas reformers). The electrical power required by the secondary loads can amount to as much as 25% of the fuel-cell output, depending on the nature of the peripherals and the size and operating point of the fuel cell. In addition to fuel-cell efficiency, the efficiency of the electric drive unit must also be taken into consideration. When considering the entire energy chain from the primary energy source to the vehicle's powered wheels, and given the technology available at present, the overall efficiency of modern diesel and fuel-cell-powered vehicles is comparable for vehicles of equal power-to-weight ratios.

No predictions can be made at this time regarding the service life of PEFCs under the dynamic conditions of motor-vehicle operation. As in all applications involving catalysts, fuel cells can also be expected to suffer from a reduction in the catalytic action of the electrodes over time. The result is a gradual decline in the voltage and efficiency of the fuel cell which is referred to as degradation. It is assumed, however, that over the long term the service life of fuel-cell drives will be similar to that of internal-combustion engines.

### References
Karl Kordesch, Günther Simander, Fuel Cells and Their Applications, VCH Weinheim 1996.

# Drivetrain

## Quantities and units

| Quantity | | Unit |
|---|---|---|
| $a$ | Acceleration | m/s² |
| $c_d$ | Drag coefficient | – |
| $e$ | Rotational inertia coefficient | – |
| $f$ | Rolling resistance coefficient | – |
| $g$ | Gravitational acceleration | m/s² |
| $i$ | Transmission ratio | – |
| $m$ | Vehicle mass | kg |
| $n$ | Rotational speed | rpm |
| $r$ | Dynamic tire radius | m |
| $s$ | Wheel slip | – |
| $v$ | Road speed | m/s |
| $A$ | Frontal area | m² |
| $D$ | System diameter | m |
| $I$ | Overall conversion range | – |
| $J$ | Mass moment of inertia | kg · m² |
| $M$ | Torque | N · m |
| $P$ | Power | kW |
| $\alpha$ | Angle of inclination | ° |
| $\varphi$ | Overdrive factor | – |
| $\eta$ | Efficiency | – |
| $\lambda$ | Performance index | – |
| $\mu$ | Conversion | – |
| $\rho$ | Density | kg/m³ |
| $\omega$ | Angular velocity | rad/s |
| $v$ | Speed ratio | – |

| Subscripts: | | eng | Engine |
|---|---|---|---|
| eff | Effective | o | Towards maximum output |
| tot | Total | dt | Drivetrain |
| hydr | Hydraulic | G | Gearbox |
| max | Maximum | P | Pump |
| min | Minimum | R | Roadwheel |
| fd | Final drive | T | Turbine |

## Function

The function of the automotive drivetrain is to provide the thrust and tractive forces required to induce motion. Energy in chemical (fuels) or electrical (batteries, solar cells) form is converted into mechanical energy in the power unit, with spark-ignition and diesel engines representing the powerplants of choice. Every power unit operates within a specific speed range as defined by two extremities: idle speed and the maximum engine speed. Torque and power are not delivered at uniform rates throughout the operating range; the respective maxima are available only within specific bands. The drivetrain's conversion ratios adapt the available torque to the momentary requirement for tractive force.

## Design

The dynamic condition of an automobile is described by the running-resistance equation. It equates the forces generated by the drivetrain with the forces required at the driving wheels (running resistance).

From the running-resistance equation, it is possible to calculate acceleration, maximum speed, climbing ability and also the overall conversion range $I$ of the transmission.

$$I = \frac{(i/r)_{max}}{(i/r)_{min}} = \frac{\tan \alpha_{max} \cdot v_o}{(P/(m \cdot g))_{eff.} \cdot \varphi}$$

### Equilibrium relation between drive forces and running resistance

The equation defining the equilibrium relation between drive forces and resistance factors is applied to determine various quantities, such as acceleration, top speed, climbing ability, etc.

Available power = Running resistance at drive wheels (power requirement)

$$M_{eng} \cdot \frac{i_{tot}}{r} \cdot \eta_{tot} = m \cdot g \cdot f \cdot \cos \alpha + m \cdot g \cdot \sin \alpha + e \cdot m \cdot \alpha + c_d \cdot A \cdot \frac{\rho}{2} \cdot v^2$$

| Driving force applied to tire footprint | Rolling resistance | Climbing resistance | Acceleration resistance | Aerodynamic drag |

Where rotational inertia coefficient $e = 1 + \dfrac{J}{m \cdot r^2}$ and mass moment of inertia $J = J_R + i_h^2 \cdot J_A + i_h^2 \cdot i_G^2 \cdot J_m$

The overdrive factor $\varphi$ is

$$\varphi = \frac{(i/r)_{min}}{\omega_o / v_o}.$$

Calculations of effective specific output should always be based on the power $P$ which is actually available for tractive application (net power minus driven ancillaries, power losses, altitude loss). Special conditions, such as trailer towing, must be factored in the weight $m \cdot g$. $\varphi = 1$ is true when the curve for cumulative running resistance in top gear directly intersects the point of maximum output. The $\varphi$ factor determines the relative positions of the curves for running-resistance and engine output in top gear. It also defines the efficiency level at which the engine operates.

$\varphi > 1$ displaces engine operation to an inefficient performance range, but also enhances acceleration reserves and hill-climbing ability in top gear. In contrast, selecting $\varphi < 1$ will increase fuel economy, but only at the price of much slower acceleration and lower climbing reserves. Minimum fuel consumption is achieved along the operating curve $\eta_{opt}$. $\varphi > 1$ reduces, $\varphi < 1$ increases the required transmission conversion range $I$.

## Drivetrain configurations

The layout of the automotive drivetrain varies according to the position of the engine and the powered axle:

| Drive configuration | Engine position | Driven axle |
|---|---|---|
| Standard rear-wheel drive | Front | Rear axle |
| Front-wheel drive | Front, longitudinal or transverse | Front axle |
| All-wheel drive | Front, occasionally rear or middle | Front axle and rear axle |
| Rear-wheel drive with rear-mounted engine | Rear | Rear axle |

## Drivetrain elements

The elements of the drivetrain must perform the following functions:
- remain stationary even with the engine running,
- achieve the transition from stationary to mobile state,
- convert torque and rotational speed,
- provide for forward and reverse motion,
- compensate for drive-wheel speed variations when cornering,
- ensure that the power unit remains within the program map that permits minimum fuel consumption and exhaust emissions.

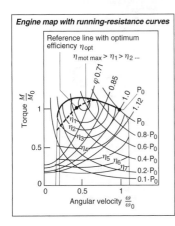

*Engine map with running-resistance curves*

Reference line with optimum efficiency $\eta_{opt}$

$\eta_{mot\,max} > \eta_1 > \eta_2 \dots$

Torque $\frac{M}{M_0}$

Angular velocity $\frac{\omega}{\omega_0}$

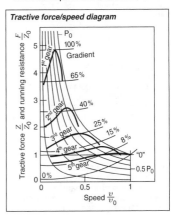

*Tractive force/speed diagram*

Tractive force $\frac{Z}{Z_0}$ and running resistance

Gradient

Speed $\frac{v}{v_0}$

Stationary idle, starting off and interruptions in the power flow are all made possible by the clutch. The clutch slips to compensate for differences in the rotational speeds of engine and the drivetrain when the vehicle is starting off from standstill. When different conditions demand a change of gear, the clutch disengages the engine from the transmission while the gearshift operation takes place. On automatic transmissions, the hydrodynamic torque converter assumes the start-off procedure. The transmission modifies the engine torque and engine speed and adapts them to the vehicle's momentary tractive requirements.

The overall conversion of the drivetrain is the product of the constant transmission ratio of the axle differential and the variable transmission ratio of the transmission – assuming there are no other transmission stages involved. Transmissions are almost always multiple fixed-ratio gearboxes, though some have continuously variable ratios.

Transmissions generally fall into one of two categories: manually shifted transmissions with spur gears in a countershaft arrangement, and load-actuated automatic transmissions with planetary-gear sets. The transmission also allows the selection of different rotational directions for forward and reverse operation.

The differential allows laterally opposed axles and wheels to rotate at varying rates when cornering to provide uniform distribution of the driving forces. Limited-slip final drives respond to slip at one of the wheels by limiting the differential effect. This shifts additional power to the wheel at which traction is available.

Torsion dampers, hydrodynamic transmission elements, controlled-slip friction clutches or mass-suspension systems dissipate high vibration amplitudes. They protect against overload and provide added ride comfort.

## Power take-up elements

### Dry-plate friction clutch

The friction clutch consists of a pressure plate, a clutch disk – featuring bonded or riveted friction linings – and a mating friction surface represented by the engine-mounted flywheel. The flywheel and pressure plate provide the thermal absorption required for friction operation of the clutch; flywheel and pressure plate are connected directly to the engine, while the clutch disk is mounted on the transmission's input shaft.

A spring arrangement, frequently in the form of a central spring plate, applies the force which joins the flywheel, pressure plate and clutch disk for common rotation; in this state, the clutch is engaged for positive torque transfer. To disengage the clutch (e.g. when gearshifting), a mechanically or hydraulically actuated throwout bearing applies force to the center of the pressure plate and releases pressure at the periphery. The clutch is controlled either by a clutch pedal or an electrohydraulic, electropneumatic or electromechanical final-control element. A single- or multi-stage torsion damper, with or without predamper, may be integrated in the clutch disk to absorb vibration.

A two-section (dual-mass) flywheel featuring a flexible intermediate element can be installed forward of the clutch for maximum insulation against vibrations. The resonant frequency of this spring/mass system is below the excitation frequency (ignition frequency) of the engine at idle speed, and is a therefore

*Clutch with dual-mass flywheel*
*1 Dual-mass flywheel, 2 Flexible element,*
*3 Pressure plate, 4 Spring plate,*
*5 Friction plate, 6 Throwout bearing.*

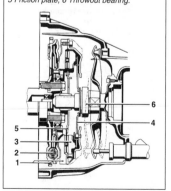

outside the operating speed range. It acts as a vibration insulating element between the engine and the other drivetrain components (low-pass filter).

When used together with electronic control units, the automatic clutch can provide either gradual engagement for start-off, or it can be applied in conjunction with a servo-operated shifting mechanism to form a fully automatic transmission unit. Traction control and disengagement of power transmission during braking are also possible.

### Wet-plate friction clutch

The wet-plate friction clutch has the advantage over the dry-plate version that its thermal performance is better as it can been flooded with oil to enhance heat dissipation. However, its drag losses when disengaged are considerably higher than for a dry clutch. Use in combination with synchromesh gearboxes presents problems due to increased synchronous load when gearshifting. The wet clutch was introduced as a standard component on continuously variable car transmissions. It has space-saving advantages, particularly when one or more friction-drive gearshift components (multiplate clutch or clutch stop) can also be used for the start-off process.

### Hydrodynamic torque converter

The hydrodynamic torque converter consists of an impeller which is the drive element, a turbine which is the driven component, and a stator which assists the torque converter function. The torque converter is filled with oil and transmits engine torque by means of the flowing forces of the oil. It compensates for speed differences between the engine and the other drivetrain components, and is therefore ideally suited for the start-off function. An impeller converts mechanical energy into fluid energy. This is converted back to mechanical energy in a second transformation that takes place in the turbine impeller.

The impeller's input torque $M_p$ and input power $P_p$ are calculated as follows:

$$M_p = \lambda \cdot \rho \cdot D^5 \cdot \omega^2_p$$
$$P_p = \lambda \cdot \rho \cdot D^5 \cdot \omega^3_p$$

$\lambda$   Performance index
$\rho$   Density of medium
   ($\approx$ 870 kg/m³ for hydraulic fluid)
$D$   Circuit diameter in m
$\omega_p$ Angular velocity of impeller

A stator located between impeller and turbine diverts the hydraulic oil back to the input side of the impeller. This raises the torque beyond the initial engine output

*Automatic clutch, limited to clutch actuation*
1 Engine, 2 Engine-speed sensor, 3 Clutch, 4 Transmission, 5 Servomotor, 6 ECU, 7 Velocity sensor, 8 Accelerator pedal, 9 Clutch pedal.

*Hydrodynamic converter with converter lockup clutch*
1 Lockup clutch, 2 Turbine, 3 Impeller, 4 Stator, 5 One-way clutch.

exerted at the impeller. Torque conversion is then:

$$\mu = -M_T/M_P$$

The factor $\nu$ is defined as the ratio of turbine speed to impeller speed; it has a determining influence on both the performance index $\lambda$ and the conversion factor $\mu$:

$$\nu = \omega_T / \omega_P.$$

The slip factor $s = 1 - \nu$ and the force conversion together determine the hydraulic efficiency:

$$\eta_{hydr} = \mu (1 - s) = \mu \cdot \nu.$$

Maximum torque multiplication is achieved at $\nu = 0$, i.e. with the turbine at stall speed. Further increases in turbine speed are accompanied by a virtually linear drop in multiplication until a torque ratio of 1:1 is reached at the coupling point. Above this point, the stator, which is housing-mounted with a one-way clutch, freewheels in the flow.

In motor-vehicle applications, the two-phase Föttinger torque converter with centripetal flow through the turbine, i.e. the "Trilok converter", has become the established design. The geometrical configuration of this unit's blades is selected to provide torque multiplication in the range of 1.7...2.5 at stall speed ($\nu = 0$). The curve defining the hydraulic efficiency factor $\eta_{hydr} = \nu \cdot \mu$ in the conversion range is roughly parabolic. Above the coupling point, which is at 10...15% slip, the efficiency is equal to the speed ratio $\nu$ and reaches levels of around 97% at high speeds.

The hydrodynamic torque converter is a fully automatic, infinitely variable transmission with virtually zero-wear characteristics; it eliminates vibration peaks and absorbs vibration with a high degree of efficiency.

However, its conversion range and efficiency, particularly at high levels of slip, are not sufficient for motor-vehicle applications. As a result, the torque converter can only be usefully employed in combination with multi-speed or continuously variable transmissions.

### Converter lockup clutch

In order to improve efficiency, the impeller and turbine can be locked together by a converter lockup clutch after startup has ended. The converter lockup clutch consists of a plunger with a friction lining that is connected to the turbine hub. The transmission-shift control regulates the direction in which the fluid flows through the converter to regulate clutch lockup.

The converter lockup clutch normally requires additional means of vibration absorption such as:
- a torsion damper
- controlled-slip operation of the converter lockup clutch at critical vibration levels, or
- a combination of both of the above

## Multi-speed gearbox

Multi-speed gearboxes have become the established means of power transmission in motor vehicles. The main reasons for its success include excellent efficiency characteristics dependent on the number of gears and engine torque characteristics, medium to good adaptation to the traction hyperbola, and easily mastered technology.

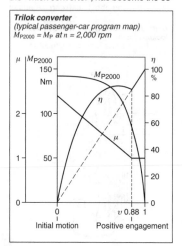

*Trilok converter*
*(typical passenger-car program map)*
$M_{P2000} = M_P$ at $n = 2,000$ rpm

Gearshifting on multi-speed gearboxes is performed using either disengagement of power transmission (positively interlocking mechanism) or under load by a friction mechanism. The first group includes manually shifted and semi-automatic transmissions, while the second group encompasses automatic transmissions.

The manually shifted transmissions installed in passenger cars and in most heavy vehicles are dual-shaft units with main shaft and countershaft. Transmissions in heavy commercial vehicles sometimes incorporate two or even three countershafts. In such cases, special design features are required in order to ensure that power is evenly distributed to all countershafts.

Automatic transmissions for cars and commercial vehicles are, in the majority of cases, planetary-gear transmissions, and only in rare cases are countershaft arrangements used. The planetary gears generally take the form of a planetary-gear link mechanism. They frequently involve the use of Ravigneaux or Simpson planetary gears.

### Planetary-gear sets

The basic planetary-gear set consists of the sun gear, internal ring gear and the planet gears with carrier. Each element can act as input or output gear, or may be held stationary. The coaxial layout of the three elements makes this type of unit ideal for use with friction clutches and brake bands, which are employed for selective engagement or fixing of individual elements. The engagement pattern can be changed – and a different conversion ratio selected – without interrupting torque flow; this capability is of particular significance in automatic transmissions.

As several gear wheels mesh under load simultaneously, planetary-gear transmissions are very compact. They have no free bearing forces, permit high torque levels, power splitting or power combination, and feature very good efficiency levels.

## Manually shifted transmissions

The basic elements of the manually-shifted transmission are:
- single or multiplate dry clutch for interrupting and engaging the power flow; actuation may be power-assisted to deal with high operating forces,
- variable-ratio gear transmission unit featuring permanent-mesh gears in one or several individual assemblies,
- shift mechanism with shift lever.

---

*Planetary-gear set with various conversion ratios*
A *Sun gear,* B *Internal ring gear,* C *Planet gears with carrier,*
Z *Number of teeth.*

Basic equation for planetary-gear sets: $n_A + (Z_B / Z_A) \cdot n_B - [1 + Z_B / Z_A] \cdot n_C = 0$

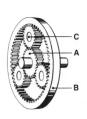

| Input | Output | Fixed | Transmission ratio | Remarks |
|---|---|---|---|---|
| A | C | B | $i = 1 + Z_B / Z_A$ | $2.5 \le i \le 5$ |
| B | C | A | $i = 1 + Z_A / Z_B$ | $1.25 \le i \le 1.67$ |
| C | A | B | $i = \dfrac{1}{1 + Z_B / Z_A}$ | $0.2 \le i \le 0.4$ overdrive |
| C | B | A | $i = \dfrac{1}{1 + Z_A / Z_B}$ | $0.6 \le i \le 0.8$ overdrive |
| A | B | C | $i = - Z_B / Z_A$ | Non-automotive with reversible direction of rotation $-0.4 \le i \le -1.5$ |
| B | A | C | $i = - Z_A / Z_B$ | Non-automotive with reversible direction of rotation $-0.25 \le i \le -0.67$ |

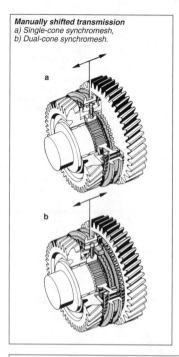

***Manually shifted transmission***
*a) Single-cone synchromesh,*
*b) Dual-cone synchromesh.*

a

b

The force required for gear selection is transmitted via shift linkage rods or cable, while dog clutches or synchronizer assemblies lock the active gears to the shafts. Before a shift can take place, it is necessary to synchronize the rotating speeds of the transmission elements to be joined. When the transmission incorporates dog clutches (of the type still sometimes used in transmissions for heavy commercial vehicles), the driver performs this task by double-clutching when upshifting and briefly touching the accelerator when downshifting.

Virtually all passenger-car transmissions, and the majority of those in commercial vehicles, employ locking synchronizer assemblies. These include a friction coupling for initial equalization of rotating speed and a lockout mechanism to prevent positive gear engagement prior to completion of the synchronization process. By far the majority use single-cone synchromesh clutches. In cases where there are particularly high demands for performance and/or reduction of gearshifting force, double-cone or even triple-cone synchromesh clutches or multi-plate synchromesh clutches are used.

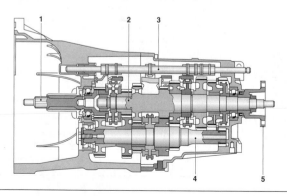

***6-speed transmission for passenger car with conventional drive layout*** *(ZF S6-37)*
*1 Input shaft, 2 Main shaft, 3 Selector rail, 4 Countershaft, 5 Output shaft.*

Most transmissions in passenger cars have 5 and increasingly 6 forward gears. The transmission-ratio range (depending on the number of gears and closeness of the ratios) is approximately between 4 and 6.3 while the transmission efficiency can be as high as 99%. The transmission layout depends on the vehicle's drive configuration (standard rear-wheel drive, front-wheel drive with inline or transverse engine, or four-wheel drive). Accordingly, the input and output shafts may share a single axis, or they may be mutually offset; the final-drive and differential assembly may also be included in the unit.

Transmissions in commercial vehicles can have between 5 and 16 gears, depending on the type of vehicle and the specific application. For up to 6 gears, the transmission consists of a single gearbox. The transmission-ratio range is between 4 and 9. Transmissions with between 7 and 9 gears are two-case transmissions in which the range-selector case is pneumatically operated. The transmission-ratio range extends to 13.

For still higher numbers of ratios – up to 16 – three transmission elements are employed: the main transmission, a splitter group and the range-selector group, with pneumatic actuation for the latter two units. The transmission-ratio range is as high as 16.

### Power take-offs

Commercial-vehicle transmissions are fitted with a variety of power take-off connections for driving ancillary equipment. A basic distinction is made between clutch and engine-driven PTO's. The individual selection depends upon the specific application.

### Retarders

Hydrodynamic or electrodynamic retarders are non-wearing auxiliary brakes for reducing the thermal load on the road-wheel brakes under continuous braking. They can be fitted on both the drive input side (primary retarders) or the drive output side (secondary retarders), either as a separate unit or integrated in the transmission. The advantages of the integrated designs are compact dimensions, low weight and fluid shared with the transmission in a single circuit. Primary retarders have specific advantages when braking at low speeds and are therefore widely used on public-transport buses. Secondary retarders have particular advantages on long-distance trucks for adjustment braking at higher speeds or when traveling downhill.

## Automatic transmissions

There are two types of automatic transmission depending on their effect on vehicle handling dynamics:

– Semi-automatic transmissions are manually shifted transmissions on which all operations normally performed by the driver when changing gear are carried out by electronically controlled actuator systems. In terms of vehicle dynamics, this means that a gear change always involves disengaging the clutch and therefore interrupting the drive to the driving wheels.

– Fully automatic transmissions, usually referred to simply as automatic transmissions, change gear under load, i.e. power continues to be transmitted to the driving wheels during a gearshift operation.

That difference in vehicle handling dynamics is the essential factor which determines the types of application for these two transmission types. Fully automatic transmissions are used in situations where disengagement of power transmission would be associated with a significant reduction in comfort (above all on cars with powerful acceleration), or where it is unacceptable for reasons of handling dynamics (mainly on off-road vehicles). Semi-automatic transmissions are equipped on long-distance trucks, tour buses and more recently on small cars, racing cars and very sporty road vehicles.

### Semi-automatic transmissions

Partially or fully automated gearshifting systems make a substantial contribution to simplifying control of the gears and increasing fuel economy. Particularly when

**16-speed multiple transmission with integrated secondary retarder for heavy trucks**
(ZF Ecosplit 16 S221)

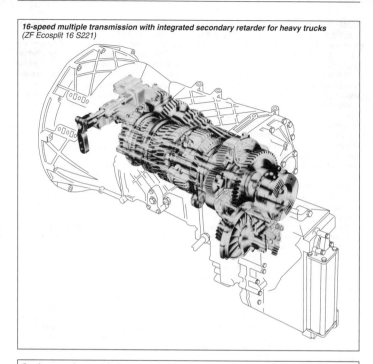

**Semi-automatic transmission** (schematic)
1 Engine electronics (EDC), 2 Transmission electronics, 3 Transmission actuator, 4 Diesel engine,
5 Dry-plate friction clutch, 6 Clutch servo unit, 7 Intarder control unit, 8 Display, 9 Gear selector,
10 ABS/TCS, 11 Gearbox, 12 Air supply.
—— Electrical, – – – – Pneumatic , —— CAN communication.

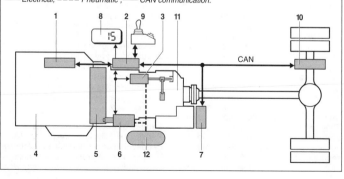

used on trucks, the disadvantages inherent in the interruption of power transmission are compensated by a number of decisive advantages:
- narrower spacing of ratios, with up to 16 gears
- enhanced efficiency power transfer
- reduced costs
- same basic transmission unit for manual and semi-automatic designs

Operating concept
An electric, hydraulic or pneumatic positioner module on the transmission shifts the individual gears and activates the clutch. The electronic transmission control generates the control signals for the gearshift operation.

Design variations
On the simplest systems, the mechanical gearshift linkage is simply replaced by a remote control system. The shift lever then merely sends out electrical signals. Start-off and clutching procedures are identical to a standard manually shifted transmission. More complex versions combine these systems with a recommended shift-point function.
Advantages are:
- reduced shifting effort
- simplified installation (no shift linkage)
- prevention of incorrect operation (over-revving of engine)

On fully automated gearshifting systems, both the transmission and the power take-up element are automated. The driver's control element consists of either a lever or pushbuttons, with an override provision in the shape of a driver-selected manual mode or +/− buttons.
Complex shift programs are required to control a multi-ratio transmission. A system which engages the gears according to a fixed pattern will not be adequate. Current running resistance (as determined by payload and road conditions) must be factored in to achieve the optimum balance between drivability and fuel economy. This task is performed by a microcomputer control system and control of synchromesh for gearshifting. Engine speed is adjusted by an electronic throttle-control system (ETC) to the speed requested by the transmission control system via the data communication bus. As a result, mechanical synchromesh systems can be partly or entirely dispensed with in the gearbox.

Advantages are:
- optimum fuel economy through automatic, computer-controlled shifting
- reduced driver stress
- lower weight and smaller dimensions
- enhanced safety for both driver and vehicle

**Fully automatic transmissions**
Fully automatic transmissions perform start-off and ratio selection (shifting) operations with no additional driver input. In the majority of cases, the power take-up unit is a hydrodynamic torque converter that generally features a mechanical converter lockup clutch. Alternatively, wet multiplate clutches are used as the power engagement facility.
The power-transmission efficiency of such fully automatic transmissions is slightly lower than that of manual and semi-automatic transmissions due to its operating principle. However, this is compensated by shift programs designed to keep engine operation inside the maximum fuel economy range.
Common fully automatic transmission components include:
- An engine-driven hydraulic-fluid pump (occasionally supplemented by a second fluid pump at the output end) provides hydraulic pressure for valve body and shift elements as well as supplying fluid to the power take-up unit. It also supports lubrication and cooling in the transmission.
- Hydraulically actuated multiplate clutches, plate or band brakes to execute shifts without interrupting the flow of power.
- A transmission-shift control system to define gear selections and shift points and to regulate demand-response shifting, as dictated by the driver-selected shift program (selector lever, tap shift), accelerator-pedal position, engine operating conditions and vehicle speed. The transmission-shift control system is an electrohydraulic system.

---

*6-speed passenger-car automatic gearbox (ZF 6 HP26)*
*1 Input shaft, 2 Controlled-slip converter lockup clutch, 3 Hydrodynamic torque converter,*
*4 6-speed planetary gears with two clutch stops, three multiplate clutches, 5 Electronic-hydraulic*
*transmission-shift control, 6 Output shaft.*

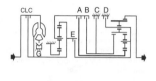

| Gear | Clutch | | | | Brake | | Over running clutch | Ratio |
|------|-----|---|---|---|---|---|---|---|
| | CLC | A | B | E | C | D | G | i |
| 1 | * | ● | | | | ● | O | 4.171 |
| 2 | * | ● | | | ● | | O | 2.340 |
| 3 | * | ● | ● | | | | O | 1.521 |
| 4 | * | ● | | ● | | | O | 1.143 |
| 5 | * | | ● | ● | | | O | 0.867 |
| 6 | * | | | ● | ● | | O | 0.691 |
| R | | | ● | | | ● | O | -3.403 |

O  Dep. on operating state
*  Dep. on shift program

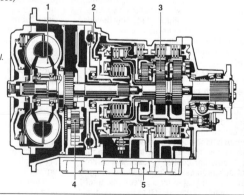

---

*Automatic transmission with integral primary retarder for buses, trucks and special vehicles (ZF Ecomat 5HP 500)*
*1 Hydrodynamic torque converter with lockup clutch,*
*2 Hydrodynamic retarders,*
*3 5-speed planetary gears,*
*4 Oil pump,*
*5 Transmission-shift control.*

Transcription design variations

Converter-type automatic transmissions feature a hydrodynamic torque converter (always used on passenger-car transmissions, while commercial vehicles generally use the Trilok design); for starting off, torque multiplication and absorbing harmonic vibrations. Several planetary-gear sets are arranged downstream of the hydrodynamic torque converter. The number and arrangement of the planetary-gear sets depend on the number of gears and transmission ratios.

Automatic car transmissions (with torque converter) normally have 4 or 5 and meanwhile even 6 and 7 gears. The mechanical transmission-ratio range goes from about 3.5 (4-speed transmission), through 5 (5-speed transmission) to 6 in 6- and 7-speed transmissions. The start-off conversion of the hydrodynamic torque converter ranges from 1.7 to 2.5. Automatic transmissions in commercial vehicles have from 3 to 6 forward gears. The mechanical transmission-ratio range extends from 2 to 8. These transmissions frequently feature integrated hydrodynamic retarders on the primary or secondary side that can use the peripheral systems, i.e. oil pump, oil pan and oil cooler, that are already in place in the transmission system.

Double clutch transmissions feature two multiplate clutches arranged on the drive side to regulate demand-response shifting and power take-off (start-off). Each clutch is connected to a synchronized reduction gear mechanism with one subunit responsible for shifting the even gears and the other for shifting the odd gears. Both subunits of the reduction gear are based on a mutually interlaced design.

To facilitate the gearshift operation, the next gear is preselected in the transmission unit currently not transmitting power, with subsequent load delivery from the other transmission part.

The first double-clutch transmission was introduced as a standard feature in a 6-speed version for front-wheel drive passenger cars with transverse-mounted engines.

## Electronic transmission control

Automatic transmissions are almost exclusively controlled by electronically operated hydraulic systems. Hydraulic actuation is retained for the clutches, while the electronics assume responsibility for gear selection and for adapting the pressures in accordance with the torque flow. The advantages are:
- a number of gearshift programs,
- smoother gearshifting,
- adaptability to different types of vehicle,
- simpler hydraulic control, and
- ability to dispense with one-way clutches.

Sensors detect the transmission output-shaft speed, the engine load and speed, the selector-lever position and the positions of the program selector and the kickdown switch. The control signal processes this information according to a predefined program and uses the results in determining the control variables to be transmitted to the gearbox. Electrohydraulic converter elements form the link between the electronic and hydraulic circuits, while standard solenoid valves activate and disengage the clutches. Analog or digital pressure regulators ensure precise control of pressure levels at the friction surfaces. A typical system includes the following:

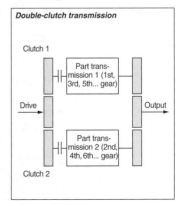

*Double-clutch transmission*

Clutch 1

Part transmission 1 (1st, 3rd, 5th... gear)

Drive → Output

Part transmission 2 (2nd, 4th, 6th... gear)

Clutch 2

### Shift-point control

In selecting the gear to be engaged, the system refers to the rotating speeds of the transmission output shaft and of the engine before triggering the appropriate solenoid valves. The driver may select from among different shift programs (e.g. for maximum fuel economy or for maximum performance). In addition, the selector lever allows manual input from the driver.

"Intelligent" shift programs improve drivability by supplementing the standard transmission-control data with additional parameters such as linear and lateral acceleration, and the speed with which accelerator and brake pedal are pressed. A complex control program selects the appropriate gear for the current operating conditions and driving style using such expedients as suppressing trailing-throttle upshifts on the approach to and during corners, or automatically responding to slow throttle openings by activating a shift program for low engine-speed upshifts. Concepts which combine the high level of convenience of such "intelligent" gearshift programs with facilities for active adaptation to individual driver preferences have become very widespread. In addition to the normal positions for neutral, drive and reverse, the selector levers for such systems have a second parallel channel in which one touch of the lever produces an immediate gear change (provided no engine-speed limits would be exceeded).

### Converter lockup

A mechanical lockup clutch can be employed to improve the efficiency of the transmission unit by eliminating torque-converter slip. The variables employed to determine when conditions are suitable for activation of the converter lockup mechanism are engine load and transmission output-shaft speed.

### Control of shift quality

The accuracy with which the pressure at the friction elements is adjusted to the level of torque being transmitted (determined with reference to engine load and speed) has a decisive influence on shift quality; this pressure is regulated by a pressure regulator. Shifting comfort can be further enhanced by briefly reducing engine torque for the duration of the shift (e.g. by retarding the ignition timing); this also reduces friction loss at the clutches and extends component service life.

### Safety circuits

Special monitoring circuits prevent transmission damage stemming from operator error, while the system responds to malfunctions in the electrical system by reverting to a backup mode.

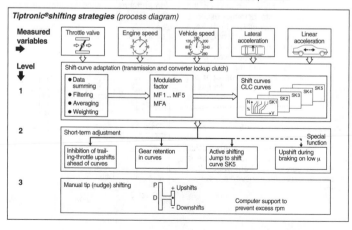

*Tiptronic® shifting strategies* (process diagram)

## Final-control elements

Electrohydraulic converter elements such as solenoid valves and pressure regulators form the interface between electronic and hydraulic circuits.

# Continuously variable transmission (CVT)

The continuously variable transmission (CVT) can convert every point on the engine's operating curve to an operating curve of its own, and every engine operating curve into an operating range within the field of potential driving conditions. Its advantage over conventional fixed-ratio transmissions lies in the potential for enhancing performance and fuel economy while reducing exhaust emissions (e.g. by maintaining the engine in the performance range for maximum fuel economy).

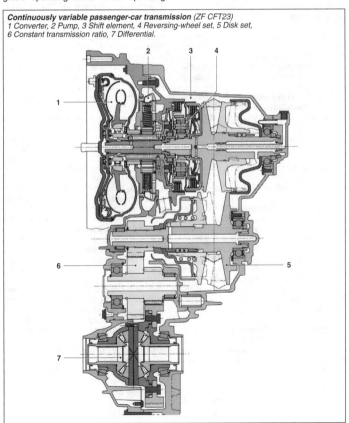

*Continuously variable passenger-car transmission* (ZF CFT23)
*1 Converter, 2 Pump, 3 Shift element, 4 Reversing-wheel set, 5 Disk set,*
*6 Constant transmission ratio, 7 Differential.*

The continuously variable transmission can operate by mechanical, hydraulic or electrical means. To date, only mechanical CVT systems have been realized for passenger vehicles, mainly in the form of a belt-wrap drive and, to a limited extent, a so-called toroidal transmission.

Belt-wrap transmissions are particularly suitable for installation in front-wheel drive vehicles with transverse-mounted engines. Either a linked thrust belt or a pull chain is used as the wrap element. The transmission ratio is between 5.5 and 6. Today transmissions for engine torque ranges between 300 Nm and 350 Nm are produced as standard.

The major elements in the continuously variable mechanical belt transmissions for passenger cars are:
– Wet engagement clutch or hydrodynamic converter as power take-up mechanism.
– Primary and secondary disk set with axially adjustable taper-disk sections and power transfer via linked thrust belt or pull chain.
– Engine-driven oil pump.
– Electronic/hydraulic transmission-shift control.
– Reversing mode for forward-reverse shift.
– Final drive unit with differential.

Toroidal transmissions belong to the group of frictional wheel and disk drives. They transmit drive power by frictional force in a punctiform friction zone. Special traction fluids are required for this purpose.

The advantages of toroidal transmissions include high transferable power, convenience as well as fast and efficient adjustability. The disadvantages compared to converter-type automatic transmissions include the required package space and higher weight.

Electrical transmissions are used on some city buses. Apart from with diesel engines, they can be combined with alternative power sources such as batteries, overhead power lines or, in the future, fuel cells. Other advantages of electrical bus transmissions on busses are nonintegrated (distributed) design of the overall power train, single-wheel drive and, in particular, simpler realization of low-floor vehicle designs.

Hydrostatic-mechanical indirect-drive transmissions are in use on production agricultural tractors. Use on road vehicles is unlikely due to the high noise levels produced.

## Final-drive units

The overall conversion ratio between engine and drive wheels is produced by several elements operating in conjunction: a transmission with several fixed ratios (automatic, manual, CVT), an intermediate transmission in some applications (AWD transfer case), and the final-drive unit.

Longer distances between transmission and final drive are bridged by the propshaft (in one piece or in several sections) with intermediate bearings. Angular offsets resulting from nonaligned connecting drive shafts are compensated for by means of universal joints, constant-velocity joints and flexible-disk joints.

The central component of a car final drive is either a hypoid bevel-gear crown wheel and pinion (inline engine) or a spur-gear crown wheel and pinion (transverse engine), while the layout of the components may take the form of a separate differential (on rear-wheel-drive and four-wheel-drive vehicles) or an integral gearbox and differential (on front-wheel-drive vehicles).

The chief components of a final drive differential are the crown wheel and pinion, the planetary gears, bearings, drive shaft and half-shaft flanges and differential housing. The final-drive transmission ratio is usually between 2.6 and 4.5 to 1.

The crown wheel is normally bolted to the differential case which holds the planetary gears, and the pinion shaft and differential case run in taper roller bearings. To reduce the transmission of structure-borne noise to the bodyshell, the final drive unit is attached to the vehicle frame by flexible (rubber) mountings.

**Direct-drive axle for buses** *(ZF A131)*
*1 Wheel hub,*
*2 Wheel bearing,*
*3 Brake caliper*
*(air-operated),*
*4 Final drive,*
*5 Differential gears.*

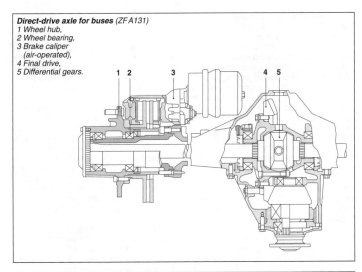

**Hub reduction axle for buses** *(ZF AV132)*
*1 Wheel bearing, 2 Brake caliper, 3 Reduction gearing, 4 Differential gears, 5 Final drive.*

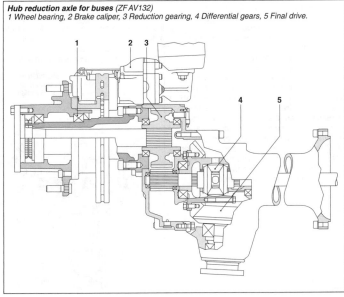

In addition to its torque transmission capabilities, mechanical efficiency and weight, the noise-producing characteristics of a final drive unit have become a decisive criterion in modern automobile development. In this regard, the crown wheel and pinion are of primary significance in terms of noise generation. The quietness of the mechanism is essentially dependent on the way in which the gears are manufactured. A distinction is made between conventional manufacturing methods and grinding of the teeth: Any imperfections produced by heat treatment (case hardening) are eliminated by appropriate grinding so that precise, reproducible tooth-profile topographies are produced (i.e. maximum possible correspondence between calculated tooth-profile topography and actual geometry produced on the machine) in contrast with conventional methods (e.g. lapping).

On commercial vehicles, direct-drive axles with hypoid bevel gears are most commonly used. The final-drive transmission ratio ranges from 3 and 6 to 1. In cases where smooth-running characteristics are particularly important, e.g. on buses, the gears are ground.

On public transport buses, which nowadays are almost always low-floor designs, hub reduction axles are used as they allow very low floor levels. In addition to the helical bevel-gear differential, there is also an indirect-drive spur-gear reducer stage. This indirect-drive arrangement allows the required high torque levels to be transmitted with the limited reducer offset.

If there are special ground clearance requirements (e.g. construction-site vehicles), planetary axles are used. Propeller shaft and half-shafts can be made smaller by splitting the power transmission, and the available space is increased.

## Differential

The differential unit compensates for differences in the rotation rates of the drive wheels: between inside and outside wheels during cornering, and between different drive axles on AWD vehicles.

Apart from a few special cases, bevel gears are the preferred design for differentials. The differential gears act as a balance arm to equalize the distribution of torque to the left and right wheels. When lateral variations in the road surface produce different coefficients of friction at the respective wheels ("μ-split"), this balance effect limits the effective drive torque to a level defined as twice the tractive force available at the wheel (tire) with the lower coefficient of friction. If torque then exceeds frictional resistance, the wheel will spin.

This undesirable effect can be eliminated by locking the differential either by a positively interlocking or friction mechanism. Positively interlocking differential locks are switched-in by the driver. Their disadvantage lies in the stress applied to the drivetrain which occurs during cornering. Friction-type differential locks operate automatically using friction plates, cones

*Passenger-car rear-axle final-drive unit* (ZF HAG210)
1 Housing (two-piece), 2 Half-shaft flange, 3 Differential-case bearings, 4 Differential gears, 5 Crown wheel and pinion, 6 Pinion bearing, 7 Propeller-shaft flange.

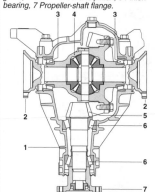

or a combination of worm and spur-gear drives and thus have a variable locking action depending on torque. The friction-type locking action can also be achieved with a viscous coupling and is then dependent on the differential speed.

Other systems employ electronically controlled multiplate clutches to produce the friction-type locking action variable up to full lock.

Today, self-locking differentials are in competition with electronic systems which slow down a spinning wheel by applying the brake and thereby transfer power transmission to the wheel with more grip (e.g. Traction Control System (TCS)).

## All-wheel drive and transfer case

All-wheel drive (AWD) improves traction on cars, off-road vehicles and commercial vehicles on wet and slippery road surfaces and rough terrain. The following types of system are available:

– Disengageable all-wheel drive with either direct transmission to front and rear axles, or with transfer case. The transfer case and final-drive differentials can also have a disengageable lock. Transfer cases for off-road vehicles incorporate an additional driver-controlled conversion range for steep gradients and low speeds.
– Permanent all-wheel drive whereby all wheels are driven at all times. Central transfer case, either non-locking or with friction-type torque-dependent locking mechanism, Torsen lock or viscous coupling. Torque distribution between front and rear axles 50:50 or asymmetrical. Additional crawler-gear ratios are also possible.

Designs with viscous coupling or electronically controlled multiplate clutch instead of the central all-wheel-drive transfer case also come under the umbrella of permanent all-wheel drive.

Some vehicles dispense with additional locks on the AWD transfer case or axle differentials in favor of intelligently controlled intervention of the brakes.

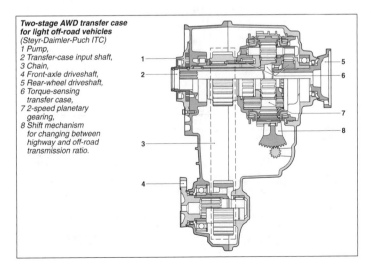

*Two-stage AWD transfer case for light off-road vehicles*
(Steyr-Daimler-Puch ITC)
1 Pump,
2 Transfer-case input shaft,
3 Chain,
4 Front-axle driveshaft,
5 Rear-wheel driveshaft,
6 Torque-sensing transfer case,
7 2-speed planetary gearing,
8 Shift mechanism for changing between highway and off-road transmission ratio.

# Suspension

## Types of oscillation

### Effects

Suspension springing and damping operate chiefly on the vertical oscillations of the vehicle. Ride comfort (vibrational loads on occupants and cargo) and driving safety (distribution of forces against the road surface as wheel-load factors fluctuate) are determined by the suspension. Several spring-damper systems will serve to illustrate the synergetic operation of vehicle components.

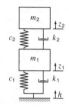

**Dual-mass model as quarter-vehicle model**
$h$ Excitation amplitude, $z$ Vibration amplitude, $c$ Spring rate, $k$ Damping factor, $m$ Mass. Subscripts. 1 Tires and axle, 2 Body.

**Table 1.**
**Impacts of design parameters on vehicle vertical oscillations**

| Design variable | Impact on body natural frequency | Impact on intermediate frequency range | Impact on suspension natural frequency |
|---|---|---|---|
| **Body specifications** Spring constant | High (ride comfort) | Medium (ride comfort) | Low (driving safety) |
| Harder | Frequency and amplitude increase, comfort decreases | | Frequency increases, amplitude decreases slightly |
| Softer | Frequency and maximum amplitude decrease, comfort increases | | Amplitude increases slightly at low excitation frequencies |
| Damper constant | Major (ride comfort) Optimization required | | Major (fluctuations in wheel load) |
| Higher (damper harder) | Acceleration decreases | Acceleration increases | No impact on ride comfort, dynamic fluctuations in wheel load decrease |
| Lower (damper softer) | Acceleration increases | Acceleration decreases | No impact on ride comfort, dynamic fluctuations in wheel load increase |
| Mass | Minor on amplification factor or wheel-load fluctuations; as payload increases, the acceleration amplification factor decreases, (ride comfort is worse, and relative wheel-load fluctuation is higher when the vehicle is unladen rather than when the vehicle is fully laden) | | |
| **Wheel and tire data** Suspension (with tires getting softer) | Natural frequency and amplitude show virtually no change | | Natural frequency and amplitude of body acceleration and fluctuations in wheel load decrease roughly in proportion to the reduction in vertical tire rigidity |
| Damping | No change in frequency and amplitude with change in tire damping | | Amplitude with body acceleration and fluctuations in wheel load decreases slightly with harder damping |
| | Due to heat generation, tire damping should be kept to a minimum in order to allow longer rebound for soft tires | | |
| Wheel mass | Reducing wheel mass hardly affects ride comfort | | Small wheel mass increases driving safety |

Ride comfort is largely determined by the degree of body oscillations. Root mean square of vertical body acceleration:

$$\vec{\ddot{z}}_2 / \vec{h}$$

Wheel-load fluctuations determine driving safety. Root mean square of dynamic wheel-load fluctuations:

$$\vec{F_{dyn}} / \vec{h}$$

Wheel-load fluctuation is derived from the sum of mass acceleration:

$$F_{dyn} = m_2 \cdot \ddot{z}_2 + m_1 \cdot \ddot{z}_1$$

Both types of motion are characterized by specific frequency relationships in the form of amplitude ratios.

Table 1 enumerates the relative impacts of parameter variations in a dual-mass model (also applicable to real vehicles).

Body-mounted springs and dampers also affect pitch and roll of the vehicle body, as well as its vertical vibration characteristics.

Pitch: Gyration about the vehicle's transverse axis, as encountered when starting from standing start (front-spring rebound and rear-spring compression). Pitching movements on starting off or braking are reduced by the axle kinematics selected (suspension-link configuration).

Roll: Gyration about a longitudinal axis, which generally runs from the lower front to the upper rear of the vehicle (roll axis is determined by the type of axis).

## Power spectral densities of body acceleration and wheel-load fluctuation

The amplification functions of body acceleration and wheel-load fluctuation during normal road traffic are excited by road-surface irregularities. On a double logarithmic scale, excitation (vibrations) coming from the road surface have a linear declining function. If this excitation (high amplitudes at low frequencies, low amplitudes at high frequencies) is linked to the vehicle response (multiplied), this produces the power spectral densities of body acceleration and dynamic wheel load, which can be measured in practical tests.

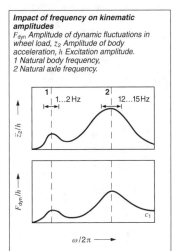

*Impact of frequency on kinematic amplitudes*
$F_{dyn}$ Amplitude of dynamic fluctuations in wheel load, $\ddot{z}_2$ Amplitude of body acceleration, $h$ Excitation amplitude.
1 Natural body frequency,
2 Natural axle frequency.

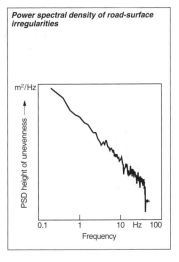

*Power spectral density of road-surface irregularities*

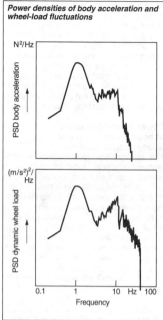

**Power densities of body acceleration and wheel-load fluctuations**

N²/Hz

↑ PSD body acceleration

(m/s²)²/Hz

↑ PSD dynamic wheel load

0.1  1  10  Hz  100

Frequency

The higher excitation amplitude of the road surface at low frequencies raises the amplitudes in the natural frequency range of the body. The low irregularity amplitudes result in a reduction of power spectral density in the natural frequency range of the axle. This means that body movement is more predominant than axle movements.

## Suspension design elements
(See Table 2)

## Controlled suspension systems

### Level-control system

Partially loaded systems

The use of soft springs (ride comfort) results in long spring travel, as encountered when the vehicle is laden. In order to maintain vehicle-body height at an acceptable level, auxiliary air springs or hydropneumatic springs are employed.

The suspension element is provided by the volume of gas, whereas the vehicle level is monitored mechanically directly from suspension parts. Valves are used to control the input or output of air or hydraulic fluid to/from the suspension

**Air-suspension level-control system**
(partially loaded system)
1 Air connection, 2 Steel spring,
3 Auxiliary air-spring element,
4 Gas volume, 5 Shock absorber.

**Hydropneumatic level-control system**
(partially loaded system)
1 Shock absorber, 2 Steel spring,
3 Accumulator, 4 Gas volume,
5 Rubber diaphragm, 6 Fluid, 7 Hose,
8 Service tee for fluid supply, 9 Fluid supply.

element; the system can also incorporate intermediate electronic level-control units acting on solenoid valves.

Advantages of the electronic system:

- Reduced energy consumption achieved by avoiding control cycles on braking, accelerating, and cornering.
- System reacts to higher vehicle speed by lowering vehicle-body ride height, resulting in fuel savings.
- Raising the vehicle-body ride height on poor road surfaces.
- Enhanced cornering stability achieved by laterally blocking the suspension elements on a given axle.

Additional advantages for commercial vehicles:

- Automatic limitation of suspension travel in order to accommodate interchangeable platform bodies and containers.
- Vehicle-body height is variably adjustable, e.g. to adjust the height of the vehicle loading area with loading platforms.
- Control of lifting axles (the ride height is raised automatically when the lifting axle is raised; it lowers automatically when the permissible drive-axle load is exceeded; the lifting axle is raised briefly (2...3 minutes) to increase the load on the powered axle (drive-away assist).

## Fully loaded suspension systems

The cushioning effect is provided by the gas suspension element alone. This dispenses with coil springs. Either a single axle (generally the rear axle) or both axles of the vehicle can be controlled. If all axles are controlled, the system must include an ECU to define a control strategy which will respond to factors such as axle-load fluctuations (in order to prevent the vehicle body from tilting), monitor control times, and detect system faults.

### Open system

The compressor draws air from the atmosphere, compresses it, and applies it to the air spring. If the ride level drops, the compressed air is blown off to the atmosphere.

Advantages: Relatively simple design and control.

Disadvantages: High compressor output required for brief periods of active control; an air drier is required; noise occurs during air intake and blow-off.

### Closed system

The compressor draws air from a pressure accumulator (which at most has a minimum required bellows pressure) of the suspension system, compresses it further, and supplies it to the air spring. If

*Level-control system* (fully loaded suspension systems)
a) Open system, b) Closed system. 1 Filter, 2 Compressor, 3 Drier, 4 Directional-control valve,
5 Bellows, 6 Non-return valve, 7 Pressure vessel, 8 Pressure switch,
9 3/2-way directional-control valve.

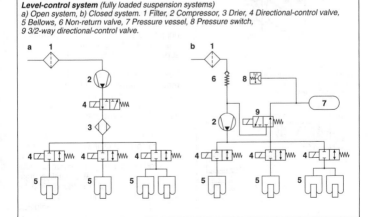

the ride height drops, it returns the compressed air to the accumulator.

Advantages: Low compressor output (low pressure differential between accumulator and spring); virtually no problems with air humidity (no need for air drier).

Disadvantages: Relatively complicated design (accumulator, pressure switch, non-return valve).

The advantages of the closed system are clearly illustrated in the *p-V* diagram. For every lift stroke, the compressor driven at admission pressure conveys a multiple of the compressed-air volume to the air spring than a compressor with the same swept volume is capable of producing in an open system (air intake from the atmosphere).

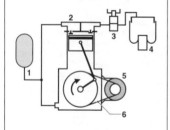

*Compressor* (view)
1 Accumulator for admission pressure,
2 Compressor, 3 Valve, 4 Air spring,
5 Electric motor, 6 Mechanical conversion ratio.

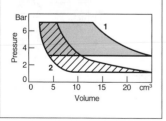

*Compressor* (p-V diagram)
Working surface with (1) and without (2) application of admission pressure.

A "reduction-gear compressor" is recommended in order to overcome adverse crankshaft positions, and this requires a high drive torque. The electric motor generates the output required for small torques at high speeds, and the torque required at the compressor crankshaft results from the resulting mechanical conversion ratio. The mass moment of inertia of the electric motor is transferred to the crankshaft, which varies as the square of the conversion ratio. This produces a sufficient mass moment of inertia to overcome the critical crankshaft angle.

## Active suspension

Active suspension controls both the "springing" and the "damping" functions. Various types of design concepts have been implemented.

### Designs incorporating a hydraulic cylinder

A source of auxiliary power generates the energy needed for rapid adjustments using high-speed hydraulic cylinders, whereas sensors provide the link between the cylinders and the vehicle body. Sensors for wheel load, travel and acceleration transmit signals to an ECU featuring a control cycle of just a few milliseconds.

The control system achieves virtually constant wheel-load factors, while maintaining a constant mean vehicle-body height. Steel springs or hydropneumatic suspension elements are employed to support the static wheel load.

### Designs incorporating hydropneumatic suspension (fluid control)

Vehicle-body movements are compensated by selective control of the hydraulic fluid in the hydropneumatic suspension circuit. The hydraulic fluid is either routed to the hydropneumatic springs, or discharged from the spring strut. In order to reduce energy requirements, the system's action is restricted to smoothing wide-spaced undulations; a gas accumulator installed adjacent to the spring strut is responsible for higher-frequency spring reaction.

The damping element can be adjusted to match wheel movements.

## Model with spring-base adjustment

It is possible to keep the vehicle body level within low-frequency ranges by adjusting the base of a conventional coil spring adjustable (either against the vehicle body or toward the axle). The base is raised for spring compression and lowered for spring rebound. Control is continuous by means of a fluid pump and proportioning valves. The coil spring must be longer than the original design. In this type of system, the shock absorbers can be fitted with constant adjustment parameters and, above all, they can be matched to the wheel dampers.

## Air-suspension systems

Coupled displacement elements are required for rapid pressure changes in the wheel-mounted air-spring bellows (pressure rises and drops), as compressor output alone would not be sufficient. Depending on the driving conditions, air is compressed into the wheel bellows located on the outside of the corner and removed from the wheel bellows on the inside of the corner. The displacement element is driven by an electric motor and/or hydraulic system, and can be linked to the steering torque.

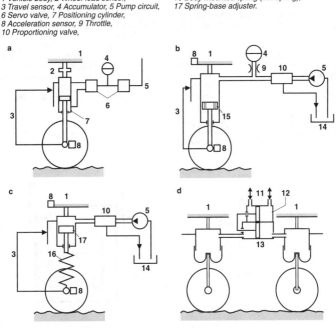

*Active suspension*
a) Hydraulic cylinder,
b) Hydropneumatic suspension,
c) Spring-base adjustment,
d) Pneumatic suspension.
1 Vehicle body, 2 Wheel-load sensor,
3 Travel sensor, 4 Accumulator, 5 Pump circuit,
6 Servo valve, 7 Positioning cylinder,
8 Acceleration sensor, 9 Throttle,
10 Proportioning valve,
11 Power supply (electric/pneumatic),
12 Displacement unit with power supply,
13 Air-volume displacement unit, 14 Tank,
15 Shock-absorber piston fitted with valve,
16 Body-mounted spring (coil spring),
17 Spring-base adjuster.

## Shock absorbers

Telescopic shock absorbers convert body and wheel oscillation energy into heat. The absorbers are attached to the body and the axle by means of resilient bearings which also help in noise insulation.

### Single-tube shock absorbers

Single-tube shock absorbers have a sliding separating piston and a pressurized compensation chamber to receive the piston rod volume that enters the shock absorber during compression.

Advantages: Easy adjustment of damping forces. No risk of cavitation due to admission pressure in the damper (> 35 bar). Sufficient space for valves and ducts. The valves on both piston sides are working valves (not non-return valves). Heat is dissipated directly via the outer tube. The shock absorber can be installed in any position.

Disadvantages: Length, otherwise the gas chamber must be located externally. The outer tube, which acts as a guide for the piston, is prone to damage caused by stone chippings, etc. Cannot be shortened in order to fit in confined spaces in the suspension geometry. The piston rod seal is subjected to the pressure in the damper, which impedes soft response.

### Twin-tube shock absorber

This type of shock absorber is available either as an atmospheric or low-pressure twin-tube type.

Advantages: Soft response, as there is little friction at the seals. Immune to stone chippings. Tube can be adapted to fit in confined spaces. This shock-absorber type is short, as the compensation chamber is located next to the working cylinder.

Disadvantages: These shock absorbers are more prone to overload than single-tube shock absorbers (no damping in the event of cavitation and vapor bubbles). Only certain specific installation positions are possible.

### Damping characteristics

The damping characteristics are the result of the cumulative function of orifice damping and the valve located at the passage orifice; the spring opens the passage orifice wider in response to mounting pressure. Piston passages and spring diaphragms can be specifically tailored to provide linear to mildly digressive damping curves. Adaptive dampers support a wide range of damping characteristics. For dampers with both fixed characteristics and program-map adjustment, the compression-mode values are only 30...50% of those for rebound mode.

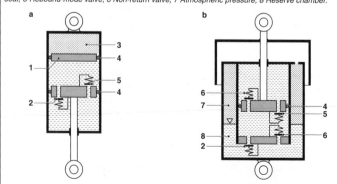

*Shock absorbers*
*a) Single-tube shock absorber, b) Twin-tube shock absorber.*
*1 Separating piston, 2 Compression-mode valve, 3 Pressurized compensation chamber, 4 Piston seal, 5 Rebound-mode valve, 6 Non-return valve, 7 Atmospheric pressure, 8 Reserve chamber.*

Objective: Ride comfort during compression mode, high damping (system calming) in rebound mode. Electronically controlled adjustable shock absorbers (active adaptation to driving conditions) can be used to enhance ride comfort and driving safety. Fixed damping parameters, on the other hand, result in defined relationships between ride comfort and driving safety.

The control law is frequently a semi-active "Skyhook" type, in which the shock absorber adjusts as a factor of body velocity.

## Vibration absorber

The vibration absorber is a supplementary mass attached to the vehicle by sprung and damped mountings. The vibration absorber assimilates the oscillations of the main system, i.e. the main system ceases to oscillate – the motion is restricted to the vibration damper (see "Oscillations", P. 44). Vibration absorbers affect body vibrations. Their impact on the suspension is minimal, at least as long as only "passive" vibration absorbers are used, i.e. no power is supplied.

*Shock-absorber curves*
1 Compression damping, 2 Rebound damping, 3 Adjustment range of adaptive dampers.

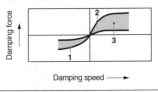

*Amplification function of axle acceleration*
1 With absorber, 2 Without absorber.
$a_1$ Amplitude of $z_1$, $h$ Excitation amplitude.

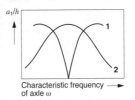

*Vibration absorption*
a) Installation on vehicle,
b) Mechanical equivalent system.
1 Spring and damper, 2 Damping mass, 3 Wheel mass, 4 Tire spring.

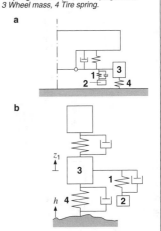

*Skyhook logic 1 Sky*

$$F_{D\,sky} = k_{sky} \cdot \dot{z}_2$$
$$F_D = k_z \cdot (\dot{z}_2 - \dot{z}_1)$$
$$\left.\right\} \quad k_2 = k_{sky} \cdot \frac{\dot{z}_2}{\dot{z}_2 - \dot{z}_1} \quad \text{variable damper "constant"}$$

for $\dot{z}_2 \cdot (\dot{z}_2 - \dot{z}_1) \geq 0$:
$$F_{D\,tot} = \left(k_{sky} \cdot \frac{\dot{z}_2}{\dot{z}_2 - \dot{z}_1} + k_2\right) \cdot (\dot{z}_2 - \dot{z}_1)$$

for $\dot{z}_2 \cdot (\dot{z}_2 - \dot{z}_1) \leq 0$: $F_{D\,tot} = k_2 \cdot (\dot{z}_2 - \dot{z}_1)$

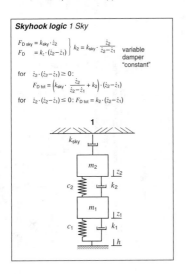

# Table 2. Suspension design elements.

| Suspension elements | Diagram | Impact of payload on body natural frequency | Properties |
|---|---|---|---|
| **Steel springs** Leaf spring $$c = \frac{b \cdot s^3}{4 \cdot l^3} \cdot E = \text{const.}$$ | Car leaf spring · Truck leaf spring with auxiliary spring | $$\frac{v_{\text{laden}}}{v_{\text{unladen}}} = \sqrt{\frac{m_{\text{unladen}}}{m_{\text{laden}}}}$$ | Single or multi-leaf Is also used to determine wheel travel in some applications. Interleaf friction in some types, can be reduced with plastic inserts (noise possible). Generally without inserts in truck, maintenance required. Good transfer of forces to chassis. $E$ Modulus of elasticity |
| Coil spring $$c = \frac{G \cdot d^4}{8 \cdot i \cdot D^3} = \text{const.}$$ | Cylindrical coil spring · Barrel-shaped coil spring | Natural frequency decreases with increase of payload. Characteristic curves are generally linear. | Progressive characteristics are achieved by change of pitch or conical coil. Shock absorber can be fitted inside spring. No self-damping, spring noise possible. Advantages: Limited space requirement, low weight, maintenance-free. Disadvantages: Special suspension links required. $G$ Shear modulus, $i$ Number of turns; $c$ nonlinear, if change to $d$, $D$ or $i$ via spring length. |
| Torsion bar $$c = \frac{G \cdot \pi \cdot d^4}{r \cdot l \cdot 32} = \text{const.}$$ | | | Made of round or flat-bar steel (round bar is lighter). Vehicle height adjustment may be possible, depending on design. Maintenance-free and wear-free. Flat-steel bundle used for additional bending stresses. $G$ Shear modulus, $d$ Torsion bar diameter (determined by shear stress) |
| **Air springs and hydropneumatic springs** $$c = \frac{A^2 \cdot n \cdot p_i}{V}$$ $$A = \frac{\pi \cdot D_w^2}{4}$$ Roll bellows · Toroid bellows | Springs with constant gas volume. 1 Chassis frame, 2 Roll bellows, 3 Piston, 4 Compressed air, 5 Mounting plate. Roll bellows · Toroid bellows | $$\frac{v_{\text{laden}}}{v_{\text{unladen}}} = 1$$ Natural frequency remains constant when vehicle is laden. Characteristic curves are dependent on gas properties, piston shape and direction of plies in the bellows. | Used as a suspension strut or spring, particularly on commercial vehicles and buses. Increasingly widespread use in passenger cars for level control at rear axle and for suspension on all wheels. Achieves high vertical compliance (increased ride comfort). Wheel travel must be defined by separate suspension arms. Low pressure (<10 bar) demands large volume. Low vertical spring rate not achievable due to geometry of the toroid bellows. $A$ Effective surface, const. or var., depending on piston shape $n$ Polytropic exponent ($n = 1.0$ isothermal line, $n = 1.4$ adiabatic line), $p_i$ Internal pressure (function of load), $V$ Volume (const.) |

| | | | |
|---|---|---|---|
| Hydropneumatic suspension<br>Hydraulic diaphragm accumulator<br>Piston accumulator | <br>Spring element with constant gas mass.<br>1 Gas, 2 Fluid, 3 Diaphragm, 4 Steel spring.<br>Hydraulic diaphragm accumulator. Piston accumulator | $\dfrac{v_{laden}}{v_{unladen}} = \sqrt{\dfrac{m_{laden}}{m_{unladen}}}$<br>Natural frequency increases with payload. Characteristics are progressive and dependent on initial charge pressure of reservoir | The gas volume in a reservoir (separated from fluid by a piston) determines its spring characteristics. The hydraulic fluid compresses the gas dependent on wheel load. Damper valves are integrated in the shock absorber and in the junction between suspension strut and reservoir. The rubber diaphragm requires maintenance due to gas diffusion.<br>$A$ Effective surface (const.), $n$ Polytropic exponent ($n = 1.0$ isothermal line, $n = 1.4$ adiabatic line), $p_i$ Inside pressure (function of payload).<br>$V$ Volume decreases as payload increases due to vol. in the hydraulic accumulator (constant gas mass). |
| **Rubber springs** | | Natural frequency is affected by payload due to the nonlinear spring rates | Vulcanized rubber compression spring between metal components, increasingly with integrated hydraulic damper. Used as engine/transmission mountings, suspension-arm mountings and as auxiliary springs. |
| **Stabilizer** | | No effect if both sides simultaneously moved in same direction. If one side is moved up/down, half of stabilizer rigidity effective, if two sides moving in opposing directions, full rigidity of stabilizer effective. | Reduces body-roll tendency and influences vehicle cornering behavior (oversteer or understeer). Generally made of U-shaped bar or tube, sides frequently flattened to cope with bending stresses. To allow stabilizers with minimum diameter, attachment points must be on the extreme outside of axle. Suspension link fulcrums must be arranged relative to the stabilizer in such a way that it is subjected only to torsion and not bending. |

# Suspension linkage

The suspension geometry employed to connect the individual wheels to the vehicle body structure defines the suspension-linkage design. The linkage allows the wheel for the most part to move vertically in order to compensate for irregularities in the road surface. In addition, the front wheels are steered, together with the rear wheels in the case of rear-wheel-steered vehicles. The front and rear suspension linkage systems differ due to the special demands imposed by the steering mechanism and the position of the longitudinal and transverse fulcrums. Appropriate design measures are taken for the suspension geometry and spring action in order to limit vertical body movements, and reduce pitch and roll.

<u>References:</u> Wolfgang Matschinsky. Radführungen der Straßenfahrzeuge. ("Suspension linkage for road vehicles"). 2nd Edition; Springer-Verlag 1998.

## Kinematics

The front wheels pivot about an inclined axis whose position is determined by the joints and the suspension linkage.

The following kinematic data are of essential importance for the wheel's response to steering input and the transfer of forces between tire and road surface:

### Toe-in $\delta_{vs}$
Toe-in is the angle between the vehicle's longitudinal axis and a plane through the center of the (steered-wheel) tire. It can also be defined as half the difference in the distance between the wheel's front and rear rim flange. Toe-in affects straight-running stability as well as steering and, in the case of front-wheel-drive vehicles, compensates for the resulting elastokinematic changes in track. For standard-drive vehicles, toe-in is approx. 5...20′. For FWD vehicles, toe-out is up to −20′ (to compensate for motive forces).

### Deflection-force lever arm $r_{st}$
The deflection-force lever arm is the shortest distance between the wheel cen-

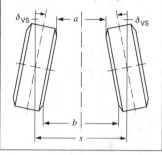

**Toe-in**
$\delta_{vs}$ Toe-in angle; distance between wheels: $a$ Front, $b$ Rear, $b-a$ Toe-in (in mm), $s$ Track.

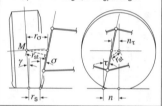

**Wheel position**
$M$ Center of wheel, $r_{st}$ Deflection-force lever arm, $n_\tau$ Caster offset, $n$ Positive caster, $\tau$ Caster angle, $r_o$ Kingpin inclination offset, $r_s$ Kingpin offset, $\gamma$ Camber angle, $\sigma$ Kingpin angle.

ter and the inclination angle of the steering axis. On FWD vehicles, its length provides an index of the effect of uneven motive forces on the right/left front wheel and on the steering.

### Caster $n$
Positive caster is the distance between the wheel contact point and the point at which the steering axis intersects the road (viewed from the side). Caster determines the degree of self-centering action in the steering and influences straight-running and steering forces when cornering.

### Caster angle $\tau$
The caster angle is defined as the angle between the steering axis and the vertical plane (viewed from the side). In conjunction with the kingpin angle, it influences

the camber change as a function of the steering angle, as well as the self-centering characteristics of the steering.

### Kingpin offset $r_s$

The kingpin offset, or steering offset, is the distance between the wheel contact point with the road surface, and the point at which the steering axis intersects the road surface. It is negative when the point of steering-axis intersection is between the wheel contact point and the outside of the vehicle. Kingpin offset combines with the effects of braking forces to generate steering motions and self-centering action at the steering wheel (driver information). Negative kingpin offset results in self-stabilizing steering angles.

### Camber angle $\gamma$

Camber angle is the inclination of the wheel axis in relation to the road surface in the vertical plane. The camber angle is negative when the top of the wheel is inclined toward the center of the vehicle. It creates minor auxiliary side forces; above all, it compensates for the effects of roll angle during cornering.

### Kingpin angle $\sigma$

The kingpin angle is the angle between the steering axis and the vehicle longitudinal plane, as measured in the vehicle transverse plane. It influences steering force (steering feel), together with caster angle and offset, and kingpin offset.

## Basic types

(see Tables on following pages.)

## Elastokinematics

Wheel track and camber are influenced by the kinematic properties of the suspension linkage, and by variations in kinematic properties during spring bounce/rebound. The forces acting on the suspension linkage (acceleration, deceleration, vertical and side forces, rolling resistance) also have an impact n the wheel's dynamic position due to compliance in mountings and in the components themselves (kinematic response due to elastic deformation: elastokinematics). The usual objective is to strive for spe-

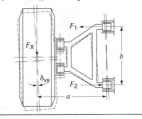

***Wheel displacement by linear force $F_x$ due to system flexibility***
$F_1$, $F_2$ Suspension-arm mounting forces, $a$ Distance between wheel and suspension-arm mountings, $b$ Suspension-arm mounting separation, $\delta_{vs}$ Toe-in angle.

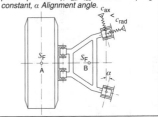

***Positioning of suspension-arm mountings to counteract steering deflection due to flexibility***
$S_F$ Center of gravity (A Reduction, B Complete equalization), $c_{ax}$, $c_{rad}$ axial/radial spring constant, $\alpha$ Alignment angle.

cific changes in wheel position by employing kinematic and elastokinematic effects. To this end, kinematic and elastokinematic properties are designed into the axle and are calculated to provide a self-compensating response to force and spring action. Specially aligned suspension-arm mountings result in cardanic angles during spring bounce/rebound. According to the design of the rubber mounts, they define the options for compensating for elastokinematic effects. Some modern rear suspensions employ elastokinematics to reduce reactions to changes in dynamic load. Different longitudinal and vertical forces at the wheels allow the flexibly mounted subframe or individual suspension arms to pivot, providing the wheels at the outside of the curve with more toe-in (stabilizing steering effect at the rear wheels).

# Basic suspension types and their characteristics

## Rigid axles

| Leaf spring | A-arm / Trailing arm | Watt linkage / A-bracket | Panhard rod / A-bracket / Trailing arm | Panhard rod / Trailing arm |
|---|---|---|---|---|

Used as rear axle with conventional (rear-wheel) drive; as front and rear axle on heavy and off-road vehicles

Track, toe-in, camber remain constant relative to road surface, even with body roll, good tracking

No lateral body movements during spring bounce/rebound, no unfavorable wheel displacement by side and linear forces or torsion, high space requirements

| Low manufacturing costs, axle tramp, high unsprung masses, unfavorable deformation under side force and torsion | Unrestricted choice of pitch fulcrum freely selectable High cost and weight | | Panhard rod causes lateral body movement when vehicle is driven | Unrestricted choice of pitch fulcrum |

## Semi-rigid axles

| Torsion-beam axle | Torsion-beam trailing-arm axle | Trailing-arm torsion-beam axle |
|---|---|---|

Used as rear suspension on FWD vehicles

Large distance between mounts minimizes structural stresses, favorable force input at rigid longitudinal members, simple manufacture, two attachment points, simple assembly, extremely robust, limited kinematic options

| RA depends on position of the Panhard rod above wheel center | RA below center of wheel (depending on link position) | RA on road surface (all RAs aligned with vehicle center) |

RA = roll axis

## Independent suspension

| Trailing arm | Semi-trailing arm | Semi-trailing arm | Swing axle | Swing axle |
|---|---|---|---|---|
| | | | | |

Rear-axle designs for front- or rear-wheel drive

| | | |
|---|---|---|
| Small space requirements, low costs, limited kinematic versatility, change in camber, large change in caster trail, position of torque fulcrum, high stresses | Low manufacturing costs, favorable options in terms of kinematics, elastokinematically poor, side force and circumferential force oversteer, high suspension link forces | Low costs, limited options in terms of kinematics, body is lifted by side force when cornering, vertical bracing effect with positive camber |

| Mc Pherson strut | Upper and lower A-arms | Lateral and transverse links |
|---|---|---|
| <br>Transverse link | | |

Used as front or rear suspension on FWD and standard RWD vehicles;

Used as front suspension on FWD and standard RWD vehicles

| | | |
|---|---|---|
| Small space requirements (vehicle width), low body forces due to large support base, small number of joints, easy to fit, lightweight, broad tolerances, limited kinematic versatility with regard to change in camber, kingpin angle, transient, and pitch fulcrum, space required for springs, tire width height | Greatest degree of kinematic latitude; high cost due to large number of suspension links; limited structural tolerances (without subframe); due to relatively small distances between mounting points, rigid mountings are required in order to prevent excessive wheel deflection (loss of ride comfort) | Force input of upper suspension arm on rigid bulkhead |

# Wheels

## Overview

Wheel size is mainly dependent on the requirements of the braking system, the axle components, and the size of the tires used.

The most important terms are:
– Rim diameter
– Rim width
– Center hole diameter (design)
– Rim offset of the wheel
– Pitrch circle diameter, wheel mounting
– Number of mounting holes
– Design of the countersink for wheel studs (spherical cap, cone)

### Rim designs

Depending on the intended purpose and the tire design, there are a range of different cross-sectional rim shapes available:
– Drop-center rim (passenger-car sector)
– Flat-base rim (special applications, multipart wheel rims)
– 5° tapered bead seat (truck sector)
– 15° tapered bead seat (truck sector, in particular with tubeless tires)

The following are the most important terms for wheel rims:
– Rim flange (rim flange shape)
– Rim bead seat
– Drop center
– Rim base
– Hump (hump shape)

### Wheel mounting

The design of the wheel and the mounting elements must meet safety requirements in all vehicle operating conditions. The wheel forces resulting from motive force, brakes, wheel load, and wheel location forces must be supported by the overall mounting system, without impairing fatigue limits or the function of the wheel and axle components.

## Passenger-car wheels

Special pressed-steel types and a range of aluminum alloys are used as the basic materials. Whereas magnesium alloys were unable to establish themselves in volume production, they are used in individual

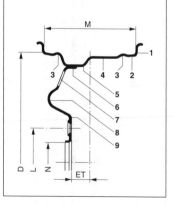

*Pressed-steel disc wheel* (e.g. 6J x 14 H 2)
1 Rim flange, 2 Rim bead seat, 3 Hump,
4 Rim, 5 Rim well, 6 Disc joint, 7 Vent hole,
8 Dish, 9 Wheel disc.
D Rim diameter, L Pitch circle diameter,
M Rim width, N Center hole, ET Rim offset.

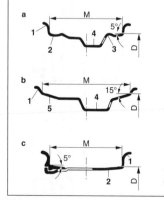

*Rim designs*
a) Car drop-center rim,
b) Truck 15° tapered bead seat (tubeless),
c) Truck 5° tapered bead seat,
1 Flange, 2 5° tapered bead seat, 3 Hump,
4 Rim well, 5 15° tapered bead seat.
M Rim width, D Diameter.

cases for special-purpose vehicles and sports cars. Wheels made of pressed aluminum were unable to prevail over pressed steel on the market for cost reasons.

Special materials and manufacturing methods offer great potential for reducing weight. The pressed aluminum wheel is also on the agenda, offering the most lightweight design and a range of different surfaces and dish designs. Further potential can also be tapped by rolling out the disc (variable wall thicknesses from wheel center to disc joint). Made from a circular aluminum blank, the "split wheel" also offers high potential cost savings depending on its intended use and wheel size. However, it soon reaches its technical and economic limits.

The production processes for pressed steel and aluminum wheels are largely identical. The only thing the conventional forged wheel and the "split wheel" have in common is the rolling process. This is a single process during which the circular blank, or a disc that is forged at its outer circumference, is rolled and split, and the rim is formed. The initial material for the forged wheel is a portioned disc of an extruded metal section. After a number of forging processes, it is fed as a preheated blank to the rolling process. Finally, it is subjected to metal-cutting processes and surface treatment. The "flow forming" process offers further weight-saving potential. The process in which a casting blank is rolled out in the rim area takes advantage of the improved material and casting properties for material savings.

Although the hollow spoke method with sand cores also offers great potential for weight saving, it requires appropriate styling. "Structural wheels" are used, among other things, as spare wheels or as road wheels with plastic wheel covers. Unrestricted by styling conditions, the aim here is to use the minimum quantity of material possible to guarantee operating and functional safety, as well as streamline production costs for these wheels.

The use of plastic as a material for wheels is still in the developmental stage due in particular to insufficient high-temperature strength and difficult wheel mounting and manufacture.

In the case of pressed-steel wheels, the wheel disc and rim are welded together, whereas forged and cast light-alloy wheels are usually produced from a single piece. Multiple-piece designs, even those which are made of different materials (e.g. magnesium disc and aluminum rim), are available only in special cases and for racing vehicles. Car-wheel rims are almost always drop-center rims with double humps H 2 (rarely with flat hump FH), tapered bead seats, and "J" section rim flange. The lower flange shape is frequently found on smaller vehicles; the higher flange shapes, JK and K, are rare on modern vehicles, and then only on heavy vehicles.

More recent rim developments, which have produced in limited series, are the TR rim (in metric dimensions). They were developed by MICHELIN for use with matching TRX tires and provide more room for the brakes. Then there is the rim with a "Denloc" groove which also requires a matching tire. The Dunlop rim-and-tire combination provides improved safety in case of loss of air. The TD rim (TRX-Denloc) brings together both wheel/tire systems. As opposed to common practice, all three if above designs incorporating different rim and tire versions are either not possible at all, only to a very limited extent.

In a completely new development, the tire grips the outside of the rim (CONTINENTAL). This design allows the brake diameter to be increased considerably, although at the same time it changes the way some tire/rim properties interreact. It allows the driver to drive at reduced speed for several hundred kilometers on a flat tire. This could eliminate the need for a spare tire. This version has not become popular on the market, and its use is confined to special applications.

Based on U.S. efforts to reduce the amount of space taken up by the spare tire as well as – to a very limited extent – to reduce overall vehicle weight, European vehicles are increasingly being fitted with a space-saving spare wheel which has a matching, low-performance tire. Opinions on the usefulness of this substandard combination vary.

Design criteria for passenger-car wheels include high component strength, efficient brake cooling, reliable wheel mounting, high concentricity, small space requirements, good corrosion protection, low weight, low cost, easy tire mounting, a good tire seat, good balance-weight attachment, and aesthetically pleasing design (particularly in the case of light-alloy wheels). Recent attention has also been given to wheel designs which reduce the vehicle drag coefficient $c_d$.

Wheels are usually mounted on the vehicle by means of three to five wheel lugs or nuts. The design of the contact surface of these lugs/nuts varies, depending on the vehicle manufacturer. The high degree of true-running is achieved by means of a central wheel mount at the wheel hub at a precise alignment shoulder. At present, wheels mounted with a central nut and interlocking driving pins are used only on racing cars.

Decorative hub or wheel trims are mainly used to improve visual appearance and are affixed to the wheels using elastic retaining spring elements, which are easily detachable (primarily used on steel wheels). Bolted solutions are also used in rare cases. These can achieve additional effects, such as reduce $c_d$ values or improve wheel ventilation for reducing the temperature of wheel bearings and brake fluid. Recently plastic wheel caps have also become much more frequent. However, in some cases, aluminum and stainless pressed steel are also used.

## Commercial-vehicle wheels

The primary requirements to be met by commercial-vehicle wheels are:
– High fatigue strength and long service life in order to maximize traffic safety.
– Lowest possible wheel weight because the wheel, as an unsprung, rotating mass, influences the overal vehicle oscillatory system.
– High load capacity by designing an appropriate wheel shape and using optimum materials.

– Reduction in wheel-disk unevenness.
– Reduction of radial and lateral run-out and wheel imbalance.
– Easy assembly of tire to rim during manufacture and in practical use.

### 15° tapered-bead seat rim
A modern engineering design is the one-piece 15° tapered-bead seat rim for tubeless commercial-vehicle tires.

Advantages:
– The one-piece wheel allows a reduction in wheel weight of up to 10% compared with a two-piece rim, and features enhanced true-running and less lateral run-out.
– Increased rim diameter.
– Sufficient free space.
– Standardized valve in a precise position and at sufficient distance from the brake drum or caliper.
– Standardized balance-weight shapes.
– Introduction of wheel centering.
– Use of fully- or semi-automatic tire-fitting equipment.

### Radial and side runout, imbalance
Radial run-out of the wheel is one of the main causes of vehicle vibrations. With today's commonly used 15° tapered-bead seat, a reduction in the permissible radial run-out to 1.25 mm (peak-to-peak) results in a noticeable improvement compared with flat-base rims. As opposed to radial run-out, side runout is a less critical problem. Wheel imbalance is not nearly as much of a problem as tire imbalance, which is much more critical. Maximum permissible static imbalance is limited to 2,000 cmg.

### Wheel centering
Bilt centering via spherical washers or solely via ball-seat nuts has been replaced by wheel centering in order to reduce excessive side runout; this arrangement also permits a range of maximum and minimum play, depending on wheel size (especially with 22.5″ wheels). This requires tolerances which are as close as possible.

**Flatness of the contact surface**

Any unevenness in the wheel contact surface (corrugation, inclination, shielding, etc.) is transmitted to the brake drum when the wheel nuts are tightened, causing fluctuations in braking force as the wheel rotates. These fluctuations, in turn, cause vibrations in the steering system. Driving tests have led to the establishment of a maximum value for corrugation of 0.15 mm, and 0.2 mm for inclination from the center of the wheel outward.

**Light-alloy wheels**

One reason for the use of light-alloy wheels is to reduce the weight of 15° tapered-bead seat wheels. Light-alloy wheels are available with cast or forged rims. In spite of weight reductions and adequate strength characteristics, light-alloy wheels are onyy used on commercial vehicles only in special cases for cost reasons.

**Commercial-vehicle wheel loading**

Prestress

Prestress occurs through the combination of stresses caused by assembling the wheel with those which result from inflating the tire.

Static nominal wheel stress

If the wheel is allowed to roll slowly on a perfectly flat road surface under static nominal wheel load, the stress in the wheel section under review will vary periodically as the wheel rotates.

Additional dynamic stresses

Similar additional stresses are caused by dynamic wheel forces which result as the vehicle is driven straight ahead over an uneven road surface. Quasi-static wheel forces are then produced and occur during maneuvers such as cornering, steering while stationary, braking, and accelerating.

The resulting complex of stresses caused by the above-mentioned types of wheel loading is used today as the basis for wheel dimensioning and testing.

**Significant weak points**

The highly stressed parts of the wheel, and therefore the parts most susceptible to cracking, are the disc flange, the vent holes, the welded joint between disc and rim, and the drop-center radius. The flange mounting is particularly prone. Hub-centered wheels most often crack tangentially above the pitch circle. With bolt-centered wheels, the cracks generally spread out radially from the bolt holes.

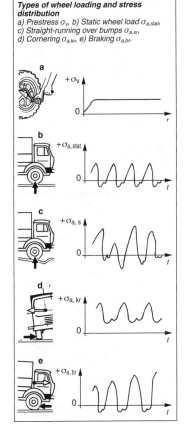

*Types of wheel loading and stress distribution*
*a) Prestress $\sigma_v$, b) Static wheel load $\sigma_{a,stat}$,*
*c) Straight-running over bumps $\sigma_{a,s}$,*
*d) Cornering $\sigma_{a,kr}$, e) Braking $\sigma_{a,br}$.*

# Tires

## Tire categories

Tire categories are classified with reference to the respective requirements of various vehicle types and sizes, and operating conditions. The essential data – tire dimensions, load ratings, specified inflation pressures, and authorized speeds – are standardized in the interests of interchangeability in the 7 tire groups or categories listed in Table 1. In addition to pneumatic tires, solid rubber tires are also permitted and are approved for speeds of up to 25 km/h (up to 16 km/h for unsprung driving wheels). The classifications in tire categories 1...4 are based on road conditions:
– "Standard" highway (summer) tires
– "Special" tires for use off-road or for mixed use on and off the road
– "M+S" (winter) tires

The same basic set of operating requirements applies to all tire categories (Table 2), although it should be noted that the emphasis shifts toward the final three criteria (in particular No. 6) on heavier vehicles.

## Tire design

Today passenger cars are equipped exclusively with radial tires. Bias-ply tires are now only fitted to motorcycles, bicycles, excavating machines, and industrial and agricultural machines. For commercial vehicles, they are increasingly becoming less important.

The once-dominant bias-ply tire received its name from the tread, where the cord threads of the tire casing run diagonally (or with a bias) so that they cross each other (cross ply). However, the more complex radial tire, with its radial design comprising two main sections, represents the only means of satisfying the increasingly varied range of operating capabilities demanded of the tires. They are now used on today's passenger cars and heavy commercial vehicles.

The cords in the radial-tire casing layers run along the shortest and most direct path – radially – from bead to bead. A belt surrounds the relatively thin, elastic casing

---

[1] The corresponding European standards can be found in the ETRTO (European Tire and Rim Technical Organization, Brussels) publication "Data Book of Tires, Rims and Valves".
[2] Guideline of the Economic Association of the German Rubber Industry, Frankfurt.

**Table 1. Tire categories and applicable standards**

| No. | Tire application | German Standards (selection) [1] | |
|---|---|---|---|
| | | DIN | WdK [2] |
| 1 | **Engine-driven, two-wheeled vehicles** Motorcycles, motor scooters, motorcycles of less than 50 cm³, Motorbicycle | 7801, 7802, 7810 | 119 |
| 2 | **Passenger cars** Including station wagons and special spare tires | 7803 | 128, 203 |
| 3 | **Light-duty trucks** Including delivery trucks | 7804 | 132, 133 |
| 4 | **Commercial vehicles** Including multipurpose vehicles | 7805, 7793 | 134, 135, 142, 143, 144, 153 |
| 5 | **Excavating machines** Transport vehicles, loaders, graders | 7798, 7799 | 145, 146 |
| 6 | **Industrial trucks** Including solid rubber tires | 7811, 7845 | 171 |
| 7 | **Agricultural vehicles and machinery** Tractors, machines, implements, trailers | 7807, 7808, 7813 | 156, 161 |

**Examples of radial-tire construction (tubeless version)**
1 Hump, 2 Rim bead seat, 3 Rim flange, 4 Casing, 5 Airtight inner liner, 6 Belt, 7 Tread,
8 Sidewall, 9 Bead, 10 Bead core, 11 Valve, 12 Cover ring, 13 Balance weight, 14 Rim shoulder.

**Passenger-car radial tires**
**Casing:** two radially oriented rayon-cord plies. **Belt:** two crossover steel-cord plies and two circumferential nylon-cord plies.

**CT tires**

**Truck radial tires**
**Casing:** one radially oriented rayon-cord plies. **Belt:** four crossover steel-cord plies.

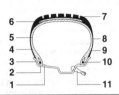
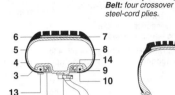

in order to provide sufficient stability. The "bias-belted" design, more widespread in the U.S. than elsewhere, incorporates an additional belt outside of the diagonal casing. The performance of this type of tire is much poorer than radial tires.

CT tires feature run-flat properties. When deflated, the tire presses against the rim shoulder and can be driven for several 100 km when flat.

Tubeless tires, already popular on passenger cars, are gradually becoming more frequent on heavy commercial vehicles. The essential requirement is a single-piece, airtight wheel rim, or a multi-piece rim capable of accepting the required flexible rim-seal rings. Tubeless tires have a vulcanized airtight inner layer instead of an inner tube.

The bead of the tubeless tire must contact the wheel rim with greater prestress in order to provide the necessary seal. Special, supplementary bead seals in the form of elastomer rings are sometimes used.

Dispensing with the inner tube reduces weight and simplifies mounting procedures.

**Diameter and design of the wheel rim**
With tire categories 3 and 4, non-sectional 15° tapered-bead seat rims (for tubeless tires) have displaced the sectional 5° tapered-bead seat rim. This type of rim is identified by the diameter code (1 unit = 25.4 mm) ending in 0.5, as in 17.5, 19.5, 22.5.

### Table 2. Service requirements

| No. | Main criteria | Sub-criteria |
|---|---|---|
| 1 | Ride comfort | Soft suspension, low noise, smooth running (low out-of-roundness) |
| 2 | Steering behavior | Steering force, steering precision[3] |
| 3 | Directional stability | Straight-running stability[3], cornering stability[3] |
| 4 | Driving safety | Tire seat on rim, tire/road adhesion[3] |
| 5 | Durability | Structural stability, high-speed performance, bursting pressure, puncture resistance |
| 6 | Economy | Expected service life (mileage), wear pattern, sidewall wear, rolling resistance, retreadability |

[3] Main criteria for driving on roads in winter.

Important codes for 5° tapered-bead seat rims are 16 and 20. For passenger-car tires, there are not only the normal drop-center rims with whole-number diameter codes 10, 12, 13, etc., but also special designs with diameter measurements in mm.

**Aspect ratio** $H/W$ (height-to-width ratio)
$H/W$ ratio = $(H/W) \cdot 100$
$H$ Tire cross-sectional height
$W$ Tire cross-sectional width

The aspect ratio ($H/W$ = height relative to width) on modern standard passenger-car tires ranges between 80 and 50; the figure ranges down to 25 for sports-car tires, and is between 100 and 45 for the tires on heavy commercial vehicles.

Passenger-car tires with low $H/W$ aspect ratios provide high levels of cornering stability. The different aspect ratios are all based on a single outside diameter in order to facilitate interchangeability. At a constant internal diameter for tire and wheel rim, a tire with a low $H/W$ aspect ratio will be wider on the same rim diameter, it will have a larger contact patch, and a more impressive appearance.

A low $H/W$ aspect ratio makes it possible to maintain the width of the footprint, while increasing the internal diameter of the wheel rim; thus providing more space for the wheel brake. The introduction of the tapered drop-center rim for commercial-vehicle tires was only made possible by the development of a suitable tubeless tire with a low $H/W$ aspect ratio. This was because a reduction in rim-base diameter was impossible since the brake-drum diameter could not be changed.

Wider tires with low H/W aspect ratios also represent the only feasible option for applications where minimum tire diameters (in other words, maximum usable height) are required, e.g. for container transport.

## Tire designation symbols

A tire's designation is stamped on the sidewall (see Table 5), and reflects standards that are mandatory in key European countries. These include ECE Regulation No. 30 for passenger-car tires; Regulation No. 54 for tires for heavy commercial vehicles (speeds of 80 km/h and above); and ECE Regulation No. 75 for tires for motorized two-wheeled vehicles (vehicles that can achieve speeds in excess of 40 km/h, or with a piston displacement exceeding 50 cm³). Regulation ECE-R 106 for tires on agricultural vehicles is not currently in force. Compliance with the regulations for remolds (ECE-R 108 for passenger-car tires; ECE-R 109 for tires used on commercial vehicles) will be mandatory in France from 2008 onwards.

Tires tested for compliance with ECE regulations are identified by the code molded into the sidewall adjacent to the bead. The code consists of a circle containing a large "E" followed by the code number of the approval agency, which is in turn followed by an approval number.

**Example:** (E4) 020 427
The small "e", which can be molded into the sidewall of passenger-car and commercial-vehicle tires in accordance with European Regulation 92/23, is of equal significance to the ECE approval mark.

**Example:** e4 00321
From August 2003 onwards new tire types must meet the noise directives of the EU. The same will apply to all tires for passenger cars and commercial vehicles from 2009 onwards, according to a specified schedule. These regulations will be published together with Directive 2001/43/EEC as Appendix 5 of the EU Tire Directive 92/23/EEC. The mark of approval on the tires looks as follows (example): e4 00687-s

The tire width, its construction (R = radial; "—" = cross-ply; B = bias-belted), and its rim diameter represent the minimum information required for tire designation. The tire diameter is also usually included on tires for industrial trucks. On tires for two-wheeled vehicles, passenger cars, and heavy commercial vehicles, this information is frequently supplemented by the $H/W$ aspect ratio in %, which is appended directly behind the width information and separated by a slash. ECE regulations require this information for all new tires. Although it is not stipulated in the ECE regulations, tires for passenger cars and two-wheeled vehicles may also feature a speed-rating code letter behind the $H/W$ aspect ratio or tire width. On bias-ply tires, the code letter replaces the horizontal line.

On VR, VB, ZR, and ZB tires, it is mandatory for the code letter to be an integral part of the tire-size designation.

The PR (Ply Rating) is displayed after the tire size, and is now employed as an optional code to distinguish the load ratings for various versions of the same size. Originally, it indicated the number of plies in the tire casing.

The service description is an additional suffix combining the load index (LI) and the speed-rating symbol (SS). ECE regulations prescribe it as a replacement for the PR number or the speed-rating letters in the tire designation. Specific values are assigned to the codes in the service description (Table 4).

For passenger-car tires:
Rated speed = top speed. On vehicles whose design only allows top speeds of 60 km/h and below, the tire load ratings may be increased as shown in the table below so that higher loads can be carried.

**Table 3. Load-rating increase**

| Speed in km/h | Load-rating increase in % | Air pressure increase in bar |
|---|---|---|
| 60 | 10 | 0.1 |
| 50 | 15 | 0.2 |
| 40 | 25 | 0.3 |
| 30 | 35 | 0.4 |
| 25 | 42 | 0.5 |

Reductions in tire load can be traded for higher top speeds on most tires for motor scooters and heavy commercial vehicles. Conversely, both types of tire may be used to carry higher loads throughout virtually the entire speed range when operated below their rated (reference) speed, provided that the vehicle can be specifically designed to operate at the lower

maximum speed. Again, increased maximum load ratings are approved for tires on passenger-car trailers for speeds up to 100 km/h, and on certain commercial vehicles used for short-distance transportation.

The correct inflation pressure for a particular tire size and PR rating or service description are specified in the standards and/or the manuals provided by the tire manufacturer (Table 1). The suffix containing the speed-rating symbol always indicates the actual rated speed.

Special passenger-car spare tires (low-weight and "space-saver" designs) are identified on the sidewall as intended for temporary use at limited speeds.

It is mot mandatory for the speed rating for M+S tires on passenger cars, heavy commercial vehicles and motorcycles, to correspond to the respective maximum speeds of the vehicles on which they are mounted. However, a sticker indicating the lower speed for which the tires are approved must be affixed inside of the vehicle within the driver's field of vision. The following tire categories may feature additional data prescribed by U.S. highway safety legislation. This data, molded into the sidewall adjacent to the bead, is also valid in Canada and in Israel:
– FMVSS 109 for passenger-car tires
– FMVSS 119 for two-wheeled and heavy commercial vehicles
This data is stamped adjacent to the letters "DOT", then come the tire identification code, the date of manufacture, and further data on maximum load rating, maximum inflation pressure, and the cord plies making up the casing and belts.

Australian Safety Regulation ADR 23, which applies to passenger-car tires, employs the identification codes from FMVSS 109 and ECE-R30.

**Table 4. Service description codes** (examples)
Load index (LI)

| LI | 50 | 51 | 88 | 89 | 112 | 113 | 145 | 149 | 157 |
|---|---|---|---|---|---|---|---|---|---|
| kg | 190 | 195 | 560 | 580 | 1,120 | 1,150 | 2,900 | 3,250 | 4,125 |

Speed-rating symbol (SS)

| SS | F | G | J | K | L | M | N | P | Q | R | S | T | H | V | W | Y |
|---|---|---|---|---|---|---|---|---|---|---|---|---|---|---|---|---|
| km/h | 80 | 90 | 100 | 110 | 120 | 130 | 140 | 150 | 160 | 170 | 180 | 190 | 210 | 240 | 270 | 300 |

## 776 Chassis systems

### Table 5. Tire identification examples

| Tire categories | Designation example | | Service designation | | Example includes details of | | | |
| Suitability | Tire designation | PR[3]) number | [4]) LI | [5]) SS | Tire Ø A | Tire width B | H/W % | Rim Ø d |
|---|---|---|---|---|---|---|---|---|
| **MC** Motorbicycle | 2¼–16 Motorbicycle | – | – | – | – | Code | – | Code |
| Small motorcycles | 3–17 reinforced[2]) | – | 51 | J | – | Code | – | Code |
| Motorcycles | 3.00–17 reinforced[2]) | – | 50 | P | – | Code | – | Code |
| | 110/80 R 18 | – | 58 | H | – | mm | 80 | Code |
| | 120/90 B 18 | – | 65 | H | – | mm | 90 | Code |
| Motor scooters | 3.50–10 | – | 51 | J | – | Code | – | Code |
| **Passenger cars** | 165 R 14 M+S | – | 84 | Q | – | mm | – | Code |
| | 195/65 R 15 reinforced[2]) | – | 95 | T | – | mm | – | Code |
| | 200/60 R 365 | – | 88 | H | – | mm | 60 | mm |
| | 205/60 ZR 15 | – | 91 | W | – | mm | 60 | Code |
| | CT 235/40 ZR 475 | – | – | – | – | mm | 40 | mm |
| **CV** Delivery vans | 185 R 14 C[1]) | 8 PR | 102/100 | M | – | mm | – | Code |
| Light-duty trucks | 245/70R 17.5 | – | 143/141 | J | – | Code | – | Code |
| Trucks | 11/70 R 22.5 | – | 146/143 | K | – | Code | 70 | Code |
| Trailers | 14/80 R 20 | – | 157 | K | – | Code | 80 | Code |
| Buses | 295/80 R 22.5 | – | 149/145 | M | – | mm | 80 | Code |
| **MPV** Multipurp. veh. | 10.5 R 20 MPV[8]) | 14 PR | 134 | G | – | Code | – | Code |
| Multipurp. veh. | 275/80 R 20 MPT[8]) | – | 134 | G | – | mm | 80 | Code |
| **EM** Transporters | 18.00–25 EM[9]) | 32 PR | – | – | – | Code | – | Code |
| Loaders | 29.5–29 EM[9]) | 28 PR | – | – | – | Code | – | Code |
| **IT** Industrial trucks | 6.50–10[6]) | 10 PR | – | – | – | Code | – | Code |
| Carts | 21 x 4[6]) | 4 PR | – | – | Code | Code | – | – |
| Industrial trucks | 28 x 9–15[7]) | 14 PR | – | – | Code | Code | – | Code |
| | 300 x 15[7]) | 18 PR | – | – | – | mm | – | Code |
| **AS** Tractors | 480/70 R 34 | – | 143 | A 8 | – | mm | – | Code |
| | 7.50–60 AS[10]) Front | 6 PR | – | – | – | Code | – | Code |
| Equipment[11]) | 11.0/65–12 Impl. | 6 PR | – | – | – | Code | 65 | Code |

Example for passenger-car tires: **175/70R13 82S**; **175** mm nominal tire width; **70**% H/W ratio; **R**adial tires; Code **13** Rim diameter (approx. 330 mm [13 inches]); Load index **82** (475 kg); Speed-rating symbol **S** = 180 km/hz

[1]) C = light-duty truck (delivery-van) tires (also for high-load-capacity motor-scooter tires). [2]) reinforced = extra load = additional designation for reinforced tires for two-wheeled vehicles and passenger-car tires. [3]) PR = load-range class. [4]) Load-range code for single/dual tires. [5]) Speed code for vehicle nominal (reference) speed. [6]) Pneumatic tires. [7]) Solid rubber tires. [8]) MPT = Multipurpose tire. [9]) EM = Excavating machines. [10]) AS = Agricultural tractors. [11]) Tires for equipment and trailers.

"IN" (together with a number for the relevant development center) and CCCs are designations for tires in Brazil and the People's Republic of China. The technical requirements of the regulations in these countries are based on those of the ECE.

## Tire applications

Tire selection based on the recommendations of the tire manufacturer is essential for obtaining satisfactory performance. Optimum operating characteristics can only be achieved when tires of one single design are mounted on all wheels (for instance, radial tires). This is obligatory for passenger cars. For commercial vehicles with a gross vehicle weight of over 2.8 t, tires on the same axle must be of identical design. During seasonal storage of the tires, inner tubes and bead bands tend to age and become brittle more rapidly when exposed to direct sunlight. Moving air promotes this process. Intact packaging is particularly important for ensuring that the tube remains in good condition. Therefore, the storage area should be cool, dry and dark. Any contact with oil or grease must be avoided. Particular care is required when mounting tires. They must never be mounted on anything other than undistorted, undamaged, rust-free wheel rims which show no signs of more than minimal wear. If a loose flange is used, that side should receive especially critical attention. New valves, and, where applicable, new tubes and bead bands, must always be installed with new tires. Caution is also advised if used inner tubes are refitted after repairs: Inner tubes expand during use, a

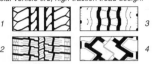

*Tire-tread examples*
1 Passenger-car tire, 2 Passenger-car M+S tire, 3 Commercial-vehicle tire, 4 Commercial-vehicle tire, high-traction tread design.

condition which can result in dangerous folds forming when the tube is reinstalled. If there are any doubts at all, new tubes should be used.

**Tire tread** (see examples)
It is illegal to regroove the tread on tires for two-wheeled vehicles and passenger cars; manufacturer regulations must be complied with for other tire categories.

Tire rotation is recommended to deal with variations in tread wear between axles. The less tread there is on the tire, the thinner is the protective layer covering the belts and casing. This aspect should be considered when planning long-term operations under demanding conditions. In addition, reduced tread depth results in a more than proportional increase in braking distances on wet road surfaces due to reduced tire adhesion. This applies in particular to passenger cars and fast commercial vehicles. For instance, for a light FWD passenger car and a heavy RWD car, the figures apply in Table 6 below when the vehicle is braked at and initial speed of 100 km/h (highly dependent on the road surface, tire tread, and the tire's rubber mixture).

**Table 6. Tread depth and braking distances** (braking at 100 km/h)

| Vehicle | | Light passenger car with front-wheel drive | | | | | Heavy passenger car with rear-wheel drive (ABS) | | | |
|---|---|---|---|---|---|---|---|---|---|---|
| Tread depth | in mm | 8 | 4 | 3 | 2 | 1 | 8 | 3 | 1.6 | 1 |
| Braking | in m | 76 | 99 | 110 | 129 | 166 | 59 | 63 | 80 | 97 |
| distance | in % | 100 | 130 | 145 | 170 | 218 | 100 | 107 | 135 | 165 |
| Increased braking distance per mm of wear | in % | 7 | | 15 | 25 | 48 | 1.4 | | 20 | 50 |

## Tire traction

### Quantities and units

| Quantity | | Unit |
|---|---|---|
| $f$ | Frequency | Hz |
| $F_B$ | Braking force | kN |
| $F_R$ | Wheel load | kN |
| $F_S$ | Side force | kN |
| $M_R$ | Aligning torque | N · m |
| $n_S$ | Caster | mm |
| $p_i$ | Tire pressure | bar |
| $v_0$ | Test velocity | km/h |
| $\alpha$ | Slip angle | ° |
| $\gamma$ | Camber angle | ° |
| $\lambda$ | Slip | – |

It is essential that accurate tire-performance maps are available to engineer and optimize the vehicle's handling, drivability, and ride comfort, and to reduce its drivetrain vibration.

Representative tire-performance maps for passenger cars and light commercial vehicles are already familiar and are available in various publications [1, 3, 4]. For this reason, the following will concen-

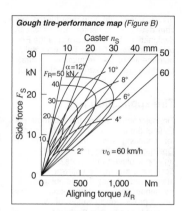

*Gough tire-performance map (Figure B)*

trate on tires for heavy-duty commercial vehicles with the dimensions 11 R 22.5. These tires are in widespread use [2].

All data in the program maps refer to the Michelin XZA 11 R 22.5 tire.

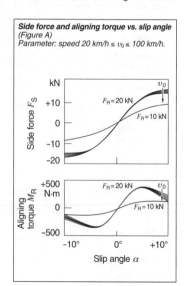

*Side force and aligning torque vs. slip angle (Figure A)*
*Parameter: speed 20 km/h ≤ $v_0$ ≤ 100 km/h.*

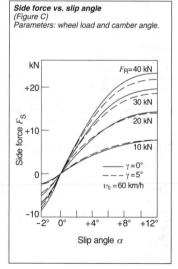

*Side force vs. slip angle (Figure C)*
*Parameters: wheel load and camber angle.*

## Tire performance with wheel rotating freely at a given slip angle

When the tire rotates at a slip angle, side forces are generated as a function of the slip angle. These side forces are accompanied by an aligning torque (Figure B). The Gough diagram [3] is frequently employed to illustrate this phenomenon. The side force is dependent on the slip angle and increases digressively as higher loads are applied to the wheel (Figure C). The maximum side force is inversely proportional to speed, while the influence of speed increases as a function of wheel load (Figure A).

When dealing with tires for passenger cars and light commercial vehicles, the situation is thus: If a wheel rotating at a given slip angle is subjected to camber, the camber and side forces cause a parallel displacement of the side-force/slip-angle curves.

Tires on heavy-duty commercial vehicles also display additional displacements of the side-force/slip-angle curves due to the side forces accompanying the camber;

this phenomenon only occurs at larger slip angles. The result is that practically all curves intersect the coordinate origin (Figure C). On dry roads, reduced tread depth results in steeper side-force/slip-angle curves, with an accompanying increase in the maximum side forces which can be transferred (Figure D).

## Tire performance under acceleration and braking with wheel rolling straight ahead

The tire's response to "slip" is similar to its reaction to slip angles (Figure E). The maximum peripheral force (braking force) will generally lie within a range of 10 to 20% slip on a dry road surface. Adhesion in the peripheral direction does not decrease as significantly with increasing wheel load as adhesion in the lateral direction. On larger tires, the influence which speed exerts at the level of the lateral coefficient of adhesion is less pronounced in the normal speed range for heavy-duty commercial vehicles than with tires similar to those used on passenger cars (Figure E).

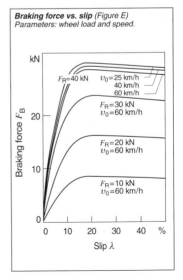

*Side force vs. slip angle* (Figure D)
Parameter: tread depth.

Side force $F_S$ (kN): +20, +10, 0, −10
— Tread depth 95%
– – Tread depth 60%
–·– Tread depth 30%
$F_R = 30$ kN
$v_0 = 60$ km/h
Slip angle $\alpha$: −2°, 0°, +4°, +8°, +12°

*Braking force vs. slip* (Figure E)
Parameters: wheel load and speed.

Braking force $F_B$ (kN): 20, 10
$F_R = 40$ kN    $v_0 = 25$ km/h, 40 km/h, 60 km/h
$F_R = 30$ kN    $v_0 = 60$ km/h
$F_R = 20$ kN    $v_0 = 60$ km/h
$F_R = 10$ kN    $v_0 = 60$ km/h
Slip $\lambda$ (%): 0, 10, 20, 30, 40

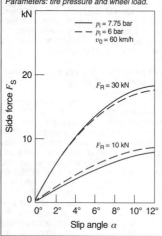

*Side force vs. slip angle on heavy-duty commercial-vehicle tires (Figure F)*
Parameters: tire pressure and wheel load.

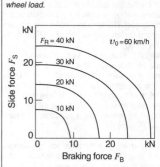

*Side force vs. braking force (Figure H)*
Maximum achievable adhesion at constant wheel load.

Tire pressure has only a minimum effect on maximum peripheral forces at low wheel loads. At higher wheel loads, reduced tire pressures result in a substantially more pronounced rate of increase in the maximum peripheral force (Figure G).

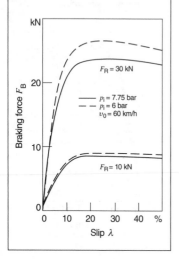

*Braking force vs. slip on heavy-duty commercial-vehicle tires (Figure G)*
Parameters: tire pressure and wheel load.

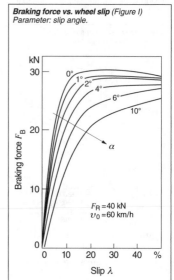

*Braking force vs. wheel slip (Figure I)*
Parameter: slip angle.

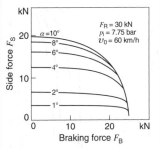

Side and circumferential forces respond to high tire loads by displaying mutually opposed reactions to variations in tire pressure (Figures F, G).

**Tire performance at slip angles and slip**
If a tire operating under peripheral forces or slip is subjected to an additional slip angle, the usable circumferential forces will decrease with increasing slip angle at all slip rates. The higher the slip angle, the more the curve for maximum peripheral force is displaced toward higher slip rates (Figure I).

The elliptical curves for side force vs. peripheral force (braking force) vary according to wheel load (Figure H). For a specific wheel load on vehicles fitted with ABS, this curve represents the maximum available adhesion limits for the vehicle dynamics.

The measured tire curves indicate the curve of the side force as a function of the braking force within a slip-angle range of 0...10°. The parameters for "wheel load", "velocity" and "tire pressure" remain constant (Figure K).

**Tires on wet road surface**
If tires are traveling on a water-covered road surface, a displacement zone A forms at the front of the tire contact patch. There is a short transitional zone B followed by an actual contact zone C at the rear of the tire contact patch. Zone A is characterized by a wedge of water which completely separates the tire from the surface of the road. If zone A affects the entire tire/road contact surface, the vehicle is aquaplaning (Figure L). The following are key influencing variables concerning the adhesion behavior of tires on wet road surfaces:
– Driving speed
– Water height
– Wheel load
– Tire width
– Tread depth
– Tire tread design
– Contact pressure distribution in the tire contact patch
– Rubber mixture
– Road surface

Each of these parameters in turn also depends on a range of further influencing variables.

*Tire contact patch dependent on state of the road surface (Figure L)*
*A Displacement zone, B Transitional zone, C Contact zone. $A_1$ Contact surface on dry road surface, $A_2$ Contact surface on wet road surface. X Direction of travel, $\omega$ Number of wheel revolutions, 1 Wedge of water.*

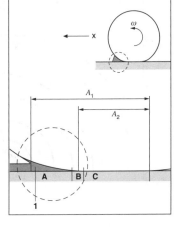

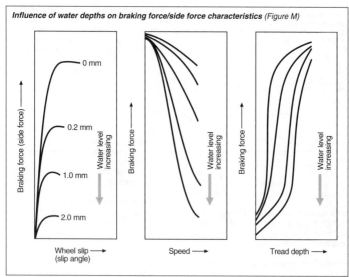

*Influence of water depths on braking force/side force characteristics (Figure M)*

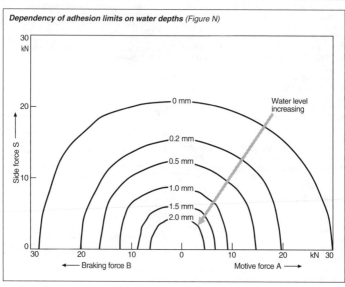

*Dependency of adhesion limits on water depths (Figure N)*

For example, the contact pressure distribution in the tire contact patch is also dependent on the tire design, the tire tread design, the camber angle, the tire belt, and sidewall design, and, in conjunction with the last two variables, on the tread curve parallel to the wheel axis.

The left diagram in Figure M shows the tire-force curves as a function of their design parameters. It is noticeable that the curve is basically the same for side force as a function of slip angle, and braking force as a function of wheel slip at different water depths. The characteristic curve shape is also the same at all water depths.

The middle diagram in Figure M shows the dependency of braking force on driving speed at different water depths. In the wet-adhesion range, i.e. at the lowest water depth, adhesion is largely influenced by the rubber mixture. However, in the aquaplaning range, i.e. at high water levels and high speeds (with otherwise identical tire parameters), the prevailing influencing variables are the tire tread design, and the contact pressure distribution in the tire contact patch.

A further major influencing parameter is the tread depth, which is part of the complex issue of tire tread design. The right diagram in Figure M shows the effect of the tread depth at different water depths.

Figure N contains a "wet program map" that shows the adhesion limits dependent on water depth.

Figure O shows the different braking forces that were achieved with different tires under aquaplaning conditions. The noticeable difference in the performance levels of tires made by different manufacturers under aquaplaning conditions is striking. They may counteract the dynamic-handling concept, drawn up in many optimization steps by the vehicle manufacturers.

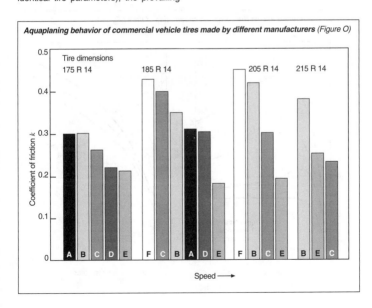

*Aquaplaning behavior of commercial vehicle tires made by different manufacturers (Figure O)*

### Tires on slippery winter road surface

The tire-performance maps on ice and snow are essentially similar to those on dry road surfaces. Key additional influencing parameters on adhesion behavior are temperature, the formation history of the ice and snow layer, the age of the ice or snow layer structure, and the degree of soiling.

Another major influencing variable for adhesion on a slippery winter road surface is the rubber mixture of the tire.

The requirements to be met by a tire are often different for ice and snow. While a high compressive load and a tread depth that is self-cleaning and provides good grip are ideal for snow conditions, a low compressive load is preferable for optimum adhesion on ice.

The side force/slip angle diagram illustrates the impact of ice surface temperature (Figure P, left diagram).

In addition to the large range of maximum side forces achievable, temperature also plays a key role in the formation of side-force maxima. Here, no side force maximum is formed on ice at around 0 °C. Similarly, no braking force maximum is formed as shown in the braking force/wheel slip diagram.

The right diagram in Figure P shows the influence of ice-surface temperature on the maximum lateral force at different speeds. As the temperature falls, the performance of the tire improves again.

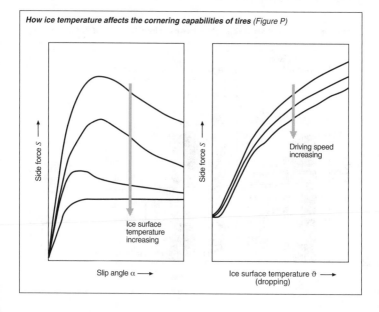

*How ice temperature affects the cornering capabilities of tires* (Figure P)

## Requirements of the "wheel/tire" system

The requirements to be met by tires in the future can be summarized as follows:
- General compliance with the overall "wheel/tire" system.
- Fewer varieties of tires currently available.
- New tire developments must either meet or exceed current requirements with regard to functional safety, economy, and service life.
- Minimized rolling resistance.
- Standardized tires on all wheels.
- Reduced tire weight.
- General compatibility with snow chains.
- Reduced tire-rolling noise.
- Significantly fewer tire irregularities.
- It is essential to produce a significant increase in tire/road-surface adhesion (both in the vehicle side and linear directions) in order to increase compatibility with other road traffic.
- Early warning of tire-performance maps to analyze and optimize dynamic handling.

The continuous adaptation of commercial vehicles to existing and foreseeable market demands – as with tires – also requires expansion of tire-performance limits.

This produces the following primary demands on tire design:
- Reduced tire weight.
- Greater load capacity.
- Reduced wheel-disk unevenness.
- Longer service life at points prone to cracking (i.e. disc flange and vent holes, welded disc/rim joint, and drop-center radius).

## Dynamic tire-performance maps

The depicted tire-performance maps are based on parameters that are only subject to gradual change during the course of the measurements, i.e. quasi-static conditions. Actual operation, on the other hand, is dependent on dynamic processes. Increases in the speed at which the influencing parameters vary will induce certain maneuver-specific changes in tire response which may no longer be neglected. The most significant influencing variables are dynamic changes in:

- Slip angle
- Track width
- Camber
- Slip
- Wheel load

Tire response to these rapidly changing influencing parameters is generally depicted as a function of frequency in program maps, i.e. frequency-dependent amplitudes and phase angles of tire forces and moments are plotted as a function of the forces acting on the tire. This includes the frequency-dependent characteristic curve for mean values for tire forces and moments [5, 6].

## References

[1] Gengenbach, W.: Experimentelle Untersuchung von Reifen auf nasser Fahrbahn (Experimental analysis of tires on wet road surface). ATZ, 1968, Volumes 3, 8, and 9,
[2] von Glasner, E.C.: Einbeziehung von Prüfstandsergebnissen in die Simulation des Fahrverhaltens von Nutzfahrzeugen (Including test-bench results in the simulation of commercial-vehicle handling). Postdoctoral thesis, University of Stuttgart, 1987.
[3] Gough, V. E.: Cornering Characteristics of Tyres. Automobile Engineer, 1954, Vol. 44.
[4] Weber R.: Beitrag zum Übertragungsverhalten zwischen Schlupf- und Reifenführungskräften (Contribution concerning the transitional behavior between slip and tire cornering forces). AI, 1981, Vol. 4.
[5] Fritz, G. Seitenkräfte und Rückstellmomente von Personenwagenreifen bei periodischer Änderung der Spurweite, des Sturz- und Schräglaufwinkels (Side forces and aligning torques of passenger-car tires under the influence of periodic changes in track width, camber, and slip angle). Doctoral thesis, University of Karlsruhe, 1978.
[6] Weber, R.: Reifenführungskräfte bei schnellen Änderungen von Schräglauf und Schlupf (Tire cornering forces as a function of rapid changes in slip angle and slip). Postdoctoral thesis, University of Karlsruhe, 1981.

# Steering

The steering mechanism converts the driver's rotational input at the steering wheel into a change in the steering angle of the vehicle's steered road wheels.

## Steering-system requirements

In accordance with European Directive 70/311/EEC, the steering system must guarantee the easy and safe steering of the vehicle. The maximum permissible operating time and operating force for a fully serviceable steering system, and for a faulty system, are contained in these regulations (see Table). They must be complied with when the vehicle is turned in a spiral path from a straight-running path at a speed of 10 km/h.

## Steering behavior

The requirements in terms of steering behavior can be summarized as follows:
1. Jolts from irregularities in the road surface must be damped as much as possible during transmission to the steering wheel. However, such damping must not cause the driver to lose contact with the road.
2. The basic design of the steering kinematics must satisfy the Ackermann conditions: When the extensions of the wheel axes on the left and right front wheels are at an angle, they intersect at an extension of the rear axle.
3. The vehicle must react to minute steering corrections by means of suitable directness of the steering system (particularly if rubber-elastic connections are used).
4. When the steering wheel is released, the wheels must return automatically to the straight-running position and must remain stable in this position.

**Regulations for steering operating force**

| Vehicle category | Fully serviceable steering system | | | Faulty steering system | | |
|---|---|---|---|---|---|---|
| | Maximum applied force in daN | Time in s | Turning radius in m | Maximum applied force in daN | Time in s | Turning radius in m |
| $M_1$ | 15 | 4 | 12 | 30 | 4 | 20 |
| $M_2$ | 15 | 4 | 12 | 30 | 4 | 20 |
| $M_3$ | 20 | 4 | 12 | 45 | 6 | 20 |
| $N_1$ | 20 | 4 | 12 | 30 | 4 | 20 |
| $N_2$ | 25 | 4 | 12 | 40 | 4 | 20 |
| $N_3$ | 20 | 4 | 12 [1] | 45 [2] | 6 | 20 |

[1]) Or steering lock in case this value is not reached.
[2]) 50 daN for non-articulated vehicles, with two or more steered axles, excluding friction-steered axles.

*Steering assembly (schematic)*
*a) Basic principle, b) Rack-and-pinion steering.*
*1 Steering arm, 2 Drag link, 3 Idler arm, 4 Tie rod/rack, 5 Steering wheel, 6 Steering shaft, 7 Steering box, 8 Pitman arm.*

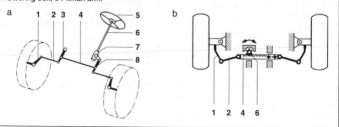

5. The steering should have as low a ratio as possible (number of steering-wheel turns from lock to lock) in order to achieve ease of handling. The steering forces involved are determined not only by the steering ratio but also by the front suspension load, the turning radius, the suspension geometry (caster angle, kingpin angle, kingpin offset), and the properties of the tire tread and the road surface.

## Types of steering box

A steering box must have the following qualities:
– no play in the straight-running position
– low friction, resulting in high efficiency
– high rigidity
– adjustability

For these reasons, only two types have become established to date:

### Rack-and-pinion steering
Basically, as the name implies, the rack-and-pinion steering consists of a rack and a pinion. The steering ratio is defined by the ratio of pinion revolutions (= steering-wheel revolutions) to rack travel. Suitable toothing of the rack allows the ratio to vary as a function of travel. This lowers the operating force or reduces the travel for steering adjustments.

### Recirculating-ball steering
The forces generated between steering worm and steering nut are transmitted via a low-friction row of recirculating balls. The steering nut acts on the steering shaft via gear teeth. A variable ratio is possible with this steering box.

## Steering kinematics

Steering kinematics and axle design must be such that, although the driver receives feedback on the adhesion between wheels and road surface, the steering wheel is not subjected to any forces from the spring motion of the wheels or from motive forces (front-wheel drive) (see P. 764).

Steering-axis inclination causes the front section of the vehicle to lift when the wheels are at an angle. This leads to a caster return torque dependent on the steering angle.

Toe-in (toe-out) is a slip angle present even during straight-running travel. This tensions the linkages and causes a rapid build-up of transverse forces when the wheels are at an angle.

Caster produces a lever arm for side forces, i.e. a speed-dependent return torque.

Kingpin offset determines the extent to which the steering system is affected by interference factors (brakes pulling unevenly, motive forces under traction/overrun in FWD vehicles). In modern designs, the aim is to achieve a steering offset which is "zero" to "slightly negative".

*Rack-and-pinion steering*
*1 Pinion, 2 Rack.*

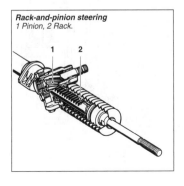

*Recirculating-ball steering*
*1 Steering worm, 2 Recirculating balls,*
*3 Steering nut, 4 Steering shaft with gear teeth.*

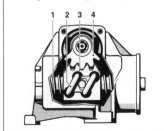

## Classification of steering systems

European Directive 70/311/EEC distinguishes between three types of steering system for front wheels:
- <u>Muscular-energy steering systems</u>, in which the steering force is produced exclusively by the driver (see Mechanical steering boxes on P. 787).
- <u>Power steering systems</u>, in which the steering force is produced exclusively by an energy source in the vehicle.
- <u>Power-assisted steering systems</u>, in which the steering force is produced by the muscular energy of the driver and by an energy source (used for high-speed vehicles).

## Hydraulic power-assisted steering

### Energy source
The energy source consists of a vane-type supply pump (generally driven by the internal-combustion engine) with an integrated oil-flow regulator, an oil reservoir, and connecting hoses and pipes.

The pump must be dimensioned so that it generates sufficient pressure to allow rotation of the steering wheel at a speed of at least 1.5 n/s, even when the engine is only idling.

The compulsory pressure-relief valve required on hydraulic systems is usually integrated.

The pump and system components must be designed so that the operating temperature of the hydraulic fluid does not rise to an excessive level (<100 °C), so that no noise is generated, and the oil does not foam.

On compact cars, electrically powered gear or roller pumps are occasionally used as well. These units are powered by the vehicle electrical system. They are more versatile with regard to their location and are conducive to modular vehicle design. An ECU achieves energy-saving effects by varying pump speed. Higher-voltage electrical systems presently under development would also allow larger cars to use this type of unit.

### Control valve
The control valve provides the steering cylinder with an oil pressure that corre-

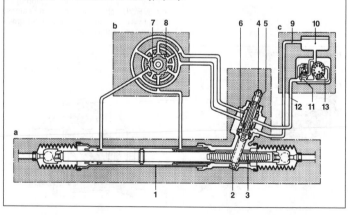

**Hydraulic rack-and-pinion steering with rotary distributor**
*a) Steering assembly, b) Rotary distributor cross-section (enlarged), c) Oil supply (energy source).*
*1 Steering cylinder, 2 Drive pinion, 3 Rack, 4 Torsion bar, 5 Steering spindle, 6 Control port,*
*7 Rotary distributor, 8 Control bushing, 9 Return line, 10 Oil reservoir, 11 Pressure and oil-flow*
*limiting valve, 12 Pressure line, 13 Vane-type pump.*

sponds to the rotary motion of the steering wheel. A flexible torque sensor (e.g. torsion bar, spiral spring, leaf spring) translates the applied torque, proportionally in most cases, precisely and without any degree of play, into as small an actuator travel as possible. The control edges, which are in the form of chamfers or bevels, move as a result of the actuator travel, and form the corresponding opening cross-section for the oil flow.

Control valves are usually built according to the "open center" principle, i.e. when the control valve is not actuated, the oil delivered by the pump flows back to the oil reservoir at zero pressure.

### Steering cylinder

The double-action steering cylinder converts the applied oil pressure into an assisting force which acts on the rack and intensifies the steering force exerted by the driver. The steering cylinder is normally integrated in the steering box. As the steering cylinder has to have extremely low friction, particularly high demands are made on the piston and rod seals.

### Parameterizable hydraulic power-assisted steering

Increasing demands regarding user-friendliness and safety have resulted in the introduction of controllable power-assisted steering systems. One example of this is the electronically controlled power-assisted rack-and-pinion steering system. It operates dependent on speed, i.e. the vehicle speed as measured by the elec-

tronic speedometer controls the actuating force of the steering system. A control unit evaluates the speed signals and determines the level of hydraulic feedback, and therefore the actuating force on the steering wheel. This level of hydraulic reaction is transmitted to the steering-system control valve via an electrohydraulic converter. This modified the hydraulic reaction in relation to vehicle speed. The special design of the steering characteristic means that, when parking, and when moving the steering wheel at standstill, only minimal forces need to be applied to the steering wheel. The level of power assistance is reduced as speed increases. In this way, precise and accurate steering is possible at high speeds. With this system, it is important that oil pressure and volumetric flow are at no time reduced, so that they can be called on immediately in emergency situations. These features permit outstanding steering precision and safety, and provide optimum steering comfort at the same time.

## Electric power-assisted steering

The SERVOLECTRIC (Bosch/ZF designation) is currently under development for medium-sized and compact cars. This electric power-assisted steering system features an electric motor which is powered by the vehicle electrical system. It can be fitted in one of three possible arrangements, either as a steering-column, pinion-drive or rack-and-pinion drive unit.

---

*Parameterizable power-assisted steering* (characteristic curves)
The characteristic curve can be adjusted to the vehicle data.

*Controllable speed-dependent power-assisted steering* (schematic)
1 Pressure-oil pump, 2 Steering-valve housing, 3 Electrohydraulic converter, 4 ECU, 5 Electronic speedometer, 6 Battery.

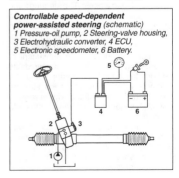

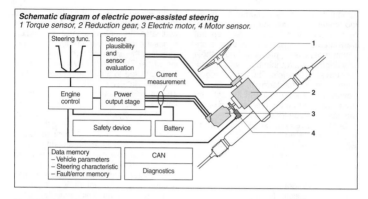

*Schematic diagram of electric power-assisted steering*
1 Torque sensor, 2 Reduction gear, 3 Electric motor, 4 Motor sensor.

The SERVOLECTRIC ECU supports parameterization (e.g. dynamic handling variables) and automatic steering-axis feedback amplification. It offers considerable potential for saving steering power (approx. 85% of hydraulic power-assisted steering with a pump driven by the vehicle engine).

The SERVOLECTRIC system allows the vehicle to be steered unassisted (using greater effort) if the power-assistance system fails.

## Power-assisted steering for commercial vehicles

### Power-assisted steering with all-hydraulic transmission

With "hydrostatic steering" there is no mechanical connection between steering wheel and road wheels. The steering force is hydraulically boosted and is transmitted exclusively by hydraulic means. Located in the ECU is a metering pump which supplies the steering cylinder with an oil pressure corresponding to the movement of the steering wheel. Owing to unavoidable leakage losses in the metering pump, the straight-running position of the steering wheel is no longer defined. This is why the use of this steering system is confined to machines.

The maximum permissible speed with this steering system is 25 km/h in many European countries; in Germany it is 50 km/h and, with dual-circuit design, could be increased to 62 km/h.

### Dual-circuit power-assisted steering system for heavy-duty commercial vehicles

Dual-circuit steering systems are required when the actuating forces needed at the steering wheel exceed 450 N if the power-assistance system fails (EEC 70/311).

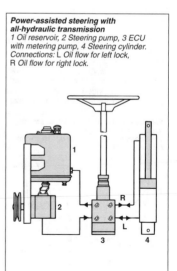

*Power-assisted steering with all-hydraulic transmission*
1 Oil reservoir, 2 Steering pump, 3 ECU with metering pump, 4 Steering cylinder.
Connections: L Oil flow for left lock, R Oil flow for right lock.

These steering systems feature hydraulic redundancy. Both steering circuits in these systems are functionally tested by means of flow indicators. The steering-circuit supply pumps must be driven in various ways (e.g. engine-dependent, vehicle-speed-dependent, or electrically). In accordance with legislation, if the engine or one of the steering circuits fails, the driver must be able to steer the vehicle with a functioning circuit.

### Single-circuit power-assisted steering system for commercial vehicles

Commercial vehicles are usually fitted with recirculating-ball hydraulic steering system. In modern systems, the control valve is integrated in the steering worm. This allows compact design and weight optimization.

Only minor modifications to the control valve components are required to permit the actuating force in modern recirculating-ball hydraulic steering systems to be adjusted. This is performed by means of control electronics in relation to vehicle speed and other parameters, such as lateral acceleration or laden state.

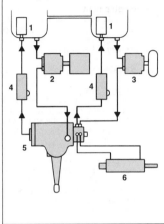

*Dual-circuit power-assisted steering system*
1 Oil reservoir, 2 Engine-driven pump,
3 Wheel-driven pump, 4 Flow indicator,
5 Dual-circuit hydraulic steering,
6 Steering cylinder.

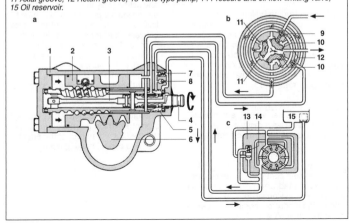

*Recirculating-ball hydraulic steering system*
a) Steering assembly, b) Rotary distributor cross-section (enlarged), c) Oil supply (energy source).
1 Housing, 2 Piston, 3 Torsion bar, 4 Rotary distributor/steering spindle, 5 Control bushing/worm,
6 Sectional shaft, 7 Pressure-relief valve, 8 Replenishing valve, 9 Inlet slot, 10 Return slot,
11 Axial groove, 12 Return groove, 13 Vane-type pump, 14 Pressure and oil-flow limiting valve,
15 Oil reservoir.

# Braking systems

## Definitions, Principles
(based on ISO 611 and DIN 70 024)

### Braking equipment
All the vehicle braking systems whose functions are to reduce vehicle speed or bring the vehicle to a halt, or to hold the vehicle stationary if already halted.

### Braking systems

#### Service-braking system
All the elements, the action of which may be regulated, allowing the driver to reduce, directly or indirectly, the speed of a vehicle during normal driving or to bring the vehicle to a halt.

#### Secondary braking system
All the elements, the action of which may be regulated, allowing the driver to reduce, directly or indirectly, the speed of a vehicle or to bring the vehicle to a halt in case of failure of the service-braking system.

#### Parking braking system
All the elements allowing the vehicle to be held stationary mechanically even on an inclined surface, and particularly in the absence of the driver.

#### Additional retarding braking system
System of components which allows the driver to reduce the vehicle's speed or descend a long downhill gradient at a virtually constant speed with practically no wear to the friction brakes. An additional retarding braking system may incorporate one or more retarders.

#### Automatic braking system
All the elements which automatically brake the trailer as a result of intended or accidental separation from the tractor vehicle.

#### Electronic braking system (EBS, EHB)
Braking system controlled by an electrical signal generated and processed by the control transmission system. An electrical output signal controls components which generate the application force.

## Component parts

#### Energy supplying device
Parts of a braking system which supply, regulate and, if necessary, condition the energy required for braking. It terminates at the point where the transmission device starts, i.e. where the various circuits of the braking systems, including the circuits of accessories if fitted, are isolated either from the energy supplying device or from each other.

The energy source is that part of an energy-supplying device which generates the energy. It may be located remotely from the vehicle (for example in the case of a compressed-air braking system for a trailer) or may be the muscular force of the driver.

#### Control device
Parts of a braking system which initiate the operation and control the effect of this braking system. The control signal can be conveyed within the control device by, for example, mechanical, pneumatic, hydraulic or electrical means, including the use of auxiliary energy or non-muscular force.

The control device is defined as starting at the component to which the control force is directly applied, and can be operated:
- by direct action of the driver, either by hand or foot
- by indirect action of the driver or without any action (only in the case of trailers)
- by varying the pressure in a connecting line, or the electric current in a cable, between the tractor vehicle and the trailer at the time when one of the braking systems on the tractor vehicle is operated, or if it fails, and
- by the inertia of the vehicle or by its weight or of one of its main component parts

The control device is defined as ending at the point at which the braking energy is distributed, or where part of the energy is diverted to control braking energy.

### Transmission device

Parts of a braking system which transmit the energy distributed by the control device. It starts either at the point where the control device terminates or at the point where the energy supplying device terminates. It terminates at those parts of the braking system in which the forces opposing the vehicle's movement, or its tendency towards movement, are generated. It can, for example, be of mechanical, hydraulic, pneumatic (pressure above or below atmospheric), electric, or combined (for example hydromechanical, hydropneumatic).

### Brake

Parts of a braking system in which the forces opposing the vehicle's movement, or its tendency towards movement, are developed, such as friction brakes (disk or drum) or retarders (hydrodynamic or electrodynamic retarders, exhaust brakes).

### Auxiliary device of the tractor vehicle for a trailer

Parts of a braking system on a tractor vehicle which are intended to supply energy to, and control, the braking systems on the trailer. It comprises the components between the energy supplying device of the tractor vehicle and the supply-line coupling head (inclusive), and between the transmission device(s) of the tractor vehicle and the control-line coupling head (inclusive).

## Braking-system types relating to the energy supplying device

### Muscular-energy braking system

Braking system in which the energy necessary to produce the braking force is supplied solely by the physical effort of the driver.

### Energy-assisted braking system

Braking system in which the energy necessary to produce the braking force is supplied by the physical effort of the driver and one or more energy supplying devices.

### Non-muscular-energy braking system

Braking system in which the energy necessary to produce the braking force is supplied by one or more energy supplying devices excluding the physical effort of the driver. This is used only to control the system.

Note: However, a braking system in which the driver can increase the braking force, in a state of totally failed energy, by muscular effort acting on the system, is not included in the above definition.

### Inertia braking system

Braking system in which the energy necessary to produce the braking force arises from the approach of the trailer to its tractor vehicle.

### Gravity braking system

Braking system in which the energy necessary to produce the braking force is supplied by the lowering of a component part of the trailer (e.g. trailer drawbar) due to gravity.

## Definitions of braking systems relating to the arrangement of the transmission device

### Single-circuit braking system

Braking system having a transmission device embodying a single circuit. The transmission device comprises a single circuit if, in the event of a failure in the transmission device, no energy for the production of the application force can be transmitted by this transmission device.

### Multi-circuit braking system

Braking system having a transmission device embodying several circuits. The transmission device comprises several circuits if, in the event of a failure in the transmission device, energy for the production of the application force can still be transmitted, wholly or partly, by this transmission device.

## Definitions of braking systems relating to vehicle combinations

Single-line braking system
Assembly in which the braking systems of the individual vehicles act in such a way that the single line is used both for the energy supply to, and for the control of, the braking system of the trailer.

Dual- or multi-line braking systems
Assembly in which the braking systems of the individual vehicles act in such a way that several lines are used separately and simultaneously for the energy supply to, and for the control of, the braking system of the trailer.

Continuous braking system
Combination of braking systems for vehicles forming a vehicle combination. Characteristics:
– From the driving seat, the driver can operate a directly operated control device on the tractor vehicle and an indirectly operated control device on the trailer by a single operation and with a variable degree of force.
– The energy used for the braking of each of the vehicles forming the combination is supplied by the same energy source (which may be the muscular effort of the driver).
– Simultaneous or suitably phased braking of the individual units of a road train.

Semi-continuous braking system
Combination of braking systems for vehicles forming a road train. Characteristics:
– The driver, from his driving seat, can operate gradually a directly operated control device on the tractor vehicle and an indirectly operated control device on the trailer by a single operation.
– The energy used for the braking of each of the vehicles forming the road train is supplied by at least two different energy sources (one of which may be the muscular effort of the driver).
– Simultaneous or suitably phased braking of the individual units of a road train.

Non-continuous braking system
Combinations of the braking systems of the vehicles forming a road train which is neither continuous nor semi-continuous.

## Braking-system control lines

Wiring and conductors: These are employed to conduct electrical energy.
Tubular lines: Rigid, semi-rigid or flexible tubes or pipes used to transfer hydraulic or pneumatic energy.

## Lines connecting the braking equipment of vehicles in a road train.

Supply line: A supply line is a special feed line transmitting energy from the tractor vehicle to the energy accumulator of the trailer.
Brake line: A control line is a special control line by which the energy essential for control is transmitted from the tractor vehicle to the trailer.
Common brake and supply line: Line serving equally as brake line and as supply line (single-line braking system).
Secondary-brake line: Special actuating line transmitting the energy from the tractor vehicle to the trailer essential for secondary braking of the trailer.

## Braking mechanics
Mechanical phenomena occurring between the start of actuation of the control device and the end of the braking action.

Gradual braking
Braking which, within the normal range of operation of the control device, permits the driver, at any moment, to increase or reduce, to a sufficiently fine degree, the braking force by operating the control device. When an increase in braking force is obtained by the increased action of the control device, an inverse action must lead to a reduction in that force.

Braking-system hysteresis: Difference in control forces between application and release at the same braking torque.

Brake hysteresis: Difference in application force between application and release at the same braking torque.

## Forces and torques

Control force $F_c$: Force exerted on the control device.

Application force $F_s$: On friction brakes, the total force applied to a brake lining and which causes the braking force by the effect of friction.

Braking torque: Product of frictional forces resulting from the application force and the distance between the points of application of these forces and the axis of rotation of the wheels.

Total braking force $F_f$: Sum of the braking forces at the tire contact patches of all the wheels and the ground, produced by the effect of the braking system, and which oppose the movement or the tendency of the vehicle to move.

Braking-force distribution: Specification of braking force according to axle, given in % of the total braking force $F_f$. Example: front axle 60%, rear axle 40%.

Brake coefficient $C^*$: Defines the relationship between the total peripheral force of a given brake and the brake's application force.

$$C^* = F_u/F_s$$

$F_u$ Total peripheral force, $F_s$ Application force. The mean is employed when there are variations in application forces at individual brake shoes ($i$ number of brake shoes).

$$F_s = \sum F_{si}/i$$

## Times (see figure)

Reaction time: The time that elapses between perception of the state or object which induces the response, and the point at which the control device is actuated ($t_0$).

Actuating time of the control device: Elapsed time between the moment when the component of the control device ($t_0$), on which the control force acts, starts to move, and the moment when it reaches its final position corresponding to the applied control force (or its travel). (This is equally true for application and release of the brakes).

Initial response time $t_1 - t_0$: Elapsed time between the moment when the component of the control device, on which the control force acts, starts to move and the moment when the braking force takes effect.

Pressure build-up time $t_{1'} - t_1$: Period that elapses between the point at which the braking force starts to take effect and the point at which a certain level is reached (75% of asymptotic pressure in the wheel-brake cylinder as per EU Directive 71/320 EEC, App. III/2.4).

Initial response and pressure build-up time: The sum of the initial response and pressure build-up times is used to assess how the braking system behaves over time until the moment at which full braking effect is reached.

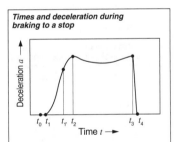

***Times and deceleration during braking to a stop***

*(Deceleration $a$ vs. Time $t$)*

| | |
|---|---|
| before $t_0$: | Reaction time |
| $t_0$: | Initial application of force on control device |
| $t_1$: | Start of deceleration |
| $t_{1'}$: | End of pressure build-up time |
| $t_2$: | Fully developed deceleration |
| $t_3$: | End of maximum retardation |
| $t_4$: | End of braking operation (vehicle stationary) |
| $t_1 - t_0$: | Initial response time |
| $t_{1'} - t_1$: | Pressure build-up time |
| $t_3 - t_2$: | "Mean maximum retardation" range |
| $t_4 - t_1$: | Active braking time |
| $t_4 - t_0$: | Total braking time |

<u>Active braking time $t_4 - t_1$</u>: Elapsed time between the moment when the braking force starts to take effect and the moment when the braking force ceases. If the vehicle stops before the braking force ceases, the time when motion ceases is the end of the active braking time.

<u>Release time</u>: Elapsed time between the moment when the control device starts to release and the moment when the braking force ceases.

<u>Total braking time $t_4 - t_0$</u>: Elapsed time between the moment when the control device, on which the control force acts, starts to move and the moment when the braking force ceases. If the vehicle stops before the braking force ceases, the time when motion ceases is the end of the active braking time.

<u>Braking distance $s$</u>: Distance traveled by the vehicle during the total braking time. If the time when motion ceases constitutes the end of the total braking time, this distance is called the "stopping distance".

<u>Braking work $W$</u>: Integral of the product of the instantaneous total braking force, $F_f$, and the elementary movement, $ds$, over the braking distance, $s$.

$$W = \int_0^s F_f \cdot ds$$

<u>Instantaneous braking power $P$</u>
Product of the instantaneous total braking force $F_f$ and the vehicle's road speed $v$:

$$P = F_f \cdot v$$

<u>Braking deceleration</u>
Reduction of speed obtained by the braking system within the considered time, $t$. A distinction is made between the following:

*Instantaneous braking deceleration*
$a = dv/dt$

*Mean braking deceleration over a period of time*
Mean braking deceleration between two points in time $t_B$ and $t_E$

$$a_{mt} = \frac{1}{t_E - t_B} \cdot \int_{t_B}^{t_E} a\,(t) \cdot dt;$$

This means that:

$$a_{mt} = \frac{v_E - v_B}{t_E - t_B},$$

where $v_B$ and $v_E$ are the vehicle speeds at the times $t_B$ and $t_E$.

*Mean braking deceleration over a specific distance*
Mean braking deceleration over the distance between two points $s_B$ and $s_E$

$$a_{ms} = \frac{1}{s_E - s_B} \cdot \int_{s_B}^{s_E} a\,(s)\,ds;$$

This means that:

$$a_{ms} = \frac{v_E^2 - v_B^2}{2 \cdot (s_E - s_B)}$$

where $v_B$ and $v_E$ are the vehicle speeds up to the points $s_B$ and $s_E$.

*Mean braking deceleration over the total braking distance*
Mean braking deceleration according to the following equation:

$$a_{ms0} = \frac{-v_0^2}{2 \cdot s_0},$$

where $v_0$ relates to the time $t_0$ (special instance of $a_{ms}$ where $s_E = s_0$).

*Mean fully developed deceleration $d_m$*
Mean fully developed deceleration over the distance determined by the conditions $v_B = 0.8 \cdot v_0$ and $v_E = 0.1 \cdot v_0$ thus:

$$d_m = \frac{v_B^2 - v_E^2}{2 \cdot (s_E - s_B)}$$

The mean fully developed deceleration is used in ECE Regulation 13 as a measure of the effectiveness of a braking system. Since positive values for $d_m$ are used here, the mathematical sign has been reversed in this case. (In order to establish a relationship between braking distance and braking deceleration, braking deceleration must be expressed as a function of the distance traveled.)

<u>Braking factor $z$</u>
Ratio between the total braking force, $F_f$, and the permissible total static weight, $G_s$, exerted on the axle or axles of the vehicle:

$$z = F_f / G_s$$

## Legal regulations

The testing of braking equipment for the purposes of issuing type approval (General Certification) to a vehicle in Europe may take place in accordance with one of the following:

- National road traffic licensing regulations and legal requirements for the testing of brakes applicable in the country of use,
- Council Directive of the European Communities: Directive 71/320/EEC and the Amending Directives and Annexes, or
- ECE Regulation 13, 13H and 78 of the UN Economic Commission in Geneva.

In Europe, the national road traffic licensing regulations in individual countries may specify compliance with the EU Directive or ECE Regulation 13 (or 13 H). Essentially, they may be very similar. ECE Regulations 13 and 13 H, however, have been further updated and also contain requirements for electrically controlled braking systems, for example, as well as requirements relating to the safety aspects of complex electronic systems such as ESP or ACC.

**Braking systems conforming
to EU Directives, and
ECE Regulations 13 and 78**
(for classification, refer to P. 885).

Category L vehicles
(less than 4 wheels)
Motorized two- and three-wheeled vehicles must be equipped with 2 mutually independent braking systems. In the case of heavy-duty Category $L_5$ 3-wheel vehicles, the two braking systems must both act on two wheels. Additionally, these vehicles must be equipped with a parking braking system.

Category M and N vehicles
Category M and N vehicles must meet the requirements which pertain to the service braking system, secondary braking system and parking braking system. These 3 braking systems may have common components. Such vehicles must have at least 2 mutually independent control devices.

The distribution of braking force between the individual axles is prescribed. Vehicles in Categories $M_2$ and $N_2$ or higher must be fitted with an antilock braking system (ABS) (some exceptions may still apply for older models).

Additional retarding braking systems can be used in order to fulfill braking requirements on long downhill gradients. Vehicles in Category $M_3$ used for local or long-distance duty must be able to meet the requirements for braking on such "descents" using the additional retarding braking system only.

Category O trailers
Category $O_1$ trailers are not required to have a braking system. However, there are requirements governing the safety connection to the tractor vehicle. Beginning with Category $O_2$, trailers must be fitted with a service braking system and a parking braking system which may have common components. It must be possible for the parking braking system to be operated by a person standing next to the vehicle. The distribution of braking force between the individual axles is prescribed.

An antilock braking system (ABS) is prescribed for some trailers in Category $O_3$ and above.

Inertia braking systems are permissible on trailers up to Category $O_2$.

The trailer must brake automatically if it becomes decoupled from the tractor vehicle while moving, or (for trailers < 1.5 t) it must be equipped with a safety connection to the tractor vehicle.

### Requirements of StVZO (Germany), EU Directive 71/320 EEC and ECE Regulations 13

| Vehicle class (for classification, refer to P. 885) | Passenger cars & motor coaches | | | Commercial vehicles | | | Trailers | | | |
|---|---|---|---|---|---|---|---|---|---|---|
| | $M_1$ | $M_2$ | $M_3$ | $N_1$ | $N_2$ | $N_3$ | $O_1$ | $O_2$ | $O_3$ | $O_4$ |
| **Service-braking system** | Acting on all wheels Prescribed braking-force distribution to the axles | | | | | | No braking system or as $O_2$ | Inertia braking system or as $O_3$ | | |
| ABS as per EC Dir. or ECE [1] ($v_{max} \geq 25$ km/h) | – | + | + | – | + | + | – | – | + | + |
| **Type O test (drive disengaged)** | | | | | | | | | | |
| Test speed    km/h | 80 | 60 | 60 | 80 | 60 | 60 | – | 60 | 60 | 60 |
| Braking distance   $\leq$ m | 50.7 | 36.7 | 36.7 | 61.2 | 36.7 | 36.7 | | $z \geq 0.50$, semitrailer: $z \geq 0.45$ | | |
| Braking distance equation | $0.1v + \dfrac{v^2}{150}$ | | | $0.15v + \dfrac{v^2}{130}$ | | | | | | |
| Mean fully developed deceleration   $\geq$ m/s² | 5.8 | | | 5.0 | | | | | | |
| Actuating force   $\leq$ N | 500 | | | 700 | | | | at $\leq$ 6.5 bar | | |
| **Type O test (drive engaged)** | Behavior of vehicle under braking from 30% – 80% $v_{max}$ and braking efficiency | | | | | | | | | |
| Test speed $v = 80\%\ v_{max}$, but   $\leq$ km/h | 160 | 100 | 90 | 120 | 100 | 90 | – | – | – | – |
| Braking distance   $\leq$ m | 212.9 | 111.6 | 91.8 | 157.1 | 111.6 | 91.8 | | | | |
| Braking distance equation | $0.1v + \dfrac{v^2}{130}$ | | | $0.15v + \dfrac{v^2}{103.5}$ | | | | | | |
| Mean fully developed deceleration   $\geq$ m/s² | 5.0 | | | 4.0 | | | | | | |
| Control force   $\leq$ N | 500 | | | 700 | | | | | | |
| **Typ I test** | Repeated braking at 3 m/s² fully laden, drive engaged | | | | | | – | Continuous braking, fully laden, 40 km/h, 7% downhill gradient, 1.7 km, $z \geq 0.36$ and $z \geq 60\%$ of the level measured in the Type O test at 40 km/h | | – |
| $v_1 = 80\%\ v_{max}$, but   $\leq$ km/h | 120 | 100 | 60 | 120 | 60 | 60 | | | | |
| $v_2 = \frac{1}{2}\,v_1$ | | | | | | | | | | |
| Number of braking cycles   $n$ | 15 | 15 | 20 | 15 | 20 | 20 | | | | |
| Braking cycle duration   s | 45 | 55 | 60 | 55 | 60 | 60 | | | | |
| Hot-brake efficiency at end of Type I test | $\geq 80\%$ of the braking efficiency specified for Type O test (drive disengaged) and $\geq 60\%$ of the braking efficiency achieved in the Type O test (drive disengaged) | | | | | | | | | |
| **Type II test** on long descents | Energy corresponding to 30 km/h, 6% downhill gradient and 6 km, fully laden, drive engaged, additional retarding braking system operated. Measured as for Type O test (drive disengaged) | | | | | | – | – | – | at 40 km/h |
| Hot-brake efficiency at end of Type II test | | | | | | | | | | |
| Braking-distance equation | $M_3$: $0.15\,v + \dfrac{1.33\,v^2}{130}$    $N_3$: $0.15\,v + \dfrac{1.33\,v^2}{115}$ | | | | | | | | | |
| Braking distance   $\leq$ m | – | – | 45.8 | – | – | 50.6 | | | | $z \geq 0.33$ |
| Mean fully developed deceleration   $\geq$ m/s² | | | 3.75 | | | 3.3 | | | | |

---

[1] Exceptions may still be allowed for older models.

| Vehicle class (for classification, refer to P. 885) | | Passenger cars & motor coaches | | | Commercial vehicles | | | Trailers | | | |
|---|---|---|---|---|---|---|---|---|---|---|---|
| | | $M_1$ | $M_2$ | $M_3$ | $N_1$ | $N_2$ | $N_3$ | $O_1$ | $O_2$ | $O_3$ | $O_4$ |
| Type IIa Test<br><br>For additional retarding braking systems | | Energy corresponding to 30 km/h, 7% downhill gradient, 6 km, laden, only additional retarding braking system in operation. Only permitted with $M_3$ [2]) and for towing $O_4$, $N_3$. | | | | | | | | | |
| Type III Test | | – | | | | | | – | – | – | [3]) |
| Residual braking effect after transmission system/brake-circuit failure, drive disengaged | | | | | | | | The brakes of the trailer must be fully or partially operable with graduated effect. | | | |
| Test speed | km/h | 80 | 60 | 60 | 70 | 50 | 40 | | | | |
| Braking distance, laden | ≤ m | 150.2 | 101.3 | 101.3 | 152.5 | 80.0 | 52.4 | | | | |
| Braking distance, unladen | ≤ m | 178.7 | 119.8 | 101.3 | 180.9 | 94.5 | 52.4 | | | | |
| Mean maximum retardation, fully laden | ≥ m/s² | 1.7 | 1.5 | 1.5 | 1.3 | 1.3 | 1.3 | | | | |
| unladen | ≥ m/s² | 1.5 | 1.3 | 1.5 | 1.1 | 1.1 | 1.3 | | | | |
| Actuating force | ≤ N | 700 | 700 | 700 | 700 | 700 | 700 | | | | |
| Secondary braking system (Tested as for Type O test, drive disengaged) | | | | | | | | The brakes of the trailer must be operable with graduated effect | | | |
| Test speed | km/h | 80 | 60 | 60 | 70 | 50 | 40 | | | | |
| Braking distance | ≤ m | 93.3 | 64.4 | 64.4 | 95.7 | 54.0 | 38.3 | | | | |
| Braking-distance formula | | $0.1v + \dfrac{2v^2}{150}$ | $0.15v + \dfrac{2v^2}{130}$ | | $0.15v + \dfrac{2v^2}{115}$ | | | | | | |
| Mean maximum retardation | ≥ m/s² | 2.9 | 2.5 | | 2.2 | | | | | | |
| Actuating force, by hand | ≤ N | 400 | 600 | | 600 | | | | | | |
| with foot | ≤ N | 500 | 700 | | 700 | | | | | | |
| Parking braking system (test in laden state) | | | | | | | | | | | |
| Holding stationary on incline (downgrade or upgrade) | ≥ % | 18 | | | 18 | | | – | | 18 | |
| Together with unbraked vehicle of class O | ≥ % | 12 | | | 12 | | | – | | – | |
| Actuating force, by hand | ≤ N | 400 | 600 | | 600 | | | – | | 600 | |
| with foot | ≤ N | 500 | 700 | | 700 | | | – | | – | |
| Type O Test [4]) (drive disengaged, laden) | | | | | | | | | | | |
| Test speed | km/h | 80 | 60 | 60 | 70 | 50 | 40 | – | | | |
| Mean maximum retardation and deceleration prior to standstill | ≥ m/s² | 1.5 | | | 1.5 | | | – | | | |
| Automatic braking system With compressed-air systems, automatic trailer braking in case of pressure loss in supply line | | | | | | | | | | | |
| Test speed | km/h | | | | | | | – | | 40 | |
| Braking factor | ≥ % | | | | | | | – | | 13.5 | |

[2]) Except city buses
[3]) Repeated braking as for Type I test for $N_3$. Afterwards, braking efficiency ≥ 40 and ≥ 60% of level achieved in Type O Test.
[4]) With parking braking system or via auxiliary control device for service-braking system.

<u>Vehicles equipped with antilock
braking systems (ABS)</u>

ABS systems must conform to Appendix
X of EU Directive 71/320/EEC or Annex
13 of ECE Regulation 13 (on Category 1
vehicles of Categories $M_2$, $M_3$, $N_2$ and $N_3$).
The essential requirements are:

– Locking of the directly controlled wheels
  under braking on any road surface at
  speeds of over 15 km/h must be prevented.
– Operating stability and steering control
  are to be maintained, and
– Grip on road surfaces offering the same
  or (in the case of Category 1) different
  levels of adhesion to wheels on different sides ($\mu$ split) must be utilized, and
– There must be a visual warning system
  to indicate electrical faults.

Only minimum standards are in force for
trailer ABS. The ABS on tractor and trailer
should be mutually compatible in order to
ensure safety and prevent excessive tire
wear.

**Tractor vehicles and trailers with
compressed-air braking systems**

The compressed-air connections must be
of the dual- or multi-line design. When the
service brakes on the tractor unit are operated, the service brakes on the trailer
must also be operated with a variable degree of force. If any fault occurs on the
service brakes of the tractor unit, that part
of the system not affected by the fault
must be capable of braking the trailer with
a variable degree of force. If one of the
lines between tractor unit and trailer is interrupted or develops a leak, it must still
be possible to brake the trailer, or it must
brake automatically.

The braking efficiency of the vehicle
when fully loaded (and when empty for
vehicles without ABS) is specified according to the pressure at the brake-line coupling head. The service-brake system of
the trailer may only be capable of operating in conjunction with the service, secondary braking or parking brake system
on the tractor vehicle.

# Design and components
of a braking system

### Basic components

A braking system consists of (Figure A):

– Energy supply,
– Control device,
– Transmission device for controling brak-
  ing force and activating the engine and
  parking brakes and retarder,
– Auxiliary devices in the tractor vehicle
  for braking a trailer,
– Wheel brakes.

Each of these components affects the
braking forces which are decisive for determining the braking factor of the vehicle
or road train.

Different applications for different vehicle types result in a wide variety of demands placed on braking systems. The
unavoidable result is a multiplicity of
highly diversified braking systems, differing from one another in both design and
application.

### Purpose

Legal regulations stipulate that the braking system on a heavy commercial vehicle must consist of:

– service-braking system,
– secondary braking system,
– parking braking system, and (in some
  cases)
– additional retarding braking system, and
– automatic braking system.

The service and parking braking systems
are equipped with separate, individual
control and transmission devices. The
service braking systems are generally applied with the foot, while the parking braking system can be actuated by either
hand or foot. The secondary braking system frequently shares components with
the service or parking braking systems.
For instance, one circuit in a dual-circuit
service-braking system may also function
as a secondary braking system. The additional retarding braking system acts as
a supplementary, wear-free braking device which relieves the load on the service
brakes, particularly when braking on
downhill gradients (see P. 846).

Automatic braking systems apply to trailers only.

**Type of energy and transmission media**
Depending on the type of energy applied to control the braking system, a distinction is made between:
– muscular-energy braking systems,
– energy-assisted braking systems,
– non-muscular-energy braking systems, and
– inertia braking systems.

The various systems can also be installed in combination. In contrast to the non-muscular-energy braking system, for instance, the energy-assisted braking system also depends to some degree on the force exerted on the pedal.

Energy-assisted and non-muscular-energy braking systems are distinguished not only by energy type, but also by the mediums used to transmit the energy. Pneumatic (vacuum, compressed air), hydraulic, and electrical energy may be used to activate the wheel brakes.

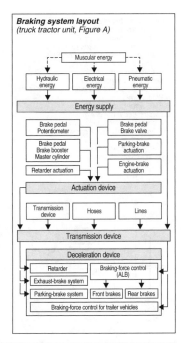

*Braking system layout*
*(truck tractor unit, Figure A)*

---

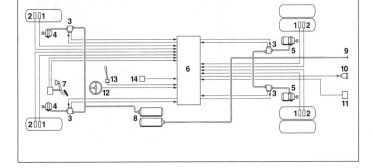

*Electronic/compressed-air braking system for two-axle truck tractor unit (Figure B)*
1 Wheel-speed sensor, 2 Brake-pad wear sensor, 3 Control valve, 4 Front-wheel cylinder,
5 Rear-wheel cylinder, 6 ECU, 7 Brake pedal, 8 Compressed-air cylinder, 9 Compressed-air
supply to trailer, 10 Trailer control line, 11 Coupling-force sensor, 12 Steering-wheel angle sensor,
13 Control for retarder and engine-braking system, 14 Yaw-rate/lateral-acceleration sensor.

*Comparison between hybrid and
fully electronic (full "brake-by-wire")
braking systems (Figure C)*
a) Electrohydraulic Brakes (EHB),
b) Electromechanical brake (EMB).
1 Hydraulic line with back-up,
2 Actuating unit with hydraulic
pedal-travel simulator,
3 Hydraulic pipe without backup,
4 Wheel brake,
5 EMB wheel modules,
6 Electric pedal-travel simulator,
7 Electrical-system management.
FW Front wheels, RW Rear wheels.

———— Supply,
– – – – Signal path.

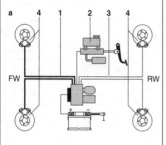

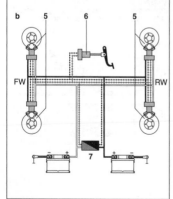

*Electromechanical brake (EMB) for full
"brake-by-wire" systems (Figure D)*

### Type of transmission device

The means employed to transmit energy within the braking system may be mechanical, hydraulic, pneumatic, or electric/electronic. Hybrid combinations may also be used to transfer the force to the wheel brakes. Electric/electronic transmission mechanisms (Figure B) are becoming increasingly important, particularly in electronic-pneumatic and electronic-hydraulic braking systems.

In fully electronic braking systems, the wheel brakes are controlled electronically and actuated by electric motors. The activities involved to make these braking systems meet the requirements demanded of them are in full swing. The first vehicles equipped with prototypes of electrically/electronically actuated wheel brakes are already undergoing trials (Figure D).

As soon as these braking systems are ready for production, they will truly deserve the term "full brake-by-wire" systems as they will only make minimal use of hydraulics and pneumatics as a media for force transmission. This is demonstrated by the comparison between hybrid braking systems and fully electronic braking systems in Figure C.

# Braking-system design

The braking system is designed with reference to both the requirements of the vehicle and the intrinsic imperatives of the system itself. In the case of the <u>vehicle-oriented design</u>, the vehicle's center of gravity and the specified distribution of braking force to the front and rear axles, determine the amount of braking force which can be applied before the wheels lock at any specific coefficient of friction between tire and road surface. The braking-force distribution diagram is used to illustrate this relationship. The coordinate axes show the braking force at front and rear axles relative to weight. The intersection of the straight lines representing equal friction coefficients at front and rear axles form the parabola defining "ideal" braking-force distribution. Lines representing constant braking complete the diagram.

If no braking-force apportioning valve is fitted, then the distribution of the braking force as installed in the unit also forms a straight line. The slope is the ratio of the braking forces at front and rear axles as determined by the dimensions of the wheel brakes. The wheels will always lock on the front axle first as long as the line for as-installed distribution remains below the ideal distribution (stable distribution of braking forces). The point at which the front wheels lock is found at the intersection of "as-installed distribution" and the lines representing the respective coefficient of friction.

The essential vehicle-related design criteria are:
- regulations governing minimum retardation required before the onset of lock, and locking sequence,
- distribution of load weight,
- influence of fading,
- engine braking torque,
- failure of a brake circuit,
- braking-force apportioning valve (if fitted),
- retarder (if fitted).

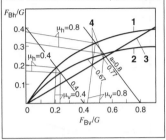

*Distribution of braking force without apportioning valve*
Ideal distribution of braking force at 1 for permissible total weight; 2 For curb weight, with driver; 3 Braking-force distribution as installed; 4 Front brakes locked. $F_{Bh}$ Rear braking force $F_{Bv}$ Front braking force, $G$ Weight, $a$ Braking factor Friction coefficients: rear $\mu_{HFH}$, front $\mu_{HFV}$.

<u>System-oriented design</u> concentrates on the dimensions for the wheel brakes and on the control devices.

Design criteria for the wheel brakes:
- brake type (disc or drum),
- durability (resistance to wear and severe use),
- space available for installation,
- acceptable pressure levels,
- rigidity (on hydraulic-actuated brakes: volume of brake fluid required for actuation).

Design criteria for the control device:
- Pedal travel and pedal force for normal braking, emergency braking, and in the event of failure of a brake circuit or the brake booster,
- comfort requirements,
- installation space,
- combination with systems for braking-force metering.

*Brake-circuit configuration: Variants*
*a) II distribution, b) X distribution,*
*c) HI distribution, d) LL distribution,*
*e) HH distribution.*
*1 Brake circuit 1, 2 Brake circuit 2.*
*← Direction of travel*

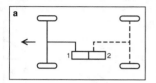

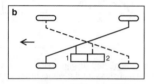

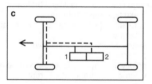

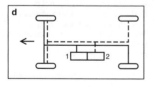

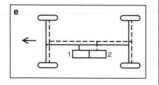

# Brake-circuit configurations

Legal regulations stipulate a dual-circuit transmission system as mandatory.

Of the five available options (DIN 74 000, see below), versions II and X have become standard. As the brake lines, hoses, connections, and static and dynamic seals remain at a low level of complication, the probability of failure due to leaks is comparable to that achieved with a single-circuit braking system. The potential response to failure of a circuit due to thermal overload in one hydraulic-actuated wheel identifies a serious weakness in the HI, LL and HH distribution patterns, where loss of both brake circuits on a wheel could lead to total brake-system failure.

Vehicles with a forward weight bias use distribution pattern X to fulfill the legal requirements with respect to secondary braking effect. The II distribution pattern is an excellent solution for vehicles with rear weight bias and mid-range and heavy-duty commercial vehicles.

II distribution pattern
Front-axle/rear-axle split. One circuit brakes the front axle and the other the rear axle.

X distribution pattern
Diagonal distribution pattern. Each circuit brakes a given front wheel and the diagonally opposite rear wheel.

HI distribution pattern
Front-axle and rear-axle/front-axle split. One circuit brakes the front and rear axles, and one circuit brakes only the front axle.

LL distribution pattern
Front-axle and rear-wheel/front-axle and rear-wheel split. Each circuit brakes the front axle and one rear wheel.

HH distribution pattern
Front-axle and rear-axle/front-axle and rear-axle split. Each circuit brakes the front axle and the rear axle.

# Braking systems for passenger cars and light utility vehicles

## Components

### Control devices

The control device consists of:
- brake pedal
- vacuum brake booster
- master cylinder
- brake-fluid reservoir
- warning systems for the failure of a brake circuit and the loss of brake fluid

In addition to the basic equipment listed above, hydraulic boosters or hydraulic non-muscular-energy braking systems may be used in certain applications. In non-muscular-energy braking systems, the brake booster and master cylinder are replaced by a brake valve. The force at the pedal is controlled to achieve the desired braking pressure. High-pressure pumps and accumulators are included to generate and store the requisite energy.

### Vacuum-operated brake booster

A vacuum brake booster is generally used due to its inexpensive and uncomplicated design. On this type of booster, the force applied at the pedal controls the pressure of outside air which is applied to a diaphragm, while vacuum remains present on the diaphragm's other side. The pres-

sure differential at the diaphragm generates force to supplement the force applied to the pedal. The simplified diagram provides a schematic illustration of the main factors which influence braking pressure; working losses and efficiency levels are not considered:
- pedal conversion
- boost factor
- diaphragm surface area
- vacuum level
- surface area of master cylinder

The braking pressure is the result of a combination of pedal force and power assistance. The proportion represented by the power assistance increases steadily up to full boost; the designed boost factor

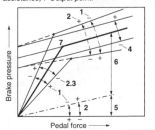

*Vacuum-operated brake booster*
Effect of design parameters.
1 Master-cylinder surface area, 2 Pedal leverage, 3 Boost factor, pedal leverage, 4 Diaphragm surface area, vacuum level, 5 Effect of pedal force, 6 Effect of power assistance, 7 Output point.

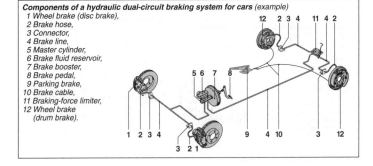

***Components of a hydraulic dual-circuit braking system for cars*** (example)
1 Wheel brake (disc brake),
2 Brake hose,
3 Connector,
4 Brake line,
5 Master cylinder,
6 Brake fluid reservoir,
7 Brake booster,
8 Brake pedal,
9 Parking brake,
10 Brake cable,
11 Braking-force limiter,
12 Wheel brake (drum brake).

determines the precise rate. At full boost, the maximum pressure differential between outside air and vacuum has been reached. Additional augmentation of the output force is only possible via an unaccustomed increase in the force applied at the pedal. Thus it is important that the booster be designed to ensure that high rates of deceleration can be achieved without exceeding full boost to any appreciable degree. The major determinant for output force is the surface area of the diaphragm. Two diaphragms in tandem are employed to meet higher pressure requirements. Technical considerations limit the maximum feasible diaphragm diameter to approx. 250 mm. The maximum negative pressure, as obtained at the intake manifold of a spark-ignition engine with the

throttle closed, is approx. 0.8 bar. A vacuum pump is required on diesel engines.

As the demand for boost pressure in heavy-duty vehicles is characteristically greater, the logical choice is a hydraulic booster, which can be designed to function on the same principles.

The energy is frequently provided by the power-steering pump, with an intermediate hydraulic accumulator incorporated in the circuit to reduce the tendency of the brakes and steering to influence each other.

### Master cylinder

A push rod carries the output force directly to the piston in the tandem master cylinder. The hydraulic pressure thus generated is transmitted to the "floating" intermediate piston, resulting in roughly equal pressures in the two chambers which supply the respective circuits.

Failure in one of the brake circuits can have one of two results: Either the push rod comes up against the intermediate piston, or hydraulic force presses the intermediate piston back against the base of the master cylinder. This condition will be felt at the pedal, which will continue moving with virtually no resistance.

A master cylinder which responds in several stages has proven a useful expedient on vehicles with the II distribution pattern. The intermediate piston, which has a smaller diameter than the push-rod piston, applies pressure to the rear-axle circuit. The system responds to failure in the front-axle circuit by increasing the pressure which is transmitted to the rear circuit at a constant pedal pressure.

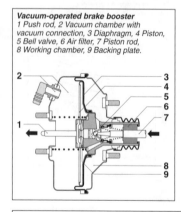

*Vacuum-operated brake booster*
1 Push rod, 2 Vacuum chamber with vacuum connection, 3 Diaphragm, 4 Piston, 5 Bell valve, 6 Air filter, 7 Piston rod, 8 Working chamber, 9 Backing plate.

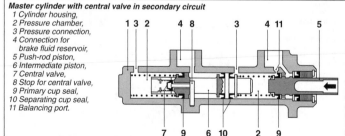

*Master cylinder with central valve in secondary circuit*
1 Cylinder housing,
2 Pressure chamber,
3 Pressure connection,
4 Connection for brake fluid reservoir,
5 Push-rod piston,
6 Intermediate piston,
7 Central valve,
8 Stop for central valve,
9 Primary cup seal,
10 Separating cup seal,
11 Balancing port.

A brake-fluid reservoir is connected to the master cylinder to compensate for the effects of brake-lining wear and leakage. When the brake is released, either a centrally positioned valve in the master-cylinder piston opens or the piston seal opens a balancing port. This ensures that the brakes are not under pressure when released and also provides compensation for brake-fluid losses. The disadvantage of this straightforward arrangement is that, if vapor bubbles form within the brake fluid due to thermal overload, the brake circuit affected empties when the brake is released. This could make it impossible to build up pressure when the brakes are applied again.

In order to prevent complete drainage in the event of a major leak, the brake-fluid reservoir is designed (at least as from a given brake-fluid level) with two circuits. One or two float-actuated switches trigger an optical display once the fluid falls below a certain level. The float-actuated switches can be replaced by differential pressure switches on the master cylinder to indicate a failure of a brake circuit.

**Wheel brakes**
The wheel brakes must meet the following requirements:
– uniform effectiveness
– smooth, graduated response
– resistance to contamination and corrosion
– extreme reliability
– durability
– resistance to wear
– ease of maintenance

Whereas, on small cars and commercial vehicles, various types of drum brake fulfill the essential demands satisfactorily, disc brakes represent the only means of achieving even response and good control on heavy cars capable of high speeds.

Gray cast-iron brake discs with bilaterally acting calipers have proven to be the most satisfactory layout. The brake disc is usually located within the well of the wheel disc. This arrangement makes it necessary to provide for adequate heat dissipation through radiation, convection and thermal conductance. Additional expedients such as internally ventilated brake discs, air

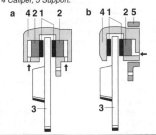

*Disc brakes*
a) Fixed caliper, b) Floating caliper.
1 Friction pads, 2 Piston, 3 Brake disc,
4 Caliper, 5 Support.

ducts and optimized-flow wheel designs are employed to reduce disc temperatures, particularly on high-performance vehicles.

Brake calipers fall into one of two categories: fixed calipers or floating calipers.

In the case of the fixed caliper, the housing is rigid and "grips" the brake disc from both sides. When the brakes are applied, two pistons in the caliper housing, one on each side of the brake disc, force the brake pads up against the brake disc.

Two basic subcategories of floating caliper have established themselves:
The sliding caliper and the so-called Mark II caliper. With both designs, the piston or pistons act directly against the brake pad on the inner side of the disc. The sliding-caliper frame or the caliper then pulls the outer pad against the disc. Compared to fixed calipers, the floating units offer the following advantages:
– Modest space requirement between brake disc and wheel nave (convenient where suspension employs small or negative steering offset).
– Reduced thermal stress on the fluid, as no fluid lines are located in the critical area directly above the brake disc.

Constructive measures effectively alleviate inherent disadvantages (tendency to rattle and squeak, uneven wear of brake pads or linings, corrosion in transmission elements).

## Braking-force apportioning valve

The braking-force apportioning valve is not a closed-loop control element, like the brake-pressure regulating valve as used for ABS, but rather an open-loop control element. The individual apportioning valves have different functions, depending whether they are acting as braking-force limiters or reducers, or different control parameters, such as braking pressure, axle load or rate of deceleration.

The braking force is apportioned between the front and rear axles in accordance with the dimensions of the particular wheel brakes. It is the job of the apportioning valve to adjust this braking-force apportionment in order to achieve a closer approximation to the ideal distribution, i.e., the parabolic curve. The ideal braking-force distribution is determined solely by the vehicle's center of gravity and the nature of the particular braking maneuver. These relationships can be shown in a dimensionless braking-force distribution diagram. The weight-related braking forces at the front and rear axles are entered on the coordinate axes. The lines for identical braking appear as straight lines with a negative slope (–1). The ideal braking-force distribution curves for the vehicle conditions "curb weight" and "permissible total weight" are in the form of parabolas. Diagram "a" is for a braking-force limiter and diagram "b" for a braking-force reducer.

Pressure-sensitive apportioning valves achieve good approximation of ideal distribution with the vehicle in the "curb weight" state. On the other hand, under "permissible total weight" conditions (upper parabola), they deviate from the ideal once the limiter or reducer becomes operative (bend in the curve), i.e. the proportion of the total braking force directed toward the rear axle decreases as the rear-axle load increases.

The load-sensitive apportioning valve responds to increased loads by displacing the triggering point upward, allowing a reasonable approximation of ideal braking-force distribution under all load conditions.

The deceleration-sensitive apportioning valve is triggered by a specific rate of deceleration, and is thus basically insensitive to load. The apportioning valve must be designed to ensure that braking-force distribution remains on or below the

*Braking-force distribution diagram*
a) Braking-force limiter,
b) Braking-force reducer.
$F_{Bh}$ Rear braking force,
$F_{Bv}$ Front braking force, G Weight.
1 Laden, 2 Unladen, 3 Laden, load-sensitive,
4 Unladen, pressure-sensitive; unladen,
deceleration-sensitive and laden; unladen,
load-sensitive, 5 Laden, pressure-sensitive.

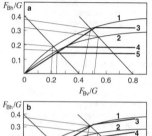

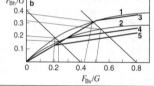

ideal curve. The potential effects of fluctuations of the pad/lining friction coefficient, as well as of engine braking torque and tolerances of the valve itself, must all be considered in preventing overbraking of the rear axle. In practice, this means that actual installed distribution (with bend in curve) should remain well below the ideal.

The criteria according to which the apportioning valve is designed include the following:
– ABS compatibility
– Complexity in split-circuit braking systems, in which each rear wheel is served by a separate circuit (e.g. diagonally split circuits (X distribution))
– Bypass function for dealing with brake-circuit failure, especially with braking-force limiters
– Facility for testing correct setting and function

Vehicles with balanced load conditions are not necessarily equipped with an apportioning valve, as the disadvantages of an undetected defect in the apportioning valve outweigh its minimal advantages.

# Vehicle stabilization systems for passenger cars

Volume-production antilock braking systems (ABS) have been in use since the end of 1978. They are now firmly established as safety systems. In Europe and North America, the equipment rates for ABS (fitting to all new vehicles) are around 80%; worldwide they are roughly 70%. In some countries, it has virtually become standard. As a result of a voluntary obligation, ABS will become standard equipment on cars in Europe as of 2004.

Bosch produced its 100 millionth system in 2003, 25 years after ABS was first introduced.

The Electronic Stability Program (ESP) went into volume production in 1995. In Europe, it has rapidly gained a foothold. The total number of Bosch systems produced exceeded the 10-million mark in 2003.

The graph below illustrates the gradual reduction in weight and size of ABS systems from 1978 to 2003.

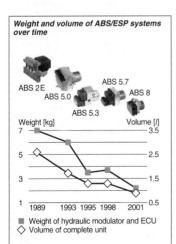

**Weight and volume of ABS/ESP systems over time**

ABS 2E
ABS 5.0
ABS 5.3
ABS 5.7
ABS 8

| Weight [kg] | | | | | Volume [*l*] |
| 7 | | | | | 3.5 |
| 5 | | | | | 2.5 |
| 3 | | | | | 1.5 |
| 1 | 1989 | 1993 | 1995 | 1998 | 2001 | 0.5 |

■ Weight of hydraulic modulator and ECU
◇ Volume of complete unit

## Antilock braking systems (ABS)

### Function

Antilock braking systems (ABS) are braking-system closed-loop control devices which prevent wheel lock when braking and, as a result, retain the vehicle's steerability and stability. In general, they also shorten braking distances compared with braking scenarios when the wheels lock completely. This is particularly the case on wet roads. The reduction in braking distance may be 10% or several times this figure, depending on how wet the conditions are and the road/tire friction coefficient.

Under certain very specific road-surface conditions, braking distances may be longer, but the vehicle still retains vehicle stability and steerability.

### Requirements

The requirements placed on an ABS system are described in the ECE Regulation 13. This regulation defines ABS as a component of a service-brake system which automatically controls wheel slip in the direction of wheel rotation on one or more wheels when braked.

ECE Regulation 13 Annex 13 defines three categories. The present generation of ABS meets the highest level of requirements (Category 1).

### Operating concept

A 2/2-way solenoid valve (inlet valve) with two hydraulic connections and two switching positions is fitted between the master cylinder and the wheel-brake cylinder of a conventional braking system (see figure overleaf). When the valve is open (normal setting for standard braking action), braking pressure can be generated in the wheel-brake cylinder. The outlet valve, also a 2/2-way solenoid valve, is closed at this point.

If the wheel-speed sensor detects an abrupt deceleration of the wheel (risk of wheel lock), the system prevents any further increase of braking pressure at the wheel concerned. The inlet and outlet valves are closed, and the braking pressure remains constant.

If the wheel deceleration rate continues to increase, the outlet valve has to be open to reduce braking pressure. The escaping brake fluid is then pumped back to the master cylinder by the return pump. The pressure in the wheel-brake cylinder then drops and the wheel is braked less heavily.

*Design of ABS*
*1 Master cylinder, 2 Wheel-brake cylinder, 3 Hydraulic modulator, 4 Pulsation-damping features, 5 Flow restrictor, 6 Return pump, 7 Inlet valve, 8 Outlet valve, 9 Accumulator.*

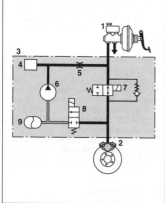

In earlier ABS systems, a 3/3-way solenoid valve was used instead of the 2/2-way solenoid valves. The three hydraulic connections and three switching positions of the valve also allows the system to perform the three functions of pressure rise, pressure retention and pressure drop.

### ABS system variants

A variety of versions are available depending upon the brake-circuit configuration (see P. 804), the vehicle's drivetrain configuration, functional requirements and cost considerations. The most common braking-force distribution is the diagonal split (X brake-circuit configuration), followed by the front-rear split (II brake-circuit configuration). The HI and HH brake-circuit configurations (e.g. in the DaimlerChrysler Maybach) are specialized applications and are rarely used in combination with ABS.

The ABS system variants are distinguished according to the number of control channels and wheel-speed sensors.

<u>4-channel/4-sensor systems</u>
These systems (see figure, Variants 1 and 2) allow individual control of the braking pressure at each wheel by the four hydraulic channels, with the brake circuits split front/rear (for type-II brake-circuit configuration) or diagonally (for type-X brake-circuit configuration). Each wheel has its own wheel-speed sensor to monitor wheel speed.

*ABS system variants*
▨ *Control channel,* ◀ *Sensor,* ◁ *Sensor (alternative to differential sensor).*

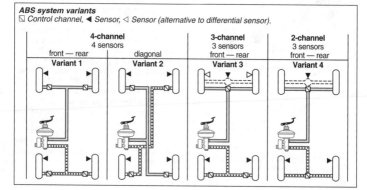

|  | 4-channel 4 sensors |  | 3-channel 3 sensors | 2-channel 3 sensors |
|---|---|---|---|---|
|  | front — rear | diagonal | front — rear | front — rear |
|  | Variant 1 | Variant 2 | Variant 3 | Variant 4 |

A much simplified ABS variant was developed for a particular section of the Japanese car market, the "midget" segment (small cars with engines < 660 cm³). It did away with damping chambers and return pumps/pump motors. The smaller number of components compared with conventional systems offers considerable cost savings but also involves significant functional tradeoffs. This type of system is now being phased out.

3-channel/3-sensor systems (Variant 3)
Instead of the familiar arrangement with a separate speed sensor on each wheel, the rear wheels with this variant share a single sensor which is fitted in the differential. Due to the characteristics of the differential, it allows the measurement of wheel-speed differences with certain restrictions. Due to the select-low control characteristic for the rear wheels, i.e. parallel connection of the two rear-wheel brakes, a single hydraulic channel is sufficient for (parallel) control of the rear braking pressures.

Hydraulic 3-channel systems require a type-II brake-circuit configuration (front/rear split).

3-sensor systems can only be used on vehicles with rear-wheel drive, i.e. primarily small commercial vehicles and light trucks. The number of vehicles fitted with such systems is generally dropping off.

2-channel/1 or 2-sensor systems
Two-channel systems were produced because of the smaller number of components required and the resulting potential for cost savings. Their popularity was limited as their functionality does not match that of "full-fledged" systems. These systems are now hardly ever used in cars.

Some light trucks sold on the American market with front/rear-split brake circuits are (still) fitted with RWAL systems (Rear wheel anti lock brake system) – special simplified versions of the 2-channel system consisting of a sensor on the rear-axle differential and a single control channel (with no return pump) which prevents the rear wheels from locking. If sufficiently high braking pressure is applied, the front wheels may still lock, i.e. loss of steerability under certain conditions is an accepted risk. This arrangement does not meet the functional requirements expected of a Category 1 ABS system, as mentioned at the start of this section.

Use of ABS on motorcycles
It has been possible to reduce the size and weight of car ABS systems substantially over recent years. As a result, volume-production ABS systems are now a very attractive option for motorcycles. Relatively widespread introduction can be expected. Consequently, this class of vehicle will also be able to benefit from the advantages of ABS as a safety system.

The car system is modified for use on motorcycles. Instead of the usual eight 2/2-way valves in the hydraulic modulator for cars (with X-configuration brake circuits), motorcycles normally only require four valves. The control algorithm also differs fundamentally from that of a car ABS system.

Other system variants have arisen from the demand for combined brake systems (CBS), i.e. systems in which both the front and rear brakes can be operated either by a foot pedal or a hand-operated lever, possibly in combination with a separate means of actuating the front brakes. This type of special case requires a 3-channel hydraulic modulator. However, the CBS variant is very model-specific in design.

### Basic closed-loop control process

#### Control processes

On initial braking, braking pressure increases; brake slip $\lambda$ rises and at the maximum point on the adhesion/slip curve, it reaches the limit between the stable and unstable ranges. From this point on, any further increase in braking pressure or braking torque does not cause any further increase in braking force $F_B$. In the stable range, brake slip is largely skidding, it increasingly tends to slipping in the unstable range.

Brake slip $\lambda = (v_F - v_R)/v_F \cdot 100\%$
Wheel speed $v_R = r \cdot \omega$
Braking force $F_B = \mu_{HF} \cdot G$
Side force $F_S = \mu_S \cdot G$
$\mu_{HF}$ Coefficient of friction,
$\mu_S$ Lateral-force coefficient.

There is a more or less sharp drop in the coefficient of friction $\mu_{HF}$, depending on the shape of the slip curve. Without ABS, the resulting excess torque causes the wheel to lock very quickly when braked and is evidenced by a sharp increase in wheel deceleration.

The wheel-speed sensor senses the state of motion of the wheel. If one of the wheels shows signs of incipient lock, there is a sharp rise in peripheral wheel deceleration and in wheel slip. If these exceed defined critical levels, the ABS controller sends commands to the solenoid-valve unit (hydraulic modulator, see P. 815) to

stop increasing or to reduce wheel brake pressure until the danger of wheel lock is averted. The braking pressure must then rise again to ensure that the wheel is not underbraked. During automatic brake control, the stability or instability of wheel motion must be detected constantly, and kept within the slip range at maximum braking force by a sequence of pressure-rise, pressure-retention and pressure-drop phases.

With reference to the front wheels, this control sequence is performed individually, i.e. separately and independently for each wheel.

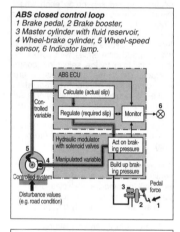

**ABS closed control loop**
1 Brake pedal, 2 Brake booster,
3 Master cylinder with fluid reservoir,
4 Wheel-brake cylinder, 5 Wheel-speed sensor, 6 Indicator lamp.

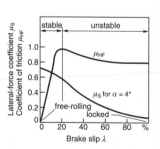

**Adhesion/slip curve**
The curve shape differs greatly as a function of road surface and tire condition.

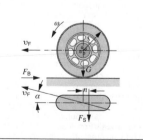

**Forces at the braked wheel**
$G$ Gravitational force, $F_B$ Braking force, $F_S$ Side force, $v_F$ Vehicle speed, $n$ Caster, $\alpha$ Slip angle, $\omega$ Angular velocity.

For reasons of handling stability, a different control strategy is required for the rear wheels. In order to be able to maintain lateral acceleration, and therefore transverse forces, on the rear wheels at full braking power when cornering, an increase in the lateral friction coefficients of the tires is required. Therefore, the slip levels of the rear wheels must be kept low, particularly the wheel on the outside of the bend. This is achieved by the select-low control characteristic for the rear wheels. That means that the rear wheel which first shows signs of incipient locking, i.e. the "low" wheel, determines the control sequence. In a 3-channel configuration for a braking system with a front/rear split, this is achieved by connecting the hydraulic circuits in parallel. On diagonally split brake circuits, however, this is attained by controling the rear-wheel valves with parallel logic.

Disturbances in the closed control loop
The ABS system must take the following disturbances into account:
– Changes in the adhesion between the tires and the road surface caused by different types of road surface and changes in wheel load, e.g. when cornering.

– Irregularities in the road surface causing the wheels and axles to vibrate.
– Out-of-roundness, brake hysteresis, brake fading.
– Variations in the pressure input to the master cylinder caused by the driver's depressing the brake pedal.
– Differences in wheel circumferences, for instance when the spare wheel is fitted.

Criteria of control quality
The following criteria for control quality must be fulfilled by efficient antilock braking systems:
– Maintain directional stability by providing sufficient lateral forces at the rear wheels.
– Maintain steerability by providing sufficient lateral forces at the front wheels.
– Reduce the stopping distance as opposed to braking with locked wheels by optimizing adhesion between tires and the road surface.
– Adapt braking pressure rapidly to different friction coefficients, for instance when driving through puddles or over patches of ice or hard snow.
– Insure low braking-torque control amplitudes to prevent vibrations in the suspension.
– Achieve a high level of comfort by using silent actuators and slight feedback through the brake pedal.

Typical control cycle
The depicted control cycle shows automatic brake control in the case of a high friction coefficient. The change in wheel speed (braking deceleration) is calculated in the ECU. After the value falls below the $(-a)$ threshold, the hydraulic modulator valve unit is switched to pressure-holding mode. If the wheel speed then also drops below the slip-switching threshold $\lambda_1$, the valve unit is switched to pressure drop; this continues as long as the $(-a)$ signal is applied. During the following pressure-holding phase, peripheral wheel acceleration increases until the $(+a)$ threshold is exceeded; the braking pressure is then kept at a constant level.

After the relatively high $(+A)$ threshold has been exceeded, the braking pressure is increased, so that the wheel is not accelerating excessively as it enters the sta-

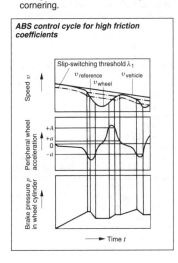

**ABS control cycle for high friction coefficients**

Slip-switching threshold $\lambda_1$

$v$ reference    $v$ vehicle

$v$ wheel

Speed $v$

Peripheral wheel acceleration: $+A$, $+a$, $0$, $-a$

Brake pressure $p$ in wheel cylinder

⟶ Time $t$

ble range of the adhesion/slip curve. After the $(+a)$ signal has dropped off, the braking pressure is slowly raised until, when the wheel acceleration again falls below the $(-a)$ threshold, the second control cycle is initiated, this time with an immediate pressure drop.

In the first control cycle, a short pressure-holding phase is necessary initially to filter out any faults. In the case of high wheel moments of inertia, low friction coefficient and slow pressure rise in the wheel-brake cylinder (cautious initial braking, e.g., on black ice), the wheel might lock

---

*Yaw-moment buildup induced by large differences in friction coefficients*
$M_{yaw}$ Yaw moment, $F_B$ Braking force,
$\mu_{HF}$ Coefficient of friction,
1 "High" wheel, 2 "Low" wheel.

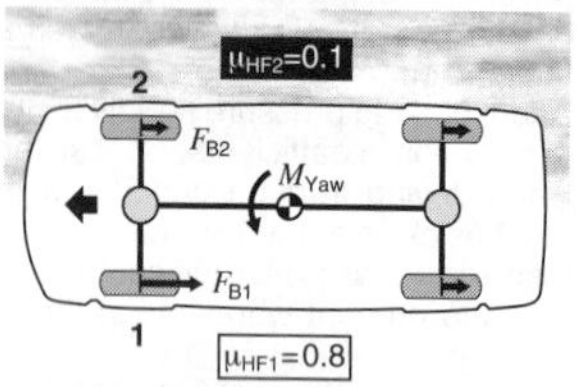

---

*Curves for braking pressure/steering-angle characteristic with yaw-moment buildup delay (GMA)*
1 Master-cylinder pressure $p_{MC}$,
2 Braking pressure $p_{high}$ w/o GMA,
3 $p_{high}$ with GMA 1, 4 $p_{high}$ with GMA 2,
5 $p_{low}$ at "low" wheel, 6 Steering angle $\alpha$ w/o GMA, 7 Steering angle $\alpha$ with GMA.

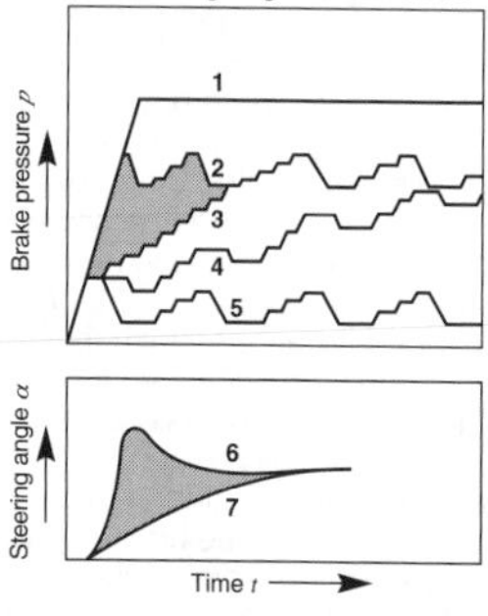

---

without any response from the deceleration switching threshold. In this case, therefore, the wheel slip is also included as a parameter in the brake control system.

Under certain road-surface conditions, passenger cars with all-wheel drive and with differential locks engaged pose problems when the ABS system is in operation; this calls for special measures to support the reference speed during the control process, lower the wheel-deceleration thresholds, and reduce the engine-drag torque.

Braking control with yaw-moment buildup delay (GMA)
When the brakes are applied on a road surface with uneven grip (for instance, left-hand wheels on dry asphalt, right-hand wheels on ice), vastly different braking forces at the front wheels result and induce a turning force (yaw moment) about the vehicle's vertical axis.

On smaller cars, ABS must be supplemented by an additional yaw-moment buildup delay device (GMA) to ensure that control is maintained during panic braking on asymmetrical road surfaces. GMA delays the pressure rise in the wheel-brake cylinder on the front wheel with the higher coefficient of friction at the road surface ("high" wheel).

The GMA concept is demonstrated in the diagram: Curve 1 represents the master-cylinder pressure $p_{MC}$. Without GMA, the braking pressure at the wheel running on asphalt quickly reaches $p_{high}$ (Curve 2), while the braking pressure at the wheel running on ice rises only to $p_{low}$ (Curve 5); each wheel brakes with the maximum transferrable braking force (individual control).

The GMA 1 System (Curve 3) is designed for use on vehicles with a less critical handling characteristics, while GMA 2 is designed for cars which display an especially marked tendency toward yaw-induced instability (Curve 4).

In all cases in which GMA comes into effect, the "high" wheel is under-braked at first. This means that the GMA must always be very carefully adapted to the vehicle in question in order to limit increases in stopping distances.

### ABS version (as at 2003)

#### Hydraulic modulator

The development of solenoid valves with two hydraulic switching positions (2/2-way valves, used in Bosch ABS systems from the ABS 5 generation onwards) allowed a complete redesign of ABS as compared with the ABS 2S/ABS 2E version which used 3/3-way valves. This rationalized design and manufacture radically. However, the basic hydraulic concept of ABS has not changed since volume production was first launched in 1978. It means that the sealed brake circuits and the return principle are unchanged.

The main hydraulic components of the hydraulic modulator are the following:
– One return pump per brake circuit
– Accumulator chamber
– Damping functions, previously performed by an accumulator chamber and a flow restrictor, are now performed both hydraulically and by control systems, i.e. software
– 2/2-way solenoid valves with two hydraulic positions and two hydraulic connections

There is one pair of solenoid valves for each wheel (except in the case of 3-channel configurations with front/rear brake-circuit split) – one of which is open when de-energized for pressure rise (inlet valve, IV) and one which is closed when de-energized for pressure drop (outlet valve, OV). In order to achieve rapid pressure relief of the wheel brakes when the pedal is released, the inlet valves each have a non-return valve which is integrated in the valve body (e.g. non-return valve sleeves or unsprung non-return valves).

The assignment of pressure-rise and pressure-drop functions to separate solenoid valves with only one active (energized) setting has resulted in compact valve designs, i.e. smaller size and weight as well as lower magnetic forces compared with the previous 3/3-way solenoid valves. This allows optimized electrical control with low electrical power loss in the solenoid coils and the control unit. In addition, the valve block can be made smaller. This results in quite significant savings in weight and size.

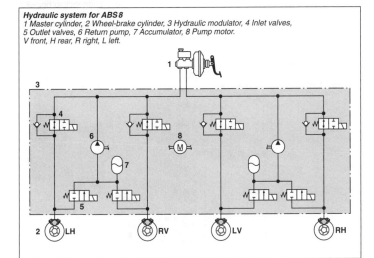

*Hydraulic system for ABS 8*
*1 Master cylinder, 2 Wheel-brake cylinder, 3 Hydraulic modulator, 4 Inlet valves,*
*5 Outlet valves, 6 Return pump, 7 Accumulator, 8 Pump motor.*
*V front, H rear, R right, L left.*

The 2/2-way solenoid valves are available in a variety of designs and specifications, and, because of their compact dimensions and excellent dynamics, they allow fast electrical switching times sufficient for pulse-width-modulated cyclic operation. In other words, they have "proportional-valve characteristics".

The ABS 8 benefits from current-signal-modulated valve control which substantially improves function (e.g. adaptation to changes in coefficient of friction) and ease of control (e.g. smaller deceleration fluctuations with the aid of pressure stages and analog pressure control). This mechatronic optimization has positive effects not only on function but also on user-friendliness, i.e. noise and pedal feedback.

ABS 8 is capable of specific adaptation to individual vehicle-class requirements by varying the components (e.g. using motors of different power ratings, varying accumulator chamber size, etc.). The power of the return motor can vary within a range of approx. 90...200 watts. The accumulator-chamber size is also variable.

Electronic control unit (ECU)

The progress achieved in the continuing development of ABS is primarily a factor of the enormous advances in the field of electronics. The times when an ABS ECU was made up of more than 1,000 components (ABS 1 generation of 1970, analog design) are long past. The integration of functions in LSI circuits, the use of high-performance microcomputers with structures as small as 15 μm and the use of hybrid ECU technology allows a high packing density and therefore further miniaturization. At the same time, this results in a significant increase in system performance and functionality. The use of microcontrollers has lead to substantial optimization of control algorithms incorporating customization to vehicle-manufacturer and model requirements.

The control unit is designed as an add-on ECU and is mounted directly on the hydraulic modulator. The advantage of this arrangement is that external wiring can be minimized. The wiring harness contains fewer wires. This results in a reduction in space requirements and less complicated installation. The design layout requires only a single plug-in connection between the ECU and the hydraulic modulator and for connecting up the return-pump motor.

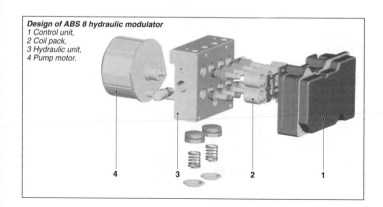

*Design of ABS 8 hydraulic modulator*
1 Control unit,
2 Coil pack,
3 Hydraulic unit,
4 Pump motor.

The ECU illustrated schematically represents a 4-channel/4-sensor version. The two microcontrollers process the control program. In ABS ECUs, they have a frequency rating of approximately 20 MHz and a ROM of around 128 KB. Memory capacities up to about 256 KB are sufficient for ABS versions with special functions.

In highly complex systems such as ESP, the ROM may be as large as < 1 MB. Depending on the required processing capacity, microcontrollers with higher timing frequencies may also be used.

The software consists of the following modules:
- the hardware-related software, i.e. the operating system
- the self-monitoring and diagnostic software
- the function-specific software, and
- the purely vehicle-manufacturer and application-specific software

Communication with other ECUs and vehicle-manufacturer-specific diagnosis takes place via a CAN.

---

**Block diagram of control unit**
1 Multifunction circuit with input circuit, speed-signal conditioning circuit, diagnostic circuit, voltage regulator, CAN, relay control circuit, etc.
2 Microcontroller 1, 3 Microcontroller 2, 4 EEPROM, 5 Output-stage module.

DS *Wheel-speed sensors*, DP *Speed-signal outputs (e.g. for instrument cluster)*, V *front*, H *rear*, R *right*, L *left*, MV *Solenoid valve*.

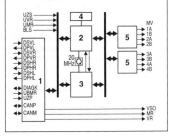

## Traction control system (TCS)

### Function and requirements

When starting off, accelerating and braking, the efficiency required to transfer forces to the road depends on the traction available between the tires and the road surface. The adhesion/slip curves for acceleration and braking have the same basic patterns (see figure on P. 812).

The vast majority of acceleration and braking operations involve only limited amounts of slip, allowing response to remain within the stable range in the diagram. Up to a certain point, any rise in slip is accompanied by a corresponding increase in useful adhesion. Beyond this point, any further increases in slip take the curves through the maxima and into the instable range where any further increase in slip generally results in a reduction in adhesion. When braking, this results in wheel lock within a few tenths of a second. When accelerating, one or both of the driven wheels start to spin more and more as the drive torque exceeds the adhesion by an ever increasing amount.

ABS responds in the first case (braking) by inhibiting wheel lock. ASR reacts to the second scenario by holding drive slip within acceptable levels to prevent wheel spin. The system actually performs two functions:
- increasing traction (electronic locking differential function), and
- maintaining vehicle stability.

These functions create the requirements demanded of TCS: It must reliably prevent wheel spin even under variable $\mu$ conditions, i.e.:
- It must prevent the driving wheels from spinning under $\mu$-split conditions and on slippery road surfaces.
- It must prevent wheel spin when the vehicle pulls out of icy parking spaces and laybys.
- It must prevent wheel spin when the vehicle accelerates in a corner.
- It must prevent wheel spin when the vehicle pulls away on a hill.
- It must improve cornering stability.

**TCS interventions**

The TCS can intervene in the following ways:

Drive-torque control (AMR): This is performed by electronic engine-performance control. Rapid intervention is achieved by blocking individual fuel-injection pulses or – on a spark-ignition engine – by retarding the ignition angle. Owing to their short duration, such methods of intervention are noncritical in terms of exhaust-gas composition and catalytic-converter load.

Slower intervention takes place on a spark-ignition engine by means of the throttle-valve actuator (electrically variable throttle valve, see P. 638). Electric throttle-valve actuators have now become standard equipment on modern engine generations.

Brake-torque control (BMR): This relates to active intervention by controled braking of the wheel that is showing incipient signs of spinning, similar to a brake-control function.

Combination of AMR and BMR: More recent systems use a combination of both methods of intervention. TCS is constantly on standby and intervenes when necessary. However, the relative proportions for applying BMR and AMR vary according to vehicle speed.

In contrast with mechanical differential locks, the tires do not scrub on tight corners. An indicator lamp on the instrument panel shows the driver when TCS is active.

A fundamental observation about this type of system (when it assumes an electronic brake-control function) is that it is not intended for continuous use on difficult offroad terrain. Since the brake-control function is achieved by braking the relevant wheel, brake heating is an inevitable consequence. The function must then be deactivated to prevent the brake from being overloaded or overheating.

In order to achieve optimized control of driven-wheel torque, the mechanical link between accelerator pedal and throttle valve on a spark-ignition engine is replaced by an electronic engine-performance control system ("EGAS" or "Electronic Throttle Control"). A pedal-travel sensor converts the position of the accelerator pedal to an electrical signal. The throttle device receives the electrical control signal via the ECU, responds by repositioning the throttle valve by means of a DC motor, and signals the new position back to the ECU. On a diesel engine, the Electronic Diesel Control (EDC) sets the engine torque in response to the accelerator-pedal position.

Brief, simultaneous activation of the wheel brakes is used to support the ETC (improved tractive performance via brake-control function).

The ABS hydraulic modulator is extended by the addition of a TCS component to provide additional hydraulic energy for intervention in the form of automatic and possibly individual brake intervention. Switchover to TCS mode allows pressure to be held or dropped to achieve rapid, precise brake-pressure modulation at the driven wheels.

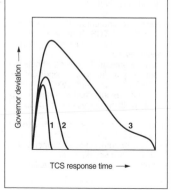

*Comparison between response times of different TCS intervention methods*
TCS using
1 Throttle-valve/brake intervention,
2 Throttle-valve/ignition intervention,
3 Throttle-valve intervention.

Governor deviation ⟶

1   2                          3

TCS response time ⟶

The ABS/TCS control unit communicates via a suitable interface (e.g. CAN) with the engine-management ECU which performs engine-torque adjustments.

Additional intervention in engine management where necessary improves the response characteristics of engine-torque control in such a way that it would not be possible to achieve using the electric throttle valve alone.

The current design of the TCS is based on the modular concept of the Generation 8. It also benefits from similar reductions in size, weight and cost. As a result, it is easily adaptable to the two most common brake-circuit configurations (II and X configurations) and drive configurations (including all-wheel drive).

As with ABS, the direct connection of the ECU to the hydraulic modulator simplifies the vehicle wiring harness and thereby reduces the number of connector contacts and leads.

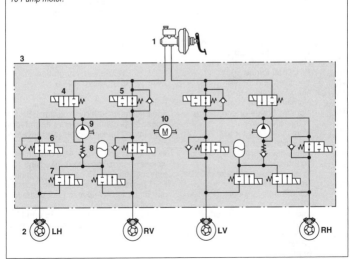

**Schematic diagram of an ABS/TCS 5 hydraulic circuit for X brake-circuit configurations**
1 Master cylinder, 2 Wheel-brake cylinder, 3 Hydraulic modulator, 4 Intake valve,
5 Changeover valve, 6 Inlet valve, 7 Outlet valves, 8 Accumulator, 9 Return pump,
10 Pump motor.

## Electronic Stability Program (ESP) for passenger cars

### Quantities and terms

| | |
|---|---|
| $a$ | Distance of front wheels from vehicle center of gravity |
| $a_x$ | Estimated vehicle longitudinal acceleration |
| $a_y$ | Measured vehicle lateral acceleration |
| $A_0, A_1, A_2$ | Parameters for calculating tire working point |
| $c$ | Distance of rear wheels from vehicle center of gravity |
| $C_p$ | Brake-torque ratio |
| $C_\lambda$ | Longitudinal tire rigidity |
| $D_T$ | Controller sampling time |
| $D_\lambda$ | Tolerance band of drive-slip difference between driven wheels |
| $F_B$ | Tire braking force |
| $F_{BF}$ | Steady-state (filtered) braking force on the tire |
| $F_N$ | Vertical tire force (normal force) |
| $F_R$ | Resultant tire force |
| $F_S$ | Lateral tire force |
| $J_{Mot}$ | Engine-drag torque |
| $J_{Whl}$ | Wheel moment of inertia |
| $K_p, K_d$, $K_i$ | Controller gains for the P, D and I components |
| $M_{Dif}$ | Desired/setpoint speed differential between the driven wheels |
| $M_{DR}$ | Driver-input engine torque |
| $M_{YwNo}$ | Vehicle yaw-moment setpoint |
| $\Delta M_{YawExp}$ | Small change in the vehicle yaw-moment setpoint |
| $M_{CaHalf}$ | Half of the propshaft torque |
| $M_{Ca}$ | Propshaft torque |
| $M_{Mot}$ | Actual engine torque |
| $M_{WhlNo}$ | Nominal braking torque |
| $M_{NoMot}$ | Nominal engine torque |
| $M_{NoLock}$ | Nominal brake-locking torque at the driven wheels |
| $M_{NoSPR}$ | Nominal engine-torque reduction by spark retard |
| $p_{Circ}$ | Brake-circuit pressure induced by the driver |
| $p_{Whl}$ | Pressure in wheel-brake cylinder |
| $p_{WhlPre}$ | Nominal pressure in wheel-brake cylinder |
| $R$ | Wheel radius |
| $T_{iOFF}$ | Injection blank-out period |
| $\ddot{U}_{Tr}$ | Transmission ratio |
| $U_{val}$ | Valve-triggering mode |
| $v_{CH}$ | Characteristic velocity of the vehicle |
| $v_{Dif}$ | Wheel-speed differential of driven wheels |
| $v_{Veh}$ | Vehicle speed |
| $v_{DS}$ | Propshaft speed |
| $v_{Whl}$ | Measured wheel speed |
| $v_{Whl3}$ | Measured wheel speed rear left |
| $v_{Whl4}$ | Measured wheel speed rear right |
| $v_{WhlFre}$ | Wheel speed (free-rolling) |
| $v_{NoDif}$ | Nominal wheel-speed difference of driven wheels |
| $v_{NoCa}$ | Nominal propshaft speed |
| $v_x$ | Vehicle linear velocity |
| $v_y$ | Vehicle lateral velocity |
| $x_1, x_2$ | Parameters of the inverse hydraulic model |
| $\alpha$ | Tire slip angle |
| $\alpha_0, \lambda_0$ | Arbitrary tire working point |
| $\beta$ | Vehicle float angle |
| $\beta_{No}$ | Nominal vehicle slip angle |
| $\delta$ | Steering-wheel angle |
| $\delta_W$ | Front-wheel steering angle |
| $\lambda$ | Tire slip |
| $\lambda_{No}$ | Nominal tire slip |
| $\lambda_{Ma}$ | Average nominal traction slip of the driven wheels |
| $\mu_{HF}$ | Coefficient of friction between tires and road |
| $\mu_{Res}$ | Resultant coefficient of friction between tire and road |
| $\dot{\psi}$ | Yaw velocity |
| $\dot{\psi}_{No}$ | Nominal yaw rate |
| m | Minimum value of the nominal driven-wheel braking torque |
| MIN | Minimum-value operator |
| SUM | Event-driven integration |
| ZWV | Spark retard (SPR) |

### Function

The Electronic Stability Program, ESP, is a closed-loop control system integrated in the vehicle's braking system and drivetrain which prevents the vehicle from breaking away to the side. While ABS prevents the wheels from locking when braked and TCS prevents the driven wheels from spinning, ESP prevents the vehicle from "pushing out" of the turn or spinning out of the turn when it is steered.

Further to the benefits of ABS and TCS, ESP improves active driving safety in the following points:

- Provides the driver with active support, even in critical lateral dynamic situations.
- Enhances directional and vehicle stability even at the vehicle's physical driving limits in all operating statuses, such as full braking, partial braking, coasting, accelerating, engine drag, and load changes.
- Enhances directional stability even in extreme steering maneuvers (fear and panic reactions), resulting in a drastic reduction in the risk of skidding.
- Improved handling also at the vehicle's physical driving limits. For the driver, handling becomes predictable as a function of the driver's driving experience. The vehicle remains fully under control even in critical traffic situations.
- Depending on the situation, enhanced utilization of the friction potential between the tires and the road when ABS and TCS intervene, and therefore improved traction and braking distances in addition to improved steerability and stability.

### Vehicle handling

The vehicle's self-steering response is defined in the description of the vehicle's lateral-motion dynamics (P. 430 onwards). This description is derived from steady-state skidpad testing and shows the dependence of tire slip angle $\alpha$ on vehicle lateral acceleration $a_y$, and therefore on lateral tire forces. Furthermore, the description of ABS (P. 809 onwards) and TCS (P. 817 onwards) also underlines the dependence of lateral tire forces on tire slip. This means that the vehicle's self-steering response can be influenced by tire slip. ESP uses this tire characteristic to implement power-assisted control for vehicle handling.

It is important for good vehicle handling that the vehicle remains safely in a lane which corresponds as far as possible to the steering-angle characteristic (see figure "Lateral dynamics of a vehicle", Curve 2). During steering maneuvers, this is the case if the lateral tire forces remain considerably below the potential of friction-coefficient matching between the tire and the road surface. The yaw-velocity curve then corresponds to that of the steering angle.

For ESP though, the mere control of the yaw motion according to the steering angle proves to be inadequate and the vehicle can become unstable (see figure, Curve 3). ESP therefore controls not only the yaw velocity but also the vehicle's float angle.

Vehicle-handling control using ESP is not restricted to ABS and TCS/MSR operations, but also extends to cover the area in which the vehicle is coasting. It also

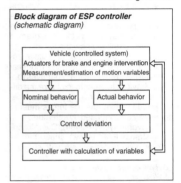

**Block diagram of ESP controller**
*(schematic diagram)*

Vehicle (controlled system)
Actuators for brake and engine intervention
Measurement/estimation of motion variables

Nominal behavior — Actual behavior

Control deviation

Controller with calculation of variables

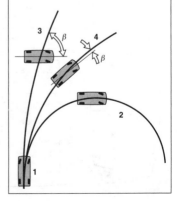

**Lateral dynamics of a vehicle**
*1 Step input at steering wheel, steering-wheel angle fixed, 2 Lane on high-road surface, 3 Lane on low-road surface with "open-loop" steering correction and yaw-rate control, 4 Lane on low-road surface when the float angle is also controlled (ESP).*

comes into action during partial braking if the vehicle is moving at its physical driving limits.

## ESP control systems

The control of the handling characteristics at the vehicle's physical driving limits must influence the vehicle's three degrees of freedom in the plane of the road (linear and lateral velocities, and yaw velocity about the vertical axis) so that vehicle handling is adapted to the driver command and the prevailing road-surface conditions. In this respect, as shown in the block diagram, it must first be defined how the vehicle is to behave at its physical driving limits in accordance with driver command (nominal behavior), and how it actually behaves (actual behavior). In order to minimize the difference between nominal and actual behavior (deviation), the tire forces must in some way be controlled by actuators.

The overall system (figure "Overall control system of ESP" below), shows the vehicle as a controlled system, with sensors (1...5) for defining the controller input variables, and actuators (6 and 7) for influencing the motive and braking forces. Also shown are the hierarchically structured controller, comprising the higher-level vehicle dynamics controller, and the lower-level slip controllers. The higher-level controllers determine the nominal values to the lower-level controllers in the form of nominal slip. The "observer" determines the controlled state variable (float angle $\beta$).

In order to determine the nominal behavior, the signals defining driver command are evaluated. These comprise the signals from the steering-wheel angle sensor (3, driver's steering input), the brake-pressure sensor (2, desired deceleration input), and the engine management (7, desired drive torque). Apart from the vehicle speed, the calculation of the nominal behavior also takes the coefficients of friction between the tires and the road into account. These are calculated from the signals sent by the wheel-speed sensors (1), the lateral-acceleration sensor (5), the yaw-rate sensor (4),

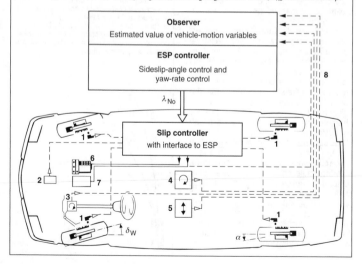

**Overall control system of ESP**
*1 Wheel-speed sensors, 2 Brake-pressure sensor, 3 Steering-wheel angle sensor, 4 Yaw-rate sensor, 5 Lateral-acceleration sensor, 6 Brake-pressure modulation, 7 Engine management, 8 Sensor signals for ESP. $\alpha$ Tire slip angle, $\delta_W$ Steering angle of the wheel, $\lambda_{No}$ Nominal tire slip.*

**Observer**
Estimated value of vehicle-motion variables

**ESP controller**
Sideslip-angle control and yaw-rate control

$\lambda_{No}$

**Slip controller**
with interface to ESP

and the brake-pressure sensor (2). Depending on the control deviation, the yaw moment, which is necessary to make the actual-state variables approach the desired-state variables, is then calculated.

In order to generate the required yaw moment, it is necessary for the changes in desired slip at the wheels to be determined by the vehicle dynamics controller. These are then set by means of the lower brake-slip and traction controllers together with the "brake-hydraulics" actuator (6), and the "engine-management actuator" (7).

The system relies on tried and proven ABS and TCS components. The TCS hydraulic modulator (6), which is described elsewhere, permits high levels of dynamic braking of all wheels throughout the complete temperature range encountered.

The necessary engine torque can be set by means of the engine management (7) and the CAN interface, so that the traction-slip values at the wheels can be adjusted accordingly.

## System components

### Vehicle dynamics controller

The relationship between steering angle, vehicle speed, and yaw velocity during steady-state skidpad testing (P. 437) is taken as the basis for desired vehicle motion during steady-state driving, and when braking and/or accelerating. By applying the "single-track (bicycle) model", the nominal yaw rate is calculated from the vehicle speed and the steering angle:

$$\dot{\psi}_{No} = \frac{v_x \cdot \delta_W}{(a + c)\left(1 + \dfrac{v_x^2}{v_{CH}^2}\right)}$$

For the float-angle control, this value is first limited according to the road-surface coefficient of friction:

$$|\dot{\psi}_{No}| \le \mu_{HF} \cdot g / v_F$$

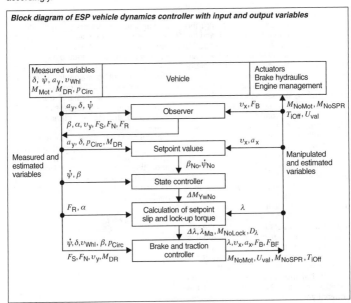

**Block diagram of ESP vehicle dynamics controller with input and output variables**

where $g$ is acceleration due to gravity, and the coefficient of friction $\mu_{HF}$ and vehicle speed $\upsilon_F$ are estimated values.

No attempt is made to directly influence lateral velocity, and thus the float angle, by means of changes in lateral forces. It is better to adjust lateral motion indirectly by means of changes in slip angle, whereby the vehicle's rotation is initiated by generating yaw moments.

A simplified block diagram is used to demonstrate the structure of the vehicle dynamics controller. The "observer" calculates the slip angle $a$, the float angle $\beta$ the vehicle lateral velocity $\upsilon_y$, the lateral and normal forces at the wheel $F_S$, $F_N$, and the resulting forces on the wheel $F_R$ from the measured variables (nominal yaw rate $\dot{\psi}_{No}$, steering-wheel angle $\delta$ and vehicle lateral acceleration $a_y$) and the estimated variables (linear vehicle speed $\upsilon_x$ and the braking forces $F_B$).

The setpoint values for the float angle $\beta_{No}$ and the yaw velocity $\dot{\psi}_{No}$ are determined from the driver input variables of steering-wheel angle $\delta$, required engine torque $M_{DR}$ (accelerator-pedal position) and braking pressure $p_{circ}$, and from the estimated linear vehicle speed $\upsilon_x$ and the friction coefficient $\mu_{HF}$, which is calculated with the aid of the estimated linear acceleration and the measured lateral acceleration. In the process, the vehicle's dynamic response, and special situations such as road camber, banks, and/or $\mu$-split road surfaces (different coefficients of friction between tires and road on the left and right side of the vehicle) are taken into account.

The vehicle dynamics controller is designed as a state controller. The controlled-state variables are the float angle and the yaw velocity. The more the float angle increases, the more it is taken into account by the vehicle dynamics controller. The state controller's output variable corresponds to a yaw moment $M_{YwNo}$.

Together with the actual slip values $\lambda$, the resultant wheel forces $F_R$, and the slip angles $\alpha$, the linearized vehicle model is now also applied to convert this yaw moment into changes in nominal slip at the appropriate wheels. For instance, presuming that the vehicle is coasting and oversteers in a right corner so that the nominal yaw rate is exceeded, a nominal

brake slip is requested at the front left wheel, among other things. This subjects the vehicle to a counterclockwise change in yaw moment that reduces the excessive yaw velocity. The nominal slip is changed by the lower-level ABS or TCS wheel controller. If the brakes have not been applied, or the driver's braking-pressure input is not sufficient to set the required nominal slip (partial-braking range), the pressure in the brake circuits is actively increased.

In TCS mode, the vehicle dynamics controller provides a mean absolute drive slip figure $\lambda_{MA}$ and a drive-slip tolerance band $D_\lambda$ as well as a nominal brake-locking torque $M_{NoLock}$ for setting the necessary vehicle yaw-moment setpoint $M_{YwNo}$. In order to achieve distinct improvements for the ABS and TCS basic functions with regard to their utilization of friction potential to suit the driving situation, all available measurement quantities and estimated variables are also applied to the full in the slip controllers.

Lower-level brake-slip controller (ABS) and engine drag-torque controller (MSR)

In order to control wheel slip to a predetermined setpoint, it must be possible to evaluate it with an adequate degree of accuracy. The vehicle's linear velocity is not measured, but is determined from the wheel speeds $\upsilon_{Whl}$. To do so, individual wheels are "under-braked" during ABS application. In other words, slip control is interrupted, and the instantaneous wheel-brake torque is reduced by a defined amount and held constant for a given period of time. Assuming that the wheel speed is stable toward the end of this period, the zero-slip (free-rolling) wheel speed $\upsilon_{WhlFre}$ can be calculated from the momentary braking force $F_B$ and the tire rigidity $C_\lambda$.

$$\upsilon_{WhlFre} = \upsilon_{Whl} \cdot \frac{C_\lambda}{C_\lambda - \dfrac{F_B}{F_N}}$$

Using the yaw velocity $\dot{\psi}$, the steering angle $\delta_w$, and lateral velocity $v_y$, together with the vehicle geometry, the (free-rolling) wheel speed is transformed to the center of gravity in order to generate the center-of-gravity velocity $v_x$ in the vehicle's linear direction. Finally, $v_x$ is transformed back to the four wheel centerpoints in order to evaluate the free-rolling speeds of all four wheels. This allows the actual slip $\lambda$ to be calculated for the control of the three remaining wheels.

$$\lambda = 1 - \frac{v_{Whl}}{v_{WhlFre}}$$

Starting from the stationary braking force $F_{BF}$ using a PID control law, the nominal torque at the wheel can be calculated as a function of slip deviation.

$$M_{WhlNo} = F_{BF} \cdot R + K_p(\lambda_{No} - \lambda)R$$
$$+ K_d\left(\frac{d}{dt}\,v_{Whl} - \frac{d}{dt}\,v_{WhlFre}\right)\frac{J_{Whl}}{R}$$
$$+ K_i \cdot C_p \cdot \text{SUM}\left\{(\lambda_{No} - \lambda) \cdot D_T\right\}$$

In the case of the driven wheels, in order to implement engine drag-torque control (MSR), the nominal braking torque $M_{WhlNo}$ can be partially set by the engine (or completely when the brakes are not applied). The driven wheel with the lower nominal wheel torque is controlled within the permissible limits by engine intervention.

The following applies for rear-wheel drive:

$$M_{NoMot} = -\frac{2m}{\ddot{U}_{Tr}} + \frac{J_{Mot} \cdot \ddot{U}_{Tr}}{R} \cdot \frac{d}{dt}\,v_x$$

$$m = \text{MIN}\,(M_{Whl3}, M_{Whl4})$$

For negative values, the nominal engine torque $M_{NoMot}$ is limited by the maximum engine-drag torque, and in the driven case (positive values), it is limited to the maximum dynamic drive torque as permitted by the manufacturer. In case of a

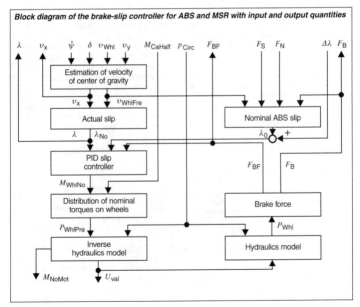

*Block diagram of the brake-slip controller for ABS and MSR with input and output quantities*

positive nominal braking torque $M_{WhlNo}$, the remaining braking torque must be adjusted by using braking pressure.

$$p_{WhlPre} = \frac{M_{WhlNo} + M_{CaHalf}}{C_p}$$

The pressure $p_{WhlPre}$ applied to the wheel-brake cylinders by the controller is adjusted by the brake hydraulics and the associated valve-triggering mode $U_{val}$. The required valve time is calculated using an inverse "hydraulic model", whose parameters $x_1$, $x_2$ have been defined beforehand and stored in the controller. Essentially, the model uses the Bernoulli theorem for incompressible media, and a pressure/volume characteristic.

$$U_{val} = \frac{p_{WhlPre} - p_{Whl}}{(x_1 + x_2 \cdot p_{Whl}) \sqrt{|p_{Circ} - p_{Whl}|}}$$

| | |
|---|---|
| $U_{val} > 0$ | Build up pressure |
| $U_{val} = 0$ | Hold pressure |
| $U_{val} < 0$ | Reduce pressure |

Since the valve-triggering mode $U_{val}$ is limited by the sampling time and quantified, the adjusted pressure $p_{Whl}$ that has actually been set must be calculated using the hydraulic model. The actual tire braking force $F_B$ and the steady-state braking force $F_{BF}$ can now be calculated by means of dynamic wheel equations, taking the known (estimated) wheel brake pressure and the measured wheel speeds:

$$F_B = C_p \cdot \frac{p_{Whl}}{R} - \frac{M_{CaHalf}}{R} + \frac{J_{Whl}}{R^2} \cdot \frac{d}{dt} v_{Whl}$$

$$F_B = T_i \cdot \frac{d}{dt} F_{BF} + F_{BF}$$

The steady-state (filtered) braking force $F_{BF}$ now serves as the reference variable for the PID controller. Using the calculated working point $\lambda_0$, and the change in slip stipulated by the vehicle dynamics controller, the ABS controller calculates the nominal tire slip $\lambda_{No}$.

$$\lambda_0 = A_0 \cdot \mu_{Res} + \frac{A_1}{v_{WhlFre}} + A_2$$

$$\mu_{Res} = \frac{\sqrt{F_B + F_S}}{F_N}$$

## Traction controller (TCS)

On rear-drive vehicles, the traction controller is used for slip control of the driven wheels only. Active intervention at the front wheels is through the brake-slip controller. Unlike ABS, the traction controller receives from the vehicle dynamics controller the nominal mean nominal traction slip $\lambda_{Ma}$ of both driven wheels and a nominal brake-locking torque value $M_{NoLock}$ to be used as reference variables for directly influencing the yaw moment. The nominal value for the differential speed of the two driven wheels $v_{NoDif}$ is the difference in their (free-rolling) speeds, whereby the vehicle dynamics controller also stipulates a tolerance band $D_\lambda$ for the difference between the two drive-slip values. This difference represents a dead zone for the control deviation in order that a nominal brake-locking torque $M_{NoLock}$ can be generated.

The TCS module calculates the nominal braking torque $M_{WhlNo}$ for both driven wheels, the nominal engine torque $M_{NoMot}$ to be set by throttle-valve intervention, the nominal value $M_{NoSPR}$ for engine-torque reduction using spark retard, and, as options, the length of time $T_{iOFF}$ during which the EFI is to be cut off, and the number of cylinders this cutoff is to be applied to.

The nominal values for the propshaft and wheel-speed differentials ($v_{NoCa}$ and $v_{NoDif}$) are calculated from nominal slip values together with the (free-rolling) wheel speeds $v_{WhlFre}$. The controlled variables $v_{Ca}$ and $v_{Dif}$ are calculated from wheel speeds $v_{Whl3}$ and $v_{Whl4}$:

$$v_{Ca} = \frac{1}{2}(v_{Whl3} + v_{Whl4})$$

$$v_{Dif} = v_{Whl3} - v_{Whl4}$$

The dynamic response depends on the highly differing operating statuses of the controlled system. It is therefore necessary to determine the operating status in order to be able to adapt the controller parameters to the controlled system's dynamic response and to nonlinearities. The large moment of inertia of the complete drivetrain (engine, gearbox, propshaft, and driven wheels) has an influence on propshaft speed $v_{Ca}$ which is therefore characterized by a relatively large time constant (low dynamic response). On the other hand, the time constant of the wheel-speed differential $v_{Dif}$ is relatively small since the dynamic response of $v_{Dif}$ is determined almost completely by the small moments of inertia of the two wheels. Apart from this, $v_{Dif}$ in contrast to $v_{Ca}$ is not directly influenced by the engine. $v_{Dif}$ and $v_{Ca}$ are used therefore as controlled variables because they permit the division of the drivetrain system (measured wheel speed, rear left and rear right, $v_{Whl3}$ and $v_{Whl4}$ respectively) in two subsystems with distinct dynamic response and distinct engine influence. The engine intervention and the "symmetrical" part of the brake intervention represent the manipulated variables of the propshaft speed controller $v_{Ca}$. The "asymmetrical" portion of the brake intervention is the command signal for the wheel-speed differential controller $v_{Dif}$.

The propshaft speed is controlled by means of a nonlinear PID controller, whereby in particular the gain of the I-component (dependent on the operating status) can vary over a wide range. At

steady state, the I-component is a measure for the torque which can be transferred to the road surface. The propshaft torque $M_{Ca}$ is the controller output.

A nonlinear PI controller is used for controlling the wheel-speed differential $v_{Dif}$. The controller parameters are dependent on the engaged gear and on influences from the engine. From the tolerance band $D_\lambda$ for the differential slip of the driven wheels, which is output by the vehicle dynamics controller, a dead zone is calculated for the control deviation. For "$\mu$-split", in order to ensure adequate traction, the vehicle dynamics controller specifies a relatively narrow dead zone. In doing so, it increases the sensitivity of the controller for the wheel-speed differential $v_{Dif}$. If the nominal brake-locking torque $M_{NoLock}$ is to be reduced, or in case of the optional select-low control, the vehicle dynamics controller defines a wider tolerance band. In these cases, the controller for the wheel-speed differential $v_{Dif}$ permits larger differences between the rotational speeds of the rear wheels. The controller output is the desired/setpoint speed differential $M_{Dif}$.

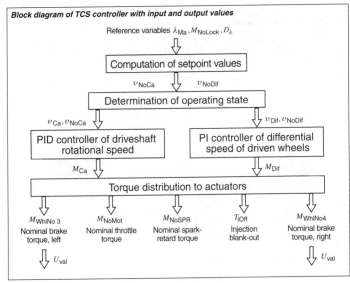

**Block diagram of TCS controller with input and output values**

Reference variables $\lambda_{Ma}$, $M_{NoLock}$, $D_\lambda$

⇩

Computation of setpoint values

$v_{NoCa}$ ⇩   $v_{NoDif}$ ⇩

Determination of operating state

$v_{Ca}$, $v_{NoCa}$ ⇩   $v_{Dif}$, $v_{NoDif}$ ⇩

PID controller of driveshaft rotational speed   |   PI controller of differential speed of driven wheels

$M_{Ca}$ ⇩   $M_{Dif}$ ⇩

Torque distribution to actuators

⇩ $M_{WhlNo\,3}$ Nominal brake torque, left   ⇩ $M_{NoMot}$ Nominal throttle torque   ⇩ $M_{NoSPR}$ Nominal spark-retard torque   ⇩ $T_{iOff}$ Injection blank-out   ⇩ $M_{WhlNo4}$ Nominal brake torque, right

⇩ $U_{val}$   ⇩ $U_{val}$

The propshaft torque $M_{Ca}$ and the desired/setpoint speed differential $M_{Dif}$ are distributed between the actuators. A corresponding valve-triggering mode $U_{val}$ in the hydraulic modulator adjusts the desired/setpoint speed differential $M_{Dif}$ via the braking-torque difference between the left and right driven wheels. The nominal propshaft torque $M_{Ca}$ is achieved by engine intervention and by means of symmetrical brake intervention. There is a relatively long delay (response time and transition response of the engine) before throttle-valve intervention comes into effect. For rapid-acting engine intervention, if optionally available, the ignition is retarded (spark retard), and fuel injection is cut off. The symmetrical brake intervention provides short-term support for the engine-torque reduction.

By means of this module, the traction controller can be relatively easily adapted to the various engine-intervention types.

## System realization

The hydraulic modulator and the wheel-speed sensors are suitable for operation in underhood conditions. The yaw-rate sensor, the lateral-acceleration sensor, the steering-wheel angle sensor, and the ECU are designed for installation in the passenger cell or in the trunk. An example of the in-vehicle installation of the components, together with their electrical and mechanical connections, is given on the opposite page.

### Sensor systems

An interface monitoring capability is a necessity, and can be implemented efficiently and at low cost with modern-day ECUs. It has a decisive effect on the architecture of the sensor interfaces (for sensors, see P. 110).

The demands reflected in the sensor requirements were ascertained by evaluating simulation studies together with an extensive program of road tests. The consequences of side-effects on ESP operation were also investigated (influence of positioning tolerances, cross-couplings, and other sensor malfunctions). The re-

---

**The ESP system with its electrical connections in the vehicle**
1 Wheel brakes, 2 Wheel-speed sensors, 3 Engine-management ECU with CAN interface,
4 Throttle-valve actuator, 5 Pre-charge pump with brake-pressure sensor, 6 Steering-wheel angle
sensor, 7 Brake booster with master cylinder, 8 Hydraulic system with brake-pressure sensor and
attached ECU, 9 Yaw sensor with integrated lateral-acceleration sensor.

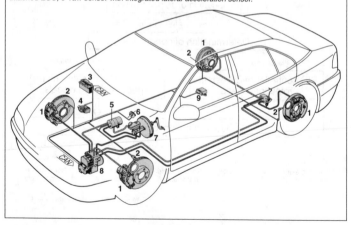

sult was a multilevel, and thus very dense monitoring network which incorporates the aspects of analytical redundancy. In order to be able to master complex systems which are relevant from the safety aspect with the necessary reliability, the aspects of analytical redundancy must be incorporated if reasons of cost forbid the application of redundant sensors.

### Electronic control unit

The ECU is constructed in conventional (4-layer) pcb technology, and in addition to two partially redundant computers, it incorporates all drivers for valve and lamp triggering, as well as the semiconductor relays for valve and pump triggering, the interface circuits for sensor-signal conditioning, and the appropriate switch inputs for auxiliary signals such as those from the brake-light switch. Furthermore, a CAN interface is integrated in order to facilitate communication with other systems in the vehicle (e.g. engine management and transmission-shift control). The large number of additional signal inputs requires the use of a special plug-in connection in order to minimize the size of the ECU housing.

### Monitoring system

A comprehensive safety-monitoring system is of fundamental importance for the ESP's reliable functioning. The system used encompasses the complete system together with all components and all their functional interactions. The safety system is based on safety methods, e.g. FMEA, ETA and error-simulation studies.

From these, measures are derived for avoiding errors which could have safety-related consequences. Extensive monitoring programs guarantee the reliable detection of all sensor errors which cannot be prevented completely. These programs are based on the well-proven safety software from the ABS and ABS/TCS systems which monitor all the components connected to the ECU together with their electrical connections, signals, and functions. The safety software was further improved by fully utilizing the possibilities offered by the additional sensors, and by adapting them to the special ESP components and functions.

The sensors are monitored at a number of stages:

In the first stage, the sensors are continuously monitored for line break and signal implausibility during vehicle operation (out-of-range check, detection of interference, physical plausibility).

In a second stage, the most important sensors are tested individually. The yaw-rate sensor is tested by intentionally detuning the sensor element and then evaluating the signal response. Even the acceleration sensor has internal background monitoring. When activated, the pressure-sensor signal must show a predefined characteristic, and the offset and amplification are compensated for internally. The steering-angle sensor is provided with "local intelligence" and has its own monitoring functions which directly deliver any error message to the ECU. In addition, the digital signal transmission to the ECU is permanently monitored.

In a third stage, analytical redundancy is applied to monitor the sensors during the steady-state operation of the vehicle. Here, a vehicle model is used to check that the relationships between the sensor signals, as determined by vehicle motion, are not violated. These models are also frequently applied to calculate and compensate for sensor offsets as long as they stay within the sensor specifications.

In case of error, the system is switched off either partially or completely depending on the type of error concerned. The system's response to errors also depends on whether the control is activated or not.

## Supplementary functions (automatic brake-system operations)

### Electronic brake balancing (EBV)

#### Function

The braking systems of vehicles used to transport people must be designed to prevent certain limits from being reached, e.g. if the rear wheels lock before the front wheels. If the rear wheels were to lock first, the vehicle would become unstable. It would turn about its vertical axis and start to skid. Preventing the rear wheels from locking before the front wheels maintains the dynamic stability of the vehicle. By using proportioning valves, it is possible to control the distribution of braking forces between the front and rear wheels to obtain the desired wheel-lock sequence.

A supplementary function of ABS achieves braking-force distribution by electronic means. This dispenses with certain components and saves costs. This electronic method of brake balancing has virtually become the standard.

#### Hydraulic (and pneumatic) braking assistant operations

Investigations into driver braking behavior in the 1990s showed that car drivers differ in the way that they respond to braking situations. The majority – the "average drivers" – do not brake hard enough when faced with an emergency situation, in other words they waste "valuable" braking distance.

This can be remedied by a system first launched in 1995, the braking assistant. Its main purposes are as follows:
- It interprets a certain rate of pedal movement (rapid application of the brakes) that fails to apply maximum braking force as an intention by the driver to carry out full braking. In this case, it generates the braking pressure required to achieve full braking effect.
- It allows the driver to "cancel" full braking operation at any time.
- The behavior of the "booster" and, therefore, the pedal feedback, is not altered under normal braking conditions.
- The basic braking system function is not diminished if the booster fails.
- The system is designed to prevent accidental activation.

#### Pneumatic/mechanical braking assistant

This system requires a modified vacuum booster which increases the level of amplification according to the rate of pedal movement. This results in faster and greater buildup of pressure in the wheel brakes.

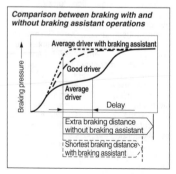

*Electronic brake balancing*
1 Ideal braking-force distribution curve,
2 Installed braking-force distribution curve,
3 Curve for electronic brake balancing,
4 Gain in braking force at rear wheels.

Braking force, rear wheels
Braking force, front wheels →

*Comparison between braking with and without braking assistant operations*

Braking pressure

Average driver with braking assistant
Good driver
Average driver
Delay
Extra braking distance without braking assistant
Shortest braking distance with braking assistant

Pneumatic/electronic braking assistant

The vacuum booster is electronically controlled to provide more opportunities to optimize definition of the trigger threshold and response characteristics.

Hydraulic braking assistant

The hydraulic braking-assistant function makes use of the hardware provided by the ESP system. A pressure sensor (standard with ESP, additional hardware requirement with TCS) detects the driver's braking intention, analyzes the signal on the basis of the defined activation criteria, and initiates the appropriate brake boosting operation using the hydraulic system. The upstream vacuum booster is a standard unit and does not require any modification.

As a general observation, it should be stated that it is an absolute requirement that all braking-assistant system variants referred to are used in conjunction with TCS or ESP due to the actively generated rapid brake-pressure rise beyond the wheel-lock limit.

**Engine drag-torque control (MSR)**

On slippery road surfaces, a downshift or sudden throttle closing can cause excessive brake slip at the driven wheels due to the engine braking effect. The wheel-slip/spin control systems, ABS and TCS, for passenger cars and light commercial vehicles can be complemented by an additional engine drag-torque control function (MSR). MSR increases engine speed by applying the accelerator appropriately, i.e. by intervening in the engine management functions, so as to keep the speed of the wheels within the optimum slip range.

MSR application is an option on vehicles which are fitted at least with ABS; with ESP it is a standard function.

**Electromechanical parking brake (EMP)**

The electromechanical parking brake (EMP) generates the force for applying the parking brake by electromechanical means. The function of the hand- or foot-operated parking-brake lever is performed by a "driver interface" with an electric-motor-and-transmission combination. When the driver operates the interface, the electric motor (actuator) is activated when the system detects that the vehicle is at standstill. When the vehicle is parked on a level surface, the brake-cable tension is set lower than when the vehicle is fully laden and parked on a gradient. Active wheel sensors are used to detect that the vehicle is parked (i.e. stationary). As an option, it is also possible for the road gradient to be detected by a tilt sensor.

The parking brake is released by means of the same driver interface. However, various safety regulations and requirements have to be met, e.g. to prevent inappropriate or inadvertent release of the parking brake by children or animals.

In addition, inadvertent or unintended operation of the parking brake while the vehicle is in motion may not cause a critical driving situation. In such cases, the TCS or ESP system takes control of braking if the vehicle is traveling at more than a set upper speed threshold and ensures safe braking even on slippery or wet road surfaces. When the vehicle's speed reaches a lower speed threshold, the vehicle is brought to a standstill by EMP.

EMP communicates with TCS/ESP via a CAN (Controller Area Network) interface.

An electromechanical parking brake of the type described here can only be used in conjunction with ESP.

### Hill-hold control (HHC)

The HHC system (<u>H</u>ill-<u>H</u>old <u>C</u>ontrol) simplifies hill starts (hill-start assistant). It prevents the vehicle from rolling back after the driver has released the brake pedal. HHC is particularly helpful on heavily laden vehicles with manual transmission and vehicles that are towing trailers. There is no need to operate the parking brake.

The HHC system detects the driver's intention to pull away. After releasing the brake pedal, there remains about 2 seconds to engage a gear and start pulling away. The brakes are automatically released as soon as the drive torque exceeds the gravitational pull of the slope.

Misuse of the HHC system as an electric parking brake is not possible because the hydraulic pressure in the wheel-brake cylinders for holding the vehicle on the gradient is only maintained by the activated solenoid valves for the specified maximum period. In addition, the system would also be deactivated by releasing the clutch pedal.

The HHC system is based on the ESP system hardware with additional sensors – a tilt sensor detects the road gradient, a gear switch detects whether the driver has shifted to first or reverse gear, and a clutch switch recognizes whether the driver has depressed the clutch pedal.

Wheel-speed sensors, brake-pedal and throttle-valve switches are required by other vehicle systems (e.g. engine management) and can be shared by the HHC.

### Hill-descent control (HDC)

The HDC system (<u>H</u>ill-<u>D</u>escent <u>C</u>ontrol) is a convenience function which assists the driver on offroad descents with gradients of approx. 8...50% by automatically operating the brakes. The driver can then concentrate fully on steering the vehicle and is not distracted by the need to operate the brakes at the same time. The brake pedal does not have to be operated.

When the HDC is activated, e.g. by pressing a button or switch, a preset speed is maintained by automatic operation of the brakes and the accelerator. It remains active until it is canceled by pressing the button or switch again, or by pressing the accelerator or brake pedal.

Misuse is prevented by presetting a maximum downhill speed and deactivating the HDC system when the vehicle is traveling on the flat or uphill.

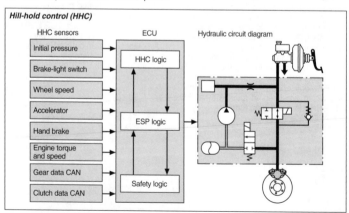

Hill-hold control (HHC)

## TIMS/DWS (Tire Inflation Monitoring System/Dunlop Warnair System)

Direct-measurement tire-pressure monitoring systems detect the absolute tire pressure using pressure sensors. They transmit the information (e.g. by wireless link) to a receiver in the vehicle for analysis or display. Indirect-measurement systems such as TIMS/DWS inform the driver if there is a significant relative difference in the pressure of one of the tires. This system is based on the principle that a tire with a lower pressure has a smaller effective circumference than a fully inflated tire. The tire pressure difference results in a measurable differential speed of the wheels and is analyzed accordingly.

The wheel-speed sensors, and therefore the wheel-speed data, are supplied by the ABS, TCS or ESP systems. They are processed in these control units (Generation 8 onwards) according to the TIMS/DWS algorithms. A pressure drop of approx. 30% typically produces an increase in wheel rotational speed of approx. 0.2...0.5%. The system detects pressure losses of more than 30% ($\pm 10\%$) relative to normal pressure. The detection time is around 3 minutes for a 30% pressure drop and > around 1 minute for a 50% pressure drop.

It must be clearly emphasized that this is a convenience system and not a safety system.

Tire-pressure monitoring systems are becoming increasingly widespread. In the U.S., for example, they are governed by the FMVSS 138 regulations. They will be introduced in several stages and will become a required standard fitting from the end of 2006.

## Rollover mitigation (ROM)

Rollover mitigation is a supplementary function designed to prevent the vehicle from turning over due to excessive lateral deceleration forces. The Electronic Stability Progam (ESP) already reduces the risk of rollover under specific circumstances, and the ROM function provides additional improvement.

The ROM function is based detecting lateral acceleration, among other things. It limits lateral acceleration to a maximum level according to the vehicle's characteristics (e.g. as determined by its center of gravity, track, mass, the combination of tires and road surface, etc.). This reduces the lateral forces acting on the vehicle. In other words, the degree of brake slip on the outer wheels is increased to allow the vehicle to slide sideways in order to prevent rollover. The proportion of transferrable lateral force diminishes and lateral acceleration is limited to the permissible level.

Owing to the rise in the number of accidents involving SUVs (Sport Utility Vehicles) and offroad vehicles, there are demands in the U.S. to redress this situation by equipping vehicles with additional functions such as ROM.

## Electronically controlled deceleration (ECD)

This function requires the ESP hardware. A "reduce speed" command, for example, is sent via the ACC (Adaptive Cruise Control) interface to the ESP, and the hydraulic systems are then adjusted to produce a certain rate of deceleration.

In the future this function will be used in suitably adapted form for various vehicle control functions.

# Electrohydraulic brakes (SBC)

## Purpose and function

The SBC (Sensotronic Brake Control) electrohydraulic braking system combines the functions of a brake booster and ABS (Antilock Braking System), including ESP (Electronic Stability Progam). Mechanical operation of the brake pedal is detected by the actuation unit by means of electronic sensors with redundant backup, and a signal is transmitted to the ECU. The ECU uses specific algorithms to calculate control commands which are converted to brake-pressure modulation for the wheel brakes. If the electronics fail, there is an automatic fallback to the hydraulic systems.

Using its "brake-by-wire" characteristics, SBC can modulate the pressure in the wheel-brake cylinders independently of the driver's actions. This allows the implementation of functions that extend beyond those of ABS (Antilock Braking System), TCS (Traction Control System) and ESP (Electronic Stability Progam). One example is straightforward braking intervention for ACC (Adaptive Cruise Control).

### Basic functions

Like a conventional braking system, the function of the electrohydraulic braking system is to:
– reduce vehicle speed
– bring the vehicle to a halt
– keep the vehicle stationary

As an active braking system, it takes control of:
– brake operation
– braking-force boosting
– braking-force metering

SBC is an electronic control system with hydraulic actuator systems. Braking-force distribution is performed electronically and individually for each wheel according to the driving situation. A vacuum for the braking-force boosting is no longer required. Self-diagnosis is an early-warning function to detect possible system faults.

*Location of SBC components in a vehicle* (Figure A)
*1 Active wheel-speed sensor with rotational direction sensing, 2 Engine-management control unit, 3 SBC control unit, 4 Yaw-rate and lateral-acceleration sensor, 5 Hydraulic modulator (for SBC, ABS, TCS, ESP), 6 Actuation unit with pedal-travel sensor, 7 Steering-angle sensor.*

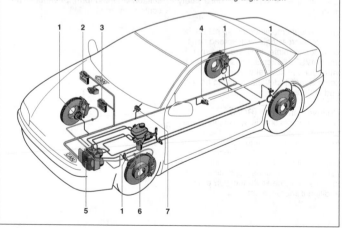

SBC uses standard hydraulic wheel brakes. Due to its fully electronic pressure control, SBC is easily integratable in a network of vehicle-control systems. SBC therefore meets all the requirements placed on future braking systems.

Due to its high-pressure accumulator, SBC has a dynamic, very rapid pressure rise, and thus provides the potential for short braking distances combined with high vehicle stability. Brake-pressure modulation and active braking are silent and generate no brake-pedal feedback. Consequently, SBC meets even high demands and expectations for user-friendliness.

The braking characteristics can be adapted to the driving situation, e.g. by adopting a "sharper" response for dynamic driving styles or high speeds. A "duller" pedal response can be used to alert the driver to a reduction in braking effect, when the brakes reach the limits of their effectiveness before overheating induces brake fading.

### SBC supplementary functions

Supplementary functions provide much greater safety and convenience when braking with SBC.

#### Drive-away assistant

After activating the drive-away assistant by a definite increase in braking force when stationary, the vehicle remains braked even when the pedal is released. The drive-away assistant is automatically canceled as soon as the driver has generated enough engine torque by pressing the accelerator. This makes it possible to perform hill starts, for instance, without the need to apply the parking brake. In other situations where the vehicle could roll from a standstill if unbraked, the driver does not need to apply the brakes constantly when the drive-away assistant is activated.

#### Extended braking-assistant functions

If the accelerator is abruptly released, the brake pads are applied slightly by automatically metering braking-pressure buildup. This function allows the brakes to "bite" faster if panic braking should follow

and achieves a shorter total braking distance.

If the system detects panic braking, the braking pressure is briefly increased to the point of optimum friction coefficient. This results in a significant reduction in total braking distance for hesitant drivers. In such situations, the rapid pressure-buildup dynamics of SBC outperform conventional systems.

#### Soft stop

If the convenience braking system is fitted, SBC allows jerk-free stopping by automatically reducing the pressure shortly before the vehicle comes to a halt. If the driver wishes to stop sooner, the function is not activated and SBC minimizes the braking distance.

#### Traffic jam assist

When the traffic-jam assist is activated, SBC generates a higher drag torque when the accelerator pedal is released. This relieves the driver of constantly switching between the gas pedal and the brake pedal in stop-start traffic. If necessary, the vehicle is automatically braked to a standstill and held stationary as well. This function can only be activated at speeds below 50 ... 60 kph.

#### Dry brake function

The dry-brake function regularly removes the film of water from the brake discs in wet conditions. This reduces the total braking distance in the wet. The signal for activating this function is derivable from the windshield-wiper signal.

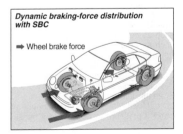

*Dynamic braking-force distribution with SBC*

➡ Wheel brake force

## Design

The SBC electrohydraulic braking system consists of the following components:
– actuation unit (Figure A, Item 6)
– vehicle-dynamics sensors (Figure A, Items 1, 4 and 7)
– SBC ECU (i.e. separate ECU) (Figure A, Item 3), and
– hydraulic modulator with an add-on ECU (Figure A, Item 5).

Those components are interlinked by electrical control lines and hydraulic high-pressure lines. Figure A shows where they are located on the vehicle.

### Actuation unit

The actuation unit consists of:
– master cylinder and brake-fluid reservoir
– pedal-travel simulator
– pedal-travel sensor

#### Pedal-travel simulation

The pedal-travel simulator produces an appropriate force/travel curve and calculates the amount of brake-pedal damping. Consequently, the driver experiences the same "brake feel" with electrohydraulic brakes as with a very well designed conventional braking system.

### SBC sensor technology

The SBC sensor system consists of the familiar vehicle-dynamics sensors from ESP and the actual SBC sensors.

#### Vehicle-dynamics sensors

The ESP sensor system consists of four wheel-speed sensors, a yaw-rate sensor, a steering-angle sensor and, where applicable, a lateral-acceleration sensor. Those sensors provide the ECU with data relating to the speed and motion of the wheels and aspects of vehicle dynamics such as cornering. The control functions such as ABS, TCS and ESP are carried out in the familiar manner.

If the vehicle is fitted with ACC (Adaptive Cruise Control), a radar system detects the distance to the vehicle in front. From this information, the SBC electronic control unit determines the amount of braking pressure to be applied if necessary, and generates it without producing pedal feedback.

#### SBC sensors

Figure B shows the SBC sensors. Four pressure sensors measure the pressure in each brake circuit. Another pressure sensor measures the pressure in the high-pressure accumulator. The driver's brake-pedal input is calculated by the pedal-travel sensor attached to the actuation unit and a pressure sensor which detects the braking pressure applied by the driver.

The pedal-travel sensor consists of two separate angle-position sensors. Together with the brake-pressure sensor for the pressure applied by the driver, this produces a threefold system for detecting driver input. The system can continue to function normally, even if one of the sensors fails.

## Operating concept

### Normal mode

Figure B shows the SBC components in a schematic diagram. An electric motor drives a hydraulic pump. This charges a high-pressure accumulator to a pressure of between approx. 90 and 130 bar, monitored by an accumulator pressure sensor. The four separate wheel-pressure modulators are supplied by the accumulator and set the required pressure separately for each wheel. The pressure modulators themselves each consist of two valves with proportional-control characteristics and a pressure sensor.

In normal mode, the isolating valves isolate the brakes from the actuation unit. The system is in "brake-by-wire" mode. It detects the driver's brake-pedal input and transmits it "by wire" to the wheel-pressure modulators. The interaction between engine, valves and pressure sensors is controlled by hybrid-technology electronic circuits in the form of an add-on ECU. This has two microcontrollers which monitor each another. The essential factor is that the electronic circuits possess self-diagnosis capability and constantly check all system statuses for plausibility. It means that any faults can be displayed to the driver before a critical condition arises. If there is a component failure, the system automatically provides the driver with an assured optimized restricted system functionality. A large fault memory allows rapid fault diagnosis and repair if problems occur.

An intelligent interface with the CAN bus provides the link to the SBC ECU. That unit integrates the following functions:
– ESP (Electronic Stability Progam)
– TCS (Traction Control System)
– ABS (Antilock Braking System)
– Calculation of driver's brake-pedal input
– SBC supplementary functions (assistant functions)

**Braking in the event of system failure**
For safety reasons, the SBC system is designed so that in the event of serious faults (e.g. power-supply failure), it switches to a state in which the driver can brake the vehicle without using the active brake-booster function. When de-energized, the isolating valves open a direct hydraulic link between the actuation unit and the wheel-brake cylinders (Figure B) so that the brakes can be directly operated.

To retain optimized functionality even in the event of system failure, the modulator plungers illustrated act as medium separators between the activated SBC circuit and the conventional brake circuit for the front wheels. They prevent any gas that might escape from the high-pressure accumulator from entering the front-wheel brake circuit, as this would reduce the braking power if the system failed.

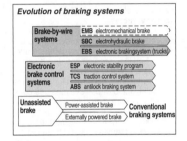

*Evolution of braking systems*

| Brake-by-wire systems | EMB electromechanical brake |
| | SBC electrohydraulic brake |
| | EBS electronic brakingsystem (trucks) |
| Electronic brake control systems | ESP electronic stability program |
| | TCS traction control system |
| | ABS antilock braking system |
| Unassisted brake | Power-assisted brake — Conventional braking systems |
| | Externally powered brake |

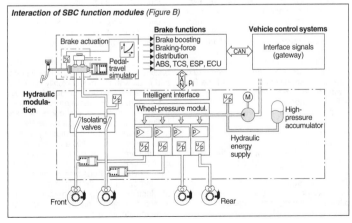

*Interaction of SBC function modules (Figure B)*

# Braking systems for commercial vehicles > 7.5 t permissible total weight

## System and configuration

Non-muscular-energy braking systems on medium-sized and heavy-duty commercial vehicles over 7.5 t permissible total weight generally use:
- compressed air as the energy-supply and force-transmission medium (Figure B)
- pneumatic-hydraulic force transmission in the service-braking system and pneumatic-force transmission in the parking-brake system (Figure C)

### Service-braking system for tractor vehicles

In medium-sized and heavy-duty commercial vehicles, the force exerted by the driver's foot is not sufficient to generate adequate braking deceleration for practical purposes. For this reason, compressed-air non-muscular-energy braking systems are mainly fitted; these systems use compressed air as a stored form of energy to control or actuate the service-braking system. Diaphragm-type cylinders produce the actuating forces required by the wheel brakes. "Air-over-hydraulic" braking systems are slowly phasing out since the air pressure required to operate the wheel brakes must be converted to hydraulic pressure by means of booster cylinders. A dual-circuit compressed-air braking system with trailer-brake connection, spring-type brake actuators, and secondary and parking-brake systems consist of the following main components:
- Energy supply
- Compressed-air reservoir
- Brake valves
- Braking-force control
- Wheel brakes
- Control and air supply for the trailer braking system (Figure D)

The energy supply comprises a compressor and pressure regulator. Antifreeze pumps, automatic water drainage, air filters, air driers, and intermediate reservoirs providing clean and well-drained air may also be included. As there may be a number of air-consuming equipment in tractor-trailer combinations apart from the braking system in modern-day commercial-vehicle operations, it is advisable to install considerably more powerful compressors than those required by EC/ECE brake regulations, for instance.

The four-circuit protection valve is located at the interface between the energy supply and the compressed-air reservoir. In the event of a fault, this protection valve assures the safety and continued air supply to the individual brake circuits and priority secondary loads. The four-circuit protection valve performs the following functions:
- Protects the brake circuits of the service-braking system in the event of a fault in the energy supply.
- Assures continued air supply to the brake circuits of the service-braking system and isolates them from one another.
- Assures continued air supply to the trailer service-braking system in the event of a fault in one of the brake circuits of the tractor service-braking system.
- Protects and assures continued air supply to the tractor service-brake circuits in the event of a brake in the trailer supply line.
- Protects the two brake circuits of the service-braking system in the event of a fault in the energy supply.
- Ensures continued air supply to secondary loads such as power-shifting system or clutch booster in the event of a fault in the service-braking system.

The control equipment for the service-braking system starts with the brake pedal and ends with the mechanically operated components of the dual-circuit brake valve.

Sometimes, on commercial vehicles, the space constraints make it necessary to fit the brake valve on the frame behind the cab instead of in the (tipping) cab itself. The problem of LHD and RHD trucks with the brake valve in the same position on the frame is solved by means of a dual-circuit hydraulic transmission device for braking-system control. In this process, an electrical warning system monitors the level of fluid in the compressed-air reservoirs of both circuits.

Additional components in the tractor-unit braking system for trailers/semitrailers with compressed-air braking systems help to supply air to the trailer/semitrailer braking system and control its braking effect (trailer control valve, coupling heads, etc.).

### Dual-line braking system for trailers

This standard European design has one line (supply line). It is permanently pressurized and connects the energy accumulators on the tractor unit to those on the trailer/semitrailer. The second line (brake line) runs from the trailer control valve in the tractor to the trailer brake valve in the trailer/semitrailer (Figure E). Braking occurs as a result of pressure rise. With this system, an automatic braking function is triggered by the supply line if the trailer becomes unhitched accidentally from the tractor unit. If it is disconnected or breaks, air escapes from the line with the result that the brake valve on the trailer/semitrailer activates the brakes. With the aid of a dual-circuit trailer control valve and the four-circuit protection valve, air can be supplied continuously to the trailer/semitrailer to control the braking effect, even if one circuit in the dual-circuit service-braking system on the tractor unit fails. Automatic shutoff of the standardized coupling heads for "supply" and "brake" opens during the hitching process.

## Automatic load-sensitive braking-force metering

The automatic load-sensitive braking-force control system (ALB) is a vital element in the transmission device of a service-braking system on a commercial vehicle. With the vehicle is partially laden or empty, braking-force metering valves permit adjustment of the braking forces to cater for the reduced axle loading, e.g. by sensing the axle ride clearances). This permits a correction of braking-force metering to the vehicle axles ("kinked load-sensitive braking-force metering"), or they permit a preselected braking force (important for vehicles in road-train or tractor-trailer operation). There are two kinds of load-sensitive braking-force metering valves (Figure A):

### Braking-force limiter

Above a given "switchover point", a braking-force limiter prevents any increase in braking force (e.g. at the rear wheels), i.e. the braking-force metering curve reaches a "plateau".

### Braking-force reducer

Even in the worst-case laden state, load-sensitive braking-force reducers allow braking-force metering which approaches the parabola of the dynamic (ideal) braking-force metering characteristic (see "Design of a braking system"). In the range above the switchover point, the braking forces on the affected axle are reduced with respect to the original braking-force metering level. Here, the installed braking-force metering is dependent on the transmission ratio and on the switchover pressure (which in turn is dependent on axle load) of the braking-force metering valve.

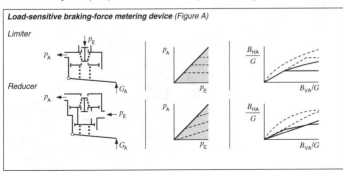

*Load-sensitive braking-force metering device* (Figure A)

*Compressed-air braking systems for commercial vehicles*

1 Compressor,
2 Pressure regulator,
3 Antifreeze pump,
4 Four-circuit protection valve (ALB),
5 Compressed-air reservoir,
6 Coupling head with automatic shutoff valve,
7 Water drain valve,
8 Non-return valve,
9 Checking valve,
10 Parking-brake valve,
11 Trailer control valve,
12 Coupling head without shutoff valve,
13 Spring-type brake cylinder,
14 Front wheels,
15 Automatic load-sensitive braking-force metering,
16 Rear wheels,
17 Service-brake valve,
18 Brake cylinder,

*Non-muscular-energy dual-circuit two-line braking system with pneumatic transmission device* (Figure B)

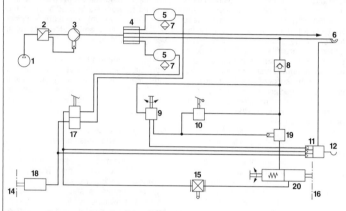

*Non-muscular-energy dual-circuit two-line braking system ("Air-over-hydraulic" braking system) with hydraulic transmission device* (Figure C)

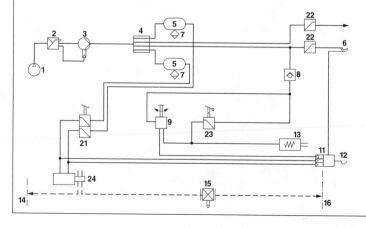

19 Relay valve,
20 Combination brake cylinder,
21 Service-brake valve with
   pressure limiter,
22 Pressure-limiting valve,
23 Parking-brake valve with
   pressure limiter,

24 Dual-circuit booster cylinder,
25 Trailer-brake valve,
26 Load/empty valve,
27 Secondary loads
   (e.g. exhaust-brake system).

### *Main components of a modern compressed-air non-muscular-energy braking system* (Figure D)

a) Energy supply, b) Reservoir, c) Brake valves, d) Control and supply for trailers,
e) Braking-force control, f) Wheel brakes.

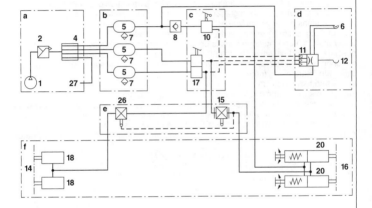

### *Dual-line braking system for trailer/semitrailer* (Figure E)

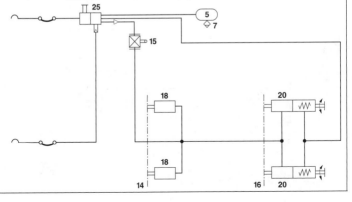

**Basic comments on "kinked" braking-force metering**

Load-sensitive braking-force metering devices adjust the installed braking-force metering to the dynamic (ideal) metering level and prevent the wheels of a given axle from locking prematurely. However, at low adhesion coefficients and low rear-axle loads, the wheels may skid because the metering device's switchover point can enter the unstable range of braking-force metering if one of the following occurs: high engine braking torque, retarder braking torque, tolerance fluctuations in the metering device, and/or high parameter fluctuations at the wheel brakes.

A braking system which works precisely under all braking conditions is only possible if load-sensitive braking-force metering is optimized. Commercial vehicles with extreme differences between empty and fully laden states require braking systems with automatic load-sensitive braking-force control (ALB) on the rear axle together with empty/load valves (in order to increase the working range of the ALB, Figure F).

# Wheel brakes

On medium-sized and heavy-duty commercial vehicles, disc brakes are becoming increasingly popular. Currently, drum brakes are in the majority worldwide.

The brake coefficient $C^*$ is an assessment criteria for brake performance and indicates the ratio of braking force to application force. This value takes into account the influence of the internal transmission ratio of the brake as well as the friction coefficient, which in turn is mainly dependent on the parameters of speed, braking pressure and temperature (Figure.

## Drum brakes

The actual construction of a drum brake depends on the requirements imposed by brake-shoe application, anchorage, and adjustment.

### Simplex drum brakes (Figure H)

These differ in particular according to their type of application (floating, fixed) and type of support or anchorage (rotating shoes, sliding shoes). Wheel brakes

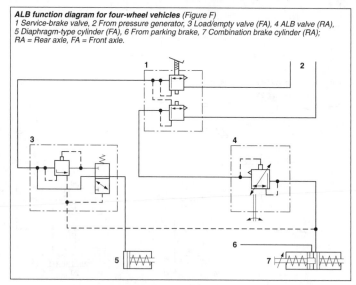

*ALB function diagram for four-wheel vehicles (Figure F)*
*1 Service-brake valve, 2 From pressure generator, 3 Load/empty valve (FA), 4 ALB valve (RA), 5 Diaphragm-type cylinder (FA), 6 From parking brake, 7 Combination brake cylinder (RA); RA = Rear axle, FA = Front axle.*

with floating-brake application and rotating-shoe support are common. In the case of hydraulic braking-force actuation, for instance, the brakes are applied by means of floating pressure pistons. Piston travel is not fixed, and they develop actuating forces which are equal in both directions. One shoe is the leading shoe and the other is the trailing shoe. In the leading shoe, the friction forces between the brake lining and the brake drum support the actuating force. In the trailing shoe, however, the friction forces oppose the actuating force.

The Simplex drum brake results in $C^*$ which is the sum of the values for the individual shoes, and is $\approx 2.0$ (referred to a coefficient of friction of $\mu = 0.38$; it always appears in the following $C^*$ considerations as the basis value). A disadvantage of this design is the considerable difference in the braking effect between the two brake shoes, and the resulting excessive wear on the leading shoe compared with the trailing shoe.

For this reason, the trailing shoe often has a much thinner lining than the leading shoe.

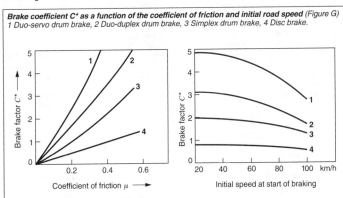

**Brake coefficient $C^*$ as a function of the coefficient of friction and initial road speed** (Figure G)
1 Duo-servo drum brake, 2 Duo-duplex drum brake, 3 Simplex drum brake, 4 Disc brake.

| Simplex drum brakes (Figure H) | | | |
|---|---|---|---|
| Design | Rotating shoe | Wedge | S-cam |
| Schematic diagram | | | |
| Brake factor | $C^* = C_1 + C_2$ | | $C^* = 4/(1/C_1 + 1/C_2)$ |
| Brake shoes | 1 Leading shoe, 2 Trailing shoe | | |

The simplex drum brake can also be actuated by means of a wedge unit (with integrated readjusting mechanism). This has become more and more prevalent, particularly on light and medium-sized commercial vehicles with compressed-air braking systems (Figures H and K).

The type of wheel brake used most often in heavy-duty commercial vehicles is the pneumatic S-cam simplex drum brake with fixed application (Figure J).

Advantages:
– Uniform lining wear on leading and trailing shoes as a result of fixed application.
– Long lining life.
– An application mechanism which is simple, reliable and insensitive to temperature. It comprises diaphragm-type cylinder, automatic slack adjuster, brake shaft, and S-cams.
– Little change in brake coefficient $C^*$.
– Simple operation of the parking-brake system via spring-type brake actuators.
– Precise adjustment by means of automatic slack adjusters.

Disadvantages:
– High internal forces and thus relatively heavy brake construction, as unequal cam forces occur and lead to high free bearing forces.
– Relatively low brake coefficient $C^*$, which means considerable application force is required when braking.

---

*Simplex drum brake with S-cam (Figure J)*
1 Diaphragm-type cylinder, 2 S-cam,
3 Brake shoes, 4 Return spring,
5 Brake drum.

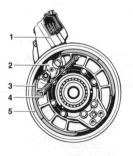

– Due to the roughly equal application travel of the leading and trailing shoes, compared to individual shoes, the actuating forces behave in the opposite manner.
– For the same coefficient of friction, the brake coefficient $C^*$ is somewhat lower than that of simplex brakes with hydraulic or pneumatic application.

### Duo-duplex drum brakes

The Duo-duplex brake with two leading shoes (with wedge-actuated control) is rarely used today (Figure K).

This brake features floating application and the associated necessity for sliding-shoe anchorage. One advantage of this brake type is that brake-lining wear is practically equal on both shoes and the internal transmission ratio is significantly higher compared with simplex drum brakes. Twin leading shoes achieve characteristics of $C^* \approx 3.0$ which, however, can not be sustained constantly for long periods due to the tendency of drum brake to fade.

### Duo-servo drum brakes

Duo-servo drum brakes: In the past, these were widely used in light commercial vehicles (particularly on the rear axle). This brake's primary feature is the fact that the support force of the primary shoe is used as the actuation force for the secondary shoe both when driving in a forward direction and when reversing. The brake coefficient is $C^* \approx 5.0$.

The popularity of the duo-servo brake lies in the fact that the high brake factors achieved allow even relatively heavy vans and light-duty trucks up to a weight of approx. 6 t to be equipped with a vacuum-assisted braking system. At the same time a muscular-force-operated parking-brake system equipped with duo-servo drum brakes generates a considerably high braking torque. However, under high thermal-stress conditions, significant brake-factor fluctuations occur. This fact limits the application range of this type of brake and requires a braking-force metering system which is precisely adapted to a particular vehicle model. Duo-servo drum brakes will hardly be used for service-braking systems in future.

## Disc brakes

The advantages of the disc brake compared with the drum brake are as follows:
- Braking effect can be applied with greater sensitivity.
- Equal wear of the inboard and outboard brake pads if the appropriate degree of thermal load is provided.
- Less tendency to develop brake noise.
- Relatively constant characteristics with minimum fading tendency.

Disadvantages:
- Shorter brake-pad life.
- Usually higher purchase and operating costs (compared with drum brakes).

The high degree of adaptive braking required at high expressway speeds is handled better by disc brakes. The brake discs are less susceptible to cracking than drum brakes. Besides, disc brakes are less subject to fading. The brake coefficient of the disc brake is $C^* \approx 0.76$, referred to a base value of $\mu = 0.38$.

Floating-caliper disc brakes are most commonly used at present. The decisive factor for this have been efforts to produce lighter and cheaper wheel brakes which are more temperature-resistant. Floating calipers have a positive effect on variability and consistency of braking effect.

## Automatic adjustment of wheel brakes

Friction-lining wear increases the clearance between brake pad/shoe and brake disc/drum, and thus increases the braking distance. If the clearance is not adjusted correctly, the piston travel in the brake cylinder may increase to such an extent in extreme cases that there is no braking effect. Automatic adjustment to the correct clearance takes place when the wheel brake is released.

When the vehicle is braked, the piston travel in the brake cylinder needed to bridge the total clearance can be divided into three sections:
- Preset constructive clearance between brake lining and brake drum/disc,
- Clearance resulting from lining wear,
- Clearance dependent on the elasticity of the brake drum/disc and of the friction lining, as well as on the transmission of force between brake cylinder and wheel brake ("elasticity clearance").

A slack adjuster automatically ensures the correct adjustment (Figure L).

| *Duo-drum brakes and disc brake* (Figure K) | | | |
|---|---|---|---|
| **Design** | **Duo-Duplex** <br> Wedge | **Duo-Servo** <br> Positive-action <br> adjustment | **Disc brake** |
| Schematic diagram | | | |
| Brake factor | $C^* = C_1 + C_2$ | $C^* = C_1 + C_2(k_1 + k_2 \cdot C_1)$ | $C^* = 2 \cdot \mu$ |
| Brake shoes | 1 Leading shoe, 2 Trailing shoe | | – |

## Parking-brake system

The braking systems with spring-type brake actuators which are usual in commercial vehicles above 6 t total weight are a convenient form of parking-brake and service-braking system. In a purely compressed-air braking system, spring-type brake cylinders from the parking-brake system and diaphragm brake cylinders from the service-braking system are combined.

In release position, the four-circuit protection valve and the handbrake valve connect the compressed-air reservoirs of the service-braking system with the spring compression chamber, and maintain the spring under tension. On vehicles with a connection for a trailer/semitrailer braking system, a buffer reservoir is also located in this line. When the handbrake valve is actuated, the pressure in the compression chamber is reduced. Consequently, partial braking occurs at first and, with the handbrake valve still actuated, a pressure drop down to the "surrounding conditions" takes place, and thus full braking of the spring-type brake actuator (secondary braking) occurs. Further actuation defines a "parking position". With the aid of a further lever setting, only the tractor is braked on road trains, and not the entire rig. As well as this test position for checking the efficiency of the mechanical parking brake

with trailer attached, EU/ECE regulations stipulate a backup emergency-air supply, nine-fold actuation and release using the energy reserve, a warning device to indicate that the spring-type brake actuator is beginning to function, and an auxiliary release device.

## Retarder braking systems (additional retarding braking systems)

The wheel brakes used in passenger cars and commercial vehicles are not designed for continuous retarding operation. In a prolonged period of braking (e.g. when driving downhill), the brakes can be thermally overloaded, causing a reduction in braking effect ("fading"). In extreme cases (particularly if the service-braking system has been badly maintained), this may even lead to complete braking system failure. In order to permit continuous downhill braking, therefore, vehicles with a high permissible total weight are frequently fitted with a wear-free supplementary retarding braking system (retarder) in addition to their normal wheel brakes. This system is independent of the wheel brakes, and is also used for braking the vehicle to comply with speed limits.

This reduces brake pad/lining wear and increases braking comfort for the driver.

**Brake clearances** (Figure L)
a Due to elasticity, b Due to wear, c Due to design. 1 Brake shoe, 2 Diaphragm-type cylinder, 3 Automatic slack adjuster.

**Braking-torque characteristics of primary and secondary retarders** (Figure M)
1 Secondary retarder, 2 Limit of cooling effect under continuous load (300 kW), 3 Primary retarder on input side of 16-speed transmission.

Retarders can be fitted between the engine and the transmission (primary retarders) or between the transmission and the driven axle(s) (secondary retarders). The disadvantage of primary retarders lies in the unavoidable interruption of power transmission, and thus braking effect, which occurs during gearshifting on manual transmissions. Primary retarders have a certain advantage over secondary retarders on steep downhill gradients negotiated at low speeds (Figures M and N).

Currently, two basic design concepts represent the state of the art:

### Primary retarders

Exhaust braking power comprises drag power together with the braking power (performed by throttling exhaust-gas flow in the exhaust stroke). The maximum drag power of standard engines is 5...7 kW/$l$ depending on engine swept volume. In contrast, standard engines with conventional exhaust brakes ("exhaust-flap brakes") achieve braking powers of 14...20 kW/$l$. A further increase in exhaust braking power is only possible by means of additional design modification. Exhaust brakes (e.g. "C-brake", "Jake brake", "Dynatard", "constant throttle", "Pritarder", "Aquatarder", etc.) can significantly improve braking power (Figure O).

#### Exhaust brake system with exhaust flap

The exhaust-flap brake is still the most common system in worldwide use today.

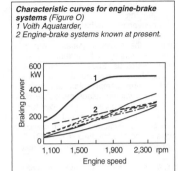

*Characteristic curves for engine-brake systems* (Figure O)
1 Voith Aquatarder,
2 Engine-brake systems known at present.

In this system, the driver closes a butterfly valve in the exhaust tract by means of compressed air (relatively little constructional outlay is involved). As a result, back-pressure is generated in the exhaust-gas system and must be overcome by each piston during its exhaust stroke (Figure P).

By the use of a pressure-control valve in the bypass, the braking effect can be increased at low and medium engine speeds by means of an exhaust flap. At higher revs, the pressure-control valve prevents pressure rises beyond the limits which could lead to valve or valve-gear damage.

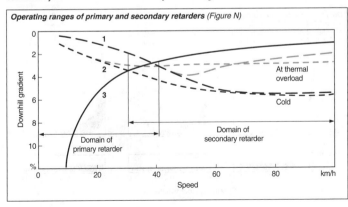

*Operating ranges of primary and secondary retarders* (Figure N)

## Exhaust brake system with constant throttle

The conventional exhaust brake with exhaust flap utilizes only the energy available in the engine's gas-exchange process, i.e. during the 4th (exhaust) and 1st (intake) strokes. Specific decompression during the 2nd and 3rd strokes releases part of the compression energy. The "pressure-volume" diagrams below show the pressure curves in a cylinder for the "exhaust flap" and "constant throttle" exhaust-brake systems, and for combinations of the two systems (Figure Q). The braking power when using the constant throttle system, as opposed to the exhaust-brake flap system, is obtained principally in the engine's high-pressure cycle.

The installation of a small restriction valve in the bypass to the exhaust valve permits an increase in braking power. This valve is actuated by compressed air, in the same way as in the positioning cylinder of the exhaust-brake flap. During exhaust-brake operation, the valve can remain open, thus providing a constant throttle cross-section (Figure R).

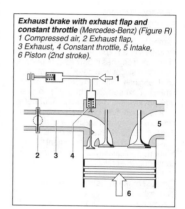

**Exhaust brake with additional pressure-control valve (Figure P)**
1 Exhaust-flap actuation (compressed air),
2 Bypass, 3 Pressure-control valve,
4 Discharge, 5 Intake, 6 Piston (4th stroke).

**Exhaust brake with exhaust flap and constant throttle (Mercedes-Benz) (Figure R)**
1 Compressed air, 2 Exhaust flap,
3 Exhaust, 4 Constant throttle, 5 Intake,
6 Piston (2nd stroke).

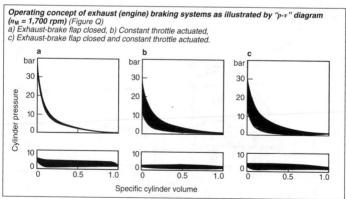

**Operating concept of exhaust (engine) braking systems as illustrated by "p-v" diagram ($n_M$ = 1,700 rpm) (Figure Q)**
a) Exhaust-brake flap closed, b) Constant throttle actuated,
c) Exhaust-brake flap closed and constant throttle actuated.

Cylinder pressure — Specific cylinder volume

In future generations of vehicles, primary retarders will offer tough competition to secondary retarders. They include, for example, crankshaft-driven water pumps with integrated retarders (Figure S), exhaust-gas turbochargers with integrated retarders, etc., which offer not only high braking power but also substantial weight savings. The high braking forces acting on the driving wheels of the vehicles require electronic monitoring of the braking effect or integration of the engine-brake systems in the electronic brake management.

### Secondary retarders

Retarders act as wear-free additional retarding braking systems in trucks and buses. This meets the legal requirements to increase active vehicle safety by reducing the stress placed on the service-braking system, and vehicle economy is increased as a result of higher average speeds and reduced brake-pad/lining wear.

#### Hydrodynamic retarders

This type of retarder works in the same way as the foettinger clutch (Figure T). A rotor converts the mechanical energy supplied by the drive shaft to kinetic energy in a fluid. This kinetic energy is in turn converted to heat at the stator, which means that the fluid used must be cooled.

*Boost retarder* (Figure T)
1 Wiring plug, 2 Proportional valve,
3 Compressed-air cylinder, 4 Stator,
5 Rotor, 6 Gearbox flange, 7 Spur gears
(transmission ratio), 8 Transmission.
A Heat exchanger, B Retarder circuit.

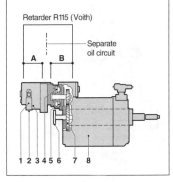

Retarder R115 (Voith)

A hand lever or the brake pedal (in the case of a retarder integrated in the EBS electronic braking system) transmits the driver's braking-power commands. In conjunction with an electronic control circuit, a defined control air pressure is set. By means of a corresponding quantity of air, this control air pressure then forces a quantity of oil into the retarder's working area between the rotor and the stator. The

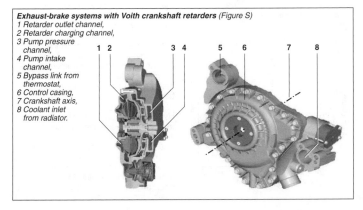

*Exhaust-brake systems with Voith crankshaft retarders* (Figure S)
1 Retarder outlet channel,
2 Retarder charging channel,
3 Pump pressure channel,
4 Pump intake channel,
5 Bypass link from thermostat,
6 Control casing,
7 Crankshaft axis,
8 Coolant inlet from radiator.

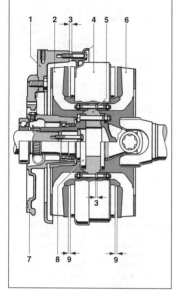

***Electrodynamic retarder*** *(Figure U)*
*1 Star-shaped bracket, 2 Rotor, transmission side, 3 Spacers (for adjusting clearance), 4 Stator with coils, 5 Intermediate flange, 6 Rotor, rear-axle side, 7 Transmission cover, 8 Transmission output shafts, 9 Clearance gap.*

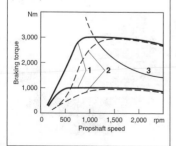

***Hydrodynamic retarder performance characteristics*** *(Figure V)*
*1 Boost retarder, 2 Conventional retarder, 3 Cooling-power limit at continuous load (300 kW).*

flow energy absorbed by the oil as a result of vehicle speed and the associated rotor motion is braked by the stator's fixed blading. This in turn brakes the rotor and thus the entire vehicle.

The main features are:
- Adequate engine cooling-circuit dimensioning is necessary in order to dissipate the heat generated by braking to the engine-cooling circuit. An oil/water heat exchanger is used.
- Relatively complex design.
- Low weight of the hydrodynamic retarder which is integrated directly in the transmission.
- High specific braking powers.
- Very sensitive control of applied braking torque.
- Fan losses occurring when the retarder is not running must also be taken into consideration in retarder design.

In the hydrodynamic secondary retarder, an almost constant braking torque is available over a broad propshaft-speed range (Figure V). Below approx. 1,000 rpm, braking torque drops abruptly. As a result of this characteristic, conventionally designed hydrodynamic retarders are particularly suited to high-speed transport vehicles (overland transport).

Modern retarder designs rectify the unfavorable braking torque characteristic of the secondary retarder design described above by providing high braking torques even at low propshaft speeds. A spur-gear stage with a transmission ratio of approx. 1:2 drives "boost retarders" which are fitted to the side of the transmission (Figure T). Even in the lower propshaft speed range, a microprocessor control ensures acceptable braking-torque levels via a proportional valve.

Hydrodynamic retarders can only be used as continuous-operation braking systems in certain situations for limited periods. The maximum cooling power of modern diesel engines is approx. 300 kW (Figure V). As a result of coupling the engine and retarder cooling circuits, there is a risk for both engine and retarder if additional safety measures are not implemented.

For this reason, thermostatic switches are used to restrict the retarder's braking power to ensure thermal equilibrium.

### Electrodynamic retarders

Common electrodynamic retarders today have a stator on which field coils are mounted (Figure U). The rotors mounted on both sides of the drive shaft are ribbed to enhance heat dissipation. In order to brake the vehicle, voltage is applied to the field coils (from the battery or alternator) to generate a magnetic field which induces eddy currents in the rotors as they pass through the field. This generates a braking-torque level which is dependent on stator excitation and on the air gap between rotor and stator.

The main features are:
– Dissipation to the atmosphere of the heat produced
– Relatively simple design
– Relatively heavy construction
– Trouble-free operation only with adequate power supply
– Heating the retarder leads to a drop in braking torque
– High braking powers even at low vehicle speeds
– Braking power influenced by rotor blading, air-flow conditions around the eddy-current brake (electrodynamic retarder), and by ambient temperature

In contrast to conventional hydrodynamic secondary retarders, electrodynamic retarders provide relatively high braking torques at low propshaft speeds (Figure W).

A significant reduction in braking torques of the electrodynamic retarder as the rotor temperature increases result from the thermal safeguard (Figure W). Vehicle deceleration is reduced as thermal stress on the electrodynamic retarder increases.

In order to prevent temperature-related destruction of the retarder when the vehicle is being braked, a bimetallic switch restricts the current supply to half of the eight coils when the stator temperature reaches approx. 250 °C (Figure X).

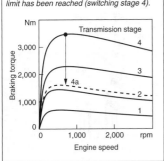

**Braking-torque characteristic of an electrodynamic retarder** (Figure W)
4a Braking power when the cooling power limit has been reached (switching stage 4).

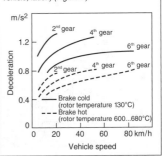

**Influence of transmission ratio and rotor temperature on the performance of electrodynamic retarders** (17 t commercial vehicle, laden) (Figure X)

## Components for compressed-air brakes

### Energy supplying device

The energy-supplying device comprises the following components:
- Energy source
- Pressure control
- Air conditioner

The <u>energy source</u> is a continuously running air compressor which is driven by the engine via V-belts or gears. It consists of:
- Crankcase and crankshaft (driver for power-steering pump at the free end of the shaft), bearing assembly and connections for circulating engine lubrication
- Cylinder with piston and connecting rod
- Intermediate plate with inlet and outlet valves
- Cylinder head with suction and pressure connections for air and, if appropriate, the fittings required for liquid-cooled versions

Energy-economy controls are in increasing use in order to reduce losses at idle (opening and flow resistances in the valves, lines, and pressure regulator). These are integrated in the valve plate

and actuated pneumatically via an actuator. At idle, either a bypass is opened from the compressor pressure chamber to the input side, or the intake bore is opened by rotating or shifting the inlet valve.

The air compressor is usually attached to the vehicle engine by means of base or flange mounting. In some cases, it is integrated in the engine block.

During its downward stroke, the piston draws in air after the inlet valve opens automatically due to vacuum. The inlet valve closes at the start of the piston's return stroke. The air is then compressed and, after reaching a set pressure, it is conveyed via the outlet valve, which also opens automatically, to the downstream compressed-air system.

In terms of delivery rate, the aim is a volumetric efficiency of 70% and, in terms of oil consumption, a maximum of 0.5 g/h is desirable.

The <u>pressure control</u> ensures that the desired pressure level is maintained. Two main types of regulation are used:
1. Regulation where the pressure regulator has no influence on the energy source (in compressors with high-idle speeds > 2,500 rpm).

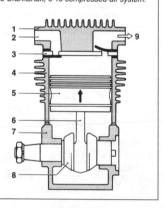

*Air compressor* (compression and discharge)
1 Cylinder head, 2 Air intake, 3 Intermediate plate (with inlet and outlet valves), 4 Cylinder, 5 Piston, 6 Connecting rod, 7 Crankcase, 8 Crankshaft, 9 To compressed-air system.

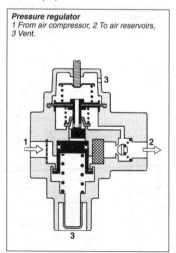

*Pressure regulator*
1 From air compressor, 2 To air reservoirs, 3 Vent.

The pressure regulator switches off when the desired maximum operating pressure is reached, and returns the air supplied by the compressor to atmosphere during the subsequent no-load period. If the pressure in the air reservoirs reaches the lower operating-pressure limit, the pressure regulator switches on again and supplies the air delivered by the compressor to the air reservoirs.

2. Regulation in which the pressure regulator influences the energy source (in compressors with high-idle speeds < 2,500 rpm).

When the desired maximum operating pressure is reached, the regulator applies pressure to a plunger in the compressor and opens its inlet valve. Without being supplied to the air reservoirs, the intake air is expelled through the inlet fitting. When the pressure in the air reservoirs reaches the lower operating-pressure limit, the regulator switches over and the inlet valve can again open and close automatically, and the air reservoirs are filled.

Pressure level: On tractor units, pressures are used ranging from max. 7 to 12.5 bar (low pressure) and from 14 to 20 bar (high pressure). In a dual-line braking system, the maximum pressure in the lines connecting the tractor unit and trailer is between 6.5 and 8.5 bar.

The purpose of <u>air conditioning</u> is to assure proper operation of downstream braking-system components. Impurities in the air can cause leaks in the control valves, and water in the compressed air leads to corrosion or icing-up in frosty weather. To combat these problems, an air drier is connected downstream of the air compressor. This type of configuration makes it unnecessary to add antifreeze to the system.

Basically, an air drier consists of a desiccant box and a housing. The housing incorporates the air passage, a bleeder valve, and a control element for granulate regeneration. Normally, the granulate is regenerated by switching in a regeneration-air reservoir with integrated regeneration throttle.

Function: When the bleeder valve is closed, compressed air from the air compressor flows through the desiccant box

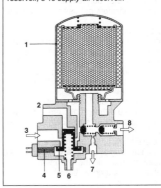

*Single-box air drier*
*1 Desiccant box, 2 From pressure regulator, 3 From air compressor, 4 Heating element, 5 Bleeder valve, 6 Vent, 7 To regeneration-air reservoir, 8 To supply-air reservoir.*

and from there to the supply-air reservoirs. At the same time a regeneration-air reservoir with a volume of approx. 4...6 liters is filled with dry compressed air. As moisture-laden compressed air flows through the desiccant box, water is removed by means of condensation and adsorption.

The granulate in the desiccant box has a limited water absorption capacity and must therefore be regenerated at regular intervals. In the reverse process, dry compressed air from the regeneration-air reservoir is reduced to atmospheric pressure via the regeneration throttle, flows back through the moist granulate from which it draws off the moisture, and flows as moist air via the open bleeder valve to the atmosphere. On air driers with an integrated pressure regulator, its control element is fitted to port 4 of the air-drier valve body.

### Control device
Normally, the control device comprises the brake pedal and all devices up to the limit of their influence on the ECUs.

### Transmission device
The transmission device comprises the following:
– Circuit isolation (e.g. multiple-circuit protection valve)

- Energy storage (e.g. air reservoirs)
- ECUs (e.g. brake valves)
- Load-sensitive braking-force metering device (e.g., automatic load-sensitive braking-force control), and
- Brake cylinders or positioning cylinders

These transmission device components interact as shown in the block diagram below of a non-muscular-energy braking system with dual-circuit service-braking system (see also the braking-system diagram on P. 840). Functions and design of components:

Circuit isolation: In the event of damage to one circuit, the circuits are separated, so the intact circuits continue to be powered.

Circuit isolation is primarily achieved by a combination of overflow valves grouped together as a unit; the operation of these valves is ensured at both low and high delivery rates.

Increasingly, the units introduced today incorporate the functions of "pressure regulation", "air conditioning" and "circuit isolation". More advanced electronically controlled units implement the functions with the aid of solenoid valves.

Energy storage: To provide the required volume of energy for all circuits in the braking system, including energy in the event of failure of the energy source. Commercially available air reservoirs are used for this purpose; these have corresponding safety allowances for excess pressure and rust.

**Control equipment**
This equipment is used to control the metering of the required pressure to the corresponding parts of the system. Mechanically, hydraulically or pneumatically actuated or controlled reaction valves are used to control pressure at the output of each valve as a function of the input variable. Due to the wide range of applications, a correspondingly large number of different components are in use. Dual-circuit control valves are also required for dual-circuit service-braking systems. Proper braking-system operation requires good control behavior, good pressure-metering capability, fast reaction times, and low braking-system hysteresis.

**Automatic load-sensitive braking-force control (ALB)**
Automatic braking-pressure control is a function of vehicle load. Load is often determined by spring compression (in the case of steel-spring suspension) and bellows pressure (in the case of pneumatic suspension). A control valve with a variable reaction-surface area reduces the output

---

*Transmission device in a non-muscular-energy braking system* (block diagram)
1 Energy supply,
2 Circuit isolation,
3 Energy storage,
4 ECUs,
5 Automatic load-sensitive braking-force metering (ALB),
6 Brake cylinders or positioning cylinders,
VA *Front wheels,*
HA *Rear wheels.*

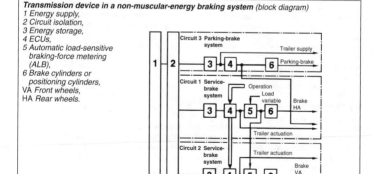

pressure in the valve in relation to the input pressure as a function of spring range or bellows pressure.

**Brake cylinders or positioning cylinders**
They convert the pressure applied to the braking system to braking force. Both plunger- and diaphragm-type cylinders are used. Diaphragm-type cylinders are primarily used for service-braking systems, while spring-type piston brake cylinders are used for the parking-brake system. In the case of axles which are subjected to both the service-braking system and the parking-brake system, combined single-chamber spring-type brake cylinders (so-called combination cylinders) are used in braking systems without hydraulic force transmission.

**Wheel brakes** (see P. 842)

**Service-brake valve**
Two tandem-arranged control valves are actuated by a common device (brake pedal with transmission). The synchronized opening of both circuits is ensured by identical spring and valve sealing forces as well as by the mechanical overcoming of the opening forces in both control valves. In the braking position, the rocking piston between the control circuits is subjected at its two ends to the currently applied braking pressure to guarantee that the circuits are synchronized. The preloaded travel-limiting spring provides small response travels of the service-brake valve. The interaction of the force of the reaction piston with the travel-limiting spring allows the system to execute the necessary control travels independently. Dual-circuit sealing of the rocking piston ensures the required safety.

**Parking-brake valve**
Today's compact design of the parking-brake valve is a direct result of the confined space on the instrument panel (where it used to be fitted). The parking-brake valve always actuates the brake cylinders via relay valves.

A hand lever (actuating lever) adjusts an internal valve seat by means of an eccentric element and a linking strap. It controls a double-seat valve in which compressed air from above and the force of compression springs from below act on a valve plunger. In brakes-applied mode, the actuating lever latches in position automatically, and the space above the valve plunger is purged of air. There are as many intermediate settings between the driving and brakes-applied modes as desired.

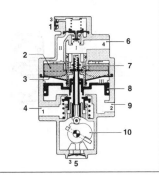

*Service-brake valve*
1 Actuation, 2 Reaction piston, 3 Brake circuit 1, 4 Rocking piston, 5 Brake circuit 2, 6 Vent, 7 Travel-limiting spring, 8 Supply circuit 1, 9 Control valves, 10 Supply circuit 2.

*Automatic load-sensing valve*
1 Vent, 2 Rake, 3 Transfer diaphragm, 4 From air reservoir, 5 Vent, 6 From service-brake valve, 7 Control valve, 8 Relay piston, 9 To brake cylinders, 10 Rotary cam.

If the actuating lever is moved beyond the brakes-applied mode position, the auxiliary (test) valve is actuated and compressed air flows from the supply-air reservoir to the connection of the trailer-control valve. This leads to retention of the tractor braking effect, although it is canceled for the trailer.

### Automatic load-sensing valve

This device is connected between the service-brake valve and the brake cylinders. Depending on vehicle payload, it regulates the applied braking pressure. The device has a transfer diaphragm with variable effective area. The diaphragm is held in two radially arranged and interlocking rakes. Depending on the vertical position of the control-valve seat, there is a large reaction area (valve position at bottom) or a small reaction area (valve position at top). Consequently, the brake cylinders are supplied via an integrated relay valve with a pressure which is lower than (unladen), or which is the same as (fully laden) the pressure coming from the service-brake valve. The regulator is mounted on the vehicle frame and senses the compression position of the axle by a rotary lever via linkages. The rotary cam moves the valve rod to the vertical direction accordingly and thus determines the

valve position. The pressure limiter which is integrated in the device at the top allows a small partial pressure to flow in to the top of the diaphragm. Thus, up to this pressure there is no reduction in brake-cylinder pressure. This results in the synchronous application of the brakes on all vehicle axles. If the rotary lever breaks, the applied pressure flows to the brake cylinders at a ratio of 2:1.

### Combination brake cylinder for wedge brakes

The combination brake cylinder consists of a single-chamber diaphragm-type cylinder for the service brakes and a spring-type brake cylinder for the parking-brake system. The cylinder- and spring-type brake cylinder are in tandem and act on a common push rod. They can be actuated independently of each other. Simultaneous actuation results in the addition of their forces. The central release screw permits tensioning the spring of the spring-type brake cylinder without compressed air having to be applied. This is the setting when installed in the vehicle. After installation, the release screw is screwed in the spring-type brake cylinder, and the spring acts via the plunger rod on the wedge mechanism. The entry of compressed air into the spring-type brake cylinder (when the parking brake is released) forces the plunger back against the action of the spring, loads the spring and releases the brake (position illustrated). When the service brakes are operated, compressed air flows into the diaphragm cylinder and exerts pressure via the plunger and the push rod on the wedge mechanism. A drop in air pressure releases the brake.

The principle described above is modified for cam-operated drum brakes and for disc brakes.

### Trailer-control valve

In dual-line braking systems, the trailer-control valve installed in the tractor controls the trailer's service brakes. This multi-circuit relay valve is triggered by both service-brake circuits and by the parking-brake system.

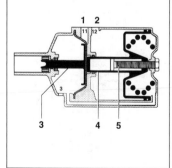

*Combination brake cylinder for wedge brakes*
1 Single-chamber cylinder control line,
2 Spring-type brake cylinder control line,
3 Push rod, 4 Plunger rod, 5 Release screw.

1  2

3      4   5

In the driving (non-braked) mode, the supply chamber and the chamber of the parking-brake circuit are each subjected to equal pressure, and the trailer brake line is vented through the central vent port. A rise in pressure upstream of the control plunger of brake circuit 1 (top) and/or of brake circuit 2 (bottom) leads to a corresponding rise in pressure in the trailer brake line. Brake circuit 1 is equipped with a larger control plunger than brake circuit 2, which means that it has priority over the control plunger of circuit 2. This priority ends when the pilot pressure is reached (pilot-spring force is exceeded). A drop in pressure in the service-brake circuits leads to an identical drop in the trailer brake line. The venting of the parking-brake circuit (braking action) increases pressure in the chamber to the trailer brake line. Application of air to the parking-brake circuit (releasing) vents the trailer brake line again.

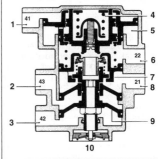

*Trailer-control valve*
1 Service-brake circuit 1, 2 Parking-brake circuit, 3 Service-brake circuit 2, 4 Pilot spring, 5 Control-plunger 1, 6 Control line to trailer, 7 Control-plunger unit, 8 Supply line to trailer, 9 Control-plunger 2, 10 Vent.

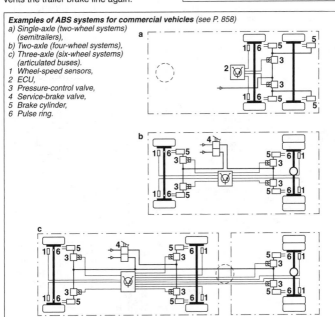

*Examples of ABS systems for commercial vehicles* (see P. 858)
a) Single-axle (two-wheel systems)
   (semitrailers),
b) Two-axle (four-wheel systems),
c) Three-axle (six-wheel systems)
   (articulated buses).
1 Wheel-speed sensors,
2 ECU,
3 Pressure-control valve,
4 Service-brake valve,
5 Brake cylinder,
6 Pulse ring.

# Vehicle stabilization systems for commercial vehicles

## Antilock braking system (ABS)

The ABS prevents the wheels from locking when the vehicle is overbraked. The vehicle therefore retains its directional stability and steerability even under emergency braking on a slippery road surface. The braking distance is often shorter than with locked wheels. ABS prevents the danger of jackknifing in the case of vehicle combinations.

In contrast to passenger cars, commercial vehicles have air-brake systems. Nevertheless, the functional description of an ABS control process for passenger cars (see P. 809 onwards) also applies in principle to commercial vehicles.

The antilock braking system as used in commercial vehicles consists of wheel-speed sensors, an electronic control unit (ECU) and pressure-control valves. ABS regulates the braking pressure in each brake cylinder by increasing the pressure, holding it constant, or reducing it by venting to atmosphere (see Figure on O. 857).

### Individual control (IR)

This process, which sets and controls the optimum braking pressure individually for each wheel, produces the shortest braking distances. Under μ-split conditions (different adhesion on right and left wheels, e.g. black ice at edge of road surface, good grip at center of road surface), braking produces a high yaw moment about the vertical axis of the vehicle, thus making short-wheelbase vehicles difficult to control. In addition, this is coupled with high steering moments as a result of the positive steering roll radii in commercial vehicles.

### Select-low control (SL)

This process reduces the yaw and steering moments to zero. It is achieved by applying the same braking pressure to both wheels on the same axle. Only one pressure-control valve is required for each axle. The pressure applied is dependent

on the wheel with less grip (select low), the wheel with more grip is braked less heavily compared to the individual control (IR) method. In μ-split conditions, braking distances are longer, but steerability and directional stability of the vehicle are enhanced. If grip conditions (friction coeffi-

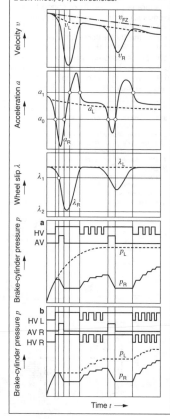

**ABS control methods**
*Example: Braking on μ-split.*
*a) IR individual control (rear axle), b) IRM individual control modified (steering axle).*
*HV Pressure-holding valve, AV Outlet valve.*
*Subscripts: FZ vehicle, R Right wheel, L Left wheel, 0, 1, 2 thresholds.*

cients) are the same on both sides of the vehicle, then braking distances, steerability and directional stability are virtually identical with individual control systems (IR).

### Select-smart control (SSM)

As with the select-low control function, select-smart control uses only one pressure-control valve for each axle. With select-smart control, however, wheel slip in μ-split conditions is increased according to a variety of physical variables, such as braking pressure and friction coefficient. The wheel with the lower friction coefficient may then lock. For this reason, SSM allows shorter braking distances in μ-split conditions than SL. Steerability and/or directional stability of the vehicle may be slightly diminished. The locked wheel does not generally suffer tire damage due to low friction coefficient.

### Individual control modified (IRM)

This process requires a pressure-control valve at each wheel of the axle. It reduces yaw and steering moments only as far as necessary, and limits braking-pressure difference between the left and right sides to permissible levels. As a result, the wheel running at a high friction coefficient is braked slightly less. This compromise results in a braking distance which is only a little longer than that for individual control (IR), but it does ensure that vehicles with critical handling characteristics remain controllable.

### ABS equipment for commercial vehicles

The current state of the art is that ABS ECUs for tractor units (commercial vehicles, tractor vehicles, buses) can be used on two and three-axle vehicles. The ECU performs a teach-in process during which it adjusts its settings to suit the particular vehicle. This involves detecting the number of axles, the ABS control method and any additional functions that may be required, such as TCS (see P. 862). A similar situation applies to ABS ECUs for trailers/semitrailers. The same ECU can be used on trailers/semitrailers with one, two or three axles, and adapts itself to the level of equipment present.

If one axle is a lifting axle, it is automatically excluded from the ABS control process when lifted.

When two axles are close together, often only one of them is fitted with wheel-speed sensors. The braking pressure of each pair of adjacent wheels is then controlled by a single pressure-control valve (combined control).

On multi-axle vehicles with a larger distance between axles, e.g. articulated buses, a three-axle control concept is preferable.

The IRM control process is most commonly used on steering axles, however, the SL method is sometimes adopted though very rarely. On tractor-unit rear axles, the IR method is normally selected, but SSM is also sometimes fitted.

The range of available control equipment permits further control combinations (not described here in detail). Example: If both axles on a semitrailer have wheel-speed sensors, but each side of the vehicle is only equipped with a single pressure-control valve, the wheels of one side of the vehicle are SL-controlled.

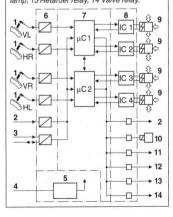

**ABS/TCS electronic control unit (ECU)**
1 Wheel-speed sensor, 2 TCS engine-management interface, 3 Self-diagnosis, 4 Vehicle power supply, 5 Power supply, protective unit, 6 Input stages,
7 Microcomputers 1 and 2, 8 Output stages, 9 Pressure-control valve, 10 TCS solenoid valve, 11 Warning lamp, 12 TCS indicator lamp, 13 Retarder relay, 14 Valve relay.

All ABS systems can be equipped with single-channel pressure-modulation valves. ABS trailer systems can also be fitted with pressure-control valves with relay action (see Figure).

In light commercial vehicles with pneumatic/hydraulic converters, ABS intervenes in the pneumatic brake circuit via single-channel pressure-modulation valves and defines the hydraulic braking pressure. In other versions, an ABS pressure modulator with integrated solenoid valves is connected in parallel to the pneumatic/hydraulic converter. The modulators are controlled by the same ECUs as the single-channel pressure-modulation valves.

When the vehicle is running on a low-friction-coefficient road surface, the operation of an additional retarding brake (exhaust brake or retarder) can lead to excessive slip at the driven wheels. This would impair vehicle stability. ABS therefore monitors brake slip and controls it to permissible levels by switching the retarder on and off.

## ABS components
### Wheel-speed sensor
Most applications today use an application-specific inductive sensor attached to the axle tube (for a description of the function, refer to P. 119). In contrast with passenger-car applications (rigidly attached sensors), the sensor on commercial vehicles is held in a spring sleeve. When the vehicle is in motion, the action of the wheel-bearing play and the flexing of the axle moves the sensor along its axis, thereby automatically adjusting the air gap between the sensor and the pulse ring. If, under exceptional circumstances, the air gap becomes excessive, the ECU switches off control for the wheel in question.

In the future, inductive sensors integrated in the wheel bearings and semiconductor wheel-speed sensors will be used more frequently for cost reasons.

### Electronic control unit (ECU)
The ECU's input stages convert the incoming near-sinusoisal signals from the wheel-speed sensors to square-wave signals. The wheel speeds are calculated from the frequency of the square-wave signals by redundant microcomputers. These speeds

are used to estimate a vehicle reference speed. The brake slip for each wheel is calculated using this reference speed and the individual wheel speed. If a wheel shows an incipient tendency to lock, this is determined from the "wheel-acceleration" and "wheel-slip signals". In this case, the microcomputer energizes (via the ECU output stages) the solenoids of the pressure-control valves which control the braking pressure in the individual wheel-brake cylinders.

The ECU contains a comprehensive program for detecting faults within the entire antilock braking system (wheel-speed sensors, ECU, pressure-control valves, wiring harness). If a fault is detected, the ECU switches off the defective part of the system and stores a fault code detailing the faulty signal path. The code is retrieved by a service technician with the aid of the diagnosis lamp (blink code) or using an intelligent testing device (e.g. personal computer) via a standardized serial interface.

The ECUs of some European ABS manufacturers include not only the ABS function, but also functions for the TCS traction control system and, in some cases, for vehicle-speed limiters (see also P. 863). The most important factor is that the ECU configures itself automatically to the required function. If a vehicle is only equipped with ABS components, the ECU only carries out the ABS function; if the vehicle is also fitted with TCS components, the ECU controls drive slip automatically as well.

### Pressure-control valve
Single-channel pressure-modulation valves are available with and without relay action. Relay-action valves are installed in semi-trailers and drawbar trailers. The standard trailer-braking system often includes relay valves which can then be replaced by ABS relay-action valves. Non-relay-action ABS valves are used in all other vehicles, i.e. in buses, trucks and tractor vehicles, as well as in trailers and special vehicles. Both types of valve have 3/2-way solenoid valves. The non-relay-action valves thereby control 2/2-way diaphragm valves, which have a sufficiently large cross-section for almost all applications. In the case of the relay-action valves, the 3/2-way solenoid valves affect

**Pressure-control valve** (schematic)
1 Pressure-holding valve, 2 Outlet valve, 3 Solenoid valve for "pressure holding",
4 Solenoid valve for "pressure drop", 5 Control plunger, 6 Valve plate, 7 Compression spring,
8 Brake cylinder, 9 Service-brake valve, 10 Supply air, 11 Vent.

**Single-channel pressure-modulation valve**    **Pressure-control valve with relay action**

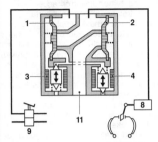    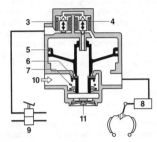

the pressure in the pilot chamber of a relay valve. The electronics control the solenoid valves in the appropriate combination so that the required function is performed (pressure holding or pressure drop). If no pilot-valve actuation takes place, "pressure rise" is the result.

When braking normally (that is, without ABS response = no incipient wheel locking), air flows through the pressure-control valves unhindered in both directions when pressure is applied to or vented from the brake cylinders. This ensures fault-free functioning of the service-braking system.

**Legal requirements**
Since October 1, 1991, ABS has been prescribed by law within the region covered by the EU member states for the first registration of commercial vehicles intended for trailer operation, and of semitrailer tractors (> 16 t), trailers (> 10 t) and buses (> 12 t). This regulation has been extended so that since October 1, 1998 all buses, and since October 1, 1999, all trucks and trailers (> 3.5 t) must be fitted with ABS.

The law stipulates 3 categories of ABS which differ from each other with respect to their specifications regarding braking factor and wheel/vehicle behavior on μ-split road surfaces. Most European ve-

hicle manufacturers only use Category 1 ABS systems. Only these must conform to all specifications of Directive 71/320/EEC.

All ABS installations must be equipped with a warning lamp which must light up for at least 2 s after switching on the driving switch. The driver must observe this lamp as part of his visual inspection. If it lights up while the vehicle is in motion, it indicates that the system's continuous self-testing facility has detected a fault. This can result in the complete deactivation of ABS.

Tractors and trailers with ABS systems from different manufacturers may be combined as required, provided there is an ABS plug-and-socket connection between the two vehicles in accordance with ISO 7638.

On all vehicle combinations (semitrailers, road trains), optimized brake control at physical driving limits is only guaranteed when both tractor and trailer are equipped with ABS. However, even without ABS on both parts of a truck combination (only on tractor or only on trailer), there are significant improvements compared to a vehicle combination which has no ABS at all.

# Traction control system (TCS)

This traction-control system is integrated within ABS ECUs for shared use of ABS components, such as wheel-speed sensors and pressure-control valves. The control system consists of a brake-control circuit and an engine-control circuit. In addition, the TCS brake-control circuit requires a two-way directional-control valve and a TCS valve (2/2-way solenoid valve). The engine-control circuit requires a final-control element for reducing the engine torque.

## Brake-control circuit

When the vehicle moves off on a road surface with a low friction coefficient or µ-split (left/right variations in traction), the wheel spin that accompanies excessive throttle is often limited to a single driving wheel. Due to the low friction coefficient at the spinning wheel, only minimal drive forces are available to move the vehicle. The brake controller responds to this situation by applying a braking torque to the spinning wheel; this force is conveyed through the differential and acts as drive torque at the (still) stationary wheel.

First, the ECU switches the TCS valve to open position for initial braking at the spinning wheel. The control circuit then uses the ABS pressure-control valve to control the pressure at the wheel-brake cylinder as a function of wheel response. The braking pressure is controlled so as to synchronize the driving wheels. The result is a differential locking effect between the two driving wheels comparable to that provided by a mechanical differential lock. In order to achieve the same forward drive, however, engine torque must be greater than required with a mechanical differential lock by an amount equivalent to the braking torque applied by the TCS brake controller.

This is one reason why mechanical differential locks are frequently employed in difficult terrain (e.g. construction sites). The brake control function is then employed under these conditions where the driver might have difficulty in determining whether differential locking between the driving wheels will provide increased traction. It is often possible to dispense with a

mechanical differential lock entirely on vehicles not used in demanding offroad conditions.

The effect of the brake controller is of greatest benefit when driving off, accelerating, or on hill stretches with "µ-split" surfaces. The control circuit must supply high braking pressure to the low-traction wheel when a fully-laden vehicle operates on extreme µ-split on uphill stretches. To prevent excessive thermal loading of the brakes, TCS incorporates two safety functions:
a) The brake controller remains inactive at speeds above 30 km/h.
b) Controller activity and wheel speed are used to estimate the thermal load at the brakes; if a defined limit is exceeded, the controller responds by de-activating TCS.

Using the brake-control function described above, the driving wheels can also be synchronized so that a mechanical differential lock, if fitted, can be engaged automatically, e.g. with the aid of a pneumatic cylinder. The ABS/TCS ECU calculates the correct point and conditions for releasing the differential lock.

## Engine-control circuit

Drive wheels on surfaces which have equal but limited traction will respond to excess throttle by spinning on both sides. The drive force available for moving the vehicle forwards is then determined by the diminishing friction coefficient in the unstable band of the adhesion/slip curve (see figure on P. 812). Attempts to accelerate a stationary or crawling vehicle on ice or snow "polish" the surface, resulting in a further, substantial reduction in traction. At the same time vehicle stability is sacrificed. The engine-control circuit responds to these conditions by reducing drive slip to an acceptable level, thus enhancing traction and vehicle stability.

Both electric and pneumatic actuators are available to control engine-torque reduction. The section below explains the principles involved by describing two options for electric control:
– an interface connected to electronic engine-control units,
– direct control of an electrical servomotor.

**Traction control system (TCS) for commercial vehicles with electronic fuel-injection pump control (EDC)**
1 Wheel-speed sensor, 2 Pulse ring, 3 ABS/TCS ECU, 4 Pressure-control valve (single circuit), 5 2/2-way solenoid valve, 6 Two-way directional-control valve, 7 Service-brake valve, 8 Load-sensing valve, 9 Wheel-brake cylinders, 10 EDC ECU, 11 Accelerator pedal, 12 Pedal-travel sensor, 13 Fuel-injection pump.

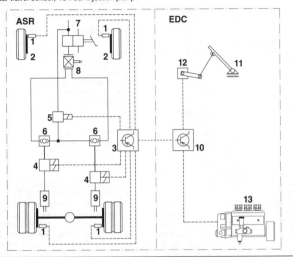

<u>Interface</u> (refer to CAN on P. 1073): An ABS/TCS ECU receives signals containing driver commands from one of the engine-management ECUs (e.g. accelerator-pedal position or desired injected-fuel quantity). The ABS/TCS ECU uses both this signal and various other data such as wheel slip to calculate the torque reduction requirement and sends the result to the engine-management ECU for implementation. Examples of engine-management ECUs are EMS (electronic engine-performance control system) and EDC (Electronic Diesel Control) units. They incorporate all engine-management functions (e.g. vehicle-speed control, engine-speed limiting, idle-speed control, etc.) and immediately carry out the TCS request to reduce engine speed with the required degree of accuracy.

<u>Servomotor:</u> An ABS/TCS ECU operates the servomotor directly. The servomotor is a direct-current device with integrated position feedback for precise closed-loop position control; regulation thus remains unaffected by variables such as positioning forces at the fuel-injection pump and friction in the accelerator-lever linkage or other disturbance values. The TCS can only use the linkage to reduce throttle, thus excluding the possibility of inadvertent opening of the throttle. A vehicle-speed limiter integrated in the ECU either holds the vehicle's road speed at a statutory speed limit ($v_{max}$ control) or at a speed set by the driver by means of a switch ($v_{set}$ control). In this case, the driver must depress the accelerator beyond the point which would otherwise be necessary to maintain the desired $v_{max}$ or $v_{set}$ speed. The ABS/TCS ECU compensates for excess throttle. Vehicle-speed limiters have been a legal requirement on buses (permissible total weight > 10 t) and commercial vehicles (permissible total weight > 12 t) since January 1, 1994.

# Electronic Stability Program (ESP) for commercial vehicles

## Function
The Electronic Stability Progam (ESP) for commercial vehicles is a dynamic-handling control system which represents a substantial extension to the Antilock Braking System (ABS) and Traction Control System (TCS).

The ABS and TCS safety systems control the dynamics of individual wheels when braked and accelerated. Wheel speeds are transmitted as measured actual data to the controller on each system, which compares them with setpoints and corrects discrepancies by modifying braking pressure and/or engine torque. As a result, critical linear-motion situations are neutralized so that the vehicle remains steerable in situations such as heavy braking.

However, since the controller does not take account of any vehicle-motion parameters, the handling stability of the vehicle depends on the matched settings between the ABS or TCS system. In the case of ABS, for example, there therefore has to be a tradeoff between braking distance and steerability. In the case of TCS, the tradeoff is between stability and traction.

ESP expands the parameters of control to include vehicle-motion variables, i.e. those relating to lateral dynamics. In addition to skidding (cf. ESP for cars on P. 820 onwards), there are other critical situations for commercial vehicles such as jackknifing and overturning which arise from their specific characteristics (scope for relative movement between tractor and trailer/semitrailer, and high center of gravity). Consequently, ESP for commercial vehicles must perform the following assignments:
- Active driver assistance in critical lateral-dynamic situations, regardless of whether the driver is braking or accelerating.

- Greater handling stability: improvement in directional stability and response of an individual vehicle or a vehicle combination (e.g. articulated road train) at physical driving limits in all operating and laden states. This includes preventing jackknifing on vehicle combinations.
- Greater directional stability: reduced risk of overturning for a vehicle or vehicle combination in both quasi-stationary and dynamic vehicle maneuvers.
- Improved utilization of the adhesion between tire and road surface and thereby optimization of ABS and TCS performance by including handling-dynamic data.

## Function groups
Deriving from these assignments, ESP requires the function groups described below.

### Stabilizing the vehicle when there is a risk of skidding or jackknifing
To stabilize the vehicle, a situation must first of all be detected as critical. The controller compares current vehicle motion in the horizontal plane with vehicle motion desired by the driver, taking account of physical driving limits. The horizontal-plane dynamics are represented for a single vehicle by three axes of motion (linear, lateral and yaw). For an articulated road train, horizontal plane motion is extended to include the articulation angle between the tractor and the trailer.

The vehicle motion intended by the driver is calculated by the ECU by means of simplified mathematical and physical models mainly based on the steering-wheel angle and vehicle speed. The nominal yaw rate $\omega_{zsoll}$ of the tractor is calculated using a single-path vehicle model as follows:

$$\omega_{zsoll} = (\delta_R \cdot v_x)/(l + EG \cdot v_x^2)$$

where:
$\delta_R$    wheel steering angle,
$v_x$    vehicle speed,
$l$    wheelbase,
$EG$    self-steering gradient which describes the vehicle's self-steering response (cf. P. 441).

ESP calculates current vehicle motion from the available measured variables for yaw rate and lateral acceleration plus the wheel speeds. Since the articulation angle is not available as a measured-variable signal, it is estimated from the available measured data. This is only possible if stable semitrailer motion is assumed.

If discrepancies are detected between current vehicle motion and motion expected by the driver, ESP firstly classifies the situation as either "oversteer" or "understeer".

"Oversteer" describes situations in which the rear of the vehicle starts to slide outwards, i.e. the vehicle rotates about its vertical axis faster than is required for the required bend radius (cf. P. 432). On articulated road trains, this type of situation frequently leads to jackknifing, and the driver is virtually unable to control this.

In "understeer" situations, the front of the vehicle slides toward the outside of the bend; this is a scenario that is often encountered by laden three-axle vehicles with a single steered axle.

After ESP has classified the situation, it calculates a yaw-moment adjustment. Yaw-moment adjustment is then implemented by braking one or more wheels to achieve the required degree of wheel slip. This is illustrated in the figure on P. 867, which depicts clearly defined oversteer and understeer situations. In addition to these clearly defined situations, there are other critical dynamic situations in which other wheels or wheel combinations are braked depending on the desired stabilization effect.

Skidding and jackknifing by a commercial vehicle primarily occur at low-to-medium coefficients of friction because of the specific characteristics of such vehicles. At high coefficients of friction, commercial vehicles tend to overturn rather than skid because of their high center of gravity.

Reducing the risk of overturning

The tip limit of a vehicle depends not only on the height of the center of gravity but also on the chassis systems (axle suspension, stabilizers, springs, etc.) and the type of payload (fixed or moving). An approximate method of calculation is described on P. 442.

The situation which causes a commercial vehicle to overturn is a relatively low tip limit combined with an excessive cornering speed.

ESP makes use of this scenario to reduce the probability of the vehicle overturning. As soon as the vehicle approaches the tip limit, it is slowed down by reducing engine torque and applying the brakes. The tip limit is estimated from the payload and load distribution, and is adjusted according to the situation.

Thus, the estimated tip limit is reduced in high-speed dynamic situations (e.g. obstacle-avoidance maneuvers) in order to permit early intervention. In very slow maneuvers, on the other hand (e.g. negotiating tight hairpin bends on uphill stretches), it is increased in order to prevent unnecessary and disruptive ESP intervention.

Estimating the tip limit is based on various assumptions regarding the height of the center of gravity and the dynamic response of the vehicle combination with a known axle-load distribution. These assumptions cover the majority of common vehicle combinations.

In order to ensure that stabilization is effective even under conditions which vary widely from these assumptions, ESP also detects when a wheel lifts on the inside of a bend. This is achieved by monitoring the wheels for implausible rotation speed. If necessary, the entire vehicle combination is then heavily decelerated by brake intervention.

A trailer wheel lifting on the inside of a bend is indicated by the trailer electronic braking system (EBS) (cf. P. 869) via the CAN communication line (SAE J 11992, cf. P. 875) by activating the ABS controller. For combinations with trailers equipped with ABS only, wheel-lift detection on the inside of a bend is limited to the tractor unit.

**Design**
The Electronic Stability Progam (ESP) for
commercial vehicles is based on the Electronic Braking System (EBS) (cf. P. 869)
and extends the system by additional dynamic-handling control functions. To do
so, ESP makes use of the EBS capability
of generating varying braking forces for
each individual wheel independently of
driver action.

<u>Sensor systems</u>
Beyond the typical EBS sensors for wheel
speed and braking pressure, ESP also
has sensors for vehicle dynamics. They
consist of a yaw-rate sensor with an integrated lateral-acceleration sensor, and a
steering-wheel angle sensor (see P. 110
onwards). Each of these sensors contains
a microcontroller with a CAN interface for
analyzing and transmitting the measured
data.

The steering-wheel angle sensor is generally mounted immediately below the
steering wheel and measures the angle of
rotation of the steering wheel.
    Vehicle lateral acceleration should be
measured as close as possible to the
tractor unit's center of gravity. For this
reason, the yaw-rate/lateral-acceleration
sensor is usually mounted on the vehicle
chassis close to the center of gravity.

<u>Electronic control unit (ECU)</u>
As well as the EBS ECU, the vehicle system now includes an additional ECU in
conventional pcb technology for the first-
generation commercial-vehicle ESP. Suc-
cessor systems incorporate ESP functions in the EBS ECU.

A CAN bus connects the ESP sensors (as
well as the electropneumatic modulators
(EPM)) to the ECU (cf. P. 869 onwards).
From the input data provided by the sensors, the ECU function groups described
above calculate braking pressure/wheel
slip for each wheel and for the trailer, and
an appropriate engine-torque reduction.
This information is then transmitted via
the braking system CAN bus to the EPMs
or via the vehicle CAN bus (general CAN
as per SAE J 1939) to the engine ECU for
implementation.

The vehicle CAN bus sends not only
requests from the ESP to the engine management to reduce engine torque, but
also information from the engine and the
retarders in the opposite direction. Essentially, this involves current and requested
engine torque and speed, retarder torque,
vehicle speed, and information from various control switches and any trailer that
may be coupled.

<u>System structure</u>
The structure of the EBS is depicted on
P. 871.

**Safety and monitoring functions**
The extensive possibilities for ESP intervention in the handling characteristics of
the vehicle or vehicle combination require
a comprehensive safety system to ensure
proper system functioning. This extends
not only to the basic EBS system but also
to the additional ESP components, including all sensors, ECUs and interfaces.

<u>Self-monitoring of components</u>
Due to system complexity and the "independent intelligence" of most components, each component monitors all of its
own internal functions, interfaces and
connected sensors. Thus, the basic EBS
incorporates monitoring routines for all
functions and components relevant to
EBS operation (see P. 871).
    ESP sensors also have internal self-
monitoring functions and signal any malfunctions that may occur to the ESP ECU
via the CAN bus.

<u>Reciprocal monitoring by microcontrollers</u>
In addition to internal monitoring functions
in each ECU, reciprocal monitoring takes
place whereby special algorithms check
the function of the microcontrollers.

<u>Monitoring the ESP sensors</u>
As well as the internal monitoring routines
in the sensors, the ESP performs a physical plausibility check of the sensor
signals (for signal gradient and mea-
sured-value range).

In addition, the sensor signals are checked with the aid of a model-based sensor-monitoring function. This uses simplified physical models and the following three sensor variables to calculate the yaw rate for the vehicle:
– speed of the front wheels
– lateral acceleration
– steering-wheel angle

The results of this calculation together with the measured yaw rate and allows an assessment of the individual sensor signals, taking account of the dynamic situation.

Response to faults
The occurrence of faults results in the shutdown either of individual function groups or the entire ESP system, depending on the nature and significance of the fault (failsafe response). This ensures that incorrect sensor signals cannot cause implausible and possibly dangerous intervention in braking operations. The occurrence a fault is indicated to the driver by suitable means (e.g. warning lamp or display) so that suitable action can be taken.

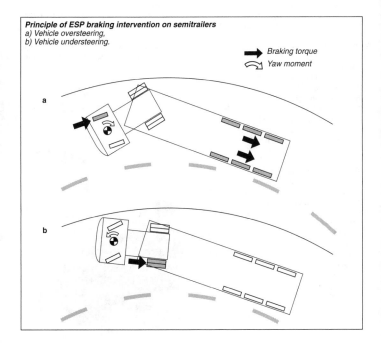

*Principle of ESP braking intervention on semitrailers*
*a) Vehicle oversteering,*
*b) Vehicle understeering.*

Braking torque
Yaw moment

**868**

# Expert Know-How on Automotive Engineering
## The Bosch Yellow Jackets

| The Complete Series | ISBN |
|---|---|
| **Automotive Electrics/** | |
| **Automotive Electronics** | |
| Motor-Vehicle Batteries | |
| and Electrical Systems | 3-934584-71-3 |
| Alternators and Starter Motors | 3-934584-69-1 |
| Automotive Lighting Technology, | |
| Windshield and | |
| Rear-Window Cleaning | 3-934584-70-5 |
| Automotive Microelectronics | 3-934584-49-7 |
| Automotive Sensors | 3-934584-50-0 |
| | |
| **Gasoline-Engine Management** | |
| Emissions-Control Technology | |
| for Gasoline Engines | 3-934584-26-8 |
| Gasoline Fuel-Injection System | |
| K-Jetronic | 3-934584-27-6 |
| Gasoline Fuel-Injection System | |
| KE-Jetronic | 3-934584-28-4 |
| Gasoline Fuel-Injection System | |
| L-Jetronic | 3-934584-29-2 |
| Gasoline Fuel-Injection System | |
| Mono-Jetronic | 3-934584-30-6 |
| Ignition Systems for | |
| Gasoline Engines | 3-934584-63-2 |
| Gasoline-Engine Management: | |
| Basics and Components | 3-934584-48-9 |
| Gasoline-Engine Management: | |
| Motronic Systems | 3-934584-75-6 |
| | |
| **Diesel-Engine Management** | |
| Diesel-Engine Management: | |
| An Overview | 3-934584-62-4 |
| Diesel In-Line Fuel-Injection | |
| Pumps | 3-934584-68-3 |
| Distributor-Type Diesel | |
| Fuel-Injection Pumps | 3-934584-65-9 |
| Diesel Accumulator Fuel- | |
| Injection System Common Rail | 3-934584-40-3 |
| Diesel Fuel-Injection Systems | |
| Unit Injector System/ | |
| Unit Pump System | 3-934584-41-1 |
| Electronic Diesel Control EDC | 3-934584-47-0 |

| **Driving and Road-Safety Systems** | |
|---|---|
| Conventional and | |
| Electronic Braking Systems | 3-934584-60-8 |
| ESP Electronic Stability Program | 3-934584-44-6 |
| Safety, Comfort and | |
| Convenience Systems | 3-934584-25-X |
| Compressed-Air Systems for | |
| Commercial Vehicles (1): Systems | |
| and Schematic Diagrams | 3-934584-45-4 |
| Compressed-Air Systems for | |
| Commercial Vehicles (2): | |
| Equipment | 3-934584-46-2 |
| Audio, Navigation and | |
| Telematics in the Vehicle | 3-934584-53-5 |
| ACC Adaptive Cruise Control | 3-934584-64-0 |
| Electronic Transmission | |
| Control ETC | 3-934584-79-9 |

The up-to-date range is available on the internet at:
**www.bosch.de/aa/de/fachliteratur/index.htm**

Conventional
and Electronic Braking
Systems

**BOSCH**

- Physical principles of braking
- Components and systems
- Antilock braking system (ABS)
- Electrohydraulic brakes (SBC)

# Electronically controlled braking system (ELB) for commercial vehicles

## Function

The electronically controlled braking system (ELB) increases and optimizes functionality under braking and under power in comparison with a conventional compressed-air braking system.

As part of the vehicle's CAN communication network, the ELB can exchange information with other systems and utilize it to implement optimum (in terms of safety, economy and convenience aspects) acceleration or braking sequences (Figure H). This "intelligent" data exchange also implemented complex functions involving the interaction of several ECUs as well as diagnostic capabilities. Despite the complexity of the functions, an ELB system can be configured more simply than a conventional braking system due to its standardized components and smaller amount of wiring.

## System design

The component groups "compressed-air supply", "compressed-air conditioning", "circuit failsafe", "energy accumulator", "brake cylinder" and "wheel brakes" are identical to conventional braking systems.

With ELB, however, the familiar air-brake system is subordinated to an electronic closed control loop which suppresses the pneumatic control functions ("backup" solenoid). The two energy supply circuits (P1 and P2) remain unchanged (Figures A and J).

The control pressure for the trailer is also controlled electronically. For communication with the ELB equipment on the trailer, there is a CAN interface compliant with ISO 11992. The diagram below shows a typical layout of the ELB pressure-control modules (Figure B).

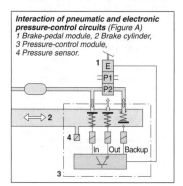

*Interaction of pneumatic and electronic pressure-control circuits* (Figure A)
1 Brake-pedal module, 2 Brake cylinder,
3 Pressure-control module,
4 Pressure sensor.

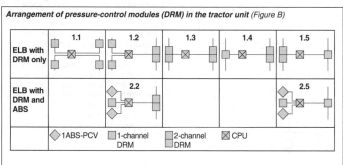

*Arrangement of pressure-control modules (DRM) in the tractor unit* (Figure B)

| | | | | | |
|---|---|---|---|---|---|
| **ELB with DRM only** | 1.1 | 1.2 | 1.3 | 1.4 | 1.5 |
| **ELB with DRM and ABS** | | 2.2 | | | 2.5 |
| | ◇ 1ABS-PCV | ▪ 1-channel DRM | ▪ 2-channel DRM | ⊠ CPU | |

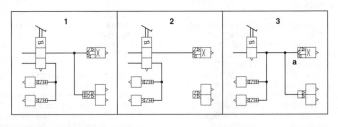

*Control of "backup circuits" (Figure C)*
1 "Backup" with two control circuits (equivalent to conventional braking system), 2 "Backup" with individual control circuits for front axle and trailer, rear axle only electrically controlled, 3 "Backup" with single-circuit pneumatic control for front axle, rear axle and trailer. a Circuit isolator.

Depending on the option selected, the braking pressure is controlled electronically for each axle or wheel. Systems with ESP require pressure control for each wheel. A fault-detection function triggers selective shutoff of functions or failed components in the electrical braking system. If electronic control of the braking system is lost, the pneumatic control functions ("backup") remain available. The "backup" system may be controlled by dual circuits (circuit configuration similar to a conventional dual-circuit braking system) or a single circuit (Figure C).

Single-circuit control of all axles requires a device for isolating the pneumatic circuits. A solution to the backup power supply problem must be found in order to achieve purely electrical ("brake-by-wire") control without pneumatic "backup" in the future.

## ELB components

### Electronic control unit (ECU)
The control center of an ELB system consists of one or more ECUs.

At present, there are both systems with a centralized structure (i.e. all software functions are run on a single control unit) and those with a decentralized configuration involving several control units.

### Brake-pedal module (FBM, Figure D)
The brake-pedal module implements two functions – first of all, two redundant electrical sensors detect the driver's braking command by measuring the travel of the brake-pedal module pushrod. They transmit the measured value to the central ECU which calculates a braking request from it. Secondly, in a similar fashion to a conventional brake-pedal valve, one or two pneumatic control circuits ("backup" circuits) are pressurized depending on the pressure applied to the brake pedal by the driver (FBV section).

*FBM brake-pedal module with two pneumatic control circuits (Figure D)*
1 Braking-level sensor, 2 Service-brake valve, 3 Supply connection (5 V), 4 Potentiometer terminal, 5 Equipment ground.

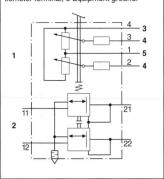

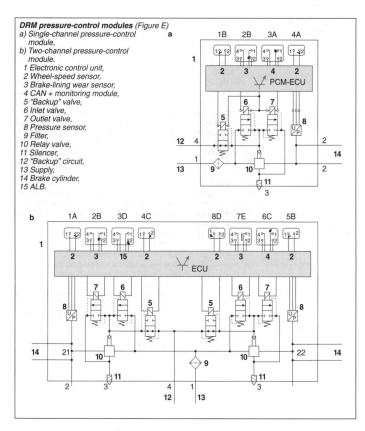

**DRM pressure-control modules** (Figure E)
a) Single-channel pressure-control module,
b) Two-channel pressure-control module.
1 Electronic control unit,
2 Wheel-speed sensor,
3 Brake-lining wear sensor,
4 CAN + monitoring module,
5 "Backup" valve,
6 Inlet valve,
7 Outlet valve,
8 Pressure sensor,
9 Filter,
10 Relay valve,
11 Silencer,
12 "Backup" circuit,
13 Supply,
14 Brake cylinder,
15 ALB.

## Pressure-control modules (DRM, Figure E)

The pressure-control modules form the interface between the electronic braking system and the pneumatic braking force. They convert the required braking pressures transmitted via the brake CAN to pneumatic pressures. Conversion is carried out by "proportional solenoids" or an inlet/outlet solenoid combination. A pressure sensor measures the braking pressure delivered. Thus, braking pressure can be controlled in a closed control loop. The electrically activated "backup" solenoid shuts off the pneumatic control circuits of the FBM in order to permit interference-free electrical pressure control.

Mounting the pressure-control modules close to the wheels means that the electrical wires for connecting the wheel-speed sensors and the brake-lining wear sensors can be kept short. The signals are transmitted to the central ECU via the braking-system CAN. This minimizes the amount of wiring required on the vehicle substantially.

### Trailer control module (ASM)

The electronic trailer control module enables modulation of the trailer control pressure according to the functional requirements of the ELB. The limits of the electrical control ranges are defined by legal requirements. The electronically specified setpoint is converted to a physical braking pressure by means of a solenoid arrangement similar to that in the pressure-control module. The "backup" pressure is shut off either by a "backup" solenoid or by pneumatic retention, depending on the type of design adopted.

Under all normal conditions, the trailer control module must be activated by two independent control signals. This may be two pneumatic signals from two control circuits, or one pneumatic and one electrical control signal. If the control signals are mixed, however, the electrical control signal must be available under all normal operating conditions.

## Electropneumatic braking (operating concept)

When the driving switch is operated, the ELB is initialized and performs a self-test. The braking system can also be initialized even if the driving switch is off and the brake-pedal module is depressed. If no faults are detected, the warning lamps go out and the ELB is ready for operation.

When the FBM is operated, the control unit calculates the braking command. At the same time the "backup" solenoids in the DRMs are activated and the pneumatic control circuits are shut off. The electronic control unit then calculates the optimum braking pressure depending on the braking command, vehicle mass, axle-load distribution, etc. That required braking pressure is transmitted to the DRMs and the ASM via the braking-system CAN (Figure F).

Depending on the configuration, the DRMs and the ASM control the supply of braking pressure to the wheel-brake cylinders separately for each axle or wheel. An appropriate braking command corresponding to the trailer control pressure is transmitted via the CAN (compliant with ISO 11992) to the trailer ELB (Figure H).

*Information transfer in an ELB* (Figure F)
1 FBM brake-pedal module, 2 Driver command, 3 ELB central ECU, 4 Pneumatic "backup",
5 Air reservoir, 6 Load data, 7 Braking-system CAN bus, 8 DRM pressure-control module,
9 Diaphragm-type cylinder, 10 Wheel-speed sensor.

For functions such as TCS (Traction Control System) or ESP (Electronic Stability Program), braking pressure is generated in the DRM, independently of the driver's braking command, and controlled in the brake cylinders.

The main basic function in an ELB system, besides electronic pressure control, ABS and TCS, is control of braking-force distribution between the individual vehicle axles. At present the following two methods of determining the required braking-force distribution are used:

### Braking-force distribution based on measuring the axle load

With this method, the axle load is determined by means of an air-spring bellows pressure sensor. For vehicles with steel springs, spring-travel sensors (distance between chassis frame and axle) can be used. Preferably, the load is measured on the powered axle.

The total vehicle mass is also determined. From these input variables, the loads on axles without load sensors are calculated. A specified braking force is then assigned to each axle according to the axle loads determined.

### Braking-force distribution based on differential wheel slip

This method is based on the assumption that the ratio between the vertical force acting on the wheel and the braking force is identical for wheels with the same degree of slip. This ensures that each wheel delivers the braking force corresponding to its vertical force. The braking pressures of individual wheels or axles are then adjusted until no further slip differential is discernible. The measured data utilized consists of the wheel speeds measured by the ABS wheel-speed sensors and the braking pressures applied by the DRMs.

## Control and management functions

In addition to the functions of a conventional braking system, ELB also offers the following additional functions:

### Deceleration control

For the deceleration control function, every brake-pedal position is assigned a set degree of vehicle deceleration. The level of braking deceleration is delivered regardless of the vehicle mass, brake condition, or road gradient. The brake-pedal "feel" is thus reproducible and independent of external parameters.

An automatic brake monitoring function provides early warning of the risk of wheel-brake overload.

### Brake-lining wear control

For the brake-lining wear control function, all wheel brakes must be fitted with continuously operating brake-lining wear sensors. The sensor signals serve as input variables for brake-lining wear control. The purpose of this function is to achieve even wear of all brake linings. The aim is, firstly, to optimize use of the available brake-lining thickness and, secondly, to reduce vehicle maintenance times. If the

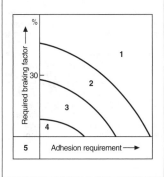

*Functional areas of brake-lining wear control in an ELB* (Figure G)
*1 ABS activity, 2 Brake optimized for adhesion, 3 Brake optimized for wear, 4 Exhaust brake, 5 TCS activity.*

sensors detect different brake-lining thicknesses on different axles, the braking pressures for individual axles are adjusted when driver inputs require only a low level of braking (e.g. $z < 30\%$, Figure G).

**Brake management and blending**

The braking force requested by the driver should be generated with the least possible degree of wear on the mechanical brake components. Consequently, the system strives to deploy the rapid-response air brakes only at the start of the braking sequence, and then transfer the remaining braking operation to the continuous-braking systems (e.g. retarders), which have a delayed braking-force response.

The transition from air brakes to retarders is referred to as "blending". For the driver, the blending process is indiscernible since vehicle deceleration remains constant during the entire operation.

Managing braking-force assignment to the various braking systems installed (exhaust brake, exhaust-flap brake, retarder, air brakes) is performed by the ELB electronics.

**Brake balancing between tractor and trailer**

The legal requirements for interaction between tractor and trailer are defined by the "compatibility diagram". However, even within these legal limits, the interaction between certain vehicle combinations can produce critical driving conditions or uneven distribution of wear between the tractor and the trailer.

For this reason, ELB attempts to determine and control the difference between actual and ideal balance. The aim is to maintain the coupling forces at the fifth-wheel load on articulated trucks, and at zero on tractor-and-trailer combinations.

If the trailer is fitted with ELB and the interface conforms to ISO 11992 (Figure H), the wheel-speed data from the trailer is available. The braking force can then be balanced on the basis of the slip differential between the tractor and the trailer/semi-trailer (see Braking-force distribution).

**Rollback limiter/"Bus-stop brake"**

The rollback limiter or bus-stop brake is operated by means of an additional switch. When the function is activated, the braking pressure applied by the driver is maintained after the vehicle has stopped, even if the brake pedal is released.

As soon as the system detects that the vehicle is pulling away (clutch position signal) and the engine is producing a drive torque equal to the braking torque produced by the braking pressure, the brake cylinders are vented. By comparing the braking torque with the drive torque, the system prevents the vehicle from rolling back on uphill gradients. The rollback limiter function must not be used as a parking brake, however.

# Monitoring and diagnostic functions

In addition to the functions already described, other monitoring and diagnostic functions are also possible.

**Additional preventative methods**

Operating the service brakes and the parking brake at the same time causes mechanical wheel-brake overload. ELB can detect simultaneous operation and reduce the load on the wheel brakes by decreasing the service-braking pressure when the parking brake is applied.

**Brake monitoring**

The load on the wheel brakes (energy consumed) is calculable from the wheel speeds and braking pressures. If the system detects that the load is approaching a critical level, it can alert the driver in good time. The driver then has more scope to avoid hazardous situations (e.g. brake fading).

***CAN networking between brake components and other vehicle systems*** *(Figure H)*
a) Tractor vehicle,
b) Trailer.
1, 2, 3 CAN nodes (e.g. information, suspension, drivetrain),
4, 5 CAN nodes (ELB ECU),
6 CAN nodes (ELB pressure-control modules),
7 ISO 7638 connector (7-pole).

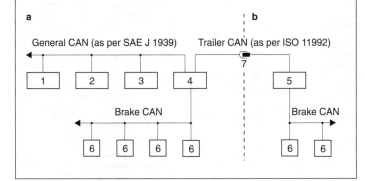

***Service-braking system components of an ELB*** *(Figure J)*
a) Tractor vehicle, b) Trailer.
1 Four-circuit protection valve, 2 Air reservoir, 3 Service-brake valve with braking-level sensor,
4 Single-channel pressure-control module (DRM), 5 Brake cylinder, 6 Wheel-speed sensor,
7 Brake-lining wear sensor, 8 ELB ECU on tractor unit, 9 Two-channel pressure-control module
(2K-DRM), 10 Pressure sensor, 11 Air-spring bellows, 12 Trailer control valve, 13 Supply
coupling head, 14 Brake coupling head, 15 ISO 7638 connector (7-pole), 16 Line filter,
17 Trailer brake valve with release device, 18 ELB ECU on trailer.

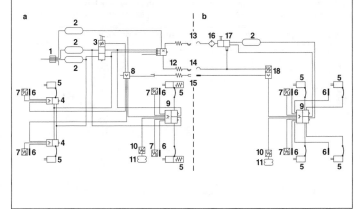

# Electronic commercial-vehicle brake management as the platform for driving-assistance systems

## Basic electronic braking system

The basic braking system consists of a dual-circuit service-braking system compliant with ECE R13 which is subordinated to an electronic braking-force control system. The brakes on the front and rear wheels are assigned to pressure-control circuits with which the required pressures calculated by the ECU are converted to actual braking pressures.

In an electronic braking system, driving-assistance systems, such as ABS or traction control, do not function as standalone systems as in conventional air-brake systems. Instead, they are directly integrated in the braking-system logic. An "intelligent" differential-slip control function ensures optimized braking-force distribution for a particular vehicle laden state. As a result, this guarantees high directional stability, good steerability and high levels of braking deceleration. Faster wheel-brake response compared with a conventional braking system makes shorter braking distances possible [1].

In contrast with a conventional service-braking system, the components in the basic electronic braking system replace the service-brake valve, the automatic load-sensitive braking-force control valve (ALB), and the ABS and TCS valves. The brake pedal and an electrical braking-level sensor transmit the driver's braking command to the electronics. ABS sensors detect the wheel speeds. Figure A shows an example of a basic electronic braking system on a two-axle truck.

With the aid of the differential-slip control function, the electronic pressure-control modules control the braking pressures at the vehicle's front and rear wheel brakes – as demanded by the driving situation – to achieve optimized braking-force distribution. If the system detects incipient over-braking of the wheels on a particular axle, the braking pressures at the front and rear wheels are readjusted to minimize speed differences between wheels on different axles, and to optimize use of the adhesion between the tires and the road surface. A braking deceleration control function integrated in the overall system has the task of precisely metering the braking effect. This means that a specific amount of pedal travel always corresponds to a specific level of braking deceleration, regardless of the payload or the road gradient.

With this type of basic braking system, driving-assistance systems can fully uti-

*Electronic/compressed-air braking system for two-axle tractor unit* (Figure A)
*1 Wheel-speed sensor, 2 Brake-lining wear sensor, 3 Control valve, 4 Front-wheel brake cylinder, 5 Rear-wheel brake cylinder, 6 ECU, 7 Brake pedal, 8 Compressed-air cylinder, 9 Compressed-air supply to trailer, 10 Trailer control line, 11 Coupling-force sensor, 12 Steering-wheel angle sensor, 13 Control for retarder and exhaust-braking system, 14 Yaw-rate/lateral-acceleration sensor.*

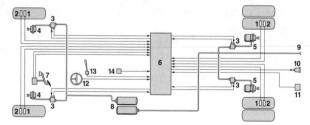

lize the following advantages of electronic brake management [1, 2, 3, 4]:
- rapid buildup of braking pressure
- optimized, load-sensitive braking-force distribution
- integrated exhaust-brake and retarder control
- optimized brake-lining wear control
- control of coupling forces between tractor and trailer
- hill-start assistance
- braking assistant
- electronic stability control including rollover mitigation

## Subsystems

### Integration of additional retarding braking systems in the service-braking system

The additional braking forces available at the rear wheels by fitting additional retarding braking systems alter the installed braking-force distribution. They primarily affect the directional stability of the vehicle when braked on wet, snow-covered, and icy roads. For this reason, the electronic brake management system must monitor and optimize the interaction between the additional retarding braking systems and the service-braking system. If necessary, the basic electronic braking system only utilizes part of the potential braking effect of the service-braking system (Figure B).

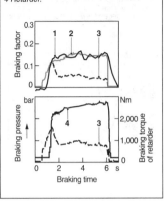

*Integration of an additional retarding braking system in the service-braking system (Figure B)*
1 Vehicle braking, 2 Driver's braking command, 3 Service-braking system, 4 Retarder.

### Stability control with integrated rollover mitigation

Stability control is an integrated subsystem in the basic electronic braking system. To detect the vehicle behavior required by the driver, the steering-wheel angle, wheel speeds, and lateral acceleration are measured (Figure C). The momentary yaw velocity is also measured to detect actual vehicle behavior. Differ-

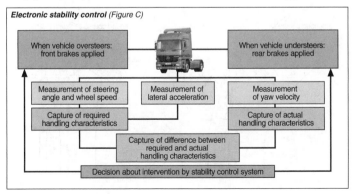

*Electronic stability control (Figure C)*

When vehicle oversteers: front brakes applied

When vehicle understeers: rear brakes applied

Measurement of steering angle and wheel speed

Measurement of lateral acceleration

Measurement of yaw velocity

Capture of required handling characteristics

Capture of actual handling characteristics

Capture of difference between required and actual handling characteristics

Decision about intervention by stability control system

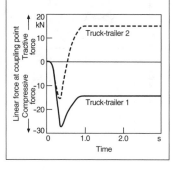

**Progression of coupling forces between tractor and trailer over time at braking deceleration of 5 m · s⁻² (Figure E)**
Road train 1 (17 t truck, fully laden, and 24 t trailer, fully laden): tractor at lower end and trailer at upper end of ECE R13 braking range Road train 2: tractor at lower end and trailer at upper end of ECE R13 braking range.

ences between "required vehicle behavior and actual vehicle behavior" result in immediate intervention by the stability control functions [1].

If the vehicle understeers, the rear wheels require brake intervention, whereas oversteer demands front-wheel brake intervention. Figure D shows the possible intervention strategies for the braking system to brake the front and rear wheels.

After detecting momentary wheel load, the basic electronic braking system controls the wheel brake on the relevant wheel individually.

Another safety-related function of stability control prevents the vehicle from overturning when cornering at high lateral acceleration on dry road surfaces. The "rollover protection" subsystem is capable of detecting when one of the wheels lifts off from the ground. If this occurs, the vehicle is prevented from overturning by immediate activation of the braking system [1].

### Compatibility between tractor and trailer
Conventional systems are not capable of achieving a satisfactory balancing of the braking effect on individual vehicles in a vehicle combination, particularly if the combination is changed frequently. Figure E shows the incompatible forces between tractor and trailer in different braking scenarios.

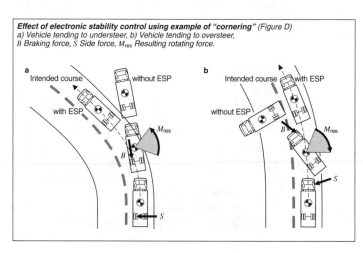

**Effect of electronic stability control using example of "cornering" (Figure D)**
a) Vehicle tending to understeer, b) Vehicle tending to oversteer,
B Braking force, S Side force, $M_{res}$ Resulting rotating force.

In order to minimize these forces, "intelligent" electronic systems can achieve compatibility by balancing the braking forces correctly. This is done by ensuring that the trailer is also involved in the braking work for the overall vehicle combination.

To the extent allowed by legally specified limits, an "intelligent" trailer control system, or a compatibility control function integrated in the basic electronic braking system of the tractor, is used to eliminate or at least minimize coupling forces between tractor and trailer to a degree that is sufficient to prevent negative effects on the stability of the vehicle combination. The braking pressure on the trailer is controlled as required (Figure F) but does not go beyond the limits specified by law [5].

### Braking assistant

The basic electronic braking system may incorporate a "braking assistant" function, which simply uses additional software functions to compensate for situations such as when the driver brakes too soft in an emergency-braking situation.

An emergency-braking situation is detected by sensing the rate of depression of the brake pedal. The required rapid increase in braking pressure is achieved by activating the maximum storage pressure (Figure G). The driver can determine how long the braking assistant function is active by releasing the brake pedal.

### Rollback prevention

Rollback prevention is designed to make hill starts easier for an inexperienced driver. It involves activating the rear-wheel brakes by storing an appropriate braking pressure using the ABS valves. Declutching provides the signal to release braking pressure. Activating the system can be made more convenient by graduating braking-pressure release using road-gradient detection and forward/reverse gear detection [1].

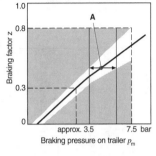

**Control of coupling forces between tractor and trailer** (Figure F)
A Scope for controlling coupling forces.

Braking factor $z$ (vertical axis, values 0, 0.3, 0.8, 1.0)
Braking pressure on trailer $p_m$ (horizontal axis, approx. 3.5, 7.5 bar)

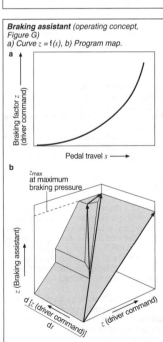

**Braking assistant** (operating concept, Figure G)
a) Curve $z = f(s)$, b) Program map.

a
Braking factor $z$ (driver command)
Pedal travel $s$ ⟶

b
$z_{max}$ at maximum braking pressure
$z$ (Braking assistant)
$\frac{d\,[z\,(\text{driver command})]}{dt}$
$z$ (driver command)

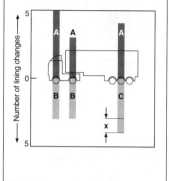

*Harmonization of brake-lining wear on different axles (Figure H)*
*Bar A: conventional braking system,*
*Bar B: electronic braking system with brake-lining wear control on tractor unit,*
*Bar C: electronic braking system on trailer.*
*x Gain in lining wear.*

## Brake-lining wear control
Uniform brake-lining wear on all axles can be achieved if only the brakes with the greatest remaining lining thickness are operated when the driver applies the wheel brakes lightly. If maximum braking power is required, all wheels are braked equally as normal. This type of brake-lining wear control can minimize vehicle maintenance costs and still retain all active safety aspects.

Figure H shows the harmonization of brake-lining wear on the tractor unit with a conventionally braked semitrailer. If the semitrailer also has an electronic braking system, overall economy can be further improved. As a result, maintenance and lining renewal times for tractor and semitrailer can be synchronized.

The electronic braking system also has a facility for keeping the driver constantly informed of the condition of the braking system and wheel brakes.

## Intelligent distance maintenance (ART)
With the aid of a radar sensor which measures the distance from, and the relative speed of, the vehicle in front, the vehicle can use a control algorithm to constantly maintain a safety distance specified by the driver.

If the distance becomes too short, the electronics intervene in the cruise control system either by activating the exhaust brake, the retarder, or even the service-braking system to make minor reductions to vehicle speed. If greater rates of braking deceleration are required, the driver receives an acoustic warning signal to operate the brakes. The legally required distance of 50 m specified for commercial vehicles under certain situations can be maintained without the driver having to adjust vehicle speed by constantly operating the brakes [1].

The active cruise control uses acceleration, road speed, distance from the vehicle in front, retarder torque, and braking pressure as the basis to control the distance. The radar sensor operates in a range of $\approx$ 77 GHz and influences the drivetrain and the braking system via the electronic control system.

The radar module transmits three radar signals at an angle of approx. 3° in each case every 20...60 ms and detects mobile objects and stationary obstacles at a distance of up to $\approx$ 120 m (Figure J). Active cruise control operates within a speed range of 35.... $\approx$ 120 kph. The function is not affected by bad weather conditions.

## Automatic vehicle handling
This system uses video images to operate an autopilot function which can identify vehicles, road markings, and road signs (Figure K).

The "lane guidance", "active cruise control", "wake-up warning" and "automated stop-and-go" subsystems substantially relieve the burden on the driver in everyday conditions [1, 6].

Another possible application for automatic vehicle handling systems is the "truck platooning function", where two or more trucks in convoy are electronically linked and driven by a single driver. In this case, an active image processing system detects even the smallest changes in distance and direction and responds accordingly. Access to all vehicle systems is electronically safeguarded (e.g. by "X-by-wire" systems). Apart from reducing the road space required, this system offers the additional advantage of reducing overall aerodynamic drag of the vehicle convoy and, therefore, fuel consumption.

## System integration and electronic networking
On future vehicle generations, all electronic systems will be internetworked. The basis for networking will be a powerful and safety-related computer communication system which "intelligently" monitors all vehicle systems.

The network will have to operate with standardized system architectures and assure error-free transmission of safety-related information regarding braking, steering, chassis system, and drivetrain.

*Intelligent distance maintenance*
*(ART, Figure J)*
*1 Radar sensor on truck, 2 Vehicle in front;*
*A/B/C Transmitted radar signals and lane widths detected by the radar module,*
*3 Symbol for "ART ON", 4 Required speed,*
*5 Actual distance from vehicle in front.*

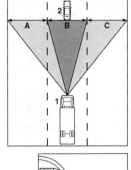

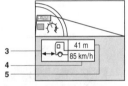

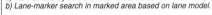

*Lane guidance (Figure K)*
*a) View of lane by camera mounted at center of windshield,*
*b) Lane-marker search in marked area based on lane model.*

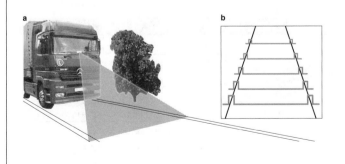

System networking will take place via high-speed and low-speed CAN buses. A master system will monitor the correct interaction between individual systems and will use a high degree of artificial intelligence to control individual subsystems (Figure L).

A good example of networked "X-by-wire" systems is the "drive-by-wire" system (Figure M), consisting of an intelligent drivetrain and suspension management system. It comprises the "power-by-wire", "clutch/shift-by-wire", "steer-by-wire", "suspension-by-wire" and "brake-by-wire" subsystems.

The development of electronic intelligence and ever expanding knowledge in vehicle dynamics allow even today to design and produce intelligent vehicle systems which can significantly increase the active safety of commercial vehicles.

By adding other subsystems linked to the basic electronic braking system in the form of software packages, there are ever increasing possibilities for introducing driving-assistant systems which can help drivers in critical situations and relieve the driving burden.

The introduction of networked electronic systems with high levels of artificial intelligence in the future will make the driver's job considerably easier and provide greater opportunity for concentrating on the driving situation. The driver will be relieved of all tasks which might distract or represent a heavy burden. This will considerably increase the active safety of commercial vehicles [1].

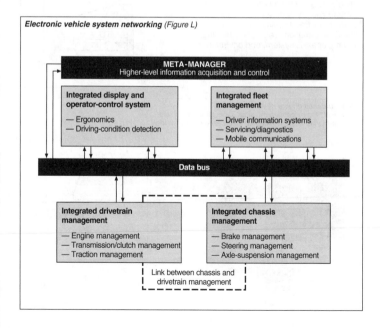

*Electronic vehicle system networking (Figure L)*

**META-MANAGER**
Higher-level information acquisition and control

**Integrated display and operator-control system**
— Ergonomics
— Driving-condition detection

**Integrated fleet management**
— Driver information systems
— Servicing/diagnostics
— Mobile communications

**Data bus**

**Integrated drivetrain management**
— Engine management
— Transmission/clutch management
— Traction management

**Integrated chassis management**
— Brake management
— Steering management
— Axle-suspension management

Link between chassis and drivetrain management

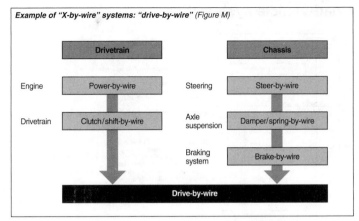

*Example of "X-by-wire" systems: "drive-by-wire"* (Figure M)

## References

[1] Breuer, B., Bill, K. H.
Bremsenhandbuch, Vieweg-Verlag, 2003.

[2] Göhring, E., von Glasner, E. C.
Fundamental Remarks on the Present Status and on Further Development of Braking Systems of Modern European Commercial Vehicles, JSAE Paper No. 911011.

[3] Povel, R., von Glasner, E. C., Wüst, K.
Electronic Systems Designed to Improve the Active Safety of Commercial Vehicles, SAE do Brazil, São Paulo, 1998.

[4] Povel, R., von Glasner, E. C.
Advanced Control Systems for Commercial Vehicles, AVEC '98, Nagoya, 1998.

[5] Pflug, H. C., von Glasner, E. C., Povel, R., Wüst, K.
The Compatibility of Tractor/Trailer Combinations during Braking Maneuvers, SAE Paper No. 97 32 82

[6] von Glasner, E. C.
Intelligent Braking System Management for Commercial Vehicles,
Braking 2002, Leeds, 2002.

# Road-vehicle systematics

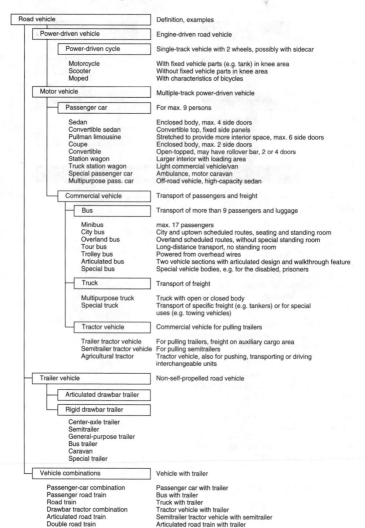

| | Definition, examples |
|---|---|
| **Road vehicle** | |
| **Power-driven vehicle** | Engine-driven road vehicle |
| **Power-driven cycle** | Single-track vehicle with 2 wheels, possibly with sidecar |
| Motorcycle | With fixed vehicle parts (e.g. tank) in knee area |
| Scooter | Without fixed vehicle parts in knee area |
| Moped | With characteristics of bicycles |
| **Motor vehicle** | Multiple-track power-driven vehicle |
| **Passenger car** | For max. 9 persons |
| Sedan | Enclosed body, max. 4 side doors |
| Convertible sedan | Convertible top, fixed side panels |
| Pullman limousine | Stretched to provide more interior space, max. 6 side doors |
| Coupe | Enclosed body, max. 2 side doors |
| Convertible | Open-topped, may have rollover bar, 2 or 4 doors |
| Station wagon | Larger interior with loading area |
| Truck station wagon | Light commercial vehicle/van |
| Special passenger car | Ambulance, motor caravan |
| Multipurpose pass. car | Off-road vehicle, high-capacity sedan |
| **Commercial vehicle** | Transport of passengers and freight |
| **Bus** | Transport of more than 9 passengers and luggage |
| Minibus | max. 17 passengers |
| City bus | City and uptown scheduled routes, seating and standing room |
| Overland bus | Overland scheduled routes, without special standing room |
| Tour bus | Long-distance transport, no standing room |
| Trolley bus | Powered from overhead wires |
| Articulated bus | Two vehicle sections with articulated design and walkthrough feature |
| Special bus | Special vehicle bodies, e.g. for the disabled, prisoners |
| **Truck** | Transport of freight |
| Multipurpose truck | Truck with open or closed body |
| Special truck | Transport of specific freight (e.g. tankers) or for special uses (e.g. towing vehicles) |
| **Tractor vehicle** | Commercial vehicle for pulling trailers |
| Trailer tractor vehicle | For pulling trailers, freight on auxiliary cargo area |
| Semitrailer tractor vehicle | For pulling semitrailers |
| Agricultural tractor | Tractor vehicle, also for pushing, transporting or driving interchangeable units |
| **Trailer vehicle** | Non-self-propelled road vehicle |
| **Articulated drawbar trailer** | |
| **Rigid drawbar trailer** | |
| Center-axle trailer | |
| Semitrailer | |
| General-purpose trailer | |
| Bus trailer | |
| Caravan | |
| Special trailer | |
| **Vehicle combinations** | Vehicle with trailer |
| Passenger-car combination | Passenger car with trailer |
| Passenger road train | Bus with trailer |
| Road train | Truck with trailer |
| Drawbar tractor combination | Tractor vehicle with trailer |
| Articulated road train | Semitrailer tractor vehicle with semitrailer |
| Double road train | Articulated road train with trailer |
| Platform road train | Truck or tractor vehicle with special trailer (dolly), the load forms the connection between the two vehicles |

# Classification[1])

## Category L
Motor vehicles with fewer than 4 wheels: motorized two-wheeled and three-wheeled vehicles.

| Category | Design | Piston displacement | Max. speed |
|---|---|---|---|
| $L_1$ | two-wheeled | $\leq 50$ cm³ | $\leq 50$ km/h |
| $L_2$ | three-wheeled | $\leq 50$ cm³ | $\leq 50$ km/h |
| $L_3$ | two-wheeled | $> 50$ cm³ | $> 50$ km/h |
| $L_4$ | three-wheeled asymmetrical to vehicle's longitudinal axis | $> 50$ cm³ | $> 50$ km/h |
| $L_5$ | three-wheeled symmetrical to vehicle's longitudinal axis | $> 50$ cm³ | $> 50$ km/h |

## Category M
Motor vehicles with at least 4 wheels and intended for passenger transport.

| Category | Total seating incl. driver | Gross veh. weight |
|---|---|---|
| $M_1$ | $\leq 9$ | |
| $M_2$ | $> 9$ | $\leq 5$ t |
| $M_3$ | $> 9$ | $> 5$ t |

The vehicle categories $M_2$ and $M_3$ are further subdivided (vehicles with seats only, vehicles with seats and standing room, Categories I...III).

## Category N
Motor vehicles with at least 4 wheels and intended for freight transport.

| Category | Total veh. weight |
|---|---|
| $N_1$ | $\leq 3.5$ t |
| $N_2$ | $> 3.5$ t $\leq 12$ t |
| $N_3$ | $> 12$ t |

## Category O
Trailers and semitrailers

| Category | Total veh. weight |
|---|---|
| $O_1$ | $\leq 0.75$ t |
| $O_2$ | $> 0.75$ t $\leq 3.5$ t |
| $O_3$ | $> 3.5$ t $\leq 10$ t |
| $O_4$ | $> 10$ t |

Vehicles in Categories M, N and O may be equipped for special purposes (e.g. caravans, ambulances).

There are further classifications for agricultural and forestry vehicles and other off-road vehicles (Category G).

---

[1]) Vehicle classification as per the Economic Commission of Europe (ECE), Consolidated Resolution on the Construction of Vehicles (R.E.3).

# Vehicle bodies (passenger cars)

## Main dimensions

### Interior dimensions

<u>Dimensional layout</u> depends on body shape, type of drive, scope of aggregate equipment, desired interior size, trunk volume, and other considerations such as driving comfort, driving safety, and operating safety. <u>Seating positions</u> are designed in accordance with ergonomic findings and with the aid of templates or 3D CAD dummy models (DIN, SAE, RAMSIS): body template as per DIN 33 408 for men (5th, 50th, and 95th percentile) and women (1st, 5th and 95th percentile). For example, the 5th percentile template represents "small" body size, i.e. only 5% of the population has smaller bodies, while 95% has larger body dimensions.

SAE H-point template in accordance with SAE J 826 (May 1987): 10th, 50th, and 95th percentile thigh segments and lower leg segments. For legal reasons, motor-vehicle manufacturers in the U.S.A. and in Canada must use the SAE H-point template for determining the seating reference point. Body templates in accordance with DIN 33 408 in accelerated form are particularly well suited to the dimensional design of seats and passenger cells. Most motor-vehicle manufacturers round the world use the 3D CAD dummy model RAMSIS (<u>computer-aided anthropological-mathematical system for passenger simulation)</u>

The hip point (H-point) is the pivot center of torso and thigh, and roughly corresponds to the hip-joint location. The seating reference point (in accordance with ISO 6549 and U.S. legislation) or R-point (ISO 6549 and EEC Directives/ECE Regulations) indicates the position of the design H-point in the rearmost normal driver seating position in the case of adjustable seats. In determining the design H-point position, many vehicle manufacturers use the 95th percentile adult-male position or, if this position is not reached, the position with the seat adjusted to its rearmost setting. In order to check the position of the measured H-point relative to the vehicle, a three-dimensional, adjustable SAE H-point machine weighing 75 kg is used. The seating reference point, heel point, vertical, and horizontal distance between these two points, and body angles specified by the vehicle manufacturer form the basis for determining the dimensions of the driver's seating position.

The seating reference point is used:
– to define the positions of the eye ellipse (SAE J 941) and the eye points (RREG 77/649) as a basis for determining the driver's direct field of view
– to define hand reach envelopes in order to correctly position controls and actuators
– to determine the <u>accelerator heel point</u> (AHP) as a reference point for positioning the pedals

The space required by the rear axle as well as location and shape of the fuel tank primarily determine the <u>rear-seating arrangement</u> (height of the seating reference point, rear seating room, head-room) and thus the shape of the roof rear portion. Depending on the type of vehicle under development, the projected main dimensions and the required passenger sizes, there are different body angles for the 2D templates or body postures (RAMSIS) and different distances between the seating reference points of the driver's and rear seats. The longitudinal dimensions are greatly influenced by the height of the seating reference point above the heel point. Lower seats require a more stretched passenger seating position, and thus greater interior length.

The <u>passenger-cell width</u> is dependent on the projected external width, the shape of the sides (curvature), and the space required for door mechanisms, passive restraint systems, and various assemblies (propshaft tunnel, exhaust-gas system, etc.).

### Trunk dimensions

The size and shape of the trunk are dependent on the design of the rear end of the vehicle, the position of the fuel tank and its volume, the position of the spare wheel, and the location of the main muffler.

Trunk capacity is determined in accordance with DIN ISO 3832 or, more commonly, with the VDA method using the

*Typical internal and external dimensions (as per DIN 70 020, Part 1)*

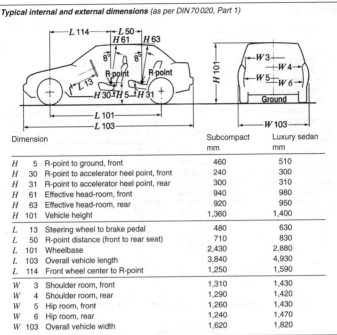

| Dimension | | | Subcompact mm | Luxury sedan mm |
|---|---|---|---|---|
| H | 5 | R-point to ground, front | 460 | 510 |
| H | 30 | R-point to accelerator heel point, front | 240 | 300 |
| H | 31 | R-point to accelerator heel point, rear | 300 | 310 |
| H | 61 | Effective head-room, front | 940 | 980 |
| H | 63 | Effective head-room, rear | 920 | 950 |
| H | 101 | Vehicle height | 1,360 | 1,400 |
| L | 13 | Steering wheel to brake pedal | 480 | 630 |
| L | 50 | R-point distance (front to rear seat) | 710 | 830 |
| L | 101 | Wheelbase | 2,430 | 2,880 |
| L | 103 | Overall vehicle length | 3,840 | 4,930 |
| L | 114 | Front wheel center to R-point | 1,250 | 1,590 |
| W | 3 | Shoulder room, front | 1,310 | 1,430 |
| W | 4 | Shoulder room, rear | 1,290 | 1,420 |
| W | 5 | Hip room, front | 1,260 | 1,430 |
| W | 6 | Hip room, rear | 1,240 | 1,470 |
| W | 103 | Overall vehicle width | 1,620 | 1,820 |

VDA unit module (a right parallelepiped measuring of 200 x 100 x 50 mm – corresponds to a volume of 1 dm³).

### External dimensions
The following factors must be taken into consideration:
- Seating arrangement and trunk
- Engine, transmission, radiator
- Auxiliary systems and special equipment
- Space required by sprung and turned wheels (allowance for snow chains)
- Type and size of powered axle
- Position and volume of fuel tank
- Front and rear fenders
- Aerodynamic considerations
- Ground clearance (approx. 100...180 mm)
- Effect of body-structure width on windshield wiper system (ADR 16, FMVSS 104)

*Key parameters of car-cockpit design*

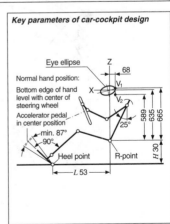

## Body design

The following technical requirements must be met in interior and exterior body design:
- Mechanical functions (lowering of side windows, opening of hood, trunk lid, and sliding sunroof, positions of lamps)
- Manufacturability and ease of repair (gap widths, bodywork assembly, window shape, protective molding rails, paint feature lines)
- Safety (position and shape of fenders, no sharp edges or points)
- Aerodynamics (air forces and moments if they affect performance, fuel consumption, and emissions as well as vehicle dynamics/directional stability, wind noise, adhesion of dirt to the outer body panels, enjoyment of open-topped driving, cabin ventilation, windshield wiper function, cooling of fluids; see also figure)
- Optics (visual distortion caused by window type and slope, glare due to reflection)
- Legal requirements (position and size of lamps, rear-view mirror, license plates)

- Design and layout of controls (positions, shapes, and surface contours)
- Visibility of vehicle extremities (parking)

## Aerodynamics

Aerodynamics encompass all the air flows that pass over, around, and through a vehicle – they can be subdivided in those affecting performance/fuel consumption, comfort (including aeroacoustics), cooling, vehicle dynamics/directional stability, and perceptibility safety (see also the section "Body design").

### Air forces and moments
With regard to performance, emissions, and fuel consumption, the aerodynamic drag coefficient $c_d$ and the frontal area of the vehicle $A$ are the determining factors which vehicle manufacturers must attempt to manipulate. The equation for aerodynamic drag $F_L$ is:

$$F_L = c_d \cdot \frac{\varrho}{2} \cdot v^2 \cdot A$$

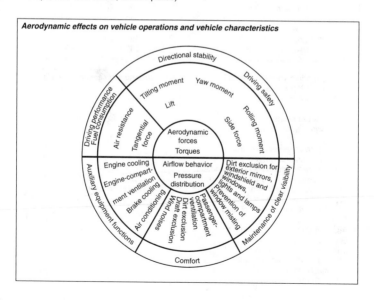

*Aerodynamic effects on vehicle operations and vehicle characteristics*

where $F_L$ is the aerodynamic drag in N; $c_d$ is the aerodynamic drag coefficient; $\varrho$ the air density in kg $\cdot$ m$^{-3}$; $v$ the vehicle speed in m $\cdot$ s$^{-1}$; $A$ the frontal area in m$^2$.

The same equation applies by analogy to the other air forces of lift $F_a$ (often subdivided in $F_{aV}$ for the front wheels, and $F_{aH}$ for the rear wheels), and crosswind force $F_S$.

As far as vehicle dynamics and directional stability are concerned, the forces of interest are the moments about the lateral axis (pitch moment $M_N$), the vertical axis (yaw moment $M_G$), and the longitudinal axis (rolling moment $M_R$). The point of reference for these moments is at the center of the vehicle, at the midpoint of the wheelbase, and at ground level. The yaw moment $M_G$ (representing the other moments) can be rendered by:

$$M_G = c_N \cdot \frac{\varrho}{2} \cdot v^2 \cdot A \cdot l$$

where $M_G$ is the yaw moment in N; $c_N$ is the yaw-moment coefficient; $\varrho$ the air density in kg $\cdot$ m$^{-3}$; $v$ the vehicle speed in m $\cdot$ s$^{-1}$; $A$ the frontal area in m$^2$; $l$ the wheelbase in m.

Ideally, aerodynamic optimization of vehicles takes place at the same time as the creation of design models to reduce the number of extra add-on parts and their associated negative side effects (cost, weight). General statements regarding the effectiveness of add-on parts are hardly possible since they are dependent on the starting point represented by the basic vehicle; nevertheless, some typical examples can be cited (see Table 1).

With the advancing optimization of vehicles, a plateau has currently been reached in terms of the drag coefficients $c_d$ achieved, also partly due to the fact that other development objectives (e.g. styling) have taken on greater importance. Table 2 contains some examples of aerodynamic drag coefficient ($c_d$) of modern vehicles in a number of vehicle categories.

**Table 1.**
**Effect of various vehicle modifications on the aerodynamic drag coefficient**

| Modification | $\Delta c_d$ [–] |
|---|---|
| Reduction of ride height by 10 mm | –0.003...–0.008 |
| Fully lined underbody | –0.010...–0.040 |
| Wheel spoilers | –0.002...–0.010 |
| Brake cooling | +0.001...+0.005 |
| Exterior mirrors | +0.004...+0.020 |
| Air flow through radiator and engine compartment | +0.010...+0.025 |
| Open side windows at front | +0.010...+0.020 |
| Open sliding sunroof | +0.005...+0.010 |
| Open soft-top | +0.040...+0.060 |
| Carrying surfboard on roof | +0.100...+0.120 |

**Table 2. Aerodynamic drag coefficients and frontal areas of modern vehicles**

| Vehicle category | Model | $c_d$ – | $A$ m$^2$ | Model | $c_d$ – | $A$ m$^2$ |
|---|---|---|---|---|---|---|
| Luxury performance | Audi A8 | 0.27 | 2.31 | MB S-Class | 0.27 | 2.29 |
| Executive | MB E-Class | 0.26 | 2.21 | BMW 5-Series | 0.27 | 2.17 |
| Mid-range | MB C-Class | 0.26 | 2.08 | Audi A4 | 0.28 | 2.06 |
| Compact | Audi A2 | 0.28 | 2.18 | MB A-Class | 0.30 | 2.30 |
| Sports car | MB SL | 0.29 | 2.00 | Porsche 911 | 0.30 | 1.94 |

**Table 3. Effect of aerodynamic drag coefficient and vehicle mass on performance and fuel consumption as illustrated by a mid-range car**

| Difference in $c_d$ | – | Basis | +0.04 | 0 | +0.04 |
|---|---|---|---|---|---|
| Difference in mass | kg | Basis | 0 | +100 | +100 |
| Mass ff/calculation | kg | 1,445/1,645 | 1,445/1,645 | 1,545/1,745 | 1,545/1,745 |
| Inertial mass for NEDC | kg | 1,590 | 1,590 | 1,700 | 1,700 |
| $c_d/A$ | 1/m² | 0.26/2.08 | 0.30/2.08 | 0.26/2.08 | 0.30/2.08 |
| $v_{max}$ | km/h | 221 | 212 | 220 | 212 |
| **Acceleration** 0...100 km/h | s | 9.8 | 9.8 | 10.2 | 10.3 |
| 60...120 km/h | s | 13.7/19.5 | 18.9/19.9 | 14.5/20.8 | 14.8/21.2 |
| (AG KD/VG) | Gear | 5th/6th | 5th/6th | 5th/6th | 5th/6th |
| **Climbing ability** at 120 km/h | % | 12.1/9.4 | 11.8/9.0 | 11.4/8.8 | 11.1/8.5 |
| | Gear | 5th/6th | 5th/6th | 5th/6th | 5th/6th |
| **Fuel consumption to** | | EU3 | EU3 | EU3 | EU3 |
| City | l/100 km | 9.5 | 9.5 | 9.7 | 9.7 |
| Highway (EUDC) | l/100 km | 5.1 | 5.2 | 5.2 | 5.4 |
| **Overall (NEDC)** | l/100 km | 6.7 | 6.8 | 6.8 | 7.0 |
| $CO_2$ overall | g/100 km | | | | |
| **Fuel consumption** at constant speed | | | | | |
| 90 km/h | l/100 km | 4.2 | 4.4 | 4.3 | 4.5 |
| 120 km/h | l/100 km | 5.3 | 5.7 | 5.4 | 5.7 |
| 150 km/h | l/100 km | 7.0 | 7.6 | 7.1 | 7.6 |
| 180 km/h | l/100 km | 9.0 | 9.9 | 9.1 | 10.0 |
| 210 km/h | l/100 km | 12.3 | 13.9 | 12.4 | 14.0 |

The effect of changing drag coefficient and vehicle mass is illustrated by the example of a mid-range car (Mercedes-Benz C220 CDI) in Table 3. The exponential increase in the effect of aerodynamic drag with increasing speed is clearly demonstrated. It is also evident that changes in aerodynamic drag only have a minimal effect on NEDC (New European Driving Cycle) results, due to the low average speed of 33.4 km/h used for the tests. Nevertheless, a change in $c_d$ of –0.001 brings about the same reduction in fuel consumption as a reduction in mass of 2 to 3 kg (even under NEDC conditions), and at a constant 210 km/h, it is equivalent to roughly 40 kg.

## Aeroacoustics

More and more attention is focused on the aspects of aerodynamics which are relevant to comfort and safety, most particularly aeroacoustics. High levels of noise inside the vehicle are increasingly perceived as indicative of poor vehicle quality and lead to customer dissatisfaction.

Wind noise is heavily dependent on vehicle speed and presents problems at high speeds in particular. At lower speeds, other sources of noise predominate (tire noise, engine noise, etc.).

There are two possible lines of attack for reducing noise levels:
- Reducing the intensity of the noise sources
- Optimizing the transmission path from the noise source to the vehicle occupants.

Efforts at reducing wind noise are now no longer limited merely to optimizing individual components (such as antennas, or door and window seals), they are directed to an increasing degree at the body design of the vehicle. Generally speaking, an air flow that remains in close contact with the body surface is better for reducing wind noise. At points where this is not possible (A-pillar area, exterior mirrors), emphasis should be placed on creating smooth detachment points, and directing turbulent flow as far away from the surface of the vehicle as possible. This prevents turbulent reattachment of the air flow as far as possible. In order to minimize transmission of noise to the vehicle interior, the seals on the doors, windows, hood, and trunk must function effectively. Equally, the design of windows in terms of thickness and laminar structure is of particular importance.

There is a growing tendency for aeroacoustic testing to be carried out in a wind tunnel (see P. 1134 onwards), rather than on the road. Wind-tunnel operators have responded to this development by building new tunnels or modifying existing facilities in order to significantly reduce base noise levels in the tunnels themselves (aeroacoustics tunnels, P. 1138). The advantages of testing in a wind tunnel are greater reproducibility, the absence of weather-related effects, and the removal of other sources of wind noise. In addition, the test cycles for each set of conditions are shorter than for road tests. In the past the conventional measure of aeroacoustic quality was the overall noise level in dB (A). However, experience has

shown that it is preferable to include an assessment of "psychoacoustic" parameters (e.g. loudness, pitch, and articulation index). These parameters measure higher-frequency noise components which take greater account of subjective perception (loudness, pitch) and speech intelligibility (articulation index).

Table 4 lists examples of the figures for modern vehicles in various categories.

## Body structure

### Unitized body
(standard design)

The unitized body consists of sheet-metal panels, hollow tubular members, and body panels that are joined together by multi-spot welding machines or welding robots. Individual components may also be bonded, riveted, or laser-welded.

Depending on vehicle type, roughly 5,000 spot welds must be made along a total flange length of 120...200 m. The flange widths are 10...18 mm. Other parts (front fenders, doors, hood, and trunk lid) are bolted to the body supporting structure. Other types of body construction include frame and sandwich designs.

Increasing use is being made of hybrid bodyshell construction, where the individual structural components of the bodyshell are made of different materials according to function and required load capacity. The bodyshell illustrated (MB W211), for example, consists of 47% high-strength steel, 42% standard steel, 10% aluminum and 1% plastic.

**Table 4. Aeroacoustic specifications of current vehicles** (140 km/h)

| Vehicle category | Example vehicle | Sound pressure dB (A) | Loudness sone | Pitch acum | Articulation index % |
|---|---|---|---|---|---|
| Luxury performance | MB S-Class | 67.1 | 21.1 | 1.23 | 74.6 |
| Executive | BMW 5-Series | 67.5 | 23.4 | 1.50 | 65.2 |
| Mid-range | Audi A4 | 68.1 | 26.4 | 1.65 | 53.2 |
| Compact | Ford Focus | 71.8 | 31.3 | 1.86 | 50.0 |
| Sports car | MB SL | 67.6 | 24.4 | 1.62 | 61.4 |

The general requirements placed on the body structure are as follows:

### Rigidity

Torsional and bending rigidity should be as high as possible in order to minimize elastic deformation of the apertures for the doors, hood, and trunk lid. The effect of body rigidity on the vibrational characteristics of the vehicle must be taken into consideration.

### Vibrational characteristics

Body vibrations as well as vibrations of individual structural components as a result of excitation by the wheels, suspension linkage, engine, and drivetrain can severely impair driving comfort if resonance occurs.

The natural frequency of the body, and of those body components which are capable of vibration, must be detuned by means of creasing, and changing the wall thicknesses and cross sections to minimize resonance and its consequences.

### Operational integrity

Alternating stresses, which can affect the body as the vehicle is driven, can lead to incipient structural cracks or spot-weld failure. Areas which are particularly susceptible are the bearing or mounting points of the suspension, the steering system, and the drivetrain assemblies.

### Body stresses due to accidents

In the event of a collision, the body must be capable of transforming as much kinetic energy as possible in the deformation process, while minimizing deformation of the passenger cell.

### Ease of repair

The components which are most susceptible to damage as a result of minor accidents ("fender-benders") must be easily replaceable or repairable (access to exterior body panels from the inside, access to bolts, favorable location of joints, feature lines for repainting individual components).

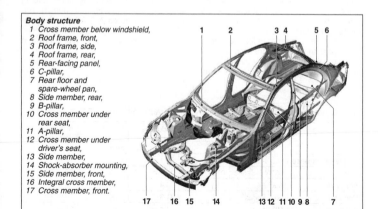

**Body structure**
1 Cross member below windshield,
2 Roof frame, front,
3 Roof frame, side,
4 Roof frame, rear,
5 Rear-facing panel,
6 C-pillar,
7 Rear floor and
   spare-wheel pan,
8 Side member, rear,
9 B-pillar,
10 Cross member under
   rear seat,
11 A-pillar,
12 Cross member under
   driver's seat,
13 Side member,
14 Shock-absorber mounting,
15 Side member, front,
16 Integral cross member,
17 Cross member, front.

## Body materials

### Sheet steel
Sheet steel of various grades (see table "Body panels" on P. 254) is customarily used for the vehicle body structure.

Sheet thicknesses range from 0.6 to 3.0 mm, and most parts range from 0.75 to 1.0 mm thick. Due to the mechanical properties of steel with regard to rigidity, strength, economy, and ductility, alternative materials for the vehicle body structure are not yet available.

High Strength Low Alloy (HSLA) sheet steel is used for high-stress structural components. The resulting high strength of these components allows their thickness to be reduced.

### Aluminum
In order to reduce weight, aluminum can be used for separate body components, such as the hood, trunk lid, etc.

Since 1994 an aluminum body has been in use on one of the German luxury sedans. The vehicle's frame is constructed from aluminum extruded sections, and the panel parts are integrated as self-supporting parts (ASF Audi Space Frame). The implementation of this principle required the use of suitable aluminum alloys, as well as new production processes and special repair facilities. According to the manufacturers, the rigidity and deformation characteristics are identical to those of steel, or are even superior.

### Plastics
Plastics replace steel in a limited number of cases for separate body components (see Table below).

### Table 5. Examples of alternative materials

| Typical applications | Material | Abbreviation | Processing method |
|---|---|---|---|
| Structural components e.g. fender cross members | Glass-fiber mat reinforced thermoplastics | PP-GMT | Injection molding |
| Moldings/ covers e.g. front apron, spoiler, front section, radiator grill, wheel-well liners, wheel covers | Glass-fiber mat reinforced thermoplastics | PP-GMT | |
| | Polyurethane | PUR | RIM (Reaction Injection Molding) RRIM (Reinforced Reaction Injection Molding) |
| Bodyshell components e.g. hood, fenders, trunk lid, sliding sunroof | Polyamide Polypropylene Polyethylene Acrylonitrile-butadiene-styrene copolymers Polycarbonate (with polybutadiene theraphthalate) | PA PP PE ABS PC-PBT | Injection molding, glass-fiber content determines elasticity |
| Flexible protective molding rails | Polyvinylchloride Ethylene-propylene-terpolymers Elastomer-modified polypropylene | PVC EPDM PP-EPDM | Injection molding/extruding |
| Energy-absorbing foam | Polyurethane Polypropylene | PUR PP | Reaction foams |
| Fenders | Thermosetting plastics with reinforcing fibers (Sheet Molding Compound) | SMC | Pressing |

## Body surface

### Corrosion protection

Allowance must be made for corrosion protection as early as the body design phase (Anti-Corrosion Code, Canada). Corrosion protection measures:
– Minimize flanged joints, sharp edges and corners.
– Avoid areas where dirt and humidity can accumulate.
– Provide holes for pretreatment and electrophoretic enameling.
– Provide good accessibility for the application of corrosion inhibitor.
– Allow for ventilation of hollow spaces.
– Prevent the penetration of dirt and water to the greatest extent possible; provide water drain openings.
– Minimize the area of the body exposed to stone-chip impact.
– Prevent contact corrosion.

Precoated sheet steel (inorganic zinc, electrolytically galvanized, hot-dip galvanized) is often used for those components at particularly high risk, such as doors and load-bearing members at the front of the vehicle. Inaccessible structural areas are coated with spot-welding paste (PVC or epoxy adhesive, approx. 10...15 m seam length per vehicle) prior to assembly.

### Painting (P. 264)

Measures subsequent to electrophoretic enameling:
– Covering the spot-welded seams (up to 90...110 m), welts and joints with PVC sealing compound.
– Coating the underbody with PVC underbody sealant to protect against stone impact (0.3...1.4 mm thick, 10...18 kg per vehicle), or alternatively lining the underbody with plastic trim panels.
– Filling cavities with penetrating, non-aging water-based wax.
– Using corrosion-resistant, attached plastic components in high-risk areas, such as the front fenders (PVC coating not used in those places).
– Sealing of underbody and engine compartment after final assembly.

## Body finishing components

### Fenders

The front and rear of the vehicle should be protected so that low-speed collisions will only damage the vehicle slightly, or not at all. Prescribed fender evaluation tests (U.S. Part 581, Canada CMVSS 215, and ECE-R 42) specify minimum requirements in terms of energy absorption and installed fender height. Compliance with fender tests in the U.S.A. to U.S. Part 581 (4 km/h barrier impact, 4 km/h pendulum tests) and in Canada (8 km/h) requires a fender system with energy absorbers that automatically regenerate. The requirements of the ECE standard are satisfied by plastic-deformable retaining elements located between the bendable bar (fender) and the vehicle body structure. In addition to sheet steel, many bendable bars are made using fiber-reinforced plastics and aluminum sections.

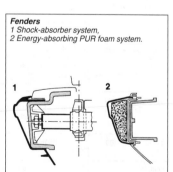

*Fenders*
1 Shock-absorber system,
2 Energy-absorbing PUR foam system.

**Table 6. Paint/coating thicknesses**

| Overall paint thickness | ≈ 120 μm |
|---|---|
| Zinc phosphate coat Electrophoretic enameling (cathodic) Filler Top coat | ≈ 2 μm<br><br>13...18 μm ≈ 40 μm 35...45 μm |
| Clear finish coat (for metallic and water-based paints only) | 40...45 μm |

**Exterior trim panels,
protective molding rails**
Plastics have become the preferred materials for external protective molding rails, trim panels, skirts, spoilers, and particularly for components whose purpose is to improve the aerodynamic characteristics of the vehicle. Criteria used in the selection of the proper material are flexibility, high-temperature shape retention, coefficient of linear expansion, notched-bar toughness, scratch resistance, chemical resistance, surface quality, and paintability.

**Glazing** (see also P. 942 onwards)
The windshield and rear window are usually retained in rubber strips, and sealed or bonded in place. The weight of the glazing is 25...35 kg per vehicle. The use of plastics (PC, PMMA) instead of glass in order to reduce weight has not yet become widely established due to a number of disadvantages. Laminated safety glass is sometimes used in door windows to provide better sound and heat insulation. Sliding sunroofs are also increasingly made of glass (usually single-pane toughened safety glass).

**Door locks** (see also P. 1028 onwards, Locking systems)
Door locks are of immense importance to passive accident safety. Various manufacturers have produced a variety of solutions to the issues of ease of operation, theft deterrence, and child safety. The legal requirements are as follows:

ECE (ECE R11)
Every lock must have a latched position and a fully closed position.
Linear force: capable of withstanding 4,440 N in latched position, 11,110 N in fully closed position.
Lateral force: capable of withstanding 4,440 N in latched position, 8,890 N in fully closed position.
Inertial force: The lock should not be forced out of the fully closed position by linear or lateral acceleration of 30 $g$ acting on the lock in both directions, and on the striker and the operating device, when the locking mechanism is not engaged.

U.S.A. (FMVSS 206)
Every lock must have a fully closed position. Doors which are attached by hinges must have a latched position.
Linear force: capable of withstanding 4,450 N in latched position, 11,000 N in fully closed position.
Lateral force: capable of withstanding 4,450 N in latched position, 8,900 N in fully closed position.
Inertial force: The lock should not be forced open from the fully closed position by linear or lateral acceleration of 30 $g$ acting on the door lock system in both directions (lock and operating device).

**Trunk locks** (excerpt from FMVSS 401, in force since 9/1/2002)

S1. Purpose and scope
These motor-vehicle safety regulations contain the requirements for a release mechanism for the trunk. Such a mechanism should allow a person locked inside the trunk of a car to free himself/herself from the trunk.

S2. Applications
These safety regulations apply to cars with a trunk. They do not apply to cars with a door at the back.

S4. Requirements
According to S4.1, every car with a trunk must have an automatic or manually operated release mechanism inside the trunk to release the trunk lid. All trunk release mechanisms must conform either to S4.2(a) and S.43, or to S4.2(b) and S4.3, depending on the choice of the manufacturer. The manufacturer must opt for one of the alternatives at the time of certification, and may not employ any other option for the vehicle in question.

According to S4.2(a), all manually operated release mechanisms fitted in accordance with S4.1 of these safety regulations for motor vehicles must be provided with a function (e.g. lighting or phosphorescence) by which the release mechanism can easily be seen inside the closed trunk.

According to S4.2(b), all automatically operated release mechanisms fitted in accordance with S4.1 of these safety regulations for motor vehicles must open the trunk lid within 5 minutes of closing if there is a person inside the trunk.

According to S4.3(a), operation of any release mechanism required by these safety regulations must release the trunk lid regardless of the position of the trunk lock.

### Seats

The strength requirements which must be met by seats in a collision pertain to the seat frame (seat cushions, backrest), the head restraints, the seat adjustment mechanism, and the seat anchors (regulations: FMVSS 207, 202; ECE-R 17, 25; RREG 74/408, 78/932, and others). One component of active safety is seating comfort. Seats must be designed so that vehicle occupants with different body dimensions are able to sit for long periods of time without becoming tired.
Parameters:
– Support of individual body areas (pressure distribution)
– Lateral support when cornering
– Seat climatic conditions
– Freedom of movement so that an occupant can change his/her sitting position without having to readjust the seat
– Vibrational and damping characteristics (matching the natural frequency within the excitation frequency band)
– Adjustability of seat cushion, backrest and head restraint

The above parameters are affected by the following:
– Dimensions and shapes of the upholstery of seat cushions and backrests
– Distribution of the spring rates of individual padded zones
– Overall spring rate and damping capacity of the seat cushions in particular
– Thermal conductivity and moisture-absorption capacity of the covering material and upholstery
– Operation and range of the seat adjustment mechanisms

### Interior trim

A section of trim consists of a dimensionally stable core (sheet steel, sheet aluminum, or plastic) with fixing elements, and energy-absorbing padding made of foam material (e.g. PUR), and a flexible surface layer. One-piece plastic trim sections made of injection-molded thermoplastic material are also used.

The headliner is made either as a stretched liner or finished liner. The materials used must be flame-retardant and slow burning (FMVSS 302).

## Safety

Active safety:
<u>Prevention</u> of accidents
Passive safety:
<u>Reduction</u> in the consequences of accidents

### Active safety

<u>Driving safety</u> is the result of a harmonious chassis and suspension design with regard to wheel suspension, springing, steering, and braking, and is reflected in optimum dynamic vehicle behavior.

<u>Conditional safety</u> results from keeping the physiological stress to which vehicle occupants are subjected by vibration, noise, and climatic conditions down to as low a level as possible. It is a significant factor in reducing the probability of misactions in traffic.

Vibrations within a frequency range of 1 to 25 Hz (stuttering, shaking, etc.) induced by wheels and drivetrain assemblies reach the occupants of the vehicle

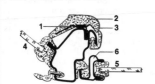

*Section through an A-pillar with trim*
(schematic)
1 Core, 2 Foam, 3 Film, 4 Windshield,
5 Side, window, 6 Door frame.

via the car body, seats, and steering wheel. The effect of these vibrations is more or less pronounced, depending on their direction, amplitude, and duration.

Noises produced as acoustical disturbances in and around the vehicle can come from internal sources (engine, transmission, propshafts, axles) or external sources (tire/road noises, wind noises), and are transmitted through the air or by structures. The sound pressure level is measured in dB(A) (see also P. 58 onwards).

Noise reduction measures are concerned, on the one hand, with the development of quiet-running components and the insulation of noise sources (e.g. engine encapsulation), and on the other hand, with noise damping by means of insulation or anti-noise materials.

Climatic conditions primarily include air temperature, air humidity, rate of air flow, and air pressure (for further details, see P. 446 onwards).

<u>Perceptibility safety</u>
Measures which increase perceptibility safety are concentrated on:
– Lighting equipment (see P. 910 onwards)
– Acoustic warning devices (see P. 1033)
– Direct and indirect visibility (driver's view: the angle of binocular obscuration – i.e. for both of the driver's eyes – caused by the A-pillars must not be more than 6 degrees).

<u>Operational safety</u>
Low driver stress, and thus a high degree of driving safety, requires optimum design of the driver's surroundings with regard to ease of operation of the vehicle controls.

**Passive safety**
<u>Exterior safety</u>
The term "exterior safety" covers all vehicle-related measures which are designed to minimize the severity of injury to pedestrians, and bicycle and motorcycle riders struck by the vehicle in an accident. The factors that determine exterior safety are:
– Vehicle-body deformation behavior
– Exterior vehicle-body shape

The primary objective is to design the vehicle so that its exterior design minimizes the consequences of a primary collision (a collision involving persons outside the vehicle and the vehicle itself).

The most severe injuries sustained by pedestrians result from impact with the front of the vehicle or the road, in addition to which the precise accident sequence greatly depends on body size. The consequences of collisions involving two-wheeled vehicles and passenger cars can only be slightly improved by passenger-car design due to the two-wheeled vehicle's often considerable inherent energy component, its high seat position, and the wide dispersion of contact points. The design features that can be incorporated in a passenger car are, for example:

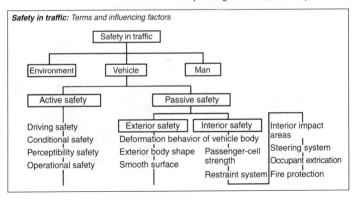

*Safety in traffic:* Terms and influencing factors

- Movable front lamps
- Recessed windshield wipers
- Recessed drip rails
- Recessed door handles

See also ECE-R26, RREG 74/483.

Interior safety

The term "interior safety" covers vehicle measures whose purpose is to minimize the acceleration and forces acting on vehicle occupants in the event of an accident, provide sufficient survival space, and ensure the operability of vehicle components critical to the extrication of occupants from the vehicle after the accident has occurred.

The determining factors for passenger safety are:
- Deformation behavior of the vehicle body.
- Passenger-cell strength, size of the survival space during and after impact.
- Restraint systems (see P. 1034 onwards).
- Impact areas in the vehicle interior (FMVSS 201).
- Steering system.
- Occupant extrication.
- Fire protection.

Laws which regulate interior safety (frontal impact) are:
- Protection of vehicle occupants in the event of an accident, in particular restraint systems (FMVSS 208 amended version, FMVSS 214, ECE R94, ECE R95, injury criteria).
- Windshield mounting (FMVSS 212).
- Penetration of the windshield by vehicle body components (FMVSS 219).
- Storage compartment lids (FMVSS 201).
- Fuel leakage prevention (FMVSS 301).

**"PRE-SAFE" systems**

Present restraint systems are primarily designed for worst-case scenarios and cannot, therefore, provide optimum occupant protection in all situations. If occupants are in an unfavorable position, restraint systems can even become a hazard.

The key to continuing improvement of occupant safety in the future is to adopt a position where active and passive safety are considered as overlapping systems, rather than separate areas. The core elements of this approach lie in networking, or even merging safety sensor systems. Furthermore, the functionality of "PRE-CRASH" sensors will no longer be viewed exclusively in terms of predicting an impact, but of activating occupant safety systems as soon as critical vehicle maneuvers are detected.

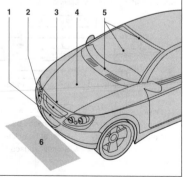

*Risk to pedestrians in collisions with passenger cars*
*Frequency of involvement of contact areas according to GIDAS (1999-2001); 100% equals 116 collisions.*

| Item | Vehicle area | Percentage of cases |
|------|-------------|---------|
| 1 | Front fender | 28% |
| 2 | Radiator grill and headlamps | 5% |
| 3 | Edge of hood | 3% |
| 4 | Hood | 8% |
| 5 | Windshield and frame | 18% |
| 6 | Ground in front of vehicle | 27% |
| – | Others | 11% |

"PRE-SAFE" systems utilize elements of active safety by preparing the vehicle, its occupants, and restraint systems for a possible accident in critical driving situations in order to improve passive safety. Such preventive systems can contribute to closing possible gaps in safety by preemptive and slower activation.

Rating tests:
– <u>N</u>ew <u>C</u>ar <u>A</u>ssessment <u>P</u>rogram (NCAP, U.S.A., Europe, Japan, Australia)
– IIHS (U.S., insurance test).

<u>Deformation behavior of vehicle body</u>
Due to the frequency of frontal collisions, an important role is played by the legal regulations for <u>frontal impact tests</u> in which a vehicle is driven at a speed of 48.3 km/h (30 mph) into a rigid barrier which is either perpendicular or inclined at an angle of up to 30° relative to the car's longitudinal axis. The chart below shows the distribution of collision types for accidents resulting in injuries to vehicle occupants. Source: GIDAS, <u>G</u>erman <u>In</u>-<u>D</u>epth <u>A</u>ccident <u>S</u>tudy (research project by BASt and FAT).

Because 50% of all frontal collisions in RHD traffic primarily involves the left half of the front of the vehicle which is either perpendicular or inclined at an angle of manufacturers worldwide conduct left-hand offset <u>frontal impact</u> tests on LHD vehicles covering 30...50% of the vehicle width.

In a frontal collision, kinetic energy is absorbed through deformation of the fender, the front of the vehicle, and in severe cases, the forward section of the passenger cell (engine compartment bulkhead). Axles, wheels (rims) and the engine limit the deformable length. Adequate deformation lengths and displaceable drivetrain assemblies are necessary, however, in order to minimize passenger-cell acceleration. Depending on vehicle design (body shape, type of drive, and engine position), vehicle mass and size, a frontal impact with a barrier at approx. 50 km/h results in permanent deformation in the forward area of 0.4...0.7 m. Damage to the passenger cell should be minimized. This concerns primarily:
– engine-bulkhead area (displacement of steering system, instrument panel, pedals, constriction of footwell),
– underbody (lowering or tilting of seats),
– the side structure (ability to open the doors after an accident).

Requirements regarding the prevention of fuel leakage must also be satisfied. Acceleration measurements and evaluations of high-speed films allow a precise analysis of deformation behavior. Dummies of various sizes are used to simulate vehicle occupants and provide measured data for forces acting on the head, neck, chest, and legs.

Head acceleration values are used to determine the <u>head injury criterion</u> (HIC). The comparison of measured data obtained from the dummies with the permissible limits as specified by FMVSS 208, e.g. for the 50th percentile male (HIC: 700, chest acceleration: 60 $g$/3 ms, thigh force: 10 kN), allows only limited conclusions to be drawn.

The <u>side impact</u>, as the next most frequent type of accident, places a high risk of injury on vehicle occupants due to the limited energy-absorption capacity of trim and structural components, and the resulting high degree of vehicle interior deformation.

The risk of injury is largely influenced by the structural strength of the side of the vehicle (pillar/door joints, top/bottom pillar points), load-carrying capacity of floorpan cross-members and seats, and the design

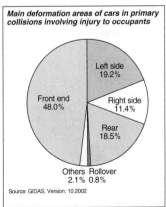

**Main deformation areas of cars in primary collisions involving injury to occupants**

Left side 19.2%
Front end 48.0%
Right side 11.4%
Rear 18.5%
Others 2.1%
Rollover 0.8%

Source: GIDAS, Version: 10.2002

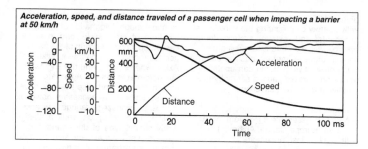

*Acceleration, speed, and distance traveled of a passenger cell when impacting a barrier at 50 km/h*

of inside door panels (FMVSS 214 and 301, ECE R95, Euro NCAP, and U.S. SINCAP). Additional airbags in the doors/seats and the headliner have considerable potential for reducing the risk of injury.

In the <u>rear impact test</u>, deformation of the passenger cell must be minor at most. It should still be possible to open the doors, the edge of the trunk lid should not penetrate the rear window or enter the vehicle interior, and fuel-system integrity must be preserved (FMVSS 301).

Roof structures are investigated by means of <u>rollover tests</u> and quasi-static car-roof crush tests (FMVSS 216).

In addition, some manufacturers subject their vehicles to the inverted vehicle drop test in order to test the fatigue strength of the roof structure (survival space) under extreme conditions (the vehicle falls from a height of 0.5 m onto the left front corner of its roof).

**Steering system** (P. 786)

Legal requirements (FMVSS 203 and 204, ECE R12) stipulate the maximum displacement of the top end of the steering column toward the driver (max. 127 mm, frontal impact at 48.3 km/h), and the limit of the impact on the steering system of a test tool (max. 1,111 daN at an impact speed of 24.1 km/h). Slotted tubes, corrugated tubes, and breakaway universal joints (among others) are used in the design of the lower section of the steering column spindle so that it can be deformed both longitudinally and transversely.

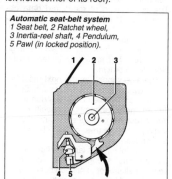

*Automatic seat-belt system*
1 Seat belt, 2 Ratchet wheel,
3 Inertia-reel shaft, 4 Pendulum,
5 Pawl (in locked position).

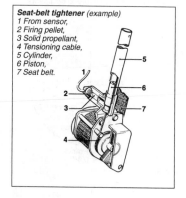

*Seat-belt tightener* (example)
1 From sensor,
2 Firing pellet,
3 Solid propellant,
4 Tensioning cable,
5 Cylinder,
6 Piston,
7 Seat belt.

### Passenger restraint systems
(P. 1034 onwards)

<u>Automatic seat belt</u> (manual systems)
The most frequently installed three-point seat belt with retractor mechanism (automatic seat belt) represents a good compromise between effective safety, ease of fastening, wearing comfort, and cost. When a specific vehicle-deceleration value is reached, a built-in, quick-response interlock inhibits the seat-belt roller.

<u>Seat-belt tightener systems</u>
There are a number of alternative seat-belt tightener designs used by the automotive industry:
– Ball tighteners
– Cable tighteners
– Rack tighteners
– Wankel tighteners

Seat-belt tightener systems represent a further development and improvement of three-point automatic seat-belt systems. By reducing seat-belt slack, they eliminate excessive forward passenger movement in serious accidents. This, in turn, reduces the differential speed between the vehicle and passengers, and also reduces the corresponding forces acting on the passengers.

Integrated belt-force limiters guarantee that controlled give of the belt takes place after it has been tightened, so as to prevent potential overloading in the chest area. These systems operate in conjunction with the front airbags.

<u>Airbag systems (P. 1036 onwards)</u>
Air bags (front air bags, side air bags, window air bags) help to prevent or reduce the impact of the occupant against interior vehicle components (steering wheel, instrument panel, doors, windows, roof pillars).

## Calculations

### Finite-Element Method
Static, dynamic and acoustic properties of components, entire vehicle bodies, and complete vehicles can be calculated using the <u>Fi</u>nite <u>E</u>lement <u>Met</u>hod (FEM) (see also P. 190 onwards). It is based on the idea that a supporting structure of any degree of complexity can be broken down into simple structural elements (beams, panels, spaces, etc.), whose elastic behavior is known and can be easily described in mathematical terms. These elements are then assembled to form an overall structure, taking into account compatibility requirements.

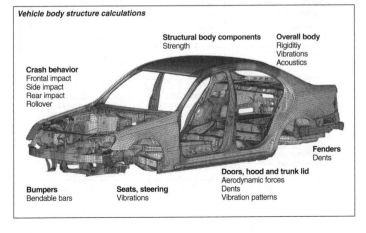

*Vehicle body structure calculations*

**Structural body components**
Strength

**Overall body**
Rigiditiy
Vibrations
Acoustics

**Crash behavior**
Frontal impact
Side impact
Rear impact
Rollover

**Fenders**
Dents

**Doors, hood and trunk lid**
Aerodynamic forces
Dents
Vibration patterns

**Bumpers**
Bendable bars

**Seats, steering**
Vibrations

This allows a mathematical model to be described in such a way that it sufficiently corresponds to the actual body in terms of its elastic characteristics. A number of systems are available for practical FE calculation, such as PERMAS, NASTRAN, ABAQUS, and DYNA3D.

Advantages of FEM:
– Characteristics of structures of any level of complexity can be calculated.
– Anisotropic and nonlinear material properties can be taken into account.
– Variants can be examined rapidly.
– Tried and tested program systems are available (easy to incorporate in the CAD/CAM chain.

Limits of FEM:
– Accuracy is dependent on element type and degree of element detailing within the structure.
– Changes in sheet-metal thicknesses and material characteristic values resulting from the deep-drawing process are not taken into account.

– Welded joints cannot be precisely replicated in the model.

**Complete body calculation**
For the calculation, the bodywork structure is broken down into elements with the required degree of detail depending on the problem to be solved (as at 2002: approx. 370,000 elements with over 1.9 million unknowns). Results under static load are supplied in the form of deformations, stresses, and deformation processes.

**Strength analysis**
Detailed analyses are carried out for individual parts and body sections which are exposed to special stresses caused by factors such as restraint systems or towed loads. The aim of these analyses is to furnish proof of adequate strength, or to reduce unacceptably high stresses by modifying the design. The definitive loads for calculating operational integrity can be determined by means of nonlinear calculations for the vehicle as a whole.

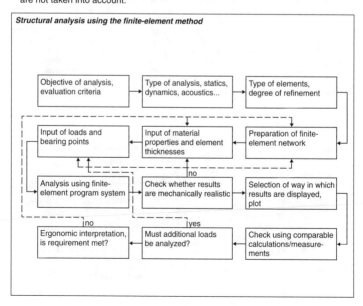

*Structural analysis using the finite-element method*

## Analysis of dynamic behavior

Dynamic analyses are carried out both for the complete body and for individual components. In these analyses, natural vibration (frequencies, forms of vibration) and the system's response to periodic or generally time-dependent excitation is determined. This allows identification of critical resonance.

For the examination of driving comfort and acoustical behavior in the vehicle interior, FE models of the chassis, engine, doors, etc., as well as a model of the interior, are added to the body model.

## Analysis of crash behavior

Accident tests carried out by automotive manufacturers (frontal, rear and side impacts, rollover, and drop tests) as well as traffic accidents, are dynamic, to a large degree, nonlinear processes which cannot be described using the commercially available FE programs. Special FE program systems (e.g. DYNA3D, PAM-CRASH) have been developed for numerical simulation of these processes, and are proving successful in the field. These systems include analysis of severe plastic deformations and determine the contact areas arising between various vehicle parts during crash processes.

## Analysis of occupant-safety systems

The following main tasks are carried out with the aid of computer simulation:
- Design/optimization of restraint systems with regard to front- and rear-end impacts by means of crash-test sled simulations in cases where the interaction between structure and dummy is negligible. The tool used for this purpose is a multibody system (e.g. Madymo-3D) in combination with an FE program system (e.g. LS-DYNA-3D).
- Design of protective components with regard to side impacts in integrated simulations, i.e. complete-vehicle simulations with dummy, seat, and trim panels. Calculation using FE program system (LS-DYNA-3D).
- Design and optimization of cushioning measures (in accordance with FMVSS 201) with regard to satisfying protective criteria. Calculation using FE program system (LS-DYNA-3D).

## Recycling, environmental protection

The automotive manufacturers are making progress in their endeavors to maintain clean water and air, prevent noise pollution, and recycle raw materials:
- Directive for handling scrap cars.
- Ban on heavy metals.
- The recycling quota for metallic materials is 95%.
- The recycling quota for plastics is approximately 14%. In cooperation with the chemical industry and the suppliers of plastic components, there are ongoing, intensive efforts to improve this figure further.
- Exhaust-gas treatment and recovery of high-value catalyst materials.
- Recycling of battery materials.
- Chlorofluorocarbons (CFCs) are no longer used as refrigerants or as expanding agents in the manufacture of plastics.
- Solvents for body degreasing are almost entirely free of chlorinated hydrocarbons; water-based paints are used in dip-priming.
- Water-based paints for top coating are in use.
- Reprocessing of consumables, e.g. oil, coolant, antifreeze.
- Recycling of some 60% of residual materials (e.g. scrap metal, waste paper, leather, textiles, and wood waste).

# Vehicle bodies (commercial vehicles)

## Commercial vehicles

Commercial vehicles are used for the safe and efficient transportation of persons and freight. In this respect, the degree of economic efficiency is determined by the ratio of usable space to overall vehicle volume, and of payload to gross vehicle weight. Dimensions and weights are limited by legal regulations.

From the design-concept viewpoint, a distinction must be made between cab-over-engine (COE) and cab-behind-engine (CBE) vehicles.

A wide variety of vehicle types meet the demands of local and long-distance transportation, as well as the demands encountered on building sites and in special applications.

Due to the wide diversity of vehicle types, the process of calculating the dimensions of the body structures (unitized body, cab, chassis, etc.) takes on a major importance right from the earliest stages of de-

sign. Building on experience with comparable vehicles, benchmark designs (volume-sales units, worst-case configurations) are defined by simulation and calculation with the aid of gradually refined complete-vehicle models using FEM or MKS+FEM. In this way, the rigidity, operational integrity, and crash characteristics of body-structure variants can be obtained to a substantial degree by computational means, even before testing starts. Structural calculations also take account of the requirements of (international) statutory safety standards.

## Light commercial vehicles

These are light-duty trucks (2...7 t) used in the transportation of persons and in local freight distribution. Light-duty trucks with more powerful engines are also increasingly deployed in pan-European long-distance transport duties involving high mileages (express delivery services, overnight courier services). In both cases, stringent demands are made on the vehicle in terms of agility, performance, user-friendliness, and safety. The design concepts are based on front-mounted engine,

| Overview of commercial vehicle types | |
|---|---|
| Light-duty trucks | |
| Truck | |
| Road train | |
| Large-capacity road train | |
| Semitrailer rig | |
| Bus | |

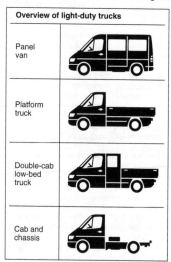

| Overview of light-duty trucks | |
|---|---|
| Panel van | |
| Platform truck | |
| Double-cab low-bed truck | |
| Cab and chassis | |

front or rear-wheel drive, independent suspension, or rigid axle and, with gross vehicle weights of 3.5 t and higher, twin tires on the rear axle.

The product range includes enclosed-body multipurpose panel vans and platform trucks, as well as low-bed and high-bed platform trucks with special superstructures and crew cabs.

In light-duty trucks (up to approx. 6 t gross vehicle weight), the bodies form an integral load-structure unit together with the chassis.

The body and chassis frameworks consist of sheet-metal pressed elements and flanged profiles. Platform trucks have a ladder-type frame with open or closed side members and cross members as the primary load-bearing structure.

Large light-duty trucks usually have a separate chassis similar to trucks (see next section) and a separate body, while for reasons of comfort and noise reduction, the cab is generally attached by flexible mountings and is thus partially isolated from chassis vibration.

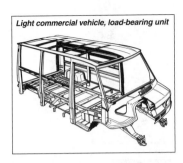

*Light commercial vehicle, load-bearing unit*

cargo, better ride) and also allows easy swapping of interchangeable bodies and decoupling of semitrailers. Three-axle vehicles (6 x 2) are fitted with either a leading or a trailing axle (in front of or behind the driven axle) to increase the payload capacity. High-traction 6 x 4 vehicles for construction-site use have a twin-axle configuration with axle-load compensation and center bearing point or air-sprung single axles (usually with pneumatic axle-load compensation).

## Medium- and heavy-duty trucks and tractor vehicles

The vehicles in this sector have either a load-bearing chassis or partially load-bearing body. In most cases, the engine is at the front. It is seldom fitted as an underfloor engine between the axles. The vehicle is driven via the twin-tire axle(s). In individual cases, the rear axle is fitted with single tires. For building-site (offroad) applications with high traction requirements, all-wheel drive with inter-axle and cross-axle differential lock technology is used.

Type of truck undercarriage (see figure below):

N x Z / L
N = Number of wheels
Z = Number of driven wheels
L = Number of steered wheels
(twin wheels count as <u>one</u> wheel)

Normal chassis have leaf- or air-sprung rigid front and rear axles. Pneumatic suspension reduces body acceleration forces (better driving comfort, less strain on the

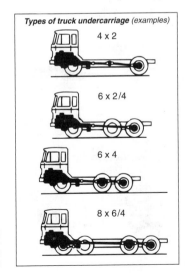

*Types of truck undercarriage (examples)*

4 x 2

6 x 2/4

6 x 4

8 x 6/4

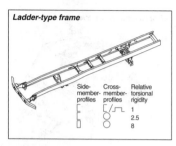

**Ladder-type frame**

| Side-member-profiles | Cross-member-profiles | Relative torsional rigidity |
|---|---|---|
| | | 1 |
| | | 2.5 |
| | | 8 |

**Frame junctions**
1 Cap cross-member, 2 U-cross-member.

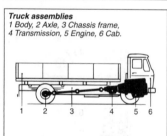

**Truck assemblies**
1 Body, 2 Axle, 3 Chassis frame,
4 Transmission, 5 Engine, 6 Cab.

**Driver's cab**
1 Cab over engine (COE),
2 Cab behind engine (CBE).

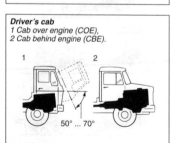

50° ... 70°

## Chassis frames

The chassis frame is the commercial vehicle's actual load-bearing element. It is designed as a ladder-type frame, consisting of side and cross members. The choice of profiles decides the level of torsional stiffness. Torsionally flexible frames are preferred in medium- and heavy-duty trucks because they allow the suspension to cope better with uneven terrain. Torsionally stiff frames are more suitable for light-duty delivery vehicles.

Apart from the force introduction points, critical points in the chassis-frame design are the side- and cross-member junctions. Special gusset plates or pressed cross-member sections form a broad connection basis. The junctions are riveted, bolted, and welded. U- or L-shaped side-member inserts provide increased frame flexural strength and reinforcement at specific points.

## Driver's cab

There are a variety of cab designs available depending on the vehicle concept. In delivery vehicles and for public-service use, low, convenient entrances are an advantage, whereas in long-distance transport applications, space and comfort are more important. Modular design concepts allow for short, medium and long cab versions while retaining the same front, rear and doors.

In the case of cab-over-engine (COE) vehicles, the bulkhead and steering system are positioned right at the front of the vehicle. The engine sits under the high-level cab (special long-distance cab with flat floor) or under an engine tunnel between the driver and co-driver. The entrance is positioned in front of or above the front axle. A mechanical (pretensioned torsion bars) or hydraulic cab-tipping mechanism provides access to the engine.

In cab-behind-engine (CBE) vehicles, the engine/transmission assembly is mounted ahead of the cab firewall under a steel or plastic hood (which is usually tiltable for reasons of accessibility). The driver enters the cab behind the front axle.

### Body structures

Specific body structures such as flatbeds, panel vans, box vans, dump-truck deep-beds, tankers, concrete mixers, etc. permit the economical and efficient transportation of a wide variety of freight and materials. The body and load-bearing chassis frame are joined sometimes by means of auxiliary frames with non-positive or positive attachments. Special design features such as sprung mountings in the forward body area are required in order to avoid critical rigidity changes along the chassis frames (which generally have low torsional strength) on rigid bodies (e.g. box-type).

Road trains and semitrailer rigs are used in long-distance transport. As the size of the transportation unit increases, the costs relative to the freight volume decrease.

Load volume is increased by reducing the empty spaces between the cab, cargo area, and trailer (high-capacity road train). Advantages of semitrailer rigs lie in the greater uninterrupted loading length of the cargo area and the shorter inoperative times of the tractor units. Measures to improve aerodynamics, such as front and side panels on the vehicle and specially adapted air deflectors from the cab to the body, are applied to minimize fuel consumption.

## Buses

The bus market offers a specific vehicle for practically every application. This has resulted in a wide range of bus types, which differ in their overall dimensions (length, height, width) and appointments (depending on the application).

### Microbuses

Microbuses carry up to approx. 19 passengers. These vehicles have been developed from light-duty trucks or vans weighing up to approx. 4.5 t.

### Minibuses

Minibuses carry up to approx. 25 passengers. These vehicles have been developed from light-duty trucks or vans weighing up to approx. 7.5 t. They are occasionally built on the ladder-type chassis of light-duty trucks. A modified suspension design and special measures carried out on the body (e.g. flexible mountings) result in optimum ride comfort and noise levels.

### Midibuses

Depending on the application, midibuses can carry up to approx. 35 passengers (in tour buses) and up to approx. 65 passengers (in city buses). These vehicles weigh up to approx. 12.5 t and are predominantly built on the ladder-type chassis of light-duty trucks. There are also integral-frame designs in operation. A modified suspension design and special measures carried out on the body result in optimum ride comfort and noise levels.

### City buses

City buses are equipped with seating and standing room for scheduled routes. The short intervals between stops in suburban passenger transportation operations require rapid passenger turnover. This is achieved by wide doors that open and close swiftly, low boarding heights (approx. 320 mm) and low floor heights (approx. 370 mm).

Overview of bus types

| Micro-bus | |
| Mini-bus | |
| Midi-bus | |
| City bus | |
| Tour bus | |

Main specifications for a 12 m standard public-service bus:
Vehicle length approx. 12 m
Gross vehicle weight 18.0 t
Number of seats 32...44
Total passenger capacity approx. 105 persons.

The use of double-decker buses (length 12 m carrying up to approx. 130 passengers), three-axle rigid buses (length up to 15 m carrying up to approx. 135 passengers) and articulated buses (approx. 160 passengers) provides increased transport capacity.

### Intercity buses or touring coaches
Depending on the application (standing passengers are not permitted at $v > 60$ km/h), either low-floor designs featuring the low boarding and floor heights of public-service buses are used, or buses are employed which, with their higher floors and small luggage compartments, are already very much like tour buses. Overland buses come in lengths of 11...15 m as rigid vehicles or in lengths of 18 m as articulated vehicles.

### Tour buses (long-distance coaches)
Tour buses are designed to provide comfortable travel over medium and long distances. They range from the low, two-axle standard bus through to the double-decker luxury bus measuring approx. 10...15 m in length.

### Body structure
Light design based on a unitized body. The body and base frames, which are firmly welded together, consist of pressed grid-type support elements and rectangular tubes.

### Undercarriage
The horizontally or vertically mounted engine drives the rear axle. Pneumatic suspension on all axles permits ride-level stabilization and a high degree of ride comfort. Intercity buses and touring coaches are mainly equipped with independent suspension on their front axles. Disk brakes, frequently supported by retarders, are used on all axles.

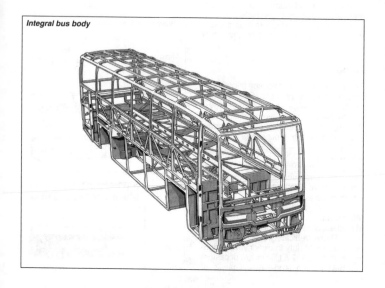

*Integral bus body*

## Passive safety in commercial vehicles

Passive safety is intended to limit the consequences of accidents and to protect other road users. Systematic recording of accidents, accident tests with complete commercial vehicles, and intensive computer optimization help to devise safety measures. Generally, the effectiveness and strength of occupant restraint systems has to be demonstrated. Therefore, the dimensioning of commercial-vehicle body structures must take account of aspects, such as the strength and rigidity of seat-belt anchor points on the seats and of the related body structures (seat rails, floor, frame, etc.).

In the event of a collision, the driver's cab and the passenger cabin must maintain the amount of room necessary for occupant survival, while at the same time deceleration must not be excessive. Depending on vehicle design, there are a variety of solutions to this problem.

In light-duty trucks and delivery vans, front-section design is energy-absorbing as in passenger cars. In spite of shorter deformation paths and higher levels of released energy, the physiologically permissible limits are not exceeded in virtually all passenger-car crash-test standards (legal requirements and rating tests).

In light-duty trucks, there must also be features which prevent injury to occupants by uncontrolled movement of the payload. The static and dynamic strength of such features (partitions, cages/nets, securing eyes) has to be demonstrated mathematically and/or by testing.

In the case of trucks, the side members extend up to the front fender and can absorb high linear forces. Such passive-safety measures are based on accident analyses and are intended to improve the structural design of the cab. Static and dynamic stress and impact tests at the front and rear of the cab, as well as on its roof, simulate the stresses involved in a frontal impact and in accidents in which the vehicle overturns, rolls over, or in which the cargo moves.

Statistical analyses have proved that the bus is one of the safest means of passenger transportation. Static roof-load tests and dynamic overturning tests provide evidence of body strength. The use of flame-retardant and self-extinguishing materials for the interior equipment of the vehicle minimizes the risk of fire.

As road traffic involves many different kinds of vehicles, collisions between light and heavy vehicles are unavoidable. As a result of the differences in vehicle weight, and incompatibility in terms of vehicle geometry and structural stiffness, the risk of injury in the lighter vehicle is greater. The equations below define the change in speed during a normal (non-oblique) plastic impact for frontal or rear collisions between two vehicles:

Vehicle 1 $\Delta c_1 = \dfrac{\mu \cdot \Delta v}{1 + \mu}$

Vehicle 2 $\Delta c_2 = \dfrac{\Delta v}{1 + \mu}$

where $\mu = m_2/m_1$

$m_1$, $m_2$ = masses of the vehicles involved, $v$ relative speed prior to impact.

Side, front and rear underride guards help to reduce the danger of the lighter vehicle driving under the heavier vehicle in the event of a collision. In other words, they serve to protect other road users.

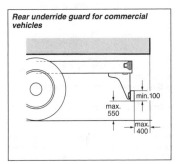

*Rear underride guard for commercial vehicles*

# Lighting

## Functions

### Vehicle front end

The primary function of the headlamps at the vehicle front end is to illuminate the roadway so that the driver can detect traffic conditions and recognize any obstacles and hazards in good time. They also serve to identify and mark out the vehicle to oncoming traffic. The turn-signal indicators serve to show the driver's intention to change direction or to indicate a hazardous situation. The headlamps and lights at the front end include the following:
– Low-beam headlamps
– High-beam headlamps
– Fog lamps
– Auxiliary driving lamps
– Turn-signal indicators
– Parking lamps
– Clearance/side-marker lamps (wide vehicles)
– Daytime running lamps (if required by law in individual countries)

### Vehicle rear end

Lights are turned on at the vehicle's rear end in accordance with the weather conditions and indicate the vehicle's position. They also indicate how the vehicle is moving and in which direction, e.g. whether it is traveling unbraked straight ahead, or whether the brakes are applied or the driver is intending to change direction, or whether a hazardous situation exists. The backup lamps illuminate the roadway while the vehicle is reversing. The lamps/lights at the rear end include the following:
– Stop lamps
– Tail lamps
– Fog warning lamps
– Turn-signal indicators
– Parking lamps
– Side-marker lamps (wide vehicles)
– Backup lamps
– License-plate lamps

### Vehicle interior

In the vehicle interior, priority over all other functions is given to the ease and reliability with which the switch elements can be reached and operated, and to provide the driver with sufficient information on the vehicle's operating states (while distracting him/her from driving as little as possible). A well-lit instrument panel (P. 1079) and discreet lighting of the various functional groups, such as the radio or navigation system, are absolutely essential to ensure relaxed and safe driving. Optical and acoustic signals must be prioritized according to their urgency and then relayed to the driver.

## Regulations and equipment

### Approval codes and symbols

Automotive lighting equipment is governed by national and international design and operating regulations, according to which the equipment in question must be manufactured and tested. For every type of lighting equipment, there is a special approval code and symbol which has to be legibly displayed on the equipment concerned. The preferred locations for approval codes and symbols are places that are directly visible when the hood is open, such as the lenses of headlamps and other lights, and the headlamp unit components. This also applies to approved replacement headlamps and lights.

If an item of equipment carries such an approval code/symbol, it has been tested by a technical inspectorate (e.g. in Germany the Lighting Technology Institute of Karlsruhe University) and approved by a licensing authority (in Germany the Federal Road Transport Office). All volume-production units which carry the approval code/symbol must conform in all respects to the type-approved unit. Examples of approval symbols:

$\textcircled{E1}$ ECE approval mark, $\boxed{e1}$ EU approval mark.

The number 1 following each letter indicates the type-approval test carried out and the award of approval according to ECE (Economic Commission for Europe) Regulations for Germany. In Europe, installation of all automotive lighting and visual signaling equipment is governed not only by national guidelines but also by the higher European directives (ECE: whole of Europe, EU, New Zealand, Australia, South Africa and Japan). In the course of the ongoing union of Europe, the implementation regulations are being increasingly simplified by the harmonization of directives and legislation. AL (Automotive Lighting) headlamps conform to the applicable ECE and EU directives and can therefore be used in all ECE and EU countries, regardless of the country in which they were purchased.

### Right-hand-drive or left-hand-drive traffic

The ECE Regulations apply by analogy to driving on the right or left. The technical requirements for lighting are mirrored around the central perpendicular of the test screen. According to the Vienna Global Treaty of 1968, when traveling in countries which drive on the other side of the road, all road users are obliged to adopt measures to prevent increased glare of oncoming traffic at night due to the asymmetrical light pattern. This can be achieved either by self-adhesive strips obtainable from the vehicle manufacturer or two-way switches in the headlamps (in the case of PES).

### U.S.A.

In the U.S., lighting equipment is governed by regulations that are very different from those in Europe. The principle of self-certification compels each manufacturer as an importer of lighting equipment to ensure, and in an emergency to furnish, proof that his products conform 100% with the regulations of FMVSS 108 laid down in the Federal Register. There is therefore no type approval in the U.S.A. The regulations of FMVSS 108 are partly based on the SAE industry standard.

### Upgrading, conversion

Vehicles imported to Europe from other regions must be modified to comply with European directives. This applies in particular to the lighting equipment. Identical components available for the European market can be used as direct replacements. Other solutions, such as retail products or, in certain cases, retention of the original equipment, require an engineer's report. In Germany, Article 22a of the StVZO (Road Traffic Licensing Regulations) requires "Approximation Certificates" for lighting equipment. Such certificates are issued by the Lighting Technology Institute of Karlsruhe University.

---

Particular attention is paid to the conversion of headlamps which use conventional filament bulbs to gas-discharge lamps. In Germany, application of the specifications is strictly regulated by the Federal Road Transport Office. Xenon headlamps have to be designed in accordance with ECE R(egulation) 98, and also fitted with automatic beam-height adjustment and a headlamp cleaning system according to Article 50 Sec. 10 of the StVZO (German Road Traffic Licensing Regulations). Subsequent alterations to type-approved headlamps and sockets invalidate the type approval and consequently the general operating license for the vehicle.

---

*Global distribution of right-hand-drive and left-hand-drive traffic*
RHD traffic (72% of total road length), ■ LHD traffic (28% of total road length).

## Definitions and terms

### Photometrical terms and definitions

Headlamp range
The distance at which the light beam continues to supply a specified luminous intensity: mostly the 1 lux line at the right side of the road (LHD traffic).

Geometric range of a headlamp
This is the distance to the horizontal portion of the light-dark cutoff on the road surface. A low-beam inclination of 1%, or 10 cm per 10 meters, results in a geometric range equal to 100 times the headlamp's fitted height (as measured between the center of the reflector and the road surface).

Visual range
Distance at which an object (vehicle, object, etc.) within the luminance distribution of the human visual field is still visible.
  The visual range is influenced by the shape, size, and reflectance of objects, the road-surface type, headlamp design and cleanliness, and the physiological condition of the driver's eyes. Due to the large number of influencing factors, it is not possible to quantify this range using precise numerical definitions. Under extremely unfavorable conditions (with RHD traffic, on the left side of a wet road surface) the visual range can fall to below 20 m. Under optimum conditions, it can extend outward to more than 100 m (with RHD traffic, on the right side of the road).

Signal identification distance
Maximum distance at which a visual signal (e.g. fog warning lamp) remains just visible in fog or other inclement weather conditions.

Disability glare
This is the quantifiable reduction in visual performance that occurs in response to light sources emitting glare. An example would be the reduction in visual range that occurs as two vehicles approach one another.

Discomfort glare
This condition occurs when a glare source induces discomfort without, however, causing an actual reduction in visual performance. Psychological glare is assessed according to a scale defining different levels of comfort and discomfort.

### Headlamp technology

Reflector focal length
Conventional reflectors for headlamps and other automotive lamps are usually parabolic in shape. The focal length $f$ (distance between the vertex of the parabola and the focal point) is 15...40 mm.

Free-form reflectors
The geometrical configurations of free-form reflectors are generated using complex mathematical calculations (HNS, Homogeneous Numerically Calculated Surface). Here, the low mean focal length $\bar{f}$ is defined relative to the distance between the reflector vertex and the center of the filament. Typical values range from 15 to 25 mm.
  In the case of reflectors partitioned with steps or facets, each partition can be created with its own mean focal length $\bar{f}$.

Reflector illuminated area
Parallel projection of the entire reflector opening on a transverse plane. The standard reference plane is perpendicular to the vehicle's direction of travel.

Effective luminous flux,
Efficiency of a headlamp
The first of the above is the portion of the light source's luminous flux that is capa-

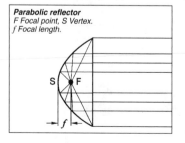

*Parabolic reflector*
*F Focal point, S Vertex.*
*f Focal length.*

ble of supplying effective illumination via its reflective or refractive components (for instance, as projected on the road surface via the headlamp reflector). A reflector with a short focal length makes efficient use of the filament bulb and has high efficiency because the reflector extends outward to encompass the bulb, allowing it to convert a large proportion of the luminous flux into a useful light beam.

### Angles of geometric visibility
These are angles that are defined relative to the axis of the lighting device, at which the illuminated area must be visible.

### Definitions of device design

#### Grouped design
A single housing, but with different lenses and bulbs.

Example: Multiple-compartment rear-lamp assemblies containing different individual light units.

#### Combined design
A single housing and bulb assembly with more than one lens.

Example: Combined tail lamp and license-plate lamp.

#### Nested design
Common housing and lens, but with individual bulbs.

Example: Headlamp assembly with nested side-marker lamp.

## Main headlamps, European system

### Low beam (dipped beam)
The high traffic density on modern roads severely restricts the use of high-beam headlamps. Under most standard conditions, the low beams are the actual driving lamps. Basic design modifications have allowed substantial improvements in low-beam performance.
- Introduction of the asymmetrical low-beam pattern, characterized (RHD traffic) by an extended visual range along the right side of the road.
- Official approval for various types of halogen lamps, making it possible to

enhance the luminance on the road surface by 50...80%.
- Introduction of new headlamp systems featuring complex geometrical configurations (PES, free-form surfaces, facetted reflectors) offering efficiency-level improvements of up to 50%.
- The "Litronic" headlamp system with gas-discharge lamps (xenon lamps with luminous arc) supplies more than twice the light generated by comparable halogen units.
- Improvement of side illumination by more than 70%, and homogeneous illumination of the road surface.

Low-beam headlamps require a light-dark cutoff in the light pattern. This is generated in halogen headlamps by H4 bulbs, and in Litronic headlamps by a D2R bulb by reflecting the cap or the light shield. In headlamps with all-round use, the light-dark cutoff is created by specifically reflecting the filaments. The "dark above/bright below" distribution pattern resulting from the light-dark cutoff furnishes acceptable visual ranges under all driving conditions. This configuration reduces glare, to which approaching traffic is exposed, within reasonable limits, and at the same time it supplies relatively high luminous intensity in the area below the light-dark cutoff.

The light-distribution pattern must combine maximum visual ranges with minimum glare effect. These demands are supplemented by other requirements affecting the area directly in front of the vehicle. For instance, the headlamps must

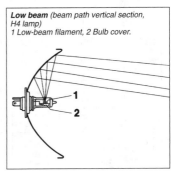

**Low beam** (beam path vertical section, H4 lamp)
1 Low-beam filament, 2 Bulb cover.

*Road perspective from driver's viewpoint*

*Measurement points relative to road perspective as per ECE R 112*

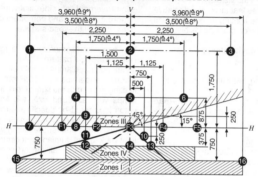

## Table 1. Measurement points and luminous intensities for headlamps

| **Low beam** (dipped beam) | | | | | | **High beam** | | | |
|---|---|---|---|---|---|---|---|---|---|
| Measurement points on graphic | | Luminous intensity | | | | Measurem. points | | Luminous intensity | |
| Item no. | RHD | LHD | Category A (lx) | Category B (lx) | | Item no. | Point | Category A (lx) | Category B (lx) |
| 01 | 8L/4U | | ≤ 0.7 | ≤ 0.7 | | | $E_{max}$ | 32 < E < 240 | 48 < E < 240 |
| 02 | V/4U | | ≤ 0.7 | ≤ 0.7 | | F1 | $E_{H-5.15°}$ | > 4 | > 6 |
| 03 | 8R/4U | | ≤ 0.7 | ≤ 0.7 | | F2 | $E_{H-2.55°}$ | > 16 | > 24 |
| 04 | 4L/2U | | ≤ 0.7 | ≤ 0.7 | | F3 | $E_{HV}$ [9] | ≥ 0.8 | ≥ 0.8 |
| 05 | V/2U | | ≤ 0.7 | ≤ 0.7 | | | | $E_{max}$ | $E_{max}$ |
| 06 | 4R/2U | | ≤ 0.7 | ≤ 0.7 | | F4 | $E_{H+2.55°}$ | > 16 | > 24 |
| 07 | 8L/H | 8R/H | ≥ 0.1; ≤ 0.7 | ≥ 0.1; ≤ 0.7 | | F5 | $E_{H+5.15°}$ | > 4 | > 6 |
| 08 | 4L/H | 4R/H | ≥ 0.2; ≤ 0.7 | ≥ 0.2; ≤ 0.7 | | | | | |
| 09 | B50L | B50R | ≤ 0.4 | ≤ 0.4 | | | | | |
| 10 | 75R | 75L | ≥ 6 | ≥ 12 | | | | | |
| 11 | 75L | 75R | ≤ 12 | ≤ 12 | | | | | |
| 12 | 50L | 50R | ≤ 15 | ≤ 15 | | | | | |
| 13 | 50R | 50L | ≥ 6 | ≥ 12 | | | | | |
| 14 | 50V | 50V | – | ≥ 6 | | | | | |
| 15 | 25L | 25R | ≥ 1.5 | ≥ 2 | | | | | |
| 16 | 25R | 25L | ≥ 1.5 | ≥ 2 | | | | | |
| Any point in Zone III | | | ≤ 0.7 | ≤ 0.7 | | | | | |
| Any point in Zone IV | | | ≥ 2 | ≥ 3 | | | | | |
| Any point in Zone I | | | ≤ 20 | ≤ 2E [1] | | | | | |

Low beam:
Total of 1 + 2 + 3 ≥ 0.3 lx
Total of 4 + 5 + 6 ≥ 0.6 lx

[1] E is the present measured figure at point 50R/50L.

provide assistance when cornering, i.e. the light-distribution pattern must extend beyond the left and right-side extremities of the road surface.

Automotive headlamp performance is subject to technical assessment and verification before they are put into volume production. Among the requirements are minimum luminous intensity, to ensure adequate road-surface visibility, and maximum intensity levels, to prevent glare (Measurement points and luminous intensities for headlamps, Table 1, P. 914).

## Cornering headlamps

Cornering headlamps have been approved for public use since the beginning of 2003. Whereas previously only high-beam headlamps were allowed to turn in response to changes in steering angle (1960s Citroën DS), swiveling low-beam headlamps are now also permitted (dynamic cornering headlamps or adaptive headlamps) and/or a supplementary light source (static cornering headlamps). Apart from the steering angle, other triggering parameters such as a GPS signal, the yaw rate, or similar are also conceivable.

## Headlamp versions

### Reflection headlamps

For conventional headlamp systems with virtually parabolic reflectors, the quality of the low beam increases in direct proportion to the size of the reflector. At the same time the geometric range increases as a function of installation height.

These factors must be balanced against the aerodynamic constraints according to which the vehicle's front-end profile must be kept as low as possible. Under these circumstances, increasing the size of the reflector results in wider headlamps.

Reflectors of a given size, but with different focal lengths, also perform differently. Shorter focal lengths are more efficient and produce wider light beams with better close-range and side illumination. This is of particular advantage during cornering.

### Stepped reflectors

Stepped reflectors are segmented reflectors consisting of paraboloid and/or parel-liptical (combined parabola and ellipse) sections designed to provide various focal lengths. These units retain the advantages of a deep reflector in a shallow unit suitable for compact installation.

### Variable-focus (stepless) reflectors

Specially designed programs (CAL, Computer Aided Lighting) assist in designing the stepless VF (Variable Focus Reflector) with its non-parabolic sectors. The focal points of the various reflector zones can change position relative to the light source. This principle can be applied to exploit the entire reflector surface.

### Headlamps with clear lenses

Developments in the area of HNS reflector technology (Homogeneous Numerically Calculated Surface) have now made it possible for headlamps to operate at efficiency levels of up to 50%. The entire light-distribution pattern is generated on the lens from the reflector surface alone, without additional optical elements. This permits unconventional headlamp design.

### Headlamps with facet-type reflectors

The reflector surface is partitioned with facets. The PD2 program provides the CAL and HNS modules for individual optimization of each individual segment. The important feature of surfaces developed with PD2 is that discontinuity and steps are permitted at all boundary surfaces of the partition. This results in freely shaped reflector surfaces with maximum homogeneity and side illumination.

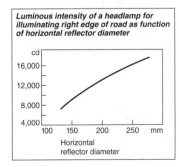

*Luminous intensity of a headlamp for illuminating right edge of road as function of horizontal reflector diameter*

**HNS or facet-type reflector**
*Filament pattern reflection with mirror optics.*

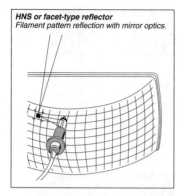

**Facet-type reflector**
a) *Vertically partitioned,*
b) *Radially and vertically partitioned.*

**PES headlamps**
The PES headlamp system (<u>P</u>oly <u>E</u>llipsoid <u>S</u>ystem) employs imaging optics and offers greater design scope than conventional headlamps, A lens aperture area with a diameter of only 40...70 mm allows the generation of light patterns previously only achievable with large-area headlamps. This result is obtained using an elliptical (CAL designed) reflector in combination with optical projection technology. A screen reflected with the objective projects precisely defined light-dark cutoffs. Depending on specific individual requirements, these transitions can be defined as sudden or gradual intensity shifts, making it possible to obtain any geometry required.

**PES reflectors** (beam path)
a) *PES, b) PES with ring parabola and lens,*
c) *PES with ring parabola and partially metallized tube body.*
1 *Reflector, 2 Objective, 3 Screen, 4 Profiled inner lens, 5 Partially metallized inner lens.*

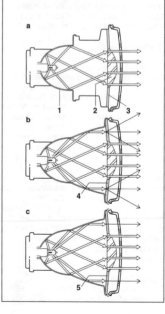

**PES reflector** (optical principle)
1 *Objective, 2 Screen, 3 Reflector, 4 Lamp.*

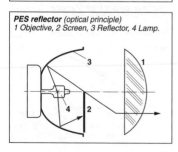

PES headlamps can be combined with conventional high beams, side-marker lamps and PES fog lamps to form lighting-strip units in which the entire headlamp is no higher than approximately 80 mm.

In PES headlamps, the beam path can be configured in such a way that the surroundings of the objective are also used in the signal image. This enlargement of the signal image is used above all with small objective diameters to reduce the psychological glare for the oncoming traffic. The annular reflector uses the portion of light which is not detected by the PES reflector, and directs it forward past the objective. An inner screen, which prevents a direct view of the lamp, can be designed as a lens or a partially metallized screen. The additional surface can also be made into a design feature with illuminated round or rectangular gaps, or illuminated three-dimensional objects.

## Litronic

The Litronic (contraction of <u>Li</u>ght and Elec<u>tronic</u>) headlamp system, with <u>xenon gas-discharge lamp</u> as its central component, generates high illumination-intensity levels with minimal frontal-area requirements, making it ideal for vehicles with aerodynamic styling. In contrast with the conventional filament bulb, light is generated by a plasma discharge inside a burner the size of a cherry stone.

The arc of the 35 W "D2S" bulb generates a luminous flux twice as intense as that produced by the H1 bulb and at a higher color temperature (4,200 K), which means that – similar to sunlight – it contains larger proportions of green and blue. Maximum luminous efficiency, corresponding to approx. 90 lm/W, is available as soon as the quartz element reaches its operating temperature of more than 900 °C. Brief high-power operation at currents of up to 2.6 A (continuous operation: approx. 0.4 A) can be used to obtain "immediate light". A service life of 2,000 hours is sufficient for the average overall operating time in cars. Since failure does not occur suddenly as with a filament bulb, fault diagnosis and timely replacement are possible.

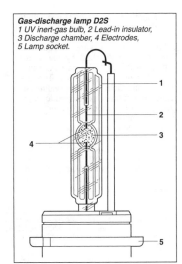

*Gas-discharge lamp D2S*
1 UV inert-gas bulb, 2 Lead-in insulator,
3 Discharge chamber, 4 Electrodes,
5 Lamp socket.

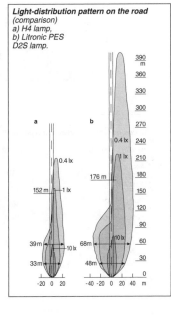

*Light-distribution pattern on the road*
(comparison)
a) H4 lamp,
b) Litronic PES
D2S lamp.

At present, gas-discharge lamps with the type designations D1x and D2x are used. In around 2005 the D3/D4-series lamps will also be fitted as standard equipment. They are distinguished by lower lamp voltage, a different plasma composition, and different arc geometries. The electronic control units for the individual lamp types are generally developed for a specific design type and are not universally interchangeable.

The D2/D4-series automotive gas-discharge lamps feature high-voltage-proof sockets and UV glass shielding elements. On the D1/D3-series models, the high-voltage electronics necessary for operation are also integrated in the lamp socket.

All systems feature two subcategories:
– the S-lamps for projection-system headlamps
– the R-lamps for reflection headlamps with an integrated light shield for producing the light-dark cutoff comparable with the bulb cover used for H4 low beams

At present the D2S lamps are the type most widely used.

An integral part of the headlamp is the electronic ballast unit responsible for activating and monitoring the lamp. Its functions include:
– Ignition of the gas discharge (voltage 10...20 kV)

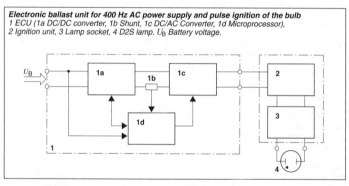

*Electronic ballast unit for 400 Hz AC power supply and pulse ignition of the bulb*
1 ECU (1a DC/DC converter, 1b Shunt, 1c DC/AC Converter, 1d Microprocessor),
2 Ignition unit, 3 Lamp socket, 4 D2S lamp. $U_B$ Battery voltage.

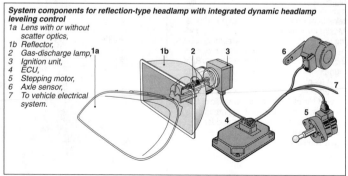

*System components for reflection-type headlamp with integrated dynamic headlamp leveling control*
1a Lens with or without scatter optics,
1b Reflector,
2 Gas-discharge lamp,
3 Ignition unit,
4 ECU,
5 Stepping motor,
6 Axle sensor,
7 To vehicle electrical system.

– Regulated power supply during the warm-up phase when the lamp is cold
– Demand-oriented supply in continuous operation

The system furnishes largely consistent levels of illumination by compensating for fluctuations in the vehicle system voltage. If the lamp goes out (for instance, due to a momentary voltage drop in the vehicle electrical system), reignition is spontaneous and automatic.

The electronic ballast unit responds to defects (such as a damaged lamp) by interrupting the power supply to help avoid injury in the event of contact.

The xenon light emitted by Litronic headlamps produces a broad carpet of light in front of the vehicle combined with a long range. This has made it possible to achieve substantially wider road-illumination patterns for lighting the edges of bends and wide roads as effectively as a halogen unit illuminates straight stretches of road. The driver enjoys substantial improvements in both visibility and orientation in difficult driving conditions and bad weather.

In accordance with ECE Regulation 48, Litronic headlamps are combined with automatic headlamp leveling control and headlamp cleaning systems. This combination ensures optimum utilization of the long headlamp range and optically unimpaired light emission at all times.

## Bi-Litronic (bi-xenon)

Bi-Litronic systems permit both the low and high beams to be generated by the arc of a single gas-discharge lamp.

## Bi-Litronic "Reflection"

The reflection version of the system uses a single D2R lamp for both headlamp functions.

When the high-/low-beam switch is operated, an electromechanical actuator moves the gas-discharge lamp in the reflector into the appropriate position for producing the high or low beam as required.

*Quad-headlamp system with Litronic*
1 Vehicle electrical system, 2 ECU,
3 Ignition unit with lamp connection,
4 Optical system (Litronic/Bi-Litronic),
5 Halogen high beam/auxiliary driving lamp.

*System components for PES-design headlamps*
1   ECU,
2   To vehicle electrical system,
3   Shielded cable,
4   Ignition unit,
5   Projection module,
5a  D2S lamp,
5b  Lens.

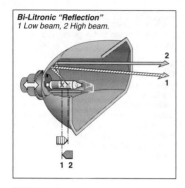

**Bi-Litronic "Reflection"**
*1 Low beam, 2 High beam.*

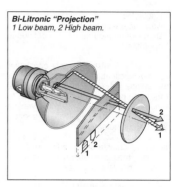

**Bi-Litronic "Projection"**
*1 Low beam, 2 High beam.*

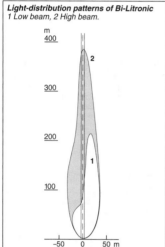

**Light-distribution patterns of Bi-Litronic**
*1 Low beam, 2 High beam.*

The main advantages are as follows:
– Xenon light for high-beam operation
– Visual guidance by continuously shifting the light pattern from close to long range
– Individual reflector shape

Special design variants of the Bi-Litronic "Reflection" lamp involve solutions in which the entire reflector is moved or individual components of the bulb cover are opened.

## Bi-Litronic "Projection" (bi-xenon)

The Bi-Litronic "Projection" system is based on a PES Litronic headlamp. The light shield for creating the light-dark cutoff is moved out of the light beam. With lens diameters of 60 and 70 mm, Bi-Litronic "Projection" allows the present highly compact headlamp design with combined high/low beam and at the same time outstanding luminous efficiency.

The essential advantages of the Bi-Litronic Projection are:
– Xenon light for high-beam operation
– Most compact solution for high and low beams
– Modular system

### High beam

The high beam is usually generated by a light source located at the focal point of the reflector (see figure on P. 912). This causes light to be reflected outward in the direction of the reflector axis. The maximum luminous intensity achievable by the high beam are largely a function of the reflector's illuminated area. In four-headlamp systems, in particular, purely paraboloid high-beam reflectors can be replaced by units with complex geometrical configurations designed to supply a "superimposed" high-beam pattern. The calculations employed to design these units seek to achieve a high-beam distribution that harmonizes with the low-beam pattern (simultaneous activation). The pure high beam is virtually "superimposed" on

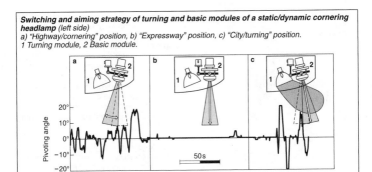

*Switching and aiming strategy of turning and basic modules of a static/dynamic cornering headlamp (left side)*
a) "Highway/cornering" position, b) "Expressway" position, c) "City/turning" position.
1 Turning module, 2 Basic module.

the low-beam projection The annoying overlap area close to the front of the vehicle is done away with in this case.

### Cornering headlamps

The "cornering headlamps" function approved since 2003 allows the vehicle to maintain visual range even when negotiating bends. This involves varying the horizontal illumination. It can be achieved essentially by switching on additional reflectors (static cornering headlamps), or by swiveling the low-beam headlamps (dynamic cornering headlamps).

### Static cornering headlamps

Static cornering headlamps are used mainly to illuminate areas close to side of the vehicle (switchbacks, turning maneuvers). For this purpose, activating additional reflector elements is generally the most effective way.

### Dynamic cornering headlamps

Dynamic cornering headlamps are used to illuminate the changing course of the road, e.g. on winding overland highways.

In contrast with the directly linked swiveling action of the cornering headlamps of the 1960s, modern high-end systems electronically control the rate of swivel and the swivel angle in response to the vehicle's speed.

*Modular system of cornering headlamps*
*Beam patterns for highways and turning off.*

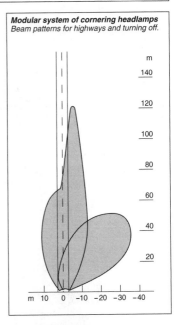

This optimizes "harmonization" between the headlamps and the vehicle attitude, and eliminates "jerky" headlamp movements.

Headlamp positioning is performed by a positioner unit (stepping motor) which

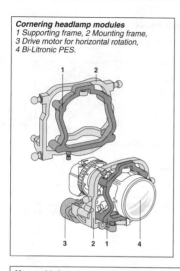

**Cornering headlamp modules**
1 Supporting frame, 2 Mounting frame,
3 Drive motor for horizontal rotation,
4 Bi-Litronic PES.

moves the basic/low-beam module or the reflector elements in response to changes in steering-wheel angle or the steering angle of the front wheels. Sensors detect those movements to prevent glare for on-coming traffic by means of failsafe algo-rithms. General legal requirements spec-ify that the headlamp beam may only be turned as far as the center line of the road at a distance of approx. 70 m in front of the vehicle to prevent glare for oncoming vehicles.

## Road safety and driving convenience
The introduction of dynamic cornering headlamps is a significant improvement in the safety and convenience of driving at night.

Compared with conventional low-beam headlamps, improvements in visual range of approximately 70% are achieved, rep-resenting an extra 1.6 seconds of travel time. With cornering headlamps, a mo-torist can assess hazards better and start

**Measurable improvement of visibility for driver with adaptive cornering headlamp light pattern**
a) Left-hand bend, dynamic cornering headlamps, b) Right turn, static cornering headlamps.
1 Halogen, 2 Xenon, 3a Adaptive light pattern: dynamic cornering headlamps,
3b Adaptive light pattern: static cornering headlamps.

**a**
- 3a
- 89 m (Adaptive light pattern)
- 65 m (Xenon)
- 1
- 53 m (Halogen)

**b**
- 2
- 3b
- 32 m (Adaptive light pattern)
- 17 m (Xenon)
- 13 m (Halogen)

braking sooner. As a result, the severity of an accident can be significantly reduced. Static cornering headlamps double the visual range for turning maneuvers.

A further ECE Regulation (AFS) is expected to come into force around 2007. In addition to cornering headlamps, it will also approve other light patterns such as expressway, city, and bad-weather headlamps.

## Designs
Global regulations mandate two headlamps for low beam and at least two (or the option of four) high-beam units for all dual-track vehicles.

### Dual headlamp system
The dual headlamp system uses lamps with two light sources (BILUX®/Duplo, halogen double-filament bulbs, U.S. sealed beam, Bi-xenon Reflection/Projection) for high and low beams using shared reflectors.

### Quad headlamp system
Two of the headlamps in a four-headlamp system provide both high and low beam, or low beam only, while the second pair only provides high-beam illumination. The light functions of projection and reflection systems can be used in any combination.

## Component groups

### Lens movable relative to body

The lens and reflector are combined in a single headlamp unit. The beam is adjusted by pivoting the complete assembly. In worst-case scenarios, this can lead to the lens shifting to an offset angle relative to the car's bodywork. The headlamp units are generally equipped with seals in the area adjacent to the bulb, and also feature special ventilation systems.

### Lens fixed relative to the body
There is no connection between the lens and the reflector, which is mounted in a housing designed to move relative to the lens for adjustment purposes (housing type). As the lens is fixed, it can be fully integrated in the vehicle's body shape. The complete headlamp is sealed or provided with ventilation elements. Aiming is carried out by integrated adjustment mechanisms which move the reflector.

## Components

### Reflector
The reflectors are made of plastic, die-cast metal or sheet steel.

Plastic reflectors are manufactured by injection molding (thermosetting plastics), which offers a considerably better precision of geometry reproduction than the deep-drawing process. Achievable geometrical tolerances are of the order of 0.01 mm. Furthermore, stepped and facetted reflectors of any design can be manufactured using this method. The base material requires no corrosion-proofing treatment.

The die-cast metal used is usually aluminum, or occasionally magnesium. The advantages are high thermal resistance and the ability to produce shapes with a high degree of complexity (shaped bulb holders, screw holes/bosses).

*Headlamp systems*
a) Dual headlamps,
b) Quad headlamps,
c) Quad headlamp system with additional fog lamp.

The surfaces of thermosetting plastic and die-cast metal reflectors are given a smooth finish by spray painting or powder-based paint before a layer of aluminum 50...150 nm thick is applied. An even thinner special coat protects the aluminum against oxidation.

Sheet-steel reflectors are manufactured as follows:

- Deep-drawing processing to obtain a paraboloid or more complex geometrical shape by multistage tools with additional punching and bending stages.
- Galvanization or powder-coating to protect against corrosion.
- Paint application to obtain a smooth surface.
- Evaporative application of aluminum to form the reflective layer.
- Evaporative application of a special protective layer onto the aluminum substrate.

This process hermetically seals the sheet steel and gives it excellent surface smoothness.

## Lens

A large proportion of contoured lenses is manufactured using high-purity glass (free of bubbles and streaks). During the lens molding process, high priority is given to surface quality in order to prevent undesirable upward light deflection in the final product – this would tend to create glare for oncoming traffic. The type and configuration of the lens prisms depend on the reflector and the desired light-distribution pattern.

The "clear" lenses used on modern headlamps are usually made of plastic. Besides reducing weight, plastic lenses provide other advantages for automotive applications, including greater freedom in headlamp and vehicle design.

There are two reasons why plastic lenses should not be cleaned with a dry cloth:

- Despite the scratch-proof coating, rubbing with a dry cloth can damage the surface of the lens.
- Rubbing with a dry cloth can produce an electrostatic charge in the lens, which can then allow dust to build up on the inside of the lens.

# Main headlamps, European regulations

## Regulations and directives

ECE R112: Headlamps for asymmetrical low beam and/or high beam that are fitted with filament bulbs (cars, buses, trucks).

ECE R112: Headlamps for symmetrical low beam and/or high beam that are fitted with filament bulbs (motorbicycles, motorcycles under 50 cm³, motorcycles over 50 cm³).

ECE R48 and 76/756/EEC: for attachment and application.

ECE R98: Headlamps with gas-discharge lamps as per ECE R99.

## Low beam, installation

Regulations prescribe 2 white-light low-beam headlamps for multiple-track vehicles.

## Low beam, lighting technology

For low-beam headlamps, there are international regulations and guidelines containing precise stipulations governing photometrical testing of the different low-beam units (with filament bulb or gas-discharge lamp).

Homologation testing is carried out under laboratory conditions using test lamps manufactured to more precise tolerances than those installed in production vehicles. The lamps are operated at the specified test luminous flux for each lamp category (filament bulbs at approx. 12 V, gas-discharge lamps at 13.5 V). The laboratory conditions apply across the board to all headlamps, but only take limited account of the specifics of individual vehicles, such as headlamp fitted height, vehicle power supply, and adjustment.

In Germany, the glare effect of a headlamp fitted to a vehicle is assessed according to StVZO §50 (6) (Road Traffic Licensing Regulations). Glare is considered to be eliminated when the luminous intensity at a height equal to that of the center of the headlamp does not exceed 1 lux at a distance of 25 m. This test is carried out with the engine running at moderate speed.

## Low beam, switching
All high-beam headlamps must extinguish simultaneously when the low beams are switched on. Dimming (gradual deactivation) is permitted, with a maximum dimming period of 5 seconds. A 2-second response delay is required to prevent the dimming feature from activating when the headlamp flashers are used. When the high-beam headlamps are switched on, the low-beam units may continue to operate (simultaneous operation). H4 bulbs are generally suitable for short periods of use with both filaments in operation.

## High beams, installation
A minimum of two and a maximum of four headlamps are prescribed for the high-beam mode.

Prescribed instrument-cluster high-beam indicator lamp: blue or yellow.

## High beams, lighting technology
High-beam light-distribution pattern is defined in the regulations and guidelines together with stipulations governing the low beams.

The most important specifications are: symmetrical distribution relative to the central perpendicular plane, maximum light along the headlamp center axis.

The maximum approved luminous intensity, a composite of the intensity ratings of all high-beam headlamps installed on the vehicle, is 225,000 cd. This value is indicated by identification codes located adjacent to the homologation code on each headlamp.

225,000 cd corresponds to the figure 75. The luminous intensity of the high beam is indicated by the number, e.g. 20, stamped next to the round ECE approval mark.

If these are the only headlamps on the vehicle (no auxiliary driving lamps), then the composite luminous intensity is in the range of 40/75 of 225,000 cd, i.e. 120,000 cd.

## Headlamp adjustment, low and high beams
The correct adjustment of vehicle headlamps is an essential factor in night-time road safety for both the driver of the vehicle concerned and for oncoming vehicles. If the beam is set only a fraction too low, there will be a substantial reduction in headlamp geometric range (see Table 2). If the beam is set only a fraction too high, oncoming traffic will suffer much greater glare.

The regulations and equipment specified for headlamp adjustment are described in the section headed "Workshop technology" (P. 1154).

*European headlamp system* (low beam)

≤ 1,200
≥ 500
≤ 400 and ≤ high beam
Dimensions in mm

**Table 2. Geometric range of the horizontal component of the low beam's light-dark cutoff.** *Headlamp installed at height of 65 cm.*

| Inclination of light-dark cutoff (1% = 10 cm/10 m) | % | 1 | 1.5 | 2 | 2.5 | 3 |
|---|---|---|---|---|---|---|
| Adjustment *e* | cm | 10 | 15 | 20 | 25 | 30 |
| Geometric range for horizontal section of light-dark cutoff | m | 65 | 43.3 | 32.5 | 26 | 21.7 |

## Headlamps, U.S.A.

### Headlamp systems

As in Europe, two and four-headlamp systems are used in the U.S.A. The fitting and use of fog lamps and additional high-beam headlamps, however, are subject to a variety of, in some cases, widely diverging local laws passed by the 50 individual states.

Up to 1983 the allowable sealed-beam headlamp sizes in the U.S.A. were as follows:

Dual-headlamp systems:
– 178 mm diameter (round)
– 200 x 142 mm (rectangular)

Quad-headlamp systems:
– 146 mm diameter (round)
– 165 x 100 mm (rectangular)

Since 1983 a supplement to FMVSS 108 has made it possible to use RBH (Replaceable Bulb Headlamps) headlamp units of various shapes and sizes.

Since 5/1/1997, however, headlamps with light-dark cutoffs have also been authorized in the U.S. but these require manual adjustment. It is now possible to develop headlamps which conform to legal requirements in both Europe and the U.S.

### Low beam (dipped beam)

The light-pattern requirements in America differ to a greater or lesser degree from the European system depending on the design type.

In particular, the minimum glare levels are higher in the U.S., and the maximum low-beam width is closer to the vehicle. The basic setting is generally higher (see measurement points, Table 3).

### High beam

The designs for high-beam headlamps are the same as in Europe. Differences exist in the required dispersion width of the light pattern, and there is a lower maximum figure on the axis of the high-beam headlamp.

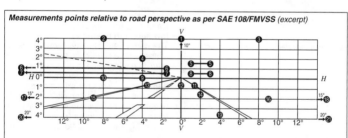

*Measurements points relative to road perspective as per SAE 108/FMVSS (excerpt)*

### Table 3. Measurement points and luminous intensities for headlamps, low beam

| Item no. | Measurement points | Luminous intensity (cd) | Item no. | Measurement points | Luminous intensity (cd) |
|---|---|---|---|---|---|
| 01 | 10U – 90U | ≤125 | 11 | 0.6D, 1.3R | ≥10,000 |
| 02 | 4U, 8L | ≥64 | 12 | 0.86D, V | ≥4,500 |
| 03 | 4U, 8R | ≥64 | 13 | 0.86D, 3.5L | ≥1,800; ≤12,000 |
| 04 | 2U, 4L | ≥135 | 14 | 1.5D, 2R | ≥15,000 |
| 05 | 1.5U, 1R-3R | ≥200 | 15 | 2D, 9L | ≥1,250 |
| 05 | 1.5U, 1R-R | ≤1,400 | 16 | 2D, 9R | ≥1,250 |
| 06 | 1U, 1.5L-L | ≤700 | 17 | 2D, 15L | ≥1,000 |
| 07 | 0.5U, 1.5L-L | ≤1,000 | 18 | 2D, 15R | ≥1,000 |
| 08 | 0.5U, 1R-3R | ≥500; ≤2,700 | 19 | 4D, 4R | ≥12,500 |
| 09 | H, 4L | ≥135 | 20 | 4D, 20L | ≥300 |
| 10 | H, 8L | ≥64 | 21 | 4D, 20R | ≥300 |

## Designs

### Sealed beam
In this design, which is no longer used, the aluminized glass reflector and the lens must be sealed gas-tight on account of the light sources that are not encapsulated. The whole unit is sealed and filled with an inert gas. If a filament burns through, the entire light source must be replaced. Units with halogen lamps are also available.

The limited range of available sealed-beam headlamps on the market severely restricted the freedom of design for vehicle front ends.

### Replaceable bulb headlamp (RBH)
European developments based on replaceable bulb technology also had an impact on the American system from 1983 onwards.

Headlamps that are adaptable in size and shape allow enhanced headlamp design (styling). Normally, plastic reflectors and lenses are used.

### Vehicle headlamp aiming device (VHAD)
This design involves RBH headlamps, which are adjusted vertically with the aid of a spirit levels integrated in each headlamp, and horizontally by means of a system comprising a needle and dial. In fact, this is equivalent to "onboard aiming".

### Headlamps for visual aiming (VOL/VOR)
These are RBH headlamps whose low beam has a light-dark cutoff line which allows visual aiming of the headlamps (as is standard in Europe).

Either the left horizontal light-dark cutoff (VOL mark on the headlamp) or, as is more often the case in the U.S., the right horizontal light-dark cutoff (VOR mark on the headlamp) is used.

There is no horizontal aiming with this type of headlamp.

## Headlamps, U.S. regulations

### Regulations and directives
The national standard is the Federal Motor Vehicle Safety Standard (FMVSS) No. 108 and the SAE Ground Vehicle Lighting Standards Manual (Standards and Recommended Practices) to which it refers.

The regulations governing installation and control circuits for headlamps are comparable to those in Europe. Since 5/1/1997 headlamps with light-dark cutoffs have likewise been authorized in the U.S.

Headlamps conforming to ECE Regulations or EEC Directives are approved for use on vehicles with two or more wheels in the U.S. if they satisfy the American requirements relating to lighting and aimability (visual).

### Headlamp aiming
Refer to the section "Headlamp aiming, U.S.A." in the chapter "Workshop technology" on P. 1157.

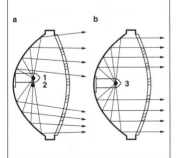

*American sealed-beam headlamps*
a) Low beam, b) High beam.
1 Low-beam filament, 2 Focal point,
3 High-beam filament (at focal point).

## Headlamp leveling control, Europe

Table 2 (P. 925) indicates the geometric ranges at various headlamp inclination angles mounted at a height of 65 cm. The inspection tolerance extends to include inclination angles of up to 2.5% (1.5% below standard setting). According to European Union regulations for headlamp leveling, the basic setting based on dimension $e$ is (10...15 cm)/10 m with the weight of one person on the driver's seat. The specifications for this setting are provided by the vehicle manufacturer.

Since 1/1/1998, an automatic or manual headlamp leveling control (beam-height adjustment) device has been mandatory in Europe for all first-time vehicle registrations, except in cases where other equipment (e.g. hydraulic suspension leveling) guarantees that light-beam inclination will remain within the prescribed tolerances. Although this equipment is not mandatory in other countries, its use is permitted.

Automatic headlamp leveling control
This must be designed to compensate for vehicle laden states by lowering or raising the low beam by between 5 cm/10 m (0.5%) and 25 cm/10 m (2.5%).

Manual headlamp leveling
This device is operated from the driver's seat and must incorporate a detent position in the base setting; beam adjustment is also performed at this position. Units with infinitely variable and graduated control must both feature visible markings in the vicinity of the hand switch for vehicle load conditions that vertical aiming.

All design variations employ an adjustment mechanism to provide vertical adjustment of the headlamp reflector (housing design).

Manually operated units employ a switch near the driver's seat to control the setting, while automatic units rely on level sensors on the vehicle axles to monitor suspension spring compression, and relay the proportional signals to the adjustment mechanisms.

### Hydromechanical systems
Hydromechanical systems operate by transmitting a fluid through the connecting hoses between the manual switch (or level sensor) and the adjustment mechanisms. The degree of adjustment corresponds to the quantity of pumped fluid.

### Vacuum systems
With vacuum systems, the hand switch (or level sensor) regulates vacuum from the intake manifold, and transmits it to the adjustment mechanisms to achieve varying degrees of adjustment.

### Electrical systems
Electric systems employ electric gear motors as the adjustment mechanisms. They are switched either by switches in the vehicle or by axle sensors.

*Automatic headlamp leveling control*
(schematic diagram)
1 Adjustment mechanism, 2 Processing unit, 3 Level sensors.

*Manual vertical-aim control*
(schematic diagram)
1 Adjustment mechanism, 2 Hand switch.

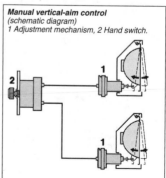

# Headlamp cleaning systems

Headlamp cleaning systems remove dirt from the lenses of the main headlamps. This ensures unimpaired illumination of the roadway and prevents glare for on-coming traffic. There are two types of cleaning system:

## Wipe/wash system

Wipe/wash systems, consisting of a wiper and a washer nozzle (sometimes integrated in the wiper), are restricted to headlamps with glass lenses, as the surface of plastic lenses is too sensitive for a mechanical cleaning system, despite their highly scratch-resistant coating.

## High-pressure washer system

High-pressure washer systems are gaining increasing acceptance as they can be used on both glass and plastic lenses. The cleaning effect is chiefly determined by the cleaning pulse of the water droplets. The decisive factors are:
– the distance between the washer nozzle(s) and the lens
– the size, contact angle, and contact velocity of the water droplets
– the amount of water

As well as fixed nozzle holders on the fenders, there are also telescopically extending nozzle holders. The telescope significantly improves the cleaning effect because it always assumes an optimum spray position. In addition, when not in use, the nozzle holder can be concealed, e.g. inside the fender.

High-pressure washer systems consist of:
– water reservoir, pump, hose, and non-return valve
– nozzle holder, which is extended by means of a telescope, with one or more nozzles

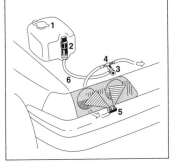

***High-pressure washer system for headlamps with fixed nozzle holder***
*1 Washer reservoir, 2 Pump, 3 Non-return valve, 4 T-joint, 5 Nozzle holder, 6 Hose.*

***Wipe/wash system for headlamps***
*1 Washer nozzle and spray pattern, 2 Wiper arm.*

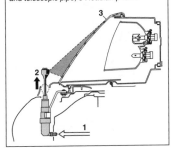

***High-pressure washer system for headlamps with telescopic nozzle holder***
*1 From washer reservoir, 2 Nozzle holder and telescopic pipe, 3 Headlamp lens.*

## Fog lamps

Fog lamps (white light) are intended to improve road-surface illumination in fog, snow, heavy rain, and dust.

### Optical concept

#### Paraboloid
A parabolic reflector featuring a light source located at the focal point reflects light along a parallel axis (as with the high-beam headlamp), and the lens extends this beam to form a horizontal band. A special bulb cover prevents the beam from being projected upward.

#### Free-form technology
Calculation methods, such as CAL (Computer Aided Lighting), can be used to design reflector shapes in such a way that they scatter light directly (i.e. without optical lens contouring) and also generate (without separate shading) a sharp light-dark cutoff. The fact that the lamp features pronounced envelopment of the bulb leads to an extremely high volume of light combined with maximum dispersion width.

#### PES fog lamps
This technology minimizes reflected glare in fog. The screen, the image of which is projected onto the road surface by the lens, provides a light-dark cutoff with minimum upward light dispersion.

### Designs
DIY and dealer-installed fog lamps are designed as individual projection units in their own housings. These are installed either upright on the fender, or suspended from it.

Stylistic and aerodynamic considerations have led to increased use of integrated fog lamps, designed either for installation within body openings or included as a component within a larger light assembly (with adjustable reflectors when the fog lamps are combined with the main headlamps).

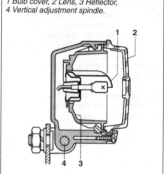

**Fog lamps**
*(parabolic reflector, upright mounting)*
1 Bulb cover, 2 Lens, 3 Reflector,
4 Vertical adjustment spindle.

**Fog lamp with free-form reflector**
*(horizontal section)*

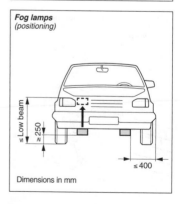

**Fog lamps**
*(positioning)*

Dimensions in mm

Present fog lamps produce white light. There is no substantive evidence that yellow lamps provide any physiological benefits. A fog lamp's effectiveness depends on the size of the illuminated area and the focal length of the reflector. Assuming the same illuminated area and focal length, the differences between round and rectangular fog lamps from the technical viewpoint are negligible.

### Regulations
Design is governed by ECE R19, installation by ECE R48 (and StVZO (Road Traffic Licensing Regulations) Article 52 in Germany); two white or yellow fog lamps are permitted. The control circuit for switching the fog lamps must be independent of the high- and low-beam circuits. In Germany, the StVZO allows fog-lamp installation in positions more than 400 mm from the widest point of the vehicle's width, provided they are wired so that they can only be switched on when the low-beam headlamps are on.

### Settings
The adjustment procedures for fog lamps are basically the same as for headlamps.

For details of regulations and aiming, refer to the chapter "Workshop technology" on P. 1154.

## Auxiliary driving lamps

Auxiliary driving lamps are used to improve the effectiveness of the high beam in standard high-beam headlamps. The optical principle is adapted to the technical lighting requirements of high-beam headlamps. Auxiliary driving lamps are often identical in shape and size to fog lamps.

Auxiliary driving lamps are mounted and aimed in the same way as standard headlamps, and the underlying lighting concepts are the same. Auxiliary driving lamps are also subject to the regulations governing maximum luminous intensity in vehicle lighting systems, according to which the sum of the reference numbers of all headlamps fitted to a vehicle must not exceed 75. For older headlamps without approval number, the number 10 is used for general assessment purposes.

## Lights and lamps

Design is governed by ECE R6, R7, R23 and R38, and mounting by ECE R48.

In the U.S., FMVSS 108 specifies the number, location, and color of signal lamps. The design and technical lighting requirements are defined in the relevant SAE standards.

These types of lamp are intended to facilitate recognition of the vehicle, and to alert other road users to any intended or present changes in direction or motion. In principle, there are a number of design-related options for satisfying the technical requirements for lamps.

### Lamps with reflector optics
Lamps with approximately parabolic reflectors or stepped reflectors direct the light from the bulb in an axial beam, and shape the beam by means of the optical dispersion elements in the lens.

Lamps with free-form reflectors achieve the required beam spread or light pattern, completely or partially, by directing the light by means of a reflector. The outer lens can thus be designed as a clear lens (see figure on P. 932, top), or supplemented by cylindrical lenses in the horizontal or vertical direction.

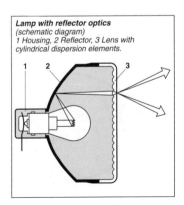

*Lamp with reflector optics*
(schematic diagram)
1 Housing, 2 Reflector, 3 Lens with cylindrical dispersion elements.

### Lamps with fresnel optics

The light from the bulb is projected directly (without diversion by a reflector) on the lens, which uses fresnel optics to shape the beam in the desired manner.

Fresnel optics are usually less efficient than reflector-optic lamps.

### Lamps combining reflector and fresnel optics

Designs combining both the above principles have also been successfully employed. The rotated-parabola (RP) reflector allows more compact units but retains the same luminous flux. They feature both shallower reflectors and smaller lenses, for example.

These designs employ a specially shaped reflector (rotated parabola) to capture the light beam emanating from the bulb at the largest possible peripheral angle. The fresnel optics then homogenize the light beam for projection along the desired path.

A free-form lamp with fresnel cap combines excellent luminous efficiency with a variety of possible stylistic implementations. It is essentially the reflector that shapes the light pattern. The fresnel lens improves luminous efficiency by diverting a proportion of the light, which would not otherwise contribute to the function of the lamp, in the desired direction. Both versions are mainly used in front turn-signal indicators.

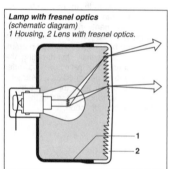

*Lamp with fresnel optics*
(schematic diagram)
1 Housing, 2 Lens with fresnel optics.

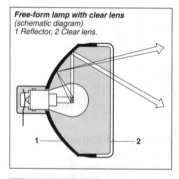

*Free-form lamp with clear lens*
(schematic diagram)
1 Reflector, 2 Clear lens.

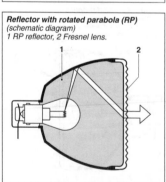

*Reflector with rotated parabola (RP)*
(schematic diagram)
1 RP reflector, 2 Fresnel lens.

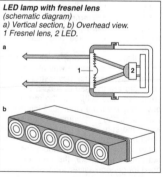

*LED lamp with fresnel lens*
(schematic diagram)
a) Vertical section, b) Overhead view.
1 Fresnel lens, 2 LED.

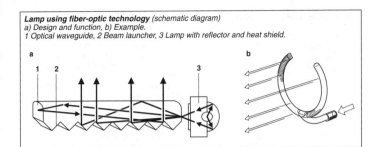

*Lamp using fiber-optic technology (schematic diagram)*
*a) Design and function, b) Example.*
*1 Optical waveguide, 2 Beam launcher, 3 Lamp with reflector and heat shield.*

Which version is actually used depends on the body shape, and thus on the available structural space, the stylistic requirements, and the luminous intensity required.

### Lamps with light-emitting diodes (LEDs)

The lights at the rear of the vehicle, in particular the auxiliary stop lamps, also use LEDs (see P. 55) as a light source. Special LEDs allow the use of a slimline design for the auxiliary stop lamps. In addition, LEDs in stop lamps provide an added safety aspect. An LED reaches maximum light output in less than 1 ms, whereas filament bulbs require about 200 ms to reach their nominal luminous flux. This means that LEDs emit the brake signal sooner, and this in turn reduces reaction time.

### Lamps with fiber-optic technology

By using optical waveguides (see P. 53), the light source can be separated from the light emission point. Suitable light sources are filament bulbs or LEDs.

The optical waveguides are usually made of glass fibers and/or transparent plastics, such as PC or PMMA. In order to obtain the desired light pattern, special beam launchers in the optical waveguides, or optically active elements on or in front of the optical fibers are required.

### Lighting technology, luminous intensity

As projected along the reference axis, minimum and maximum luminous intensities for all lamps must remain within a range calculated to guarantee signal recognition without, however, causing glare nuisance for other road users.

Luminous intensity levels to the sides, and above and below the reference axis, may be lower than along the axis itself. This deviation has been quantified on a percentile basis ("unified spatial light-distribution pattern").

### Color filters

Depending on their application (e.g. stop lamps, turn-signal indicators, or fog warning lamps), motor-vehicle lamps must display uniform, distinctive colors in the red or yellow color range. These colors are defined in specific ranges of a standardized color scale (color location).

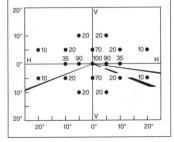

*ECE lamp test screen*
*Schematic representation of tail-lamp light pattern viewed to the rear (figures in %).*

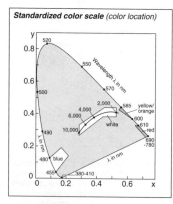

*Standardized color scale (color location)*

Since white light is composed of various colors, filters can be used to weaken or filter out the emission of undesirable spectral ranges (colors) completely. The color-filter functions may be performed by either the tinted lenses of the lamp, or a colored coating on the glass bulb of the lamp (e.g. yellow lamp in turn-signal indicators with clear lens).

Filter technology can also be used to design lamp lenses in such a way that, when the lamp is switched off, the color is matched to the vehicle's paintwork. Nevertheless, existing homologation regulations are complied with when the lamp is on. Color locations have been laid down in the EU/ECE region. They correspond to a wavelength of approximately 592 nm for "yellow/orange" turn-signal indicators, for example, and to a wavelength of approximately 625 nm for "red" stop and tail lamps (see figure).

## Turn-signal indicators (ECE R6)

ECE R48 and 76/756/EEC specify Group 1 (front), Group 2 (rear), and Group 5 (side) turn-signal indicators for vehicles with three or more wheels. For motorcycles, Group 2 turn-signal indicators are sufficient. Any color may be used for the function lamp. The flash frequency is defined as $90 \pm 30$ cycles per minute.

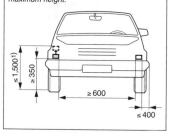

*Front turn-signal lamps (ECE)*
*(positioning, dimensions in mm)*
*[1] Less then 2,100 mm if vehicle body type prohibits compliance with regulations on maximum height.*

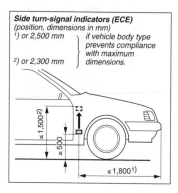

*Rear turn-signal indicators (ECE)*
*(position, dimensions in mm)*
*1 Tail lamp.*
*Height and width as for front turn-signal indicators.*

*Side turn-signal indicators (ECE)*
*(position, dimensions in mm)*
*[1] or 2,500 mm — if vehicle body type prevents compliance with maximum dimensions.*
*[2] or 2,300 mm*

### Front turn-signal indicators
Two yellow turn-signal indicators are stipulated. An indicator is required inside the vehicle.

### Rear turn-signal indicators
Two yellow turn-signal indicators are stipulated.

### Side-mounted turn-signal indicators
Two yellow turn-signal indicators are stipulated. U.S.A.: SAE J588 Nov.1984.

## Hazard-warning and turn-signal flashers

### Regulations
Both the StVZO (Road Traffic Licensing Regulations) (FMVSS/CUR), and EU Directive EEC 76/756 stipulate that standard lighting must be supplemented by visual signaling devices for indicating turns, and for use as hazard-warning flashers on all vehicles at top speeds exceeding 25 km/h.

Flashing signals
Signals at a frequency of 60...120 flashes per minute and a relative illumination period of 30...80%. Light must be emitted within 1.5 s of lamp switch-on. If one lamp fail, the remaining lamps must continue to generate visible light.

Turn-signal flashing
Synchronized signal generated by all turn-signal indicators on one side of the vehicle. The lamps are electrically monitored.

Malfunctions are indicated.

Hazard-warning flashers
Synchronous flashing of all turn-signal indicators, also operational with the ignition off.

An operation indicator is mandatory.

### Hazard-warning and turn-signal flashers for vehicles without trailer
The electronic hazard-warning and turn-signal flashers include a pulse generator designed to switch on the lamps via a relay, and a current-controlled monitoring circuit to modify the flashing frequency in response to bulb failure. The turn-signal indicator stalk controls the turn signals, whereas the hazard flashers are operated using a separate switch.

*Hazard-warning and turn-signal flashers for passenger cars*
*1 Hazard-warning and turn-signal flasher unit with integrated circuit (IS) or pulse generator G and control circuit H, 2 Turn-signal indicator stalk, 3 Indicator lamp, 4 Turn-signal indicators, 5 Hazard-warning switch with indicator.*

### Hazard-warning and turn-signal flashers for vehicles with/without trailer

This type of hazard-warning and turn-signal flasher differs from those employed on vehicles without trailers in the way that the function of the turn-signal indicators is controlled when they flash to indicate a change in direction.

<u>Single-circuit monitoring</u>
The tractor and trailer share a single monitoring circuit designed to activate the two indicator lamps at the flashing frequency. This type of unit cannot be used to localize lamp malfunctions. The flashing frequency remains constant.

<u>Dual-circuit monitoring</u>
Tractor and trailer are equipped with separate monitoring circuits. The malfunction is localized by means of the indicator lamp. The flashing frequency remains constant.

## Side-marker, clearance, and tail lamps

### Tail and side-marker lamps (ECE R7)
According to ECE R48 and 76/756/EEC, vehicle and trailer combinations wider than 1,600 mm require side-marker lamps (facing forwards). Tail lamps (at rear) are mandatory equipment on vehicles of all widths. Vehicles wider than 2,100 mm (e.g. trucks) must also be equipped with side-marker lamps visible from the front and rear.

### Side-marker lamps (ECE R7)
Two white-light side-marker lamps are stipulated.
U.S.A.: SAE J222 Dec. 1970.

### Tail lamps (ECE R7)
Two red tail lamps are stipulated. When the tail and stop lamps are combined in a nested design, the luminous-intensity ratio for the individual functions must be at least 1:5. Tail lamps must operate together with the side-marker lamps.
U.S.A.: SAE J585e Sept. 77.

### Side-marker lamps (ECE R7)
Vehicles wider than 2,100 mm require two white lamps facing forward, and two red lamps facing to the rear.
Position: As far outward and as high as possible.
U.S.A.: SAE J592e

### Side-marker lamps (ECE R91)
According to ECE R48, vehicles of any length exceeding 6 m must have yellow side-marker lights (SML) except on vehicles with cab and chassis only.
Type SM1 side-marker lights may be used on vehicles of all categories; type SM2 side-marker lights, on the other hand, may only be used on cars. On all other types of vehicle (e.g. buses, trailers), SMLs of both types are permitted.
U.S.A.: SAE J592e

### Reflectors (ECE R3)
According to ECE R48, <u>two red, non-triangular, rear reflectors</u> are required on motor vehicles (one on motorcycles and motorbicycles).
Additional reflective items (red reflective tape) are permitted if they do not impair the function of the legally required lighting and signaling equipment.

<u>Two colorless, non-triangular front reflectors</u> are required on trailers and on vehicles on which all forward-facing lamps with reflectors are concealed (e.g. retractable headlamps). There are permitted on all other types of vehicle.

<u>Yellow, non-triangular, side reflectors</u> are required on all vehicles with a length exceeding 6 m, and on all trailers. There are permitted on vehicles shorter than 6 m.

<u>Two red triangular rear reflectors</u> are required on trailers, but are banned on motor vehicles.
There may be no light fitted inside the triangle.
U.S.A.: SAE J594f.

## Parking lamps (ECE R77)

ECE R48 permits either two parking lamps at the front and rear, or one parking lamp on each side. The prescribed colors are white facing forwards and red facing rearwards. Yellow may also be used at the rear if the parking lamps have been designed as single units together with the side turn-signal indicators.

The parking lamps must be designed to operate even when no other vehicle lights (headlamps) are on. The parking-lamp function is usually assumed by the tail and side-marker lamps.
   U.S.A.: SAE J222 Dec. 1970.

## License-plate lamp (ECE R4)

According to ECE R48, the rear license-plate must be illuminated so as to be legible at a distance of 25 m at night.

The minimum luminance at all points on the surface of the license plate is 2.5 cd/m$^2$. The luminance gradient of 2 x $B_{min}$/cm should not be exceeded between any of the test points distributed across the surface of the license plate. $B_{min}$ is defined as the smallest luminance measured at the test point.
   U.S.A.: SAE J587 Oct. 1981.

## Stop lamps (ECE R7)

According to ECE R48, all cars must be fitted with two type S1 or S2 stop lamps, and one type S3 stop lamp, colored red in each case.

When a nested design with stop and tail lamps is used, the luminous-intensity ratio between individual functions must be at least 5:1.

The category S3 stop lamp (central high-level stop lamp) must not be a combined unit incorporating any other lamp.
   U.S.A.: SAE J586 Feb. 1984,
           SAE J186a Sept. 1977.

## Rear fog warning lamps (ECE R38)

For EU/ECE countries, ECE R48 prescribes one or two red rear fog warning lamps for all new vehicles. They must be distanced at least 100 mm from the stop lamp.

The visible illuminated area along the reference axis may not exceed 140 cm$^2$. The circuit must be designed to ensure that the fog warning lamp operates only in conjunction with the low beam, high beam and/or front fog lamp. It must also be possible to switch off the fog warning lamps independently of the front fog lamps.

---

*Stop lamps (ECE)*
*(position, dimensions in mm)*
*1 Central high-level stop lamp (category S3),*
*2 Two stop lamps (category S1/S2).*
*¹) 400 mm if width < 1,300 mm,*
*²) 2,100 mm if compliance with max. height*
*  not possible,*
*³) 150 mm below bottom edge of rear window,*
*⁴) However, the lower edge of the central*
*  high-mounted stop lamp must be higher*
*  than the upper edge of the (main) stop lamps.*

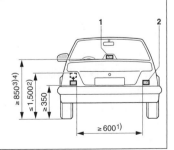

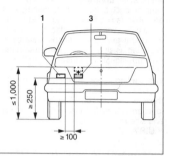

*Rear fog warning lamps (ECE)*
*(position, dimensions in mm)*
*1 Stop lamp, 2 Two rear fog warning lamps, 3 One rear fog warning lamp for driving on right.*

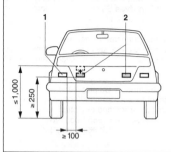

*Reversing lamps (ECE)*
*(position, dimensions in mm)*
*Quantity: 1 or 2*

*Daytime running lamps (ECE)*
*(position, dimensions in mm)*

Rear fog warning lamps may only be used when the visual range is less than 50 m due to <u>fog</u>. Responsible drivers are careful to observe this restriction because rear fog warning lamps can cause glare for following vehicles in clear visibility conditions due to their high luminous intensity.

Required indicator lamp: yellow.

## Reversing lamps (ECE R23)

According to ECE R48, one or two white reversing lamps are permitted.

The switching circuit must be designed to ensure that the reversing lamps operate only when reverse gear is engaged and the ignition on.

U.S.A.: SAE J593c Feb. 1968.

## Daytime running lamps

ECE R87 authorizes the installation of daytime running lamps in Europe. Their use, or the use of low-beam headlamps for daytime driving, is required by law in Denmark, Norway, Finland, Sweden, Lithuania, Estonia, Latvia, Hungary, Poland, Slovakia, Slovenia, Spain (out-of-town areas), and Italy (out-of-town areas).

## Other lighting devices

### Identification lamps
According to ECE R65, identification lamps must be visible from any direction, and create the impression of flashing. The required flashing frequency is 2...5 Hz. Blue identification lamps are intended for installation on official vehicles. Yellow identification lamps are designed to warn of dangers or the transport of dangerous freight.

### Spot lamps
Spot lamps generate a narrow beam of light of high luminous intensity, making it possible to illuminate a small area from a substantial distance.

### Floodlamps
On a moving vehicle, floodlamps may be switched on only when the vehicle's motion represents an integral part of the operation being performed, for instance, when tractors are used in agriculture and forestry, on self-propelled machinery, on rescue vehicles, etc.

### Convenience lamps
Lights for use when the vehicle is stationary are increasingly being fitted. Typical applications are the illumination of areas immediately outside the doors when the doors are open or closed, lights that identify the vehicle outline in the underbody area, or lights which identify the door handles.

Combinations of such lights with side-marker lamps or fog lamps are referred to as "coming home" functions, which are activated when the doors are unlocked, for instance.

### Table 4. Specified minimum flash intensities for identification lamps

| Measurement range | | Flash intensity cd | |
|---|---|---|---|
| | | blue | yellow |
| Parallel to road surface | | > 20 | > 40 |
| Within of light beam Angle to road surface | ± 4° | > 10 | |
| | ± 8° | | > 30 |

## Motor-vehicle bulbs

Bulbs for automotive lighting in accordance with ECE R37 are available in 6-V, 12-V and 24-V versions (see Table 5 on following pages). To help avoid mix-ups, different bulb types are identified by different base shapes. Bulbs of differing operating voltages are labeled with this voltage in order to avoid mix-ups in the case of identical bases. The bulb type suitable in each case must be indicated on the equipment. A voltage increase of 10% results in a 75% difference in service life, and a 30% difference in light output (see figure).

The luminous efficiency (lumens per watt) represents the bulb's photometrical efficiency relative to its power input. The luminous efficiency of vacuum bulbs is 10...18 lm/W. The higher luminous efficiency of halogen bulbs of 22...26 lm/W is primarily the result of higher filament temperature. D2S and D2R gas-discharge bulbs (Litronic) provide a luminous efficiency in the order of 85 lm/W for substantial improvements in low-beam performance.

Replaceable bulbs must be type-approved in accordance with ECE R37. Other light sources which do not conform to this regulation (LED, neon, filament bulbs) can only be installed as a fixed component part of a lamp. In the event of repair work, the entire unit must be replaced.

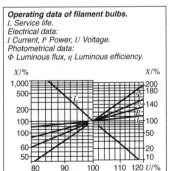

*Operating data of filament bulbs.*
$L$ Service life.
Electrical data:
$I$ Current, $P$ Power, $U$ Voltage.
Photometrical data:
$\Phi$ Luminous flux, $\eta$ Luminous efficiency.

**Table 5. Specifications for the main motor-vehicle bulbs (not including motorcycle bulbs)**

| Application | Category | Voltage rating V | Power rating W | Luminous flux Lumen | IEC Base type | Illustration |
|---|---|---|---|---|---|---|
| High beam, low beam | R2 | 6<br>12<br>24 | 45/40[1]<br>45/40<br>55/50 | 600 min/<br>400–550[1] | P 45 t-41 | |
| Fog lamp, high beam, low beam in 4 HL | H1 | 6<br>12<br>24 | 55<br>55<br>70 | 1,350[2]<br>1,550<br>1,900 | P14.5 e | |
| Fog lamp, high beam | H3 | 6<br>12<br>24 | 55<br>55<br>70 | 1,050[2]<br>1,450<br>1,750 | PK 22s | |
| High beam/ low beam | H4 | 12<br><br>24 | 60/55<br><br>75/70 | 1,650/<br>1,000[1], [2]<br>1,900/1,200 | P 43 t – 38 | |
| High beam, low beam in 4 HL, fog lamp | H7 | 12<br>24 | 55<br>70 | 1,500[2]<br>1,750 | PX 26 d | |
| Fog lamp, static cornering headlamp | H8 | 12 | 35 | 800 | PGJ 19-1 | |
| High beam | H9 | 12 | 65 | 2,100 | PGJ 19-5 | |
| Low beam, fog lamp | H11 | 12<br>24 | 55<br>70 | 1,350<br>1,600 | PGJ 19-2 | |
| Fog lamp | H10 | 12 | 42 | 850 | PY 20 d | |
| Low beam in 4-HL systems | HB4 | 12 | 55 | 1,100 | P 22 d | |
| High beam in 4-HL systems | HB3 | 12 | 60 | 1,900 | P 20 d | |
| Low beam, high beam | D1S | 85<br>12[5] | 35<br>approx.<br>40[5] | 3,200 | PK 32 d-2 | |
| Low beam, high beam | D2S | 85<br>12[5] | 35<br>approx.<br>40[5] | 3,200 | P 32 d-2 | |
| Low beam, high beam | D2R | 85<br>12[5] | 35<br>approx.<br>40[5] | 2,800 | P 32 d-3 | |

**Table 5. Continued**

| Application | Category | Voltage rating V | Power rating W | Luminous flux Lumen | IEC Base type | Illustration |
|---|---|---|---|---|---|---|
| Stop, turn-signal, rear fog, reversing lamp | P 21 W PY 21 W[6]) | 6, 12, 24 | 21 | 460[3]) | BA 15 s | |
| Stop lamp/ tail lamp | P 21/5 W | 6 12 24 | 21/5[4]) 21/5 21/5 | 440/35[3]), [4]) 440/35[3]), [4]) 440/40[3]) | BAY 15d | |
| Side-marker lamp, tail lamp | R 5 W | 6 12 24 | 5 | 50[3]) | BA 15 s | |
| Tail lamp | R 10 W | 6 12 24 | 10 | 125[3]) | BA 15 s | |
| Stop lamp, turn-signal ind. | P 19 W PY 19 W | 12 12 | 19 19 | 350[3]) 215[3]) | PGU 20/1 PGU 20/2 | |
| Rear fog, reversing lamp, front turn-signal ind. | P 24 W PY 24 W | 12 12 | 24 24 | 500[3]) 300[3]) | PGU 20/3 PGU 20/4 | |
| Stop, turn-signal, rear fog, reversing lamp | P 27 W | 12 | 27 | 475[3]) | W 2.5 x 16 d | |
| Stop lamp/ tail lamp | P 27/7 W | 12 | 27/7 | 475/36[3]) | W 2.5 x 16 q | |
| License-plate lamp, tail lamp | C 5 W | 6 12 24 | 5 | 45[3]) | SV 8.5 | |
| Reversing lamp | C 21 W | 12 | 21 | 460[3]) | SV 8.5 | |
| Side-marker lamp | T 4 W | 6 12 24 | 4 | 35[3]) | BA 9 s | |
| Side-marker lamp, License-plate lamp | W 5 W | 6 12 24 | 5 | 50[3]) | W 2.1 x 9.5 d | |
| Side-marker lamp, License-plate lamp | W 3 W | 6 12 24 | 3 | 22[3]) | W 2.1 x 9.5 d | |

[1]) High/low beam. [2]) Specifications at test voltage of 6.3; 13.2 or 28.0 V.
[3]) Specifications at test voltage of 6.75; 13.5 or 28.0 V. [4]) Main/secondary filament.
[5]) With ballast unit. [6]) Yellow-light version.

# Automotive windshield and window glass

## The material properties of glass

Window panes for automotive use are made of silica glass. The basic chemical constituents and their proportions are as follows:
- 70...72% silicic acid ($SiO_2$) as the basic component of glass
- approx. 14% sodium oxide ($Na_2O$) as flux
- approx. 10% calcium oxide (CaO) as stabilizer

These substances are mixed in the form of quartz sand, soda ash, and limestone. Other oxides such as magnesium and aluminum oxide are added to the mixture in proportions of up to 5%. The additives improve the physical and chemical properties of glass.

### Manufacturing flat glass

The glass panes are made out of the basic product, flat glass. Flat glass that is cast using the float-glass process is used. This process involves melting the mixture at a temperature of 1,560 °C. The melt then passes through a refining zone at 1,500 °C to 1,100 °C, and is then floated on a float bath of molten tin. The molten glass is heated from above (fire-finished). The flat surface of the molten tin creates flat glass with flat parallel surfaces of a very high quality (tin bath underneath, fire-finishing on top). The glass is then cooled to about 600 °C. After a further period of slow, non-stress cooling, the glass is cut into sheets measuring 6.10 x 3.20 m².

Tin is suitable for the float-glass process because it is the only metal that does not produce any vapor pressure at 1,000 °C and is liquid at 600 °C.

### Material properties and physical data of automotive glass (finished windshields and windows)

| Property | Dimension | TSG | LSG |
|---|---|---|---|
| Density | kg/m³ | 2,500 | 2,500 |
| Surface hardness | Mohs | 5...6 | 5...6 |
| Compressive strength | MN/m² | 700...900 | 700...900 |
| Modulus of elasticity | MN/m² | 68,000 | 70,000 |
| Bending strength | | | |
| before prestressing | MN/m² | 30[2] | 30[1] |
| after prestressing | MN/m² | 50[2] | |
| Specific heat | kJ/kgK | 0.75...0.84 | 0.75...0.84 |
| Coefficient of thermal conductivity | W/mK | 0.70...0.87 | 0.70...0.87 |
| Coefficient of thermal expansion | m/mK | $9.0 \cdot 10^{-6}$ | $9.0 \cdot 10^{-6}$ |
| Dielectric constant | | 7...8 | 7...8 |
| Light transmittance (DIN 52 306) transparent[3] | % | ≈ 90 | ≈ 90[1] |
| Refractive index[3] | | 1.52 | 1.52[1] |
| Deviation angle due to wedge[3] | Arc | < 1.0 flat | ≤ 1.0 flat[1] |
| | minute | <1.5 curved | ≤ 1.5 curved[1] |
| Dioptric divergence DIN 52 305[3] | Dptr. | < 0.03 | ≤ 0.03[1] |
| Temperature resistance | °C | 200 | 90[1] |
| | | | (max. 30´) |
| Resistance to temperature shocks | K | 200 | |

[1] Properties of finished laminated safety glass (LSG). In calculating the permissible bending stress, the coupling effect of PVB film is to be disregarded.

[2] Calculated values; these values already contain the necessary safety margins.

[3] Figures for optical properties depend very heavily on the type of window.

# Automotive glazing

Glass used for automotive glazing is of two types:
- Single-pane toughened safety glass (TSG), which is chiefly used for side-window, rear-window and sunroof glazing.
- Laminated safety glass (LSG), which is used primarily for windshields and rear windows, but also for sunroofs. LSG is also increasingly being fitted in vehicle side and rear windows.

The materials from which TSG and LSG panes are made are the basic glass types:
- Transparent float glass: This glass offers the best possible light transmittance.
- Tinted float glass: This glass has a homogeneous green or gray tint within the material; the tint blocks heat from the sun.
- Coated float glass: The glass is coated on one side with noble-metal and metal oxides; the coating reduces heat and UV radiation entering the vehicle, thus providing thermal insulation.

## TSG panes
TSG panes differ from LSG panes as they have greater mechanical and thermal strength, and their breaking and shattering behavior is different. They pass through a toughening process which greatly pre-stresses the surface of the glass. In case of breakage, these panes break into many small blunt-edged pieces.

Post-processing (grinding, drilling) is not possible.

The standard thicknesses for TSG panes are 3, 4, and 5 mm.

## LSG panes
An LSG pane is made of a crack-proof, flexible plastic intermediate layer of polyvinyl butyral (PVB) bonded between two sheets of glass. When subjected to impact or shock, the glass splits into web-like crack patterns. The plastic intermediate layer holds the broken pieces of glass together. The laminate retains its integrity and transparency when the glass is shattered.

The standard thicknesses for LSG panes are 4.5...5.6 mm.

The formation of many small blunt fragments when broken (in the case of TSG) and lamination with a plastic layer (in the case of LSG) reduce the risk of injury from glass breakage in accidents.

## Optical properties
The requirements for the optical quality of automotive glazing are as follows:
- unimpeded vision,
- flawless vision,
- undistorted vision.

Achievement of optimum optical quality has to be balanced against structural requirements and the vehicle-body design, taking account of such factors as
- glazing with large surface areas,
- glazing that is fitted in a horizontal position,
- cylindrical or spherical glazing,
- glazing with a high degree of curvature.

Possible quality impairments arise from:
- optical deflection,
- optical distortion,
- double imaging.

Optical deflection increases with:
- increasing obliqueness of the angle of incidence, i.e. increasing slope of the window,
- increasing pane thickness,
- reducing radius of curvature (increasing degree of bend),
- increasing divergence from perfect surface parallelism of the original glass sheet.

Green- or gray-tinted glass is used as heat absorption glass because it blocks the transmission of infrared rays (heat radiation) more strongly than shorter wavelengths. On the other hand, it also reduces transmittance within the visual spectrum. The PVB film in LSG absorbs light in the ultraviolet range.

The optical properties of TSG and LSG panes are roughly the same because the optical properties of the intermediate plastic layer in LSG are very similar to those of glass in the visible spectrum.

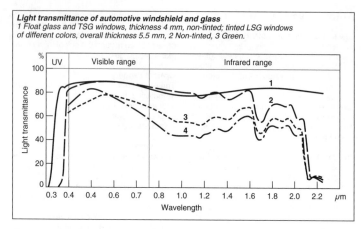

**Light transmittance of automotive windshield and glass**
1 Float glass and TSG windows, thickness 4 mm, non-tinted; tinted LSG windows of different colors, overall thickness 5.5 mm, 2 Non-tinted, 3 Green.

## Functional design glazing

The demands made of glazing are continually increasing. The flat panes used in the past simply served to protect occupants from wind and weather. Now, automotive glazing performs a wide variety of functions.

### Tinted glazing

This is made from glass which is tinted within the material, and reduces the direct penetration of solar radiation into the vehicle interior.

The reduction in the transmittance of solar energy occurs chiefly in the long wavelength spectrum (infrared), and this mainly lowers the transmittance of energy, thus reducing the heat transmitted to the vehicle interior. The degree to which light transmittance within the visible spectrum is affected depends on the degree of color tinting and the thickness of the glass.

For windshields, light transmittance must be at least 75%. Strongly tinted glass with a light transmittance of less than 70% can be used in windows from the B-pillar to the rear, if the vehicle has two exterior mirrors. For sunroof glazing, tinted glass with a significantly lower light transmittance and a UV transmittance of ≤ 2% is used.

### Coated glazing

This type of glazing uses glass with a metal or metal-oxide coating. Depending on the production process, the coating may be carried out before or after the sheet of glass is bent and prestressed. The coating is applied to the inner glass surface of an LSG pane.

This type of coated glazing has a light transmittance of less than 70%. Consequently, it can be fitted from the B-pillar to the rear, if the vehicle has two exterior mirrors.

Coated glass can also be used for sunroof glazing. Another type of sunroof glazing uses pyrolytically coated windows which are post-processed after the coating has been applied.

Coated glazing reduces direct solar radiation into the vehicle interior and absorbs solar energy in the infrared and ultraviolet ranges.

## Windshields with sunshield coating

A coating is applied to the inner surface of the outer or inner layer of glass in a laminated glass pane. The coating is a multilayer interference system with silver as its base layer. As the coating is on the inside of the laminate, it is permanently protected against corrosion and scratching.

The purpose of the coating is to reduce the transmittance of solar energy by more than 50%. This reduces heating of the vehicle interior. Transmittance is reduced primarily in the infrared range so that visible light transmittance is altered negligibly. The reduction is achieved largely by reflection, so that secondary reflection into the interior is low. The light transmittance of this glass in the UV range is very low, i.e. less than 1%.

## Printed sunroof glazing

Before bending and prestressing, the pattern is printed on the flat, tinted sunroof glass using the screen-printing process. The subsequent bending and prestressing process fires the screen-printed ink so that it forms a permanent bond with the glass.

The glass is printed with a pattern of dots, whose size and spacing determine the final optical effect.

## Sunroof glazing made from laminated safety glass

The bent laminated safety glass consists of two tinted-glass layers which are thermally partially prestressed in order to increase mechanical strength. They are bonded to either side of a highly crack-resistant and specially tinted film. The overall thickness depends on the surface area of the glass, and the overall design of the sunroof.

The absorption of solar energy mainly in the infrared range guarantees minimum heat penetration. The coating also provides low light transmittance and complete filtering of UV light.

## Automotive insulation glass

Automotive insulation glass is made of two flat or curved sheets of single-pane toughened safety glass (3 mm) separated by an air gap (3 mm). This type of insulation glass reduces heating of the vehicle interior, particularly in combination with a tinted coating. Transmittance is reduced primarily in the infrared range so that visible light transmittance is altered negligibly.

Insulation glass also provides better thermal insulation in the winter and improves sound insulation.

## Heated laminated safety glass

Heated laminated safety glass can be used for windshields or rear windows. They prevent icing and misting of the glass pane, even in extreme winter temperatures, and ensure clear visibility.

Heated laminated safety glass is made up of two more sheets of glass with a PVB film bonded between them. Inside the PVB film, there are heater filaments which may be less than 20 µm thick, depending on the heat output required. The heater filaments may be laid in a waveform pattern or in straight lines. They may also run vertically or horizontally. The heated area may cover the whole of the pane or may be divided into separate zones with varying heat outputs. In this way, the windshield wipers can be prevented from freezing to the windshield in subzero temperatures.

Heated windows can also be created by layering.

## Automotive antenna glass

This type of glass has antenna wire embedded in it. In the case of windows made of single-pane toughened safety glass (roof and side windows), the antenna is printed on the glass and is located – almost invisibly – on the inner surface of the window. With laminated safety glass windows (windshields), the antenna wiring system is embedded or printed onto the inner film.

# Windshield and rear-window cleaning systems

Systems for cleaning the vehicle's windshield, headlamps, and rear window are needed in order to comply with legal stipulations for all-round visibility at all times. Such systems can be subdivided as follows:
- Windshield wiper systems
- Rear-window wiper systems
- Headlamp wiper systems
- Headlamp washer systems
- Combination wipe/wash systems

## Windshield wiper systems

The following are the most important windshield-cleaning systems, using the passenger car as an example. These systems are based on the legally prescribed areas of vision (Europe, U.S.A., and Australia). The wipe patterns areas may be changed by additional controls acting on the wiper blades (parallelogram, general four-bar mechanism).

The windshield wiper system must meet the following requirements:
- Remove water and snow
- Remove dirt (mineral, organic or biological)
- Operate at high temperature (+80 °C) and low temperature (−30 °C)
- Be corrosion-resistant against acids, alkalis, salts (240 h), ozone (72 h)
- Service life: passenger cars $1.5 \cdot 10^6$ wipe cycles commercial vehicles, $3 \cdot 10^6$ wipe cycles,
- Pass a stall test

**Mechanical wiper mechanism**
Series- or parallel-coupled four-bar mechanisms are used, with transversely jointed linkage or additional controlled four-bar linkages for large wiping angles or difficult mechanical transmission configurations.

Optimizing the mechanism is important. Smooth operation can be achieved by matching the maximum values of angular acceleration and/or the force-transmission angles near to the wiper reversal points.

*Windshield cleaning systems*

Tandem system

Opposed-pattern system

Tandem system, with aerodynamic characteristics

Single-arm wiper system, not controlled

Single-arm wiper system, controlled

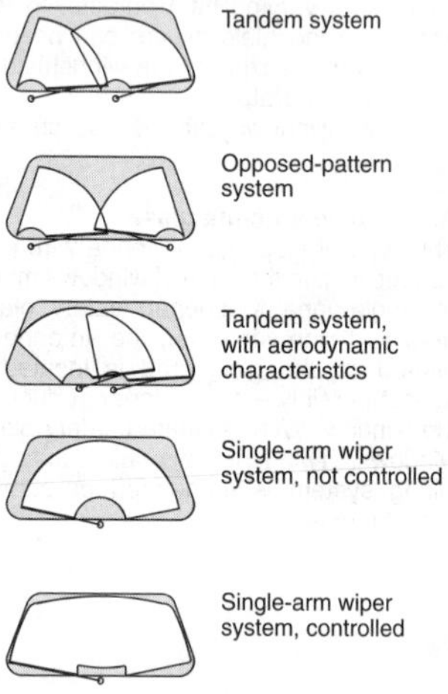

*Principle of the mechanical wiper mechanism*
1 Series-coupled, 2 Parallel-coupled.
$\alpha$ Crank angle. $\beta$, $\gamma$ Wiping angle.
$\nu_T$ Tangential force-transmission angle.

1 — Oscillating crank 1, Crank 2, Couple rod 1, $\nu_T$, Couple rod 2, Oscillating crank 2, Crank 1

2 — Oscillating crank 2, Oscillating crank 1, Crank 1, Couple rod 1, Crank 2, Couple rod 2, $\nu_T$

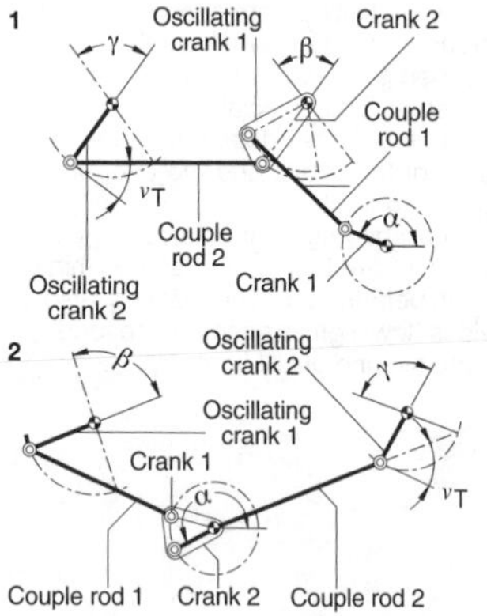

The trend is no longer to allow the crank to rotate fully, but to allow it to complete only (barely) a half rotation (reversing system). This significantly reduces the space needed by the linkage for movement. For this purpose, the drive motor is electronically controlled, and its direction of rotation is reversed in line with the wiping motion.

With minimum extra outlay, it is also possible to achieve an "extended parking position", "protection against snow overload", infinitely variable wiping speed and, despite varying operating conditions, a wipe pattern of constant area.

If problems are experienced in accommodating the linkage, the above-mentioned technology permits a large linkage to be replaced by two significantly smaller units, each with its own (smaller) drive motor (two-motor wiper system).

A second optimization step involves the work position of the wiper-element lip relative to the surface of the windshield or rear window. By positioning the wiper bearings at the proper angle to the windshield, and by applying additional torsion to the wiper arms, the position of the wiper blades can be defined so that, at their reversal points, they are inclined laterally towards the wipe-pattern bisector, thus assisting the wiper-blade elements to swivel into their new work position when reversal takes place.

**Wiper arms**

The wiper arm is the connecting link between the wiper drive mechanism and the wiper blade. It holds the wiper blade and directs its movement across the windshield. It is screwed to the tapered wiper arm pivot shaft by its mounting end, which is usually made of die-cast aluminum or zinc. The other end is generally a steel strip bent into a hook shape ("hook-type fastening") and bears the wiper blade. In addition to the standard wiper-arm design, there are a number of design variations. There are also special designs which perform additional functions, such as:

– wiper arm with quadruple-link reciprocating action
– wiper arm with wiper-blade control
– parallelogram wiper arm

---

*Tandem-pattern wiper system* (series-coupled)
Right-hand part of wiper mechanism designed as: 1 Oscillating crank, 2 Transversely jointed linkage, 3 Additional controlled four-bar linkage, 4 Controlled crank with attached coupling link.

Direction of rotation

2      3

4

---

*Wiper arm* (top and side views)
1 Steel strip with hook-type fastening, 2 Joint section, 3 Tension spring, 4 Attachment part with taper for mounting on wiper arm pivot shaft.

### Wiper arm with quadruple-link reciprocating action

The wiper arm with quadruple-link reciprocating action effectively extends the length of the wiper arm at a certain point in its passage over the windshield so as to reduce the size of the unwiped area to one corner of the windshield.

### Wiper arm with wiper-blade control

The wiper arm with wiper-blade control normally makes an additional rotation of the wiper blade relative to the wiper arm in order to produce a visually "pleasing" wiped-area border parallel to the A-pillar, for example.

### Parallelogram wiper arm

The parallelogram wiper arm is a special type with wiper-blade control. It holds the wiper blade in a fixed position, e.g. vertical to the windshield surface, over the entire wipe movement (e.g. for local-transport buses).

### Wiper blades

The wiper blade holds the wiper-blade element and directs its movement across the windshield. Wiper blades are used in lengths of 260...1,000 mm. Their dimensions for mounting (e.g., snap-in or hook fastening) are standardized. Low-wear operation is achieved by compensating the play in their mountings and linkages. The tops of the center brackets are perforated to prevent blade liftoff at high speeds. In special cases, wind deflectors are integrated in the wiper arms or blades to press the blades against the windshield.

### Rubber wiper-blade elements

The most important component of a wiper system is the rubber element. It is retained by the claws of the bracket system, and supported by sprung rails. Its double microedge is pressed against the windshield, and at its point of contact, it has a width of only 0.01...0.015 mm. When moving across the windshield, the wiper-blade element must overcome coefficients of dry friction of 0.8...2.5 (depending on air humidity), and coefficients of wet friction of 0.6...0.1 (depending on frictional velocity). The correct combination of wiper-element profile and rubber properties must be chosen so that the wiper lip can cover the complete wipe pattern on the windshield surface at an angle of approx. 45°.

The "twin wiper", with a two-component wiper-blade element made of synthetic rubber, consists of a specially hardened,

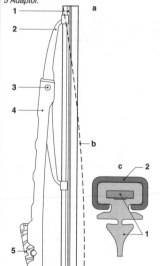

*Conventional wiper blade*
a) Wiper blade under load, b) At zero load, c) Cross-section.
1 Wiper-blade element with sprung rail, 2 Claw bracket, 3 Joint, 4 Center bracket, 5 Adaptor.

*Rubber wiper-blade element in working position*
1 Claw, 2 Sprung rail, 3 Wiper-element lip, 4 Windshield, 5 Double microedge.

abrasion-resistant wiper-element lip which merges into an extra-soft spine. The soft spine ensures that the wiper element has optimum reversing characteristics and wipes smoothly.

**Flat wiper blade** (aero-wiper blade)
The flat wiper blade (aero-wiper blade) is the present trend in wiper-blade design. The contact pressure over the wiper-blade element is no longer distributed by the claws of the wiper bracket, but by two preshaped spring strips (sprung rails) specially adapted to the shape of the windshield. They press the wiper-element lip more evenly against the windshield. This reduces wear on the wiper-element lip and increases wipe quality. In addition, the elimination of the bracket system means that there is no linkage wear, the overall height of the wiper system is substantially reduced, the weight is lower, and the wiper is quieter (there is also less wind noise).

The top edge of the wiper blade is in the shape of a spoiler (air deflector) and can cope with very high speeds without any modification. The flexible material of the spoiler is also much less likely to cause injury to pedestrians in the event of an accident.

An adapted, simplified connection to the wiper arm provides reliable attachment of the wiper blade when the wipers are in operation, and also allow easy replacement when required.

**Rain sensors**
The advent of rain sensors represents the completion of another step in the direction of a "fully automatic wiper system". The rain sensor detects how heavy the rain is, and converts this data into an appropriate signal that is sent to the wiper motor. The motor is then automatically switched on and set to speed 2, speed 1, or intermittent mode as required.
However, the full potential of the rain sensor can only be fully realized in conjunction with an electronic motor, whose speed is infinitely variable to match the level of rainfall (see also P. 110, "Sensors").

## Rear-window wiper systems

The operating characteristics of wiper systems for rear windows are the same as for windshield cleaning systems. However, their service life is limited to $0.5 \cdot 10^6$ wipe cycles. In RHD vehicles, the wipe pattern is preferred with park position on the right-hand side (viewed in the direction of travel). The 180°-system is used.

The gearing is generally integrated in the wiper motor so that the wiper pivot itself has an oscillating action. The wiper arm is attached directly to the pivot, usually by means of a knurled tapered fixing.
In order to ensure uniform appearance, the wiper arms and wiper blades of rear-window wiper systems are often both made of plastic.

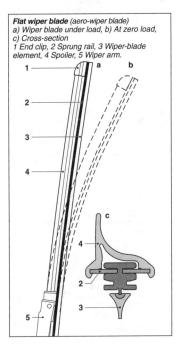

*Flat wiper blade* (aero-wiper blade)
a) Wiper blade under load, b) At zero load,
c) Cross-section
1 End clip, 2 Sprung rail, 3 Wiper-blade element, 4 Spoiler, 5 Wiper arm.

## Headlamp washer systems

Two types of headlamp washer system have become established: the wipe/wash system, and the wash-only system (PP. 951, 929). For the wipe/wash system, a wiper arm is driven directly by a motor with a step-down gear unit; the water required to clean the headlamps is taken from the windshield washer-fluid reservoir.

The advantages of the headlamp washer system lie in its simplicity, and the fact that it is often easier to adapt to the vehicle styling concept. It is important that the nozzles are positioned correctly so that the water jets properly cover the headlamps at all driving speeds.

Legislation requires that a dirty headlamp achieving only 20% of its luminosity must be restored to 80% of its luminosity within 8 s. The system must be able to complete at least 50 cycles on one charge of washer fluid.

## Wiper motors

Permanent-magnet DC motors are used as wiper motors. For normal use in windshield-wiper systems, they incorporate a worm-gear unit, but when used in rear-window and headlamp washer systems, they often incorporate an additional gear unit for translating rotary motion into oscillating motion (four-bar linkage, rack-and-pinion mechanism or crank-wheel mechanism).

The output of wiper motors for windshield and rear-window cleaning systems is rated differently from that of common electric motors. Statutory legislation and implementing regulations generally require that the motor operating speed for the lower wipe frequency is generally set at $n_{B1}$ = 45 rpm and for the higher wipe frequency at $n_{B2}$ = 65 rpm. Taking into account the maximum friction between rubber element and window, there is a torque level for each wiper arm which the wiper motor must produce at a minimum speed of $n_A$ = 5 rpm. The tightening torque $M_{An}$ in Nm for operation of <u>one</u> wiper arm is calculated as follows:

$$M_{An} = F_{WFN} \cdot \mu_{max} \cdot f_S \cdot f_T \cdot L_A \cdot (\omega_{Hmax}/\omega_{mot.}) \cdot (1/\eta_{trans.}) \cdot (R_{Aw}/R_{Ak}).$$

$F_{WFN}$    Downward nominal contact force of wiper arm in N (approx. 15 N per m of wiper-blade length when moving toward window).

$\mu_{max}$    Maximum coefficient of dry friction of wiper-blade element (2.5 at $\varphi$ = 93% relative air humidity).

$f_S$    Multiplier to account for joint friction of wiper arm (usually 1.15).

$f_T$    Tolerance factor to account for wiper-arm load tolerance (usually 1.12).

$L_A$    Wiper-arm length in m.

*Rear-window wipe patterns*
The shaded areas (here, LHD vehicle) represent impaired visibility when vehicles are overtaking.

*Layout of headlamp washer systems*
(wash system/motor and wiper arm)

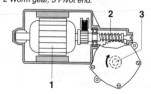

*Wiper motor with worm gear*
1 Permanent-magnet DC motor,
2 Worm gear, 3 Pivot end.

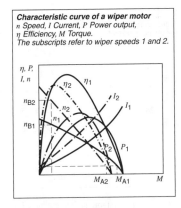

**Characteristic curve of a wiper motor**
$n$ Speed, $I$ Current, $P$ Power output,
$\eta$ Efficiency, $M$ Torque.
The subscripts refer to wiper speeds 1 and 2.

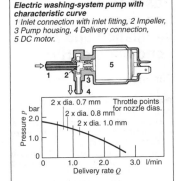

**Electric washing-system pump with characteristic curve**
1 Inlet connection with inlet fitting, 2 Impeller,
3 Pump housing, 4 Delivery connection,
5 DC motor.

| $\omega_{Hmax}$ | Maximum angular velocity of wiper arm. |
| $\omega_{mot.}$ | Mean angular velocity of wiper-motor crank. $\omega_{Hmax}/\omega_{mot.} \approx 0.15 \cdot (0.01 \cdot \omega_W)^2 + \sin(\omega_W/2)$. $\omega_W$ = Wiping angle $\beta$ or $\gamma$. |
| $\eta_{trans.}$ | Efficiency of gear unit, usually assumed to be 0.8; must be separately measured if using special gearing mechanisms (e.g. transversely jointed linkage, additional controlled four-bar linkage, multiple O-ring seal). |
| $R_{Aw}$ | Electrical resistance of armature winding heated by operation at rated speed. |
| $R_{Ak}$ | Electrical resistance of cold armature winding. |

$R_{Aw}/R_{Ak}$ typically 1.25.

The motor short-circuit strength is another important factor in its design. This is defined as the length of time during which the stalled motor must withstand the full test voltage without its windings overheating (usually specified as $t_K$ = 15 min).

Together, the frictional load and the gear ratio result in an operating torque on wet glass which is 0...20% of the tightening torque. In the case of very large wiper systems operating on nearly vertical windshields (e.g. on buses), the torque of the wiper arm resulting from its own weight must also be taken into consideration (separately calculated allowance).

In the case of drive motors with pendulum drive mechanisms (rear-window cleaning system and headlamp washer system), the required torque is determined at the oscillating pivot.

It is calculated as:

$$M_H = F_{WFN} \cdot \mu_{max} \cdot f_S \cdot f_T \cdot L_A \cdot (R_{Aw}/R_{Ak})$$

# Washing systems

To ensure good visibility in the wipe pattern, it is imperative that the wiper system is backed by a washing system. Electrical centrifugal pumps of simple design are used (characteristic pump curve) to pump the washer fluid through 2 to 4 nozzles onto the windshield in a narrow spray pattern. The capacity of the washer-fluid reservoir is usually 1.5...2 $l$. If the same washer-fluid reservoir is also used to supply the headlamp washers, a capacity of up to 7 $l$ may be required.

A separate reservoir may be provided for the rear-window cleaning system. The washing system is often linked to the wiper system by means of an electronic control system so that water is sprayed onto the rear window or windshield for as long as a pushbutton remains pressed. The wiper system then continues to operate for several additional cycles after the pushbutton is released.

# Passenger-compartment heating ventilation and air conditioning (HVAC)

## Function

The vehicle's air-conditioning system provides for the following:
- a comfortable climate for all passengers
- an environment calculated to minimize driver stress and fatigue
- more recent units use filters to remove particulate matter (pollen, dust) and even odors from the air
- good visibility through all windows and windshield

In many countries, the performance of the heater unit is governed by legal requirements, with emphasis on the defroster's ability to maintain clear windows and windshields (such as EEC Directive 78/317 within the European Community, and MVSS 103 in the U.S.).

## Systems deriving heat from the engine

On vehicles with liquid-cooled engines, the engine heat (byproduct of the combustion process) contained in the coolant is used to warm the passenger compartment. With air-cooled engines, engine heat is taken from the exhaust gas or, in some cases, from the engine's lubrication circuit. The heater core consists of tubes and fins, and has the same basic design as the engine radiator. Coolant flows through the core's tubes, while air flows through its fins. Two design concepts are available for regulating the heater's thermal output.

### Coolant-side heater control

In these systems, the entire air flow is usually directed through the heater core, while a valve controls the heating output by regulating the flow of coolant through the unit. Extreme precision is required from the valves, which must be capable of

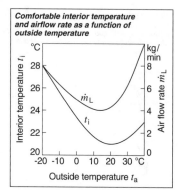

*Comfortable interior temperature and airflow rate as a function of outside temperature*

providing consistent, stable settings for accurate control at the minimal flow rates necessary for maintaining low heat levels (important between seasons). A disadvantage lies in the fact that the heating output varies according to the coolant's pressure and temperature, which means that heater performance is affected by engine speed and load.

### Air-side heater control

In this type of system, the flow of coolant through the heater core is unrestricted. The heat is regulated by dividing the air flow before it reaches the core. A portion of the air flows through the core, while the rest is directed around it. The two air flows are then reunited in the plenum chamber. An air flap can be used to regulate the distribution of the two air flows, thus determining the amount of heat taken from the coolant. This type of control arrangement is less sensitive to fluctuations in engine load, and air-temperature adjustments take effect immediately. Water and/or air-side blocks prevent undesirable residual warmth from emerging from the hot core when the heater is not in operation.

One disadvantage of the air-side control layout lies in the larger installation volume required for housing the bypass duct and the plenum chamber.

The ventilation air flow is provided by a constant-speed or adjustable-speed electric blower, where aerodynamic pressure can also become a significant factor as vehicle speed increases. The minimum hourly airflow rate should be 30 m³ per person (figure for reference purposes only). Factors such as passenger-compartment temperature, outside temperature, air flow, and (to a certain extent) heat radiation, all affect the process of achieving a comfortable climate (see figure). Since the precise data on these variables vary considerably from one vehicle to the next, actual figures must be derived empirically.

As motor vehicles have relatively small passenger compartments, drafts and sunlight entering through windshield and windows confront the heating, ventilation and air-conditioning (HVAC) systems with extreme challenges. In order to enhance passenger comfort, an attempt should be made to maintain the temperature in the footwell 4...8 °C above that of the air around the upper body.

### Electronic heater control

Variations in outside-air temperature and vehicle speed cause fluctuations in the temperature of the passenger compartment. On standard systems, the heater controls must be constantly readjusted by hand in order to maintain an agreeable temperature. Electronic heater control dispenses with this requirement by maintaining the interior temperature at the desired level automatically.

On heater units featuring water-side regulation, sensors monitor the temperatures of the vehicle's interior and of the emerging air. The control unit processes this information and compares it with the preselected temperature. Meanwhile, a solenoid valve installed in the cooling circuit opens and closes at a given frequency in response to the signals which it receives from the control unit. Adjustments in open/close ratio in the cycle periods regulate the flow rate from the closed position up to the maximum. A servo-actuated adjustment flap is usually employed to provide infinitely variable temperature regulation in air-side systems (pneumatic linear adjusters are also occasionally used). Sophisticated systems allowing separate adjustment for the left and right sides of the vehicle are also available.

## Air conditioners

The heater unit alone is not capable of providing a comfortable environment at all times. When the outside temperature climbs beyond 20 °C, the air must be cooled to achieve the required interior temperatures. Here, compressor-driven refrigeration units with R 134a refrigerant are in use (up to 1992, R 12 refrigerant).

The engine-driven compressor compresses the vaporous refrigerant, which heats up in the process and is then directed to the condenser where it cools and liquefies. The energy supplied in the compressor and the heat absorbed in the evaporator are dissipated to the environment here.

An expansion valve sprays the cooled liquid into the evaporator where the evaporation process extracts the required evaporation heat from the incoming stream of fresh air, thereby cooling the air. Moisture is extracted from the cooled air as condensate, and the air's humidity is reduced to the desired level. Evaporators and condensers are generally designed as tube-and-fin heat exchangers. The evaporator is located before the heater core in the fresh-air stream and cools the air to approx. 3...5 °C. The dehumidified air is reheated in the heater core to the desired temperature.

### Automatic climate control

Automatic climate control is particularly useful for vehicles in which both air conditioner and heater are installed, because the constant monitoring and adjustment required to maintain a temperate climate presents the occupants with a complicated task. This rule applies to bus drivers in particular, as they are exposed only to the conditions at the front of the vehicle. An automatic climate control system incorporating a preselection feature can automatically maintain the correct temperature, air flow, and air distribution in the passenger compartment. These parameters are mutually interdependent, and changes to one will affect the others. At the center of the system is a temperature-control circuit for interior temperature. The electronic control unit records all significant influencing and disturbance variables, as well as the temperature setting selected by the occupants, and uses this information to constantly calculate a required temperature, $t_i$. The required temperature is compared with the actual temperature, and the difference between them is used as the basis for producing reference variables for controlling the heating, air conditioning, and air flow. Another function controls the position of the air-distribution flaps with reference to the program which the occupants have selected. Meanwhile, all control circuits continue to respond to manual inputs.

The setpoint temperature determined by the control unit is achieved by means of water or air-side adjustments (as described in "Electronic heater control").

Infinitely variable or stepped blower control is used to adjust the air flow to the specified level. There is generally no setpoint processing involved in this opera-

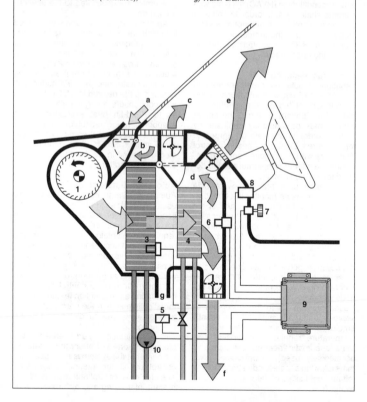

*Air conditioner with electronic water-side control* (schematic)
1 Fan, 2 Evaporator, 3 Evaporator temperature sensor, 4 Heater matrix, 5 Solenoid valve, 6 Air exit-temperature sensor, 7 Temperature control, 8 Interior sensor (ventilated),
9 Control unit, 10 Compressor.
a) Fresh air, b) Recirculated air, c) Defroster,
d) A/C bypass, e) Ventilation, f) Footwell,
g) Water drain.

tion. This type of arrangement is inadequate for dealing with increases in flow rate caused by aerodynamic pressure at high speeds. Here, a special control function can compensate by responding to increasing vehicle speeds, initially by reducing the blower speed to zero, and then, if the flow continues to rise, by using a restriction flap to throttle the flow of incoming air.

Air distribution to the three levels – defroster, upper compartment, and footwell – is controlled manually, with preselection, or with a fully-automatic program. Most popular are units featuring program control buttons, in which each button provides a specific air-distribution pattern for the three levels.

The defroster represents a special case. In order to clear the windows as rapidly as possible, the temperature control must revert to maximum heat and maximum blower speed, while the air flow is directed through the upper defroster outlets. On systems with program switches and fully automatic units, this operating mode is selected with a single button; at temperatures above 0 °C, the refrigeration unit is also activated to extract humidity from the air. To prevent unheated air from causing drafts, the blower is switched off electronically after cold starts in winter, except when "DEF" and the cooling function are in operation.

The variations described above are used in both passenger cars and trucks. Buses require more complicated layouts. The passenger compartment can be divided into several control zones, in which the temperature is controlled by electronically regulating the speed of the zone's individual water pump.

**Coolant circuit of an air-conditioning system**
1 Compressor, 2 Electric clutch (for compressor on/off function), 3 Condenser, 4 Auxiliary fan, 5 High-pressure switch, 6 Fluid reservoir with desiccant insert, 7 Low-pressure switch, 8 Temperature switch or on/off control (for compressor on/off function), 9 Temperature sensor, 10 Condensate drip pan, 11 Evaporator, 12 Evaporator fan, 13 Fan switch, 14 Expansion valve.

━━━ High pressure, liquid    ▭▭▭ Suction pressure, liquid
━▬━ High pressure, gaseous    ═══ Suction pressure, gaseous

## Auxiliary heater systems

### Function and designs

The fuel for auxiliary heater systems is supplied by the standard vehicle tank (or, on very large vehicles, by a separate fuel supply). An electric pump delivers the fuel via an evaporator or atomizer to the burner, where it is mixed with air and burned.

Whether the unit is an <u>air heater</u> or a <u>coolant heater</u> depends on the manner in which the heat produced is distributed. Both types of heater heat the vehicle interior without using heat from the vehicle engine, whereas coolant heaters also heat the engine.

The advantages of auxiliary heater systems are as follows:
- By deicing windows, they reduce the risk of accidents by ensuring better visibility.
- The vehicle is comfortably warm at all times.
- A preheated engine suffers less wear and produces lower emissions when first started.
- The catalytic converter reaches maximum efficiency faster and the engine uses less fuel.

### Air heaters

Applications

Air heaters are the most common type of auxiliary heater in trucks and buses. Their main advantages are:
- low cost
- ease of installation
- low power and fuel consumption

Operating concept

Air heaters operate independently of the vehicle's standard heater system. A combustion-air impeller draws the air required for combustion from the surrounding atmosphere, and blows it into the burner. The heating-air impeller draws in the air required, blows it through a heat exchanger, and into the vehicle cabin.

An important safety aspect is that the combustion air and the cabin air must be kept entirely separate. This prevents exhaust gas from entering the cabin.

Temperature regulators and sensors control the thermal output. If the detected temperature is lower that the setting on the temperature control (potentiometer), the thermal output is increased in gentle increments to its maximum level. When the desired temperature is reached, the thermal output is regulated accordingly. The control unit also detects any problems that may occur (e.g. overheating), and switches the heater off in good time.

Installation

Air heaters for commercial vehicles can usually be fitted directly inside the cab. In trucks, for instance, the preferred locations are in the co-driver's footwell, on the rear cab wall, under the bunk bed, on the outside of the cab wall, or in a stowage compartment. The exhaust pipe always runs under the floor (either into the wheel arch, or out of the rear cab wall). A large proportion of fuel sender units fitted in vehicle fuel tanks already have a spare connection for the fuel supply. If necessary, an extra tank sender unit is fitted. A fuel reserve for the vehicle's engine must be retained.

### Coolant heaters

Applications

Coolant heaters are the common choice for use in cars. They are connected directly to the engine's cooling system (flow pipe between engine and heat exchanger for passenger cell). They also make use of existing equipment, such as fans, air flaps, and air outlets. A distinction is made between <u>auxiliary heaters and booster heaters</u>.

Operating concept

Auxiliary heaters:

The circulation pump in auxiliary heaters pumps engine coolant to the system's heat exchanger where it is heated up. The heated coolant preheats the engine. It also passes through the vehicle's heat exchanger, where it transfers its heat. The heated air is blown controllably through the existing ventilation system into the vehicle cabin. Operation is controlled by a programmable timer (for immediate man-

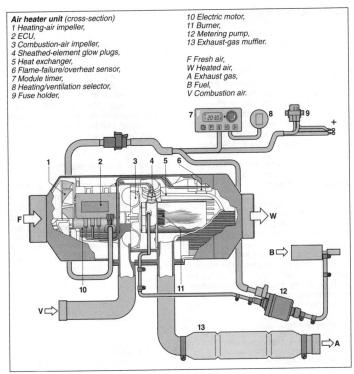

**Air heater unit** (cross-section)
1 Heating-air impeller,
2 ECU,
3 Combustion-air impeller,
4 Sheathed-element glow plugs,
5 Heat exchanger,
6 Flame-failure/overheat sensor,
7 Module timer,
8 Heating/ventilation selector,
9 Fuse holder,

10 Electric motor,
11 Burner,
12 Metering pump,
13 Exhaust-gas muffler.

F Fresh air,
W Heated air,
A Exhaust gas,
B Fuel,
V Combustion air.

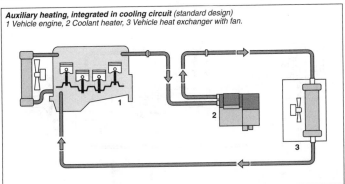

**Auxiliary heating, integrated in cooling circuit** (standard design)
1 Vehicle engine, 2 Coolant heater, 3 Vehicle heat exchanger with fan.

ual operation and preprogrammed automatic operation at switch-on times and for set periods), or by a radio remote control, and recently even by cellular phone or landline telephone.

Booster heaters:
Direct-injection diesel engines are efficiency-optimized, and therefore produce too little surplus heat for heating the vehicle cabin. Fuel-fired booster heaters are used to make up the resulting heat deficit. They only operate when the engine is running and the outside temperature is below +5°C.

However, booster heaters can easily be converted into auxiliary heaters with a few additional components.

Installation
Coolant heaters are usually fitted in the engine compartment. The simplest method of integrating them in the vehicle's cooling system is to connect them in series between the engine and the heat exchanger (primary circuit). A disadvantage with engines over approx. 2.5 l is that engine heating makes heating the passenger compartment much slower. In such cases, the passenger cell can be heated by a secondary circuit comprising a non-return valve and a temperature regulator, and the engine is only heated when the temperature regulator reaches a predetermined coolant temperature.

In Germany, all auxiliary heaters and fuel-fired booster heaters must have general type approval from the Federal Road Transport Office. The installation instructions provided by the manufacturer must be observed, and installation must be inspected by an expert.

Regulations
The use of auxiliary heating systems in vehicles transporting hazardous materials is governed by ADR/TRS 003 / TMD. The heater must be switched off before the vehicle enters a hazardous area (e.g. refinery or filling station). In addition, the heater switches off automatically as soon as the vehicle engine is switched off, an ancillary system (e.g. auxiliary drive for discharge pump or similar) is switched on, or a vehicle door is opened.

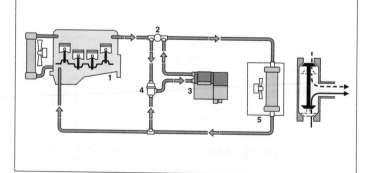

*Auxiliary heating system integrated in the cooling system*
*(divided into "primary" and "secondary" circuits)*
*1 Vehicle engine, 2 Non-return valve, 3 Coolant heater, 4 Heater temperature regulator, 5 Vehicle heat exchanger with fan.*

*Separated by heater thermostat and non-return valve to secondary circuit (priority for passenger compartment heating) and primary coolant circuit (including engine).*

# Cabin filters for passenger cars

Heating and air-conditioning systems in motor vehicles draw in air from the outside. After conditioning, the air passes into the passenger compartment together with any particles or gaseous pollutants it may contain. Such air pollution can cause allergic reactions. Therefore, it makes sense to filter out the critical particles and gases. A filter also reduces the amount of dirt that builds up on the fan, in the heating system, on the instrument panel, and on the inside of the windshield.

Depending on the particular requirements, either particle or combination filters are used. Combination filters have the advantage that, besides filtering out particles, they can also prevent unpleasant odors from entering the passenger compartment. That is achieved by carefully embedding activated charcoal granules (up to 300 g/m²) on the particle filter medium to eliminate aromatic substances. The activated charcoal also removes ozone, benzene, and toluene, for instance.

### Filter media
Whereas in the past filter media were primarily paper-based, the situation has now changed as a result of the greater demands placed on the filter system (removal of particles smaller than 0.001 mm). Present-day filter media generally consist of polyester or polypropylene-based nonwoven materials. The particle filter consists of three graduated fiber layers: the preliminary filter, the microfiber nonwoven layer with electrostatically spun microfibers, and the base nonwoven material. An activated charcoal filter also has an activated charcoal layer in addition to the three fiber layers.

When the filter material is made into a filter, a number of specific parameters must be considered. There is a complex interrelationship between the filter material used, the depth of the filter-element folds, and the distance between the folds. The interaction between these parameters is important in determining the filter performance in service.

### Design
Basically, cabin filters are optimized in three ways:
- for filtration
- for pressure loss
- for dust storage capacity

The specifics of the application determine which of these three considerations is given precedence.

The "best" filter may, for example, be a filter that achieves the highest possible filtration efficiency at the expense of tradeoffs in pressure loss and dust storage capacity. Another filter design may be one where a long service life is achieved by a high dust storage capacity at a defined level of filtration.

The service life of filters used in passenger cars is around 20,000 km, i.e. with today's servicing intervals, they are replaced each time the car is taken for a scheduled service.

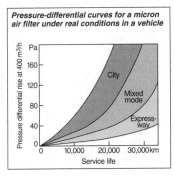

*Prevailing particle sizes x encountered in road traffic*

*Pressure-differential curves for a micron air filter under real conditions in a vehicle*

# Vehicle electrical systems

## Electrical power supply in a conventional vehicle electrical system

The electrical system in a motor vehicle essentially consists of an energy accumulator (battery), an energy converter (alternator), and energy consumers (electrical/electronic equipment).

The vehicle engine is started by the starter (load) using energy drawn from the battery (accumulator), and is adapted to suit the operating requirements during sustained operation by engine-specific control equipment (loads).

When the engine is running, the alternator (converter) supplies power which, depending on the voltage level of the vehicle electrical system (dependent on alternator speed and electrical equipment switched on and drawing power from the system), is sufficient under ideal operating conditions to supply the electrical equipment and also charge the battery. If the electrical equipment connected to the system draws power higher than the power generated by the alternator, the vehicle system voltage falls to battery voltage level, and the battery is discharged accordingly. A specific selection of battery, starter, alternator, and vehicle electrical system equipment insures an even charge balance in the battery:
– This guarantees that the internal-combustion engine can always be started.
– It allows operation of specific electrical equipment for a reasonable period of time when the engine is off.

The prime criteria for finding the optimized design combination are low weight, compact size, low fuel consumption, and the associated reduction in pollutant emission caused by energy conversion in the alternator. The following factors must receive special consideration:

### Minimum starting temperature

The lowest temperature at which the engine can be started depends on a number of factors, including the battery (capacity, low-temperature test current, state of charge, internal resistance, etc.) and the starter (design, size, and performance). If the engine is started at a temperature of –20 °C for example, the battery must have a given minimum state of charge $p$.

### Alternator output

The current output of the alternator varies as a function of engine speed. For an engine idling speed of $n_L$, the alternator can only supply some of its rated current if it has a conventional turns ratio ranging from 1:2 to 1:3 (crankshaft to alternator).

*Possible starting temperature as a function of battery charge state*
*$p$ Minimum charge.*

*Minimum starting temperature*

Battery
— 44 Ah
— 55 Ah

$p55$ $p44$

empty — State of battery charge — full

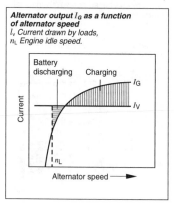

*Alternator output $I_G$ as a function of alternator speed*
*$I_v$ Current drawn by loads,*
*$n_L$ Engine idle speed.*

Battery discharging    Charging

Current

$I_G$
$I_V$

$n_L$

Alternator speed ⟶

**Installed loads as a function of duty cycle (examples)**

| Load | Power consumption | Average power output |
|---|---|---|
| Motronic, electric fuel pump | 250 W | 250 W |
| Radio | 20 W | 20 W |
| Side-marker lamps | 8 W | 7 W |
| Low-beam headlamps | 110 W | 90 W |
| License-plate lamp, tail lamps | 30 W | 25 W |
| Indicator lamp, instruments | 22 W | 20 W |
| Heated rear window | 200 W | 60 W |
| Interior heating, fan | 120 W | 50 W |
| Electric radiator blower | 120 W | 30 W |
| Windshield wipers | 50 W | 10 W |
| Stop lamps | 42 W | 11 W |
| Turn-signal lamps | 42 W | 5 W |
| Front fog lamps | 110 W | 20 W |
| Fog warning lamp | 21 W | 2 W |
| Total Electrical-load requirements | 1,145 W | |
| Average electrical-load requirements | | 600 W |

The rated current is defined at an alternator speed of 6,000 rpm.

If the equipment current draw $I_v$ in the vehicle electrical system is greater than the power supplied by the alternator $I_G$ (e.g. when the engine is idling), the battery is discharged. The vehicle system voltage falls to the voltage level of the battery from which current is drawn.

On the other hand, if the equipment current draw $I_v$ is less than the current supplied by the alternator $I_G$, some of the current difference is used for battery charging $I_B$.

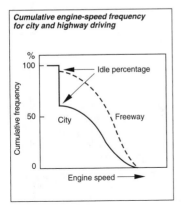

**Cumulative engine-speed frequency for city and highway driving**

**Driving**
The rotational speed supplied to the alternator (and therefore the alternator output) depends on the vehicle application.

The cumulative engine speed frequency distribution shows how often a certain engine speed is achieved or exceeded in a specific type of vehicle application.

Owing to traffic congestion or stopping at traffic lights, a passenger car driven in city commuter traffic runs at idle for a high percentage of the time. Under expressway driving conditions, on the other hand, the percentage of time the engine runs at idle is generally lower. A city bus running on scheduled routes has a high idle percentage time due to interruptions in driving at bus stops. The charge balance of the battery is also adversely affected by electrical equipment which is operated when the engine is off (e.g. electrical equipment which cannot be switched off at the depot). Tour buses in general only run at idle for a small percentage of the time. However, electrical equipment may draw a high level of current when the vehicle is at a standstill during stops.

**Electrical loads**
Electrical loads have a variety of duty cycles. A differentiation is made between continuous loads (ignition, fuel injection, etc.), long-term loads (lighting, heated rear window, etc.), and short-term loads (turn signals, stop lamps, etc.). Use of some

electrical loads is seasonal (air conditioners in summer, seat heating in winter). The on-time of electrical radiator blowers depends on the ambient temperature and vehicle operation. In winter, lights are generally used when driving in commuter traffic. The electrical load requirements encountered during vehicle operation are not constant. The first minutes after startup are generally characterized by high demand, followed by a sharp drop in electrical load requirements:

1. In future the electrical windshield heating will require up to 2 kW for 1...3 mins after the engine starts up to defrost the windshield.

2. The secondary-air pump is responsible for supplying air immediately downstream of the combustion chambers for exhaust-gas afterburning. It operates for up to 3 mins after the engine starts up.

3. Other electrical equipment such as heaters (rear window, seats, mirrors, etc.), blower, and lighting systems draw current for various periods of time, while the engine-management system remains in continuous operation.

## Charge voltage

The battery charge voltage must be higher in cold weather and lower in warm weather in order to accommodate the chemical processes which take place inside the battery. The gassing voltage curve indicates the maximum permissible charge voltage at which the battery does not "gas".

Electrical loads require a voltage which is as constant as possible. The voltage applied to filament bulbs must have very close tolerances so that bulb service life and luminous intensity remain within specified limits. The governor therefore limits the maximum voltage if the potential alternator current $I_G$ is larger than the sum of the required equipment current draw $I_V$ and potential battery charge current $I_B$. Governors are normally mounted on the alternator.

If there is a significant deviations between the temperatures of the voltage regulator and the battery electrolyte, it is better to monitor the voltage-regulation temperature directly at the battery. It is possible to compensate for voltage drop in the charging cable between the alternator and the battery by using a regulator to monitor actual voltage directly at the battery (via an additional wire).

## Dynamic system characteristics

The interrelationships between the battery, alternator, loads, temperature, engine speed, and engine/alternator speed ratio define the system's dynamic response pattern. It is dynamic because it varies with each combination of parameters and each set of operating conditions. Measuring systems can be connected to the battery terminals to plot dynamic system characteristics.

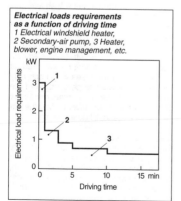

*Electrical loads requirements as a function of driving time*
1 Electrical windshield heater,
2 Secondary-air pump, 3 Heater, blower, engine management, etc.

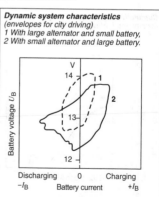

*Dynamic system characteristics* (envelopes for city driving)
1 With large alternator and small battery,
2 With small alternator and large battery.

### Charge-balance calculation

The charge-balance calculation must take the above-mentioned influencing variables into consideration. A computer program is used to determine the state of battery charge state at the end of a typical driving schedule. A typical passenger-car cycle consists of vehicle operation in commuter traffic (engine speeds are low) combined with winter operation (when charge-current consumption by the battery is low). Summer operation may place even greater loads on the system when the vehicle is equipped with an air conditioner (high current draw). The battery charge state at the end of the driving schedule must – at the very least – be sufficient to allow the engine to start at the ambient temperature.

### Vehicle electrical system simulation

In contrast with this non-analytical approach to charge-balance calculations, the situation in relation to the vehicle-electrical-system energy supply can be calculated at any time during operation using model-based simulations. This can also take vehicle electrical-system management systems into account and assess their effectiveness.

In addition to adjusting current levels in the battery, it is possible to record the vehicle-system voltage characteristic curve and the battery cycle at any time during a trip. Calculations performed using vehicle electrical-system simulations are always useful for comparing electrical-system typologies and assessing the effectiveness of electrical equipment with a high dynamic response or electrical equipment with short operating times.

### Vehicle electrical-system design

The voltage level in the vehicle electrical system, and thus the battery charge state, are also affected by the wiring between alternator, battery, and electrical loads. The total current $I_G = I_B + I_V$ flows through the charging cable if all electrical equipment is connected to the battery.

The charging voltage is less due to the high voltage drop. If all loads are connected on the alternator side, the voltage drop is less and the charging voltage is higher. This could be difficult to loads (such as electronics) that are sensitive to voltage peaks or voltage ripple. Electrical devices which feature high current draw and relative insensitivity to overvoltage should therefore be connected close to the alternator, whereas voltage-sensitive loads with low current draw should be connected close to the battery.

Voltage drops can be minimized by suitable conductor cross-sections and good connections with low contact resistance, even after a long service life.

## Future vehicle electrical systems

### Two-battery vehicle electrical systems

As part of a standard 12-V vehicle electrical system, the battery represents a compromise between (to some extent) conflicting requirements: Its capacity must be selected with reference to starting requirements as well as on-board current supply. During the engine starting sequence, the battery is subjected to high current loads (300...500 A). The associated voltage drop has an adverse effect on certain electrical equipment (e.g. units with microcontroller) and should be as low as possible. By contrast, current draw during standard vehicle operation – where battery capacity is the salient factor – is comparatively low. It is not possible to optimize both criteria within a single battery at the same time.

*Vehicle electrical system with loads connected to alternator and battery*
*1 Alternator, 2 High-draw electrical loads, 3 Low-draw electrical loads, 4 Battery.*

Future vehicle electrical systems will feature two batteries (starter battery and general-purpose battery); the "high power for starting" and "general-purpose electrical supply" functions will be separated. This will make it possible to avoid the voltage drop during the starting process, while ensuring reliable cold starts, even when the charge level of the general-purpose battery is low.

### Vehicle electrical-system ECU

The ECU in a two-battery vehicle electrical system separates the starter battery and the starter from the rest of the vehicle electrical system. It therefore prevents the voltage drop that occurs during starting, affecting the performance of the vehicle electrical system.

When the vehicle is parked, this prevents the starter battery from becoming discharged electrical equipment that draws current when switched on when the engine is switched off and standstill-draw devices.

In principal, due to the complete separation of the starting system from the rest of the vehicle electrical system, there is no limit to the potential level of charge in the starter battery. This means that the starter battery can be optimized and adjusted to suit the battery using a DC/DC converter, i.e. recharged in the shortest possible time.

If there is no charge in the general-purpose battery, the ECU is capable of provisionally connecting both vehicle electrical systems. This means that the vehicle electrical system can be sustained using the fully-charged starter battery. In addition, information can be sent over a CAN interface for storage on the on-board computer.

Another possible variation allows the ECU to connect only the electrical equipment required for starting to the corresponding fully-charged battery.

### Starter battery

The starter battery must supply a high amount of current for only a limited period of time (during starting). Compact dimensions allow installation in the immediate vicinity of the starter motor with short connecting cables. Capacity can also be reduced.

### General-purpose battery

This battery only supplies the vehicle electrical system (excluding the starter). It supplies relatively low currents (e.g. roughly 20 A for the engine-management system), but is also designed to cater for highly cyclical variations; i.e. this unit can store and furnish substantial amounts of energy if it has the right capacity and it is above the deep-discharge limit. Design dimensions are selected based on capac-

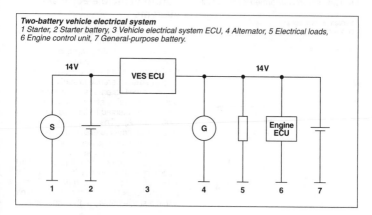

*Two-battery vehicle electrical system*
*1 Starter, 2 Starter battery, 3 Vehicle electrical system ECU, 4 Alternator, 5 Electrical loads, 6 Engine control unit, 7 General-purpose battery.*

ity reserves for electrical equipment (e.g. parking lamps, hazard-warning flashers), constant-draw devices, and maximum specified discharge level.

### 42-V vehicle electrical systems

In vehicle electrical systems, the complex interaction of energy generators and loads requires coordination. The fuel is used not only to produce kinetic energy, but also to obtain electrical energy. The aim of development activities is to make the management of all energy generated and consumed by the vehicle as efficient as possible. For example, hydraulic energy consumers (such as power-assisted steering systems) can be replaced by electrical systems which use energy more efficiently.

Increases in safety, fuel economy, and comfort cause greater electrical loads. Examples include heated windshields for increased safety, and PTC heating in the passenger cabin, which provides greater comfort when driving with high-efficiency diesel engines. The consequence of this is that electrical peak performance, which rises to more than 10 kW, is increased by nearly fivefold. Electrical loads of this magnitude can no longer be managed using 14-V vehicle electrical systems.

The Association of German Automobile Manufacturers (VDA) working together with suppliers, universities, and international bodies have therefore specified a system voltage of 42 V for future vehicle electrical systems.

<u>Two-voltage vehicle electrical system with Electrical Energy Management (EEM)</u>

The first step towards achieving a higher vehicle system voltage is the two-voltage vehicle electrical system with 14-V and 42-V subnetworks. Advantage: Continued use of existing low-cost components based on 14-V systems. In this vehicle electrical system, the alternator supplies current directly to the 42-V high-performance electrical equipment. The remaining electrical equipment is connected to the 14-V subnetwork by means of a DC voltage converter. The separate batteries for each subnetwork can be dimensioned in such a way that their combined weight does not greatly exceed the weight of conventional batteries used today.

The Electrical Energy Management (EEM) coordinates the interaction of the alternator, voltage converter, batteries, and electrical equipment when the vehicle is in operation. When the vehicle is parked, the EEM monitors the batteries, and switches standstill-draw and constant-draw equipment off as soon as the battery charge reaches a critical limit. The EEM coordinator governs the overall electrical energy balance. It compares the power requirements of electrical equipment with the power available in the vehi-

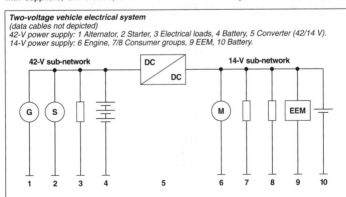

*Two-voltage vehicle electrical system*
*(data cables not depicted)*
*42-V power supply: 1 Alternator, 2 Starter, 3 Electrical loads, 4 Battery, 5 Converter (42/14 V).*
*14-V power supply: 6 Engine, 7/8 Consumer groups, 9 EEM, 10 Battery.*

cle electrical system, and establishes in each case an equilibrium between the generation and output of power. The EEM coordinator can prevent power peaks, which arise when several electrical loads are switched on simultaneously, by supplying the power required in timed stages.

However, the two-voltage vehicle electrical system is merely regarded by many as a temporary solution. A 42-V-only vehicle electrical system is regarded as the ideal solution.

Starter alternators

For 42-V vehicle electrical systems with high energy requirements, starter alternators are an alternative to individual alternator and starter machines. They generate and consume energy at the same time.

The integrated crankshaft-starter alternator (ICSA) increases the efficiency of the electrical system. This electric motor is designed as a permanent-field synchronous machine and is located between the internal-combustion engine and transmission.

When the vehicle is in operation, the ICSA generates electrical energy. The high efficiency of the starter alternator contributes to a reduction in fuel consumption by approx. 0.5%. This potential for fuel savings can be increased to 4...6% if the ICSA is equipped to include start-stop operations. These operations switch the engine off automatically when the car is at a standstill (e.g. at traffic lights). When the driver depresses the clutch, the engine starts quickly and smoothly again by means of the ICSA.

When the vehicle brakes and the engine is switched off, the alternator can transform the residual kinetic energy into electrical energy (recuperation). This energy can be used, for example, to power an electrical drive-away assistance. This results in further potential savings.

## Influence on fuel consumption

Only a small portion of the fuel used by the vehicle is used to drive the alternator and transport the combined weight of starter, battery, and alternator (approx. 5% in a mid-range car).

Average fuel consumption per 100 km: for a weight of 10 kg, approx. 0.1 $l$, for 100 W of drive power: approx. 0.1 $l$.

Alternators with high levels of efficiency at part load, therefore, help to reduce fuel consumption, despite the fact that they are slightly heavier.

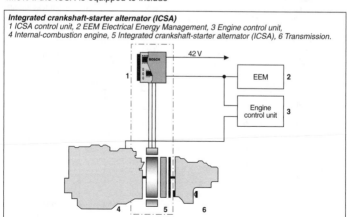

*Integrated crankshaft-starter alternator (ICSA)*
*1 ICSA control unit, 2 EEM Electrical Energy Management, 3 Engine control unit,*
*4 Internal-combustion engine, 5 Integrated crankshaft-starter alternator (ICSA), 6 Transmission.*

# Starter batteries

## Requirements

The performance requirements for starter batteries in modern motor vehicles are constantly increasing:

- Diesel engines and large-volume gasoline engines have high cold-starting power requirements (high starting currents, particularly at low temperatures).
- Electrical systems in vehicles with a comprehensive range of electrical equipment require large amounts of energy from the battery if the supply from the alternator is temporarily insufficient or – not to be underestimated – when the engine is at a standstill.

The total output power of all installed electrical equipment, which draws electrical energy from the battery for several minutes at a time, often exceeds 2 kW. In addition, the peak quiescent current, which the battery is required to deliver for days and weeks at a time, amounts to many thousand milliamperes.

In addition to these aspects requiring uniform energy supply, the battery in the vehicle electrical system must increasingly support tasks which require dynamic, high-current impulses which cannot be delivered by the alternator as quickly (for "transient" operations). Furthermore, due to the very high inherent natural capacitance of the double-layer capacitor – several farad (F) – the battery has a superb inherent smoothing function on ripples in the current supplied by the vehicle electrical system. This helps to minimize and eliminate EMC problems. Recently, new demands have arisen for increasing the reliability of the electrical power supply for safety-relevant electrical equipment, e.g. electrohydraulic brakes and/or electric steering.

Taking all these requirements into consideration, it is easy to understand why so much effort is invested into optimizing the properties of batteries during production and ensuring their operation in service. The most advanced batteries are those that not only have the required electrical properties but are also maintenance-free, environment-friendly, and especially safe to handle. It is anticipated that more 2-battery systems and devices or measuring electronic battery charge states will be fitted to vehicles as greater reliability of the energy supply is achieved by preventing batteries from fully discharging, and by replacing spent batteries in good time.

*Influence of temperature on starter speed and minimum initial engine speed*
Example: 1a Starter speed, 20% battery discharge; 1b Starter speed, heavy battery discharge; 2 Minimum initial engine speed $S_1$, $S_2$ Cold-start limit.

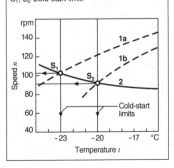

*Electrical parameters inside and on the battery*
$I_E$ Discharge current, $R_i$ Internal resistance, $R_V$ Load resistance, $U_0$ Steady-state voltage, $U_K$ Terminal voltage, $U_i$ Voltage drop across internal resistance.

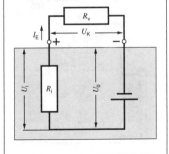

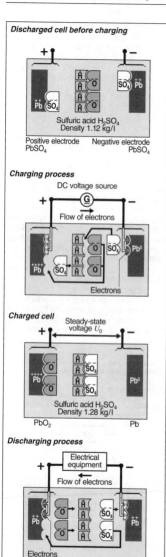

*Discharged cell before charging*

+       −

Sulfuric acid $H_2SO_4$
Density 1.12 kg/l

Positive electrode    Negative electrode
$PbSO_4$             $PbSO_4$

*Charging process*

DC voltage source

Flow of electrons

Electrons

*Charged cell*

Steady-state voltage $U_0$

+       −

Sulfuric acid $H_2SO_4$
Density 1.28 kg/l

$PbO_2$            $Pb$

*Discharging process*

Electrical equipment

+       −

Flow of electrons

Electrons

Despite all the technical advances, it is still the driver's responsibility to make sure that the battery, and in turn the vehicle electrical system, remains in good function. The excellent charge acceptance properties of modern starter batteries would be useless if a positive battery charge balance cannot be achieved during regular, short trips through the city in winter (involving high power consumption and low engine speed). Generally, charge states that are consistently low for long periods of time shorten storage-battery service life. This shifts the engine starting speed toward the critical cold-start limit.

Batteries must be specifically designed to meet the requirements of individual vehicle electrical systems for starting power, capacity, and charge-current storage at temperatures ranging from approx. −30 °C to +70 °C. There are also additional specifications which must be satisfied for particular applications (e.g. maintenance-free, vibration-proof). Typical system voltages are 12 V for passenger cars, and 24 V for commercial vehicles (achieved by connecting two 12-V batteries in series).

### Lead-acid batteries
#### Charging and discharging

The active materials in a lead-acid battery are lead oxide ($PbO_2$) on the positive plates, spongy, highly porous lead ($Pb$) on the negative plates, and electrolyte composed of diluted sulfuric acid ($H_2SO_4$). The electrolyte is simultaneously an ion conductor for charging and discharging. Compared with the electrolyte, $PbO_2$ and $Pb$ adopt typical electrical voltages (individual potentials). Their magnitudes (disregarding the electrical sign) are equal to the sum of the cell voltages measurable from the outside. At rest, cell voltage is approx. 2 V. It must rise during the charging process and fall when current is drawn in order to compensate for the voltage drop across the internal resistance (see figure). When the cell discharges, $PbO_2$ and $Pb$ combine with $H_2SO_4$ to form $PbSO_4$ (lead sulfate). This conversion causes the electrolyte to lose $SO_4$ (sulfate) ions, and its specific gravity decreases. During the charging process, the active materials $PbO_2$ and $Pb$ are reconstituted from the $PbSO_4$.

**Specific gravity and freezing point of diluted sulfuric acid.**

| State of charge | Battery design | Specific gravity of electrolyte kg/l[1] | Freezing point °C |
|---|---|---|---|
| Charged | Standard | 1.28 | −68 |
| | For tropical regions | 1.23 | −40 |
| Half-charged | Standard | 1.16/1.20[2] | −17...−27 |
| | For tropical regions | 1.13/1.16[2] | −13...−17 |
| Discharged | Standard | 1.04/1.12[2] | −3...−11 |
| | For tropical regions | 1.03/1.08[2] | −2...−8 |

[1] At 20°C: The specific gravity of electrolyte reduces as temperature rises and increases as temperature drops at a rate of about 0.01 kg/l for every 14 K difference in temperature.

[2] Lower figure: High electrolyte consumption.
Higher figure: Low electrolyte consumption.

If the charge voltage continues to be applied after the cell has reached a state of full charge, only the electrolytic decomposition of water occurs. This produces oxygen at the positive plate and hydrogen at the negative plate (oxyhydrogen gas). The specific gravity of electrolyte can be used to indicate the state of charge of the battery. The accuracy of this relationship depends on battery design (see table below showing "Density and freezing point of diluted sulfuric acid"), electrolyte stratification, and battery wear with a certain degree of irreversible sulfating and/or a high degree of shedding of plate material.

The following individual processes take place (diagram sequence on left):

Discharged cell before charging: $PbSO_4$, which is made up of the ions $Pb^{++}$ and $SO_4^{--}$, is on both electrodes. The electrolyte consists of low specific-gravity $H_2SO_4$ due to previous current demand resulting in the formation of $H_2O$.

Charging: $Pb^{++}$ is converted to $Pb^{++++}$ at the positive electrode due to electron "stripping". This combines with $O_2$ from $H_2O$ to form $PbO_2$. On the other hand, Pb is formed at the negative electrode. The $SO_4^{--}$ ions released from $PbSO_4$ on both electrodes and $H^+$ ions from $H_2O$ create new $H_2SO_4$ and increase the specific gravity of the electrolyte.

Charged cell: $PbSO_4$ on the positive electrode is converted to $PbO_2$, and $PbSO_4$ on the negative diode is converted to Pb. There is no further rise in charge voltage or the specific gravity of the electrolyte.

Discharging: The direction of current flow and the electrochemical processes during discharging are reversed in relation to charging. This results in a combination of $Pb^{++}$ and $SO_4^{--}$ ions on both electrodes to form the discharge product $PbSO_4$.

Behavior at low temperatures

Basically, the chemical reactions in a storage battery take place more slowly at lower temperatures. The starting power even of a fully charged battery, therefore, decreases as the temperature drops. The more the battery discharges, the more diluted the electrolyte becomes. This means that electrolyte has a greater probability of freezing in a discharged battery. A discharged battery can only supply a low current which is not sufficient to start the vehicle.

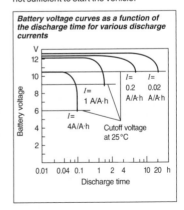

*Battery voltage curves as a function of the discharge time for various discharge currents*

## Battery characteristics

### Designation

In addition to mechanical parameters, such as physical dimensions, attachment, and terminal design, batteries are primarily characterized by electrical ratings measured according to specific testing standards (e.g. DIN EN 60 096-1, previously DIN 43 539-2). Starter batteries manufactured in Germany are identified by a 9-digit type number, nominal voltage, nominal capacity, and low-temperature test current in compliance with DIN EN 60 095-1/A11. Example: 555 059 042 indicates 12 V, 55 A · h, a special construction (059), and a low-temperature test current of 420 A. In future this European (EN) standard will become a more widely used starter-battery identification convention.

### Capacity

Battery capacity, rated in A · h, is the current which can be drawn from the battery under specified conditions. Capacity decreases as discharge current increases and temperature decreases.

### Nominal capacity $K_{20}$

As defined by DIN EN, nominal capacity is the charge which a battery can deliver within 20 h at constant discharge current down to a cutoff voltage of 10.5 V (1.75 V/cell) at 25 °C. The battery nominal capacity depends on the quantities of ac-

tive material used (positive material, negative material, electrolyte), and is relatively unaffected by the number of plates.

### Low-temperature test current $I_{CC}$ (previously $I_{KP}$)

This figure provides an index of the battery's current-supply capability at low temperatures. According to DIN EN standards, the terminal voltage when discharging at $I_{CC}$ and −18 °C must be at least 7.5 V (1.25 V/cell) 10 s after start of discharge. Further details relating to discharge duration are specified in the above standard. The short-term response of the battery when discharged at $I_{CC}$ is largely determined by the number of plates, their surface area, the gap between plates, and the separator material. Another variable which characterizes starting response is internal resistance $R_i$.

The following equation applies to a fully charged battery (12 V) at −18 °C: $R_i \leq 4{,}000/I_{CC}$ (mΩ), where $I_{CC}$ is given in A. The battery internal resistance and other resistances in the starter circuit determine the cranking speed.

## Battery design

The 12-volt starter battery contains six series-connected, individually partitioned cells in a polypropylene case. Each cell consists of a positive and negative plate set. These sets, in turn, are composed of plates (lead grid and active materials) and microporous material (separators) which insulates the plates of opposite polarities. The electrolyte is in the form of diluted sulfuric acid which permeates the pores in the plates and separators, and the voids in the cells. The terminal posts, cells, and plate straps are made of lead; the openings in the partitions for the cell connectors are tightly sealed. A hot-sealing process is employed to permanently bond the one-piece cover to the battery case, providing the battery's upper seal. On conventional batteries, each cell is sealed by its own vent plug, which, when removed, permits initial battery filling and topping-up during service. When screwed in, the ventilation openings allow charge gases to escape. Maintenance-free batteries frequently appear to be completely sealed units, but they also require escape vents.

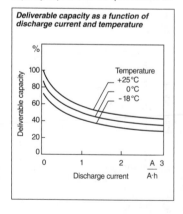

**Deliverable capacity as a function of discharge current and temperature**

Deliverable capacity (%) vs. Discharge current (A · h)

Temperature +25 °C, 0 °C, −18 °C

### Battery designs
#### Maintenance-free battery

According to DIN standards, due to the greatly reduced levels of antimony in the lead alloy used to make the grid, the maintenance-free battery incurs low water loss during charging, and therefore produces less gas. Electrolyte inspections are therefore limited to:

- Every 15 months or 25,000 km for a low-maintenance battery
- Every 25 months or 40,000 km for a maintenance-free battery (according to DIN)

The fully maintenance-free battery (lead-calcium battery) no longer requires electrolyte checks (and generally provides no means of doing so); it is, with the exception of two ventilation openings, completely sealed. Under normal vehicle electrical-system operating conditions ($U =$ constant), water decomposition is reduced to such an extent that the supply of electrolyte above the plates will last for the entire service life of the battery. Another advantage of this type of lead-calcium battery is its extremely low self-discharge rate. This makes it possible to store the battery for months, provided its is fully charged to start with. Where a maintenance-free battery is recharged outside the vehicle electrical system, the charge voltage of 2.3 to 2.4 V per cell may not be exceeded. The reason for this is

that, for all lead storage batteries, overcharging using continuous current, or battery chargers using the W-curve automatically leads to water loss.

Further enhancements to the lead alloy for the grid on the positive plate includes the addition of silver, reduced calcium content, and increased levels of tin. This alloy has proven to be very durable when subjected to high temperatures which accelerate corrosive deterioration. The alloy has proven resistant not only to the damaging effects of overcharging at a high electrolyte specific gravity, but also to periods of inactivity at low electrolyte specific gravity, which are equally to be avoided. This effect was further intensified by fitting a cast grid designed as a supporting structure and optimized with additional electric conductivity. This technology allows an even thinner (but stronger) plate design and increases the number of plates. This improves cold-start performance even further without any quality tradeoffs.

#### Deep-cycle resistant battery

Due to their design (thin plates, lightweight separator material), starter batteries are less suitable for applications which involve repeated exhaustive discharging, as this results in heavy wear on the positive plates (mainly caused by a loosening and shedding of active materials). A deep-cycle resistant starter battery has separators with glass mats that support relatively

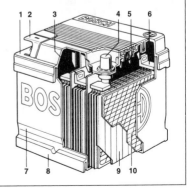

*Maintenance-free starter battery*
1 One-piece cover,
2 Terminal-post cover,
3 Cell connector,
4 Terminal post,
5 Frit,
6 Plate strap,
7 Battery case,
8 Bottom rail,
9 Positive plates, inserted
  in film-separator pockets,
10 Negative plates.

thick plates containing positive material and therefore prevent premature shedding. Service life measured in charge/discharge cycles is nearly twice as long as a standard battery. A deep-cycle resistant starter battery with pocket separators and nonwoven lining has an even longer service life.

Vibration-proof battery

In a vibration-proof battery, the plate block is fixed to the battery case by means of cast resin and/or plastic to prevent any relative movement between the two components. According to DIN regulations, this battery type must pass a 20-hour sinusoidal vibration test (at a rate of 22 Hz), and it must be capable of withstanding a maximum acceleration of $6 \cdot g$. Requirements are therefore about 10 times greater than for standard batteries. A vibration-proof battery, which carries the designation "Rf", is mainly used in commercial vehicles, construction machines, tractor vehicles, etc.

Heavy-duty battery

A heavy-duty battery combines the attributes of the deep-cycle resistant and vibration-proof types. It is used in commercial vehicles which are subjected to extreme vibrations, and where cyclic discharge patterns are commonplace. Designation: "HD".

"Kt" battery

The Kt (or "S") battery shares the basic design of a deep-cycle resistant unit, but has thicker and fewer plates. Although no low-temperature test current is specified for the "Kt" battery, its starting power lies well below (35 to 40%) starter batteries of the same size. This battery type is used in applications that are subjected to extreme cyclic variations, e.g. traction battery (see P. 723).

## Operating states

Charging

In vehicle electrical systems, the battery is charged using voltage limitation. This corresponds to the IU charging method, where the battery charge current reduces automatically as the steady-state voltage rises. The IU charging method prevents damage due to overcharging, and makes sure that the battery has a long service life.

Battery chargers, on the other hand, still operate using constant current or the W-characteristic (see figure "Battery charging using the W curve"). In both cases, once the full state of charge has been reached, charging continues with only a slightly reduced, or possibly a constant current. This leads to high water consumption and to subsequent corrosion of the positive grid.

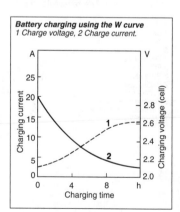

**Battery charging using the IU curve**
1 Charge voltage, 2 Charge current.

**Battery charging using the W curve**
1 Charge voltage, 2 Charge current.

Discharging

Shortly after discharging begins, the voltage in the storage battery drops to a value which, in contrast to a capacitor, only changes relatively slowly if discharging continues. Only shortly before the end of the discharging process will the voltage collapse sharply due to exhaustion of one or more of the active components (positive material, negative material, electrolyte).

Self-discharge
(see also "Battery maintenance")
Batteries discharge over a period of time – even if they are not subjected to loads, i.e. when no electrical equipment is connected. Modern batteries with low amounts of antimony lose approx. 0.1 to 0.2% of their charge daily when new. As battery ages, this value can increase by up to 1% or more each day due to the migration of antimony to the negative plate and other impurities, until a point is reached when the battery finally stops functioning. A rule of thumb for the impact of temperature: the self-discharge rate doubles for every 10 °C rise in temperature.

Lead-calcium batteries have a considerably lower rate of self-discharge (by a factor of 1:5). This remains virtually constant throughout their entire service life.

**Battery maintenance**

On low-maintenance batteries, the electrolyte level should be inspected in accordance with the manufacturer's operating instructions; when required, it should be replenished to the MAX mark with distilled or demineralized water. The battery should be kept clean and dry to minimize self-discharge. It is also advisable to test the electrolyte's specific gravity before the onset of winter or, if this is impossible, measure the battery voltage. The battery should be recharged when the specific gravity is below 1.20 g/ml, or the battery voltage is under 12.2 V. Terminal posts, terminal clamps, and fixings should be coated with acid-protection grease.

Batteries temporarily removed from service should be stored in a cool, dry place. The electrolyte's specific gravity and/or the battery voltage should be checked every 3 to 4 months. The battery should be recharged whenever the electrolyte specific gravity drops below 1.20 g/ml or the battery voltage is below 12.2 V. Low-maintenance and maintenance-free batteries are best recharged with the IU method (see "Charging") at a maximum voltage of 14.4 V. This method allows adequate charging times in the order of 24 hours without any risk of overcharging. If a constant-current or W-characteristic battery charger is used, the current (in A) should be reduced to max. 1/10 of the nominal capacity when gassing is first observed, i.e. at a current of 6.6 A on a 66 Ah battery. The battery charger should be switched off about 1 hour afterwards. The charging area should be well ventilated (oxyhydrogen gas, risk of explosion, no naked flames, or sparks), and the operator should wear protective goggles.

**Battery malfunctions**

Battery failures which are traceable to internal faults (such as short-circuits caused by separator wear, or loss of active material, broken cell connectors or plate straps) can rarely be rectified by repair. The battery has to be replaced. Internal short-circuits are indicated by major fluctuations in specific-gravity readings between cells (difference between max. and min. >0.03 g/ml). It is often possible to charge and discharge a battery with defective cell connectors, provided that the currents remain small, but attempts to start the engine will result immediately in total voltage collapse, even if the battery is fully charged.

If no defects can be found in a battery which consistently loses its charge (indication: low specific gravity in all cells, no starting power), or is overcharged (indication: high water loss), this suggests a malfunction in the vehicle electrical system (faulty alternator, electrical equipment remains on when the engine is switched off due to faulty relays for instance, voltage regulator set too high or too low, or regulator completely inoperative). When a battery remains severely discharged for a relatively long period, the $PbSO_4$ crystals in the active material become coarse, making the battery more difficult to recharge. A battery in this state should be recharged by applying a minimal charge current (approx. 1/40 of the nominal capacity in A) for roughly 50 hours.

# Alternators

### Electrical-energy generation
The alternator must furnish the vehicle electrical system with a sufficient supply of current under all operating conditions in order to ensure that the state of charge in the energy storage device (battery) is always maintained at an adequate level. The object is to achieve balanced charging, i.e. the characteristics for performance and speed-frequency response must be selected to ensure that the amount of current generated by the alternator under actual operating conditions is at least equal to the consumption of all electrical equipment within the same period.

The alternator actually produces alternating current. The vehicle electrical system, on the other hand, requires direct current to recharge the battery and operate the electrical equipment. It is thus direct current that must ultimately be supplied to the electrical system. A bridge rectifier integrated in the alternator converts the three-phase alternating current. The essential requirements are:

– Maintenance of a direct-current supply to all electrical equipment in the system.
– Supplementary charging reserves for (re)charging the battery, even at a constant load from electrical devices in continuous operation.
– Maintenance of a constant alternator voltage throughout the entire ranges of engine speed and load conditions.
– Robust design capable of withstanding external stresses, such as vibration, high ambient temperatures, temperature cycles, dirt, moisture, etc.
– Low weight, compact dimensions, and long service life.
– Minimized operating noise.
– High level of efficiency.

### Design factors

#### Rotational speed
The alternator's operating efficiency (its power-to-weight ratio expressed as the ratio of energy generated to component mass in kg) increases as a function of rotational speed. This factor alone would dictate as high a conversion ratio as possible between the engine crankshaft and the alternator. The following factors must also be considered:
– Centrifugal forces at high engine speeds.
– Alternator and fan noise.
– Efficiency fall-away at high speeds.
– Effect of high speeds on the service lives of wearing parts (bearings, collector rings, carbon brushes).
– Mass moment of inertia of the alternator relative to the crankshaft, and the resulting stress on the belt drive.

Typical conversion factors for automotive applications lie within a range of 1:2 to 1:3, with ratios of up to 1:5 in large commercial vehicles. In extreme cases (e.g. in commuter traffic), the alternator runs for up to two-thirds of total operating time when the engine is idling, i.e. in the speed range with the lowest performance efficiency.

#### Temperatures
The losses that accompany energy conversion in any machine lead to high component temperatures.

High alternator temperatures are also a result of heat radiation from engine components and ancillaries (such as exhaust-gas systems and turbochargers); the amount of heat depends on the relative installation positions, and is greatest when the engine operates at high speeds and at wide-open throttle. Cooling air is generally drawn in from the engine compartment by the alternator.

In view of the trend toward engine-compartment encapsulation, which is becoming more and more common as a means of suppressing noise, the ducting of fresh air toward the alternator is an appropriate method of reducing component temperature. Generators with liquid cooling are available for situations where engine-compartment temperatures are extreme.

#### External influences
Installing the alternator on an IC engine means exposing it to extreme mechanical stresses. Depending on the installation configuration and the engine's vibration characteristics, the alternator may be subjected to vibration levels of 500 to 800 m·s$^{-2}$. This applies extreme forces to the alternator mountings and components,

and it is essential to avoid critical natural frequencies in the alternator design.

Further detrimental influences include spray water, dirt, oil, fuel mist, and road salt in winter. These factors expose all components to the risk of corrosion. It is important to prevent leakage paths from forming between conducting parts, as electrolysis could otherwise lead to the early failure of vital operating components.

### Features and operating concept
In order to maintain an adequate charge in 12-V, 24-V or 36-V batteries, automotive alternators are designed to supply charge voltages of 14 V, 28 V for heavy commercial vehicles, and in future 42 V.

As direct current is required to charge the battery, a diode rectifier must be provided to convert the alternator's three-phase alternating current into direct current. The alternator is also subjected to battery voltage when the engine is at a standstill. This allows the rectifier diodes to prevent the battery discharging.

The maximum current-generation curve has a sharp bend. There is no current generation until after the so-called "zero-ampere speed" is exceeded. At high speeds, the effect of the reverse magnetization field generated by the load current prevents the characteristic from climbing any higher. This characteristic means that even over-

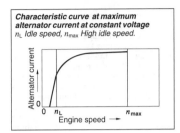

*Characteristic curve at maximum alternator current at constant voltage*
$n_L$ Idle speed, $n_{max}$ High idle speed.

loading cannot result in any further increases in alternator current, thereby protecting the alternator from thermal damage associated with electrical overload.

Alternators used in motor vehicles are designed as 12- or 16-pole three-phase synchronous generators with claw-pole rotors (in most cases, self-exciting). The three-phase winding is wound in the stator's slots, while the excitation winding is housed within the rotor. The DC excitation current required by the excitation winding is conducted to the rotating rotor via sliding contacts (carbon brushes). The current produced in the three-phase winding is channeled in two directions. Most of it flows through the positive diodes of the main rectifier bridge to the vehicle electrical system, from where it returns via the negative diodes.

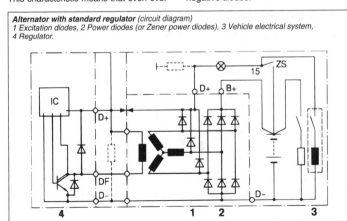

*Alternator with standard regulator (circuit diagram)*
1 Excitation diodes, 2 Power diodes (or Zener power diodes), 3 Vehicle electrical system, 4 Regulator.

Depending on the design of the alternator and regulator, the excitation current flows:
a) via excitation diodes in the case of standard regulators.
b) directly from the B+ terminal in the case of multifunction regulators.

With standard regulators, some of the current generated acts as excitation current, flowing via the three excitation diodes to terminal D+, via the regulator and collector rings to the rotating field winding, and from there back via the three negative diodes of the main rectifier.

On alternators with multifunction regulators, there are no excitation diodes, and the excitation current branches off immediately downstream of the main rectifier. The voltage regulator switches on the excitation current only when the engine is started (this is detected by means of alternator rotation). This prevents battery discharge when the engine is not running.

Alternator output is adjusted by the alternator regulator which varies the excitation current to supply demand from the vehicle electrical system. It is controlled by pulse-width modulation on the basis of constant terminal voltage. This means, it sets a specific pulse duty factor (= duty cycle/period) to achieve the nominal voltage.

The D+ terminal assumes several functions: Firstly, the alternator is pre-excited via battery terminal B+, via the alternator

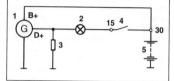

*Symbol for standard regulator with fault indication in the event of break in the excitation circuit*
1 Alternator, 2 Alternator indicator lamp, 3 Resistor R, 4 Ignition and starting switch, 5 Battery.

indicator lamp and terminal D+. Secondly, terminal D+ is at a similar voltage level to B+ after excitation of the alternator. Specific consumer groups can be supplied with power via a relay.

The pre-excitation current determines the self-excitation speed at which initial excitation occurs when the engine is started. This speed is well above the "zero-ampere speed" and, in the case of alternators with excitation diodes, the precise figure is largely determined by the power of the indicator lamp.

The indicator lamp should come on when the ignition is switched before starting (lamp test), and go out as the engine runs up to speed.

*Alternator with multifunction regulator*
Supply connections L, DFM
1 Regulator IC, 2 Casing, 3 Alternator, 4 Vehicle electrical system, 5 Evaluation/monitoring circuits.

## Design variants

### Claw-pole alternators

The very familiar mechanical concept embodied in this alternator type has completely replaced the earlier DC generator as the standard design in automotive applications. Based on equal outputs for both concepts, a claw-pole alternator weighs 50% less, and is also less expensive to manufacture. Large-scale application only became feasible with the availability of compact, powerful, inexpensive, and reliable silicone diodes.

In order to increase output, two systems can be combined within the same housing in certain cases.

The <u>classic alternator design</u> is characterized by the external fan that provides single-flow axial ventilation (compact-diode design).

### Compact alternator (air-cooled)

The compact alternator is a new variant of the claw-pole concept based on double-flow ventilation with two smaller internal fan elements. Cooling air is drawn from the surrounding air in the axial plane, and exits the alternator radially in the vicinity of the stator winding heads, at the drive and collector-ring end shields. The major advantages of the compact alternator are:

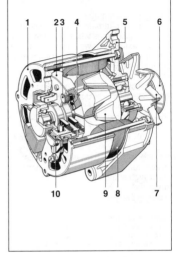

*Claw-pole alternator* (compact-diode design)
1 Collector-ring end shield, 2 Rectifier heat sink, 3 Power diode, 4 Excitation diode, 5 Drive end shield with mounting flanges, 6 Belt pulley, 7 External fan, 8 Stator, 9 Claw-pole rotor, 10 Transistor regulator.

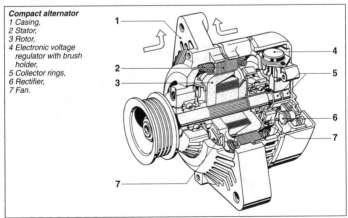

*Compact alternator*
1 Casing,
2 Stator,
3 Rotor,
4 Electronic voltage regulator with brush holder,
5 Collector rings,
6 Rectifier,
7 Fan.

– Higher maximum operating speeds for enhanced efficiency.
– Smaller fan diameters for reduced aerodynamic noise.
– Substantial reduction in magnetic noise.
– Longer carbon-brush life due to smaller collector-ring diameter.

## Salient-pole alternator

Salient-pole alternators are required in special applications which are characterized by extreme power demands (as in tour buses). The rotor is equipped with individual magnetic poles, each of which is provided with its own field winding. This layout allows the stator to be substantially longer (relative to its diameter) than would be possible with a claw-pole alternator. This means that higher outputs can be achieved without increasing diameter. The high idle speeds achievable, however, are lower than with claw-pole designs. Since the excitation currents required for salient-pole alternators are much higher than for claw-pole alternators, and cause considerable energy losses in the governor, the higher temper-

atures mean that the electronic regulator must be mounted in a special housing remote from the alternator.

## Alternators with windingless rotors

The windingless-rotor alternator is a special design variant of the claw-pole alternator where only the claw poles rotate, while the excitation winding remains stationary. Instead of being connected directly to the shaft, one of the pole wheels is held in place by the opposite pole wheel via a nonmagnetic intermediate ring. The magnetic flux must cross two additional air gaps beyond the normal working gap. With this design, the rectifier supplies current to the excitation winding directly through the regulator; sliding contacts are not required. This arrangement obviates the wear factor represented by the collector-ring and carbon-brush assemblies, making it possible to design alternators for a much longer service life (important for construction equipment and railroad generators). The units weigh somewhat more than claw-pole alternators with collector rings due to the fact that additional iron and copper is required to conduct the magnetic flux through two additional air gaps.

**Salient-pole alternator**
*1 Collector-ring end shield, 2 Contact brushes, 3 Excitation winding, 4 Casing, 5 Stator, 6 Drive end shield, 7 Belt pulley, 8 Radial blower, 9 Salient-pole rotor, 10 Collector rings, 11 Power diode, 12 Heat sink, 13 Suppression capacitor, 14 Socket for connecting wires, to governor.*

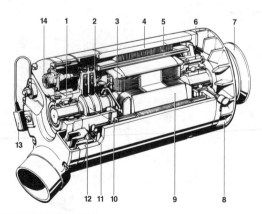

The windingless-rotor design is also designed as a liquid-cooled version (type LIF-B). Engine coolant flows around the complete jacket and rear of the alternator casing. The electronic components are mounted on the drive-end shield.

### Operational limits

#### Cooling
Air-cooled passenger-car alternators are almost always cooled by a flow of air supplied by an integrated or attached radial fan. In certain cases where engine-compartment temperatures are very high, air is drawn in from outside. The dimensions of the cooling arrangement must be adequate to ensure that component temperatures remain below the specified limits under all conceivable operating conditions.

On alternators for heavy-duty vehicles, the entire collector-ring and carbon-brush assembly is usually encapsulated in order to prevent the entry of dust, dirt, and water. Fresh-air induction is almost always beneficial, especially when higher outputs are required. In certain cases, sealed alternators have cooling fins on the outer casing to cool the surface. Other special applications may require the use of sealed alternators with liquid cooling (e.g. oil).

Liquid-cooled alternators with a water jacket around the alternator casing are characterized in particular by:
– No flow noise (–20 dB A)
– Suitable for use in engine compartments with high temperatures
– Integratable in the engine block
– Suitable for fording due to complete encapsulation
– Help to warm up the engine coolant using heat dissipated by the alternator

By contrast to air-cooled alternators, the electrical connections are on the belt-pulley end. If a liquid-cooled alternator is fitted to the engine as a separate unit with its own housing, there must be some means of connecting it to the cooling system (e.g. by means of hoses). A reliable coolant supply must be included in the design during general application-engineering work.

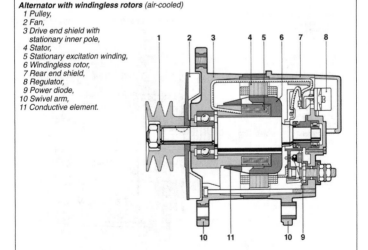

**Alternator with windingless rotors** (air-cooled)
1 Pulley,
2 Fan,
3 Drive end shield with stationary inner pole,
4 Stator,
5 Stationary excitation winding,
6 Windingless rotor,
7 Rear end shield,
8 Regulator,
9 Power diode,
10 Swivel arm,
11 Conductive element.

Installation in the vehicle

Virtually all engine-powered alternators that are driven by standard V-belts are installed on bracket assemblies which allow the belt to be tensioned by pivoting the alternator. If ribbed V-belts are used (poly-grooved belts), the alternator mounting is generally rigid, and belt tension is maintained by a separate mechanism. Larger alternators can be attached directly to the engine in special cradle-shaped mounts. The load imposed by the V-belt is the decisive factor in selecting the rolling bearing dimensions for the alternator drive side. The belt forces are determined by both the geometry of the belt drive and the electrical load requirements of all the other assemblies driven by the belt. Yet another factor is the effective radius of the pulley; larger radii can produce a substantial lever effect between the pulley's load-bearing surface and the drive-side rolling bearings. The stresses from these static factors the dynamic forces associated with torque and speed fluctuations are compounded by another factor that must be considered when dimensioning the rolling bearing and tearing the alternator.

Belt pulleys with freewheel mechanisms allow the alternator shaft to be isolated from crankshaft vibration, thus making the belt drive much smoother for larger alternators with a greater mass moment of inertia.

Drive layout

Although standard V-belts are usually employed to drive the alternator, ribbed V-belts are becoming increasingly more frequent in automotive applications. As this design allows tighter bend radii, smaller alternator pulleys and higher conversion ratios can be achieved. Railroad alternators are operated by helical-gear assemblies driven directly from the axle. It is imperative that special measures be taken to dampen rotational oscillations when direct mechanical drive is used to power the alternator without an intermediate V-belt (e.g. centrally at the crankshaft or via gears).

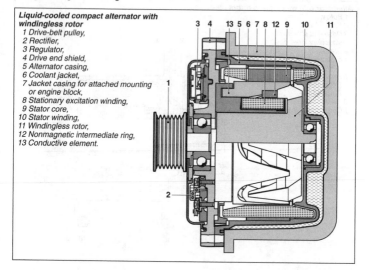

Liquid-cooled compact alternator with windingless rotor
1 Drive-belt pulley,
2 Rectifier,
3 Regulator,
4 Drive end shield,
5 Alternator casing,
6 Coolant jacket,
7 Jacket casing for attached mounting or engine block,
8 Stationary excitation winding,
9 Stator core,
10 Stator winding,
11 Windingless rotor,
12 Nonmagnetic intermediate ring,
13 Conductive element.

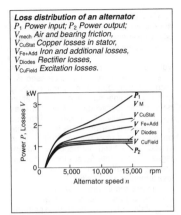

**Loss distribution of an alternator**
$P_1$ Power input; $P_2$ Power output;
$V_{mech}$ Air and bearing friction,
$V_{CuStat}$ Copper losses in stator,
$V_{Fe+Add}$ Iron and additional losses,
$V_{Diodes}$ Rectifier losses,
$V_{CuField}$ Excitation losses.

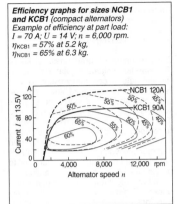

**Efficiency graphs for sizes NCB1
and KCB1** (compact alternators)
Example of efficiency at part load:
$I = 70$ A; $U = 14$ V; $n = 6,000$ rpm.
$\eta_{KCB1} = 57\%$ at 5.2 kg,
$\eta_{NCB1} = 65\%$ at 6.3 kg.

## Efficiency

Losses are an unavoidable byproduct of all processes in which mechanical or kinetic energy is converted into electrical energy. The efficiency rating is the ratio between the power which is supplied to the unit and the actual power output. Iron losses result from hysteresis and eddy currents produced by alternating magnetic fields in the iron of the stator and rotor. Copper losses are produced by resistance in the rotor and stator windings. Their extent is proportional to the power-to-weight ratio, i.e. the ratio of generated electrical power to the mass of the effective components. Mechanical losses include frictional loss in the rolling bearings and at the contact brushes, air resistance encountered by the rotor and, above all, fan resistance which rises dramatically as speed increases.

In regular automotive operation, the alternator operates in the part-load range. Efficiency at medium speeds is then about 50%. The use of a larger (and heavier) alternator allows it to operate in a more favorable part-load efficiency band for the same electrical load. The efficiency gains provided by the larger alternator more than compensate for losses in fuel economy associated with greater weight. However, the higher mass moment of inertia must be taken into consideration.

The alternator is a typical example of an assembly which is in permanent operation, but when reviewing design measures regarding maximum fuel economy, more emphasis should be placed on optimizing its efficiency, rather than on optimizing its mass.

## Noise

The quieter the modern-day vehicle becomes, the more the noise developed by the alternator becomes noticeable. The alternator's noise consists of a magnetic and an aerodynamic component.

The magnetically induced high-pitched noise is audible mainly at low speeds (< 4,000 rpm). It can be attenuated by optimizing the alternator's magnetic circuit, and its oscillation and radiation characteristics.

Aerodynamic noise becomes particularly noticeable at high speeds. It can be reduced by optimizing fan design (e.g. using an asymmetrical fan) and refining air-channel design.

### Alternator (voltage) regulation

Here again, there are two options:
– standard regulator
– multifunction regulator

Each option has different basic purposes. The standard voltage regulator maintains the alternator at constant voltage to counteract the wide range of fluctuations in alternator speed and load. The setpoint value is usually temperature-dependent. The voltage is somewhat higher in winter to compensate for the fact that the battery is more difficult to charge when cold. In summer the voltage regulator maintains vehicle system voltage at a lower level to prevent the battery from overcharging.

Voltage regulators were formerly produced using discrete components. Today they incorporate hybrid or monolithic circuits. When monolithic technology is applied, the control and regulator IC, the power transistor, and the freewheeling diode are all accommodated on a single chip.

Multifunction regulators perform special functions in addition to the basic task of voltage regulation.

The load-response (LR) function is worthy of special mention. It helps to improve the running and exhaust-gas characteristics of the IC engine by means of a limited rate of output increase over time. A distinction is made between load response while the engine is running, and load response when the engine is started (alternator inactive for a specific period after starting).

Voltage regulators with digital interfaces are the response to increased demands for greater mutual compatibility between engine-management and alternator-regulation systems. The interfaces used are chiefly of the bit-synchronous type. Coding is performed by way of signal period instead of signal amplitude, and is stored with a fixed protocol. The advantages for the interface electronics are greater immunity from interference and less temperature sensitivity.

Interface regulators allows a fine-tuning of load-response functions to engine operating state, optimization of torque patterns to reduce fuel consumption, and adjustment of charging voltage to improve the battery charge state.

### Overvoltage protection

The electric strength of alternators and voltage regulators usually suffices to ensure that their semiconductor components will operate reliably when the vehicle battery is operating. Emergency operation without the battery is characterized by extreme voltage peaks. Especially critical is the load-dump phenomenon when the current to major consumers is suddenly

*Function of regulator*
$I_{err}$ Excitation current, $I_m$ Mean excitation current, $T_E$ Duty cycle, $T_A$ Off period, $n_1$ Lower speed, $n_2$ Higher speed.

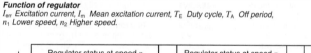

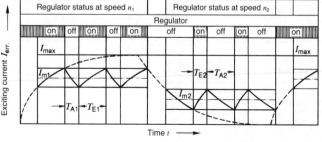

interrupted. Additional measures are therefore necessary to ensure complete reliability in these cases.

There are three options available for protecting against overvoltage:

### Zener diodes

Zener power diodes can be used in the rectifier as an alternative to power diodes, which have a high-blocking capacity. Zener diodes limit the high-energy voltage peaks to levels which are harmless for the alternator or the regulator. In addition, Zener diodes can be used to provide remote protection for other voltage-sensitive equipment in the vehicle electrical system. When using a 14-V alternator, the response voltage of a rectifier fitted with Zener diodes ranges from 25 to 30 V. Compact alternators are all fitted with Zener diodes without exception.

### Alternators and regulators with enhanced electric strength

The semiconductor components in these alternators and regulators have higher electric-strength ratings. Enhanced electric strength only protects the units themselves, but provide no additional protection for other electrical equipment in the system.

### Overvoltage-protection devices

These semiconductors are connected to the alternator's D+ and D- (ground) terminals. The system responds to voltage peaks by short-circuiting the alternator at the excitation winding. Overvoltage protection devices primarily protect the alternator and regulator, and only provide secondary protection to other voltage-sensitive equipment in the electrical system. Overvoltage-protection devices can be combined with other units specially designed to inhibit consequential damage, e.g. if the battery boils off its electrolyte when a regulator malfunctions and remains in the "on" position.

Normally, alternators are not provided with reverse-polarity protection. Reversal of battery polarity (e.g. when using an external battery to start the vehicle) leads to destruction of the alternator diodes and poses a critical threat to the semiconductor components of other assemblies in the vehicle.

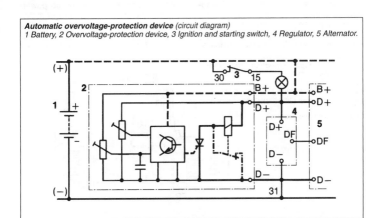

*Automatic **overvoltage-protection device*** *(circuit diagram)*
*1 Battery, 2 Overvoltage-protection device, 3 Ignition and starting switch, 4 Regulator, 5 Alternator.*

# Starting systems

## Requirements

Internal-combustion engines in motor vehicles require start assistance before they can run autonomously. Starting systems consist of the following assemblies:
– DC motor (starter)
– Switchgear and ECUs
– Battery
– Wiring

The starter speed, which is much higher than the engine speed, is matched to the engine speed by means of a suitable gear ratio (between 1/10 and 1/20) arranged between the starter pinion and the engine-flywheel ring gear. A small starter is capable of achieving the required rotational speed for sustained operation of the engine (for spark-ignition (Otto-cycle) engines, between 60 and 100 rpm; for diesel engines, between 80 and 200 rpm).

## Design factors

To achieve the necessary air/fuel (A/F) mixture for spark-ignition (Otto-cycle) engines and the auto-ignition temperature for diesel engines, the starter must drive the internal-combustion engine at a minimum speed (cranking speed). The cranking speed largely depends on the characteristics of the internal-combustion engine (engine type, engine swept volume, number of cylinders, compression, bearing friction, engine oil, fuel-management system, additional loads driven by the engine), and the ambient temperature.

In general, starting torque and starting rotational speed require a gradual increase in starting power as temperatures decline. However, the power supplied by a starter battery falls as temperatures drop because its internal resistance increases. This opposing relationship of electrical load requirements and available power means that the least favorable operating conditions which a starting system must be capable of dealing with is a cold start.

## Starter design and operation

A starter consists of the following assemblies: electric motor, pinion-engaging system, roller-type overrunning clutch, pinion, and possibly reduction gear set. During the start, the starter pinion engages with the ring gear by means of a solenoid switch. The starter is either coupled to the starter pinion directly or by means of a reduction gear set, which reduces the rotational speed of the DC motor ($i \approx 3...6$). The starter pinion drives the internal-combustion engine via the engine flywheel ring gear until the engine can run at sustained operation. After the engine starts, it can acceleration quickly to high rotational speeds. After only several ignitions, the engine accelerates so powerfully that the starter can no longer match its speed. The internal-combustion engine "overruns" the starter and would then accelerate the armature to extremely high

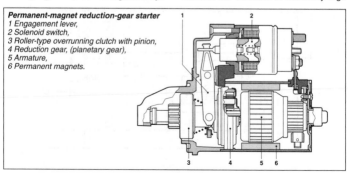

*Permanent-magnet reduction-gear starter*
1 Engagement lever,
2 Solenoid switch,
3 Roller-type overrunning clutch with pinion,
4 Reduction gear, (planetary gear),
5 Armature,
6 Permanent magnets.

speeds if the overrunning clutch installed between the pinion and armature did not cancel the non-positive lock. When the ignition key is released, the starting-motor relay drops out, and the demeshing spring disengages the pinion from the ring gear.

## Electric motor

The magnetic materials available today have allowed the development of starters which are resistant to demagnetization, and have a highly effective magnetic flux to deliver a high starting power. Permanent-magnet excitation of passenger-car starters has now become more or less standard.

The objective is to minimize the weight and dimensions of the starter by reducing the volume of the electric motor. In order to achieve the same starting power at the same time, a higher armature speed is required to compensate for the existing lower armature torque. The torque is adjusted to match the rotation rate of the internal-combustion engine crankshaft by increasing the overall gear ratio of the crankshaft/starter armature. This is achieved with the assistance of an additional gear stage (reduction gear), which is incorporated in the starter. This usually consists of a planetary gear.

Permanently excited reduction-gear starters with a starting power of up to approx. 2.5 kW are generally used in cars today. They have advantages in terms of weight and volume when compared to electrically excited direct-drive versions.

Direct-drive starters and series-wound reduction-gear starters are ideal solutions to produce starting power in the range of 3 kW to 7 kW. Besides direct-drive starters with a series-wound motor, higher starting power can be provided by shunt-wound starters that feature smoother startup and limit the armature no-load speed.

## Pinion-engaging systems

The pinion-engaging drive assembly ensures that the pinion meshes with the ring gear. It consists of a pinion, a roller-type overrunning clutch, a meshing spring, and a solenoid switch.

### Inertia-drive starters

The inertia drive (as employed in lawn mowers, for example) is the simplest form of pinion-engaging system. A helical spline in the shaft slides the overrunning clutch forward when the armature rotates. When the starter is switched on, the unloaded armature begins to rotate freely. The pinion and overrunning clutch do not yet rotate due to their mass moment of inertia, but are pushed along the helical spline. When the pinion meshes with the ring gear, the overrunning clutch begins to transmit the armature torque to the ring gear via the pinion. The starter then begins to crank the internal-combustion engine.

When the internal-combustion engine overruns, the overrunning clutch releases the non-positive connection. The overrunning torque caused by the friction of the overrunning clutch generates an axial

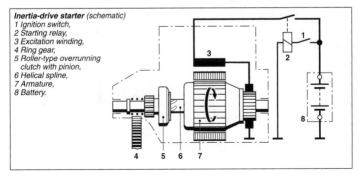

*Inertia-drive starter* (schematic)
1 Ignition switch,
2 Starting relay,
3 Excitation winding,
4 Ring gear,
5 Roller-type overrunning clutch with pinion,
6 Helical spline,
7 Armature,
8 Battery.

force in conjunction with the helical spline, which disengages the pinion from the ring gear. This demeshing operation is assisted by the return spring.

### Pre-engaged-drive starter
The pre-engaged-drive starter has become the worldwide standard. The meshing travel of the pre-engaged-drive starter consists of pinion travel and helical travel. During pinion travel, the solenoid-switch relay armature pushes the pinion toward the ring gear via the engagement lever. If a pinion tooth meshes directly with a tooth space on the ring gear (tooth-gap positioning), the pinion engages as far as the movement of the relay allows.

If the pinion tooth strikes a tooth on the ring gear (tooth-tooth positioning) – this occurs approx. 80% of the time – the relay armature tensions the meshing spring via the engagement lever. When the pinion travel limit generated by the solenoid switch has been reached, the relay-armature contact bridge closes the main starter current, and the starter armature begins to rotate. In the case of tooth-gap positioning, the rotating electric motor screws the pinion fully into the ring gear via the helical spline (helical travel). Starting from a tooth-tooth position, the electric motor turns the pinion in front of the ring gear until a pinion tooth finds a ring-gear gap. The pretensioned meshing spring then pushes the pinion and overrunning clutch forward. The rotating electric motor screws the pinion fully into the ring gear via the helical spline.

When the solenoid winding is de-energized, the return spring pushes the relay armature – and the pinion and overrunning clutch via the engagement lever – back into the rest position. This demeshing operation is assisted by the helical spline when the internal-combustion engine speed overruns the starter speed.

### Sliding-gear starters
The sliding-gear drive switches the starter on in two stages. When the ignition switch is closed, the magnetic force of the solenoid switch moves the starter pinion against the ring gear by means of a fork lever and a helical spline, and meshes it smoothly with the ring gear. At the same time the starter armature starts to function. Smooth meshing is possible as the starter series winding is not yet fully supplied with current during this first switching stage.

The solenoid switch connects the full excitation and armature current in the second switching stage, shortly before the meshing-travel limit of the pinion is reached. The starter now begins to crank the internal-combustion engine via the pinion with integrated overrunning clutch. When the internal-combustion engine starts, the roller-type overrunning clutch comes into effect; when the ignition switch is released, the return spring pushes the pinion back to its initial position. The shunt field (limited idling speed) ensures that the armature comes to a standstill as quickly as possible so that any necessary repeat start can be carried out within a short space of time.

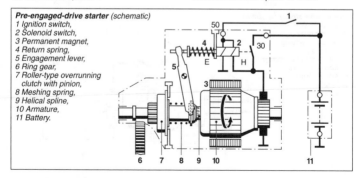

**Pre-engaged-drive starter** *(schematic)*
1 Ignition switch,
2 Solenoid switch,
3 Permanent magnet,
4 Return spring,
5 Engagement lever,
6 Ring gear,
7 Roller-type overrunning clutch with pinion,
8 Meshing spring,
9 Helical spline,
10 Armature,
11 Battery.

## Overrunning clutch types

In all starter designs, the drive torque is transmitted by an overrunning clutch. This overrunning clutch is installed between the starter and the pinion. Its purpose is to drive the pinion while the starter is cranking the internal-combustion engine, and then release the connection between the pinion and drive shaft as soon as the internal-combustion engine is turning faster than the starter. The overrunning clutch therefore prevents the internal-combustion engine from accelerating the starter-motor armature to an excessive speed as it runs up.

### Roller-type overrunning clutch

Pre-engaged-drive starters normally incorporate a roller-type overrunning clutch. The "roller-type overrunning clutch" assembly comprises: driver with clutch shell, roller race, rollers, springs, pinion, pinion shaft with helical spline, and end cap. The roller-type overrunning clutch pushes individual sprung rollers into wedge-shaped pockets.

When the starter armature shaft is driven, the cylindrical rollers are clamped in the constricting roller race and create a non-positive connection between the internal shaft and the driver.

When overrunning takes place, the rollers are released against the force of the compression springs and move into the expanding section of the race. The clamping non-positive force is canceled.

### Multiplate overrunning clutch

The multiplate overrunning clutch is used in large commercial-vehicle starters (torque-dependent coupling). The assembly comprises: driver, outer-plate package, disc spring, clutch race, stop ring, and helical spline. The design of this overrunning clutch is mainly characterized by the individual axially adjustable plates, which transmit the force and are mounted on the clutch race. The clutch race on the drive shaft is also axially adjustable by means of a helical spline. As the load increases, the clutch race is displaced by the helical spline toward the compression and disc springs, and their tension increases accordingly.

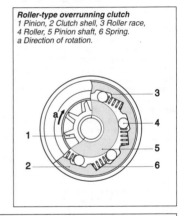

*Roller-type overrunning clutch*
1 Pinion, 2 Clutch shell, 3 Roller race,
4 Roller, 5 Pinion shaft, 6 Spring.
a Direction of rotation.

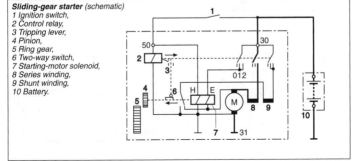

*Sliding-gear starter* (schematic)
1 Ignition switch,
2 Control relay,
3 Tripping lever,
4 Pinion,
5 Ring gear,
6 Two-way switch,
7 Starting-motor solenoid,
8 Series winding,
9 Shunt winding,
10 Battery.

The multiplate overrunning clutch therefore transmits greater torques as the load applied by the starter increases.

If the rotational speed of the starter pinion overruns the speed of the starter armature when the internal-combustion engine starts (overrunning), the plate overrunning clutch, in reverse motion, releases the non-positive force between the starter pinion and starter armature. The clutch plates slip.

Radial-tooth overrunning clutch

The radial-tooth overrunning clutch is also used in large commercial-vehicle starters. It comprises: pinion with spur gear, flyweights, conical compression ring, clutch component with spur gear, springs, and a set of rubber components. The overrunning clutch transfers positive torque by means of a spur gear.

When the overrunning process starts, the internal-combustion engine ring gear drives the pinion, which is connected to the clutch component by a spur gear. Due to the saw-tooth form of the spur gear, the clutch component is pushed inward in the direction of the starter motor onto the helical teeth as the pinion overruns. The outer ring moves axially due to the centripetal force of the flyweights and hold the spur gear open.

## Triggering the starter

### Conventional control

During conventional starts, the driver connects the battery voltage (ignition key in starting position) to the starter relay. The relay current (approx. 30 A for passenger cars to approx. 70 A for commercial vehicles) generates power in the relay. This pushes the pinion toward the engine-flywheel ring gear and activates the starter primary current (200...1,000 A for passenger cars, approx. 2,000 A for commercial vehicles).

The starter is switched off when the ignition key is turned back. The ignition switch opens and interrupts the starter relay voltage.

### Automatic starting systems

The high demands on the latest generation of vehicles with regard to convenience, safety, quality, and low noise levels have resulted in an increase in the use of automatic starting systems.

An automatic starting system differs from a conventional system due to additional components:

One or more ballast relays (see figure 2) as well as hardware and software components (e.g. an engine control unit, see figure 3) to control the starting sequence.

*Multiplate overrunning clutch*
*1 Drive shaft (connected to pinion),*
*2 Compression spring, 3 Driver with outer plates, 4 Inner clutch race with inner plates,*
*5 Helical spline, 6 Drive end (connected to armature).*

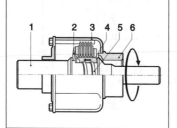

*Radial-tooth overrunning clutch*
*1 Pinion, 2 Flyweight, 3 Spur gear,*
*4 Disengaging ring, 5 Clutch nut, 6 Spring,*
*7 Helical spline, 8 Damper, 9 Bearing sleeve,*
*10 Straight gear.*

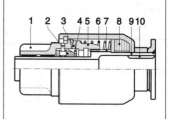

The driver no longer controls the starter relay current directly. Instead, the driver sends a "start message" to the ECU by turning the ignition key. The ECU then performs a safety check before initiating the starting sequence.

The safety check comprises a wide range of options and can verify any of the following:
– Is the driver authorized to start the vehicle (theft-deterrence feature)?
– Is the internal-combustion engine stationary (prevents the pinion from meshing with the moving ring gear)?
– Is the state of charge (in relation to engine temperature) sufficient to carry out the start?
– For automatic transmissions, is the selector lever in neutral or, for on manually shifted transmissions, is the clutch disengaged?

When the check has been completed successfully, the ECU initiates the start. On starting, the starting system compares the engine speed (which the ECU also detects) with a sustained operation speed of the engine (which may also depend on the engine temperature). Once the engine reaches sustained operation speed, the ECU switches the starter off. This always achieves the shortest possible starting time, reduces the perceived noise levels, and lessens starter wear.

This process can also be used as the basis to implement "start-stop" operation. Here, the internal-combustion engine is switched off when the vehicle is not in motion, e.g. at traffic lights, and restarts automatically when required. The results are considerable fuel savings – particularly in city traffic.

A start-stop system requires a higher-level control system to implement the switchoff and restart strategy. A start-stop system requires an electrical energy management system that incorporates battery-charge detection. Measures may also be required to stabilize the vehicle electrical system during the starting phase to avoid unacceptable voltage drops. The control equipment and starting system must therefore be matched. The level and duration of voltage drop must be limited, and the control equipment must also remain functional even if the supply voltage drops significantly.

At the same time, the internal-combustion engine must also be optimized for quick-start response. What is needed is a starter that incorporates service-life prolonging features in order to meet service-life requirements and also guarantee quicker, low-noise starts. The design of the pinion and ring-gear geometry must be optimized to reduce wear and noise emissions.

The drive to reduce fuel consumption and emissions on the one hand, combined with increasing demand for comfort and safety on the other, is leading to the introduction of this type system in motor vehicles. For example, the New European Driving Cycle (NEDC) specifies that idle periods may amount to approx. 28%. The NEDC thus predicts fuel savings of around 4% using a start-stop function.

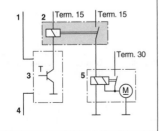

*Automatic starting system* (circuit diagram)
1 Starting signal from driver, 2 Ballast relay, 3 ECU, 4 Park-neutral position/clutch signal, 5 Starter.

# Symbols used in vehicle electrical systems

Standards: DIN 40 900

**General symbols** (selection from circuit diagrams on P. 995 onwards)

| Connections | Mechanical Function | |
|---|---|---|
| Conductor; conductor cross-over, without/with connection  | Switch positions (basic position: solid line)  | Variability/adjustability, not intrinsic (external), general  |
| Conductor; conductor cross-over, without/with connection  | | Variability/adjustability, intrinsic, caused by applied physical variable, linear/non-linear  |
| Mechanical linkage; electrical conductor (laid at later stage)  | | |
| Crossovers (without/with connections) 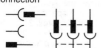 | Manual actuation, actuation by follower (cam), thermal (bimetallic strip) | Variability/adjustability, general  |
| | | **Switches** |
| Connection, general; separable connection (if indication necessary)  | Detent; non-automatic/automatic return in direction of arrow (pushbutton) | Momentary switch, NO/NC contact |
| Plug-in connection; socket; connector; triple plug-in connection | Actuation, general (mech., pneum., hydraul.); piston actuation | Detent switch, NO/NC contact |
| Ground (equipment/vehicle ground) | Actuation by rotational speed $n$, pressure $p$, quantity $Q$, time $t$, temperature $t°$ 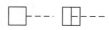 | Changeover contact, non-bridging/bridging |

| Switches | Various components | |
|---|---|---|
| Two-way make contact with neutral position (e.g. turn-signal switch)  | Actuators with one winding  | Resistor  |
| NO/NC contact  | Actuators with two windings acting in same direction  | Potentiometer (with three connections) 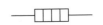 |
| Contact with two makes  | Actuators with two windings acting in opposing directions  | Heating resistor, glow plug, flame plug, heated rear window  |
| Multiple-position switch  | Electrothermal actuator, thermal relay  | Antenna/aerial  |
| Cam-operated switch (e.g. contact breaker)  | Electrothermal actuator, solenoid  | Fuse  |
| Thermostatic switch  | Solenoid valve, closed  | Permanent magnets  |
| Release/trip device | Relay (actuator and switch) example: non-delayed-break NC contact and delayed-break NO contact  | Winding, inductive |

| **Various components** | **Devices in motor vehicle** | |
|---|---|---|
| PTC resistor  | Dotted/dashed line used to delineate or group together associated circuit sections  | Battery  |
| NTC resistor  | Shielded device, dashed line connected to ground  | Plug-and-socket connection  |
| Diode, general, current in direction of triangle tip  | Regulator, general  | Light, headlamp  |
| PNP transistor<br>NPN transistor<br><br>E=Emitter (arrow points in direction of flow<br>C=Collector, positive<br>B=Base (horizontal), negative<br> | Electronic control units  | Horn, fanfare horn  |
| | | Heated rear window (general heating resistor)  |
| Light-emitting diode (LED)  | Indicating instrument, general; voltmeter; clock   | Switch, general; without indicator lamp  |
| Hall generator  | Rotational-speed indicator; temperature indicator; linear-speed indicator    | Switch, general; with indicator lamp  |

## Devices in motor vehicle

| Pressure switch | Spark plug | Motor with blower, fan |
|---|---|---|
|  |  |  |
| Relay, general | Ignition coil | Starter motor with solenoid switch (without/with internal circuitry) |
|  |  |  <br>  |
| Solenoid valve, fuel injector, cold-start valve | Ignition distributor, general | |
|  |  | Wiper motor (one/two wiper speeds) |
| Thermo-time switch | Voltage regulator |  <br>  |
|  |  | |
| Throttle-valve switch | Alternator with regulator (without/with internal circuitry) | |
|  |  | Intermittent-wiper relay <br>  |
| Rotary actuator | | |
|  | | |
| Auxiliary-air valve with electrothermal actuator | Electric fuel pump, motor drive for hydraulic pump | Car radio |
|  |  |  |

## Devices in motor vehicle

| | | |
|---|---|---|
| Speaker  | Piezoelectric sensor  | Linear-speed sensor  |
| Voltage stabilizer  | Resistance sensor  | ABS rotational-speed sensor  |
| Inductive sensor, controlled with reference mark  | Air-flow sensor  | Hall sensor  |
| Turn-signal flasher, pulse generator, intermittent relay  | Air-mass meter  | Converter (rate, voltage)  |
| Lambda oxygen sensor (unheated/heated)   | Flow-quantity sensor, fuel-level sensor  | Inductive sensor  |
| | Temperature switch, temperature sensor  | |

Instrument-cluster device (dashboard)

N1   P2   P3   P4   P5   H1 H2   H3   H4   H5   H6

## Circuit diagrams

A circuit diagram is a drawn representation of electrical devices by means of symbols, and includes illustrations or simplified design drawings as necessary.

A circuit diagram illustrates the relationship between the various devices and shows how they are connected to each other. A circuit diagram may be supplemented by tables, graphs, or descriptions. The type of circuit diagram actually used is determined by its particular purpose (e.g. illustrating the operation of a system), and by the way in which the circuit is represented.

A circuit diagram must comply with the requirements of the appropriate standards, and deviations must be explained.

Current paths should be arranged so that current flow or mechanical action takes place from left to right and/or from top to bottom.

In automotive electrical systems, block diagrams are usually produced with single inputs and outputs, and internal circuitry is omitted.

## Schematic diagrams

### Function

A schematic diagram is the detailed representation of a circuit diagram. By clearly showing the individual current paths, it explains the operation of an electric circuit. In a schematic diagram, the clear presentation of the circuit's operation, which makes the diagram easy to read, must not be interfered with by the presentation of the individual circuit components and their spatial relationships.

### Design

The following schematic diagrams show examples of automotive circuits. They only serve as explanations of the text and cannot be used as the basis for design or installation.

### Examples of identification

**G1** Equipment identification (DIN 40719)
15 Terminal designation (DIN 72 552)
*1* Section designation (DIN 40 719)

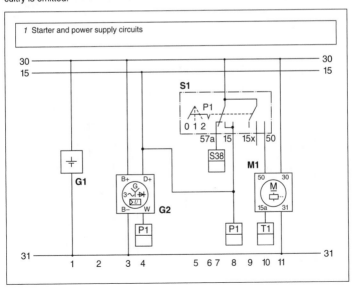

*1* Starter and power supply circuits

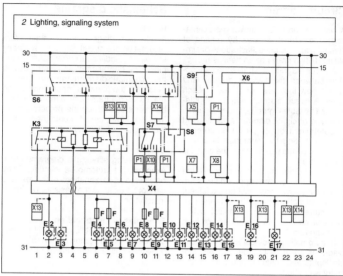

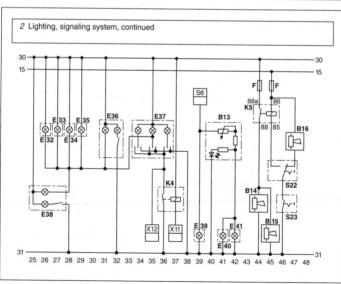

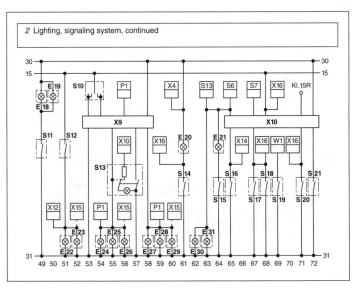

2 Lighting, signaling system, continued

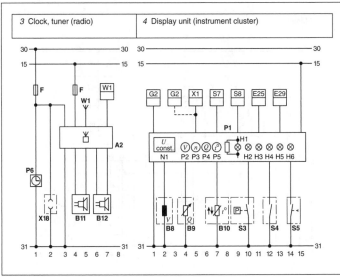

3 Clock, tuner (radio)

4 Display unit (instrument cluster)

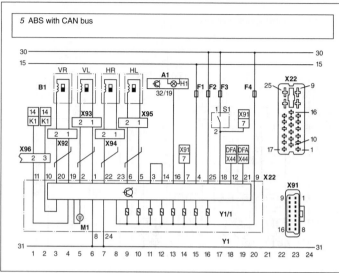

*5* ABS with CAN bus

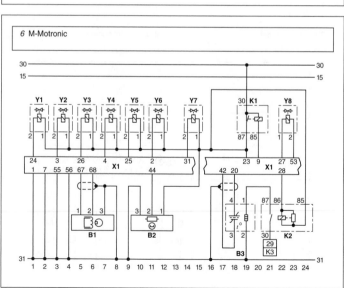

*6* M-Motronic

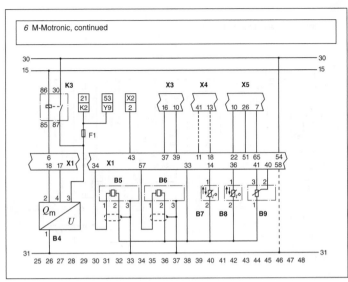

6 M-Motronic, continued

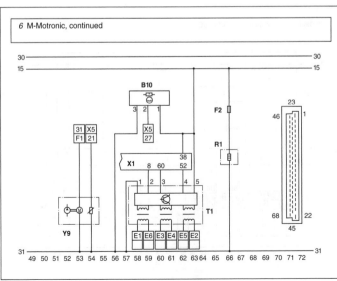

6 M-Motronic, continued

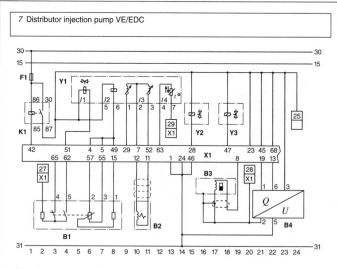

7 Distributor injection pump VE/EDC

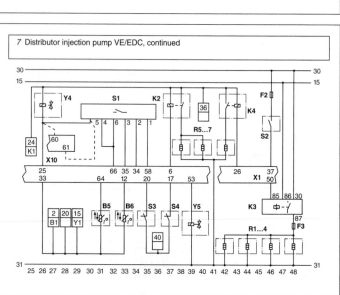

7 Distributor injection pump VE/EDC, continued

**7** Distributor injection pump VE/EDC, continued

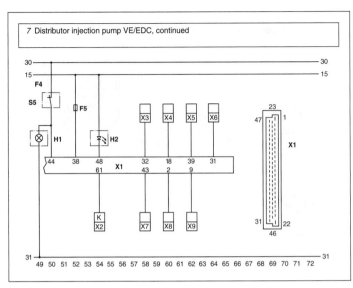

**8** Start-assist system, diesel engine | **9** Car alarm

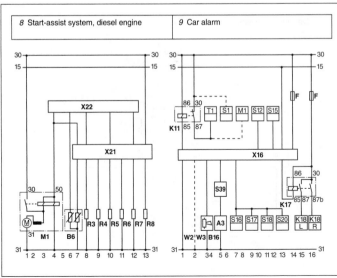

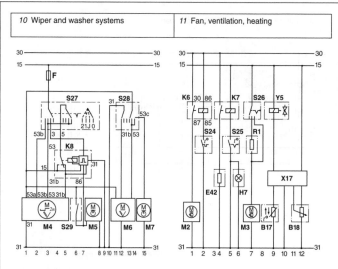

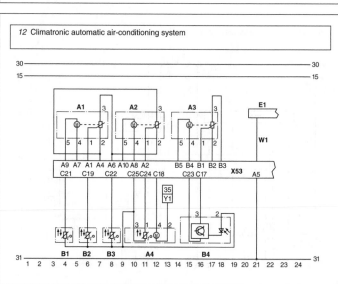

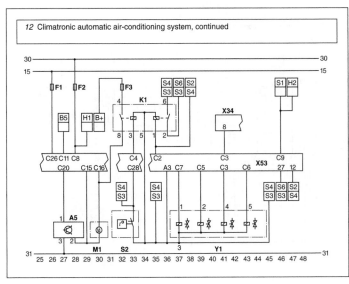

*12* Climatronic automatic air-conditioning system, continued

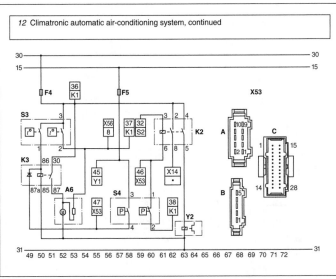

*12* Climatronic automatic air-conditioning system, continued

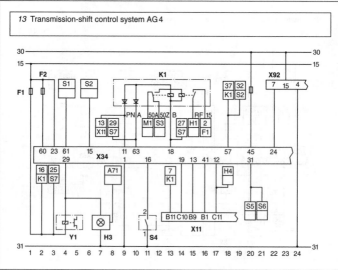

13 Transmission-shift control system AG 4

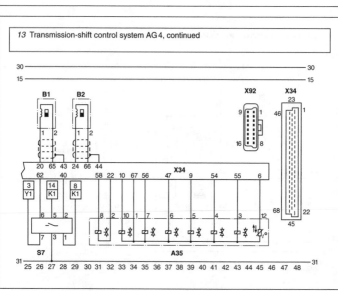

13 Transmission-shift control system AG 4, continued

## Section designation and device identification

Table 1 details all section designations as listed in "Schematic diagrams" (P. 995 onwards). The sections identify defined areas of the schematic diagrams which represent a particular system.

Table 2 lists electrical devices and their identification codes along with the number of the schematic-diagram section in which they appear.

**Table 1 Sections**

| Section | System |
|---------|--------|
| 1 | Starting and power supply |
| 2 | Lighting and signaling system |
| 3 | Clock, tuner (radio) |
| 4 | Display unit (instrument cluster) |
| 5 | ABS with CAN bus |
| 6 | M Motronic |
| 7 | Distributor injection pump VE/EDC |
| 8 | Start-assist system, diesel engine |
| 9 | Car alarm |
| 10 | Wiper and washer systems |
| 11 | Blower, ventilation, heating |
| 12 | Climatronic automatic air-conditioning system |
| 13 | AG4 Transmission-shift control system |

**Table 2 Device identification**

| ID Code | Device | Section |
|---------|--------|---------|
| A1 | Display-unit warning lamp | 5 |
| A1 | Servomotor for center flap | 12 |
| A2 | Tuner (radio) | 3 |
| A2 | Servomotor for dynamic-pressure flap | 12 |
| A3 | Ignition system with knock control (EZK) | 9 |
| A3 | Servomotor for temperature flap | 12 |
| A4 | Instrument-panel temperature sensor and fan | 12 |
| A5 | Blower control unit | 12 |
| A6 | Radiator fan | 12 |
| A35 | Transmission unit, electrical | 13 |
| B1 | Engine-speed/reference-mark sensor | 5, 6 |
| B1 | Accelerator-pedal sensor | 7 |
| B1 | Coolant-temperature sensor | 12 |
| B1, 2 | Vehicle-speed sensor | 6, 13 |

| ID Code | Device | Section |
|---------|--------|---------|
| B2 | Needle-motion sensor | 7 |
| B2 | Ambient-temperature sensor | 12 |
| B2 | Transmission input-shaft speed sensor | 13 |
| B3 | Lambda oxygen sensor | 6 |
| B3 | Engine-speed/reference-mark sensor | 7 |
| B3 | Intake-air temperature sensor | 12 |
| B4 | Air-mass meter | 6, 7 |
| B4 | Photosensor | 12 |
| B5 | Knock sensor 1 | 6 |
| B5, 7 | Coolant-temperature sensor | 6, 7 |
| B6 | Knock sensor 2 | 6 |
| B6 | Fuel-temperature sensor | 7, 8 |
| B8 | Linear-speed sensor | 4 |
| B8 | Intake-air temperature sensor | 6 |
| B9 | Fuel-level sensor | 4 |
| B9 | Throttle-valve potentiometer | 6 |
| B10 | Coolant-temperature sensor | 4 |
| B10 | Cylinder identification sensor | 6 |
| B11, 12 | Speaker | 3 |
| B13 | Dimmer for instrument lighting | 2 |
| B14, 15 | Supertone horn | 2 |
| B16 | Standard horn | 2, 9 |
| B17 | Cabin-temperature sensor | 11 |
| B18 | Setting adjuster | 11 |
| E1 | Climatronic display unit | 12 |
| E2, 3 | Fog warning lamp, L/R | 2 |
| E4, 5 | High-beam headlamp, L/R | 2 |
| E6, 7 | Fog lamp, L/R | 2 |
| E8, 9 | Low-beam headlamp, L/R | 2 |
| E10, 11 | Side-marker lamp, L/R | 2 |
| E12, 13 | License-plate lamp, L/R | 2 |
| E14, 17 | Stop lamp L/R | 2 |
| E15, 16 | Tail lamp L/R | 2 |
| E18 | Trunk-lid lamp, L/R | 2 |
| E19 | Trunk lamp | 2 |
| E20 | Glove-box lamp | 2 |
| E21 | Engine-compartment lamp | 2 |
| E22, 23 | Backup lamp, L/R | 2 |
| E24, 26 | Turn-signal lamp FL/RL | 2 |
| E25, 28 | Auxiliary turn-signal lamp, L/R | 2 |
| E27, 29 | Turn-signal lamp FR/RR | 2 |
| E30, 31 | Ashtray lamp, F/R | 2 |
| E32, 33 | Footwell lamp, FL/RL | 2 |
| E34, 35 | Footwell lamp, FR/RR | 2 |
| E36, 38 | Rear reading lamp, R/L | 2 |
| E37 | Front reading lamp | 2 |
| E39 | Vanity-mirror lamp | 2 |
| E40 | Instrument lighting | 2 |
| E41 | Instrument-panel lighting | 2 |
| E42 | Rear-window heating | 11 |
| F.. | Fuses | |

| ID Code | Device | Section |
|---------|--------|---------|
| G1 | Battery | 1 |
| G2 | Alternator | 1 |
| H1 | Charge-indicator lamp | 4 |
| H1 | ABS warning lamp | 5 |
| H1 | Indicator lamp | 7 |
| H2 | Oil-pressure warning lamp | 4 |
| H2 | Stop lamp | 7 |
| H3 | Handbrake warning lamp | 4 |
| H3 | Selector-lever illumination | 13 |
| H4 | Brake-lining wear warning lamp | 4 |
| H5 | High-beam indicator lamp | 4 |
| H6 | Turn-signal indicator lamp | 4 |
| H7 | Indicator lamp for rear-window heating | 11 |
| K1 | Main relay | 6, 7 |
| K1 | Air-conditioner relay | 12 |
| K1 | Starter locking relay | 13 |
| K2 | Relay for lambda-oxygen sensor heater | 6 |
| K2 | Relay for small heater filament | 7 |
| K2 | Air-conditioner compressor relay | 12 |
| K3 | Side-marker lamp scanning relay | 2 |
| K3 | Electric fuel pump relay | 6 |
| K3 | Glow-plug relay | 7 |
| K3 | Radiator-fan runon relay | 12 |
| K4 | Interior-light control relay | 2 |
| K4 | Heater-filament relay | 7 |
| K5 | Supertone-horn relay | 2 |
| K6 | Engine-fan relay | 11 |
| K7 | Rear-window heating relay | 11 |
| K8 | Intermittent-wiper relay | 10 |
| K11 | Starter locking/immobilizer relay | 9 |
| K17 | Visual alarm relay | 9 |
| M1 | Starter | 1, 8 |
| M1 | Pump motor, hydraulic modulator | 5 |
| M1, 3 | Ventilation-blower motor | 11, 12 |
| M2 | Cooling-fan motor | 11 |
| M4 | Wiper motor | 10 |
| M5 | Windshield-washer motor | 10 |
| M6 | Engine-fan relay | 10 |
| M7 | Rear-window washer motor | 10 |
| N1 | Voltage stabilizer | 4 |
| P1 | Instrument cluster | 4 |
| P2 | Electric speedometer | 4 |
| P3 | Revcounter | 4 |
| P4 | Fuel gauge | 4 |
| P5 | Engine-temperature display | 4 |
| P6 | Clock | 3 |

| ID Code | Device | Section |
|---------|--------|---------|
| R1 | Heating resistor | 6 |
| R1..4 | Glow plugs | 7 |
| R1 | Blower resistor | 11 |
| R5..7 | Auxiliary heating (manual transmission) | 7 |
| R3..8 | Sheathed-element glow plugs | 8 |
| S1 | Ignition switch | 1 |
| S1 | Stop-lamp switch | 5 |
| S1 | Operator unit for cruise control | 7 |
| S1 | Light switch | 12 |
| S2 | Air-conditioner switch | 7 |
| S2 | Evaporator thermostatic switch | 12 |
| S3 | Oil-pressure switch | 4 |
| S3 | Brake-pedal switch | 7 |
| S3 | Radiator-fan thermostatic switch | 12 |
| S4 | Handbrake switch | 4 |
| S4 | Clutch-pedal switch | 7 |
| S4 | Air-conditioner pressure switch | 12 |
| S4 | Kickdown switch | 13 |
| S5 | Brake-lining wear detector contact | 4 |
| S5 | Stop-lamp switch | 7 |
| S6 | Light switch | 2 |
| S7 | Fog-lamp switch | 2 |
| S7 | Multifunction switch | 13 |
| S8 | Dipswitch | 2 |
| S9 | Stop-lamp switch | 2 |
| S10 | Turn-signal switch | 2 |
| S11 | Switch for trunk-lid lamps | 2 |
| S12 | Switch for backup lamps | 2 |
| S13 | Hazard-warning and turn-signal system switch | 2 |
| S14 | Switch for glove-box lamp | 2 |
| S15 | Switch for engine-compartment lamp | 2 |
| S16...18 | Door position switch, FL, RR, RL | 2 |
| S19 | Impact switch | 2 |
| S20 | Door position switch, FR | 2 |
| S21 | Door-handle switch | 2 |
| S22 | Horn changeover switch | 2 |
| S23 | Horn button | 2 |
| S24 | Thermostatic switch | 11 |
| S25 | Rear-window heating switch | 11 |
| S26 | Blower switch | 11 |
| S27 | Wiper switch | 10 |
| S28 | Rear-window wiper/washer switch | 10 |
| S29 | Washer switch | 10 |
| S39 | Alarm-system encoding switch | 9 |
| T1 | Ignition coil | 6 |
| W1 | Vehicle antenna | 3 |

| ID Code | Device | Section |
|---------|--------|---------|
| **W1** | Connector for 16-core ribbon cable | 12 |
| **W2, 3** | Encoding wire | 9 |
| **X1** | ECU connector for Motronic/VE/EDC | 6, 7 |
| **X3** | ECU connector for air conditioner | 6 |
| **X4** | Connector, lamp-test module | 2 |
| **X4** | ECU connector for transmission-shift control | 6 |
| **X5** | Connector for instrument cluster | 6 |
| **X6** | Plug, check control | 2 |
| **X9** | Plug-in base, hazard-warning and turn-signal relay | 2 |
| **X10** | Connector for central bodyshell electronics basic module | 2, 7 |
| **X11** | ECU connector for engine management | 13 |
| **X16** | ECU connector for alarm system | 9 |
| **X17** | ECU connector for air conditioner/heater control | 11 |

| ID Code | Device | Section |
|---------|--------|---------|
| **X18** | Diagnosis socket | 3 |
| **X21** | Connector for glow-plug control unit | 8 |
| **X22** | ECU connector for ABS/ABD[1] | 5 |
| **X22** | Diagnosis socket | 8 |
| **X34** | ECU connector for transmission-shift control | 12, 13 |
| **X44** | Navigation-system connector | 5 |
| **X53** | Connector for automatic air-conditioning system | 12 |
| **X91, 92** | Diagnosis socket | 5, 13 |
| **Y1** | Hydraulic modulator | 5 |
| **Y1** | Fuel injector 1 | 6, 7 |
| **Y1** | Valve block | 12 |
| **Y1** | Shift-lock solenoid | 13 |
| **Y2** | Air-conditioning output control | 7 |
| **Y2** | Air-conditioner compressor solenoid-operated coupling | 12 |
| **Y2..5** | Fuel injectors 2..5 | 6, 7 |
| **Y5** | Hot-water valve | 11 |
| **Y6** | Fuel injector 6 | 6 |
| **Y7** | Canister-purge valve | 6 |
| **Y8** | Idle actuator | 6 |
| **Y9** | Electric fuel pump | 6 |

[1] ABS = Antilock Braking System
ABD = Automatic Braking Differential

## Wiring diagram: Detached representation

In the detached method of representation, the continuous connecting lines between the individual devices are omitted. The individual devices are represented by squares, rectangles, circles, symbols, or illustrations, and designated in accordance with DIN 40 719 Part 2. The terminal designation of the device is also indicated. Each outgoing conductor from a device receives a code containing the terminal designation of the destination device as well as the device designation. If necessary, the wire color code is also given.

**Example: Alternator**
a) Device designation (code letter and codenumber),
b) Terminal designation on device,
c) Device to ground,
d) Destination, (code letter and code number, terminal designation, wire color code).

Device diagram    Destination designation

D+ o— H1/sw
B+ o— G2:+/rt
B– ●—|
sw = black
rt = red

G1

a          b   c   d

## Terminal designations

The purpose of the terminal-designation system for automotive electrical systems specified by DIN 72 552 is to allow easy and correct connection of the wires to the various devices in the event of repairs and equipment replacement. The terminal designations do not identify the wires because devices with different terminal designations can be connected at the two ends of each wire. For this reason, the terminal designations need not be written on the wires. In addition to the terminal designations listed, designations according to DIN VDE standards may also be used on electrical machines.

Multiple connectors, for which the number of terminal designations as per DIN 72 552 no longer suffice, are numbered by consecutive numbers or letters whose function assignment is not specified by standards.

### Terminal designations: Examples

| Term. | Definition |
|---|---|
| | **Ignition coil, ignition distributor** |
| 1 | Low voltage |
| | Ignition distributor with two separate circuits |
| 1a | to contact breaker I |
| 1b | to contact breaker II |
| | Ignition coil, ignition distributor |
| 4 | High voltage |
| | Ignition distributor with two separate circuits |
| 4a | from ignition coil I, terminal 4 |
| 4b | from ignition coil II, terminal 4 |
| 15 | Switched (+) downstream of battery (output of ignition/starting switch) |
| 15a | Output on series resistor to ignition coil and to starter motor |
| | **Glow-plug and starter switch** |
| 17 | Start |
| 19 | Preheat |
| | **Battery** |
| 30 | Input from battery positive (direct) |
| | Battery changeover 12/24 V |
| 30a | Input from battery II positive |
| | Return from battery |
| 31 | Negative or ground (direct) |
| | Return to battery |
| 31b | Negative or ground via switch or relay (switched negative) |
| | Battery changeover relay 12/24 V |
| 31a | Return to battery II negative |
| 31c | Return to battery I negative |
| | **Electric motors** |
| 32 | Return line [1] |
| 33 | Main terminal [1] |

| Term. | Definition |
|---|---|
| 33a | Self-parking switchoff |
| 33b | Shunt field |
| 33f | For second lower-speed level |
| 33g | For third lower-speed level |
| 33h | For fourth lower-speed level |
| 33L | Counterclockwise rotation |
| 33R | Clockwise rotation |
| | **Starters** |
| 45 | Separate starter relay, output; starter, input (primary current) |
| | Two-starter parallel operation |
| | Starting relay for engagement current |
| 45a | Output, starter I, Input, starters I and II |
| 45b | Output, starter II |
| 48 | Terminal on starter and on start-repeating relay for monitoring starting procedure |
| | **Turn-signal flashers (pulse generators)** |
| 49 | Input |
| 49a | Output |
| 49b | Output, second flasher circuit |
| 49c | Output, third flasher circuit |
| | **Starters** |
| 50 | Starter control (direct) |
| | Battery changeover relay |
| 50a | Output for starter control |
| | Starter control |
| 50b | For parallel operation of two starters with sequential control |
| | Starting relay for sequential control of engagement current during parallel operation of two starters |
| 50c | Input to starting relay for starter I |

[1] Polarity reversal terminal 32/33 possible

| Term. | Definition |
|-------|------------|
| 50d | Input to starting relay for starter II |
| | Start-locking relay |
| 50e | Input |
| 50f | Output |
| | Start-repeating relay |
| 50g | Input |
| 50h | Output |
| | **Wiper motors** |
| 53 | Wiper motor, input (+) |
| 53a | Wiper (+), self-parking |
| 53b | Wiper (shunt winding) |
| 53c | Electric windshield-washer pump |
| 53e | Wiper (brake winding) |
| 53i | Wiper motor with permanent magnet and third brush (for higher speed) |
| | **Lighting** |
| 55 | Fog lamp |
| 56 | Headlamp |
| 56a | High beam and high-beam indicator |
| 56b | Low beam |
| 56d | Headlamp-flasher contact |
| 57a | Parking lamp |
| 57L | Parking lamp, left |
| 57R | Parking lamp, right |
| 58 | Side-marker lamps, tail lamps, license-plate lamps and instrument-panel lamps |
| 58L | ditto, left |
| 58R | ditto, right |
| | **Alternators and voltage regulators** |
| 61 | Alternator charge-indicator lamp |
| B+ | Battery positive |
| B– | Battery negative |
| D+ | DC generator positive |
| D– | DC generator negative |
| DF | DC generator field |
| DF1 | DC generator field 1 |
| DF2 | DC generator field 2 |
| U,V,W | Alternator terminals |
| | **Audio systems** |
| 75 | Tuner (radio), cigarette lighter |
| 76 | Loudspeakers |
| | **Switches** |
| | NC/changeover switch |
| 81 | Input |
| 81a | 1st output, NC switch side |
| 81b | 2nd output, NC switch side |
| | NO switch |
| 82 | Input |
| 82a | 1st output |

| Term. | Definition |
|-------|------------|
| 82b | 2nd output |
| 82z | 1st input |
| 82y | 2nd input |
| | Multi-position switch |
| 83 | Input |
| 83a | Output, position 1 |
| 83b | Output, position 2 |
| 83L | Output, left position |
| 83R | Output, right position |
| | **Current relays** |
| 84 | Input, actuator and relay contact |
| 84a | Output, actuator |
| 84b | Output, relay contact |
| | **Switching relays** |
| 85 | Output, actuator (winding end negative or ground) |
| 86 | Input, actuator (winding start) |
| 86a | Winding start or 1st winding |
| 86b | Winding tap or 2nd winding |
| | Relay contact for break (NC) and changeover contacts: |
| 87 | Input |
| 87a | 1st output (NC switch side) |
| 87b | 2nd output |
| 87c | 3rd output |
| 87z | 1st input |
| 87y | 2nd input |
| 87x | 3rd input |
| | Relay contact for make (NO) contact: |
| 88 | Input |
| | Relay contact for make (NO) and changeover contacts (NO side): |
| 88a | 1st output |
| 88b | 2nd output |
| 88c | 3rd output |
| | Relay contact for make (NO) contact |
| 88z | 1st input |
| 88y | 2nd input |
| 88x | 3rd input |
| | **Turn-signal indicators** (turn-signal flashers) |
| C | Indicator lamp 1 |
| C0 | Main terminal for monitoring circuits separate from flasher |
| C2 | Indicator lamp 2 |
| C3 | Indicator lamp 3 (e.g. when towing two trailers) |
| L | Turn-signal lamps, left |
| R | Turn-signal lamps, right |

## Assembled-representation diagrams

For troubleshooting on complex and extensively networked systems with self-diagnosis function, Bosch has developed system-specific schematic diagrams. For other systems on a wide variety of vehicles, Bosch provides the assembled-representation diagrams on a "P" CD-ROM. They are fully integrated in ESI, the Electronic Service Information system from Bosch. This provides automotive repair shops with a useful tool for locating faults or wiring retrofit equipment. An assembled-representation diagram is shown on the opposite page.

In contrast with other schematic diagrams, the assembled-representation diagrams use U.S. symbols that are supplemented by additional descriptions (see figure below). Those include component codes, such as "A28" (theft-deterrence system) that are explained in Table 1, and wire color codes (explained in Table 2). The two tables are available on the "P" CD-ROM.

**Table 1.**
**Explanation of component codes.**

| Code | Description |
|------|-------------|
| A1865 | Electrically adjustable seat system |
| A28 | Theft-deterrence system |
| A750 | Fuse/relay box |
| F53 | Fuse C |
| F70 | Fuse A |
| M334 | Fuel-supply pump |
| S1178 | Warning-buzzer switch |
| Y157 | Vacuum actuator |
| Y360 | Actuator, front right door |
| Y361 | Actuator, front left door |
| Y364 | Actuator, rear right door |
| Y365 | Actuator, rear left door |
| Y366 | Actuator, fuel filler flap |
| Y367 | Actuator, trunk lid/tailgate |

**Table 2.**
**Explanation of wire color codes.**

| Code | Description |
|------|-------------|
| BLK | Black |
| BLU | Blue |
| BRN | Brown |
| CLR | Clear |
| DKBLU | Dark blue |
| DKGRN | Dark green |
| GRN | Green |
| GRY | Gray |
| LTBLU | Light blue |
| LTGRN | Light green |
| NCA | Color not known |
| ORG | Orange |
| PNK | Pink |
| PPL | Purple |
| RED | Red |
| TAN | Tan |
| VIO | Violet |
| WHT | White |
| YEL | Yellow |

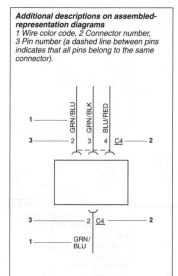

*Additional descriptions on assembled-representation diagrams*
*1 Wire color code, 2 Connector number, 3 Pin number (a dashed line between pins indicates that all pins belong to the same connector).*

*Assembled-representation diagram of a door locking system* (example)

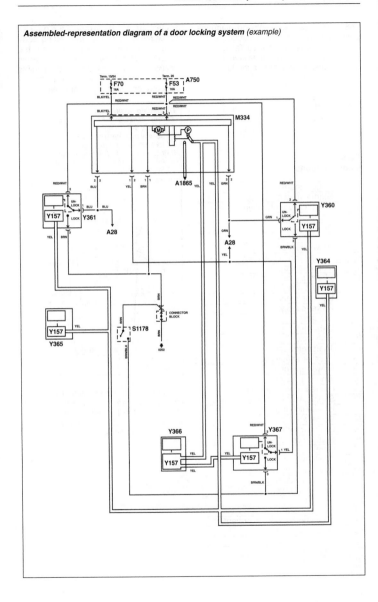

The assembled-representation diagrams are subdivided into system circuits and, if applicable, subsystems (see Table 3). As with other systems in ESI, system circuits are also allocated to one of the four vehicle assemblies:
– Engine
– Bodyshell
– Suspension
– Drivetrain

**Table 3.**
**System circuits**

| | |
|---|---|
| 1 | Engine management |
| 2 | Starting/charging |
| 3 | Air conditioner/heating (HVAC) |
| 4 | Radiator blower |
| 5 | ABS |
| 6 | Cruise control |
| 7 | Power windows |
| 8 | Central locking system |
| 9 | Instrument panel |
| 10 | Washer/wiper system |
| 11 | Headlamps |
| 12 | Exterior lights |
| 13 | Power supply |
| 14 | Grounding |
| 15 | Data wire |
| 16 | Shift lock |
| 17 | Theft deterrence |
| 18 | Passive-safety systems |
| 19 | Power antenna |
| 20 | Warning system |
| 21 | Heated windshield/mirrors |
| 22 | Supplementary safety systems |
| 23 | Interior lighting |
| 24 | Power steering |
| 25 | Mirror adjuster |
| 26 | Soft-top controls |
| 27 | Horn |
| 28 | Trunk, tailgate |
| 29 | Seat adjustment |
| 30 | Electronic damping |
| 31 | Cigarette lighter, socket |
| 32 | Navigation |
| 33 | Transmission |
| 34 | Active bodyshell components |
| 35 | Suspension control |
| 36 | Cellular phone |
| 37 | Radio tuner/sound system |
| 38 | Immobilizer |

It is important to be aware of the grounding points, particularly when fitting additional accessories. For this reason, the "P" CD-ROM includes the vehicle-specific location diagram for the grounding points (see figure below) in addition to the assembled-representation diagrams.

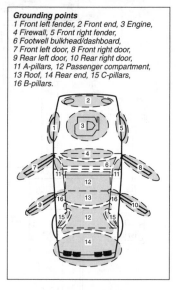

**Grounding points**
1 Front left fender, 2 Front end, 3 Engine,
4 Firewall, 5 Front right fender,
6 Footwell bulkhead/dashboard,
7 Front left door, 8 Front right door,
9 Rear left door, 10 Rear right door,
11 A-pillars, 12 Passenger compartment,
13 Roof, 14 Rear end, 15 C-pillars,
16 B-pillars.

The assembled-representation diagrams use U.S. diagram symbols which are different from the DIN/IEC symbols. A selection of the U.S. diagram symbols is shown on the opposite page.

*Selection of U.S. diagram symbols*

| Symbol | Description |
|--------|-------------|
| | Relay |
| | Normally closed contact |
| | Normally open contact |
| | Two-way switch with zero position |
| | Fuse |
| | Power fuse |
| | LED (light-emitting diode) |
| | Incandescent lamp (bulb) |
| | Resistor |
| | Plug, screw or soldered connection |
| | Component with fixed wiring harness |
| | Connection box with ground terminal |
| | Ground cable |
| | Line connection |
| | Dotted line: indicates a single connecting point |
| | Circuit is continued in another circuit diagram |
| | Circuit is continued at another point. Identical letters indicate the connecting point |
| | The entire component is illustrated |
| | Only the part of the component relevant to the system is illustrated |
| | Potentiometer |
| | Motor |
| | Coil |

## Conductor dimensions

### Quantities and units

| Symbol | | Unit |
|---|---|---|
| $A$ | Conductor cross-section | mm² |
| $I$ | Electric current | A |
| $l$ | Conductor length | m |
| $P$ | Electrical load requirements | W |
| $R$ | Resistance (ohmic) (loads) | Ω |
| $S$ | Current density of conductor | A/mm² |
| $U_N$ | Nominal voltage | V |
| $U_{vl}$ | Permissible voltage drop along insulated wire | V |
| $U_{vg}$ | Permissible voltage drop across complete circuit | V |
| $\varrho$ | Resistivity | Ω · mm²/m |

### Calculations

In determining the conductor cross-section, allowance must be made for voltage drop and the effect of elevated temperatures.

1. Determine the current $I$ of load

$$I = P/U_N = U_N/R$$

2. Calculate conductor cross-sectional area $A$ using parameters for $U_{vl}$ given in Table 2 (for copper $\varrho = 0.0185$ Ω · mm²/m).

$$A = I \cdot \varrho \, l/U_{vl}$$

3. Round up the value for $A$ to the next larger conductor cross-section in accordance with Table 1.

Individual conductors with a cross-sectional area of less than 1 mm² are not recommended due to their low mechanical strength.

4. Calculate the actual voltage drop $U_{vl}$

$$U_{vl} = I \cdot \varrho \, l/A \text{ and}$$

5. Check current density $S$ to ensure thermal stability (for short-duty operation $S < 30$ A/mm², see Table 1 for nominal conductor cross-sectional areas).

$$S = I/A$$

### Table 1.1. Electrical copper conductor for motor vehicles
Single-core, untinned, PVC-insulated conductor with normal wall thickness, FLY type

| Nominal cross-sectional area mm² | Approx. number of individual strands[1] | Maximum resistance per meter[1] at +20 °C mΩ/m | Maximum conductor wire diameter[1] mm | Nominal wall thickness of insulation[1] mm | Maximum diameter external wire[1] mm |
|---|---|---|---|---|---|
| 0.5 | 16 | 37.1 | 1.1 | 0.6 | 2.3 |
| 0.75 | 24 | 24.7 | 1.3 | 0.6 | 2.5 |
| 1 | 32 | 18.5 | 1.5 | 0.6 | 2.7 |
| 1.5 | 30 | 12.7 | 1.8 | 0.6 | 3.0 |
| 2.5 | 50 | 7.60 | 2.2 | 0.7 | 3.6 |
| 4 | 56 | 4.71 | 2.8 | 0.8 | 4.4 |
| 6 | 84 | 3.14 | 3.4 | 0.8 | 5.03 |
| 10 | 80 | 1.82 | 4.5 | 1.0 | 6.5 |
| 16 | 126 | 1.16 | 6.3 | 1.0 | 8.3 |
| 25 | 196 | 0.743 | 7.8 | 1.3 | 10.4 |
| 35 | 276 | 0.527 | 9.0 | 1.3 | 11.6 |
| 50 | 396 | 0.368 | 10.5 | 1.5 | 13.5 |
| 70 | 360 | 0.259 | 12.5 | 1.5 | 15.5 |
| 95 | 475 | 0.196 | 14.8 | 1.6 | 18.0 |
| 120 | 608 | 0.153 | 16.5 | 1.6 | 19.7 |

[1] According to DIN ISO 6722, Part 3.

Supply lines are normally FLY-type PVC cables with normal wall thickness, or FLRY type with reduced wall thickness. These can be used in applications at temperatures of up to +105 °C. FLRY conductors are mainly used up to 2.5 mm² and FLY conductors mainly for over 2.5 mm².

The design of FLY conductors is detailed in Table 1.1., and the design of FLRY conductors is detailed in Table 1.2. (see also figure on right).

In most new vehicles, with the exception of the starter, most electrical equipment is fused.

Starter lines cannot be protected using conventional fuses due to the current curves of the starter. Starter lines are therefore either unfused, or are de-energized by a pyrotechnical disconnector in the event of a crash.

In addition, the starter cable requires a special design because the voltage drop across the line has a much greater impact on the cold-starting characteristics of the engine with respect to anticipated peak/continuous current than the normal design.

All other electrical equipment is protected by fuses or, if they are fitted with electronic triggers, they are protected electronically.

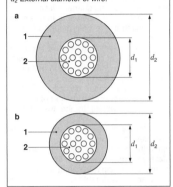

*Comparison of wire cross-sections for automotive electrical copper conductors*
a) FLY type with normal wall thickness,
b) FLRY type with reduced wall thickness.
1 Insulation,
2 Conductor with individual strands.
$d_1$ Wire diameter,
$d_2$ External diameter of wire.

The type of protection must be taken into consideration when dimensioning standard supply lines.

For fuses, the maximum continuous current of the electrical equipment should be less than 0.8 times the rated current of the fuse.

**Table 1.2. Electrical copper conductors for motor vehicles**
Single-core, untinned, PVC-insulated conductor with reduced wall thickness, FLRY type

| Nominal cross-sectional area mm² | Approx. number of individual strands[2] | Maximum resistance per meter[2] at +20 °C mΩ/m | Maximum conductor wire diameter[2] mm | Nominal wall thickness of insulation[2] mm | Maximum external diameter of insulated wire[2] mm |
|---|---|---|---|---|---|
| 0.35 | 12 | 52 | 0.9 | 0.25 | 1.4 |
| 0.5 | 16 | 37.1 | 1 | 0.3 | 1.6 |
| 0.75 | 24 | 24.7 | 1.2 | 0.3 | 1.9 |
| 1 | 32 | 18.5 | 1.35 | 0.3 | 2.1 |
| 1.5 | 30 | 12.7 | 1.7 | 0.3 | 2.4 |
| 2.5 | 50 | 7.6 | 2.2 | 0.35 | 3.0 |
| 4 | 56 | 4.7 | 2.75 | 0.4 | 3.7 |
| 6 | 84 | 3.1 | 3.3 | 0.4 | 4.3 |

[2] According to DIN ISO 6722, Part 4.

Table 2 provides typical protection values for standard PVC lines.

The peak current should not exceed the rated current of the fuse in order to avoid premature triggering – or possible aging – of the fuse. If this is the case, however, the duration of the maximum potential peak current must be well below the characteristic triggering characteristic or tolerance band of the fuse used. In this situation, testing is the only means of determining the level of safety.

For electronically protected lines, the dimensioning of supply lines is much simpler. They allow features such as current limitation, specific triggering characteristics, and short-circuit detection. This results in greater approximation of continuous current values to the fuse ratings listed in Table 2.

Factors that also have an impact on fuse design or conductor dimensions include the contact systems selected, special layout requirements in the vehicle, or combined routing with supply lines. These can place considerable restrictions on the current-carrying capacity which must be verified in each individual case.

In addition to the current-carrying capacity, the maximum voltage drop across the line is also important. Table 3 lists some recommended figures. In many cases, however, precise specifications by the component manufacturers are re-quired in order to ensure safe operation. The voltage drop across the overall electric circuit is much higher, particularly where high-resistance power semiconductors are used instead of relays.

All information is provided for guidance and recommendation only. In-house standards may well vary from one automotive manufacturer to another. In every case, the in-house standards of a particular automotive manufacturer must be observed.

***Current vs. time characteristics***
*The current vs. time characteristic of a line must be above the characteristic of a fuse installed upstream and below the equipment current draw.*
*1 Fuse characteristic (with dispersion range),*
*2 Line characteristic.*

**Table 2. Typical protection values for fuses**
These apply to untinned, PVC-insulated, single-core FLY-type and FLRY-type conductors with a maximum continuous temperature resistance of +105 °C at a maximum ambient temperature of +70 °C.

| Conductor cross-section mm² | Fuse rating A | Maximum continuous current A |
|---|---|---|
| 0.35 | 5 | 4 |
| 0.5 | 7.5 | 6 |
| 0.75 | 10 | 8 |
| 1 | 15 | 12 |
| 1.5 | 20 | 16 |
| 2.5 | 30 | 24 |
| 4 | 40 | 32 |
| 6 | 50 | 40 |
| 10 | 70 | 56 |
| 16 | 100 | 80 |
| 25 | 125 | 100 |
| 35 | 150 | 120 |
| 50 | 200 | 160 |
| 70 | 250 | 200 |

The figures given for $U_{vl}$ in Table 3 are used to calculate the dimensions of the positive line. The voltage drop across the ground return is not taken into account. In the case of insulated ground cables, the total cable length in both directions should normally be used.

The $U_{vg}$ figures given in the table are test values and cannot be used for conductor-size calculations because they also include the contact resistance of switches, fuses, etc.

**Notes**

1 *In special cases where the main starter line is very long and the minimum starting temperature has been reduced, the $U_{vl}$ figure may be exceeded.*
2 *In cases where the starter return line has been insulated, the voltage drop across the return line should not exceed the voltage drop across the supply line – maximum values are 4% of the nominal voltage in each case, i.e. a total of 8%.*
3 *The $U_{vl}$ figures apply to solenoid-switch temperatures from 50 °C to 80 °C.*
4 *Allowance may also have to made for the line upstream of the ignition/starting switch.*

**Table 3. Recommended max. voltage drop.**

| Type of conductor | Voltage drop across positive conductor $U_{vl}$ | | Voltage drop across complete electric circuit $U_{vg}$ | | Remarks |
|---|---|---|---|---|---|
| Nominal voltage $U_N$ | 12 V | 24 V | 12 V | 24 V | |
| **Lighting wires** From light switch terminal 30 to bulbs < 15 W to trailer socket From trailer socket to lights | 0.1 V | 0.1 V | 0.6 V | 0.6 V | Current at rated voltage and rated power |
| From light switch terminal 30 to bulbs > 15 W to trailer socket | 0.5 V | 0.5 V | 0.9 V | 0.9 V | |
| From light switch terminal 30 to headlamps | 0.3 V | 0.3 V | 0.6 V | 0.6 V | |
| **Charging cable** From 3-phase alternator terminal B + to battery | 0.4 V | 0.8 V | — | — | Current at rated voltage and rated power |
| **Starter power cable** | 0.5 V | 1.0 V | — | — | Starter short-circuit current at + 20 °C (Notes 1 and 2) |
| **Starter control cable** From ignition/starting switch to starter terminal 50 Solenoid switch with simple winding Solenoid switch with pull-in and hold-in windings | 1.4 V 1.5 V | 2.0 V 2.2 V | 1.7 V 1.9 V | 2.5 V 2.8 V | Maximum control current (Notes 3 and 4) |
| **Other control cables** From switch to relay, horn, etc. | 0.5 V | 1.0 V | 1.5 V | 2.0 V | Current at rated voltage |

# Connectors

## Function and requirements

Electrical connectors must provide a reliable electrical connection between different system components, and thereby ensure safe and reliable operation of the systems concerned under all operating conditions. They are designed to withstand the various stresses to which they will be subjected during the service life of the vehicle. Examples of such stresses are:
- vibration
- temperature fluctuation
- extreme temperatures
- humidity and splash water
- corrosive fluids and gases
- micro-movement between contacts resulting from fretting corrosion

Such stresses can increase contact resistance and even cause complete loss of conduction. Insulation resistance can also decrease, thereby causing short-circuits between adjacent conductors.

Electrical connectors, therefore, must have the following characteristics:
- low contact resistance between current-carrying components
- high insulation strength between current-carrying components with different electrical potentials
- high sealing capabilities against water, humidity and saline spray

In addition to their physical properties, connectors must also satisfy further requirements specific to their particular area of application such as:
- simple, foolproof connection/disconnection in vehicle assembly/servicing situations, reliable polarity-reversal protection
- secure, perceptible locking action, simple disconnection
- toughness and suitability for automated wiring-harness manufacture and transport

## Design and types

There is a range of design series spanning the variety of applications for Bosch electrical connectors. The various designs incorporate the types of contact specifically suited to the conditions in which they are used. Below are examples of two types of contact and their characteristics.

### Bosch micro-contact

This tin or gold-plated contact, which fits a 0.6 mm contact pin, has been specially designed for a pin spacing of 2.5 mm, high thermal resistance (155°C), and high vibration strength. It is suited to use in multi-pin connectors because it allows very compact connector dimensions.

The contact consists of two parts. One performs the conducting function and the other (steel spring sleeve) provides the contact pressure (normal contact force).

The steel spring sleeve maintains the contact pressure even at high temperatures and for the complete service life of the vehicle. The higher forces that are then required to connect and disconnect the connector are reduced by a special connector-locating facility. This also ensures the connector is precisely aligned so that the contacts or pins cannot be damaged by twisting or bending.

*Bosch micro-contact*
*1 Steel spring sleeve, 2 Locking spring (primary spring), 3 Single core, 4 Insertion radius, 5 Contact body, 6 Conductor crimp, 7 Insulation crimp.*

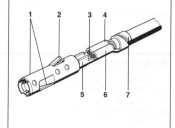

The complete connector is sealed against the male connector on the ECU concerned by a circumferential radial seal in the connector casing. This, together with three sealing lips, ensures a reliable seal against the ECU sealing collar.

The contacts are protected against the ingress of humidity along the cable by a flat seal, through which the contacts are inserted and the wire crimped to them. The flat seal is made of a silicon gel and replaces the conventional individual core seal. At the same time it allows a substantial reduction in connector size and variations in pin assignment (different numbers of contacts used).

The flat seal forms a reliable seal on its inner surface against the insulation of the wires.

When the connector is assembled, the contact with the wire attached is inserted through the flat seal that is already in the connector, and the contact slides home into its position in the contact holder. There, it automatically locks into position by means of the locking spring. When all contacts are in position, a sliding plate provides a secondary locking mechanism. This is a supplementary locking facility and increases security if the connector is inadvertently withdrawn from the wire and contact by force.

## Bosch sensor/actuator contact

The Bosch sensor/actuator contact is used for 2- to 7-pin compact connectors which connect engine-compartment components (sensors and actuators) with the ECU. The pin spacing of 5 mm allows for the physical strength required.

The Bosch sensor/actuator contact has an internal meander-shaped design which reliably prevents vibration transmission from the cable to the contacts. This ensures that there is no relative movement of the contact surfaces that might lead to corrosion.

The compact connector has individual core seals which prevent the ingress of humidity into the contact area. Three sealing lips on the connector casing provide the contact force to ensure there is an adequate seal against splash-water and other sources of humidity.

The self-locking snap-on connectors with additional release facility allow simple connection and disconnection in vehicle assembly and servicing situations. The connector is released by pressing a point marked by a ribbed surface.

The typical uses for this type of contact include connectors on diesel-engine components (e.g. common-rail pressure sensor, fuel injectors) and gasoline-engine components (e.g. fuel injectors, knock sensor).

*Multi-pole connection with micro-contacts* (section)
1 Pressure plate, 2 Sealing plate, 3 Radial seal, 4 Sliding pin (secondary locking mechanism), 5 Contact holder, 6 Contact.

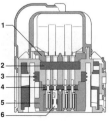

*Bosch sensor/actuator contact*
1 Steel spring sleeve, 2 Single core, 3 Conductor crimp, 4 Insulation crimp, 5 Meander.

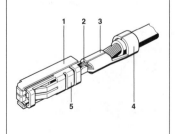

# Electromagnetic compatibility (EMC) and interference suppression

## Requirements

The expression "electromagnetic compatibility" (EMC) defines an electrical system's ability to remain neutral in the vicinity of other systems. In automotive applications, this means that the various electrical and electronic systems, such as the ignition system, electronic fuel-injection system, ABS/TCS, airbags, car tuner, car phone, navigation system, etc., must function in close physical proximity without interfering with each other beyond a permissible level (internal suppression). It also means that the vehicle as a system must remain neutral within its environment, i.e. it should not interfere electrically with other vehicles, or with radio/TV broadcasts, or with any other radio services (radiated interference). At the same time the vehicle must itself remain fully operational when exposed to strong external electromagnetic fields, e.g. in the vicinity of radio transmitters (interference immunity).

It is in view of these considerations that automotive electrical systems and complete vehicles are designed to ensure electromagnetic compatibility.

## Sources of interference

### Vehicle electrical system, ripple

The alternator supplies the vehicle electrical system with rectified three-phase current. Although the current is smoothed by the battery, a residual ripple remains. Its amplitude depends on the load applied to the vehicle electrical system and the wiring. Its frequency does not change according to alternator or engine speed, and the fundamental oscillation is in the kHz range. It can penetrate into the vehicle sound systems – either directly (conductive) or by inductance – where ripple is heard as a howl in the loudspeakers.

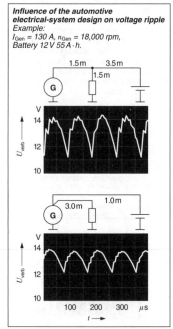

*Influence of the automotive electrical-system design on voltage ripple*
Example:
$I_{Gen}$ = 130 A, $n_{Gen}$ = 18,000 rpm,
Battery 12 V 55 A · h.

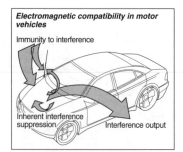

*Electromagnetic compatibility in motor vehicles*

Immunity to interference

Inherent interference suppression

Interference output

## Vehicle electrical system, pulses

Interference pulses are generated on the supply lines when electrical equipment is switched on and off. They are routed to adjacent systems directly through the power supply (conductive coupling) and indirectly by coupling from connecting lines (inductive and capacitive coupling). If there is no compatibility between the interference source and the receiving system, the pulses can cause anything from a malfunction through to total destruction of the adjacent systems.

The wide variety of pulses that occur in the vehicle can be classified in five basic groups. To prevent any unacceptable functions from occurring in the vehicle electrical system, an optimized solution must be found to make the interference sources compatible with interference sinks (susceptible devices).

Pulse amplitudes (which are different for 12-V and 24-V vehicle electrical systems) are divided into categories. When defining the permissible level of radiated interference, the pulse sources, and the necessary immunity of the interference sinks, a compatibility process is carried out by classifying all interference sources in a vehicle by at least one category lower than all the interference sinks (e.g. ECUs), and including a signal-to-interference ratio. The selection of an interference-suppression category is made according to the effort required to either suppress the interference sources, or to protect the susceptible devices.

## Vehicle electrical system, high frequencies

High-frequency oscillations are generated inside many electromechanical and electronic components when voltages and currents are switched (digital circuits, controlling output stages, commutation). These oscillations travel through the component circuits – especially along power-supply lines – and back into the vehicle electrical system, where they arrive at different attenuated intensities.

Depending on whether the interference-voltage spectrum measured is continuous or composed of individual curves, a distinction is drawn between two kinds of interference source: broadband inter-

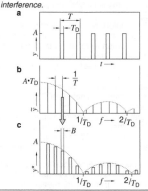

*Sources of broadband and narrowband interference*
a) Signal curve as a function of time $y(t)$,
b) Associated spectrum $\bar{y}(f)$,
c) Spectrum observed using measuring instrument of bandwidth $B$: Where $B \cdot T < 1$ (as shown in diagram), single bars indicate "narrowband" interference; where $B \cdot T > 1$, continuous curve indicates "broadband" interference.

ferers (electric motors, as used for wipers, fans, fuel pump, alternator, and specific electronic components) or "narrowband" interferers (ECUs comprising microprocessors). This classification depends on the bandwidth of the measuring instrument used in relation to the signal characteristics.

High-frequency oscillations can represent a permanent source or interference for communication systems within the vehicle; they are located within the same frequency and amplitude as useful signals, and can easily enter the vehicle's communication system, either directly at the sensor (antenna) or through the antenna cable. Narrowband interference is highly critical as they have signal characteristics that are very similar to the spectrum of transmitters.

For broadband interference, such as electric motors, fans, etc., the radiated interference is assessed on the basis of the interference voltages traveling along power-supply lines in a standardized test setup. It is also partially assessed according to CISPR 25 or DIN/VDE 0879-2 by means of antenna measurements in anechoic chambers lined with high-frequency absorbers. The interference voltage gradings and interference-field strengths caused by interference-suppression levels defined in these standards simplify the electromagnetic compatibility of interference sources and susceptible devices included in the vehicle's original equipment (OE).

If the interference level originally approved for the vehicle's OE proves to be too high when retrofitting additional communication system, the interference suppression measures that can then be taken are limited:

- If the interference source is powered directly from terminal 15 or 30, the interference level can be attenuated by means of suppression capacitors and filters that are designed to function in motor vehicles. The capacitors are generally connected directly to the interference-source terminal with the shortest possible ground cable. Coupling that crosses over from conductors carrying interference voltage to other conductors can be reduced by routing to a braided metal shield which is shorted to ground at both ends.
- If the interference source is controlled by an ECU, it is generally forbidden to retrofit any wiring to the interference source as this would modify the ECU switching response.
- Clock signals from the microprocessors in ECUs act as narrowband interference sources. It is normally not possible to retrofit interference suppression with these components. Radiated interference can therefore be minimized as far as possible by designed circuits and devices appropriately (e.g. suppression capacitors), and locating and routing components and conductors suitably within the layout. If such interference-

**Permissible interference levels in dbμV for interference-suppression levels in individual frequency bands according to DIN/VDE 0879, Part 2, or CISPR 25 for broadband interferers, measured with quasi-peak detector (B), and narrowband interference, measured with peak detector (S).**

| Interference-suppression levels | Interference level | | | | | | | | | | | |
|---|---|---|---|---|---|---|---|---|---|---|---|---|
| | 0.15...0.3 MHz (LW) | | 0.53...2.0 MHz (MW) | | 5.9...6.2 MHz (SW) | | 30...54 MHz | | 68...87 MHz | | 76...108 MHz (FM) | |
| | B | S | B | S | B | S | B | S | B | S | B | S |
| 1 | 100 | 90 | 82 | 66 | 64 | 57 | 64 | 52 | 48 | 42 | 48 | 48 |
| 2 | 90 | 80 | 74 | 58 | 58 | 51 | 58 | 46 | 42 | 36 | 42 | 42 |
| 3 | 80 | 70 | 66 | 50 | 52 | 45 | 52 | 40 | 36 | 30 | 36 | 36 |
| 4 | 70 | 60 | 58 | 42 | 46 | 39 | 46 | 34 | 30 | 24 | 30 | 30 |
| 5 | 60 | 50 | 50 | 34 | 40 | 33 | 40 | 28 | 24 | 18 | 24 | 24 |

**Permissible radio interference-field strength levels in dbμV/m for interference-suppression levels in individual frequency bands according to DIN/VDE 0879, Part 2, or CISPR 25 for broadband interferers, measured with quasi-peak detector (B), and narrowband interference, measured with peak detector (S).**

| Interference-suppression levels | Interference field strength | | | | | | | | | | | | | | | | | |
|---|---|---|---|---|---|---|---|---|---|---|---|---|---|---|---|---|---|---|
| | 0.15...0.3 MHz (LW) | | 0.53...2.0 MHz (MW) | | 5.9...6.2 MHz (SW) | | 30...54 MHz | | 68...87 MHz | | 76...108 MHz (FM) | | 142...175 MHz | | 380...512 MHz | | 820...960 MHz | |
| | B | S | B | S | B | S | B | S | B | S | B | S | B | S | B | S | B | S |
| 1 | 83 | 61 | 70 | 50 | 47 | 46 | 47 | 46 | 36 | 36 | 36 | 42 | 36 | 36 | 43 | 43 | 49 | 49 |
| 2 | 73 | 51 | 62 | 42 | 41 | 40 | 41 | 40 | 30 | 30 | 30 | 36 | 30 | 30 | 37 | 37 | 43 | 43 |
| 3 | 63 | 41 | 54 | 34 | 35 | 34 | 35 | 34 | 24 | 24 | 24 | 30 | 24 | 24 | 31 | 31 | 37 | 37 |
| 4 | 53 | 31 | 46 | 26 | 29 | 28 | 29 | 28 | 18 | 18 | 18 | 24 | 18 | 18 | 25 | 25 | 31 | 31 |
| 5 | 43 | 21 | 38 | 18 | 23 | 22 | 23 | 22 | 12 | 12 | 12 | 18 | 12 | 12 | 19 | 19 | 25 | 25 |

suppression measures are not sufficient, an attempt must be made to solve the situation by appropriately designing the vehicle electrical system, selecting the best position for the antenna, and routing the antenna cable.

In the laboratory, the interference response of electronic components is also assessed by means of line-bound methods (e.g. measuring the interference voltage level along power-supply lines) and antenna measurements in anechoic chambers. The final verdict as to whether reception (radio or mobile communications) will be possible in the vehicle depends on interference-voltage measurements carried out at the receiver terminal of the antenna cable. This is done by means of a suitable test circuit to match the input impedance of the test receiver to the input impedance of the receiver unit. In order to obtain realistic results, the tests are best performed using the original antenna in its original installation location. In order to decouple them from the external electromagnetic transmitter and interference signals, such measurements are carried out in shielded EMC anechoic chambers equipped with high-frequency absorbers.

### The vehicle as interference source
The ignition system is a major source of radiated interference in the vehicle as a whole. The maximum permissible radiation from motor vehicles is limited by law (EU Directive 95/54/EC) in order to ensure that there is no interference with radio and TV reception by other vehicles and roadside residents. Maximum limits are specified for both broadband and narrowband interference.

The levels specified in the directive represent the minimum requirements. Keeping interference to a level only just within the specified limits is not normally sufficient in practice to ensure interference-free reception in the same vehicle. For this reason, suppression has to be enhanced for each specific vehicle type in order to achieve acceptable radio reception by vehicle systems, e.g. radio tuner, cellular phone, etc. Radiated interference by ignition systems can be reduced by us-

ing suitable suppression components (such as resistors in the ignition coils or HT connectors) and resistance spark plugs. For special vehicles (e.g. equipped with two-way radio for emergency services), it may even be necessary to shield the ignition system partially or completely. Such interference-suppression measures may have an impact on the ignition system's power supply. In such cases, therefore, a detailed feasibility study must be made to ensure that the measures taken are permissible.

## Potentially susceptible devices

ECUs and sensors are susceptible to interference signals entering the system from outside. The interference signals emanate either from adjacent systems within the vehicle itself, or from sources in the immediate vicinity (such as a powerful radio transmitter). Malfunctions start to occur at the point where the system loses the ability to distinguish between interference signals and useful signals.

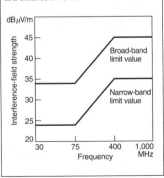

*Limits for interference radiation by vehicles as per CISPR 12 and 95/54/EC*
Broadband and narrowband limits, tested at a distance of 10 m.

The possibility of taking effective measures depends on the characteristics of the useful and the interference signals.

The ECU is unable to distinguish between useful and interference signals if the characteristic of an interference signal is similar to that of a useful signal. This is the case, for instance, when a pulse-shaped interference signal is at the same frequency as the signal from a wheel-speed sensor. Particularly critical here are frequencies in the vicinity of the useful-signal frequency ($f_S \approx f_N$) and within the same range as some of the useful-frequency harmonics.

Non-modulated (or AF-modulated) sinusoidal HF signals (transmitter field strengths) can be demodulated at the p-n junctions in the electronic circuits. This can lead to level shifts caused by DC components, or to the superposition of transient interference signals as a result of demodulated AF components in the interference signal. Normally, the carrier frequency is a multiple of the useful frequency ($f_{S,HF} \gg f_N$). The AF components in the interference signal are particularly critical if it is in the vicinity of the useful-signal frequencies ($f_{S,AF} = f_N$). Interference signals at far lower frequencies than the useful signals ($f_S \ll f_N$) can also lead to malfunctions due to intermodulation.

The necessary interference immunity from electromagnetic fields is also defined by EU Directive 95/54/EC. The directive specifies the field strengths to which a vehicle must be immune, as well as radiated-interference requirements and minimum requirements. In practice, vehicle manufacturers and suppliers provide much higher levels of interference immunity.

## Interference coupling

Signals from interference sources penetrate susceptible devices in any of three ways:

Conductive coupling occurs when the interference source and susceptible device share common current paths, a condition which can hardly be avoided with a common power supply. The vehicle's wiring harness should be designed with the lowest possible level of conductive coupling. Whether a parallel, serial, or multipoint structure is best for the supply lines will depend on the current intensity, the frequency band, component impedance, and the general design of the connected system.

Crossover occurs on connecting lines when they are routed in parallel from the interference source to the susceptible device. In the model, the voltage $U_b$, which is coupled to the susceptible device, is calculated using the formula below with the following parameters:

$$k = C/C_0; \quad k_a = (C_a + C)/C_0; \quad k_b = (C_b + C)/C_0$$
$$C_0 = \sqrt{C_a \cdot C_b + C \cdot (C_a + C_b)}$$

$$\gamma \cdot l = j(\omega/c) \cdot l; \quad W = 1/(c \cdot C_0)$$
$$c = 3 \cdot 10^8 \text{ m/s (speed of light)}$$

$U_b$ consists of two parts: a capacitive component dependent on the voltage $U$, and an inductive component dependent on the current $I$. If the wavelength of the interference signal is greater than the geometrical conductor length $I$, then the formula is simplified as follows:

$$U_b \approx k \cdot (\gamma \cdot l) \cdot [U(R_1 \cdot R_2)/(R_1 + R_2) - W \cdot I \cdot R_2/(R_1 + R_2)]$$

$$U_b = \frac{k \cdot R_2 \cdot \sinh(\gamma \cdot l)}{(R_1 + R_2) \cdot \cosh(\gamma \cdot l) + W \left(k_a + \frac{R_1 \cdot R_2}{W^2} \cdot k_b\right) \cdot \sinh(\gamma \cdot l)} \cdot \left(\frac{R_1}{W} \cdot U - W \cdot I\right)$$

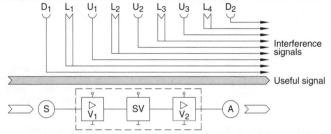

**Interference model**
*Electronic system: S Sensor(s); V₁ Signal amplification and conditioning;
SV Signal processing; V₂ Power amplification; A Actuator(s).
An interference-signal flow is superimposed on the useful-signal flow. (U₁...U₃) conductive
coupling; (L₁...L₄) crossover on connecting lines; (D₁, D₂) direct coupling into sensor and actuator.*

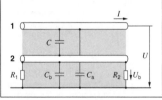

**Model of coupling mechanism of
line-conducted electromagnetic waves**
1 *Conductor along which an electromagnetic
wave generated by a radio-interference
source propagates,*
2 *Target conductor (component of susceptible
device).*

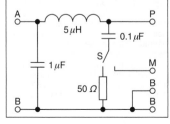

**Schematic diagram of the equivalent
circuit of an automotive electrical system
according to DIN/VDE 0879-2**
*Connections: P–B Unit under test;
A–B Power supply; M–B Radio-interference
monitor; S Switch; B Reference ground
(sheet-metal plate, shield for artificial
network).*

This indicates that crossover can be minimized, the shorter the length $l$, and the lower the standardized coupling capacity $k$.

$k$ decreases as the distance between conductors increases. It can be further reduced by shorting a shield to ground at both ends.

<u>Direct interference coupling</u> may occur if the sensor (S) or the actuator (A) reacts directly to electromagnetic fields. For example, "S" may be a receiving antenna, a microphone, or the magnetic head of a cassette player, or a sensor which has the same operating principle used to detect an electromagnetic field. Here, the aim is to reduce coupling by increasing the physical distance between the interference source and the susceptible device until the interference disappears.

For high frequencies, in particular, the architecture on printed-circuit boards and integrated circuits in electronic equipment can act directly as receiving antennas. In these cases, unacceptable interference coupling must be prevented by selecting appropriate components, a suitable design and, most significantly, an EMC-compliant printed-circuit board design.

## Electrostatic discharge

The subject of potential danger to components and electronic circuits from electrostatic discharge (ESD) also falls under the umbrella of EMC. Here, it is a case of protecting components and equipment from damage by static discharge from humans or from machinery on the production line. On the one hand, it involves adopting appropriate methods for handling equipment and, on the other, designing equipment in such a way that the extremely high voltages (several thousand volts) produced by electrostatic discharges are reduced to acceptable levels.

## Measuring techniques

A wide variety of test methods are in common use for testing radiated interference and interference immunity. Depending on the methods used to assess interference phenomena, they can be roughly divided into methods operating in the timing range (pulse generators, oscilloscopes), and those operating in the frequency band (sine-wave generators, test receivers, spectrum analyzers).

**Test pulse as per ISO 7637, Part 2 for 12-V and 24-V automotive electrical systems**

| Test pulse | |
|---|---|
| Pulse shape | Cause |
| 1 | Switch off inductive loads, e.g. relay or valve. |
| 2 | Switch off electric-motor loads, e.g. fan motor, which generate positive overvoltage when running on. |
| 3a<br>3b | Steep overvoltages resulting from switching operations. |
| 4 | Supply-voltage curve during engine startup. |
| 5 | Alternator load dump [1] |

[1] "Load dump", i.e. when the alternator is feeding high current to the battery and the connection to the battery is suddenly interrupted.

In measurement engineering, interference signals are generally specified for radiated interference as reference values in dB (decibels). The reference value is 1 μV for interference voltages, 1 μV/m for electric field strength, and 1 mW for power. This means:

$$u^* = 20 \cdot \lg U; \quad u^* \text{ in dB}, \quad U \text{ in μV}$$
$$e^* = 20 \cdot \lg E; \quad e^* \text{ in dB}, \quad E \text{ in μV/m}$$
$$p^* = 10 \cdot \lg P; \quad p^* \text{ in dB}, \quad P \text{ in mW}$$

In measurement engineering, parameters (pulse amplitude and transmitter field strengths) used for interference suppression are usually specified directly ($E$ in V/m; $U$ in V; $I$ in A).

EMC measurements are performed on individual systems in the laboratory and in the vehicle.

**Laboratory test procedures**
Under standardized conditions, artificial networks are used to examine pulses or high-frequency interference voltages radiated from a device.

Immunity to pulsed interference is tested using special pulse generators which produce test pulses according to ISO 7637, Part 2. The coupling of pulsed interference on signal and control lines is reproduced using capacitive coupling pliers according to ISO 7637, Part 3.

Line-borne interference waves injected into the wiring harness of the electrical system under test are produced either with the aid of a stripline, a TEM (Transverse Electromagnetic Mode) cell, or BCI (Bulk Current Injection). In the case of a stripline, the wiring harness is arranged in line with the direction of propagation of the electromagnetic wave between a strip conductor and a base plate. When a TEM cell is used, the ECU and a section of the wiring harness are arranged at right angles to the propagation direction of the electromagnetic waves. The BCI method involves superimposing a current on the wiring harness by means of a current clamp.

For higher frequencies (> 400 MHz), the unit under test and the wiring harness are irradiated by antennas and thus directly exposed to an electromagnetic field.

All of these measurement methods are described in various sections of ISO 11 452. Emitted interference radiation is measured with <u>broadband antennas</u> in shielded anechoic chambers lined with absorbers, according to CISPR 25.

<u>Selection of EMC tests</u>
The EMC tests carried out on an electric or electronic device depend on the component's area of application and its internal design. Simple electromechanical devices, which do not contain electronic components, are not tested for interference immunity using electromagnetic fields. On the other hand, a variety of individual tests must be specified in test plans for components containing electronic components.

**Vehicle testing procedures**
The immunity of electronic systems to electromagnetic fields radiated by high-power transmitters is tested inside of the vehicle in a special anechoic chambers. Here, high electrical and magnetic field strengths can be generated, and the complete vehicle can be exposed to them (ISO 11 451).

The interference effects of the vehicle electrics and electronics on radio reception are measured using highly sensitive test receivers. As far as possible, the original vehicle antenna is left in place, and measurements are taken at the receiver input terminal (CISPR 25).

## Regulations and standards

Automotive interference suppression (protection of non-mobile, permanently installed radio reception) has been mandatory in Europe since 1972 (EC Regulation ECE 10 / EU Directive 72/245/EEC). Since January 1 1996 binding legal regulations have been in place concerning electromagnetic compatibility (EU/EEC Directive or German EMC laws) for all electrical products and installations in circulation on the market. For motor vehicles, the special EC Directive 95/54/EC, which supersedes Directive 72/245/EEC, governs the protection of fixed-installation radio reception and the immunity of motor vehicles to interference from electromagnetic fields. In addition to regulations governing the design of vehicles and components brought into circulation, this directive also specifies test methods and maximum limits.

EMC measuring methods are defined in a number of German and international standards. Essentially, national German standards (DIN/VDE) conform with international standards (ISO/IEC-CISPR) and cover all aspects of automotive EMC.

**Standards**
<u>Interference immunity</u>
ISO 7637-1/-2/-3
ISO 11 451/11 452
ISO/TR 10 605

<u>Interference suppression</u>
DIN/VDE 0879-1/-2
CISPR 12
CISPR 25

# Locking systems

## Function, structure, operating principle

The function of locking systems is to ensure and maintain access authorization at all times. Although lock mechanisms in motor vehicles are subject to substantial wear and tear as a result of prolonged cold, wet and dirty conditions over several years, their main design feature must be to reliably protect the vehicle and its occupants while ensuring smooth and efficient operation.

A locking system comprises the following components (based on the example of the driver's door):
- Locking bars on the body pillars
- Side doors, door lock mechanisms, and the associated mechanical and electrical parts
- Electrical components that make up the access authorization facility and radio remote control – features frequently assigned to locking systems

Depending on their location in the vehicle, a further distinction is made between the following assemblies (with differing scope of functions):
- Side door assembly,
- Trunk assembly and
- Hood assembly.

The most important component in the locking system is the door lock mechanism. Its primary functions include:
- To transmit the structural forces between the door and the vehicle body
- To open and close the locking mechanism reliably
- To evaluate the mechanical or electrical commands, and
- To store the logic statuses (mechanical computer)

Accordingly, the lock mechanism is made up of assemblies that perform the following functions:
The locking mechanism is responsible for transmitting forces to initiate the opening and closing functions. It consists of a spagnolet, pawl and latch.

---

**Structure** (example side door)
■  Mechanical connection,
—  Electrical signals.

```
Side door
 ┌──────────────┐      ┌──────────────┐
 │ Lock         │      │ Locking      │
 │ barrel       │      │ element      │
 │ (key)        │      │ (knob)       │
 └──────────────┘      └──────────────┘
 ┌──────────┐ ┌──────────┐
 │ Exterior │ │ Interior │
 │ operating│ │ operating│
 │ element  │ │ element  │
 │ (handle) │ │          │
 └──────────┘ └──────────┘
 ┌──────────┐        ┌──────────────┐
 │ Door lock│        │ Electronics  │
 │          │        │ (option)     │
 │          │        └──────────────┘
 │          │        ┌──────────────┐
 │          │        │ Actuators    │
 │          │        └──────────────┘
 │          │        ┌──────────────┐
 │          │        │ Mechanical   │
 │          │        │ logic unit   │
 └──────────┘        └──────────────┘
 ┌──────────┐ ┌──────┐ ┌──────────┐
 │ Lock     │ │ Data │ │ Power    │
 │ stirrup  │ │ bus  │ │ supply   │
 │(B-pillar)│ │      │ │          │
 └──────────┘ └──────┘ └──────────┘
```

---

**Mechanical door lock**
1 Backplate with locking mechanism,
2 Spagnolet, 3 Electrical interface,
4 Cable assembly to inner handle.

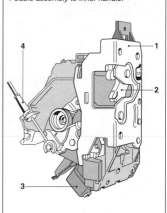

The corresponding door lock striker is mounted on the body pillar. During the closing procedure, the door lock striker engages in the latch. This centers the door, while the spagnolet holds it in the closed position (main catch). In turn, the pawl then positively locks the spagnolet in position.

This lock status is initially canceled to initiate the opening procedure. For this purpose, the actuating forces applied at the inner or outer door handles are transmitted to the pawl. The pawl now releases the spagnolet to allow the door to be opened. The door lock striker is fixed in position while the spagnolet swivels into the open position.

## Mechanical locking system

**Logic statuses of the lock mechanism**

The logic unit of the lock mechanism permits the mechanical decoupling or isolation of the outer door handle, the inner opener and the locking element. For instance, with the door locked, the outer door handle can be freely pulled with no response, and it is consequently not possible to open the door from the outside.

In addition, the inner opener (opening from inside) and the locking element (unlocking from inside) are inoperative in connection with a theft-deterrence system.

The rear door locks cannot be opened from the inside when the child-proof lock is engaged. However, the occupants are able to unlock the door from the inside to allow a person providing assistance to open the door from the outside. (Note the difference compared to the theft-deterrence system!) The following status matrix illustrates the basic functions of a typical rear door.

Table 1: Basic function of rear door variant (type "Single-stroke ejection")

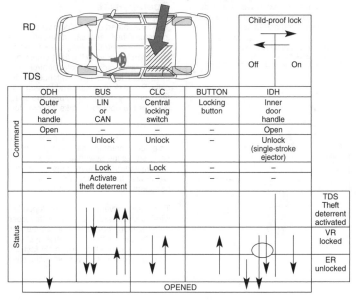

| | | ODH | BUS | CLC | BUTTON | IDH | |
|---|---|---|---|---|---|---|---|
| | | Outer door handle | LIN or CAN | Central locking switch | Locking button | Inner door handle | |
| Command | | Open | – | – | – | Open | |
| | | – | Unlock | Unlock | – | Unlock (single-stroke ejector) | |
| | | – | Lock | Lock | – | – | |
| | | – | Activate theft deterrent | – | – | – | |
| Status | | | | | | | TDS Theft deterrent activated |
| | | | | | | | VR locked |
| | | | | | | | ER unlocked |
| | | | OPENED | | | | |

**Design features**

The lock mechanism is installed in the wet area inside door. The adverse effects of water and dust, the considerable impact load that occurs when the door is slammed, and the theft-deterrence requirements necessitate a sturdy, tough design.

Today the typical locking parts and lever mechanisms are made of steel materials (precision punched parts, springs, riveted connections). Plastic components are being used to an ever greater extent. However, they must fulfill their function even after a side impact or in the event of a vehicle fire. Corrosion, friction and wear dictate that the metal components undergo a comprehensive surface treatment process (trowalizing, galvanizing, coating).

The parts of the locking mechanism are sheathed in plastic materials to provide effective sound-deadening in order to satisfy requirements to minimize closing noise. Higher-grade lock mechanisms normally feature extensive sound deadening measures incorporated in the lever mechanisms and actuators.

*Locking mechanism* (schematic)
1 Pawl, 2 Spagnolet in lock,
3 Door lock striker on B-pillar or C-pillar.

In the past, operation of automotive locks was purely mechanical. Central locking was then introduced in the form of flange-mounted locking actuators (electrically and pneumatically operated control elements).

These actuators are now integrated in the housing of more recent lock mechanisms. Miniature motors carry out the electrical commands from the access authorization facility in the form of mechanical actuating movements. The locking status is stored mechanically in the lever mechanisms.

The output from the high-speed drive units is converted in worm-gear, multistage spur-gear or planetary-gear mechanisms (plastic materials). Spindle drive systems are also used.

Sensors in the lock mechanism permit the electrical evaluation of the lock status. Hall-effect sensors and microswitches have proven to be particularly suitable for this purpose.

# Open-by-wire

The widespread use of electrical systems in motor vehicle applications initially gave rise to the central locking system, which was soon followed by the theft-deterrence system and radio remote control. The child-proof lock is now switched electrically. Some door closing and locking systems employ motors to actuate the spagnolet or the door lock striker (servo closing).

The obvious next step is therefore to use an electric motor for the opening function, i.e. to swivel the pawl ("open-by-wire"). Consequently, development of the "x-by-wire" function for lock mechanisms has been pursued consistently.

The main advantage of the "open-by-wire" function is its interaction with access authorization, particularly in connection with the use of "passive entry" systems, as they require either extremely fast unlocking actuators or "overtake" solutions.

Based on the "overtake principle", the actuator begins the opening procedure in the locking mechanism before the lock logic has been completely released. This function is intended to avoid waiting times for the user. Corresponding design measures reliably rule out the possibility of being locked in.

## Electrical locking system

Demands for quality and reliability as well as the pressures of rising costs render it necessary in future to minimize the number of mechanical parts in the locking system and replace them by electrical components. This development will finally culminate in an electrical locking system.

The lock then consists of only the locking mechanism, opening actuator and the associated electronics. The door handles and other operating elements are equipped with sensors. Electrical wires replace the mechanical connections to the lock.

The advantages of an electrical locking system are considerable:
– Reduced size and weight of the lock
– Symmetrical design
– Only one lock variant per vehicle (variant coding at the end of the assembly line)
– Door handles no longer move (or handles can be dispensed with completely)

Auxiliary functions such as interior lighting, status indicators and a whole range of other functions will then be easy to implement in electrical locking systems, as the lock is equipped with electronics that can perform these functions.

Communication with the locks, access authorization and power supply all take place via the data bus interfaces. Prognoses using fault-tree analysis indicate that the electrical locking system is just as reliable as conventional systems. Economically feasible systems can be expected with the introduction of the 42-V vehicle electrical system at the latest (active redundant power supply).

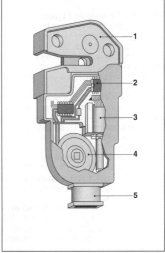

*Electromechanical door lock* (principle)
1 Locking mechanism, 2 Electronics,
3 Electric motor, 4 Gear mechanism,
5 Electrical interface.

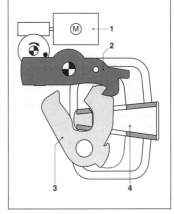

*Open-by-wire* (principle)
1 Electric motor, 2 Pawl, 3 Spagnolet,
4 Door lock striker.

# Central locking system

The central locking and unlocking of the vehicle doors, trunk and fuel filler flap are an integral part of the convenience system in motor vehicles. Electric or pneumatic actuators operate the mechanisms in the individual locking devices.

In pneumatic systems, a central electric dual-pressure pump (vacuum/gage pressure) and dimensionally stable lines leading to the diaphragms of the individual actuators provide the opening and closing movement of the actuators.

The electromechanical central locking system features an electric servomotor to drive the locking function at each point in the system. This electric motor with a reduction-gear drive unit actuates a mechanical connection (rod, lever) responsible for the locking device.

All central locking systems feature a control unit for signal processing. The control unit is integrated in the housing in pneumatic dual-pressure pump systems. In electromechanical systems, it is located centrally, or to minimize wiring, decentrally in the door modules in connection with multiplex systems. The lines associated with decentral or distributed door multiplex systems have multiple functions, i.e. they are also used for the power-window drive units and door-mirror adjustment.

Electromechanical and pneumatic central locking systems are actuated via electrical contact switches in the actuators or locking cylinders in the driver's door, passenger's door, trunk lid, and operating switches in the vehicle interior. Infrared and radio remote control systems enhance operating convenience.

In newer comfort and convenience systems, the central locking system is locked on starting off (vehicle speed signal) to prevent the vehicle from being opened from the outside. The system is unlocked in the event of an accident (crash sensor).

A distinction is made between opening, closing and locking. In connection with the opening and closing functions, manual operation from the inside (e.g. occupants) is possible at any time. When the system is locked, the locking mechanism is blocked as theft deterrence and can only be operated with the vehicle key from the outside or with the remote control.

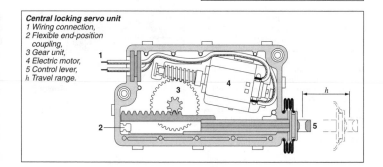

*Central locking with electric motor*
1 Central switch, 2 Contacts in door-lock mechanisms, 3 Control unit, 4 Servomotors.

*Central locking servo unit*
1 Wiring connection,
2 Flexible end-position coupling,
3 Gear unit,
4 Electric motor,
5 Control lever,
h Travel range.

# Acoustic signaling devices

## Applications

The internationally applicable ECE Regulation No. 28 specifies that acoustic signals produced by motor vehicles must maintain a uniform sound quality with no perceptible frequency fluctuations during operation. Operation is permitted only as a hazard warning function. In countries where this regulation does not apply, the acoustic signaling device is a wearing part subject to heavy use.

The use of sirens, bells and the like is not permitted, nor is the playing of melodies by means of sonic generators operating in a given sequence.

Signaling devices must be installed facing forward in the vehicle and must produce the signal at a sufficient loudness level at a distance of 2 m. They are subjected to temperatures ranging from −40°C to +90°C and must be designed to be resistant to moisture, salt spray as well as mechanical shock and vibration. Elastic couplings must be used to decouple electric horns and fanfare horns from the vehicle body, as the horn would otherwise induce sympathetic oscillations in the adjacent bodywork. The resulting feedback would diminish both loudness level and tone quality. Both electric and electropneumatic horns and fanfare horns are sensitive to series resistors in their control circuits. When horns are installed in pairs, they should be triggered by relays.

The warning produced by the impact horn is more conspicuous; it is therefore the better choice for vehicles which are frequently used for long-distance overland truck traffic instead of fanfare horns. Alternatively, the fanfare horn is superior for city driving, as pedestrians often find the standard horn excessively loud and unpleasant. Both sets of requirements can be fulfilled by installing the two horn types together in a single system with a selector switch for city or overland traffic. Standard and fanfare horns both operate at standardized frequencies. High and low tones can be combined to produce a harmonious dual-tone sound.

## Horns

The mass of the armature together with the flexible diaphragm forms an oscillating system within the standard horn. When voltage is applied to the solenoid coil controlled by a contact breaker, the armature impacts against the magnetic core at the horn's basic frequency. A fixed tone disk, directly attached to the armature, responds to these intense periodic impacts by radiating harmonic waves. Legal regulations stipulate that the maximum sound energy must lie within a band of 1.8...3.55 kHz. This frequency explains the horn's relatively piercing sound. This sound, which is essentially emitted along the horn's axis and outwards to the front, can be heard above the background noise in traffic, even over longer distances. The horn's size is one of the factors which determine the basic frequency and loudness level.

As well as increased diameters, supertone horns have a higher electrical power input. Their warning signals can therefore still be heard under extreme conditions (e.g. truck driver's cab).

## Fanfare horns

The electropneumatic fanfare horn employs the same basic actuating system as its standard counterpart. The main difference is that the armature is allowed to vibrate freely in front of the coil with no impact occurring. The oscillating diaphragm induces vibration of an air column within a tube. The resonant frequency of the diaphragm and the air column are tuned to each other and determine the signal pitch. The tube is in the shape of a funnel, with a wide opening to enhance the efficiency of sound propagation. The funnel tube is generally coiled to minimize the unit's size.

The presence of upper harmonics in the lower range of the frequency spectrum provides the fanfare horn with a rich, melodious sound. The tone is less penetrating than that of a standard horn due to the more consistent distribution of sound energy over a wide spectrum.

# Occupant safety systems

## Active and passive safety in motor vehicles

Active safety systems help to prevent accidents and thus make a preventive contribution to safety in road traffic. One example of an active driving safety system is the Antilock Braking System (ABS) with Electronic Stability Program (ESP) from Bosch, which stabilizes the vehicle even in critical braking situations and maintains steerability in the process.

Passive safety systems help to protect the occupants against serious or even fatal injuries. An example of passive safety are the airbags, which protect the occupants after an unavoidable impact.

## Seat belts and seat-belt tighteners

### Function

The function of seat belts is to restrain the occupants of a vehicle in their seats when the vehicle impacts against an obstacle. Seat-belt tighteners improve the restraining characteristics of a three-point inertia-reel belt and increase protection against

injury. In the event of a frontal impact, they pull the seat belts tighter against the body and hold the upper body as closely as possible against the seat backrest. This prevents excessive forward displacement of the occupants caused by mass inertia (see figure).

### Operating concept

In a frontal impact with a solid obstacle at a speed of 50 km/h, the seat belts must absorb a level of energy comparable to the kinetic energy of a person dropping in free fall from the fourth floor of a building.

Due to the seat-belt slack, seat-belt stretch and the delayed effect of the belt retractor ("film-reel effect"), three-point inertia-reel belts provide only limited protection in frontal impacts against solid obstacles at speeds of over 40 km/h because they can no longer safely prevent the head and body from impacting against the steering wheel or the instrument panel. An occupant experiences extensive forward displacement without restraint systems (see figure on next page).

In an impact, the <u>shoulder-belt tightener</u> compensates for seat-belt slack and the "film-reel effect" by retracting and tightening the seat belt. At an impact speed of 50 km/h, this system achieves its full effect within the first 20 ms of impact; this supports the airbag which needs

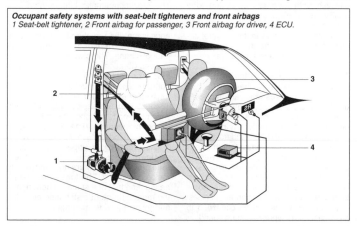

*Occupant safety systems with seat-belt tighteners and front airbags*
1 Seat-belt tightener, 2 Front airbag for passenger, 3 Front airbag for driver, 4 ECU.

approx. 40 ms to inflate completely. After that, an occupant continues to move forwards by a certain amount, thereby expelling the gas ($N_2$) from the airbag so that the occupant's kinetic energy is dissipated in a relatively gradual manner. This protects occupants from injury because it prevents impact with rigid parts of the vehicle structure.

A prerequisite for optimum protection is that the occupants' forward movement away from their seats must be minimal as they decelerate with the vehicle. Activation of the seat-belt tighteners takes care of this virtually from the moment of impact, and ensures restraint of occupants as early as possible. The maximum forward displacement with tightened seat belts is approx. 2 cm and the duration of mechanical tightening is 5...10 ms.

On activation, the system electrically detonates a pyrotechnical propellant charge. The rising pressure acts on a piston, which turns the belt reel via a steel cable in such a way that the belt is held tightly against the body (see figure "Shoulder-belt tightener").

### Variants

In addition to the described shoulder-belt tighteners for rewinding the belt-reel shaft, there are variants which pull the seat-belt buckle back (buckle tighteners) and simul-taneously tighten the shoulder and lap belts. Buckle tighteners further improve the restraining effect and the protection to prevent occupants from sliding forward under the lap belt ("submarining effect"). The tightening process in these two systems takes place in the same period of time as for shoulder-belt tighteners.

A larger degree of tightener travel for achieving a better restraining effect is provided by the combination of two seat-belt tighteners for each (front) seat which, on the Renault Laguna for instance, consist of a shoulder-belt tightener and a belt-buckle tightener. The belt-buckle tightener is activated either only in an impact above a certain degree of severity, or with a certain time lag (e.g. approx. 7 ms) relative to activation of the shoulder-belt tightener.

Apart from pyrotechnical seat-belt tighteners, there are also mechanical versions. In the case of a mechanical tightener, a mechanical or electrical sensor releases a pretensioned spring, which pulls the seat-belt buckle back. The sole advantage of these systems is that they are cheaper. However, their deployment characteristics are not so well synchronized with the deployment of the airbag as pyrotechnical seat-belt tighteners which, of course, have the same electronic impact-sensing equipment as the front airbags.

---

*Deceleration to standstill and forward displacement of an occupant at an impact speed of 50 km/h*
① Impact, ② Firing of seat-belt tightener/airbag, ③ Seat belt tightened, ④ Airbag inflated.
– – – without/ —— with restraint systems.

*Shoulder-belt tightener*
1 Firing wire,
2 Firing element,
3 Propellant charge,
4 Piston,
5 Cylinder,
6 Metal cable,
7 Belt reel,
8 Seat belt.

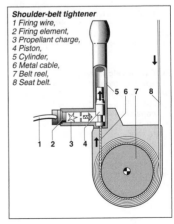

In order to achieve optimum protection, the response of all components of the complete occupant-protection system, comprising seat-belt tighteners and airbags for frontal impacts, must be adapted to one another. Seat belts and seat-belt tighteners provide the greater part of the protective effect since they absorb 50...60% of impact energy alone. With front airbags, the energy absorption is about 70% if deployment timing is properly synchronized.

A further improvement, above all, prevention of collarbone and rib fractures and the resulting internal injuries to more elderly occupants, can be achieved by belt-force limiters. In this case, the set-belt tighteners initially tighten fully (using the maximum force of approx. 4 kN, for example) and restrain the occupants to maximum possible effect. If a certain belt tension is exceeded, the belt gives and allows a greater degree of forward movement. The kinetic energy is converted into deformation energy so that acceleration peaks are avoided. Examples of deformation elements include:
– torsion bar (belt-reel shaft),
– rip-seam in the belt,
– seat-belt buckle with deformation element,
– machining element.

DaimlerChrysler, for example, has an electronically controlled single-stage belt-force limiter which reduces the belt tension to 1...2 kN by deploying a detonator a specific period after deployment of the second front-airbag stage and after a specific extent of forward movement is reached.

### Further developments

The performance of pyrotechnical seat-belt tighteners is constantly being improved. "High-performance tighteners" are capable of retracting an extended belt length of about 15 cm in roughly 5 ms. In future there will also be two-stage belt-force limiters consisting of two torsion bars with staggered response or a single torsion bar combined with an extra deformation plate in the retractor.

## Front airbag

### Function

The function of front airbags is to protect the driver and front passenger against head and chest injuries in a vehicle impact with a solid obstacle at speeds of up to 60 km/h. In a frontal impact between two vehicles, the front airbags afford protection at relative speeds of up to 100 km/h. A seat-belt tightener alone cannot prevent the head from hitting the steering wheel in response to severe impact. In order to fulfill this function, airbags have different filling capacities and shapes to suit varying vehicle requirements, depending on where they are fitted, the vehicle type, and its structure-deformation characteristics.

In a few vehicle types, front airbags also operate in conjunction with "inflatable knee pads", which safeguard the "ride down benefit", i.e. the speed decrease of the occupants together with the speed decrease of the passenger cell. This ensures that the upper body and head describe the rotational forward motion which is needed for the airbag to provide optimum protection, and is of particular benefit in countries where seat-belt usage is not mandatory.

### Operating concept

To protect driver and front passenger, pyrotechnical gas inflators inflate the driver and passenger airbags using dynamic pyrotechnics after a vehicle impact detected by sensors. In order for the affected occupant to enjoy maximum protection, the airbag must be fully inflated before the occupant comes into contact with it. On contact with the upper body, the airbag partly deflates in order to "gently" absorb impact energy acting on the occupant with non-critical (in terms of injury) surface pressures and declaration forces. This concept significantly reduces or even prevents head and chest injuries.

The maximum permissible forward displacement before the driver's airbag is fully inflated is approx. 12.5 cm, corresponding to a period of approx. 10 ms + 30 ms = 40 ms after the initial impact (at 50 km/h with a solid obstacle) (see Fig. "Deceleration to standstill"). It needs 10 ms for electronic firing to take place and 30 ms for the airbag to inflate.

In a 50 km/h crash, the airbag takes approx. 40 ms to inflate fully and a further 80...100 ms to deflate through the deflation holes. The entire process takes little more than a tenth of a second, i.e. the bat of an eyelid.

### Impact detection

Optimum occupant protection against the effects of frontal, offset, oblique or pole impact is obtained – as already mentioned – through the precisely coordinated interaction of electronically detonated pyrotechnical front airbags and seat-belt tighteners. To maximize the effect of both protective devices, they are activated with optimized time response by a common ECU (trigger unit) installed in the passenger cell. This involves the electronic control unit using one or two electronic linear-acceleration sensors to measure the deceleration occurring on impact and calculate the change in velocity. In order to be able to better detect oblique and offset impacts, the deployment algorithm can also take account of the signal from the lateral-acceleration sensor.

The impact must also be analyzed. The airbag should not trigger from a hammer blow in the workshop, gentle impacts, bottoming out, driving over a curbstone or a pothole. With this end in mind, the sensor signals are processed in digital-analysis algorithms whose sensitivity parameters have been optimized with the aid of crash-data simulations. The first seat-belt-tightener trigger threshold is reached within 8...30 ms depending on the type of impact, and the first front-airbag trigger threshold after approx. 10...50 ms.

The acceleration signals, which are influenced for instance by the vehicle equipment and the body's deformation characteristics, are different for each vehicle. They determine the setting parameters which are of crucial importance for sensitivity in the analysis algorithm (computing process) and, ultimately, for triggering the airbag and seat-belt tightener. Depending on the vehicle-manufacturer's production concept, the deployment parameters and the vehicle's equipment level can also be programmed into the ECU at the end of the assembly line ("end-of-line programming").

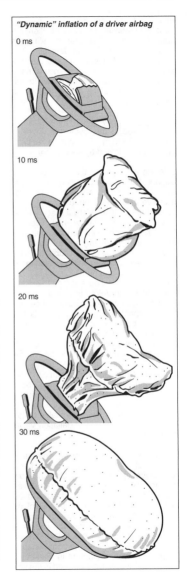

*"Dynamic" inflation of a driver airbag*

0 ms

10 ms

20 ms

30 ms

In order to prevent injuries caused by airbags or fatalities to "out-of-position" occupants or to small children in child seats with automatic child-seat detection, it is essential that the front airbags are triggered and inflated in accordance with the particular situations. The following improvement measures are available for this purpose:

1. <u>Deactivation switches</u>. These switches can be used to deactivate the driver or passenger airbag. The airbag function states are indicated by special lamps.

2. In the U.S., where there are currently approx. 160 fatalities caused by airbags, attempts are being made to reduce aggressive inflation by introducing "<u>depowered airbags</u>". These are airbags whose gas-inflator power has been reduced by 20...30%, which itself reduces inflation speed, inflation severity and the risk of injury to "out-of-position" occupants. "Depowered airbags" can be depressed more easily by large and heavy occupants, i.e. they have a reduced energy-absorption capacity. It is therefore essential – above all with regard to the possibility of severe frontal impacts – for occupants to fasten their seat belts. In the U.S., the "low-risk" deployment method is currently preferred. This means that, in "out-of-position" situations, only the first front-airbag stage is triggered. In heavy impacts, the full gas-inflator output can then be brought into effect by triggering both inflator stages. Another way of implementing "low-risk" deployment with single-stage inflators and controllable deflation vents is to keep the deflation valve constantly open.

3. "<u>Intelligent airbag systems</u>". The introduction of improved sensing functions and control options for the airbag inflation process, with the accompanying improvement in protective effect, is intended to result in a gradual reduction in the risk of injury. Such functional improvements are:
– Impact severity detection by improvements in the deployment algorithm or the use of one or two upfront sensors (see the system diagram in "<u>Restraint System Electronics</u>") installed in the vehicle's crumple zone (e.g. on the radiator cross-member). These are acceleration sensors which facilitate early detection of impacts that are difficult to sense centrally, e.g. ODB (<u>O</u>ffset <u>D</u>eformable <u>B</u>arrier crashes, offset against soft crash barriers), pole or underride impacts. They also allow an assessment of the impact energy.
– Selt-belt usage detection
– Occupant presence, position and weight detection
– Seat-position and backrest-inclination detection
– Use of front airbags with two-stage gas inflators or with single-stage gas inflators and pyrotechnically triggered gas-discharge valves (see also "low-risk" deployment method)
– Use of seat-belt tighteners with occupant-weight-dependent belt-force limiters
– CAN bus networking of the occupant-protection system for communication and synergy utilization of data from "slow" sensors (switches) in other systems (data on vehicle speed, brake operation, seat-belt buckle and door-switch status) and for activation of warning lamps and transmission of diagnostic data.

For transmission of emergency calls after a crash and for activation of "secondary-safety systems" (hazard-warning signals, central-locking release, fuel-supply pump shutoff, battery disconnection, etc.) the "crash output" is used (see figure "Airbag control unit 9").

## Side airbag

### Function

Side impacts make up approx. 30% of all accidents. This makes the side collision the second most common type of impact after the frontal impact. An increasing number of vehicles are therefore being fitted with side airbags in addition to seat-belt tighteners and front airbags. Side airbags, which inflate along the length of the roof lining for the purposes of head protection are designed to cushion the occupants and protect them from injury in the event of a side impact (e.g. inflatable tubular systems, window bags, inflatable curtains) or from the door or the seat backrest (thorax bags, upper body protection).

### Operating concept

Due to the lack of a crumple zone, and the minimum distance between the occupants and the vehicle's side structural components, it is particularly difficult for side airbags to inflate in time. In the case of severe impacts, therefore, the time needed for impact detection and activation of the side airbags must be approx. 5...10 ms and the time needed to inflate the approx. 12 *l* thorax bags must not exceed 10 ms.

Bosch offers the following option to meet the above requirements: an instrument-cluster ECU, which processes the input signals of peripheral (mounted at suitable points on the body), side-sensing acceleration sensors, and which can trigger side airbags as well as the seat-belt tighteners and the front airbags.

## Components

### Acceleration sensors

Acceleration sensors for impact detection are integrated directly in the control unit (seat-belt tighteners, front airbag), and mounted in selected positions on both sides of the vehicle on supporting structural components such as seat cross-members, sills, B and C-pillars (side airbags) or in the crumple zone at the front of the vehicle (upfront sensors for "intelligent airbag systems"). The precision of these sensors is crucial in saving lives. Nowadays, those acceleration sensors are surface-micromechanical sensors consisting of fixed and moving finger structures and spring pins. A special process is used to incorporate the "spring/mass system" on the surface of a silicon wafer. Since the sensors only have low working capacitances (≈ 1 pF), it is necessary to accommodate the evalua-

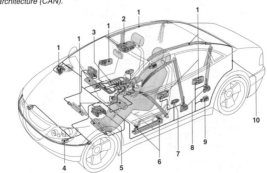

*Electronic impact-protection system "Restraint System Electronics" (RSE)*
1 Airbag with gas inflator, 2 iVision™ passenger-compartment camera, 3 OC mat, 4 Upfront sensor, 5 Central control unit with integral rollover sensor, 6 iBolt™, 7 Peripheral pressure sensor (PPS), 8 Seat-belt tightener with propellant charge, 9 Peripheral acceleration sensor (PAS), 10 Bus architecture (CAN).

tion electronics in the same housing in the immediate proximity of the sensor element so as to avoid stray capacitance and other forms of interference.

## Combined ECUs for belt tighteners, front and side airbags and rollover protection equipment

The central ECU, also called the trigger unit, incorporates the following functions (current status):
- Impact detection by acceleration sensor and safety switch, or by two acceleration sensors with no safety switch (redundant, fully electronic sensing).

### Airbag 9 central combined control unit

| | |
|---|---|
| Terminal 30 | Direct battery positive, not fed through ignition switch, |
| Terminal 15R | Switched battery positive when ignition switch in "radio", "ignition on" or "starter" position, |
| Terminal 31 | Body ground (at one of the device mounting points). |
| CROD | Crash Output Digital, |
| OC/ACSD | Occupant Classification/Automatic Child-Seat Detection, |
| SOS/ACSD | Seat-Occupancy Sensing/Automatic Child-Seat Detection, |
| CAN low | Controller Area Network, low level, |
| CAN high | Controller Area Network, high level, |
| CAHRD | Crash Active Head Rest Driver |
| CAHRP | Crash Active Head Rest Passenger, |
| UFSD | UpFront Sensor Driver, |
| PASFD | Peripheral Acceleration Sensor Front Driver, |
| PASFP | Peripheral Acceleration Sensor Front Passenger, |

(Block diagram)

| | |
|---|---|
| BLFD | Belt Lock (Switch) Front Driver, |
| BLFP | Belt Lock (Switch) Front Passenger, |
| BLRL | Belt Lock (Switch) Rear Left, |
| BLRC | Belt Lock (Switch) Rear Center, |
| BLRR | Belt Lock (Switch) Rear Right, |
| BL3SRL | Belt Lock (Switch) 3rd Seat Row Left, |
| BL3SRR | Belt Lock (Switch) 3rd Seat Row Right, |
| PPSFD | Peripheral Pressure Sensor Front Driver, |
| PPSFP | Peripheral Pressure Sensor Front Passenger, |
| UFSP | UpFront Sensor Passenger, |
| PPSRD | Peripheral Pressure Sensor Rear Driver, |
| PPSRP | Peripheral Pressure Sensor Rear Passenger, |
| FP | Firing Pellets 1...4 / 21...24. |

Other abbreviations:

| | |
|---|---|
| FLIC | Firing Loop Integrated Circuit, |
| PIC | Periphery Integrated Circuit, |
| SCON | Safety Controller, |
| μC | Micro Controller. |

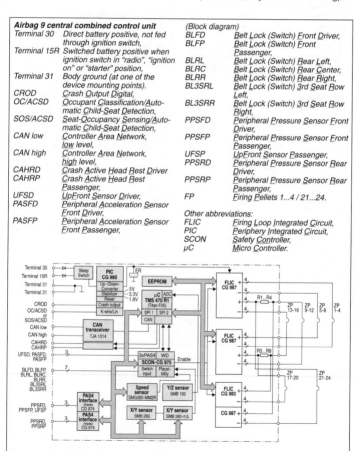

- Rollover detection by yaw-rate and low $g$-y- and z-acceleration sensors (see section "Rollover sensing").
- Prompt activation of front airbags and seat-belt tighteners in response to different types of impact in the vehicle longitudinal direction (e.g. frontal, oblique, offset, pole, rear-end).
- Control of rollover protection equipment.
- For the side airbags, the ECU operates in conjunction with a central lateral sensor and two or four peripheral acceleration sensors. The Peripheral Acceleration Sensors (PAS) transmit the triggering command to the central ECU via a digital interface. The central ECU triggers the side airbags provided the internal lateral sensor has confirmed a side impact by means of a plausibility check. Since the central plausibility confirmation arrives too late in the case of impacts into the door or above the sill, Peripheral Pressure Sensors (PPS) inside the door cavity are to be used in the future to measure the adiabatic pressure changes caused by deformation of the door. This will result in rapid detection of door impacts. Confirmation of "plausibility" is now provided by PAS mounted on supporting peripheral structural components. This is now unquestionably faster than the central lateral-acceleration sensors.
- Voltage transformer and energy accumulator in case the supply of power from the vehicle battery should fail.
- Selective triggering of the seat-belt tighteners, depending on monitored belt-buckle status: firing only takes place if key is in the ignition switch. At present, proximity-type seat-belt buckle switches are used, i.e. Hall-effect IC switches which detect the change in the magnetic field when the buckle is fastened.
- Setting of multiple triggering thresholds for two-stage seat-belt tighteners and two-stage front airbags depending on the status of belt use and seat occupation.

- Watchdog (WD): Airbag triggering units must meet high safety standards with regard to false activation in non-crash situations and correct activation when needed (crashes). For this reason, ninth-generation (AB 9) airbag triggering units incorporate three independent intensive-monitoring hardware watchdogs (WDs):
  WD1 uses its own independent oscillator to monitor the 2-MHz system clock.
  WD2 monitors the realtime processes (time base 500 µs) for correct and complete sequence. For this reason, the safety controller (SCON, see AB 9 block diagram) sends the microcomputer 8 digital messages to which it must respond by sending 8 correct replies to the SCON within a time window of $1 \pm 0.3$ ms.
  WD3 monitors the "background" processes such as the "built-in self-test" routines of the ARM core for correct operation. The microcomputer's response to the SCON in this case must be provided within a period of 100 ms.
  On AB 9, sensors, analyzer modules and output stages are linked by two SPIs (Serial Peripheral Interfaces). The sensors have digital outputs whose signals can be transmitted directly via SPIs. Signal changes can then be detected by line connections on the printed-circuit board, or else they have no effect and a high level of functional reliability is achieved. Deployment is only permitted if an independent hardware plausibility channel also detects an impact and enables the output stages for a limited period.
- Diagnosis of internal and external functions and of system components.
- Storage of failure modes and durations with crash recorder; readout via the diagnostic or CAN-bus interface.
- Warning-lamp activation.

### Gas inflators

The pyrotechnical propellant charges of the gas inflators for generating the airbag inflation gas (mainly nitrogen) and for actuating belt tighteners are activated by an electrically operated firing element.

The gas inflator in question inflates the airbag with nitrogen. The driver airbag built in the steering-wheel hub (volume approx. 60 *l*) or, as the case may be, the passenger airbag fitted in the glove-box space (approx. 120 *l*) is inflated in approx. 30 ms from detonation.

### AC firing

In order to prevent inadvertent triggering through contact between the firing element and the vehicle system voltage (e.g. faulty insulation in the wiring harness), AC firing is used. This involves firing by alternating-current pulses at approx. 80 kHz. A small capacitor with a capacitance of 470 nF incorporated in the firing circuit in the firing-element plug electrically isolates the firing element from the DC current. This isolation from the vehicle system voltage prevents inadvertent triggering, even after an accident when the airbag remains untriggered and the occupants have to be freed from the deformed passenger cell by emergency services. It may even be necessary to cut through the (permanent +) firing-circuit wires in the steering-column wiring harness.

### Passenger-compartment sensing

Occupant-classification mats ("OC mats"), which measure the pressure profile on the seat, are used to distinguish whether the seat is occupied by a person or by an object. In addition, the pressure distribution and the pelvic-bone spacing are used to indicate the occupant's size and thus indirectly the occupant's weight. The mats consist of individually addressable force-sensing points which reduce their resistance according to the FSR principle (Force Sensing Resistor) as pressure increases.

In addition, absolute-weight measurement using four piezoresistive sensors or wire strain gages on the seat frame is also under development. Instead of using deformation elements, the Bosch strategy for weight measurement involves the use

of "iBolts" ("intelligent" bolts) for fixing the seat frame (seat cradle) to the sliding base. These force-sensing "iBolts" (see detail and system diagram of RSE Restraint System Electronics) replace the four fixing bolts otherwise used. They measure the weight-dependent change in the gap between the bolt sleeve and the internal bolt with integral Hall-element IC connected to the sliding base.

Four different concepts are under consideration for detecting "out-of-position" situations:
- Determining the position of the occupant's center of gravity from the weight distribution on the seat detected by the four weight sensors.
- Using the following optical processes: "Time of Flight" (TOF) principle. This system sends out infrared light signals and measures the time taken for the reflected signals to be received back, which is dependent on the distance to the occupant. The time intervals being

***Force-sensing "iBolt"*** (functional principle)
a) Resting position, b) Functioning position.
1 Sliding base, 2 Sleeve, 3 Magnet holder,
4 Double flexing rod (spring), 5 Hall-effect IC,
6 Seat frame.

measured are of the order of picoseconds!

"Photonic Mixer Device" (PMD) method. A PMD imaging sensor sends out "ultrasonic light" and enables spatial vision and triangulation.

"iVision" passenger-compartment stereo video camera using CMOS technology (the option favored by Bosch, see system diagram of RSE Restraint System Electronics). This detects occupant position, size and restraint method and can also control convenience functions (seat, mirror and radio settings) to suit the individual occupant.

No unified standard for passenger-compartment sensing has yet been able to establish itself. Jaguar, for example, uses occupant classification mats combined with ultrasonic sensors.

# Rollover protection systems

### Function

In the event of an accident where the vehicle rolls over, open-top vehicles such as convertibles, off-road vehicles, etc., lack the protecting and supporting roof structure of closed-top vehicles. Initially, therefore, rollover sensing and protection systems were only installed in convertibles and roadsters without fixed rollover bars.

*Start of a rollover*
*1 Airbag control unit with integral rollover sensing for deployment of seat-belt tighteners and head airbags.*

Now engineers are developing rollover sensing for use in closed passenger cars. If a car turns over, there is the danger that non-belted occupants may be thrown through the side windows and crushed by their own vehicle, or the arms, heads or torsos of belted occupants may protrude from the vehicle and be seriously injured.

To provide protection in such eventualities, existing restraint systems, such as seat-belt tighteners and head airbags, are activated. In convertibles, the extendable rollover bars or the extendable head restraints, are triggered.

### Operating concept

The earlier sensing concepts (from mid-1989) started out with an omnidirectional sensing function, In other words, a rollover in any direction from the horizontal should be detectable. For this purpose, manufacturers used all-round-sensing acceleration sensors and tilt sensors (AND-wired) or else level-gage (spirit-level principle) and gravitation sensors (sensor closes a spring-assisted reed switch when contact with the ground is lost).

Current sensing concepts no longer trigger the system at a fixed threshold but rather at a threshold that conforms to a situation and only for the most common rollover situation, i.e. about the longitudinal axis. The Bosch sensing concept involves a surface-micromechanical yaw sensor (see figure) and high-resolution acceleration sensors in the vehicle's transverse and vertical axes (y- and z-axes).

The yaw-rate sensor is the main sensor, while the y- and z-axis acceleration sensors are used both to check plausibility and to detect the type of rollover (slope, gradient, curb-impact or "soil-trip" rollover). On Bosch systems, these sensors are incorporated in the airbag triggering unit.

Deployment of occupant-protection systems is adapted to the situation according to the type of turnover, the yaw rate and the lateral acceleration, i.e. systems are triggered at between 30...3,000 ms by automatic selection and use of the algorithm module appropriate to the type of rollover.

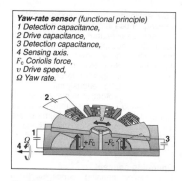

***Yaw-rate sensor*** *(functional principle)*
1 Detection capacitance,
2 Drive capacitance,
3 Detection capacitance,
4 Sensing axis.
$F_c$ Coriolis force,
$v$ Drive speed,
$\Omega$ Yaw rate.

## Outlook

In addition to front-airbag shutoff using de-activation switches, in the near future there will also be seats with standardized anchorages ("ISOFIX child seats"). Switches integrated in the anchoring locks initiate an automatic passenger-airbag shutoff, which must be indicated by a special lamp.

For further improvement of the deployment function and better advance detection of the type of impact ("precrash" detection), microwave radar or LIDAR sensors (optical system using laser light) will be used to detect relative speed, distance and angle of impact for frontal impacts.

In connection with precrash sensing, reversible seat-belt pretensioners are being developed. They are electromechanically actuated, i.e. they take longer to tighten, and must be triggered earlier, i.e. 150 ms before initial impact, by precrash sensing alone (prefire function).

A further improvement in the restraining effect will be provided by airbags integrated in the thorax section of the seat belt ("air belts", "inflatable tubular torso restraints" or "bag-in-belt" systems) which will reduce the risk of broken ribs in older occupants.

The same path for improving protective functions is being pursued by engineers developing "inflatable headrests" (adaptive head restraints for preventing whiplash trauma and cervical-vertebra injuries), "inflatable carpets" (prevention of foot and ankle injuries), two-stage seat-belt tighteners and "active seats". In the case of "active seats", an airbag made of thin steel sheet (!) is inflated to prevent occupants sliding forwards under the lap belt ("submarining effect").

To reduce wiring-harness size and complexity, firing-circuit networking is being developed. The "safe-by-wire" bus (originally developed by Philips) is an example of a product for such applications. More recently, a consortium of companies has been formed with the aim of developing a volume-production "safe-by-wire" firing bus. There is also the DSI bus (developed by Motorola for TRW) and the BST bus (joint development by Bosch, Siemens and Temic). As it is still entirely uncertain whether a firing-bus concept will become established, the BST project has been suspended.

Signals from "slow" sensors or switches (e.g. the seat-belt buckle or ISOFIX switches) can also be transmitted by the firing bus.

There are efforts currently in progress in the U.S.A. to standardize the "safe-by-wire firing bus" concept. Standardization is imperative in order to ensure market penetration and the potential usability of standardized firing elements with standardized bus-user electronics. Efforts are underway to integrate the receiver electronics in the firing elements, without increasing diameter and while maintaining a maximum cap extension of 5 mm. This would increase the usability of standard gas inflators.

In addition to the "firing bus", there will also be a "sensor bus" for networking the signals of "fast" sensors. This will make it possible to combine inertial sensors, for instance, in a "sensor cluster". The overall picture of vehicle dynamics can then be made available via CAN to the evaluation chips of various vehicle systems. Conceivable sensor buses include TT CAN (Time Triggered CAN), TTP (Time Triggered Protocol) and FlexRay, the option currently favored by Bosch. The requirements of a sensor bus regarding transmission reliability and speed are extremely high.

The first phase of legally required measures for improving pedestrian protection can be expected in 2005. Therefore, vehicle manufacturers urgently need to develop solutions for their new models to meet the pedestrian-trauma limits which will then be in force and which in most cases will be achievable by passive design features (body shape, impact-damping materials). Enactment of the second stage of the legislation (around 2010) providing for even lower trauma limits will then require active safety features, i.e. pedestrian impact will have to be detected and protective actuators actuated.

Pedestrian-impact sensing will initially be implemented by deformation or force sensors in the fender and possibly the front of the hood, e.g. in the form of
– double-shielded piezoelectric wires,
– pressure hoses,
– fiber-optic cables which utilize the "microbending" effect,
– film pressure sensors (as in occupant classification mats), and
– acceleration sensors or knock sensors on the fender cross-members.

At a later date contactless sensors will be used to reliably distinguish between a pedestrian and an object. These might, for instance, be:
– short-range radar,
– ultrasonic sensors, or
– external stereo video cameras.

The protective actuators consist of A-pillar airbags and hoods which can be raised by approx. 10 cm so that, if impacted by a pedestrian's head, they are not depressed far enough to come in contact with the rigid engine components due to the greater clearance. As a result, the trauma suffered is less severe.

In Europe, 7,000 pedestrians are killed every year. That figure represents 20% of the total number of road-accident fatalities. In Japan, for example, there are 17,000 pedestrian deaths a year. For this reason, legislators in Japan are deliberating whether to make safety features for pedestrians a legal requirement as in Europe.

The following additional improvements for softer cushioning of occupants are also likely:
1. Airbags with active ventilation system: These airbags have a controllable deflation valve to maintain the internal pressure of the airbag constant even if an occupant falls against it and to minimize occupant trauma. A simpler version is an airbag with "intelligent vents". These vents remain closed (so that the airbag does not deflate) until the pressure increase resulting from the impact of the occupant causes them to open and allow the airbag to deflate. As a result, the airbag's energy-absorption capacity is fully maintained until the point at which its motion-damping function comes into effect.
2. Adaptive, pyrotechnically triggered steering-column release.
   This allows the steering wheel to move forward in a severe impact so that the occupant can be more softly cushioned over a greater distance of travel.
3. Networking of passive and active safety features.
   The first example of the synergetic use of sensors in different safety systems will be implemented in ROSE II (Rollover Sensing II). ROSE II will utilize the signals available on the CAN from the speed-vector sensor for improved detection of soil-trip rollover situations. The speed-vector sensor is part of the ESP system and is used to measure the deviation of the vehicle motion vector from the vehicle's longitudinal axis. The ESP, on the other hand, can utilize the signals from the ROSE II low-$g$ acceleration sensors (y and z axes) for improved detection of unstable dynamic-handling situations.

# Power windows

Power windows have mechanisms that are driven by electric motors. There are two types of system in use. The available installation space assumes a prominent place among the criteria applied in determining which system to install.
– Rod-linkage regulator mechanism: The drive motor pinion engages with a quadrant gear which is connected to a rod linkage. The use of this type of window regulator mechanism is decreasing.
– Cable regulator mechanism: The drive motor turns a cable reel which operates the cable regulator mechanism.

## Power-window motors

Space limitations inside the door make narrow drive units imperative (flat motors). The reduction gearing is a self-inhibiting worm-gear design. This prevents the window from opening inadvertently of its own accord or being opened by force.

Dampers integrated in the gearing mechanism provide good damping characteristics at the end positions.

## Power-window control

Window operation is controlled manually by means of a rocker switch. For greater convenience, power windows can be linked to a central or decentralized closing system which, when the vehicle is locked, closes the windows automatically or sets them to a predefined partially open position for ventilation purposes.

When the windows are closed, a force-limitation device comes into effect. The device serves to prevent human limbs from being caught by the closing window. In Germany, paragraph 30 of the StVZO (Road Traffic Licensing Regulations) stipulates that the force-limitation device must be effective when the window is moving upwards within a range of 200...4 mm from the upper edge of the window aperture.

The power-window drive units include integral Hall-effect sensors to monitor motor speed during operation. If a reduction in speed is detected, the motor's direction of rotation is immediately reversed. The

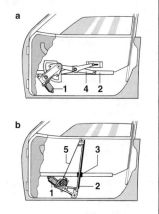

*Power-window drives*
*a) System with regulator mechanism,*
*b) System with flexible cable.*
*1 Electric gear motor, 2 Guide rail,*
*3 Driver, 4 Regulator mechanism,*
*5 Flexible drive cable.*

**a**

**b**

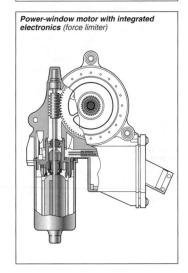

*Power-window motor with integrated electronics (force limiter)*

window closing force must not exceed 100 N at a spring rate of 10 N/mm. The unit automatically overrides the force-limitation function immediately before the window enters the door seal, allowing the motor to run to its end position and permitting complete closure of the window. The window position is monitored over its entire range of movement.

Electronic control may be concentrated in a central control unit, or the control elements may be dispersed among the individual power-window motors in order to reduce the complexity of the wiring. Future decentralized electronics will be networked via bus interfaces (LIN bus/CAN bus). The advantages offered are fault diagnosis for the electronics and further reduction of the amount of wiring.

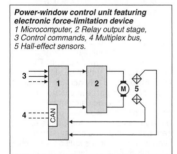

*Power-window control unit featuring electronic force-limitation device*
*1 Microcomputer, 2 Relay output stage, 3 Control commands, 4 Multiplex bus, 5 Hall-effect sensors.*

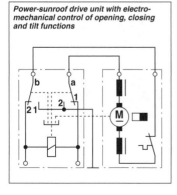

*Power-sunroof drive unit with electromechanical control of opening, closing and tilt functions*

# Power sunroofs

Power sunroofs can combine tilting and sliding sunroof functions. This requires the use of special control systems that may be electronic or electromechanical in design. With electromechanical control (see figure), mechanical interlocks on limit switches a) and b) ensure that the roof can either slide or tilt open from the closed position, depending on the polarity applied to Terminals 1 and 2. Once the sunroof has been tilted or opened, a polarity changeover will initiate the lowering or closing process. An electronic control unit featuring integral force limitation allows the sliding/tilting sunroof to be incorporated in a central-locking system. The electronic control system includes a microcomputer responsible for evaluating incoming signals and monitoring sliding sunroof position. The closed and end-positions for the sliding action of the sunroof are monitored with the aid of microswitches or Hall-effect sensors. Supplementary functions can all be included in the package at relatively modest expense. These include:
– preset position control
– closing via rain sensor
– motor-speed control, and
– electronic motor protection

Drive for the roof is provided by Bowden cables or other torsion- and pressure-resistant control cables. The drive motor is usually installed in the roof or at the rear of the vehicle (e.g. in the trunk). Permanently energized worm-drive motors with outputs of approx. 30 W are used to drive the sunroof mechanism. They are protected against thermal overload by a thermostatic switch (phasing out) or (most frequently) by a software thermal-protection switch.

Provision must also be made for ensuring that the roof can be closed using simple on-board tools (e.g. wheel-nut wrench or similar) if the electrical system fails.

# Seat and steering-column adjustment

Electric power seats are still essentially restricted to passenger cars in the mid- and high-price ranges. The primary function of these systems is to enhance comfort, but multiple adjustment options combined with space restrictions and difficult access to the controls limit the practicality of manually operated mechanisms. Up to seven motors control the following functions:
– seat-cushion height, front/rear,
– seat fore-aft adjustment,
– seat-cushion length angle,
– backrest tilt adjustment,
– lumbar support, height/curvature,
– shoulder-support tilt angle,
– head-restraint height adjustment.

A common seat-bottom frame includes four motors which drive the height adjustment gearing or the combined fore/aft and height-adjustment gearing. The unit for adjusting the seat height is not included on simpler seat designs. Another concept features three identical motor-and-gear assemblies with four height and two fore/aft-adjustment gear sets. The motor-and-gear assemblies drive the gear sets via flexible shafts. This is a highly universal system and can be installed on any seat design.

Modern seats (especially for sportscars) do not merely affix the lap belt to the seat frame, they also attach the shoulder strap – together with its height adjustment, inertia reel and seat-belt tightener mechanism – to the backrest. This type of seat design ensures optimized seat-belt positioning for a wide range of different occupant sizes at all available seat positions, and makes an important contribution to occupant safety. The seat frame must be reinforced for this type of design, while both the gearset components and their connections to the frame must be strengthened.

The optional programmable electric seat adjustment ("memory seat") can recall several preset seat positions. Potentiometers or Hall-effect sensors provide seat-position feedback. On two-door vehicles, a feature designed to slide the front seat to its extreme forward position can be incorporated to help rear passengers enter the vehicle.

Electrically adjustable steering columns are also on the increase as another means of enhancing driver comfort. The adjustment mechanism, consisting of a single electric motor and self-inhibiting gearset for each adjustment plane, forms an integral part of the steering column. The gear set for linear adjustment must be capable of absorbing all impact forces (crash forces) which might be applied to the steering column. The adjustment can be triggered in either of two ways, by the manual position switch or by the programmable seat adjustment. The column can also be tilted upward when the ignition is switched off to help the driver enter or exit the vehicle.

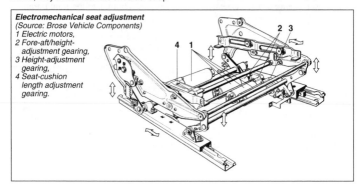

***Electromechanical seat adjustment***
*(Source: Brose Vehicle Components)*
*1 Electric motors,*
*2 Fore-aft/height-*
*adjustment gearing,*
*3 Height-adjustment*
*gearing,*
*4 Seat-cushion*
*length adjustment*
*gearing.*

# Expert Know-How on Automotive Engineering
## The Bosch Yellow Jackets

The up-to-date range is available on the internet at:
**www.bosch.de/aa/de/fachliteratur/index.htm**

The Bosch Yellow Jackets  Edition 2001  Technical Instruction  Automotive Electrical and Electronic Systems

Automotive
Microelectronics

**BOSCH**   Automotive Technology

· Basic principles
· Components
· Development
  and production

# Biometric systems

## Function

"Biometric systems" have the task of determining or confirming the identity of persons on the basis of "biometric" features.

At present about ten biometric processes are known, including
– fingerprint identification,
– face identification,
– iris identification, and
– voice identification.

## Biometric systems in motor vehicles

Fingerprint identification is becoming established in automotive applications since criminology has developed a fundamental understanding of the techniques of fingerprint distinction.

As fingerprint identification will in future replace passwords on computers, in time-management and access-control systems, and on mobile phones as well, the development of sensors and algorithms has already become widespread. Due to the confined space available on board a motor vehicle, there is also limited space for installing the sensor.

## Biometric features

Biometric features are features that are uniquely characteristic to a particular person. They may either be physiological features (such as the pattern of a fingerprint) or behavioral characteristics (such as the way a person walks or writes his/her signature).

The advantage of biometric systems is, firstly, for the greater convenience of the user. Since biometric features are part of a person's individuality, they are carried by the person at all times, i.e. they cannot be forgotten or lost. There is no need to carry a key or a transponder card.

Secondly, they offer the advantage of an attainable enhancement in security. Since biometric features are intrinsic and unique to a particular individual, they can neither be deliberately given to others nor stolen in the traditional sense of the word. Therefore, a high level of reliance can be placed on whether the vehicle really is being driven by a known driver.

## Enrollment

In order to be able to recognize a user, a biometric system must first of all learn the fingerprint pattern of that person. This process is known as "enrollment". It involves the user placing his/her finger on a fingerprint sensor that generates a grayscale image (typical size: 64,000...96,000 pixels at a resolution of 8 bits/pixel).

Using signal-processing algorithms, a processor calculates the characteristics features within that image, e.g. branches or nodal points in the line pattern. The biometric system then stores these features – but not as an actual fingerprint pattern – in a permanent database, typically in an EEPROM memory (capacity requirement: 250...600 bytes per fingerprint).

When the biometric system checks a person's fingerprint pattern the next time, it again identifies the characteristic features of the fingerprint and then searches the database for a matching set of features. If it finds a match, the person is recognized as an authorized user.

## Typical applications

Many vehicles already have programmable seat-adjustment functions. The control panel typically has three numbered memory buttons, which can be assigned to three different drivers, and a teach-in button. The drivers of the vehicle will have to select a memory button for each driver and then remember which button contains their own settings. The number of drivers that can use the system is limited by the number of memory buttons.

The use of a biometric system significantly enhances the level of personalized convenience. A fingerprint sensor replaces the memory buttons for the programmable seat-adjustment system. Instead of pressing a memory button to recall his/her personal settings, the driver places a finger on the sensor.

Since biometric features are intrinsic to a particular individual, the biometric system can always identify a particular driver reliably and apply the correct personal settings.

If a previously unknown driver places his/her finger on the sensor to store his/her personal settings, the biometric system automatically performs an enrollment sequence and then memorizes the current settings. Once a driver is known to the biometric system, only the current settings are stored.

The advantage for the user lies in the simplified human-machine interface. Users no longer have to agree on the allocation of memory buttons, nor do they have to remember which button is theirs. In addition, the maximum number of users is not limited to the number of memory buttons available. Ultimately, the number of users is limited by the biometric system's memory capacity for user identities and personal settings.

Personalization can be extended beyond seat-adjustment, mirror-adjustment and steering-column adjustment functions. Theoretically, all configurable vehicle systems can be connected to the biometric personalization system. It could be conceivable to personalize air-conditioning and automatic-transmission settings (sports/economy). For the radio, a set of personal favorite stations and preferred volume and tone settings could be selected, while there could be a list of favorite destinations for the navigation system. Similarly, if the vehicle has configurable displays, a driver's personal preferences for the display elements could be recalled.

In the case of self-teaching assistance systems which adapt to the driver's driving patterns, the "last known settings" regarding driver characteristics could be retrieved by the personalization system before starting off.

Biometric systems can also be used even before starting the engine as a means of implementing a vehicle immobilizer and for vehicle access. Vehicles equipped with this technology could then be driven entirely without the use of keys. With regard to the use as a vehicle immobilizer, it has not yet been definitively demonstrated that the same degree of security is attainable as with the present transponder-based immobilizers.

For vehicle-access applications, the sensors for identifying the fingerprint pattern would have to be integrated in the vehicle's outer skin. The technical challenge is then to design a sufficiently resilient sensor system that is adequately protected against external conditions so that effective usability is guaranteed at all times – including in winter.

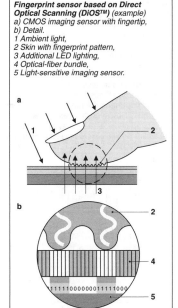

*Fingerprint sensor based on Direct Optical Scanning (DiOS™) (example)*
*a) CMOS imaging sensor with fingertip,*
*b) Detail.*
*1 Ambient light,*
*2 Skin with fingerprint pattern,*
*3 Additional LED lighting,*
*4 Optical-fiber bundle,*
*5 Light-sensitive imaging sensor.*

# Driving-assistance systems

### Critical driving situations

On average, someone dies every minute somewhere in the world as a result of a traffic accident. Bosch pursues the aim of reducing the frequency and the severity of accidents by developing active and passive driving-assistance systems. Driving-assistance systems aim to make the vehicle capable of perceiving its surroundings, interpret them, identify critical situations, and assist the driver in performing driving maneuvers. The object is, at best, to prevent accidents completely and, at worst, to minimize the consequences of an accident for those concerned.

In critical driving situations, fractions of a second are often decisive in determining whether an accident occurs or not. According to various studies, approximately 60% of rear-end collisions and virtually a third of frontal impacts could have been avoided if the driver had reacted only half a second earlier. Every second accident at an intersection could be prevented by faster driver reaction.

At the end of the 1980s, when the vision of highly efficient and partially automated road traffic was presented as part of the "Prometheus" project, the electronic components for this task was not in existence. However, the highly sensitive

sensors and extremely powerful micro-computers now available have brought the "sensitive" vehicle a step nearer to realization. Sensors scan the vehicle's surroundings, and systems generate warnings based on the objects identified, or directly perform the maneuvers required. All this takes place at those decisive fractions of a second faster than even a fully attentive and experienced driver would be capable of.

### Causes of accidents and possible action

In 2000 a total of more than 91,000 people were killed in road-traffic accidents in Europe, the U.S.A. and Japan. The resulting cost to the various national economies totaled more than € 600 billion.

The fact that the capabilities of many motorists are overburdened by the complexities of road-traffic situations is borne out by recent statistics – in Germany, for example, there were 2.37 million road accidents in 2001, 375,345 of which resulted in personal injury. In nine out of ten cases, the cause was human error.

A statistical analysis of accident causes outside built-up areas in Germany (see figure) shows more than a third of the total number are caused by drivers changing lanes or unintentionally failing to keep in lane. Systems which can see the "blind spot" and lane-change alarms offer a means of reducing the number of acci-

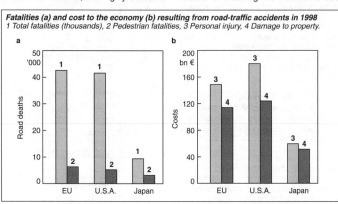

*Fatalities (a) and cost to the economy (b) resulting from road-traffic accidents in 1998*
1 Total fatalities (thousands), 2 Pedestrian fatalities, 3 Personal injury, 4 Damage to property.

dents caused in this way. About another third of accidents result from "rear-ending" and frontal collisions.

Collision-warning systems can represent a first line of defense in combatting such accidents. A second level can be provided by collision-avoidance systems which actively intervene in the control of the vehicle. A first step in this direction has already been taken through the development of ACC (<u>A</u>daptive <u>C</u>ruise <u>C</u>ontrol, see P. 1058 and P. 1060).

Accidents involving pedestrians and at intersections have a high level of complexity. Only networked sensor systems with scenario-interpretation capabilities can master such complicated accident situations. This is one of the issues currently occupying researchers.

### Applications

Driving-assistance systems with multiple applications (see figure) can be divided in:
- safety systems aimed at preventing accidents, and
- comfort and convenience systems with the long-term aim of "semi-automated driving".

A further distinction is made between:
- active systems which intervene in vehicle dynamics, and
- passive, i.e. informative systems, which do not intervene in vehicle control.

### Convenience and safety functions

<u>Passive safety</u> (lower left quadrant of diagram) consists of features for lessening the consequences of accidents, such as precrash functions and pedestrian-protection features.

Systems for <u>driver support</u> without intervention in vehicle control represent a precursor to vehicle-handling functions. Such systems merely warn the driver or recommend maneuvers.

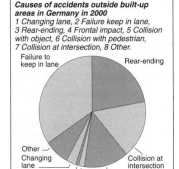

*Causes of accidents outside built-up areas in Germany in 2000*
*1 Changing lane, 2 Failure keep in lane, 3 Rear-ending, 4 Frontal impact, 5 Collision with object, 6 Collision with pedestrian, 7 Collision at intersection, 8 Other.*

Failure to keep in lane

Rear-ending

Other
Changing lane
Collision with object
Collision with pedestrian

Collision at intersection

Frontal impact

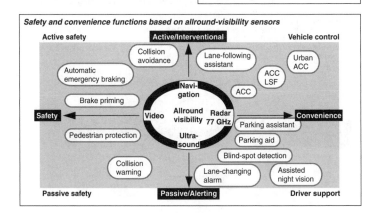

*Safety and convenience functions based on allround-visibility sensors*

Active safety — **Active/Interventional** — Vehicle control

Collision avoidance
Automatic emergency braking
Brake priming

Lane-following assistant

ACC LSF
ACC

Urban ACC

**Safety**

Navigation
Video — Allround visibility — Radar 77 GHz
Ultrasound

**Convenience**

Pedestrian protection

Parking assistant
Parking aid
Blind-spot detection

Collision warning

Lane-changing alarm

Assisted night vision

Passive safety — **Passive/Alerting** — Driver support

Examples: The parking assistant first measures the length of the parking space and indicates to the driver whether it will be easy or difficult to park in the space, or if the space is too small. In the next stage, the system offers the driver recommendations for steering the vehicle during the parking maneuver based on the measurement it has taken of the parking space. The long-term aim for Bosch in the development of parking systems is the autonomous parking assistant – in other words a system that actively intervenes in vehicle handling and automatically maneuvers the vehicle into the parking space.

Detection of potentially dangerous objects in the blind spot is performed by close-range sensors (ultrasound sensors, radar sensors or Lidar sensors). Video sensors can be effectively used to improve visibility for the driver at night. Lane-change alarms use a video camera to extrapolate the course of the lane in front of the vehicle and warn the driver if the vehicle leaves its lane and the direction indicators have not been operated. The warning can be an acoustic signal through the sound-system speakers or a mechanical indication in the form of a small turning force applied to the steering wheel.

ACC is among the vehicle-handling systems (upper right quadrant of diagram) already fitted to vehicles. A further development of this system aims to relieve the burden on the driver in slow-moving traffic congestions – firstly by braking the vehicle to a standstill, and then by moving it forward again at low speed (ACC LSF: ACC Low Speed Following).

A later stage of development aims to utilize interaction between a number of different sensors to enable complete linear control even in city areas (ACC Stop & Go) and at high vehicle speeds. The basis for this is a complex fusion of radar and video data. By combining the linear-control system with a (similarly video-based) lateral-control (lane-following assistance) system, an autonomous vehicle-handling system is conceivable in theory. The lane-following assistance system is a further development of the lane-changing alarm.

The active safety functions (top left quadrant of diagram) encompass all features intended to prevent accidents. The demanding requirements placed on them regarding functionality and reliability extend from the simple parking-assistance brake, which automatically brakes the vehicle before it hits an obstruction, to the computer-aided execution of driving maneuvers for the purpose of avoiding collisions. Intermediate stages are repre-

*Vehicle allround visibility, detection range of sensors*
*1 Long-range radar, 77 GHz, standard (range 1...120 m), 2 Long-range/close-range infrared vision system (night-vision range 0...100 m), 3 Exterior video range (night vision, medium range 0...80 m), 4 Close-range sensor (range 0.2...20 m), 5 Interior video, 6 Ultrasound, standard (ultra-close range 0.2...1.5 m).*

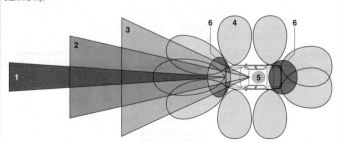

sented by "Predictive Safety Systems" (PSS). They extend from pre-pressurizing the brakes when a potential hazard is detected, to brief sharp application of the brakes, through to automatic emergency braking which always triggers full braking force if the vehicle computer detects that a collision is unavoidable.

Comfort and convenience systems and driver-support systems (such as Parkpilot and ACC Adaptive Cruise Control) are the foundations on which Bosch will be developing safety systems to full production maturity over the next few years. In the medium term the aim of these systems is to reduce the severity of accidents, while the longer-term objective is to prevent accidents altogether.

**Sensors for allround electronic visibility**

Using electronic "allround visibility", numerous driving-assistance systems are achievable – both for warning and for active-intervention purposes. The diagram shows the protection areas covered by present and future allround-visibility sensors.

Close range

Due to the limited availability of sensors, only a few driving-assistance systems have been able to become established on the marketplace so far. One of them is "Parkpilot" (see P. 1086) which uses ultrasound technology to monitor the close-range area. Ultrasound sensors integrated in the vehicle's fenders ensure that the driver is given an acoustic or optical warning if the vehicle approaches an obstruction. The sensors have a range of ≤ 1.5 m. The next (fourth) generation of ultrasonic sensors will have a range of ≈ 2.5 m. These sensors will then be suitable for the future, more demanding, advanced functions of "parking-space measurement" and "parking assistant".

The close-range system now in widespread use has been well accepted by users and is already standard equipment on some models.

Long range

For long-range applications, ACC systems with Long-Range Radar (LRR) sensors are already in use. They have an operating frequency of 76.5 GHz and a range of ≈ 120 m. A very narrow-beam radar lobe scans the area in front of the vehicle in order to determine the distance to the vehicle in front. The driver specifies the required speed and safety distance. If a slow-moving vehicle is detected in front by the sensors scanning the vehicle's surroundings, the ACC automatically applies the brakes to maintain the distance previously specified by the driver. As soon as the scanned area is clear of vehicles, ACC accelerates the vehicle again up to the preset cruising speed. In this way, the vehicle integrates harmoniously within the traffic flow. It not only allows the driver to reach his/her destination in a more relaxed state, it also increases the level of attention that can be devoted to traffic conditions. The ACC data can also be used to warn the driver if the vehicle is approaching too close to the vehicle in front.

The current Bosch ACC version (see P. 1058) meets these requirements by actively intervening in the braking and engine-management systems automatically at speeds of > 30 km/h. At lower speeds, the system is deactivated.

The second generation (ACC2) will be launched in 2004. Not only has the horizontal scanning range been doubled to ± 8°, the size of the radar module has also been reduced substantially. The device will be the smallest radar distance control system with integrated ECU.

ACC is the first driving-assistance system which not only warns the driver but also actively intervenes in vehicle dynamics. The current version of ACC is designed particularly for use on expressways. Due to its larger beam width, ACC2 will be able to assess the traffic situation better, in particular when negotiating bends or filtering in, and will also be usable on highways with tight bends.

## Virtual safety shield

Close-range sensors can form a "virtual safety shield" around the vehicle. It can be used to implement a number of functions. The signals from that safety shield firstly warn the driver of potentially dangerous situations, and secondly, it acts as a data source for safety and convenience systems. Even the driver's "blind spot" can be monitored by these sensors.

## Video sensors

Video sensors perform a major role in driving-assistance systems because they specifically assist with the interpretation of visual information (object classification). In the near future, Bosch will be able to offer this type of sensor for use in vehicles. This will open the way for a wide range of new functions.

Rear-end video sensors (in their simplest form) can assist the ultrasound-based Parkpilot system during parking maneuvers.

Greater benefit is offered by a rear-end camera if the detected objects can be interpreted by image-processing software and the driver is alerted in critical situations. Such a situation might be one where an intended lane change would be dangerous because a vehicle is approaching fast in the outside lane.

The use of a front-end camera is necessary to implement functions for night-vision enhancement, for instance. To this end, the system illuminates the road ahead of the vehicle with infrared light. A display shows the image recorded by an infrared-sensitive camera. Visibility is enhanced for the driver without dazzling oncoming vehicles, and obstructions and hazards can be identified more quickly in the dark.

A day-and-night sensitive front-end camera allows several assistance functions. For example, Bosch is currently developing systems for lane-detection and road-sign recognition based on this technology.

The "lane-detection system" can identify the lane boundaries and the lane direction ahead. If the vehicle is about to move out of its lane unintentionally, the system alerts the driver. At a later stage, Bosch is planning to expand lane detection into a lane-following assistance system which can move the vehicle back to its lane by actively turning the steering wheel. Combined with ACC, this will make an ideal system for relieving driver stress in stop-and-go traffic.

Another function that makes use of data from the video sensor is "road-sign recognition". This system is capable of recognizing ("reading") road signs (e.g. speed-limit or no-overtaking signs). The instrument cluster then displays the last road signs recognized.

The front-end camera also assists the ACC sensor by providing the capability of not only measuring the distance from an object, but of classifying it as well. By combining the video system with long-range radar, there are synergetic benefits – the visible range of the ACC is extended significantly, and object detection is even more reliable.

Video technology will initially be used in information-providing driving-assistance systems. Current video sensors are still a long way from imitating the capabilities of the human eye in terms of resolution, sensitivity and light-intensity response. However, advanced methods of image processing combined with recently developed dynamic imaging sensors already demonstrate the enormous potential of these sensors.

CMOS technology with nonlinear luminance conversion will be capable of covering a very wide range of brightness dynamics and will be far superior to conventional CCD sensors. Since the brightness of images in the automotive environment is not controllable, the dynamic range of conventional imaging sensors is inadequate; for this reason, highly dynamic imagers are required.

The video signals from the camera in a video system are transmitted to an image processor which extracts individual image features (see figure and schematic diagram). This information can also be sent over a data bus to other ECUs or information units (HMI: Human Machine Interface), where it can be used as the basis for initiating intervention in vehicle control or for driver information.

### Sensor-data fusion

To ensure that assistance functions are as fault-resistant as possible but remain capable of detecting and classifying several objects simultaneously, the signals of multiple sensors must be combined and analyzed. Sensor-data fusion allows systems to create an overall, realistic picture of the vehicle's surroundings. In this way, information about the vehicle's surroundings is much more reliable than if it was detected by individual sensors.

Future driving-assistance systems will incorporate the functions of gradually more sensors and actuators and will have more complex connections to other vehicle systems. Bosch is developing all the components and functions based on the "Cartronic" system architecture (see P. 1066) and intends to network all control and regulation tasks in the vehicle. It consists of a clearly structured function architecture and modular software with open, standardized interfaces.

### Summary and outlook

The development of sensors for detecting the vehicle's surroundings is progressing at a fast pace. New functions are quickly being integrated according to their relevance to safety and convenience.

Close-range sensors represent the next milestone in this development. They will form a "virtual safety shield" around the vehicle and provide the signals that will firstly alert the driver to potentially critical situations, and secondly act as a data source for active safety and convenience systems.

At the same time (and as the high-performance sensor chips become available for volume production), video sensors will enter the world of automotive technology and open up a multiplicity of opportunities. This will open up the way for information systems that are based on highly complex image analysis using high-performance processors and which can be used as data sources by several driving-assistance systems.

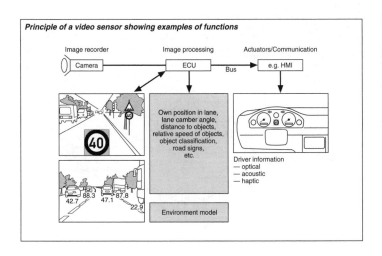

*Principle of a video sensor showing examples of functions*

Image recorder — Camera → Image processing — ECU — Bus → Actuators/Communication — e.g. HMI

Own position in lane, lane camber angle, distance to objects, relative speed of objects, object classification, road signs, etc.

40

88.3  87.8
42.7  47.1  22.9

Driver information
— optical
— acoustic
— haptic

Environment model

# Adaptive Cruise Control (ACC) for passenger cars

## Function
The basic function of Adaptive Cruise Control relies on the conventional cruise-control system (vehicle-speed controler), which maintains a desired speed specified by the driver. In addition, ACC can adapt vehicle speed to changing traffic conditions by means of automatic acceleration, throttle closing or braking. This system thus maintains the vehicle's distance to the vehicle driving in front as a function of road speed.

## Distance sensor
The most important component in an ACC system is a sensor which measures the distance, the relative speed and the relative position of the preceding vehicles. Maximum performance is achieved – even in poor weather conditions – with a radar sensor.

The radar sensor (see P. 117) operates at a frequency of 76...77 GHz which has been specially allocated to ACC. Three beams are emitted simultaneously for measurement purposes. The beams reflected by the preceding vehicles are analyzed regarding their propagation time, Doppler shift and amplitude ratio. From these factors, the distance, relative speed, and relative position are calculated (for details, refer to PP. 117...119).

## Course setting
To ensure reliable ACC operation no matter what the situation – e.g. also on curves/bends – it is essential that the preceding vehicles can be allocated to the correct lane(s). For this purpose, the information from the ESP sensor system (yaw rate, steering-wheel angle, wheel speeds and lateral acceleration) is evaluated with regard to the ACC-equipped vehicle's actual curve status. Further information on the traffic flow is obtained from the radar signals. To assist with course setting, data from the navigation system is used. In future, information from video image processing systems will also be utilized.

## Engine intervention
Speed control requires an electronic engine-performance control system (ETC or EDC). This system allows the vehicle to be accelerated to the required speed or, if an obstacle appears, to be decelerated by means of automatic throttle closing.

## Active brake intervention
Experience has shown that deceleration by means of throttle closing is not sufficient for ACC operation. Only the inclusion of brake intervention makes it possible for longer follow-up control operations

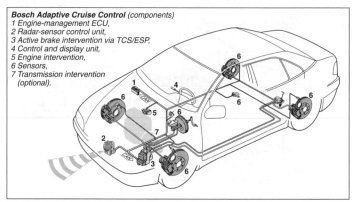

*Bosch Adaptive Cruise Control* (components)
1 Engine-management ECU,
2 Radar-sensor control unit,
3 Active brake intervention via TCS/ESP,
4 Control and display unit,
5 Engine intervention,
6 Sensors,
7 Transmission intervention (optional).

with ACC without the need for frequent driver intervention. ESP provides the possibility of braking without driver intervention.

ACC permits only "soft" brake intervention. Panic braking due to the sudden appearance of obstacles (e.g. a slow-moving vehicle in front suddenly changes its lane) is therefore not possible.

### Setting options
The driver inputs the required speed and the required time gap; the time gap available to the driver ranges from 1 to 2 s.

### Display elements
The driver must be provided with at least the following information:
- indication of the required speed
- indication of the switch-on status
- indication of the required time gap selected by the driver
- indication of the follow-up mode, which informs the driver as to whether the system is controlling the distance to a detected target object or not.

### Aim of ACC
The aim of ACC is to relieve the driver of the stress associated with "mindless" driving tasks such as maintaining speeds and driving behind other vehicles in congested traffic. This system helps to improve road safety as well as driver comfort.

### System limits
Even with this form of driver support, the driver remains fully responsible for handling the vehicle. He/she remains responsible for complex decisions relating to straight-ahead driving and control of the vehicle – and obviously for steering as well. The orientation of the function towards driver convenience draws a clear boundary between the tasks which are the responsibility of ACC and those which are the responsibility of the driver. Thus, safety functions such as panic braking are not featured in this system and are postponed to future generations of the technology. These functions, together with selecting the required speed and the required time gap, are the sole responsibility of the driver.

ACC does not yet permit control operations in city environments. This system can only be activated at speeds in excess of 30 km/h.

Expanding functions for operation in city areas would require considerably higher performance on the part of the sensors responsible for monitoring the environment. This level of performance cannot be achieved by the 76.5 GHz radar alone.

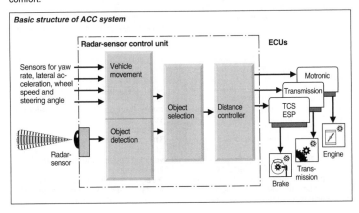

*Basic structure of ACC system*

# Adaptive Cruise Control (ACC) for commercial vehicles

## Design and function

Like the basic cruise-control system that has been available as a standard feature for many years, ACC can be categorized as a driving-assistance system. In addition to the basic cruise-control function, ACC measures the distance to the vehicle in front and its relative speed, and uses this information together with other collected data to regulate the time gap between the vehicles.

ACC is a convenience system which relieves the driver of routine tasks, but not of his/her responsibility to maintain control of the vehicle. Therefore, the driver can override or deactivate the ACC function at any time.

The ACC systems currently available consist of a 77-GHz radar sensor (see P. 117) as also used in ACC systems for cars (see P. 1058). The evaluation and control electronics are integrated in the sensor housing. The radar module sends and receives data via a CAN data bus (see P. 1072) to and from other electronic control units which regulate engine torque and vehicle braking (by means of retarders, exhaust brakes and service brakes).

The time gap to the vehicle in front is calculated from the radar signals and compared with the required time gap specified by the driver. If the time gap is <u>shorter</u> than the required gap, the ACC system responds in a manner appropriate to the traffic situation by initially reducing engine torque, and only if necessary by automatically braking the vehicle using the retarder or the exhaust brake.

The service brakes are only brought into action if, for example, the retarder is not capable of generating the deceleration required by the ACC due to its limited and speed-dependent braking capacity. This may be the case at low speeds or if the vehicle is fully laden. On average, the

braking systems are not operated any more frequently by ACC than by a driver with proper anticipation.

If the time gap is <u>longer</u> than the required gap, the vehicle is accelerated. If the traffic situation changes and there is no longer a vehicle ahead within the range of the ACC, the vehicle is accelerated up to the required speed set in the cruise control.

The required deceleration calculated by the ACC is limited to approx. 2 m/s² so that full braking cannot be initiated automatically on dry roads. Acceleration operations are computed on the basis of energy efficiency.

On slippery road surfaces, vehicle braking or acceleration may trigger the ABS (see P. 858) or TCS (see P. 862) in the usual way.

## Applications

Fundamentally, the same type of ACC system can be used for buses and trucks or tractor vehicles. It caters for varying requirements with regard to drivetrain and braking systems, and manual, semiautomatic or fully automatic transmissions. The exacting user-friendliness requirements demanded for buses are also satisfied.

ACC for commercial vehicles has to meet different requirements than those demanded of ACC for passenger cars (see P. 117):
- Regulation of braking and acceleration must take account of the widely variable parameters of "payload/engine size".
- Overtaking and filtering maneuvers follow a different dynamic pattern on trucks than on cars, and therefore result in different control requirements and settings.
- The control dynamics must be capable of handling a situation where several vehicles equipped with ACC are driving in a platoon.
- A degree of simplification is provided by the fact that trucks have a more limited speed range than cars.

**ACC for commercial vehicles** (function modules)
1 Possible functions of radar sensor with integrated electronics. Block 4 may be implemented on external control units.
1...3 Identical functions for passenger-car and commercial-vehicle applications.

4 Specific functions for commercial vehicles and vehicle types.
5 External control units for drivetrain and brake-control systems.

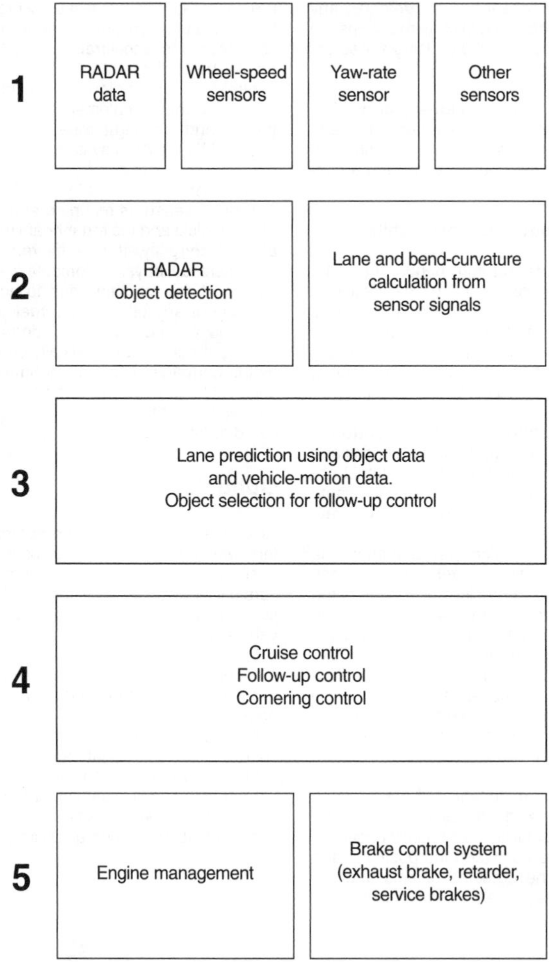

| 1 | RADAR data | Wheel-speed sensors | Yaw-rate sensor | Other sensors |

| 2 | RADAR object detection | Lane and bend-curvature calculation from sensor signals |

**3** Lane prediction using object data and vehicle-motion data. Object selection for follow-up control

**4** Cruise control
Follow-up control
Cornering control

| 5 | Engine management | Brake control system (exhaust brake, retarder, service brakes) |

# Control algorithms

The control system for trucks (as for cars) basically consists of three control modules:

**Control module 1: cruise control**
If the radar sensor has not detected any vehicles in front, the system maintains the vehicle's speed at the cruising speed set by the driver.

**Control module 2: follow-up control**
The radar sensor has detected vehicles in front. Control essentially maintains the time gap to the nearest vehicle at a constant setting.

**Control module 3: control while cornering**
When negotiating tight bends, the radar sensor can "lose sight" of the vehicle in front because of the limited width of its "field of vision". Until the vehicle comes in sight of the radar again, or until the system is switched to normal cruise control, special measures come into effect.

**Object detection and lane allocation**
The central task of the radar sensor and its integrated electronics is to detect objects and allocate them either to the same lane as the one on which the truck is traveling, or to a different lane.

Firstly, lane allocation demands the precise detection of vehicles ion front, and secondly, a precise knowledge of the motion of the system's own vehicle. Vehicle motion is calculated from the signals sent by sensors also used for the Electronic Stability Program (see P. 864). This includes the wheel-speed sensors for all the wheels, the yaw-rate and lateral-acceleration sensors, and the steering-angle sensor.

The decision as to which of the detected objects is used as the reference for adaptive cruise control is essentially based on a comparison between the positions and motion of the detected objects and the motion of the system's own vehicle.

**Electronic structure**
Apart from the sensor data outlined above, ACC requires additional data from the engine, retarder, transmission and brake control units and which is transmitted via CAN data bus. These control units are allocated different tasks according to their particular functions. Regulating deceleration and acceleration can, for example, be controlled by a central vehicle control unit. The engine and braking control units then implement the engine-torque and braking-torque adjustments required by the ACC system.

**Alignment**
The radar sensor is mounted at the front of the vehicle and the radar beam must be aligned correctly. If it is moved out of alignment by physical force, e.g. deformation of the mounting due to accident damage or any other effect, realignment must be carried out. Small degrees of misalignment are automatically corrected by the permanently active alignment routines implemented in the software. If manual realignment is required, this is indicated to the driver.

# Outlook

ACC is a measurement and control system which, for the first time, uses a "visual" sensor. A characteristic of the sensors currently available is their limited object-detection range, particularly in the vehicle's close range.

In order to improve close-range performance, sensors are under development to allow additional functions such as stop-and-roll and stop-and-go.

If the object-detection range using "visual" sensors (i.e. radar, laser and ultrasonic sensors and video cameras) is extended to the vehicle's entire surrounding area, other driving-assistance systems besides ACC will become possible.

Future advances might take the form of:
- Assistance systems which provide the driver with information and hazard alerts. Example: While the ACC controls vehicle motion in the direction of travel, a lane-detection system can alert the driver if the vehicle is about to leave its lane.
- Assistance systems which actively support the driver. Example: If a radar sensor or another sensor detects that a collision cannot be avoided, emergency braking can be automatically initiated in order to minimize damage. ACC is an assistance system of this type.
- Assistance systems which automatically intervene in order to prevent accidents in situations that are recognized as critical. Example: Steering adjust-

ments and/or braking operations are initiated automatically if obstructions are detected in the "blind spot" when the vehicle is cornering and are not immediately perceived by the driver.

The development of ACC was started as part of the European research project PROMETHEUS. Under the auspices of the European research project CHAUFFEUR, a study is being conducted on the automated control of trucks driving in platoons (where only the leading vehicle has a driver). Commercial use of such a function would at least require the addition of radio links between the vehicles as well as additional equipment for traffic management.

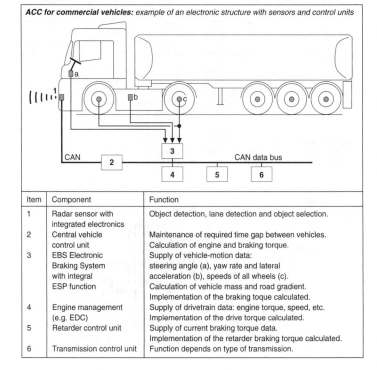

*ACC for commercial vehicles:* example of an electronic structure with sensors and control units

| Item | Component | Function |
|---|---|---|
| 1 | Radar sensor with integrated electronics | Object detection, lane detection and object selection. |
| 2 | Central vehicle control unit | Maintenance of required time gap between vehicles. Calculation of engine and braking torque. |
| 3 | EBS Electronic Braking System with integral ESP function | Supply of vehicle-motion data: steering angle (a), yaw rate and lateral acceleration (b), speeds of all wheels (c). Calculation of vehicle mass and road gradient. Implementation of the braking toque calculated. |
| 4 | Engine management (e.g. EDC) | Supply of drivetrain data: engine torque, speed, etc. Implementation of the drive torque calculated. |
| 5 | Retarder control unit | Supply of current braking torque data. Implementation of the retarder braking torque calculated. |
| 6 | Transmission control unit | Function depends on type of transmission. |

# Data processing and communication networks in motor vehicles

## Requirements

Highly sophisticated state-of-the-art open-loop and closed-loop control concepts are essential for meeting the demands for function, safety, environmental compatibility and convenience associated with the wide range of automotive subsystems installed in modern-day vehicles. Sensors monitor reference and controlled variables, which an electronic control unit (ECU) then converts to the signals required to adjust the final-control elements/actuators. The input signals can be analog (e.g. voltage characteristic at pressure sensor), digital (e.g. switch position) or pulse-shaped (i.e. information content as a function of time, e.g. engine-speed signal). These input signals are processed after appropriate conditioning (filtering, amplification, pulse-shape modification) and converted (analog/digital), preferably by digital signal-processing methods.

With modern semiconductor technology, powerful microcomputers can be integrated on relatively few chips together with their accompanying program and data memories, and special peripheral circuits designed specifically for real-time applications.

Modern vehicles are equipped with 20 to 60 electronic control units, e.g. for engine management, Antilock Braking System (ABS), and transmission-shift control. Improved performance and additional functions are obtained by synchronizing the processes controlled by the individual ECUs and by mutual real-time adaptation of the respective parameters. An example of this type of function is traction control (TCS), which reduces the drive torque if the driving wheels spin.

Originally, data exchange between the ECUs (in the example cited above, ABS/TCS and engine management ) took place via separate wires. However, this type of point-to-point connection is only suitable for a limited number of signals. The introduction of automotive-compatible communication networks for serial transmission of information and data between ECUs has expanded the data transfer capabilities and represents the logical development of autonomous "microcomputers" in motor vehicles.

---

*Signal processing in the ECU*
1 Digital input signals, 2 Analog input signals, 3 Protective circuit, 4 Amplifier, filter,
5 A/D converter, 6 Digital signal processing, 7 D/A converter, 8 Circuit breaker, 9 Power amplifier.

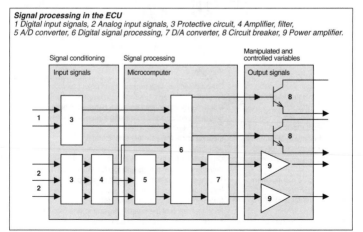

## Electronic control unit (ECU)

ECUs developed for use in motor vehicles all have a similar design. Their structure can be subdivided in the conditioning of input signals, the logic processing of these signals in the microcomputer, and the output of logic and power levels as regulation or control signals (see figure).

### Digital input signals
Detect a switch position or digital sensor signals (e.g. rotational-speed pulses from a Hall-effect sensor).

### Analog input signals
Signals from analog sensors (lambda sensor, pressure sensor).

### Pulse-shaped input signals
Signals from inductive wheel-speed sensors. After signal conditioning, they are then processed as digital signals.

### Initial conditioning of input signals
Protective circuits (passive: R and RC circuits; active: special surge-proof semiconductor components) are used to limit the voltage of the input signals to acceptable levels (operating voltage of the microcomputer). Filters remove most of the superimposed noise from the useful signals, which are then amplified to the microcomputer's input voltage.

### Signal processing
ECUs generally process signals in digital form. Rapid, periodic, real-time signals are processed in hardware modules specifically designed for the particular function. Results, e.g. a counter reading or the time of an event, are sent in registers to the CPU for further processing. This procedure substantially reduces the CPU's interrupt-response time ($\mu$s range).

The amount of time available for calculations is determined by the controlled system (e.g. milliseconds in the case of engine management) The software contains the actual control algorithms. Depending on the data, almost any logical operation can be implemented, and any data records can be stored and processed in the form of parameters, characteristic curves, or multidimensional program maps. For more complex requirements in the field of image processing, the use digital-signal processors (DSP) is becoming more widespread.

### Manipulated and controlled variables
Manipulated and controlled variables in the output module provide the required signals or power levels for peripheral actuators (e.g. electric motors for seat adjustment, power windows or power-assisted steering). Circuit breakers and amplifiers raise the microcomputer's output-signal levels (0...5 V, a few mA) to the power levels required for the actuators concerned (e.g. up to 100 A for short periods for engine cooling).

## Architecture

The structural building blocks are assembled in hardware platforms or modular kits by using identical components (chipsets). These modules are also increasingly used for multiple applications (e.g. engine management for gasoline and diesel engines).

The same procedure is also suitable for function modules for control algorithms, which then become modular, reusable components within the overall system. Essentially, there are two elements that are important for implementing this type of methodology transfer:
- A concept for configuring and structuring functionality within the vehicle (CARTRONIC).
- Communication networks over which ECUs can interexchange information.

The building plan for assembling functions, network hardware and software is referred to as the architecture. System architecture describes the entirety of the structural and dynamic characteristics of distributed systems.

## CARTRONIC®

### Networked vehicle systems
The continuing development of automotive electronic systems is influenced by ever increasing demands. These include safety, convenience and environmental compatibility, tougher legal requirements and directives, integration of information and entertainment-system functions ("infotainment"), and communication with external computers and data services via mobile radio.

Driven by these demands combined with the continuing downward spiral of prices, individual vehicle systems (fuel injection, ABS, radio) have become a composite, networked system in which information is exchanged via data buses (e.g. CAN), and reciprocal interaction is possible. Cross-marque standardization of individual components, subsystems and subfunctions within such a composite system is the basic requirement if development times are to be shortened. At the same time, reliability and system availability must be increased, and the number of components required must be reduced by sharing information between different vehicle systems.

### Composite systems (examples)
Present-day vehicles already have composite systems, such as the traction control system (TCS) and the electronic stability program (ESP), which is an extension of it. The cross-system functions of these two systems are carried out by the TCS electronic control unit (ECU) that informs the engine ECU when the wheels start to spin so that the latter can reduce drive torque accordingly. Similarly, the air-conditioning system may inform the engine-management system that it is about to switch on, which will result in the need to increase engine torque or speed.

### Requirements
The implementation of such cross-system functions through the interaction of subsystems requires agreement on the standardization of interfaces and subsystem functions. Definitions must be drawn up to specify what information a subsystem re-

quires and what variables are to be controlled on the basis of that information. This is all the more important in view of the fact that the subsystems are developed separately (often by several different suppliers), and modifications to suit a particular vehicle model or the requirements of a specific manufacturer are costly and error-prone.

The increasing implementation of functionality through software requires applying interface compatibility and standardization to the software.

### Concept
The above demands have resulted in the development of CARTRONIC, a classification and specification concept for all vehicle control and management systems. It contains fixed rules for interaction between subsystems as well as expandable modular architectures for "function", "safety", and "electronics" on the basis of these formal rules. It thus provides the means for a description of the vehicle as an overall system. On this basis, suppliers can harmonize interaction between their products without having to be familiar with the internal processes of subsystems, and without causing large-scale manufacturer- or model-related modifications.

### Structuring and architecture
What is required is a universal structuring system and practical implementation methods within a derivative, formalized structure. The function architecture at vehicle level encompasses all control and management tasks that arise within the vehicle. Logic components are defined to represent the tasks of the composite system. The links and interfaces between components and the way they interact are specified by a requirements analysis. The implementation-independent system architecture thus created has to be supplemented by a safety architecture which provides additional elements in order to ensure safe and reliable operation of the system as a whole. The composite system is then created by transforming various logic and functional components produces a hardware form (electronic circuits, ECUs, microcomputers). The resulting optimized hardware topology is

characterized by the specifics of the vehicle model (e.g. specified dimensions and physical location of components).

## Architecture rules

The rules for the function or domain architecture are designed to derive a definition and layout organization for the composite system based on requirements, independently of the specific hardware or network topology. It is created exclusively on the basis of logic, functional, and nonfunctional aspects (e.g. costs, reliability). For this reason, the rules essentially define components and the permissible interaction in the sense of communication interrelationships.

## Requirements analysis

Conceptually, the requirements analysis for a planned or existing composite system starts by analyzing the functionality and other general parameters (qualities) of the previously autonomous individual systems and their environment (e.g. fault tolerance in the case of safety-related systems). The secondary conditions are termed "nonfunctional requirements". As

this also takes place at functional level (separate from final hardware development and partitioning), the descriptions are still independent of vehicle-specific design variations and therefore permit universally valid statements. Basic structuring at this level makes it possible to restrict the diversity of hardware and software and to use identical electronic modules (basic modules) for the basic functions of a large number of vehicle types.

## Structuring elements

Architecture elements are systems, components and communication interrelationships which formally describe a composite system and also include the structuring and modeling rules for designing interaction and defining interdependencies. The degree to which components are detailed is chiefly determined by their reusability in other systems (as general as possible, as specific as necessary).

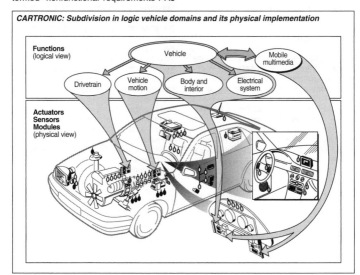

**CARTRONIC: Subdivision in logic vehicle domains and its physical implementation**

Functions (logical view)

Vehicle — Mobile multimedia

Drivetrain — Vehicle motion — Body and interior — Electrical system

Actuators Sensors Modules (physical view)

## Systems, components, interfaces

In these terms, a system is a combination of components that are interlinked by means of communication mechanisms and which perform a higher-level function beyond their individual functions. The term "component" is not explicitly limited to a physical unit but is understood as a unit of function. CARTRONIC recognizes three types of component:

- components whose function is primarily coordination
- components whose function is primarily operative
- components whose function is exclusively to generate, supply and forward information

Component interfaces refer to possible communication interrelationships that can be established with other components. Wherever possible, physical variables are defined as interfaces (e.g. drive or engine torque).

## System description

Therefore, a system is described by the representation of all functional components, their communication interrelationships, and modes of reciprocal interaction.

## Structuring rules

Structuring rules describe permissible communication interrelationships between different components within the system architecture. A hierarchical system concept is created according to the structure which starts with the vehicle as an entity and extends as far as the individual components. Accordingly, there are structuring rules for communication interrelationships between components at the same level and at different levels. There are also structuring rules for transferring communications from one subsystem to another.

## Modeling rules

The modeling rules consist of patterns which combine components and communication interrelationships for solving specific tasks which arise more than once within a vehicle system. These patterns can then be repeated at various points within the vehicle structure.

## Architectural features

A structure represented by means of the specified structuring and modeling rules displays standardized features and characteristics:

- a hierarchical work flow (jobs are accepted only at the same or a higher level)
- a clear distinction between coordinators and information suppliers (operating controls and sensors)
- clear delimitation of individual components based on the black-box principle (as visible as necessary and as concealed as possible)

## Integration in the development process

In the development process (see figure), the CARTRONIC concept systematically supports the integration of the vehicle manufacturer's requirements in the function structures with simple communication relationships (requirements analysis). A second stage involves more precise detailing of the function structure by converting it to a behavior model (analysis model) using a modeling language (e.g. Unified Modeling Language (UML)). As the analysis model is further refined, functional requirements (e.g. control times) and nonfunctional requirements (such as costs, safety, etc.) are incorporated in an object-oriented design model. Implementation can be represented by code-framework generation, or code generation using application-oriented development tools (e.g. Statemate, ASCET, Matlab/Simulink).

### Consequences

CARTRONIC represents a standardized concept for describing all vehicle functions. By virtue of the facility for defining generic functions, it can describe all commonly used vehicle control and management systems using standardized terminology. New functions will require appropriate extension of these function categories. The next step required is a cross-marque definition of interfaces between components or subsystems at functional and physical levels. This allows the implementation of complex function networks within the vehicle involving collaboration between several suppliers.

### Outlook

The functional capabilities of present-day vehicle systems are determined to an increasing degree by software, and composite systems are becoming computer networks. The standardization of operating systems is making software applications portable, i.e. they can be used on different ECUs. Software architecture is thus becoming independent of hardware topology. In order to keep individual software modules interchangeable and reusable, the CARTRONIC architecture and interface rules will require further refinement and more precise definition. As in the field of computer applications, interfaces between different functions will be defined by "APIs" (application programming interfaces) which will then precisely define the CARTRONIC communication interrelationships. This course requires agreement on industry standards between the different manufacturers and suppliers. CARTRONIC has established the basic foundations for such a development.

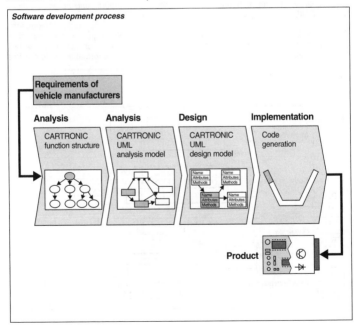

*Software development process*

## Communication networks

Present-day motor vehicles are equipped with a large number of electronic control units (ECUs) which interexchange large volumes of data in order to perform their various functions. The conventional method of communication over dedicated data lines for each link is now reaching the limits of its capabilities. On the one hand, it makes wiring harnesses so complex that they become unmanageable, and on the other, the finite number of pins on the connectors becomes the limiting factor for ECU development. The solution lies in the use of specific, vehicle-compatible serial bus systems. Once system that has become a widespread standard is CAN (Controller Area Network). The communication networks and their layout – the network architecture – represent one of the most important components in the creation of modern automotive electronic systems, besides the function architecture (CARTRONIC).

There are four areas of application in motor vehicles, each with its own set of requirements:

## Multimedia networking

Mobile communications applications link components such as navigation systems, phones, or audio/video systems with central display and operator units. The aim is to standardize processes as far as possible and to summarize status information in order to minimize distraction of the driver. In order to protect other vehicle systems from unauthorized access and external interference (CD, mobile channel, Internet), the network domains are separated by access restrictions (firewalls).

The data transfer rates for controlling components in this "infotainment" domain are of the order of 125 kbit/s. Direct transmission of audio or video data requires bandwidths ranging from 10 Mbit/s to more than 100 Mbit/s.

### Networking concept

With the entry of multimedia systems to the automotive world, more and more aspects of computer and communications technology are finding their way in motor vehicles (e.g. mobile radio components, such as GSM equipment or modules, computer-similar architectures in navigation, and driver-information systems). In a

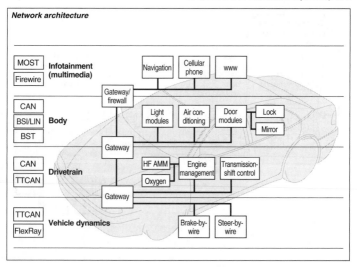

*Network architecture*

| MOST | Infotainment |
| Firewire | (multimedia) |

| CAN | Body |
| BSI/LIN | |
| BST | |

| CAN | Drivetrain |
| TTCAN | |

| TTCAN | Vehicle dynamics |
| FlexRay | |

Navigation — Cellular phone — www

Gateway/firewall

Light modules — Air conditioning — Door modules — Lock — Mirror

Gateway

HF AMM — Engine management — Transmission-shift control

Oxygen

Gateway

Brake-by-wire — Steer-by-wire

well equipped vehicle, therefore, there has to be a double DIN slot instead of the normal single DIN slot for the radio. For higher-specification systems or for system expandability over the life cycle of the vehicle, (e.g. for devices such as DVD players, CDC, rear-seat units), the introduction of a powerful network is required.

In addition, the enormous divergence between the product life cycles of computers and communications equipment (in extreme cases only a few months) and of motor vehicles (over ten years) gives rise to the possibility of upgrading equipment easily. Standardized networking via cable, or in some cases using wireless radio systems, is therefore indispensable. For this reason, the development of specialized multimedia data buses was started a number of years ago. Such buses must be able to transmit control data as well as audio and video signals, while the characteristics of data (band-width, continuous/variable bit rates, compressed/noncompressed) vary widely.

The large number of different types of data places particular requirements on the networking concept.

**Multiplex applications**

Multiplex applications are suitable for controlling components in the area of bodywork and convenience electronics, such as air-conditioning, central locking, and seat adjustment. Bit rates typically range from 1 kbit/s to 125 kbit/s. Owing to the considerable pressure on prices in this application sector, a number of different alternatives have been pursued. Cost-effective point-to-point connection, such as Bit-Synchronous Interface (BSI), can be installed between the alternator and the engine-management ECU, and local subnetworks, such as driver doors, can be created with the Local Interface Network (LIN) with bit rates up to 20 kbit/s.

*Automotive networking*

| Body/multiplex systems: | Infotainment/multimedia: | Driving-related functions: |
|---|---|---|
| 1 Lighting, | 10 Human-machine interface | 19 Chassis system, |
| 2 Air conditioning, | (e.g. display instruments), | 20 Environment sensors, |
| 3 Anti-theft alarm, | 11 Gateway/firewall, | Adaptive Cruise Control |
| 4 Actuators and sensors, | 12 Audio/video, | (ACC), |
| 5 Doors, locks, mirrors, | 13 Mobile communications, | 21 Driver-restraint systems |
| 6 Passenger-compartment | 14 Other options, | (airbags, seat-belt |
| sensing, | 15 Engine management, | tighteners, etc.), |
| 7 Energy management, | 16 Brake management | 22 Other options, |
| 8 Other options, | (e.g. ESP), | 23 Diagnosis interface. |
| 9 Navigation, location | 17 Transmission-shift control, | |
| detection/gateway/firewall, | 18 Steering, | |

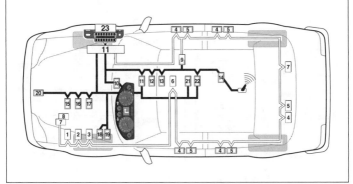

Based on performance and versatility, the upper end of the application range including vehicle diagnostics is represented by the Controller Area Network (CAN).

## Multiplex applications

Multiplex applications are used to control the drivetrain and vehicle motion. These applications include internetworked electronic systems, such as Motronic, transmission-shift control, and Electronic Stability Program. Typical bit rates range from 125 kbit/s to 1 Mbit/s in order to guarantee the required application operation.

## Controller Area Network (CAN)

The CAN is a bus system which has established itself as the standard for automotive applications. With this system, the control units of the various electronic systems are not interconnected by multiple separate cables, but are networked by a data bus instead. This does away with a large number of electrical connections and results in a reduced likelihood of failure of the device network.

### Bus topology

CAN operates according to the multi-master principle, in which a linear bus topology connects several ECUs of equal priority rating. The advantage of this type of topology lies in the fact that a malfunction at one node does not impair bus-system access for the other devices. Thus, the probability of total system failure is substantially lower than with other logic architectures (such as ring or active-star topologies). When a ring or active-star topology is employed, failure at a single node or at the CPU is sufficient to cause total system failure.

### Content-based addressing

CAN uses message-based addressing. This involves assigning a fixed identifier to each message. The identifier classifies the content of the message (e.g. engine speed). Each station processes only messages whose identifiers are stored in its acceptance list (message filtering). Thus, CAN requires no station addresses for data transmission, and the nodes are not involved in managing the system configuration. This facilitates adaptation to variations in equipment levels.

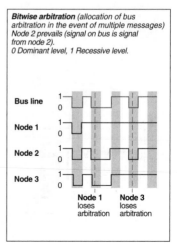

*Addressing and acceptance checking*
Node 2 sends, nodes 1 and 4 receive the data.

CAN node 1 | CAN node 2 | CAN node 3 | CAN node 4

Adoption | Provision | | Adoption
Selection | Message transmission | Selection | Selection
Reception | | Reception | Reception

Bus

*Bitwise arbitration* (allocation of bus arbitration in the event of multiple messages)
Node 2 prevails (signal on bus is signal from node 2).
0 Dominant level, 1 Recessive level.

Bus line
Node 1
Node 2
Node 3

Node 1 loses arbitration | Node 3 loses arbitration

## Logic bus states

The CAN protocol is based on two logic states: The bits are either "recessive" (logic 1) or "dominant" (logic 0). When at least one station transmits a dominant bit, it overwrites the recessive bits simultaneously sent by other stations.

## Priority assignments

The identifier labels both data content and the message priority when the message is sent. Identifiers corresponding to low binary numbers enjoy a high priority and vice versa.

## Bus arbitration

Each station can begin transmitting its most important data as soon as the bus is unoccupied. When several stations start to transmit simultaneously, the system responds by employing "wired-and" arbitration to sort out the resulting contentions over bus access. The message with the highest priority is assigned first access, without any bit loss or delay. Transmitters respond to failure to gain bus access by automatically switching to receive mode; they then repeat the transmission attempt as soon as the bus is free again.

## Message format

CAN supports two different data-frame formats, where the only difference is the length of the identifier (ID). The standard-format ID is 11 bits, while the extended version consists of 29 bits. Thus, the transmission data frame contains a maximum of 130 bits in standard format, or 150 bits in the extended format. This ensures minimum waiting time until the next transmission (which could be urgent). The data frame consists of seven consecutive bit fields:

<u>Start of Frame</u> indicates the beginning of a message and synchronizes all stations.

The <u>arbitration field</u> consists of the message's identifier and an additional control bit. While this field is being transmitted, the transmitter accompanies the transmission of each bit with a check to ensure that no higher-priority message is being transmitted (which would cancel the access authorization). The control bit determines whether the message is classified under "data frame" or "remote frame".

The <u>control field</u> contains the code indicating the number of data bytes in the data field.

The <u>data field</u> information content comprises 0 to 8 bytes. A message of data length 0 can be used to synchronize distributed processes.

The <u>CRC field</u> (Cyclic Redundancy Check) contains the check word for detecting possible transmission interference.

The <u>Ack field</u> contains the acknowledgement signals with which all receivers indicate the error-free receipt of messages.

<u>End of Frame</u> marks the end of the message.

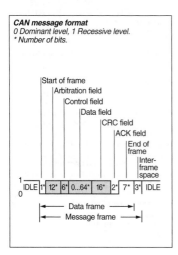

*CAN message format*
*0 Dominant level, 1 Recessive level.*
*\* Number of bits.*

Start of frame
Arbitration field
Control field
Data field
CRC field
ACK field
End of frame
Inter-frame space

| 1 0 IDLE | 1* | 12* | 6* | 0...64* | 16* | 2* | 7* | 3* | IDLE |

|← Data frame →|
|← Message frame →|

### Transmitter initiative
The transmitter will usually initiate a data transmission by sending a data frame. However, the receiver can also request data from the transmitter. This involves the receiver sending out a "remote frame". The data frame and the corresponding remote frame have the same identifier. They are distinguished by the bit that follows the identifier.

### Error detection
CAN incorporates a number of monitoring features for detecting errors. These include:

15-bit CRC (Cyclic Redundancy Check): Each receiver compares the CRC sequence which it receives with the calculated sequence.

Monitoring: Each transmitter compares transmitted and scanned bit.

Bit stuffing: between "start of frame" and the end of the CRC field, each data frame or remote frame may contain a maximum of 5 consecutive bits of the same polarity. The transmitter follows up a sequence of 5 bits of the same polarity by inserting a bit of the opposite polarity in the bit stream; the receivers eliminate these bits as the messages arrive.

Frame check: The CAN protocol contains several bit fields with a fixed format for verification by all stations.

### Error handling
When a CAN controller detects an error, it aborts the current transmission by sending an error flag. An error flag consists of 6 dominant bits; it functions by deliberately violating the stuffing convention and/or formats.

### Fault confinement with local failure
Defective stations can severely impair the ability to process bus traffic. Therefore, the CAN controllers incorporate mechanisms which can distinguish between intermittent and permanent errors, and local station failures. This process is based on statistical evaluation of error conditions.

### Implementations
In order to provide proper CPU support for a wide range of different requirements, semiconductor manufacturers have introduced implementations representing a broad range of performance levels. The various implementations differ neither in the message format they produce, nor in their error-handling methods. The difference lies solely in the type of CPU support required for message administration.

As the demands placed on the ECU's processing capacity are extensive, the interface controller should be able to administer a large number of messages, and expedite data transmission without overloading the CPU. Powerful CAN controllers are generally used in this type of application.

The demands placed on the controllers by multiplex systems and the control tasks of current mobile communications are more modest. For this reason, more basic and less expensive chips are preferred.

### Standardization
CAN for data exchange in automotive applications has been standardized both by ISO and SAE – in ISO 11519-2 for low-speed applications up to 125 kbit/s, and in ISO 11898 and SAE J 22584 (cars), and SAE J 1939 (trucks and buses) for high-speed applications greater than 125 kbit/s. There is also an ISO standard for diagnosis via CAN (ISO 15765) in preparation.

### Extensions for time-based systems (new)
The current development trend for systems related to vehicle dynamics, such as brakes and steering, means that mechanical and hydraulic components are becoming increasingly replaced by electronic systems (x-by-wire). In order to meet the demands for reliability, safety and fault tolerance, networks with demonstrable time-response characteristics are required. With this type of protocol, the control units (nodes) within the communication network and communication between them are allocated time windows within a communication matrix in the network planning process.

This means that the age of the data and the availability of the nodes can be determined at any time, and the communicating nodes can be synchronized with one another with minimal time differences. Such protocols are referred to as time-triggered as distinct from event-driven protocols. They support separate development by different developers through the "combinability" of individual systems and predictable behavior of the overall system.

The extension of the CAN protocol to include the capability of operating in time-triggered mode is called "Time-Triggered CAN" (TTCAN). It is fully configurable with regard to the proportion of time-triggered to event-driven communication components, and is therefore fully compatible with CAN networks. Application has been made to ISO for standardization of TTCAN (ISO 11 898-4).

Expansion of the bandwidth to up to 10 Mbit/s and of the protocol (e.g. FlexRay) are presently under development in consortiums consisting of members of the automotive industry and their suppliers.

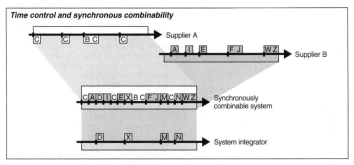

*Time control and synchronous combinability*

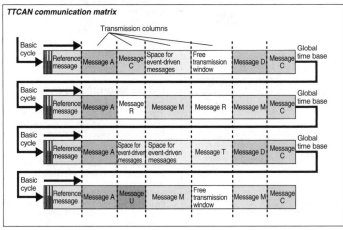

*TTCAN communication matrix*

# Instrumentation

Drivers have to process a constantly increasing stream of information originating from their own and other vehicles, from the road, and from telecommunication equipment. All this information must be conveyed to drivers in the information and communications areas of the vehicle on suitable display and indicating equipment that comply with ergonomic requirements. In future, in-car cellular phones, navigation systems, and distance control systems will join automative sound systems and vehicle monitoring systems as standard equipment in motor vehicles.

***Driver information area*** *(development)*
*1 Needle instrument, 2 Needle instrument with TN LCD and separate AMLCD in center console, 3 Needle instrument with (D)STN and integrated AMLCD, 4 Programmable instrument with two AMLCD components.*

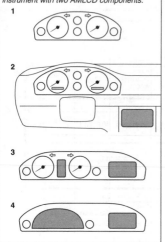

## Information and communication areas

In any vehicle, there are four information and communication areas which must satisfy different requirements in terms of their display features:
– the instrument cluster
– the windshield
– the center console
– the vehicle rear compartment

The display features in these areas are determined by the available range of information and the necessary, useful, or desirable information for the occupants.

Dynamic information and monitoring information (e.g. fuel level), to which the driver should respond, is displayed on the <u>instrument cluster</u>, i.e. as close as possible to the driver's primary field of vision.

A head-up display (HUD), which reflects the information on the <u>windshield</u>, is ideally suited to engage the driver's attention (e.g. in the case of warnings from a radar distance control system (ACC) or route directions). The display is supplemented acoustically by voice output.

Status information or dialog prompts are mainly displayed in the vicinity of the control unit in the <u>center console</u>.

Information of an entertainment nature is featured in the <u>vehicle rear compartment</u>, away from the primary field of vision. This is also the ideal location for a mobile office. The backrest of the front-passenger seat is a suitable installation location for the monitor and operator unit of a laptop computer.

## Driver information systems

The driver information area in the vehicle cockpit and the display technologies used have gone through the following stages of development:

### Individual and combined instruments
Conventional individual instruments for the optical output of information were initially superseded by more cost-effective instrument clusters (combination of several information units in a single housing) with good illumination and antireflection

qualities. The passage of time, with the continual increase in information, saw the creation of the modern instrument cluster in the existing space available, with several needle instruments and numerous indicator lamps (see figure, 1).

### Digital displays
#### Digital instruments
The digital instruments fitted up to the 1990s displayed information using vacuum fluorescence display (VFD) technology and, later, liquid crystal (LCD) technology, but they have now largely disappeared. Instead, conventional analog needle instruments are used in combination with displays. At the same time, there is an increase in the size, resolution and color representation of the displays.

#### Central display and operator unit in the center console
With the advent of automotive information, navigation, and telematic systems (see PP. 1082/1112/1114), screens and keyboards on the center console are now becoming widespread. Such systems combine all the additional information in a central display and operator unit, from functional units and information components (e.g. cellular phone, car radio/CD, controls for heating/air conditioning (HVAC) and – important for Japan – the "TV" function). The components are interconnected in a network and are capable of interactive communication.

Positioning this terminal, which is of universal use to driver and passenger, in the center console is effective and necessary from both ergonomic and technical standpoints. The optical information appears in a graphics display. The demands placed by TV reproduction and the navigation system on the video/map display determine its resolution and color reproduction (see figure, 2).

### Graphics modules
Fitting vehicles with a driver's airbag and power-assisted steering as standard has resulted in a reduction in the view through the top half of the steering wheel. At the same time the amount of information that has to be displayed in the installation space available has increased. This cre-

ates the need for additional display modules with graphics capabilities and display areas that can show any information flexibly and in prioritized form.

This tendency results in instrumentation featuring a classical needle instrument but supplemented by a graphics display. The central screen is also at the level of the instrument cluster (see figure, 3). The important issue for all visual displays is that they can be easily read within the driver's primary field of vision or its immediate vicinity without the driver having to look away from the road for long periods, as is the case, for instance, if the displays are positioned in the lower area of the center console.

The graphics modules in the instrument cluster permit mainly the display of driver- and vehicle-related functions such as service intervals, check functions covering the vehicle's operating state, and also vehicle diagnostics as needed for the workshop. They can also show route-direction information from the navigation system (no digitized map excerpts, only route-direction symbols such as arrows as turnoff instructions or intersection symbols). The originally monochrome units are now being superseded on higher-specification vehicles by color displays (usually TFT screens) which can be read more quickly and easily because of their color resolution.

For the central display monitor with an integrated information system, the tendency is now to switch from a 4:3 aspect ratio to a wider format with a 16:9 aspect ratio (cinema-film format), which allows additional route-direction symbols to be displayed as well as the map.

### Individual module with computer monitor
In about 2006 TFT displays will be used to represent analog instruments for the first time (see figure, 4). For cost reasons, however, this technology will only gradually replace conventional displays.

## Instrument clusters

### Design

Microcontroller technology and the ongoing networking of motor vehicles have meanwhile transformed instrument clusters from precision-mechanical instruments to electronically dominated devices. A typical instrument cluster (LED-illuminated, with TN-type conductive-rubber-contacted segment LCDs, see Figure) is a very flat component (electronics, flat stepping motors), and virtually all the components (mainly SMT) are directly contacted on a printed-circuit board.

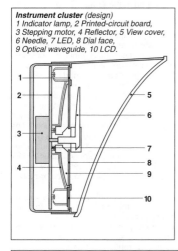

*Instrument cluster* (design)
1 Indicator lamp, 2 Printed-circuit board,
3 Stepping motor, 4 Reflector, 5 View cover,
6 Needle, 7 LED, 8 Dial face,
9 Optical waveguide, 10 LCD.

### Operating concept

While the basic functions are the same in most instrument clusters (see typical block diagram), the partitioning of the function modules in (partly application-specific) microcontrollers, ASICs, and standard peripherals sometimes differs significantly (product range, display scope, display types).

Electronic instrument clusters indicate measured variables with high accuracy thanks to stepping-motor technology, and also take over "intelligent" functions such as speed-dependent oil-pressure warning, prioritized fault display in matrix displays, or service-interval indicator. Even online diagnostic functions are standard and take up a significant part of the program memory.

Since instrument clusters are part of the basic equipment of any vehicle, and all bus systems come together here in any case, they also incorporate gateway functions to a certain degree; in other words, they act as bridges between different bus systems in the vehicle (e.g. engine CAN, body CAN, and diagnostics bus).

### Measuring instruments

The vast majority of instruments operates with a mechanical needle and a dial face. Initially, the compact, electronically triggered moving-magnet quotient measuring instrument replaced the bulky eddy-current speedometer. Nowadays, more durable geared stepping motors, which are very slim-fitting, have become the preferred choice. Due to a compact magnetic circuit and (mostly) 2-stage gearing

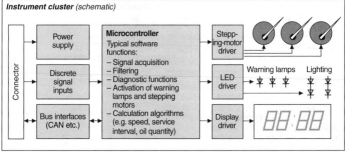

*Instrument cluster* (schematic)

with a power output of only approx. 100 mW, these motors permit swift and highly accurate needle positioning.

## Lighting

Instrument clusters were originally lit by frontlighting technology in the form of incandescent lamps. Backlighting technology has meanwhile gained acceptance on account of its attractive appearance. Incandescent lamps have been replaced by long-lasting light-emitting diodes (LEDs, see P. 55). LEDs are also suitable as warning lamps and for backlighting scales, displays and (via plastic optical waveguides) needles (refer to table headed "Overview of lighting sources").

The efficient yellow, orange, and red InAlGaP technology LEDs are now in widespread use. The more recent InGaN technology has produced significant efficiency improvements for the colors green, blue, and white. Here, the color white is obtained by combining a blue LED chip with an orange-emitting luminescent material (yttrium-aluminum granulate).

However, special technologies are also being used for specialized configurations: CCFLs (Cold Cathode Fluorescent Lamps): Mainly for "black screen" instruments which appear black when they are deactivated. The combination of a tinted view cover (e.g. 25% transmission) with these very bright lamps (high luminance, high voltage) produces a brilliant appearance with outstanding contrast. Since color LCDs have very low transmission (typically approx. 6%), it is imperative that CCFLs are used to backlight them in order to obtain good contrast, even in daylight.

EL (electroluminescent) film: This flat film, which lights up when an alternating voltage is applied and achieves an extremely even light pattern, has only been available in automobile-compatible form since about the year 2000. It offers extensive freedom of design for color combinations and/or for superimposing dial faces on display surfaces.

## Overview of lighting sources

| Illumination method | Possible colors | Typical data [1] | Technical suitability for | Conventional inst. clust. | Black-screen inst. | Service life [2] in hrs | Activation |
|---|---|---|---|---|---|---|---|
| Bulb | White (any color poss. with filter) | 2 lm/W 65 mA 14 V | Dial face Needle Display | + o o | − − − | $B_3 \approx 4,500$ | No special activation required |
| SMD LED luminescence diode | Red, orange, yellow (AlInGaP) | 20 lm/W 25 mA 2 V | Dial face Needle Display | + + + | o + − | $B_3 \gg 10,000$ | Series resistors or regulation required |
| | Blue, green (InGaN), White (with converter) | 3...12 lm/W 15 mA 3.6 V | Dial face Needle Display | + + o | o + − | $B_3 > 10,000$ | |
| EL film electro- luminescence | Blue, violet, yellow, green, orange, white | 2 lm/W 100 V~ 400 Hz | Dial face Needle Display | + − o | − − − | approx. 10,000 | High voltage required |
| CCFL cold cathode lamp | White (any color poss. depending on fluorescent material | 25 mA 2 kV~ 50...100 kHz | Dial face Needle Display | + − + | o o + | $B_3 > 10,000$ | High voltage required |

[1] Efficiency in lm/W (lumen per watt), current in mA, voltage in V or kV, activation frequency in kHz.

[2] $B_3$ time at which 3% of the components can have failed. Suitability: + Preferred, o Qualified, − Not suitable

# Display types

## TN LCD

With its high status of development, TN LCD technology ("Twisted Nematic Liquid-Crystal Display", see P. 55) is the most commonly used form of display. The term stems from the twisted arrangement of the elongated liquid-crystal molecules between the locating glass plates with transparent electrodes. A layer of this type forms a "light valve", which blocks or passes polarized light depending on whether voltage is applied to it or not. It can be used in the temperature range of $-40\,°C...+85\,°C$. The switching times are relatively long at low temperatures on account of the high viscosity of the liquid-crystal material.

TN LCDs can be operated in positive contrast (dark characters on a light background) or negative contrast (light characters on a dark background). Positive-contrast cells are ideal for frontlighting or backlighting modes, but negative-contrast cells can only be read with sufficient contrast if they receive strong backlighting. TN technology is suitable not only for smaller display modules but also for larger display areas in modular, or even full-size, LCD instrument clusters.

*Thin-film transistor LCD (TFT LCD)*
*1 Row conductor, 2 Thin-film transistor,*
*3 Column conductor, 4 Front plane electrode,*
*5 Color layers, 6 Black matrix,*
*7 Glass substrate, 8 Pixel electrode.*

## Graphics displays for instrument clusters

Dot-matrix displays with graphics capabilities are needed to display infinitely variable information. They are activated by line scanning and therefore require multiplex characteristics. Under the conditions prevailing in a motor vehicle, conventional TN LCDs can today produce multiplex rates of up to 1:4 with good contrast and up to 1:8 with moderate contrast. Other LCD display technologies are needed to achieve higher multiplex rates. STN and DSTN technologies are in current use for modules with moderate resolution. DSTN technology can be implemented to provide monochrome or multicolor displays.

## STN LCD and DSTN LCD

The molecule structure of a super-twisted nematic (STN) display is more heavily twisted within the cell than in a conventional TN display. STN LCDs permit only monochrome displays; usually in blue-yellow contrast. Neutral color can be obtained by applying "retarder film", but this is not effective throughout the entire temperature range encountered in the vehicle.

DSTN LCDs (Double-layer STN) feature considerably improved characteristics, which permit neutral black-and-white reproduction over wide temperature ranges with negative and positive contrast. Color is created by backlighting with colored LEDs. Multicolor reproduction is created by incorporating red, green, and blue thin-film color filters on one of the two glass substrates. Under automotive conditions, shades of gray are only possible to a very limited extent. The result of this is that the range of colors is limited to black, white, the primary colors red, green, and blue, and their secondary colors yellow, cyan, and magenta.

## AMLCD

The task of the visually sophisticated and rapidly changing display of complex information in the area of the instrument cluster and the center console can only be performed effectively by an active-matrix liquid-crystal display (AMLCD) which has high-resolution liquid-crystal monitors with video capabilities.

The best developed and mostly widely used are the thin-film transistor LCDs (TFT LCDs) addressed by thin-film transistors. Display monitors with diagonals of 4"...7" in the center-console area and an extended temperature range (–25°C...+85°C) are available for motor vehicles. Formats of 10"...14" with an even wider temperature range (–40°C...+95°C) are planned for programmable instrument clusters.

TFT LCDs consist of the "active" glass substrate and the opposing plate with the color-filter structures. The active substrate accommodates the pixel electrodes made from tin-indium oxide, the metallic row and column conductors, and semiconductor structures. At each intersecting point of the row and column conductors, there is a field-effect transistor which is etched in several masking steps from a previously applied sequence of layers. A capacitor is also generated at each pixel.

The opposite glass plate accommodates the color filters and a "black-matrix" structure, which improves display contrast. These structures are applied to the glass in a sequence of photolithographic processes. A continuous counter-electrode is applied on top of them for all the pixels. The color filters are applied either in the form of continuous strips (good reproduction of graphics information) or as mosaic filters (especially suitable for video pictures).

**Head-up display (HUD)**

Conventional instrument clusters have a viewing distance of 0.8...1.2 m. In order to read information in the area of the instrument cluster, the driver must adjust his vision from infinity (observing the road ahead) to the short viewing distance for the instrument. This process of adjustment usually takes 0.3...0.5 s. Older drivers find this process strenuous and in some cases impossible, depending on their constitution. HUD, a technology involving projection, can eliminate this problem. Its optical system generates a virtual image at such a viewing distance that the human eye can remain adjusted to infinity. This distance begins at approx. 2 m, and the driver can read the information with very little distraction, without having to divert his eyes from the road to the instrument cluster.

Design

A typical HUD features an activated display for generating the image, a lighting facility, an optical imaging unit, and a "combiner", which reflects the image to the driver's eyes. The untreated windshield can also take the place of the combiner.

Green vacuum fluorescence displays (VFDs) are most commonly used for HUDs with modest levels of information content, whereas more sophisticated displays generally use TFTs based on polysilicon technology. There are also projection systems under development which allow a wider field of vision, and therefore permit a step toward contact-analogous display – i.e. warning of an obstacle below the line of sight below which the driver would also see the obstacle, for instance.

Display of HUD information

The virtual image should not cover the road ahead so that the driver is not distracted from the traffic or road conditions. It is therefore displayed in a region with a low road- or traffic-information content.

In order to prevent the driver from being overwhelmed with stimuli in his primary field of vision, the HUD should not be overloaded with information, and is therefore not a substitute for the conventional instrument cluster. It is, however, particularly well suited for displaying safety-related information, such as warnings, safety distance, and route directions.

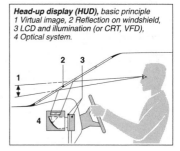

**Head-up display (HUD),** *basic principle*
*1 Virtual image, 2 Reflection on windshield,*
*3 LCD and illumination (or CRT, VFD),*
*4 Optical system.*

# Vehicle information system

In addition to the display and control elements for mainly vehicle-related functions, there is an increasing array of information, communication, and convenience applications in a modern-day motor vehicle. Radio and audio functions are already standard equipment. Phone, navigation, Telematics services, and multimedia applications are in widespread use. Each of these functions requires a large variety of operator controls and display elements. For ergonomic and safety reasons, therefore, many of these controls and displays are combined in a single information system which offers users (driver and passengers) a simple and uniform user interface.

Controls and displays are separately positioned in optimum locations within the vehicle. For example, almost all information is presented on a centrally positioned monitor, while the few controls are located within easy reach on the center console between the driver and front-passenger seats.

Whereas emphasis in the past was placed on expanding functionality, the main focus today is mainly on design, ergonomics, and user-friendliness.

LCD screens up to 9 inches in size and with resolutions up to 1200 x 800 pixels allow the display of TV and video films in the vehicle. Information specifically intended for the driver is presented on projection displays (head-up displays, see P. 1081) which project images in front of the vehicle. The driver can then assimilate the information without having to look away from the road. Navigation directions are an example of information that can be displayed in this way.

Online services, which offer the driver a wide variety of information and services, such as hotel room booking, service-center locations, traffic reports, and even stock-exchange bulletins, also play an ever-increasing role.

A voice-output facility can supplement the visual displays and help to reduce the burden on the driver. A further improvement in user convenience is provided by voice input for many functions. In the future it will be possible to enter telephone numbers by voice, as well as destinations for the navigation system, radio stations, or instructions for air-conditioner settings, for example.

Due to the large amount of information and the high bit rates (e.g. video images) between information sources (e.g. DVD drive for navigation maps) and displays, high-speed bus links are required. The launch of the MOST bus (Media Oriented Systems Transport) in 2002 made bandwidths of 22 Mbit/s possible. This permits the simultaneous transfer of digital audio, video, and control data between the various devices. A vehicle information system is frequently a complex system made up of a large number of individual components linked together in a network.

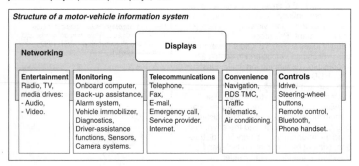

*Structure of a motor-vehicle information system*

| Networking | | Displays | | |
|---|---|---|---|---|
| **Entertainment** | **Monitoring** | **Telecommunications** | **Convenience** | **Controls** |
| Radio, TV, media drives: <br> - Audio, <br> - Video. | Onboard computer, Back-up assistance, Alarm system, Vehicle immobilizer, Diagnostics, Driver-assistance functions, Sensors, Camera systems. | Telephone, Fax, E-mail, Emergency call, Service provider, Internet. | Navigation, RDS TMC, Traffic telematics, Air conditioning. | Idrive, Steering-wheel buttons, Remote control, Bluetooth, Phone handset. |

# Trip recorders

## Applications

Trip recorders show the vehicle speed, the distance covered (odometer), the clock times, and they also have a warning lamp for indicating that the vehicle is exceeding a set speed (e.g. the legal speed limit or the maximum speed that allows economical driving). They also record the vehicle's speed-vs.-time graph, driving hours, rest periods, and distances covered on a tachograph chart – all mapped against the time of day. The driver's name and the vehicle registration number also have to be entered on the tachograph chart. All EU member states require the use of tachographs in trucks and buses. There are also regulations requiring the use of tachographs in a number of other countries.

## Operating concept

### EC tachographs
Recording and display

EC tachographs not only record the driving hours and rest periods, they also record the driving, working, idle, and rest periods (time-category recording), and do so for one or two drivers depending on the design. The EC tachograph meets all the requirements specified in EEC Regulation 3821/85, i.e. the EC tachograph charts serve as the driver's official daily record. In the countries of the EU, the EC tachograph is compulsory equipment on specific types of vehicle and monitors compliance with the driving time rest periods prescribed in EEC Regulation 3820/85. The supplementary features on the EC tachograph include a clock-function display and an indicator lamp, which tells the driver that the charts are installed and that all styluses are functioning properly. Some tachographs also display and record engine speed. Faults and other functions can also be recorded

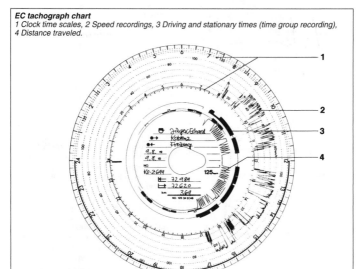

**EC tachograph chart**
*1 Clock time scales, 2 Speed recordings, 3 Driving and stationary times (time group recording), 4 Distance traveled.*

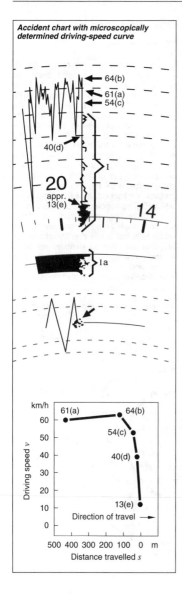

*Accident chart with microscopically determined driving-speed curve*

if the appropriate auxiliary devices are installed. These include a two-stage auxiliary stylus (e.g. for recording fuel consumption), and contacts which trigger other warning and control devices in response to vehicle and engine speed.

All tachographs are subject to strict operating tolerances defined by calibration regulations (in Germany, Article 57b of the StVZO (Road Traffic Licensing Regulations) and in EEC Regulation 3821/85. These regulations also extend to periodic inspection of tachograph and related equipment by authorized centers.

The tachograph chart can be interpreted using any of several methods, including visual, electronic, and microscopic evaluation.

### Visual evaluation

Visual evaluation is the simplest method, as the chart disk makes it possible to appraise and check an entire day's operation at a glance. Systematic visual evaluation encompasses the following checks:
- handwritten entries
- hours worked
- breaks
- rest periods
- assessment of driving style
- fuel consumption and engine speed
- falsified or incorrect recordings

### Microscopic examination

Microscopic examination uses a special microscope to analyze the recording with an accuracy that is precise to the meter and second. The data gathered can be entered in a time/distance graph (see figure) for precise reconstruction, e.g. of the events preceding an accident. Within the framework of a fleet-management system, tachograph charts can also be subjected to semi- or fully automatic evaluation, and the data can be processed in a computer.

### Electronic measuring system

Pulse drive is employed on tachographs featuring electronic measuring systems. It runs on signals produced by a pulse generator, installed either in the vehicle or at the transmission's speedometer-drive gear, which converts the mechanical rotation of the speedometer pinion to electronic pulses.

The most modern electronic tachographs incorporate an integrated conversion feature without separate means of conversion to adapt the unit for variations in the number of pulses per kilometer traveled. On vehicles with variable rear-axle ratios, a conversion-gear unit modifies the ratio of the tachograph's drive signal to maintain synchronization with vehicle conditions.

<u>Separate recording and display</u>

More recent EC tachographs consist of a recorder unit, which records the required information on a conventional tachograph chart, and a display unit which shows speed and odometer readings. The recorder unit with its own display, controls, and drawer for inserting the tachograph charts, fits in a standard DIN radio slot, while the display unit can be incorporated in a vehicle-specific instrument cluster, for example. The two units are connected by means of "K" line communication or, preferably, a CAN communication link.

The separation of recording and display functions firstly simplifies standardization of the actual tachograph depending on manufacturer and model, and secondly, allows vehicle manufacturers more scope for individual design of the instrument panel.

The pioneer tachograph system since 1999 has been the MTCO modular tachograph. Another innovation involved the use of KITAS pulse sensors to transmit not only the drive-speed realtime signal, but a cryptologically ciphered data signal. This allowed the omission of a physically protected armored cable for tamper-proofing.

## Digital tachographs

The Technical Appendix 1B of the 2002 amendment of the EU Recording Equipment Directive defines a new generation of "digital tachographs". Electronic recording of the specified data by such devices represents a crucial change.

The tachograph records the relevant data for the last 365 days, and in addition, each driver has an individual digital identity card (SmartCard) which stores the data relating to his/her last 28 work days. The printer incorporated in the tachograph prints out check logs when required. Other interfaces for monitoring, calibration, electronic archiving, etc. are provided.

The display of the digital tachographs shows the vehicle speed, although a suitable CAN bus can also transmit this information to an instrument cluster, for example.

Communication with the pulse generator is also encoded cryptologically. In general, the tamper-proofing requirements are very high.

Compulsory fitting of the digital tachograph on all new commercial vehicles that are subject to tachograph regulations is expected to come to force in August 2004. A general requirement to upgrade existing vehicles is not planned at present.

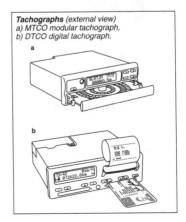

*Tachographs* (external view)
a) MTCO modular tachograph,
b) DTCO digital tachograph.

# Parking systems

## Parking aid with ultrasonic sensors

### Applications
On virtually all motor vehicles, the bodies have been designed and developed in such a way as to achieve the lowest possible drag-coefficient values in order to reduce fuel consumption. Generally speaking, this trend has resulted in a gentle wedge shape which greatly restricts the driver's view when maneuvering. Obstacles can only be poorly discerned – if at all.

Parking aids with ultrasonic sensors provide drivers with effective support when parking. They monitor an area of approx. 30 cm to 150 cm behind or in front of the vehicle. Obstacles are detected and brought to the driver's attention by optical and/or acoustic means.

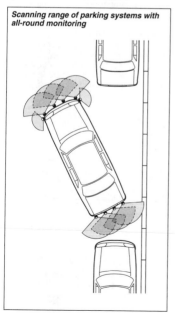

*Scanning range of parking systems with all-round monitoring*

### System
The system comprises the following components: ECU, warning element and ultrasonic sensors.

Vehicles with rear-end protection normally have only 4 ultrasonic sensors in the rear fender. Additional front-end protection is provided by a further 4 to 6 ultrasonic sensors in the front fender.

The system is activated automatically when reverse gear is engaged or, in the case of systems with additional front-end protection, when the vehicle speed drops below a threshold of approx. 15 km/h. The system's self-test function ensures that all the system components are permanently monitored during operation.

### Ultrasonic sensor
Following a principle that is similar to echo depth sounding, the sensors transmit ultrasonic pulses at a frequency of approx. 40 kHz, and measure the time taken for the echo pulses to be reflected back from obstacles. The distance of the vehicle to the nearest obstacle is calculated from the propagation time of the first echo pulse to be received back according to the equation:

$$a = 0.5 \cdot t_e \cdot c$$

$t_e$ propagation time of ultrasonic signal (s)
$c$ velocity of sound in air (approx. 340 m/s).

The sensors themselves consist of a plastic housing with integrated plug-in connection, an aluminum diaphragm on the inner side of which a piezoceramic wafer is attached, and a printed-circuit board with transmit and evaluation electronics. They are electrically connected to the ECU by three wires, two of which supply the power. The third, bidirectional signal line is responsible for activating the transmit function and returning the evaluated received signal to the ECU. When the sensor receives a digital transmit pulse from the ECU, the electronic circuit excites the aluminum diaphragm with square-wave pulses at the resonant frequency so that it vibrates, and ultrasound is emitted. The diaphragm, which has meanwhile returned to rest, is made to vibrate again by the sound reflected back from the obstacle. These vibrations are converted by the piezoceramic wafer to an analog electrical signal which is then amplified and converted to a digital signal by the sensor electronics.

In order to cover as extensive a range as possible, the detection characteristic must fulfill special requirements. In the horizontal range, a wide detection angle is desirable. In the vertical range, however, it is necessary to have a smaller angle in order to avoid interference from ground reflections. A compromise is needed here so that obstacles can be reliably detected.

Specifically adapted mounting brackets secure the sensors in their respective positions in the fender.

### Electronic control unit

The ECU contains a voltage stabilizer for the sensors, an integrated microprocessor, and all the interface circuits needed to adapt the different input and output signals. The software assumes the following functions:
- activates the sensors and receives the echo
- evaluates the propagation time and calculates the obstacle distance
- activates the warning elements
- evaluates the input signals from the vehicle
- monitors the system components including fault storage
- provides diagnostic functions

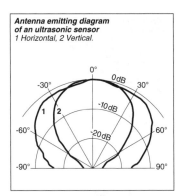

*Antenna emitting diagram of an ultrasonic sensor*
1 Horizontal, 2 Vertical.

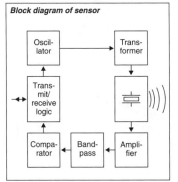

*Block diagram of sensor*

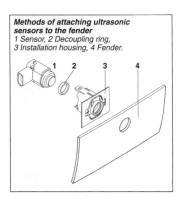

*Methods of attaching ultrasonic sensors to the fender.*
1 Sensor, 2 Decoupling ring, 3 Installation housing, 4 Fender.

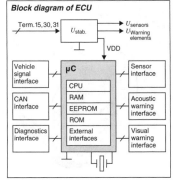

*Block diagram of ECU*

**Warning elements**

The warning elements display the distance from an obstacle. Their design is vehicle-specific, and they usually provide for a combination of acoustic signal and optical display. Both LEDs and LCDs are currently used for optical displays.

In the example of a warning element shown here, the indication of the distance from the obstacle is divided into 4 main ranges (see figure and table).

**Protection area**

The protection area is determined by the range and number of sensors and by their emission characteristic.

Previous experience has shown that 4 sensors are sufficient for rear-end protection, and 4 to 6 for front-end protection. The sensors are integrated in the fenders, which means that the distance from the ground is already fixed.

The installation angle of, and the gaps between, the sensors are vehicle-specific. This data is taken into account in the ECU's calculation algorithms. At the time of going to press, application engineering had already been carried out on more than 200 different vehicle types. Thus, even older vehicles can be retrofitted.

---

*Calculating the distance from a single obstacle (example)*
*a Fender/obstacle distance,*
*b Sensor 1/obstacle distance,*
*c Sensor 2/obstacle distance,*
*d Sensor 1/sensor 2 distance.*
*1 Transmit/receive sensor,*
*2 Receive sensor,*
*3 Obstacle.*

$$a = \sqrt{c^2 - \frac{(d^2 + c^2 - b^2)^2}{4d^2}}$$

---

*Example of a warning element*
*1 LED warning lamps,*
*2 Slits for audible signal.*

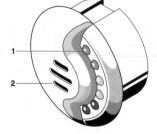

| Range | Distance $s$ | Opt. display LED | Acoustic signal |
|-------|----------|------------------|-----------------|
| I | < 1.5 m | green | Intermittent |
| II | < 1.0 m | green + yellow | Intermittent |
| III | < 0.5 m | green + yellow + red | Continuous tone |
| IV | < 0.3 m | All LEDs flashing | Continuous tone |

# Further development

### Extended range
The present sensor range of about 150 cm is sometimes perceived to be too short by accustomed parkers. For this reason, a new sensor with a range up to 250 cm is currently under development. Due to greater levels greater packaging density of the electronics, it is also much smaller in size than the present generation of devices. This is a welcome improvement, particularly with regard to increased pedestrian-safety requirements for fenders.

### Parking-space measurement
Another possible application for ultrasonic sensors is measuring the size of a parking space.

After the driver activates the system, a sensor mounted on the side of the vehicle measures the length of the parking space. After comparing the measured length with the signals from the wheel-speed sensor in order to check plausibility, the system indicates to the driver whether the parking space is long enough.

A further refinement will make it possible for the system to suggest to the driver the optimum amount of steering lock required in order to complete the parking maneuver with the least effort.

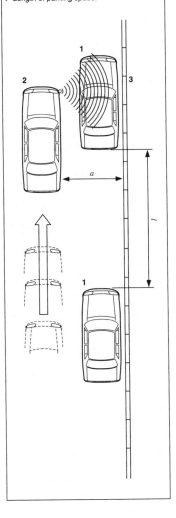

*Measuring a parking space*
1 Parked vehicles,
2 Parking vehicle,
3 Parking-space boundary.
*a* Measured distance,
*l* Length of parking space.

# Analog signal transmission

Analog wireless transmission technology permits the simultaneous broadcasting of information to large populations. In fact, wireless transmission is of major significance to mobile radio reception as used in motor vehicles. At present the importance of digital transmission methods is also growing. The wireless section of the transmission chain also uses analog signal transmission, so the two technologies are basically identical.

## Wireless signal transmission, TV and radio broadcasting

Analog radio and TV broadcasting is primarily used for terrestrial transmissions. Analog radio broadcasting modulates the audio signal on the high-frequency signal. The receiver then converts the received high-frequency signal to the baseband frequency and demodulates it. The final signal obtained in this way is identical to the useful signal.

### Vibration and oscillation

Oscillations are changes to the physical state of a wave that recur at regular intervals. The maximum value of an oscillation is called its amplitude and is a measure of its intensity. The way in which an oscillation travels is called wave propagation. Telecommunications uses the propagation of an electromagnetic wave to transmit information.

### Frequency and wavelength

Frequency is measured in Hertz (Hz) and is the number of oscillations per second. The following commonly used frequency units are all multiples of the Hertz:

Kilohertz (kHz): 1 kHz = 1,000 Hz
Megahertz (MHz): 1 MHz = 1,000 kHz
Gigahertz (GHz): 1 GHz = 1,000 MHz

The range within which sound waves are audible to the human ear extends from about 20 Hz to a maximum of 20 kHz. The frequencies commonly used in radio and TV broadcasting, by contrast, span a range from a few kHz to 100 GHz. Table 1 lists some of the most common frequency ranges. The use of frequency bands is subject to legal control (in Germany by Article 45 of the Telecommunication Act of July 1996). Each country's frequency allocation plan is based on international agreements that are set out in Article S5 of the *Radio Regulations* of the ITU International Telecommunications Union).

The shortest distance between two points at which a propagating wave has the same state is called the "wavelength $\lambda$" (expressed in meters). It is calculated from the propagation velocity [1] (in m · s$^{-1}$) and the frequency (in s$^{-1}$):

$$\lambda = c/f$$

---

[1] In air, an electromagnetic wave travels at a speed of about $c = 2.998 \cdot 10^8$ m · s$^{-1}$.

**Table 1. Frequency ranges for TV/radio broadcasting** (general overview)

| Wavebands | Classification | Frequency $f$ (MHz) | Wavelength $\lambda$ (m) |
|---|---|---|---|
| Long wave (LW)<br>Medium wave (MW)<br>Short wave (SW) | Radio broadcasting | 0.148...0.283<br>0.526...1.606<br>3.95...26.10 | $\approx 2,000...\approx 1,000$<br>$\approx 1,000...\approx 100$<br>$\approx 100...\approx 10$ |
| Very high frequency<br>Band 1 (TV)<br>Band 2 (VHF)<br>Band 3 (TV) | VHF | 30...300<br>47...68<br>87.5...108<br>174...223 | $\approx 10...\approx 1$ |
| Ultra high frequency<br>Band 4 (TV)<br>Band 5 (TV)<br>L-Band | UHF | 300...3,000<br>470...582<br>610...790<br>1,453...1,491 | $\approx 1...\approx 0.1$ |
| Super high frequency<br>(e.g. radio relay) | SHF | 3,000...30,000 | $\approx 0.1...\approx 0.01$ |

## Information transmission using high-frequency waves

The variation in a high-frequency signal used to transmit a useful signal from a transmitter to a receiver is called modulation. An antenna emits the modulated high-frequency signal within a precisely determined, narrowly defined frequency band. The receiver selects precisely that frequency band from the large number of frequencies received by the antenna. In this way, wave propagation between transmitter and receiver is a link within the signal transmission chain.

In contrast with the high-frequency carrier signal, the useful signal is made up of various frequencies ranging up to a maximum of 20 kHz. The low-frequency sound wave is converted by a microphone to an electrical signal, which is used to modulate the high-frequency carrier. A transmitter antenna beams out the carrier wave.

The maximum distance at which the signal can still be received and reception quality depend on the frequency, among other things. Short-wave and long-wave have very long ranges, in some cases intercontinental, whereas the reception range of VHF transmissions is hardly any further than the line of sight.

The receiver station demodulates the signal. A loudspeaker then converts the resulting low-frequency electrical oscillation to sound waves.

### Amplitude modulation (AM)
Amplitude modulation (AM) is the change in amplitude $A_H$ of the high-frequency oscillation at frequency $f_H$ in synchronization with the low-frequency oscillation ($A_L$, $f_L$). Amplitude modulation is used in the short-wave, medium-wave and long-wave bands, for example.

### Frequency modulation (FM)
Frequency modulation (FM) is the change in frequency $f_H$ of the high-frequency oscillation in synchronization with the low-frequency oscillation. Frequency modulation is used for FM radio and the sound channel of TV transmissions, for example. Amplitude-modulation interference (e.g. caused by the ignition systems of

spark-ignition engines) impair the transmissions of frequency-modulation transmitters to a lesser degree than the signals of amplitude-modulation transmitters.

## Propagation of high-frequency waves

The propagation of high-frequency waves depends on their frequency. Long-wave signals travel along the earth's surface as ground waves, whereas short-wave and, in some cases, medium-wave signals propagate as sky waves. Sky waves can propagate over long distances by reflecting off the ionosphere. By contrast, VHF wave propagation is virtually linear since there is no ionospheric reflection. As a result, the various wavebands have different ranges.

The high-frequency electromagnetic waves produced by radio transmitters are not dependent on the transmission medium, as is the case with sound waves, and can therefore be used for satellite links, for example. If electromagnetic

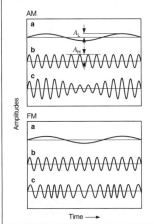

*Amplitude modulation AM (top), and frequency modulation FM (bottom)*
a) Low-frequency oscillation at amplitude $A_L$ and frequency $f_L$,
b) Unmodulated high-frequency oscillation,
c) Modulated high-frequency oscillation.

waves come in contact with a conductor, such as a receiving antenna, there is a change in current and voltage characteristics in the conductor.

Within its transmission range, the transmitter alters the electromagnetic state of space. The range is also referred to as the transmitter's electromagnetic field. Field strength is measured in V/m and diminishes as a function of its distance from the transmitter. The propagation characteristics depend on wavelength.

### Long-wave (LW) signals

Long-wave signals are AM signals and propagate along the earth's surface as ground waves. They can be received over long distances (approx. 600 km), regardless of the time of day. Atmospheric or localized interference (e.g. caused by engines, motor vehicles, or trams) have a very pronounced impact on transmissions in this waveband.

### Medium-wave (MW) signals

Medium-wave signals are also AM signals and partly propagate along the earth's surface as ground waves. The remaining component is transmitted as a sky wave. This component can be reflected by the Kennelly-Heaviside layers (commonly known as Heaviside layers) of the ionosphere which are located at a distance of 80...400 km above the earth's surface. The altitude of the Heaviside layers and their degree of reflectivity depend on atmospheric conditions, in particular solar radiation. As a result, long-distance reception is better at dusk or dawn, or at night, rather than during the daytime.

In poor conditions, medium-wave reception can suffer from fluctuations in the signal ("fading") if the ground and sky waves interact by amplifying or attenuating each other.

### Short-wave (SW) signals

Short-wave signals are also AM signals and are absorbed more easily by the earth's surface than medium-wave signals. However, they can travel very long distances. The reception conditions for these waves vary considerably due to the changing reflectivity of the Heaviside layers. There also zones in which no reception is

possible at all because sky waves are only reflected up to a certain limit angle.

### Very high frequency (VHF) signals

Very high frequency signals are FM signals which have virtually linear propagation. They follow the curvature of the earth, and can be blocked or reflected by buildings and topographical features. It is not possible to achieve long-distance reception by bouncing them off the Heaviside layers. Similarly, reception of a ground wave is impossible due to the high level of the attenuation of the ground. Their range over flat terrain is not much further than the human eye's line of sight (up to approx. 100 km).

### Reception problems

VHF signals have virtually a linear propagation. As a result, a car radio may lose the signal from a VHF transmitter that is only 30 km away if there is high ground between the car and the transmitter. On the other hand, reception may be unimpaired at a location twice as far away if there is a clear "line of sight" between the car and the transmitter. Such "radio shadows" are thus often covered by a "fill-in transmitter"

Signals may be reflected off the sides of valleys or high-rise buildings. The reflected signals then arrive at the receiving antenna with a time delay and are superimposed on the signals received directly from the transmitter. This produces what is known as "multi-channel reception". It causes multipath interference and results in the deterioration of sound quality in radio reception.

Conductors within the transmitter's radiation field (e.g. steel masts or power lines) and even nearby forests, houses, or locations in deep valleys, impair the propagation and reception of electromagnetic waves. The characteristics of wave propagation very briefly described above are important when it comes to suppressing interference in motor vehicles effectively. Interference-free reception is impossible if the signals received from the transmitter are too weak. Thus, reception of an interference-free signal will break down suddenly when a car enters a tunnel. This can be explained by the shielding effect of the reinforced-concrete tunnel walls which reduce the useful field strength of the transmitter signal to which the radio is tuned. At the same time the interference-field strength remains the same. Under certain conditions, it may not be possible at all to continue to receive the radio-station signal. Similar phenomena can also be experienced when traveling in mountains, for example.

## Radio interference

### Origin
Radio interference is caused by undesirable high-frequency waves which are received by the receiver together with the desired signal. They occur wherever electrical currents are suddenly interrupted or switched on. For example, the ignition system of a spark-ignition engine, the operation of a switch, or the switching operations on the commutator of an electric motor produce high-frequency interference signals. Such rapid changes of current generate high-frequency waves which interfere with radio reception by receivers located close by. The effect of the interference depends on the steepness of the signal pulse and its amplitude, among other things.

Radio interference caused by such steeply rising current pulses can be reduced or completely eliminated by EMC measures (Electromagnetic compatibility, see P. 1020).

### Propagation
Interference can travel to the receiver in two different ways – directly through wires connecting the interference source and the receiver, or by wireless transmission of electromagnetic radiation, or by capacitative or inductive coupling. Strictly speaking, the last three sources cannot be separated from one another.

## Signal-to-noise ratio

Reception quality depends on the strength of the electromagnetic field generated by the transmitter. This should be substantially greater than the strength of the interference field. In other words, the ratio between the strength of the transmitter signal and the strength of the interference signal – the signal-to-noise ratio – should be as large as possible.

A receiver close to the interference source receives not only the useful signal from the desired transmitter, but also the undesired interference signal, if it is transmitted at the same frequency. Nevertheless, good-quality reception is still possible provided that the field strength of the desired transmitter signal at the point of reception is very high in comparison with the strength of the electromagnetic field generated by the interference source. The useful field strength of the signal from the transmitter depends on transmitter power, transmitter frequency, the distance between the transmitter and the receiver, and the propagation characteristics of the electromagnetic waves described previously.

In the case of medium-wave and long-wave signals, the field strength of the transmitter signal can be weakened by difficult topology to such an extent that the signals of even powerful transmitters have low useful field strengths at some reception locations. VHF signals may be subject to heavy fluctuations in useful field strength under certain conditions. Receivers in motor vehicles may also suffer from relatively low useful voltages at the receiver input due to the short effective height of the antenna. Accordingly, the opportunities for improving the signal-to-noise ratio in the receiver are very limited.

By optimizing antenna positioning, the available useful voltage at the receiver input can be increased, thereby improving the signal-to-noise ratio, which is the decisive factor in reception quality. Frequently, however, a compromise is made between design considerations and technical demands. Another means of improving signal-to-noise ratio is by reducing the strength of the radiated interference signals.

Receiver design also has an impact on reception quality. In addition to metallic shielding, which prevents the direct entry of radiated interference, and filters on the power source input, some receivers have circuits fitted with automatic interference suppression (ASU) (see "Automotive sound systems", P. 1096).

# Digital signal transmission

## Applications

Since the 1980s the replacement of vinyl discs (LP records) by CDs as the medium for recording music has brought about a change in the methods of transmitting signal and, therefore, data from analog to digital systems. It was followed by a parallel change in mobile radio networks. Satellite TV transmissions now use the digital DVB-S system increasingly. Cable TV networks have yet to be converted.

The digital DAB system has been introduced for TV and radio broadcasting. It was specially developed for radio, TV and multimedia applications (see "Multimedia systems", P. 1118). In contrast with analog systems (see "Analog signal transmission", P. 1090), data is modulated digitally and is thus not susceptible to interference.

Measures allowing reception in motor vehicles and for counteracting the effects of multipath propagation have also been adopted.

## The Digital Audio Broadcasting (DAB) system

The DAB system is essentially based on three components:
- Audio-data compression method in accordance with MPEG-1 (ISO 11 172-3) or MPEG-2 (ISO 13818-3), Layer II in each case.
- Transmission process Coded Orthogonal Frequency Division Multiplexing (COFDM) and
- Flexible distribution of the transmission capacity to a variety of subchannels which, independently of each other, can transmit audio and data programs with differing data rates and differing error-protection levels (DAB multiplexing).

The block diagram shows the structure and interaction of the various components of the DAB system and the process for generating the DAB signal.

Audio encoders compress the data in each of the radio broadcasts. Channel coding then provides the redundancy required for error correction in the receiver. Several data services can be combined within a packet multiplexer. The packet-

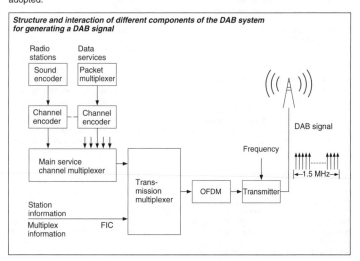

Structure and interaction of different components of the DAB system for generating a DAB signal

multiplex signal is then routed to the channel encoder.

The channel-encoded data in the sub-channels is combined with the Fast Information Channel data, which contains the multiplex and broadcast-data structure, and is then modulated using COFDM. This is generally performed digitally by Fast Fourier Transform (FFT). The signal is then converted from digital to analog, mixed at the corresponding transmit frequency, amplified, filtered, and finally transmitted.

Transmission takes place in Band 3 and the L-Band.

## Measures for reliable transmission in the mobile channel

The COFDM transmission process contains several measures to guarantee the difficult task of reliable transmission to mobile receivers. Thus, groups of 3072 bits are combined to form a "symbol" and modulated on 1536 carrier frequencies at a spacing of 1 kHz (frequency division), i.e. 2 bits per carrier using differential quartenary phase shift keying (DQPSK).

Since different frequencies suffer different levels of interference in the mobile channel (frequency selectivity), this ensures that a sufficient number of carriers can always be received. An error correction function can reconstruct the bits from carriers affected by interference.

As a means of counteracting the effects of multipath propagation, a "buffer period" was introduced. This means that a proportion (1/4 or 250 ms) of the symbol referred to above is repeated at the end.

If signal components then reach the receiver later due to reflection, they are still part of the same symbol or data record. This prevents "intersymbol interference" and achieves reliable demodulation. Another advantage of this strategy is the possibility for DAB transmitters to operate

within a single-frequency network. Normally, radio and TV transmitters that transmit at the same frequency interfere with each other's signals because their signals arrive at the receiver with time delays. The buffer period solves this problem, with the result that transmission at the same frequency is possible nationwide.

As a means of overcoming high levels of transient interference, a process known as "time interleaving" was introduced. This involves spreading the data over a longer period (384 ms). If transient interference occurs (bundle errors), they are mixed with correctly received bits over time so that the error correction procedures can take effect.

## The Digital radio broadcasting system (DRM) for the long, medium and short wavebands

In analogy to DAB, the DRM "Digital Radio Mondial" system will be used in future to digitize transmission in the long, medium and short wavebands. The advantage of these frequency bands is their long transmission range which allows extremely economical broadcasting of radio programs. Unfortunately, the propagation conditions in these wavebands are even more difficult than in the VHF band.

The DRM system adopts similar measures to those used by DAB to minimize the effects of interference.

In addition, it uses very effective audio encoding based on the MPEG-4 AAC method with an expanded audio bandwidth (SBR). This means that good sound quality can be obtained even in narrow short-wave channels.

# Automotive sound systems

The term "automotive sound systems" refers not only to a radio tuner but to devices with a large number of integrated information and entertainment functions. These include, for instance, the analysis of supplementary information (e.g. traffic news), players for reproducing from storage media (e.g. CDs and hard disks), and integrated cellular phones. In the past few years conventional analog transmission technology has developed new systems at ever shorter product cycles. For this reason, present-day car tuners are capable of receiving a wide variety of radio broadcast systems worldwide. Among these systems are DAB, SDARS and DRM, as well as conventional radio broadcasting.

## Radio tuners

The conventional radio tuner has an analog signal path from the antenna to the audio signal. Car tuners with the highest "reception performance", on the other hand, process signals digitally. The IF signal supplied by the tuner is digitized by an analog-digital converter (see P. 102), and then processed accordingly.

## Conventional tuners

### Signal processing
To begin with, the antenna picks up the electromagnetic signal transmitted through the air. Initially, it consists of different channels with a fixed frequency spacing. The tuner receives and processes the high-frequency alternating voltage generated at the base of the antenna.

Most car tuners basically contain two signal paths (see block diagram of typical conventional tuner):
– one path for processing amplitude-modulated (AM) signals, and
– one path for processing frequency-modulated (FM) signals.

### AM input stage
A bandpass filter limits the amplitude-modulated signal in the LW, MW and SW bands, and the resulting signal is amplified in the following stage.

### VHF/FM input stage
A separate input stage receives the VHF signal. The input filter is tuned to the receive frequency so that the desired channel can be extracted from the received band.

The received signal level is then adjusted to the desired input level for the following mixer stage by an automatically controlled amplifier.

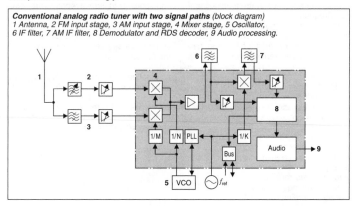

**Conventional analog radio tuner with two signal paths** (block diagram)
1 Antenna, 2 FM input stage, 3 AM input stage, 4 Mixer stage, 5 Oscillator, 6 IF filter, 7 AM IF filter, 8 Demodulator and RDS decoder, 9 Audio processing.

### Voltage-controlled oscillator (VCO)

The oscillator, whose frequency is controlled by a phase-locked loop (PLL), generates a high-frequency oscillation with which the input signal is converted to a constant intermediate frequency by the mixer stage. A quartz-stabilized signal serves as reference frequency.

### Mixer stage

The mixer stage converts the input signal to a constant intermediate frequency (IF). Often there are different mixer stages for receiving FM and AM signals. On the other hand, however, the method of frequency conversion with which some receivers convert the IF AM signal a second time to a second intermediate frequency is the same.

### IF filter and amplifier

The IF signal recovered in the mixer stage is then fed to an IF filter and a regulated amplifier.

### Demodulator

The demodulator extracts the low-frequency audio signal, which is basically the same as the microphone output signal at the transmitter end, from the high-frequency IF signal.

### Decoder

Additional information, such as RDS data (Radio Data System), is decoded by the decoder and passed on to a processor for processing.

### Audio processing

After demodulation, the audio signal may be adapted to the conditions prevailing in the vehicle and the listener's preferences. This can be achieved by using the appropriate controls for tone, volume, and balance between right and left, or between front and rear speakers.

### AF pre-amplifier and output stage

The AF pre-amplifier and output stage are used to amplify the audio signal.

## Digital receivers
(DigiCeivers)

### Signal processing

DigiCeivers are high-integration receiver modules. They convert the analog IF input signal to a digital signal, and then process it in digital form. This digital technology allows a type of signal processing that would not be possible using analog technology. It produces IF filters which achieve exceptionally good distortion-factor levels, while its variable bandwidth can be adapted to the reception conditions. In addition, it has a large number of other means of processing the received signal to reduce interference in the audio signal substantially. The section below on "Reception improvements" also outlines other important functions that only digital technology can deliver. This includes SHARX, DDA, and DDS.

### Digital equalizer (DEQ)

The digital equalizer (DEQ) consists of a multiband parametric equalizer which provides separate adjustment features for the mid-frequency, and the amplification/attenuation of individual filters. The suppression of unwanted resonances thus obtained optimizes sound quality inside the vehicle. The frequency response of the speakers can also be linearized. Some devices also have preset equalizer filters which can be activated according to music genre or vehicle type (jazz, pop, van, or sedan, etc.).

### Digital Sound Adjustment (DSA)

The Digital Sound Adjustment (DSA) system analyzes and corrects frequency response in in-car systems automatically. A microphone and a DSP are used to pick up and analyze a test signal produced by the speakers. The optimum sound curve for the vehicle is then set on the equalizer.

### Dynamic Noise Covering (DNC)

While the vehicle is in motion, Dynamic Noise Covering (DNC) uses a microphone to constantly detect and analyze the vehicle-noise spectrum that is blocking out the audio signal and impairing the perceived sound quality. It selectively amplifies the frequencies that are blocked out, and maintains sound quality at a constant level, regardless of vehicle noise.

### TwinCeiver

The latest generation of digital car tuners produced by Blaupunkt incorporates a high-integration receiver chip called the TwinCeiver. It has two digital signal paths and an analog-digital converter. This receiver system can calculate a new antenna aperture from the two received signals. This substantially improves reception quality (Digital Directional Antenna, DDA). Among other things, this minimizes interference caused by multipath propagation.

## Reception quality

Analog radio broadcasting is primarily used for terrestrial transmissions. The transmission path is not always ideal, with the result that reception quality may be impaired, depending on the transmitter/receiver constellation and environmental conditions. In the case of VHF reception, reception locations may be critical because of the transmission-path problems described below.

### Fading

Fading is caused by fluctuations in signal reception level due to obstacles in the signal path, such as tunnels, high-rise buildings, and mountains.

### Multipath reception

Multipath reception, caused by the reflection of signals off buildings, trees, or water, can easily lead to substantial loss of reception signal field strength, and even total signal loss. The differences in the strength of the received signal field strength occur within a few centimeters of each other. Such fluctuations have a particularly detrimental effect on mobile receivers, such as car tuners.

### Adjacent channel

Adjacent-channel interference occurs when there is another receivable channel with a high field strength close to the channel received.

### High-level signal interference

High-level signal interference occurs close to the transmitter at high field strength. The receiver protects its input by reducing the field strength. This has the effect of attenuating the weaker signals from other transmitters, i.e. they become quieter.

### Overmodulation

Some transmitters increase the modulation level in order to achieve a greater range or higher loudness level. The disadvantages of this process are greater distortion factor and greater susceptibility to multipath interference.

### Ignition interference

High-frequency interference sources (such as the ignition system of a spark-ignition engine, the operation of a switch, or switching operations on the commutators of electric motors) produce reception interference.

## Reception improvement

Present-day car tuners have a large number of functions for improving reception performance. The most important of these functions are the following:

### RDS (Radio Data System)

RDS is a digital transmission system for FM radio. This format is standardized throughout Europe. It provides the tuner with extra information in addition to the desired audio signal by using alternative receive frequencies with the same modulation. This means, for example, that the tuner can switch continuously to the frequency with the least interference. The sections below briefly outline the categories of information transmitted.

#### PS code

The PS code represents the name of the radio station received.

#### AF code

The AF code contains a list of alternative frequencies on which the station also broadcasts.

PI code
The PI code uniquely identifies the broadcast station.

TP and TA codes
The TP and TA codes allow identification of stations which broadcast traffic announcements.

PTY code
The PTY code identifies the station type, while PTY31 is a special control signal reserved for public warning announcements.

EON code
EON signals traffic announcements on a parallel station. The frequency can then be changed for the duration of the announcement.

TMC code
The TMC code transmits standardized traffic information. The information is communicated in the appropriate local language by means of a language generator. Navigation systems can take such information into account when computing routes.

CT code
The CT code contains the time and date.

RT code
RT consists of text transmissions (e.g. the title of the current track) for the tuner.

**DDA** (Digital Directional Antenna)
This system developed by Blaupunkt uses the signals from two antennas to calculate a balanced antenna with a different directional characteristic. This permits suppression of interference caused by multipath reception (see figure).

**DDS** (Digital Diversity System)
The reception characteristics of FM radio are heavily dependent on location. A diversity system has a number of antennas at its disposal so that it can switch between them in order to enhance reception. The DDS integrated in the DigiCeiver uses exactly the same signal for its switching strategy and the signal is available as the audio signal after demodulation.

**High Cut**
Interference caused by such effects as fading and multipath reception has a greater effect on higher frequencies. For this reason, modern car tuners have a facility for detecting such interference and reducing the level of the audio signal at higher audio frequencies when there is interference.

**SHARX**
SHARX is a function which automatically adjusts the bandwidth of the digital intermediate frequency filter for FM reception to suit reception conditions. If different stations transmit at frequencies that are very close to one another, this function significantly increases the clarity of separation and allows virtually interference-free reception. If there are no adjacent channels, it can expand bandwidth and thus reduce the distortion factor.

**ASU** (automatic interference suppression)
ASU suppresses interference both from interference sources on the vehicle itself and from external sources to improve reception. At the instant when the interference occurs, ASU scans the demodulated signal which contains interference pulses as well as the useful signal, i.e. it interrupts the signal momentarily.

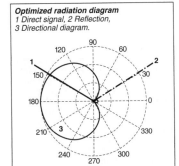

*Optimized radiation diagram*
*1 Direct signal, 2 Reflection,*
*3 Directional diagram.*

## Auxiliary equipment

### Amplifier

This is a separate power amplifier (with integrated transformers) which the car tuner controls via the pre-amplifier output. The much higher output power achieves a significant improvement in the tone and dynamic sound of music, particularly in the bass range.

### Equalizer

The equalizer is an auxiliary device for standard car tuners or a digital module in high-end automotive sound systems that is used to control tone. It allows selective amplification or attenuation of individual tone channels (frequency bands). It counterbalances the emphasis distortions (nonlinearities) caused by the specific acoustic properties of the vehicle cabin.

### CD changer

The CD changer is a playback device for CDs (Compact Discs) which is fitted in the trunk. It is loaded by a CD changer, which is usually capable of holding up to ten CDs. The CDs and the individual tracks are selected using either a suitably equipped tuner, or a separate remote-control unit.

### FM modulator

The FM modulator acts like a small radio transmitter by converting incoming signals (e.g. from a CD changer) to radio waves at a selectable frequency. An adaptor connected between the antenna input and the antenna jack feeds the signals to the car tuner. This allows a CD changer to be connected to any car tuner.

### MP3 player

This highly compact device can be connected to virtually any car tuner. It can play up to 18 hours of MP3 recordings from its mini hard drive (MP3 Compact Drive). The MP3 data compression method can compress audio data without discernible loss of sound quality so that recordings can be downloaded from the Internet to a home PC. The Microdrive hard disk is a universal re-recordable storage medium and at present has enough capacity for around 250 music tracks.

### Digital signal processor with integrated MP3 changer

The digital signal processor with integrated MP3 player function performs extensive equalizer functions and supplements them with preprogrammed settings for genres ranging from pop to classical. Individual adjustment of frequency bands is possible, as well as adjustment of the loudness boost level. Compressed MP3 music data is loaded to the device from a chip card. The storage medium is an MMC (MultiMediaCard) which can be re-recorded any number of times on a PC. The device simultaneously accepts up to 5 cards of any storage capacity and can play individual track or card selections.

### Automotive speakers

Automotive speakers convert the low-frequency electrical signals obtained after demodulation by the receiver back to sound waves that are audible to the human ear (30...20,000 Hz). They consist of a diaphragm, that is flexibly held by an elastic bead around its outer perimeter. Its apex is moved in and out by the vibrating coil of an electromagnetic driver system. For low and midrange frequencies, the diaphragm is usually conical, whereas speakers for high-frequency sounds normally have dome-shaped diaphragms. They are made of stiff paper or, in high-quality speakers, of polypropylene, SAC aluminum, or a ceramic material.

A dynamic speaker (see figure) consists of a permanent magnet which has a circular air gap inside which a coil attached to the diaphragm oscillates. The capacitor speaker for high frequencies > 5,000 Hz is based on the electrostatic attraction between two opposing metal surfaces carrying an electrical potential. The crystal speaker utilizes the piezo-electric effect. In an ionic speaker, ionized air particles are made to vibrate instead of a diaphragm. There are various categories according to the frequency band as follows:

– tweeters
– midrange speakers
– woofers
– subwoofers

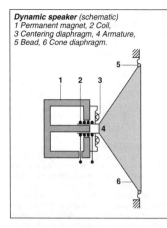

***Dynamic speaker*** *(schematic)*
*1 Permanent magnet, 2 Coil,*
*3 Centering diaphragm, 4 Armature,*
*5 Bead, 6 Cone diaphragm.*

The acoustic properties of the vehicle interior, the speakers, and their locations determine the reproduction quality. The larger the speakers, the better the bass reproduction. As a single speaker cannot reproduce the full range of audible sound, high-fidelity systems divide the entire frequency spectrum among a number of speakers.

The precondition for well-balanced stereo reproduction is a series of specially positioned speakers, together with a digital signal processor (DSP, e.g. in conjunction with sound systems). They create the effect of a stereophonic panorama at any point within the vehicle interior. The audible "landscape" then appears to extend far beyond the spatial limits of the vehicle interior.

## Vehicle antennas

Vehicle antennas pick up the high-frequency carrier waves broadcast by radio transmitters and pass them on to the receiver (tuner, car cellular phone, or radio navigation unit) for demodulation. The operating frequency for radios and cellular phones covers the range from 150 kHz to 1.9 GHz. It would require a large number of antennas to fully cover such a wide frequency range under mobile reception conditions. For this reason, there is a trend toward combination antennas which can receive several radio services at the same time.

The received power of a radio antenna depends on its location and the distance from the receiver. The further it is from smooth metal surfaces and the vehicle's windows, the more effective it is. The amplifier in the antenna base increases the received power of an active antenna. Good results can be obtained with telescopic, freestanding rod antennas (which may also extend and retract automatically driven by an electric motor). An alternative is the window antenna which, because of its directional characteristics, is slightly inferior, but has the advantage of being wear-and maintenance-free. The flexible short rod antenna is a technical compromise.

The cellular phone antenna on a motor vehicle uses two tuned RF frequencies for simultaneous bidirectional digital data transmission between the base station and the cellular phone. The simple $\lambda/4$ rod antenna is well suited to the purpose due to its directional diagram. In weak cellular-phone network cells, a $\lambda/4 + \lambda/2$ or a $\lambda/4 + 2 \times \lambda/2$ "gain antenna" is a better alternative. Combination antennas are used for receiving as many radio services as possible. "On-glass" and clamp-on window antennas are suitable for quick and easy fitting or conversion.

The horizontal patch navigation antenna with an amplifier for increasing gain-to-noise temperature ratio is particularly suited to use as a circular-polarized antenna for GPS satellite reception. Combination antennas with antenna filters can also be used for radio, communication, and cellular-phone services, etc. A line of sight prevents reception losses caused by radio shadow.

# Mobile and data radio

## Telecommunications networks

Telecommunications networks consist of terminals and an infrastructure. Mobile radiocommunications networks can be classified as belonging to telecommunications networks based on the mobility of the terminals and the method these terminals use to access the infrastructure.

|  |  | Access method | |
|---|---|---|---|
|  |  | Wired | **Wireless** |
| Mobility | Fixed | – Traditional phone network<br>– Internet, LAN | – Radio relay |
|  | Mobile | | – **Mobile/data radio**<br>– Private mobile radio<br>– Radio broadcasting<br>– Marine/aeronautical radio<br>– Cordless phones |

## Components and structure

Mobile radiocommunications networks can be subdivided in mobile radio telephones and infrastructure.

### Mobile radio telephones

Mobile radio telephones include cellular phones and automotive radiocommunication devices. A mobile radio telephone is made up of three functional components:
– an operator unit (microphone, speaker, display, and keypad)
– Radio modem (modem, modulator/demodulator) to convert voice and data signals to electrical signals
– a radio transmitter/receiver unit.

Data terminal devices without radio transmitter/receiver units such as laptop computers or PDAs (Personal Digital Assistants) can communicate with a mobile radio communication system through an internal or external radio modem.

### Mobile radiocommunications infrastructure

The mobile radiocommunications infrastructure consists of the fixed radio transmitter/receiver stations and the radio system control. A radio transmitter/receiver station consists of a base station, which provides radio coverage of an area, and a base-station control system. The positioning of base stations depends on several considerations, including topographical constraints and expected communications traffic levels (maximum subscriber capacity). A cellular network structure allows the few radio frequencies available to be reused in adjacent cells.

### Radio system control

The mobile radio switching office controls call connection between mobiles that are in the same or even in different radio cells. It also controls the switching of radio traffic to the wire-line telephone network. In order to control call switching automatically, the mobile radio switching office must know the location of all mobiles within the radio cells at all times. The is made possible by continuously exchanging an identification signal between the mobiles and the base stations. A base station can detect when a mobile moves to an adjacent cell by the drop in field strength or quality of the received signal.

The subscriber database performs the job of authenticating subscribers, and stores each subscriber's location within the radio cells.
A maintenance and control system continuously monitors network operation.

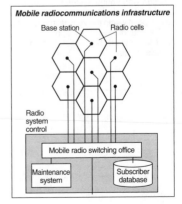

*Mobile radiocommunications infrastructure*

Base station    Radio cells

Radio system control

Mobile radio switching office

Maintenance system    Subscriber database

# Mobile radiocommunications networks

## GSM and DCS 1800 mobile radio networks

The standardized digital mobile communications network for Europe, GSM (<u>G</u>lobal <u>S</u>ystem for <u>M</u>obile Communication), has been in operation since 1992. In contrast to analog radio networks, it transmits voice and control data in digital form. GSM radio networks operate in the 900 MHz band, and each has a capacity of around 2 million subscribers. The similar DCS 1800 (<u>D</u>igital <u>C</u>ellular <u>S</u>ystem) network operates using identical technology in the 1800 MHz band ,and has been in service since 1994. Each radio cell has several high-frequency channels, each with a bandwidth of 200 kHz. Each high-frequency channel transmits seven voice channels (traffic channels) and one control channel in succession in short time slots within a time frame. When a call is set up, the high-frequency channel is available to each cellular phone every 4.6 ms for the duration of the time slot (time-division multiplexing). The time delay of 4.6 ms between two consecutive identical time slots is short enough to guarantee perfect speech quality.

Each traffic channel can transmit a maximum gross data stream of 22.8 kbit/s. To compensate for errors during radio transmission, digitized speech is only transferred at a data rate of 9.6 kbit/s. The difference between this and 22.8 kbit/s is used for error correction. Instead of speech, a traffic channel can also transfer data (e.g. a fax transmission).

A time slot between the terminals is permanently reserved for the duration of a mobile radio connection (line connection), regardless of whether the connection carries speech or data.

## Short Message Service (SMS)

SMS (<u>S</u>hort <u>M</u>essage <u>S</u>ervice) offers economical data transmission within GSM mobile radio networks for text messages of up to 160 characters in length. The text in an SMS message is transmitted without occupying a separate voice channel by using unused capacity in the control channels. SMS messages can be sent from one mobile to another or from a PC to a mobile via the Internet. After an SMS message is sent, it is temporarily stored on the mobile radio network, and automatically sent out as soon as the receiving mobile is switched on ("store and forward" principle).

## HSCSD data transmission procedure

The HSCSD (<u>H</u>igh <u>S</u>peed <u>C</u>ircuit <u>S</u>witched <u>D</u>ata) data transmission procedure involves GSM networks combining up to four adjacent traffic channels for data-transmission purposes (line connection). With a net data transmission rate of 14.4 kbit/s per traffic channel, channel bundling provides an overall data rate of 57.6 kbit/s. The cost of an HSCSD connection is calculated on the basis of the connection time and the number of traffic channels used.

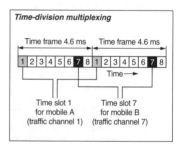

*Time-division multiplexing*

Time frame 4.6 ms    Time frame 4.6 ms

| 1 | 2 | 3 | 4 | 5 | 6 | 7 | 8 | 1 | 2 | 3 | 4 | 5 | 6 | 7 | 8 |

Time →

Time slot 1 for mobile A (traffic channel 1)

Time slot 7 for mobile B (traffic channel 7)

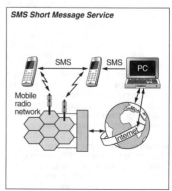

*SMS Short Message Service*

SMS    SMS    PC

Mobile radio network

Internet

## GPRS data transmission procedure

In 2001 the packet-based data transmission procedure GPRS (General Packet Radio Service) was introduced to complement the GSM radio network. GPRS data channels and normal voice channels share the time slots in a time frame. GPRS data channels are dynamically allocated according to voice-channel priority. During transmission pauses in GPRS connections, other GPRS connections can use the temporarily "unused" time slots. In contrast with the HSCSD procedure, a data stream is subdivided in individual consecutively numbered data packets for transmission. The data packets are transmitted independently of one another. The receiving mobile rearranges the data packets into the correct order on the basis of their consecutive numbering. Transmission costs are calculated on the basis of the data volume transmitted. A mobile equipped with a GPRS module can connect to data networks (e.g. the Internet).

## WAP data service

The WAP (Wireless Application Protocol) service in GSM radio networks is based on a special data-transmission protocol derived from the widely adopted Internet protocol. This service has been defined independently of mobile radio standards. Therefore, it can be used not only in GSM networks, but also in the future 3G/UMTS radio network. A microbrowser integrated in the mobile can access data from the Internet (World Wide Web, e-mail, etc.). In contrast with the SMS and MMS services, access to stored data/messages (WAP pages or e-mails) on the Internet is actively initiated by the user ("store and retrieve" principle). In order to display WAP pages on a small cellular phone or PDA screen, they are specially adapted for the small display format, and are frequently stored in parallel to the regular web pages on the Internet. Typical applications are the transmission of messages (e-mail), weather, traffic, and stock-exchange bulletins.

## i-Mode wireless data service

The i-Mode wireless data service ("i" stands for Internet or interactive) in Europe is part of the DC1800 mobile radio network and has been very successful in Japan as an alternation to the WAP service. Both services use GPRS data-transmission technology.

## MMS data service

MMS (Multimedia Messaging Service) allows the transmission of images, graphics, video clips, audio files, etc. to or from a mobile. The MMS service was defined for the transmission of MMS messages in GSM networks, using GPRS/WAP technology, and in the UMTS radio network. Before transmitting multimedia objects to a mobile, the display format must be adapted. Special computers in the mobile-radio networks therefore configure the multimedia data. Any combination of individual multimedia objects can also be created and reproduced on the mobile based on a specific time plan. In addition to "fun applications" (sending photos live on vacation), there are also possible business uses, such as sending presentations, product data, or directions to field staff on their mobiles.

## G3/UMTS mobile radiocommunication network

The future mobile radiocommunications network is G3/UMTS (G3: 3rd generation; Universal Mobile Telecommunication System) is an advance development of the GSM network. The radio communication interface has been optimized for multimedia applications, such as voice, data, music, images, video, games, etc., and packet-based data transmission. The G3/UMTS radio network operates in Europe in the 1.9...2.2 GHz frequency band. The radiocommunications infrastructure is divided into three levels as follows:

1. The macrocellular network, as the highest network level, consists of radio transmitter/receiver stations with a cell size of approx. 2 km. It provides nationwide network coverage. The maximum data transmission rate is 144 kbit/s.
2. The microcellular network, as the middle network level, supplies smaller areas (cell size approx. 1 km, primarily for large conurbations). The maximum data transmission rate is 384 kbit/s.

3. The picocellular network (cell size approx. 60 m, max. data transmission rate 2 Mbit/s) primarily supplies buildings (e.g. airports).

In contrast with GSM time-division multiplexing, G3/UMTS transmits all data within a radio cell simultaneously on the same radio channel.

WCDMA (Wideband Code-Division Multiple-Access) codes separate data for different mobiles in a high-frequency channel. The base station and the mobile negotiate these codes with each other. WCDMA technology allows more efficient utilization of radio channels compared with GSM technology. Thus, the data-transmission capacity for a connection can be flexibly adapted to suit the service in use. Voice transmission, for example, requires a lower data rate than the transmission of multimedia applications, such as images and video clips.

## Data radio networks

Special data radiocommunications networks, such as Bluetooth and WLAN, provide a data link between mobile terminals, or within a data network such as the Internet.

### Bluetooth
Bluetooth is an alternative to infrared links, and is used to provide wireless connection between PCs and external devices, such as printers, digital cameras, etc.

The Bluetooth network operates in the unlicensed 2.4 GHz frequency band (like appliances such as microwave ovens). "Bluetooth" is derived from the name of a Viking king called Harald Blåtand (meaning "Bluetooth") in recognition of the leading contribution to the development of the technology by Danish companies. The transmitter output is 1 mW over a range of approx. 10 m. In order to eliminate errors in transmission as far as possible, the frequency is changed 1,600 times a second (frequency hopping). The individual frequency divisions transmit the data sequentially as data packets. If a frequency division experiences a fault during data transmission, an error correction procedure can completely reconstruct a frequency division on the receiver side.

The maximum data rate is 721 kbit/s. In Bluetooth networks, no particular data-encryption method is employed. Data security is limited simply to synchronizing the frequency hopping procedure between devices.

### WLAN
WLAN networks (Wireless Local Area Network) offer mobile telephones and Bluetooth networks a wireless link to computer networks in the 2.4 GHz frequency band. In contrast with Bluetooth, the frequency is changed only every 2.5 seconds. The transmit output is up to 100 mW, which allows a range of up to 100 m in buildings. Using WLAN, data links to the Internet with a maximum data rate of 11 Mbit/s can be created at a low investment cost. As distinct from Bluetooth, WLAN radio networks also employ an effective data-encryption process.

The terminals used are laptop computers or PDAs equipped with an appropriate radio LAN interface module. WLANs replace or complement cable-based LANs in enterprises, universities, and airports, etc. In order to allow billing in public WLANs (airports, railway stations, etc.), the mobiles must be fitted with a SIM (Security Identify Module) for identification.

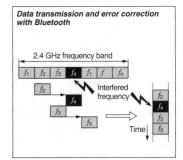

*Data transmission and error correction with Bluetooth*

2.4 GHz frequency band

$f_1$ $f_2$ $f_3$ $f_4$ $f_1$ $f$ $f_n$

$f_2$
$f_4$ — Interfered frequency
$f_3$
$f_5$

$f_2$
$f_4$
$f_3$
$f_5$

Time

# Mobile information services

Whereas the chapter "Mobile and data radio" (P. 1102) dealt with the various transmission technologies used in mobile radio, this chapter will focus on the information transmitted and the services provided.

## Transmission systems for mobile information services

Transmission systems, in the telecommunications sense, are the major factor in the ability to send information over almost any distance. Voice, images, and text are the main types of information transmitted at present. Whereas voice, in the form of telephony, video, in the form of television, and text, in the form of fax and telex, all date back some considerable time, the Internet (a network made up of autonomous servers and clients) is a comparatively new information communication medium. In the simplest terms, it merely offers a quick and easy means of exchanging digital information between connected systems. But its essential innovation in comparison with older systems is the way in which it separates applications (such as voice, text, images, and video) from the transmission of information as digital data without any knowledge of the content.

Existing transmission systems have also been progressively digitized in the course of development. One example of this is the development of the mobile radiocommunications network in Germany from its origins in analog mobile radio. With the introduction of the "C" network in 1985, followed by the "D" network in 1992, voice could be transmitted as digital information with the aid of analog-digital conversion. Up to this point, applications and the mode of transmission were inextricably linked. As technology continued to advance, the transmission of text messages became popular, and since 2001 and the introduction of GPRS, the use of mobile or cellular phones has become established as a data interface with the Internet.

## Basic functions

Basically, transmission systems can be divided into two categories:
- Unidirectional systems, such as radio broadcasting and satellite radio
- Bidirectional systems, such as mobile radio, the Internet, and WLAN spots (Wireless Local Area Networks with a range of about 100 m).

Unidirectional transmission systems are designed to broadcast information at low cost to large numbers of receivers at the same time. Bidirectional systems, by contrast, are optimized to allow two-way communication between information providers and receivers.

Therefore, bidirectional transmission systems require that the user is directly addressable for responses from the provider, that the loss of data along the transmission path can be detected, that data can be protected against corruption by third parties, and that a query will definitely initiate a response. The complexity of data transmission is therefore quite considerable.

## Layer architecture

The OSI (Open Systems Interconnections) ISO 7498 standard was published in 1984. It divides the task of information transmission within a distributed system into "layers". This represents a further subdivision of the general communication tasks required in terms of separating information usage and transmission. Tasks that are more user-related are placed higher up the hierarchy of levels.

### Application layer

The application layer encompasses all the tasks that are directly related to the user or the user process. For example, an e-mail program might notify the user that an e-mail has been received or allow the user to compose a new message; on the other hand, it may also automatically reply with an "out-of-office" announcement.

## Presentation layer

The presentation layer is concerned with presenting data transmitted, i.e. compression, character-set encoding, and encryption. Encryption functions are, to some extent, also accommodated below the session or transport layer, as this allows better implementation with regard to security. In the Internet equivalent, this includes the encryption layers such as the SSL (Secure Socket Layer) or TLS (Transport Layer Security). They are positioned between the session and transport layers.

## Session layer

The job of the session layer includes the communication control and communication management between communicating parties. In the fields of WAP (Wireless Application Protocol) and WWW (World Wide Web), a format has become established to divide data into question-and-answer pairs without regard to status, i.e. without the server having to memorize queries after they have been responded to. HTTP (Hyper Text Transfer Protocol) is the best-known Internet standard for this.

## Transport layer

The transport layer provides a data connection independent of the network in the lower hierarchy layers. The Internet usually uses the widely familiar TCP (Transfer Control Protocol) protocol for this.

## Network layer

The English term is aptly named: This layer has the task of routing data into the network. A distributed infrastructure consisting of a large number of individual computing systems has to manage and interconnect routes and data packets, e.g. where to contact which subscriber or server. The Internet uses the IP (Internet Protocol) among others to do this.

## Physical layer

The transmission of data is then further subdivided into two more layers:
- the security layer
- the physical layer

This will not be discussed any further at this point.

# Components

The transmission systems referred to above have a number of components which perform functions within the transmission chain and which are described below.

### Server

A server is the terminal point in an information chain and is the machine that stores and provides the information. It can be queried for the information using standardized functions and it responds appropriately to information requests, depending on the application.

### Client

A client is the other terminal point in the chain. It is usually the machine operated by the user. The client initiates queries to the server, thus establishing an active connection. It is entirely possible for client and server to be combined on a single machine.

Term assignment must be regarded from the viewpoint of the communication process as a whole because, in a certain situation, a server may act as a client in order to contact another server.

### Proxy

A proxy, frequently combined with a firewall, is a break point within the communication chain. It uses the same transmission protocol on both sides. Its functions are:
- to encode or decode content into readable formats for the terminal device
- to manage terminal-device profiles
- to allocate IP addresses
- to cache, i.e. temporarily store, previously requested data in order to speed up later requests for the same data

### Firewall

A firewall is a security system that distinguishes between an internal and external zone. It protects internal communication and data against unauthorized access from external sources. It does so by veiling or masking the internal addresses (network address translation) or using various other mechanisms. It also scans data for known viruses and "disinfects" it where necessary.

### Gateway

A gateway is used to translate communication from one protocol to another. It attempts to allow the application to communicate through the gateway with as little interference as possible. Nevertheless, certain restrictions exist, since only functions which can be represented on both sides are available. One of the more undesirable effects occurs with the WAP security layer WTLS. On the Internet, the corresponding encryption function exists in a different form. Therefore, if a terminal wishes to set up a WTLS access to the Internet, the gateway must open the data and decrypt it, and then re-encrypt it for the Internet by other means. Since it is precisely the operation of opening data packets which is regarded as critical, the encryption functions used on the Internet were added to "WAP 2.0" devices.

### Access point

An access point is the point at which semipermanent connections are made between the wireless and line communication infrastructures. It is also the point at which protocol conversion takes place so that, ultimately, access points are usually also gateways.

## Challenges

Mobile radio transmission systems are used to communicate and display information at the instigation of the user. However, a number of circumstances complicate this process as explained under the various headings below.

### Error tolerance

In comparison with line systems, the user is able to move around and change reception quality while transmission is taking place (either by entering a radio shadow or by leaving the reception range of the transmitter).

When a user moves beyond the range of one transmitter and into the range of an adjacent transmitter, the connection is automatically switched over. In order to make this possible, the first transmitter passes a data record containing all the required details of the connection ("visitor location register") to the second transmitter. This operation is referred to as "handover". A handover is a complex procedure which represents a considerable time delay at high transmission frequencies. Cars traveling at high speeds may temporarily cause a break in the connection as a result. It is then the job of the

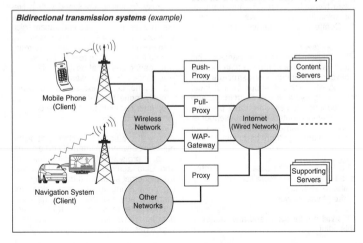

*Bidirectional transmission systems (example)*

Mobile Phone (Client)

Navigation System (Client)

Wireless Network

Other Networks

Push-Proxy

Pull-Proxy

WAP-Gateway

Proxy

Internet (Wired Network)

Content Servers

Supporting Servers

transport layer to detect the situation unnoticed to the user and reestablish the connection if possible.

Interference in the radio network can also lead to errors, however. GSM DCS, for example, guarantees an error rate of 1%, which is not reliable enough for some types of data. In contrast with speech encoding, a program cannot tolerate any errors whatsoever, otherwise it would crash.

### Availability/connection failure

In Germany, mobile radio coverage is virtually 100%. Nevertheless, there are still locations where a terminal cannot connect to a transmitter (e.g. in the cellar of a house). It would be annoying for the user if a very brief break in communication resulted in termination of the communication, and all the data transmitted since the start of the communication were lost. Therefore, the session layer opens a connection to a special service so that the process can continue to run for a relatively long period without receiving a response (depending on the service, the period may even extend to several hours). As soon as the device reenters an area where reception is possible, the connection can be reactivated.

### Equipment characteristics

Another difference between a home PC and a mobile terminal is the question of format. Whereas PCs represent a quasi standard (800 x 600 pixels, 102-key keyboard and mouse), mobile terminals differ widely in terms of input and output. In addition to the number of keys and the screen size, color reproduction, and resolution, they also differ with regard to area of application. To allow service providers to deliver information to terminals in the appropriate format, the type of terminal using the service can be automatically negotiated for each session. Appropriate conversion of the information then ensures that it is optimized for the user's device.

### Billing

Billing for chargeable services is a problem that has been solved in many different ways on the Internet. Since advertising is hardly a suitable means of financing services for mobiles because of the small screen size, this feature is attracting more and more interest. Interfaces for EC cards (Eurocheque card), for example, would make the terminal unnecessarily expensive. For this reason, future solutions will be capable of managing electronic payment and identification ("signatures") and allow them to be transported over the network to a terminal. Another aspect of billing is the data connection itself. There already far-reaching solutions in this area. The term "roaming" relates to movement of users between networks of different network operators. Network operators exchange details of the connected users using the visitor location register, so that a user can move his/her terminal from one network to another. Charges are then collected on the home mobile radio bill.

### Location-based services

A PC or laptop generally remains in one location while in use. The usual size of mobile terminals means that they are mobile and easy to use. They open up the possibility for another type of service that is dependent on location ("location-based service") and, in addition to the information already referred to, essentially projects the geographical position of a terminal on a digital road map. A "yellow pages service", for example, could then dispense with a large number of the required entries (relating to the user's location) normally needed to display local businesses. Help with finding a local destination might be another service that could make use of such information.

## Service classes

As already indicated, a large number of possible applications arise from the special functions of mobile radio. Below is a brief outline of the various services that are possible with mobile terminals. From the user's viewpoint, the meanings of the terms "application" and "service" begin to merge. A service can be an application in its own right or may use another application, such as a browser, in order to interface with the user. In either case, it is primarily the service itself which is of interest to the user.

### POI service
A POI (Point of Interest) is a location which in itself offers a function or a service of interest to the user. POIs may be tourist attractions, department stores, or filling stations (P. 1112), for example. POI services frequently offer responses to inquiries such as "Where is the nearest post office?".

### Remote diagnosis
Remote diagnosis and telecontrol are services which can be used to examine the condition of a vehicle or make adjustments over a communication link. If, for example, a vehicle has broken down or is signaling an alert, the user can use this service to obtain advice on what to do next.

A diagnosis service can also check whether windows and doors are closed, the auxiliary heating is switched, on or the immobilizer is armed. Conversely, the telecontrol service can make adjustments to vehicle systems (after user authentication).

### Traffic management
Traffic management services (in the true sense) are primarily used for the control and management of traffic networks. From the user's viewpoint, they can provide traffic reports or route recommendations for avoiding traffic holdups. The information can not only be displayed or announced, it can also be taken into account by navigation systems (P. 1112), for instance, when calculating routes.

### Online shopping
If the requirements for identification and payment are satisfied, then it is possible for mobile terminals to be used as payment channels. An agency service processes the bank transaction and credits the amount to the trader's account.

### Software updates
With Java, it is now possible to download small Java programs ("mid-lets") to terminals. Games or tools, such as special calculators or chat programs, belong to this class of service.

### General information exchange
Information exchange using browsers is a service in its own right which is used by many other services to interface with the user. At the same time it will continue to exist as a separate service. Over 8 million WAP pages were already available to users by the year 2000, and numbers have continued to grow ever since. The majority of them can be accessed free of charge. However, there are also "premium content" concepts where pages of a guaranteed content quality are financed by charging a small access fee.

## Alternative mobile information services

Examples of alternative mobile information services offered by various providers are:

### WWW
In the WWW digital marketplace, large numbers of providers disseminate their information using a variety of business models. The vast majority of services presupposes the availability of a "standard" PC (processor with a capacity of several 100 MIPS), a monitor screen with a resolution of approx. 800 x 600 pixels, a keyboard, and a mouse. In addition, a large number of service providers are primarily interested in offering "attractive" or appealing content. Due to the landline transmission path offered by the Internet, they use very large data volumes for images and animations. The WWW is largely financed by advertising, which is dependent on such visual effects.

The WWW is not limited by national boundaries in the conventional sense. All languages are spoken simultaneously all over the world. Virtually every country in the world has access to the "Web".

## OMA/WAP

By contrast, mobile radio systems have adopted a variety of different and mutually incompatible solutions on the various continents. This is due to the use of different frequencies or modulation methods, or differences in the configuration of the infrastructures or the security concepts used. Such barriers have to be overcome if mobile radio systems are to become part of the network.

OMA/WAP is the international initiative on the part of the mobile radio industry to bring together mobile radio networks and the landline Internet. This course has been pursued by an industrial forum since 1998. The primary aim is to establish the use of mobile information services on mobile radio terminals. In the early days the forum was essentially concerned with the definition and standardization of the transmission system.

Since it was reformed as the "Open Mobile Alliance" in 2002, the focus has shifted to applications based on that system. There are a large number of different models for access to existing, web-based services. They appear to the user as such things as inboxes for multimedia messages (text messages combined with images, animations, and music clips), for example. They also include services that send photographs that have just been taken to the user's home mailbox. The mobile browser now has active elements ("scripts" or Java programs) which can be executed.

The Open Mobile Alliance incorporates many smaller forums, such as MGIF (Mobile Gaming Interoperability Forum) which use the new platform for communicative games.

OMA/WAP functions on virtually all mobile radio systems such as GSM, CDMA, PDC, and UMTS, and many other types of network such as WLAN, Bluetooth, or DECT. It therefore provides a basic function similar to the Internet and allows a similar system solution across the various radio systems.

## i-Mode

In Japan, one mobile network provider has a majority share of the market, and can therefore create quasi-standards for Japan on its own. Although this company is involved with OMA/WAP, it decided to continue with the proprietary solution in Japan.

i-Mode has now penetrated the European and German markets as a result of international participation by other mobile radio operators. The concept is aimed less at the technical quality of the transmission solution than at the ability to offer high-quality and "premium content" presented in an appealing way.

The company operates the entire information portfolio and places emphasis on a standard operating concept and useful recognition effects. Chargeable services are offered on the basis of a simple and easily understandable pricing system that provides for charges that are collected or canceled on a monthly basis.

The present i-Mode programs of German service providers contain a large number of service in the fields of news, weather, sports, mailing, chat, leisure, games, sounds, logos, navigation, finances, knowledge, price comparisons, and looking up information.

Migration paths are already discernible for future generations of terminals, and this is being pursued by OMA and i-Mode service providers.

# Navigation systems

Navigation systems have become extremely popular in recent years. Whereas the first systems on the market were mainly retrofit equipment, the present systems are original equipment fitted as standard or as an option. Integration in the vehicle allows shared use of sensors for various systems and networking with other components. In this way, displays on the instrument cluster can place important route-guidance information in the driver's primary field of vision.

On many types of vehicle, navigation has been integrated in an overall driver-information system that includes audio and telephone functions. This development trend is set to continue.

Common to all systems is a combination of the basic functions of position locating, destination selection, route computation, and route guidance. Systems in the upper performance range also offer a color map display. All functions require a digital map of the road network which – except in the case of offboard navigation systems (see "Traffic telematics") – is normally stored on a CD-ROM or DVD.

## Position location

Position location is achieved by means of compound navigation. Route elements are added cyclically (compounded) according to magnitude and angle. However, this process tends to accumulate errors. They are compensated for by constantly comparing the vehicle's location with the route of the road on the digital map (map matching). The satellite positioning system GPS (Global Positioning System) has gained in importance since the artificial scrambling of the signal for military purposes has been discontinued. GPS allows trouble-free system operation to resume, even after short excursions beyond the boundaries of the digitized road map, or after the vehicle has been transported by sea or rail.

### Sensors

For position-locating purposes, two wheel-speed sensors (see P. 119) were frequently used to determine the distance traveled and changes in direction, while a geomagnetic sensor was used to determine the absolute direction of travel. Essentially, the GPS positioning system served to correct heavy sensor interference, or to locate the correct point of reentry to the stored road network after trips outside the range of the digital map.

Current systems only need a simple travel signal, which is already often used for speed-dependent volume control of car tuners. Changes in direction are detected by a yaw-rate sensor (oscillation gyrometer, see P. 121 onwards). The absolute direction of travel is determined by the Doppler effect of the GPS signals.

## Destination entry

The digital map contains directories so that a destination can be entered as an address. Lists of all known place names are required for this purpose. In turn, all locations are allocated lists containing the names of the stored street names. To pinpoint a destination even further, the user can also select road/street intersections, or the number of a building.

Drivers rarely know the addresses of destinations, such as airports, railroad stations, filling stations, multi-story parking lots, etc. Therefore, in order to make them easier to find, subject directories are often provided listing the POIs (Points-of-Interest). These directories also make it possible to locate a nearby filling station, for instance.

Marking a destination in the map display, or calling up destinations which were previously stored in a destination memory, are further selection options.

### Travel guides

A logical consequence of selecting points of interests is the publication of data carriers containing travel guides produced as the result of joint ventures between publishing houses and the producers of digital maps. These guides provide functions such as locating hotels in the vicinity of the destination. They also contain the size, prices, and facilities offered by points of interest.

## Route computation

### Standard computation

The way in which the route is calculated can be adapted to suit the driver's preferences. These may include the choice between route optimization based on driving time or distance, or preferences for the type of route (e.g. whether to avoid expressways, ferry crossings, or toll roads). Route recommendations are expected in less than half a minute after entering the destination.

A more time-critical scenario is recomputing the route if the driver departs from the recommended route. The system must be capable of supplying new directions before the driver reaches the next intersection. A "tailback" button is used to indicate that the road ahead is blocked and that computation of an alternative route is required.

### Dynamic routing

Processing RDS TMC-coded traffic announcements (see P. 869) is a means of avoiding traffic holdups. Traffic announcements can be received by RDS or GSM. The TMC codes required for this are limited to expressways and major highways.

Advanced possibilities for dynamic routing based on new processes are under development.

## Route guidance

Route guidance is performed by comparing the present position with the computed route. The system can decide whether the driver must turn off the road he/she is on or remain on it by following the route already traveled and calculating the remaining route.

### Route direction recommendation

Route direction recommendations are mainly reproduced acoustically. This allows the driver to follow the directions without being distracted from the task of driving. Simple graphics, preferably positioned in the primary field of vision (instrument cluster), support the driver in understanding the directions. The conciseness of these acoustic and graphic directions is the main factor governing the quality of route guidance.

Expecting the driver to identify the route direction from a map on the display is not considered a primary option due to the risk of distraction.

## Map display

Depending on the system, the map can be displayed on a color monitor at a scale ranging from approx. 1:8,000 to 1:16 million. This is helpful for obtaining a general overview of the route in the immediate locality or over a wider area.

Some topographical background information showing bodies of water, rivers, built-up areas, railroads, and forests provides added orientation.

## Road-map memory

CDs are widely used as the medium for road-map storage. As DVDs have a storage capacity that is seven times larger than CDs, they can accommodate road maps covering substantially larger areas, and they are now superseding CDs to an increasing extent.

The structures of data stored on CD and DVD are proprietary know-how, and this is a prime factor affecting system function and performance. For this reason, the CDs and DVDs for the systems produced by different manufacturers are not generally intercompatible.

In the future, automotive-compatible hard disks for use as road-map storage media will offer not only greater capacity but also the facility for regular map updates.

# Traffic telematics

Traffic telematics refers to systems that transmit traffic-related information to and from vehicles and, generally, which analyze this information automatically.

The term "telematics" is essentially derived from the German words for telecommunications and information technology.

## Transmission paths

At present the main transmission paths for telecommunications are provided by radio broadcasting and mobile radiocommunications networks.

Radio broadcasting only allows the one-way path to the vehicle and cannot communicate individual messages. With GSM, information can be exchanged in both directions between vehicles and control centers operated by service providers.

The amount of information exchanged is restricted in each case by the bandwidth of the available transmission channels. As a result, the coding must be as free as possible of redundant information. With GPRS, the available bandwidth is considerably greater and will increase even further when G3/UMTS services are introduced.

## Standardization

The standardization of content allows not only compact coding, which is one of the initial objectives, but also the use of information from different sources and by different terminals.

In the case of traffic-holdup announcements, standardization of content refers to the type of holdup (e.g. "tailback" or "road closure"), causes (e.g. "accident" or "black ice"), the expected duration, and identification of the road sections affected.

The coding for geographical regions, long freeway sections (segments), and individual interchanges (locations) already exists in many countries for transmission over the Traffic Message Channel (TMC) of the Radio Data System (RDS, see P. 869 onwards).

However, GSM-network service providers also use the same coding.

GATS, the Global Automotive Telematics Standard, is used for breakdown calls, emergency calls, information services, and traffic data collection according to the "floating car data" principle explained below.

## Referencing

The use of predefined interchanges and road sections within the road network presupposes that they are known to the on-board equipment. To date this has been limited to the major roads (expressways and highways). This method also requires considerable updating work. For these reasons, an EU-wide project (AGORA) has developed a method which allows messages for any road to be coded without transmitters and receivers having to use identical-version reference tables.

## Selection

The on-board terminal filters out the relevant messages from those available using the vehicle location and, if necessary, its movement along a route.

## Decoding of traffic messages

The facility for decoding and selecting TMC-coded traffic announcements is already integrated in 1-block car tuners. A voice-output chip converts messages into audible announcements. As the messages are standardized, there is no difficulty in converting them to different languages.

## Telematics services

Equipment, such as the Blaupunkt "Gemini GPS 148", contain a GSM module and a Global Positioning System (GPS) receiver. As well as normal telephone functions, the GSM module also permits bidirectional message transmission via SMS (text messaging). It allows the vehicle's location to be pinpointed to within approximately 100 meters. With this type of device, Telematics services such as "Traffic information", "Breakdown call", and "Assistance call" can be used.

Traffic announcements can be selected on the basis of the vehicle's present location and direction of travel, or by specifying expressways and highways. In the event of a breakdown, the driver can establish a telephone link to a control center at the touch of a button. At the same time the vehicle's position is transmitted via SMS.

For future GSM services, it will be possible to expand equipment functions by loading new software.

## Dynamic route guidance

The most extensively automated evaluation of traffic information is performed for the purposes of dynamic route guidance. Owing to the standardized coding of locations (see the paragraph headed "Standardization"), events, their physical extent, and expected duration allow computers in route-guidance systems to assess the impact of a traffic holdup on a particular route. They can then calculate whether there is a better alternative route. In this case, the driver is instructed that the route has been recalculated on account of traffic announcements received. Further route recommendations will follow in accordance with the new route.

For this purpose, the CDs that contain digital road maps for route-guidance systems require a reference table containing the location codes used in traffic announcements.

Systems with dynamic route guidance have been on the market since 1998, and have rapidly become popular because of their driver convenience.

## Offboard navigation

Offboard navigation offers route guidance through a GSM-network service provider. The vehicle requires only an input device for destinations, an output device for displaying route recommendations, and a position-locating device. Routes and directions are computed at a central location by a service provider and transmitted to the vehicle via GSM. The route also includes a display of the roads along the route, and this can be used to support the position-locating function. There is no need for a CD or other storage medium containing map data.

## Information recording

The benefit of traffic telematics is dependent on the quality of the messages and how up-to-date they are.

### Information collection by way of road infrastructure

For many years information about traffic flow on important stretches of road has been recorded by induction loops inserted in the road surface. Induction loops indicate the number and speed of the vehicles passing over them, and the figures can be used to calculate traffic density (vehicles per km), and traffic flow (vehicles per hour). There has been a marked step-up in the installation of such loops in recent years, but this is a time-consuming and expensive process.

Service providers have also installed sensors which transmit data by radio on expressway bridges. They are cheap to install, but are also limited to counting vehicles and roughly classifying their speed.

### Floating car data

Traffic information is also collected using the "floating car data" principle. A car "floats" along in the traffic flow and transmits its position and speed to a control center at regular intervals. Statistical analysis of this data is employed to generate up-to-date messages about the traffic situation.

This statistical method depends on whether a sufficient number of vehicles is fitted with position-locating and transmitting equipment (GSM SMS).

# Fleet management

## Definition

The term "fleet management" in this particular context refers to the use of traffic telematics services in commercially operated vehicle fleets.

Whereas the flow of traffic telematics information takes place only between an individual vehicle and a service provider in a private-transport scenario, fleet management can connect almost any number of links to the information chain.

Fleet Management Systems (FMS) comprise mobile and fixed components which exchange information over a wireless communication medium.

## Services

### Applications

Just as the term "traffic telematics" covers a number of applications for transmitting information relevant for the individual motorist, specific function blocks can also be defined for fleet management. They are recurring components of telematics applications in commercial vehicles. Basically, there are two types of service used:

– Operations-related fleet-management services which assist in the deployment of vehicles as a business resource. These services benefit the fleet operator, whose aim is to manage the fleet as efficiently as possible.
– Services which focus on the vehicle itself as a business resource. These can be used by the vehicle manufacturer, for instance, to carry out diagnoses of all major mechanical assemblies and electronic control units over the entire operating life of the vehicle, and initiate appropriate fault-rectification measures.

### Position location

Vehicle-location information is usually obtained on board by means of the GPS satellite positioning system and is transmitted to the fleet control center. Depending on the application, it may then be displayed on electronic maps for visualization purposes, or used as the basis for comparing the expected and actual progress of a vehicle according to its tour plan. In this way, problems within a logistic chain can be identified at an early stage and appropriate remedial action initiated.

### Communication

The exchange of short, concise messages between fleet control center and the vehicles is always preferable to voice communication.

The messages themselves may take a number of forms. In addition to user-definable text messages, there are usually standardized status messages (e.g. arrival at delivery/collection point, start of duty, break time), and even formatted job orders which may include the main way-bill information.

### Navigation

As a logical extension to the transmission of job orders to vehicles, geographical coordinates of the tour destination can be added to the message data records. In this way, the navigation system can automatically direct the driver to the required destinations without any driver input.

### Diagnosis

The benefit of mobility management systems is not only limited to the basic functions of "communication", "position location", and "navigation". In the highly competitive logistics market, fleet operators and leasing companies have gradually come to value the integration of information relating to fuel consumption, component wear, utilization profiles, maintenance planning, and operating data, and the associated opportunities for more efficient planning and the resulting cost and time savings.

At present, systems fitted on new vehicles can analyze vehicle deployment by collecting vehicle operating data and producing vehicle utilization profiles. Systems for telediagnosis and maintenance planning have been announced for the next vehicle generations.

## Transmission paths

Essential to the choice of a suitable transmisssion medium are, firstly, its availability over a wide area, and secondly, the cost of using the medium.

### Mobile-telephone systems
In general, the GSM (Groupe Spécial Mobile: Global System for Mobile communication) cellular telephone system available throughout Europe is used. The system used here is usually the Short Message Services (SMS), which allow the transmission of messages up to 160 characters long.

As tariff structures are changing in favor of new transmission services in GSM networks, such as GPRS (General Packet Radio System), a trend is developing for the use of such technologies in FMS applications in the near future. This will then allow the exchange of larger data volumes between vehicles and control centers.

### Trunked radio networks
For applications used by the police, fire, and other emergency services, the digital trunked radio network TETRA (Trans European Trunked Radio), and the alternative TETRAPOL, have been defined for use across Europe and are destined to replace the analog voice communication media. TETRA terminals have the technological requirements for integrating external components in these FMS applications via the PEI Peripheral Equipment Interface).
The use of private mobile radio or analog trunked radio networks for FMS applications only plays a minor role in practice.

## Standardization

### Components and subsystems
In fleet-management systems, an information network is made up of a large number of very different components. Information passes through a large number of interfaces between individual components and subsystems. Standardization of the interfaces is a desirable aim for a number of reasons.

From the user's viewpoint, components that can be incorporated in fleet management systems via standardized interfaces carry a low investment risk, and the certainty that the system will be capable of operating over a long period. The system can then be expanded as requirements grow, and individual components can be replaced if more suitable technology becomes available at a later date. The widely diverging product life cycles of individual system components further strengthen the desirability of this objective.

### Vehicle interfaces
In order to use the wide variety of applications and functions, the manufacturer-specific instruments and controls in the vehicle must be able to interact with FMS components.
In addition, vehicle operating data is indispensable for analyzing vehicle deployment, or diagnosis, or maintenance-planning applications that may be available later on.

The leading commercial-vehicle manufacturers in Europe have agreed on a common interface for truck data. A whole collection of basic information, such as vehicle speed, fuel consumption, or operating hours can be read from the vehicle via this interface. Access takes place via the CAN (J1939). The protocol used in the application is specified as an "FMS standard" (www.fms-standard.com).

### Air interface
A standardized transmission protocol for fleet-management applications does not exist at present. Providers of FMS components are therefore operating with a wide variety of proprietary interface definitions.

Efforts to achieve a standard, such as expanding GATS (Global Auto-motive Telematics Standard), or agreement on a service portfolio, or a protocol, have so far been unable to gain acceptability on the market.

# Multimedia systems

Multimedia means the combination of different media. All known media are internetworked and are available for use.

Various sound and information sources, and communication installations can form a common mobile driver-information system consisting of radio, cassette player, CD player, phone, navigation and traffic telematics equipment, and even computer, video player, and TV.

## Multimedia broadcasting

The digital audio broadcasting systems developed in recent years (DAB, DRM) allow the transmission of any type of data at high bit rates so that the radio of the past is currently developing into a genuine multimedia system for the future. It permits transmission of audio data (music, news), textual information (messages), and video data (from individual images through to TV broadcasts). With such capabilities, DAB becomes DMB (<u>D</u>igital <u>M</u>ultimedia <u>B</u>roadcasting). This is illustrated by the following conceivable examples:

### Traffic and travel information
Traffic and travel information may encompass the following services:
– <u>Traffic announcements</u> may be transmitted as audio (synthetic voice), or as text, or map extracts (on a display).
– TMC or TPEG-coded traffic announcements may be transmitted for <u>navigation devices</u>, thus allowing dynamic route guidance. In addition, updated digital road maps may be transmitted to ensure that route guidance by navigation systems is based on information that is completely up-to-date.
– <u>Travel guides</u> may use maps to provide directions to vacation destinations, or to business appointments, and offer information about the locality, the hotel, (photos, room prices, and vacancies), local events, parking facilities (with details of parking lots with free spaces), filling stations, timetables, local stores, etc. Along with the information about the "<u>P</u>oints <u>o</u>f Interest" (POI), details of their location (references) may also be

transmitted so that the navigation system can locate them automatically without any driver input.

### Transmission of text and images
Text data is an extension of radio broadcasts, and may contain a large amount of additional information, such as title and composer of a music track currently being played, information about the present station tuned, including phone number/address to request additional information, or even an electronic program listing. The DAB standard offers the following modes for transmitting text:
– <u>Station name and type.</u>
– <u>Dynamic label</u> for the station, the speed of the label is controlled by the transmitting station.
– <u>Interactive text pages</u> in HTML or XML format, which can be displayed in various formats.

## Mobile Internet

Combination with mobile communication media, such as GSM and UMTS, permits interaction with servers on the Internet so that interactive services can be offered. <u>W</u>ireless <u>A</u>pplication <u>P</u>rotocol (WAP) is the name of the internationally established protocol which links the two worlds together.

The aim is to integrate the various communication elements such as navigation system, car tuner, mobile radiocommunications, digital audio broadcasting, and Internet.

For mobile access to the Internet from a motor vehicle (or on board a train), it must be possible to receive over the air interface, even when traveling at high speeds. In addition, there is certainly a challenge in meeting the demands for consistent Internet-access quality while moving between city and rural surroundings, with the resulting wide variations in transmission conditions.

The Internet is an open medium or market-place for users and information providers and has a wide variety of services for the mobile consumer. International bodies, such as the <u>O</u>pen <u>M</u>obile <u>A</u>lliance (OMA), the <u>W</u>orld <u>W</u>ide <u>W</u>eb <u>C</u>onsortium (W3C), or the <u>I</u>nternational <u>E</u>ngineering <u>T</u>ask <u>F</u>orce (IETF) define interfaces and protocols so that the new services can be used anywhere at any time:

- A hotel or restaurant may encode its geographical coordinates on its website so that they can be accessed by a navigation system. This would then direct the driver automatically to the desired destination. A reservation inquiry could be made and confirmed in advance over the mobile radiocommunications channel.
- Vehicle functions, such as remote diagnosis and remote maintenance support, could connect automatically to a service center via the Internet in case of a breakdown or accident. The service center would then produce a diagnosis of the vehicle's condition, and accompany the vehicle to the workshop, or inform the breakdown assistance or emergency services.

- Future traffic management systems will take account of traffic flow in city areas as well. The number of organizations involved will be so large that coordination over the Internet will become necessary, as this is the medium accessible to everyone. Traffic flow in selected areas will be shown online on graphical displays, or will be distributed in machine-readable form as network lists. The navigation system will then be able to use this information to compute the best route.
- In addition, other specially prepared services may be accessible over the Internet. This include e-mails, e-commerce, or news, weather, and sports announcements, or online transactions with banks, hotels, cinemas, or travel agents.
- With the ever shorter development cycles in the fields of information and communications technology, software updates via the Internet will allow the longer-lasting components of motor vehicles to be kept up-to-date.

*Mobile Internet services* (examples)
*a) Traffic-holdup maps (with forecast), b) Parking information and parking guidance system,*
*c) Dynamic navigation, d) Public transport information, e) Camera shots of traffic situation,*
*f) Information about events.*

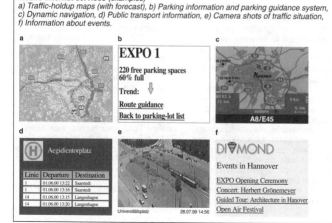

# Methods and tools

## Function and requirements

Every development has the aim of creating a new function or improving an existing function of the vehicle. We use the word "functions" to include all working features of the vehicle. These functions are appreciated by drivers, as they represent a value or a benefit for the user of the vehicle. The technical realization of a function is of secondary importance, i.e. whether it is a mechanical, hydraulic, electric, or electronic system.

In combination with mechanical, electrical, or hydraulic parts, electronic components can offer many advantages for the technical realization, whether it is to achieve improvements in reliability, weight, installation space, or costs. Electronics, therefore, are the most important technology achieving many innovations in vehicle construction. At present nearly all functions in the vehicle are controlled, regulated, or monitored electronically. Ongoing advances in the technology and performance of electronics hardware allow the realization of many new, more powerful functions through the use of software.

The increasing number of these software functions, their integration, rising demands with regard to reliability and security, the expanding variety of vehicle variants, and the different life cycles of software, hardware, and vehicles all represent requirements and conditions that have a considerable impact on the development of software for the electronic systems of a motor vehicle.

Mastering the resulting complexity is a challenge for vehicle manufacturers and automotive suppliers alike. Precautions must be taken during development to guarantee the safe controllability of software and electronic systems. The methods and tools described below contribute to this safety, and they focus on the application areas of the drivetrain, suspension, and body shell.

## Model-based development of vehicle functions

Collaboration between the various disciplines in development (e.g. cooperation between drivetrain and electronics engineering) requires a mutual understanding and overall comprehension of the problems involved. For example, when designing the open-loop and closed-loop control functions of a vehicle, it is also necessary to maintain an overview of overall reliability and safety requirements, as well as the aspects of software realization in embedded systems.

A graphics-based function model considers all system component and can be used as the basis for a general understanding. In software development, therefore, the use of model-based development methods, with notations such as block diagrams or finite state machines, is replacing written software specifications to an increasing extent. This method of <u>modeling</u> software functions has other advantages. If the specification model is formal, i.e. clear and unambiguous, the specification can be reproduced by <u>simulation</u> on computer, and "experienced" in the vehicle itself by means of <u>rapid prototyping</u>.

Methods of automated <u>code generation</u> can be used to model the specified function models on software components for electronic control units (ECUs). The function models, therefore, need to contain additional software design information, which may include optimization measures, depending on the product characteristics required by the electronic system.

In the next step, <u>working vehicles</u> simulate the ECU environment, thus allowing ECUs to be tested in the laboratory. Compared to test bench and road tests, this increases flexibility, thereby making test cases easier to reproduce.

<u>Calibrating</u> software functions in the electronic system must consider the vehicle-specific settings, for example, parameters stored in the form of characteristic values,

characteristic curves, and program maps of these functions. In many cases, these cannot be matched until a later stage in the development process, and sometimes only directly in the vehicle once the system is running. Making the settings requires the support of suitable procedures and tools.

In this model-based development process for software functions, a distinction is made between development methods, as illustrated in the figure.

This procedure can also be applied to the development of function networks and ECU networks. In these cases, however, additional degrees of freedom are introduced, such as:
– Combinations of modeled, virtual, and realized functions
– Combinations of modeled, virtual, and realized technical components

It is useful, therefore, to distinguish between functions at an abstract level, and technical realization at a more concrete level.

The concept of a separate abstract and concrete approach can be applied to all vehicle components, the driver, and the environment. The abstract view, in this case, is called the <u>logical system architecture</u> (displayed in gray in the figures), and the concrete view of the realization is called the <u>technical system architecture</u> (displayed in white in the diagrams). This procedure is described in terms of open-loop and closed-loop control functions, but is also suitable for general realization – for example, for monitoring and diagnostic functions.

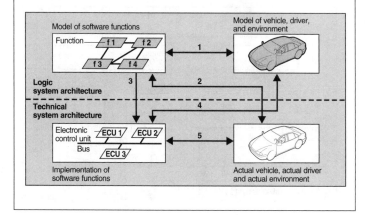

*Development methods in the model-based development of software functions*
*1 Computer modeling and simulation of software functions as well as the vehicle, driver, and environment,*
*2 Rapid prototyping of the software functions in the real vehicle,*
*3 Realization of software functions on a network of electronic control units (ECU),*
*4 Integration and testing of ECUs with working vehicles and test benches,*
*5 Testing and calibration of the software functions of the ECUs in the vehicle.*

Model of software functions

Function — f 1 — f 2
f 3 — f 4

Model of vehicle, driver, and environment

1

**Logic system architecture**

3

2

- - - - - - - - - - - - - - - - - - - - - -

**Technical system architecture**

4

Electronic control unit — ECU 1 / ECU 2
Bus — ECU 3

5

Implementation of software functions

Actual vehicle, actual driver and actual environment

## Software architecture and standardized software components

Standardization measures have been successfully introduced for the software architecture of microcontrollers integrated in ECUs. For example, the architecture is divided into the "actual" software functions of the application software, and platform software, which may depend on the hardware (see figure below)

One layer of the platform software, the (hardware abstraction layer, HAL) groups software components that cover hardware-related aspects of the input and output units (I/O units) of a microcontroller. As displayed in the figure, the following description excludes the input and output units from this "hardware abstraction layer" required for communication with other systems via buses. The bus drivers required for this are dealt with separately.

Platform software also includes the software components from the above layers that are required for communication with other ECUs in the network, or for communication with diagnostic testers.

Examples of standardized software components are real-time operating systems, network management according to OSEK [2], or diagnostic protocols according to ISO [3, 4]. These software components have standardized interfaces for application software (application programming interfaces, API). The platform software can therefore be standardized for different applications. Most of the functions in application software can be developed independently of the hardware.

## Modeling and simulation of software functions

Block diagrams should be used where possible to model open-loop and closed-loop control systems. These diagrams use blocks to represent the response of components, and arrows represent the flow of signals between the blocks (right side of top figure). As most of the systems are multivariable systems, all signals are generally in vector form. These are classified into:

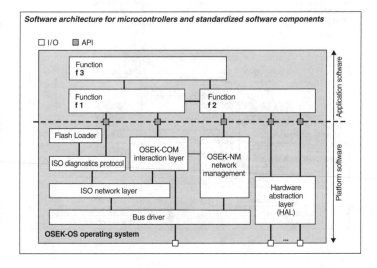

*Software architecture for microcontrollers and standardized software components*

- Measurement and
  feedback variables     **R**
- Open or closed-loop control
  output variables     **U**
- Reference or setpoint variables   **W**
- Driver setpoint values     **W\***
- Open or closed-loop
  control variables     **X**
- Manipulated variables     **Y**
- Disturbance values     **Z**

The blocks are classified into:
- Open or closed-loop control model
- Model of actuators
- Road model
- Models of desired-value generators
  and sensors
- Model of the driver and the
  environment

The driver can influence the functions of the open or closed-loop controller by defining setpoint values. All components for entering setpoint values for the driver (for example, switches or pedals), are known as desired-value generators. Sensors, in contrast, record signals from the route. In this example, the driver is representative of all users of vehicle functions, including, for example, other vehicle occupants.

A model of this type can be executed on a simulation system (for example, a PC), thus allowing it to be analyzed in more detail.

## Rapid prototyping of software functions

Rapid prototyping in this context includes all methods for the early implementation of specifications of open-loop and closed-loop control functions in the real vehicle. To allow this, the modeled open or closed-loop control functions must be implemented as a prototype. Experimental systems can be used as an implementation platform for the software controls of the open-loop and closed-loop control functions (see figure below).

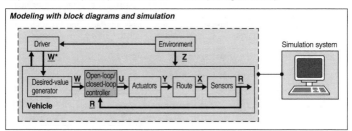

*Modeling with block diagrams and simulation*

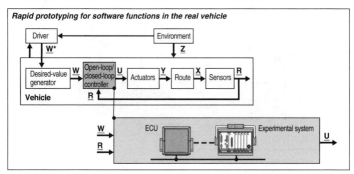

*Rapid prototyping for software functions in the real vehicle*

The software controls are then connected to the desired-value generators, sensors, and actuators, as well as the vehicle ECUs. The interfaces to the real vehicle mean that the software functions in the experimental system – and in the ECU – are implemented taking into account real-time considerations.

Real-time computer systems with considerably higher computing power are usually deployed as ECUs in experimental systems. This allows the model of a software function to be automatically converted from a specification into an implementable model using a rapid-prototyping tool that is subject to standardized rules. The specified behavior can then be modeled as accurately as possible.

Experimental systems with a modular structure can be configured specifically for the application, for example, in terms of the required interfaces for input and output signals. The overall system is designed for deployment in the vehicle, and is operated using a computer, e.g. a PC. This allows the testing of software-function specifications directly in the vehicle at an early stage. The specifications can then be changed as required.

When using experimental systems, there is a choice between bypass and fullpass applications.

**Bypass applications**

Bypass development is suitable for early testing of an additional or modified software function of an ECU in the vehicle.

The new or modified software function is defined by a model and run on the experimental system. This requires an ECU that can run the basic functionality of the software system, support all the necessary desired-value generators, sensors, and actuators, and provide a <u>bypass interface</u> to the experimental system. The new or modified software function is developed using a rapid prototyping tool. It is then run "in bypass" on the experimental system (see figure below).

This approach is also suitable for further developments to existing ECU functions. In this case, the existing functions in the ECU are still used, but they are modified to the extent that the input values are sent via the bypass interface, and the output values from the newly developed bypass

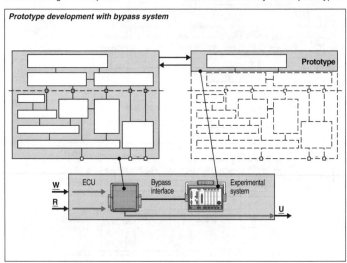

*Prototype development with bypass system*

function are used. The required software modifications to the ECU are called the bypass outsourcing.

For the essential synchronization of functional computing between the ECU and the experimental system, a procedure is normally adopted in which the ECU triggers computation of the bypass function on the experimental system via a control flow interface. The ECU monitors the output values of the bypass function for plausibility.

### Fullpass application

If a completely new function is to be tested in the vehicle, and an ECU with a bypass interface is not available, the test can be carried out using a "fullpass" development. In this case, the experimental system must support all the desired-value generators, sensors, and actuator interfaces for the function. The real-time behavior of the function must also be defined and guaranteed by the experimental system (see figure below). In general, this is performed by a real-time operating system on the fullpass computer.

### Bypass or fullpass application

Bypass applications are mainly used if only a few software functions are under development, and an ECU with tried-and-true basic functionality is available – for example, from a previous project. Bypass applications are also suitable if the sensor and actuator functions of an ECU are very complex, and supporting them requires significant effort on the part of the experimental system (for example, in the case of engine control units).

Fullpass applications are more suitable if an ECU of this type is not available, if additional desired-value generators, sensors, and actuators also need to be tested, and if the scope of the ECU is of manageable complexity.

It is also possible to use a combination of bypass and fullpass applications. This has the advantage of increased flexibility.

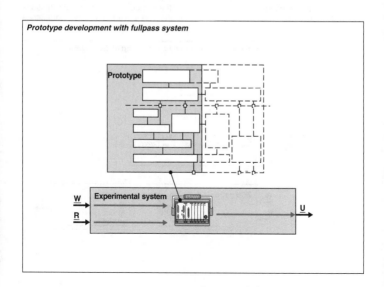

**Prototype development with fullpass system**

## Design and implementation of software functions

Based on the data specifications, the behavior, and the real-time behavior of a software function, all the technical details of the ECU network, the implemented microcontroller, and the software architecture must be taken into account at the design stage. The final implementation of the software functions can then be defined and executed on the basis of software components (see figure below).

In addition to decisions regarding the design and behavior of a software function, that takes the time- and value-related functions of the microcontrollers into consideration, an implementation includes design decisions regarding real-time behavior, distribution and integration of microcontrollers and ECUs, and reliability and safety requirements of the electronic systems.

For cost reasons, ECUs often contain microcontrollers with limited computing power and limited memory space. In many cases, this requires optimization measures in software development to reduce the hardware resources required for a software function.

An example of this is the implementation in fixed-point arithmetic.

All requirements for electronic systems and vehicles from the production and service viewpoints must also be taken into account (for example, monitoring and diagnostics concepts, the parameterization of software functions, or software updates for ECUs in the field).

## Integration and testing of software and ECUs

In the integration and test phase, simulation models can be used as the basis for working vehicles and test benches. The particular specifications for development, integration, and test functions must be taken into account. This is often the same for all companies.

This is why prototype vehicles are therefore often available only in limited numbers. It means that a component supplier often does not have a complete or up-to-date integration and test environment for the components supplied. Restrictions in the test environment can sometimes limit the possible test steps.

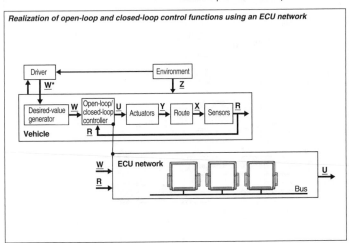

*Realization of open-loop and closed-loop control functions using an ECU network*

Component integration is a synchronization point for all the individual component developments involved. The integration test, system test, and acceptance test cannot be carried out until all the components are available. Any delays in individual components also delay the integration phase, and hence all downstream test steps.

For control units, this means that the software functions can only be tested when all the components in a vehicle system are available (ECUs, desired-value generators, sensors, actuators, and route). The use of working vehicles allows early verifications on ECUs in a virtual test environment in the absence of actual peripheral components (see figure below).

This allows tests to be performed and automated under reproducible laboratory conditions with a high level of flexibility. In contrast to tests on the test bench or in the real vehicle, the full, unrestricted range of operating states can be tested (for example, an engine ECU can be tested at the highest load and rpm). Vehicle wear and breakdown situations are easy to simulate, and allow testing of the monitoring, diagnostic, and safety functions of the ECU. Component tolerances (for example, in desired-value generators, sensors, and actuators) can be simulated to allow a verification of the sturdiness of open-loop and closed-loop control functions.

This procedure can also be applied to testing actual desired-value generators, sensors, and actuators. The interfaces of the working vehicle need to modified accordingly. Any intermediate steps can also be incorporated in the procedure.

A structure as illustrated in the figure below depicts the ECUs in the form of a black box. The behavior of the ECU functions can only be assessed on the basis of the input and output signals **W**, **R**, and **U**. This procedure is sufficient for simple software functions, but testing more complicated functions requires the integration of a measurement procedure for internal ECU intermediate variables. This type of measuring technique is also known as instrumentation. The testing of diagnostic functions also requires access to the error memory via the ECU diagnosis interface, and this requires the integration of a measurement and diagnostics system.

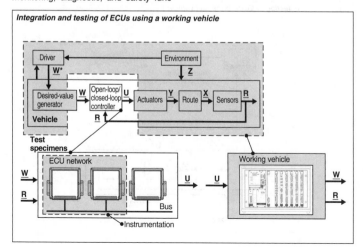

*Integration and testing of ECUs using a working vehicle*

## Calibration of software functions

The integration and testing of electronic systems in the real vehicle requires the instrumentation to cover all the affected system components in the vehicle. In addition to a measurement and diagnostics system, a calibration system is often required to calibrate internal ECU parameters (such as characteristic curves and program maps).

In the calibration, the parameter values must be changeable (as they cannot be stored in a changeable format in a read-only memory, such as ROM, EEPROM, or Flash). A calibration system, therefore, consists of one or more ECUs with a suitable interface to a measurement and calibration tool (see figure below). In addition to their deployment in vehicles, measurement, calibration and diagnostics systems can also be used in working vehicles and on test benches.

The calibration tool contains editors, which work either at the implementation level or the physical specification level,

and facilitate changes to parameter values, such as the values of a characteristic curve.

Accordingly, the measurement tool converts recorded values into a physical representation or an implementation display. The figure at the bottom right shows an example of the physical and the implementation levels for a characteristic curve and a recorded measurement signal.

When working with calibration systems, it is usually possible to choose between offline and online calibration.

In offline calibration, the execution of open-loop control, closed-loop control, and monitoring functions of the "driving schedule" are interrupted to modify or adjust parameter values. Offline calibration therefore leads to many restrictions. In particular when deployed on test benches and during in-vehicle testing, it always causes an interruption to the test-bench or road test.

It is, therefore, preferable to use a procedure that supports online calibration.

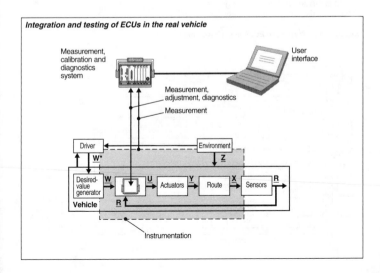

*Integration and testing of ECUs in the real vehicle*

Measurement, calibration and diagnostics system

User interface

Measurement, adjustment, diagnostics

Measurement

Driver

Environment

Desired-value generator — W → U → Actuators — Y → Route — X → Sensors — R

W*

Z

R

Vehicle

Instrumentation

In online calibration, the parameter values can be adjusted by the microcontrollers during driving-schedule execution. It is, therefore, possible to adjust parameter values while executing open-loop control, closed-loop control, and monitoring functions at the same time, and hence during regular use of the test bench or vehicle.

Online calibration places higher demands on the stability of the open-loop control, closed-loop control, and monitoring functions, since the driving schedule must remain stable during all adjustment procedures if exceptions occur, for example, if the distribution of interpolation points in characteristic curves fails to rise monotonically for short periods of time.

Online calibration is suitable for long-term modification of less dynamic parameters (for example, tuning of engine control functions on the engine test bench).

For calibrating more dynamic functions or safety-critical functions (for example, setting the software functions of an ABS system for braking maneuvers during a test drive), the settings are not made during actual access to the governor. In this case, online calibration can still save time by avoiding any interruptions in the driving schedule, thus reducing the interval between two test drives.

## References

[1] Jörg Schäuffele, Thomas Zurawka: Automotive Software Engineering. Grundlagen, Prozesse, Methoden und Werkzeuge (Basic principles, processes, methods, and tools). Vieweg-Verlag. 2003.
[2] OSEK Open systems and the corresponding interfaces for automotive electronics. http://www.osekvdx.org
[3] ISO International Organization for Standardization: ISO 14230 – Road Vehicles – Diagnostic Systems – Keyword Protocol 2000. 1999.
[4] ISO International Organization for Standardization: ISO 15765 – Road Vehicles – Diagnostic Systems – Diagnostics on CAN. 2000.

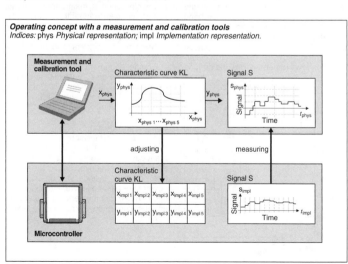

***Operating concept with a measurement and calibration tools***
*Indices:* phys *Physical representation;* impl *Implementation representation.*

# Sound design

## Definition

Sound design is the controlled and recordable change of a sound. To some extent, sounds are assessed subjectively, but they can also be visualized by computer programs. These programs can be used to analyze sounds precisely, and identify the areas where changes can be made. Since the end of the 1980s sound design, a specialist field of acoustics and vibration engineering, has gradually become an important tool to describe technical developments in terms of acoustics.

Sound design, in collaboration with sound engineering, is an important field not only in motor-vehicle design, but also for manufacturers of household appliances and even potato chips ("crunching" sounds.)

## Implementation

### Sound perception

Many appliances generate vibrations from their drive motors, which emit sound when they are within a frequency band of 20 Hz to 20 kHz (the range audible to the human ear). The decisive factors in terms of loudness level are amplitude (the strength of the oscillation), noise-emission level (determined by the surface characteristics of the component), and frequency. Volume is measured using the logarithmic decibel scale (dB) (see P. 56 onward). This measurement is based on the human ear, which can perceive a range of sound intensities from very small to very wide apart (factor $10^0...10^{12}$).

### Sources of noise and emissions limits

There are several hundred sources of noise in a motor vehicle. In acoustics, these are described as "loudspeaker areas". A distinction is made between exterior and interior noise levels.

When creating new sounds, acoustics experts must pay careful attention to international laws governing exterior noise levels. In the EU, for example, the limit is currently 74 dB (A). This limit has been subject to several reductions since 1970.

By comparison: Ten vehicles of a current model combined produce approximately the same level of noise as one vehicle from the end of the 1960s. The loudest single source of noise from a modern vehicle is normally the sound of the tires rolling on the road.

### Design concept

A vehicle sound is mainly formed by its design concept ("inherited characteristics") The decisive factors are:
– Diesel or spark-ignition engine
– Number of cylinders and number of windows
– Engine alignment (inline engine, flat engine, V-engine, or Wankel engine)
– Structure of the drivetrain (front, mid, rear engine, front-wheel, rear-wheel, all-wheel drive)

### Sound harmonization

The most important sources of noise to design a sound (the "sound orchestra") are located in the engine. The crankshaft drive, camshaft drive, crankcase structure, oil pan, cylinder heads, auxiliary power take-offs, belt drive, and the intake and exhaust-gas mufflers: All of these elements contribute to making a typical "sound".

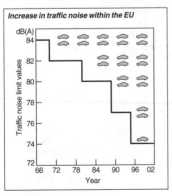

*Increase in traffic noise within the EU*

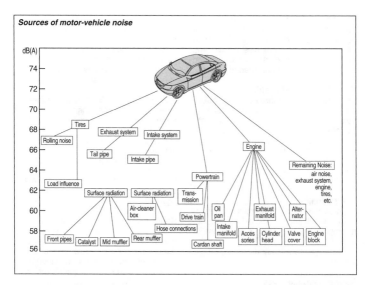

*Sources of motor-vehicle noise*

The basic task of an acoustics engineer is to detect the individual sources of noise in the engine and their combined effect, record these noises, and make the appropriate technical changes to bring about a harmonization of all the noises in the engine. The differences between the engine speeds "idle" and "wide-open throttle" are important. The differences must not become too small, as the sound of the vehicle "lives" from the load placed on the engine.

The basic work involved in harmonizing engine acoustics is very complex. The acoustics engineer can take the following approaches:

– Deciding on the concept
– Measuring tolerances/clearances/structures
– Calculating thermal expansion in clearances
– Avoiding torsional resonance
– Using appropriate materials for components
– Amplifying and damping vibration modes in the engine/transmission unit and the mufflers

Positioning and designing the engine/transmission bearings is also an important sound path that affects sounds level inside the vehicle. In modern vehicles, highly insulating, hydraulically dampened elements are used to support the engine/transmission unit on elastic mountings. This produces the a certain "softness" of noise inside the vehicle, and the vibration perceived for the whole vehicle when driving at road speed is still acceptable.

### External sound

Airborne sound radiation from the drive unit determines the external sound. This can vary greatly depending on the noise-shadowing effects of the engine's installation location within the body shell. Front-mounted engines are easier to control acoustically than rear-engine vehicles. In rear-mounted engines, all the main sources of noise are located in the rear. It is not possible to separate the sources acoustically or spatially.

The position of the mufflers (in the air-intake and exhaust-gas sections) in relation to surface and orifice noise, combined with engine noise, transmission ratio, and tire noise, all contribute to the required load-dependency of the external sound.

### Sound level inside vehicle

The figure shows a three-dimensional visualization of the sound level inside a sports car at low and high revs. In high-performance vehicles, particularly "soft" noise levels can be achieved at low engine speeds. At full speed, the internal sound level rises considerably, which is perceived as a positive feature by sports-car drivers.

### Load dynamics

Load dynamics play an important role in terms of both internal and external sound. It provides drivers with a spectrum of sound experiences which they can influence personally by their driving style (see figure).

### Assessment methods

#### From noise to sound

Up to the 1960s the decibel scale was the only factor considered in objective noise assessment. This value has been gradually replaced by the values of "frequency" (Hz) and "loudness" (sones).

The assessment of loudness considers the following factors:

There are two sources of noise with the same volume (dB). One produces very frequencies that are very close together; in the other, the frequencies are spaced at wide intervals. The human ear perceives that noises have different loudness levels, although their intensity may be identical on the dB(A) scale.

A <u>tone</u> represents an audible oscillation of a particular frequency. On the other hand, a <u>complex tone</u> consists of several tones that occur at the same time.

<u>Noise</u> is a mixture of different tones of varying amplitudes. "Sound" is a (desirable) noise that changes noticeably depending on the operating state of the vehicle, and raises or lowers suitable frequencies appropriate to the product (see figure below).

#### Sound recording/sound studio

Tone recordings for assessment are made with the help of artificial-head or dummy-head technology. In the sound studio, sound samples are then presented to several test subjects over separate headphones or loudspeaker systems. The visualization of noise recordings supports the elementary design of sound tests. A computer program is used to suggest acoustic variants of the recorded sound. When a variant is selected, the virtual sound is converted into real sound by sound engineering (technical alterations to the product).

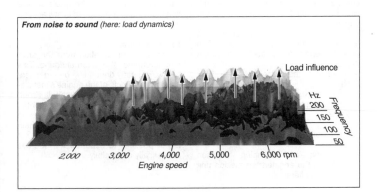

*From noise to sound* (here: load dynamics)

Load influence

Hz
200
150
100
50
Frequency

2,000    3,000    4,000    5,000    6,000 rpm
Engine speed

## Psychoacoustics

As acoustic assessment methods become more refined, more subjective factors become involved. This field, known as psychoacoustics, provides a more accurate picture of a desirable vehicle noise, and this contributes to greater brand identity that is associated with vehicle appeal.

The appeal or desirability of a product, particularly a sports car, is closely linked to emotional factors, which can be decisive in the popularity of a particular type of vehicle. Vehicle manufacturers need to pay careful attention to this requirement.

The psychoacoustic assessment of generated sounds plays an important supporting role (see the figure on the right).

Several test subjects assess a designed noise according to various criteria within a specified period, and assign it a grade. The "grades" are entered by keyboard and are immediately evaluated by a computer program.

## Sound engineering

Sound engineering is the science of technically influencing internal or external sound through specialized component design.

Sound engineering requires experienced acoustics engineers who can visualize the technical functions of components in terms of vibrational vehicle physics.

If sound engineering is used in the development of a vehicle body shell, the result is a body with structural features, membrane surface connections, and sources of structure-borne noise (from the engine/transmission unit to the acoustic bypass ducts, seals and acoustic housing), which have all been sound-optimized.

These modifications mainly affect the sound level inside the vehicle, which is also influenced by tire rolling and wind noise.

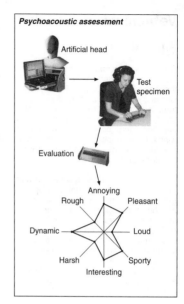

*Psychoacoustic assessment*

Artificial head

Test specimen

Evaluation

Annoying
Rough
Pleasant
Dynamic
Loud
Harsh
Sporty
Interesting

# Vehicle wind tunnels

## Applications

A vehicle wind tunnel is used to represent the air flow affecting a vehicle traveling on the road in an environment that is as realistic and reproducible as possible. By nature, however, the road environment is totally inhomogeneous and transient. The direction and consistency of natural winds, for example, is constantly changing due to factors such as natural wind, buildings, and traffic.

The advantages of using a vehicle wind tunnel as an experimental development tool compared with road measurements are the reproducibility of test conditions, the uncomplicated, reliable, and fast measuring technology, and the ability to isolate certain effects that do not occur alone in the natural environment (for example, driving noise). Design prototypes that are not yet roadworthy can be optimized aerodynamically in a wind tunnel with guaranteed secrecy.

## Aerodynamic parameters

Table 1 shows the main parameters, i.e. the forces, moments, and coefficients that apply in aerodynamic vehicle development (also see P. 888).

### Aerodynamic drag

The drag coefficient $c_d$ describes the aerodynamic shape of the body in an air flow. Multiplying this by the dynamic pressure of the air flow:
$q = 0.5 \cdot \varrho \cdot v^2$ and the vehicle frontal area $A_{fx}$ results in the drag $W$.

In contrast to the meaning of drag $W$, the rolling moment $L$ about the x-axis is not as important.

### Lift

The curved shape of the car roof makes the air flow faster across this surface than along the underside of the vehicle. This generates an undesirable lifting force, reducing the tire contact forces, and thus directional stability.

**Table 1. Aerodynamic forces, moments, and coefficients**

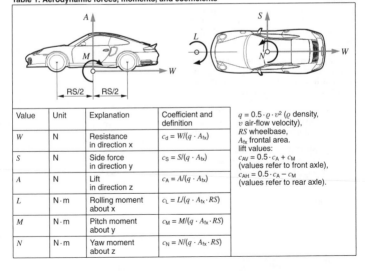

| Value | Unit | Explanation | Coefficient and definition | |
|---|---|---|---|---|
| $W$ | N | Resistance in direction x | $c_d = W/(q \cdot A_{fx})$ | $q = 0.5 \cdot \varrho \cdot v^2$ ($\varrho$ density, $v$ air-flow velocity), $RS$ wheelbase, $A_{fx}$ frontal area. lift values: $c_{AV} = 0.5 \cdot c_A + c_M$ (values refer to front axle), $c_{AH} = 0.5 \cdot c_A - c_M$ (values refer to rear axle). |
| $S$ | N | Side force in direction y | $c_S = S/(q \cdot A_{fx})$ | |
| $A$ | N | Lift in direction z | $c_A = A/(q \cdot A_{fx})$ | |
| $L$ | N·m | Rolling moment about x | $c_L = L/(q \cdot A_{fx} \cdot RS)$ | |
| $M$ | N·m | Pitch moment about y | $c_M = M/(q \cdot A_{fx} \cdot RS)$ | |
| $N$ | N·m | Yaw moment about z | $c_N = N/(q \cdot A_{fx} \cdot RS)$ | |

The lift coefficient $c_A$ is the sum of the lift coefficients on the front axle $c_{AV}$ and the rear axle $c_{AH}$. The difference between front- and rear-axle lift is referred to as "lift balance", and is a variable that influences directional stability.

The pitch moment $M$, which pivots about the y axis, is often used as a reference value in design instead of lift. A positive pitch moment requires understeer, and a negative pitch moment requires oversteer.

### Side force

A car has an almost symmetrical shape when viewed from the front, which means that side forces generated by air flows are small. As soon as the approaching air flow deviates from the x-axis (i.e. in a crosswind), the air flow generates side forces that can affect vehicle behavior considerably.

The yaw moment $N$, which acts about the z-axis, is also used as an indication for measuring the effects of side winds. This value is taken to derive the yaw-angle velocity and yaw-angle acceleration, which are an indication for the strength of the side wind.

## Wind tunnel designs

### Types of wind tunnel

Aerodynamic specifications are calculated in wind tunnels. They vary in the type of air guidance, test section, size, and road-surface simulation (Table 2).

Closed-jet wind tunnels with return flow are called "Göttinger wind tunnels", and systems with return flow are called "Eiffel wind tunnels" (see figure below).

### Standard wind tunnel equipment

The <u>test section</u> can be open-circuit, have slotted walls, or can be a closed circuit. A wind tunnel is characterized by the exit area of the diffusers, the cross-section of the collector, and the length of the test section (Table 2, P. 1136, layout of a wind tunnel, P. 1139).

Obstruction $\varphi_N = A_{fx}/A_N$ is also an important parameter. This is the ratio between the frontal area of the vehicle $A_{fx}$ and the diffuser cross-section $A_N$. On the road, this ratio $\varphi_N = 0$, therefore it should also be as small as possible in the wind tunnel. Taking the construction and operating costs of a wind tunnel into account, $\varphi_N = 0.1$ is a common figure in practice. This requires a diffuser cross-section of approx. 20 m².

---

**Wind tunnel designs**
a) Eiffel wind tunnel, b) Göttinger wind tunnel, c) Open-circuit test section,
d) Closed-circuit test section, e) test section with slotted walls.

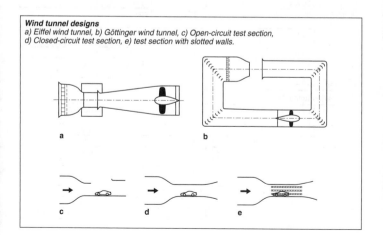

a

b

c

d

e

The contraction and contours of a diffuser determine the velocity and steadiness of the wind-tunnel air flow. A large contraction ratio $\varkappa$ from the cross-sectional areas of the prechamber to the diffuser outlet ($\varkappa = A_V/A_D$) leads to uniform velocity distribution and low turbulence, as well as to fast acceleration of the air flow.

The diffuser contour can influence the steadiness of the velocity profile at the diffuser outlet in the test section, and parallelism in relation to the geometrical tunnel axis.

The settling chamber or prechamber is positioned upstream of the diffuser and in the largest cross-sectional area of the wind tunnel. The prechamber contains flow rectifiers, filters, and heat exchangers that improve the quality of the air flow in terms of steadiness and direction, and keep the channel temperature constant.

For vehicle aerodynamics, Göttinger tunnels with open-circuit test sections or with slotted walls are the main designs used.

The fan in most wind tunnels can generate wind speeds of well over 200 km/h. Speeds of this size are only rarely used, for example, for testing the functional safety and stability of bodyshell components under wind loads. This is because such tests require the full fan capacity of up to 5,000 kW.

Normal measurements are taken at 140 km/h. At this speed, the aerodynamic coefficients can be determined reliably and at low operating cost. The wind speed is regulated either by changing the fan speed, or by adjusting the fan blades at a constant speed (Table 3).

A wind tunnel balance records the aerodynamic forces at work on the test vehicle and the moments of all four tire contact surfaces, and uses them to calculate the aerodynamic parameters for components x, y and z.

**Table 2. Vehicle wind tunnels in Germany** (examples)

| Wind tunnel operator | Diffuser cross-section m² | Collector cross-section m² | Test section length m | Test section version | Simulation of road traveled |
|---|---|---|---|---|---|
| Audi | 11.0 | 37.4 | 9.5...9.93 | open | with 5 moving belts |
| BMW | 20.0 | 22.1 | 10.0 | open | – |
| Daimler Chrysler | 32.0 | 53.6 | 12.2 | open | – |
| IVK Stuttgart | 22.5 | 26.5 | 9.9 | open | with 5 moving belts |
| Ford | 23.8 | 28.2 | 9.7 | open | – |
| Porsche | 22.3 | 37.7 | 13.5 | slotted walls/ open | – |
| Volkswagen | 37.5 | 44.8 | 10.0 | open | – |

**Table 3. Wind tunnel fans**

| Wind tunnel | Drive power kW | Fan diameter m | Control |
|---|---|---|---|
| Audi | 2,600 | 5.0 | rpm |
| BMW | 2 x 900 [1] | 2 x 4.97 [1] | rpm |
| Daimler Chrysler | 5,000 | 8.5 | rpm |
| IVK Stuttgart | 2,950 | 7.1 | rpm |
| Ford | 1,650 | 6.3 rpm | |
| Porsche | 2,600 | 7.4 | rpm |
| Volkswagen | 2,600 | 9.0 | Blade adjustment |

[1] The BMW tunnel uses two synchronized fans.

A wind tunnel balance is normally positioned below a turning platform, which is used to turn the vehicle in relation to the wind direction, and thus simulate the effect of side winds.

In contrast to a real situation, the vehicle is stationary in the wind tunnel, and is exposed to the air flowing over it. The influence of the relative movement between the vehicle and the road cannot be taken into account. More recent developments have therefore resulted in several wind tunnels that use <u>moving belts</u> incorporated in the floor to reproduce road motion and turning wheels (see figure). The quality of the air flow between the vehicle and the road can thus be improved and made significantly more realistic.

## Wind-tunnel auxiliary systems

The <u>frontal-area measuring system</u> (laser or CCD system) measures the frontal area of the vehicle by optical means. The results are then used to calculate the aerodynamic coefficients from the forces measured in the wind tunnel.

A time-related <u>pressure transducer system</u> in the wind tunnel can record pressure changes at min. 100 pressure points simultaneously, for example, to measure pressure distribution using flat sensors on the bodyshell surface. The miniature (quartz) pressure sensors used for each measuring point have no wearing parts, and can therefore supply electronic information at a relatively high frequency (see figure).

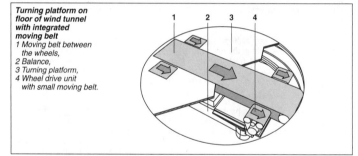

*Turning platform on floor of wind tunnel with integrated moving belt*
1 Moving belt between the wheels,
2 Balance,
3 Turning platform,
4 Wheel drive unit with small moving belt.

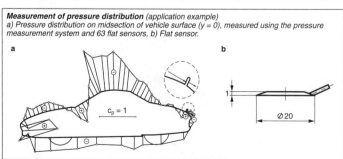

*Measurement of pressure distribution* (application example)
a) Pressure distribution on midsection of vehicle surface (y = 0), measured using the pressure measurement system and 63 flat sensors, b) Flat sensor.

a

$c_p = 1$

b

1

Ø 20

The traversing cradle allows the measurement of the complete vehicle airflow field. Each position in the test section can be located by coordinates and reproduced. According to the sensors present at each point, the pressure, velocity, or noise sources at each location can then be determined.

Smoke lances are used to visualize the air flow which is otherwise not visible. The smoke pattern detects any irregularities in the air flow which may worsen the coefficients as a result of energy-sapping turbulence. The nontoxic "smoke" is usually created by heating a glycol mixture in an oil-vapor generator.

Other methods for visualizing the air flow include:
– Tufts on the vehicle surface
– Tuft sensors
– Photographs of flow patterns from quick-drying liquid mixture of kerosene and talc
– Helium bubble generators
– Laser sheet

The "pollutant dispersion system" can be used to spray the vehicle in the wind tunnel with water from light mist to heavy rain. The flow patterns can be visualized and documented by mixing chalk or a fluorescent agent to the pollutant.

The hot-water unit provides heated water at a constant rate for measuring radiator cooling capacity in prototypes that are not yet roadworthy.

## Wind tunnel variants

A vehicle wind tunnel is a major investment. This investment, combined with high operating costs, make it an expensive test environment with a high hourly rate. Only very frequent utilization of vehicle wind tunnels for aerodynamic, aeroacoustic, and thermal experiments can justify the construction of several wind tunnels specialized for different tasks.

A model wind tunnel can considerably reduce operating costs, due to the lower construction requirements and technical complexity. Depending on the scale (1:5 to 1:2), changing the shape of vehicle models is easier to perform, faster, and more cost-effective to implement.

Model tests are primarily used in the early development phase for optimizing the basic aerodynamic shape. With the support of designers, "plasticine" models are used to make shape optimizations or form complete alternative shape variants before testing their aerodynamic potential.

Using new production methods (rapid prototyping), the models can be quickly and accurately produced in every detail and to any scale. This allows important investigations of the models in order to optimize details, even after the shaping phase.

In an acoustic wind tunnel, extensive sound insulation measures mean that the sound pressure level is approximately ≈30 dB (A) lower than in a standard wind tunnel. This provides a sufficiently large signal-to-noise ratio of ≥10 dB (A) from the useful signal of the vehicle to allow identification and evaluation of wind noises generated by the air circulation and throughflow.

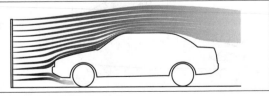

*Use of smoke rake and smoke lances to visualize air flow*

Climate-controlled wind tunnels are used for thermal analysis and protection of vehicles in defined temperature ranges at different load conditions.

Large-scale heat exchangers are used to set a temperature range, e.g. from −40 °C to +70 °C at a low control tolerance limit of approx. ±1 K.

The vehicle is positioned on dynamometer rollers and driven at the required load condition or load cycle. Wind speed and roller speed must be exactly synchronized, even at low speeds. If necessary, uphill or downhill gradients can be simulated to introduce realistic road factors to the vehicle operating cycle.

Optionally, the air humidity can be regulated, or solar radiation can be simulated by switching on banks of lamps.

The extensive aerodynamic challenges in vehicle design are not all covered by enhanced test-bench simulations as described above. In addition to experimental testing, manufacturers are therefore making increasing use of CFD models (Computational Fluid Dynamics). They allow preliminary decisions to be made to reduce the test workload.

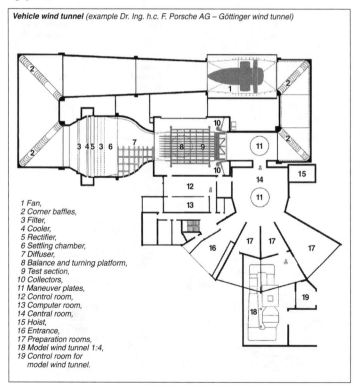

**Vehicle wind tunnel** (example Dr. Ing. h.c. F. Porsche AG – Göttinger wind tunnel)

1 Fan,
2 Corner baffles,
3 Filter,
4 Cooler,
5 Rectifier,
6 Settling chamber,
7 Diffuser,
8 Balance and turning platform,
9 Test section,
10 Collectors,
11 Maneuver plates,
12 Control room,
13 Computer room,
14 Central room,
15 Hoist,
16 Entrance,
17 Preparation rooms,
18 Model wind tunnel 1:4,
19 Control room for
   model wind tunnel.

# Environmental management

## Overview

An environmental management system is used for setting up and maintaining an organizational structure for implementing a company's environmental policy.

### Environmental management systems

Basically, an environmental management system can be structured according to two systems:
– In accordance with Regulation (EC) No. 761/2001 of the European Parliament and of the Council allowing voluntary participation by organizations in a Community environmental management and audit scheme (EMAS, referred to below as the Eco-Audit Regulation)
– In accordance with DIN EN ISO 14 001

The structures of the two environmental management systems are almost identical.

The main differences lie in their validity and interface with the public:

The Eco-Audit Regulation only applies within the European Union. It requires the company to publish an annual environmental statement to inform the public and other interested parties about its environmental impacts, its environmental performance and the continuous improvement of its environmental performance.

ISO 14 001 is a worldwide standard. Unlike the Eco-Audit Regulation, it does not require public participation.

### System elements

An environmental management system consists of eleven elements and should be described in detail in an environmental manual:
– Environmental policy
– Legal principles
– Organization and managerial tasks
– Suppliers and service providers
– Technical development
– Procurement of environment-friendly materials
– Production
– System monitoring
– Corrective measures
– Eco-management system audit
– Education and training

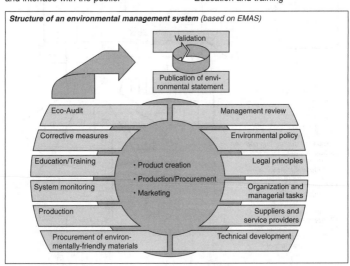

*Structure of an environmental management system* (based on EMAS)

Validation

Publication of environmental statement

Eco-Audit
Corrective measures
Education/Training
System monitoring
Production
Procurement of environmentally-friendly materials

· Product creation
· Production/Procurement
· Marketing

Management review
Environmental policy
Legal principles
Organization and managerial tasks
Suppliers and service providers
Technical development

**Documentation**
The documentation of an environmental management system comprises the following elements:
- Environmental policy
- Environmental manual
- Procedural instructions
- Work instructions

# Environmental policy

A company's environmental policy lays down operational principles at top management level for continuously improving the environmental compatibility of its products and production facilities, and for the environment-compatible use of natural resources.

# Legal principles

Due to the significance of legal standards, official regulations and internal rules on environmental protection, an environmental management system must also provide information about compliance with legal standards, such as laws, ordinances, administrative regulations, and technical directives.

# Organization and management tasks

Environment-conscious management means that responsibility for environmental protection starts at management level. Environmental protection should, however, be regarded as a responsibility that involves all parts of the company. This requires the proper organization of corporate environmental protection and the precise definition of the various tasks and responsibilities within the company.

# Suppliers and service providers

A large proportion of components required for automotive production are procured externally. Therefore, a company's environmental protection also lies partly in the hands of external business part-

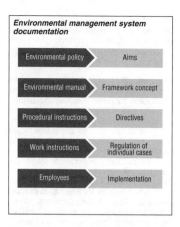

*Environmental management system documentation*

| Environmental policy | Aims |
| Environmental manual | Framework concept |
| Procedural instructions | Directives |
| Work instructions | Regulation of individual cases |
| Employees | Implementation |

ners. To make sure external partners also work to high environmental standards, Audi, for example, has issued a "Vehicle Environmental Standard", which contains clear guidelines.

This standard, which applies to the whole of the VW Group, defines substances whose use is prohibited by Audi, and stipulates emission limits for permissible (but critical) substances. It regulates the use of recycled materials and the labeling of parts for recycling.

Environmental aspects are taken into account in service contracts for cleaning, assembly and dismantling work.

Before concluding a disposal contract, it is essential to check the legitimacy, reliability and technical competence of the disposal company in every case.

# Technical development

An appropriate starting point for environmental protection within a company is product development. It is possible to make a major contribution to successful environmental protection within a company even at this early stage. Developing new, environment-compatible processes and products helps the company to substitute environmentally hazardous substances, minimize its consumption of water, energy, and other resources, and reduce environmental pollution from exhaust-gas emissions, wastewater, garbage and waste materials.

More than 80% of a car's environmental impacts, for example, arise outside of the production facilities – during the extraction and use of raw materials, and during disposal. However, the decision concerning how a car and its components are built, used, repaired and disposed of is made at the car plant.

In the product development stage, developers perform life-cycle analyses and analyze material flows, energy consumption and emissions for alternative product systems. This allows decisions to be made on aspects such as when it makes environmental sense to use aluminum.

It is in the product development phase that the course is set for producing cars that are less polluting, have longer service lives and are more suitable for recycling.

In order to make it as easy as possible to separate the individual materials during disposal, the different kinds of plastics must be identified. Wherever possible, compounds that are difficult to recycle should not be used.

## Procurement of environment-friendly materials

The use of raw materials is a crucial starting point in preventive environmental protection. By using a less pollutant material, it is often possible to avoid using additional cleaning equipment, filters, etc. at the end of the production process.

Before using chemical products, a check is always made whether safe or less dangerous alternatives are available.

The procurement process at Audi, for example, is regulated by a directive issued by the board of management. A materials evaluation committee, consisting of members from fire protection, environmental, occupational health and safety, health protection, and process engineering/chemical safety departments, evaluates the technical and chemical safety of all chemical products. Once a material has been assessed positively, it is approved for use. The committee compiles instructions for handling the materials and hands them over to the user.

## Production

Production processes are usually relevant to the environment, due to the generation of byproducts such as exhaust air, wastewater, waste materials, and noise.

The aim is to minimize these byproducts, as well as the energy consumed, or to prevent them from being created in the first place by implementing environment-compatible production methods, and to recycle the byproducts as usefully as possible. Some examples in a car workshop include:

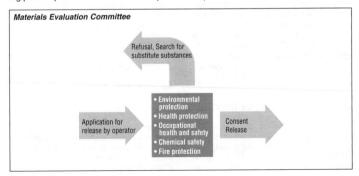

*Materials Evaluation Committee*

Refusal, Search for substitute substances

Application for release by operator

- Environmental protection
- Health protection
- Occupational health and safety
- Chemical safety
- Fire protection

Consent Release

**Heating systems**
Energy-saving central-heating boiler technology, insulated hot water pipes, burning non-polluting fuels such as natural gas.

**Paintwork repair shop**
Low-solvent or water-soluble painting systems, low-overspray application technology.

Spot repair technology for minor repairs, dry filter mats in the cabin exhaust-air line to prevent emission of paint particles.

**Wastewater**
Cleaning wastewater from the washing station in a wastewater treatment system to remove emulgated oil. Recycling water used for washing.

Workshop drainage and surface water from the filling station via oil separator/coalescence separator.

**Energy savings**
Heat exchanger in exhaust-air line in paint spraying cabins, building insulation, thermal glazing, high-speed gates, solar-powered system for process water, photovoltaic system. Feasibility study required for each individual measure.

**Water protection**
Vessels with water-polluting liquids secured with collecting trays. Fuels are only stored underground in double-walled tanks with leak monitoring.

**Waste**
All packaging waste collected separately and recycled.

Special waste collected separately and disposed of by authorized, specialized disposal firms.

## System monitoring

Monitoring production, disposal and storage facilities is one of the most important tasks in environmental protection. These tasks are the responsibility of line managers.

Systematic self-checks must be performed in order to guarantee that operational tasks, procedures and activities have as little impact on the environment as possible.

Failure to perform these tests, or performing them incorrectly, can have serious consequences in terms of criminal law and legal liability.

Monitoring programs can simplify work processes, remind employees of their legal obligations and prevent them from missing regular monitoring tasks during day-to-day business. Monitoring programs for workshops can contain details of the extent of inspection since this is listed in a monitoring program (see next page).

Monitoring programs should specify the names of the people responsible and monitoring dates.

Any shortcomings identified are logged and operators are instructed to rectify them.

The log should contain information such as the date, time, area checked, the persons involved, the inspected items such as storage of substances harmful to water, waste separation, or the function of environmental systems, the shortcomings identified, and the signatures of the persons responsible.

## Corrective measures

An environmental management system also regulates the reporting paths and procedures for identifying improper operation or environmental risks, and the measures to be taken to rectify them.

Potentially dangerous substances, such as flammable liquids and substances harmful to water, are often stored and handled.

The aim is to rectify shortcomings quickly and effectively in order to avoid pollution altogether or at least to restrict it to a minimum.

Examples of improper operation:
– Escape of vessel content as a result of leakage
– Failure of waste water treatment system
– Transport accident with negative impact on the environment

Hazard protection measures are defined by means of a flowchart.

**Table 1: Monitoring program (example for the year 2003)**

| Check | Check interval | Person responsible | 01 | 02 | 03 | 04 | 05 | 06 | 07 | 08 | 09 | 10 | 11 | 12 |
|---|---|---|---|---|---|---|---|---|---|---|---|---|---|---|
| Storage of liquids harmful to water | Every 6 months | A.N. Other | | | | X | | | | | X | | | |
| Waste disposal<br>– Separate collection of hazardous waste<br>– Separate collection of garbage/recyclable materials | Every 4 months | T.B. T.B. | | X | | | | X | | | | X | | |
| Workshop inspection<br>– Items worthy of observation | Every 12 months | T.B. T.B. | | | | | | | X | | | | | |
| Visual examination of underground tanks | Every 12 months | T.B. T.B. | | | | | X | | | | | | | |
| Check emissions from painting system | Every 3 years | T.B. T.B. | | | | | | Next check 2005 | | | | | | |
| Check painting process<br>– Process changes<br>– Material changes | Every 12 months | T.B. T.B. | | | | | | | | X | | | | |
| Wastewater disposal<br>– Leak tightness of pump sumps<br>– Operation of wastewater treatment plant | Every 3 months | T.B. T.B. | | | X | | | X | | | X | | | X |
| Check oil separator<br>– Function | Every 6 months | T.B. T.B. | | | | X | | | | | | | X | |

*Month*

## Eco-management system audit

The eco-audit is a comprehensive audit of the environmental issues associated with a company's activities and their impact at corporate locations.

The Eco-Audit Regulation describes two kinds of eco-audits:
– The technical eco-audit
– The eco-management audit

The technical eco-audit checks compliance in practice with environmental regulations, the company's environmental policy, and its environmental program in production divisions. The emphasis is on aspects of technical environmental protection.

The eco-management audit checks whether the company's environmental management system is suitable for ensuring compliance with the company's environmental policy and environmental program, and whether it does so effectively. For this purpose, documents are analyzed and facilities are inspected. All managerial staff who are in any way involved in environmental management are interviewed.

Eco-audits can be performed by specially trained, inhouse audit teams, or by independent external experts.

After every eco-audit, an appropriate written report is compiled as a formal presentation of all of the observations and conclusions of the audit. Corporate management is officially notified of the results.

The report also contains any appropriate corrective measures and the names of the people responsible for implementing them. The existing environmental program is amended or supplemented accordingly and is updated on an ongoing basis.

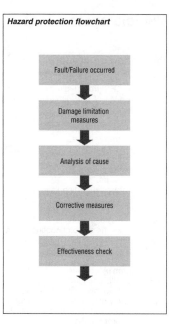

*Hazard protection flowchart*

## Education and training

Motivating the staff to take the initiative and encouraging environmental awareness are elementary tasks.

Procedures should be introduced to ensure that staff are aware of the significance of complying with environmental policy and the main impacts which their work can affect the environment.

Education, instruction and training must be provided for staff who are assigned specific environment-relevant tasks.

Training requirements must therefore be defined and training courses implemented for certain groups of people.

# Vehicle system test

## Workshop equipment

### Workshop software

The Bosch ESI[tronic] diagnostics software is a suite of programs that assists workshop technicians with vehicle testing, diagnosis, and selection of spare parts. The main "Vehicle Diagnosis" product covers areas such as:

– The Service Information System (SIS), which guides the user through troubleshooting procedures to allow successful repairs.
– ECU-Diagnosis, which allows quick and reliable fault diagnosis in conjunction with a system tester (see P. 1147).
– Computer Aided Service (CAS[plus]), which links the troubleshooting procedures directly to ECU diagnostics, thus optimizing the vehicle repair sequence.

The ESI[tronic] software suite also includes the following information:

– Spare-part identification data with exploded-view diagrams (vehicle-specific lists and cross-references to vehicle-manufacturer numbers).
– Labor units and labor times.
– Vehicle-specific troubleshooting sequences and repair instructions.
– Vehicle diagnosis.
– Vehicle-engine wiring diagrams (location of components, wiring and hose-connection diagrams, etc.).
– Servicing data and service schedules including details of mechanical settings.
– Wiring diagrams for convenience electrics.
– Test specifications.

### Instruments and testing equipment

Servicing and maintenance requirements for motor vehicles are declining steadily; electronic systems are essentially maintenance-free. But malfunctions can still occur. Factors such as wear, contamination and corrosion can impair the operation of engine and electronic systems, and settings can drift over time. Rapid and reliable diagnosis of malfunctions is among the most important functions of any customer service. It is important to distinguish between "testing" and "diagnosis".

"Testing" involves taking specific readings or measurements in order to compare them with setpoint values. "Diagnosis" (e.g. engine diagnosis) involves relating divergences from specified levels to system functions, fault scenarios, and empirical knowledge with the aim of identifying the failure mode or the defective components.

Effective system testing requires the use of suitable instruments and testing equipment. Whereas in the past an electronic system could be tested with relatively simple instruments (e.g. a multimeter), complex testing equipment is now indispensable due to the continuous advance of electronic systems (e.g. Motronic, EDC, ABS).

### Hand-held testers

Hand-held testers are small and relatively uncomplicated testing devices. Examples include:

– Multimeters: for measuring electrical current, voltage and resistance.
– Multimeters with scope function: with an additional function for displaying the progress of measured variables over time.
– Scan tools (e.g. Bosch KTS 100 and KTS 115): for reading and clearing the fault storage of the ECU for exhaust-related systems.

### Engine analyzers

The "traditional" engine analyzer is designed for checking and indicating the operating status of the engine and associated mechanical units for vehicle systems without self-diagnosis capability. Measured variables include:

– Engine speed
– Ignition primary and secondary-circuit voltage
– Dwell and ignition angles
– Current, voltage and resistance
– Injection time
– On/off ratio
– Start of delivery/timing devices on diesel engines
– Oil temperature
– Air temperature and vacuum measurement in the air-intake port

### ECU diagnostic testers

The Bosch range of ECU diagnostic testers is the KTS Series Designs range from modules, such as the KTS 520/KTS 550 which require a PC or laptop to operate, to standalone testers, such as the portable KTS 650 or the FIS 550 fixed unit. These system testers can be combined with the ESI[tronic] software to provide fast and reliable vehicle diagnosis.

KTS system testers are suitable for use with all modern diagnostic protocols (ISO systems for European vehicles, SAE systems for American and Japanese vehicles, CAN protocols for CAN bus systems). The KTS 520 incorporates a multimeter for measuring signals and testing components on vehicles. The KTS 550 and KTS 650 offer extended testing capabilities by way of a two-channel multimeter and a two-channel oscilloscope (for details of other functions, see P. 1148). The KTS 650 is operated by means of a touch screen and two membrane-sealed keys.

### Vehicle system analysis

Vehicle system analysis is a component of a universal workshop testing station and combines the functionality of the traditional engine analyzer and the KTS testers. In addition, it offers other capabilities such as:

– Electronic component testing (e.g. sensors, CAN bus)
– Measuring battery quiescent current
– Voltage and current analysis
– Signal generation to simulate sensor signals
– Ignition analysis (primary and secondary circuits)

## System test using KTS tester

### ECU diagnostics

Since the dominant role is assumed by electronic systems in the vehicle, this requires greater attention to the problems associated with service. In addition, as essential vehicle functions are becoming increasingly dependent on electronics, these systems must satisfy stringent reliability requirements. Emergency default programs are required in case of any errors occurring.

ECU diagnostics (see P. 582 onwards) of the electronic system can use its "intelligence" to monitor itself constantly, detect faults, record them, and analyze them diagnostically. The results of this "onboard" diagnosis can be evaluated by "offboard" testing equipment.

The communication interface establishes the link between the system tester and the ECU. The serial interface, with a variable transmission rate of 10 Baud...10 kBaud, takes the form of either a single- or two-wire interface which is designed to analyze several ECUs (e.g. ABS, Motronic/EDC) on one central diagnosis connector. A transmitted trigger address is addressed to all connected ECUs. An addressed system recognizes its own address and automatically sets itself accordingly. The key bytes that follow (In Germany assigned by the DIN Technical Committee for Motor Vehicles) specify the protocol for subsequent data communications. The system tester converts the data subsequently transmitted to diagnosis sequences and plaintext tailored specifically for the system under test.

In future the CAN bus will play a greater role in data exchange between tester and ECUs.

*System test with ECU diagnostics*
1 Engine ECU (Motronic/EDC),
2 ABS ECU,
3 Transmission ECU,
4 Diagnosis interface,
5 System tester (e.g. KTS 650).

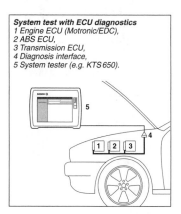

## KTS tester functions

There are a number of system testers that are suitable for system-testing functions. In combination with the ESI[tronic] software, the KTS Series testers provide efficient test procedures.

When the tester is connected to the diagnosis interface, diagnosis can begin. ECU diagnostics using a KTS tester allows functions such as:

Identification: The KTS tester automatically adjusts its settings to suit the ECU under test.

Reading and clearing the fault storage: The KTS tester can read the faults detected and stored by the control unit's self-diagnosis function (see P. 582), and show the fault text in plaintext on the display or PC monitor. Afterwards, it clears the ECU's fault storage.

Reading actual data: Current data that is calculated by the ECU can be represented as physical quantities (e.g. engine speed in rpm).

Multimeter function: Measurement and display of currents, voltages and resistances as on a conventional multimeter.

Oscilloscope function: Graphic display of continuously recorded readings as signal progress over time as on an oscilloscope.

Actuator diagnosis: Electrical actuators can be activated in order to check that they are functioning. This means that it is possible to activate and visually or acoustically check the function of actuators independently of the operating conditions.

Engine test: The KTS tester initiates programmed test procedures to check the engine management or the engine itself (e.g. analysis of speed fluctuations while the engine is being turned by the starter motor with the fuel injection disabled for the compression test).

Additional information: Specific additional details relating to the faults or components displayed (e.g. component locations and testing specifications, electrical circuit diagrams) can be displayed with the aid of the ESI[tronic] software.

Printout: Commercially available PC printers can print out all data (e.g. list of actual data).

Coding: The KTS tester can be used to recode the ECU's program memory.

**Examples of KTS tester functions**
a) Multimeter display,
b) Circuit diagram (data from ESI[tronic]),
c) Volume comparison.

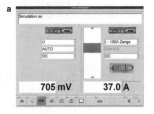

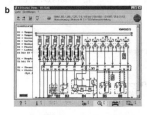

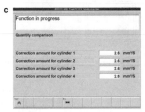

# Engine-test technology

### Test procedures

Complex systems control the engine, the ignition, and the mixture formation. Universal, automated and objective procedures are thus the essential components of computer-controlled testing equipment in vehicle service-center workshops.

Fault diagnosis is carried out by means of an engine analyzer (e.g. Bosch FSA). The component connector can be disconnected to take readings on components. Vehicle-specific 'Y' adaptors allow components to be connected to the engine analyzer.

Fault diagnosis includes:
- Comparing individual cylinder outputs by analyzing engine smooth-running at a given engine speed.
- Comparing individual cylinder compressions by analyzing starter-motor current pattern.
- Measuring selected HCs to determine mixture distribution in the exhaust gas.
- Analyzing ignition primary and secondary voltage patterns with relation to faults, such as breaks in high-tension ignition cables, short-circuits to ground, defective spark plugs, and defective ignition coils.
- Measuring electrical currents (e.g. battery charge current, battery quiescent current), voltages (e.g. battery voltage, signal patterns from sensors, and actuator control signals), and resistances (e.g. throttle-valve potentiometer resistance, contact resistances of connectors).
- Measuring fuel-injection signals (injection time, start of injection, signal pattern).
- Checking output signals from sensors which produce signal levels indicating the pulse duty factor of digital signals.
- Checking start of delivery and timing adjustment of diesel fuel-injection pumps with the aid of a "clamp sensor" on high-pressure delivery lines.
- Measuring oil temperature with the aid of an oil-temperature sensor inserted in place of the dipstick.
- Measuring air temperature with the aid of a temperature sensor (e.g. in the intake port, or in the passenger cabin, in order to check air conditioners).
- Testing electrical components (e.g. throttle-valve sensor, intake-manifold pressure sensor) by means of the signal pattern.

### Adaptation using vehicle-specific adaptors

The measurement of secondary ignition signals on static HT distribution systems requires vehicle-specific adaptors for different vehicles. After the adaptor has been placed on the ignition coil, measurement is performed by capacitative or inductive coupling.

### Testing electrical components in the vehicle

The engine analyzer can test electrical components (alternator, starter motor) while they are still fitted to the vehicle. The charge-current and charge-voltage patterns can be tested on the alternator, for example. To test component function under a defined load, however, the component has to be removed from the vehicle and mounted on a test bench (see P. 1152 onwards).

### Exhaust-gas diagnosis

With the addition of an exhaust-gas testing module, the FSA can measure the composition of the exhaust gas.

On spark-ignition engines, exhaust-gas diagnosis consists of measuring the engine speed, the oil temperature, and the levels of $CO$, $CO_2$, HC, $O_2$ and NO in the exhaust gas. Using the Brettschneider equation, the excess-air factor $\lambda$ (lambda) can be calculated from the exhaust-gas readings.

When diagnozing the exhaust gas from diesel engines, the idle and breakaway speeds are first checked. The oil temperature must have risen beyond a certain threshold. The breakaway speed, engine speed curve, acceleration response, opacity, and opacity progression during acceleration bursts are then analyzed.

# Electrical tests

## Testing and charging starter batteries

The specifications and test procedures for standard automotive starter batteries are defined in DIN EN 60 095-1. These tests are suitable for determining and monitoring the quality of new starter batteries, but do not claim in any way to fully reproduce the enormous variety of possible demands to which a battery might be subjected in practical use.

### Handling

Before fitting a new starter battery, the manufacturer's instructions should be carefully read in order to avoid safety hazards resulting from incorrect handling. The possible dangers originate from the sulfuric acid in the battery and the explosive gas (mixture of hydrogen and oxygen) formed when the battery is being charged. If the battery is kept tilted for any length of time, or if the electrolyte checked without taking the proper precautions, the result can be acid burns from the sulfuric acid. Extra caution should be taken when charging the battery, or connecting and disconnecting jumper cables immediately after charging, due to the danger of oxyhydrogen gas exploding.

The explosive gas mixture created by the charging process can be ignited by a sufficiently high level of thermal energy. For this reason, naked flames must not be permitted in the vicinity of batteries. What should be avoided is sparking, e.g. by suddenly opening or closing electrical circuits, should be avoided, or generating static electricity (by walking on carpets), or rubbing the battery with woolen or artificial fabrics. For these reasons, battery-charging areas should always be well-ventilated, and persons should wear protective goggles and gloves when handling the battery.

In order to prevent sparks when the battery is connected or disconnected, all electrical equipment must be switched off, and the terminals must be connected in the proper sequence. The rules are as follows:

- When installing the battery, always connect the positive cable first, and the negative cable last. When removing the battery, first disconnect the negative, and only then the positive cable (assuming that negative is ground).
- When connecting a charger or an external battery to boost an undercharged battery which remains installed in the vehicle, always start by connecting the positive terminal of the battery under charge to the positive terminal of the external booster. Then connect the negative cable from the external charger or booster battery to an exposed metallic surface on the vehicle, at least 0.5 m away from the battery.
- Always disconnect the cable from the negative terminal before commencing work in the vicinity of the battery or on the vehicle's electrical system. Short-circuits (and tools) generate sparks, and can also cause injury.

### Battery testers

The purpose of a battery test is to measure the starting power, condition, charge level, and voltage of a battery. Testers for starter batteries make a distinction between the no-load test and the under-load test.

#### Under-load test

In the case of the under-load test, the battery is subjected to a current load comparable to one which occurs when the engine is started (up to several 100 A). The voltage drop $\Delta U$ while this load is applied, and the voltage rise $\Delta U$ during the recovery phase after the load is removed, are criteria for assessing the starting power and the condition of the battery. In order to provide a percentage figure for starting power, the $\Delta U$ level measured is compared with the setpoint value for a correctly functioning battery. The setpoint value is dependent on the size of the battery and is preselected by the user by entering the battery capacity or the low-temperature test current. The charge level is measured from the battery voltage.

The advantage of the under-load test is the reliable detection of even the finest hairline cracks in the battery's cell connectors and lead plates.

The under-load period of around 30 seconds corresponds to the current demand for several starting attempts, and this has a negative effect on the battery charge level.

No-load test

In the no-load test, the battery is subjected for only a few seconds to a low-frequency, square-wave current of about 0.25 A to 2 A. This load superimposes an alternating millivolt-range current on the battery direct current. An assessment of the starting power and the condition of the battery can then be made on the basis of the signal amplitude and signal waveform of this AC voltage. In order to assess battery condition and starting power using the no-load test, the low-temperature test current of the battery under test must be entered in the tester.

The advantages of the no-load test are minimal discharge of the battery under test, and the speed of the test.

**Battery chargers**

Charging curves

The most commonly used charging characteristic is the "W" curve (see P. 972). The chargers in such cases are generally uncontrolled . Due to the battery's and the charger's internal resistances, the chargers respond to increasing battery voltage by steadily lowering the charge current (charging times 12...24 hours).

Since these W-curve chargers do not incorporate any means for limiting the charge voltage, they are only suitable with restrictions for use on maintenance-free batteries. In this case, chargers which operate using IU (see P. 972), IWU, or WU curves should be used.

With the IU curve, the lead-acid battery (2.4 V per cell) is supplied with a constant-charge current (to protect the charger against overload) until gassing commences. The charge voltage is then held constant and the charge current reduced sharply (to protect the battery against overcharging).

If the initial charge current is high enough, charging times (to 80% of full charge) of < 5 hours can be achieved with IU chargers.

Special variations of both the IU and the W charging curves are available (e.g. Wa, WoW, IUW, etc.). These can be applied in combination to meet individual demands for charging time/electrolyte level, and freedom from maintenance.

Charge current and voltage settings

On chargers with controlled charging patterns (e.g. IU curve), a controller monitors the momentary actual charge current and voltage levels continuously (and also the ambient temperature, if necessary). It compares the monitored (actual-value) data with battery-specific setpoint values, and uses a final-control element to reduce the deviation to 0. This type of unit also compensates for fluctuations in its input power voltage, which could otherwise lead to variations in charge current. This has a beneficial effect on battery life and maintenance intervals, among other things.

Charge current

During normal charging ($I_L = 1 \cdot I_{10}$), the battery is supplied with current corresponding to approximately 10% of its capacity in A · h. Several hours are required to charge the battery completely. Boost charging ($I_L = 5 \cdot I_5$) can be used to bring a depleted battery back up to about 80% of its rated capacity without damaging it. If the gassing voltage is reached, the charge current must either be switched off (e.g. Wa curve), or reduced to a lower level (e.g. IU curve). These current-switching functions are controlled by an adjustable charge limiter or an automatic switchoff device. By using special electronic monitoring circuits, the full-charge point can also be determined on the basis of battery-specific voltage patterns in conjunction with the charging time (the battery voltage starts to drop again if it is overcharged).

## Test technology for alternators

### Testing directly on the vehicle

A visual inspection centers on the drive belt, wiring and the alternator indicator lamp. Basically, electrical testing is carried using with a motor tester or a voltmeter/ammeter for measuring the following measured variables:

– Oscillograph of DC voltage with low harmonics component (between D+, B+ and B–)
– Alternator voltage (between B+ and B–)
– Quiescent current
– Battery voltage
– Breaks in wires
– Contact resistances of wires

### Repairing alternators

Test equipment used: alternator tester and coil-winding short-circuit testers. In addition, each alternator type requires special tools for locating the fault within the alternator and repairing it correctly.

### Testing the alternator on the combination test bench

After repair, the alternator is fixed to the alternator test bench on the combination test bench (see Figure on next page). Depending on the alternator type, it is normally possible to drive it directly at test speeds up to 6,000 rpm. For higher speeds, the drive is transmitted via a drive belt.

After setting the position of the alternator and tensioning the drive belt on the clamping fixture, the speed sensor is adjusted. The wires are then connected to the alternator.

In order to test an alternator, it is driven to two points on its output curve; in other words, at two different test speeds within its output curve, the alternator is subjected to the required load current by means of a variable load resistance. The alternator voltage must remain above a specified limit. If it does, the alternator is ready for service.

*Combination test bench for starters and alternators*
*1 Control panel for alternator and starter testing, 2 Variable load resistance (alternator testing),*
*3 Handwheel for test-bench vertical adjustment (alternator testing), 4 Alternator test bench,*
*5 Protection hood (alternator testing), 6 Storage compartment, 7 Display unit, 8 Lighting console,*
*9 Socket for speed sensor (starter and alternator testing), 10 Starter test bench,*
*11 Starter terminals, 12 Battery compartment with door, 13 Pedal for starter load (drum brake).*

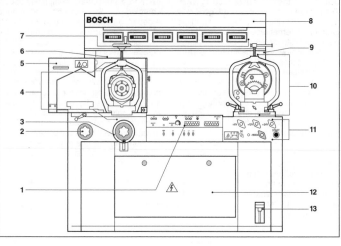

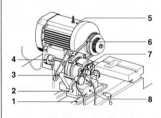

*Alternator mounted on test bench*
1 Guide, 2 Clamping fixture, 3 Swivel arm,
4 Speed sensor, 5 Drive motor, 6 Drive belt,
7 Alternator, 8 Test bench.

## Test technology for starters

### Testing directly on the vehicle

First of all, the battery voltage must be tested under load, and the electrolyte level and specific gravity must be checked. The following faults can be identified by listening to the sound of the starter when it is turning:
– Unusual noises when starting.
– Starter engages but either only turns the engine slowly or fails to turn it at all.
– No starter-engagement sound.
– Starter fails to disengage or disengages too slowly.

If unusual noises occur when starting, the fault can be traced to either the starter itself, the way it has been fitted, or the flywheel ring gear. Other problems require systematic electrical testing of the starting system (e.g. using an engine analyzer). The following tests are carried out with the starter at rest:
– Voltage at terminal 30
– Continuity of wires
– Contact resistances of wires

The tests carried out during the starting sequence are:
– Voltage at terminal 50
– Voltage at terminal 30
– Starter power consumption

### Repairing starters

First of all, the starter pinion is checked for damage (broken or worn teeth, etc.) and replaced if necessary. Various testers are then used as specified by the relevant servicing instructions. In addition, each starter type requires special tools for disassembly and reassembly, and for locating and correctly repairing faults inside the starter.

### Testing the starter on the combination test bench

After the starter has been fixed to the starter test bench on the combination test bench (see Figure below), the speed sensor is adjusted, and the wires are connected to the starter. The tests essentially consist of:
– a no-load test,
– a short-circuit or load test With more recent types of starter, the short-circuit test is no longer permissible and has therefore been replaced by a load test.

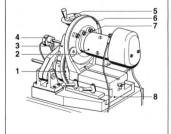

*Starter motor mounted on test bench*
1 Ring gear, 2 Starter, 3 Guard,
4 Speed sensor, 5 Handwheel,
6 Clamping bracket, 7 Clamping flange,
8 Test bench.

# Headlamp adjustment Europe

## Regulations and procedure

Correct adjustment of motor-vehicle headlamps should ensure the best possible illumination of the roadway at the same time as minimizing glare for other traffic. The EU Directives (and therefore the requirements of Article 50 of the StVZO (Road Traffic Licensing Regulations) in Germany) specify the required horizontal and vertical alignment of the headlamp beams. Low-beam glare is regarded as eliminated if the luminous intensity is not more than 1 lux at a distance of 25 m in front of each headlamp when the beam is projected on a surface vertical to the road surface at the height of the center of the headlamp and above. If, however, the vehicle is subject to extreme variations in attitude due to changes in payload, the headlamps must be adjusted so that the desired aim is achieved.

ECE R48 and EEC 76/756 define the basic setting or the adjustment dimension required on the vehicle. For vehicle categories not covered by these directives, the regulations contained in ECE R48 or ECE R53 shall apply.

Preparations for adjustment

Laden state of vehicle:
- Motor vehicles excluding motorcycles: unladen, 75 kg (one person in driver's seat).
- Motorcycles: for EC (as per 93/92/EEC) unladen, without rider on driving seat; for ECE/StVZO (Road Traffic Licensing Regulations) unladen, 75 kg (one person on the driving seat).

Tire pressure: as specified by the manufacturer for the laden state in question.
Suspension:
- Vehicles without suspension leveling: roll the vehicle for a short distance or rock it so that the suspension settles to a level position.
- Vehicles with suspension leveling: set suspension to correct level according to the operating instructions.
- If the vehicle is fitted with a manual headlamp-range adjuster, the adjuster should be set to the required setting.

Compulsory function checks on headlamp-range adjustment systems
- Systems that operate automatically should be set or operated according to the manufacturer's instructions.
- On vehicles registered before 1/1/1990, a positively locating adjuster position is not required.
- Manually operated systems with two positively locating adjuster positions: On vehicles on which the headlamp beam is raised as the vehicle payload is increased, the adjuster must be set to the position at which the beam is at its highest (smallest degree of dip). On vehicles on which the headlamp beam is lowered as the vehicle payload is increased, the adjuster must be set to the position at which the beam is at its lowest (greatest degree of dip).

Surface and testing environment
- The vehicle and headlamp tester must be standing on a flat surface (based on ISO 10604).
- Adjustments and tests should be carried out in an enclosed space where the lighting conditions are not too bright.

Adjusting and testing with a headlamp aiming device
- The headlamp aiming device should be aligned at the specified distance in front of the headlamp under test (except in the case of automatic adjustment).
- In the case of headlamp aiming devices which do not run on tracks, vertical alignment relative to the vehicle's longitudinal center axis should be carried out separately for each headlamp. The test should then be carried out without moving the unit sideways again.
- In the case of headlamp aiming devices which run on tracks (or the like), alignment with the vehicle's longitudinal center axis need only be carried out once at the most favorable position (e.g. in a central position in front of the vehicle).
- The specified adjustment dimension for the headlamp concerned should then be set on the headlamp aiming device, and the headlamp adjustment checked and/or the headlamp adjusted to the correct setting.

Adjusting and testing with a test surface
- The test surface must be vertical to the surface on which the vehicle is standing and at right angles to the vehicle's longitudinal center axis.
- The test surface should be finished in a light color, adjustable vertically and horizontally, and marked with the markings shown in the figure.
- The test surface should be positioned at a distance of 10 m in front of the vehicle so that the center mark is aligned with the center of the headlamp under test/ adjustment. In the case of lamps with very low beams (e.g. fog lamps), a shorter distance can be chosen by calculating the adjustment dimension accordingly.
- Each headlamp must be set individually. Therefore, the other headlamp(s) must be covered over.
- The vertical position of the test surface must be set so that the top cutoff (parallel to the ground) is at the height $h = H - e$. If the surface is not 10 m from the vehicle, the setting $e$ must be converted accordingly.

Notes on adjustment
In the case of headlamps with asymmetrical lower beams and fog lamps, the highest position of the light-dark cutoff must be on the top cutoff and run as horizontally as possible across the minimum width of the test surface. The lateral adjustment of the headlamps must be such that the light pattern is positioned as symmetrically as

possible about the perpendicular line running through the center mark.

In the case of headlamps for asymmetrical lower beam, the light-dark cutoff must touch the top cutoff to the left of center. The intersection between the left section (which should be as horizontal as possible) and the sloping section on the right of the light-dark cutoff must be located at the perpendicular line passing through the center mark.

The center of the high beam must be on the center mark.

In the case of headlamps where the low beam and fog lamps, or the high/low beams and fog lamps, are adjusted to-

**Table 1. Headlamp adjustment**
(excerpt from StVZO (Road Traffic Licensing Regulations))

| Vehicle type: Motor veh., > 2 whs. Headlamp position: Height above road surface | Adj. dimension "$e$" | |
|---|---|---|
| | Dipped beam | Fog lamp |
| Approved to 76/756/EEC or ECE R48 and StVZO first registered 1/1/1990 or later, < 1,200 mm | Setting on vehicle e.g. $\leqq \bigcirc 1.0\%$ | –2.0% |
| First registered 31/12/1989 or earlier, 1,400 mm and first registered after 31/12/1989, > 1,200 mm, but 1,400 mm | –1.2% | –2.0% |

*Test surface for headlamp beam*
*1 Top cutoff, 2 Center mark, 3 Test surface, 4 Break point.*
*$H$   Height of headlamp center above standing surface in cm,*
*$h$   Height of test-surface top cutoff above standing surface in cm,*
*$e = H - h$ Adjustment dimension.*

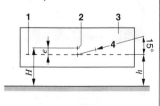

*Relative positions of test surface and vehicle longitudinal axis*
*1 Center mark, 2 Test surface.*
*A Distance between headlamp centers.*

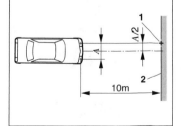

gether, adjustment should always be made on the basis of the low-beam setting.

Refer to Table 1 (see P. 1156) for adjustment dimension $e$.

### Headlamp aiming devices

Function
Correct adjustment of motor-vehicle headlamps should ensure the best possible illumination of the roadway by the low beam while minimizing glare for oncoming traffic at the same time. For this purpose, the inclination of the headlamp beams with respect to a level base surface, and their direction to the vertical longitudinal center plane of the vehicle, must satisfy official directives.

Equipment design
Headlamp aiming devices are portable imaging chambers. They comprise a single lens and an aiming screen located in the focal plane of the lens, and are rigidly connected to it. The aiming screen has markings to facilitate correct headlamp adjustment, and can be viewed by the equipment operator using suitable devices such as windows and adjustable refraction mirrors. The prescribed headlamp adjustment dimension $e$, i.e. the inclination relative to the centerline of the headlamp in cm at a fixed distance of 10 m, is set by turning

a knob to move the aiming screen (see Tables 1 and 2).

The aiming device is aligned with the vehicle axis using a sighting device, such as a mirror with an orientation line. It is turned and aligned so that the orientation line uniformly touches two external vehicle-reference marks. The imaging chamber can be moved vertically and clamped at the level of the vehicle headlamp.

Headlamp testing
The headlamp can be tested after the equipment has been correctly positioned at the front of the lens. An image of the light pattern emitted by the headlamp appears on the aiming screen. Some test devices are also equipped with photodiodes and a display to measure the luminous intensity.

On headlamps with asymmetrical lower-beam patterns, the light-dark cutoff should touch the horizontal top cutoff; the intersection between the horizontal and sloping sections must be located on the perpendicular line running through the center mark. After adjusting the lower-beam light-dark cutoff in accordance with the regulations, the center of the upper beam (assuming that high and low beam are adjusted together) should be located within the rectangular border about the center mark.

**Headlamp test and adjustment device**
1 Alignment mirror, 2 Handle,
3 Luxmeter, 4 Refraction mirror,
5 Markings for center of lens.

**Viewing window in aiming device**
a) Top cutoff for light-dark cutoff for asymmetrical lower beam, b) Center mark for middle of upper-beam pattern.

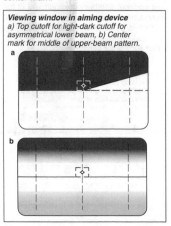

**Table 2. Geometric range for horizontal section of low beam light-dark cutoff**
(fitted height of headlamps 65 cm)

| Slope of light-dark cutoff (1% = 10 cm/10 m) | % | 1 | 1.5 | 2 | 2.5 | 3 |
|---|---|---|---|---|---|---|
| Adjustment dimension $e$ | cm | 10 | 15 | 20 | 25 | 30 |
| Geometric range for horizontal section of light-dark cutoff | m | 65 | 43.3 | 32.5 | 26 | 21.7 |

## Headlamp adjustment, U.S.A.

For headlamps compliant with U.S. Federal legislation, visual (vertical only) adjustment as permitted since 1/5/1997 has become increasingly widespread in the U.S. since mid-1997. There is no horizontal aiming here.

Whereas headlamps in Europe have always been adjusted on the basis of visual assessment of the light beam, the use of mechanical aiming devices was the most common method of headlamp adjustment in the U.S. The headlamp units were equipped with three pads on the lenses – one for each of the three adjustment planes. A calibrating unit is placed against these pads. Aiming is checked using spirit levels.

With the VHAD (Vehicle Headlamp Aiming Device) method permitted since 1993, the headlamps are adjusted relative to a fixed vehicle reference axis. This procedure is carried out using a spirit level firmly attached to the headlamp. As a result, the three lens pads were no longer required.

# Testing diesel fuel-injection pumps

## Testing on test benches

Thorough testing and precise adjustment are indispensable if fuel-injection pumps and governors are to assist the diesel engine in achieving its optimum fuel consumption and output, while at the same time allowing it to comply with today's increasingly stringent emission-control legislation. This is where the fuel-injection pump test bench is essential. The basic specifications for test procedures and the test bench are stipulated in ISO standards, which place very strict demands on the rigidity and uniform stability of the drive unit.

The fuel-injection pump under test is clamped to the test bench, and its drive side is connected to the test-bench coupling. The test-bench drive unit comprises a special motor attached directly to the flywheel. Test-bench control is by means of a frequency converter with a vector control loop. Calibrating oil supply and return lines connect the fuel-injection pump to the calibrating oil supply on the test bench. High-pressure lines provide the link with the delivery-quantity measuring device. This consists of calibrating nozzles set to a precise opening pressure, which inject calibrating oil directly in the measuring system via injection dampers. The supply pressure and temperature of the calibrating oil can be adjusted to comply with test specifications.

### Continuous-flow delivery-quantity measurement

Using the continuous-flow method of delivery-quantity measurement (Figure A), the 12 measurement inputs are connected to two precision measurement cells via a hydraulic multiplexing device (Figure B).

Using the multiplexing device, two fuel-injection pump outlets are tested at intervals of approx. 10 seconds apart. Solenoid valves perform the job of switching between the various pump outlets. The outlets are connected to the measurement cells via dampers. Each measurement cell incorporates a precision gear pump. The speed of each gear pump is regulated so that the volume of calibrating oil that it delivers per unit of time is equal to the volume of calibrating oil delivered by the fuel-injection pump. The speed of the gear pump is thus a measure of the fuel-injection pump delivery quantity per unit of time. A microprocessor analyzes the measurement results and converts them to bar-graph form for display on a monitor. This test method is characterized by a high degree of accuracy and consistently reproducible test results.

### Quantity measurement using measuring glasses

Quantity measurement with measuring glasses starts with the calibrating oil from the test nozzles routed past the measuring glasses and back to the calibrating-oil reservoir. The control unit waits until the prescribed number of strokes has been entered in the stroke counter before starting the actual test by the shutoff slide switching the calibrating-oil flow to the measuring glasses. The flow is interrupted again when the prescribed number of strokes has been completed. The quantity of calibrating oil which has been discharged by the test nozzles can be read on the measuring glasses.

### Tester for solenoid-valve-controlled distributor injection pumps

Testing and adjustment of solenoid-valve-controlled distributor injection pumps requires a special set of testing devices in conjunction with the fuel-injection pump test bench (Figure C).

The existing control PC on the test bench has specially developed hardware and software for the purpose. An interface module connects the pump or pump ECU to the control PC. The control PC contains all the data required for programming the pump ECU, and for testing and adjusting the pump.

The testing and adjustment sequence for the fuel-injection pump is largely automated. It is based on communication between the test software, the quantity measurement system or test-bench control system and the pump ECU. All delivery quantity levels are recorded and automatically corrected if the pump requires adjustment. At the end of the pump adjustment sequence, the test program calculates a pump map and programs the pump ECU with it.

A printable test report documents the pump settings.

The range of tester functions includes:
– testing and adjustment of the fuel-injection pump
– blocking start of delivery
– reading and clearing the fault storage

To protect the pump ECU against unauthorized access, every instance of data access is documented by a code on the pump ECU.

### Measuring the delivery quantity of common-rail high-pressure pumps (CR/CP)

By virtue of the control PC on the fuel-injection pump test bench (Figure D), tests on CR high-pressure pumps are more or less automated.

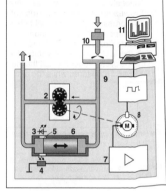

*Continuous volume measurement system*
(precision measurement cell, Figure A)
1 Return line to calibrating oil container,
2 Gear pump, 3 LED, 4 Photoelectric cell,
5 Window, 6 Control piston,
7 Amplifier with control electronics,
8 Electric motor, 9 Pulse counter,
10 Test nozzle-holder assembly,
11 Monitor (PC).

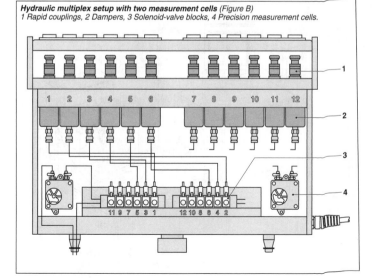

*Hydraulic multiplex setup with two measurement cells* (Figure B)
1 Rapid couplings, 2 Dampers, 3 Solenoid-valve blocks, 4 Precision measurement cells.

In conjunction with the Bosch CRS 845 upgrade test set, various operating situations are simulated during the course of the test (e.g. specified delivery quantity of CR high-pressure pump during the start, maximum delivery quantity of CR high-pressure pump at wide-open throttle).

In order to simulate the driving conditions as closely as possible, the pressure-control valves on the test bench recreate the supply pressure (from the fuel tank to the CR high-pressure pump), and the return pressure (from the CR high-pressure pump to the fuel tank) of the vehicle fuel system. The pressures are set at the start of the test and monitored while the test is in progress.

The CR high-pressure pump delivers the fuel to the high-pressure fuel rail (2). The high-pressure fuel rail, with its pressure sensors, acts as a pressure accumulator and pressure regulator. The fuel distributor (3) distributes the fuel delivered by the CR high-pressure pump before it is cooled in the heat exchanger (5), and the continuous delivery quantity is measured in up to 12 measurement channels.

The actuator (6) controls the pressure in the high-pressure fuel rail and the valves of the CR high-pressure pump, and checks that the splash guard (7) doors are closed while the test is in progress. The splash guard is required for safety reasons because pressures up to 16 MPa (1,600 bar) are generated in the CR high-pressure pump during the test.

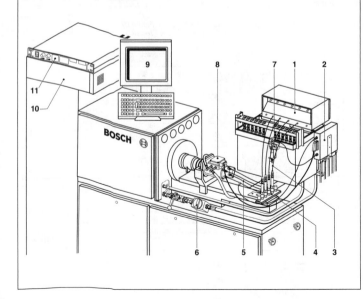

*Fuel-injection pump test bench* (e.g. Bosch EPS 815 with VPM 844 upgrade set for testing distributor injection pumps, Figure C)
1 Heat exchanger, 2 Interface module, 3 Connecting hose and connector, 4 Test nozzle-holder assembly with holder, 5 Test pressure lines, 6 Adjuster valve for heat exchanger, 7 Pressure sensor, 8 Solenoid-valve-controlled distributor injection pump, 9 TFT display and keyboard, 10 PC CPU, 11 Voltage stabilizer.

## Testing in the vehicle

A diesel system can also be tested while fitted to the vehicle. However, thorough testing of the pump is only possible on the test benches described above.

In the case of electronic diesel systems, a large amount of actual data can be read off via the vehicle's diagnostic interface and compared with the setpoint values. A comparison permits various conclusions with regard to the mechanical adjustment of the pump.

In the case of older, non-electronic diesel systems, the pump can be adjusted precisely to the engine by means of an engine analyzer. The engine analyzer can check the start of delivery, injection timing and the corresponding engine speed, without having to disconnect the high-pressure delivery lines. An inductive clamp sensor is attached to the fuel-injection line for cylinder #1. The sensor produces a signal as the high-pressure line expands when fuel is delivered at high pressure. The engine analyzer then determines the start of delivery and the injection timing by means of a stroboscope or TDC sensor for monitoring crankshaft position.

If a start-of-delivery sensor system is used, an inductive sensor is screwed to the governor housing instead. The sensor receives pulses from a pin when the pin moves past the sensor. This pin is attached to the governor flyweight housing. The pulses trail the signals from the TDC sensor at a specific interval which is used by the unit to calculate the start of delivery.

*CR upgrade test set CRS 845 on EPS 815* test bench (Figure D)
1 High-pressure hose, 2 High-pressure fuel rail, 3 Fuel distributor, 4 Pressure-control valve, 5 Heat exchanger, 6 Actuator, 7 Splash guard.

# Brake testing

Braking systems are vitally important in maintaining high technical standards of vehicle safety; it is therefore imperative that the brake system be inspected on a regular basis. Such testing of vehicles for compliance with the prevailing statutory regulations (e.g. Article 29 of the StVZO (Road Traffic Licensing Regulations) in Germany), and in vehicle servicing in repair workshops or repairs by brake repair services, the brake tests are carried out on brake dynamometers (usually chassis dynamometers). The braking forces monitored at the wheel's circumference provide the basis for evaluating the operation and effectiveness of the braking system. In Germany, the brake dynamometers used for the tests required by Article 29 of the StVZO must comply with the "Directives for the Use, Specifications and Testing of Brake Dynamometers" issued by the German Federal Transport Ministry.

## Brake test stands

### Design

The brake dynamometer's main components are two roller sets, for the left and right sides of the vehicle respectively. The vehicle is driven on the test stand so that the wheels of the axle under test rest on the roller sets.

A stable frame supports the roller sets, on which the drive roller and a secondary roller are mounted in parallel in rolling bearings. A chain drive provides the positive dynamic connection between the two rollers. An AC motor powers the drive roller via a gear set with an upward conversion ratio, while the drive unit itself is suspended on an extension of the drive roller's shaft. Pressure exerted against a torque lever flanged to the gear-drive unit is transferred via a load sensor, with the frame providing positive support for the entire assembly. Measurement of the braking force $F_{Br}$ is based on the measurement of the reaction torque $M_R$. The electric motors drive the rollers at a certain peripheral velocity and maintain that speed at a virtually constant level, even when an opposing braking torque is applied by vehicle wheels running on the rollers. The suspended drive unit with a lever arm transmits the braking torque to the load sensor when the wheel is braked. The load sensor takes the form of a flexural sensor with a wire strain gage.

The system's computer employs digital technology in evaluating the various data derived from braking-force testing, such as fluctuations or differences in braking force. When processed, the information is presented in either analog or digital form, depending on the specific system, while a printer can be connected to provide a hardcopy test report.

### Operation

The drive motors for the test-bench roller sets may be activated in one of two ways, either by remote control or by an integrated automatic on/off switch. An automatic-activation test stand features sensor rollers that are located between the main test rollers of each roller set. When the vehicle is driven on the test stand, the wheels push down the sensor rollers and activate the stand. When the vehicle leaves the stand, the pressure-sensitive rollers are released, and the unit is switched off. If the applied braking force starts to exceed the available friction force between the tires and the test rollers, the wheel will respond by starting to slip and will then lock. Tire slip, however, makes it impossible to perform useful measurements of braking force. Under these conditions, it is the slip resistance between tire and roller (as a function of wheel load) that is measured, and this is of no use for the brake test. Here, assistance is provided by an automatic override device which recognizes this kind of wheel slip by monitoring the sensor-roller speed, and which responds to it by switching off the test stand when a given maximum figure is exceeded. This avoids both false measurements and possible tire damage. The display, meanwhile, continues to show the maximum braking force achieved before the override device was activated. An electronic memory circuit ensures that the final reading remains displayed long enough to be noted down by the operator.

In addition, the vehicle and/or axle weight can also be measured on the test stand or entered remotely; the test stand can then use this information to calculate the effective braking factor.

The brake dynamometer employs specific test sequences to provide extremely rationalized test procedures, allowing the operator to carry out complete testing of both front and rear brakes without getting out of the vehicle.

Vehicles with permanent all-wheel drive and variable torque distribution are tested on special stands. The stands are constructed to prevent the forces generated at the test axle from being transferred to the axle which is at rest.

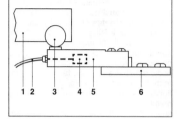

*Brake test stand: measuring sensor*
1 Torque lever,
2 Electrical connection,
3 Thrust block,
4 Measuring sensor,
5 Flexural sensor with wire strain gage,
6 Adjustment plate.

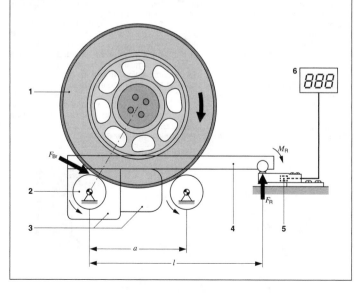

*Determining braking force $F_{Br}$ by measuring reaction torque $M_R$*
1 Vehicle tire,
2 Roller set with spacing $a$,
3 Motor with gear set,
4 Torque lever with length $l$,
5 Measuring sensor,
6 Display unit.

# German emissions inspection

## Regulations

The European Union (EU) has passed a Directive which defines the general conditions for exhaust-gas emissions testing. The member states of the EU adopt the requirements arising from it as national law. The national legislatures then demand regular testing of exhaust-gas emissions from vehicles in circulation (periodic exhaust emissions testing). Arising from these requirements, there are national test procedures in each of the member states, e.g. the Emissions Inspection in Germany (which has been required by law since 1993).

In Germany, for example, cars have to undergo an emissions inspection three years after they are first registered, and then every two years after that. The test checks whether the exhaust-gas emissions of the tested vehicle can be classed as "satisfactory" for the technology in operation.

With the introduction of "<u>On</u>board <u>Di</u>agnosis" (OBD), the emissions-related vehicle components and systems are constantly monitored. The periodic emissions inspection has thus been adapted to the new vehicle requirements and the test procedure extended to include OBD functionality.

The ermissions inspection establishes whether the OBD system is operating correctly and meets the specified requirements over the entire service life of the vehicle.

## Test procedure

### Vehicles with spark-ignition engines

The test procedure for a vehicle with OBD encompasses the following stages:
- Vehicle identification, i.e. entry of the vehicle registration number, vehicle manufacturer, odometer reading, etc., selection of vehicle type by means of test type (based on the type of catalytic converter and whether the vehicle is equipped with OBD), or using the vehicle specification database (option, available in Germany only).
- Visual examination of the exhaust-gas system: visual inspection for the presence and completeness of the system, damage and leaks.
- "Onboard diagnosis" (OBD). Visual inspection using the MI lamp when the ignition is on and when the engine is running. Read-out of the MI lamp status from the ECU via the OBD interface. Read-out of the fault storage and status of test readiness codes (see P. 587). If there is a fault recorded in the fault storage, the vehicle fails the emissions inspection. If one or more readiness tests are not completed, the CO level is measured at idle, followed by the lambda-sensor voltage (voltage measurement if the vehicle is fitted with a

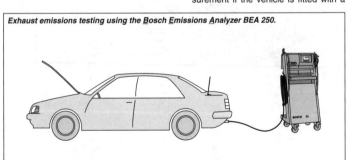

*Exhaust emissions testing using the <u>B</u>osch <u>E</u>missions <u>A</u>nalyzer BEA 250.*

two-point sensor; voltage, current, or lambda measurement if the vehicle is fitted with a broadband sensor). If the measured levels are not within the required tolerance band, the vehicle fails the emission inspection.
– Testing engine speed and temperature.
– Testing CO and oxygen levels within a defined engine-speed window (raised idle speed).
– Test passed? Yes/No.
  Entry of tester's remarks.
– Automatic printout of test report.

### Vehicles with diesel engines

The test procedure encompasses the following stages:
– Vehicle identification, i.e. entry of the vehicle registration number, vehicle manufacturer, odometer reading, etc., selection of the vehicle type by means of the test type (diesel), or using the vehicle specification database (option, available in Germany only).
– Visual examination of the exhaust-gas system: visual inspection for presence, completeness, damage, and leaks.
– Testing engine speed and temperature.
– Recording the idle speed measured.
– Recording the breakaway speed measured.
– Initiating at least three accelerator bursts (unrestricted acceleration) to determine exhaust-gas opacity. If the opacity levels are below the specified limit (naturally aspirated engines $<2.5$ m$^{-1}$, turbocharged engines $<3.0$ m$^{-1}$), and all three readings are within a bandwidth of $<0.5$ m$^{-1}$, the vehicle passes the emissions inspection.
– Test passed? Yes/No.
  Entry of tester's remarks.
– Automatic printout of test report.

## Test equipment

### Test equipment for exhaust-gas emissions testing on spark-ignition engines

The individual exhaust-gas components have to be measured with the utmost accuracy. In laboratories, complex procedures are adopted. In vehicle service centers, the NDIR (Non-Dispersive InfraRed) method has become generally established for emissions testing (see P. 575 onwards). It is based on the fact that particular exhaust-gas components absorb infrared light at different specific rates, according to their characteristic wavelengths.

The various designs include both single-component analyzers (e.g. for CO only) and multi-component analyzers (for CO/HC, CO/$CO_2$, CO/HC/$CO_2$, etc.). The multicomponent analyzers have several measuring chambers through which the exhaust gas passes.

### Test equipment for soot-emission testing on diesel engines

The testing of soot emissions on diesel engines is carried out in the workshop using turbidity meters (opacimeters) which operate according to the absorption method (see P. 579 onwards).

# Motorsports

## Motronic in motor racing

At the same time as Motronic was introduced on standard production vehicles, modified versions were used on racing engines. Whereas the development objectives for production models focus on user-convenience, safety, long service life, emission limits, and fuel economy, motorsport applications emphasize short-term high performance. Production costs are a secondary issue in the choice of materials and dimensioning of motorsport components.

Even now the two varieties of the Motronic system still have a common foundation because both systems have similar functions to achieve opposite aims. The lambda (oxygen) closed-loop control system and the knock control systems are two examples of this.

Environmental regulations have become an increasingly important consideration in motor racing. The cars used in the German Touring Car Championship, for example, are now fitted with catalytic converters. Noise and fuel-consumption limits must to be observed in more and more racing categories. Consumption-reducing developments from production vehicles quickly find their way to motor racing where shorter/less frequent refueling stops can prove decisive. Thus, in 2001, the Le Mans 24-hour race was won for the first time by a car equipped with Bosch gasoline direct injection.

### ECU/software

The casings of motorsport ECUs are specially strengthened designs made of carbon fiber or aluminum. Additional design features for making them dustproof, moistureproof, and for absorbing vibration increase their resistance to thermal and mechanical stresses. Numerous inputs, outputs, and communication interfaces for sensors and actuators provide the capability for highly complex applications. The high ECU clock rate required by the high revving speeds of racing engines and the large volume of data to be processed increasingly need the use of multiprocessor systems.

The software of the motorsport version of the Motronic system offers the capability of switching between user-programmable data maps for a large number of functions while the vehicle is in motion. In this way, the car can easily be adapted to different drivers, racing circuits, and weather conditions. In addition, Motronic for motorsports has an unlimited number of displayable software functions.

Another special feature, specifically for V-engines, are the multibank systems. This is an arrangement whereby the two banks of cylinders are treated separately for control purposes. In other words, each cylinder bank has its own fuel system, lambda closed-loop control system, and boost-pressure control systems. Changes in operating parameters (specifically the airbox pressure, here) may result in separate adjustments to the injected-fuel quantity for each cylinder bank.

### Sensors/wiring harness

In terms of function, the sensor systems of a racing car differ very little from those of a standard production model. The only difference is that more suspension and handling data is collected. The sensors are optimized for lightness and maximum resistance to high levels of vibration and high temperatures to withstand racing applications. The numbers produced are usually very small, and frequently, sensors are one-off prototypes.

The transmission of signals from the sensors to the ECUs on racing cars requires wiring harnesses that sometimes do not exist on standard production vehicles. For this reason, the wiring harnesses for racing models are very often customized.

The best-quality connection between sensor/actuator and wiring harness is provided by quadruple military-standard connectors which can be easily, quickly, and frequently plugged and unplugged without any deterioration in contact quality.

## Display page

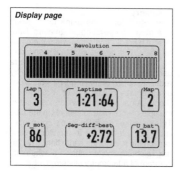

## Display

The display in the cockpit provides the driver with up-to-the-second information about the car. Since not all the data can be displayed on the small screen at once, the display can be switched between different pages – even while the car is moving. The figure *Display page* shows an example.

## Data storage and analysis

Depending on the equipment and requirements, the data detected by sensors can be stored on small memory cards with a maximum capacity of currently about 250 MB and/or transmitted by radio to the pits. The detection rate, the number of operating parameters detected, and the detection limit are user-definable.

In the pits, the data for different drivers or training sessions can be compared on a computer on a lap-by-lap basis using specially developed data analysis tools. The figure *Data analysis* shows an excerpt from the data for a training session with reference to the current section of the circuit.

## Data analysis

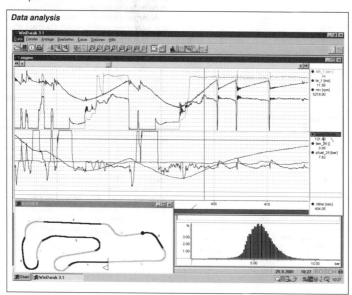

### Vehicle components (actuators)

The high revving speeds of racing engines severely restricts the amount of time available per operating cycle. This means that not only the ECU but also the ignition and fuel-injection components have to operate at very high speeds. In turn, this requires ignition coils with very fast charging times, and fuel-system components that are capable of faster throughput and higher pressures. Spark plugs with smaller-diameter threads made of materials capable of withstanding the higher operating temperatures help to achieve higher compression ratios. Starter motors are adapted to special racing requirements in terms of their weight and cranking speeds, and may be combined with a reduction gear, depending on the engine design. The alternators are modified in a similar fashion, with particular attention again paid to vibration and heat resistance.

### Telemetry

Telemetry refers to the online transmission of a range of operating parameters. Data is sent by radio to the pits when the car is on track. This allows constant monitoring of pressures and temperatures. Drivers can then react quickly to abnormalities by reducing speed or making a pit stop. Modern telemetry systems have a radio LAN (Local Area Network) which can serve multiple clients via a teleserver in the pits. This increases flexibility for pit crews, especially when they have to monitor several cars on the track at the same time. The figure *Telemetry system* shows a schematic diagram of a telemetry system.

### Competition rules

Every motor-racing category has rule books that are updated every year by the relevant motorsports governing body. At national level in Germany, for example, this would be the Deutsche Motorsportbund (German Motorsports Association), whereas international competition is governed by the FIA (Fédération Internationale de l'Automobile).

A large number of technical features are very precisely defined for cars that race in a particular category. As an example, an excerpt from the technical rules for the German Touring Car Championship for 2001 appears below. This section specifies the installation position of the crankshaft.

*"6.1.1.: The crankshaft axis of rotation must, when viewed from above, run parallel to the longitudinal axis of the car. The mandatory numbering of the cylinders is specified in Drawing B10.*

*In addition, the engine must be positioned in such a way that the center of the crankshaft relative to the car's longitudinal axis is 1,075 mm in front of the center of the wheelbase. The allowable tolerance is ± 5 mm. The position of the center of the crankshaft must be indicated by a clearly visible and accessible mark (e.g. casting lug) on the engine block."*

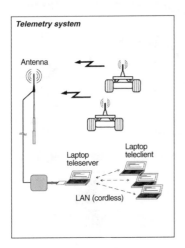

*Telemetry system*

Antenna

Laptop
teleclient

Laptop
teleserver

LAN (cordless)

## Super Race Trucks

Motor racing is not restricted merely to purpose-built racing cars or modified production cars powered by gasoline engines. There is also a branch of the sport in which trucks are raced. The diesel engines and fuel-injection systems used for the "Super Race Trucks" are specially adapted for racing conditions. For example, production truck engines which develop about 300 kW (410 bhp) are tuned to produce nearly four times the power (roughly 1,100 kW/1,500 bhp). This means:
– higher engine speeds
– higher cylinder charge (air mass)
– greater injected-fuel quantities with shorter injection times.

### Modifying the mechanical components

For racing purposes, the engines run at an air/fuel ratio ($\lambda$) that is only marginally > 1. Therefore, larger pump elements and special nozzles are used. The injection cams – if used – must also have a steeper profile.

In order to obtain enough air, the engines have two turbochargers whose turbines glow at the extremely high exhaust temperatures of about 1,100 °C. These conditions also demand specially welded exhaust pipes. The charge-air pressure is about 4 bar at wide-open throttle. Consequently, very exacting demands are placed on the charge-air cooling system.

Racing modifications to the vehicles are naturally made at the expense of fuel consumption, exhaust-emission levels and service life of all components. Black smoke is not produced because all racing trucks are fitted with particulate filters.

### EDC requirements

The electronic systems have to operate with high precision, just as they do on production vehicles. The competition rules stipulate that the maximum speed of 160 kph may not be exceeded by more than 2 kph (1.25%!). This requires special control functions that come into operation near the cutoff speed. Otherwise, the electronic diesel control (EDC) is the same as the standard version.

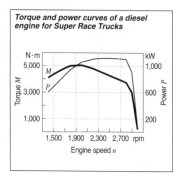

*Torque and power curves of a diesel engine for Super Race Trucks*

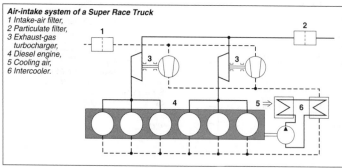

*Air-intake system of a Super Race Truck*
1 Intake-air filter,
2 Particulate filter,
3 Exhaust-gas turbocharger,
4 Diesel engine,
5 Cooling air,
6 Intercooler.

# Automotive hydraulics

## Quantities and units[1]

| Symbols | | Units |
|---|---|---|
| $A$ | Area of flow cross section | cm² |
| $A_D$ | Cross-sect. area of restriction | cm² |
| $A_K$ | Piston area | cm² |
| $A_R$ | Cross-sectional area of line | cm² |
| $b$ | Gap width | mm |
| $d$ | Line diameter | mm, cm |
| $E_{Fl}$ | Modulus of elasticity, fluid | N · mm⁻² |
| $E_{Oil}$ | Bulk modulus, oil | N · mm⁻² |
| $e$ | Eccentricity offset | mm |
| $F$ | Force | N |
| $g$ | Gravitational acceleration | m · s⁻² |
| $H$ | Cylinder stroke length | cm, mm |
| $h$ | Gap height | μm, mm |
| $l$ | Gap length, line length | mm, m |
| $l_o$ | Output length | cm |
| $M_1$ | Input torque | N · m |
| $M_2$ | Output torque | N · m |
| $M_{th}$ | Theoretical input or output torque | N · m |
| $M_{verl}$ | Torque loss | N · m |
| $n$ | Rotational speed | rpm |
| $P_{an}$ | Input power | kW |
| $P_{ab}$ | Output power | kW |
| $p_z$ | Cylinder pressure | bar |
| $\Delta p$ | Pressure difference | bar |
| $Q$ | Delivery rate of hydraulic pump, or intake rate of hydraulic motor or hydraulic cylinder | l · rpm |
| $Q_1$ | Delivery rate | l · rpm |
| $Q_2$ | Intake rate | l · rpm |
| $Q_L$ | Leakage rate | l · rpm |
| $Q_{th}$ | Theoretical delivery or Intake rate | l · rpm |
| $Re$ | Reynolds number | — |
| $r$ | Line radius | mm |
| $t$ | Stroke time of hydraulic cyl. | s |
| $U$ | Perimeter of flow cross section | cm |
| $V_{Fl}$ | Fluid volume | cm³ |
| $V_H$ | Displacement of hydraulic cyl. | cm³ |
| $V_o$ | Output volume | cm³ |
| $V_{th}$ | Theoretical delivery/intake volume per revolution | cm³ |
| $v$ | Line flow rate | m · s⁻¹ |
| $v_1$ | Stroke rate | m · s⁻¹ |
| $\alpha_D$ | Flow coefficient of e.g. flow restrictors | — |
| $\eta$ | Dynamic viscosity | Ns · m⁻² |
| $\eta_{hm}$ | Hydromechanical Efficiency | — |
| $\eta_{vol}$ | Volumetric efficiency | — |
| $\lambda$ | Coefficient of flow resistance | — |
| $\nu$ | Kinematic viscosity | m² · s⁻¹ |
| $\varrho$ | Density | kg · dm⁻³ |
| $\omega$ | Angular velocity | s⁻¹ |

## Terms and formulas

Calculation of coefficient of flow resistance $\lambda$

$\lambda = \dfrac{64}{Re}$ for laminar flow and isothermal change of state

$\lambda = \dfrac{75}{Re}$ for laminar flow and adiabatic change of state

$\lambda = \dfrac{0.316}{Re^{0.25}}$ for turbulent flow up to $Re = 80{,}000$ and smooth lines

$Re = v \cdot D_H/\nu$ where $D_H = A/U$

### Hydraulic pump
Delivery rate
$$Q_1 = V_{th} \cdot n \cdot \eta_{vol}$$
Output power
$$P_{ab} = Q_1 \cdot \Delta p$$
Input torque
$$M_1 = \frac{V_{th} \cdot \Delta p}{2\pi} \cdot \frac{1}{\eta_{hm}}$$
Input power
$$P_{an} = M_1 \cdot \omega$$
Volumetric efficiency
$$\eta_{vol} = \frac{Q_1}{Q_{th}} = \frac{Q_{th} - Q_L}{Q_{th}} = 1 - \frac{Q_L}{Q_{th}}$$
Hydromechanical efficiency Efficiency
$$\eta_{hm} = \frac{M_{th}}{M_1} = \frac{M_{th}}{M_{th} + M_{verl}}$$

### Hydraulic motor
Intake rate
$$Q_2 = V_{th} \cdot n/\eta_{vol}$$
Output power
$$P_{ab} = M_2 \cdot \omega$$
Output torque
$$M_2 = \frac{V_{th} \cdot \Delta p}{2\pi} \cdot \eta_{hm}$$
Volumetric efficiency
$$\eta_{vol} = \frac{Q_{th}}{Q_2} = \frac{Q_{th}}{Q_{th} + Q_L}$$
Hydromechanical efficiency Efficiency
$$\eta_{hm} = \frac{M_2}{M_{th}} = \frac{M_{th} - M_{verl}}{M_{th}}$$

### Hydraulic cylinder
Cylinder pressure $p_z = F/(A_K \cdot \eta_{hm})$
Swept volume $V_H = A_K \cdot H$
Stroke time $t = V_H/Q_1$
Stroke rate $v_1 = Q_1/A_K$

---

[1] These are commonly used units, not SI-units.

## Flow rates in lines and gaps

Required line cross section

$A_R = Q_1/v$

Pressure loss in straight lines

$$\Delta p = \lambda \cdot \frac{l}{d} \cdot \frac{\varrho}{2} \cdot v^2$$

Flow through a pipe
(according to Hagen-Poiseuille)

$$Q = \frac{\pi \cdot r^4}{8 \cdot \eta \cdot l} \cdot \Delta p$$

Flow (laminar) through
a smooth gap

$$Q = \frac{b \cdot h^3}{12 \cdot \eta \cdot l} \cdot \Delta p$$

Flow (laminar) through
an eccentric sealing gap

$$Q = \frac{d \cdot \pi \cdot \Delta r^3}{12 \cdot \eta \cdot l} \cdot \left[ 1 + 1.5 \cdot \left( \frac{e}{\Delta r} \right)^2 \right] \cdot \Delta p$$

($2 \cdot \Delta r$ = clearance between piston and bore)

Flow through restrictors and orifices

$$Q = \alpha_D \cdot A_D \cdot \sqrt{2 \, \Delta p/\varrho}$$

($\alpha_D$ at control slide valves: 0.6 to 0.8)

## Compressibility of a hydraulic fluid

$\Delta V_{Fl} = A_K \cdot \Delta l = V_o \cdot \Delta p/E_{Fl}$,

where the initial volume is

$V_o = A_K \cdot l_o$

and the bulk modulus for oil is

$E_{Oil} \approx 1.6 \cdot 10^9 \; N \cdot m^{-2}$

## Gear pumps

Gear pumps are designed either with one external-toothed and one internal-toothed gear or with two external-toothed gears. External-toothed pumps are cheaper to manufacture and are therefore in much more common use. The displacement per revolution is constant, and is determined by the gear diameter, the center-to-center distance and the width of the teeth. The rotating (meshed) gears transport the hydraulic fluid in the spaces between the teeth from the low-pressure to the high-pressure side, and the teeth immersed in the fluid force it into the delivery line. There is almost no clearance between the housing and the tips of the teeth; thus the pump exhibits good radial sealing properties. The pump chamber is axially sealed by plates or bushings which are hydraulically pressed against the gears. These plates or bushings also act as bearings for the gears. This design achieves the high efficiency characteristic of high-pressure pumps. Drive speeds of up to 4,000 rpm, maximum pressures of up to approx. 300 bar and high power densities (6 kW/kg) make gear pumps particularly well suited for use in automotive hydraulic systems. The span of delivery rates required, which ranges from 0.5...300 l/min, is covered by a range of 4 to 5 pump sizes.

---

*Gear pumps and motors*
*(Direction of fluid flow and gear rotation shown for pump operation)*

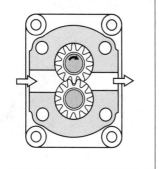

---

*High-pressure gear pump*
Volumetric efficiency $\eta_v$ and overall efficiency $\eta_t$ according to delivery rate at $\Delta p = 210$ bar.

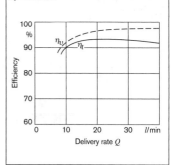

## Gear motors

Like gear pumps, the simplest gear motors are designed to operate in only one direction of rotation. In gear motors, oil flows from the high-pressure to the low-pressure side, and the gears rotate in a direction opposite to the direction in which they would rotate if the device were a pump. Motors suitable for use as vehicle drives, i.e. motors which can be operated in both directions of rotation and which can be loaded in the reverse direction, have also been derived from gear pumps through appropriate design of the axial pressure field and the leakage fluid passages. The advantages of external toothed pumps such as high power density, small installation-space requirements and low manufacturing costs also apply to gear motors. They are therefore chosen for road vehicles, construction equipment and agricultural machinery for driving cooling and cleaning fans, screw conveyors, sweepers, spreading plates, vibrators, etc. The excellent starting behavior of gear motors is utilized in driving pumps and compressors, as well as in motive drives.

## Piston pumps and motors

The drive mechanism of hydraulic piston pumps and motors differs significantly from the classical piston-machine design. The high pressure level (standard pressure for hydrostatic drives 350...400 bar) results in high piston forces which necessitate sturdy and rigid mechanical drive systems. The drive mechanisms of modern machines are nevertheless highly compact, particularly due to the hydrostatic transmission of force between the two primary reciprocating components. The good lubricating and cooling qualities of the hydraulic fluid promote such space-saving designs. Hydraulic piston machines are thus able to achieve a maximum power density of more than 5 kW/kg.

In order to achieve a uniform volumetric flow rate, hydraulic piston machines are designed with an odd number of piston elements. A differentiation is made between radial- and axial-piston machines, depending upon the configuration of the drive mechanism. Both types are available as either pumps or motors with constant or variable displacement, suitable for use in open and closed circuits. Since the phase control of hydraulic machines did not prove itself in practice, continuous control is only possible by varying the piston stroke. Rotating, stroke-generating mechanisms, such as eccentric shaft or crankshaft (radial), and swashplate (axial), are unsuitable for stroke adjustment and are only used in some fixed-capacity machines. All variable-displacement units and many constant-displacement units use other drive mechanisms specific to the hydraulic system. These types incorporate a rotating cylinder assembly. To-

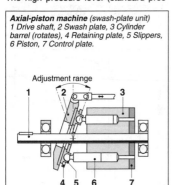

**Axial-piston machine** (swash-plate unit)
1 Drive shaft, 2 Swash plate, 3 Cylinder barrel (rotates), 4 Retaining plate, 5 Slippers, 6 Piston, 7 Control plate.

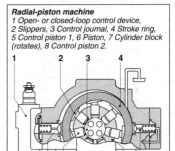

**Radial-piston machine**
1 Open- or closed-loop control device, 2 Slippers, 3 Control journal, 4 Stroke ring, 5 Control piston 1, 6 Piston, 7 Cylinder block (rotates), 8 Control piston 2.

gether with a stationary control plate or control journal, the cylinder assembly forms a rotary slide valve which alternately exhausts and fills the cylinders. <u>Axial-piston machines</u> are designed as swashplate units.

The centrally-ported machine has been adopted as the standard <u>radial design</u>. The cylinder block rotates on the control journal. The bearing forces are supported by hydrostatic pressure fields on the journal. Similar pressure fields transmit the forces between the rotating piston slippers and the stationary cam ring. The ring's variable eccentric position relative to the control journal generates the piston stroke. In the case of pumps in which the delivery direction can be reversed, the stroke ring can be moved in both directions via its adjustment piston. All control elements are located in the stator, allowing rapid and precise adjustments in flow volume using hydraulic or electronic servo elements and controllers. The hydraulic adjustable piston unit can be integrated within the electronic control circuit using either proportional valves in the control circuit or an electrohydraulic adjustment system.

## Electrohydraulic pumps and small units

An electrohydraulic pump is a combination of a hydraulic pump and an electric motor. A DC motor is used in most mobile hydraulics applications, however AC and three-phase motors are also used in stationary operation. Gear pumps are characterized by a low degree of pulsation and quiet operation.

As such, these hydraulic components have proven their worth for generating pressure in electrohydraulic pumps. Sizes B and F with capacities of 1...22.5 cm³ per revolution are used, and generate operating pressures of up to approx. 280 bar. Together with size I to T electric motors which generate a maximum nominal output of 8 kW, they are used in a number of different mobile-hydraulics applications.

Electrohydraulic pumps provide the hydraulic energy for lifting and steering functions on vehicles of all types, but particu-

larly for factory/warehouse transport vehicles (fork-lift trucks, pallet stackers ), mobile lifting platforms, heavy goods vehicles, specialized construction, transport and rescue vehicles, and cars. In the latter case, electrohydraulic pumps and, increasingly, small and mini-pumps are used for auxiliary functions such as suspension levelling and power assisted steering/parking. Safety-related braking and acceleration control represent a special area of application. A hydraulic unit is at the heart of the ABS and ASR systems, and generates the oil pressure needed when these come into operation.

In addition to electrohydraulic pumps, various valves or valve assemblies must be installed in motor vehicles in order to implement a wide variety of control functions. This has led to the development of small, compact units with outputs of up to 4 kW. In these units, the electric motor and hydraulic pump are supplemented by a valve block, a hydraulic-fluid tank, and fluid and air filters. The design concept accommodates individual modifications for specific control functions. Sleeve and seat valves can be combined in a compact control block or at unions in the system. Small and miniaturized units are used in those applications where high power is required despite limited space being available. Examples include municipal vehicles (street sweepers, rotary snow plows, utility tractors, industrial trucks, special-purpose vehicles, and passenger-transport vehicles with lifts and pivoting equipment for carrying handicapped persons).

New applications include functions for cars. The most advanced convertibles utilize hydraulic mechanisms to operate the softtop; these devices fold the top, stow it in a specified manner, and lock it into place.

## Valves

### Directional-control valves

<u>OC valves (open-center)</u>
When the valve unit is in the neutral position, the flow from the pump is directed through up to 10 valves (neutral circulation pattern). The fluid flow is restricted when a valve is actuated prior to the

opening of the line to the servo unit.
Disadvantages:
- High pressure loss = Energy loss in neutral position,
- Control precision affected by load pressure.

### LS Valves (load-sensing)

Used in systems with variable-capacity pumps or constant-capacity pumps and auxiliary pressure compensator. In the neutral position, the LS control line removes the pressure from the pump and pressure compensator. When the valve unit is actuated, the pump controller/pressure regulator maintains the pressure differential at the valve spool at a constant level. The result: The flow of hydraulic fluid to the servo unit is not affected by the load pressure.

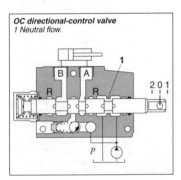

**OC directional-control valve**
1 Neutral flow.

**LS directional-control valve**
1 Metering restrictor, 2 Pressure balance,
3 Constant-capacity pump, 4 Variable-capacity pump.

Advantages:
- Minimal neutral-position loss,
- Improved precision control independent of load pressure.

### Flow-control valves

#### Throttle valves

Throttle valves are used to adjust the fluid flow rate by altering the cross-sectional area of the flow. According to the laws of rheological science, this flow-limiting function is pressure-dependent; it is therefore used only for simple flow adjustment. Pressure-independent adjustment requires the use of control valves. Flow-pressure-compensated control

#### Flow-control valve

In order to be able to set the fluid flow $Q$ independently of the load pressure $p_3$ at 2-way flow-control valves, the pressure difference at the metering orifice $(p_1 - p_2)$ is held constant by a variable restrictor (pressure compensator). The pressure difference $p_1 - p_2$ corresponds to the spring force acting on the pressure compensator. In this type of control, the surplus fluid flows via the pressure-relief valve in the system.

Losses can be reduced by using 3-way flow-control valves which have an additional drain through which the surplus fluid flows back to the tank or to other hydraulic devices.

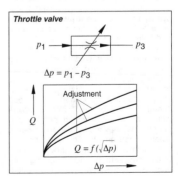

**Throttle valve**

$$\Delta p = p_1 - p_3$$

$$Q = f(\sqrt{\Delta p})$$

### Pressure-control valves

#### Pressure-relief valve

Hydraulic circuits incorporate a pressure-relief valve in order to protect the components as well as to ensure the operational safety of the system. If the pressure acting on the seat diameter exerts a force equal to the force exerted by the precompressed spring, the valve cone lifts off its seat and the fluid flows to the tank. Pilot-operated pressure-relief valves are used for greater flow volumes and to achieve valve characteristics which are independent of the flow rate. The pilot valve relieves the spring chamber of the main valve which controls return flow to the tank.

#### Electric proportional directional-control valves

Nowadays, agricultural and industrial vehicles such as tractors and fork-lift trucks increasingly use electrically operated directional-control valves. The reasons for this are higher productivity, lower demands on the driver and more economical installation costs as a result of the greater scope in the choice of valve location on the vehicle. Electronic circuitry provides for easy-to-use, safe and reliable control systems which in some cases extend up to automatic movement sequences.

#### Direct solenoid actuation

In applications involving small to medium hydraulic powers (e.g. positioning movements on combine harvesters, tilting function on fork-lift trucks), the directional-control-valve spool is displaced by a solenoid against the action of a spring by an amount proportional to the excitation current. The application limit is determined by the available solenoid force, e.g. 30 l/min, 200 bar. The short stroke of the solenoid limits application of this principle to 3-position valves.

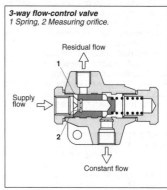

*3-way flow-control valve*
1 Spring, 2 Measuring orifice.

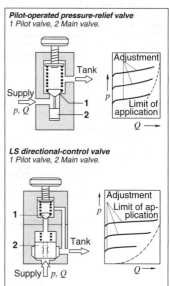

*Pilot-operated pressure-relief valve*
1 Pilot valve, 2 Main valve.

*LS directional-control valve*
1 Pilot valve, 2 Main valve.

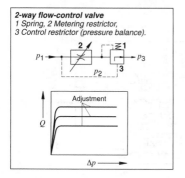

*2-way flow-control valve*
1 Spring, 2 Metering restrictor,
3 Control restrictor (pressure balance).

### Electrohydraulic actuation

The new EHS electrohydraulic positioner (EHSe) generates a high actuation force for high-performance control such as is required for the front lifter on agricultural tractors or the jib on a truck loading crane. A positioning piston which moves the valve armature to the position specified by the setpoint generator is used to amplify the force. A position control loop compensates for interference from flow forces thereby providing low hysteresis. The 4/3 pilot-operated directional-control valve with double solenoid is supplied with a control pressure of approx. 20 bar. An inductive travel sensor detects the spool position for the purposes of position control. It also performs the same function for diagnosis and safety purposes.

### Electronic control circuitry

The electronic analyzer circuitry of the travel sensor (ASIC) and the digital control electronics with serial CAN bus interface are housed inside the positioner unit casing. The use of a microcontroller with an EEPROM means that the valve characteristics are programmable. The valve and timing characteristics can be chosen and modified according to application. Static characteristics which define the relationship between input signal and flow volume (precision control), and time gradients for defined acceleration and deceleration of hydraulic drive units are stored.

In addition to the primary control option using the CAN bus, control by means of analog or pulse-width-modulated (PWM) voltage signal is also possible. In the event of malfunctions on the part of the directional-control valve, e.g. sticking valve armature, loss of control pressure, etc., depending on the seriousness of the fault it is indicated (coded flashing signal, CAN message) and/or the actuator unit is switched off.

## Cylinders

Cylinders convert hydraulic power (pressure, oil flow) into rectilinear motion (force, velocity). They are characterized by high power density and relatively simple design. Cylinder efficiency is determined by the seals, the operating pressure and the piston surface quality. In addition to force and speed, resistance to buckling is also an important design criterion. It determines the dimensions and the extension of the cylinder piston. Types of cylinder mounting at the head and bottom include holes, clevises, pivoting bearings and threads.

---

**SB23LS directional-control valve with electrohydraulic positioning unit EHS**
*1 Inductive travel sensor, 2 Digital electronics module, 3 Control input: CAN, PWM or potentiometer signal, 4 Diagnostics output: fault signal, 5 Diagnostics output: visual indicator, 6 Pilot valve, 7 Check valve, 8 Pressure compensator.*

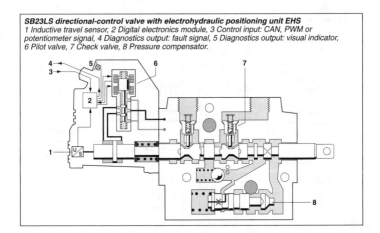

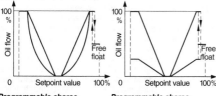 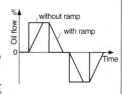

**EHS electrohydraulic positioner for mobile directional control valves**
*Programmable characteristics.*

**Programmable charac-teristic-curve shape**
– Linear (x) to progressive (x³)
– Individual for both directions
– For adjustment of fine control characteristics

**Programmable charac-teristic-curve gradient**
– 0...100%
– Individual for both directions
– For adjustment to hydraulic motor or cylinder

**Programmable timing characteristics**
– Timing gradients from 0.07...4 s
– Individual for both directions
– For adjustment of acceleration and deceleration to varying load conditions

---

*Cylinder*
1 Sealing element, 2 Wiper, 3 Pivoting head,
4 Piston, 5 Cylinder barrel, 6 Guide sleeve,
7 Piston rod.

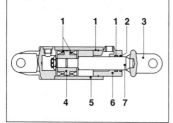

| Design | Remarks |
|---|---|
| Single-action | Performs work only in one direction |
| Double-action | Performs work in two directions, different surface areas on which pressure is acting on piston and piston-rod sides |
| Double-action | Performs work in two directions, identical surface areas, straight-through piston rod |

## Tractor hydraulics

A hydraulic system transforms the tractor into a universal mobile device for agricultural and forestry applications. With the aid of hydraulics, the wide variety of implements used can be quickly mounted to the tractor at the front, rear and between the axles, and moved into their appropriate operating positions by means of open or closed-loop control systems. Quick-disconnect hydraulic couplings are used to control additional linear and rotary motors on the implement itself. Operation of the tractor is facilitated by means of hydraulic power-assisted steering (see also the section on steering systems), brakes, clutches and gear-shifting systems. Pressure relief valves prevent the tractor from being overloaded by the attachments. Trailers pulled by the tractor and matched to its braking system can be hydraulically braked.

High power density and flexibility account for the wide use of hydraulics in tractors. The wide variety of applications ranging from small vineyard tractors rated at approximately 20 kW to large center-pivot-steered tractors rated at roughly 300 kW, and including tool carriers, standard tractors, forestry tractors and construction-work tractors, represent a number of different requirements in terms of hydraulic power, hydraulic systems and system operation.

### Hydraulic systems for tractors

Tractor hydraulic systems generally have three pressure circuits:
- the high-pressure or work circuit with pressures of up to 250 bar and flow rates of up to 120 l/min for steering, trailer brake, control of lifting equipment and other loads,
- the control circuit which has a pressure of approx. 20 bar and a flow rate of around 30 l/min for power-shift transmission, PTO, locking differential, etc.
- the lubrication circuit with a pressure of approx. 3...5 bar.

There are considerable differences in the high-pressure circuit as described below. The essential criteria for choice of design are function, cost, energy losses, complexity and ease of operation.

Constant flow system/Open Center (OC) system ($Q$ constant, $p$ variable)
This system is the most common owing to its favorable price-performance ratio. The pressure is most frequently provided by gear pumps. With all valves in their neutral positions, the hydraulic fluid circulates around the neutral circuit to the tank, and its volumetric flow rate is variable only as a function of pump speed. In order to operate one or more loads, the neutral-flow channel in the valve is constricted, and hydraulic fluid is supplied to the working ports according to the valve-spool displacement. Priority valves are used to ensure that precedence is given to the pressure supply for safety-related functions such as steering and trailer-brake operation. The inherent high levels of power loss in the neutral circulation system can be counteracted by appropriate splitting of the work circuit and the use of two or more pumps to provide the pressure.

Constant pressure system/Closed center (CC) system ($Q$ variable, $p$ constant)
A pump with variable volumetric flow rate operates at a regulated constant pressure. When the valves are in their neutral positions, the pump reduces its delivery volume to the rate of leakage loss. When

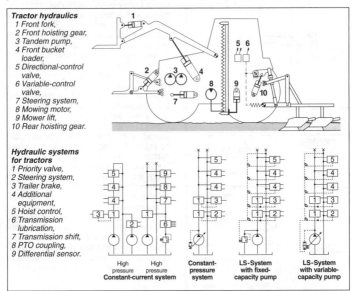

**Tractor hydraulics**
1 Front fork,
2 Front hoisting gear,
3 Tandem pump,
4 Front bucket loader,
5 Directional-control valve,
6 Variable-control valve,
7 Steering system,
8 Mowing motor,
9 Mower lift,
10 Rear hoisting gear.

**Hydraulic systems for tractors**
1 Priority valve,
2 Steering system,
3 Trailer brake,
4 Additional equipment,
5 Hoist control,
6 Transmission lubrication,
7 Transmission shift,
8 PTO coupling,
9 Differential sensor.

High pressure · High pressure **Constant-current system** · **Constant-pressure system** · **LS-System with fixed-capacity pump** · **LS-System with variable-capacity pump**

a valve is operated, the pump automatically adjusts its flow volume to that required by the load. Priority valves are used to give precedence to safety-related functions. This type of system is insignificant in terms of automotive hydraulics.

Load-compensating system with constant-displacement pump/Open center load sensing (OCLS) system
($Q$ constant, $p$ variable)
In this type of system, the differential pressure is kept constant with the aid of a control element (pressure compensator) using the variable valve cross-section (measuring diaphragm). Thus, the flow of hydraulic fluid directed to the consumer unit is proportional to the valve opening and unaffected by the load pressure. The highest load pressure within the control system is selected and directed to the pressure compensator by shuttle valves and control lines. The excess pump flow is returned to the tank via the pressure compensator. If load compensation is also to be maintained for all consumer units in parallel operation, a second 2-way flow regulator (individual pressure compensator) is used for each consumer unit.

This system is technically very involved but is becoming increasingly popular in mobile hydraulics (materials flow/agricultural applications) due to its ease of operation. The energy losses are only negligibly lower than with the constant-flow system.

Load-compensating system with variable-displacement pump/Closed center load sensing (CCLS) system
($Q$ variable, $p$ variable)
This system is similar to the OCLS system. The difference, however, is that the pressure is supplied by a variable-displacement pump with regulated pressure and flow, instead of by a constant-displacement pump with pressure compensator. In addition to the gains in convenience, this system also offers substantially reduced energy losses at partial load. This type of system is being increasingly used in applications involving high-power hydraulics (construction machinery, large tractors).

**Rear hoisting-gear control**
The rear hoisting gear with its standardized 3-point coupling is the most frequently used type of mount for implements. The attached implements can be raised, lowered and held in position. In addition, the tractive force in the hitch linkage can be held constant, or the position of the implement with respect to the tractor can be held constant. Tractive-force regulation is primarily used in working the soil, e.g., plowing (a constant tractive force produces a constant working depth in homogeneous soil). High control quality, i.e. small fluctuations in tractive force, is required for full utilization of engine characteristics and small fluctuations in depth. Because the implements are guided and thus largely supported by the hoisting-gear control, the resistance associated with the implement's movement through the soil generates additional downward force at the drive wheels. This reduces wheel slip, and thus energy losses. Position control is used primarily for implements which do not penetrate the ground. In addition, in the case of highly variable soil resistance, a certain percentage of the position control can be mixed with the tractive-force control (mixed control) in order to limit depth fluctuations.

---

*Electronic hoist-control mechanism (EHR–D)*
*1 Electronics, 2 Control panel, 3 Position sensor, 4 Force-sensor pins, 5 Rear actuation, 6 Pump, 7 Control valve, 8 Cylinder, 9 External sensor, 10 Radar sensor, 11 RPM sensor.*

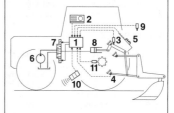

Mechanical hoisting-gear control (MHR)

The sensor signals are monitored and processed as mechanical travel. The tractive force is measured in the form of the spring travel on the upper or lower control arms. The actual position can be read from a cam disc on the lifting shaft. A control rod relays the signals to the control valve according to the selected ratio. At the control valve, the actual values are compared with those selected by the operator. The hoisting mechanism is then raised or lowered to compensate for any control deviations.

Electronic hoisting-gear control (EHR)

The salient feature of EHR lies in the fact that the monitored and control signals are derived, transmitted and processed electronically. The tractive force is measured directly by force-sensor pins at the hitch coupling point. It is possible to supplement position and force control with other functions by expanding the electronic controller and the number of sensors. Rear activation eases attachment of implements. An external sensor can be installed to monitor the travel height of an attached implement (e.g., beet lifter). A speed sensor (radar) and a wheel-speed sensor make it possible to determine slip, providing the basis for a slip-control feature. Active suspension control is useful for enhancing safety and comfort when heavy attachments are being towed.

Hoisting-gear control with hydraulic signal transmission

The basis of this hydraulic signal-transmission system is a hydraulic bridge. The setpoint and actual values of the controlled variable are applied via throttle elements to the bridge's arms and, if the setpoint and actual values do not coincide, this causes the control valve to be shifted against the force of a spring by the diagonally tapped-off differential pressure.

**Directional-control valves for tractors**

Depending upon the type of hydraulic system, directional-control valves for the high-pressure circuit have either open or closed neutral positions with load sensing. For holding heavy loads for long periods – and for safety reasons – poppet valves or slide valves (see section on directional-control valves) with mechanically or hydraulically releasable poppet valves connected to the work port are frequently used. In addition to the three positions for load extension, retraction and holding, the valves often have a fourth position (free-floating position) in order to permit the implement to be guided on the soil, for example by means of supporting wheels. Detent mechanisms with hydraulic maximum-pressure release automatically reset a valve which has moved past its neutral position in response to overload, or if a cylinder reaches its limit position (operating convenience). Integrated flow regulators allow pressure-independent parallel connections and constant speed of linear and rotary motors. Built-in shock absorbers protect the tractor from overload if the cylinder port is closed.

Solenoid valves are used to actuate a number of hydraulic functions on the implement, and are controlled from the tractor by means of cables (e.g. beet lifters).

The hydraulic energy is supplied by way of hydraulic connectors or a separate pump driven by the tractor's PTO shaft. Electromagnetic switching valves for gear-shifting purposes, and for actuating the various clutches on the tractor, are increasingly being incorporated in the low-pressure circuit.

For trailer braking, a braking valve is included in the high-pressure circuit. It is actuated by the tractor brake, and supplies a correspondingly controlled brake pressure to the trailer.

# Hydraulic accumulators

Objectives: Energy storage, impact and pulsation damping, operation as spring element.

The hydraulic accumulator consists of a shell, the interior of which is separated by a solid or flexible barrier. On one side of the barrier is gas, on the other fluid. There are three basic types of units: The bladder, the diaphragm and the piston accumulator.

Nitrogen is employed as the gas medium. During operation, the pressure from the fluid compresses the gas. The minimum operating pressure $p_1$ should lie at least 10% above the initial gas pressure $p_0$. The pressure variation between the initial gas pressure and the maximum operating pressure $p_2$ should not exceed the following: 1:4 in diaphragm and bladder accumulators; 1:10 in piston accumulators. The three operating states illustrated in the diagram are governed by the laws of polytropic changes in state:

$$p_0 \cdot V_0^n = p_1 \cdot V_1^n = p_2 \cdot V_2^n$$

For nitrogen, the polytropic exponent for isothermal changes of state is n = 1 and for adiabatic changes of state, n = 1.4. The available fluid volume between operating pressures is equivalent to the volume difference:

$$\Delta V = V_1 - V_2.$$

## Auxiliary drives

Electrohydraulic devices are employed as drive units in numerous automotive applications. The advantages associated with a positive power-to-weight ratio are accompanied by flexibility in installation. Electrohydraulic devices are used to control hoists and trailing axles, and for raising tractor axles. They are also used for controlling the steering and lifting mechanisms on industrial trucks and other vehicles. Platform lifts for loads of 500 kg to 5,000 kg represent a major area of application for electrohydraulic devices.

The motion of the platform is divided into both lowering and raising. While the upward or downward stroke is controlled by a single central or two outside cylinders, the tilt function is usually governed by two cylinders. These are either single-action cylinders with return springs, or double-action cylinders. The tilt-control functions are generally governed hydraulically. In addition to the "raise" and "lower" functions, other important features are a "floating" position for loading at fixed-position docks, positioning at an optional height (tilting under full load), and compliance with specified "raising" and "lowering" speeds.

## Hydrostatic fan drives

Air-cooling of engine coolant is regulated by thermostatic control of radiator-fan speed. In situations which demand greater scope in the siting of the radiator (due to space constraints, engine encapsulation) in positions where it is not in close proximity to the engine, hydrostatic fan drive systems are generally used for higher-power applications (busses, trucks, construction and agricultural machinery, fixed plant). Aside from the flexibility in positioning the radiator, these units also have the advantages of high power-to-weight ratios (low weight, compact component dimensions), uncompli-

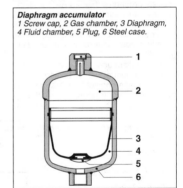

***Diaphragm accumulator***
*1 Screw cap, 2 Gas chamber, 3 Diaphragm, 4 Fluid chamber, 5 Plug, 6 Steel case.*

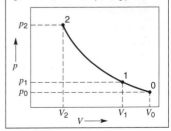

***Operating states of hydraulic accumulator***
*$p_0$ Initial gas pressure, $p_1$ Minimum operating pressure, $p_2$ Maximum operating pressure, $V_0$ Volume at initial gas pressure, $V_1$ Volume at minimum operating pressure, $V_2$ Volume at maximum operating pressure.*

cated control and regulation, reliability, and the reduced component wear which results from the hydraulic fluid's lubrication effect.

The essential components of the hydrostatic fan drive are the hydraulic pump, the motor (high-pressure gear or piston units), and the temperature-controlled valve in the bypass line to the hydraulic motor for controlling fan speed. The hydraulic pump is driven by the engine either directly or indirectly using a V-belt drive (conversion ratio).

The pump, in turn, powers the hydraulic motor in the fan assembly. The motor speed depends on the fan's specific response properties ($n_L \sim \sqrt{\Delta p_M}$) and the effective pressure differential ($\Delta p_M$). If losses associated with transmitting the power are discounted, the speed will be directly proportional to system pressure ($p$).

Both continuous-action and discontinuous-action control are employed to govern the engine-coolant temperature. With two-point control (discontinuous), the bypass valve is in the form of an electrically triggered directional-control valve, with actuation controlled by a thermo-switch in the engine's coolant circuit. A pressure valve mounted in a parallel circuit determines the maximum fan speed – and thus cooling power – which will be obtained when the directional-control valve is closed. The precise regulating response is a function of the system pressure to which the valve is set (usually 200 bar). Continuous-control systems feature a bypass valve in the form of a pressure valve or throttle valve with a supplementary bypass-pressure valve for limiting system pressure. The unit is adjusted by a temperature-sensitive control mechanism with proportional response characteristics. It provides continuous, progressive control of system pressure (in the case of the throttle valve via outgoing bypass flow). The control mechanism can be a thermostatic element (expansion element with wax) located in the coolant stream. Electrohydraulic systems in which the valve is adjusted by a solenoid (proportional solenoid or solenoid with pulse-modulated switching) are becoming increasingly important. The output signal of

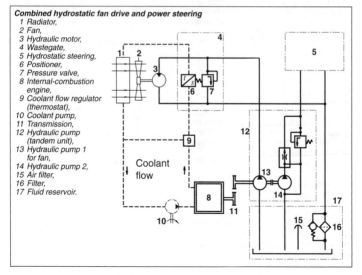

**Combined hydrostatic fan drive and power steering**
1 Radiator,
2 Fan,
3 Hydraulic motor,
4 Wastegate,
5 Hydrostatic steering,
6 Positioner,
7 Pressure valve,
8 Internal-combustion engine,
9 Coolant flow regulator (thermostat),
10 Coolant pump,
11 Transmission,
12 Hydraulic pump (tandem unit),
13 Hydraulic pump 1 for fan,
14 Hydraulic pump 2,
15 Air filter,
16 Filter,
17 Fluid reservoir.

Coolant flow

an electrical temperature sensor in the coolant circuit controls that solenoid. Within the control range of ± 2.5°C, that temperature-related change in system pressure effects infinitely variable adjustment of the fan speed to the required cooling effect. The proportion of operating time during which the fan operates at maximum speed is only roughly 5%. meaning that the fan rotates at reduced speed most of the time. Reductions in fuel consumption and noise emissions are the result. The inherent system losses with this type of slip regulation, a maximum of roughly 15% are commensurate with the requirements of economy. In order to ensure adequate ventilation in the engine compartment beyond the base speed – of particular importance with compartments for encapsulated engines on low-noise vehicles – there is also a limit on minimum system pressure. The control electronics can also be expanded to process additional analog (such as internal and external temperature) and digital input signals. These can serve as the basis for generating output signals to the control solenoid, allowing additional adjustment of fan speed. An example is the combined application of the fan drive to regulate coolant, boost-air, and engine-compartment temperatures, and to switch the fan to maximum rpm during retarder operation. Electrohydraulic systems can be integrated within the engine-management system. Hydrostatic fan-drive systems can also supply other systems or combine with additional ancillary drive systems such as clutch, transmission, compressor, water pump, alternator, hydraulic power steering, rear-axle steering, hydraulic systems for tippers, etc. By means of suitable system design or multiple pump combinations, function prioritization and safety-related demands can be satisfied.

**Electrohydraulic fan drive**
*1 Gear motor with proportional pressure valve, 2 Control unit, 3 Current regulator,*
*4 Voltage regulator, 5 Retarder operation.*
*Temperature sensors for: 6 Coolant, 7 Boost air, 8 Outside air.*
$U_B$ *Battery voltage.*

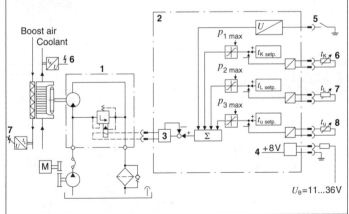

## Hydrostatic drives

If the pressure outlet of an adjustable hydraulic pump is connected to a constant-speed or adjustable hydraulic motor (piston or gear motor), the result is an infinitely variable power-transmission device. The mechanical input power (torque × rpm) emerges as mechanical output at another point. The specific conversion ratio is determined by the quotients of the preset pump flow volume and the motor's displacement volume. Parallel layouts incorporating several motors (differential effect) and series layouts (constant velocity) are also possible. However, a basic transmission within an open circuit can neither change direction nor apply braking force without the assistance of auxiliary mechanisms. Nevertheless, this type of layout is well suited to variable ancillary drive systems, such as fans, spreader plates, etc.

### Main drives

Hydrostatic drive systems for automotive application must be able to cope with turning under power and with braking. For this reason, it is the closed circuit which has gained predominance. The main (reversible) pump is combined with a charge pump, which is usually flange-mounted. The flow from the charge pump into the low-pressure line compensates for leakage and losses in compression volume. Because there is always pressure on the low-pressure side, the main pump's maximum permissible speed is higher than in suction operation. At a constant conversion ratio, this type of transmission provides almost the same degree of positive drive as a mechanical unit. It is especially well-suited as a device for powering machinery. Meanwhile, "automotive" controls have been developed to provide drive characteristics similar to those of cars (for industrial trucks, etc.). In these, the vehicle's IC engine and the transmission are governed by a single pedal. Most fa-

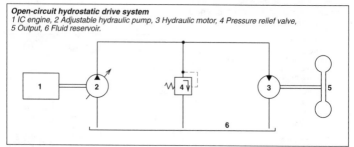

**Open-circuit hydrostatic drive system**
1 IC engine, 2 Adjustable hydraulic pump, 3 Hydraulic motor, 4 Pressure relief valve,
5 Output, 6 Fluid reservoir.

**Basic layout for closed circuit**
1 IC engine, 2 Adjustable hydraulic pump, 3 Charge pump, 4 Charge-pressure relief valve,
5 High-pressure relief valve, 6 Charge non-return valve, 7 Reversible hydraulic motor, 8 Output.

miliar are the circuits in which the operator uses the pedal to control the engine speed only. The engine power is directed through an auxiliary pump and a throttle circuit (generally incorporating several stages) to generate the control pressure which corresponds to the specific engine speed. This pressure, in turn, determines the main pump's flow volume via a control mechanism with proportional pressure response. This control concept is uncomplicated, and prevents the engine from stalling, as the pump responds to losses in input rpm by switching down to lower flow rates requiring lower torques. However, more complicated circuits are required to satisfy more stringent demands for power control and fuel economy. Electrically adjustable pumps and modern sensor technology provide for elegant solutions using electronics.

## Auxiliary drive systems

Yet another application for hydrostatic drives is as auxiliary units on otherwise free-wheeling truck axles for slow operation in difficult terrain. When required, this unit acts as a hydrostatic substitute for drive shaft and transfer case. For normal road operation, some form of low-loss switchoff is required for the unit. The solution is provided by a constant-displacement pump at the engine; this pump features variable ratios, and can also be disengaged completely. On the auxiliary-drive axle, there are slow-running hub motors whose pistons are retracted by springs when driving on the road. Thus the hydraulic system can be dimensioned for slow vehicle speeds. Neither rotating losses nor substantial friction losses are encountered under normal operating conditions.

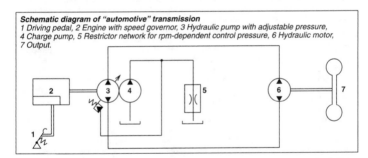

*Schematic diagram of "automotive" transmission*
*1 Driving pedal, 2 Engine with speed governor, 3 Hydraulic pump with adjustable pressure,*
*4 Charge pump, 5 Restrictor network for rpm-dependent control pressure, 6 Hydraulic motor,*
*7 Output.*

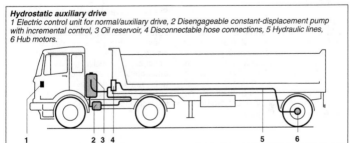

*Hydrostatic auxiliary drive*
*1 Electric control unit for normal/auxiliary drive, 2 Disengageable constant-displacement pump*
*with incremental control, 3 Oil reservoir, 4 Disconnectable hose connections, 5 Hydraulic lines,*
*6 Hub motors.*

# Automotive pneumatics

Pneumatic systems are used in motor vehicles as sources of energy for
- Opening, closing and locking doors, hatches, etc.,
- Operation and control of braking systems (braking equipment) p. 838 ff, and
- Suspension levelling p. 756 ff.

## Operation of bus doors

Bus doors are operated by double-acting control cylinders. The action of the piston is transmitted to the door leaf. Alternating pressurization and depressurization of the two cylinder chambers opens and closes the door. Three drive systems are in use:
- The working cylinder's piston rod is connected to a lever attached to the door pivot. The door pivot is attached to the door. The extended piston rod responds to cylinder actuation by rotating the spindle to open the door.
- The piston cylinder is axially flange-mounted to the door spindle. The reciprocating motion of the cylinder piston is converted into rotary motion in the door spindle. This rotating motion opens and closes the flange-mounted door by pivoting it outward.
- The control cylinder (rotary drive) is actually a combined cylinder and rotary spindle. The piston stroke is transmitted to the door in the form of a rotating motion at the flange axis.

The doors should reach their travel limits without violent impacts and sudden stops. In order to damp the movement of the door during opening and closing, a pressure- or travel-sensitive cushioning device can be installed in the cylinder to reduce the speed of the door shortly before it reaches either end position. The end-position cushioning effect can be adjusted using a throttle screw.

To cite an example, a 4/2-way solenoid valve can be used to reverse the door's travel as follows. The driver triggers a current pulse by pushing the door-control button, causing the solenoid armature to move the rocker into the opposite position via a rod. The rocker responds by closing the supply valve and opening the discharge on one end of the cylinder, while the discharge is opened and the supply closed on the other end. Additional valve and control functions are specified in Germany by the requirements of the vehicle manufacturers as well as the safety requirements contained in § 35 e of the StVZO Road Licensing Regulations (FMVSS/CUR), the ZH 1/494 guidelines for power windows, doors and hatches defined by the professional trade association, and the guidelines of the Association of Public Transport Services (VÖV) for standard city buses.

Power to closing doors must be deactivated or its direction reversed in response to any travel resistance (in Germany, VÖV standard city bus). The opening force must be limited to 150 N or be interrupted upon encountering resistance. After the emergency valve has been operated, the opening or closing force of the door must be canceled, so that the door can be operated by hand. After the emergency valve has been returned to its normal position, door movement must not begin until a separate pushbutton (located on the driver's console or in a box above the door) is pressed or adequate failsafe conditions have been satisfied. Abrupt door movements must be prevented.

### Systems in urban buses
The doors in urban buses rely on any of several methods for travel reversal. These include pressure devices in the weather-stripping, differential-pressure switches, photocells, flexible doorshafts and potentiometers. Should a passenger get caught in the door the system responds by generating an electrical switching signal to reverse the door valve.

During opening the system can react by depressurizing the control mechanism or, alternatively, by pressurizing both door-control cylinders simultaneously. In buses with more than two doors, the rear third door must be controlled automatically. The driver only releases the door for operation. Door opening, open time and closing are electronically controlled on the basis of driver and passenger information.

It is often desirable for the front half of the front door to open while the other half remains closed. This function is achieved by a 2/2-way solenoid valve located in the closing line of the cylinder for the second door section.

### Systems in touring coaches

Where the emergency valve is located upstream of the door valve (see diagram), the door-control button activates a solenoid to release the pushrod for the return mechanism.

When this power operation is triggered, violent closing is prevented by a flow restrictor. In normal operation the flow restrictor is kept open by secondary pressure.

If the emergency valve is installed downstream of the door valve in the line leading to the closing chamber of the door cylinder, the emergency-valve lock is pneumatically actuated. Once a mean pressure is reached, the control rod is pneumatically released and the valve reverses position.

### Door and hatch locking

In large tour-bus doors which swing outward, it is essential that the doors remain locked during the journey. This is done either by lifting the door immediately after the closing process or by additional locking devices, with single-acting actuating cylinders installed in the door frame. At the conclusion of the door-closing process, these are activated by the door itself, for instance by way of a 3/2 shuttle control valve, and thus assist the door drive at the end of the closing process. This closure assistance and locking system is designed in such a way that it unlocks in the event of pressure loss. The door is then held only by the door lock which can be opened by hand in an emergency.

In contrast, springs engage the locking mechanisms for luggage-bay hatches when the control system is depressurized.

---

**Door operating system (circuit diagram)**
1 Air tank, 2 Emergency valve with solenoid release mechanism, 3 Flow restrictor, 4 Door valve, 5 Pressure-relief valve, 6 Control cylinder, 7 Push button, 8 Electric switch for acoustic signal.

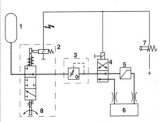

---

**Closing and locking device for touring coaches**
1 Locking bolt, 2 Swinging door, 3 Safety catch, 4 Rocker arm, 5 Actuating cylinder.

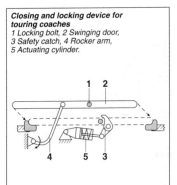

## International registration plates

| | | | |
|---|---|---|---|
| **A** | Austria | **GB** | United Kingdom |
| **AFG** | Afghanistan | **GBA** | Alderney |
| **AL** | Albania | **GBG** | Guernsey |
| **AND** | Andorra | **GBJ** | Jersey |
| **ANG** | Angola | **GBM** | Isle of Man |
| **AUS** | Australia | **GBZ** | Gibraltar |
| **AZ** | Azerbaijan | **GCA** | Guatemala |
| | | **GE** | Georgia |
| **B** | Belgium | **GH** | Ghana |
| **BD** | Bangladesh | **GR** | Greece |
| **BDS** | Barbados | **GUY** | Guyana |
| **BF** | Burkina-Faso | | |
| **BG** | Bulgaria | **H** | Hungary |
| **BH** | Belize | **HK** | Hong Kong |
| **BIH** | Bosnia and Herzegovina | **HN** | Honduras |
| **BOL** | Bolivia | **HR** | Croatia |
| **BR** | Brazil | | |
| **BRN** | Bahrain | **I** | Italy |
| **BRU** | Brunei Darussalam | **IL** | Israel |
| **BS** | Bahamas | **IND** | India |
| **BY** | Belarus | **IR** | Iran |
| | | **IRL** | Ireland |
| **C** | Cuba | **IRQ** | Iraq |
| **CD** | Democratic Republic of the Congo | **IS** | Iceland |
| **CDN** | Canada | | |
| **CH** | Switzerland | **J** | Japan |
| **CI** | Ivory Coast | **JA** | Jamaica |
| **CO** | Columbia | **JOR** | Jordan |
| **CR** | Costa Rica | | |
| **CY** | Cyprus | **K** | Cambodia |
| **CZ** | Czech Republic | **KS** | Kyrgyzstan |
| | | **KSA** | Kingdom of Saudi Arabia |
| **D** | Germany | **KWT** | Kuwait |
| **DK** | Denmark | **KZ** | Kazakhstan |
| **DOM** | Dominican Republic | | |
| **DZ** | Algeria | **L** | Luxembourg |
| | | **LAO** | People's Democratic Republic of Laos |
| **E** | Spain | | |
| **EAK** | Kenya | **LS** | Lesotho |
| **EAT** | Tanzania | **LT** | Lithuania |
| **EAU** | Uganda | **LV** | Latvia |
| **EC** | Ecuador | | |
| **ER** | Eritrea | **M** | Malta |
| **ES** | El Salvador | **MA** | Morocco |
| **EST** | Estonia | **MAL** | Malaysia |
| **ET** | Egypt | **MC** | Monaco |
| **ETH** | Ethiopia | **MD** | Moldova |
| | | **MEX** | Mexico |
| **F** | France | **MGL** | Mongolia |
| **FIN** | Finland | **MK** | Macedonia (former Yugoslavian Republic) |
| **FJI** | Fiji | | |
| **FL** | Liechtenstein | **MOC** | Mozambique |
| **FR** | Faeroes | **MS** | Mauritius |

| | |
|---|---|
| MW | Malawi |
| MYA | Myanmar |
| | |
| N | Norway |
| NA | Netherlands Antilles |
| NAM | Namibia |
| NIC | Nicaragua |
| NL | Netherlands |
| NZ | New Zealand |
| | |
| OM | Oman |
| | |
| P | Portugal |
| PA | Panama |
| PE | Peru |
| PK | Pakistan |
| PL | Poland |
| PY | Paraguay |
| | |
| Q | Qatar |
| | |
| RA | Argentina |
| RB | Botswana |
| RC | Republic of China (Taiwan) |
| RCA | Central African Republic |
| RCB | Congo |
| RCH | Chile |
| RH | Haiti |
| RI | Indonesia |
| RIM | Mauritania |
| RL | Lebanon |
| RM | Madagascar |
| RMM | Mali |
| RN | Niger |
| RO | Romania |
| ROK | Korea (Republic) |
| ROU | Uruguay |
| RP | Philippines |
| RSM | San Marino |
| RT | Togo |
| RUS | Russian Federation |
| RWA | Rwanda |
| | |
| S | Sweden |
| SD | Swaziland |
| SGP | Singapore |
| SK | Slovakia |
| SLO | Slovenia |
| SME | Surinam |
| SN | Senegal |
| SP | Somalia |
| SU | Soviet Union (former) |
| SY | Seychelles |
| SYR | Syria |

| | |
|---|---|
| THA | Thailand |
| TJ | Tajikistan |
| TM | Turkmenistan |
| TN | Tunisia |
| TR | Turkey |
| TT | Trinidad and Tobago |
| | |
| UA | Ukraine |
| UAE | United Arab Emirates |
| USA | United States of America |
| UZ | Uzbekistan |
| | |
| V | Vatican City |
| VN | Vietnam |
| | |
| WAG | The Gambia |
| WAL | Sierra Leone |
| WAN | Nigeria |
| WD | Dominica |
| WG | Grenada |
| WL | Santa Lucia |
| WS | Samoa |
| WV | St. Vincent and the Grenadines |
| | |
| YU | Yugoslavia (Serbia/Montenegro) |
| YV | Venezuela |
| | |
| Z | Zambia |
| ZA | South Africa |
| ZW | Zimbabwe |

Source: German Federal Ministry for Transport, Building and Housing, Verkehrsblatt (Official Bulletin and Gazette) (VkBl. Official Section, Vol. 24 – 1999, No. 204)
Present Edition: December 1999

## Alphabets and numbers

### German alphabet

Gothic type

| | | | | | | | | | |
|---|---|---|---|---|---|---|---|---|---|
| 𝔄 | a | a | | ℑ | j | j | | 𝔖 | s | s |
| 𝔅 | b | b | | 𝔎 | k | k | | 𝔗 | t | t |
| ℭ | c | c | | 𝔏 | l | l | | 𝔘 | u | u |
| 𝔇 | d | d | | 𝔐 | m | m | | 𝔙 | v | v |
| 𝔈 | e | e | | 𝔑 | n | n | | 𝔚 | w | w |
| 𝔉 | f | f | | 𝔒 | o | o | | 𝔛 | x | x |
| 𝔊 | g | g | | 𝔓 | p | p | | 𝔜 | y | y |
| 𝔥 | h | h | | 𝔔 | q | q | | ℨ | z | z |
| ℑ | i | i | | ℜ | r | r | | | | |

### Greek alphabet

| Letter | | Name | Letter | | Name |
|---|---|---|---|---|---|
| $A$ | $\alpha$ | alpha | $N$ | $\nu$ | nu |
| $B$ | $b$ | beta | $\Xi$ | $\xi$ | xi |
| $\Gamma$ | $\gamma$ | gamma | $O$ | $o$ | omicron |
| $\Delta$ | $\delta$ | delta | $\Pi$ | $\pi$ | pi |
| $E$ | $\varepsilon$ | epsilon | $P$ | $\varrho$ | rho |
| $Z$ | $\zeta$ | zeta | $\Sigma$ | $\sigma\,\varsigma$ | sigma |
| $H$ | $\eta$ | eta | $T$ | $\tau$ | tau |
| $\Theta$ | $\vartheta$ | theta | $Y$ | $\upsilon$ | upsilon |
| $I$ | $\iota$ | iota | $\Phi$ | $\varphi$ | phi |
| $K$ | $\kappa$ | kappa | $X$ | $\chi$ | chi |
| $\Lambda$ | $\lambda$ | lambda | $\Psi$ | $\psi$ | psi |
| $M$ | $\mu$ | mu | $\Omega$ | $\omega$ | omega |

### Phonetic alphabets

| | German | International | Voice radio |
|---|---|---|---|
| A | Anton | Amsterdam | Alpha |
| Ä | Ärger | – | – |
| B | Berta | Baltimore | Bravo |
| C | Cäsar | Casablanca | Charlie |
| CH | Charlotte | – | – |
| D | Dora | Denmark | Delta |
| E | Emil | Edison | Echo |
| F | Friedrich | Florida | Foxtrot |
| G | Gustav | Gallipoli | Golf |
| H | Heinrich | Havana | Hotel |
| I | Ida | Italy | India |
| J | Julius | Jerusalem | Juliet |
| K | Kaufmann | Kilogram | Kilo |
| L | Ludwig | Liverpool | Lima |
| M | Martha | Madagascar | Mike |
| N | Nordpol | New York | November |
| O | Otto | Oslo | Oscar |
| Ö | Ökonom | – | – |
| P | Paula | Paris | Papa |
| Q | Quelle | Quebec | Quebec |
| R | Richard | Rome | Romeo |
| S | Samuel | Santiago | Sierra |
| Sch | Schule | – | – |
| T | Theodor | Tripoli | Tango |
| U | Ulrich | Uppsala | Uniform |
| Ü | Übermut | – | – |
| V | Viktor | Valencia | Victor |
| W | Wilhelm | Washington | Whiskey |
| X | Xanthippe | Xanthippe | X-ray |
| Y | Ypsilon | Yokohama | Yankee |
| Z | Zeppelin | Zurich | Zulu |

### Russian alphabet

| Letter | | Pro-nounced | Letter | | Pro-nounced |
|---|---|---|---|---|---|
| А | а | a | Р | р | r |
| Б | б | b | С | с | ss |
| В | в | w | Т | т | t |
| Г | г | g | У | у | u |
| Д | д | d | Ф | ф | f |
| Е | е | je | Х | х | ch |
| Ё | ё | jo | Ц | ц | zh |
| Ж | ж | sh | Ч | ч | ch |
| З | з | s | Ш | ш | sh |
| И | и | i | Щ | щ | shch |
| Й | й | i (short) | Ъ | ъ | hard mark |
| К | к | k | Ы | ы | ü |
| Л | л | l | Ь | ь | soft mark |
| М | м | m | Э | э | ä |
| Н | н | n | Ю | ю | yu |
| О | о | o | Я | я | ya |
| П | п | p | | | |

### Roman numerals

| | | | |
|---|---|---|---|
| I | 1 | XXX | 30 |
| II | 2 | XL | 40 |
| III | 3 | L | 50 |
| IV | 4 | LX | 60 |
| V | 5 | LXX | 70 |
| VI | 6 | LXXX | 80 |
| VII | 7 | XC | 90 |
| VIII | 8 | C | 100 |
| IX | 9 | CC | 200 |
| X | 10 | CD | 400 |
| XI | 11 | D | 500 |
| XX | 20 | DC | 600 |
| XXI | 21 | M | 1000 |
| XXIX | 29 | MVM | 1995 |

# Index

# Abbreviations

## A:

| | |
|---|---|
| **A/D:** | **A**nalog/**D**igital Converter |
| **ABD:** | **A**utomatic **B**raking **D**ifferential |
| **ABG:** | **A**llgemeine **B**auart**g**enehmigung (General Type Approval) |
| **ABS:** | **A**ntilock **B**raking **S**ystem |
| **AC:** | **A**lternating **C**urrent |
| **ACC:** | **A**daptive **C**ruise **C**ontrol |
| **ACC LSF:** | **ACC L**ow **S**peed **F**ollowing |
| **ACEA:** | **A**ssociation des **C**onstructeurs **E**uropéens de l'**A**utomobile (Association of European Automobile Manufacturers) |
| **ADA(1):** | **A**tmosphärend**r**uck**a**bhängiger (Volllastanschlag) (Atmospheric-pressure sensitive full load stop) |
| **ADA(2):** | **A**uto-**D**irectional **A**ntenna |
| **ADR:** | **A**ustralian **D**esign **R**ule |
| **AFC:** | **A**nti-**F**riction-**C**oating (Lubricants) |
| **AF Code:** | **A**lternative **F**requencies Code |
| **AGR:** | **A**bgas**r**ückführung (EGR: Exhaust-Gas Recirculation) |
| **AHP:** | **A**ccelerator **H**eel **P**oint |
| **AKSE:** | **A**utomatische **K**indersitz**e**rkennung (Automatic child-seat recognition) |
| **AL:** | **A**utomotive **L**ighting |
| **ALB:** | **A**utomatic **l**oad-sensitive **b**raking-force |
| **AM:** | **A**mplitude **m**odulation |
| **AM-LCD:** | **A**ctive **M**essage **L**iquid **C**rystal **D**isplay |
| **AMR:** | **A**ntriebs**m**oment**r**egelung (Drive-torque control) |
| **AMR sensor:** | **S**ensor made of thin anisotropic **m**agneto**r**esistive NiFe layers |
| **AOS:** | **A**utomotive **O**ccupancy **S**ensing |
| **API:** | **A**pplication **P**rogrammer **I**nterface |
| **API Classification:** | **A**merican **P**etroleum **I**nstitute Classification |
| **ARF:** | **A**bgas**r**ückführung (EGR: Exhaust-Gas Recirculation) |
| **ARI:** | **A**utofahrer-**R**undfunk-**I**nformation (Driver information via broadcast radio) |
| **ART:** | **A**bstandsregeltempomat (Active cruise control) |
| **AS:** | **A**cker**s**chlepper (Agricultural tractors) |
| **ASF:** | **A**udi **S**pace **F**rame |
| **ASIC:** | **A**pplication **S**pecific **I**ntegrated **C**ircuit |
| **ASM:** | **A**nhänger**s**teuer**m**odul (Trailer control module) |
| **ASR:** | **A**cceleration **S**lip **C**ontrol (Traction control) |
| **ASSP:** | **A**pplication **S**pecific **S**tandard **P**roduct |
| **ASTM:** | **A**merican **S**ociety of **T**esting and **M**aterials |
| **ASU:** | **A**utomatische **S**törunterdrückung (Automatic interference suppression) |
| **AT:** | **A**ufkohltiefe (Carburizing depth) |
| **ATF:** | **A**utomatic-**T**ransmission **F**luid |
| **ATL:** | **A**bgasturbolader (Exhaust-gas turbocharger) |
| **AU:** | **A**bgas**u**ntersuchung (German emissions inspection) |
| **AV:** | **A**bbau**v**entil (ABS) (Discharge valve, made of ABS rubber) |

## B:

| | |
|---|---|
| **BA:** | **B**raking **A**ssistant |
| **BCD-Mischprozess:** | **B**ipolar/**C**MOS/**D**MOS-Mischprozess (Mixed production process for bipolar CMOS/DMOS devices) |
| **BCI:** | **B**ulk **C**urrent **I**njection |
| **BDC:** | **B**ottom **D**ead **C**enter |
| **BDE:** | **B**enzin-**D**irekteinspritzung (GDI: Gasoline Direct injection) |
| **BEM:** | **B**oundary-**E**lement **M**ethod |
| **BiCMOS:** | **Bi**polar **C**omplementary **MOS** Transistor |
| **BIP-Signal:** | **B**eginning of **I**njection **P**eriod Signal |
| **BK:** | **B**ereichs**k**ennung (Group code) |
| **BLCD:** | **B**rushless **E**lectronically **C**ommutated **DC** motor |
| **BLFD:** | **B**elt **L**ock (Switch) **F**ront **D**river |
| **BLFP:** | **B**elt **L**ock (Switch) **F**ront **P**assenger |
| **BLRC:** | **B**elt **L**ock (Switch) **R**ear **C**enter |
| **BLRL:** | **B**elt **L**ock (Switch) **R**ear **L**eft |
| **BLRR:** | **B**elt **L**ock (Switch) **R**ear **R**ight |

**BL3SRL:** Belt Lock (Switch) 3rd Seat Row Left
**BL3SRR:** Belt Lock (Switch) 3rd Seat Row Right
**BMD:** Bag Mini Diluter
**BMK:** Bosch micro-contact
**BMM:** Bulk micromechanics (Etching process for the reverse side of a wafer)
**BMR:** Bremsmomentregelung (Braking-torque control)
**BOTE-ACT:** Bosch-Temic-Aktuatorenbusprinzip (Bosch-Temic actuator bus principle)
**BSK:** Bosch-Sensor/Steller-Kontakt (Bosch sensor/transistor actuator contact)
**BSS:** Bit-Synchrone Schnittstelle (Bit-synchronous interface)
**BZ:** Brennstoffzelle (fuel cell)

**C:**

**CAD:** Computer-Aided Design
**CAE:** Computer-Aided Engineering
**CAFE:** Corporate Average Fuel Economy
**CAHRD:** Crash Active Head Rest Driver
**CAHRP:** Crash Active Head Rest Passenger
**CAL:** Computer-Aided Lighting
**CAN:** Controller Area Network
**CARB:** California Air Resource Board
**CARTRONIC:** Concept for organizing and describing all control systems in an automobile
**CBS:** Combined Brake System
**CCD:** Charge-Coupled Device
**CCFL:** Cold-Cathode Fluorescence Lamp
**CC-LS-System:** Closed-Center Load Sensing System
**CCMC:** Comité des Constructeurs d'Automobile du Marché Commun (Committee of Automobile Manufacturers in the Common Market)
**CC-System:** Closed-Center System
**CD(1):** Cathodic deposition
**CD(2):** Compact Disc
**CDC:** Compact Disc Charger
**CET:** Central European Time
**CFD:** Computational Fluid Dynamics
**CFI:** Central (Single-Point) Fuel Injection
**CFPP:** Cold Filter Plugging Point

**CFV:** Critical Flow Venturi
**CGPM:** Conférence Générale des Poids et Mésures (General conference on wieghts and measures)
**CISC:** Complex-Instruction-Set Computing
**CLD:** ChemiLuminescence Detector
**CMOS:** Complementary MOS-Transistors (PMOS and NMOS transistors produced in pairs in the same silicon chip)
**CMVSS:** Canadian Motor Vehicle Safety Standard
**CN:** Cetane Number
**CNG:** Compressed Natural Gas
**COB:** Chip on Board
**COFDM:** Coded Orthogonal Frequency Division Multiplexing
**COP:** Conformity of Production
**CPU:** Central Processing Unit
**CRC:** Cyclic Redundancy Check
**CROD:** Crash Output Digital
**CRS:** Common Rail System
**CRT:** Continuously Regenerating Trap
**CT-Code:** Clock/Time Code
**CVD:** Chemical Vapor Deposition
**CVS:** Constant Volume Sampling
**CVT:** Continuously Variable Transmission
**CZ:** Cetanzahl (CN: Cetane Number)

**D:**

**D/F-Verhältnis:** Dampf-/Flüssigkeits-Verhältnis (Vapor/fluid ratio)
**DAB:** Digital Audio Broadcasting
**DBV:** Druckbegrenzungsventil (Pressure-relief valve)
**DC:** Direct Current
**DCS:** Digital Cellular System
**DDA:** Digital Directional Antenna
**DDS:** Digital Diversity System
**DEQ:** Digital Equalizer
**DFPM:** Diagnosis Fault Path Management
**DFS:** Dauerfestigkeitsschaubild (Fatigue-limit diagram)
**DFV:** Dampf-Flüssigkeits-Verhältnis (Kraftstoffe) (Vapor/liquid ratio for fuels)
**DHK:** Düsenhalterkombination (Nozzle-holder assembly)
**DI:** Direct Injection
**DI-Motronic:** Motronic für Benzin-Direkteinspritzung (Direct Injection)

**DigiCeiver:** Digital Receiver
**DIN:** Deutsches Institut für Normung (German Standardization Institute)
**DK(1):** Dielektrizitätskonstante (Dielectric constant)
**DK(2):** Durchsagekennung (Announcement code)
**DKA:** Drosselklappenansteller (Throttle-valve actuator)
**DKG:** Drosselklappengeber (Throttle-valve sensor)
**DLC:** Diamond like Carbon
**DMB:** Digital Multimedia Broadcasting
**DME:** Dimethylether
**DMOS:** Digital MOS Transistor
**DMS:** Dehnmessstreifen (Strain gage)
**DMSB:** Deutscher Motorsportbund (German Motorsports Association)
**DNC:** Dynamic Noise Covering
**DOHC:** Double Overhead Camshaft
**DOT:** Department of Transportation
**DPE:** Digital Parametric Equalizing
**DPR:** Dual Port RAM
**DRAM:** Dynamic RAM
**DRM(1):** Druckregelmodul (Pressure-control module)
**DRM(2):** Digital Radio Mondial
**DRO:** Dielectric Resonance Oscillator
**DSA:** Digital Sound Adjustment
**DSCHED:** Diagnostic Function Scheduler
**DS-L:** Ladedrucksensor (Boost-pressure sensor)
**DSM:** Diagnostic System Management
**DSP:** Digital Signal Processor
**DS-S:** Saugrohrdrucksensor (Intake-manifold pressure sensor)
**DSTN-LCD:** Double Super Twisted Nematic-Liquid Crystal Display
**DS-U:** Umgebungsdrucksensor (Ambient-pressure sensor)
**DTM:** Deutsche Tourenwagen Masters (German Touring Car Championships)
**DVAL:** Diagnosis Validator
**DVD:** Digital Versatile Disc
**DWS(1):** Drehwinkelsensor (Angle-of-rotation sensor)
**DWS(2):** Dunlop Warnair System

**E:**
**E/A:** Eingabe-/Ausgabeeinheit (I/O: input/output device)
**EBS:** Elektronisches Bremssystem (ELB: Electronically controlled braking system)
**EBV:** Elektronische Bremskraftverteilung (Electronic brake balancing)
**ECD:** Elektronisch geregelte Verzögerung (Electronically controlled deceleration)
**ECE:** Economic Commission for Europe
**ECL:** Emitter-Coupled Logic (Bipolar integrated digital circuit)
**EC-Motor:** Electrically Commutated Direct Current Motor
**EDC:** Electronic Diesel Control
**EEC:** European Economic Community
**EEPROM:** Electrically Erasable Programmable Read Only Memory
**EET:** East European Time
**EEV:** Enhanced Environmentally Friendly Vehicle
**EG(1):** Europäische Gemeinschaft (EU: European Union)
**EG(2):** Eigenlenkgradient (Self-steering gradient)
**EGAS:** Electronic Throttle Control
**EGR:** Exhaust-Gas Recirculation
**EHB:** Electrohydraulic Brakes
**EHR:** Elektronische Hubwerksregelung (Electronic hoisting-gear control)
**EHSe:** Elektrohydraulische Stelleinheit für Mobilwegeventile (Electrohydraulic positioner unit for mobile directional-control valves)
**EHT:** Einsatzhärtungstiefe (Case-hardening depth)
**EHVS:** Elektrohydraulisch betätigte Ventilsteuerungen (Electrohydraulically operated valve controls)
**EIR:** Emissions Information Report
**EIS:** Electrochemical Impedance Spectroscopy
**EKP:** Elektrokraftstoffpumpe (Electric fuel pump)
**EL-Folie:** Elektroluminiszenz-Folie (Electroluminescence foil)

**ELB:** Electronically controlled braking system
**ELPI:** Electrical Low Pressure Impactor
**ELR:** European Load Response
**EM(1):** Einmodenfaser (MMF: Monomode fiber)
**EM(2):** Erdbewegungsmaschine (Earthmoving machine)
**EMF:** Electromotive force
**EMK:** Elektromotorische Kraft (EMF: Electromotive force)
**EMP:** Elektromechanische Parkbremse (Electromechanical parking brake)
**EMS:** Elektronische Motorsteuerung (Electronic engine-management system)
**EMC:** Electromagnetic compatibility
**EN:** Euronorm (European standard)
**EOBD:** European On-Board Diagnosis
**EON code:** Enhanced Other Networks
**EP:** Extreme Pressure (Lubricants)
**EPA:** Environment Protection Agency
**EPM:** Electropneumatic Modulator
**EPROM:** Erasable Programmable Read Only Memory
**EP lubricant:** Extreme Pressure lubricant
**ESC:** European Steady-State Cycle
**ESI[tronic]:** Electronic Service Information
**ESD:** Electrostatic Discharge
**ESG:** Einscheiben-Sicherheitsglas (Single-pane toughened safety glass)
**ESP:** Electronic Stability Program
**ESV(1):** Experimental Safety Vehicle
**ESV(2):** Elektronische Spätverstellung (Electronic retard device)
**ETC:** European Transient Cycle
**ETRTO:** European Tire and Rim Technical Organization
**ETSI:** European Telecommunication Standards Institute
**EU:** European Union
**EUATL:** Elektrisch unterstützte Abgasturboaufladung (Electrically supported exhaust-gas turbocharging)
**EUDC:** Extra Urban Driving Cycle
**EV(1):** Einlassventil (ABS) (Intake valve)
**EV (2):** Einspritzventil (Injector)

**EVG:** Elektronisches Vorschaltgerät (Electronic ballast unit)
**EWG:** Europäische Wirtschaftsgemeinschaft (EEC: European Economic Community)
**EWIR:** Emissions Warranty Information Report

**F:**

**FAME:** Fatty Acid Methyl Ester (alternative fuel)
**FBG:** Förderbeginngeber (Port-closing sensor)
**FBM:** Fußbremsmodul (Brake-pedal module)
**FDMA:** Frequency Division Multiplex Access
**FE:** Finite Element
**FEM:** Finite-Element Method
**FET:** Field-Effect Transistor
**FFT:** Fast Fourier Transformation
**FGB:** Fahrgeschwindigkeitsbegrenzer (Vehicle-speed limitation)
**FH-Felge:** Flathump-Felge (Flat-hump rim)
**FIA:** Fédération Internationale de l'Automobile (International Automobile Association)
**FIC:** Fast Information Channel
**FID:** Flame Ionization Detector
**FIFO:** First In First Out
**FIR:** Field Information Report
**FIS:** Fahrer-Informations-System (Driver information system)
**Flash memory:** Flash EEPROM (Flash Electrically Erasable Programmable Read Only Memory)
**FLIC:** Firing Loop Integrated Circuit
**FM:** Frequency Modulation
**FMCW:** Frequency-Modulated Continuous Wave
**FMEA:** Failure Mode and Effects Analysis
**FMS:** Fleet Management System
**FMVSS:** Federal Motor Vehicle Safety Standard
**FPK:** Frei programmierbares Kombiinstrument (Freely programmable instrument cluster)
**FR:** First Registration
**FSI:** Fuel Stratified Injection
**FSR(1):** Full-Scale Range
**FSR(2):** Force-Sensing Resistor

**FTA:** Fault Tree Analysis
**FTIR:** Fourier Transform Infrared (spectroscopy)
**FTP:** Federal Test Procedure

## G:

**GATS:** Global Automotive Telematics Standard
**GC:** Gas Chromatographic column
**GDI:** Gasoline Direct Injection
**GH:** Gestaltänderungsenergie-hypothese (Deformation-energy hypothesis; strength of materials)
**GIDAS:** German In-Depth Accident Study
**GKZ:** Glühen auf körnigem Zementit (Annealing on coarse-grain cementite)
**GMA:** Giermomentaufbauverzögerung (Yaw-moment buildup delay)
**GOT:** Gaswechsel-OT (Top dead center in exhaust cycle)
**GP:** Gedrehte Parabel (Inverse parabolic reflector)
**GPRS:** General Packet Radio Service
**GPS:** Global Positioning System
**GSK:** Glühstiftkerze (Sheathed-element glow plug)
**GSM:** Global System for Mobile Communication
**GSY:** Geschwindigkeitssymbol (Tire speed-rating symbol)
**GTO:** Gate Turn-Off

## H:

**HAL:** Hardware Abstraction Layer
**H/B-Verhältnis:** Höhe-/Breite-Verhältnis des Reifenquerschnitts (Height/width ratio of tire cross-section)
**HDC:** Hill-Descent Control
**HDEV:** Hochdruck-Einspritzventil (High-pressure injector)
**HDG:** Hell-Dunkel-Grenze (Light-dark cutoff)
**HD-Öl:** Heavy-Duty Oil
**HDP:** Hochdruckpumpe (High-pressure pump)
**HD-Stufe:** Hochdruck-Stufe (High-pressure stage)
**HF:** Hochfrequenz (High frequency)
**HFM:** Hot-film air-mass meter

**HHC:** Hill-Hold Control
**HIC:** Head Injury Criterion
**HKZ:** Hochspannungs-Kondensator-zündung (Capacitor-discharge ignition)
**HNS:** Homogeneous Numerically Calculated Surface
**HSCSD:** High Speed Circuit Switched Data
**HSLA:** High Strength Low Alloy
**HTTP:** Hyper Text Transfer Protocol
**HUD:** Head-up Display

## I:

**I/O:** Input/Output
**I²L:** Integrated Injection Logic
**IC:** Integrated Circuit
**ID:** Identifier
**IDB-M:** Intelligent Data Bus Multimedia
**IDI:** Indirect Injection
**IEC:** International Electrotechnical Commission
**IETF:** International Engineering Taskforce
**IF:** Intermediate Frequency
**IR(1):** Infrared
**IR(2):** Individualregelung der Räder durch das ABS (Individual wheel control by ABS)
**IRM:** Individualregelung modifiziert (Individual wheel control, modified)
**IP:** Internet Protocol
**IS:** Integrierte Schaltung (IC: Integrated Circuit)
**ISO:** International Organization for Standardization
**ITU:** International Telecommunications Union

## J:

**JFET:** Junction Field-Effect Transistor

## K:

**KE-Jetronic:** Mechanisch gesteuerte kontinuierliche Einzelein-spritzung mit elektronischem Steuergerät (Continuous multi-point fuel injection with electronic control unit)

**KE-Motronic:** Motormanagementsystem Motronic auf Basis
der kontinuierlichen Einzelein-
spritzung **KE**-Jetronic (Engine
management based on continuous multipoint fuel injection)
**Kfz:** Kraftfahrzeug (Motor vehicle)
**KI:** Kombiinstrument
(Instrument cluster)
**K-Jetronic:** Mechanisch gesteuerte
kontinuierliche Einzelein-
spritzung (Mechanically controlled continuous multipoint
fuel injection)
**KOM:** Kraftomnibus (Omnibus)
**KTL:** Kathodische Tauchlackierung
(CD: Cathodic deposition)
**KW(1):** Kurbelwelle (Crankshaft)
**KW(2):** Kurzwellen (SW: Short Wave)

**L:**

**LAN:** Local Area Network
**LBK:** Ladungsbewegungsklappe
(Turbulence flap)
**LCD:** Liquid Crystal Display
**LCF:** Low Cycle Fatigue
**LDA:** Ladedruckabhängiger
Volllastanschlag (Manifold-
pressure compensator)
**LED:** Light-Emitting Diode
**LGS:** Luftgütesteuergerät
(Air-quality ECU)
**LH-Jetronic:** Elektronisch gesteuerte
Einzeleinspritzung mit Hitzdraht-
Luftmassenmesser
(Electronically controlled multi-
point fuel injection with hot-wire
air-mass meter)
**LI:** Last-Index (Tyres)
**LIN:** Local Interface Network
**Lidar:** Licht des nahen Infrarotbereiches
(LIDAR: Light Identification
Detection and Ranging)
**Litronic: Light** and **Electronic**
**L-Jetronic:** Elektronisch gesteuerte
intermittierende Einzelein-
spritzung (Electronically con-
trolled intermittent multipoint
fuel injection)
**LKE:** Ladekolbeneinheit
(Charging-piston unit)
**Lkw:** Lastkraftwagen (Truck)
**LLK:** Ladeluftkühlung (Intercooling
(charge-air cooling))

**LNG:** Liquified Natural Gas
**LPG:** Liquified Petroleum Gas
**LR:** Load-Response function
**LRR-Sensor:** Long-Range Radar
Sensor
**LSB:** Least Significant Bit
**LSF:** Lambda-Sonde (Fingersonde)
(Two-point oxygen sensor)
**LSI:** Large Scale Integration
**LSU:** Lambda-Sonde (Universal-
bzw. Breitbandsonde)
(Broadband oxygen sensor)
**LS-Ventil:** Load-Sensing Valve
(Pump or pressure compensator
relieved in neutral position)
**LW:** Long Wave
**LWL:** Lichtwellenleiter
(Optical fibers/waveguides)

**M:**

**M+S-Reifen:** „Matsch-und-Schnee"-
Reifen (Snow tyres)
**MCM:** Multi-Chip Module
**MDPV:** Medium-Duty Passenger Vehicle
**ME:** Miner Elementar (Wöhler curve,
strength of materials)
**MED-Motronic:** Motormanagement-
system Motronic mit EGAS
und Benzin-Direkteinspritzung
(Engine management with
electronic throttle control and
gasoline direct injection)
**MEMO:** Multimedia Environment for
Mobiles
**ME-Motronic:** Motormanagement-
system Motronic mit EGAS
(Engine management with
electronic throttle control)
**MEZ:** Mitteleuropäische Zeit
(CET: Central European Time)
**MGIF:** Mobile Gaming Interoperability
Forum
**MHR:** Mechanische Hubwerksregelung
(Mechanical hoisting-gear
control)
**MI:** Main Injection
**MIL:** Malfunction Indicator Lamp
**MIL-Spezifikation:** Militär-Spezifikation
(MIL specifications)
**MIN:** Minimaloperator (ESP)
(Minimum operator (ESP))
**MKL:** Mechanischer Kreisellader
(Centrifugal supercharger)

**ML:** Miner Liu/Zenner (Wöhler curve, strength of materials)
**MM(1):** Mehrmodenfaser
(MMF: Multimode Fiber)
**MM(2):** Miner Modifiziert (Wöhler curve, strength of materials)
**MMC:** MultiMediaCard
**MMF(1):** Monomode fiber
**MMF(2):** Multimode Fiber
**MMS:** Multimedia Messaging Service
**M-Motronic:** Motormanagementsystem Motronic auf Basis der Einzeleinspritzung L-Jetronic (Engine management based on L-Jetronic multipoint fuel injection)
**MNEDC:** Modified New European Driving Cycle
**MNEFZ:** Modifizierter Neuer Europäischer Fahrzyklus (MNEDC: Modified New European Driving Cycle)
**Mono-Jetronic:** Elektronisch gesteuerte Zentraleinspritzung (Electronically controlled single-point fuel injection)
**MO:** Miner Original (Wöhler curve, strength of materials)
**Modem:** Modulator/Demodulator
**MON:** Motor Octane Number
**Mono-Motronic:** Motormanagementsystem Motronic auf Basis der intermittierenden Zentraleinspritzung **Mono**-Jetronic (Engine management based on intermittent single-point fuel injection)
**MOS:** Metal-Oxide Semiconductor
**MOSFET:** MOS Field Effect Transistor
**MOST:** Media-Oriented Systems Transport
**MOZ:** Motor-Oktanzahl (MON: Motor Octane Number)
**MPT(1):** Multi-Purpose Tire
**MPT(2):** Ministry of Post and Telecommunications
**MSB:** Most Significant Bit
**MSI:** Medium-Scale Integration
**MTBE:** Methyl Tertiary Butyl Ether
**MTTF:** Mean Time To Failure
**MVL:** Mechanischer Verdrängerlader (Positive-displacement supercharger)
**MVSS:** Motor Vehicle Safety Standard
**MW:** Mittelwellen (Medium Wave)

**N:**

**NA:** Numerical Aperture (Optical waveguides)
**NBF:** Nadelbewegungsfühler (NBS: Needle-motion sensor)
**NBS:** Nadelbewegungssensor (NBS: Needle-motion sensor)
**NCAP:** New Car Assessment Program
**NDIR:** Non-Dispersive Infrared Analyzer
**ND-Stufe:** Niederdruck-Stufe (Low-pressure stage)
**NEDC:** New European Driving Cycle
**NEFZ:** Neuer Europäischer Fahrzyklus (NEDC: New European Driving Cycle)
**NH:** Normalspannungshypothese (Direct-stress hypothesis)
**NHT:** Nitrierhärtetiefe (Nitriding Depth)
**NLEV:** National Low Emission Vehicle
**NMHC:** Non-Methane Hydrocarbon
**NMOG:** Non-Methane Organic Gases
**NMOS:** N-Kanal-MOS-Transistor (N-channel MOST transistor)
**NTC:** Negative Temperature Coefficient
**NYCC:** New York City Cycle

**O:**

**OBD:** On-Board Diagnosis
**OC:** Occupant Classification
**OC-LS-System:** Open-Center Load Sensing System
**OC-System:** Open-Center System
**OC-Ventil:** Open-Center Valve
**ODB:** Offset Deformable Barrier Crash
**OEZ:** Osteuropäische Zeit (EET: East European Time)
**OHC:** Overhead Camshaft
**OHV:** Overhead Valves
**OMA:** Open Mobile Alliance
**OMM:** Oberflächen-Mikromechanik (Surface micromechanics)
**OP:** Operational Amplifier
**OP:** Operationsverstärker (Operational amplifier)
**OSI:** Open Systems Interconnections
**OT:** Oberer Totpunkt (Kolben des Verbrennungsmotors) (TDC: Top Dead Center)
**OTP:** One-Time Programmable ROM

**P:**

**PA:** Polyamid (Polyamide)
**PAS:** Peripheral Acceleration Sensor
**PASFD:** Peripheral Acceleration Sensor Front Driver
**PASFP:** Peripheral Acceleration Sensor Front Passenger
**PASS:** Photo-acoustic Soot Sensor
**PC:** Personal Computer
**PDA:** Personal Digital Assistant
**PDE:** Pumpe-Düse-Einheit (UIS: Unit Injector System)
**PDLC:** Passive-Display Liquid Crystal
**PDP:** Positive Displacement Pump
**PE:** Polyethylene
**PEI:** Peripheral Equipment Interface
**PE-Pumpe:** Reiheneinspritzpumpe mit Eigenantrieb (In-line fuel-injection pump with separate drive)
**PES:** Poly-Ellipsoid System
**PF-Pumpe:** Einzeleinspritzpumpe mit Fremdantrieb (Discrete fuel-injection pump with external drive)
**P-Grad:** Regelkennlinie für Drehzahlregler (Control curve for governor)
**PI:** Pilot Injection
**PIC:** Periphery Integrated Circuit
**PI-Code:** Program Identifying Code
**Pkw:** Personenkraftwagen (Passenger car)
**PLD(1):** Pumpe-Leitung-Düse (Unit Pump System)
**PLD(2):** Programmable Logic Devices
**PMD(1):** ParaMagnetic Detector
**PMD(2):** Photonic Mixer Device
**PMOS:** P-Kanal-MOS-Transistor (P-channel MOS transistor)
**POI(1):** Points of Interest
**POI(2):** Post Injection
**PP:** Polypropylene
**PPS:** Peripheral Pressure Sensor
**PPSFD:** Peripheral Pressure Sensor Front Driver
**PPSFP:** Peripheral Pressure Sensor Front Passenger
**PPSRD:** Peripheral Pressure Sensor Rear Driver
**PPSRP:** Peripheral Pressure Sensor Rear Passenger
**Preact:** Precrash Engagement of Active Safety Devices

**Prefire:** Precrash-Firing of Reversible Restraints
**Preset:** Precrash-Setting of Algorithm Thresholds
**PROM:** Programmable Read Only Memory
**PR number:** Ply Rating number (Tire load-carrying capacity)
**PS-Code:** Program Service Code
**PSS:** Prädiktive Sicherheitssysteme (Predicative safety systems)
**PTC:** Positive Temperature Coefficient
**PTFE:** PolyTetraFluor Ethylene (Teflon)
**PTY-Code:** Program Type Code
**PUR:** PolyURethane
**PVC:** PolyVinyl Chloride
**PVD:** Physical Vapor Deposition
**PWM:** Pulse-width Modulation

**Q:**

**QM:** Quality Management

**R:**

**RAM:** Random Access Memory
**RAMSIS:** Rechnerunterstütztes anthropologisch-mathematisches System zur Insassensimulation (Computer-assisted anthropological and mathematical system for occupant simulation)
**RBH:** Replaceable Bulb Headlamp
**RDS:** Radio Data System
**RFP:** Rückförderpumpe (Return pump)
**RG-Management:** Reliability-Growth Management
**RIM:** Reaction-Injection Molding
**RISC:** Reduced Instruction-Set Computing
**RLFS:** Rücklauffreies Kraftstoffsystem (Returnless Fuel System)
**RME:** Rape-seed Methyl Ester (alternative fuel)
**RNT:** Radio Nuclide Testing
**ROM(1):** Read Only Memory
**ROM(2):** Rollover Mitigation
**RON:** Research Octane Number
**ROV:** Rotierende Hochspannungsverteilung (Rotating high-voltage distribution)

**ROZ:** Research Oktanzahl (RON: Research Octane Number)

**RREG:** Richtlinie des Rates der Europäischen Gemeinschaft (Directive of the Council of the European Union)

**RRIM:** Reinforced Reaction-Injection Molding

**RSE:** Restraint System Electronics

**RT-Code:** Radio Text Code

**RUV:** Ruhende Spannungsverteilung (Stationary voltage distribution)

**RWAL:** Rear Wheel Anti Lock Brake System

**RWG:** Regelweggeber (Control-rack travel sensor)

## S:

**SAE:** Society of Automotive Engineers

**SBC:** Sensotronic Brake Control

**SCB:** Semiconductor Base Bridge Wires (Ignition resistors integrated in silicon)

**SCON:** Safety Controller

**SCR(1):** Silicon Controlled Rectifier (Thyristor triode)

**SCR(2):** Selective Catalytic Reduction

**SEP:** Scheinwerfer-Einstellprüfgerät (Headlight aiming device)

**SERVOLECTRIC:** Elektrische Hilfskraftlenkung (Electronic power-assisted steering)

**SH:** Schubspannungshypothese (Shear-stress theory, strength of materials)

**SI:** Système International d'Unités (International Unit System)

**SIM:** Security Identify Module

**SK:** Signalkennung (Signal code)

**SL:** Select-Low control

**SMC:** Sheet Moulding Compound

**SMD:** Surface-Mounted Device

**SMK:** Schwungmassenklasse (Flywheel class)

**SMPS:** Scanning Mobility Particle Sizer

**SMS:** Short-Message Service

**SMT:** Surface-Mount Technology

**SoC:** System on a Chip

**SPC:** Statistic Process Control

**SPI:** Single-Point Injection

**SRAM:** Static RAM

**SRET:** Scanning Reference-Electrode Techniques

**SRR-Sensor:** Short-Range Radar Sensor

**SSI:** Small-Scale Integration

**SSL:** Secure Socket Layer

**SSM:** Select-Smart-Regelung (Select-smart control)

**STN-LCD:** Super Twisted Nematic Liquid Crystal Display

**StVZO:** Straßenverkehrszulassungsordnung (German Road Traffic Licensing Regulations)

**SUM:** Ereignisgesteuerte Integration (ESP) (Event-driven integration)

**SW:** Short Wave

## T:

**TA:** Type Approval

**TA-Code:** Traffic Announcement Code

**TAS:** Temperaturabhängiger Startmengenanschlag (Temperature-compensating start-quantity stop)

**TBI:** Throttle-Body Injection

**TDC:** Top Dead Center

**TDMA:** Time-Division Multiplex Access

**TEM:** Transverse Electromagnetic Mode

**TETRA:** Trans European Trunked Radio

**TFT-LCD:** Thin-Film Transistor Liquid-Crystal Display

**TIMS:** Tire Inflation Monitoring System

**TLS:** Transport Layer Security

**TMC Code:** Traffic Message Channel Code

**TME:** Tallow Methyl Ester

**TN-LCD:** Twisted Nematic Liquid Crystal Display

**TOF:** Time Of Flight (principle)

**TP-Code:** Traffic Program Code

**Triac:** Triode Alternating Current Switch

**TSZ-K:** Kontaktgesteuerte Transistor-Spulenzündung (Breaker-triggered transistorized coil ignition)

**TTCAN:** Time Triggered CAN

**TTL:** Transistor-Transistor Logic (Bipolar integrated digital circuit)

**TTP:** Time Triggered Protocol

**TÜA:** Technische Überwachungs-Anstalt (Technical Supervisory Agency)

**TÜV:** Technischer Überwachungs-Verein (Technical Inspectorate)

## U:

| | |
|---|---|
| **UDC:** | **U**rban **D**riving **C**ycle |
| **UDDS:** | **U**rban **D**ynamometer **D**riving **S**chedule |
| **UFOME:** | **U**sed **F**rying **O**il **M**ethyl **E**ster |
| **UFSD:** | **U**p**F**ront **S**ensor **D**river |
| **UFSP:** | **U**p**F**ront **S**ensor **P**assenger |
| **UIS:** | **U**nit **I**njector **S**ystem |
| **UKW:** | **U**ltra**k**urz**w**ellen (VHF: Very High Frequency/ FM: Frequency Modulation) |
| **ULSI:** | **U**ltra **L**arge **S**cale **I**ntegration |
| **UMTS:** | **U**niversal **M**obile **T**elecomunication **S**ystem |
| **ÜOT:** | **Ü**berschneidungs-**OT** (Top Dead Center in the exhaust cycle) |
| **UPS:** | **U**nit **P**ump **S**ystem |
| **USV:** | **U**m**s**chalt**v**entil (Changeover valve) |
| **UT(1):** | **U**niversal **T**ime |
| **UT(2):** | **U**nterer **T**otpunkt (BDC: Bottom Dead Center) |
| **UTC:** | **U**niversal **T**ime **C**oordinated |
| **UV:** | **U**ltra**v**iolet |

## V:

| | |
|---|---|
| **VCI:** | **V**olatile **C**orrosion **I**nhibitor |
| **VDA:** | **V**erband **d**eutscher **A**utomobil-hersteller (Association of German Automobile Manufacturers) |
| **VDE:** | **V**erband **D**eutscher **E**lektrotechniker (Association of German Electrical Engineers) |
| **VDI:** | **V**erein **D**eutscher **I**ngenieure (Association of German Engineers) |
| **VE-Pumpe:** | **V**erteiler**e**inspritzpumpe (Distributor injection pump) |
| **VFD:** | **V**acuum **F**luorescence **D**esign |
| **VHAD:** | **V**ehicle **H**eadlamp **A**iming **D**evice |
| **VHD:** | **V**ertical **H**all **D**evice |
| **VHF:** | **V**ery **H**igh **F**requency |
| **VLI:** | **V**apor-**L**ock **I**ndex |
| **VLP:** | **V**or**l**ade**p**umpe (Pre-charge pump) |
| **VLSI:** | **V**ery **L**arge **S**cale **I**ntegration |
| **VÖV:** | **V**erband der **ö**ffentlichen **V**erkehrsbetriebe (Association of German Public Transport Companies) |
| **VPI:** | **V**apor-**P**hase **I**nhibitor |

| | |
|---|---|
| **VRAM:** | **V**ideo **RAM** |
| **VSG:** | **V**erbund-**S**icherheits**g**las (Laminated safety glass) |
| **VST:** | Turbine mit **v**er**st**ellbarem Regelschieber (Variable Sleeve Turbine) |
| **VTG:** | **V**ariable **T**urbinen-**G**eometrie (Turbolader) (Variable Turbine Geometry) |
| **VVT:** | **V**ariable **V**alve **T**iming |

## W:

| | |
|---|---|
| **WAP:** | **W**ireless **A**pplication **P**rotocol |
| **WCDMA:** | **W**ideband **C**ode **D**ivision **M**ultiplexing **A**ccess |
| **WD:** | **W**atch**d**og |
| **WET:** | **W**est **E**uropean **T**ime |
| **WEZ:** | **W**est**e**uropäische **Z**eit (WET: West European Time) |
| **WLAN:** | **W**ireless **L**ocal **A**rea **N**etwork |
| **WS:** | **W**ork **S**tation |
| **WWW:** | **W**orld **W**ide **W**eb |
| **W3C:** | **W**orld **W**ide **W**eb **C**onsortium |

## Z:

| | |
|---|---|
| **ZF:** | **Z**wischen**f**requenz (IF: Intermediate Frequency) |
| **ZOT:** | **Z**ünd-**OT** (Top Dead Center in the power cycle) |
| **ZP:** | **Z**ünd**p**ille (Firing pellet) |
| **ZRAM:** | **Z**ero-Power **RAM** |
| **ZWV:** | **Z**ünd**w**inkel**v**erstellung (Spark retard) |

| | |
|---|---|
| **µC:** | **M**icro**c**ontroller |

# Bosch reference books –
# First-hand technical knowledge

## Diesel-Engine Management

There is a lot of movement – also in a figurative sense – when it comes to the diesel engine and diesel-fuel injection, in particular. These developments are now described in the completely revised and updated 3rd Edition of the "Diesel-Engine Management" reference book. The electronics that control the diesel engine are explained in easy detail. It provides a comprehensive description of all conventional diesel fuel-injection systems. It also contains a competent and detailed introduction to the modern common-rail system, Unit Injector System (UIS) and Unit Pump System (UPS), including the radial-piston distributor injection pump.

## Contents

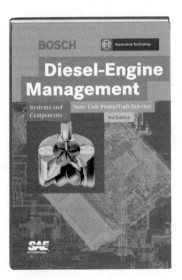

Hardcover,
17 x 24 cm format,
3rd Edition, completely revised and extended,
489 pages, hardback,
with numerous illustrations.

ISBN
0-7680-1343-7

# Bosch reference books –
# First-hand technical knowledge

## Gasoline-Engine Management

Starting with a brief review of the beginnings of automotive history, this book dis-
cusses the basics relating to the method
of operation of gasoline-engine control
systems. The descriptions of cylinder-
charge control systems, fuel-injection
systems (intake manifold and gasoline
direct injection), and ignition systems provide a comprehensive, firsthand overview
of the control mechanisms indispensable
for operating a modern gasoline engine.
The practical implementation of engine
management and control is described by
the examples of various Motronic variants, and of the control and regulation
functions integrated in this particular
management system. The book concludes with a chapter describing how
a Motronic system is developed.

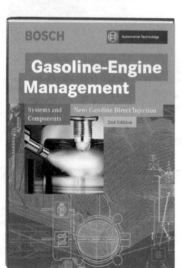

## Contents

Hardcover,
17 x 24 cm format,
2nd Edition, completely revised
and extended,
418 pages, hardback,
with numerous illustrations.

ISBN
0-8376-1052-4

# Bosch reference books –
# First-hand technical knowledge

## Automotive Electrics/ Automotive Electronics

The rapid pace of development in automotive electrics and electronics has had
a major impact on the equipment fitted to
motor vehicles. This simple fact necessi-
tated a complete revision and amendment of this authoritative technical reference work. The 4th Edition goes into
greater detail on electronics and their
application in the motor vehicle. The
book was amended by adding sections
on "Microelectronics" and "Sensors". As
a result, the basics and the components
used in electronics and microelectronics
are now part of this book. It also includes
a review of the measured quantities,
measuring principles, a presentation
of the typical sensors, and finally a description of sensor-signal processing.

## Contents

– Automotive electrical systems, includ-
  ing calculation of wire dimensions,
  plug-in connections, circuit diagrams
  and symbols
– Electromagnetic compatibility and
  interference suppression
– Batteries
– Alternators
– Starters
– Lighting technology
– Windshield and rear-window cleaning
– Microelectronics
– Sensors
– Data processing and transmission in
  motor vehicles.

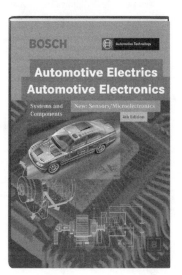

Hardcover,
17 x 24 cm format,
4th Edition, completely revised
and extended,
503 pages, hardback,
with numerous illustrations.

**ISBN**
0-8376-1050-8